PROJECT

MANAGEMENT

Dr. Kerzner's 16 Points to Project Management Maturity

1. Adopt a project management methodology and use it consistently.

2. Implement a philosophy that drives the company toward project management maturity and communicate it to everyone.

3. Commit to developing effective plans at the beginning of each project.

4. Minimize scope changes by committing to realistic objectives.

5. Recognize that cost and schedule management are inseparable.

6. Select the right person as the project manager.

7. Provide executives with project sponsor information, not project management information.

8. Strengthen involvement and support of line management.

9. Focus on deliverables rather than resources.

10. Cultivate effective communication, cooperation, and trust to achieve rapid project management maturity.

11. Share recognition for project success with the entire project team and line management.

12. Eliminate non-productive meetings.

13. Focus on identifying and solving problems early, quickly, and cost effectively.

14. Measure progress periodically.

15. Use project management software as a tool—not as a substitute for effective planning or interpersonal skills.

16. Institute an all-employee training program with periodic updates based upon documented lessons learned.

PROJECT

MANAGEMENT

A Systems Approach to Planning, Scheduling, and Controlling

SEVENTH EDITION

HAROLD KERZNER, Ph.D.

Division of Business Administration
Baldwin-Wallace College
Berea, Ohio

John Wiley & Sons, Inc.

New York   Chichester   Weinheim   Brisbane   Singapore   Toronto

Copyright © 2001 by John Wiley & Sons. All rights reserved.

Published simultaneously in Canada.

Library of Congress Cataloging-in-Publication Data:

Kerzner, Harold.
    Project management : a systems approach to planning, scheduling, and controlling / by Harold Kerzner.--7th ed.
        p. cm.
    Includes indexes.
    ISBN 0-471-39342-8 (cloth : alk. paper)
    1. Industrial project management.   I. Title.

HD69.P75 K47 2000
658.4′04--dc21   00-036802

Printed in the United States of America.

10   9   8   7   6   5   4   3   2   1

To
Dr. Herman Krier,
my Friend and Guru,
who taught me well the
meaning of the word "persistence"

Contents

PREFACE

As we enter the twenty-first century, our perception of project management has changed. Project management, once considered nice to have, is now recognized as a necessity for survival. Organizations that were opponents of project management are now advocates. Management educators of the 1970s and 1980s, who preached that project management could not work, are now staunch supporters. Project management is here to stay.

This text discusses the principles of project management. Students who are interested in advanced topics in project management, as well as in best practices in implementation, may wish to read one of my others texts, *Applied Project Management,* (New York: Wiley, 2000).

This book is addressed not only to those undergraduate and graduate students who wish to understand and improve upon their project management skills, but also to those functional managers and upper-level executives who must provide continuous support to all projects. During the past several years, management's knowledge and understanding of project management has matured to the point where almost every company and industry is using project management in one form or another. These companies have come to the realization that project management and productivity are related. Project management coursework is now consuming more and more of training budgets than ever before.

General reference is provided in the text to engineers. However, the reader should not consider project management as strictly engineering-related. The engineering examples are the result of the fact that project management first appeared in the engineering disciplines, and we should be willing to learn from their mistakes, regardless of the industry that we are in.

The textbook is designed for undergraduate and graduate courses in both business and engineering. The structure of the text is based upon my belief that project management is much more behavioral than quantitative. The first five chapters are part of the basic core of knowledge needed to understand project management. Chapters 6 through 8 deal with the support functions of time management, conflicts, and other special topics. Chapters 9 and 10 describe executive involvement and the critical success factors for predicting project success. It may seem strange that ten chapters on organizational behavior and structuring are needed prior to the "hard-core" chapters of planning, scheduling, and controlling. These first ten chapters are framework chapters needed to develop the cultural environment for all projects and systems. These chapters are necessary for the reader to understand the difficulties in achieving cross-functional cooperation on projects and why the people involved, all of whom may have different backgrounds, cannot simply be forged into a cohesive work-unit without any friction. Chapters 11 through 15 are the quantitative chapters on planning, scheduling, cost control, and estimating. Chapter 16 deals with trade-offs on time, cost, and performance. Chapters 17 through 24 cover the more advanced topics in project management, as well as future trends.

The text contains forty-six case studies, and more than 340 discussion questions. In addition, there is a supplemental workbook that contains more than 600 multiple choice questions, additional case studies, challenging problems, and crossword puzzles. The workbook and the textbook are ideal as a self-study tool for the Project Management Institute's Certification Exam. An instructor's manual is available *only* to college and university faculty members by contacting your local Wiley sales representative or by visiting the Wiley web site at www.wiley.com/kerzner.

One-day, two-day, and three-day seminars on project management and PMI certification training using the text are offered by contacting me at 216-765-8090 (E-mail address: hkerzner@hotmail.com).

The problems and case studies at the end of each chapter cover a variety of industries. Almost all of the case studies are real-world situations taken from my consulting practice. Feedback from colleagues who are using the text has provided me with fruitful criticism, most of which has been incorporated into the sixth edition.

The majority of the articles on project management that have become classics have been referenced in the textbook throughout the first eleven chapters. These articles were the basis for most of the modern developments in project management and are therefore identified throughout the text.

Valuable criticism was made by many colleagues. In particular, I am indebted to those industrial/government training managers whose dedication and commitment to quality project management education and training have led to valuable changes in this edition.

To Dr. Mark Collier, President of Baldwin-Wallace College, I again express my deepest appreciation and respect for his never-ending support and encouragement toward conducting meaningful research for this text.

Harold Kerzner
Baldwin-Wallace College

PROJECT

MANAGEMENT

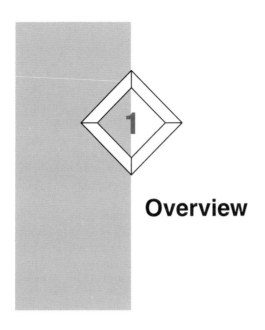

Overview

1.0 INTRODUCTION

Executives will be facing increasingly complex challenges during the next decade. These challenges will be the result of high escalation factors for salaries and raw materials, increased union demands, pressure from stockholders, and the possibility of long-term, high inflation accompanied by a mild recession and a lack of borrowing power with financial institutions. These environmental conditions have existed before, but not to the degree that they do today.

In the past, executives have attempted to ease the impact of these environmental conditions by embarking on massive cost-reduction programs. The usual results of these programs have been early retirement, layoffs, and a reduction in manpower, through attrition. As jobs become vacant, executives pressure line managers to accomplish the same amount of work with fewer resources, either by improving efficiency or by upgrading performance requirements to a higher position on the learning curve. Because people costs are more inflationary than the cost of equipment or facilities, executives are funding more and more capital equipment projects in an attempt to increase or improve productivity without increasing labor.

Unfortunately, modern executives are somewhat limited in how far they can go to reduce manpower without running a high risk to corporate profitability. Capital equipment projects are not always the answer. Thus, executives have been forced to look elsewhere for the solutions to their problems.

Almost all of today's executives are in agreement that the solution to the majority of corporate problems involves obtaining better control and use of existing corporate resources. Emphasis is being placed on looking internally rather than externally for the solution to these problems. As part of the attempt to achieve an internal solution, executives are taking a hard look at the ways corporate activities are being managed. Project management is one of the techniques now under consideration.

The project management approach is relatively modern. It is characterized by new methods of restructuring management and adapting special management techniques, with the purpose of obtaining better control and use of existing resources. Thirty years ago project management was confined to U.S. Department of Defense contractors and construction companies. Today, the concept behind project management is being applied in such diverse industries and organizations as defense, construction, pharmaceuticals, chemicals, banking, hospitals, accounting, advertising, law, state and local governments, and the United Nations.

The rapid rate of change in both technology and the marketplace has created enormous strains on existing organizational forms. The traditional structure is highly bureaucratic, and experience has shown that it cannot respond rapidly enough to a changing environment. Thus, the traditional structure must be replaced by project management, or other temporary management structures that are highly organic and can respond very rapidly as situations develop inside and outside the company.

Project management has long been discussed by corporate executives and academics as one of several workable possibilities for organizational forms of the future that could integrate complex efforts and reduce bureaucracy. The acceptance of project management has not been easy, however. Many executives are not willing to accept change and are inflexible when it comes to adapting to a different environment. The project management approach requires a departure from the traditional business organizational form, which is basically vertical and which emphasizes a strong superior–subordinate relationship.

1.1 UNDERSTANDING PROJECT MANAGEMENT

In order to understand project management, one must begin with the definition of a project. A project can be considered to be any series of activities and tasks that:

- Have a specific objective to be completed within certain specifications
- Have defined start and end dates
- Have funding limits (if applicable)
- Consume human and nonhuman resources (i.e., money, people, equipment)
- Be multifunctional (i.e., cut across several functional lines)

Project management, on the other hand, involves project planning and project monitoring and includes such items as:

- Project planning
  - Definition of work requirements
  - Definition of quantity and quality of work
  - Definition of resources needed
- Project monitoring
  - Tracking progress
  - Comparing actual outcome to predicted outcome
  - Analyzing impact
  - Making adjustments

Successful project management can then be defined as having achieved the project objectives:

- Within time
- Within cost

- At the desired performance/technology level
- While utilizing the assigned resources effectively and efficiently
- Accepted by the customer

The potential benefits from project management are:

- Identification of functional responsibilities to ensure that all activities are accounted for, regardless of personnel turnover
- Minimizing the need for continuous reporting
- Identification of time limits for scheduling
- Identification of a methodology for trade-off analysis
- Measurement of accomplishment against plans
- Early identification of problems so that corrective action may follow
- Improved estimating capability for future planning
- Knowing when objectives cannot be met or will be exceeded

Unfortunately, the benefits cannot be achieved without overcoming obstacles such as:

- Project complexity
- Customer's special requirements and scope changes
- Organizational restructuring
- Project risks
- Changes in technology
- Forward planning and pricing

Project management can mean different things to different people. Quite often, people misunderstand the concept because they have ongoing projects within their company and feel that they are using project management to control these activities. In such a case, the following might be considered an appropriate definition:

> Project management is the art of creating the illusion that any outcome is the result of a series of predetermined, deliberate acts when, in fact, it was dumb luck.

Although this might be the way that some companies are running their projects, this is not project management. Project management is designed to make better use of existing resources by getting work to flow horizontally as well as vertically within the company. This approach does not really destroy the vertical, bureaucratic flow of work but simply requires that line organizations talk to one another horizontally so work will be accomplished more smoothly throughout the organization. The vertical flow of work is still the responsibility of the line managers. The horizontal flow of work is the responsibility of the project managers, and their primary effort is to communicate and coordinate activities horizontally between the line organizations.

Figure 1–1 shows how many companies are structured. There are always "class or prestige" gaps between various levels of management. There are also

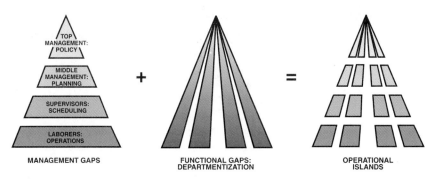

FIGURE 1–1. Why are systems necessary?

functional gaps between working units of the organization. If we superimpose the management gaps on top of the functional gaps, we find that companies are made up of small operational islands that refuse to communicate with one another for fear that giving up information may strengthen their opponents. The project manager's responsibility is to get these islands to communicate cross-functionally toward common goals and objectives.

The following would be an overview definition of project management:

> Project management is the planning, organizing, directing, and controlling of company resources for a relatively short-term objective that has been established to complete specific goals and objectives. Furthermore, project management utilizes the systems approach to management by having functional personnel (the vertical hierarchy) assigned to a specific project (the horizontal hierarchy).

The above definition requires further comment. Classical management is usually considered to have five functions or principles:

- Planning
- Organizing
- Staffing
- Controlling
- Directing

You will notice that, in the above definition, the staffing function has been omitted. This was intentional because the project manager does not staff the project. Staffing is a line responsibility. The project manager has the right to request specific resources, but the final decision of what resources will be committed rests with the line managers.

We should also comment on what is meant by a "relatively" short-term project. Not all industries have the same definition for a short-term project. In engineering, the project might be for six months or two years; in construction, three to five years; in nuclear components, ten years; and in insurance, two weeks.

FIGURE 1–2. Overview of project management.

Long-term projects, which consume resources full-time, are usually set up as a separate division (if large enough) or simply as a line organization.

Figure 1–2 is a pictorial representation of project management. The objective of the figure is to show that project management is designed to manage or control company resources on a given activity, within time, within cost, and within performance. Time, cost, and performance are the constraints on the project. If the project is to be accomplished for an outside customer, then the project has a fourth constraint: good customer relations. The reader should immediately realize that it is possible to manage a project internally within time, cost, and performance and then alienate the customer to such a degree that no further business will be forthcoming. Executives often select project managers based on who the customer is and what kind of customer relations will be necessary.

1.2 DEFINING PROJECT SUCCESS

In the previous section, we defined project success as the completion of an activity within the constraints of time, cost, and performance. This was the definition that has pertained for the past twenty years or so. Today, the definition of project success has been modified to include completion:

● Within the allocated time period
● Within the budgeted cost

- At the proper performance or specification level
- With acceptance by the customer/user
- When you can use the customer's name as a reference
- With minimum or mutually agreed upon scope changes
- Without disturbing the main work flow of the organization
- Without changing the corporate culture

The last three elements require further explanation. Very few projects are completed within the original scope of the project. Scope changes are inevitable and have the potential to destroy not only the morale on a project, but the entire project itself. Scope changes *must* be held to a minimum and those that are required *must* be approved by both the project manager and the customer/user.

Project managers must be willing to manage (and make concessions/trade-offs, if necessary) such that the company's main work flow is not altered. Most project managers view themselves as self-employed entrepreneurs after project go-ahead, and would like to divorce their project from the operations of the parent organization. This is not always possible. The project manager must be willing to manage within the guidelines, policies, procedures, rules, and directives of the parent organization.

All corporations have corporate cultures, and even though each project may be inherently different, the project manager should not expect his assigned personnel to deviate from cultural norms. If the company has a cultural standard of openness and honesty when dealing with customers, then this cultural value should remain in place for all projects, regardless of who the customer/user is or how strong the project manager's desire for success is.

As a final note, it should be understood that simply because a project is a success does not mean that the company as a whole is successful in its project management endeavors. Excellence in project management is defined as a continuous stream of successfully managed projects. Any project can be driven to success through formal authority and strong executive meddling. But in order for a continuous stream of successful projects to occur, there must exist a strong corporate commitment to project management, and this commitment *must be visible.*

1.3 THE PROJECT MANAGER–LINE MANAGER INTERFACE

We have stated that the project manager must control company resources within time, cost, and performance. Most companies have six resources:

- Money
- Manpower
- Equipment
- Facilities
- Materials
- Information/technology

Actually, the project manager does *not* control any of these resources directly, except perhaps money (i.e., the project budget).[1] Resources are controlled by the line managers, functional managers, or, as they are often called, resources managers. Project managers must, therefore, negotiate with line managers for all project resources. When we say that project managers control project resources, we really mean that they control those resources (which are temporarily loaned to them) *through line managers.*

It should become obvious at this point that successful project management is strongly dependent on:

- A good daily working relationship between the project manager and those line managers who directly assign resources to projects
- The ability of functional employees to report vertically to their line manager at the same time that they report horizontally to one or more project managers

These two items become critical. In the first item, functional employees who are assigned to a project manager still take technical direction from their line managers. Second, employees who report to multiple managers will always favor the manager who controls their purse strings. Thus, most project managers appear always to be at the mercy of the line managers.

Classical management has often been defined as a process in which the manager does not necessarily perform things for himself, but accomplishes objectives through others in a group situation. This basic definition also applies to the project manager. In addition, a project manager must help himself. There is nobody else to help him.

If we take a close look at project management, we will see that the project manager actually works for the line managers, not vice versa. Many executives do not realize this. They have a tendency to put a halo around the head of the project manager and give him a bonus at project termination, when, in fact, the credit should really go to the line managers, who are continually pressured to make better use of their resources. The project manager is simply the agent through whom this is accomplished. So why do some companies glorify the project management position?

To illustrate the role of the project manager, consider the time, cost, and performance constraints shown in Figure 1–2. Many functional managers, if left alone, would recognize only the performance constraint: "Just give me another $50,000 and two more months, and I'll give you the ideal technology."

The project manager, as part of these communicating, coordinating, and integrating responsibilities, reminds the line managers that there are also time and cost constraints on the project. This is the starting point for better resource control.

Project managers depend on line managers. When the project manager gets in trouble, the only place he can go is to the line manager because additional re-

---

1. Here we are assuming that the line manager and project manager are not the same individual.

sources are almost always required to alleviate the problems. When a line manager gets in trouble, he usually goes first to the project manager and requests either additional funding or some type of authorization for scope changes.

To illustrate this working relationship between the project and line managers, consider the following situation:

Project Manager: (addressing the line manager): "I have a serious problem. I'm looking at a $150,000 cost overrun on my project and I need your help. I'd like you to do the same amount of work that you are currently scheduled for but in 3,000 less man-hours. Since your organization is burdened at $60/hour, this would more than compensate for the cost overrun."

Line Manager: "Even if I could, why should I? You know that good line managers can always make work expand to meet budget. I'll look over my manpower curves and let you know tomorrow."

The following day . . .

Line Manager: "I've looked over my manpower curves and I have enough work to keep my people employed. I'll give you back the 3,000 hours you need, but remember, *you owe me one!"*

Several months later . . .

Line Manager: "I've just seen the planning for your new project that's supposed to start two months from now. You'll need two people from my department. There are two employees that I'd like to use on your project. Unfortunately, these two people are available now. If I don't pick these people up on your charge number right now, some other project might pick them up in the interim period, and they won't be available when your project starts."

Project Manager: "What you're saying is that you want me to let you sandbag against one of my charge numbers, knowing that I really don't need them."

Line Manager: "That's right. I'll try to find other jobs (and charge numbers) for them to work on temporarily so that your project won't be completely burdened. Remember, you owe me one."

Project Manager: "O.K. I know that I owe you one, so I'll do this for you. Does this make us even?"

Line Manager: "Not at all! But you're going in the right direction."

When the project management–line management relationship begins to deteriorate, the project almost always suffers. Executives must promote a good working relationship between line and project management. One of the most common ways of destroying this relationship is by asking, "Who contributes to profits—the line or project manager?" Project managers feel that they control all project profits because they control the budget. The line managers, on the other hand, argue that they must staff with appropriately budgeted-for personnel, supply the resources at the desired time, and supervise the actual performance. Actually, both the vertical and horizontal lines contribute to profits. These types of conflicts can destroy the entire project management system.

The previous examples should indicate that project management is more behavioral than quantitative. Effective project management requires an understanding of:

- Quantitative tools and techniques
- Organizational structures
- Organizational behavior

Most people understand the quantitative tools for planning, scheduling, and controlling work. It is imperative that project managers understand totally the operations of each line organization. In addition, project managers must understand their own job description, especially where their authority begins and ends. During an in-house seminar on engineering project management, the author asked one of the project engineers to provide a description of his job as a project engineer. During the discussion that followed, several project managers and line managers said that there was a great deal of overlap between their job descriptions and that of the project engineer.

Organizational behavior is important because the functional employees at the interface position find themselves reporting to more than one boss—a line manager and one project manager for each project they are assigned to. Executives must provide proper training so functional employees can report effectively to multiple managers.

1.4 DEFINING THE PROJECT MANAGER'S ROLE

The project manager is responsible for coordinating and integrating activities across multiple, functional lines. In order to do this, the project manager needs strong communicative and interpersonal skills, must become familiar with the operations of each line organization, and should have a general knowledge of the technology being used (unless he is managing R&D activities, in which case a command of technology is more important than a general understanding).

An executive with a computer manufacturer stated that his company was looking externally for project managers. When asked if he expected candidates to have a command of computer technology, the executive remarked: "You give me an individual who has good communicative skills and interpersonal skills, and I'll give that individual a job. I can teach people the technology and give them technical experts to assist them in decision making. But I cannot teach somebody how to work with people."

The project manager's job is not an easy one. Project managers may have increasing responsibility, but very little authority. This lack of authority can force them to "negotiate" with upper-level management as well as functional management for control of company resources, as shown in Figure 1–3. They may often

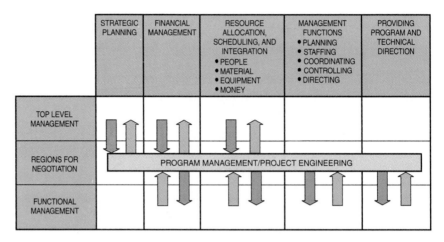

FIGURE 1–3. The negotiation activities of systems management.

be treated as outsiders by the formal organization. Yet, even with these problems and roadblocks, they have managed to survive.

In the project environment, everything seems to revolve about the project manager. Although the project organization is a specialized, task-oriented entity, it cannot exist apart from the traditional structure of the organization. The project manager, therefore, must walk the fence between the two organizations. The term *interface management* is often used for this role, which can be described as:

- Managing human interrelationships within the project team
- Managing human interrelationships between the project team and the functional organizations
- Managing human interrelationships between the project team and senior management
- Managing human interrelationships between the project team and the customer's organization, whether an internal or external organization

Organizational restraints have a tendency to develop into organizational conflict, often requiring that top management take an active role in conflict resolution by:

- Setting a selection criterion for projects
- Establishing priorities among projects

To be effective as a project manager, an individual must have management as well as technical skills. Unfortunately, businesspeople sometimes find it difficult to think as businesspeople. Executives have found that it is usually easier to train engineers rather than businesspeople to fill project management positions.

Because engineers often consider their careers limited in the functional disciplines, they look toward project management and project engineering as career path opportunities. But becoming a manager entails learning about psychology, human behavior, organizational behavior, interpersonal relations, and communications. MBA programs have come to the rescue of individuals desiring the background to be effective project managers.

The average age of project managers in industry is between thirty and forty. The major reason is risk. The younger individual in most cases is willing to take more risks than the older individual in order to meet the project objective. Furthermore, the younger individual is often willing to work long hours including overtime and weekends.

One final comment should be made concerning the young project manager's desire to take risks. Frequently the young risk taker does not fully understand the extent of the risk being taken, because of a lack of experience or a lack of objectivity when implementing one's creative ideas. Although this is a problem, it has a positive aspect if it reflects youth's positive attitude and aggressiveness; an almost innocent view that "it won't or can't happen to me." Far less positive is the rationale on which risk decisions are frequently made by the younger person. When a risk is taken primarily to further an individual's career, rather than for the betterment of the project (or business); or when the risk taker, if successful, seeks immediate recognition, or is willing to look for a new job if the risk becomes a reality; the risk decision-making process has become flawed and poor decisions can result.

Actually, the age of the project manager varies from industry to industry. Information systems project managers are usually younger than average because current knowledge of computer technology is a necessity. R&D project managers may span the entire age range because of technology requirements. Manufacturing and construction project managers are often older because their experience is important.

In the past, executives motivated and retained qualified personnel primarily with financial incentives. Today other ways are being used. Some people are more title-oriented than money-oriented. For example, a change in title sometimes motivates people to stay with a company simply because they want to put the new title on their resume at a later date. Another method, and by far the best, is work challenge. Perhaps the lowest turnover rates of any professions in the world are in project management and project engineering. In a project environment, the project managers and project engineers get to see their project through from "birth to death." Being able to see the fruits of one's efforts is highly rewarding. A senior project manager in a construction company commented on why he never accepted a vice presidency that had been offered to him: "I can take my children and grandchildren into ten countries in the world and show them facilities that I have built as the project manager. What do I show my kids as an executive? The size of my office? My bank account? A stockholder's report?"

Work challenge and other nonmonetary rewards are becoming increasingly important today, so people are refusing to leave project management positions.

The project manager is actually a general manager and gets to know the total operation of the company. In fact, project managers get to know more about the total operation of a company than most executives know. That is why project management is often used as a training ground to prepare future general managers who will be capable of filling top management positions. That is not a bad idea provided that executives know the general management aspect is the result of experience in integrating work horizontally. Placing an individual into project management for the sole purpose of training a future general manager is not recommended unless the company is willing to risk the failure of the project to provide such training.

1.5 DEFINING THE FUNCTIONAL MANAGER'S ROLE

Assuming that the project and functional managers are not the same person, we can identify a specific role for the functional manager. There are two elements to this role:

- The functional manager has the responsibility to define *how* the task will be done and *where* the task will be done (i.e., the technical criteria).
- The functional manager has the responsibility to provide sufficient resources to accomplish the objective within the project's constraints (i.e., *who* will get the job done).
- The functional manager has the responsibility for the deliverable.

In other words, once the project manager identifies the requirements for the project (i.e., what work has to be done and the constraints), it becomes the line manager's responsibility to identify the technical criteria. Except perhaps in R&D efforts, the line manager should be the recognized technical expert. If the line manager believes that certain technical portions of the project manager's requirements are unsound, then the line manager has the right, by virtue of his expertise, to take exception and plead his case to a higher authority.

In Section 1.1 we stated that all resources (including personnel) are controlled by the line manager. The project manager has the right to request specific staff, but the final appointments rest with line managers. Project managers view line managers as rather shady characters (see Figure 1–4) who never keep their promises. In a project environment, line managers are under tremendous pressure to live up to their commitments. Unfortunately, project managers do not realize the line manager's problems. The line manager has to cope with:

- Unlimited work requests (especially during competitive bidding)
- Predetermined deadlines
- All requests having a high priority
- Limited number of resources
- Limited availability of resources

FIGURE 1–4. Do functional managers live up to commitments?

- Unscheduled changes in the project plan
- Unpredicted lack of progress
- Unplanned absence of resources
- Unplanned breakdown of resources
- Unplanned loss of resources
- Unplanned turnover of personnel

Only in a very few industries will the line manager be able to identify to the project manager in advance exactly what resources will be available when the project is scheduled to begin. Actually, it is not important for the project manager to have the best available resources. Functional managers should not commit to certain people's availability. Rather, the functional manager should commit to achieving his portion of the objective within time, cost, and performance even if he has to use average or below-average personnel. If the project manager is unhappy with the assigned functional resources, then the project manager should closely track that portion of the project. Only if and when the project manager is convinced by the evidence that the assigned resources are unacceptable should he then confront the line manager and demand better resources.

Just the fact that a project manager is assigned does not relieve the line manager of his functional responsibility to perform. If a functional manager assigns resources such that the constraints are not met, then *both* the project and functional managers will be blamed. One company is even considering evaluating line managers for merit increases and promotion based on how often they have lived up to their commitments to the project managers. Therefore, it is extremely valuable to everyone concerned to have all project commitments *made visible to all.*

Some companies carry the concept of commitments to extremes. An aircraft components manufacturer has a Commitment Department headed up by a second-level manager. The function of the Commitment Department is to track how well the line managers keep their promises to the project managers. The department manager reports directly to the vice president of the division. In this company, line managers are extremely careful and cautious in making commitments, but do everything possible to meet deliverables. This same company has gone so far as to tell both project and line personnel that they run the risk of being discharged from the company for burying a problem until such time that options for solving it become limited rather than bringing the problem to the surface *immediately* where help can be found.

Project management is not designed to be a unity of command methodology. It is designed to have shared authority and responsibility between the project and line managers. Project managers plan, monitor, and control the project, whereas functional managers perform the work. Table 1–1 shows this shared responsibility. The one exception to Table 1–1 occurs when the project and line managers are the same person. This situation, which happens more often than not, creates a conflict of interest. If a line manager has to assign resources to six projects, one of which is under his direct control, he might save the best resources for his project. In this case, his project will be a success at the expense of all of the other projects.

The exact relationship between project and line managers is of paramount importance in project management where multiple-boss reporting prevails. Table 1–2 shows that the relationship between project and line managers is not always in balance and thus, of course, has a bearing on who exerts more influence over the assigned functional employees.

TABLE 1–1. DUAL RESPONSIBILITY

	Responsibility	
Topic	**Project Manager**	**Line Manager**
Rewards	Give recommendation: Informal	Provide rewards: Formal
Direction	Milestone (summary)	Detailed
Evaluation	Summary	Detailed
Measurement	Summary	Detailed
Control	Summary	Detailed

TABLE 1–2. REPORTING RELATIONSHIPS

Type of Project Manager	Type of Matrix Structure*	Project Manager (PM)/Line Manager (LM)/Employee Relationship			
		PM Negotiates For	Employees Take Technical Direction From	PM Receives Functional Progress From	Employee Performance Evaluations Made By
Lightweight no	Weak	Deliverables	LMs	Primarily LMs	LMs only with input from PM
Heavyweight	Strong	People who report informally to PM but formally to LMs	PM and LMs	Assigned employees who report to LMs	LMs with input from PM
Tiger teams	Very strong	People who report entirely to PM full-time for duration of project	PM only	Assigned employees who now report directly to PM	PM only

*The types of organizational structures are discussed in Chapter 3.

1.6 DEFINING THE FUNCTIONAL EMPLOYEE'S ROLE

Once the line managers commit to the deliverables, it is the responsibility of the assigned functional employees to achieve the functional deliverables. For years the functional employees were called subordinates. Although this term still exists in textbooks, industry prefers to regard the assigned employees as "associates" rather than subordinates. The reason for this is that in project management the associates can be a higher pay grade than the project manager. The associates can even be a higher pay grade than their functional manager.

In most organizations, the assigned employees report on a "solid" line to their functional manager, even though they may be working on several projects simultaneously. The employees are usually a "dotted" line to the project but solid to their function. This places the employees in the often awkward position of reporting to multiple individuals simultaneously. This situation is further complicated when the project manager has more technical knowledge than the line manager. This occurs during R&D projects.

The functional employee is expected to accomplish the following activities when assigned to projects:

- Accept responsibility for accomplishing the assigned deliverables within the project's constraints
- Complete the work at the earliest possible time
- Periodically inform both the project and line manager of the project's status
- Bring problems to the surface quickly for resolution
- Share information with the rest of the project team

1.7 DEFINING THE EXECUTIVE'S ROLE

In a project environment there are new expectations of and for the executives, as well as a new interfacing role.[2] Executives are expected to interface a project as follows:

- In project planning and objective-setting
- In conflict resolution
- In priority-setting
- As project sponsor[3]

Executives are expected to interface with projects very closely at project initiation and planning, but to remain at a distance during execution unless needed for priority-setting and conflict resolution. One reason why executives "meddle" during proj-ect execution is that they are not getting accurate information from the project manager as to project status. If project managers provide executives with meaningful status reports, then the so-called meddling may be reduced or even eliminated.

1.8 WORKING WITH EXECUTIVES

Success in project management is like a three-legged stool. The first leg is the project manager, the second leg is the line manager, and the third leg is senior management. If any of the three legs fail, then even delicate balancing may not prevent the stool from toppling down.

The critical node in project management is the project manager–line manager interface. At this interface, the project and line managers must view each other as equals and be willing to share authority, responsibility, and accountability. In excellently managed companies, project managers do not negotiate for resources but simply ask for the line manager's commitment to executing his portion of the work within time, cost, and performance. Therefore, in excellent companies, it should not matter who the line manager assigns as long as the line manager lives up to his commitments.

Since the project and line managers are "equals," senior management involvement is necessary to provide advice and guidance to the project manager, as well as to provide encouragement to the line managers to keep their promises. When executives act in this capacity, they assume the role of project sponsors, as shown in Figure 1–5,[4] which also shows that sponsorship need not always be at the executive levels. The exact person appointed as the project sponsor is based on the dollar value of the project, the priority of the project, and who the customer is.

---

2. The expectations are discussed in Section 9.3.

3. The role of the project sponsor is discussed in Section 10.1.

4. Section 10.1 describes the role of the project sponsor in more depth.

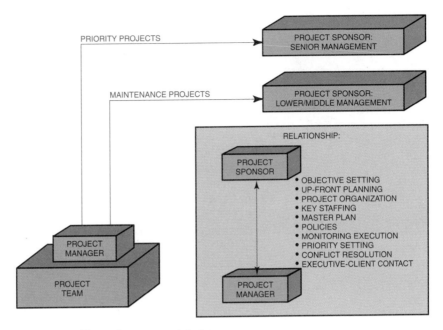

FIGURE 1–5. The project sponsor interface.

The ultimate objective of the project sponsor is to provide behind-the-scenes assistance to project personnel for projects both "internal" to the company, as well as "external," as shown in Figure 1–5. Projects can still be successful without this commitment and support, as long as all work flows smoothly. But in time of crisis, having a "big brother" available as a possible sounding board will surely help.

When an executive is required to act as a project sponsor, then the executive has the responsibility to make effective and timely project decisions. To accomplish this, the executive needs timely, accurate, and complete data for such decisions. The project manager must be made to realize that keeping management informed serves this purpose, and that the all-too-common practice of "stonewalling" will prevent an executive from making effective decisions related to the project.

1.9 THE PROJECT MANAGER AS THE PLANNING AGENT

The major responsibility of the project manager is planning. If project planning is performed correctly, then it is conceivable that the project manager will work himself out of a job because the project can run itself. This rarely happens, however. Few projects are ever completed without some conflict or trade-offs for the project manager to resolve.

In most cases, the project manager provides overall or summary definitions of the work to be accomplished, but the line managers (the true experts) do the detailed planning. Although project managers cannot control or assign line resources, they must make sure that the resources are adequate and scheduled to satisfy the needs of the project, not vice versa. As the architect of the project plan, the project manager must provide:

- Complete task definitions
- Resource requirement definitions (possibly skill levels)
- Major timetable milestones
- Definition of end-item quality and reliability requirements
- The basis for performance measurement

These factors, if properly established, result in:

- Assurance that functional units will understand their total responsibilities toward achieving project needs.
- Assurance that problems resulting from scheduling and allocation of critical resources are known beforehand.
- Early identification of problems that may jeopardize successful project completion so that effective corrective action and replanning can be taken to prevent or resolve the problems.

Project managers are responsible for project administration and, therefore, must have the right to establish their own policies, procedures, rules, guidelines, and directives–provided these policies, guidelines, and so on, conform to overall company policy. Companies with mature project management structures usually have rather loose company guidelines, so project managers have some degree of flexibility in how to control their projects. However, there are certain administrative requirements project managers cannot establish. As an example, the project manager cannot make any promises to a functional employee concerning:

- Promotion
- Grade
- Salary
- Bonus
- Overtime
- Responsibility
- Future work assignments

These seven items can be administered by line managers only, but the project manager can have indirect involvement by telling the line manager how well an employee is doing (and putting it in writing), requesting overtime because the project budget will permit it, and offering individuals the opportunity to perform work above their current pay grade. However, such work above pay grade can cause severe managerial headaches if coordination with the line manager does not take place, because the individual will expect immediate rewards if he performs well.

The establishment of project administrative requirements is part of project planning. Executives must either work with the project managers at project initiation or act as resource persons. Improper project administrative planning can create a situation that requires:

- A continuous revision and/or establishment of company and/or project policies, procedures, and directives
- A continuous shifting in organizational responsibility and possible unnecessary restructuring
- A need for staff to acquire new knowledge and skills

If these situations occur simultaneously on several projects, there can be confusion throughout the organization.

1.10 PROJECT CHAMPIONS

Corporations encourage employees to think up new ideas that, if approved by the corporation, will generate monetary and nonmonetary rewards for the idea generator. One such reward is to identify the individual as a "project champion." Unfortunately, all too often the project champion becomes the project manager, and, although the idea was technically sound, the project fails.

Table 1–3 provides a comparison between project managers and project champions. The conclusion to be drawn from Table 1–3 is that the project champions may become so attached to the technical side of the project that they become derelict in their administrative responsibilites. Perhaps, therefore, the project champion might function best as a project engineer rather than the project manager.

TABLE 1–3. PROJECT MANAGERS VERSUS PROJECT CHAMPIONS

Project Managers	Project Champions
• Prefer to work in groups	• Prefer working individually
• Committed to their managerial and technical responsibilities	• Committed to technology
• Committed to the corporation	• Committed to the profession
• Seek to achieve the objective	• Seek to exceed the objective
• Are willing to take risks	• Are unwilling to take risks; try to test everything
• Seek what is possible	• Seek perfection
• Think in terms of short time spans	• Think in terms of long time spans
• Manage people	• Manage things
• Are committed to and pursue material values	• Are committed to and pursue intellectual values

This comparison does not mean that technically oriented project managers-champions will fail. Rather, it implies that the selection of the "proper" project manager should be based on *all* facets of the project.

1.11 THE DOWNSIDE RISK OF PROJECT MANAGEMENT

Project management is much too often recognized only as a high-salaried, highly challenging position whereby the project manager receives excellent training in general management.

For projects that are done for external sources, the project manager is first viewed as starting out with a pot of gold (see Figure 1–6) and then as having to manage the project so that sufficient profits will be made for the stockholders (see Figure 1–7). If the project manager performs well, then the expected result is as shown in Figure 1–8.

For projects external to the company, the project manager's responsibility is shown in Figure 1–7. Unfortunately, in going from Figure 1–6 to Figure 1–7, the project manager may experience a change in health (as shown in Figure 1–9), especially if he falls in love with his project.

FIGURE 1–6. Project initiation and funding.

FIGURE 1–7. Booking profits for the stockholders.

FIGURE 1–8. Successful project completion.

Project Initiation

Project Completion

FIGURE 1–9. Project manager's health.

There are severe downside risks that are not always evident. Some project management positions may require not only a sixty-hour workweek, but also extensive time away from home (see Figures 1–10 through 1–13). When a project manager begins to fall in love more with the job than with his family, the result is usually lack of friends, a poor home life, and possibly divorce. During the birth of the missile and space programs, companies estimated that the divorce rate among project managers and project engineers was probably twice the national average. Accepting a project management assignment is not always compatible with raising a young family. The following have been found to be characteristic of the workaholic project manager:

- Every Friday he thinks that there are only two more working days until Monday.
- At 5:00 P.M. he considers the working day only half over.
- He has no time to rest or relax.
- He always takes work home from the office.
- He takes work with him on vacations.

FIGURE 1–10. Effective project management: no pressure.

FIGURE 1–11. Effective project management: good home life.

FIGURE 1–12. Effective project management: meet new people.

1.12 PROJECT-DRIVEN VERSUS NON–PROJECT-DRIVEN ORGANIZATIONS

On the micro level, virtually all organizations are either marketing-, engineering-, or manufacturing-driven. But on the macro level, organizations are either project- or non–project-driven. In a project-driven organization, such as construction or

FIGURE 1–13. Effective project management: limited travel.

aerospace, all work is characterized through projects, with each project as a separate cost center having its own profit-and-loss statement. The total profit to the corporation is simply the summation of the profits on all projects. In a project-driven organization, everything centers around the projects.

In the non–project-driven organization, such as low-technology manufacturing, profit and loss are measured on vertical or functional lines. In this type of organization, projects exist merely to support the product lines or functional lines. Priority resources are assigned to the revenue-producing functional line activities rather than the projects.

Project management in a non–project-driven organization is generally more difficult for these reasons:

- Projects may be few and far between.
- Not all projects have the same project management requirements, and therefore they cannot be managed identically. This difficulty results from poor understanding of project management and a reluctance of companies to invest in proper training.
- Executives do not have sufficient time to manage projects themselves, yet refuse to delegate authority.
- Projects tend to be delayed because approvals most often follow the vertical chain of command. As a result, project work stays too long in functional departments.
- Because project staffing is on a "local" basis, only a portion of the organization understands project management and sees the system in action.
- There exists heavy dependence on subcontractors and outside agencies for project management expertise.

Non–project-driven organizations may also have a steady stream of projects, all of which are usually designed to enhance manufacturing operations. Some projects may be customer-requested, such as:

- The introduction of statistical dimensioning concepts to improve process control
- The introduction of process changes to enhance the final product
- The introduction of process change concepts to enhance product reliability

If these changes are not identified as specific projects, the result can be:

- Poorly defined responsibility areas within the organization
- Poor communications, both internal and external to the organization
- Slow implementation
- A lack of a cost-tracking system for implementation
- Poorly defined performance criteria

Figure 1–14 shows the tip-of-the-iceberg syndrome, which can occur in all types of organizations but is most common in non–project-driven organizations.

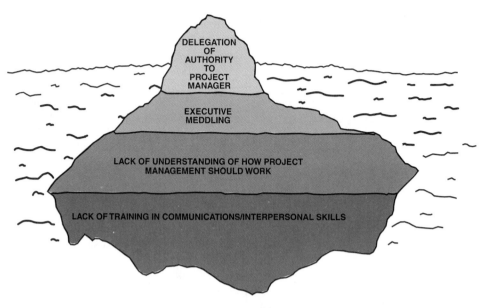

MANY OF THE PROBLEMS SURFACE MUCH LATER IN
THE PROJECT AND RESULT IN A MUCH HIGHER COST
TO CORRECT AS WELL AS INCREASE PROJECT RISK

FIGURE 1–14. The tip-of-the-iceberg syndrome for matrix implementation.

On the surface, all we see is a lack of authority for the project manager. But beneath the surface we see the causes; there is excessive meddling due to lack of understanding of project management, which, in turn, resulted from an inability to recognize the need for proper training.

In the previous sections we stated that project management could be handled on either a formal or an informal basis. As can be seen from Figure 1–15, informal project management most often appears in non–project-driven organizations. It is doubtful that informal project management would work in a project-driven organization where the project manager has profit-and-loss responsibility.

1.13 MARKETING IN THE PROJECT-DRIVEN ORGANIZATION

To the realistic manager, winning new concepts is the lifeblood of any project-oriented business. The practices of the project-oriented company are, however, substantially different from traditional product businesses and require highly specialized and disciplined team efforts among marketing, technical, and operating personnel, plus significant customer involvement. Projects are different from products in many respects, especially marketing. Marketing projects require the

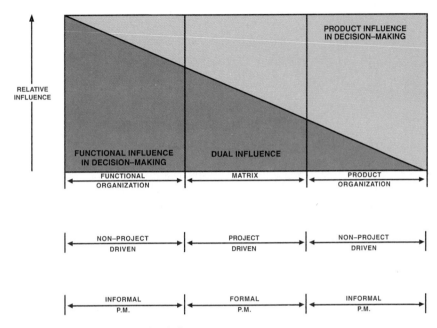

FIGURE 1–15. Decision-making influence.

ability to identify, pursue, and capture one-of-a-kind business opportunities, and are characterized by:

- *A systematic effort.* A systematic approach is usually required to develop a new program lead into an actual contract. The project acquisition effort is often highly integrated with ongoing programs and involves key personnel from both the potential customer and the performing organization.
- *Custom design.* While traditional businesses provide standard products and services for a variety of applications and customers, projects are custom-designed items to fit specific requirements of a single-customer community.
- *Project life cycle.* Project-oriented businesses have a well-defined beginning and end and are not self-perpetuating. Business must be generated on a proj-ect-by-project basis rather than by creating demand for a standard product or service.
- *Marketing phase.* Long lead times often exist between the product definition, start-up, and completion phases of a project.
- *Risks.* There are risks present, especially in the research, design, and production of programs. The program manager not only has to integrate the multidisciplinary tasks and project elements within budget and schedule constraints, but also has to manage inventions and technology while working with a variety of technically oriented prima donnas.
- *The technical capability to perform.* Technical ability is critical to the successful pursuit and acquisition of a new project.

In spite of the risks and problems, profits on projects are usually very low in comparison with commerical business practices. One may wonder why companies pursue project businesses. Clearly, there are many reasons why projects are good business:

- Although immediate profits (as a percentage of sales) are usually small, the return on capital investment is often very attractive. Progress payment practices keep inventories and receivables to a minimum and enable companies to undertake projects many times larger in value than the assets of the total company.
- Once a contract has been secured and is being managed properly, the project may be of relatively low financial risk to the company. The company has little additional selling expenditure and has a predictable market over the life cycle of the project.
- Project business must be viewed from a broader perspective than motivation for immediate profits. Projects provide an opportunity to develop the company's technical capabilities and build an experience base for future business growth.
- Winning one large project often provides attractive growth potential, such as (1) growth with the project via additions and changes; (2) follow-on work; (3) spare parts, maintenance, and training; and (4) being able to compete effectively in the next project phase, such as nurturing a study program into a development contract and finally a production contract.

Customers come in various forms and sizes. For small and medium size businesses particularly, it seems to be a true challenge to compete for contracts from large industrial or governmental organizations. Although the contract to a firm may be relatively small, it is often subcontracted via a larger organization. Selling to such a diversified heterogeneous customer is a true marketing challenge that requires a highly sophisticated and disciplined approach.

The first step in a new business development effort is to define the market to be pursued. The market segment for a new program opportunity is normally in an area of relevant past experience, technical capability, and customer involvement. Good marketeers in the program business have to think as product line managers. They have to understand all dimensions of the business and be able to define and pursue market objectives that are consistent with the capabilities of their organizations.

Program businesses operate in an opportunity-driven market. It is a common mistake, however, to believe that these markets are unpredictable and unmanageable. Market planning and strategizing is important. New project opportunities develop over periods of time, sometimes years for larger projects. These developments must be properly tracked and cultivated to form the bases for management actions such as (1) bid decisions, (2) resource commitment, (3) technical readiness, and (4) effective customer liaison. This strategy of winning new business is supported by systematic, disciplined approaches, which are illustrated in Figure 1–16.

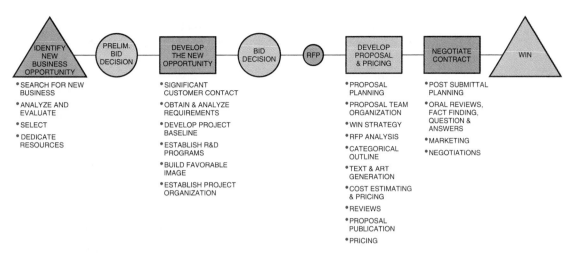

FIGURE 1–16. The phases of winning new contracts in project-oriented businesses.

1.14 CLASSIFICATION OF PROJECTS

The principles of project management can be applied to any type of project and to any industry. However, the relative degree of importance of these principles can vary from project to project and industry to industry. Table 1–4 shows a brief comparison of certain industries/projects.

For those industries that are project-driven, such as aerospace and large construction, the high dollar value of the projects mandates a much more rigorous

TABLE 1–4. CLASSIFICATION OF PROJECTS/CHARACTERISTICS

	Type of Project/Industry					
	In-house R&D	Small Construction	Large Construction	Aerospace/ Defense	MIS	Engineering
Need for interpersonal skills	Low	Low	High	High	High	Low
Importance of organizational structure	Low	Low	Low	Low	High	Low
Time management difficulties	Low	Low	High	High	High	Low
Number of meetings	Excessive	Low	Excessive	Excessive	High	Medium
Project manager's supervisor	Middle management	Top management	Top management	Top management	Middle management	Middle management
Project sponsor present	Yes	No	Yes	Yes	No	No
Conflict intensity	Low	Low	High	High	High	Low
Cost control level	Low	Low	High	High	Low	Low
Level of planning/scheduling	Milestones only	Milestones only	Detailed plan	Detailed plan	Milestones only	Milestones only

project management approach. For non–project-driven industries, projects may be managed more informally than formally, especially if no immediate profit is involved.

1.15 LOCATION OF THE PROJECT MANAGER

The success of project management could easily depend on the location of the project manager within the organization. Two questions must be answered:

- What salary should the project manager earn?
- To whom should the project manager report?

Figure 1–17 shows a typical organizational hierarchy (the numbers represent pay grades). Ideally, the project manager should be at the same pay grade as the

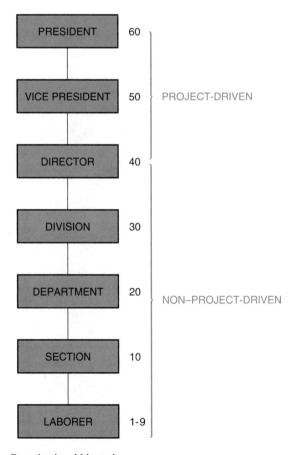

FIGURE 1–17. Organizational hierarchy.

individuals with whom he must negotiate on a daily basis. Using this criterion, and assuming that the project manager interfaces at the department manager level, the project manager should earn a salary between grades 20 and 25. A project manager earning substantially more or less money than the line manager will usually create conflict.

The ultimate reporting location of the project manager (and perhaps his salary) is heavily dependent on whether the organization is project- or non–project-driven, and whether the project manager is responsible for profit or loss. In addition, Martin has shown other good reasons for having project managers report either high or low:[5]

> Projects should be located wherever in the organization they can function most effectively. Several reasons for having the project manager report directly to a high level in the organization may be mentioned:
>
> - The project manager is charged with getting results from the coordinated efforts of many functions. He should, therefore, report to the man who directs all those functions.
> - The project manager must have adequate organizational status to do his job effectively.
> - To get adequate and timely assistance in solving problems that inevitably appear in any important project, the project manager needs direct and specific access to an upper echelon of management.
> - The customer, particularly in a competitive environment, will be favorably impressed if his project manager reports to a high organizational echelon.
>
> Good reasons may also exist for having the project manager report to a lower echelon:
>
> - It is organizationally and operationally inefficient to have too many projects, especially small ones, diverting senior executives from more vital concerns.
> - Although giving a small project a high place in the organization may create the illusion of executive attention, its real result is to foster executive neglect of the project.
> - Placing a junior project manager too high in the organization will alienate senior functional executives on whom he must rely for support.

Project managers can end up reporting both high and low in an organization during the life cycle of the project. During the planning phase of the project, the project manager may report high, whereas during implementation, he may report low. Likewise, the positioning of the project manager may be dependent on the risk of the project, the size of the project, or the customer.

---

5. Reprinted, with permission of the publisher, from Charles Martin, *Project Management: How to Make It Work* (p. 80). Copyright © 1976 AMACOM, a division of the American Management Association. All rights reserved.

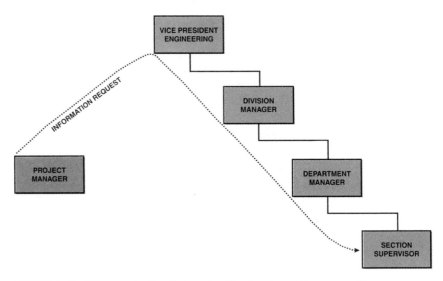

FIGURE 1–18. The organizational hierarchy: for planning and/or approval?

Finally, it should be noted that even if the project manager reports low, he should still have the right to interface with top executives during project planning although there may be two or more reporting levels between the project manager and executives. At the opposite end of the spectrum, the project manager should have the right to go directly into the depths of the organization instead of having to follow the chain of command downward, especially during planning. As an example, see Figure 1–18. The project manager had two weeks to plan and price out a small project. Most of the work was to be accomplished within one section. The project manager was told that all requests for work, even estimating, had to follow the chain of command from the executive down through the section supervisor. By the time the request was received by the section supervisor, twelve of the fourteen days were gone, and only an order-of-magnitude estimate was possible. The lesson to be learned here is:

The chain of command should be used for approving projects, not planning them.

Forcing the project manager to use the chain of command (in either direction) for project planning can result in a great deal of unproductive time and idle time cost.

1.16 DIFFERING VIEWS OF PROJECT MANAGEMENT

Many companies, especially those with project-driven organizations, have differing views of project management. Some people view project management as an excellent means toward achieving objectives, while others view it as a threat. In project-driven organizations, there are three career paths that lead to executive management:

- Through project management
- Through project engineering
- Through line management

In project-driven organizations, the fast-track position is in project management, whereas in a non–project-driven organization, it would be line management. Even though line managers support the project management approach, at the same time they resent the project manager because his promotions and top-level visibility are greater. In one construction company, a department manager was told that he had no chance for promotion above his present department manager position unless he went into project management or project engineering. As the vice president for engineering stated, "In order to get promoted higher up, you must go into project management or project engineering so as to get to know the operation of the total company." A second construction company requires that individuals aspiring to become even a department manager first spend a "tour of duty" as an assistant project manager or proj-ect engineer.

Executives may also dislike project managers because more authority and control must be delegated. However, once executives realize that it is a necessary methodology to do business, project management becomes important, as shown in the following letter:[6]

> In order to sense and react quickly and to insure rapid decision-making, lines of communication should be the shortest possible between all levels of the organization. People with the most knowledge must be available at the source of the problem, and they must have decision-making authority and responsibility. Meaningful data must be available on a timely basis and the organization must be structured to produce this environment.
>
> In the aerospace industry, it is a serious weakness to be tied to fixed organization charts, plans, and procedures. With regard to organization, we successfully married the project concept of management with a central function concept. What we came up with is an organization within an organization—one to ramrod the day-to-day problems; the other to provide support for existing projects and to anticipate the requirements for future projects.
>
> The project system is essential in getting complicated jobs done well and on time, but it solves only part of the management problem. When you have your nose to the project grindstone, you are often not in a position to see much beyond that project. This is where the central functional organization comes in. My experience has been that you need this central organization to give you depth, flexibility, and perspective. Together, the two parts permit you to see both the woods and the trees.

---

6. Letter from J. Donald Rath, vice president of Martin-Marietta Corporation, Denver Division, to J. E. Webb, of NASA, October 18, 1963.

TABLE 1–5. BENEFITS OF PROJECT MANAGEMENT

Past View	Present View
• Project management will require more people and add to the overhead costs.	• Project management allows us to accomplish more work in less time and with less people.
• Profitability may decrease.	• Profitability will increase.
• Project management will increase the amount of scope changes.	• Project management will provide better control of scope changes.
• Project management creates organizational instability and increases conflicts.	• Project management makes the organization more efficient and effective through better organizational behavior principles.
• Project management is really "eye wash" for the customer's benefit.	• Project management will allow us to work more closely with our customers.
• Project management will create problems.	• Project management provides a means for solving problems.
• Only large projects need project management.	• All projects will benefit from project management.
• Project management will increase quality problems.	• Project management increases quality.
• Project management will create power and authority problems.	• Project management will reduce power struggles.
• Project management focuses on suboptimization by looking at only the project.	• Project management allows people to make good company decisions.
• Project management delivers products to a customer.	• Project management delivers solutions.
• The cost of project management may make us noncompetitive.	• Project management will increase our business.

Initiative is essential at all levels of the organization. We try to press the level of decision to the lowest possible rung of the managerial ladder. This type of decision-making provides motivation and permits recognition for the individual and the group at all levels. It stimulates action and breeds dedication.

With this kind of encouragement, the organization can become a live thing—sensitive to problems and able to move in on them with much more speed and understanding than would be normally expected in a large operation. In this way, we can regroup or reorganize easily as situations dictate and can quickly focus on a "crisis." In this industry a company must always be able to reorient itself to meet new objectives. In a more staid, old-line organization, frequent reorientation usually accompanied by a corresponding shift of people's activities, could be most upsetting. However, in the aerospace industry, we must be prepared for change. The entire picture is one of change.

In the past several years, almost all of the differing views of project management have concluded that project management will benefit the firm. Table 1–5 shows how individuals and organizations tend to view project management today.

1.17 CONCURRENT ENGINEERING: A PROJECT MANAGEMENT APPROACH

In the past decade, organizations have become more aware of the fact that America's most formidable weapon is its manufacturing ability, and yet more and more work seems to be departing for Southeast Asia and the Far East. If America as well as other countries are to remain competitive, then survival into the twenty-first century may depend entirely on the manufacturing of a quality product together with a rapid introduction into the marketplace. Today, companies are under tremendous pressure to rapidly introduce new products into the marketplace because existing product life cycles are becoming shorter. As a result, organizations no longer have the luxury of performing work in series.

Concurrent or simultaneous engineering is an attempt to accomplish work in parallel rather than in series. This requires that marketing, R&D, engineering, and production are all actively involved in the early project phases and making plans even before the product design has been finalized. This concept of current engineering will accelerate product development, but it does come with serious and potentially costly risks, the largest one being the cost of rework.

Today, almost everyone is in agreement that the best way of reducing or minimizing the risks is for the organization to perform better planning than they have ever accomplished in the past. Since project management is one of the best methodologies available to foster better planning, it is little wonder that more and more organizations are accepting project management as a way of life.

1.18 TOTAL QUALITY MANAGEMENT (TQM): A PROJECT MANAGEMENT APPROACH

During the past decade, the concept of total quality management (TQM) has revolutionized the operations and manufacturing functions of companies. Previously, we stated that non–project-driven companies (such as those that are primarily manufacturing-oriented) were slow to accept and mature in project management. But today, companies have shown that project management can be used effectively both to support and administer TQM programs.

As an example, the Automotive Division of a multinational corporation had maintained continuous competitive success by being a leader in both quality and customer service. To keep pace with the rapidly changing dynamics of the marketplace, the company found that it had to adopt a TQM program. The factors influencing this need were:

- Progressively higher demand for quality products
- Increasing reliance on vendors and subcontractors to provide higher quality engineering and technical support
- Rapid industrial growth, both domestically and internationally
- Extremely competitive pricing, causing pressure on costs and, in particular, quality costs
- Demand for shorter time cycles for both design and development of products and processes

For the past several years, the company had made improvements in many of these areas. Unfortunately, the results were fragmented and had not kept pace with expectations as shown in Figure 1–19.

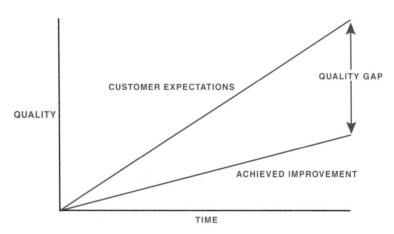

FIGURE 1–19. Present quality pattern.

With the increased complexity of the business, the cost of maintaining a meaningful level of quality had been steadily increasing. To reverse this trend, the company decided to use TQM in order to achieve a major competitive advantage (see Figure 1–20).

The TQM program was established to accomplish the following:

- Improve competitive quality leadership.
- Respond to business objectives and effect results that maximize quality and profitability.
- Improve productivity and cash flow.
- Minimize unproductive demands for engineering changes, rework, and other quality failures.
- Improve management planning and control.

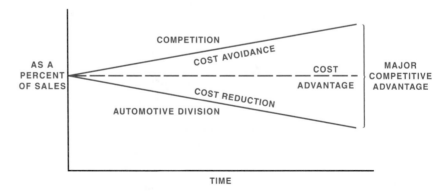

FIGURE 1–20. Quality cost trend.

The company recognized that quality results from all organizational functions and departments performing the quality-related portions of their work on schedule and in a way that is supportive of others in the organization. All departments do play a part in the production of a quality product. From the sensing of customer requirements through product planning, engineering, manufacturing, etc., all organizational functions play an important part in providing customer satisfaction (see Figure 1–21). The Quality Department alone cannot produce quality products. Therefore, the company decided that project management was the only viable alternative for the execution and integration of a TQM system.

Once the commitment to project management was made, the company established an operating quality cost program. Quality costs can be broken down into the following four areas:

- *Prevention costs* are the up-front costs oriented toward the satisfaction of customer's requirements with the first and all succeeding units of product produced without defects. Included in this are such costs as design review, training, quality planning, and related preventive activities.

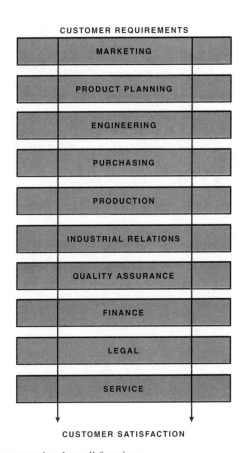

FIGURE 1–21. The system involves all functions.

- *Appraisal costs* are costs associated with evaluation of product or process to ascertain how well all of the requirements of the customer have been met. Included in this are typically such costs as inspection of product, lab tests, vendor control, and in-process testing.
- *Internal failure costs* are those costs associated with the failure of the processes to make products acceptable to the customer, before leaving the control of the organization. Included in this area are scrap, rework, repair, downtime, defect evaluation, evaluation of scrap, and corrective actions.
- *External failure costs* are those costs associated with the determination by the customer that requirements have not been satisfied. Included are customer returns and allowances, evaluation of customer complaints, inspection by the customer, customer visits to resolve quality complaints, and necessary corrective action.

An estimate of current quality costs was made using the results of existing systems, surveys to various parts of the organization, and available financial information. The distribution of these costs to the four areas is shown in Figure 1–22. The total amount of quality costs is approximately equal to the amount of direct labor used in production. Note that the external failure costs are much lower than the internal failure costs. This indicates that most of the failures are discovered before they leave the functional areas or plants.

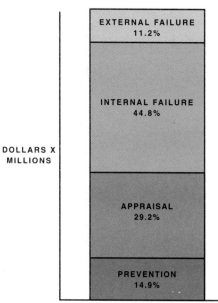

FIGURE 1–22. Total quality cost.

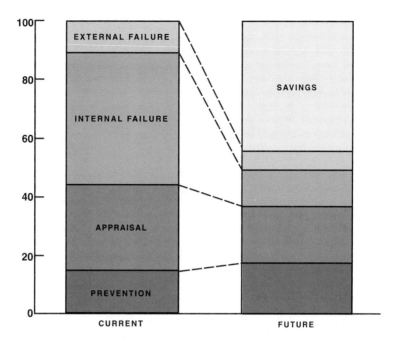

FIGURE 1–23. Total quality cost.

Figure 1–23 shows the expected results of the TQM system on quality costs. Prevention costs are expected to actually rise as more time is spent in prevention activities throughout the organization. As processes improve over the long run, the appraisal costs will go down as the need to inspect quality decreases. The biggest savings will come from the internal failure areas of rework, scrap, reengineering, redo, etc. The additional time spent in up-front design and development will really pay off here. And, finally, the external costs will also come down as processes yield first-time quality on a regular basis. The improvements will continue to impact the company on a long-term basis in both improved quality and lower costs. Also, as project management begins to mature, there should be further decreases in both the cost of maintaining quality and developing products.

PROBLEMS

1–1 In the project environment, cause-and-effect relationships are almost always readily apparent. Good project management will examine the effect in order to better understand the cause and possibly prevent it from occurring again. Below are causes and effects. For each one of the effects, select the possible cause or causes that may have existed to create this situation:

Effects
1. Late completion of activities
2. Cost overruns

3. Substandard performance
4. High turnover in project staff
5. High turnover in functional staff
6. Two functional departments performing the same activities on one project

Causes

a. Top management not recognizing this activity as a project
b. Too many projects going on at one time
c. Impossible schedule commitments
d. No functional input into the planning phase
e. No one person responsible for the total project
f. Poor control of design changes
g. Poor control of customer changes
h. Poor understanding of the project manager's job
i. Wrong person assigned as project manager
j. No integrated planning and control
k. Company resources are overcommitted
l. Unrealistic planning and scheduling
m. No project cost accounting ability
n. Conflicting project priorities
o. Poorly organized project office

(This problem has been adapted from Russell D. Archibald, *Managing High-Technology Programs and Projects,* New York: John Wiley, 1976, p. 10.)

1–2 Because of the individuality of people, there always exists differing views of what management is all about. Below are lists of possible perspectives and a selected group of organizational members. For each individual select the possible ways that this individual might view project management:

Individuals

1. Upper-level manager
2. Project manager
3. Functional manager
4. Project team member
5. Scientist and consultant

Perspectives

a. A threat to established authority
b. A source for future general managers
c. A cause of unwanted change in ongoing procedures
d. A means to an end
e. A significant market for their services
f. A place to build an empire
g. A necessary evil to traditional management
h. An opportunity for growth and advancement
i. A better way to motivate people toward an objective
j. A source of frustration in authority
k. A way of introducing controlled changes
l. An area of research
m. A vehicle for introducing creativity

    n. A means of coordinating functional units

    o. A means of deep satisfaction

    p. A way of life

1–3 Consider an organization that is composed of upper-level managers, middle- and lower-level managers, and laborers. Which of the groups should have first insight that an organizational restructuring toward project management may be necessary?

1–4 How would you defend the statement that a project manager must help himself?

1–5 Will project management work in all companies? If not, identify those companies in which project management may not be applicable and defend your answers.

1–6 In a project organization, do you think that there might be a conflict in opinions over whether the project managers or functional managers contribute to profits?

1–7 What attributes should a project manager have? Can an individual be trained to become a project manager? If a company were changing over to a project management structure, would it be better to promote and train from within or hire from the outside?

1–8 Do you think that functional managers would make good project managers?

1–9 What types of projects might be more appropriate for functional management rather than project management, and vice versa?

1–10 Do you think that there would be a shift in the relative degree of importance of the following terms in a project management environment as opposed to a traditional management environment?

    a. Time management

    b. Communications

    c. Motivation

1–11 Classical management has often been defined as a process in which the manager does not necessarily perform things for himself, but accomplishes objectives through others in a group situation. Does this definition also apply to project management?

1–12 Which of the following are basic characteristics of project management?

    a. Customer problem

    b. Responsibility identification

    c. Systems approach to decision making

    d. Adaptation to a changing environment

    e. Multidisciplinary activity in a finite time duration

    f. Horizontal and vertical organizational relationships

1–13 Project managers are usually dedicated and committed to the project. Who should be "looking over the shoulder" of the project manager to make sure that the work and requests are also in the best interest of the company? Does your answer depend on the priority of the project?

1–14 Is project management designed to transfer power from the line managers to the project manager?

1–15 Explain how career paths and career growth can differ between project-driven and non–project-driven organizations. In each organization, is the career path fastest in project management, project engineering, or line management?

1–16 Explain how the following statement can have a bearing on who is ultimately selected as part of the project team:
"There comes a time in the life cycle of all projects when one must shoot the design engineers and begin production."

1–17 How do you handle a situation where the project manager has become a generalist, but still thinks that he is an expert?

CASE STUDIES

JACKSON INDUSTRIES

"I wish the hell that they had never invented computers," remarked Tom Ford, president of Jackson Industries. "This damn computer has been nothing but a thorn in our side for the past ten years. We're gonna resolve this problem now. I'm through watching our people fight with one another. We must find a solution to this problem."

In 1982, Jackson Industries decided to purchase a mainframe computer, primarily to handle the large, repetitive tasks found in the accounting and finance functions of the organization. It was only fitting, therefore, that control of the computer came under the director of finance, Al Moody. For two years, operations went smoothly. In 1984, the computer department was reorganized in three sections: scientific computer programming, business computer programming, and systems programming. The reorganization was necessary because the computer department had grown into the fifth largest department, employing some thirty people, and was experiencing some severe problems working with other departments.

After the reorganization, Ralph Gregg, the computer department manager, made the following remarks in a memo distributed to all personnel:

The Computer Department has found it increasingly difficult to work with engineering and operations functional departments, which continue to permit their personnel to write and document their own computer programs. In order to maintain some degree of consistency, the Computer Department will now assume the responsibility for writing all computer programs. All requests should be directed to the department manager. My people are under explicit instructions that they are to provide absolutely no assistance to any functional personnel attempting to write their own programs without authorization from me. Company directives in this regard will be forthcoming.

The memo caused concern among the functional departments. If engineering wanted a computer program written, they would now have to submit a formal request and then have the person requesting the program spend a great deal of time explaining the problem to the scientific programmer assigned to this effort. The department managers were reluctant to have their people "waste time" in training the scientific programmers to be engineers. The computer department manager countered this argument by stating that once the programmer was fully familiar with the engineering problem, then the engineer's time could be spent more fruitfully on other activities until the computer program was ready for implementation.

This same problem generated more concern by department managers when they were involved in computer projects that required integration among several departments. Although Jackson Industries operated on a traditional structure, the new directive implied that the computer department would be responsible for managing all projects involving computer programming even if they crossed into other departments. Many people looked on this as a "baby" project management structure within the traditional organization.

In June 1992, Al Moody and Ralph Gregg met to discuss the deterioration of working relationships between the computer department and other organizations.

Al Moody: "I'm getting complaints from the engineering and operations departments that they can't get any priorities established on the work to be done in your group. What can we do about it?"

Ralph Gregg: "I set the priorities as I see fit, for what's best for the company. Those guys in the engineering and operations have absolutely no idea how long it takes to write, debug, and document a computer program. Then they keep feeding me this crap about how their projects will slip if this computer program isn't ready on time. I've told them what problems I have, and yet they still refuse to let me participate in the planning phase of their activities."

Al Moody: "Well, you may have a valid gripe there. I'm more concerned about this closed shop you've developed for your department. You've built a little empire down there and it looks like your people are unionized where the rest of us are not. Furthermore, I've noticed that your people have their own informal organization and tend to avoid socializing with the other employees. We're supposed to be one big, happy family, you know. Can't you do something about that?"

Ralph Gregg: "The problem belongs to you and Tom Ford. For the last three years, the average salary increase for the entire company has been 7.5 percent and our department has averaged a mere 5 percent because you people upstairs do not feel as though we contribute anything to company profits. My scientific programmers feel that they're doing engineering work and that they're making the same contribution to profits as is the engineer. Therefore, they should be on the engineering pay structure and receive an 8 percent salary increase."

Al Moody: "You could have given your scientific programmers more money. You had a budget for salary increases, the same as everyone else."

Ralph Gregg: "Sure I did. But my budget was less than everyone else's. I could have given the scientific people 7 percent and everyone else 3 percent. That would be an easy way to tell people that we think they should look for another job. My people do good work and do, in fact, contribute to profits. If Tom Ford doesn't change his impression of us, then I expect to lose some of my key people. Maybe you should tell him that."

Al Moody: "Between you and me, all of your comments are correct. I agree with your concerns. But my hands are tied, as you know.

"We are contemplating the installation of a management information system for all departments and, especially, for executive decision making. Tom is contemplating creating a new position, Director of Information Services. This would move the computer out of a department under finance and up to the directorate level. I'm sure this would have an impact on yearly salary increases for your people.

"The problem that we're facing involves the managing of projects under the new directorate. It looks like we'll have to create a project management organization just for this new directorate. Tom likes the traditional structure and wants to leave all other directorates intact. We know that this new directorate will have to integrate the new computer projects across multiple departments and divisions. Once we solve the organizational structure problem, we'll begin looking at implementation. Got any good ideas about the organizational structure?"

Ralph Gregg: "You bet I do. Make me director and I'll see that the work gets done."

KOMBS ENGINEERING

In June 1993, Kombs Engineering had grown to a company with $25 million in sales. The business base consisted of two contracts with the U.S. Department of Energy (DOE), one for $15 million and one for $8 million. The remaining $2 million consisted of a variety of smaller jobs for $15,000–$50,000 each.

The larger contract with DOE was a five-year contract for $15 million per year. The contract was awarded in 1988 and was up for renewal in 1993. DOE had made it clear that, although they were very pleased with the technical performance of Kombs, the follow-on contract must go through competitive bidding by law. Marketing intelligence indicated that DOE intended to spend $10 million per year for five years on the follow-on contract with a tentative award date of October 1993.

On June 21, 1993, the solicitation for proposal was received at Kombs. The technical requirements of the proposal request were not considered to be a problem for Kombs. There was no question in anyone's mind that on technical merit alone, Kombs would win the contract. The more serious problem was that DOE required a separate section in the proposal on how Kombs would manage the $10 million/year project as well as a complete description of how the project management system at Kombs functioned.

When Kombs won the original bid in 1988, there was no project management requirement. All projects at Kombs were accomplished through the traditional organizational structure. Line managers acted as project leaders.

In July 1993, Kombs hired a consultant to train the entire organization in project management. The consultant also worked closely with the proposal team in responding to the DOE project management requirements. The proposal was submitted to DOE during the second week of August. In September 1993, DOE provided Kombs with a list of questions concerning its proposal. More than 95 percent of the questions involved project management. Kombs responded to all questions.

In October 1993, Kombs received notification that they would not be granted the contract. During a post-award conference, DOE stated that they had no "faith" in the Kombs project management system. Kombs Engineering is no longer in business.

    a.   What was the reason for the loss of the contract?

    b.   Could it have been averted?

    c.   Does it seem realistic that proposal evaluation committees could consider project management expertise to be as important as technical ability?

WILLIAMS MACHINE TOOL COMPANY

For seventy-five years, the Williams Machine Tool Company had provided quality products to its clients, becoming the third largest U.S.-based machine tool company by 1980. The company was highly profitable and had an extremely low employee turnover rate. Pay and benefits were excellent.

Between 1970 and 1980, the company's profits soared to record levels. The company's success was due to one product line of standard manufacturing machine tools. Williams spent most of its time and effort looking for ways to improve its bread-and-butter product line rather than to develop new products. The product line was so successful that companies were willing to modify their production lines around these machine tools rather than asking Williams for major modifications to the machine tools.

By 1980, Williams Company was extremely complacent, expecting this phenomenal success with one product line to continue for twenty to twenty-five more years. The recession of 1979–1983 forced management to realign their thinking. Cutbacks in production had decreased the demand for the standard machine tools. More and more customers were asking for either major modifications to the standard machine tools or a completely new product design.

The marketplace was changing and senior management recognized that a new strategic focus was necessary. However, lower-level management and the work force, especially engineering, were strongly resisting a change. The employees, many of them with over twenty years of employment at Williams Company, refused to recognize the need for this change in the belief that the glory days of yore would return at the end of the recession.

By 1985, the recession had been over for at least two years yet Williams Company had no new product lines. Revenue was down, sales for the standard product (with and without modifications) were decreasing, and the employees were still resisting change. Layoffs were imminent.

In 1986, the company was sold to Crock Engineering. Crock had an experienced machine tool division of its own and understood the machine tool business. Williams Company was allowed to operate as a separate entity from 1985 to 1986. By 1986, red ink had appeared on the Williams Company balance sheet. Crock replaced all of the Williams senior managers with its own personnel. Crock then announced to all employees that Williams would become a specialty machine tool manufacturer and that the "good old days" would never return. Customer demand for specialty products had increased threefold in just the last twelve months alone. Crock made it clear that employees who would not support this new direction would be replaced.

The new senior management at Williams Company recognized that eighty-five years of traditional management had come to an end for a company now committed to specialty products. The company culture was about to change, spearheaded by project management, concurrent engineering, and total quality management.

Senior management's commitment to product management was apparent by the time and money spent in educating the employees. Unfortunately, the seasoned twenty-year-plus veterans still would not support the new culture. Recognizing the problems, management provided continuous and visible support for project management in addition to hiring a project management consultant to work with the people. The consultant worked with Williams from 1986 to 1991.

From 1986 to 1991, the Williams Division of Crock Engineering experienced losses in twenty-four consecutive quarters. The quarter ending March 31, 1992, was the first profitable quarter in over six years. Much of the credit was given to the performance and maturity of the project management system. In May 1992, the Williams Division was sold. More than 80 percent of the employees lost their jobs when the company was relocated over 1,500 miles away.

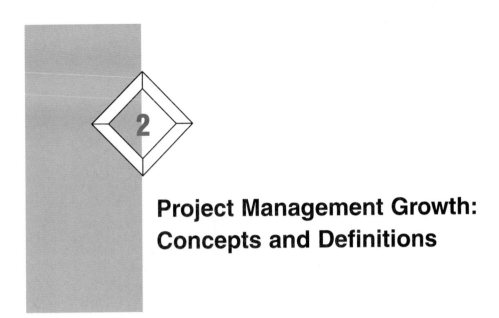

Project Management Growth: Concepts and Definitions

2.0 INTRODUCTION

The growth and acceptance of project management has changed significantly over the past forty years, and these changes are expected to continue well into the twenty-first century, especially in the area of multinational project management. It is interesting to trace the evolution and growth of project management from the early days of systems management to what some people call "modern project management."

The growth of project management can be traced through topics such as roles and responsibilities, organizational structures, delegation of authority and decision-making, and especially corporate profitability. Twenty years ago, companies had the choice of whether or not to accept the project management approach. Today, several companies foolishly think that they still have the choice. Nothing could be further from the truth. The survival of the firm may very well rest upon how well project management is implemented, and how quickly.

2.1 GENERAL SYSTEMS MANAGEMENT

Organizational theory and management philosophies have undergone a dramatic change in recent years with the emergence of the project management approach to management. Because project management is an outgrowth of systems management, it is only fitting that the underlying principles of general systems theory be described. Simply stated, general systems theory can be classified as a management approach that attempts to integrate and unify scientific information across many fields of knowledge. Systems theory attempts to solve problems by looking at the total picture, rather than through an analysis of the individual components.

General systems theory has been in existence for more than four decades. Unfortunately, as is often the case with new theory development, the practitioners require years of study and analysis before implementation was deemed feasible and finally accepted as a way of life. General systems theory is still being taught in graduate programs. Today, project management is viewed as applied systems management.

In 1951, Ludwig von Bertalanffy, a biologist, described so-called open systems using anatomy nomenclature. The body's muscles, skeleton, circulatory system, and so on, were all described as subsystems of the total system (the human being). Dr. von Bertalanffy's contribution was important in that he identified how specialists in each subsystem could be integrated so as to get a better understanding of the interrelationships, thereby contributing to the overall knowledge of the operations of the system. Thus, the foundation was laid for the evolution and outgrowth of project management.

In 1956, Kenneth Boulding identified the communications problems that can occur during systems integration. Professor Boulding was concerned with the fact that subsystem specialists (i.e., physicists, economists, chemists, sociologists, etc.) have their own languages. He advocated that, in order for successful integration to take place, all subsystem specialists must speak a common language, such as mathematics. Today we use the PMBOK™ to satisfy this need for project management.

General systems theory implies the creation of a management technique that is able to cut across many organizational disciplines—finance, manufacturing, engineering, marketing, and so on—while still carrying out the functions of management. This technique has come to be called systems management, project management, or matrix management (the terms are used interchangeably).

2.2 PROJECT MANAGEMENT: 1960–1985

The growth of project management has come about more through necessity than through desire. Its slow growth can be attributed mainly to lack of acceptance of the new management techniques necessary for its successful implementation. An inherent fear of the unknown acted as a deterrent for those managers wishing to change over.

Between the middle and late 1960s, more and more executives began searching for new management techniques and organizational structures that could be quickly adapted to a changing environment. The table below and Figure 2–1 identify two major variables that executives consider with regard to organizational restructuring.

Type of Industry	Tasks	Environment
A	Simple	Dynamic
B	Simple	Static
C	Complex	Dynamic
D	Complex	Static

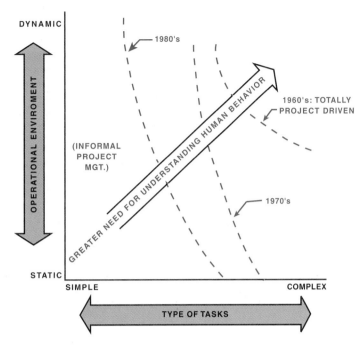

FIGURE 2–1. Matrix implementation scheme.

Almost all type C and most type D industries have project management–related structures. The key variable appears to be task complexity. Companies that have complex tasks and that also operate in a dynamic environment find project management mandatory. Such industries would include aerospace, defense, construction, high-technology engineering, computers, and electronic instrumentation.

Other than aerospace, defense, and construction, the majority of the companies in the 1960s maintained an informal method for managing projects. In informal project management, just as the words imply, the projects were handled on an informal basis whereby the authority of the project manager was minimized. Most projects were handled by functional managers and stayed in one or two functional lines, and formal communications were either unnecessary or handled informally because of the good working relationships between line managers. Many organizations today, such as low-technology manufacturing, have line managers who have been working side by side for ten or more years. In such situations, informal project management may be effective on capital equipment or facility development projects.

By 1970 and again during the early 1980s, more and more companies departed from informal project management and restructured to formalize the project management process, mainly because the size and complexity of their activities had grown to a point where they were unmanageable within the current structure. Figure 2–2 shows what happened to one such construction company.

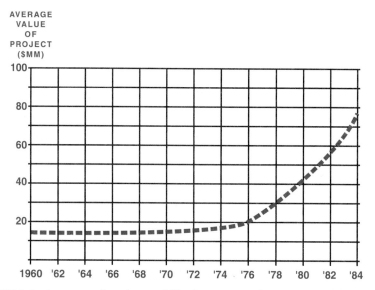

FIGURE 2–2. Average project size capability for a construction company, 1960–1984.

The following five questions normally give some insight as to whether formal project management is necessary:

- Are the jobs complex?
- Are there dynamic environmental considerations?
- Are the constraints tight?
- Are there several activities to be integrated?
- Are there several functional boundaries to be crossed?

If any of these questions are answered yes, then some form of formalized project management may be necessary. It is possible for formalized project management to exist in only one functional department or division, such as for R&D or perhaps just for certain types of projects. Some companies have successfully implemented both formal and informal project management concurrently, but these companies are few and far between. Today we realize that the last two questions may be the most important.

The moral here is that not all industries need project management, and executives must determine whether there is an actual need before making a commitment. Several industries with simple tasks, whether in a static or a dynamic environment, do not need project management. Manufacturing industries with slowly changing technology do not need project management, unless of course they have a requirement for several special projects, such as capital equipment activities, that could interrupt the normal flow of work in the routine manufacturing operations. The slow growth rate and acceptance of project management were related to the fact that the limitations of project management were readily apparent, yet the advantages were not completely recognizable. Project management requires organizational restructuring. The question, of course, is "How much restructuring?" Executives have avoided the subject of project management for fear that "revolutionary" changes must be made in the organization. As will be seen in Chapter 3, project management can be achieved with little departure from the existing traditional structure.

Project management restructuring permitted companies to:

- Accomplish tasks that could not be effectively handled by the traditional structure
- Accomplish onetime activities with minimum disruption of routine business

The second item implies that project management is a "temporary" management structure and, therefore, causes minimum organizational disruption. The major problems identified by those managers who endeavored to adapt to the new system all resolved about conflicts in authority and resources.

Three major problems were identified by Killian:[1]

- Project priorities and competition for talent may interrupt the stability of the organization and interfere with its long-range interests by upsetting the normal business of the functional organization.
- Long-range planning may suffer as the company gets more involved in meeting schedules and fulfilling the requirements of temporary projects.
- Shifting people from project to project may disrupt the training of new employees and specialists. This may hinder their growth and development within their fields of specialization.

Another major concern was the fact that project management required upper-level managers to relinquish some of their authority through delegation to the middle managers. In several situations, middle managers soon occupied the power positions, even more so than upper-level managers.

Despite these limitations, there were several driving forces behind the project management approach. According to John Kenneth Galbraith, these forces stem from "the imperatives of technology." The six imperatives are the following:[2]

- The time span between project initiation and completion appears to be increasing.
- The capital committed to the project prior to the use of the end item appears to be increasing.

---

1. William P. Killian, "Project Management—Future Organizational Concepts," *Marquette Business Review,* Vol. 2, 1971, pp. 90–107.

2. Excerpt from John Kenneth Galbraith, *The New Industrial State,* 3rd ed. Copyright © 1967, 1971, 1978, by John Kenneth Galbraith. Reprinted by permission of Houghton Mifflin Company. All rights reserved.

- As technology increases, the commitment of time and money appears to become inflexible.
- Technology requires more and more specialized manpower.
- The inevitable counterpart of specialization is organization.
- The above five "imperatives" identify the necessity for more effective planning, scheduling, and control.

As the driving forces overtook the restraining forces, project management began to mature. Executives began to realize that the approach was in the best interest of the company. Project management, if properly implemented, can make it easier for executives to overcome such internal and external obstacles as:

- Unstable economy
- Shortages
- Soaring costs
- Increased complexity
- Heightened competition
- Technological changes
- Societal concerns
- Consumerism
- Ecology
- Quality of work

Project management may not eliminate these problems, but may make it easier for the company to adapt to a changing environment.

If these obstacles are not controlled, the results can be:

- Decreased profits
- Increased manpower needs
- Cost overruns, schedule delays, and penalty payments occurring earlier and earlier
- An inability to cope with new technology
- R&D results too late to benefit existing product lines
- New products introduced into the marketplace too late
- Temptation to make hasty decisions that prove to be costly
- Management insisting on earlier and greater return on investment
- Greater difficulty in establishing on-target objectives in real time
- Problems in relating cost to technical performance and scheduling during the execution of the project

Project management became a necessity for many companies. They began to expand into multiple product lines, many of which were often dissimilar, and organizational complexities grew almost without bound. This growth can be attributed to:

- Technology increasing at an astounding rate
- More money invested in R&D

- More information available
- Shortening of project life cycles

To satisfy the requirements imposed by the above four factors, management was "forced" into organizational restructuring; the traditional organizational form that had survived for so many decades was found to be inadequate for integrating activities across functional "empires."

By 1970, the environment began to change rapidly. Companies such as aerospace, defense, and construction pioneered in implementing project management, and other industries soon followed, some with great reluctance. NASA and the Department of Defense "forced" subcontractors into accepting project management. The 1970s also brought much more published data on project management. As an example:[3]

> Project teams and task forces will become more common in tackling complexity. There will be more of what some people call temporary management systems as project management systems where the men [and women] who are needed to contribute to the solution meet, make their contribution, and perhaps never become a permanent member of any fixed or permanent management group.

The definition simply states that the purpose of project management is to put together the best possible team to achieve the objective, and, at termination, the team is disbanded. Nowhere in the definition do we see the authority of the project manager or his rank, title, or salary.

Because current organizational structures are unable to accommodate the wide variety of interrelated tasks necessary for successful project completion, the need for project management has become apparent. It is usually first identified by those lower-level and middle managers who find it impossible to control their resources effectively for the diverse activities within their line organization. Quite often middle managers feel the impact of a changing environment more than upper-level executives.

Once the need for change is identified, middle management must convince upper-level management that such a change is actually warranted. If top-level executives cannot recognize the problems with resource control, then project management will not be adopted, at least formally. Informal acceptance, however, is another story.

In 1978, the author received a request from an automobile equipment manufacturer who was considering formal project management. The author was permitted to speak with several middle managers. The following comments were made:

- "Here at ABC Company (a division of XYZ Corporation), we have informal project management. By this, I mean that work flows the same as it would in formal project management except that the authority, responsibility, and accountability are implied rather than rigidly defined. We

---

3. Reprinted from the October 17, 1970 issue of *BusinessWeek* by special permission, © 1970 by McGraw-Hill, Inc., New York, New York 10020. All rights reserved.

have been very successful with this structure, especially when you consider that the components we sell cost 30 percent more than our competitors, and that our growth rate has been in excess of 12 percent each year for the past six years. The secret of our success has been our quality and our ability to meet schedule dates."

- "Our informal structure works well because our department managers do not hide problems. They aren't afraid to go into another department manager's office and talk about the problems they're having controlling resources. Our success is based upon the fact that all of our department managers do this. What's going to happen if we hire just one or two people who won't go along with this approach? Will we be forced to go to formalized project management?"
- "This division is a steppingstone to greatness in our corporation. It seems that all of the middle managers who come to this division get promoted either within the division, to higher management positions in other divisions, or to a higher position at corporate headquarters."

At this point, the author conducted two three-day seminars on engineering project management for seventy-five of the lower-, middle-, and upper-level managers. The seminar participants were asked whether they wanted to adopt formal project management. The following concerns were raised by the participants:

- "Will I have more or less power and/or authority?"
- "How will my salary be affected?"
- "Why should I permit a project manager to share the resources in my empire?"
- "Will I get top management visibility?"

Even with these concerns, the majority of the attendees felt that formalized project management would alleviate a lot of their present problems.

Although the middle levels of the organization, where resources are actually controlled on a day-to-day basis, felt positive about project management, convincing the top levels of management was another story. If you were the chief executive officer of this division, earning a salary in six figures, and looking at a growth rate of 12 percent per year for the last five years, would you "rock the boat" simply because your middle managers want project management?

This example highlights three major points:

- The final decision for the implementation of project management does (and will always) rest with executive management.
- Executives must be willing to listen when middle management identifies a crisis in controlling resources. This is where the need for project management should first appear.
- Executives are paid to look out for the long-range interest of the corporation and should not be swayed by near-term growth rate or profitability.

Today, ABC Company is still doing business the way it was done in the past—with informal project management. The company is a classic example of how informal project management can be made to work successfully. The author agrees with the company executives that, in this case, formal project management is not necessary.

William C. Goggin, board chairman and chief executive officer of Dow Corning, describes a situation in his corporation that was quite different from the one at ABC:[4]

> Although Dow Corning was a healthy corporation in 1967, it showed difficulties that troubled many of us in top management. These symptoms were, and still are, common ones in U.S. business and have been described countless times in reports, audits, articles and speeches. Our symptoms took such forms as:
>
> - Executives did not have adequate financial information and control of their operations. Marketing managers, for example, did not know how much it cost to produce a product. Prices and margins were set by division managers.
> - Cumbersome communications channels existed between key functions, especially manufacturing and marketing.
> - In the face of stiffening competition, the corporation remained too internalized in its thinking and organizational structure. It was insufficiently oriented to the outside world.
> - Lack of communications between divisions not only created the antithesis of a corporate team effort but also was wasteful of a precious resource—people.
> - Long range corporate planning was sporadic and superficial; this was leading to overstaffing, duplicated effort and inefficiency.

Once the need for project management has been defined, the next logical question is, "How long a conversion period will be necessary before a company can operate in a project management environment?" To answer this question we must first look at Figure 2–3. Technology, as expected, has the fastest rate of change, and the overall environment of a business must adapt to rapidly changing technology.

In an ideal situation, the organizational structure of a company would immediately adapt to the changing environment. In a real situation, this will not be a smooth transition but more like the erratic line shown in Figure 2–3. This erratic line is a trademark or characteristic of the traditional structure. Project management structures, however, can, and often do, adapt to a rapidly changing environment with a relatively smooth transition.

Even though an executive can change the organizational structure with the stroke of a pen, people are responsible for its implementation. However, it can be

---

4. William C. Goggin, "How the Multidimensional Structure Works at Dow Corning," *Harvard Business Review,* January–February 1974, p. 54. Copyright © 1973 by the President and Fellows of Harvard College; All rights reserved.

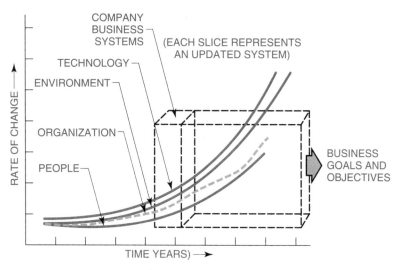

FIGURE 2–3. Systems in a changing environment.

seen in Figure 2–3 that people have the slowest rate of change. Edicts, documents signed by executives, and training programs will not convince employees that a new organizational form will work. Employees will be convinced only after they see the new system in action, and this takes time.

As a ground rule, it often takes two to three years to convert from a traditional structure to a project management structure. The major reason for this is that in a traditional structure the line employee has one, and only one, boss; in a project management structure the employee reports vertically to his line manager and horizontally to every project manager to whose activities he is assigned, either temporarily or full-time. This situation often leads to a cultural shock condition. Employees will perform in a new system because they are directed to do so but will not have confidence in it or become dedicated until they have been involved in several different projects and believe that they can effectively report to more than one boss.

When an employee is told that he will be working horizontally as well as vertically, his first concern is his take-home pay. Employees always question whether they can be evaluated fairly if they report to several managers during the same time period. One of the major reasons why project management fails is that top-level executives neglect to consider that any organizational change must be explained in terms of the wage and salary administration program.[5] This must occur *before* change is made. If change comes first, and employees are not con-

---

5. The mechanisms for employee evaluation in a project environment are discussed further in Section 8.1.

vinced that they can be evaluated correctly, they may very likely try to sabotage the whole effort. From then on, it will probably be a difficult, if not impossible, task to rectify the situation. However, once the organizational employees accept project management and the procedure of reporting in two directions, the company can effectively and efficiently convert from one project management organizational form to another. After all, weren't most of us educated throughout our childhood on how to report to two bosses—a mother and a father?

Not all companies need two to three years to convert to project management. The ABC Company described earlier would probably have very little trouble in converting because informal project management is well accepted. In the early 1960s, TRW was forced to convert to a project management structure almost overnight. The company was highly successful in this, mainly because of the loyalty and dedication of the employees. The TRW employees were willing to give the system a chance. Any organizational structure, no matter how bad, will work if the employees are willing to make it work. Yet other companies can spend three to five years trying to implement change and drastically fail. The literature describes many cases where project management has failed because:

- There was no need for project management.
- Employees were not informed about how project management should work.
- Executives did not select the appropriate projects or project managers for the first few projects.
- There was no attempt to explain the effect of the project management organizational form on the wage and salary administration program.
- Employees were not convinced that executives were in total support of the change.

Some companies (and executives) are forced into project management before they realize what has happened, and if recognition at the top levels of management does not occur soon afterward, chaos seems inevitable. As an example, consider a highly traditional company that purchased a computer a few years ago. The company has five divisions: engineering, finance, manufacturing, marketing, and personnel. Not knowing where to put the computer, the chief executive officer created an electronic data processing (EDP) department and placed it under finance and accounting. The executive's rationale was that since the purpose for buying the computer was to eliminate repetitive tasks and the majority of these were in accounting and finance, that was where EDP belonged. The vice president for accounting and finance might not be qualified to manage the EDP department, but that seemed beside the point.

The EDP department has a staff of scientific and business computer programmers and systems analysts. The scientific programmers spend almost all their time working in the engineering division writing engineering programs; they must learn engineering in order to do this. In this company, the engineer does not consider himself to be a computer programmer, but does the computer programmer consider himself to be an engineer?

The company's policy is that merit and cost-of-living increases are given out in July of each year. This year the average salary increase will be 7 percent. However, the president wants the increase given according to merit, and not as a flat rate across the board. After long hours of deliberation, it was decided that engineering, manufacturing, and marketing would receive 8 percent raises, and finance and personnel 5.5 percent.

After announcement of the salary increases, the scientific programmers began to complain because they felt they were doing engineering-type work and should therefore be paid according to the engineering pay scale. Management tried to resolve this problem by giving each division its own computer and personnel. However, this resulted in duplication of effort and inefficient use of personnel.

With the rapid advancements in computer technology of recent years, management realized the need for timely access to information for executive decision making. In a rather bold move, executives created a new division called management information systems (MIS). The MIS division now has full control of all computer operations and gives the EDP personnel the opportunity to show that they actually contribute to corporate profits.

Elevating the computer to the top levels of the organization was a significant step toward project management. Unfortunately, many executives did not fully realize what had happened. Because of the need for a rapid information retrieval system that can integrate data from a variety of line organizations, the MIS personnel soon found that they were working horizontally, not vertically. Today, MIS packages cut across every division of the company. Thus, the project management concept for handling a horizontal flow of work emerged.

With the emergence of data processing project management, executives were forced to find immediate answers to such questions as:

- Can we have project management strictly for data processing projects?
- Should the project manager be the programmer or the user?
- How much authority should be delegated to the project manager, and will this delegated authority cause a shift in the organizational equilibrium?

The answers to these questions have not been and still are not easy to solve. Today, IBM provides its customers with the opportunity to hire IBM as the in-house data processing project management team. This partially eliminates the necessity for establishing internal project management relationships that could easily become permanent.

In TRW Nelson Division,[6] data processing project management began with MIS personnel acting as the project leaders. However, after two years, the company felt that the people best qualified to be the project leaders were the techni-

---

6. The TRW Nelson Division case study is found in the workbook that accompanies this text.

cal experts (i.e., users). Therefore, the MIS personnel now act as team members and resource personnel rather than as the project managers.

There are many different types of projects. Each of these projects can have its own organizational form and can operate concurrently with other active projects. This diversity of projects has contributed to the implementation of full project management in several industries.

J. Robert Fluor, chairman, chief executive officer, and president of the Fluor Corporation, commented on twenty years of operations in a project environment:[7]

> The need for flexibility has become apparent since no two projects are ever alike from a project management point of view. There are always differences in technology; in the geographical locations; in the client approach; in the contract terms and conditions; in the schedule; in the financial approach to the project; and in a broad range of international factors, all of which require a different and flexible approach to managing each project. We found the task force concept, with maximum authority and accountability resting with the project manager, to be the most effective means of realizing project objectives. And while basic project management principles do exist at Fluor, there is no single standard project organization or project procedure yet devised that can be rigidly applied to more than one project.
>
> Today, our company and others and their project managers are being challenged as never before to achieve what earlier would have been classified as "unachievable" project objectives. Major projects often involve the resources of a large number of organizations located on different continents. The efforts of each must be directed and coordinated toward a common set of project objectives of quality performance, cost and time of completion as well as many other considerations.

As project management developed, some essential factors in its successful implementation were recognized. The major factor was the role of the project manager, which became the focal point of integrative responsibility. The need for integrative responsibility was first identified in research and development activities:[8]

> Recently, R&D technology has broken down the boundaries that used to exist between industries. Once-stable markets and distribution channels are now in a state of flux. The industrial environment is turbulent and increasingly hard to predict. Many complex facts about markets, production methods, costs and scientific potentials are related to investment decisions.
>
> All of these factors have combined to produce a king-size managerial headache. There are just too many crucial decisions to have them all processed

---

7. J. Robert Fluor, "Development of Project Managers," keynote address to the Project Management Institute, Ninth International Seminar Symposium, Chicago, Illinois, October 24, 1977.

8. Paul R. Lawrence and Jay W. Lorsch, "New Management Job: The Integrator," *Harvard Business Review,* November–December 1967, p. 142. Copyright © 1967 by the President and Fellows of Harvard College. All rights reserved.

and resolved through regular line hierarchy at the top of the organization. They must be integrated in some other way.

Providing the project manager with integrative responsibility resulted in:

- Total accountability assumed by a single person
- Project rather than functional dedication
- A requirement for coordination across functional interfaces
- Proper utilization of integrated planning and control

Without project management, these four elements have to be accomplished by executives, and it is very questionable whether these activities should be part of an executive's job description. An executive in a Fortune 500 corporation stated that he was spending seventy hours a week acting as an executive and as a project manager, and he did not feel that he was performing either job to the best of his abilities. During a presentation to the CEO staff, the executive stated what he expected of the organization after project management implementation:

- Push decision making down in the organization
- Eliminate the need for committee solutions
- Trust the decisions of peers

Those executives who chose to accept project management soon found the advantages of the new technique:

- Easy adaptation to an ever-changing environment
- Ability to handle a multidisciplinary activity within a specified period of time
- Horizontal as well as vertical work flow
- Better orientation toward customer problems
- Easier identification of activity responsibilities
- A multidisciplinary decision-making process
- Innovation in organizational design

2.3 PROJECT MANAGEMENT: 1985–2000

By the 1990s, companies had begun to realize that implementing project management was a necessity, not a choice. The question was not how to implement project management, but how fast could it be done?

Table 2–1 shows the typical life-cycle phases that an organization goes through to implement project management. In the first phase, the Embryonic Phase, the organization recognizes the apparent need for project management.

TABLE 2-1. LIFE-CYCLE PHASES FOR PROJECT MANAGEMENT MATURITY

Embryonic Stage	Executive Management Acceptance Stage	Line Management Acceptance Stage	Growth Stage	Maturity Stage
• Recognize need	• Visible executive support	• Line management support	• Use of life-cycle phases	• Development of a management cost/schedule control system
• Recognize benefits	• Executive understanding of project management	• Line management commitment	• Development of a project management methodology	• Integrating cost and schedule control
• Recognize applications	• Project sponsorship	• Line management education	• Commitment to planning	• Developing an educational program to enhance project management skills
• Recognize what must be done	• Willingness to change way of doing business	• Willingness to release employees for project management training	• Minimization of "creeping scope"	
			• Selection of a project tracking system	

This recognition normally takes place at the lower and middle levels of management where the project activities actually take place. The executives are then informed of the need and assess the situation. It is the exception, rather than the norm, for the need for project management to be first identified at the executive levels of management.

There are six driving forces that lead executives to the recognition of the need for project management:

- Capital projects
- Customer expectations
- Competitiveness
- Executive understanding
- New project development
- Efficiency and effectiveness

Manufacturing companies are driven to project management either because of large capital projects or because of a multitude of simultaneous projects. Executives soon realize the impact on cash flow and that slippages in the schedule could end up idling workers.

Companies that sell products or services to their clients and that also wish to be responsible for installation activities must have good project management practices. These companies are usually non–project-driven but function as though they were project-driven. These companies now sell solutions to their customers rather than products. It is almost impossible to sell complete solutions to customers without having superior project management practices because what you are actually selling is your project management expertise.

There are two situations where competitiveness becomes the driving force: internal projects and external (outside customer) projects. Internally, companies get into trouble when the organization realizes that much of the work can be outsourced for less than it would cost to perform the work themselves. Externally, companies get into trouble when they are no longer competitive on price or quality, or simply cannot increase their market share.

Executive understanding is the driving force in those organizations that have a rigid traditional structure that performs routine, repetitive activities. These organizations are quite resistant to change unless driven by the executives. This driving force can exist in conjunction with any of the other driving forces.

New product development is the driving force for those organizations that are heavily invested in R&D activities. Given the fact that only a small percentage of R&D projects ever make it into commercialization where the R&D costs can be recovered, project management becomes a necessity. Project management can also be used as an early warning system that a project should be cancelled.

Efficiency and effectiveness, as a driving force, can exist in conjunction with any other driving forces. Efficiency and effectiveness take on paramount importance for small companies that are enduring growing pains. Project management can be used to help such companies remain competitive during periods of growth and to assist in determining capacity constraints.

Because of the interrelatedness of these driving forces, some people contend that the only true driving force is survival. This is illustrated in Figure 2–4. When the company recognizes that survival of the firm is at stake, the implementation of project management becomes easier.

The speed by which companies reach some degree of maturity in project management is most often based upon how important they perceive the driving

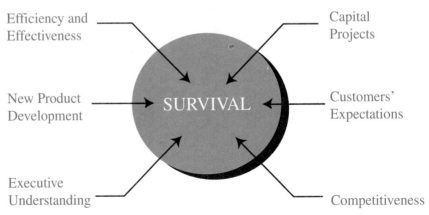

FIGURE 2–4. The components of survival. *Source:* Reprinted from H. Kerzner, *In Search of Excellence in Project Management.* New York: Wiley, 1998, p. 51.

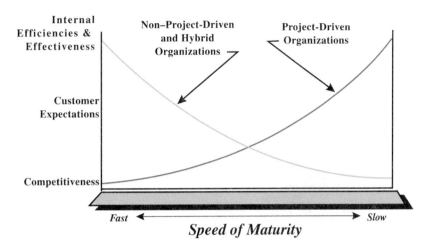

FIGURE 2–5. The speed of maturity.

forces to be. This is illustrated generically in Figure 2–5. Non–project-driven and hybrid organizations move quickly to maturity if increased internal efficiencies and effectiveness are needed. Competitiveness is the slowest path because these types of organizations do not recognize project management as affecting their competitive position directly. For project-driven organizations, the path is reversed. Competitiveness is the name of the game and the vehicle used is project management.

Once the organization perceives the need for project management, the organization enters the second life-cycle phase of Table 2–1, Executive Support. Project management cannot be implemented rapidly in the near term without executive support. Furthermore, the support must be visible to all.

The third life-cycle phase is Line Management Support. It is highly unlikely that any line manager would actively support the implementation of project management without first recognizing the same support coming from above. Even minimal line management support will still cause project management to struggle.

The fourth life-cycle phase is the Growth Phase where the organization becomes committed to the development of the corporate tools for project management. This includes the project management methodology for planning, scheduling, and controlling, as well as selection of the appropriate supporting software. Portions of this phase can begin during earlier phases.

The fifth life-cycle phase is Maturity. In this phase, the organization begins using the tools developed in the previous phase. Here, the organization must be totally dedicated to project management. The organization must develop a reasonable project management curriculum to provide the appropriate training and education in support of the tools, as well as the expected organizational behavior.

By the 1990s, companies finally began to recognize the benefits of project management, and the fact that these benefits could be realized. Table 2–2 shows

TABLE 2–2. BENEFITS OF PROJECT MANAGEMENT

Past View	Present View
• Project management will require more people and add to the overhead costs.	• Project management allows us to accomplish more work in less time and with less people.
• Profitability may decrease.	• Profitability will increase.
• Project management will increase the amount of scope changes.	• Project management will provide better control of scope changes.
• Project management creates organizational instability and increases conflicts.	• Project management makes the organization more efficient and effective through better organizational behavior principles.
• Project management is really "eye wash" for the customer's benefit.	• Project management will allow us to work more closely with our customers.
• Project management will create problems.	• Project management provides a means for solving problems.
• Only large projects need project management.	• All projects will benefit from project management.
• Project management will increase quality problems.	• Project management increases quality.
• Project management will create power and authority problems.	• Project management will reduce power struggles.
• Project management focuses on suboptimization by looking at only the project.	• Project management allows people to make good company decisions.
• Project management delivers products to a customer.	• Project management delivers solutions.
• The cost of project management may make us noncompetitive.	• Project management will increase our business.

the benefits of project management. Also shown in Table 2–2 is a comparison of how our past view of project management has changed.

Recognizing that the organization can benefit from the implementation of project is just the starting point. The question now becomes, "How long will it take us to achieve these benefits?" This question can be partially answered from Figure 2–6. In the beginning of the implementation process, there will be added

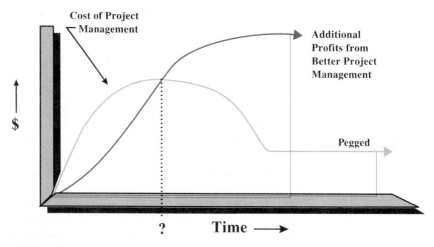

FIGURE 2–6. Project management costs versus benefits.

expenses to develop the project management methodology and establish the support systems for planning, scheduling, and control. Eventually, the cost will level off and become pegged. The question mark in Figure 2–6 is the point at which the benefits equal the cost of implementation. This point can be pushed to the left through training and education.

2.4 RESISTANCE TO CHANGE

Why was project management so difficult for companies to accept and implement? The answer is shown in Figure 2–7. Historically, project management resided only in the project-driven sectors of the marketplace. In these sectors, the project managers were given the responsibility for profit and loss. This profit and loss (P&L) responsibility virtually forced companies to treat project management as a profession.

In the non–project-driven sectors of the marketplace, corporate survival was based upon products and services, rather than upon a continuous stream of projects. Profitability was identified through marketing and sales, with very few projects having an identifiable P&L. As a result, project management in these firms was never viewed as a profession.

In reality, most firms that believed that they were non–project-driven were actually hybrids. Hybrid organizations are typically non–project-driven firms with one or two divisions that are project-driven. Historically, hybrids have functioned as though they were non–project-driven, as shown in Figure 2–7, but today they are functioning like project-driven firms. Why the change? Management

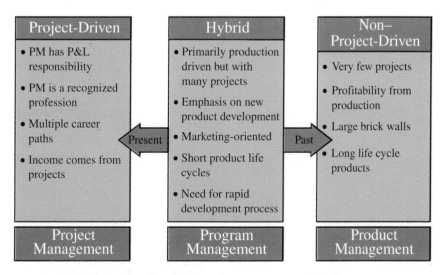

FIGURE 2–7. Industry classification (by project management utilization).

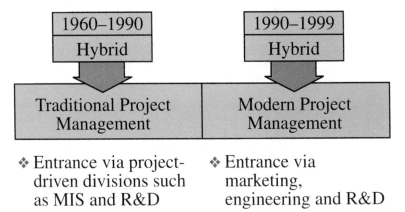

FIGURE 2–8. From hybrid to project-driven.

has come to the realization that they can most effectively run their organization on a "management by project" basis, and thereby achieve the benefits of both a project management organization and a traditional organization. The rapid growth and acceptance of project management during the last ten years has taken place in the non–project-driven/hybrid sectors. Now, project management is being promoted by marketing, engineering, and production, rather than only by the project-driven departments (see Figure 2–8).

A second factor contributing to the acceptance of project management was the economy, specifically the recessions of 1979–1983 and 1989–1993. This can be seen from Table 2–3. By the end of the recession of 1979–1983, companies recognized the benefits of using project management but were reluctant to see it implemented. Companies returned to the "status quo" of traditional management.

TABLE 2–3. RECESSIONARY EFFECTS

	Characteristics				
Recession	Layoffs	R&D	Training	Solutions Sought	Results of the Recessions
1979–1983	Blue collar	Eliminated	Eliminated	Short-term	• Return to status quo • No project management support • No allies for project management
1989–1993	White collar	Focused	Focused	Long-term	• Change way of doing business • Risk management • Examine lessons learned

There were no allies or alternative management techniques that were promoting the use of project management.

The recession of 1989–1993 finally saw the growth of project management in the non–project-driven sector. This recession was characterized by layoffs in the white collar/management ranks. Allies for project management were appearing and emphasis was being placed upon long-term solutions to problems. Project management was now here to stay.

The allies for project management began surfacing in 1985 and continued throughout the recession of 1989–1993. This is seen in Figure 2–9.

- *1985:* Companies recognize that they must compete on the basis of quality as well as cost. There exists a new appreciation for total quality management (TQM). Companies begin using the principles of project management for the implementation of TQM. The first ally for project management surfaces with the "marriage" of project management and TQM.
- *1990:* During the recession of 1989–1993, companies recognize the importance of schedule compression and being the first to market. Advocates of concurrent engineering begin promoting the use of project management to obtain better scheduling techniques. Another ally for project management is born.
- *1991–1992:* Executives realize that project management works best if decision-making and authority are decentralized. Executives recognize that control can still be achieved at the top by functioning as project sponsors.
- *1993:* As the recession of 1989–1993 comes to an end, companies begin "re-engineering" the organization, which really amounts to elimination of organizational "fat." The organization is now a "lean and mean" machine. People are asked to do more work in less time and with fewer people; executives recognize that being able to do this is a benefit of project management.

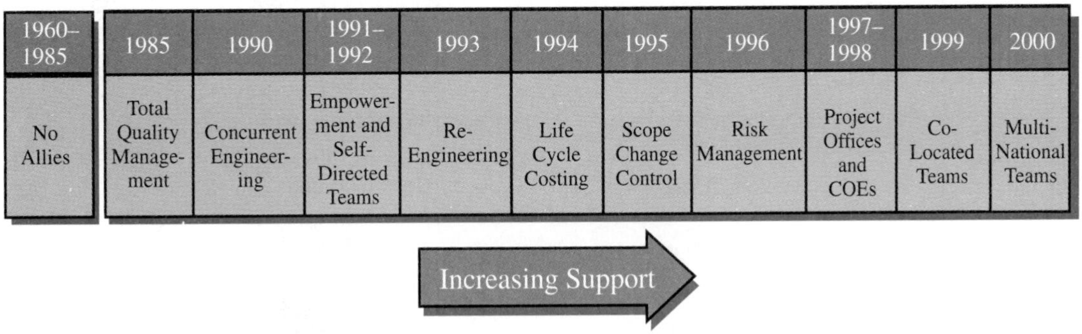

1960–1985	1985	1990	1991–1992	1993	1994	1995	1996	1997–1998	1999	2000
No Allies	Total Quality Management	Concurrent Engineering	Empowerment and Self-Directed Teams	Re-Engineering	Life Cycle Costing	Scope Change Control	Risk Management	Project Offices and COEs	Co-Located Teams	Multi-National Teams

Increasing Support →

FIGURE 2–9. New processes supporting project management.

- *1994:* Companies recognize that a good project cost control system (i.e., horizontal accounting) allows for improved estimating and a firmer grasp of the real cost of doing work and developing products.
- *1995:* Companies recognize that very few projects are completed within the framework of the original objectives without scope changes. Methodologies are created for effective change management.
- *1996:* Companies recognize that risk management involves more than padding an estimate or a schedule. Risk management plans are now included in the project plans.
- *1997-1998:* The recognition of project management as a professional career path mandates the consolidation of project management knowledge and a centrally located project management group. Benchmarking for best practices forces the creation of centers for excellence in project management.
- *1999:* Companies that recognize the importance of concurrent engineering and rapid product development find that it is best to have dedicated resources for the duration of the project. The cost of overmanagement may be negligible compared to risks of undermanagement. More and more organizations can be expected to use colocated teams all housed together.
- *2000:* Mergers and acquisitions are creating more multinational companies. Multinational project management will become the major challenge for the next decade.

As project management continues to grow and mature, more allies will appear. In the twenty-first century, second and third world nations will come to recognize the benefits and importance of project management. Worldwide standards for project management will occur.

The reason for the early resistance to project management was that the necessity for project management was customer-driven rather than internally driven, despite the existence of allies. Project management was being implemented, at least partially, simply to placate customer demands. By 1995, however, project management had become internally driven and a necessity for survival. Project management benchmarking was commonplace, and companies recognized the importance of achieving excellence in project management.

If a company wishes to achieve excellence in project management, then that company must go through a successful implementation process. The speed by which implementation occurs will dictate how quickly the full benefits of project management will be realized. This can be illustrated with Situation 2–1.

Situation 2–1: The aerospace division of a Fortune 500 company had been using project management for over thirty years. Everyone in the organization had attended courses in the principles of project management. From 1985 to 1994, the division went through a yearly ritual of benchmarking themselves against other aerospace and defense organizations. At the end of the benchmarking period, the staff would hug and kiss one another, believing that they were performing project management as well as could be expected.

In 1995, the picture changed. The company decided to benchmark itself against organizations that were not in the aerospace or defense sector. The company soon learned that there were companies that had been using project management for less than five or six years but whose skills at implementation had surpassed the aerospace/defense firms who had been using project management for more than thirty years. It was a rude awakening to see how quickly several non–profit-driven firms had advanced in project management.

Another factor that contributed to a resistance to change was senior management's preference for the status quo. More often than not, this preference was based upon what was in the executives' best interest rather than the best interest of the organization as a whole. This led to frustration for those in the lower and middle levels of management, who supported the implementation of project management for the betterment of the firm.

It was also not uncommon for someone to attend basic project management programs and then discover that his or her organization would not allow full implementation of project management. To illustrate this problem, consider Situation 2–2 below:

Situation 2–2: The largest division of a Fortune 500 company recognized the need for project management. Over a three-year period, 200 people were trained in the basics of project management, and 18 people passed the national certification exam for project management. The company created a project management division and developed a methodology for project management. As project management began to evolve in this division, the project managers quickly realized that the organization would not allow their "illusions of grandeur" to materialize. The executive vice president made it clear that the functional areas, rather than the project management division, would have budgetary control. Project managers would *not* be empowered with authority or critical decision-making opportunities. Simply stated, the project managers were being treated as expediters and coordinators, rather than real project managers. There were roadblocks that had to be overcome before theory could be turned into practice. How to overcome these obstacles had not been discussed in the basic courses on project management.

Even though project management has been in existence for more than forty years, there are still different views and misconceptions about what project management really is. Textbooks on operations research or management science still have chapters that are entitled, "Project Management" but that discuss only PERT scheduling techniques. A textbook on organizational design recognized project management as simply another organizational form. Even among educators, differing views are still prevalent.

All companies sooner or later understand the basics of project management. But those companies that have achieved excellence in project management have done so through successful implementation and execution of processes and methodologies.

2.5 SYSTEMS, PROGRAMS, AND PROJECTS: A DEFINITION

In the preceding sections the word "systems" has been used rather loosely. The exact definition of a system depends on the users, environment, and ultimate goal. Modern business practitioners define a system as:

> A group of elements, either human or nonhuman, that is organized and arranged in such a way that the elements can act as a whole toward achieving some common goal, objective, or end.

Systems are collections of interacting subsystems that either span or interconnect all schools of management. Systems, if properly organized, can provide a synergistic output.

Systems are characterized by their boundaries or interface conditions. For example, if the business firm system were completely isolated from the environmental system, then a *closed system* would exist, in which case management would have complete control over all system components. If the business system does in fact react with the environment, then the system is referred to as *open*. All social systems, for example, are categorized as open systems. Open systems must have permeable boundaries.

If a system is significantly dependent on other systems for its survival, then the system can be further defined as an *extended system*. Not all open systems are extended systems. Extended systems are ever-changing ones and can impose great hardships on individuals who desire to work in a regimented atmosphere.

Military and government organizations were the first to attempt to define clearly the boundaries of systems, programs, and projects. Below are two such definitions for systems:

- *Air Force Definition:* A composite of equipment, skills, and techniques capable of performing and/or supporting an operational role. A complete system includes related facilities, equipment, material services, and personnel required for its operation to the degree that it can be considered as a self-sufficient unit in its intended operational and/or support environment.
- *NASA Definition:* One of the principal functioning entities comprising the project hardware within a project or program. The meaning may vary to suit a particular project or program area. Ordinarily a "system" is the first major subdivision of project work (spacecraft systems, launch vehicle systems).

Systems tend to imply an infinite lifetime, but with constant upgrading.

Programs can be construed as the necessary first-level elements of a system. Two representative definitions of programs are given below:

- *Air Force Definition:* The integrated, time-phased tasks necessary to accomplish a particular purpose.
- *NASA Definition:* A relative series of undertakings that continue over a period of time (normally years) and that are designed to accomplish a broad, scientific or technical goal in the NASA long-range plan (lunar and planetary exploration, manned spacecraft systems).

Programs can be regarded as subsystems. However, programs are generally defined as time-phased efforts, whereas systems exist on a continuous basis.

Projects are also time-phased efforts (much shorter than programs) and are the first level of breakdown of a program. A typical definition would be:

- *NASA/Air Force Definition:* A project is within a program as an undertaking that has a scheduled beginning and end, and that normally involves some primary purpose.

As shown in Table 2–4, the government sector tends to run efforts as programs, headed by a program manager. The majority of the industrial sector, on the other hand, prefers to describe efforts as projects, headed by a project manager. Whether we call our undertaking project management or program management is inconsequential because the same policies, procedures, and guidelines that regulate programs most often apply to projects also. For the remainder of this text, programs and projects will be discussed interchangeably. However, the reader should be aware that projects are normally the first-level subdivision of a program. This breakdown will be discussed in more detail in Chapter 11.

Once a group of tasks is selected and considered to be a project, the next step is to define the kinds of project units. There are four categories of projects:

- *Individual projects:* These are short-duration projects normally assigned to a single individual who may be acting as both a project manager and a functional manager.
- *Staff projects:* These are projects that can be accomplished by one organizational unit, say a department. A staff or task force is developed from

TABLE 2–4. DEFINITION SUMMARY

Level	Sector	Title
System*	—	—
Program	Government	Program managers
Project	Industry	Project managers

*Definitions, as used here, do not include in-house industrial systems such as management information systems or shop floor control systems.

each section involved. This works best if only one functional unit is involved.

- *Special projects:* Very often special projects occur that require certain primary functions and/or authority to be assigned temporarily to other individuals or units. This works best for short-duration projects. Long-term projects can lead to severe conflicts under this arrangement.
- *Matrix or aggregate projects:* These require input from a large number of functional units and usually control vast resources.

Each of these categories of projects can require different responsibilities, job descriptions, policies, and procedures.

Project management may now be defined as the process of achieving project objectives through the traditional organizational structure and over the specialties of the individuals concerned. Project management is applicable for any ad hoc (unique, one-time, one-of-a-kind) undertaking concerned with a specific end objective. In order to complete a task, a project manager must:

- Set objectives
- Establish plans
- Organize resources
- Provide staffing
- Set up controls
- Issue directives
- Motivate personnel
- Apply innovation for alternative actions
- Remain flexible

The type of project will often dictate which of these functions a project manager will be required to perform.

2.6 PRODUCT VERSUS PROJECT MANAGEMENT: A DEFINITION

For all practical purposes, there is no basic difference between program management and project management. But what about product management? Project management and product management are similar, with one major exception: The project manager focuses on the end date of his project, whereas the product manager is not willing to admit that his product line will ever end. The product manager wants his product to be as long-lived and profitable as possible. Even when the demand for the product diminishes, the product manager will always look for spin-offs to keep his product alive.

Figure 2–10 shows the relationship between project and product management. When the project is in the R&D phase, a project manager is involved. Once the product is developed and introduced into the marketplace, control is taken over by the product manager. In some situations, the project manager can become

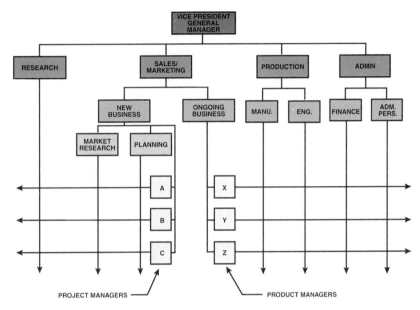

FIGURE 2–10. Organizational chart.

the product manager. Both product and project management can, and do, exist concurrently within companies.

Figure 2–10 shows that product management can operate horizontally as well as vertically. When a product is shown horizontally on the organizational chart, the implication is that the product line is not big enough to control its own resources full-time and therefore shares key functional resources similarly to project management. If the product line were large enough to control its own resources full-time, it would be shown as a separate division or a vertical line on the organization chart.

Also shown in Figure 2–10 is the remarkable fact that the project manager (or project engineer) is reporting to a marketing-type person. Should executives permit project managers and project engineers to report to a marketing-type individual even if the project entails a great amount of engineering? Many executives today would attest that the answer is "yes." The reason for this is that technically oriented project leaders get too involved with the technical details of the project and lose insight into when and how to "kill" a project. Remember, most technical leaders have been trained in an academic rather than a business environment. Their commitment to success often does not take into account such important parameters as return on investment, profitability, competition, and marketability.

To alleviate these problems, project managers and project engineers, especially on R&D-type projects, are now reporting to marketing so that marketing input will be included in all R&D decisions. Many executives have been forced into this position because of the high costs incurred during R&D, especially since, in case of a severe need to reduce costs, the R&D organization is usually the first to feel the pinch. Executives must exercise caution with regard to this structure in which both product and project managers report to the marketing function. The marketing executive could become the focal point of the entire organization, with the capability of building a very large empire.

2.7 MATURITY AND EXCELLENCE: A DEFINITION

Some people contend that maturity and excellence in project management are the same. Unfortunately, this is not the case. Consider the following definition:

> Maturity in project management is the implementation of a standard methodology and accompanying processes such that there exists a high likelihood of repeated successes.

This definition is supported by the life-cycle phases shown in Table 2–1. Maturity implies that the proper foundation of tools, techniques, processes, and even culture, exists. When projects come to an end, there is usually a debriefing with senior management to discuss how well the methodology was used and to recommend changes. This debriefing looks at "key performance indicators," which are shared learning topics, and allows the organization to maximize what it does right and to correct what it did wrong.

The definition of excellence can be stated as:

> Organizations excellent in project management are those that create the environment in which there exists a *continuous* stream of successfully managed projects and where success is measured by what is in the best interest of *both* the company and the project (i.e., customer).

Excellence goes well beyond maturity. You must have maturity to achieve excellence. Figure 2–11 shows that once the organization completes the first four life-cycle phases in Table 2–1, it may take two years or more to reach some initial levels of maturity. Excellence, if achievable at all, may take an additional five years or more.

Figure 2–11 also brings out another important fact. During maturity, more successes than failures occur. During excellence, we obtain a continuous stream of successful projects. Yet, even after having achieved excellence, there will still be some failures.

Executives who always make the right decision are not making enough decisions. Likewise, organizations in which all projects are completed successfully are not taking enough risks and are not working on enough projects.

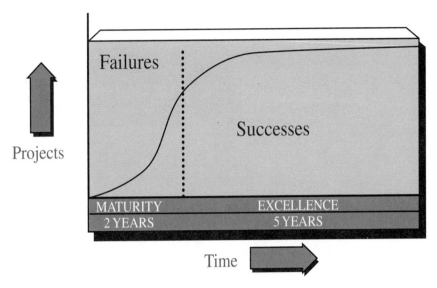

FIGURE 2–11. The growth of excellence.

It is unrealistic to believe that all projects will be completed successfully. Some people contend that the only true project failures are the ones from which nothing is learned. Failure can be viewed as success if the failure is identified early enough such that the resources can be reassigned to other more opportunistic activities.

2.8 INFORMAL PROJECT MANAGEMENT: A DEFINITION

Companies today are managing projects more on an informal basis than on a formal one. Informal project management does have some degree of formality but emphasizes managing the project with a minimum amount of paperwork. A reasonable amount of formality still exists. Furthermore, informal project management is based upon guidelines rather than the policies and procedures that are the basis for formal project management. This was shown previously to be a characteristic of a good project management methodology. Informal project management mandates:

- Effective communications
- Effective cooperation
- Effective teamwork
- Trust

These four elements are absolutely essential for informal project management to work effectively.

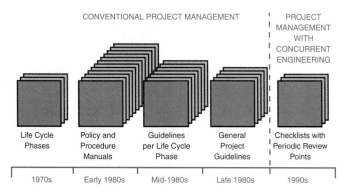

FIGURE 2–12. Evolution of policies, procedures, and guidelines. *Source:* Reprinted from H. Kerzner, *In Search of Excellence in Project Management.* New York: Wiley, 1998, p. 196.

Figure 2–12 shows the evolution of project documentation over the years. As companies become mature in project management, emphasis is on guidelines and checklists. Figure 2–13 shows the critical issues as project management matures toward more informality.

As a final note, not all companies have the luxury of using informal project management. Customers often have a strong voice in whether formal or informal project management will be used.

2.9 PROJECT LIFE CYCLES

Every program, project, or product has certain phases of development. A clear understanding of these phases permits managers and executives to better control total corporate resources in the achievement of desired goals. The phases of development are known as life-cycle phases. However, the breakdown and terminology of these phases differ, depending on whether we are discussing products or projects.

During the past few years, there has been at least partial agreement about the life-cycle phases of a product. They include:

● Research and development
● Market introduction
● Growth
● Maturity
● Deterioration
● Death

Today, there is no agreement among industries, or even companies within the same industry, about the life-cycle phases of a project. This is understandable because of the complex nature and diversity of projects.

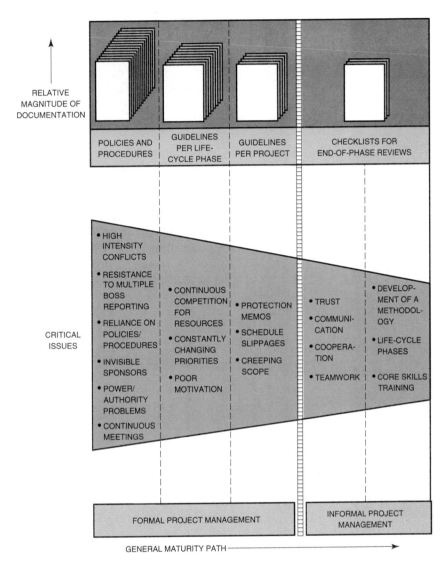

FIGURE 2–13. Maturity path.

The theoretical definitions of the life-cycle phases of a system can be applied to a project. These phases include:

- Conceptual
- Planning
- Testing
- Implementation
- Closure

The first phase, the conceptual phase, includes the preliminary evaluation of an idea. Most important in this phase is a preliminary analysis of risk and the resulting impact on the time, cost, and performance requirements, together with the potential impact on company resources. The conceptual phase also includes a "first cut" at the feasibility of the effort.

The second phase is the planning phase. It is mainly a refinement of the elements described under the conceptual phase. The planning phase requires a firm identification of the resources to be required together with the establishment of realistic time, cost, and performance parameters. This phase also includes the initial preparation of all documentation necessary to support the system. For a project based on competitive bidding, the conceptual phase would include the decision of whether to bid, and the planning phase would include the development of the total bid package (i.e., time, schedule, cost, and performance).

Because of the amount of estimating involved, analyzing system costs during the conceptual and planning phases is not an easy task. As shown in Figure 2–14, most project or system costs can be broken down into operating (recurring) and implementation (nonrecurring) categories. The implementation costs include one-time expenses such as construction of a new facility, purchasing computer hardware, or detailed planning. Operating costs, on the other hand, include recurring expenses such as manpower. The operating costs may be reduced as shown in Figure 2–14 if personnel perform at a higher position on the learning curve. The identification of a learning curve position is vitally important during the planning phase when firm cost positions must be established. Of course, it is not always possible to know what individuals will be available or how soon they can perform at a higher learning curve position.

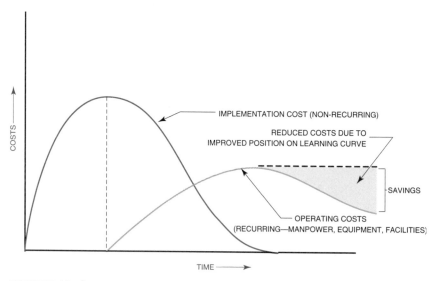

FIGURE 2–14. System costs.

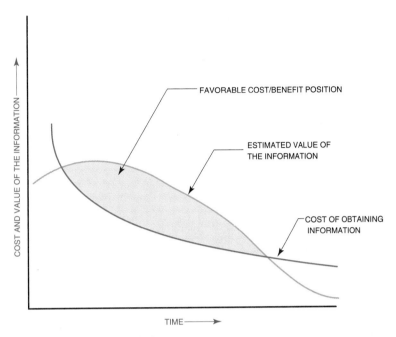

COST AND VALUE OF THE INFORMATION

FAVORABLE COST/BENEFIT POSITION

ESTIMATED VALUE OF
THE INFORMATION

COST OF OBTAINING
INFORMATION

TIME

FIGURE 2–15. Cost-benefit analysis.

Once the approximate total cost of the project is determined, a cost-benefit analysis should be conducted (see Figure 2–15) to determine if the estimated value of the information obtained from the system exceeds the cost of obtaining the information. This analysis is often included as part of a feasibility study. There are several situations, such as in competitive bidding, where the feasibility study is actually the conceptual and definition phases. Because of the costs that can be incurred during these two phases, top-management approval is almost always necessary before the initiation of such a feasibility study.

The third phase—testing—is predominantly a testing and final standardization effort so that operations can begin. Almost all documentation must be completed in this phase.

The fourth phase is the implementation phase, which integrates the project's product or services into the existing organization. If the project was developed for establishment of a marketable product, then this phase could include the product life-cycle phases of market introduction, growth, maturity, and a portion of deterioration.

The final phase is closure and includes the reallocation of resources. The question to be answered is, "Where should the resources be reassigned?" Consider a company that sells products on the open consumer market. As one product begins the deterioration and death phases of its life cycle (i.e., the divestment phase of a system), then new products or projects must be established. Such a company would, therefore, require a continuous stream of projects as a ne-

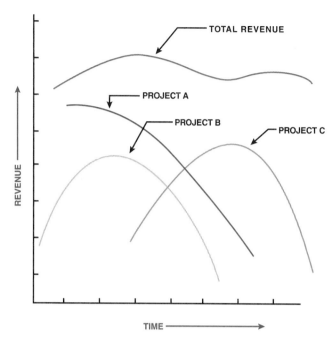

FIGURE 2–16. A stream of projects.

cessity for survival, as shown in Figure 2–16. As projects A and B begin their decline, new efforts (project C) must be developed for resource reallocation. In the ideal situation these new projects will be established at such a rate that total revenue will increase and company growth will be clearly visible.

The closure phase evaluates the efforts on the total system and serves as input to the conceptual phases for new projects and systems. This final phase also has an impact on other ongoing projects with regard to priority identification.

Thus far no attempt has been made to identify the size of a project or system. Large projects generally require full-time staffs, whereas small projects, although they undergo the same system life-cycle phases, may require only part-time people. This implies that an individual can be responsible for multiple projects, possibly with each project existing in a different life-cycle phase. The following questions must be considered in multiproject management:

- Are the project objectives the same?
  - For the good of the project?
  - For the good of the company?
- Is there a distinction between large and small projects?
- How do we handle conflicting priorities?
  - Critical versus critical projects

- Critical versus noncritical projects
- Noncritical versus noncritical projects

Later chapters discuss methods of resolving conflicts and establishing priorities.

The phases of a project and those of a product are compared in Figure 2–17. Notice that the life-cycle phases of a product generally do not overlap, whereas the phases of a project can and often do overlap.

Table 2–5 identifies the various life-cycle phases that are commonly used. Even in mature project management industries such as construction, one could survey ten different construction companies and find ten different definitions for the life-cycle phases.

The life-cycle phases for computer programming, as listed in Table 2–5, are also shown in Figure 2–18 which illustrates how manpower resources can build up and decline during a project. In Figure 2–18, PMO stands for the present method of operations, and PMO′ will be the "new" present method of operations after conversion. This life cycle would probably be representative of a twelve-month activity. Most executives prefer short data processing life cycles because computer technology changes at a very rapid rate. An executive of a major utility commented that his company was having trouble determining how to terminate a computer programming project to improve customer service because by the time a package is ready for full implementation, an updated version appears on the scene. Should the original project be canceled and a new project begun? The solution appears to lie in establishing short data processing project life-cycle phases, perhaps through segmented implementation. In any case, we can conclude that:

Top management is responsible for the periodic review of major projects. This should be accomplished, at a minimum, at the completion of each life-cycle phase.

More and more companies are preparing procedural manuals for project management and for structuring work using life-cycle phases. There are several reasons for this trend:

- Clear delineation of the work to be accomplished in each phase may be possible.
- Pricing and estimating may be easier if well-structured work definitions exist.
- There exist key decision points at the end of each life-cycle phase so that incremental funding is possible.

As a final note, the reader should be aware that not all projects can be simply transposed into life-cycle phases (e.g., R&D). In such a case it might be possible (even in the same company) for different definitions of life-cycle phases to exist because of schedule length, complexity, or just the difficulty of managing the phases.

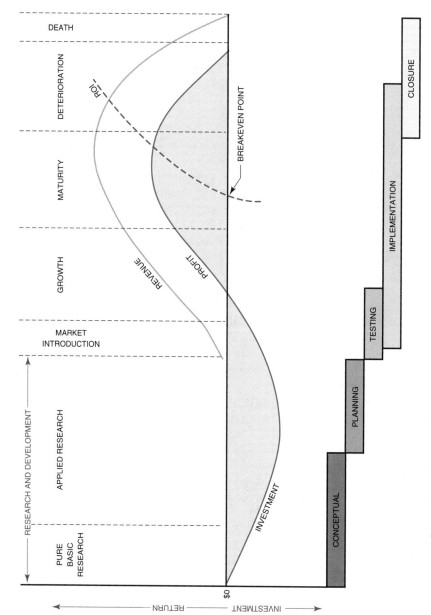

FIGURE 2–17. System/product life cycles.

TABLE 2–5. LIFE-CYCLE PHASE DEFINITIONS

Engineering	Manufacturing	Computer Programming	Construction
• Start-up • Definition • Main • Termination	• Formation • Buildup • Production • Phase-out • Final audit	• Conceptual • Planning • Definition and design • Implementation • Conversion	• Planning, data gathering and procedures • Studies and basic engineering • Major review • Detail engineering • Detail engineering/ construction overlap • Construction • Testing and commissioning

2.10 PROJECT MANAGEMENT METHODOLOGIES: A DEFINITION

Achieving project management excellence, or even maturity, may not be possible without a repetitive process that can be used on each and every project. This repetitive process is referred to as the project management methodology. Continuous use of the methodology will drastically improve a company's chances for success.

If at all possible, companies should maintain and support a single methodology for project management. Good methodologies integrate other processes into

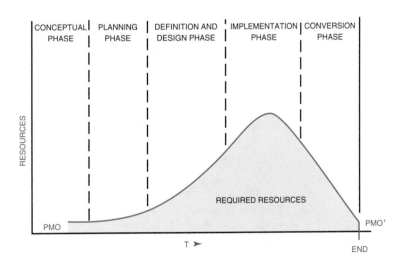

FIGURE 2–18. Definition of a project life cycle.

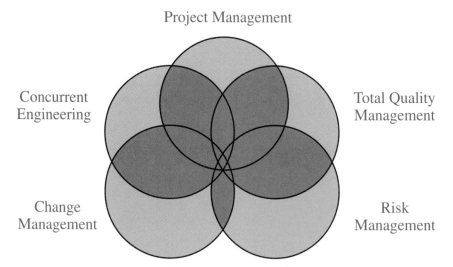

FIGURE 2–19. Integrated processes for the twenty-first century.

the project management methodology, as shown in Figure 2–19. Companies such as Nortel, Ericsson, and Johnson Controls Automotive have all five of these processes integrated into their project management methodology.

During the 1990s, the following processes were integrated into a single methodology:

- *Project Management:* The basic principles of planning, scheduling, and controlling work
- *Total Quality Management:* The process of ensuring that the end result will meet the quality expectations of the customer
- *Concurrent Engineering:* The process of performing work in parallel rather than series in order to compress the schedule without incurring serious risks
- *Scope Change Control:* The process of controlling the configuration of the end result such that value added is provided to the customer
- *Risk Management:* The process of identifying, quantifying, and responding to the risks of project without any material impact on the project's objectives

In the next century, companies can be expected to integrate more of their business processes in the project management methodology. This is shown in Figure 2–20. Managing off of a single methodology lowers cost, reduces resource requirements for support, minimizes paperwork, and eliminates duplicated efforts. When a company feels the need to have multiple methodologies, time is wasted up front arguing on which methodology to use.

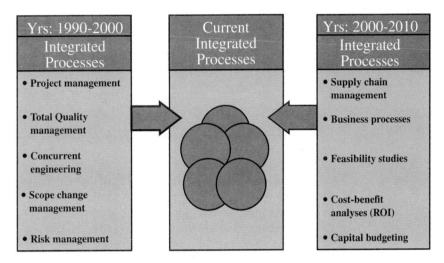

FIGURE 2–20. Integrated processes (past, present, and future).

The characteristics of a good methodology based upon integrated processes include:

- A recommended level of detail
- Use of templates
- Standardized planning, scheduling, and cost control techniques
- Standardized reporting format for both in-house and customers' use
- Flexibility for application to all projects
- Flexibility for rapid improvements, as needed
- Easy for the customer to understand and follow
- Readily accepted and used throughout the entire company
- Use of standardized life-cycle phases (which can overlap) and end of phase reviews (Section 2.9)
- Based upon guidelines rather than policies and procedures (Section 2.8)
- Based upon a good work ethic

Methodologies do not manage projects; people do. It is the corporate culture that executes the methodology. Senior management must create a corporate culture that supports project management and demonstrates faith in the methodology. If this is done successfully, then the following benefits can be expected:

- Faster "time to market" through better control of the project's scope
- Lower overall project risk
- Better decision-making process
- Greater customer satisfaction, which leads to increased business
- More time available for value-added efforts, rather than internal politics and internal competition

One company found that their customers liked their methodology so much and that the projects were so successful, that the relationship between the contractor and the customer improved to the point where the customers began treating the contractor as a partner rather than as a supplier.

2.11 SYSTEMS THINKING

Ultimately, all decisions and policies are made on the basis of judgments; there is no other way, and there never will be. In the end, analysis is but an aid to the judgment and intuition of the decision maker. These principles hold true for project management as well as for systems management.

The systems approach may be defined as a logical and disciplined process of problem-solving. The word *process* indicates an active ongoing system that is fed by input from its parts.

Systems approach definitions should be considered. The systems approach:

- Forces review of the interrelationship of the various subsystems
- Is a dynamic process that integrates all activities into a meaningful total system
- Systematically assembles and matches the parts of the system into a unified whole
- Seeks an optimal solution or strategy in solving a problem

The systems approach to problem-solving has phases of development similar to the life-cycle phases shown in Figure 2–17. These phases are defined as follows:

- *Translation:* Terminology, problem objective, and criteria and constraints are defined and accepted by all participants.
- *Analysis:* All possible approaches to or alternatives to the solution of the problem are stated.
- *Trade-off:* Selection criteria and constraints are applied to the alternatives to meet the objective.
- *Synthesis:* The best solution in reaching the objective of the system is the result of the combination of analysis and trade-off phases.

Other terms essential to the systems approach are as follows:

- *Objective:* The function of the system or the strategy that must be achieved.
- *Requirement:* A partial need to satisfy the objective.
- *Alternative:* One of the selected ways to implement and satisfy a requirement.

- *Selection criteria:* Performance factors used in evaluating the alternatives to select a preferable alternative.
- *Constraint:* An absolute factor that describes conditions that the alternatives *must* meet.

A common error by potential decision makers (those dissatisfied individuals with authority to act) who base their thinking solely on subjective experience, judgment, and intuition is that they fail to recognize the existence of alternatives. Subjective thinking is inhibited or affected by personal bias resulting from conditions within the brain and sense organs.

Objective thinking, on the other hand, is a fundamental characteristic of the systems approach and is exhibited or characterized by emphasis on the tendency to view events, phenomena, and ideas as external and apart from self-consciousness. Objective thinking is unprejudiced and exists independent of the mind.

The systems analysis process, as shown in Figure 2–21, begins with systematic examination and comparison of those alternative actions that are related to the accomplishment of the desired objective. The alternatives are then compared on the basis of the resource cost and the associated benefits. The inputs from the constraints and limitations identify the explicit consideration of the uncertainty variables. The loop is then completed using feedback in order to determine how compatible each alternative is with the objectives of the organization.

The above analysis can be arranged in steps:

- Input data to mental process
- Analyze data
- Predict outcomes
- Evaluate outcomes and compare alternatives
- Choose the best alternative
- Take action
- Measure results and compare them with predictions

The systems approach to thinking is most effective if individuals can be trained to be ready with alternative actions that directly tie in with the prediction of outcomes. The basic tool is the outcome array, which represents the matrix of all possible circumstances. This outcome array can be developed only if the decision maker thinks in terms of the wide scope of possible outcomes. Outcome descriptions force the decision maker to spell out clearly just what he is trying to achieve (i.e., his objectives).

Systems thinking is vital for the success of a project. Project management systems urgently need new ways of strategically viewing, questioning, and analyzing project needs for alternative nontechnical as well as technical solutions. The ability to analyze the total project, rather than the individual parts, is the first prerequisite for successful project management.

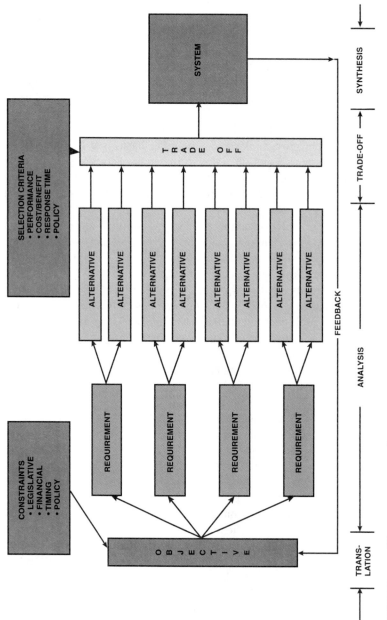

FIGURE 2-21. The systems approach.

PROBLEMS

2–1 Can the organizational chart of a company be considered as a systems model? If so, what kind of systems model?

2–2 Do you think that someone could be a good systems manager but a poor project manager? What about the reverse situation? State any assumptions that you may have to make.

2–3 Can we consider R&D as a system? If so, under what circumstances?

2–4 For each of the following projects, state whether we are discussing an open, closed, or extended system:

    a. A high-technology project
    b. New product R&D
    c. An on-line computer system for a bank
    d. Construction of a chemical plant
    e. Developing an in-house cost accounting reporting system

2–5 Can an entire organization be considered as a model? If so, what type?

2–6 Systems can be defined as a combination or interrelationship of subsystems. Does a project have subsystems?

2–7 If a system can, in fact, be broken down into subsystems, what problems can occur during integration?

2–8 How could suboptimization occur during systems thinking and analysis?

2–9 Would a cost-benefit analysis be easier or harder to perform in a traditional or project management organizational structure?

2–10 What impact could the product life cycle have on the selection of the project organizational structure?

2–11 In the development of a system, what criteria should be used to determine where one phase begins and another ends and where overlap can occur?

2–12 Consider the following expression: "Damn the torpedoes: full-speed ahead." Is it possible that this military philosophy can be applied to project management and lead to project success?

CASE STUDIES

L. P. MANNING CORPORATION

In March 1991, the Marketing Division of the L. P. Manning Corporation performed a national survey to test the public's reaction to a new type of toaster. Manning had achieved success in the past and established itself as a leader in the home appliance industry.

Although the new toaster was just an idea, the public responded favorably. In April of the same year, the vice presidents for planning, marketing, engineering, and manufacturing all met to formulate plans for the development and ultimately the production of the new toaster. Marketing asserted that the manufacturing cost must remain below $70 per unit or else Manning Corporation would not be competitive. Based on the specifications drawn up in the meeting, manufacturing assured marketing that this cost could be met.

The engineering division was given six months to develop the product. Manning's executives were eager to introduce the product for the Christmas rush. This might give them an early foothold on a strong market share.

During the R&D phase, marketing continually "pestered" engineering with new designs and changes in specifications that would make the new product easier to market. The ultimate result was a one-month slip in the schedule.

Pushing the schedule to the right greatly displeased manufacturing personnel. According to the vice president for manufacturing, speaking to the marketing manager: "I've just received the final specifications and designs from engineering. This is not what we had agreed on last March. These changes will cause us to lose at least one additional month to change our manufacturing planning. And because we're already one month behind, I don't see any way that we could reschedule our Christmas production facilities to accommodate this new product. Our established lines must come first. Furthermore, our estimating department says that these changes will increase the cost of the product by at least 25 to 35 percent. And, of course, we must include the quality control section, which has some questions as to whether we can actually live with these specifications. Why don't we just cancel this project or at least postpone it until next year?"

PROJECT FIRECRACKER

"Don, project management is the only way to handle this type of project. With $40 million at stake we can't afford not to use this approach."

"Listen, Jeff, your problem is you take seminars given by these ivory tower professors and you think you're an expert. I've been in this business for forty years and I know how to handle this job—and it isn't through project management."

History and Background

Jeff Pankoff, a registered professional engineer, came to work for National Corporation after receiving a mechanical engineering degree. After he arrived at National, he was assigned to the engineering department. Soon thereafter, Jeff realized that he needed to know more about statistics, and he enrolled in the graduate school of a local university. When he was near completion of his master of science degree, National transferred Jeff to one of its subsidiaries in Ireland to set up an engineering department. After a successful three years, Jeff returned to National's home office and was promoted to chief engineer. Jeff's department increased to eighty engineers and technicians. Spending a considerable time in administration, Jeff decided an MBA would be useful, so he enrolled in a program at a nearby university. At the time when this project began, Jeff was near the end of the MBA program.

National Corporation, a large international corporation with annual sales of about $600 million, employs 8,000 people worldwide and is a specialty machine, component, and tool producer catering to automotive and aircraft manufacturers. The company is over a hundred years old and has a successful and profitable record.

National is organized in divisions according to machine, component, and tool production facilities. Each division is operated as a profit center (see Exhibit 2–1). Jeff was assigned to the Tool Division.

National's Tool Division produces a broad line of regular tools as well as specials. Specials amounted to only about 10 percent of the regular business, but over the last five years had increased from 5 percent to the current 10 percent. Only specials that were similar to the regular tools were accepted as orders.

National sells all its products through about 3,000 industrial distributors located throughout the United States. In addition, National employs 200 sales representatives who work with the various distributors to provide product seminars.

The traditional approach to project assignments is used. The engineering department, headed by Jeff, is basically responsible for the purchase of capital equipment and the selection of production methods used in the manufacture of the product. Project assignments to evaluate and purchase a new machine tool or to determine the production routing for a new product are assigned to the engineering department. Jeff assigns the project to the appropriate section, and, under the direction of a project engineer, the project is completed.

The project engineer works with all the departments reporting to the vice president, including production, personnel, plant engineering, product design (the project engineer's link to sales), and time study. As an example of the working relationship, the project engineer selects the location of the new machine and devises instructions

Exhibit 2–1. The Tool Division of National Corporation

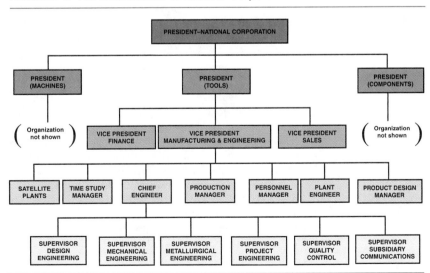

for its operation with production. With personnel the engineer establishes the job descriptions for the new jobs as well as for the selection of people to work on the new machine. The project engineer works with plant engineering on the moving of the machine to the proper location and instructs plant engineering on the installation and services required (air, water, electricity, gas, etc.). It is very important that the project engineer work very closely with the product design department, which develops the design of the product to be sold. Many times the product designed is too ambitious an undertaking or cannot be economically produced. Interaction between departments is essential in working out such problems.

After the new machine is installed, an operator is selected and the machine is ready for production. Time study, with the project engineer's help, then establishes the incentive system for the job.

Often a customer requests certain tolerances that cannot be adhered to by manufacturing. In such a case, the project engineer contacts the product design department, which contacts the sales department, which in turn contacts the customer. The communication process is then reversed, and the project engineer gets an answer. Based on the number of questions, the total process may take four to five weeks.

As the company is set up, the engineering department has no authority over time study, production, product design, or other areas. The only way that the project engineer can get these departments to make commitments is through persuasion or through the chief engineer, who could go to the vice president of manufacturing and engineering. If the engineer is convincing, the vice president will dictate to the appropriate manager what must be done.

Salaries in all departments of the company are a closely guarded secret. Only the vice president, the appropriate department manager, and the individual know the exact salary. Don Wolinski, the vice president of manufacturing and engineering, pointed out that this approach was the "professional way" and an essential aspect of smooth business operations.

The Ill-Fated Project

Jeff Pankoff, the chief engineer for National, flew to Southern California to one of National's (tool) plants. Ben Ehlke, manager of the Southern California plant, wanted to purchase a computer numerical controlled (CNC) machining center for $250,000. When the request came to Jeff for approval, he had many questions and wanted some face-to-face communication.

The Southern California plant supplied the aircraft industry, and one airplane company provided 90 percent of the Southern California plant's sales. Jeff was mainly concerned about the sales projections used by Ehlke in justifying the machining center. Ehkle pointed out that his projections were based on what the airplane company had told him they expected to buy out the next five years. Since this estimate was crucial to the justification, Jeff suggested that a meeting be arranged with the appropriate people at the airplane company to explore these projections. Since the local National sales representative was ill, the distributor salesman, Jack White, accompanied Jeff and Ben. While at the airplane company (APC), the chief tool buyer of APC, Tom Kelly, was informed that Jeff was there. Jeff received a message from the receptionist that Tom Kelly wanted to see him before he left the building. After the sales projections were reviewed and Jeff was convinced that they were as accurate and as reliable as they possibly could be, he asked the receptionist to set up an appointment with Tom Kelly.

When Jeff walked into Kelly's office the fireworks began. He was greeted with, "What's wrong with National? They refused to quote on this special part. We sent them a print and asked National for their price and delivery, indicating it could turn into a sizable order. They turned me down flat saying that they were not tooled up for this business. Now I know that National is tops in the field and that National can provide this part. What's wrong with your sales department?"

All this came as a complete surprise to Jeff. The distributor salesman knew about it but never thought to mention it to him. Jeff looked at the part print and asked, "What kind of business are you talking about?" Kelly said, without batting an eye, "$40 million per year."

Jeff realized that National had the expertise to produce the part and would require only one added machine (a special press costing $20,000) to have the total manufacturing capability. Jeff also realized he was in an awkward situation. The National sales representative was not there, and he certainly could not speak for sales. However, a $40 million order could not be passed over lightly. Kelly indicated that he would like to see National get 90 percent of the order if they would only quote on the job. Jeff told Kelly that he would take the information back and discuss it with the vice presidents of sales, manufacturing, and engineering and that most likely the sales vice president would contact him next.

On the return flight, Jeff reviewed in his mind his meeting with Kelly. Why did Bob Jones, National's sales vice president, refuse to quote? Did he know about the possible $40 million order? Although Jeff wasn't in sales, he decided that he would do whatever possible to land this order for National. That evening Jack White called from California. Jack said he had talked to Kelly after Jeff left and told Kelly that if anybody could make this project work, it would be Jeff Pankoff. Jeff suggested that Jack White call Bob Jones with future reports concerning this project.

The next morning, before Jeff had a chance to review his mail, Bob Jones came storming into his office. "Who do you think you are committing National to accept an order on your own without even a sales representative present? You know that all communication with a customer is through sales."

Jeff replied, "Let me explain what happened."

After Jeff's explanation, Jones said, "Jeff, I hear what you're saying, but no matter what the circumstances, all communications with any customer must go through proper channels."

Following the meeting with Jones, Jeff went to see Wolinski, his boss. He filled Wolinski in on what had happened. Then he said, "Don, I've given this project considerable thought. Jones is agreeable to quoting this job. However, if we follow our normal channels, we will experience too many time delays and problems. Through the various stages of this project, the customer will have many questions and changes and will require continuous updating. Our current system will not allow this to happen. It will take work from all departments to implement this project, and unless all departments work under the same priority system, we won't have a chance. What we need, Don, is project management. Without this approach where one man heads the project with authority from the top, we just can't make it work."

Wolinski looked out the window and said, "We have been successful for many years using our conventional approach to project work. I grant you that we have not had an order of this magnitude to worry about, but I see no reason why we should change even if the order were for $100 million."

"Don, project management is the only way to handle this type of project. With $40 million at stake we can't afford not to use this approach."

"Listen Jeff, your problem is you take seminars given by these ivory tower professors and you think you're an expert. I've been in this business for forty years and I know how to handle this job—and it isn't through project management. I'll call a meeting of all concerned department managers so we can get started on quoting this job."

That afternoon, Jeff and the other five department managers were summoned to a meeting in Wolinski's office. Wolinski summarized the situation and informed the assembled group that Jeff would be responsible for the determination of the methods of manufacture and the associated manufacturing costs that would be used in the quotation. The method of manufacture, of course, would be based on the design of the part provided by product design. Wolinski appointed Jeff and Waldo Novak, manager of product design, as coheads of the project. He further advised that the normal channels of communication with sales through the product design manager would continue as usual on this project.

The project began. Jeff spent considerable time requesting clarification of the drawings submitted by the customer. All these communications went through Waldo. Before the manufacturing routing could be established for quotation purposes, questions concerning the drawings had to be answered. The customer was getting anxious to receive the quotation because its management had to select a supplier within eight weeks. One week was already lost owing to communication delay. Wolinski decided that to speed up the quoting process he would send Jeff and Waldo along with Jones, the sales vice president, to see the customer. This meeting at APC helped clarify many questions. After Jeff returned, he began laying out the alternative routing for the parts. He assigned two of his most creative technicians and an engineer to run isolated tests on the various methods of manufacturing. From the results he would then finalize the routing that would be used for quoting. Two weeks of the eight were gone, but Jeff was generally pleased until the phone rang. It was Waldo.

"Say, Jeff, I think if we change the design on the back side of the part, it will add to its strength. In fact, I've assigned one of my men to review this and make this change, and it looks good."

While this conversation was going on, Wolinski popped into Jeff's office and said that sales had promised that National would ship APC a test order of 100 pieces in two weeks. Jeff was irate. Product design was changing the product. Sales was promising delivery of a test order that no one could even describe yet.

Needless to say, the next few days were long and difficult. It took three days for Jeff and Waldo to resolve the design routing problem. Wolinski stayed in the background and would not make any position statement except that he wanted everything "yesterday." By the end of the third week the design problem was resolved, and the quotation was prepared and sent out to the customer. The quotation was acceptable to APC pending the performance of the 100 test parts.

At the start of the fourth week, Jeff, with the routing in hand, went to Charlie Henry, the production manager, and said he needed 100 parts by Friday. Charlie looked at the routing and said, "The best I can do is a two-week delivery."

After discussing the subject for an hour, the two men agreed to see Wolinski. Wolinski said he'd check with sales and attempt to get an extension of one week. Sales asked the distributor salesman to request an extension. Jack White was sure it would be okay so he replied to Bob Jones without checking that the added week was in fact acceptable.

The 100 pieces went out in three weeks rather than two. That meant the project was at the end of the sixth week and only two remained. Inspection received the test pieces on Monday of the seventh week and immediately reported them not to be in specification. Kelly was upset. He was counting heavily on National to provide these parts. Kelly had received four other quotations and test orders from National's competitors. The prices were similar, and the test parts were to specification. However, National's parts, although out of specification, looked better than their competitors'. Kelly reminded Jones that the customer now had only nine days left before the contract would be let. That meant the 100 test parts had to be made in nine days. Jones immediately called Wolinski, who agreed to talk to his people to try to accomplish this.

The tools were shipped in eleven days, two days after the customer had awarded orders to three of National's competitors. Kelly was disappointed in National's performance but told Jones that National would be considered for next year's contract, at least a part of it.

Jeff, hearing from Waldo that National lost the order, returned to his office, shut the door, and thought of the hours, nearly round the clock, that were spent on this job. Hours were wasted because of poor communications, nonuniform priorities, and the fact that there was no project manager. "I wonder if Wolinski learned his lesson; probably not. This one cost the company at least $6 million in profits, all because project management was not used." Jeff concluded that his work was really cut out for him. He decided that he must convince Wolinski and others of the advantages of using project management. Although Wolinski had attended a one-day seminar on project management two years ago, Jeff decided that one of his objectives during the coming year would be to get Wolinski to the point where he would, on his own, suggest becoming more knowledgeable concerning project management. Jeff's thought was that if the company was to continue to be profitable it must use project management.

The phone rang, it was Wolinski. He said, "Jeff, do you have a moment to come down to my office? I'd like to talk about the possibility of using, on a trial basis, this project management concept you mentioned to me a few months ago."

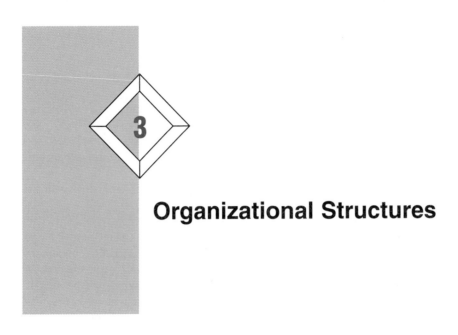

Organizational Structures

3.0 INTRODUCTION

During the past thirty years there has been a so-called hidden revolution in the introduction and development of new organizational structures. Management has come to realize that organizations must be dynamic in nature; that is, they must be capable of rapid restructuring should environmental conditions so dictate. These environmental factors evolved from the increasing competitiveness of the market, changes in technology, and a requirement for better control of resources for multiproduct firms. More than thirty years ago, Wallace identified four major factors that caused the onset of the organizational revolution:[1]

- The technology revolution (complexity and variety of products, new materials and processes, and the effects of massive research)
- Competition and the profit squeeze (saturated markets, inflation of wage and material costs, and production efficiency)
- The high cost of marketing
- The unpredictability of consumer demands (due to high income, wide range of choices available, and shifting tastes)

Much has been written about how to identify and interpret those signs that indicate that a new organizational form may be necessary. According to Grinnell and Apple, there are five general indications that the traditional structure may not be adequate for managing projects:[2]

---

1. W. L. Wallace, "The Winchester-Western Division Concept of Product Planning" (New Haven: Olin Mathieson Corporation, January 1963), pp. 2–3.

2. S. K. Grinnell and H. P. Apple, "When Two Bosses Are Better Than One," *Machine Design,* January 1975, pp. 84–87.

- Management is satisfied with its technical skills, but projects are not meeting time, cost, and other project requirements.
- There is a high commitment to getting project work done, but great fluctuations in how well performance specifications are met.
- Highly talented specialists involved in the project feel exploited and misused.
- Particular technical groups or individuals constantly blame each other for failure to meet specifications or delivery dates.
- Projects are on time and to specifications, but groups and individuals aren't satisfied with the achievement.

Unfortunately, many companies do not realize the necessity for organizational change until it is too late. Management continually looks externally (i.e., to the environment) rather than internally for solutions to problems. A typical example would be that new product costs are continually rising while the product life cycle may be decreasing. Should emphasis be placed on lowering costs or developing new products?

If we assume that an organizational system is composed of both human and nonhuman resources, then we must analyze the sociotechnical subsystem whenever organizational changes are being considered. The social system is represented by the organization's personnel and their group behavior. The technical system includes the technology, materials, and machines necessary to perform the required tasks.

Behavioralists contend that there is no one best structure to meet the challenges of tomorrow's organizations. The structure used, however, must be one that optimizes company performance by achieving a balance between the social and the technical requirements. According to Sadler:[3]

> Since the relative influence of these (sociotechnical) factors change from situation to situation, there can be no such thing as an ideal structure making for effectiveness in organizations of all kinds, or even appropriate to a single type of organization at different stages in its development.
>
> There are often real and important conflicts between the type of organizational structure called for if the tasks are to be achieved with minimum cost, and the structure that will be required if human beings are to have their needs satisfied. Considerable management judgment is called for when decisions are made as to the allocation of work activities to individuals and groups. High standardization of performance, high manpower utilization and other economic advantages associated with a high level of specialization and routinization of work have to be balanced against the possible effects of extreme specialization in lowering employee attitudes and motivation.

Organizations can be defined as groups of people who must coordinate their activities in order to meet organizational objectives. The coordination function requires strong communications and a clear understanding of the relationships and interdependencies among people. Organizational structures are dictated by such factors as technology and its rate of change, complexity, resource availability, products and/or services, competition, and decision-making requirements. The reader must keep in mind that *there is no such thing as a good or bad organizational structure; there are only appropriate or inappropriate ones.*

Even the simplest type of organizational change can induce major conflicts. The creation of a new position, the need for better planning, the lengthening or shortening of the span of control, the need for additional technology (knowledge), and centralization or decentralization can result in major changes in the sociotechnical subsystem. Argyris has defined five conditions that form the basis for organizational change requirements:[4]

---

3. Philip Sadler, "Designing an Organizational Structure," *Management International Review,* Vol. 11, No. 6, 1971, pp. 19–33.

4. Chris Argyris, "Today's Problems with Tomorrow's Organizations," *The Journal of Management Studies,* February 1967, pp. 31–55.

These requirements . . . depend upon (1) continuous and open access between individuals and groups, (2) free, reliable communication, where (3) independence is the foundation for individual and departmental cohesiveness and (4) trust, risk-taking and helping each other is prevalent so that (5) conflict is identified and managed in such a way that the destructive win-lose stances with their accompanying polarization of views are minimized. . . . Unfortunately these conditions are difficult to create. . . . There is a tendency toward conformity, mistrust and lack of risk-taking among the peers that results in focusing upon individual survival, requiring the seeking out of the scarce rewards, identifying one's self with a successful venture (be a hero) and being careful to avoid being blamed for or identified with a failure, thereby becoming a "bum." All these adaptive behaviors tend to induce low interpersonal competence and can lead the organization, over the long-run, to become rigid, sticky, and less innovative, resulting in less than effective decisions with even less internal commitment to the decision on the part of those involved.

Today, organizational restructuring is a compromise between the traditional (classical) and the behavioral schools of thought; management must consider the needs of individuals as well as the needs of the company. After all, is the organization structured to manage people or to manage work?

There is a wide variety of organizational forms for restructuring management. The exact method depends on the people in the organization, the company's product lines, and management's philosophy. A poorly restructured organization can sever communication channels that may have taken months or years to cultivate; cause a restructuring of the informal organization, thus creating new power, status, and political positions; and eliminate job satisfaction and motivational factors to such a degree that complete discontent is the result.

Sadler defines three tasks that must be considered because of the varied nature of organizations: control, integration, and external relationships.[5] If the company's position is very sensitive to the environment, then management may be most concerned with the control task. For an organization with multiple products, each requiring a high degree of engineering and technology, the integration task can become primary. Finally, for situations with strong labor unions and repetitive tasks, external relations can predominate, especially in strong technological and scientific environments where strict government regulations must be adhered to.

In the sections that follow, a variety of organizational forms will be presented. Obviously, it is an impossible task to describe all possible organizational structures. Each of the organizational forms included is used to describe how the project management organization evolved from the classical theories of management. For each organizational form, advantages and disadvantages are listed in terms of both technology and social systems. Sadler has prepared a six-question checklist that explores a company's tasks, social climate, and relationship to the environment.[6]

- To what extent does the task of organization call for close control if it is to be performed efficiently?
- What are the needs and attitudes of the people performing the tasks? What are the likely effects of control mechanisms on their motivation and performance?
- What are the natural social groupings with which people identify themselves? To what extent are satisfying social relationships important in relation to motivation and performance?
- What aspect of the organization's activities needs to be closely integrated if the overall task is to be achieved?

---

5. Philip Sadler, "Designing an Organizational Structure," *Management International Review,* Vol. 11, No. 6, 1971, pp. 19–33.

6. See note 5.

- What organizational measures can be developed that will provide an appropriate measure of control and integration of work activities, while at the same time meeting the needs of people and providing adequate motivation?
- What environmental changes are likely to affect the future trend of company operations? What organizational measures can be taken to insure that the enterprise responds to these effectively?

The answers to these questions are not easy. For the most part, they are a matter of the judgment exercised by organizational and behavioral managers.

3.1 ORGANIZATIONAL WORK FLOW

Organizations are continually restructured to meet the demands imposed by the environment. Restructuring can produce a major change in the role of individuals in both the formal and the informal organization. Many researchers believe that the greatest usefulness of behavioralists lies in their ability to help the informal organization adapt to changes and resolve the resulting conflicts. Unfortunately, behavioralists cannot be totally effective unless they have an input into the formal organization as well. Conflicts arise out of changes in the formal structure. Whatever organizational form is finally selected, formal channels must be developed so that each individual has a clear description of the authority, responsibility, and accountability necessary for the flow of work to proceed.

In the discussion of organizational structures, the following definitions will be used:

- *Authority* is the power granted to individuals (possibly by their position) so that they can make final decisions for others to follow.
- *Responsibility* is the obligation incurred by individuals in their roles in the formal organization in order to effectively perform assignments.
- *Accountability* is the state of being totally answerable for the satisfactory completion of a specific assignment. (Accountability = authority + responsibility.)

Authority and responsibility can be delegated (downward) to lower levels in the organization, whereas accountability usually rests with the individual. Accountability is the summation of authority and responsibility. Yet, many executives refuse to delegate and argue that an individual can have total accountability just through responsibility.

Even with these clearly definable divisions of authority, responsibility, and accountability, establishing good interface relationships between project and functional managers can take a great deal of time, especially during the conversion from a traditional to a project organizational form. Trust is the key to success here; it can overcome any problems in authority, responsibility, or accountability. When trust exists, the normal progression in the growth of the project-functional interface bond is as follows:

- Even though a problem exists, both the project and functional managers deny that any problem exists.
- When the problem finally surfaces, each manager blames the other.
- As trust develops, both managers readily admit responsibility for several of the problems.
- The project and functional managers meet face-to-face to work out the problem.
- The project and functional managers begin to formally and informally anticipate the problems that can occur.

For each of the organizational structures described in the following sections, advantages and disadvantages are listed. Many of the disadvantages stem from possible conflicts arising from problems in authority, responsibility, and accountability. The reader should identify these conflicts as such.

3.2 TRADITIONAL (CLASSICAL) ORGANIZATION

The traditional management structure has survived for more than two centuries. However, recent business developments, such as the rapid rate of change in technology and position in the marketplace, as well as increased stockholder demands, have created strains on existing organizational forms. Fifty years ago companies could survive with only one or perhaps two product lines. The classical management organization, as shown in Figure 3–1, was found to be satisfactory for control, and conflicts were at a minimum.[7]

However, with the passing of time, companies found that survival depended on multiple product lines (i.e., diversification) and vigorous integration of technology into the existing organization. As organizations grew and matured, managers found that company activities were not being integrated effectively, and that new conflicts were arising in the well-established formal and informal channels. Managers began searching for more innovative organizational forms that would alleviate the integration and conflict problems.

Before a valid comparison can be made with the newer forms, the advantages and disadvantages of the traditional structure must be shown. Table 3–1 lists the advantages of the traditional organization. As seen in Figure 3–1, the general manager has beneath him all of the functional entities necessary to either perform R&D or develop and manufacture a product. All activities are performed within the functional groups and are headed by a department (or, in some cases, a division) head. Each department maintains a strong concentration of technical expertise. Since all projects must flow through the functional departments, each project can benefit from the most advanced technology, thus making this

---

7. Many authors refer to classical organizations as pure functional organizations. This can be seen from Figure 3–1. Also note that the department level is below the division level. In some organizations these titles are reversed.

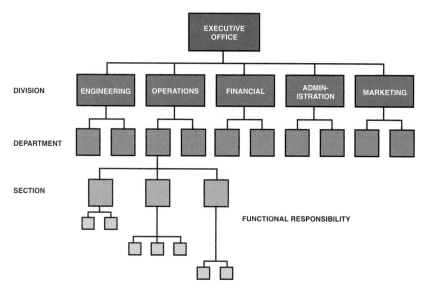

FIGURE 3–1. The traditional management structure.

organizational form well suited to mass production. Functional managers can hire a wide variety of specialists and provide them with easily definable paths for career progression.

The functional managers maintain absolute control over the budget. They establish their own budgets, on approval from above, and specify requirements for additional personnel. Because the functional manager has manpower flexibility and a broad base from which to work, most projects are normally completed within cost.

TABLE 3–1. ADVANTAGES OF THE CLASSICAL TRADITIONAL ORGANIZATION

- Easier budgeting and cost control are possible.
- Better technical control is possible.
  - Specialists can be grouped to share knowledge and responsibility.
  - Personnel can be used on many different projects.
  - All projects will benefit from the most advanced technology (better utilization of scarce personnel).
- It provides flexibility in the use of manpower.
- It provides a broad manpower base to work with.
- It provides continuity in the functional disciplines; policies, procedures, and lines of responsibility are easily defined and understandable.
- It readily admits mass production activities within established specifications.
- It provides good control over personnel, since each employee has one and only one person to report to.
- Communication channels are vertical and well established.
- Quick reaction capability exists, but may be dependent upon the priorities of the functional managers.

Both the formal and informal organizations are well established, and levels of authority and responsibility are clearly defined. Because each person reports to only one individual, communication channels are well structured. If a structure has this many advantages, then why are we looking for other structures?

For each advantage, there is almost always a corresponding disadvantage. Table 3–2 lists the disadvantages of the traditional structure. The majority of these disadvantages are related to the fact that there is no strong central authority or individual responsible for the total project. As a result, integration of activities that cross functional lines becomes a difficult chore, and top-level executives must get involved with the daily routine. Conflicts occur as each functional group struggles for power. The strongest functional group dominates the decision-making process. Functional managers tend to favor what is best for their functional groups rather than what is best for the project. Many times, ideas will remain functionally oriented with very little regard for ongoing projects. In addition, the decision-making process is slow and tedious.

Because there exists no customer focal point, all communications must be channeled through upper-level management. Upper-level managers then act in a customer-relations capacity and refer all complex problems down through the vertical chain of command to the functional managers. The response to the customer's needs therefore becomes a slow and aggravating process because the information must be filtered through several layers of management. If problem-solving and coordination are required to cross functional lines, then additional lead time is required for the approval of decisions. All trade-off analyses must be accomplished through committees chaired by upper-level management.

Projects have a tendency to fall behind schedule in the classical organizational structure. Completing all projects and tasks on time, with a high degree of quality and efficient use of available resources, is all but impossible without continuous involvement of top-level management. Incredibly large lead times are required. Functional managers attend to those tasks that provide better benefits to themselves and their subordinates first. Priorities may be dictated by requirements of the informal as well as formal departmental structure.

TABLE 3–2. DISADVANTAGES OF THE TRADITIONAL/CLASSICAL ORGANIZATION

- No one individual is directly responsible for the total project (i.e., no formal authority; committee solutions).
- It does not provide the project-oriented emphasis necessary to accomplish the project tasks.
- Coordination becomes complex, and additional lead time is required for approval of decisions.
- Decisions normally favor the strongest functional groups.
- There is no customer focal point.
- Response to customer needs is slow.
- There is difficulty in pinpointing responsibility; this is the result of little or no direct project reporting, very little project-oriented planning, and no project authority.
- Motivation and innovation are decreased.
- Ideas tend to be functionally oriented with little regard for ongoing projects.

With the growth of project management in the late 1960s, executives began to realize that many of the problems that had surfaced to the executive levels of management were the result of weaknesses in the traditional structure. William Goggin identified the problems that faced Dow Corning:[8]

> Although Dow Corning was a healthy corporation in 1967, it showed difficulties that troubled many of us in top management. These symptoms were, and still are, common ones in U.S. business and have been described countless times in reports, audits, articles and speeches. Our symptoms took such form as:

- Executives did not have adequate financial information and control of their operations. Marketing managers, for example, did not know how much it cost to produce a product. Prices and margins were set by division managers.
- Cumbersome communications channels existed between key functions, especially manufacturing and marketing.
- In the face of stiffening competition, the corporation remained too internalized in its thinking and organizational structure. It was insufficiently oriented to the outside world.
- Lack of communications between divisions not only created the antithesis of a corporate team effort but also was wasteful of a precious resource—people.
- Long-range corporate planning was sporadic and superficial; this was leading to over-staffing, duplicated effort and inefficiency.

Executive analyses of the traditional structure, identified by Carlisle, are:[9]

- Functional organizations tend to emphasize the separate functional elements at the expense of the whole organization.
- Under functional departmentation there is no group that effectively integrates the various functions of an organization and monitors them from the "big picture standpoint."
- Functional organizations do not tend to develop "general managers."
- Functional organizations emphasize functional relationships based on the vertical organizational hierarchy.
- Functional organizations tend to fragment other management processes.
- Functional organizations develop a strong resistance to change.
- Functional segregation through the formal organization process encourages conflict among the various functions.
- The emphasis on the various operating functions focuses attention on the internal aspects and relations of the company to the detriment of its external relations.
- Functional organizations tend to be closed systems.

---

8. William C. Goggin, "How the Multidimensional Structure Works at Dow Corning," *Harvard Business Review,* January–February 1974, p. 54. Copyright © 1973 by the President and Fellows of Harvard College. All rights reserved.

9. Howard M. Carlisle, "Are Functional Organizations Becoming Obsolete?" Reprinted, by permission of the publisher, from *Management Review* (pp. 4–6), January/1969 © 1969. American Management Association, New York. All rights reserved.

3.3 DEVELOPING WORK INTEGRATION POSITIONS

As companies grew in size, more emphasis was placed on multiple ongoing programs with high-technology requirements. Organizational pitfalls soon appeared, especially in the integration of the flow of work. As management discovered that the critical point in any program is the interface between functional units, the new theories of "interface management" developed.

Because of the interfacing problems, management began searching for innovative methods to coordinate the flow of work between functional units without modification to the existing organizational structure. This coordination was achieved through several integrating mechanisms:[10]

- Rules and procedures
- Planning processes
- Hierarchical referral
- Direct contact

By specifying and documenting management policies and procedures, management attempted to eliminate conflicts between functional departments. Management felt that, even though many of the projects were different, the actions required by the functional personnel were repetitive and predictable. The behavior of the individuals should therefore be easily integrated into the flow of work with minimum communication necessary between individuals or functional groups.

Another means of reducing conflicts and minimizing the need for communication was detailed planning. Functional representation would be present at all planning, scheduling, and budget meetings. This method worked best for non-repetitive tasks and projects.

In the traditional organization, one of the most important responsibilities of upper-level management was the resolution of conflicts through "hierarchical referral." The continuous conflicts and struggle for power between the functional units consistently required that upper-level personnel resolve those problems resulting from situations that were either nonroutine or unpredictable and for which no policies or procedures existed.

The fourth method is direct contact and interactions by the functional managers. The rules and procedures, as well as the planning process method, were designed to minimize ongoing communications between functional groups. The quantity of conflicts that executives had to resolve forced key personnel to spend a great percentage of their time as arbitrators, rather than as managers. To alleviate problems of hierarchical referral, upper-level management requested that all conflicts be resolved at the lowest possible levels. This required that functional managers meet face-to-face to resolve conflicts.

---

10. Jay R. Galbraith, "Matrix Organization Designs." Reprinted with permission from *Business Horizons,* February 1971, pp. 29–40. Copyright © 1971 by the Board of Trustees at Indiana University. Used with permission. Galbraith defines a fifth mechanism, liaison departments, that will be discussed later in this section.

In many organizations, these new methods proved ineffective, primarily because there still existed a need for a focal point for the project to ensure that all activities would be properly integrated.

When the need for project managers was acknowledged, the next logical question was that of where in the organization to place them. Executives preferred to keep project managers as low as possible in the organization. After all, if they reported to someone high up, they would have to be paid more and would pose a continuous threat to management.

The first attempt to resolve this problem was to develop project leaders or coordinators within each functional department, as shown in Figure 3–2. Section-level personnel were temporarily assigned as project leaders and would return to their former positions at project termination. This is why the term "project leader" is used rather than "project manager," as the word "manager" implies a permanent relationship. This arrangement proved effective for coordinating and integrating work within one department, provided that the correct project leader was selected. Some employees considered this position as an increase in power and status, and conflicts occurred about whether assignments should be based on experience, seniority, or capability. Some employees wanted the title merely so they could use it on their resumes. Furthermore, the project leaders had almost no authority, and section-level managers refused to take directions from them. Many

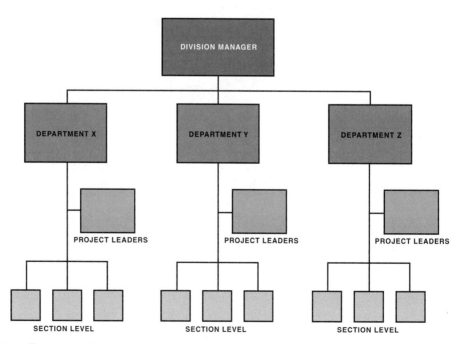

FIGURE 3–2. Departmental project management.

section managers were afraid that if they did take direction, they were admitting that the project leaders were next in line for the department manager's position.

When the activities required efforts that crossed more than one functional boundary, say, two or more sections or departments, conflicts arose. The project leader in one department did not have the authority to coordinate activities in any other department. Furthermore, the creation of this new position caused internal conflicts within each department. As a result, many employees refused to become dedicated to project management and were anxious to return to their "secure" jobs. Quite often, especially when cross-functional integration was required, the division manager was forced to act as the project manager. If the employee enjoyed the assignment of project leader, he would try to "stretch out" the project as long as possible.

Even though we have criticized this organizational form, it does not mean that it cannot work. Any organizational form (yes, any form) will work if the employees want it to work. As an example, a computer manufacturer has a midwestern division with three departments within it, as in Figure 3–2, and approximately fourteen people per department. When a project comes in, the division manager determines which department will handle most of the work. Let us say that the work load is 60 percent department X, 30 percent department Y, and 10 percent department Z. Since most of the effort is in department X, the project leader is selected from that department. When the project leader goes into the other two departments to get resources, he will almost always get the resources he wants. There are two reasons why this organizational form works in this case:

- The other department managers know that they may have to supply the project leader on the next activity.
- There are only three functional boundaries or departments involved (i.e., a small organization).

This structure works best in small organizations where minimal cross-communication is necessary.

The next step in the evolution of project management was the task force concept. The rationale behind the task force concept was that integration could be achieved if each functional unit placed a representative on the task force. The group could then jointly solve problems as they occurred, provided that budget limitations were still adhered to. Theoretically, decisions could now be made at the lowest possible levels, thus expediting information and reducing, or even eliminating, delay time.

The task force was composed of both part-time and full-time personnel from each department involved. Daily meetings were held to review activities and discuss potential problems. Functional managers soon found that their task force employees were spending more time in unproductive meetings than in performing functional activities. In addition, the nature of the task force position caused many individuals to shift membership within the informal organization. Many functional managers then placed nonqualified and inexperienced individuals on task forces. The result was that the group soon became ineffective because they either did not have the information necessary to make the decisions, or lacked the authority (delegated by the functional managers) to allocate resources and assign work.

Development of the task force concept was a giant step toward conflict resolution: Work was being accomplished on time, schedules were being maintained, and costs were usually within budget. But integration and coordination were still problems because there were no specified authority relationships or individuals to oversee the entire project through completion. Many attempts were made to overcome this by placing various people in charge of the task force: Functional managers, division heads, and even upper-level management had opportunities to direct task forces. However, without formal project authority relationships, task force members maintained loyalty to their functional organizations, and when conflicts came about between the project and functional organization, the project always suffered.

Although the task force concept was a step in the right direction, the disadvantages strongly outweighed the advantages. A strength of the approach was that it could be established very rapidly and with very little paperwork. Integration, however, was complicated; work flow was difficult to control; and functional support was difficult to obtain because it was almost always strictly controlled by the functional manager. In addition, task forces were found to be grossly ineffective on long-range projects.

The next step in the evolution of work integration was the establishment of liaison departments, particularly in engineering divisions that perform multiple projects involving a high level of technology (see Figure 3–3). The purpose of the liaison department was to handle transactions between functional units within the (engineering) division. The liaison personnel received their authority through

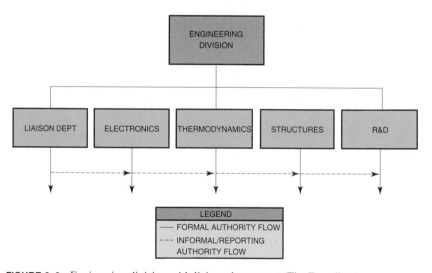

FIGURE 3–3. Engineering division with liaison department (The Expeditor).

the division head. The liaison department did not actually resolve conflicts. Their prime function was to assure that all departments worked toward the same requirements and goals. Liaison departments are still in existence in many large companies and typically handle engineering changes and design problems.

Unfortunately, the liaison department is simply a scaleup of the project coordinator within the department. The authority given to the liaison department extends only to the outer boundaries of the division. If a conflict came about between the manufacturing and engineering divisions, for example, hierarchical referral would still be needed for resolution. Today, liaison departments are synonymous with project engineering and systems engineering departments, and the individuals in these departments have the authority to span the entire organization.

3.4 LINE–STAFF ORGANIZATION (PROJECT COORDINATOR)

It soon became obvious that control of a project must be given to personnel whose first loyalty is directed toward the completion of the project. For this purpose, the project management position must be separated from any controlling influence of the functional managers. Figure 3–4 shows a typical line–staff organization.

Two possible situations can exist with this form of line–staff project control. In the first situation, the project manager serves only as the focal point for activity control, that is, a center for information. The prime responsibility of the project manager is to keep the division manager informed of the status of the project and to "harass" or attempt to "influence" managers into completing activities on time. Referring to such early project managers, Galbraith stated, "Since these men had no formal authority, they had to resort to their technical competence and their interpersonal skills in order to be effective."[11]

The project manager in the first situation maintained monitoring authority only, despite the fact that both he and the functional manager reported to the same individual. Both work assignments and merit reviews were made by the functional managers. Department managers refused to take direction from the project managers because to do so would seem an admission that the project manager was next in line to be the division manager.

The amount of authority given to the project manager posed serious problems. Almost all upper-level and division managers were from the classical management schools and therefore maintained serious reservations about how much authority to relinquish. Many of these managers considered it a demotion if they had to give up any of their long-established powers.

---

11. Jay R. Galbraith, "Matrix Organization Designs." Reprinted with permission from *Business Horizons*, February 1971, pp. 29–40. Copyright © 1971 by the Board of Trustees at Indiana University. Used with permission.

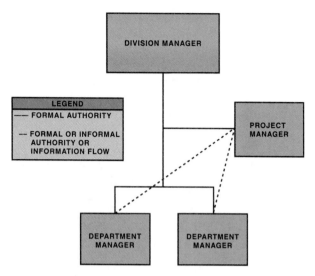

FIGURE 3–4. Line–staff organization (Project Coordinator).

In the second situation, the project manager is given more authority; using the authority vested in him by the division manager, he can assign work to individuals in the functional organizations. The functional manager, however, still maintains the authority to perform merit reviews, but cannot enforce both professional and organizational standards in the completion of an activity. The individual performing the work is now caught in a web of authority relationships, and additional conflicts develop because functional managers are forced to share their authority with the project manager.

Although this second situation did occur during the early stages of matrix project management, it did not last because:

- Upper-level management was not ready to cope with the problems arising from shared authority.
- Upper-level management was reluctant to relinquish any of its power and authority to project managers.
- Line–staff project managers who reported to a division head did not have any authority or control over those portions of a project in other divisions; that is, the project manager in the engineering division could not direct activities in the manufacturing division.

3.5 PURE PRODUCT (PROJECTIZED) ORGANIZATION

The pure product organization, as shown in Figure 3–5, develops as a division within a division. As long as there exists a continuous flow of projects, work is

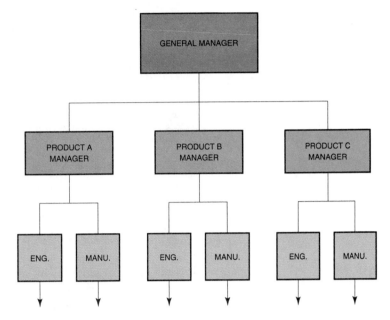

FIGURE 3–5. Pure product structure.

stable and conflicts are at a minimum. The major advantage of this organizational flow is that one individual, the program manager, maintains complete line authority over the entire project. Not only does he assign work, but he also conducts merit reviews. Because each individual reports to only one person, strong communication channels develop that result in a very rapid reaction time.

In pure product organizations, long lead times became a thing of the past. Trade-off studies could be conducted as fast as time would permit without the need to look at the impact on other projects (unless, of course, identical facilities or equipment were required). Functional managers were able to maintain qualified staffs for new product development without sharing personnel with other programs and projects.

The responsibilities attributed to the project manager were entirely new. First of all, his authority was now granted by the vice president and general manager. The program manager handled all conflicts, both those within his organization and those involving other projects. Interface management was conducted at the program manager level. Upper-level management was now able to spend more time on executive decision making than on conflict arbitration.

The major disadvantage with the pure project form is the cost of maintaining the organization. There is no chance for sharing an individual with another project in order to reduce costs. Personnel are usually attached to these projects long after they are needed because once an employee is given up, the project manager might never be able to get him back. Motivating personnel becomes a problem. At project completion, functional personnel do not "have a home" to return to.

TABLE 3–3.   ADVANTAGES OF THE PRODUCT ORGANIZATIONAL FORM

- It provides complete line authority over the project (i.e., strong control through a single project authority).
- The project participants work directly for the project manager. Unprofitable product lines are easily identified and can be eliminated.
- There are strong communications channels.
- Staffs can maintain expertise on a given project without sharing key personnel.
- Very rapid reaction time is provided.
- Personnel demonstrate loyalty to the project; better morale with product identification.
- A focal point develops for out-of-company customer relations.
- There is flexibility in determining time (schedule), cost, and performance trade-offs.
- Interface management becomes easier as unit size is decreased.
- Upper-level management maintains more free time for executive decision making.

Many organizations place these individuals into an overhead labor pool from which selection can be made during new project development. People still in the labor pool for a certain period of time may be laid off indefinitely. As each project comes to a close, people become uneasy and often strive to prove their worth to the company by overachieving, a condition that is only temporary. It is very difficult for management to convince key functional personnel that they do, in fact, have career opportunities in this type of organization.

In pure functional (traditional) structures, technologies are well developed, but project schedules often fall behind. In the pure project structure, the fast reaction time keeps activities on schedule, but technology suffers because without strong functional groups, which maintain interactive technical communication, the company's outlook for meeting the competition may be severely hampered. The engineering department for one project might not communicate with its counterpart on other projects, and duplication of efforts can easily occur.

The last major disadvantage of this organizational form lies in the control of facilities and equipment. The most frequent conflict is that which occurs when two projects require use of the same piece of equipment or facilities at the same time. Hierarchical referral is required to alleviate this problem. Upper-level management can assign priorities to these projects. This is normally accomplished by

TABLE 3–4. DISADVANTAGES OF THE PRODUCT ORGANIZATION FORM

- Cost of maintaining this form in a multiproduct company would be prohibitive due to duplication of effort, facilities, and personnel; inefficient usage.
- There exists a tendency to retain personnel on a project long after they are needed. Upper-level management must balance workloads as projects start up and are phased out.
- Technology suffers because, without strong functional groups, outlook of the future to improve company's capabilities for new programs would be hampered (i.e., no perpetuation of technology).
- Control of functional (i.e., organizational) specialists requires top-level coordination.
- There is a lack of opportunities for technical interchange between projects.
- There is a lack of career continuity and opportunities for project personnel.

defining certain projects as strategic, tactical, or operational—the same definitions usually given to plans.

Table 3–3 summarizes the advantages of this organizational form, and Table
3–4 lists the disadvantages.

3.6 MATRIX ORGANIZATIONAL FORM

The matrix organizational form is an attempt to combine the advantages of the
pure functional structure and the product organizational structure. This form is ideally suited for companies, such as construction, that are "project-driven." Figure
3–6 shows a typical matrix structure. Each project manager reports directly to the
vice president and general manager. Since each project represents a potential profit
center, the power and authority used by the project manager come directly from
the general manager. The project manager has total responsibility and accountability for project success. The functional departments, on the other hand, have
functional responsibility to maintain technical excellence on the proj-ect. Each
functional unit is headed by a department manager whose prime responsibility is
to ensure that a unified technical base is maintained and that all available information can be exchanged for each project. Department managers must also keep
their people aware of the latest technical accomplishments in the industry.

Project management is a "coordinative" function, whereas matrix management is a collaborative function division of project management. In the coordi-

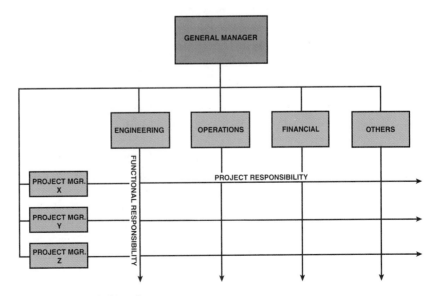

FIGURE 3–6. Typical matrix structure.

native or project organization, work is generally assigned to specific people or units who "do their own thing." In the collaborative or matrix organization, information sharing may be mandatory, and several people may be required for the same piece of work. In a project organization, authority for decision making and direction rests with the project leader, whereas in a matrix it rests with the team.

Certain ground rules exist for matrix development:

- Participants must spend full time on the project; this ensures a degree of loyalty.
- Horizontal as well as vertical channels must exist for making commitments.
- There must be quick and effective methods for conflict resolution.
- There must be good communication channels and free access between managers.
- All managers must have input into the planning process.
- Both horizontally and vertically oriented managers must be willing to negotiate for resources.
- The horizontal line must be permitted to operate as a separate entity except for administrative purposes.

These ground rules simply state some of the ideal conditions that matrix structures should possess. Each ground rule brings with it advantages and disadvantages.

Before describing the advantages and disadvantages of this structure, the organization concepts must be introduced. The basis for the matrix approach is an attempt to create synergism through shared responsibility between project and functional management. Yet this is easier said than done. *No two working environments are the same, and, therefore, no two companies will have the same matrix design.* The following questions must be answered before successful operation of a matrix structure can be achieved:

- If each functional unit is responsible for one aspect of a project, and other parts are conducted elsewhere (possibly subcontracted to other companies), how can a synergistic environment be created?
- Who decides which element of a project is most important?
- How can a functional unit (operating in a vertical structure) answer questions and achieve project goals and objectives that are compatible with other projects?

The answers to these questions depend on mutual understanding between the project and functional managers. Since both individuals maintain some degree of authority, responsibility, and accountability on each project, they must continuously negotiate. Unfortunately, the program manager might only consider what is best for his project (disregarding all others), whereas the functional manager might consider his organization more important than each project.

In Chapter 1 we stated that project management is more behavioral than quantitative and that interpersonal skills and communicative skills are extremely important attributes of the project manager. Figure 3–7 shows why these skills are so important in matrix management.

In the matrix:

- There should be no disruption due to dual accountability.
- A difference in judgment should not delay work in progress.

FIGURE 3–7. Matrix humor. (Source unknown)

In order to get the job done, project managers sometimes need adequate organizational status and authority. A corporate executive contends that the organization chart shown in Figure 3–6 can be modified to show that the project managers have adequate organizational authority by placing the department manager boxes at the tip of the functional responsibility arrowheads. The executive further contends that, with this approach, the project managers appear to be higher in the organization than their departmental counterparts but are actually equal in status. Executives who prefer this method must exercise due caution because the line and project managers may not feel that there still exists an equality in the balance of power.

Problem solving in this type of environment is a fragmented and diffused process. The project manager acts as a unifying agent for project control of resources and technology. He must maintain open channels of communication between himself and functional units as well as between functional units themselves to prevent suboptimization of individual projects. The problems of routine administration can and do become a cost-effective requirement.

In many situations, functional managers have the power and means of making a project manager look good, provided that they can be motivated enough to think in terms of what is best for the project. Unfortunately, this is not always accomplished. As stated by Mantell:[12]

> There exists an inevitable tendency for hierarchically arrayed units to seek solutions and to identify problems in terms of scope of duties of particular units rather than looking beyond them. This phenomenon exists without regard for the competence of the executive concerned. It comes about because of authority delegation and functionalism.

Such tunnel vision can exist at all levels of management.

The project environment and functional environment cannot be separated; they must interact. The location of the project and functional unit interface is the focal point for all activities.

The functional manager controls departmental resources (i.e., people). This poses a problem because, although the project manager maintains the maximum control (through the line managers) over all resources including cost and personnel, the functional manager must provide staff for the project's requirements. It is therefore inevitable that conflicts occur between functional and project managers:

> These conflicts revolve about items such as project priority, manpower costs, and the assignment of functional personnel to the project manager. Each project manager will, of course, want the best functional operators assigned to his program. In addition to these problems, the accountability for profit and loss is much more difficult in a matrix organization than in a project organization.

---

12. Leroy H. Mantell, "The Systems Approach and Good Management." Reprinted with permission from *Business Horizons,* October 1972 (p. 50). Copyright © 1972 by the Board of Trustees at Indiana University. Used with permission.

Project managers have a tendency to blame overruns on functional managers, stating that the cost of the function was excessive. Whereas functional managers have a tendency to blame excessive costs on project managers with the argument that there were too many changes, more work required than defined initially and other such arguments.[13]

The individual placed at the interface position has two bosses: He must take direction from both the project manager and the functional manager. The merit review and hiring and firing responsibilities still rest with the department manager. Merit reviews are normally made by the functional manager after discussions with the program manager. The functional manager may not have the time necessary to measure the progress of this individual continuously. He must rely on the word of the program manager for merit review and promotion. The interface members generally give loyalty to the person signing their merit review. This poses a problem, especially if conflicting orders are given by the functional and project managers. The simplest solution is for the individual at the interface to ask the functional and project managers to communicate with each other to resolve the problem. This type of situation poses a problem for project managers:

- How does a project manager motivate an individual working on a project (either part-time or full-time) so that his loyalties are with the project?
- How does a project manager convince an individual to perform work according to project direction and specifications when these requests may be in conflict with department policy, especially if the individual feels that his functional boss may not regard him with much favor?

There are many advantages to matrix structures, as shown in Table 3–5. Functional units exist primarily as support for a project. Because of this, key people can be shared and costs can be minimized. People can be assigned to a variety of challenging problems. Each person, therefore, has a "home" after project completion. Each person can be shown a career path in the company. People in these organizations are especially responsive to motivation and end-item identification. Functional managers find it easy to develop and maintain a strong technical base and can, therefore, spend more time on complex problem solving. Knowledge can be shared for all projects.

The matrix structure can provide a rapid response to changes, conflicts, and other project needs. Conflicts are normally minimal, but those requiring resolution are easily resolved using hierarchical referral.

This rapid response is a result of the project manager's authority to commit company resources, provided that scheduling conflicts with other projects can be eliminated. Furthermore, the project manager has the authority independently to establish his own project policies and procedures, provided that they do not con-

---

13. William P. Killian, "Project Management—Future Organizational Concepts," *Marquette Business Review,* Vol. 2, 1971, pp. 90–107.

TABLE 3–5. ADVANTAGES OF A PURE MATRIX ORGANIZATIONAL FORM

- The project manager maintains maximum project control (through the line managers) over all resources, including cost and personnel.
- Policies and procedures can be set up independently for each project, provided that they do not contradict company policies and procedures.
- The project manager has the authority to commit company resources, provided that scheduling does not cause conflicts with other projects.
- Rapid responses are possible to changes, conflict resolution, and project needs (as technology or schedule).
- The functional organizations exist primarily as support for the project.
- Each person has a "home" after project completion. People are susceptible to motivation and end-item identification. Each person can be shown a career path.
- Because key people can be shared, the program cost is minimized. People can work on a variety of problems; that is, better people control is possible.
- A strong technical base can be developed, and much more time can be devoted to complex problem-solving. Knowledge is available for all projects on an equal basis.
- Conflicts are minimal, and those requiring hierarchical referrals are more easily resolved.
- There is a better balance between time, cost, and performance.
- Rapid development of specialists and generalists occurs.
- Authority and responsibility are shared.
- Stress is distributed among the team (and the functional managers).

flict with company policies. This can do away with much red tape and permit a better balance between time, cost, and performance.

The matrix structure provides us with the best of two worlds: the traditional structure and the matrix structure. The advantages of the matrix structure eliminate almost all of the disadvantages of the traditional structure. The word "matrix" often brings fear to the hearts of executives because it implies radical change, or at least they think that it does. If we take a close look at Figure 3–6, we can see that the traditional structure is still there. The matrix is simply horizontal lines superimposed over the traditional structure. The horizontal lines will come and go as projects start up and terminate, but the traditional structure will remain forever.

Matrix structures are not without their disadvantages, as shown in Table 3–6. The first three elements in Table 3–6 are due to the horizontal and vertical work flow requirements of a matrix. Actually the flow may even be multidimensional if the project manager has to report to customers or corporate or other personnel in addition to his superior and the functional line managers.

Most companies believe that if they have enough resources to staff all of the projects that come along, then the company is "overstaffed." As a result of this philosophy, priorities may change continuously, perhaps even daily. Management's goals for a project may be drastically different from the project's goals, especially if executive involvement is lacking during the definition of a project's requirements in the planning phase. In a matrix, conflicts and their resolution may be a continuous process, especially if priorities change continuously. Regardless of how mature an organization becomes, there will always exist difficulty in monitoring and control because of the complex, multidirectional work flow. Another

TABLE 3–6. DISADVANTAGES OF A PURE MATRIX ORGANIZATIONAL FORM

- Multidimensional information flow.
- Multidimensional work flow.
- Dual reporting.
- Continuously changing priorities.
- Management goals different from project goals.
- Potential for continuous conflict and conflict resolution.
- Difficulty in monitoring and control.
- Company-wide, the organizational structure is not cost-effective because more people than necessary are required, primarily administrative.
- Each project organization operates independently. Care must be taken that duplication of efforts does not occur.
- More effort and time are needed initially to define policies and procedures, compared to traditional form.
- Functional managers may be biased according to their own set of priorities.
- Balance of power between functional and project organizations must be watched.
- Balance of time, cost, and performance must be monitored.
- Although rapid response time is possible for individual problem resolution, the reaction time can become quite slow.
- Employees and managers are more susceptible to role ambiguity than in traditional form.
- Conflicts and their resolution may be a continuous process (possibly requiring support of an organizational development specialist).
- People do not feel that they have any control over their own destiny when continuously reporting to multiple managers.

disadvantage of the matrix organization is that more administrative personnel are needed to develop policies and procedures, and therefore both direct and indirect administrative costs will increase. In addition, it is impossible to manage projects with a matrix if there are steep horizontal or vertical pyramids for supervision and reporting, because each manager in the pyramid will want to reduce the authority of the managers operating within the matrix. Each project organization operates independently. This poses a problem in that duplication of effort can easily occur; for example, two projects might be developing the same cost accounting procedure, or functional personnel may be doing similar R&D efforts on different projects. Both vertical and horizontal communication is a must in a project matrix organization.

Functional managers are human and, therefore, may be biased according to their own sets of priorities. Project managers, however, must realize that their projects are not the only ones, and that a proper balance is needed; this includes a balance of power between functional and project units as well as a proper balance between time, cost, and performance.

One of the advantages of the matrix is a rapid response time for problem resolution. This rapid response generally applies to slow-moving projects where problems occur within each functional unit. On fast-moving projects, the reaction time can become quite slow, especially if the problem spans more than one functional unit. This slow reaction time exists because the functional employees assigned to the project do not have the authority to make decisions, allocate functional resources, or change schedules. Only the line managers have this authority. Therefore, in times of crisis, functional managers must be actively brought into the "big picture" and invited to team meetings.

Middleton has listed four additional undesirable results that can develop from the use of matrix organizations and that can affect company capabilities:[14]

- Project priorities and competition for talent may interrupt the stability of the organization and interfere with its long-range interests by upsetting the traditional business of functional organizations.
- Long-range plans may suffer as the company gets more involved in meeting schedules and fulfilling the requirements of temporary projects.
- Shifting people from project to project may disrupt the training of employees and specialists, thereby hindering the growth and development within their fields of specialization.
- Lessons learned on one project may not be communicated to other projects.

In addition to the above-mentioned disadvantages, Davis and Lawrence have identified nine matrix pathologies:[15]

- Power struggles: The horizontal versus vertical hierarchy.
- Anarchy: Formation of organizational islands during periods of stress.
- Groupitis: Confusing the matrix as being synonymous with group decision making.
- Collapse during economic crunch: Flourishing during periods of growth and collapsing during lean times.
- Excessive overhead: How much matrix supervision is actually necessary?
- Decision strangulation: Too many people involved in decision making.
- Sinking: Pushing the matrix down into the depths of the organization.
- Layering: A matrix within a matrix.
- Navel gazing: Becoming overly involved in the internal relationships of the organization.

The matrix structure therefore becomes a compromise in an attempt to obtain the best of two worlds. In pure product management, technology suffered because there did not exist any single group for planning and integration. In the pure functional organization, time and schedule are sacrificed. Matrix project management is an attempt to obtain maximum technology and performance in a cost-effective manner and within time and schedule constraints.

We should note that with proper executive-level planning and control, all of the disadvantages can be eliminated. This is the only organizational form where such control is possible. However, care must be taken with regard to the first dis-

---

14. C. J. Middleton, "How to Set Up a Project Organization," *Harvard Business Review,* March–April 1967. Copyright © 1967 by the President and Fellows of Harvard College. All rights reserved.

15. Stanley M. Davis and Paul R. Lawrence, *Matrix* (adapted from pp. 129–144), © 1977 by Addison Wesley Longman Publishing, Inc. Reprinted by permission of Addison Wesley Longman, Inc.

advantage listed in Table 3–6. There is a natural tendency when going to a matrix to create more positions in executive management than are actually necessary in order to get better control, and this will drive up the overhead rates. This may be true in some companies, but there is a point where the matrix will become mature and fewer people will be required at the top levels of management. When executives wish to reduce cost, they normally begin at the top by combining positions when slots become vacant. This is a natural fallout of having mature project and line managers with less top-level interference.

Previously we identified the necessity for the project manager to be able to establish his own policies, procedures, rules, and guidelines. Obviously, with personnel reporting in two directions and to multiple managers, conflicts over administration can easily occur. According to Shannon:[16]

> When operating under a matrix management approach, it is obviously extremely important that the authority and responsibility of each manager be clearly defined, understood and accepted by both functional and program people. These relationships need to be spelled out in writing. It is essential that in the various operating policies, the specific authority of the program direction, and the authority of the functional executive be defined in terms of operational direction.

Most practitioners consider the matrix to be a two-dimensional system where each project represents a potential profit center and each functional department represents a cost center. (This interpretation can also create conflict because functional departments may feel that they no longer have an input into corporate profits.) For large corporations with multiple divisions, the matrix is no longer two-dimensional, but multidimensional.

William C. Goggin has described geographical area and space and time as the third and fourth dimensions of the Dow Corning matrix:[17]

> Geographical areas . . . business development varied widely from area to area, and the profit-center and cost-center dimensions could not be carried out everywhere in the same manner. . . . Dow Corning area organizations are patterned after our major U.S. organizations. Although somewhat autonomous in their operation, they subscribe to the overall corporate objectives, operating guidelines, and planning criteria. During the annual planning cycle, for example, there is a mutual exchange of sales, expense, and profit projections between the functional and business managers headquartered in the United States and the area managers around the world.
>
> Space and time. . . . A fourth dimension of the organization denotes fluidity and movement through time. . . . The multidimensional organization is far from

---

16. Robert Shannon, "Matrix Management Structures," *Industrial Engineering,* March 1972, pp. 27–28. Published and copyright © 1972 by the Institute of Industrial Engineers, 25 Technology Park, Norcross, Georgia 30092 (770-449-0461). Reprinted with permission.

17. William C. Goggin, "How the Multidimensional Structure Works at Dow Corning," *Harvard Business Review,* January–February 1974, pp. 56–57. Copyright © 1973 by the President and Fellows of Harvard College. All rights reserved.

rigid; it is constantly changing. Unlike centralized or decentralized systems that are too often rooted deep in the past, the multidimensional organization is geared toward the future: Long-term planning is an inherent part of its operation.

Goggin then went on to describe the advantages that Dow Corning expected to gain from the multidimensional organization:

- Higher profit generation even in an industry (silicones) price-squeezed by competition. (Much of our favorable profit picture seems due to a better over-all understanding and practice of expense controls through the company.)
- Increased competitive ability based on technological innovation and product quality without a sacrifice in profitability.
- Sound, fast decision making at all levels in the organization, facilitated by stratified but open channels of communications, and by a totally participa-tive working environment.
- A healthy and effective balance of authority among the businesses, func-tions, and areas.
- Progress in developing short- and long-range planning with the support of all employees.
- Resource allocations that are proportional to expected results.
- More stimulating and effective on-the-job training.
- Accountability that is more closely related to responsibility and authority.
- Results that are visible and measurable.
- More top-management time for long-range planning and less need to be-come involved in day-to-day operations.

Obviously, the matrix structure is the most complex of all organizational forms. Careful consideration must be given as to where and how the matrix or-ganization fits into the total organization. Grinnell and Apple define four situa-tions where it is most practical to consider a matrix:[18]

- When complex, short-run products are the organization's primary output.
- When a complicated design calls for both innovation and timely completion.
- When several kinds of sophisticated skills are needed in designing, building, and testing the products—skills then need constant updating and develop-ment.
- When a rapidly changing marketplace calls for significant changes in prod-ucts, perhaps between the time they are conceived and delivered.

Matrix implementation requires:

- Training in matrix operations
- Training in how to maintain open communications
- Training in problem solving

---

18. S. K. Grinnell and H. P. Apple, "When Two Bosses Are Better Than One," *Machine Design,* January 1975, pp. 84–87.

- Compatible reward systems
- Role definitions

An excellent report on when the matrix will and will not work was made by Wintermantel:[19]

- Situational factors conducive to successful matrix applications:
  - Similar products produced in common plants but serving quite different markets.
  - Different products produced in different plants but serving the same market or customer and utilizing a common distribution channel.
  - Short-cycle contract businesses where each contract is specifically defined and essentially unrelated to other contracts.
  - Complex, rapidly changing business environment which required close multifunctional integration of expertise in response to change.
  - Intensive customer focus businesses where customer responsiveness and solution of customer problems is considered critical (and where the assigned matrix manager represents a focal point within the component for the customer).
  - A large number of products/projects/programs which are scattered over many points on the maturity curve and where limited resources must be selectively allocated to provide maximum leverage.
  - Strong requirement for getting into and out of businesses on a timely and low cost basis. May involve fast buildup and short lead times. Frequent situations where you may want to test entrance into a business arena without massive commitment of resources and with ease of exit assured.
  - High technology businesses where scarce state-of-the-art technical talent must be spread over many projects in the proposal/advanced design stage, but where less experienced or highly talented personnel are adequate for detailed design and follow-on work.
  - Situations where products are unique and discrete but where technology, facilities or processes have high commonality, are interchangeable or are interdependent.
- Situational factors tending toward nonviable matrix applications:
  - Single product line or similar products produced in common plants and serving the same market.
  - Multiple products produced in several dedicated plants serving different customers and/or utilizing different distribution channels.
  - Stable business environment where changes tend to be glacial and relatively predictable.
  - Long, high volume runs of a limited number of products utilizing mature technology and processes.
  - Little commonality or interdependence in facilities, technology or processes.

---

19. Richard E. Wintermantel, "Application of the Matrix Organization Mode in Industry," *Proceedings of the Eleventh Project Management Institute Seminar Symposium,* 1979, pp. 493–497. Original data source is *General Electric Organization Planning Bulletin,* No. 6, November 3, 1976.

- Situations where only one profit center can be defined and/or small businesses where critical mass considerations are unimportant.
- Businesses following a harvest strategy wherein market share is being consciously relinquished in order to maintain high prices and generate maximum positive cash flow.
- Businesses following a heavy cost take-out strategy where achieving minimum costs is critical.
- Businesses where there is unusual need for rapid decisions, frequently on a sole-source basis, and wherein time is not usually available for integration, negotiation and exploration of a range of action alternatives.
- Heavy geographic dispersion wherein time/distance factors make close interpersonal integration on a face-to-face recurrent basis quite difficult.

3.7 MODIFICATION OF MATRIX STRUCTURES

The matrix can take many forms, but there are basically three common varieties. Each type represents a different degree of authority attributed to the program manager and indirectly identifies the relative size of the company. As an example, in the matrix of Figure 3–6 all program managers report directly to the general manager. This type of arrangement works best for small companies that have a minimum number of projects and assumes that the general manager has sufficient time to coordinate activities between his project managers. In this type of arrangement, all conflicts between projects are hierarchically referred to the general manager for resolution.

As companies grew in size and the number of projects, the general manager found it increasingly difficult to act as the focal point for all projects. A new position was created, that of director of programs, or manager of programs or projects. This is shown in Figure 3–8. The director of programs was responsible for all program management. This freed the general manager from the daily routine of having to monitor all programs himself.

Beck has elaborated on the basic role of this new position, the manager of project managers (M.P.M.):[20]

> One difference in the roles of the M.P.M. and the project manager is that the M.P.M. must place a great deal more emphasis on the overview of a project than on the nuts and bolts, tools, networks and the details of managing the project. The M.P.M. must see how the project fits into the overall organizational plan and how projects interrelate. His perspective is a little different from the project manager who is looking at the project on its own merits rather than how it fits into the overall organization.

---

20. Dale R. Beck, "The Role of the Manager of Project Managers," *Proceedings of the Ninth Annual International Seminar/Symposium on Project Management,* October 24–26, 1977, Chicago, Illinois, pp. 139–141.

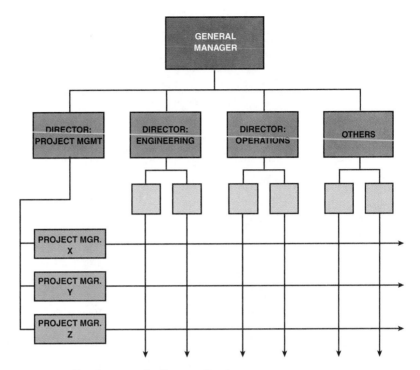

FIGURE 3–8. Development of a director of project management.

The M.P.M. is a project manager, a people manager, a change manager and a systems manager. In general, one role cannot be considered more important than the other. The M.P.M. has responsibilities for managing the projects, directing and leading people and the project management effort, and planning for change in the organization. The Manager of Project Managers is a liaison between the Project Management Department and upper management as well as functional department management and acts as a systems manager when serving as a liaison.

Executives contend that an effective span of control is five to seven people. Does this apply to the director of project management as well? Consider a company that has fifteen projects going on at once. There are three projects over $5 million, seven are between $1 and $3 million, and five projects are under $700,000. Each project has a full-time project manager. Can all fifteen project managers report to the same person? The company solved this problem by creating a deputy director of project management. All projects over $1 million reported to the director, and all projects under $1 million went to the deputy director. The director's rationale soon fell by the wayside when he found that the more severe problems that were occupying his time were occurring on projects with a smaller dollar volume, where flexibility in time, cost, and performance was nonexistent and trade-offs were almost impossible. If the project manager is actually a general manager, then the director of project management should be able to supervise effectively more than seven project managers. The desired span of control, of course, will vary from company to company and must take into account:

- The demands imposed on the organization by task complexity
- Available technology
- The external environment
- The needs of the organizational membership
- The types of customers and/or products

These variables influence the internal functioning of the company. Executives must realize that there is no one best way to organize under all conditions. This includes span of control.

As companies expand, it is inevitable that new and more complex conflicts arise. The control of the engineering functions poses such a problem:

Should the project manager have ultimate responsibility for the engineering functions of a project, or should there be a deputy project manager who reports to the director of engineering and controls all technical activity?

Although there are pros and cons for both arrangements, the problem resolved itself in the company mentioned above when projects grew so large that the project manager became unable to handle both the project management and project engineering functions. Then, as shown in Figure 3–9, a chief project engineer was assigned to each project as deputy project manager, but remained functionally assigned to the director of engineering. The project manager was now responsible for time and cost considerations, whereas the project engineer was concerned with technical performance. The project engineer can be either "solid" vertically and "dotted" horizontally, or vice versa. There are also situations where the project engineer may be "solid" in both directions. The decision usually rests with the director of engineering. Of course, in a project where the project engineer would be needed on a part-time basis only, he would be solid vertically and dotted horizontally.

Engineering directors usually demand that the project engineer be solid vertically in order to give technical direction. As one director of engineering stated, "Only engineers that report to me will have the authority to give technical direction to other engineers. After all, how else can I be responsible for the technical integrity of the product when direction comes from outside my organization?"

This subdivision of functions is necessary in order to control large projects adequately. However, for small projects, say $100,000 or less, it is quite common on R&D projects for an engineer to serve as the project manager as well as the project engineer. Here, the project manager must have technical expertise, not merely understanding. Furthermore, this individual can still be attached to a functional engineering support unit other than project engineering. As an example, a mechanical engineering department receives a government contract for $75,000 to perform tests on a new material. The proposal is written by an engineer attached to the department. When the contract is awarded, this individual, although not in

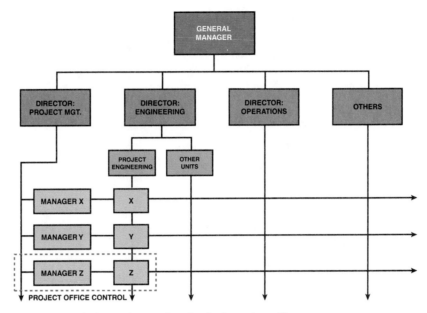

FIGURE 3–9. Placing project engineering in the project office.

the project engineering department, can fulfill the role of project manager and project engineer while still reporting to the manager of the mechanical engineering department. This arrangement works best (and is cost-effective) for short-duration projects that cross a minimum number of functional units.

Finally, we must discuss the characteristics of a project engineer. In Figure 3–10, most people would place the project manager to the right of center with

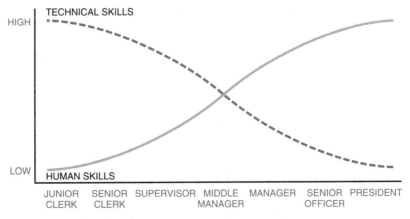

FIGURE 3–10. Philosophy of management.

Project Management	*Project Engineering*
• Total project planning	• Total project planning
• Cost control	• Cost control
• Schedule control	• Schedule control
• System specifications	• System specifications
• Logistics support	• Logistics support

• Contract control	• Configuration control
• Report preparation and distribution	• Fabrication, testing, and production technical leadership support
• Procurement	
• Identification of reliability and maintainability requirements	
• Staffing	
• Priority scheduling	
• Management information systems	

stronger human skills than technical skills, and the project engineer to the left of center with strong technical skills than human skills. The question, of course, is, "How far from the center point will the project manager and project engineer be?" Today, many companies are merging project management and project engineering into one position. This can be seen on the list above. The project manager and project engineer have similar functions above the line but different ones below the line.[21] The main reason for separating project management from project engineering is so that the project engineer will remain "solid" to the director of engineering in order to have the full authority to give technical direction to engineering.

3.8 CENTER FOR PROJECT MANAGEMENT EXPERTISE

In project-driven companies, the creation of a project management division is readily accepted as a necessity to conduct business. Organizational restructuring can quite often occur based on environmental changes and customer's needs. In non–project-driven organizations, employees are less tolerant of organizational change. Power, authority, and turf become important. The implementation of a separate division for project management is extremely difficult. Resistance can become so strong that the entire project management process can suffer.

Recently, non–project-driven companies have created centers for project management expertise. These centers are not necessarily formal line organizations, but

---

21. Procurement, reliability, and maintainability may fall under the responsibility of the project engineer in some companies.

more informal committees whose membership may come from each functional unit of the company. The assignment to the center for expertise can be part-time or full-time; it may be only for six months to a year, and it may or may not require the individual to manage projects. Usually, the center for expertise has as its charter:

- To develop and update a methodology for project management. The methodology usually advocates informal project management.
- To act as a facilitator or trainer in conducting project management training programs.
- To provide project management assistance to any employee who is currently managing projects and requires support in planning, scheduling, and controlling projects.
- To develop or maintain files on "lessons learned" and to see that this information is made available to all project managers.

Since these centers pose no threat to the power and authority of line managers, support is usually easy to obtain.

3.9 MATRIX LAYERING

Matrix layering can be defined as the creation of one matrix within a second matrix. For example, a company can have a total company matrix, and each division or department (i.e., project engineering) can have its own internalized matrix. In the situation of a matrix within a matrix, all matrices are formal operations.

Matrix layering can also be a mix of formal and informal organizations. The for-

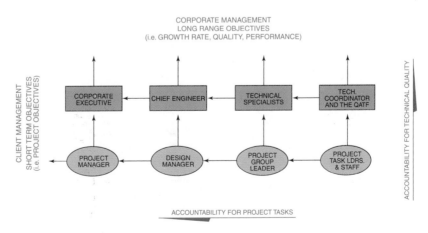

FIGURE 3–11. The design matrix. *Source:* Marc S. Caspe, "An Overview of Project Management and Project Management Services," *Proceedings of the Ninth Annual Seminar Symposium on Project Management,* 1979, pp. 8–9.

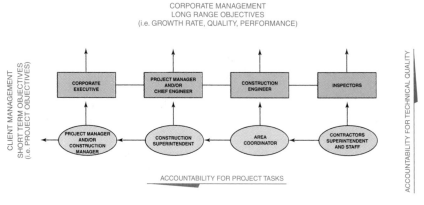

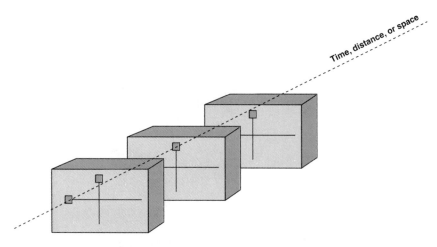

FIGURE 3–12. The construction matrix. *Source:* Marc S. Caspe, "An Overview of Project Management and Project Management Services," *Proceedings of the Ninth Annual Seminar Symposium on Project Management,* 1979, pp. 8–9.

mal matrix exists for work flow, but there can also exist an informal matrix for information flow. There are also authority matrices, leadership matrices, reporting matrices, and informal technical direction matrices. Figures 3–11 and 3–12 identify the design matrix and construction matrix that can exist within the total company matrix.

Another example of layering would be the multidimensional matrix, shown in Figure 3–13, where each slice represents either time, distance, or geographic area. For example, a New York bank utilizes a multinational matrix to control operations in foreign countries. In this case, each foreign country would represent a different slice of the total matrix.

FIGURE 3–13. The multidimensional matrix.

3.10 SELECTING THE ORGANIZATIONAL FORM

Project management has matured as an outgrowth of the need to develop and produce complex and/or large projects in the shortest possible time, within anticipated cost, with required reliability and performance, and (when applicable) to realize a profit. Granted that modern organizations have become so complex that traditional organizational structures and relationships no longer allow for effective management, how can executives determine which organizational form is best, especially since some projects last for only a few weeks or months while others may take years?

To answer such a question, we must first determine whether the necessary characteristics exist to warrant a project management organizational form. Generally speaking, the project management approach can be effectively applied to a onetime undertaking that is:[22]

- Definable in terms of a specific goal
- Infrequent, unique, or unfamiliar to the present organization
- Complex with respect to interdependence of detailed tasks
- Critical to the company

Once a group of tasks is selected and considered to be a project, the next step is to define the kinds of projects, described in Section 2.5. These include individual, staff, special, and matrix or aggregate projects.

Unfortunately, many companies do not have a clear definition of what a project is. As a result, large project teams are often constructed for small projects when they could be handled more quickly and effectively by some other structural form. All structural forms have their advantages and disadvantages, but the project management approach appears to be the best possible alternative.

The basic factors that influence the selection of a project organizational form are:

- Project size
- Project length
- Experience with project management organization
- Philosophy and visibility of upper-level management
- Project location
- Available resources
- Unique aspects of the project

This last item requires further comment. Project management (especially with a matrix) usually works best for the control of human resources and thus may be more applicable to labor-intensive projects rather than capital-intensive

---

22. John M. Stewart, "Making Project Management Work." Reprinted with permission from *Business Horizons*, Fall 1965 (p. 54). Copyright © 1964 by the Board of Trustees at Indiana University. Used with permission.

projects. Labor-intensive organizations have formal project management, whereas capital-intensive organizations may use informal project management. Figure 3–14 shows how matrix management was implemented by an electric equipment manufacturer. The company decided to use fragmented matrix management for facility development projects. After observing the success of the fragmented matrix, the executives expanded matrix operations to include interim and ongoing capital equipment projects. The first three levels were easy to implement. The fourth level, ongoing business, was more difficult to convert to matrix because of functional management resistance and the fear of losing authority.

Four fundamental parameters must be analyzed when considering implementation of a project organizational form:

- Integrating devices
- Authority structure
- Influence distribution
- Information system

Project management is a means of integrating all company efforts, especially research and development, by selecting an appropriate organizational form. Two questions arise when we think of designing the organization to facilitate the work of the integrators:[23]

- Is it better to establish a formal integration department, or simply to set up integrating positions independent of one another?
- If individual integrating positions are set up, how should they be related to the larger structure?

Informal integration works best if, and only if, effective collaboration can be achieved between conflicting units. Without any clearly defined authority, the

---

23. William P. Killian, "Project Management—Future Organizational Concepts," *Marquette Business Review,* Vol. 2, 1971, pp. 90–107.

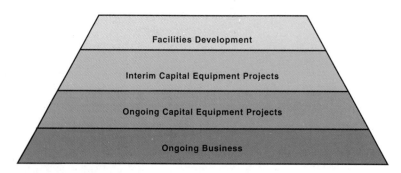

FIGURE 3–14. Matrix development in manufacturing.

role of the integrator is simply to act as an exchange medium across the interface of two functional units. As the size of the organization increases, formal integration positions must exist, especially in situations where intense conflict can occur (e.g., research and development).

Not all organizations need a pure matrix structure to achieve this integration. Many problems can be solved simply through the scalar chain of command, depending on the size of the organization and the nature of the project. The organization needed to achieve project control can vary in size from one person to several thousand people. The organizational structure needed for effective project control is governed by the desires of top management and project circumstances.

Unfortunately, integration and specialization appear to be diametrically opposed. As described by Davis:[24]

> When organization is considered synonymous with structure, the dual needs of specialization and coordination are seen as inversely related, as opposite ends of a single variable, as the horns of a dilemma. Most managers speak of this dilemma in terms of the centralization-decentralization variable. Formulated in this manner, greater specialization leads to more difficulty in coordinating the differentiated units. This is why the (de)centralization pendulum is always swinging, and no ideal point can be found at which it can come to rest.
>
> The division of labor in a hierarchical pyramid means that specialization must be defined either by function, by product, or by area. Firms must select one of these dimensions as primary and then subdivide the other two into subordinate units further down the pyramid. The appropriate choice for primary, secondary and tertiary dimensions is based largely upon the strategic needs of the enterprise.

Top management must decide on the authority structure that will control the integration mechanism. The authority structure can range from pure functional authority (traditional management), to product authority (product management), and finally to dual authority (matrix management). This range is shown in Figure 3–15. From a management point of view, organizational forms are often selected based on how much authority top management wishes to delegate or surrender.

Integration of activities across functional boundaries can also be accomplished by influence. Influence includes such factors as participation in budget planning and approval, design changes, location and size of offices, salaries, and so on. Influence can also cut administrative red tape and develop a much more unified informal organization.

Matrix structures are characterized as strong or weak based on the relative influence that the project manager possesses over the assigned functional resources. When the project manager has more "relative influence" over the performance of the assigned resources than does the line manager, the matrix structure is a strong matrix. In this case, the project manager usually has the

---

24. Stanley M. Davis, "Two Models of Organization: Unity of Command versus Balance of Power," *Sloan Management Review*, Fall 1974, p. 30. Reprinted by permission of the publisher. Copyright © 1974 by the Sloan Management Review Association. All rights reserved.

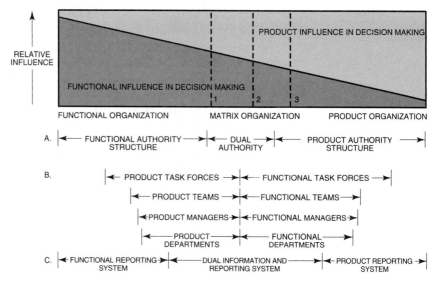

FIGURE 3–15. The range of alternatives. *Source:* Jay R. Galbraith, "Matrix Organization Designs." Reprinted with permission from *Business Horizons,* February 1971 (p. 37). Copyright © 1971 by the Board of Trustees at Indiana University. Used with permission.

knowledge to provide technical direction, assign responsibilities, and may even have a strong input into the performance evaluation of the assigned personnel. If the balance of influence tilts in favor of the line manager, then the matrix is referred to as a weak matrix.

Information systems also play an important role. Previously we stated that one of the advantages of several project management structures is the ability to make both rapid and timely decisions with almost immediate response to environmental changes. Information systems are designed to get the right information to the right person at the right time in a cost-effective manner. Organizational functions must facilitate the flow of information through the management network.

Galbraith has described additional factors that can influence organizational selection. These factors are:[25]

- Diversity of product lines
- Rate of change of the product lines
- Interdependencies among subunits

---

25. Jay R. Galbraith, "Matrix Organization Designs." Reprinted with permission from *Business Horizons,* February 1971, pp. 29–40. Copyright © 1971 by the Board of Trustees at Indiana University. Used with permission.

- Level of technology
- Presence of economies of scale
- Organizational size

A diversity of project lines requires both top-level and functional managers to maintain knowledge in all areas. Diversity makes it more difficult for managers to make realistic estimates concerning resource allocations and the control of time, cost, schedules, and technology. The systems approach to management requires sufficient information and alternatives to be available so that effective trade-offs can be established. For diversity in a high-technology environment, the organizational choice might, in fact, be a trade-off between the flow of work and the flow of information. Diversity tends toward strong product authority and control.

Many functional organizations consider themselves as companies within a company and pride themselves on their independence. This attitude poses a severe problem in trying to develop a synergistic atmosphere. Successful project management requires that functional units recognize the interdependence that must exist in order for technology to be shared and schedule dates to be met. Interdependency is also required in order to develop strong communication channels as well as coordination.

The use of new technologies poses a serious problem in that technical expertise must be established in all specialties, including engineering, production, material control, and safety. Maintaining technical expertise works best in strong functional disciplines, provided the information is not purchased outside the organization. The main problem, however, is that of how to communicate this expertise across functional lines. Independent R&D units can be established, as opposed to integrating R&D into each functional department's routine efforts. Organizational control requirements are much more difficult in high-technology industries with ongoing research and development than with pure production groups.

Economies of scale and size can also affect organizational selection. The economies of scale are most often controlled by the amount of physical resources that a company has available. For example, a company with limited facilities and resources might find it impossible to compete with other companies on production or competitive bidding for larger dollar-volume products. Such a company must rely heavily on maintaining multiple projects (or products), each of low cost or volume, whereas a larger organization may need only three or four projects large enough to sustain the organization. The larger the economies of scale, the more the organization tends to favor pure functional management.

The size of the organization is important in that it can limit the amount of technical expertise in the economies of scale. While size may have little effect on the organizational structure, it does have a severe impact on the economies of scale. Small companies, for example, cannot maintain large specialist staffs and therefore, incur a larger cost for lost specialization and lost economies of scale.

The four factors described above for organizational form selections together with the six alternatives of Galbraith can be regarded as universal in nature.

Beyond these universal factors, we must look at the company in terms of its product, business base, and personnel. Goodman has defined a set of subfactors related to R&D groups:[26]

- Clear location of responsibility
- Ease and accuracy of communication
- Effective cost control
- Ability to provide good technical supervision
- Flexibility of staffing
- Importance to the company
- Quick reaction capability to sudden changes in the project
- Complexity of the project
- Size of the project with relation to other work in-house
- Form desired by customer
- Ability to provide a clear path for individual promotion

Goodman asked various managers to select from the above list and rank the factors from most important to least important in terms of how they would be considered in designing an organization. Both general management and project management personnel were queried. With one exception—flexibility of staffing—the response from both groups correlated to a coefficient of 0.811. Clear location of responsibility was seen as the most important factor, and a path for promotion the least important.

Middleton conducted a mail survey to aerospace firms in an attempt to determine how well the companies using project management met their objectives. Forty-seven responses were received. Tables 3–7 and 3–8 identify the results. Middleton stated, "In evaluating the results of the survey, it appears that a company taking the project organization approach can be reasonably certain that it will improve controls and customer (out-of-company) relations, but internal operations will be more complex."[27]

The way in which companies operate their project organization is bound to affect the organization, both during the operation of the project and after the project has been completed and personnel have been disbanded. The overall effects on the company must be looked at from a personnel and cost control standpoint. This will be accomplished, in depth, in later chapters. Although project management is growing, the creation of a project organization does not necessarily ensure that an assigned objective will be accomplished successfully. Furthermore, weaknesses can develop in the areas of maintaining capability and structural changes.

---

26. Richard A. Goodman, "Organizational Preference in Research and Development," *Human Relations*, Vol. 3, No. 4, 1970, pp. 279–298.

27. C. J. Middleton, "How to Set Up a Project Organization," *Harvard Business Review*, March–April 1967, pp. 73–82. Copyright © 1967 by the President and Fellows of Harvard College. All rights reserved.

TABLE 3–7. MAJOR COMPANY ADVANTAGES OF PROJECT MANAGEMENT

Advantages	Percent of Respondents
• Better control of projects	92%
• Better customer relations	80%
• Shorter product development time	40%
• Lower program costs	30%
• Improved quality and reliability	26%
• Higher profit margins	24%
• Better control over program security	13%

Other Benefits

- • Better project visibility and focus on results
- • Improved coordination among company divisions doing work on the project
- • Higher morale and better mission orientation for employees working on the project
- • Accelerated development of managers due to breadth of project responsibilities

Reprinted by permission of *Harvard Business Review.* An exhibit from "How to Set Up a Project Organization," by C. J. Middleton, March–April, 1967 (pp. 73–82). Copyright © 1967 by the President and Fellows of Harvard College, all rights reserved.

Project management structures have been known to go out of control:[28]

When a matrix appears to be going out of control, executives revert back to classical management. This results in:

- ● Reduced authority for the project manager
- ● All project decision making performed at executive levels
- ● Increase in executive meddling in projects
- ● Creation of endless manuals for job descriptions

This can sometimes be prevented by frequently asking for authority/responsibility clarification and by the use of linear responsibility charts.

An almost predictable result of using the project management approach is the increase in management positions. Killian describes the results of two surveys:[29]

One company compared its organization and management structure as it existed before it began forming project units with the structure that existed afterward. The number of departments had increased from 65 to 106, while total employ-

---

28. Adapted from L. E. Greiner, and V. E. Schein, "The Paradox of Managing a Project-Oriented Matrix: Establishing Coherence within Chaos," *Sloan Management Review,* Winter 1981, p. 17, by permission of the publisher. Copyright © 1981 by the Sloan Management Review Association. All rights reserved.

29. William P. Killian, "Project Management—Future Organizational Concepts," *Marquette Business Review,* Vol. 2, 1971, pp. 90–107.

TABLE 3–8. MAJOR COMPANY DISADVANTAGES OF PROJECT MANAGEMENT

Disadvantages	Percent of Respondents
• More complex internal operations	51%
• Inconsistency in application of company policy	32%
• Lower utilization of personnel	13%
• Higher program costs	13%
• More difficult to manage	13%
• Lower profit margins	2%

Other Disadvantages

- Tendency for functional groups to neglect their job and let the project organization do everything
- Too much shifting of personnel from project to project
- Duplication of functional skills in project organization

Reprinted by permission of *Harvard Business Review*. An exhibit from "How to Set Up a Project Organization," by C. J. Middleton, March–April, 1967 (pp. 73–82). Copyright © 1967 by the President and Fellows of Harvard College, all rights reserved.

ment remained practically the same. The number of employees for every supervisor had dropped from 13.4 to 12.8. The company concluded that a major cause of this change was the project groups [see footnote 27 for reference article].

Another company uncovered proof of its conclusion when it counted the number of second-level and higher management positions. It found that it had 11 more vice presidents and directors, 35 more managers, and 56 more second-level supervisors. Although the company attributed part of this growth to an upgrading of titles, the effect of the project organization was the creation of 60 more management positions.

Although the project organization is a specialized, task-oriented entity, it seldom, if ever, exists apart from the traditional structure of the organization.[30] All project management structures overlap the traditional structure. Furthermore, companies can have more than one project organizational form in existence at one time. A major steel product, for example, has a matrix structure for R&D and a product structure elsewhere.

Accepting a project management structure is a giant step from which there may be no return. The company may have to create more management positions without changing the total employment levels. In addition, incorporation of a project organization is almost always accompanied by the upgrading of jobs. In any event, management must realize that whichever project management structure is selected, a dynamic state of equilibrium will be necessary.

30. Allen R. Janger, "Anatomy of the Project Organization," *Business Management Record*, November 1963, pp. 12–18.

3.11 STRUCTURING THE SMALL COMPANY

Small and medium-sized companies generally prefer to have the project manager report fairly high up in the chain of command, even though the project manager may be working on a relatively low-priority project. Project managers are usually viewed as less of a threat in small organizations than in the larger ones, thus creating less of a problem if they report high up.

Organizing the small company for projects involves two major questions:

- Where should the project manager be placed within the organization?
- Are the majority of the projects internal or external to the organization?

These two questions are implicitly related. For either large, complex projects or those involving outside customers, project managers generally report to a high level in the organization. For small or internal projects, the project manager reports to a middle or lower-level manager.

Small and medium-sized companies have been very successful in managing internal projects using departmental project management (see Figure 3–2), especially when only a few functional groups must interface with one another. Quite often, line managers are permitted to wear multiple hats and also act as project managers, thereby reducing the need for hiring additional project managers.

Customers external to the organization are usually favorably impressed if a small company identifies a project manager who is dedicated and committed to their project, even if only on a part-time basis. Thus, outside customers, particularly through a competitive bidding environment, respond favorably toward a matrix structure, even if the matrix structure is simply eyewash for the customer. For example, consider the matrix structure shown in Figure 3–16. Both large and small companies that operate on a matrix usually develop a separate organizational chart for each customer. Figure 3–16 represents the organizational chart that would be presented to Alpha Company. The Alpha Company project would be identified with bold lines and would be placed immediately below the vice president, regardless of the priority of the project. After all, if you were the Alpha Company customer, would you want your project to appear at the bottom of the list?

Figure 3–16 also identifies two other key points that are important to small companies. First, only the name of the Alpha Company project manager, Bob Ray, need be identified. The reason for this is that Bob Ray may also be the project manager for one or more of the other projects, and it is usually not a good practice to let the customer know that Bob Ray will have split loyalties among several projects. Actually, the organization chart shown in Figure 3–16 is for a machine tool company employing 280 people, with five major and thirty minor projects. The company has only two full-time project managers. Bob Ray manages the projects for Alpha, Gamma, and Delta Companies; the Beta Company project has the second full-time project manager; and the IBM project is being

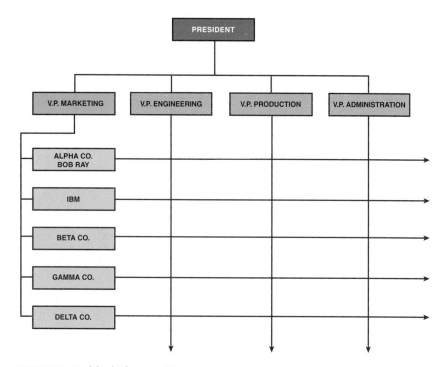

FIGURE 3–16. Matrix for a small company.

managed personally by the vice president of engineering, who happens to be wearing two hats.

The second key point is that small companies generally should not identify the names of functional employees because:

- The functional employees are probably part-time.
- It is usually best in small companies for all communications to be transmitted through the project manager.

Another example of how a simple matrix structure can be used to impress customers is shown in Figure 3–17. The company identified here actually employs only thirty-eight people. Very small companies normally assign the estimating department to report directly to the president, as shown in Figure 3–17. In addition, the senior engineers, who appear to be acting in the role of project managers, may simply be the department managers for drafting, startup, and/or design engineering. Yet, from an outside customer's perspective, the company has a dedicated and committed project manager for the project.

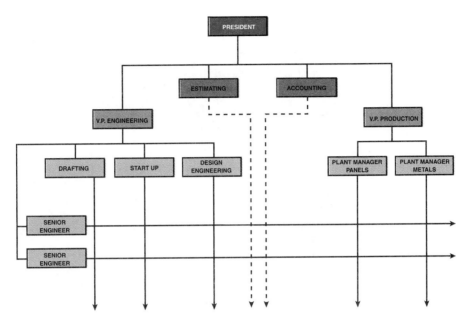

FIGURE 3–17. Matrix for a small company.

3.12 STRATEGIC BUSINESS UNIT (SBU) PROJECT MANAGEMENT

During the past ten years, large companies have restructured into strategic business units (SBUs). An SBU is a grouping of functional units that have the responsibility for profit (or loss) of part of the organization's core businesses. Figure 3–18 shows how one of the automotive suppliers restructured into three SBUs; one each for Ford, Chrysler, and General Motors. Each strategic business unit is large enough to maintain its own project and program managers. The executive in charge of the strategic business unit may act as the sponsor for all of the program and project managers within the SBU. The major benefit of these types of project management SBUs is that it allows the SBU to work more closely with the customer. It is a customer-focused organizational structure.

It is possible for some resources to be shared across several SBUs. Manufacturing plants can end up supporting more than one SBU. Also, corporate may provide the resources for cost accounting, human resource management, and training.

A more recent organizational structure, and a more complex one, is shown in Figure 3–19. In this structure, each SBU may end up using the same platform (i.e., powertrain, chassis, and other underneath components). The platform managers are responsible for the design and enhancements of each platform, whereas

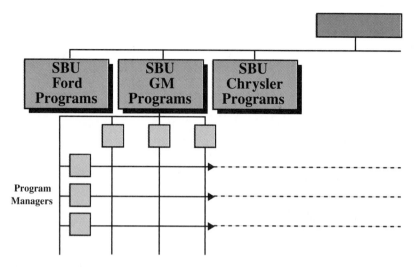

FIGURE 3–18. Strategic business unit project management.

the SBU program managers must adapt this platform to a new model car. This type of matrix is multidimensional inasmuch as each SBU could already have an internal matrix. Also, each manufacturing plant could be located outside of the continental United States, making this structure a multinational, multidimensional matrix.

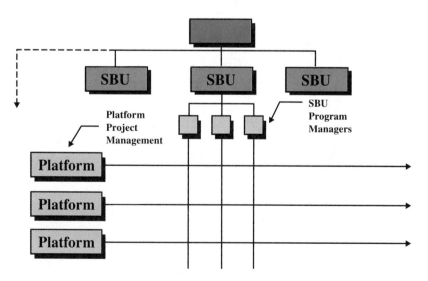

FIGURE 3–19. SBU project management using platform management.

3.13 TRANSITIONAL MANAGEMENT[31]

Organizational redesign is occurring at a rapid rate because of shorter product life cycles, rapidly changing environments, accelerated development of sophisticated information systems, and increased marketplace competitiveness. Because of these factors, more and more companies are considering project management organizations as a solution.

The obvious question is, "Why have some companies been able to implement this change in a short period of time while other companies require years?" The answer is that successful implementation requires good transitional management.

Transitional management is the art and science of managing the conversion period from one organizational design to another. Transitional management necessitates an understanding of the new goals, objectives, roles, expectations, and fears that people consider.

- *Senior management:* Maintain or increase current power and authority and delegate as little as possible.
- *Line management:* Minimize the project manager's involvement and impact on the functional empire.
- *Project managers:* Accept and adapt to the newer responsibilities with minimum disruption to the organization.
- *Employees:* Receive additional monetary and nonmonetary rewards, be evaluated correctly, and obtain more visibility with management.

Some people fear change, while others look at it as a chance to demonstrate their creativity. It is the responsibility of the transitional managers to remove personnel fears and stimulate creativity and the desire to achieve in line with corporate objectives.

A survey was conducted of executives, managers, and employees in thirty-eight companies that had implemented matrix management. Almost all executives felt that the greatest success could be achieved through proper training and education, both during and after transition. In addition to training, executives stated that the following fifteen challenges must be accounted for during transition:

- *Transfer of power.* Some line managers will find it extremely difficult to accept someone else managing their projects, whereas some project managers will find it difficult to give orders to workers who belong to someone else.
- *Trust.* The secret to a successful transition without formal executive authority will be trust between line managers, between project managers, and between project and line managers. It takes time for trust to develop. Senior management should encourage it throughout the transition life cycle.

---

31. Adapted from Harold Kerzner and David I. Cleland, "Transitional Management: The Key to Successful Implementation of Project Management," *Proceedings of the 1984 Project Management Institute Seminar/Symposium on Project Management*, Oct. 8–10, 1984, pp. 181–194.

- *Policies and procedures.* The establishment of well-accepted policies and procedures is a slow and tedious process. Trying to establish rigid policies and procedures at project initiation will lead to difficulties.
- *Hierarchical consideration.* During transition, every attempt should be made to minimize hierarchical considerations that could affect successful organizational maturity.
- *Priority scheduling.* Priorities should be established only when needed, not on a continual basis. If priority shifting is continual, confusion and disenchantment will occur.
- *Personnel problems.* During transition there will be personnel problems brought on by moving to new locations, status changes, and new informal organizations. These problems should be addressed on a continual basis.
- *Communications.* During transition, new channels of communications should be built but not at the expense of old ones. Transition phases should show employees that communication can be multidirectional, for example, a project manager talking directly to functional employees.
- *Project manager acceptance.* Resistance to the project manager position can be controlled through proper training. People tend to resist what they do not understand.
- *Competition.* Although some competition is healthy within an organization, it can be detrimental during transition. Competition should not be encouraged at the expense of the total organization.
- *Tools.* It is common practice for each line organization to establish their own tools and techniques. During transition, no attempt should be made to force the line organizations to depart from their current practice. Rather, it is better for the project managers to develop tools and techniques that can be integrated with those in the functional groups.
- *Contradicting demands.* During transition and after maturity, contradicting demands will exist as a way of life. When they first occur during transition, they should be handled in a "working atmosphere" rather than a crisis mode.
- *Reporting.* If any type of standardization is to be developed, it should be for project status reporting, regardless of the size of the project.
- *Teamwork.* Systematic planning with strong functional input will produce teamwork. Using planning groups during transition will not obtain the necessary functional and project commitments.
- *Theory X–Theory Y.* During transition, functional employees may soon find themselves managed under either Theory X or Theory Y approaches. People must realize (through training) that this is a way of life in project management, especially during crises.
- *Overmanagement costs.* A mistake often made by executives is that projects can be managed with less resources. This usually leads to disaster because undermanagement costs may be an order of magnitude greater than overmanagement costs.

Transition to a project-driven matrix organization is not easy. Several caveats are in order for managers and professionals contemplating such a move:

- Proper planning and organization of the transition on a life-cycle basis will facilitate a successful change.
- Training of the executives, line managers, and employees in project management knowledge, skills, and attitudes is critical to a successful transition and probably will shorten the transition time.
- Employee involvement and acceptance may be the single most important function during transition.
- The strongest driving force toward success during transition is a demonstration of commitment to and involvement in project management by senior executives.
- Organizational behavior becomes important during transition.
- It is extremely important that commitments made by senior executives prior to transition be preserved both during and following transition.
- Major concessions by senior management will come slowly.
- Schedule or performance compromises are not acceptable during transition; cost overruns may be acceptable.
- Conflict intensity among participants increases during transition.
- If project managers are willing to manage with only implied authority during transition, then the total transition time may be drastically reduced.
- It is not clear how long transition will take.

Transition from a classical or product organization to a project-driven organization is not easy. With proper understanding, training, demonstrated commitment, and patience, transition will have a good chance for success.

PROBLEMS

3–1 Much has been written about how to identify and interpret signs that indicate that a new organizational form is needed. Grinnell and Apple have identified five signs in addition to those previously described in Section 3.6:[32]

- Management is satisfied with its technical skills, but projects are not meeting time, cost, and other project requirements.
- There is a high commitment to getting project work done, but great fluctuation in how well performance specifications are met.
- Highly talented specialists involved in the project feel exploited and misused.
- Particular technical groups or individuals constantly blame each other for failure to meet specifications or delivery dates.

32. See note 18.

- Projects are on time and to specification, but groups and individuals aren't satisfied with the achievement.

Grinnell and Apple state that there is a good chance that a matrix structure will eliminate or alleviate these problems. Do you agree or disagree? Does your answer depend on the type of project? Give examples or counterexamples to defend your answers.

3–2 One of the most difficult problems facing management is that of how to minimize the transition time between changeover from a purely traditional organizational form to a project organizational form. Managing the changeover is difficult in that management must consistently "provide individual training on teamwork and group problem solving; also, provide the project and functional groups with assignments to help build teamwork."[33]

TRW Systems Group tried to make almost an instantaneous conversion from a traditional to a matrix organizational form. Managing the conversion was accomplished through T-groups and special study sessions. Describe the problems associated with new organizational form conversion. Which project form should be easiest to adapt to? State how long a period you might need for conversion from a traditional structure to a product structure, matrix structure, and task force structure. (Note: The TRW Systems Group Studies can be found in cases 9-476-117, 9-413-066, and 9-413-069 distributed by the Intercollegiate Case Clearing House.)

3–3 Do you think that personnel working in a project organizational structure should undergo "therapy" sessions or seminars on a regular basis so as to better understand their working environment? If yes, how frequently? Does the frequency depend upon the project organizational form selected, or should they all be treated equally?

3–4 Which organizational form would be best for the following corporate strategies?[34]

     a. Developing, manufacturing, and marketing many diverse but interrelated technological products and materials
     b. Having market interests that span virtually every major industry
     c. Becoming multinational with a rapidly expanding global business
     d. Working in a business environment of rapid and drastic change, together with strong competition

3–5 Robert E. Shannon ["Matrix Management Structures," *Industrial Engineering*, March 1972, pp. 27–29. Published and copyright © 1972 by the Institute of Industrial Engineers, 25 Technology Park, Norcross, GA 30092 (770-449-0461), reprinted with permission] made the following remarks:

> When operating under a matrix management approach, it is obviously extremely important that the responsibility and authority of each manager be clearly defined, understood, and accepted by both functional and program people. These relationships need to be spelled out in writing. It is essential that in the various operating policies, the specific authority of the program manager be clearly defined in terms of program direction, and that the authority of the functional executive be defined in terms of operational direction.

---

33. See note 18.

34. See note 17.

Do you think that documenting relationships is necessary in order to operate effectively in any project organizational structure? How would you relate Shannon's remarks to a statement made in the previous chapter that each project can set up its own policies, procedures, rules, and directives as long as they conform to company guidelines?

3–6 In general, how could each of the following parameters influence your choice for an organizational structure? Explain your answers in as much depth as possible.

    a. The project cost
    b. The project schedule
    c. The project duration
    d. The technology requirements
    e. The geographical locations
    f. The required working relationships with the customer

3–7 In general, what are the overall advantages and disadvantages of superimposing one organizational form over another?

3–8 In deciding to go to a new organizational form, what impact should the capabilities of the following groups have on your decision?

    a. Top management
    b. Middle management
    c. Lower-level management

3–9 Should a company be willing to accept a project that requires immediate organizational restructuring? If so, what factors should it consider?

3–10 Figure 2–7 identifies the different life cycles of programs, projects, systems, and products. For each of the life cycles' phases, select a project organizational form that you feel would work best. Defend your answer with examples, advantages, and disadvantages.

3–11 A major steel producer in the United States uses a matrix structure for R&D. Once the product is developed, the product organizational structure is used. Are there any advantages to this setup?

3–12 A major American manufacturer of automobile parts has a division that has successfully existed for the past ten years with multiple products, a highly sophisticated R&D section, and a pure traditional structure. The growth rate for the past five years has been 12 percent. Almost all middle and upper-level managers who have worked in this division have received promotions and transfers to either another division or corporate headquarters. According to "the book," this division has all the prerequisites signifying that they should have a project organizational form of some sort, and yet they are extremely successful without it. Just from the amount of information presented, how can you account for their continued success? What do you think would be the major obstacles in convincing the personnel that a new organizational form would be better? Do you think that continued success can be achieved under the present structure?

3–13 Several authors contend that technology suffers in a pure product organizational form because there is no one group responsible for long-range planning, whereas the pure functional organization tends to sacrifice time and schedule. Do you agree or disagree with this statement? Defend your choice with examples.

3–14 Below are three statements that are often used to describe the environment of a matrix. Do you agree or disagree? Defend your answer.

  a. Project management in a matrix allows for fuller utilization of personnel.
  b. The project manager and functional manager must agree on priorities.
  c. Decision making in a matrix requires continual trade-offs on time, cost, technical risk, and uncertainty.

3–15 Assume that you have to select a project organizational form for a small company. For each form described in this chapter, discuss the applicability and state the advantages and disadvantages as they apply to this small company. (You may find it necessary to first determine the business base of the small company.)

3–16 How would each person identified below respond to the question, "How many bosses do you have?"

  a. Project manager
  b. Functional team member
  c. Functional manager

(Repeat for each organizational form discussed in this chapter.)

3–17 If a project were large enough to contain its own resources, would a matrix organizational form be acceptable?

3–18 One of the most common reasons for not wanting to adopt a matrix is the excessive administrative costs and accompanying overhead rates. Would you expect the overhead rates to decrease as the matrix matures? (Disregard other factors that can influence the overhead rates, such as business base, growth rate, etc.)

3–19 Which type of organizational structure is best for R&D personnel to keep in touch with other researchers?

3–20 Which type of organizational form fosters teamwork in the best manner?

3–21 Canadian bankers have been using the matrix organizational structure to create "banking general managers" for all levels of a bank. Does the matrix structure readily admit itself to a banking environment in order to create future managers? Can we consider a branch manager as a matrix project manager?

3–22 A major utility company in Cleveland has what is commonly called "fragmented" project management, where each department maintains project managers through staff positions. The project managers occasionally have to integrate activities that involve departments other than their own. Each project normally requires involvement of several people. The company also has product managers operating out of a rather crude project (product) organizational structure. Recently, the product managers and project managers were competing for resources within the same departments.

   To complicate matters further, management has put a freeze on hiring. Last week top management identified 120 different projects that could be undertaken. Unfortunately, under the current structure there are not enough staff project managers available to handle these projects. Also, management would like to make better use of the scarce functional resources.

   Staff personnel contend that the solution to the above problems is the establishment of a project management division under which there will be a project management department and a product management department. The staff people feel that under this arrangement better utilization of line personnel will be made, and that each project can be run with fewer staff people, thus providing the opportunity for more projects. Do you agree or disagree, and what problems do you foresee?

3–23 Some organizational structures are considered to be "project-driven." Define what is meant by "project-driven." Which organizational forms described in this chapter would fall under your definition?

3–24 Are there any advantages to having a single project engineer as opposed to having a committee of key functional employees who report to the director of engineering?

3–25 The major difficulty in the selection of a project organizational form involves placement of the project manager. In the evolutionary process, the project manager started out reporting to a department head and ultimately ended up reporting to a senior executive. In general, what were the major reasons for having the project manager report higher and higher in the organizational structure?

3–26 Ralph is a department manager who is quite concerned about the performance of the people beneath him. After several months of analysis, Ralph has won the acceptance of his superiors for setting up a project management structure in his department. Out of the twenty-three departments in the company, his will be the only one with formalized project management. Can this situation be successful even though several projects require interfacing with other departments?

3–27 A large electronics corporation has a multimillion dollar project in which 90 percent of the work stays within one division. The division manager wants to be the project manager. Should this be allowed even though there exists a project management division?

3–28 The internal functioning of an organization must consider:

- The demands imposed on the organization by task complexity
- Available technology
- The external environment
- The needs of the organizational membership

Considering these facts, should an organization search for the one best way to organize under all conditions? Should managers examine the functioning of an organization relative to its needs, or vice versa?

3–29 Project managers, in order to get the job accomplished, need adequate organizational status and authority. One corporate executive contends that an organizational chart such as that in Figure 3–6 can be modified to show that the project managers have adequate authority by placing the department managers in boxes at the top of the functional responsibility arrowheads. The executive further contends that, with this approach, the project managers appear to be higher in the organization than their departmental counterparts but are actually equal in status. Do you agree or disagree with the executive's idea? Will there be a proper balance of power between project and department managers with this organizational structure?

3–30 Defend or attack the following two statements concerning the operation of a matrix:

- There should be no disruption due to dual accountability.
- A difference in judgment should not delay work in progress.

3–31 A company has fifteen projects going on at once. Three projects are over $5 million, seven projects are between $1 million and $3 million, and five projects are between $500,000 and $700,000. Each project has a full-time project manager. Just based upon this information, which organizational form would be best? Can all the project managers report to the same person?

3–32 A major insurance company is considering the implementation of project management. The majority of the projects in the company are two weeks in duration, with very few existing beyond one month. Can project management work here?

3–33 The definition of project management in Section 1.9 identifies project teams and task forces. How would you distinguish between a project team and a task force, and what industries and/or projects would be applicable to each?

3–34 Can informal project management work in a structured environment at the same time as formal project management and share the same resources?

3–35 Several people believe that the matrix structure can be multidimensional (as shown in Figure 3–13). Explain the usefulness of such a structure.

3–36 Many companies have informal project management where work flows horizontally, but in an informal manner. What are the characteristics of informal project management? Which types of companies can operate effectively with informal project management?

3–37 Some companies have tried to develop a matrix within a matrix. Is it possible to have a matrix for formal project control and an internal authority matrix, communication matrix, responsibility matrix, or a combination of several of these?

3–38 Is it possible for a matrix to get out of control because of too many small projects, each competing for the same shared resources? If so, how many projects are too many? How can management control the number of projects? Does your answer depend on whether the organization is project-driven or non–project-driven?

3–39 A government subcontractor operates with a pure specialized product management organizational structure and has four product lines. All employees are required to have a top secret security clearance. The subcontractor's plant is structured such that each of the four product lines occupies a secured area in the building. Employees wear security badges that give them access to the different areas. Most of the employees are authorized to have access only to their area. Only the executives have access to all four areas. For security reasons, functional employees are not permitted to discuss the product lines with each other.

Many of the projects performed in each of the product lines are identical, and severe duplication of efforts exist. Management is interested in converting over to a matrix structure to minimize the duplication of effort. What problems must be overcome before and during matrix implementation?

3–40 A company has decided to go to full project management utilizing a matrix structure. Can the implementation be done in stages? Can the matrix be partially implemented, say, in one portion of the organization, and then gradually expanded across the rest of the company?

3–41 A company has two major divisions, both housed under the same roof. One division is the aerospace group, where all activities are performed within a formal matrix. The second division is the industrial group, which operates with pure product management, except for the MIS department, which has an informal matrix. If both divisions have to share common corporate resources, what problems can occur?

3–42 Several Fortune 100 corporations have a corporate engineering group that assumes the responsibility of the project management-project engineering function for all major capital projects in all divisions worldwide. Explain how the corporate engineering function should work, as well as its advantages and disadvantages.

CASE STUDIES

JONES AND SHEPHARD ACCOUNTANTS, INC.

By 1970, Jones and Shephard Accountants, Inc. (J&S) was ranked eighteenth in size by the American Association of Accountants. In order to compete with the larger firms, J&S formed an Information Services Division designed primarily for studies and analyses. By 1975, the Information Services Division (ISD) had fifteen employees.

In 1977, the ISD purchased three minicomputers. With this increased capacity, J&S expanded its services to help satisfy the needs of outside customers. By September 1978, the internal and external work loads had increased to a point where the ISD now employed over fifty people.

The director of the division was very disappointed in the way that activities were being handled. There was no single person assigned to push through a project, and outside customers did not know who to call to get answers regarding project status. The director found that most of his time was being spent on day-to-day activities such as conflict resolution instead of strategic planning and policy formulation.

The biggest problems facing the director were the two continuous internal projects (called Project X and Project Y, for simplicity) that required month-end data collation and reporting. The director felt that these two projects were important enough to require a full-time project manager on each effort.

In October 1978, corporate management announced that the ISD director would be reassigned on February 1, 1979, and that the announcement of his replacement would not be made until the middle of January. The same week that the announcement was made, two individuals were hired from outside the company to take charge of Project X and Project Y. Exhibit 3–1 shows the organizational structure of the ISD.

Within the next thirty days, rumors spread throughout the organization about who would become the new director. Most people felt that the position would be filled from within the division and that the most likely candidates would be the two new project managers. In addition, the associate director was due to retire in December, thus creating two openings.

On January 3, 1979, a confidential meeting was held between the ISD director and the systems manager.

ISD Director: "Corporate has approved my request to promote you to division director. Unfortunately, your job will not be an easy one. You're going to have to restruc-

Exhibit 3–1. ISD Organizational Chart

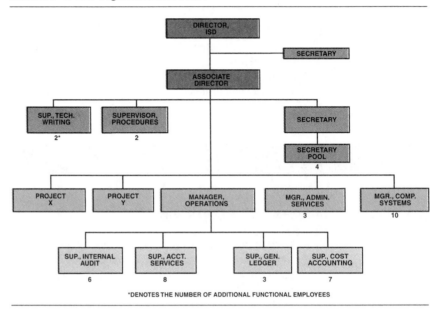

*DENOTES THE NUMBER OF ADDITIONAL FUNCTIONAL EMPLOYEES

ture the organization somehow so that our employees will not have as many conflicts as they are now faced with. My secretary is typing up a confidential memo for you explaining my observations on the problems within our division.

"Remember, your promotion should be held in the strictest confidence until the final announcement later this month. I'm telling you this now so that you can begin planning the restructuring. My memo should help you." (See Exhibit 3–2 for the memo.)

The systems manager read the memo and, after due consideration, decided that some form of matrix would be best. To help him structure the organization properly, an outside consultant was hired to help identify the potential problems with changing over to a matrix. The following problem areas were identified by the consultant:

1. The operations manager controls more than 50 percent of the people resources. You might want to break up his empire. This will have to be done very carefully.
2. The secretary pool is placed too high in the organization.
3. The supervisors who now report to the associate director will have to be reassigned lower in the organization if the associate director's position is abolished.
4. One of the major problem areas will be trying to convince corporate management that their change will be beneficial. You'll have to convince them that this change can be accomplished without having to increase division manpower.

Exhibit 3–2. Confidential Memo

From: ISD Director
To: Systems Manager
Date: January 3, 1979

Congratulations on your promotion to division director. I sincerely hope that your tenure will be productive both personally and for corporate. I have prepared a short list of the major obstacles that you will have to consider when you take over the controls.

1. Both Project X and Project Y managers are highly competent individuals. In the last four or five days, however, they have appeared to create more conflicts for us than we had previously. This could be my fault for not delegating them sufficient authority, or could be a result of the fact that several of our people consider these two individuals as prime candidates for my position. In addition, the operations manager does not like other managers coming into his "empire" and giving direction.
2. I'm not sure that we even need an associate director. That decision will be up to you.
3. Corporate has been very displeased with our inability to work with outside customers. You must consider this problem with any organizational structure you choose.
4. The corporate strategic plan for our division contains an increased emphasis on special, internal MIS projects. Corporate wants to limit our external activities for a while until we get our internal affairs in order.
5. I made the mistake of changing our organizational structure on a day-to-day basis. Perhaps it would have been better to design a structure that could satisfy advanced needs, especially one that we can grow into.

---

5. You might wish to set up a separate department or a separate project for customer relations.
6. Introducing your employees to the matrix will be a problem. Each employee will look at the change differently. Most people have the tendency of looking first at the shift in the balance of power—have I gained or have I lost power and status?

The systems manager evaluated the consultant's comments and then prepared a list of questions to ask the consultant at their next meeting:

1. What should the new organizational structure look like? Where should I put each person, specifically the managers?
2. When should I announce the new organizational change? Should it be at the same time as my appointment or at a later date?
3. Should I invite any of my people to provide input to the organizational restructuring? Can this be used as a technique to ease power plays?
4. Should I provide inside or outside seminars to train my people for the new organizational structure? How soon should they be held?

FARGO FOODS*

Fargo Foods is a $2 billion a year international food manufacturer with canning facilities in 22 countries. Fargo products include meats, poultry, fish, vegetables, vitamins, and cat and dog foods. Fargo Foods has enjoyed a 12.5 percent growth rate each of the past eight years primarily due to the low overhead rates in the foreign companies.

During the past five years, Fargo had spent a large portion of retained earnings on capital equipment projects in order to increase productivity without increasing labor. An average of three new production plants have been constructed in each of the last five years. In addition, almost every plant has undergone major modifications each year in order to increase productivity.

In 1985, the president of Fargo Foods implemented formal project management for all construction projects using a matrix. By 1989, it became obvious that the matrix was not operating effectively or efficiently. In December 1989, the author consulted for Fargo Foods by interviewing several of the key managers and a multitude of functional personnel. Below are the several key questions and responses addressed to Fargo Foods:

Q. Give me an example of one of your projects.

A. "The project begins with an idea. The idea can originate anywhere in the company. The planning group picks up the idea and determines the feasibility. The planning group then works 'informally' with the various line organizations to determine rough estimates for time and cost. The results are then fed back to the planning group and to the top management planning and steering committees. If top management decides to undertake the project, then top management selects the project manager and we're off and running."

Q. Do you have any problems with this arrangement?

A. "You bet! Our executives have the tendency of equating rough estimates as detailed budgets and rough schedules as detailed schedules. Then, they want to know why the line managers won't commit their best resources. We almost always end up with cost overruns and schedule slippages. To make matters even worse, the project managers do not appear to be dedicated to the projects. I really can't blame them. After all, they're not involved in planning the project, laying out the schedule, and establishing the budget. I don't see how any project manager can become dedicated to a plan in which the project manager has no input and may not even know the assumptions or considerations that were included. Recently, some of our more experienced project managers have taken a stand on this and are virtually refusing to accept a project assignment unless they can do their own detailed planning at the beginning of the project in order to verify the constraints established by the planning group. If the project managers come up with different costs and schedules (and you know that they will), the planning group feels that they have just gotten slapped in the face. If the costs and schedules are the same, then the planning group runs upstairs to top management asserting that the project managers are wasting money by continuously wanting to replan."

*Disguised case.

Q. Do you feel that replanning is necessary?

A. "Definitely! The planning group begins their planning with a very crude statement of work, expecting our line managers (the true experts) to read in between the lines and fill in the details. The project managers develop a detailed statement of work and a work breakdown structure, thus minimizing the chance that anything would fall through the crack. Another reason for replanning is that the ground rules have changed between the time that the project was originally adopted by the planning group and the time that the project begins implementation. Another possibility, of course, is that technology may have changed or people can be smarter now and can perform at a higher position on the learning curve."

Q. Do you have any problems with executive meddling?

A. "Not during the project, but initially. Sometimes executives want to keep the end date fixed but take their time in approving the project. As a result, the project manager may find himself a month or two behind scheduling before he even begins the project. The second problem is when the executive decides to arbitrarily change the end date milestone but keep the front end milestone fixed. On one of our projects it was necessary to complete the project in half the time. Our line managers worked like dogs to get the job done. On the next project, the same thing happened, and, once again, the line managers came to the rescue. Now, management feels that line managers cannot make good estimates and that they (the executives) can arbitrarily change the milestones on any project. I wish that they would realize what they're doing to us. When we put forth all of our efforts on one project, then all of the other projects suffer. I don't think our executives realize this."

Q. Do you have any problems selecting good project managers and project engineers?

A. "We made a terrible mistake for several years by selecting our best technical experts as the project managers. Today, our project managers are doers, not managers. The project managers do not appear to have any confidence in our line people and often try to do all of the work themselves. Functional employees are taking technical direction from the project managers and project engineers instead of the line managers. I've heard one functional employee say, 'Here come those project managers again to beat me up. Why can't they leave me alone and let me do my job?' Our line employees now feel that this is the way that project management is supposed to work. Somehow, I don't think so."

Q. Do you have any problems with the line manager—project manager interface?

A. "Our project managers are technical experts and therefore feel qualified to do all of the engineering estimates without consulting with the line managers. Sometimes this occurs because not enough time or money is allocated for proper estimating. This is understandable. But when the project managers have enough time and money and refuse to get off their ivory towers and talk to the line managers, then the line managers will always find fault with the project manager's estimate even if it is correct. Sometimes I just can't feel any sympathy for the project managers. There is one special case that I should mention. Many of our project managers do the estimating themselves but have courtesy enough to ask the line manager for his blessing. I've seen line managers who were so loaded with work that they look the estimate over for two seconds and say, 'It looks fine to me. Let's do it.' Then when the cost overrun appears, the project manager gets blamed."

Q. Where are your project engineers located in the organization?

A. "We're having trouble deciding that. Our project engineers are primarily responsible for coordinating the design efforts (i.e., electrical, civil, HVAC, etc). The design manager wants these people reporting to him if they are responsible for coordinating efforts in his shop. The design manager wants control of these people even if they have their name changed to assistant project managers. The project managers, on the other hand, want the project engineers to report to them with the argument that they must be dedicated to the project and must be willing to complete the effort within time, cost, and performance. Furthermore, the project managers argue that project engineers will be more likely to get the job done within the constraints if they are not under the pressure of being evaluated by the design manager. If I were the design manager, I would be a little reluctant to let someone from outside of my shop integrate activities that utilize the resources under my control. But I guess this gets back to interpersonal skills and the attitudes of the people. I do not want to see a 'brick wall' set up between project management and design."

Q. I understand that you've created a new estimating group. Why was that done?

A. "In the past we have had several different types of estimates such as first guess, detailed, 10 percent complete, etc. Our project managers are usually the first people at the job site and give a shoot-from-the-hip estimate. Our line managers do estimating as do some of our executives and functional employees. Because we're in a relatively slowly changing environment, we should have well-established standards, and the estimating department can maintain uniformity in our estimating policies. Since most of our work is approved based on first-guess estimates, the question is, 'Who should give the first-guess estimate?' Should it be the estimator, who does not understand the processes but knows the estimating criteria, or the project engineer, who understands the processes but does not know the estimates, or the project manager, who is an expert in project management? Right now, we are not sure where to place the estimating group. The vice president of engineering has three operating groups beneath him—project management, design, and procurement. We're contemplating putting estimating under procurement, but I'm not sure how this will work."

Q. How can we resolve these problems that you've mentioned?

A. "I wish I knew!"

QUASAR COMMUNICATIONS, INC.

Quasar Communications, Inc. (QCI), is a thirty-year-old, $350 million division of Communication Systems International, the world's largest communications company. QCI employs about 340 people of which more than 200 are engineers. Ever since the company was founded thirty years ago, engineers have held every major position within the company, including president and vice president. The vice president for accounting and finance, for example, has an electrical engineering degree from Purdue and a master's degree in business administration from Harvard.

QCI, up until 1986, was a traditional organization where everything flowed up and down. In 1986, QCI hired a major consulting company to come in and train *all* of their personnel in project management. Because of the reluctance of the line managers to accept formalized project management, QCI adopted an informal, fragmented project management structure where the project managers had lots of responsibility but very little authority. The line managers were still running the show.

In 1989, QCI had grown to a point where the majority of their business base revolved around twelve large customers and thirty to forty small customers. The time had come to create a separate line organization for project managers, where each individual could be shown a career path in the company and the company could benefit by creating a body of planners and managers dedicated to the completion of a project. The project management group was headed up by a vice president and included the following full-time personnel:

- Four individuals to handle the twelve large customers
- Five individuals for the thirty to forty small customers
- Three individuals for R&D projects
- One individual for capital equipment projects

The nine customer project managers were expected to handle two to three projects at one time if necessary. Because the customer requests usually did not come in at the same time, it was anticipated that each project manager would handle only one project at a time. The R&D and capital equipment project managers were expected to handle several projects at once.

In addition to the above personnel, the company also maintained a staff of four product managers who controlled the profitable off-the-shelf product lines. The product managers reported to the vice president of marketing and sales.

In October 1989, the vice president for project management decided to take a more active role in the problems that project managers were having and held counseling sessions for each project manager. The following major problem areas were discovered.

R&D Project Management

Project Manager: "My biggest problem is working with these diverse groups that aren't sure what they want. My job is to develop new products that can be introduced into the marketplace. I have to work with engineering, marketing, product management, manufacturing, quality assurance, finance, and accounting. Everyone wants a detailed schedule and product cost breakdown. How can I do that when we aren't even sure what the end-item will look like or what materials are needed? Last month I prepared a detailed schedule for the development of a new product, assuming that everything would go according to the plan. I worked with the R&D engineering group to establish what we considered to be a realistic milestone. Marketing pushed the milestone to the left because they wanted the product to be introduced into the marketplace earlier. Manufacturing then pushed the milestone to the right, claiming that they would need more time to verify the engineering specifications. Finance and accounting then pushed the milestone to the left asserting that management wanted a quicker return on investment. Now, how can I make all of the groups happy?"

Vice President: "Whom do you have the biggest problems with?"

Project Manager: "That's easy—marketing! Every week marketing gets a copy of the project status report and decides whether to cancel the project. Several times marketing has canceled projects without even discussing it with me, and I'm supposed to be the project leader."

Vice President: "Marketing is in the best position to cancel the project because they have the inside information on the profitability, risk, return on investment, and competitive environment."

Project Manager: "The situation that we're in now makes it impossible for the project manager to be dedicated to a project where he does not have all of the information at hand. Perhaps we should either have the R&D project managers report to someone in marketing or have the marketing group provide additional information to the project managers."

Small Customer Project Management

Project Manager: "I find it virtually impossible to be dedicated to and effectively manage three projects that have priorities that are not reasonably close. My low-priority customer always suffers. And even if I try to give all of my customers equal status, I do not know how to organize myself and have effective time management on several projects."

Project Manager: "Why is it that the big projects carry all of the weight and the smaller ones suffer?"

Project Manager: "Several of my projects are so small that they stay in one functional department. When that happens, the line manager feels that he is the true project manager operating in a vertical environment. On one of my projects I found that a line manager had promised the customer that additional tests would be run. This additional testing was not priced out as part of the original statement of work. On another project the line manager made certain remarks about the technical requirements of the project. The customer assumed that the line managers's remarks reflected company policy. Our line managers don't realize that only the project manager can make commitments (on resources) to the customer as well as on company policy. I know this can happen on large projects as well, but it is more pronounced on small projects."

Large Customer Project Management

Project Manager: "Those of us who manage the large projects are also marketing personnel, and occasionally, we are the ones who bring in the work. Yet, everyone appears to be our superior. Marketing always looks down on us, and when we bring in a large contract, marketing just looks down on us as if we're riding their coattails or as if we were just lucky. The engineering group outranks us because all managers and executives are promoted from there. Those guys never live up to commitments. Last month I sent an inflammatory memo to a line manager because of his poor response to my requests. Now, I get no support at all from him. This doesn't happen all of the time, but when it does, it's frustrating."

Project Manager: "On large projects, how do we, the project managers, know when the project is in trouble? How do we decide when the project will fail? Some of our large projects are total disasters and should fail, but management comes to the rescue and pulls the best resources off of the good projects to cure the ailing projects. We then end up with six marginal projects and one partial catastrophe as opposed to six excellent projects and one failure. Why don't we just let the bad projects fail?"

Vice President: "We have to keep up our image for our customers. In most other companies, performance is sacrificed in order to meet time and cost. Here at QCI, with our professional integrity at stake, our engineers are willing to sacrifice time and cost in order to meet specifications. Several of our customers come to us because of this. Last year we had a project where, at the scheduled project termination date, engineering was able to satisfy only 75 percent of the customer's performance specifications. The project manager showed the results to the customer, and the customer decided to change his specification requirements to agree with the product that we designed. Our engineering people thought that this was a 'slap in the face' and refused to sign off the engineering drawings. The problem went all the way up to the president for resolution. The final result was that the customer would give us an additional few months if we would spend our own money to try to meet the original specification. It cost us a bundle, but we did it because our integrity and professional reputation were at stake."

**Capital Equipment
Project Management**

Project Manager: "My biggest complaint is with this new priority scheduling computer package we're supposedly considering to install. The way I understand it, the computer program will establish priorities for *all* of the projects in-house, based on the feasibility study, cost-benefit analysis, and return on investment. Somehow I feel as though my projects will always be the lowest priority, and I'll never be able to get sufficient functional resources."

Project Manager: "Every time I lay out a reasonable schedule for one of our capital equipment projects, a problem occurs in the manufacturing area and the functional employees are always pulled off of my project to assist manufacturing. And now I have to explain to everyone why I'm behind schedule. Why am I always the one to suffer?"

The vice president carefully weighed the remarks of his project managers. Now came the difficult part. What, if anything, could the vice president do to amend the situation given the current organizational environment?

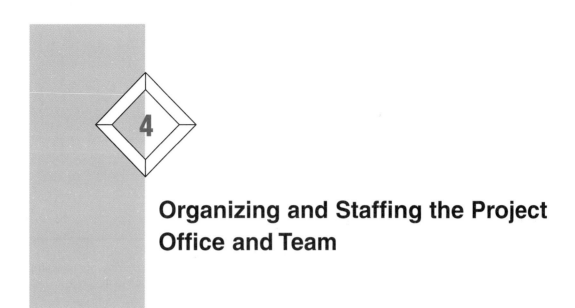

Organizing and Staffing the Project Office and Team

4.0 INTRODUCTION

Successful project management, regardless of the organizational structure, is only as good as the individuals and leaders who are managing the key functions. Project management is not a one-person operation; it requires a group of individuals dedicated to the achievement of a specific goal. Project management includes:

- A project manager
- An assistant project manager
- A project (home) office
- A project team

Generally, project office personnel are assigned full-time to the project and work out of the project office, whereas the project team members work out of the functional units and may spend only a small percentage of their time on the project. Normally, project office personnel report directly to the project manager, but they may still be solid to their line function just for administrative control. A project office usually is not required on small projects, and sometimes the project can be accomplished by just one person who may fill all of the project office positions.

Before the staffing function begins, five basic questions are usually considered:

- What are the requirements for an individual to become a successful project manager?
- Who should be a member of the project team?
- Who should be a member of the project office?

- What problems can occur during recruiting activities?
- What can happen downstream to cause the loss of key team members?

On the surface, these questions may not seem especially complex. But when we apply them to a project environment (which is by definition a "temporary" situation) where a constant stream of projects is necessary for corporate growth, the staffing problems become overly complex, especially if the organization is understaffed. Conflicts and priority setting become a way of life during the staffing functions.

4.1 THE STAFFING ENVIRONMENT

For a full understanding of the problems that occur during staffing, we must first investigate the characteristics of project management, including the project environment, the project management process, and the project manager.

Two major kinds of problems are related to the project environment: personnel performance problems and personnel policy problems. Personnel performance is difficult for many individuals in the project environment because it represents a change in the way of doing business. Individuals, regardless of how competent they are, find it difficult to adapt continually to a changing situation in which they report to multiple managers. As a result, some people have come to resent change. Most individuals prefer a stable situation, and projects, by definition, are temporary assignments. On the other hand, many individuals thrive on temporary assignments because it gives them a "chance for glory." These individuals are usually highly creative and enjoy challenging work. The challenge is more important than the cost of failure.

Unfortunately, in some situations the line employees might consider the chance for glory more important than the project. For example, an employee pays no attention to the instructions of the project manager and performs the task his own way. When the project manager asks why, the employee asks, "Well, isn't my way better?" In this situation, the employee wants only to be recognized as an achiever and really does not care if the project is a success or failure. If the project fails, the employee still has a functional home to return to. Even the instructions of the line manager can be ignored if the individual wants that "one chance for glory" where he will be identified as an achiever with good ideas.

The second major performance problem lies in the project–functional interface, where an individual suddenly finds himself reporting to two bosses, the functional manager and the project manager. If the functional manager and the project manager are in total agreement about the work to be accomplished, then performance at the interface may not be hampered. But if conflicting directions are received, then the individual at the interface, regardless of his capabilities and experience, may let his performance suffer because of his compromising position. In this case, the employee will "bend" in the direction of the manager who controls his purse strings.

Personnel policy problems can create havoc in an organization, especially if the "grass is greener" in a project environment than in the functional environment. Functional organizations are normally governed by unit manning documents that specify grade and salary for the employees. Project offices, on the other hand, have no such regulations because, by definition, projects are different from each other and, therefore, require different structures. It is a fact, however, that opportunities for advancement are greater in the project office than in the functional organization. The functional organization may be regulated by a unit manning document regardless of how well employees perform, whereas the project office promotes according to achievement. The difficulty here rests in the fact that one can distinguish between employees in grades 7, 8, 9, 10, and 11 in a line organization, whereas for a project manager the distinction might appear only in the size of the project or the amount of responsibility. Bonuses for outstanding performance are easier to obtain in the project office than in the line organization; but, although bonuses may create the illusion of stimulating competition, the real result is creation of conflict and jealousy between the horizontal and vertical elements.

Many of the characteristics of the project management process have already been discussed. Project management is organized:

- To achieve a single set of objectives
- Through a single project of a finite lifetime
- To operate as a separate company entity except for administrative purposes

Because each project is different, the project management process allows each project to have its own policies, procedures, rules, and standards, provided they fall within broad company guidelines. Each project must be recognized as a project by top management so that the project manager has the delegated authority necessary to enforce the policies, procedures, rules, and standards.

Project management is successful only if the project manager and his team are totally dedicated to the successful completion of the project. This requires each team member of the project team and office to have a good understanding of the fundamental project requirements, which include:

- Customer liaison
- Project direction
- Project planning
- Project control
- Project evaluation
- Project reporting

Every member of the project office (and sometimes the project team) must have the ability to satisfy these requirements. Since these requirements cannot generally be fulfilled by single individuals, members of the project office, as well as functional representatives, must work together as a team. This teamwork concept is vital to the success of a project.

Ultimately, the person with the greatest influence during the staffing phase is the project manager. The personal attributes and abilities of project managers will either attract or deter highly desirable individuals. Project managers must like trouble. They must be capable of evaluating risk and uncertainty. Other basic characteristics include:

- Honesty and integrity
- Understanding of personnel problems
- Understanding of project technology
- Business management competence
  - Management principles
  - Communications
- Alertness and quickness
- Versatility
- Energy and toughness
- Decision-making ability

Project managers must exhibit honesty and integrity with their subordinates as well as line personnel, thus fostering an atmosphere of trust, as shown in Figure 4–1. They should not make impossible promises, such as immediate promotions for everyone if a follow-on contract is received. Honesty, integrity, and an understanding of personnel problems can often eliminate any problems or con-

FIGURE 4–1. Deal from the top of the deck.

flicts that detract from the creation of a truly dedicated environment. Most project managers have "open-door" policies for project as well as line personnel. On temporarily assigned activities, such as a project, managers cannot wait for personnel to iron out their own problems for fear that time, cost, and performance requirements will not be satisfied. As an example, a line employee is having problems at home, and it is beginning to affect his performance on the project. The project manager talks to his line manager and is greeted with the statement, "Just give him a little time, and he'll work out the problem himself." In this situation, the line manager may not recognize the time constraint on the project.

Project managers should have both business management and technical expertise. They must understand the fundamental principles of management, especially those involving the rapid development of temporary communication channels. Project managers must understand the technical implications of a problem, since they are ultimately responsible for all decision making. They may have a staff of professionals to assist them. However, many good technically oriented managers have failed because they have become too involved with the technical side of the project rather than the management side. There are several strong arguments for having a project manager who has more than just an understanding of the necessary technology. Technical expertise is ideal, but it is not always possible because the individual tends to become a generalist, and a general understanding without business management sense can become a major problem, as illustrated in the following example. A young woman with a computer manufacturer was responsible for managing all projects involving a specific product line. Marketing came to her stating that they had found a customer for the product line, but major modifications had to be made. Since she had only an understanding of technology, she met with the true experts, the line managers, who informed her that the modifications were impossible. She had the authority to spend up to $1 million to make the modifications, but if the line managers were correct, the $1 million would be wasted. She called a meeting between engineering and marketing, but each held their ground and no final decision was reached. She ultimately called a meeting between line managers and the vice president for engineering. The line managers held their ground with the vice president, and the project was eventually rejected.

Because a project has a relatively short time duration, decision making must be rapid and effective. Managers must be alert and quick in their ability to perceive "red flags" that can eventually lead to serious problems. They must demonstrate their versatility and toughness in order to keep subordinates dedicated to goal accomplishment. Executives must realize that the project manager's objectives during staffing are to:

- Acquire the best available assets and try to improve them
- Provide a good working environment for all personnel
- Make sure that all resources are applied effectively and efficiently so that all constraints are met, if possible

4.2 SELECTING THE PROJECT MANAGER: AN EXECUTIVE DECISION

Probably the most difficult decision facing upper-level management is the selection of project managers. Some managers work best on long-duration projects where decision making can be slow; others may thrive on short-duration projects that can result in a constant-pressure environment. Upper-level management must know the capabilities and shortcomings of their project managers. A director was asked whom he would choose for a key project manager position—an individual who had been a project manager on previous programs in which there were severe problems and cost overruns, or a new aggressive individual who might have the capability to be a good project manager but had never had the opportunity. The director responded that he would go with the seasoned veteran assuming that the previous mistakes would not be made again. The argument here is that the project manager must learn from his own mistakes so they will not be made again. The new individual is apt to make the same mistakes the veteran made. However, executives cannot always go with the seasoned veterans without creating frustrating career path opportunities for the younger personnel. Stewart has commented on this type of situation:[1]

> Though the project manager's previous experience is apt to have been confined to a single functional area of business, he must be able to function on the project as a kind of general manager in miniature. He must not only keep track of what is happening but also play the crucial role of advocate for the project. Even for a seasoned manager, this task is not likely to be easy. Hence, it is important to assign an individual whose administrative abilities and skills in personal relations have been convincingly demonstrated under fire.

Charles Martin has commented on the fact that project manager selection is a general management responsibility:[2]

- A project manager is given license to cut across several organizational lines. His activities, therefore, take on a flavor of general management, and must be done well.
- Project management will not succeed without good project managers. Thus, if general management sees fit to establish a project, it should certainly see fit to select a good man as its leader.
- A project manager is far more likely to accomplish desired goals if it is obvious that general management has selected and appointed him.

---

1. John M. Stewart, "Making Project Management Work." Reprinted with permission from *Business Horizons,* Fall 1965, p. 63. Copyright © by the Board of Trustees at Indiana University.

2. Reprinted with permission of the publisher, from *Project Management: How to Make It Work* (p. 234) by Charles Martin, © 1976 AMACOM, a division of the American Management Association. All rights reserved.

The selection process for project managers is not an easy one. Five basic questions must be considered:

- What are the internal and external sources?
- How do we select?
- How do we provide career development in project management?
- How can we develop project management skills?
- How do we evaluate project management performance?

Project management cannot succeed unless a good project manager is at the controls. The selection process is an upper-level management responsibility because the project manager is delegated the authority of the general manager to cut across organizational lines in order to accomplish the desired objectives successfully. It is far more likely that project managers will succeed if it is obvious to the subordinates that the general manager has appointed them. Usually, a brief memo to the line managers will suffice. The major responsibilities of the project manager include:

- To produce the end-item with the available resources and within the constraints of time, cost, and performance/technology
- To meet contractual profit objectives
- To make all required decisions whether they be for alternatives or termination
- To act as the customer (external) and upper-level and functional management (internal) communications focal point
- To "negotiate" with all functional disciplines for accomplishment of the necessary work packages within the constraints of time, cost, and performance/technology
- To resolve all conflicts, if possible

If these responsibilities were applied to the total organization, they might reflect the job description of the general manager. This analogy between project and general managers is one of the reasons why future general managers are asked to perform functions that are implied, rather than spelled out, in the job description. As an example, you are the project manager on a high-technology project. As the project winds down, an executive asks you to write a paper so that he can present it at a technical meeting in Tokyo. His name will appear first on the paper. Should this be a part of your job? As this author sees it, you really don't have much of a choice.

In order for project managers to fulfill their responsibilities successfully, they are constantly required to demonstrate their skills in interface, resource, and planning and control management. These implicit responsibilities are shown below:

- Interface Management
  - Product interfaces
    - —Performance of parts or subsections
    - —Physical connection of parts or subsections

- Project interfaces
- Customer
- Management (functional and upper-level)
- Change of responsibilities
- Information flow
- Material interfaces (inventory control)
- Resource Management
  - Time (schedule)
  - Manpower
  - Money
  - Facilities
  - Equipment
  - Material
  - Information/technology
- Planning and Control Management
  - Increased equipment utilization
  - Increased performance efficiency
  - Reduced risks
  - Identification of alternatives to problems
  - Identification of alternative resolutions to conflicts

Consider the following advertisement for a facilities planning and development project manager (adapted from *The New York Times*, January 2, 1972):

Personable, well-educated, literate individual with college degree in Engineering to work for a small firm. Long hours, no fringe benefits, no security, little chance for advancement are among the inducements offered. Job requires wide knowledge and experience in manufacturing, materials, construction techniques, economics, management and mathematics. Competence in the use of the spoken and written English is required. Must be willing to suffer personal indignities from clients, professional derision from peers in the more conventional jobs, and slanderous insults from colleagues.

Job involves frequent extended trips to inaccessible locations throughout the world, manual labor and extreme frustration from the lack of data on which to base decisions.

Applicant must be willing to risk personal and professional future on decisions based upon inadequate information and complete lack of control over acceptance of recommendations by clients. Responsibilities for the work are unclear and little or no guidance is offered. Authority commensurate with responsibility is not provided either by the firm or its clients.

Applicant should send resume, list of publications, references and other supporting documentation to . . .

Fortunately, these types of job descriptions are very rare today as maturity in project management continues.

Finding the person with the right qualifications is not an easy task because the selection of project managers is based more on personal characteristics than on the job description. In Section 4.1 a brief outline of desired characteristics was presented. Russell Archibald defines a broader range of desired personal characteristics:[3]

- Flexibility and adaptability
- Preference for significant initiative and leadership
- Aggressiveness, confidence, persuasiveness, verbal fluency
- Ambition, activity, forcefulness
- Effectiveness as a communicator and integrator
- Broad scope of personal interests
- Poise, enthusiasm, imagination, spontaneity
- Able to balance technical solutions with time, cost, and human factors
- Well organized and disciplined
- A generalist rather than a specialist
- Able and willing to devote most of his time to planning and controlling
- Able to identify problems
- Willing to make decisions
- Able to maintain proper balance in the use of time

Figure 4–2 is a humorous summation of these elements.

This ideal project manager would probably have doctorates in engineering, business, and psychology, and experience with ten different companies in a variety of project office positions, and would be about twenty-five years old. Good

---

3. Russell D. Archibald, *Managing High-Technology Programs and Projects* (New York: Wiley, 1976), p. 55. Copyright © 1976 by John Wiley & Sons, Inc. Reprinted by permission of the publisher.

FIGURE 4–2. Keep your nose to the grindstone.

project managers in industry today would probably be lucky to have 70 to 80 percent of these characteristics. The best project managers are willing and able to identify their own shortcomings and know when to ask for help. Project managers who believe that they can do it all themselves may end up as shown in Figure 4–3.

Figures 4–4 and 4–5 show the basic knowledge and responsibilities that construction project managers should possess. It is understandable that the apprenticeship program for training construction project managers could easily be ten years.

The difficulty in staffing, especially for project managers or assistant project managers, is in determining what questions to ask during an interview to see if an individual has the necessary or desired characteristics. There are numerous situations in which individuals are qualified to be promoted vertically but not horizontally. An individual with poor communication skills and interpersonal skills can be promoted to a line management slot because of his technical expertise, but this same individual is not qualified for project management promotion.

Most executives have found that the best way to interview is by reading each element of the job description to the potential candidate. Many individuals want a career path in project management but are totally unaware of what the project manager's duties are.

So far we have discussed the personal characteristics of the project manager. There are also job-related questions to consider, such as:

FIGURE 4–3. Let the experts do it.

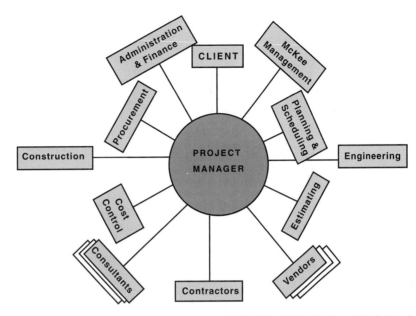

FIGURE 4–4. McKee project services. *Source:* V. E. Cole, W. B. Ball, and D. S. Barrie, "Managing the Project," *Proceedings of the Ninth International Seminar/Symposium on Project Management,* The Project Management Institute, 1977, p. 57.

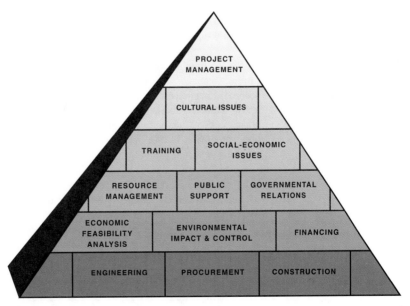

FIGURE 4–5. Project management responsibilities. *Source:* L. J. Weber, W. Riethmeier, A. F. Westergard, and K. O. Hartley, "The Project Sponser's View," *Proceedings of the Ninth International Seminar/Symposium on Project Management,* The Project Management Institute, 1977, p. 76.

- Are feasibility and economic analyses necessary?
- Is complex technical expertise required? If so, is it within the individual's capabilities?
- If the individual is lacking expertise, will there be sufficient backup strength in the line organizations?
- Is this the company's or the individual's first exposure to this type of project and/or client? If so, what are the risks to be considered?
- What is the priority for this project, and what are the risks?
- With whom must the project manager interface, both inside and outside the organization?

Most good project managers generally know how to perform feasibility studies and cost-benefit analyses. Sometimes this capability can create organizational conflict. A major utility company begins each computer project with a feasibility study in which a cost-benefit analysis is performed. The project managers, all of whom report to a project management division, perform the study themselves without any direct functional support. The functional managers argue that the results are grossly inaccurate because the functional experts are not involved. The project manager, on the other hand, argues that they never have sufficient time or money to perform a complete analysis. This type of conflict requires executive attention. Some companies resolve this by having a special group simply to perform these types of analyses.

Most companies would prefer to find project managers from within. Unfortunately, this is easier said than done. The following remarks by Robert Fluor illustrate this point:[4]

> On-the-job training is probably the most important aspect in the development of a project manager. This includes assignments to progressively more responsible positions in engineering and construction management and project management. It also includes rotational assignments in several engineering department disciplines, in construction, procurement, cost and scheduling, contract administration, and others. . . . We find there are great advantages to developing our project managers from within the company. There are good reasons for this:
>
> - They know the corporate organization, policies, procedures, and the key people. This allows them to give us quality performance quicker.
> - They have an established performance record which allows us to place them at the maximum level of responsibility and authority.
> - Clients prefer a proven track record within the project manager's present organization.

---

4. J. Robert Fluor, "Development of Project Managers—Twenty Years' Study at Fluor," Keynote address to Project Management Institute Ninth International Seminar/Symposium, Chicago, Illinois, October 24, 1977.

There are also good reasons for recruiting from outside the company. A new project manager hired from the outside would be less likely to have strong informal ties to any one line organization and thus could show impartiality on the project. Some companies further require that the individual spend an apprenticeship period of twelve to eighteen months in a line organization to find out how the company functions, to become acquainted with some of the people, and to understand the company's policies and procedures.

One of the most important but often least understood characteristics of good project managers is their ability to understand and know both themselves and their employees in terms of strengths and weaknesses. They must understand human behavior. Each manager must understand that in order for employees to perform efficiently:

- They must know what they are supposed to do, preferably in terms of an end product.
- They must have a clear understanding of authority and its limits.
- They must know what their relationship with other people is.
- They should know what constitutes a job well done in terms of specific results.
- They should know where and when they are falling short.
- They must be made aware of what can and should be done to correct unsatisfactory results.
- They must feel that their superior has an interest in them as individuals.
- They must feel that their superior believes in them and is anxious for their success and progress.

4.3 SKILL REQUIREMENTS FOR PROGRAM MANAGERS

Programs are often complex and multifaceted. Managing these programs represents a challenge requiring skills in team building, leadership, conflict resolution, technical expertise, planning, organization, entrepreneurship, administration, management support, and the allocation of resources. This section examines these skills relative to program management effectiveness. A key factor to good program performance is the program manager's ability to integrate personnel from many disciplines into an effective work team.

To get results, the program manager must relate to (1) the people to be managed, (2) the task to be done, (3) the tools available, (4) the organizational structure, and (5) the organizational environment, including the customer community.

All work factors are interrelated and operate under the limited control of the program manager. With an understanding of the interaction of corporate organization and behavior elements, the manager can build an environment conducive to the working team's needs. The internal and external forces that impinge on the organization of the project must be reconciled to mutual goals. Thus the program manager must be both socially and technically aware to understand how the organization functions and how these functions will affect the program organization of the particular job to be done. In addition, the program manager must understand the culture and value system of the organization he is working with. Research and experience show that effective program management performance is directly related to the level of proficiency at which these skills are mastered.

Ten specific skills are identified (in no particular order) and discussed in this section:

- Team building
- Leadership
- Conflict resolution
- Technical expertise
- Planning
- Organization
- Entrepreneurship
- Administration
- Management support
- Resource allocation

It is important that the personal management traits underlying these skills operate to form a homogeneous management style. The right mixture of skill levels depends on the project task, the techniques employed, the people assigned, and the organizational structure. To be effective, program managers must consider all facets of getting the job done. Their management style must facilitate the integration of multidisciplinary program resources for synergistic operation. The days of the manager who gets by with technical expertise alone or pure administrative skills are gone.

Team-Building Skills

Building the program team is one of the prime responsibilities of the program manager. Team building involves a whole spectrum of management skills required to identify, commit, and integrate the various task groups from the traditional functional organization into a single program management system.

To be effective, the program manager must provide an atmosphere conducive to teamwork. He must nurture a climate with the following characteristics:

- Team members committed to the program
- Good interpersonal relations and team spirit
- The necessary expertise and resources
- Clearly defined goals and program objectives
- Involved and supportive top management

- Good program leadership
- Open communication among team members and support organizations
- A low degree of detrimental interpersonal and intergroup conflict

Three major considerations are involved in all of the above factors aimed toward integration of people from many disciplines into an effective team: (1) effective communications, (2) sincere interest in the professional growth of team members, and (3) commitment to the project.

Leadership Skills

An absolutely essential prerequisite for program success is the program manager's ability to lead the team within a relatively unstructured environment. It involves dealing effectively with managers and supporting personnel across functional lines with little or no formal authority. It also involves information processing skills, the ability to collect and filter relevant data valid for decision making in a dynamic environment. It involves the ability to integrate individual demands, requirements, and limitations into decisions that benefit overall project performance. It further involves the program manager's ability to resolve intergroup conflicts, an important factor in overall program performance.

Perhaps more than in any other position below the general manager's level, quality leadership depends heavily on the program manager's personal experience and credibility within the organization. An effective management style might be characterized this way:

- Clear project leadership and direction
- Assistance in problem solving
- Facilitating the integration of new members into the team
- Ability to handle interpersonal conflict
- Facilitating group decisions
- Capability to plan and elicit commitments
- Ability to communicate clearly
- Presentation of the team to higher management
- Ability to balance technical solutions against economic and human factors

The personal traits desirable and supportive of the above skills are:

- Project management experience
- Flexibility and change orientation
- Innovative thinking
- Initiative and enthusiasm
- Charisma and persuasiveness
- Organization and discipline

**Conflict Resolution
Skills**

Conflict is fundamental to complex task management. It is often determined by the interplay of the program organization and the larger host organization and its multifunctional components. Understanding the determinants of conflicts is important to the program manager's ability to deal with conflicts effectively. When conflict becomes dysfunctional, it often results in poor program decision making, lengthy delays over issues, and a disruption of the team's efforts, all negative influences to program performance. However, conflict can be beneficial when it produces involvement and new information and enhances the competitive spirit.

A number of suggestions have been derived from various research studies aimed at increasing the program manager's ability to resolve conflict and thus improve overall program performance. Program managers must:

- Understand interaction of the organizational and behavioral elements in order to build an environment conducive to their team's motivational needs. This will enhance active participation and minimize unproductive conflict.
- Communicate effectively with all organizational levels regarding both project objectives and decisions. Regularly scheduled status review meetings can be an important communication vehicle.
- Recognize the determinants of conflict and their timing in the project life cycle. Effective project planning, contingency planning, securing of commitments, and involving top management can help to avoid or minimize many conflicts before they impede project performance.

The value of the conflict produced depends on the ability of the program manager to promote beneficial conflict while minimizing its potential hazardous consequences. The accomplished manager needs a "sixth sense" to indicate when conflict is desirable, what kind of conflict will be useful, and how much conflict is optimal for a given situation. In the final analysis, he has the sole responsibility for his program and how conflict will contribute to its success or failure.

Technical Skills

The program manager rarely has all the technical, administrative, and marketing expertise needed to direct the program single-handedly. Nor is it necessary or desirable. It is essential, however, for the program manager to understand the technology, the markets, and the environment of the business to participate effectively in the search for integrated solutions and technological innovations. More important, without this understanding, the integrated consequences of local decisions on the total program, the potential growth ramifications, and relationships to other business opportunities cannot be foreseen by the manager. Further technical expertise is necessary to evaluate technical concepts and solutions, to communicate effectively in technical terms with the project team, and to assess risks and make trade-offs between cost, schedule, and technical issues. This is why in complex problem-solving situations so many project managers must have an engineering background.

Taken together, technical expertise is important to the successful management of engineering projects. It is composed of an understanding of the:

- Technology involved
- Engineering tools and techniques employed
- Specific markets, their customers, and requirements
- Product applications
- Technological trends and evolutions
- Relationship among supporting technologies
- People who are part of the technical community

The technical expertise required for effective management of engineering programs is normally developed through progressive growth in engineering or supportive project assignments in a specific technology area. Frequently, the project begins with an exploratory phase leading into a proposal. This is normally an excellent testing ground for the future program manager. It also allows top management to judge the new candidate's capacity for managing the technological innovations and integration of solutions needed for success.

Planning Skills

Planning skills are helpful for any undertaking; they are absolutely essential, however, for the successful management of large complex programs. The project plan is the road map that defines how to get from the start to the final results.

Program planning is an ongoing activity at all organizational levels. However, the preparation of a project summary plan, prior to project start, is the responsibility of the program manager. Effective project planning requires particular skills far beyond writing a document with schedules and budgets. It requires communication and information processing skills to define the actual resource requirements and administrative support necessary. It requires the ability to negotiate the necessary resources and commitments from key personnel in various support organizations with little or no formal authority, including the definition of measurable milestones.

Effective planning requires skills in the areas of:

- Information processing
- Communication
- Resource negotiations
- Securing commitments
- Incremental and modular planning
- Assuring measurable milestones
- Facilitating top management involvement

In addition, the program manager must assure that the plan remains a viable document. Changes in project scope and depth are inevitable. The plan should reflect necessary changes through formal revisions and should be the guiding document throughout the life cycle of the program. Nothing is more useless than an obsolete or irrelevant plan.

Finally, program managers need to be aware that planning can be overdone. If not controlled, planning can become an end in itself and a poor substitute for innovative work. Individuals retreat to the utopia of no responsibility where innovative actions cannot be taken "because it is not in the plan." It is the responsibility of the program manager to build flexibility into the plan and police it against such misuse.

Organizational Skills

The program manager must be a social architect, that is, he must understand how the organization works and how to work with the organization. Organizational skills are particularly important during project formation and startup when the program manager establishes the program organization by integrating people from many different disciplines into an effective work team. It requires far more than simply constructing a project organization chart. At a minimum, it requires defining the reporting relationships, responsibilities, lines of control, and information needs. Supporting skills in the area of planning, communication, and conflict resolution are particularly helpful. A good program plan and a task matrix are useful organizational tools. In addition, the organizational effort is facilitated by clearly defined program objectives, open communication channels, good program leadership, and senior management support.

Entrepreneurial Skills

The program manager also needs a general management perspective. For example, economic considerations are one important area that normally affects the organization's financial performance. However, objectives often are much broader than profits. Customer satisfaction, future growth, cultivation of related market activities, and minimum organizational disruptions of other programs might be equally important goals. The effective program manager is concerned with all these issues.

Entrepreneurial skills are developed through actual experience. However, formal MBA-type training, special seminars, and cross-functional training programs can help to develop the entrepreneurial skills needed by program managers.

Administrative Skills

Administrative skills are essential. The program manager must be experienced in planning, staffing, budgeting, scheduling, and other control techniques. In dealing with technical personnel, the problem is seldom to make people understand administrative techniques such as budgeting and scheduling, but to impress on them that costs and schedules are just as important as elegant technical solutions.

Particularly on larger programs, managers rarely have all the administrative skills required. While it is important that program managers understand the company's operating procedures and available tools, it is often necessary for the program manager to free himself from administrative details regardless of his ability to handle them. He has to delegate considerable administrative tasks to support groups or hire a project administrator.

Some helpful tools for the manager in the administration of his program include: (1) the meeting, (2) the report, (3) the review, and (4) budget and schedule controls. Program managers must be thoroughly familiar with these available tools and know how to use them effectively.

Management Support Building Skills

The program manager is surrounded by a myriad of organizations that either support him or control his activities. An understanding of these interfaces is important to program managers as it enhances their ability to build favorable relationships with senior management. Management support is often an absolute necessity for dealing effectively with interface groups. Project organizations are shared-power systems with personnel of many diverse interests and "ways of doing things." These power systems have a tendency toward imbalance. Only a strong leader backed by senior management can prevent the development of unfavorable biases.

Four key variables influence the project manager's ability to create favorable relationships with senior management: (1) his ongoing credibility, (2) the visibility of his program, (3) the priority of his program relative to other organizational undertakings, and (4) his own accessibility. All these factors are interrelated and can be developed by the individual manager. Furthermore, senior management can aid such development significantly.

Resource Allocation Skills

A program organization has many bosses. Functional lines often shield support organizations from direct financial control by the project office. Once a task has been authorized, it is often impossible to control the personnel assignments, priorities, and indirect manpower costs. In addition, profit accountability is difficult owing to the interdependencies of various support departments and the often changing work scope and contents.

Effective and detailed program planning may facilitate commitment and reinforce control. Part of the plan is the "Statement of Work," which establishes a basis for resource allocation. It is also important to work out specific agreements with all key contributors and their superiors on the tasks to be performed and the associated budgets and schedules. Measurable milestones are not only important for hardware components, but also for the "invisible" program components such as systems and software tasks. Ideally, these commitments on specs, schedules, and budgets should be established through involvement by key personnel in the early phases of project formation, such as the proposal phase. This is the time when requirements are still flexible, and trade-offs among performance, schedule, and budget parameters are possible. Further, this is normally the time when the competitive spirit among potential contributors is highest, often leading to a more cohesive and challenging work plan.

4.4 SPECIAL CASES IN PROJECT MANAGER SELECTION

Thus far we have assumed that the project is large enough for a full-time project manager to be appointed. This is not always the case. There are four major problem areas in staffing projects:

- Part-time versus full-time assignments
- Several projects assigned to one project manager
- Projects assigned to functional managers
- The project manager role retained by the general manager

The first problem is generally related to the size of the project. If the project is small (in time duration or cost), a part-time project manager may be selected. Many executives have fallen into the trap of letting line personnel act as part-time project managers while still performing line functions. If the employee has a conflict between what is best for the project and what is best for his line organization, the project will suffer. It is only natural that the employee will favor the place the salary increases come from.

It is a common practice for one project manager to control several projects, especially if they are either related or similar. Problems come about when the projects have drastically different priorities. The low-priority efforts will be neglected.

If the project is a high-technology effort that requires specialization and can be performed by one department, then it is not unusual for the line manager to take on a dual role and act as project manager as well. This can be difficult to do, especially if the project manager is required to establish the priorities for the work under his supervision. The line manager may keep the best resources for the project, regardless of the priority. Then that project will be a success at the expense of every other project he must supply resources to.

Probably the worst situation is that in which an executive fills the role of project manager for a particular effort. The executive may not have the time necessary for total dedication to the achievement of the project. He cannot make effective decisions as a project manager while still discharging normal duties. Additionally, the executive may hoard the best resources for his project.

4.5 SELECTING THE WRONG PROJECT MANAGER

Even though executives know the personal characteristics and traits that project managers should possess, and even though job descriptions are often clearly defined, management may still select the wrong person. Below are several common criteria by which the wrong person may be selected.

Maturity

Some executives consider gray hair and baldness to be a sure indication of maturity, but this is not the type of maturity needed for project management. Maturity in project management generally comes from exposure to several types of projects in a variety of project office positions. In aerospace and defense, it is possible for a project manager to manage the same type of project for ten years or more. When placed on a new project, the individual may try to force personnel and project requirements to adhere to the same policies and procedures that existed on the ten-year project. The project manager may know only one way of managing projects. Perhaps, in this case, the individual would best function as an assistant project manager on a new project.

Hard-Nosed Tactics

Applying hard-nosed tactics to subordinates can be very demoralizing. Project managers must give people sufficient freedom to get the job done, without providing continuous supervision and direction. A line employee who is given "freedom" by his line manager but suddenly finds himself closely supervised by the project manager will be a very unhappy individual. Employees must be trained to understand that supervised pressure will occur in time of crisis. If the project manager provides continuous supervised pressure, then he may find it difficult to obtain a qualified staff for the next project.

Maturity in project management means maturity in dealing with people. Line managers, because of their ability to control an employee's salary, need only one leadership style and can force the employees to adapt. The project manager, on the other hand, cannot control salaries and must have a wide variety of leadership styles. The project manager must adapt a leadership style to the project employees, whereas the reverse is true in the line organization.

Availability

Executives should not assign individuals as project managers simply because of availability. People have a tendency to cringe when you suggest that project managers be switched halfway through a project. For example, manager X is halfway through his project. Manager Y is waiting for an assignment. A new project comes up, and the executive switches managers X and Y. There are several reasons for this. The most important phase of a project is planning, and, if it is accomplished correctly, the project could conceivably run itself. Therefore, manager Y should be able to handle manager X's project.

There are several other reasons why this switch may be necessary. The new project may have a higher priority and require a more experienced manager. Second, not all project managers are equal, especially when it comes to planning. When an executive finds a project manager who demonstrates extraordinary talents at planning, there is a natural tendency for the executive to want this project manager to plan all projects. An experienced project manager once commented to the author, "Once, just once, I'd like to be able to finish a project." There are other reasons for having someone take over a project in midstream. The director of project management calls you into his office and tells you that one of your fellow project managers has had a heart attack midway through the project. You will be taking over his project, which is well behind schedule and overrunning costs. The director of project management then "orders" you to complete the project within time and cost. How do you propose to do it? Perhaps the only viable solution to this problem is to step into a phone booth and begin taking off your clothes in order to expose the big "S" on your chest.

Technical Expertise   Executives quite often promote technical line managers without realizing the consequences. Technical specialists may not be able to divorce themselves from the technical side of the house and become project managers rather than project doers. There are also strong reasons to promote technical specialists to project managers. These people often:

- Have better relationships with fellow researchers
- Can prevent duplication of effort
- Can foster teamwork
- Have progressed up through the technical ranks
- Are knowledgeable in many technical fields
- Understand the meaning of profitability and general management philosophy
- Are interested in training and teaching
- Understand how to work with perfectionists

As described by Taylor and Watling:[5]

> It is often the case, therefore, that the Project Manager is more noted for his management technique expertise, his ability to "get on with people" than for his sheer technical prowess. However, it can be dangerous to minimize this latter talent when choosing Project Managers dependent upon project type and size. The Project Manager should preferably be an expert either in the field of the project task or a subject allied to it.

Promoting an employee to project management because of his technical expertise may be acceptable if, and only if, the project requires this expertise and technical direction, as in R&D efforts. For projects in which a "generalist" is acceptable as a project manager, there may be a great danger in assigning highly technical personnel. According to Wilemon and Cicero:[6]

- The greater the project manager's technical expertise, the higher the propensity that he will overly involve himself in the technical details of the project.
- The greater the project manager's difficulty in delegating technical task responsibilities, the more likely it is that he will overinvolve himself in the technical details of the project. (Depending upon his expertise to do so.)

---

5. W. J. Taylor and T. F. Watling, *Successful Project Management* (London: Business Books Limited, 1972), p. 32.

6. D. L. Wilemon and J. P. Cicero, "The Project Manager—Anomalies and Ambiguities," *Academy of Management Journal,* Vol. 13, 1970, pp. 269–282.

- The greater the project manager's interest in the technical details of the project, the more likely it is that he will defend the project manager's role as one of a technical specialist.
- The lower the project manager's technical expertise, the more likely it is that he will overstress the non-technical project functions (administrative functions).

If an expert is selected, then the individual must learn how to use people effectively. As an example, in 1972 a company (with $100 million in sales today) implemented project management with the adoption of a matrix. The decision was made that the best technical experts would staff the project management slots. The technical experts then began usurping the authority of the line managers by giving continuous technical direction to the line people. Unfortunately, management felt that this was the way the system should operate. When an employee was assigned to a project, the employee knew that the project manager would not stand behind him unless he followed the project manager's directions. Today management is trying to clear up the problem of who are the true technical experts—the project managers or the line managers.

Customer Orientation

Executives quite often place individuals as project managers simply to satisfy a customer request. Being able to communicate with the customer does not guarantee project success, however. If the choice of project manager is simply a concession to the customer, then the executive must insist on providing a strong supporting team. This is often an unavoidable situation and must be lived with.

New Exposure

Executives run the risk of project failure if an individual is appointed project manager simply to gain exposure to project management. An executive of a utility company wanted to rotate his line personnel into project management for twelve to eighteen months and then return them to the line organization where they would be more well-rounded individuals and better understand the working relationship between project management and line management. There are two major problems with this. First, the individual may become technically obsolete after eighteen months in project management. Second, and more important, individuals who get a taste of project management will generally not want to return to the line organization.

Company Exposure

The mere fact that individuals have worked in a variety of divisions does not guarantee that they will make good project managers. Their working in a variety of divisions may indicate that they couldn't hold any one job. In that case, they have reached their true level of incompetency, and putting them into project management will only maximize the damage they can do to the company. Some executives contend that the best way to train a project manager is by rotation through the various functional disciplines for two weeks to a month in each or-

TABLE 4–1. METHODS AND TECHNIQUES FOR DEVELOPING PROJECT MANAGERS

  I. Experiential training/on-the-job
     Working with experienced professional leader
     Working with project team member
     Assigning a variety of project management responsibilities, consecutively
     Job rotation
     Formal on-the-job training
     Supporting multifunctional activities
     Customer liaison activities
 II. Conceptual training/schooling
     Courses, seminars, workshops
     Simulations, games, cases
     Group exercises
     Hands-on exercises in using project management techniques
     Professional meetings
     Conventions, symposia
     Readings, books, trade journals, professional magazines
III. Organizational development
     Formally established and recognized project management function
     Proper project organization
     Project support systems
     Project charter
     Project management directives, policies, and procedures

ganization. Other executives maintain that this is useless because the individual cannot learn anything in so short a period of time.

Tables 4–1 and 4–2 identify current thinking on methods for training project managers.

Finally, there are three special points to consider:

- Individuals should not be promoted to project management simply because they are at the top of their pay grade.
- Project managers should be promoted and paid based on performance, not on the number of people supervised.
- It is not necessary for the project manager to be the highest ranking or salaried individual on the project team with the rationale that sufficient "clout" is needed.

TABLE 4–2. HOW TO TRAIN PROJECT MANAGERS

Company Management Say Project Managers Can Be Trained in a Combination of Ways:

Experiential learning, on-the-job	60%
Formal education and special courses	20%
Professional activities, seminars	10%
Readings	10%

4.6 NEXT GENERATION PROJECT MANAGERS

The skills needed to be an effective, twenty-first century project manager have changed from those needed during the 1980s. Historically, only engineers were given the opportunity to become project managers. The belief was that the project manager had to have a command of technology in order to make all of the technical decisions. As project management began to grow and as projects became larger and more complex, it became obvious that project managers might need simply an understanding rather than a command of technology. The true technical expertise would reside with the line managers, except for special situations such as R&D project management.

As project management began to grow and mature, the project manager was converted from a technical manager to a business manager. This trend will become even more pronounced in the twenty-first century. The primary skills needed to be an effective project manager in the twenty-first century will be:

- Knowledge of the business
- Risk management
- Integration skills

The critical skill is risk management. However, to perform risk management effectively, a sound knowledge of the business is required. Figure 4-6 shows the changes in project management skills needed between 1985 and 2000. Training in these business skills is on the increase.

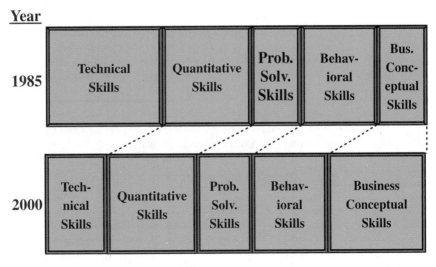

FIGURE 4–6. Project management skills.

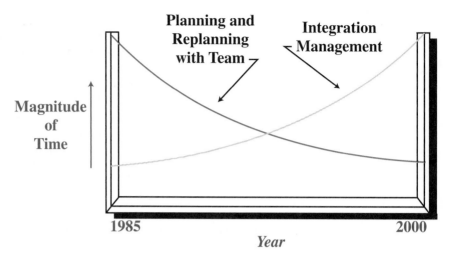

FIGURE 4–7. How do project managers spend their time?

As projects become larger and larger, the complexities of integration management become more pronounced. Figure 4-7 illustrates the importance of integration management. In 1985, project managers spent most of their time planning and replanning with their team. This was a necessity for the project manager since the project manager was the technical expert. Today, line managers are the technical experts and perform the majority of the planning and replanning efforts within their line. The project manager's efforts are now heavily oriented toward integration of the function plans into a total project plan. Some people contend that, with the increased risks and complexities of integration management, the project manager of the future will become an expert in damage control.

4.7 DUTIES AND JOB DESCRIPTIONS

Since projects, environments, and organizations differ from company to company as well as project to project, it is not unusual for companies to struggle to provide reasonable job descriptions of the project manager and associated personnel. Below is a simple list identifying the duties of a project manager in the construction industry:[7]

- Planning
  - Become completely familiar with all contract documents
  - Develop the basic plan for executing and controlling the project

---

7. Source unknown.

- Direct the preparation of project procedures
- Direct the preparation of the project budget
- Direct the preparation of the project schedule
- Direct the preparation of basic project design criteria and general specifications
- Direct the preparation of the plan for organizing, executing, and controlling field construction activities
- Review plans and procedures periodically and institute changes if necessary
- Organizing
  - Develop organization chart for project
  - Review project position descriptions, outlining duties, responsibilities, and restrictions for key project supervisors
  - Participate in the selection of key project supervisors
  - Develop project manpower requirements
  - Continually review project organization and recommend changes in organizational structure and personnel, if necessary
- Directing
  - Direct all work on the project that is required to meet contract obligations
  - Develop and maintain a system for decision making within the project team whereby decisions are made at the proper level
  - Promote the growth of key project supervisors
  - Establish objectives for project manager and performance goals for key project supervisors
  - Foster and develop a spirit of project team effort
  - Assist in resolution of differences or problems between departments or groups on assigned projects
  - Anticipate and avoid or minimize potential problems by maintaining current knowledge of overall project status
  - Develop clear written strategy guidelines for all major problems with clear definitions of responsibilities and restraints
- Controlling
  - Monitor project activities for compliance with company purpose and philosophy and general corporate policies
  - Interpret, communicate, and require compliance with the contract, the approved plan, project procedures, and directives of the client
  - Maintain personal control of adherence to contract warranty and guarantee provisions
  - Closely monitor project activities for conformity to contract scope provisions. Establish change notice procedure to evaluate and communicate scope changes
  - See that the plans for controlling and reporting on costs, schedule, and quality are effectively utilized
  - Maintain effective communications with the client and all groups performing project work

A more detailed job description of a construction project manager (for a utility company) appears below:

DUTIES

Under minimum supervision establishes the priorities for and directs the efforts of personnel (including their consultants or contractors) involved or to be involved on project controlled tasks to provide required achievement of an integrated approved set of technical, manpower, cost and schedule requirements.

1. Directs the development of initial and revised detailed task descriptions and forecasts of their associated technical, manpower, cost, and schedule requirements for tasks assigned to the Division.
2. Directs the regular integration of initial and revised task forecasts into Divisional technical, manpower, cost, and schedule reports and initiates the approval cycle for the reports.
3. Reviews conflicting inter- and extra-divisional task recommendations or actions that may occur from initial task description and forecast development until final task completion and directs uniform methods for their resolution.
4. Evaluates available and planned additions to Division manpower resources, including their tasks applications, against integrated technical and manpower reports and initiates actions to assure that Division manpower resources needs are met by the most economical mix of available qualified consultant and contractor personnel.
5. Evaluates Divisional cost and schedule reports in light of new tasks and changes in existing tasks and initiates actions to assure that increases or decreases in task cost and schedule are acceptable and are appropriately approved.
6. Prioritizes, adjusts and directs the efforts of Division personnel (including their consultants and contractors) resource allocations as necessary to both assure the scheduled achievement of state and federal regulatory commitments and maintain Divisional adherence to integrated manpower, cost and schedule reports.
7. Regularly reports the results of Divisional manpower, cost and schedule evaluations to higher management.
8. Regularly directs the development and issue of individual task and integrated Project programs reports.
9. Recommends new or revised Division strategies, goals and objectives in light of anticipated long-term manpower and budget needs.
10. Directly supervises project personnel in the regular preparation and issue of individual task descriptions and their associated forecasts, integrated Division manpower, cost and schedule reports and both task and Project progress reports.
11. Establishes basic organizational and personnel qualification requirements for Division (including their consultants or contractors) performance on tasks.
12. Establishes the requirements for, directs the development and approves control programs to standardize methods used for controlling similar types of activities in the Project and in other Division Departments.

13. Establishes the requirements for, directs the development of and approves administrative and technical training programs for Divisional personnel.
14. Approves recommendations for the placement of services or material purchase orders by Division personnel and assures that the cost and schedule data associated with such orders is consistent with approved integrated cost and schedule reports.
15. Promotes harmonious relations among Division organizations involved with Project tasks.
16. Exercises other duties related to Divisional project controls as assigned by the project manager.

QUALIFICATIONS

1. A Bachelor of Science Degree in Engineering or a Business Degree with a minor in Engineering or Science from an accredited four (4) year college or university.
2. a) (For Engineering Graduate) Ten (10) or more years of Engineering and Construction experience including a minimum of five (5) years of supervisory experience and two (2) years of management and electric utility experience.
   b) For Business Graduate) Ten (10) or more years of management experience including a minimum of five (5) years of supervisory experience in an engineering and construction related management area and two (2) years of experience as the manager or assistant manager of major engineering and construction related projects and two (2) recent years of electric utility experience.
3. Working knowledge of state and federal regulations and requirements that apply to major design and construction projects such as fossil and nuclear power stations.
4. Demonstrated ability to develop high level management control programs.
5. Experience related to computer processing of cost and schedule information.
6. Registered Professional Engineer and membership in appropriate management and technical societies is desirable (but not necessary).
7.[8] At least four (4) years of experience as a staff management member in an operating nuclear power station or in an engineering support on- or off-site capacity.
8.[8] Detailed knowledge of federal licensing requirement for nuclear power stations.
9.[8] Reasonably effective public speaker.

Because of the potential overlapping nature of job descriptions in a project management environment, some companies try to define responsibilities for each project management position, as shown in Table 4–3.

---

8. Qualifications 7 through 9 apply only for Nuclear Project Directors.

TABLE 4–3.   PROJECT MANAGEMENT POSITIONS AND RESPONSIBILITIES

Project Management Position	Typical Responsibility	Skill Requirements
• Project Administrator • Project Coordinator • Technical Assistant	Coordinating and integrating of subsystem tasks. Assisting in determining technical and manpower requirements, schedules, and budgets. Measuring and analyzing project performance regarding technical progress, schedules, and budgets.	• Planning • Coordinating • Analyzing • Understanding the organization
• Task Manager • Project Engineer • Assistant Project Manager	Same as above, but stronger role in establishing and maintaining project requirements. Conducting trade-offs. Directing the technical implementation according to established schedules and budgets.	• Technical expertise • Assessing trade-offs • Managing task implementation • Leading task specialists
• Project Manager • Program Manager	Same as above, but stronger role in project planning and controlling. Coordinating and negotiating requirements between sponsor and performing organizations. Bid proposal development and pricing. Establishing project organization and staffing. Overall leadership toward implementing project plan. Project profit. New business development.	• Overall program leadership • Team building • Resolving conflict • Managing multidisciplinary tasks • Planning and allocating resources • Interfacing with customers/sponsors
• Executive Program Manager	Title reserved for very large programs relative to host organization. Responsibilities same as above. Focus is on directing overall program toward desired business results. Customer liaison. Profit performance. New business development. Organizational development.	• Business leadership • Managing overall program businesses • Building program organizations • Developing personnel • Developing new business
• Director of Programs • V.P. Program Development	Responsible for managing multiprogram businesses via various project organizations, each led by a project manager. Focus is on business planning and development, profit performance, technology development, establishing policies and procedures, program management guidelines, personnel development, organizational development.	• Leadership • Strategic planning • Directing and managing program businesses • Building organizations • Selecting and developing key personnel • Identifying and developing new business

Occasionally, an attempt is made to create specialized definitions for the project manager. As described by Shah:[9]

> Like a physician, a project manager must be an expert diagnostician; he must guard his project from infection, detect symptoms, diagnose causes and prescribe cures for a multitude of afflictions.

4.8 THE ORGANIZATIONAL STAFFING PROCESS

Staffing the project organization can become a long and tedious effort, especially on large and complex engineering projects. Three major questions must be answered:

- What people resources are required?
- Where will the people come from?
- What type of project organizational structure will be best?

To determine the people resources required, the types of individuals (possibly job descriptions) must be decided on, as well as how many individuals from each job category are necessary and when these individuals will be needed.

Consider the following situation: As a project manager, you have an activity that requires three separate tasks, all performed within the same line organization. The line manager promises you the best available resources right now for the first task but cannot make any commitments beyond that. The line manager may have only below-average workers available for the second and third tasks. However, the line manager is willing to make a deal with you. He can give you an employee who can do the work but will only give an average performance. If you accept the average employee, the line manager will guarantee that the employee will be available to you for all three tasks. How important is continuity to you? There is no clearly definable answer to this question. Some people will always want the best resources and are willing to fight for them, whereas others prefer continuity and dislike seeing new people coming and going. The author prefers continuity, provided that the assigned employee has the ability to do the up-front planning needed during the first task. The danger in selecting the best employee is that a higher-priority project may come along, and you will lose the employee; or if the employee is an exceptional worker, he may simply be promoted off your project.

Sometimes, a project manager may have to make concessions to get the right people. For example, during the seventh, eighth, and ninth months of your proj-

---

9. Ramesh P. Shah, "Cross Your Bridges Before You Come to Them," *Management Review*, December 1971, p. 21.

ect you need two individuals with special qualifications. The functional manager says that they will be available two months earlier, and that if you don't pick them up then, there will be no guarantee of their availability during the seventh month. Obviously, the line manager is pressuring you, and you may have to give in. There is also the situation in which the line manager says that he'll have to borrow people from another department in order to fulfill his commitments for your project. You may have to live with this situation, but be very careful—these employees will be working at a low level on the learning curve, and overtime will not necessarily resolve the problem. You must expect mistakeshere.

Line managers often place new employees on projects so they can be upgraded. Project managers often resent this and immediately go to top management for help. If a line manager says that he can do the work with lower-level people, then the project manager must believe the line manager. After all, the line manager, not the assigned employees, make the commitment to do the work, and it is the line manager's neck that is stuck out.

Mutual trust between project and line managers is crucial, especially during staffing sessions. Once a project manager has developed a good working relationship with employees, the project manager would like to keep those individuals assigned to his activities. There is nothing wrong with a project manager requesting the same administrative and/or technical staff as before. Line managers realize this and usually agree to it.

There must also be mutual trust between the project managers themselves. Project managers must work as a total team, recognize each other's needs, and be willing to make decisions that are in the best interest of the company.

Once the resources are defined, the next question must be whether staffing will be from within the existing organization or from outside sources, such as new hires or consultants. Outside consultants are advisable if, and only if, internal manpower resources are being fully utilized on other programs, or if the company does not possess the required project skills. The answer to this question will indicate which organizational form is best for achievement of the objectives. The form might be a matrix, product, or staff project management structure.

Not all companies permit a variety of project organizational forms to exist within the main company structure. Those that do, however, consider the basic questions of classical management before making a decision. These include:

- How is labor specialized?
- What should the span of management be?
  - How much planning is required?
  - Are authority relationships delegated and understood?
  - Are there established performance standards?
  - What is the rate of change of the job requirements?
- Should we have a horizontal or vertical organization?
  - What are the economics?
  - What are the morale implications?
- Do we need a unity-of-command position?

As in any organization, the subordinates can make the superior look good in the performance of his duties. Unfortunately, the project environment is symbolized by temporary assignments in which the main effort put forth by the project manager is to motivate his (temporary) subordinates toward project dedication and to make them fully understand that:

- Teamwork is vital for success.
- Esprit de corps contributes to success.
- Conflicts can occur between project and functional tiers.
- Communication is essential for success.
- Conflicting orders may be given by the:
    - Project manager
    - Functional manager
    - Upper-level manager
- Unsuccessful performance may result in transfer or dismissal from the project as well as disciplinary action.

Earlier we stated that a project operates as a separate entity but remains attached to the company through company administration policies and procedures. Although project managers can establish their own policies, procedures, and rules, the criteria for promotion must be based on company standards. Therefore, we can ask:

- What commitments can a project manager make to his prospective subordinates?
- What promises can a project manager make regarding an individual's assignment after termination?

The first question involves salary, grade, responsibility, evaluation for promotion, bonuses, and overtime pay. There are many documented cases of project managers promising subordinates "the world" as a means of motivating them, when in fact the managers knew that these promises could not be kept.

The second question deals with the equity principle of job reassignment. According to Martin:[10]

> After reassignment at the end of his tour on a project, a person should have the same prospects for the future that he would have had if he had performed equally well (or badly) in a normal assignment not connected with the project during the same period.

---

10. Charles C. Martin, *Project Management: How to Make It Work* (New York: AMACOM, A Division of American Management Associations, 1976), p. 41. Reprinted with permission of the publisher, from *Project Management: How to Make It Work* (p. 41) by Charles Martin, © 1976 AMACOM, a division of the American Management Association. All rights reserved.

After unkept promises on previous projects, a project manager will find it very difficult to get top-quality personnel to volunteer for another project. Even if top management orders key individuals to be assigned to his project, they will always be skeptical about any promises that he may make.

Selecting the project manager is only one-third of the staffing problem. The next step, selecting the project office personnel and team members, often can be a time-consuming chore. The project office consists of personnel who are usually assigned as full-time members of the project. In selecting the project office staff, the project manager first must evaluate all potential candidates, whether or not they are assigned to another project. This evaluation process should include active project team members, functional team members available for promotion or transfer, and outside applicants.

Upon completion of the evaluation process, the project manager meets with upper-level management. This coordination is required to assure that:

- All assignments fall within current policies on rank, salary, and promotion.
- The individuals selected can work well with both the project manager (formal reporting) and upper-level management (informal reporting).
- The individuals selected have good working relationships with the functional personnel.

Good project office personnel cannot be trained overnight. Good training is usually identified as experience with several types of projects. Project managers do not "train" project office members, primarily because time constraints do not often permit this luxury. Project office personnel must be self-disciplined, especially during the first few assignments.

The third and final step in the staffing of the project office is a meeting between the project manager, upper-level management, and the project manager on whose project the requested individuals are currently assigned. Project managers are very reluctant to give up qualified personnel to the staff of other project offices, but unfortunately, this procedure is a way of life in a project environment. Upper-level management attends these meetings to show all negotiating parties that top management is concerned with maintaining the best possible mix of individuals from available resources and to help resolve staffing conflicts. Staffing from within is a negotiation process in which upper-level management establishes the ground rules and priorities.

The selected individuals are then notified of the anticipated change and asked their opinions. If individuals have strong resentment to being transferred or reassigned, alternate personnel may be selected because projects cannot operate effectively under discontented managers. Upper-level managers, however, have the authority to direct changes regardless of the desires of the individuals concerned.

Figure 4–8 shows the major concern that project managers have in employee selection. In order to avoid the loss of key people, project managers should seek

FIGURE 4–8. What happens to your project if you lose a key employee?

employees who have the necessary (not superior) skills and use these resources only when needed. Hoarding good talent unnecessarily creates organizational conflict.

Figure 4–9 shows the typical staffing pattern as a function of time. There is a manpower buildup in the early phases and a manpower decline in the later stages. This means that the project manager should bring people on board as *needed* and release them as *early* as possible.

There are several psychological approaches that the project manager can use during the recruitment and staffing process. Consider the following:

- Line managers often receive no visibility or credit for a job well done. Be willing to introduce line managers to the customer.
- Be sure to show people how they can benefit by working for you or on your project.
- Any promises made during recruitment should be documented. The functional organization will remember them long after your project terminates.
- As strange as it may seem, the project manager should encourage conflicts to take place during recruiting and staffing. These conflicts should be brought to the surface and resolved. It is better for conflicts to be resolved during the initial planning stages than to have major confrontations later.

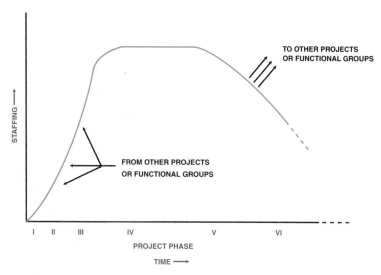

FIGURE 4–9. Staffing pattern versus time.

Most companies have both formal and informal guidelines for the recruiting and assigning of project personnel. Below are examples of such guidelines as defined by Charles Martin:[11]

- Unless some other condition is paramount, project recruiting policies should be as similar as possible to those normally used in the organization for assigning people to new jobs.
- Everyone should be given the same briefing about the project, its benefits, and any special policies related to it. For a sensitive project, this rule can be modified to permit different amounts of information to be given to different managerial levels, but at least everyone in the same general classification should get the same briefing. It should be complete and accurate.
- Any commitments made to members of the team about treatment at the end of the project should be approved in advance by general management. No other commitments should be made.
- Every individual selected for a project should be told why he or she was chosen.
- A similar degree of freedom should be granted all people, or at least all those within a given job category, in the matter of accepting or declining a project assignment.

This last one is a major consideration in the recruiting process: How much discretion is to be given to the employee concerning the proposed assignment? Several degrees of permissiveness appear possible:

- The project is explained and the individual is asked to join and given complete freedom to decline, no questions asked.
- The individual is told he will be assigned to the project. However, he is invited to bring forward any reservations he may have about joining. Any sensible reason he offers will excuse him from the assignment.
- The individual is told he is assigned to the project. Only a significant personal or career preference is accepted as a reason for excusing him from joining the project.
- The individual is assigned to the project as he would be to any other work assignment. Only an emergency can excuse him from serving on the project team.

The recruitment process is not without difficulties. What is unfortunate is that problems of recruiting and retaining good personnel are more difficult in a project organizational structure than in one that is purely traditional. Clayton Reeser identifies nine potential problems related to personnel that can exist in project organizations:[12]

- Personnel connected with project forms of organization suffer more anxieties about possible loss of employment than members of functional organizations.
- Individuals temporarily assigned to matrix organizations are more frustrated by authority ambiguity than permanent members of functional organizations.
- Personnel connected with project forms of organization that are nearing their phase-out are more frustrated by what they perceive to be "make work" assignments than members of functional organizations.
- Personnel connected with project forms of organization feel more frustrated because of lack of formal procedures and role definitions than members of functional organizations.
- Personnel connected with project forms of organization worry more about being set back in their careers than members of functional organizations.
- Personnel connected with project forms of organization feel less loyal to their organization than members of functional organizations.
- Personnel connected with project forms of organization have more anxieties in feeling that there is no one concerned about their personal development than members of functional organizations.
- Permanent members of project forms of organization are more frustrated by multiple levels of management than members of functional organizations.
- Frustrations caused by conflict are perceived more seriously by personnel connected with project forms of organization than members of functional organizations.

Grinnell and Apple have identified four additional major problems associated with staffing:[13]

---

12. Clayton Reeser, "Some Potential Human Problems of the Project Form of Organization," *Academy of Management Journal*, Vol. XII, 1969, pp. 462–466.

13. S. K. Grinnell and H. P. Apple, "When Two Bosses Are Better Than One," *Machine Design*, January 1975, pp. 84–87.

- People trained in single line-of-command organizations find it hard to serve more than one boss.
- People may give lip service to teamwork, but not really know how to develop and maintain a good working team.
- Project and functional managers sometimes tend to compete rather than cooperate with each other.
- Individuals must learn to do more "managing" of themselves.

Thus far we have discussed staffing the project. Unfortunately, there are also situations in which employees must be terminated from the project because of:

- Nonacceptance of rules, policies, and procedures
- Nonacceptance of established formal authority
- Professionalism being more important to them than company loyalty
- Their stressing technical competency at the expense of the budget and schedule
- Incompetency

There are three possible solutions for working with incompetent personnel. First, the project manager can provide an on-the-spot appraisal of the employee. This includes identification of weaknesses, corrective action to be taken, and threat of punishment if the situation continues. The second solution for incompetency is reassignment of the employee to less critical activities. This solution is usually not preferred by project managers. The third solution, and the most frequent one, is the removal of the employee.

Project managers have the right to get people removed from their projects, especially for incompetence. However, although project managers can get project office people (who report to the project manager) removed directly, the removal of a line employee is an indirect process and must be accomplished through the line manager. The removal of the line employee should be made to look like a transfer; otherwise the project manager will be branded as an individual who gets people fired from his projects.

Executives must be ready to cope with the staffing problems that can occur in a project environment. C. Ray Gullett has summarized these major problems:[14]

- Staffing levels are more variable in a project environment.
- Performance evaluation is more complex and more subject to error in a matrix form of organization.
- Wage and salary grades are more difficult to maintain under a matrix form of organization. Job descriptions are often of less value.
- Training and development are more complex and at the same time more necessary under a project form of organization.
- Morale problems are potentially greater in a matrix organization.

---

14. C. Ray Gullett, "Personnel Management in the Project Environment," *Personnel Administration/Public Personnel Review,* November–December 1972, pp. 17–22.

4.9 THE PROJECT OFFICE

The project team is a combination of the project office and functional employees as shown in Figure 4–10. Although the figure identifies the project office personnel as assistant project managers, some employees may not have any such title. The advantage of such a title is that it entitles the employee to speak directly to the customer. For example, the project engineer might also be called the assistant project manager for engineering. The title is important because when the assistant project manager speaks to the customer, he represents the company, whereas the functional employee represents himself.

The project office is an organization developed to support the project manager in carrying out his duties. Project office personnel must have the same dedication toward the project as the project manager and must have good working relationships with both the project and functional managers. The responsibilities of the project office include:

- Acting as the focal point of information for both in-house control and customer reporting
- Controlling time, cost, and performance to adhere to contractual requirements
- Ensuring that all work required is documented and distributed to all key personnel
- Ensuring that all work performed is both authorized and funded by contractual documentation

The major responsibility of the project manager and the project office personnel is the integration of work across the functional lines of the organization. Functional units, such as engineering, R&D, and manufacturing, together with

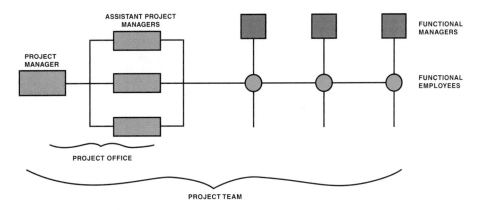

FIGURE 4–10. Project organization.

extra-company subcontractors, must work toward the same specifications, designs, and even objectives. The lack of proper integration of these functional units is the most common cause of project failure. The team members must be dedicated to all activities required for project success, not just their own functional responsibilities. The problems resulting from lack of integration can best be solved by full-time membership and participation of project office personnel. Not all team members are part of the project office. Functional representatives, performing at the interface position, also act as integrators but at a closer position to where the work is finally accomplished (i.e., the line organization).

One of the biggest challenges facing project managers is determining the size of the project office. The optimal size is determined by a trade-off between the maximum number of members necessary to assure compliance with requirements and the maximum number for keeping the total administrative costs under control. Membership is determined by factors such as project size, internal support requirements, type of project (i.e., R&D, qualification, production), level of technical competency required, and customer support requirements. Membership size is also influenced by how strategic management views the project to be. There is a tendency to enlarge project offices if the project is considered strategic, especially if follow-on work is possible.

On large projects, and even on some smaller efforts, it is often impossible to achieve project success without permanently assigned personnel. The four major activities of the project office, shown below, indicate the need for using full-time people:

- Integration of activities
- In-house and out-of-house communication
- Scheduling with risk and uncertainty
- Effective control

These four activities require continuous monitoring by trained project personnel. The training of good project office members may take weeks or even months, and can extend beyond the time allocated for a project. Because key personnel are always in demand, project managers should ask themselves and upper-level management one pivotal question when attempting to staff the project office:

Are these any projects downstreamdgrfdause me to lose key members of my team?

If the answer to this question is yes, then it might benefit the project to have the second- or third-choice person selected for the position or even to staff the position on a part-time basis. Another alternative, of course, would be to assign the key members to activities that are not so important and that can be readily performed by replacement personnel. This, however, is impractical because such personnel will not be employed efficiently.

Program managers would like nothing better than to have all of their key personnel assigned full-time for the duration of the program. Unfortunately, this is undesirable, if not impossible, for many projects because:[15]

- Skills required by the project vary considerably as the project matures through each of its life-cycle phases.
- Building up large permanently assigned project offices for each project inevitably causes duplication of certain skills (often those in short supply), carrying of people who are not needed on a full-time basis or for a long period, and personnel difficulties in reassignment.
- The project manager may be diverted from his primary task and become the project engineer, for example, in addition to his duties of supervision, administration, and dealing with the personnel problems of a large office rather than concentrating on managing all aspects of the project itself.
- Professionally trained people often prefer to work within a group devoted to their professional area, with permanent management having qualifications in the same field, rather than becoming isolated from their specialty peers by being assigned to a project staff.
- Projects are subject to sudden shifts in priority or even to cancellation, and full-time members of a project office are thus exposed to potentially serious threats to their job security; this often causes a reluctance on the part of some people to accept a project assignment.

All of these factors favor keeping the full-time project office as small as possible and dependent on established functional departments and specialized staffs to the greatest extent possible for performance of the various tasks necessary to complete the project. The approach places great emphasis on the planning and control procedures used on the project. On the other hand, there are valid reasons for assigning particular people of various specialties to the project office. These specialties usually include:

- Systems analysis and engineering (or equivalent technical discipline) and product quality and configuration control, if the product requires such an effort
- Project planning, scheduling, control, and administrative support

Many times a project office is staffed by promotion of functional specialists. Unless careful examination of individual qualifications is made, disaster can easily result. This situation is quite common to engineering firms with a high percentage of technical employees.

In professional firms, personnel are generally promoted to management on the basis of their professional or technical competence rather than their managerial

---

15. Russell D. Archibald, *Managing High-Technology Programs and Projects* (New York: Wiley, 1976), p. 82. Copyright © 1976 by John Wiley & Sons, Inc. Reprinted by permission of the publisher.

ability. While this practice may be unavoidable, it does tend to promote men with insufficient knowledge of management techniques and creates a frustrating environment for the professional down the line.[16]

With regard to the training needed by technicians who aspire to high positions in a world of increasing professionalism in management, more than half of the technically trained executives studied . . . wished that they had had "more training in the business skills traditionally associated with the management function." In fact, 75 percent admitted that there were gaps in their nontechnical education. . . . Essentially, the engineer whose stock in trade has always been "hard skills" will need to recognize the value of such "soft skills" as psychology, sociology, and so forth, and to make serious and sustained efforts to apply them to his current job.[17]

There is an unfortunate tendency today for executives to create an environment where line employees feel that the "grass is greener" in project management and project engineering than in the line organization. How should an executive handle a situation where line specialists continually apply for transfer to project management? The solution being incorporated today is the development of a dual ladder system, as shown in Figure 4–11, with a pay scale called "consultant." This particular company created the consultant position because:

- There were several technical specialists who were worth more money to the company but who refused to accept a management position to get it.
- Technical specialists could not be paid more money than line managers.

Promoting technical specialists to a management slot simply to give them more money can:

- Create a poor line manager
- Turn a specialist into a generalist
- Leave a large technical gap in the line organization

Line managers often argue that they cannot perform their managerial duties and control these "prima donnas" who earn more money and have a higher pay grade than the line managers. That is faulty reasoning. Every time the consultants do something well, it reflects on the entire line organization, not merely on themselves.

The concept of having functional employees with a higher pay grade than the line manager can also be applied to the horizontal project. It is possible for a junior project manager suddenly to find that the line managers have a higher pay

16. William P. Killian, "Project Management—Future Organizational Concept," *Marquette Business Review,* 1971, pp. 90–107.

17. Richard A. Koplow, "From Engineer to Manager—And Back Again," *IEEE Transactions on Engineering Management,* Vol. EM-14, No. 2, June 1967, pp. 88–92. © 1967 IEEE.

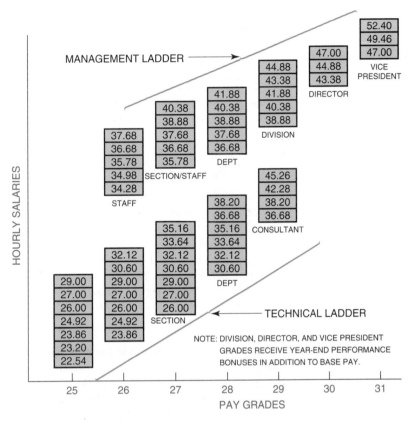

FIGURE 4–11. Exempt, upper-level pay structure.

grade than the project manager. It is also possible for assistant project managers (as project engineers) to have a higher pay grade than the project manager. Project management is designed to put together the best mix of people to achieve the objective. If this best mix requires that a grade 7 report to a grade 9 (on a "temporary" project), then so be it. Executives should not let salaries, and pay grades, stand in the way of constructing a good project organization.

Another major concern is the relationship that exists between project office personnel and functional managers. In many organizations, membership in the project office is considered to be more important than in the functional department. Functional members have a tendency to resent an individual who has just been promoted out of a functional department and into project management. Killian has described ways of resolving potential conflicts:[18]

---

18. William P. Killian, "Project Management—Future Organizational Concept," *Marquette Business Review,* 1971, pp. 90–107.

It must be kept in mind that veteran functional managers cannot be expected to accept direction readily from some lesser executive who is suddenly labelled a Project Manager. Management can avoid this problem by:

- Selecting a man who already has a high position of responsibility or placing him high enough in the organization.
- Assigning him a title as important-sounding as those of functional managers.
- Supporting him in his dealings with functional managers.

If the Project Manager is expected to exercise project control over the functional departments, then he must report to the same level as the departments, or higher.

Executives can severely hinder project managers by limiting their authority to select and organize (when necessary) a project office and team. According to Cleland:[19]

> His [project manager's] staff should be qualified to provide personal administrative and technical support. He should have sufficient authority to increase or decrease his staff as necessary throughout the life of the project. The authorization should include selective augmentation for varying periods of time from the supporting functional areas.

Sometimes, a situation occurs in the project office in which the assistant project manager does not fully understand the intentions of the project manager. For example, an assistant project manager became convinced that the project manager was making decisions that were not in the best interest of the project. Unfortunately, what is in the best interest of the company may not be in the best interest of the project. The cause of this problem was a communication breakdown in the project office.

Many executives have a misconception concerning the makeup and usefulness of the project office. People who work in the project office should be individuals whose first concern is project management, not the enhancement of their technical expertise. It is almost impossible for individuals to perform for any extended period of time in the project office without becoming cross-trained in a second or third project office function. For example, the project manager for cost could acquire enough expertise eventually to act as the assistant to the assistant project manager for procurement. This technique of project office cross-training is an excellent mechanism for creating good project managers.

People who are placed in the project office should be individuals who are interested in making a career out of project management. These dedicated individuals must realize that there may not be bigger and better projects for them to manage downstream, and they may have to take a step backward and manage a smaller project or simply be assistant project managers. It is not uncommon for

---

19. David I. Cleland, "Why Project Management?" Reprinted with permission from *Business Horizons*, Winter 1964 (p. 85). Copyright © 1964 by the Board of Trustees at Indiana University.

an individual to rotate back and forth between project management and assistant project management.

We have mentioned two important facts concerning the project management staffing process:

- The individual who aspires to become a project manager must be willing to give up technical expertise and become a generalist.
- Individuals can be qualified to be promoted vertically but not horizontally.

Let us elaborate on these two points. Once an employee has demonstrated the necessary attributes to be a good project manager, there are three ways the individual can become a project manager or part of the project office. The executive can:

- Promote the individual in salary and grade and transfer him into project management.
- Laterally transfer the individual into project management without any salary or grade increase. If, after three to six months, the employee demonstrates that he can perform, he will receive an appropriate salary and grade increase.
- Give the employee a small salary increase without any grade increase or a grade increase without any salary increase, with the stipulation that additional awards will be forthcoming after the observation period, assuming that the employee can handle the position.

Many executives believe in the philosophy that once an individual enters the world of project management, there are only two places to go: up in the organization or out the door. If an individual is given a promotion and pay increase and is placed in project management and fails, his salary may not be compatible with that of his previous line organization, and now there is no place for him to go. Most executives, and employees, prefer the second method because it actually provides some protection for the employee. Of course, the employee might not want to return having been branded a failure in project management.

Many companies don't realize until it is too late that promotions to project management may be based on a different set of criteria from promotions to line management. Promotions on the horizontal line are strongly based on communicative skills, whereas line management promotions are based on technical skills. An employee was interviewed for promotion to a project management position. The following two questions were asked by the executive:

- Can you write, and I really mean it, can you write?
- Are you willing to give up your car pool?

Almost every corporation has line managers who are extremely poor communicators but were promoted to their positions to reward them for technical excellence.

4.10 THE FUNCTIONAL TEAM

The project team consists of the project manager, the project office (whose members may or may not report directly to the project manager), and the functional or interface members (who must report horizontally as well as vertically for information flow). Functional team members are often shown on organizational charts as project office team members. This is normally done to satisfy customer requirements.

Upper-level management can have an input into the selection process for functional team members just as with project office membership. However, executives should not take an active role unless the project and functional managers cannot come to an agreement. If executives continually step in and tell line managers how to staff a project, then the line managers will feel that the executives are usurping the line managers' authority, and, of course, the project will suffer. Functional management must be represented at all staffing meetings. Functional staffing is directly dependent on project requirements and, therefore, must include functional management because:

- Functional managers generally have more expertise and can identify high-risk areas.
- Functional managers must develop a positive attitude toward project success. This is best achieved by inviting their participation in the early activities of the planning phase.

Functional team members are not always full-time. They can be full-time or part-time for either the duration of the project or only specific phases.

The selection process for both the functional team member and the project office must include evaluation of any special requirements. The most common special requirements develop from:

- Changes in technical specifications
- Special customer requests
- Organizational restructuring because of deviations from existing policies
- Compatibility with the customer's project office

Each of these factors has a direct impact on whether an individual should be assigned to the project office or the functional interface.

A typical project office may include between ten and thirty members, whereas the total project team may be in excess of a hundred people. Large staffs inherently create additional work and increase communication channel noise to such a degree that information reporting may become a slow process. Large staffs also create difficult problems with regard to customer relations.

For large projects, it is desirable to have a full-time functional representative from each major division or department assigned permanently to the project, and perhaps even to the project office. Such representation might include:

- Program management
- Project engineering
- Engineering operations
- Manufacturing operations
- Procurement
- Quality control
- Cost accounting
- Publications
- Marketing
- Sales

Both the project manager and team members must understand fully the responsibilities and functions of each other team member so that total integration can be achieved as rapidly and effectively as possible. On high-technology programs the chief project engineer assumes the role of deputy project manager. Project managers must understand the problems that the line managers have when selecting and assigning the project staff. Line managers try to staff with people who understand the need for teamwork. Unfortunately, these people may simply be the average or below-average employees because the senior people may consider themselves to be gods and may not have any respect for other disciplines. As an example, a department manager hired a fifty-four-year-old engineer who had two master's degrees in engineering disciplines. For the past thirty years, the new employee was a true loner, never having worked in a project management organization. How should the department manager handle this situation?

First, the department manager gave the individual an overload of work so that he would ask for help. Instead, the individual worked overtime and did a good job. Next, the manager put the individual in charge of a line project and assigned two people to report to him. These two people were idle most of the time because the individual was still doing all the work himself (and quite well). The department manager did not want to lose this employee. Today, the employee is assigned only those tasks that he can do himself.

When employees are attached to a project, the project manager must identify the "star" employees. These are the employees who are vital for the success of the project and who can either make or break the project manager. Most of the time, star employees are found in the line organization, not the project office.

As a final point, we should discuss the responsibilities that the project manager can assign to an employee. Project managers can assign line employees added responsibilities within the scope of the project. If the added responsibilities can result in upgrading, then the project manager should consult with the line manager before such situations are initiated. Quite often, line managers (or even personnel representatives) send "check" people into the projects to verify that employees are performing at their proper pay grade. This is very important when working with blue-collar workers who, by union contractual agreements, must be paid at the grade level at which they are performing.

Also, project managers must be willing to surrender resources when they are no longer required. If the project manager constantly cries wolf in a situation where a problem really does not exist or is not as severe as the project manager makes it out to be, the line manager will simply pull away the resources (this is the line manager's right), and a deteriorating working relationship will result.

4.11 THE PROJECT ORGANIZATIONAL CHART

One of the first requirements of the project startup phase is to develop the organizational chart for the project and determine its relationship to the parent organizational structure. Figure 4–12 shows, in abbreviated form, the six major programs at Dalton Corporation. Our concern is with the Midas Program. Although the Midas Program may have the lowest priority of the six programs, it is placed at the top, and in boldface, to give the impression that it is the top priority. This type of representation usually makes the client or customer feel that his program is important to the contractor.

The employees shown in Figure 4–12 may be part-time or full-time, depending upon the project's requirements. Perturbations on Figure 4–12 might include one employee's name identified on two or more vertical positions (i.e., the project engineer on two projects) or the same name in two horizontal boxes (i.e., for a small project, the same person could be the project manager and project engineer). Remember, this type of chart is for the customer's benefit and may not show the true "dotted/solid" reporting relationships in the company.

The next step is to show the program office structure, as illustrated in Figure 4–13. Note that the chief of operations and the chief engineer have dual reporting responsibility; they report directly to the program manager and indirectly to the directors. Again, this may be just for the customer's benefit with the real reporting structure being reversed. Beneath the chief engineer, there are three positions. Although these positions appear as solid lines, they might actually be dotted lines. For example, Ed White might be working only part-time on the Midas Program but is still shown on the chart as a permanent program office member. Jean Flood, under contracts, might be spending only ten hours per week on the Midas Program.

If the function of two positions on the organizational chart takes place at different times, then both positions may be shown as manned by the same person. For example, Ed White may have his name under both engineering design and engineering testing if the two activities are far enough apart that he can perform them independently.

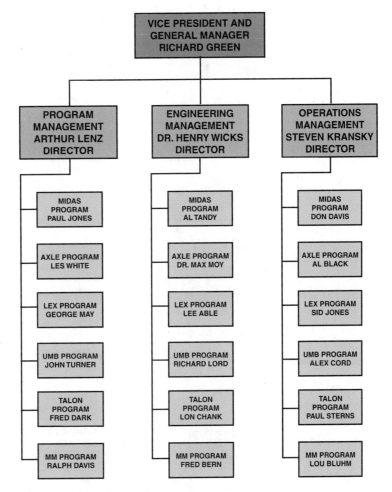

FIGURE 4–12. Dalton Corporation.

The people shown in the project office organizational chart, whether full-time or part-time, may not be physically sitting in the project office. For full-time, long-term assignments, as in construction projects, the employees may be physically sitting side by side (see Figure 4–14), whereas for part-time assignments, it may be imperative for them to sit in their functional group. Remember, these types of charts may simply be eyewash for the customer.

Most customers realize that the top-quality personnel may be shared with other programs and projects. Project manning charts, such as the one shown in Figure 4–15, can be used for this purpose. These manning charts are also helpful in preparing the management volume of proposals to show the customer that key personnel will be readily available on his project.

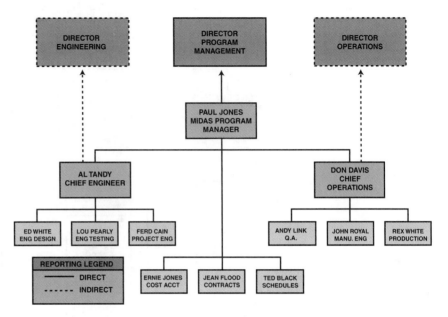

FIGURE 4–13. Midas Program office.

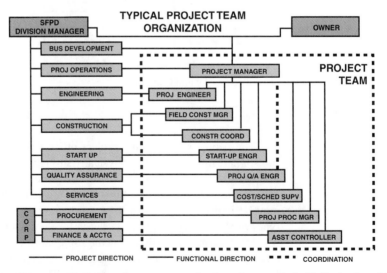

FIGURE 4–14. Typical project team organization. *Source:* F. A. Hollenbach and D. P. Schultz, "The Organization and Controls of Project Management," *Proceedings of the Ninth Annual Seminar/Symposium on Project Management,* 1977.

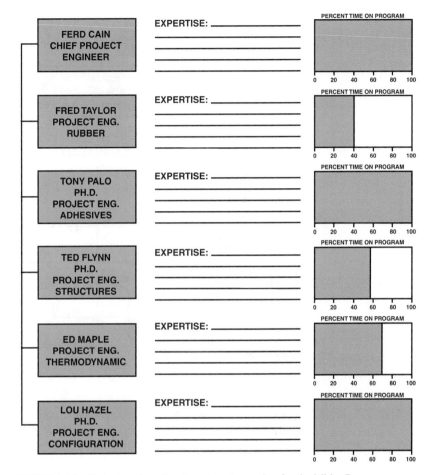

FIGURE 4–15. Project engineering department manning for the Midas Program.

4.12 SPECIAL PROBLEMS

There are always special problems that influence the organizational staffing process. For example, the department shown in Figure 4–16 has a departmental matrix. All activities stay within the department. Project X and project Y are managed by line employees who have been temporarily assigned to the projects, whereas project Z is headed by supervisor B. The department's activities involve high-technology engineering as well as R&D.

The biggest problem facing the department managers is that of training their new employees. The training process requires nine to twelve months. The employees become familiar with the functioning of all three sections, and only after training is an employee assigned to one of the sections. Line managers claim that

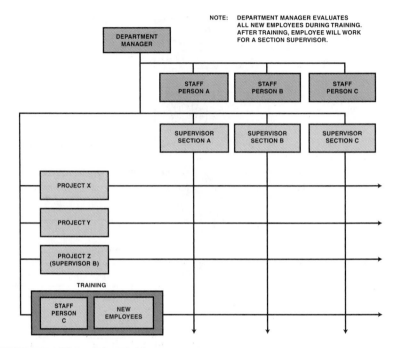

FIGURE 4–16. The training problem.

they do not have sufficient time to supervise training. As a result, the department manager in the example found staff person C to be the most competent person to supervise training. A special department training project was set up, as shown in Figure 4–16.

At the end of six months, all new employees were up for their first performance evaluation. The staff person signed the evaluation forms. Within forty-eight hours, the personnel department began screaming that only managers could sign evaluation forms, and since the staff person was not a manager, personnel could not accept the evaluations. There were now four options available to the department manager:

- Request that the personnel department be disbanded.
- Request personnel to change their procedures.
- Speed up training and, before six months were up, assign the employees to one of the sections.
- Continue as before, but with the department manager to sign the evaluation forms after staff person C filled them out.

The first two choices were found to be impossible, and the third was impractical. The company is now using the fourth approach.

Figure 4–17 shows a utility company that has three full-time project managers controlling three projects, all of which cut across the central division.

Unfortunately, the three full-time project managers cannot get sufficient resources from the central division because the line managers are also acting as divisional project managers and saving the best resources for their own projects, regardless of the priority.

The obvious solution to the problem is that the central division line managers not be permitted to wear two hats. Instead, one full-time project manager can be added to the left division to manage all three central division projects. It is usually best for all project managers to report to the same division for priority setting and conflict resolution.

Line managers have a tendency to feel demoted when they are suddenly told that they can no longer wear two hats. For example, Mr. Adams is a department manager with thirty years of experience in a company. For the last several years, he has worn two hats and acted as both project manager and functional manager on a variety of projects. He is regarded as an expert in his field. The company decided to incorporate formal project management and established a project man-

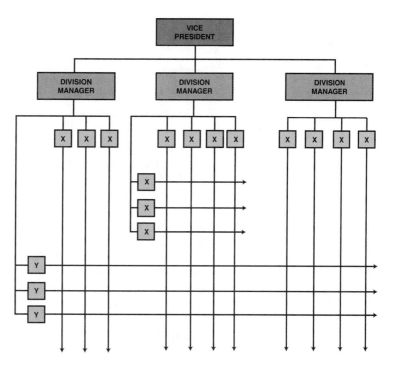

NOTE: X INDICATES FULL–TIME FUNCTIONAL MANAGERS
         Y INDICATES FULL–TIME PROJECT MANAGERS

FIGURE 4–17. Utility service organization.

agement department. Mr. Bell, a thirty-year-old employee with three years of experience with the company, was assigned as the project manager. In order to staff his project, Bell asked Adams for Mr. Cane (Bell's friend) to be assigned to the project as the functional representative. Cane has been with the company for two years. Adams agreed to the request and informed Cane of his new assignment, closing with the remarks, "This project is yours all the way. I don't want to have anything to do with it. I'll be busy with paperwork as a result of the new organizational structure. Just send me a memo once in a while telling me what's happening."

During the project kickoff meeting, it became obvious to everyone that the only person with the necessary expertise was Adams. Without his support, the time duration of the project could be expected to double.

The real problem here was that Adams wanted to feel important and needed, and was hoping that the project manager would come to him asking for his assistance. The project manager correctly analyzed the situation but refused to ask for the line manager's help. Instead, the project manager asked an executive to step in and force the line manager to help. The line manager gave his help, but with great reluctance. Today, the line manager provides poor support to the projects that come across his line organization.

4.13 SELECTING THE PROJECT MANAGEMENT IMPLEMENTAITON TEAM

The implementation of project management within an organization requires strong executive support and an implementation team that is dedicated to making project management work. Selecting the wrong team players can either lengthen the implementation process or reduce employee morale to a point where the organization will no longer support project management. Some employees may play destructive roles on a project team. These roles, which undermine project management implementation, are shown in Figure 4–18 and described below:

- The aggressor
  - Criticizes everybody and everything on project management
  - Deflates the status and ego of other team members
  - Always acts aggressively
- The dominator
  - Always tries to take over
  - Professes to know everything about project management
  - Tries to manipulate people
  - Will challenge those in charge for leadership role
- The devil's advocate
  - Finds fault in all areas of project management
  - Refuses to support project management unless threatened

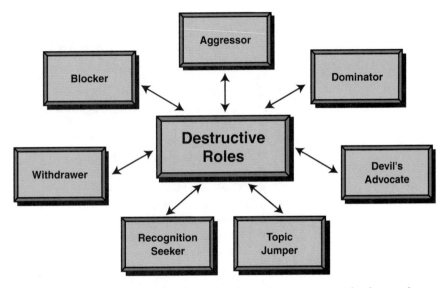

FIGURE 4–18. Roles people play that undermine project management implementation.

- Acts more of a devil than an advocate
- The topic jumper
  - Must be the first one with a new idea/approach to project management
  - Constantly changes topics
  - Cannot focus on ideas for a long time unless it is their idea
  - Tries to keep project management implementation as an action item forever
- The recognition seeker
  - Always argues in favor of his/her own ideas
  - Always demonstrates status consciousness
  - Volunteers to become the project manager if status is recognized
  - Likes to hear himself/herself talk
  - Likes to boast rather than provide meaningful information
- The withdrawer
  - Is afraid to be criticized
  - Will not participate openly unless threatened
  - May withhold information
  - May be shy
- The blocker
  - Likes to criticize
  - Rejects the views of others
  - Cites unrelated examples and personal experiences
  - Has multiple reasons why project management will not work

These types of people should not be assigned to project management implementation teams. The types of people who should be assigned to implementation teams are shown in Figure 4-19 and described below. Their roles are indicated by their words:

- The initiators
  - "Is there a chance that this might work?"
  - "Let's try this."
- The information seekers
  - "Have we tried anything like this before?"
  - "Do we know other companies where this has worked?"
  - "Can we get this information?"
- The information givers
  - "Other companies found that . . ."
  - "The literature says that . . ."
  - "Benchmarking studies indicate that . . ."
- The encouragers
  - "Your idea has a lot of merit."
  - "The idea is workable, but we may have to make small changes."
  - "What you said will really help us."
- The clarifiers
  - "Are we saying that . . . ?"
  - "Let me state in my own words what I'm hearing from the team."
  - "Let's see if we can put this into perspective."
- The harmonizers

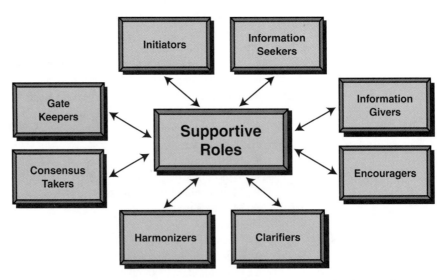

FIGURE 4–19. Roles people play that support project management implementation.

- "We sort of agree, don't we?"
- "Your ideas and mine are close together."
- "Aren't we saying the same thing?"
- The consensus takers
  - "Let's see if the team is in agreement."
  - "Let's take a vote on this."
  - "Let's see how the rest of the group feels about this."
- The gate keepers
  - "Who has not given us their opinions on this yet?"
  - "Should we keep our options open?"
  - "Are we prepared to make a decision or recommendation, or is there additional information to be reviewed?"

PROBLEMS

4–1 From S. K. Grinnell and H. P. Apple ("When Two Bosses Are Better Than One," *Machine Design,* January 1975, pp. 84–87):

- People trained in single-line-of-command organizations find it hard to serve more than one boss.
- People may give lip service to teamwork, but not really know how to develop and maintain a good working team.
- Project and functional managers sometimes tend to compete rather than cooperate with each other.
- Individuals must learn to do more "managing" of themselves.

The authors identify the above four major problems associated with staffing. Discuss each problem and identify the type of individual most likely to be involved (i.e., engineer, contract administrator, cost accountant, etc.) and in which organizational form this problem would be most apt to occur.

4–2 David Cleland ("Why Project Management?" Reprinted from *Business Horizons,* Winter 1964, p. 85. Copyright ficr 1964 by the Foundation for the School of Business at Indiana University. Used with permission) made the following remarks:

> His [project manager's] staff should be qualified to provide personal administrative and technical support. He should have sufficient authority to increase or decrease his staff as necessary throughout the life of the project. This authorization should include selective augmentation for varying periods of time from the supporting functional areas.

Do you agree or disagree with these statements? Should the type of project or type of organization play a dominant role in your answer?

4–3 The contractor's project office is often structured to be compatible with the customer's project office, sometimes on a one-to-one basis. Some customers view the contractor's project organization merely as an extension of their own company. Below are three statements concerning this relationship. Are these statements true or false? Defend your answers.

- There must exist mutual trust between the customer and contractor together with a close day-to-day working relationship.
- The project manager and the customer must agree on the hierarchy of decision that each must make, either independently or jointly. (Which decisions can each make independently or jointly?)
- Both the customer and contractor's project personnel must be willing to make decisions as fast as possible.

4–4   C. Ray Gullet ("Personnel Management in the Project Organization," *Personnel Administration/Public Personnel Review,* November–December 1972, pp. 17–22) has identified five personnel problems. How would you, as a project manager, cope with each problem?

- Staffing levels are more variable in a project environment.
- Performance evaluation is more complex and more subject to error in a matrix form of organization.
- Wage and salary grades are more difficult to maintain under a matrix form of organization. Job descriptions are often of less value.
- Training and development are more complex and at the same time more necessary under a project form of organization.
- Morale problems are potentially greater in a matrix organization.

4–5   Ramesh P. Shah ("Project Management: Cross Your Bridges Before You Come to Them," *Management Review,* December 1971, pp. 21–27) states, "Like a physician, a project manager must be an expert diagnostician; he must guard his project from infection, detect symptoms, diagnose causes and prescribe cures for a multitude of afflictions." What is intended by the words "infection, symptoms, diagnose causes, and affliction?"

4–6   Paul is a project manager for an effort that requires twelve months. During the seventh, eighth, and ninth months he needs two individuals with special qualifications. The functional manager has promised that these individuals will be available two months before they are needed. If Paul does not assign them to his project at that time, they will be assigned elsewhere and he will have to do with whomever will be available later. What should Paul do? Do you have to make any assumptions in order to defend your answer?

4–7   Some of the strongest reasons for promoting functional engineers to project engineers are:

- Better relationships with fellow researchers
- Better prevention of duplication of effort
- Better fostering of teamwork

These reasons are usually applied to R&D situations. Could they also be applied to product life-cycle phases other than R&D?

4–8   The following have been given as qualifications for a successful advanced-technology project manager:

- Career has progressed up through the technical ranks
- Knowledgeable in many engineering fields
- Understands general management philosophy and the meaning of profitability
- Interested in training and teaching his superiors
- Understands how to work with perfectionists

Can these same qualifications be modified for non-R&D project management? If so, how?

4–9 W. J. Taylor and T. F. Watling (*Successful Project Management,* London: Business Books, 1972, p. 32) state:

> It is often the case, therefore, that the Project Manager is more noted for his management technique expertise, his ability to "get things done" and his ability to "get on with people" than for his sheer technical prowess. However, it can be dangerous to minimize this latter talent when choosing Project Managers dependent upon project type and size. The Project Manager should preferably be an expert either in the field of the project task or a subject allied to it.

How dangerous can it be if this latter talent is minimized? Will it be dangerous under all circumstances?

4–10 Frank Boone is the most knowledgeable piping engineer in the company. For five years, the company has turned down his application for transfer to project engineering and project management stating that he is too valuable to the company in his current position. If you were a project manager, would you want this individual as part of your functional team? How should an organization cope with this situation?

4–11 Tom Weeks is manager of the insulation group. During a recent group meeting, Tom commented, "The company is in trouble. As you know, we're bidding on three programs right now. If we win just one of them, we can probably maintain our current work level. If, by some slim chance, we were to win all three, you'll all be managers tomorrow." The company won all three programs, but the insulation group did not hire anyone, and there were no promotions. What would you, as a project manager on one of the new projects, expect your working relations to be with the insulation group?

4–12 You are a project engineer on a high-technology program. As the project begins to wind down, your boss asks you to write a paper so that he can present it at a technical meeting. His name goes first on the paper. Should this be part of your job? How do you feel about this situation?

4–13 Research has indicated that the matrix structure is often confusing because it requires multiple roles for people, with resulting confusion about these roles (Keith Davis, *Human Relations at Work,* New York: McGraw-Hill, 1967, pp. 296–297). Unfortunately, not all program managers, project managers, and project engineers possess the necessary skills to operate in this environment. Stuckenbruck has stated, "The path to success is strewn with the bodies of project managers who were originally functional line managers and then went into project management" (Linn Stuckenbruck, "The Effective Project Manager," *Project Management Quarterly,* Vol. VII, No. 1, March 1976, pp. 26–27. What do you feel is the major cause for this downfall of the functional manager?

4–14 For each of the organizational forms shown below, who determines what resources are needed, when they are needed and how they will be employed? Who has the authority and responsibility to mobilize these resources?

    a. Traditional organization

    b. Matrix organization

    c. Product line organization
    d. Line/staff project organization

4–15 Do you agree or disagree that project organizational forms encourage peer-to-peer communications and dynamic problem-solving?

4–16 The XYZ Company operates on a traditional structure. The company has just received a contract to develop a new product line for a special group of customers. The company has decided to pull out selected personnel from the functional departments and set up a single product organizational structure to operate in parallel with the functional departments.

    a. Set up the organizational chart.
    b. Do you think this setup can work? Does your answer depend on how many years this situation must exist?

4–17 You are the project engineer on a program similar to one that you directed previously. Should you attempt to obtain the same administrative and/or technical staff that you had before?

4–18 A person assigned to your project is performing unsatisfactorily. What should you do? Will it make a difference if he is in the project office or a functional employee?

4–19 You have been assigned to the project office as an assistant project engineer. You are to report to the chief project engineer who reports formally to the project manager and informally to the vice president of engineering. You have never worked with this chief project engineer before. During the execution of the project, it becomes obvious to you that the chief project engineer is making decisions that do not appear to be in the best interest of the project. What should you do about this?

4–20 Should individuals be promoted to project management because they are at the top of their functional pay grade?

4–21 Should one functional department be permitted to "borrow" (on a temporary basis) people from another functional department in order to fulfill project manning requirements? Should this be permitted if overtime is involved?

4–22 Should a project manager be paid for performance or for the number of people he supervises?

4–23 Should a project manager try to upgrade his personnel?

4–24 Why should a functional manager assign his best people to you on a long-term project?

4–25 A coal company has adopted the philosophy that the project manager for new mine startup projects will be the individual who will eventually become the mine superintendent. The coal company believes that this type of "ownership" philosophy is good. Do you agree?

4–26 Can a project manager be considered as a "hired gun?£

4–27 Manufacturing organizations are using project management/project engineering strictly to give new employees exposure to total company operations. After working on one or two projects, each approximately one to two years in duration, the employee is transferred to line management for his career path and opportunities for advancement. Can a situation such as this, where there is no career path in either project management or project engineering, work successfully? Could there be any detrimental effects on the projects?

4-28 Can a project manager create dedication and a true winning spirit and still be hated by all?

4-29 Can anyone be trained to be a project manager?

4-30 A power and light company has part-time project management in which an individual acts as both a project manager and a functional employee at the same time. The utility company claims that this process prevents an employee from becoming "technically obsolete," and that when the employee returns to full-time functional duties, he is a more well-rounded individual. Do you agree or disagree? What are the arrangement's advantages and disadvantages?

4-31 Some industries consider the major criterion for promotion and advancement to be gray hair and/or baldness. Is this type of maturity advantageous?

4-32 In Figure 4–13 we showed that Al Tandy and Don Davis (as well as other project office personnel) reported directly to the project manager and indirectly to functional management. Could this situation be reversed, with the project office personnel reporting indirectly to the project manager and directly to functional management?

4-33 Most organizations have "star" people who are usually identified as those individuals who are the key to success. How does a project manager identify these people? Can they be in the project office, or must they be functional employees or managers?

4-34 Considering your own industry, what job-related or employee-related factors would you wish to know before selecting someone to be a project manager or a project engineer on an effort valued at:

    a. $30,000?
    b. $300,000?
    c. $3,000,000?
    d. $30,000,000?

4-35 One of the major controversies in project management occurs over whether the project manager needs a command of technology in order to be effective. Consider the following situation:

    You are the project manager on a research and development project. Marketing informs you that they have found a customer for your product and that you must make major modifications to satisfy the customer's requirements. The engineering functional managers tell you that these modifications are impossible. Can a project manager without a command of technology make a viable decision as to whether to risk additional funds and support marketing, or should he believe the functional managers, and tell marketing that the modifications are impossible? How can a project manager, either with or without a command of technology, tell whether the functional managers are giving him an optimistic or a pessimistic opinion?

4-36 As a functional employee, you demonstrate that you have exceptionally good writing skills. You are then promoted to the position of special staff assistant to the division manager and told that you are to assume full responsibility for all proposal work that must flow through your division. How do you feel about this? Is it a promotion? Where can you go from here?

4-37 Government policymakers content that only high-ranking individuals (high GS grades) can be project managers because a good project manager needs sufficient "clout" to make the project go. In government, the project manager is generally the highest grade on the project team. How can problems of pay grade be overcome? Is the government's policy effective?

4-38 A major utility company is worried about the project manager's upgrading functional employees. On an eight-month project that employs four hundred full-time project employees, the department managers have set up "check" people whose responsibility is to see that functional employees do not have unauthorized (i.e., not approved by the functional manager) work assignments above their current grade level. Can this system work? What if the work is at a position below their grade level?

4-39 A major utility company begins each computer project with a feasibility study in which a cost-benefit analysis is performed. The project managers, all of whom report to a project management division, perform the feasibility study themselves without any functional support. The functional personnel argue that the feasibility study is inaccurate because the functional "experts" are not involved. The project managers, on the other hand, stipulate that they never have sufficient time or money to involve the functional personnel. Can this situation be resolved?

4-40 How would you go about training individuals within your company or industry to be good project managers? What assumptions are you making?

4-41 Should project teams be allowed to evolve by themselves?

4-42 At what point or phase in the life cycle of a project should a project manager be appointed?

4-43 Top management generally has two schools of thought concerning project management. One school states that the project manager should be used a means for coordinating activities that cut across several functional departments. The second school states that the project management position should be used as a means of creating future general managers. Which school of thought is correct?

4-44 Some executives feel that personnel working in a project office should be cross-trained in several assistant project management functions. What do you think about this?

4-45 A company has a policy that employees wishing to be project managers must first spend one to one-and-a-half years in the functional employee side of the house so that they can get to know the employees and company policy. What do you think about this?

4-46 Your project has grown to a point where there now exist openings for three full-time assistant project managers. Unfortunately, there are no experienced assistant project managers available. You are told by upper-level management that you will fill these three positions by promotions from within. Where in the organization should you look? During an interview, what questions should you ask potential candidates? Is it possible that you could find candidates who are qualified to be promoted vertically but not horizontally?

4–47 A functional employee has demonstrated the necessary attributes of a potentially successful project manager. Top management can:

- Promote the individual in salary and grade and transfer him into project management.
- Laterally transfer the employee into project management without any salary or grade increase. If, after three to six months, the employee demonstrates that he can perform, he will receive an appropriate salary and grade increase.
- Give the employee either a grade increase without any salary increase, or a small salary increase without any grade increase, under the stipulation that additional awards will be given at the end of the observation period, assuming that the employee can handle the position.

If you were in top management, which method would you prefer? If you dislike the above three choices, develop your own alternative. What are the advantages and disadvantages of each choice? For each choice, discuss the ramifications if the employee cannot handle the project management position.

CASE STUDIES

GOVERNMENT PROJECT MANAGEMENT

A major government agency is organized to monitor government subcontractors as shown in Exhibit 4–1. Below are the vital characteristics of certain project office team members:

- *Project manager:* Directs all project activities and acts as the information focal point for the subcontractor.
- *Assistant project manager:* Acts as chairman of the steering committee and interfaces with both in-house functional groups and contractor.
- *Department managers:* Act as members of the steering committee for any projects that utilize their resources. These slots on the steering committee must be filled by the department managers themselves, not by functional employees.
- *Contracts officer:* Authorizes all work directed by the project office to in-house functional groups and to the customer, and ensures that all work requested is authorized by the contract. The contracts officer acts as the focal point for all contractor cost and contractual information.

1. Explain how this structure *should* work.
2. Explain how this structure *actually* works.
3. Can the project manager be a military type who is reassigned after a given tour of duty?
4. What are the advantages and disadvantages of this structure?
5. Could this be used in industry?

Exhibit 4–1. Project Team Organizational Structure

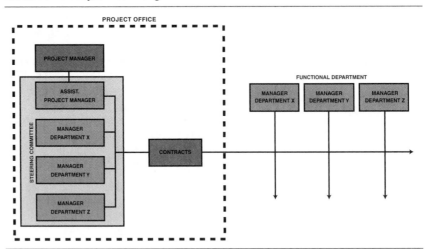

FALLS ENGINEERING

Located in New York, Falls Engineering is a $250-million chemical and materials operation employing 900 people. The plant has two distinct manufacturing product lines: industrial chemicals and computer materials. Both divisions are controlled by one plant manager, but direction, strategic planning, and priorities are established by corporate vice presidents in Chicago. Each division has its own corporate vice president, list of projects, list of priorities, and manpower control. The chemical division has been at this location for the past twenty years. The materials division is, you might say, the tenant in the landlord–tenant relationship, with the materials division manager reporting dotted to the plant manager and solid to the corporate vice president (see Exhibit 4–2).

The chemical division employed 3,000 people in 1968. By 1983, there were only 600 employees. In 1984, the materials division was formed and located on the chemical division site with a landlord–tenant relationship. The materials division has grown from $50 million in 1985 to $120 million in 1989. Today, the materials division employs 350 people.

All projects originate in construction or engineering but usually are designed to support production. The engineering and construction departments have projects that span the entire organization directed by a project coordinator. The project coordinator is a line employee who is temporarily assigned to coordinate a project in his line organization in addition to performing his line responsibilities. Assignments are made by the division managers (who report to the plant manager) and are based on technical expertise. The coordinators have monitoring authority only and are not noted for being good planners or negotiators. The coordinators report to their respective line managers.

Basically, a project can start in either division with the project coordinators. The coordinators draw up a large scope of work and submit it to the project engineering group, who arrange for design contractors, depending on the size of the project.

Exhibit 4–2. Falls Engineering Organizational Chart

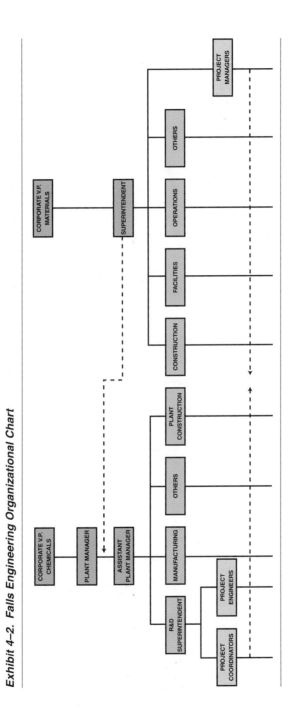

Project engineering places it on their design schedule according to priority and produces prints and specifications, and receives quotes. A construction cost estimate is then produced following 60–75 percent design completion. The estimate and project papers are prepared, and the project is circulated through the plant and in Chicago for approval and authorization. Following authorization, the design is completed, and materials are ordered. Following design, the project is transferred to either of two plant construction groups for construction. The project coordinators than arrange for the work to be accomplished in their areas with minimum interference from manufacturing forces. In all cases, the coordinators act as project managers and must take the usual constraints of time, money, and performance into account.

Falls Engineering has 300 projects listed for completion between 1993 and 1995. In the last two years, less than 10 percent of the projects were completed within time, cost, and performance constraints. Line managers find it increasingly difficult to make resource commitments because crises always seem to develop, including a number of fires.

Profits are made in manufacturing, and everyone knows it. Whenever a manufacturing crisis occurs, line managers pull resources off the projects, and, of course, the projects suffer. Project coordinators are trying, but with very little success, to put some slack onto the schedules to allow for contingencies.

The breakdown of the 300 plant projects is shown below:

Number of Projects	$ Range
120	less than $50,000
80	50,000–200,000
70	250,000–750,000
20	1–3 million
10	4–8 million

Corporate realized the necessity for changing the organizational structure. A meeting was set up between the plant manager, plant executives, and corporate executives to resolve these problems once and for all. The plant manager decided to survey his employees concerning their feelings about the present organizational structure. Below are their comments:

- "The projects we have the most trouble with are the small ones under $200,000. Can we use informal project management for the small ones and formal project management on the large ones?"
- Why do we persist in using computer programming to control our resources? These sophisticated packages are useless because they do not account for firefighting."
- "Project coordinators need access to various levels of management, in both divisions."
- "Our line managers do not realize the necessity for effective planning of resources. Resources are assigned based on emotions and not need."
- "Sometimes a line manager gives a commitment but the project coordinator cannot force him to keep it."
- "Line managers always find fault with project coordinators who try to develop detailed schedules themselves."
- "If we continuously have to 'crash' project time, doesn't that indicate poor planning?"

- "We need a career path in project coordination so that we can develop a body of good planners, communicators, and integrators."
- "I've seen project coordinators we have no interest in the job, cannot work with diverse functional disciplines, and cannot communicate. Yet, someone assigned them as a project coordinator."
- "Any organizational system we come up with has to be better than the one we have now."
- "Somebody has to have total accountability. Our people are working on projects and, at the same time, do not know the project status, the current cost, the risks, and the end date."
- "One of these days I'm going to kill an executive while he's meddling in my project."
- "Recently, management made changes requiring more paperwork for the project coordinators. How many hours a week do they expect me to work?"
- "I've yet to see any documentation describing the job description of the project coordinator."
- "I have absolutely no knowledge about who is assigned as the project coordinator until work has to be coordinated in my group. Somehow, I'm not sure that this is the way the system should work."
- "I know that we line managers are supposed to be flexible, but changing the priorities every week isn't exactly my idea of fun."
- "If the projects start out with poor planning, then management does not have the right to expect the line managers always to come to the rescue."
- "Why is it the line managers always get blamed for schedule delays, even if it's the result of poor planning up front?"
- "If management doesn't want to hire additional resources, then why should the line managers be made to suffer? Perhaps we should cut out some of these useless projects. Sometimes I think management dreams up some of these projects simply to spend the allocated funds."
- "I have yet to see a project I felt had a realistic deadline."

After preparing alternatives and recommendations as plant manager, try to do some role playing by putting yourself in the shoes of the corporate executives. Would you, as a corporate executive, approve the recommendation? Where does profitability, sales, return on investment, and so on enter in your decision?

WHITE MANUFACTURING

In 1985, White Manufacturing realized the necessity for project management in the manufacturing group. A three-man project management staff was formed. Although the staff was shown on the organizational chart as reporting to the manufacturing operations manager, they actually worked for the vice president and had sufficient authority to integrate work across all departments and divisions. As in the past, the vice president's position was filled by the manufacturing operations manager. Manufacturing operations was directed by the former manufacturing manager who came from manufacturing engineering (see Exhibit 4–3).

In 1988, the manufacturing manager created a matrix in the manufacturing department with the manufacturing engineers acting as departmental project managers.

Exhibit 4–3. White Manufacturing Organizational Structure

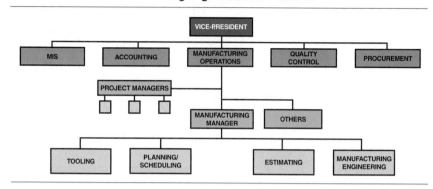

This benefited both the manufacturing manager and the group project managers since all information could be obtained from one source. Work was flowing very smoothly.

In January 1989, the manufacturing manager resigned his position effective March, and the manufacturing engineering manager began packing his bags ready to move up to the vacated position. In February, the vice president announced that the position would be filled from outside. He said also that there would be an organizational restructuring and that the three project managers would now be staff to the manufacturing manager. When the three project managers confronted the manufacturing operations manager, he said, "We've hired the new man in at a very high salary. In order to justify this salary, we have to give him more responsibility."

In March 1989, the new manager took over and immediately made the following declarations:

1. The project managers will never go "upstairs" without first going through him.
2. The departmental matrix will be dissolved and he (the department manager) will handle all of the integration.

How do you account for the actions of the new department manager? What would you do if you were one of the project managers?

MARTIG CONSTRUCTION COMPANY

Martig Construction was a family-owned mechanical subcontractor business that had grown from $5 million in 1986 to $25 million in 1988. Although the gross profit had increased sharply, the profit as a percentage of sales declined drastically. The question was, "Why the decline?" The following observations were made:

1. Since Martig senior died in July of 1988, Martig junior has tried unsuccessfully to convince the family to let him sell the business. Martig junior, as company president, has taken an average of eight days of vacation per month for the past year. Although the project managers are supposed to report to Martig, they ap-

pear to be calling their own shots and are in a continuous struggle for power.

2. The estimating department consists of one man, John, who estimates all jobs. Martig wins one job in seven. Once a job is won, a project manager is selected and is told that he must perform the job within the proposal estimates. Project managers are not involved in proposal estimates. They are required, however, to provide feedback to the estimator so that standards can be updated. This very seldom happens because of the struggle for power. The project managers are afraid that the estimator might be next in line for executive promotion since he is a good friend of Martig.

3. The procurement function reports to Martig. Once the items are ordered, the project manager assumes procurement responsibility. Several times in the past, the project manager has been forced to spend hour after hour trying to overcome shortages or simply to track down raw materials. Most project managers estimate that approximately 35 percent of their time involves procurement.

4. Site superintendents believe they are the true project managers, or at least at the same level. The superintendents are very unhappy about not being involved in the procurement function and, therefore, look for ways to annoy the project managers. It appears that the more time the project manager spends at the site, the longer the work takes; the feedback of information to the home office is also distorted.

THE CARLSON PROJECT

"I sympathize with your problems, Frank," stated Joe McGee, Manager of Project Managers. "You know as well as I do that I'm supposed to resolve conflicts and coordinate efforts among all projects. Staffing problems are your responsibility."

Frank: "Royce Williams has a resume that would choke a horse. I don't understand why he performs with a lazy, I-don't-care attitude. He has fifteen years of experience in a project organizational structure, with ten of those years being in project offices. He knows the work that has to be done."

McGee: "I don't think that it has anything to do with you personally. This happens to some of our best workers sooner or later. You can't expect guys to give 120 percent all of the time. Royce is at the top of his pay grade, and being an exempt employee, he doesn't get paid for overtime. He'll snap out of it sooner or later."

Frank: "I have deadlines to meet on the Carlson Project. Fortunately, the Carlson Project is big enough that I can maintain a full-time project office staff of eight employees, not counting myself.

"I like to have all project office employees assigned full-time and qualified in two or three project office areas. It's a good thing that I have someone else checked out in Royce's area. But I just can't keep asking this other guy to do his own work and that of Royce's. This poor guy has been working sixty to seventy hours a week and Royce has been doing only forty. That seems unfair to me."

McGee: "Look, Frank, I have the authority to fire him, but I'm not going to. It doesn't look good if we fire somebody because they won't work free overtime. Last year we had a case similar to this, where an employee refused to work on Monday and Wednesday evenings because it interfered with his MBA classes. Everyone knew he was going to resign the instant he finished his degree, and yet there was nothing that I could do."

Frank: "There must be other alternatives for Royce Williams. I've talked to him as well as to other project office members. Royce's attitude doesn't appear to be demoralizing the other members, but it easily could in a short period of time."

McGee: "We can reassign him to another project, as soon as one comes along. I'm not going to put him on my overhead budget. Your project can support him for the time being. You know, Frank, the grapevine will know the reason for his transfer. This might affect your ability to get qualified people to volunteer to work with you on future projects. Give Royce a little time and see if you can work it out with him. What about this guy, Harlan Green, from one of the functional groups?"

Frank: "Two months ago, we hired Gus Johnson, a man with ten years of experience. For the first two weeks that he was assigned to my project, he worked like hell and got the work done ahead of schedule. His work was flawless. That was the main reason why I wanted him. I know him personally, and he's one great worker.

"During weeks three and four, his work slowed down considerably. I chatted with him and he said that Harlan Green refused to work with him if he kept up that pace."

McGee: "Did you ask him why?"

Frank: "Yes. First of all, you should know that for safety reasons, all men in that department must work in two- or three-men crews. Therefore, Gus was not allowed to work alone. Harlan did not want to change the standards of performance for fear that some of the other employees would be laid off.

By the end of the first week, nobody in the department would talk to Gus. As a matter of fact, they wouldn't even sit with him in the cafeteria. So, Gus had to either conform to the group or remain an outcast. I feel partially responsible for what has happened, since I'm the one who brought him here.

"I know that has happened before, in the same department. I haven't had a chance to talk to the department manager as yet. I have an appointment to see him next week."

McGee: "There are solutions to the problem, simple ones at that. But, again, it's not my responsibility. You can work it out with the department manager."

"Yeah," thought Frank. "But what if we can't agree?"

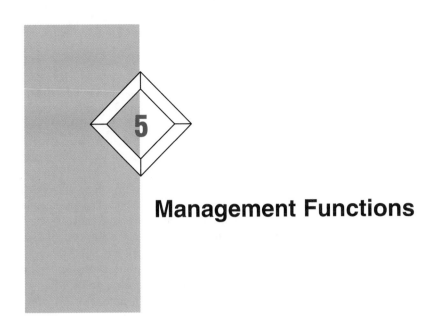

Management Functions

5.0 INTRODUCTION

As we have stated, the project manager measures his success by how well he can negotiate with both upper-level and functional management for the resources necessary to achieve the project objective. Moreover, the project manager may have a great deal of delegated authority but very little power. Hence, the managerial skills he requires for successful performance may be drastically different from those of his functional management counterparts.

The difficult aspect of the project management environment is that individuals at the project–functional interface must report to two bosses. Functional managers and project managers, by virtue of their different authority levels and responsibilities, treat their people in different fashions depending on their "management school" philosophies. There are generally five management schools, as described below:

- *The classical/traditional school:* Management is the process of getting things done (i.e., possibly achieving objectives) by working both with and through people operating in organized groups. Emphasis is placed on the end-item or objective, with little regard for the people involved.
- *The empirical school:* Managerial capabilities can be developed by studying the experiences of other managers, whether or not the situations are similar.
- *The behavioral school:* Two classrooms are considered within this school. First, we have the human relations classroom in which we emphasize the interpersonal relationship between individuals and their work. The second classroom includes the social system of the individual. Management is considered to be a system of cultural relationships involving social change.
- *The decision theory school:* Management is a rational approach to decision making using a system of mathematical models and processes, such as operations research and management science.

231

- *The management systems school:* Management is the development of a systems model, characterized by input, processing, and output, and directly identifies the flow of resources (money, equipment, facilities, personnel, information, and material) necessary to obtain some objective by either maximizing or minimizing some objective function. The management systems school also includes contingency theory, which stresses that each situation is unique and must be optimized separately within the constraints of the system.

In a project environment, functional managers are generally practitioners of the first three schools of management, whereas project managers utilize the last two. This imposes hardships on both the project managers and functional representatives. The project manager must motivate functional representatives toward project dedication on the horizontal line using management systems theory and quantitative tools, often with little regard for the employee. After all, the employee might be assigned for a very short-term effort, whereas the end-item is the most important objective. The functional manager, however, expresses more concern for the individual needs of the employee using the traditional or behavioral schools of management.

Modern practitioners still tend to identify management responsibilities and skills in terms of the principles and functions developed in the early management schools, namely:

- Planning
- Organizing
- Staffing
- Controlling
- Directing

Although these management functions have generally been applied to traditional management structures, they have recently been redefined for temporary management positions. Their fundamental meanings remain the same, but the applications are different.

5.1 CONTROLLING

Controlling is a three-step process of measuring progress toward an objective, evaluating what remains to be done, and taking the necessary corrective action to achieve or exceed the objectives. These three steps—measuring, evaluating, and correcting—are defined as follows:

- *Measuring:* determining through formal and informal reports the degree to which progress toward objectives is being made.
- *Evaluating:* determining cause of and possible ways to act on significant deviations from planned performance.
- *Correcting:* taking control action to correct an unfavorable trend or to take advantage of an unusually favorable trend.

The project manager is responsible for ensuring the accomplishment of group and organizational goals and objectives. To effect this, he must have a thorough knowledge of standards and cost control policies and procedures so that a comparison is possible between operating results and preestablished standards. The project manager must then take the necessary corrective actions. Later chapters provide a more in-depth analysis of control, especially the cost control function.

In Chapter 1, we stated that project managers must understand organizational behavior in order to be effective and must have strong interpersonal skills. This is especially important during the controlling function. As stated by Doering:[1]

> The team leader's role is crucial. He is directly involved and must know the individual team members well, not only in terms of their technical capabilities but also in terms of how they function when addressing a problem as part of a group. The technical competence of a potential team member can usually be determined from information about previous assignments, but it is not so easy to predict and control the individual's interaction within and with a new group, since it is related to the psychological and social behavior of each of the other members of the group as a whole. What the leader needs is a tool to measure and characterize the individual members so that he can predict their interactions and structure his task team accordingly.

5.2 DIRECTING

Directing is the implementing and carrying out (through others) of those approved plans that are necessary to achieve or exceed objectives. Directing involves such steps as:

- *Staffing:* seeing that a qualified person is selected for each position.
- *Training:* teaching individuals and groups how to fulfill their duties and responsibilities.
- *Supervising:* giving others day-to-day instruction, guidance, and discipline as required so that they can fulfill their duties and responsibilities.
- *Delegating:* assigning work, responsibility, and authority so others can make maximum utilization of their abilities.
- *Motivating:* encouraging others to perform by fulfilling or appealing to their needs.
- *Counseling:* holding private discussions with another about how he might do better work, solve a personal problem, or realize his ambitions.
- *Coordinating:* seeing that activities are carried out in relation to their importance and with a minimum of conflict.

---

1. Robert D. Doering, "An Approach Toward Improving the Creative Output of Scientific Task Teams," *IEEE Transactions on Engineering Management.* February 1973, pp. 29–31. © 1973 IEEE.

Directing subordinates is not an easy task because of both the short time duration of the project and the fact that employees might still be assigned to a functional manager while temporarily assigned to your effort. The luxury of getting to "know" one's subordinates may not be possible in a project environment.

Project managers must be decisive and move forward rapidly whenever directives are necessary. It is better to decide an issue and be 10 percent wrong than it is to wait for the last 10 percent of a problem's input and cause a schedule delay and improper use of resources. Directives are most effective when the KISS (keep it simple, stupid) rule is applied. Directives should be written with one simple and clear objective so that subordinates can work effectively and get things done right the first time. Orders must be issued in a manner that expects immediate compliance. Whether people will obey an order depends mainly on the amount of respect they have for you. Therefore, never issue an order that you cannot enforce. Oral orders and directives should be disguised as suggestions or requests. The requestor should ask the receiver to repeat the oral orders so that there is no misunderstanding.

Project managers must understand human behavior, perhaps more so than functional managers. The reason for this is that project managers must continually motivate people toward successful accomplishment of project objectives. Motivation cannot be accomplished without at least a fundamental knowledge of human behavior.

Douglas McGregor advocated that most workers can be categorized according to two theories.[2] The first, often referred to as Theory X, assumes that the average worker is inherently lazy and requires supervision. Theory X further assumes that:

- The average worker dislikes work and avoids work whenever possible.
- To induce adequate effort, the supervisor must threaten punishment and exercise careful supervision.
- The average worker avoids increased responsibility and seeks to be directed.

The manager who accepts Theory X normally exercises authoritarian-type control over workers and allows little participation during decision making. Theory X employees generally favor lack of responsibility, especially in decision making.

According to Theory Y, employees are willing to get the job done without constant supervision. Theory Y further assumes that:

- The average worker wants to be active and finds the physical and mental effort on the job satisfying.
- Greatest results come from willing participation, which will tend to produce self-direction toward goals without coercion and control.
- The average worker seeks opportunity for personal improvement and self-respect.

---

2. Douglas McGregor, *The Human Side of Enterprise* (New York: McGraw-Hill, 1960), pp. 33–34.

The manager who accepts Theory Y normally advocates participation and a management–employee relationship. However, in working with professionals, especially engineers, special care must be exercised because these individuals often pride themselves on their ability to find a better way to achieve the end result regardless of cost. The risk of this happening rises with the numbers of professional degrees that one possesses. The problem with this is that it is the responsibility of the functional manager to determine "how" the job will be done once the project manager states "what" must be done. Project management has the right to insist that an individual who is given free rein to accomplish an objective will also fully understand the necessity of time, cost, and performance constraints. This situation holds true for several engineering disciplines in which engineers consistently strive to exhibit their individuality by seeking new and revolutionary solutions to problems for which well-established solutions already exist. Under these conditions, project managers must become authoritarian leaders and treat Theory Y employees as though they are Theory X. Employees must be trained in how to report to two bosses at the same time. This problem occurs when the employee's line manager treats him as though he is a Theory Y employee, but the project manager treats him as if he is Theory X. Employees must realize that this situation will occur.

Many psychologists have established the existence of a prioritized hierarchy of needs that motivate individuals toward satisfactory performance. Maslow was the first to identify these needs.[3] The first level is that of the basic or physiological needs, namely, food, water, clothing, shelter, sleep, and sexual satisfaction. Simply speaking, human primal desire to satisfy these basic needs motivates him to do a good job. However, once a need becomes satisfied, humans are no longer motivated unless there is a lower-level need to be fulfilled. Fulfilled needs are not motivators.

After an employee has fulfilled his physiological needs, he turns to the next lower need, safety. Safety needs include economic security and protection from harm, disease, and violence. Safety needs must be considered on projects that may include handling of dangerous materials or anything else that could produce bodily harm. Safety can also include security. It is important that project managers realize this because these managers may find that as a project nears termination, functional employees are more interested in finding a new role for themselves than in giving their best to the current situation.

The next level contains the social needs, including love, belonging, togetherness, approval, and group membership. At this level, the informal organization plays a dominant role. Many people refuse promotions to project management (as project managers, project office personnel, or functional representatives) because they fear that they will lose their "membership" in the informal organization. This problem can occur even on short-duration projects. In a project environment, project managers generally do not belong to any informal organization and, there-

---

3. Abraham Maslow, *Motivation and Personality* (New York: Harper and Brothers, 1954).

fore, tend to look outside the organization to fulfill this need. Project managers consider authority and funding to be very important in gaining project support. Functional personnel, however, prefer friendship and work assignments. In other words, the project manager can use the project itself as a means of helping fulfill the third level for the line employees (i.e., team spirit).

The two lowest needs are esteem and self-actualization. The esteem need includes self-esteem (self-respect), reputation, the esteem of others, recognition, and self-confidence. Highly technical professionals are often not happy unless esteem needs are fulfilled. For example, many engineers strive to publish and invent as a means of satisfying these needs. These individuals often refuse promotions to project management because they believe that they cannot satisfy esteem needs in this position. Being called a project manager does not carry as much importance as being considered an expert in one's field by one's peers. The lowest need is self-actualization and includes doing what one can do best, desiring to utilize one's potential, full realization of one's potential, constant self-development, and a desire to be truly creative. Many good project managers find this level to be the most important and consider each new project as a challenge by which they can achieve self-actualization.

Project managers must motivate temporarily assigned individuals by appealing to their desires to fulfill the lowest two levels. Of course, the motivation process should not be developed by making promises that the project manager knows cannot be met. Project managers must motivate by providing:

- A feeling of pride or satisfaction for one's ego
- Security of opportunity
- Security of approval
- Security of advancement, if possible
- Security of promotion, if possible
- Security of recognition
- A means for doing a better job, not a means to keep a job

Understanding professional needs is an important factor in helping people realize their true potential. Such needs include:

- Interesting and challenging work
- Professionally stimulating work environment
- Professional growth
- Overall leadership (ability to lead)
- Tangible rewards
- Technical expertise (within the team)
- Management assistance in problem-solving
- Clearly defined objectives
- Proper management control
- Job security

- Senior management support
- Good interpersonal relations
- Proper planning
- Clear role definition
- Open communications
- A minimum of changes

Motivating employees so that they feel secure on the job is not easy, especially since a project has a finite lifetime. Specific methods for producing security in a project environment include:

- Letting people know why they are where they are
- Making individuals feel that they belong where they are
- Placing individuals in positions for which they are properly trained
- Letting employees know how their efforts fit into the big picture

Since project managers cannot motivate by promising material gains, they must appeal to each person's pride. The guidelines for proper motivation are:

- Adopt a positive attitude
- Do not criticize management
- Do not make promises that cannot be kept
- Circulate customer reports
- Give each person the attention he requires

There are several ways of motivating project personnel. Some effective ways include:

- Giving assignments that provide challenges
- Clearly defining performance expectations
- Giving proper criticism as well as credit
- Giving honest appraisals
- Providing a good working atmosphere
- Developing a team attitude
- Providing a proper direction (even if Theory Y)

5.3 PROJECT AUTHORITY

Project management structures create a web of relationships that can cause chaos in the delegation of authority and the internal authority structure. Four questions must be considered in describing project authority:

- What is project authority?
- What is power, and how is it achieved?

- How much project authority should be granted to the project manager?
- Who settles project authority interface problems?

One form of the project manager's authority can be defined as the legal or rightful power to command, act, or direct the activities of others. The breakdown of the project manager's authority is shown in Figure 5–1. Authority can be delegated from one's superiors. Power, on the other hand, is granted to an individual by his subordinates and is a measure of their respect for him. A manager's authority is a combination of his power and influence such that subordinates, peers, and associates willingly accept his judgment.

In the traditional structure, the power spectrum is realized through the hierarchy, whereas in the project structure, power comes from credibility, expertise, or being a sound decision-maker.

Authority is the key to the project management process. The project manager must manage across functional and organizational lines by bringing together activities required to accomplish the objectives of a specific project. Project authority provides the way of thinking required to unify all organizational activities toward accomplishment of the project regardless of where they are located. The project manager who fails to build and maintain his alliances will soon find opposition or indifference to his project requirements.

The amount of authority granted to the project manager varies according to project size, management philosophy, and management interpretation of potential conflicts with functional managers. There do exist, however, certain fundamental

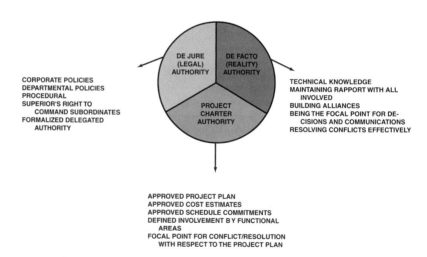

FIGURE 5–1. Project authority breakdown. *Source.* Bill Eglinton, "Matrix Project Management Myths and Realities," *Proceedings of the PMI Seminar/Symposium on Project Management,* Toronto, Ontario, Canada, p. IV-G.33.

elements over which the project manager must have authority in order to maintain effective control. According to Steiner and Ryan:[4]

> The project manager should have broad authority over all elements of the project. His authority should be sufficient to permit him to engage all necessary managerial and technical actions required to complete the project successfully. He should have appropriate authority in design and in making technical decisions in development. He should be able to control funds, schedule and quality of product. If subcontractors are used, he should have maximum authority in their selection.

Generally speaking, a project manager should have more authority than his responsibility calls for, the exact amount of authority usually depending on the amount of risk that the project manager must take. The greater the risk, the greater the amount of authority. A good project manager knows where his authority ends and does not hold an employee responsible for duties that he (the project manager) does not have the authority to enforce. Some projects are directed by project managers who have only monitoring authority. These project managers are referred to as influence project managers.

Failure to establish authority relationships can result in:

- Poor communication channels
- Misleading information
- Antagonism, especially from the informal organization
- Poor working relationships with superiors, subordinates, peers, and associates
- Surprises for the customer

The following are the most common sources of power and authority problems in a project environment:

- Poorly documented or no formal authority
- Power and authority perceived incorrectly
- Dual accountability of personnel
- Two bosses (who often disagree)
- The project organization encouraging individualism
- Subordinate relations stronger than peer or superior relationships
- Shifting of personnel loyalties from vertical to horizontal lines
- Group decision making based on the strongest group
- Ability to influence or administer rewards and punishment
- Sharing resources among several projects

---

4. Reprinted from George A. Steiner and William G. Ryan, *Industrial Project Management* (1968), p. 24. Copyright © 1968 by the Trustees of Columbia University in the City of New York. Reprinted with permission of The Free Press, a division of Simon and Schuster.

The project management organizational structure is an arena of continuous conflict and negotiation. Although there are many clearly defined authority boundaries between functional and project management responsibilities, the fact that each project can be inherently different from all others almost always creates new areas where authority negotiations are necessary.

The project manager does not have unilateral authority in the project effort. He frequently negotiates with the functional manager. The project manager has the authority to determine the "when" and "what" of the project activities, whereas the functional manager has the authority to determine "how the support will be given." The project manager accomplishes his objectives by working with personnel who are largely professional. For professional personnel, project leadership must include explaining the rationale of the effort as well as the more obvious functions of planning, organizing, directing, and controlling.

Certain ground rules exist for authority control through negotiations:

- Negotiations should take place at the lowest level of interaction.
- Definition of the problem must be the first priority:
  - The issue
  - The impact
  - The alternative
  - The recommendations
- Higher-level authority should be used if, and only if, agreement cannot be reached.

The critical stage of any project is planning. This includes more than just planning the activities to be accomplished; it also includes the planning and establishment of the authority relationships that must exist for the duration of the project. Because the project management environment is an ever-changing one, each project establishes its own policies and procedures, a situation that can ultimately result in a variety of authority relationships. It is therefore possible for functional personnel to have different responsibilities on different projects, even if the tasks are the same.

During the planning phase the project team develops a responsibility assignment matrix (RAM) that contains such elements as:

- General management responsibility
- Operations management responsibility
- Specialized responsibility
- Who must be consulted
- Who may be consulted
- Who must be notified
- Who must approve

The responsibility matrix is often referred to as a linear responsibility chart (LRC) or responsibility assignment matrix (RAM). Linear responsibility charts identify the participants, and to what degree an activity will be performed or a decision

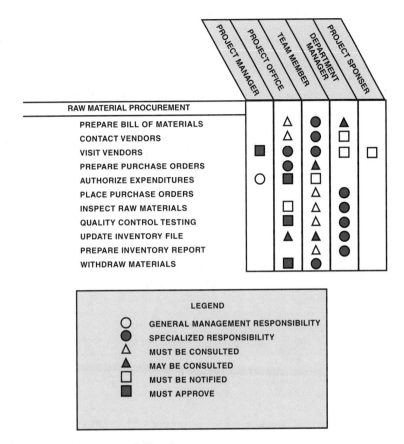

FIGURE 5–2. Linear responsibility chart.

will be made. The LRC attempts to clarify the authority relationships that can exist when functional units share common work. As described by Cleland and King:[5]

> The need for a device to clarify the authority relationships is evident from the relative unity of the traditional pyramidal chart, which (1) is merely a simple portrayal of the overall functional and authority models and (2) must be combined with detailed position descriptions and organizational manuals to delineate authority relationships and work performance duties.

Figure 5–2 shows a typical linear responsibility chart. The rows, which indicate the activities, responsibilities, or functions required, can be all of the tasks in the

5. From David I. Cleland and William Richard King, *Systems Analysis and Project Management* (New York: McGraw-Hill), p. 271. Copyright © 1968, 1975 McGraw-Hill Inc. Used with permission of McGraw-Hill Book Company.

| | REPORTED TO | | | | | | | | | | | | |
| | INTERNAL | | | | | | EXTERNAL (CUSTOMER)** | | | | | | |
INITIATED FROM	PROJECT MANAGER	PROJECT OFFICE	TEAM MEMBER	DEPARTMENT MEMBERS	FUNCTIONAL EMPLOYEES	DIVISION MANAGER	EXECUTIVE MANAGEMENT	PROJECT MANAGER	PROJECT OFFICE	TEAM MEMBER	DEPARTMENT MEMBERS	FUNCTIONAL EMPLOYEES	DIVISION MANAGER	EXECUTIVE MANAGEMENT
PROJECT MANAGER	▧	○	◆	△	▲	▲	◆	○	○	■	■	■	■	△
PROJECT OFFICE	○	▧	○	○	▲	▲	▲	○	○	△	△	■	■	△
TEAM MEMBER	◆	○	▧	◆	◯	■	■	■	■	▲	▲	▲	■	■
DEPARTMENT MEMBERS	▲	△	○	▧	○	◆	■	△	△	△	△	△	■	■
FUNCTIONAL EMPLOYEES	▲	▲	○	○	▧	■	■	▲	▲	▲	▲	▲	■	■
DIVISION MANAGERS	△	▲	▲	▲	▲	▧	△	■	■	■	■	■	△	△
EXECUTIVE MANAGEMENT	△	▲	▲	▲	▲	▲	▧	△	△	▲	▲	■	△	△

*CAN VARY FROM TASK TO TASK AND CAN BE WRITTEN OR ORAL
** DOES NOT INCLUDE REGUARLY SCHEDULED INTERCHANGE MEEINGS

LEGEND
○ DAILY
◆ WEEKLY
◯ MONTHLY
▲ AS NEEDED
△ INFORMAL
■ NEVER

FIGURE 5–3. Communications responsibility matrix.*

work breakdown structure. The columns identify either positions, titles, or the people themselves. If the chart will be given to an outside customer, then only the titles should appear, or the customer will call the employees directly without going through the project manager. The symbols indicate the degrees of authority or responsibility existing between the rows and columns.

Another example of an LRC is shown in Figure 5–3. In this case, the LRC is used to describe how internal and external communications should take place. This type of chart can be used to eliminate communications conflicts. Consider a customer who is unhappy about having all of his information filtered through the project manager and requests that his line people be permitted to talk to your line people on a one-on-one basis. You may have no choice but to permit this, but you should make sure that the customer understands that:

- Functional employees cannot make commitments for additional work or resources.
- Functional employees give their own opinion and not that of the company.
- Company policy comes through the project office.

Linear responsibility charts can be used to alleviate some of these problems.

DATA ITEM DISTRIBUTION MATRIX

		CUSTOMER AND CONTRACTOR'S PERSONNEL				
DATA ITEM	REPORT DESCRIPTION	PROJECT MANAGER	PROJECT OFFICE	TEAM MEMBER	LINE MANAGER	EXECUTIVE MANAGEMENT
1	MONTHLY COST SUMMARIES	X	X			X
2	MILESTONE REPORTS	X	X	X	X	X
3	MANPOWER CURVES	X	X		X	
4	INVENTORY UTILIZATION	X	X			
5	PRESSURE TEST REPORT	X	X		X	
6	HUMIDITY TESTS	X	X		X	
7	HOTLINE REPORTS	X	X	X	X	X
8	SCHEDULING SUMMARIES	X	X	X	X	

FIGURE 5–4. Data distribution matrix.

Figures 5–4 and 5–5 are examples of modified LRCs. Figure 5–4 is used to show the distribution of data items, and Figure 5–5 identifies the skills distribution in the project office.

The responsibility matrix attempts to answer such questions as: "Who has signature authority?" "Who must be notified?" "Who can make the decision?" The questions can only be answered by clear definitions of authority, responsibility, and accountability:

- *Authority* is the right of an individual to make the necessary decisions required to achieve his objectives or responsibilities.
- *Responsibility* is the assignment for completion of a specific event or activity.
- *Accountability* is the acceptance of success or failure.

The linear responsibility chart, although a valuable tool for management, does have a weakness in that it does not describe how people interact within the program. The LRC must be considered with the organization for a full understanding of how interactions between individuals and organizations take place. As described by Karger and Murdick, the LRC has merit:[6]

6. D. W. Karger and R. G. Murdick, *Managing Engineering and Research* (New York: Industrial Press, 1963), p. 89.

FUNCTIONAL AREAS OF EXPERTISE \ PROJECT TEAM	ABLE, J.	BAKER, P.	COOK, D.	DIRK, L.	EASLEY, P.	FRANKLIN, W.	GREEN, C.	HENRY, L.	IMHOFF, R.	JULES, C.	KLEIN, W.	LEDGER, D.	MAYER, O.	NEWTON, A.	OLIVER, G.	PRATT, L.
ADMINISTRATIVE MANAGEMENT		a				a		a			a	a			a	
COST CONTROL		b	b		b	b	b				b	b		b	b	
ECONOMIC ANALYSIS	c			c				c	c				c			c
ENERGY SYSTEMS		d	d		d		d			d			d		d	d
ENVIROMENTAL IMPACT ASSESSMENT	e	e	e						e		e		e			
INDUSTRIAL ENGINEERING	f				f					f						
INSTRUMENTATION	g			g		g					g				g	
PIPING AND DESIGN LAYOUT	h		h		h	h				h			h			
PLANNING AND SCHEDULING		i		i	i							i		i		i
PROJECT MANAGEMENT	j			j		j					j				j	
PROJECT REPORTING		k	k		k			k	k			k		k		k
QUALITY CONTROL		l	l	l		l	l	l	l							
SITE EVALUATION		m				m			m	m				m		
SPECIFICATION PREPARATION			n	n			n				n		n			n
SYSTEM DESIGN		o	o		o		o	o		o		o			o	

FIGURE 5–5. Personal skills matrix.

244

Obviously the chart has weaknesses, of which one of the larger ones is that it is a mechanical aid. Just because it says that something is a fact does not make it true. It is very difficult to discover, except generally, exactly what occurs in a company—and with whom. The chart tries to express in specific terms relationships that cannot always be delineated so clearly; moreover, the degree to which it can be done depends on the specific situation. This is the difference between the formal and informal organizations mentioned. Despite this, the Linear Responsibility Chart is one of the best devices for organization analysis known to the authors.

Linear responsibility charts can result from customer-imposed requirements above and beyond normal operations. For example, the customer may require as part of its quality control that a specific engineer supervise and approve all testing of a certain item or that another individual approve all data released to the customer over and above program office approval. Customer requirements similar to those identified above necessitate LRCs and can cause disruptions and conflicts within an organization.

Several key factors affect the delegation of authority and responsibility, both from upper-level management to project management and from project management to functional management. These key factors include:

- The maturity of the project management function
- The size, nature, and business base of the company
- The size and nature of the project
- The life cycle of the project
- The capabilities of management at all levels

Once agreement has been reached as to the project manager's authority and responsibility, the results must be documented to clearly delineate his role in regard to:

- His focal position
- Conflict between the project manager and functional managers
- Influence to cut across functional and organizational lines
- Participation in major management and technical decisions
- Collaboration in staffing the project
- Control over allocation and expenditure of funds
- Selection of subcontractors
- Rights in resolving conflicts
- Voice in maintaining integrity of the project team
- Establishment of project plans
- Providing a cost-effective information system for control
- Providing leadership in preparing operational requirements
- Maintaining prime customer liaison and contact
- Promoting technological and managerial improvements
- Establishment of project organization for the duration
- Cutting red tape

Documenting the project manager's authority is necessary because:

- All interfacing must be kept as simple as possible.
- The project manager must have the authority to "force" functional managers to depart from existing standards and possibly incur risk.
- The project manager must gain authority over those elements of a program that are not under his control. This is normally achieved by earning the respect of the individuals concerned.
- The project manager should not attempt to fully describe the exact authority and responsibilities of his project office personnel or team members. Instead, he should encourage problem solving rather than role definition.

5.4 INTERPERSONAL INFLUENCES

There exist a variety of relationships (although they are not always clearly definable) between power and authority. These relationships are usually measured by "relative" decision power as a function of the authority structure, and are strongly dependent on the project organizational form.

Consider the following statements made by project managers:

- "I've had good working relations with department X. They like me and I like them. I can usually push through anything ahead of schedule."
- "I know it's contrary to department policy, but the test must be conducted according to these criteria or else the results will be meaningless" (remark made to a team member by a research scientist who was temporarily promoted to project management for an advanced state-of-the-art effort).

These two statements reflect the way two project managers get the job done.

Project managers are generally known for having a lot of delegated authority but very little formal power. They must, therefore, get jobs done through the use of interpersonal influences. There are five such interpersonal influences:

- *Legitimate power:* the ability to gain support because project personnel perceive the project manager as being officially empowered to issue orders.
- *Reward power:* the ability to gain support because project personnel perceive the project manager as capable of directly or indirectly dispensing valued organizational rewards (i.e., salary, promotion, bonus, future work assignments).
- *Penalty power:* the ability to gain support because the project personnel perceive the project manager as capable of directly or indirectly dispens-

ing penalties that they wish to avoid. Penalty power usually derives from the same source as reward power, with one being a necessary condition for the other.

- *Expert power:* the ability to gain support because personnel perceive the project manager as possessing special knowledge or expertise (that functional personnel consider as important).
- *Referent power:* the ability to gain support because project personnel feel personally attracted to the project manager or his project.

The following six situations are examples of referent power (the first two are also reward power):

- The employee might be able to get personal favors from the project manager.
- The employee feels that the project manager is a winner and the rewards will be passed down to the employee.
- The employee and the project manager have strong ties, such as the same foursome for golf.
- The employee likes the project manager's manner of treating people.
- The employee wants identification with a specific product or product line.
- The employee has personal problems and believes that he can get empathy or understanding from the project manager.

Figure 5–6 shows how project managers perceive their influence style.

Like relative power, interpersonal influences can be identified with various project organizational forms as to their relative value. This is shown in Figure 5–7.

For any temporary management structure to be effective, there must exist a rational balance of power between functional and project management. Unfortunately, a balance of equal power is often impossible to obtain because each project is inherently different from others, and the project managers possess different leadership abilities. Organizations, nevertheless, must attempt to obtain such a balance so that trade-offs can be effectively accomplished according to the merit of the individuals and not as a result of some established power structure.

Achievement of this balance is a never-ending challenge for management. If time and cost constraints on a project cannot be met, the project influence in decision making increases, as can be seen in Figure 5–7. If the technology or performance constraints need reappraisal, then the functional influence in decision making will dominate.

Regardless of how much authority and power a project manager develops over the course of the project, the ultimate factor in his ability to get the job done is usually his leadership style. Project managers, because of the inherent authority gaps that develop at the project–functional interface, must rely heavily on sup-

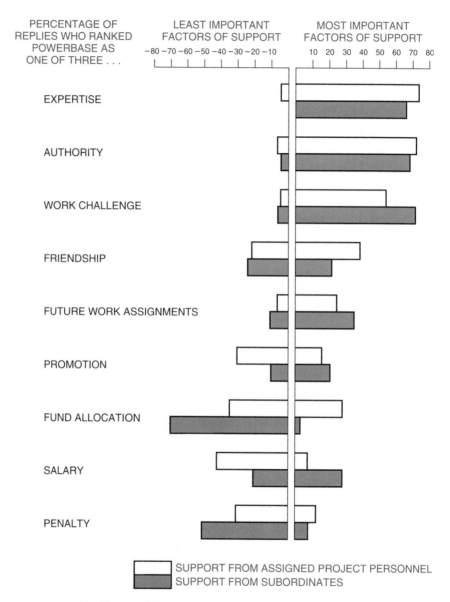

FIGURE 5–6. Significance of factors of support to project management. *Source. Seminar in Project Management Workbook,* © 1979 by Hans J. Thamhain. Reproduced by permission.

plementary techniques for getting the job done. These supplementary techniques include factors that directly affect the leadership style, such as developing bonds of trust, friendship, and respect with the functional workers. Of course, the relative importance of these techniques can vary depending on the size and scope of the project.

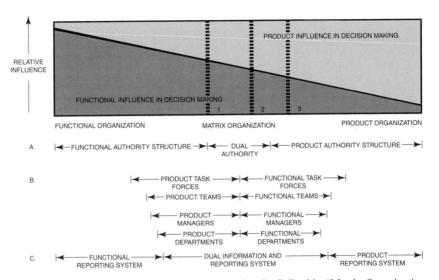

FIGURE 5–7. The range of alternatives. *Source.* Jay R. Galbraith, "Matrix Organization Designs." Reprinted with permission from *Business Horizons,* February 1971 (p. 37). Copyright © 1971 by the Board of Trustees at Indiana University. Used with permission.

5.5 BARRIERS TO PROJECT TEAM DEVELOPMENT

Most people within project-driven and non–project-driven organizations have differing views of project management. Table 5–1 compares the project and functional viewpoints of project management. These differing views can create severe barriers to successful project management operations.

Perhaps the most common barriers occur as a result of the need to delegate. The following results, identified by MacKenzie, apply to project management:[7]

- Barriers in the Delegator
  - Preference for operating
  - Demand that everyone "know all the details"
  - "I can do it better myself" fallacy
  - Lack of experience in the job or in delegating
  - Insecurity
  - Fear of being disliked
  - Refusal to allow mistakes
  - Lack of confidence in subordinates

---

7. R. Alec MacKenzie, *The Time Trap* (New York: McGraw-Hill, 1972), p. 135. Reprinted, with permission of the publisher, from *The Time Trap* © 1972 R. Alec MacKenzie. Published by AMA-COM, a division of the American Management Association. All rights reserved.

- Perfectionism, leading to overcontrol
- Lack of organizational skill in balancing workloads
- Failure to delegate authority commensurate with responsibility
- Uncertainty over tasks and inability to explain
- Disinclination to develop subordinates
- Failure to establish effective controls and to follow up
- Barriers in the Delegatee
  - Lack of experience
  - Lack of competence
  - Avoidance of responsibility
  - Overdependence on the boss
  - Disorganization
  - Overload of work
  - Immersion in trivia
- Barriers in the Situation
  - One-man-show policy
  - No toleration of mistakes
  - Criticality of decisions
  - Urgency, leaving no time to explain (crisis management)
  - Confusion in responsibilities and authority
  - Understaffing

The understanding of barriers to project team building can help in developing an environment conducive to effective team work. The following barriers to team building were identified and analyzed in a field study by Thamhain and Wilemon.[8] They are typical for many project environments.

Differing outlooks, priorities, and interests. A major barrier exists when team members have professional objectives and interests that are different from the project objectives. These problems are compounded when the team relies on support organizations that have different interests and priorities.

Role conflicts. Team development efforts are thwarted when role conflicts exist among the team members, such as ambiguity over who does what within the project team and in external support groups.

Project objectives/outcomes not clear. Unclear project objectives frequently lead to conflict, ambiguities, and power struggles. It becomes difficult, if not impossible, to define roles and responsibilities clearly.

Dynamic project environments. Many projects operate in a continual state of change. For example, senior management may keep changing the project scope, objectives, and resource base. In other situations, regulatory changes or client demands can drastically affect the internal operations of a project team.

---

8. For detailed discussion see H. J. Thamhain and D. L. Wilemon, "Team Building in Project Management," *Proceedings of the Annual Symposium of the Project Management Institute,* October 1979.

TABLE 5–1. COMPARISON OF THE FUNCTIONAL AND THE PROJECT VIEWPOINTS

Phenomena	Project Viewpoint	Functional Viewpoint
Line–staff organizational dichotomy	Vestiges of the hierarchical model remain: the line functions are placed in a support position. A web of authority and responsibility exists.	Line functions have direct responsibility for accomplishing the objectives; line commands, and staff advises.
Scalar principle	Elements of the vertical chain exist, but prime emphasis is placed on horizontal and diagonal work flow. Important business is conducted as the legitimacy of the task requires.	The chain of authority relationships is from superior to subordinate throughout the organization. Central, crucial, and important business is conducted up and down the vertical hierarchy.
Superior–subordinate relationship	Peer-to-peer, manager-to-technical expert, associate-to-associate, etc., relationships are used to conduct much of the salient business.	This is the most important relationship; if kept healthy, success will follow. All important business is conducted through a pyramiding structure of superiors and subordinates
Organizational objectives	Management of a project becomes a joint venture of many relatively independent organizations. Thus, the objective becomes multilateral.	Organizational objectives are sought by the parent unit (an assembly of suborganizations) working within its environment. The objective is unilateral.
Unity of direction	The project manager manages across functional and organizational lines to accomplish a common interorganizational objective.	The general manager acts as the one head for a group of activities having the same plan.
Parity of authority and responsibility	Considerable opportunity exists for the project manager's responsibility to exceed his authority. Support people are often responsible to other managers (functional) for pay, performance reports, promotions, etc.	Consistent with functional management; the integrity of the superior–subordinate relationship is maintained through functional authority and advisory staff services.
Time duration	The project (and hence the organization) is finite in duration.	Tends to perpetuate itself to provide continuing facilitative support.

Source: David I. Cleland, "Project Management," in David I. Cleland and William R. King, eds., *Systems Organizations, Analysis, Management: A Book of Readings* (New York: McGraw-Hill, Inc., 1969), pp. 281–290. © 1969 by McGraw-Hill Inc. Reprinted with permission of the publisher.

Competition over team leadership. Project leaders frequently indicated that this barrier most likely occurs in the early phases of a project or if the project runs into severe problems. Obviously, such cases of leadership challenge can result in barriers to team building. Frequently, these challenges are covert challenges to the project leader's ability.

Lack of team definition and structure. Many senior managers complain that teamwork is severely impaired because it lacks clearly defined task responsibilities and reporting structures. We find this situation is most prevalent in dynamic, organizationally unstructured work environments such as computer systems and R&D projects. A common pattern is that a support department is charged with a task but no one leader is clearly delegated the responsibility. As a consequence, some personnel are working on the project but are not entirely clear on the extent of their responsibilities. In other cases, problems result when a project is supported by several departments without interdisciplinary coordination.

Team personnel selection. This barrier develops when personnel feel unfairly treated or threatened during the staffing of a project. In some cases, project personnel are assigned to a team by functional managers, and the project manager has little or no input into the selection process. This can impede team development efforts, especially when the project leader is given available personnel versus the best, hand-picked team members. The assignment of "available personnel" can result in several problems (e.g., low motivation levels, discontent, and uncommitted team members). We've found, as a rule, that the more power the project leader has over the selection of his team members, and the more negotiated agreement there is over the assigned task, the more likely it is that team-building efforts will be fruitful.

Credibility of project leader. Team-building efforts are hampered when the project leader suffers from poor credibility within the team or from other managers. In such cases, team members are often reluctant to make a commitment to the project or the leader. Credibility problems may come from poor managerial skills, poor technical judgments, or lack of experience relevant to the project.

Lack of team member commitment. Lack of commitment can have several sources. For example, the team members having professional interests elsewhere, the feeling of insecurity that is associated with projects, the unclear nature of the rewards that may be forthcoming upon successful completion, and intense interpersonal conflicts within the team can all lead to lack of commitment.

Lack of team member commitment may result from suspicious attitudes existing between the project leader and a functional support manager, or between two team members from two warring functional departments. Finally, low commitment levels are likely to occur when a "star" on a team "demands" too much effort from other team members or too much attention from the team leader. One team leader put it this way: "A lot of teams have their prima donnas and you learn to live and function with them. They can be critical to overall success. But some stars can be so demanding on everyone that they'll kill the team's motivation."

Communication problems. Not surprisingly, poor communication is a major enemy to effective team development. Poor communication exists on four major levels: problems of communication among team members, between the project leader and the team members, between the project team and top management, and between the project leaders and the client. Often the problem is caused by team members simply not keeping others informed on key project developments. Yet the "whys" of poor communication patterns are far more difficult to determine. The problem can result from low motivation levels, poor morale, or carelessness. It was also discovered that poor communication patterns between the team and support groups result in severe team-building problems, as does poor communication with the client. Poor communication practices often lead to unclear objectives and poor project control, coordination, and work flow.

Lack of senior management support. Project leaders often indicate that senior management support and commitment is unclear and subject to waxing and waning over the project life cycle. This behavior can result in an uneasy feeling among team members and lead to low levels of enthusiasm and project commitment. Two other common problems are that senior management often does not help set the right environment for the project team at the outset, nor do they give the team timely feedback on their performance and activities during the life of the project.

Project managers who are successfully performing their role not only recognize these barriers but also know when in the project life cycle they are most likely to occur. Moreover, these managers take preventive actions and usually foster a work environment that is conducive to effective teamwork. The effective team builder is usually a social architect who understands the interaction of organizational and behavior variables and can foster a climate of active participation and minimal conflict. This requires carefully developed skills in leadership, administration, organization, and technical expertise on the project. However, besides the delicately balanced management skills, the project manager's sensitivity to the basic issues underlying each barrier can help to increase success in developing an effective project team. Specific suggestions for team building are advanced in Table 5–2.

5.6 SUGGESTIONS FOR HANDLING THE NEWLY FORMED TEAM

A major problem faced by many project leaders is managing the anxiety that usually develops when a new team is formed. The anxiety experienced by team members is normal and predictable. It is a barrier, however, to getting the team quickly focused on the task. In other words, if team members are suffering from anxiety, their attention will be consciously or subconsciously focused on resolution of their own anxieties rather than the needs of the project.

This anxiety may come from several sources. For example, if the team members have never worked with the project leader, they may be concerned about his

TABLE 5–2. BARRIERS TO EFFECTIVE TEAM BUILDING AND SUGGESTED HANDLING APPROACHES

Barrier	Suggestions for Effectively Managing Barriers (How to Minimize or Eliminate Barriers)
Differing outlooks, priorities, interests, and judgments of team members	Make effort early in the project life cycle to discover these conflicting differences. Fully explain the scope of the project and the rewards that may be forthcoming on successful project completion. Sell "team" concept and explain responsibilities. Try to blend individual interests with the overall project objectives.
Role conflicts	As early in a project as feasible, ask team members where they see themselves fitting into the project. Determine how the overall project can best be divided into subsystems and subtasks (e.g., the work breakdown structure). Assign/negotiate roles. Conduct regular status review meetings to keep team informed on progress and watch for unanticipated role conflicts over the project's life.
Project objectives/outcomes not clear	Assure that all parties understand the overall and interdisciplinary project objectives. Clear and frequent communication with senior management and the client becomes critically important. Status review meetings can be used for feedback. Finally, a proper team name can help to reinforce the project objectives.
Dynamic project environments	The major challenge is to stabilize external influences. First, key project personnel must work out an agreement on the principal project direction and "sell" this direction to the total team. Also educate senior management and the customer on the detrimental consequences of unwarranted change. It is critically important to forecast the "environment" within which the project will be developed. Develop contingency plans.
Competition over team leadership	Senior management must help establish the project manager's leadership role. On the other hand, the project manager needs to fulfill the leadership expectations of team members. Clear role and responsibility definition often minimizes competition over leadership.
Lack of team definition and structure	Project leaders need to sell the team concept to senior management as well as to their team members. Regular meetings with the team will reinforce the team notion as will clearly defined tasks, roles, and responsibilities. Also, visibility in memos and other forms of written media as well as senior management and client participation can unify the team.

(continues)

TABLE 5–2. BARRIERS TO EFFECTIVE TEAM BUILDING AND SUGGESTED HANDLING APPROACHES (*Continued*)

Barrier	Suggestions for Effectively Managing Barriers (How to Minimize or Eliminate Barriers)
Project personnel selection	Attempt to negotiate the project assignments with potential team members. Clearly discuss with potential team members the importance of the project, their role in it, what rewards might result on completion, and the general "rules of the road" of project management. Finally, if team members remain uninterested in the project, then replacement should be considered.
Credibility of project leader	Credibility of the project leader among team members is crucial. It grows with the image of a sound decision-maker in both general management and relevant technical expertise. Credibility can be enhanced by the project leader's relationship to other key managers who support the team's efforts.
Lack of team member commitment	Try to determine lack of team member commitment early in the life of the project and attempt to change possible negative views toward the project. Often, insecurity is a major reason for the lack of commitment; try to determine why insecurity exists, then work on reducing the team members' fears. Conflicts with other team members may be another reason for lack of commitment. It is important for the project leader to intervene and mediate the conflict quickly. Finally, if a team member's professional interests lie elsewhere, the project leader should examine ways to satisfy part of the team member's interests or consider replacement.
Communication problems	The project leader should devote considerable time communicating with individual team members about their needs and concerns. In addition, the leader should provide a vehicle for timely sessions to encourage communications among the individual team contributors. Tools for enhancing communications are status meetings, reviews schedules, reporting system, and colocation. Similarly, the project leader should establish regular and thorough communications with the client and senior management. Emphasis is placed on written and oral communications with key issues and agreements in writing.

(*continues*)

TABLE 5–2. BARRIERS TO EFFECTIVE TEAM BUILDING AND SUGGESTED HANDLING
APPROACHES (*Continued*)

Barrier	Suggestions for Effectively Managing Barriers (How to Minimize or Eliminate Barriers)
Lack of senior management support	Senior management support is an absolute necessity for dealing effectively with interface groups and proper resource commitment. Therefore, a major goal for project leaders is to maintain the continued interest and commitment of senior management in their projects. We suggest that senior management become an integral part of project reviews. Equally important, it is critical for senior management to provide the proper environment for the project to function effectively. Here the project leader needs to tell management at the onset of the program what resources are needed. The project manager's relationship with senior management and ability to develop senior management support is critically affected by his own credibility and the visibility and priority of his project.

leadership style and its effect on them. In a different vein, some team members may be concerned about the nature of the project and whether it will match their professional interests and capabilities. Other team members may be concerned about whether the project will help or hinder their career aspirations. Further, team members can be highly anxious about life-style/work-style disruptions that the project may bring. As one project manager remarked, "Moving a team member's desk from one side of the room to the other can sometimes be just about as traumatic as moving someone from Chicago to Manila." As the quote suggests, seemingly minor changes can cause unanticipated anxiety among team members.

Another common concern among newly formed teams is whether there will be an equitable distribution of the workload among team members and whether each member is capable of pulling his own weight. In some newly formed teams, members not only must do their own work, but also must train other team members. Within reason this is bearable, necessary, and often expected. However, when it becomes excessive, anxiety increases, and morale can fall.

Certain steps taken early in the life of a team can be effective in terms of handling the above problems. First, we recommend that the project leader at the start of the project talk with each team member on a one-to-one basis about the following:

1. What the objectives are for the project.
2. Who will be involved and why.
3. The importance of the project to the overall organization or work unit.
4. Why the team member was selected and assigned to the project. What role he will perform.

5. What rewards might be forthcoming if the project is successfully completed.
6. What problems and constraints are likely to be encountered.
7. The rules of the road that will be followed in managing the project (e.g., regular status review meetings).
8. What suggestions the team member has for achieving success.
9. What the professional interests of the team member are.
10. What challenge the project will present to individual members and the entire team.
11. Why the team concept is so important to project management success and how it should work.

A frank, open discussion of the above questions with each team member is likely to reduce his initial anxiety. Consequently, the team member is likely to be more attentive to the needs of the project. Of course, the opposite reaction is possible, too. A frank discussion, for example, may actually increase a team member's anxiety level. Often, however, the source of the anxiety can be identified and dealt with in a timely manner.

Dealing with these anxieties and helping team members feel that they are an integral part of the team can yield rich dividends. First, as noted in Figure 5–8, the more effective the project leader is in developing a feeling of team membership, the higher the quality of the information that is likely to be contributed by team members. Team members will openly share their ideas and approaches. By contrast, when a team member does not feel part of the team and does not trust others in team deliberations, information will not be shared willingly or openly. One project leadership emphasized this point:

> There's nothing worse than being on a team when no one trusts anyone else. . . . Such situations lead to gamesmanship and a lot of watching what you say because you don't want your own words to bounce back in your face.

Second, the greater the feeling of team membership and the better the information exchange among team members, the more likely it is that the team will be able to develop effective decision-making processes. The reason is that team members feel committed to the project, and they feel free to share their information and develop effective problem-solving approaches. Third, the team is likely to develop more effective project control procedures. Project control procedures can be divided into two basic types. The first type is the quantitative control procedures traditionally used to monitor project performance (PERT/CPM, networking, work breakdown structures, etc.). The second is represented by the willingness and ability of project team members to give feedback to each other regarding performance. Again, trust among the project team members makes the feedback process easier and more effective. Without a high level of trust, project personnel are often reluctant to give constructive feedback to fellow team members.

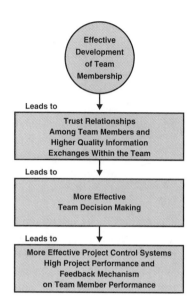

FIGURE 5–8. Team-building outcomes.

5.7 TEAM BUILDING AS AN ONGOING PROCESS

While proper attention to team building is critical during early phases of a project, it is a never-ending process. The project manager is continually monitoring team functioning and performance to see what corrective action may be needed to prevent or correct various team problems. Several barometers provide good clues of potential team dysfunctioning. First, noticeable changes in performance levels for the team and/or for individual team members should always be investigated. Such changes can be symptomatic of more serious problems (e.g., conflict, lack of work integration, communication problems, and unclear objectives). Second, the project leader and team members must be aware of the changing energy levels of team members. These changes, too, may signal more serious problems or that the team is tired and stressed. Sometimes changing the work pace, taking time off, or selling short-term targets can serve as a means to reenergize team members. More serious cases, however, can call for more drastic action (e.g., reappraising project objectives and/or the means to achieve them). Third, verbal and nonverbal clues from team members may be a source of information on team functioning. It is important to hear the needs and concerns of team members (verbal clues) and to observe how they act in carrying out their responsibilities (nonverbal clues). Finally, detrimental behavior of one team member toward another can be a signal that a problem within the team warrants attention.

We highly recommend that project leaders hold regular meetings to evaluate overall team performance and deal with team functioning problems. The focus of these meetings can be directed toward "what we are doing well as team" and "what areas need our team's attention." This approach often brings positive surprises in that the total team is informed of progress in diverse project areas (e.g., a breakthrough in technology development, a subsystem schedule met ahead of the original target, or a positive change in the client's behavior toward the project). After the positive issues have been discussed, attention should be devoted to areas needing team attention. The purpose of this part of the review session is to focus on actual or potential problem areas. The meeting leader should ask each team member for his observations on these issues. Then, an open discussion should be held to ascertain how significant the problems really are. Assumptions should, of course, be separated from the facts of each situation. Next, assignments should be agreed on for best handling of these problems. Finally, a plan for problem follow-up should be developed. The process should result in better overall performance and promote a feeling of team participation and high morale.

Over the life of a project, the problems encountered by the project team are likely to change, and as old problems are identified and solved, new ones will emerge.

In summary, effective team building is a critical determinant of project success. While the process of team building can entail frustrations and energy on the part of all concerned, the rewards can be great.

Social scientists generally agree that there are several indicators of effective and ineffective teams, which are summarized in Table 5–3.

In the next decade, we anticipate important developments in team building. As shown in Figure 5–8, these developments will lead to higher performance levels, increased morale, and a pervasive commitment to final results that can withstand almost any kind of adversity.

TABLE 5–3. EFFECTIVENESS–INEFFECTIVENESS INDICATOR

The Effective Team's Likely Characteristics	The Ineffective Team's Likely Characteristics
• High performance and task efficiency • Innovative/creative behavior • Commitment • Professional objectives of team members coincident with project requirements • Team members highly interdependent, interface effectively • Capacity for conflict resolution, but conflict encouraged when it can lead to beneficial results • Effective communication • High trust levels • Results orientation • Interest in membership • High energy levels and enthusiasm • High morale • Change orientation	• Low performance • Low commitment to project objectives • Unclear project objectives and fluid commitment levels from key participants • Unproductive gamesmanship, manipulation of others, hidden feelings, conflict avoidance at all costs • Confusion, conflict, inefficiency • Subtle sabotage, fear, disinterest, or foot-dragging • Cliques, collusion, isolation of members • Lethargy/unresponsiveness

5.8 LEADERSHIP IN A PROJECT ENVIRONMENT

Leadership can be defined as a style of behavior designed to integrate both the organizational requirements and one's personal interests into the pursuit of some objective. All managers have some sort of leadership responsibility. If time permits, successful leadership techniques and practices can be developed.

Leadership is composed of several complex elements, the three most common being:

- The person leading
- The people being led
- The situation (i.e., the project environment)

Project managers are often selected or not selected because of their leadership styles. The most common reason for not selecting an individual is his inability to balance the technical and managerial project functions. Wilemon and Cicero have defined four characteristics of this type of situation:[9]

- The greater the project manager's technical expertise, the higher his propensity to overinvolve himself in the technical details of the project.
- The greater the project manager's difficulty in delegating technical task responsibilities, the more likely it is that he will overinvolve himself in the technical details of the project (depending on his ability to do so).
- The greater the project manager's interest in the technical details of the project, the more likely it is that he will defend the project manager's role as one of a technical specialist.
- The lower the project manager's technical expertise, the more likely it is that he will overstress the nontechnical project functions (administrative functions).

There have been several surveys to determine what leadership techniques are best. The following are the results of a survey by Richard Hodgetts:[10]

- Human relations–oriented leadership techniques
  - "The project manager must make all the team members feel that their efforts are important and have a direct effect on the outcome of the program."
  - "The project manager must educate the team concerning what is to be done and how important its role is."
  - "Provide credit to project participants."
  - "Project members must be given recognition and prestige of appointment."

9. D. L. Wilemon and John P. Cicero, "The Project Manager: Anomalies and Ambiguities," *Academy of Management Journal*, Vol. 13, pp. 269–282, 1970.

10. Richard M. Hodgetts, "Leadership Techniques in Project Organizations," *Academy of Management Journal*, Vol. 11, pp. 211–219, 1968.

- "Make the team members feel and believe that they play a vital part in the success (or failure) of the team."
- "By working extremely close with my team I believe that one can win a project loyalty while to a large extent minimizing the frequency of authority-gap problems."
- "I believe that a great motivation can be created just by knowing the people in a personal sense. I know many of the line people better than their own supervisor does. In addition, I try to make them understand that they are an indispensable part of the team."
- "I would consider the most important technique in overcoming the authority-gap to be understanding as much as possible the needs of the individuals with whom you are dealing and over whom you have no direct authority."
- Formal authority–oriented leadership techniques
  - "Point out how great the loss will be if cooperation is not forthcoming."
  - "Put all authority in functional statements."
  - "Apply pressure beginning with a tactful approach and minimum application warranted by the situation and then increasing it."
  - "Threaten to precipitate high-level intervention and do it if necessary."
  - "Convince the members that what is good for the company is good for them."
  - "Place authority on full-time assigned people in the operating division to get the necessity work done."
  - "Maintain control over expenditures."
  - "Utilize implicit threat of going to general management for resolution."
  - "It is most important that the team members recognize that the project manager has the charter to direct the project."

5.9 LIFE-CYCLE LEADERSHIP

Perhaps the best model for analyzing leadership in a project management environment was developed by Hersey and Blanchard.[11] The model, as shown in Figure 5–9, is the life-cycle theory of leadership. Hersey and Blanchard contend that leadership styles must change according to the maturity of the employees, with *maturity* defined as job-related experience, willingness to accept job responsibility, and desire to achieve. This definition of maturity is somewhat different from other behavioral management definitions, which define maturity as age or emotional stability.

As shown in Figure 5–9, the subordinates enter the organization in quadrant S1, which is high task and low relationships behavior. In this quadrant, the leadership style is almost pure task-oriented behavior and is an autocratic approach,

---

11. Paul Hersey and Kenneth Blanchard, *Management of Organizational Behavior* (Englewood Cliffs, NJ: Prentice-Hall, 1979), p. 165.

TASK BEHAVIOR—
The extent to which the leader engages in defining roles i.e. telling what, how, when, where, and if more than one person, who is to do what in:
• Goal Setting
• Organizing
• Establishing Time Lines
• Directing
• Controlling

RELATIONSHIP BEHAVIOR—
The extent to which a leader engages in two-way (multi-way) communication, listening, facilitating behaviors, socioemotional support:
• Giving Support
• Communicating
• Facilitating Interactions
• Active Listening
• Providing Feedback

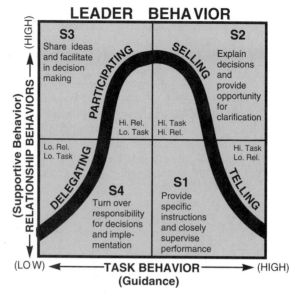

LEADER BEHAVIOR

(HIGH)

(Supportive Behavior)
RELATIONSHIP BEHAVIORS

S3
Share ideas and facilitate in decision making

PARTICIPATING

S2
Explain decisions and provide opportunity for clarification

SELLING

Hi. Rel. Lo. Task | Hi. Task Hi. Rel.

Lo. Rel. Lo. Task | Hi. Task Lo. Rel.

DELEGATING

S4
Turn over responsibility for decisions and implementation

S1
Provide specific instructions and closely supervise performance

TELLING

(LOW) ◄——— **TASK BEHAVIOR** ———► (HIGH)
(Guidance)

FOLLOWER READINESS

HIGH	MODERATE		LOW
R4	**R3**	**R2**	**R1**
Able and Willing or Confident	Able but Unwilling or Insecure	Unable but Willing or Confident	Unable and Unwilling or Insecure

FOLLOWER DIRECTED | LEADER DIRECTED

DECISION STYLES

1
Leader-Made Decision

2
Leader-Made Decision with Dialogue and/or Explanation

3
Leader & Follower-Made Decision or Follower-Made Decision with Encouragement from Leader

4
Follower-Made Decision

ABILITY: has the necessary knowlege, experience, and skill

WILLINGNESS: has the necessary confidence, commitment, motivation

When a Leader Behavior is used appropriately with its corresponding level of readiness, it is termed a High Probability Match.

FIGURE 5–9. Expanded Situational Leadership Model. Adapted from Paul Hersey, *Situational Selling* (Escondido, Calif.: Center for Leadership Studies, 1985), p. 35. Reproduced by permission of the Center for Leadership Studies.

where the leader's main concern is the accomplishment of the objective, often with very little concern for the employees or their feelings. The leader is very forceful and relies heavily on his own abilities and judgment. Other people's opinions may be of no concern. Hersey and Blanchard assume that, in the initial stage, there is anxiety, tension, and confusion among new employees, so that relationship behavior is inappropriate.

In quadrant S2, employees begin to understand their tasks and the leader tries to develop strong behavioral relationships. The development of trust and understanding between the leader and subordinates becomes a driving force for the strong behavioral relationships. However, although the leader begins utilizing behavioral relationships, there still exists a strong need for high task behavior as

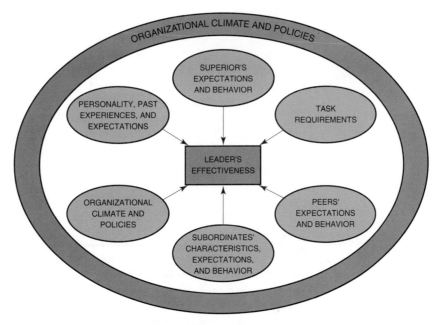

FIGURE 5–10. Personality and situational factors that influence effective leadership. *Source.* James A. F. Stoner, *Management,* 2nd ed. Englewood Cliffs, NJ: Prentice-Hall Inc. Used by permission.

well, since employees may not have achieved the level of competency to assume full responsibility.

Quadrant S3 is often regarded as pure relationship behavior, where the leader is perhaps more interested in gaining the respect of the employees than in achieving the objectives. Referent power becomes extremely important. This behavior can be characterized by delegation of authority and responsibility (often excessive), participative management, and group decision making. Hersey and Blanchard believe that, in this phase, employees no longer need directives and are knowledgeable enough about the job and self-motivated to the extent that they are willing to assume more responsibility for the task. Therefore, the leader can try to straighten his relationships with subordinates.

In quadrant S4, employees are experienced in the job, confident about their own abilities, and trusted to handle the work themselves. The leader demonstrates low task and low relationship behavior as the employees mature.

This type of life-cycle approach to leadership is extremely important to project managers, because it implies that effective leadership must be dynamic and flexible rather than static and rigid (see Figure 5–10). Effective leaders are neither pure task or relationship behavioralists, but maintain a balance between them. However, in time of crisis, a leader may be required to demonstrate a pure behavioral style or a pure task style.

In pure project management, the situation is even more complex. Line managers have *sufficient time* to develop a meaningful relationship with subordinates to the point that they get to know each other quite well. The line manager can then "train" his subordinates to adapt to the line manager's leadership style.

Project managers, on the other hand, are under a severe time constraint and may have to develop a different leadership style for each team member. To illustrate this graphically, the quadrants in Figure 5–9 should be three-dimensional, with the third axis being the life-cycle phase of the project. In other words, the leadership style is dependent not only on the situation, but on the life-cycle phase of the project.

5.10 ORGANIZATIONAL IMPACT

In most companies, whether or not project-oriented, the impact of management emphasis on the organization is well known. In the project environment there also exists a definite impact due to leadership emphasis. The leadership emphasis is best seen by employee contributions, organizational order, employee performance, and the project manager's performance:

- Contributions from People
  - A good project manager encourages active cooperation and responsible participation. The result is that both good and bad information is contributed freely.
  - A poor project manager maintains an atmosphere of passive resistance with only responsive participation. This results in information being withheld.
- Organizational Order
  - A good project manager develops policy and encourages acceptance. A low price is paid for contributions.
  - A poor project manager goes beyond policies and attempts to develop procedures and measurements. A high price is normally paid for contributions.
- Employee Performance
  - A good project manager keeps people informed and satisfied (if possible) by aligning motives with objectives. Positive thinking and cooperation are encouraged. A good project manager is willing to give more responsibility to those willing to accept it.
  - A poor project manager keeps people uninformed, frustrated, defensive, and negative. Motives are aligned with incentives rather than objectives. The poor project manager develops a "stay out of trouble" atmosphere.

- Performance of the Project Manager
  - A good project manager assumes that employee misunderstandings can and will occur, and therefore blames himself. A good project manager constantly attempts to improve and be more communicative. He relies heavily on moral persuasion.
  - A poor project manager assumes that employees are unwilling to cooperate and therefore blames subordinates. The poor project manager demands more through authoritarian attitudes and relies heavily on material incentives.

Management emphasis also impacts the organization. The following four categories show this management emphasis resulting for both good and poor project management:

- Management Problem-Solving
  - A good project manager performs his own problem-solving at the level for which he is responsible through delegation of problem-solving responsibilities.
  - A poor project manager will do subordinate problem-solving in known areas. For areas that he does not know, he requires that his approval be given prior to idea implementation.
- Organizational Order
  - A good project manager develops, maintains, and uses a single integrated management system in which authority and responsibility are delegated to the subordinates. In addition, he knows that occasional slippages and overruns will occur, and simply tries to minimize their effect.
  - A poor project manager delegates as little authority and responsibility as possible, and runs the risk of continual slippages and overruns. A poor project manager maintains two management information systems: one informal system for himself and one formal (eyewash) system simply to impress his superiors.
- Performance of People
  - A good project manager finds that subordinates willingly accept responsibility, are decisive in attitude toward the project, and are satisfied.
  - A poor project manager finds that his subordinates are reluctant to accept responsibility, are indecisive in their actions, and seem frustrated.
- Performance of the Project Manager
  - A good project manager assumes that his key people can "run the show." He exhibits confidence in those individuals working in areas in which he has no expertise, and exhibits patience with people working in areas where he has a familiarity. A good project manager is never too busy to help his people solve personal or professional problems.

- A poor project manager considers himself indispensable, is overcautious with work performed in unfamiliar areas, and becomes overly interested in work he knows. A poor project manager is always tied up in meetings.

5.11 EMPLOYEE–MANAGER PROBLEMS

The two major problem areas in the project environment are the "who has what authority and responsibility" question, and the resulting conflicts associated with the individual at the project–functional interface. Almost all project problems in some way or another involve these two major areas. Other problem areas found in the project environment include:

- The pyramidal structure
- Superior–subordinate relationships
- Departmentalization
- Scalar chain of command
- Organizational chain of command
- Power and authority
- Planning goals and objectives
- Decision making
- Reward and punishment
- Span of control

The two most common employee problems involve the assignment and resulting evaluation processes. Personnel assignments were discussed in Chapter 4. In summary:

- People should be assigned to tasks commensurate with their skills.
- Whenever possible, the same person should be assigned to related tasks.
- The most critical tasks should be assigned to the most responsible people.

The evaluation process in a project environment is difficult for an employee at the functional–project interface, especially if hostilities develop between the functional and project managers. In this situation, the interfacing employee almost always suffers owing to a poor rating by either the project manager or his supervisor. Unless the employee continually keeps his superior abreast of his performance and achievements, the supervisor must rely solely on the input received from project office personnel. This can result in a performance evaluation process that is subject to error.

Three additional questions must be answered with regard to employee evaluation:

- Of what value are job descriptions?
- How do we maintain wage and salary grades?
- Who provides training and development, especially under conditions where variable manloading can exist?

If each project is, in fact, different from all others, then it becomes an almost impossible task to develop accurate job descriptions. In many cases, wage and salary grades are functions of a unit manning document that specifies the number, type, and grade of all employees required on a given project. Although this might be a necessity in order to control costs, it also is difficult to achieve because variable manloading changes project priorities. Variable manloading creates several difficulties for project managers, especially if new employees are included. Project managers like to have seasoned veterans assigned to their activities because there generally does not exist sufficient time for proper and close supervision of the training and development of new employees. Functional managers, however, content that the training has to be accomplished on someone's project, and sooner or later all project managers must come to this realization.

On the manager level, the two most common problems involve personal values and conflicts. Personal values are often attributed to the "changing of the guard." New managers have a different sense of values from that of the older, more experienced managers. Miner identifies some of these personal values attributed to new managers:[12]

- Less trust, especially of people in positions of authority.
- Increased feelings of being controlled by external forces and events, and thus belief that they cannot control their own destinies. This is a kind of change that makes for less initiation of one's own activities and a greater likelihood of responding in terms of external pressures. There is a sense of powerlessness, although not necessarily a decreased desire for power.
- Less authoritarian and more negative attitudes toward persons holding positions of power.
- More independence, often to the point of rebelliousness and defiance.
- More freedom, less control in expressing feelings, impulses, and emotions.
- Greater inclination to live in the present and to let the future take care of itself.
- More self-indulgence.
- Moral values that are relative to the situation, less absolute, and less tied to formal religion.
- A strong and increasing identification with their peer and age groups, with the youth culture.
- Greater social concern and greater desire to help the less fortunate.

---

12. John B. Miner, "The OD-Management Development Conflict." Reprinted with permission from *Business Horizons,* December 1973, p. 32. Copyright © 1973 by the Board of Trustees at Indiana University. Used with permission.

- More negative attitude toward business, the management role in particular. A professional position is clearly preferred to managing.
- A desire to contribute less to an employing organization and to receive more from the organization.

Previously, we defined one of the attributes of a project manager as liking risks. Unfortunately, the amount of risk that today's managers are willing to accept varies not only with their personal values but also with the impact of current economic conditions and top management philosophies. If top management views a specific project as vital for the growth of the company, then the project manager may be directed to assume virtually no risks during the execution of the project. In this case the project manager may attempt to pass all responsibility to higher or lower management claiming that "his hands are tied." Wilemon and Cicero identify problems with risk identification:[13]

- The project manager's anxiety over project risk varies in relation to his willingness to accept final responsibility for the technical success of his project. Some project managers may be willing to accept full responsibility for the success or failure of their projects. Others, by contrast, may be more willing to share responsibility and risk with their superiors.
- The greater the length of stay in project management, the greater the tendency for project managers to remain in administrative positions within an organization.
- The degree of anxiety over professional obsolescence varies with the length of time the project manager spends in project management positions.

The amount of risk that managers will accept also varies with age and experience. Older, more experienced managers tend to take few risks, whereas the younger, more aggressive managers may adopt a risk-lover policy in hopes of achieving a name for themselves.

Conflicts exist at the project–functional interface regardless of how hard we attempt to structure the work. Authority and responsibility relationships can vary from project to project. In general, however, there does exist a relatively definable boundary between the project and functional manager. According to Cleland and King, this interface can be defined by the following relationships:[14]

- Project Manager
  - *What* is to be done?
  - *When* will the task be done?
  - *Why* will the task be done?
  - *How much* money is available to do the task?
  - *How well* has the total project been done?

---

13. D. L. Wilemon and John P. Cicero, "The Project Manager: Anomalies and Ambiguities," *Academy of Management Journal,* Vol. 13, 1970, pp. 269–282.

14. From David I. Cleland and William Richard King, *Systems Analysis and Project Management* (New York: McGraw-Hill), p. 237. Copyright © 1968, 1975 by McGraw-Hill, Inc. Used with permission of McGraw-Hill Book Company.

- Functional Manager
  - *Who* will do the task?
  - *Where* will the task be done?
  - *How* will the task be done?
  - *How well* has the functional input been integrated into the project?

Another difficulty arises from the way the functional manager views the proj-ect. Many functional managers consider the project as simply a means toward an end and therefore identify problems and seek solutions in terms of their immediate duties and responsibilities rather than looking beyond them. This problem also exists at the horizontal hierarchy level. The problem comes about as a result of authority and responsibility relationships, and may not have anything at all to do with the competence of the individuals concerned. This situation breeds conflicts that can also have an impact on the amount of risk that a manager wishes to accept. William Killian defined this inevitable conflict between the functional and project manager:[15]

> The conflicts revolve about items such as project priority, manpower costs, and the assignment of functional personnel to the project manager. Each project manager will, of course, want the best functional operators assigned to his project. In addition to these problems, the accountability for profit and loss is much more difficult in a matrix organization than in a project organization. Project managers have a tendency to blame overruns on functional managers, stating that the cost of the function was excessive. Whereas functional managers have a tendency to blame excessive costs on project managers with the argument that there were too many changes, more work required than defined initially, and other such arguments.

Another major trouble area is in problem reporting and resolution. Major conflicts can arise during problem resolution sessions, not only for the above-mentioned reasons, but also because the time constraints imposed on the project often prevent both parties from taking a logical approach. Project managers tend to want to make immediate decisions, after which the functional manager asserts that his way is "the only way" the problem can be resolved. One of the major causes for prolonged problem-solving is a lack of pertinent information. In order to ease potential conflicts, all pertinent information should be made available to all parties concerned as early as possible. The following information should be reported by the project manager:[16]

- The problem
- The cause
- The expected impact on schedule, budget, profit, or other pertinent area

---

15. William P. Killian, "Project Management—Future Organizational Concepts," *Marquette Business Review,* Vol. 2, 1971, pp. 90–107.

16. Russell D. Archibald, *Managing High-Technology Programs and Projects* (New York: Wiley, 1976), p. 230.

- The action taken or recommended and the results expected of that action
- What top management can do to help

5.12 MANAGEMENT PITFALLS

The project environment offers numerous opportunities for project managers and team members to get into trouble. These activities that readily create problems are referred to as management pitfalls. Lack of planning, for example, can be considered a management pitfall. Other common types of management pitfalls are:

- Lack of self-control (knowing oneself)
- Activity traps
- Managing versus doing
- People versus task skills
- Ineffective communications
- Time management
- Management bottlenecks

Knowing oneself, especially one's capabilities, strengths, and weaknesses, is the first step toward successful project management. Too often, managers will assume that they are jacks-of-all-trades and indispensable to the organization. The ultimate result is that such managers tend to "bite off more than they can chew," and then find that insufficient time exists for training additional personnel. (This, of course, assumes that the project budget provided sufficient funding for additional positions that were never utilized.)

The following lines illustrate self-concept:

> The "me" I think I am
> The "me" I wish I were
> The "me" I really am
> The "me" I try to project
> The "me" others perceive
> The "me" I used to be
> The "me" others try to make me.
> *Author unknown*

> *Four Men*
> It chanced upon a winter's night
> Safe sheltered from the weather.
> The board was spread for only one,
> Yet four men dined together.
> There sat the man I meant to be
> In glory, spurred and booted.
> And close beside him, to the right
> The man I am reputed.

The man I think myself to be
His seat was occupying
Hard by the man I really am
To hold his own was trying.
And all beneath one roof we met
Yet none called his fellow brother
No sign of recognition passed
They knew not one another.
Author unknown

Activity traps result when the means become the end, rather than the means to achieve the end. The most common activity traps are team meetings and customer technical interchange meetings. Another common activity trap is the development of special schedules and charts that cannot be used for customer reporting but are used to inform upper-level management of project status. Managers must always evaluate whether the time spent to develop these charts is worth the effort. Sign-off documents, such as manufacturing plans, provide yet another activity trap by requiring that the project manager and/or several key project team members sign off all documentation. Proper project planning and the delegation of authority and responsibility can reduce this activity trap.

We previously defined one of the characteristics of poor leadership as the inability to obtain a balance between management functions and technical functions. This can easily develop into an activity trap where the individual becomes a doer rather than a manager. Unfortunately, there often exists a very fine line between managing and doing. As an example, consider a project manager who was asked by one of his technical people to make a telephone call to assist him in solving a problem. Simply making the phone call is doing work that should be done by the project team members or even the functional manager. However, if the person being called requires that someone in absolute authority be included in the conversation, then this can be considered managing instead of doing.

There are several other cases where one must become a doer in order to be an effective manager and command the loyalty and respect of subordinates. Assume a special situation where you must schedule subordinates to work overtime, say on special holidays or even weekends. By showing up at the plant during these times, just to make a brief appearance before the people in question, you can create a better working atmosphere and understanding with the subordinates.

Another major pitfall is the decision to utilize either people skills or task skills. Is it better to utilize subordinates with whom you can obtain a good working relationship or to employ highly skilled people simply to get the job done? Obviously, the project manager would like nothing better than to have the best of both worlds. Unfortunately, this is not always possible. Consider the following situations:

- There exists a task that will take three weeks to complete. John has worked for you before, but not on such a task as this. John, however, understands how to work with you. Paul is very competent but likes to work alone. He can get the job done within constraints. Should you employ people or task skills? (Would your answer change if the task were three months instead of three weeks?)

- There exist three tasks, each one requiring two months of work. Richard has the necessary people skills to handle all three tasks, but he will not be able to do so as efficiently as a technical specialist. The alternate choice is to utilize three technical specialists.

- In both situations there should be more information made available to assist in the final decision. However, based on the amount of information given, the author prefers task skills so as not to hinder the time or performance constraints on the project. Generally speaking, for long-duration projects that require constant communications with the customer, it might be better to have permanently assigned employees who can perform a variety of tasks. Customers dislike seeing a steady stream of new faces.

- Highly technical industries are modifying the marketing function because of this distinction between people and task skills. In the past, people skills were considered to be of extreme importance in marketing technology. Today the trend is toward giving more importance to the task skill. The result has been that the project manager and project engineer must undertake marketing efforts in addition to their everyday duties. The marketing function has, therefore, moved down to middle management.

- It is often said that a good project manager must be willing to work sixty to eighty hours a week to get the job done. This might be true if he is continually fighting fires or if budgeting constraints prevent employing additional staff. The major reason, however, is the result of ineffective time management. Prime examples might include the continuous flow of paperwork, unnecessary meetings, unnecessary phone calls, and acting as a tour guide for visitors. Improper time management becomes an activity trap whereby the project manager becomes controlled by the job rather than controlling the job himself. The final result is that the project manager must work long and arduous hours in order to find time for creative thinking.

- To be effective, the project manager must establish time management rules and then ask himself four questions:
  - What am I doing that I don't have to be doing at all?
  - What am I doing that can be done better by someone else?
  - What am I doing that could be done sufficiently well by someone else?
  - Am I establishing the right priorities for my activities?
- Rules for Time Management
  - Conduct a time analysis (time log)
  - Plan solid blocks for important things
  - Classify your activities
  - Establish priorities
  - Establish opportunity cost on activities
  - Train your system (boss, subordinate, peers)

- Practice delegation
- Practice calculated neglect
- Practice management by exception
- Focus on opportunities—not on problems

This type of time management analysis can greatly reduce such proverbial "time robbers" is:

- Incomplete work
- A job poorly done (must be done over)
- Delayed decisions
- Poor communications channels
- Uncontrolled telephone calls
- Casual visitors
- Waiting for people
- Failure to delegate
- Poor retrieval system

5.13 COMMUNICATIONS

Effective project communications is needed to ensure that we get the right information to the right person at the right time and in a cost-effective manner. Typical literature definitions of effective communications include:

- An exchange of information
- An act or instance of transmitting information
- A verbal or written message
- A technique for expressing ideas effectively
- A process by which meanings are exchanged between individuals through a common system of symbols

Proper communication is vital to the success of the project. Communications is the process by which information is exchanged. Communications can be:

- Written formal
- Written informal
- Oral formal
- Oral informal (preferred by project managers)

Oral communications come with a high degree of flexibility. Oral communications use the medium of personal contact, group meetings, or the telephone. Written communications are precise. They are transmitted through the medium of correspondence (minutes, letters, memos, and reports), electronic mail, and the project management information system. Some people consider nonverbal/visual communications, such as gestures and body language, as an acceptable process.

The process selected will obviously depend on with whom we are communicating. Figures 5–11 and 5–12 show typical communications patterns. Some people consider Figure 5–11 "politically incorrect" because project managers should not be identified as talking "down" to people. Actually, it is acceptable for communications to project office personnel to be horizontal as well, since the people in the project office could easily be a higher pay grade than the project manager. Most project managers communicate laterally, whereas line managers communicate vertically downward to subordinates. Figure 5–13 shows the complete communication model. The screens or barriers are from one's perception, personality, attitudes, emotions, and prejudices.

- *Perception barriers* occur because individuals can view the same message in different ways. Factors influencing perception include the individual's level of education and region of experience. Perception problems can be minimized by using words that have precise meaning.
- *Personality and interests,* such as the likes and dislikes of individuals, affect communications. People tend to listen carefully to topics of interest but turn a deaf ear to unfamiliar or boring topics.
- *Attitudes, emotions, and prejudices* warp our sense of interpretation. Individuals who are fearful or have strong love or hate emotions will tend to protect themselves by distorting the communication process. Strong emotions rob individuals of their ability to comprehend.

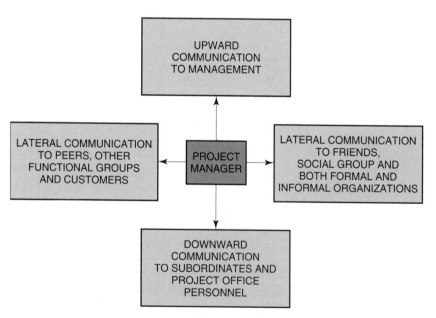

FIGURE 5–11. Communication channels. *Source.* D. I. Cleland and H. Kerzner, *Engineering Team Management* (Melbourne, Florida: Krieger, 1986), p. 39.

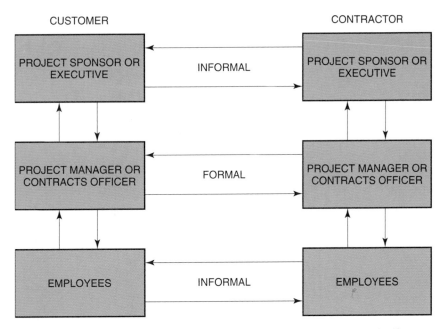

FIGURE 5–12. Customer communications. *Source.* D. I. Cleland and H. Kerzner, *Engineering Team Management* (Melbourne, Florida: Krieger, 1986), p. 64.

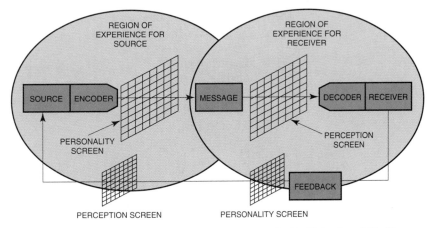

FIGURE 5–13. Total communication process. *Source.* D. I. Cleland and H. Kerzner, *Engineering Team Management* (Melbourne, Florida: Krieger, 1986), p. 46.

Typical barriers that affect the encoding process include:

- Communication goals
- Communication skills
- Frame of reference
- Sender credibility
- Needs
- Personality and interests
- Interpersonal sensitivity
- Attitude, emotion, and self-interest
- Position and status
- Assumptions (about receivers)
- Existing relationships with receivers

Typical barriers that affect the decoding process include:

- Evaluative tendency
- Preconceived ideas
- Communication skills
- Frame of reference
- Needs
- Personality and interest
- Attitudes, emotion, and self-interest
- Position and status
- Assumptions about sender
- Existing relationship with sender
- Lack of responsive feedback
- Selective listening

The receiving of information can be affected by the way the information is received. The most common ways include:

- Hearing activity
- Reading skills
- Visual activity
- Tactile sensitivity
- Olfactory sensitivity
- Extrasensory perception

The communications environment is controlled by both the internal and external forces, which can act either individually or collectively. These forces can either assist or restrict the attainment of project objectives.

Typical internal factors include:

- Power games
- Withholding information

- Management by memo
- Reactive emotional behavior
- Mixed messages
- Indirect communications
- Stereotyping
- Transmitting partial information
- Blocking or selective perception

Typical external factors include:

- The business environment
- The political environment
- The economic climate
- Regulatory agencies
- The technical state-of-the-art

The communications environment is also affected by:

- Logistics/geographic separation
- Personal contact requirements
- Group meetings
- Telephone
- Correspondence (frequency and quantity)
- Electronic mail

Noise tends to distort or destroy the information within the message. Noise results from our own personality screens, which dictate the way we present the message, and perception screens, which may cause us to "perceive" what we thought was said. Noise therefore can cause ambiguity:

- Ambiguity causes us to hear what we want to hear.
- Ambiguity causes us to hear what the group wants.
- Ambiguity causes us to relate to past experiences without being discriminatory.

In a project environment, a project manager may very well spend 90 percent or more of his or her time communicating. Typical functional applications include:

- Providing project direction
  - Decision making
  - Authorizing work
  - Directing activities
  - Negotiating
  - Reporting (including briefings)

- Attending meetings
- Overall project management
- Marketing and selling
- Public relations
- Records management
  - Minutes
  - Memos/letters/newsletters
  - Reports
  - Specifications
  - Contract documents

Project managers are required to provide briefings for both internal and external customers. Visual aids can greatly enhance a presentation. Their advantages include:

- Enlivening a presentation, which helps to capture and hold the interest of an audience.
- Adding a visual dimension to an auditory one, which permits an audience to perceive a message through two separate senses, thereby strengthening the learning process.
- Spelling out unfamiliar words by presenting pictures, diagrams, or objects, and by portraying relations graphically, which helps in introducing material that is difficult or new.
- Remaining in view much longer than oral statements can hang in the air, which can serve the same purpose as repetition in acquainting an audience with the unfamiliar and bringing back listeners who stray from the presentation.

Minutes can be classified according to their frequency of occurrence:

- The daily meeting where people work together on the same project with a common objective and reach decisions informally by general agreement.
- The weekly or monthly meeting where members work on different but parallel projects and where there is a certain competitive element and greater likelihood that the chairman will make the final decision himself or herself.
- The irregular, occasional, or special-project meeting, composed of people whose normal work does not bring them into contact and whose work has little or no relationship to that of the others. They are united only by the project the meeting exists to promote and motivated by the desire that the project succeed. Though actual voting is uncommon, every member effectively has a veto.

There are three types of written media used in organizations:

- Individually oriented media: These include letters, memos, and reports.
- Legally oriented media: These include contracts, agreements, proposals, policies, directives, guidelines, and procedures.
- Organizationally oriented media: These include manuals, forms, and brochures.

Because of the time spent in a communications mode, the project manager may very well have as his or her responsibility the process of *communications management*. Communications management is the formal or informal process of conducting or supervising the exchange of information either upward, downward, laterally or diagonally. In short, the main business of project managers may be communications. There appears to be a direct correlation between the project manager's ability to manage the communications process and project performance.

The communications process is more than simply conveying a message; it is also a source for control. Proper communications let the employees in on the act because employees need to know and understand. Communication must convey both information and motivation. The problem, therefore, is how to communicate. Below are six simple steps:

- Think through what you wish to accomplish.
- Determine the way you will communicate.
- Appeal to the interest of those affected.
- Give playback on ways others communicate to you.
- Get playback on what you communicate.
- Test effectiveness through reliance on others to carry out your instructions.

Knowing how to communicate does not guarantee that a clear message will be generated. There are techniques that can be used to improve communications. These techniques include:

- Obtaining feedback, possibly in more than one form
- Establishing multiple communications channels
- Using face-to-face communications if possible
- Determining how sensitive the receiver is to your communications
- Being aware of symbolic meaning such as expressions on people's faces
- Communicating at the proper time
- Reinforcing words with actions
- Using a simple language
- Using redundancy (i.e., saying it two different ways) whenever possible

Techniques can vary from project to project. For example, on one project the customer may require that all test data be made available, in writing, as soon as testing occurs and possibly before your own people have had a chance to examine the results. This type of clear and open communication cannot exist indefinitely because the customer might form his own opinion of the data before hearing the project office position. Similarly, project managers should not expect functional managers to provide them with immediate raw test data until functional analysis is conducted.

With every effort to communicate there are always barriers. The barriers include:

- Receiver hearing what he wants to hear. This results from people doing the same job so long that they no longer listen.
- Sender and receiver having different perceptions. This is vitally important in interpreting contractual requirements, statements of work, and proposal information requests.
- Receiver evaluating the source before accepting the communications.
- Receiver ignoring conflicting information and doing as he pleases.
- Words meaning different things to different people.
- Communicators ignoring nonverbal cues.
- Receiver being emotionally upset.

The scalar chain of command can also become a barrier with regard to in-house communications. The project manager must have the authority to go to the general manager or counterpart to communicate effectively. Without direct upward communication, it is possible that filters can develop such that the final message gets distorted.

Three important conclusions can be drawn about communications techniques and barriers:

- Don't assume that the message you sent will be received in the form you sent it.
- The swiftest and most effective communications take place among people with common points of view. The manager who fosters good relationships with his associates will have little difficulty in communicating with them.
- Communications must be established early in the project.

Communication problems in project management require answering the following three questions:

- What are the channels of communication?
- What information is really important?
- Will I be punished for bringing forth bad news?

In a project environment, communications are often filtered. There are several reasons for the filtering of upward communications:

- Unpleasantness for the sender
- Receiver cannot obtain information from any other source
- To embarrass a superior
- Lack of mobility or status for the sender
- Insecurity
- Mistrust

Information filtering can occur through:

- Methods
- Blocking
- Withholding
- Partial transmittal

Communication is also listening. Good project managers must be willing to listen to their employees, both professionally and personally. The advantages of listening properly are that:

- Subordinates know you are sincerely interested
- You obtain feedback
- Employee acceptance is fostered.

The successful manager must be willing to listen to an individual's story from beginning to end, without interruptions. The manager must be willing to see the problem through the eyes of the subordinate. Finally, before making a decision, the manager should ask the subordinate for his solutions to the problem.

Project managers should ask themselves four questions:

- Do I make it easy for employees to talk to me?
- Am I sympathetic to their problems?
- Do I attempt to improve human relations?
- Do I make an extra effort to remember names and faces?

The project manager's communication skills and personality screen often dictates the communication style. Typical communication styles include:

- Authoritarian: gives expectations and specific guidance
- Promotional: cultivates team spirit
- Facilitating: gives guidance as required, noninterfering
- Conciliatory: friendly and agreeable, builds compatible team
- Judicial: uses sound judgment
- Ethical: honest, fair, by the book

- Secretive: not open or outgoing (to project detriment)
- Disruptive: breaks apart unity of group, agitator
- Intimidating: "tough guy," can lower morale
- Combative: eager to fight or be disagreeable

Team meetings are supposedly meetings of the mind where information-giving, receiving, and listening take place. Team meetings must be effective, or else they become time management pitfalls. It is the responsibility of the project manager to ensure that meetings are valuable and necessary for the exchange of information. The following are general guides for conducting a more effective meeting:

- Start on time. If you wait for people, you reward tardy behavior.
- Develop agenda "objectives." Generate a list and proceed; avoid getting hung up on the order of topics.
- Conduct one piece of business at a time.
- Allow each member to contribute in his own way. Support, challenge, and counter; view differences as helpful; dig for reasons or views.
- Silence does not always mean agreement. Seek opinions: "What's your opinion on this, Peggy?"
- Be ready to confront the verbal member: "Okay, we've heard from Mike on this matter; now how about some other views?"
- Test for readiness to make a decision.
- Make the decision.
- Test for commitment to the decision.
- Assign roles and responsibilities (only after decision making).
- Agree on follow-up or accountability dates.
- Indicate the next step for this group.
- Set the time and place for the next meeting.
- End on time.
- Was the meeting necessary?

Team meetings quite often provide individuals with means of exhibiting suppressed ideas. The following three humorous quotations identify these:

- "In any given meeting, when all is said and done, 90 percent will be said—10 percent will be done."—Orben's *Current Comedy*
- "A committee meeting provides a great chance for some people who like to hear their own voices talk and talk, while others draw crocodiles or a lady's legs. It also prevents the men who can think and make quick decisions from doing so."—Lin Yutang, *The Pleasures of Nonconformist (World)*
- "Having served on various committees, I have drawn up a list of rules: Never arrive on time or you will be stamped a beginner. Don't say anything until the meeting is half over; this stamps you as being wise. Be as

TABLE 5–4. COMMUNICATIONS POLICY

Program Manager	Functional Manager	Relationship
The program manager utilizes existing authorized communications media to the maximum extent rather than create new ones.		Communications up, down, and laterally are essential elements to the success of programs in a multiprogram organization, and to the morale and motivation of supporting functional organizations. In principle, communication from the program manager should be channeled through the program team member to functional managers.
Approves program plans, subdivided work description, and/or work authorizations, and schedules defining specific program requirements.	Assures his organization's compliance with all such program direction received.	Program definition must be within the scope of the contract as expressed in the program plan and work breakdown structure.
Signs correspondence that provides program direction to functional organizations. Signs correspondence addressed to the customer that pertains to the program except that which has been expressly assigned by the general manager, the function organizations, or higher management in accordance with division policy.	Assures his organization's compliance with all such program direction received. Functional manager provides the program manager with copies of all "Program" correspondence released by his organization that may affect program performance. Ensures that the program manager is aware of correspondence with unusual content, on an exception basis, through the cognizant program team member or directly if such action is warranted by the gravity of the situation.	In the program manager's absence, the signature authority is transferred upward to his reporting superior unless an acting program manager has been designated. Signature authority for correspondence will be consistent with established division policy.
Reports program results and accomplishments to the customer and to the general manager, keeping them informed of significant problems and events.	Participates in program reviews, being aware of and prepared in matters related to his functional specialty. Keeps his line or staff management and cognizant program team member informed of significant problems and events relating to any program in which his personnel are involved.	Status reporting is the responsibility of functional specialists. The program manager utilizes the specialist organizations. The specialists retain their own channels to the general manager but must keep the program manager informed.

283

vague as possible; this prevents irritating the others. When in doubt, suggest that a subcommittee be appointed. Be the first to move for adjournment; this will make you popular—it's what everyone is waiting for."—Harry Chapman, quoted in *Think*

Many times, company policies and procedures can be established for the development of communications channels for project personnel. Table 5–4 illustrates such communications guidelines.

5.14 PROJECT REVIEW MEETINGS

Project review meetings are necessary to convince key personnel that orderly progress is being made on a project. There are three types of review meetings:

- Project team review meetings
- Executive management review meetings
- Customer project review meetings

Most projects have weekly, bimonthly, or monthly meetings in order to keep the project manager and his team informed about the project's status. These meetings are flexible and should be called only if positive benefits will result. Team meetings should not be called just for the sake of having meetings. Having both too many or too few meetings can prove detrimental.

Executive management has the right to require monthly status review meetings. However, if the project manager believes that other meeting dates are better (because they occur at a point where progress can be identified), then he should request changes in date from top management.

Customer review meetings are often the most critical and most inflexibly scheduled. Every attempt must be made to adhere to the requirements for such meetings. Project managers often overlook the fact that their project is simply one of several interrelated projects for the customer. Project managers must allow time to prepare handouts and literature well in advance of the meeting. This preparation and/or travel time must be accounted for in the budget.

5.15 PROJECT MANAGEMENT BOTTLENECKS

Poor communications can easily produce communications bottlenecks. These bottlenecks can occur in both the parent and client organizations. The most common bottleneck occurs when all communications between the customer and the parent organization must flow through the project office. There are two major disadvantages to this type of arrangement. First, requiring that all information pass through the project office may be a necessity but develops slow reaction times. Second, regardless of the qualifications of the project office members, the client always fears that the information he receives will be "filtered" prior to disclosure.

Customers not only like firsthand information, but also prefer that their technical specialists be able to communicate directly with the parent organization's technical specialists. Many project managers dislike this arrangement, for they fear that the technical specialists may say or do something contrary to project strategy or thinking. These fears can be allayed by telling the customer that this situation will be permitted if, and only if, the customer realizes that the remarks made by the technical specialists do not, in any way, shape, or form, reflect the position of the project office or company. Furthermore, only the project office can authorize commitment of resources or the providing of information for a customer request. This will alleviate the necessity for having a project representative present during all discussions, but will require that records be provided to the project office of all communications with the customer.

For long-duration projects the customer may require that the contractor have an established customer representative office in the contractor's facilities. The idea behind this is sound in that all information to the customer must flow through the customer's project office at the contractor's facility. This creates a problem in that it attempts to sever direct communications channels between the customer and contractor project managers. The result is that in many situations, the establishment of a local project office is merely an eyewash situation to satisfy contractual requirements, whereas actual communications go from customer to contractor as though the local project office did not exist. This creates an antagonistic local customer project office.

The last bottleneck to be discussed occurs when the customer's project manager considers himself to be in a higher position than the contractor's project manager and, therefore, seeks some higher authority with which to communicate. As an example, the customer has a $130 million program and subcontracts $5 million out to you. Even though you are the project manager and report to either the vice president and general manager or the director of program management, the customer's project manager may wish to communicate directly with the vice president or one of the directors. Project managers who seek status can often jeopardize the success of the project by creating rigid communications channels.

Figure 5–14 identifies why communications bottlenecks such as these occur. There almost always exist a minimum of two paths for communications flow to and from the customer. Many times, strategic project planning is accomplished between the customer and contractor at a level above the respective project managers. This type of situation can have a strongly demoralizing effect.

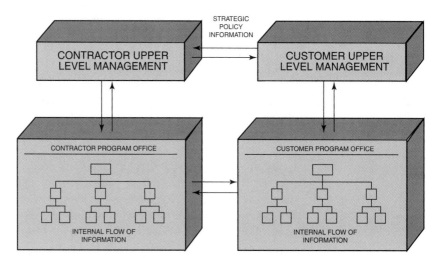

FIGURE 5–14. Information flow pattern from contractor program office.

5.16 COMMUNICATION TRAPS

Projects are run by communications. The work is defined by the communications tool known as the work breakdown structure. Actually, this is the easy part of communications, where everything is well defined. Unfortunately, project managers cannot document everything they wish to say or relate to other people, regardless of the level in the company. The worst possible situation occurs when an outside customer loses faith in the contractor. When a situation of mistrust prevails, the logical sequence of events would be:

- More documentation
- More interchange meetings
- Customer representation on your site

In each of these situations, the project manager becomes severely overloaded with work. This situation can also occur in-house when a line manager begins to mistrust a project manager, or vice versa. There may suddenly appear an exponential increase in the flow of paperwork, and everyone is writing "protection" memos. Previously, everything was verbal.

Communication traps occur most frequently with customer–contractor relationships. The following are examples of this:

- Phase I of the program has just been completed successfully. The customer, however, was displeased because he had to wait three weeks to a month after all tests were completed before the data were presented. For

Phase II, the customer is insisting that his people be given the raw data at the same time your people receive it.

● The customer is unhappy with the technical information that is being given by the project manager. As a result, he wants his technical people to be able to communicate with your technical people on an individual basis without having to go through the project office.

● You are a subcontractor to a prime contractor. The prime contractor is a little nervous about what information you might present during a technical interchange meeting where the customer will be represented, and therefore wants to review all material before the meeting.

● You are a subcontractor to a prime contractor. During negotiations between the customer and the prime contractor, your phone rings. You find out that it is the customer asking for certain information.

● The customer has asked to have a customer representative office set up in the same building as the project office.

● During an interchange meeting with the customer, one of your company's functional employees presents data to the customer and concludes with the remarks, "I personally disagree with our company's solution to this problem, and I think that the company is all wet in their approach. Let me show you my solution to this problem."

● Functional employees are supposed to be experts. In front of the customer (or even your top management) an employee makes a statement that you, the project manager, do not believe is completely true or accurate.

● On Tuesday morning, the customer's project manager calls your project manager and asks him a question. On Tuesday afternoon, the customer's project engineer calls your project engineer and asks him the same question.

Communication traps can also occur between the project office and line managers. Below are several examples:

● The project manager can hold too many "useless" team meetings.
● The project manager can hold too few team meetings.
● People refuse to make decisions, and ultimately the team meetings are flooded with agenda items that are irrelevant.
● Last month, Larry completed an assignment as an assistant project manager on an activity where the project manager kept him continuously informed as to project status. Now, Larry is working for a project manager who tells him only what he needs to know to get the job done.

In a project environment, the line manager is not part of any project team; otherwise he would spend forty hours per week simply attending team meetings. Therefore, how does the line manager learn of the true project status? Written memos will not do it. The information must come firsthand from either the project manager or the assigned functional employee. Line managers would rather hear it from the project manager because line employees have the tendency to censor bad news from the respective line manager. Line managers must be provided true status by the project office. Consider the following example:

> John is a functional support manager with fourteen highly competent individuals beneath him. John's main concern is performance. He has a tendency to leave scheduling and cost problems up to the project managers. During the past two months, John has intermittently received phone calls and casual visits from upper-level management and senior executives asking him about his department's costs and schedules on a variety of projects. Although he can answer almost all of the performance questions, he has found great difficulty in responding to time and cost questions. John is a little nervous that if this situation continues it may affect his evaluation and merit pay increase.

Sometimes, project managers expect too much from their employees during problem-solving or brainstorming sessions, and communications become inhibited. There are several possible causes for having unproductive team meetings:

- Because of superior–subordinate relationships (i.e., pecking orders), creativity is inhibited.
- Criticism and ridicule have a tendency to inhibit spontaneity.
- Pecking orders, unless adequately controlled, can inhibit teamwork and problem solving.
- All seemingly crazy or unconventional ideas are ridiculed and eventually discarded. Contributors do not wish to contribute anything further.
- Many lower-level people, who could have good ideas to contribute, feel inferior and, therefore, refuse to contribute.
- Meetings are dominated by upper-level management personnel.
- The meetings are held at an inappropriate place and time.
- Many people are not given adequate notification of meeting time and subject matter.

5.17 PROVERBS

Below are twenty project management proverbs that show you what can go wrong:[17]

- You cannot produce a baby in one month by impregnating nine women.
- The same work under the same conditions will be estimated differently by ten different estimators or by one estimator at ten different times.
- The most valuable and least used word in a project manager's vocabulary is "NO."

---

17. Source unknown.

- You can con a sucker into committing to an unreasonable deadline, but you can't bully him into meeting it.
- The more ridiculous the deadline, the more it costs to try to meet it.
- The more desperate the situation, the more optimistic the situatee.
- Too few people on a project can't solve the problems—too many create more problems than they solve.
- You can freeze the user's specs but he won't stop expecting.
- Frozen specs and the abominable snowman are alike: They are both myths, and they both melt when sufficient heat is applied.
- The conditions attached to a promise are forgotten, and the promise is remembered.
- What you don't know hurts you.
- A user will tell you anything you ask about—nothing more.
- Of several possible interpretations of a communication, the least convenient one is the only correct one.
- What is not on paper has not been said.
- No major project is ever installed on time, within budget, with the same staff that started it.
- Projects progress quickly until they become 90 percent complete; then they remain at 90 percent complete forever.
- If project content is allowed to change freely, the rate of change will exceed the rate of progress.
- No major system is ever completely debugged; attempts to debug a system inevitably introduce new bugs that are even harder to find.
- Project teams detest progress reporting because it vividly demonstrates their lack of progress.
- Parkinson and Murphy are alive and well—in your project.

5.18 MANAGEMENT POLICIES AND PROCEDURES

Although project managers have the authority and responsibility to establish project policies and procedures, they must fall within the general guidelines established by top management. Table 5–5 identifies sample top-management guidelines. Guidelines can also be established for planning, scheduling, controlling, and communications.

PROBLEMS

5–1 A project manager finds that he does not have direct reward power over salaries, bonuses, work assignments, or project funding for members of the project team with whom he interfaces. Does this mean that he is totally deficient in reward power? Explain your answer.

TABLE 5–5. FALLS ENGINEERING ORGANIZATIONAL CHART

Program Manager	Functional Manager	Relationship
The program manager is responsible for overall program direction, control, and coordination; and is the principal contact with the program management of the customer.	The functional organization managers are responsible for supporting the program manager in the performance of the contract(s) and in accordance with the terms of the contract(s) and are accountable to their cognizant managers for the total performance.	The program manager determines what will be done: he obtains, through the assigned program team members, the assistance and concurrence of the functional support organizations in determining the definitive requirements and objectives of the program.
To achieve the program objectives, the program manager utilizes the services of the functional organizations in accordance with the prescribed division policies and procedures affecting the functional organizations.		The functional organizations determine *how* the work will be done.
He establishes program and technical policy as defined by management policy.	The functional support organizations perform all work within their functional areas for all programs within the cost, schedule, quality, and specifications established by contract for the program so as to assist the program manager in achieving the program objectives.	The program manager operates within prescribed division policies and procedures except where requirements of a particular program necessitate deviations or modifications as approved by the general manager. The functional support organizations provide strong, aggressive support to the program managers.
The program manager is responsible for the progress being made as well as the effectiveness of the total program.		
Integrates research, development, production, procurement, quality assurance, product support, test, and financial and contractual aspects.		
Approves detailed performance specifications, pertinent physical characteristics, and functional design criteria to meet the program's development or operational requirements.	The functional support organization management seeks out or initiates innovations, methods, improvements, or other means that will enable that function to better schedule commitments, reduce cost, improve quality, or otherwise render exemplary performance as approved by the program manager.	The program manager relies on the functional support program team members for carrying out specific program assignments.
Ensures preparation of, and approves, overall plan, budgets, and work statements essential to the integration of system elements.		Program managers and the functional support program team members are jointly responsible for ensuring that unresolved conflicts between requirements levied on functional organizations by different program managers are brought to the attention of
Directs the preparation and maintenance of a time, cost, and performance schedule to ensure the orderly progress of the program.		

Coordinates and approves subcontract work statement, schedules, contract type, and price for major "buy" items.

Coordinates and approves vendor evaluation and source selections in conjunction with procurement representative to the program team.

Program decision authority rests with the program manager for all matters relating to his assigned program, consistent with division policy and the responsibilities assigned by the general manager.

management.

Program managers do not make decisions that are the responsibility of the functional support organizations as defined in division policies and procedures and/or as assigned by the general manager.

Functional organization managers do not request decisions of a program manager that are not within the program manager's delineated authority and responsibility and that do not affect the requirements of the program.

Functional organizations do not make program decisions that are the responsibility of the program manager.

Joint participation in problem solution is essential to providing satisfactory decisions that fulfill overall program and company objectives, and is accomplished by the program manager and the assigned program team members.

In arriving at program decisions, the program manager obtains the assistance and concurrence of cognizant functional support managers, through the cognizant program team member, since they are held accountable for their support of each program and for overall division functional performance.

5–2 For each of the remarks made below, what types of interpersonal influences could exist?

    a. "I've had good working relations with department X. They like me and I like them. I can usually push through anything ahead of schedule."

    b. A research scientist was temporarily promoted to project management for an advanced state-of-the-art effort. He was overheard making the following remark to a team member: "I know it's contrary to department policy, but the test must be conducted according to these criteria or else the results will be meaningless."

5–3 Do you agree or disagree that scientists and engineers are likely to be more creative if they feel that they have sufficient freedom in their work? Can this condition backfire?

5–4 Should the amount of risk and uncertainty in the project have a direct bearing on how much authority is granted to a project manager?

5–5 Some projects are directed by project managers who have only monitoring authority. These individuals are referred to as influence project managers. What kind of projects would be under their control? What organizational structure might be best for this?

5–6 As a project nears termination, the project manager may find that the functional people are more interested in finding a new role for themselves than in giving their best to the current situation. How does this relate to Maslow's hierarchy of needs, and what should the project manager do?

5–7 Richard M. Hodgetts ("Leadership Techniques in the Project Organization," *Academy of Management Journal,* June 1968, pp. 211–219) conducted a survey on aerospace, chemical, construction, and state government workers as to whether they would rate the following leadership techniques as very important, important, or not important:

- Negotiation
- Personality and/or persuasive ability
- Competence
- Reciprocal favors

How do you think each industry answered the questionnaires?

5–8 Robert D. Doering ("An Approach Toward Improving the Creative Output of Scientific Task Teams," *IEEE Transactions on Engineering Management,* February 1973, pp. 29–31, © 1973 IEEE) commented that:

> The team leader's role is crucial. He is directly involved and must know the individual team members well, not only in terms of their technical capabilities but also in terms of how they function when addressing a problem as part of a group. The technical competence of a potential team member can usually be determined from information about previous assignments, but it is not so easy to predict and control the individual's interaction within and with a new group, since it is related to the psychological and social behavior of each of the other members of the group as a whole. What the leader needs is a tool to measure and characterize the individual members so that he can predict their interactions and structure his task team accordingly.

Is such a test possible for people working in a project environment? Are there any project organizational forms that would be conducive for such testing?

5–9 Project managers consider authority and funding as being very important in gaining support. Functional personnel, however, prefer friendship and work assignments. How can these two outlooks be related to the theories of Maslow and McGregor?

5–10 Lloyd A. Rogers ("Guidelines for Project Management Teams," *Industrial Engineering,* December 1974, p. 12. Published and copyright 1974 by the Institute of Industrial Engineers, 25 Technology Park, Norcross, GA 30092) has commented that:

> The technical planners, whether they are engineers or systems analysts, must be experts at designing the system, but seldom do they recognize the need to "put on another hat" when system design specifications are completed and design the project control or implementation plan. If this it not done, setting a project completion target date or a set of management checkpoint milestones is done by guesswork at best. Management will set the checkpoint milestones, and the technical planners will hope they can meet the schedule.

How can this planning problem be effectively resolved on a continuing basis?

5–11 What kind of working relationships would result if the project manager had more reward power than the functional managers?

5–12 For each of the following remarks, state the possible situation and accompanying assumptions that you would make.

    a. "A good project manager should manage by focusing on keeping people happy."
    b. "A good project manager must be willing to manage tension."
    c. "The responsibility for the success or failure rests with upper-level management. This is their baby."
    d. Remarks by functional employee: "What if I fail on this project? What can he (the project manager) do to me?"

5–13 Can each of the following situations lead to failure?

    a. Lack of expert power
    b. Lack of referent power
    c. Lack of reward and punishment power
    d. Not having sufficient authority

5–14 One of your people comes into your office and states that he has a technical problem and would like your assistance by making a phone call.

    a. Is this managing or doing?
    b. Does your answer depend on who must be called? (That is, is it possible that authority relationships may have to be considered?)

5–15 On the LRC, can we structure the responsibility column to primary and secondary responsibilities?

5–16 Discuss the meaning of each of the two poems listed below:

> We shall have to evolve
> Problem solvers galore
> Since each problem they solve
> Creates ten problems more.
> *Author unknown*

> Jack and Jill went up the hill
>   To fetch a pail of water
> Jack fell down and broke his crown
>   And Jill came tumbling after.

> Jack could have avoided this awful lump
>   By seeking alternative choices
> Like installing some pipe and a great big pump
>   And handing Jill the invoices.[18]

5–17 What is the correct way for a project manager to invite line managers to attend team meetings?

5–18 Can a project manager sit and wait for things to happen, or should he cause things to happen?

5–19 The company has just hired a fifty-four-year-old senior engineer who holds two masters degrees in engineering disciplines. The engineer is quite competent and has worked well as a loner for the past twenty years. This same engineer has just been assigned to the R&D phase of your project. You, as project manager or project engineer, must make sure that this engineer works as a team member with other functional employees, not as a loner. How do you propose to accomplish this? If the individual persist in wanting to be a loner, should you fire him?

5–20 Suppose the linear responsibility chart is constructed with the actual names of the people involved, rather than just their titles. Should this chart be given to the customer?

5–21 How should a functional manager handle a situation where the project manager:

  a. Continually cries wolf concerning some aspect of the project when, in fact, the problem either does not exist or is not as severe as the project manager makes it out to be?
  b. Refuses to give up certain resources that are no longer needed on the project?

5–22 How do you handle a project manager or project engineer who continually tries to "bite off more than he can chew?" If he were effective at doing this, at least temporarily, would your answer change?

---

18. Stacer Holcomb, OSD (SA), as quoted in *The C/E Newsletter,* publication of the cost effectiveness section of the Operations Research Society of America, Vol. 2, No. 1, January 1967.

5–23 A functional manager says that he has fifteen people assigned to work on your project next week (according to the project plan and schedule). Unfortunately, you have just learned that the prototype is not available and that these fifteen people will have nothing to do. Now what? Who is at fault?

5–24 Manpower requirements indicate that a specific functional pool will increase sharply from eight to seventeen people over the next two weeks and then drop back to eight people. Should you question this?

5–25 Below are several sources from which legal authority can be derived. State whether each source provides the project manager with sufficient authority from which he can effectively manage the project.

    a. The project or organizational charter
    b. The project manager's position in the organization
    c. The job description and specifications for project managers
    d. Policy documents
    e. The project manager's "executive" rank
    f. Dollar value of the contract
    g. Control of funds

5–26 Is this managing or doing?[19]

MANAGING	DOING	
_____	_____	1. Making a call with one of your people to assist him in solving a technical problem.
_____	_____	2. Signing a check to approve a routine expenditure.
_____	_____	3. Conducting the initial screening interview of a job applicant.
_____	_____	4. Giving one of your experienced people your solution to a new problem without first asking for his recommendation.
_____	_____	5. Giving your solution to a recurring problem that one of your new people has just asked you about.
_____	_____	6. Conducting a meeting to explain to your people a new procedure.
_____	_____	7. Phoning a department to request help in solving a problem that one of your people is trying to solve.
_____	_____	8. Filling out a form to give one of your people a pay increase.
_____	_____	9. Explaining to one of your people why he is receiving a merit pay increase.
_____	_____	10. Deciding whether to add a position.

---

19. From Raymond O. Leon, *Manage More by Doing Less* (New York: McGraw-Hill), p. 4. Copyright © 1971 by McGraw-Hill, Inc., New York. Used with permission of McGraw-Hill Book Company.

_____	_____	11. Asking one of your people what he thinks about an idea you have that will affect your people.
_____	_____	12. Transferring a desirable assignment from employee A to employee B because employee A did not devote the necessary effort.
_____	_____	13. Reviewing regular written reports to determine your people's progress toward their objectives.
_____	_____	14. Giving a regular progress report by phone to your supervisor.
_____	_____	15. Giving a tour to an important visitor from outside of your organization.
_____	_____	16. Drafting an improved layout of facilities.
_____	_____	17. Discussing with your key people the extent to which they should use staff services during the next year.
_____	_____	18. Deciding what your expense-budget request will be for your area of responsibility.
_____	_____	19. Attending a professional or industrial meeting to learn detailed technical developments.
_____	_____	20. Giving a talk on your work activities to a local community group.

5–27 Below are three broad statements describing the functions of management. For each statement, are we referring to upper-level management, project management, or functional management?

   a. Acquire the best available assets and try to improve them.
   b. Provide a good working environment for all personnel.
   c. Make sure that all resources are applied effectively and efficiently such that all constraints are met, if possible.

5–28 Decide whether you agree or disagree that, in the management of people, the project manager:

   ● Must convert mistakes into learning experiences.
   ● Acts as the lubricant that eases the friction (i.e., conflicts) between the functioning parts.

5–29 Functional employees are supposed to be the experts. A functional employee makes a statement that the project manager does not believe is completely true or accurate. Should the project manager support the team member? If so, for how long? Does your answer depend on who the remarks are being addressed to, such as upper-level management or the customer? At what point should a project manager stop supporting his team members?

5–30 Below are four statements: two statements describe a function, and two others describe a purpose. Which statements refer to project management and which refer to functional management?

- Function
  - Reduce or eliminate uncertainty
  - Minimize and assess risk
- Purpose
  - Create the environment (using transformations)
  - Perform decision making in the transformed environment

5–31 Manager A is a department manager with thirty years of experience in the company. For the last several years, he has worn two hats and acted as both project manager and functional manager on a variety of projects. He is an expert in his field. The company has decided to incorporate formal project management and has established a project management department. Manager B, a thirty-year-old employee with three years of experience with the company, has been assigned as project manager. In order to staff his project, manager B has requested from manager A that manager C (a personal friend of manager B) be assigned to the project as the functional representative. Manager C is twenty-six years old and has been with the company for two years. Manager A agrees to the request and informs manager C of his new assignment, closing with the remarks, "This project is yours all the way. I don't want to have anything to do with it. I'll be too busy with paperwork as the result of our new organizational structure. Just send me a memo once in a while telling me what's happening."

During the project kickoff meeting it became obvious to both manager B and manager C that the only person with the necessary expertise was manager A. Without the support of manager A, the time duration for project completion could be expected to double.

This situation is ideal for role playing. Put yourself in the place of managers A, B, and C and discuss the reasons for your actions. How can this problem be overcome? How do you get manager A to support the project? Who should inform upper-level management of this situation? When should upper-level management be informed? Would any of your answers change if manager B and manager C were not close friends?

5–32 Is it possible for a product manager to have the same degree of tunnel vision that a project manager has? If so, under what circumstances?

5–33 Your company has a policy that employees can participate in an educational tuition reimbursement program, provided that the degree obtained will benefit the company and that the employee's immediate support gives his permission. As a project manager, you authorize George, your assistant project manager who reports directly to you, to take courses leading to an MBA degree.

Midway through your project, you find that overtime is required on Monday and Wednesday evenings, the same two evenings that George has classes. George cannot change the evenings that his classes are offered. You try without success to reschedule the overtime to early mornings or other evenings. According to company policy, the project office must supervise all overtime. Since the project office consists of only you and George, you must perform the overtime if George does not. How should you handle this situation? Would your answer change if you thought that George might leave the company after receiving his degree?

5–34 Establishing good interface relationships between the project manager and functional manager can take a great deal of time, especially during the conversion from a traditional to a project organizational form. Below are five statements that represent the different stages in the development of a good interface relationship. Place these statements in the proper order and discuss the meaning of each one.

  a. The project manager and functional manager meet face-to-face and try to work out the problem.
  b. Both the project and functional managers deny that any problems exist between them.
  c. The project and functional managers begin formally and informally to anticipate the problems that can occur.
  d. Both managers readily admit responsibility for several of the problems.
  e. Each manager blames the other for the problem.

5–35 John is a functional support manager with fourteen highly competent individuals beneath him. John's main concern is performance. He has a tendency to leave scheduling and cost problems up to the project managers. During the past two months, John has intermittently received phone calls and casual visits from upper-level management and senior executives asking him about his department's costs and schedules on a variety of projects. Although he can answer almost all of the performance questions, he has experienced great difficulty in responding to time and cost questions. John is a little apprehensive that if this situation continues, it may affect his evaluation and merit pay increase. What are John's alternatives?

5–36 Projects have a way of providing a "chance for glory" for many individuals. Unfortunately, they quite often give the not-so-creative individual an opportunity to demonstrate his incompetence. Examples would include the designer who always feels that he has a better way of laying out a blueprint, or the individual who intentionally closes a door when asked to open it, or vice versa. How should a project manager handle this situation? Would your answer change if the individual were quite competent but always did the opposite just to show his individuality? Should these individuals be required to have close supervision? If close supervision is required, should it be the responsibility of the functional manager, the project office, or both?

5–37 Are there situations in which a project manager can wait for long-term changes instead of an immediate response to actions?

5–38 Is it possible for functional employees to have performed a job so long or so often that they no longer listen to the instructions given by the project or functional managers?

5–39 On Tuesday morning, the customer's project manager calls the subcontractor's project manager and asks him a question. On Tuesday afternoon, the customer's project engineer calls the contractor's project engineer and asks him the same question. How do you account for this? Could this be "planned" by the customer?

5–40 Below are eight common methods that project and functional employees can use to provide communications:

  a. Counseling sessions   e. Project office memo
  b. Telephone conversation   f. Project office directive
  c. Individual conversation   g. Project team meeting
  d. Formal letter   h. Formal report

For each of the following actions, select one and only one means of communication from the above list that you would utilize in accomplishing the action:

1. Defining the project organizational structure to functional managers
2. Defining the project organizational structure to team members
3. Defining the project organizational structure to executives
4. Explaining to a functional manager the reasons for conflict between his employee and your assistant project managers
5. Requesting overtime because of schedule slippages
6. Reporting an employee's violation of company policy
7. Reporting an employee's violation of project policy
8. Trying to solve a functional employee's grievance
9. Trying to solve a project office team member's grievance
10. Directing employees to increase production
11. Directing employees to perform work in a manner that violates company policy
12. Explaining the new indirect project evaluation system to project team members
13. Asking for downstream functional commitment of resources
14. Reporting daily status to executives or the customer
15. Reporting weekly status to executives or the customer
16. Reporting monthly or quarterly status to executives or the customer
17. Explaining the reason for the cost overrun
18. Establishing project planning guidelines
19. Requesting a vice president to attend your team meeting
20. Informing functional managers of project status
21. Informing functional team members of project status
22. Asking a functional manager to perform work not originally budgeted for
23. Explaining customer grievances to your people
24. Informing employees of the results of customer interchange meetings
25. Requesting that a functional employee be removed from your project because of incompetence

5–41 Last month, Larry completed an assignment as chief project engineering on project X. It was a pleasing assignment. Larry, and all of the other project personnel, were continually kept informed (by the project manager) concerning all project activities. Larry is now working for a new project manager who tells his staff only what they have to know in order to get their job done. What can Larry do about this situation? Can this be a good situation?

5–42 Phase I of a program has just been completed successfully. The customer, however, was displeased because he always had to wait three weeks to a month after all tests were complete before data were supplied by the contractor.

For Phase II of the program, the customer is requiring that advanced quality control procedures be adhered to. This permits the customer's quality control people to observe all testing and obtain all of the raw data at the same time the contractor does. Is there anything wrong with this arrangement?

5–43 You are a subcontractor to company Z, who in turn is the prime contractor to company Q. Before any design review or technical interchange meeting, company Z requires that they review all material to be presented both in-house and with company Q prior to the meeting. Why would a situation such as this occur? Is it beneficial?

5–44 Referring to Problem 5–43, during contract negotiations between company Q and company Z, you, as project manager for the subcontractor, are sitting in your office when the phone rings. It is company Q requesting information to support its negotiation position. Should you provide the information?

5–45 How does a project manager find out if the project team members from the functional departments have the authority to make decisions?

5–46 One of your functional people has been assigned to perform a certain test and document the results. For two weeks you "hound" this individual only to find out that he is continually procrastinating on work in another program. You later find out from one of his co-workers that he hates to write. What should you do?

5–47 During a crisis, you find that all of the functional managers as well as the team members are writing letters and memos to you, whereas previously everything was verbal. How do you account for this?

5–48 Below are several problems that commonly occur in project organizations. State, if possible, the effect that each problem could have on communications and time management:

    a. People tend to resist exploration of new ideas
    b. People tend to mistrust each other in temporary management situations.
    c. People tend to protect themselves.
    d. Functional people tend to look at day-to-day activities rather than long-range efforts.
    e. Both functional and project personnel often look for individual rather than group recognition.
    f. People tend to create win-or-lose positions.

5–49 How can executives obtain loyalty and commitments from horizontal and vertical personnel in a project organizational structure?

5–50 What is meant by polarization of communications? What are the most common causes?

5–51 Many project managers contend that project team meetings are flooded with agenda items, many of which may be irrelevant. How do you account for this?

5–52 Paul O. Gaddis ("The Project Manager," *Harvard Business Review,* May–June 1959, p. 90, copyright © 1959 by the President and Fellows of Harvard College. All rights reserved) has stated that:

> In learning to manage a group of professional employees, the usual boss–subordinate relationship must be modified. Of special importance, the how—the details or methods of work performance by a professional employee—should be established by the employee. It follows that he must be given the facts necessary to permit him to develop a rational understanding of the why of tasks assigned to him.

How would you relate this information to the employee?

5–53 The customer has asked to have a customer representative office set up in the same building as the project office. As project manager, you put the customer's office at the opposite end of the building from where you are, and on a different floor. The customer states that he wants his office next to yours. Should this be permitted, and, if so, under what conditions?

5–54 During an interchange meeting from the customer, one of the functional personnel makes a presentation stating that he personally disagrees with the company's solution to the particular problem under discussion and that the company is "all wet" in its approach. How do you, as a project manager, handle this situation?

5–55 Do you agree or disagree with the statement that documenting results "forces" people to learn?

5–56 Should a project manager encourage the flow of problems to him? If yes, should he be selective in which ones to resolve?

5–57 Is it possible for a project manager to hold too few project review meetings?

5–58 If all projects are different, should there exist a uniform company policies and procedures manual?

5–59 Of the ten items below, which are considered as part of directing and which are controlling?

      a. Supervising
      b. Communicating
      c. Delegating
      d. Evaluating
      e. Measuring
      f. Motivating
      g. Coordinating
      h. Staffing
      i. Counseling
      j. Correcting

5–60 Which of the following items is not considered to be one of the seven Ms of management?

      a. Manpower
      b. Money
      c. Machines
      d. Methods
      e. Materials
      f. Minutes
      g. Mission

5–61 Match the following leadership styles (source unknown):

1. Management by inaction	_____	a. Has an executive who manages with flair, wisdom, and vision. He listens to his
2. Management by detail	_____	
3. Management by invisibility	_____	

4. Management by consensus   _____
5. Management by manipulation   _____
6. Management by rejection   _____
7. Management by survival   _____
8. Management by depotism   _____
9. Management by creativity   _____
10. Management by leadership   _____

people, prods them, and leads them.

b. Grows out of fear and anxiety.

c. Can be fair or unfair, effective or ineffective, legitimate or illegitimate. Some people are manipulators of others for power. People are not puppets.

d. Is the roughly negative style. Executive always has ideas; devil's advocate. Well-prepared proponents can win—so such a boss can be stimulating.

e. Has an executive who needs every conceivable fact; is methodical and orderly; often is timid, inappropriate, or late.

f. Is good as long as it is based on reality. The executive has a trained instinct.

g. Has an executive who will do anything to survive—the jungle fighter. If it is done constructively, the executive will build instead of destroy.

h. Is totalitarian. There are no clashes of ideas. The organization moves. Creative people flee. Employees always know who is boss.

i. Has an executive who is not around, has good subordinates, and works in an office, offstage.

j. Can be important in dealing with the unknown (R&D projects). Subordinates are independent and powerful. This style could be a substitute for decision making. It is important for setting policy.

CASE STUDIES

WYNN COMPUTER EQUIPMENT (WCE)

In 1965, Joseph Wynn began building computer equipment in a small garage behind his house. By 1982, WCE was a $1 billion a year manufacturing organization employing 900 people. The major success found by WCE has been attributed to the nondegreed workers who have stayed with WCE over the past fifteen years. The nondegreed personnel account for 80 percent of the organization. Both the salary structure and fringe benefit packages are well above the industry average.

CEO Presentation

In February 1982, the new vice president and general manager made a presentation to his executive staff outlining the strategies he wished to see implemented to improve productivity:

> Our objective for the next twelve months is to initiate a planning system with the focus on strategic, developmental, and operational plans that will assure continued success of WCE and support for our broad objectives. Our strategy is a four-step process:
>
> - To better clarify expectations and responsibility
> - To establish cross-functional goals and objectives
> - To provide feedback and performance results to all employees in each level of management
> - To develop participation through teamwork
>
> The senior staff will merely act as a catalyst in developing long- and short-term objectives. Furthermore, the senior staff will participate and provide direction and leadership in formulating an integrated manufacturing strategy that is both technology-and human-resources-driven. The final result should be an integrated project plan that will:
>
> - Push decision making down
> - Trust the decision of peers and people in each organization
> - Eliminate committee decisions
>
> Emphasis should be on communications that will build and convey ownership in the organization and a *we* approach to surfacing issues and solving problems.

In April 1982, a team of consultants interviewed a cross section of Wynn personnel to determine the "pulse" of the organization. The following information was provided:

- "We have a terrible problem in telling our personnel (both project and functional) exactly what is expected on the project. It is embarrassing to say that we are a computer manufacturer and we do not have any computerized planning and control tools."
- "Our functional groups are very poor planners. We, in the project office, must do the planning for them. They appear to have more confidence in and pay more attention to our project office schedules than to their own."

- "We have recently purchased a $65,000 computerized package for planning and controlling. It is going to take us quite a while to educate our people. In order to interface with the computer package, we must use a work breakdown structure. This is an entirely new concept for our people."

- "We have a lack of team spirit in the organization. I'm not sure if it is simply the result of poor communications. I think it goes further than that. Our priorities get shifted on a weekly basis, and this produces a demoralizing effect. As a result, we cannot get our people to live up to either their old or new commitments."

- "We have a very strong mix of degreed and nondegreed personnel. All new, degreed personnel must 'prove' themselves before being officially accepted by the nondegreed personnel. We seem to be splitting the organization down the middle. Technology has become more important than loyalty and tradition and, as a result, the nondegreed personnel, who believe themselves to be the backbone of the organization, now feel cheated. What is a proper balance between experience and new blood?"

- "The emphasis on education shifts with each new executive. Our nondegreed personnel obviously are paying the price. I wish I knew what direction the storm is coming from."

- "My department does not have a database to use for estimating. Therefore, we have to rely heavily on the project office for good estimating. Anyway, the project office never gives us sufficient time for good estimating so we have to ask other groups to do our scheduling for us."

- "As line manager, I am caught between the rock and the hard spot. Quite often, I have to act as the project manager and line manager at the same time. When I act as the project manager I have trouble spending enough time with my people. In addition, my duties also include supervising outside vendors at the same time."

- "My departmental personnel have a continuous time management problem because they are never full-time on any one project, and all of our projects never have 100 percent of the resources they need. How can our people ever claim ownership?"

- "We have trouble in conducting up-front feasibility studies to see if we have a viable product. Our manufacturing personnel have poor interfacing with advanced design."

- "If we accept full project management, I'm not sure where the project managers should report. Should we have one group of project managers for new processes/products and a second group for continuous (or old) processes/products? Can both groups report to the same person?"

THE TROPHY PROJECT

The ill-fated Trophy Project was in trouble right from the start. Reichart, who had been an assistant project manager, was involved with the project from its conception. When the Trophy Project was accepted by the company, Reichart was assigned as the project manager. The program schedules started to slip from day one, and expenditures were excessive. Reichart found that the functional managers were charging direct labor time to his project but working on their own "pet" projects. When Reichart complained of this, he was told not to meddle in the functional manager's allocation of resources and budgeted expenditures. After approximately six months, Reichart was requested to make a progress report directly to corporate and division staffs.

Reichart took this opportunity to bare his soul. The report substantiated that the project was forecasted to be one complete year behind schedule. Reichart's staff, as supplied by the line managers, was inadequate to stay at the required pace, let alone make up any time that had already been lost. The estimated cost at completion at this interval showed a cost overrun of at least 20 percent. This was Reichart's first opportunity to tell his story to people who were in a position to correct the situation. The result of Reichart's frank, candid evaluation of the Trophy Project was very predictable. Nonbelievers finally saw the light, and the line managers realized that they had a role to play in the completion of the project. Most of the problems were now out in the open and could be corrected by providing adequate staffing and resources. Corporate staff ordered immediate remedial action and staff support to provide Reichart a chance to bail out his program.

The results were not at all what Reichart had expected. He no longer reported to the project office; he now reported directly to the operations manager. Corporate staff's interest in the project became very intense, requiring a 7:00 A.M. meeting every Monday morning for complete review of the project status and plans for recovery. Reichart found himself spending more time preparing paperwork, reports, and projections for his Monday morning meetings than he did administering the Trophy Project. The main concern of corporate was to get the project back on schedule. Reichart spent many hours preparing the recovery plan and establishing manpower requirements to bring the program back onto the original schedule.

Group staff, in order to closely track the progress of the Trophy Project, assigned an assistant program manager. The assistant program manager determined that a sure cure for the Trophy Project would be to computerize the various problems and track the progress through a very complex computer program. Corporate provided Reichart with twelve additional staff members to work on the computer program. In the meantime, nothing changed. The functional managers still did not provide adequate staff for recovery, assuming that the additional manpower Reichart had received from corporate would accomplish that task.

After approximately $50,000 was spent on the computer program to track the problems, it was found that the program objectives could not be handled by the computer. Reichart discussed this problem with a computer supplier and found that $15,000 more was required for programming and additional storage capacity. It would take two months for installation of the additional storage capacity and the completion of the programming. At this point, the decision was made to abandon the computer program.

Reichart was now a year and a half into the program with no prototype units completed. The program was still nine months behind schedule with the overrun projected at 40 percent of budget. The customer had been receiving his reports on a timely basis and was well aware of the fact that the Trophy Project was behind schedule. Reichart had spent a great deal of time with the customer explaining the problems and the plan for recovery. Another problem that Reichart had to contend with was that the vendors who were supplying components for the project were also running behind schedule.

One Sunday morning, while Reichart was in his office putting together a report for the client, a corporate vice president came into his office. "Reichart," he said, "in any project I look at the top sheet of paper and the man whose name appears at the top of the sheet is the one I hold responsible. For this project your name appears at the top of the sheet. If you cannot bail this thing out, you are in serious trouble in this corporation." Reichart did not know which way to turn or what to say. He had no control over the functional managers who were creating the problems, but he was the person who was being held responsible.

After another three months the customer, becoming impatient, realized that the Trophy Project was in serious trouble and requested that the division general manager and his entire staff visit the customer's plant to give a progress and "get well" report within a week. The division general manager called Reichart into his office and said, "Reichart, go visit our customer. Take three or four functional line people with you and try to placate him with whatever you feel is necessary." Reichart and four functional line people visited the customer and gave a four-and-a-half-hour presentation defining the problems and the progress to that point. The customer was very polite and even commented that it was an excellent presentation, but the content was totally unacceptable. The program was still six to eight months late, and the customer demanded progress reports on a weekly basis. The customer made arrangements to assign a representative in Reichart's department to be "on-site" at the project on a daily basis and to interface with Reichart and his staff as required. After this turn of events, the program became very hectic.

The customer representative demanded constant updates and problem identification and then became involved in attempting to solve these problems. This involvement created many changes in the program and the product in order to eliminate some of the problems. Reichart had trouble with the customer and did not agree with the changes in the program. He expressed his disagreement vocally when, in many cases, the customer felt the changes were at no cost. This caused a deterioration of the relationship between client and producer.

One morning Reichart was called into the division general manager's office and introduced to Mr. "Red" Baron. Reichart was told to turn over the reins of the Trophy Project to Red immediately. "Reichart, you will be temporarily reassigned to some other division within the corporation. I suggest you start looking outside the company for another job." Reichart looked at Red and asked, "Who did this? Who shot me down?"

Red was program manager on the Trophy Project for approximately six months, after which, by mutual agreement, he was replaced by a third project manager. The customer reassigned his local program manager to another project. With the new team the Trophy Project was finally completed one year behind schedule and at a 40 percent cost overrun.

LEADERSHIP EFFECTIVENESS (A)

Instructions

This form is concerned with a comparison of personal supervisory styles. Indicate your preference to the two alternatives after each item by writing appropriate figures in the blanks. Some of the alternatives may seem equally attractive or unattractive to you. Nevertheless, please attempt to choose the alternative that is relatively more characteristic of you. For each question given, you have three (3) points that you may distribute in any of the following combinations:

A. If you agree with alternative (a) and disagree with (b), write 3 in the top blank and 0 in bottom blank.
   a. $\underline{3}$
   b. $\underline{0}$

B. If you agree with (b) and disagree with (a), write:
   a. $\underline{0}$
   b. $\underline{3}$

   C. If you have a slight preference for (a) over (b), write:
   a. $\underline{2}$
   b. $\underline{1}$

D. If you have a slight preference for (b) over (a), write:
   a. $\underline{1}$
   b. $\underline{2}$

Important—Use only the combinations shown above. Try to relate each item to your own personal experience. Please make a choice from every pair of alternatives.

1. On the job, a project manager should make a decision and . . .

   a. _____ tell his team to carry it out.

   b. _____ "tell" his team about the decision and then try to "sell" it.

2. After a project manager has arrived at a decision . . .

   a. _____ he should try to reduce the team's resistance to his decision by indicating what they have to gain.

   b. _____ he should provide an opportunity for his team to get a fuller explanation of his ideas.

3. When a project manager presents a problem to his subordinates . . .

   a. _____ he should get suggestions from them and then make a decision.

   b. _____ he should define it and request that the group make a decision.

4. A project manager . . .

   a. _____ is paid to make all the decisions affecting the work of his team.

   b. _____ should commit himself in advance to assist in implementing whatever decision his team selects when they are asked to solve a problem.

5. A project manager should . . .

   a. _____ permit his team an opportunity to exert some influence on decisions but reserve final decisions for himself.

   b. _____ participate with his team in group decision making but attempt to do so with a minimum of authority.

6. In making a decision concerning the work situation, a project manager should . . .

    a. _____ present his decision and ideas and engage in a "give-and-take" session with his team to allow them to fully explore the implications of the decision.

    b. _____ present the problem to his team, get suggestions, and then make a decision.

7. A good work situation is one in which the project manager . . .

    a. _____ "tells" his team about a decision and then tries to "sell" it to them.

    b. _____ calls his team together, presents a problem, defines the problem, and requests they solve the problem with the understanding that he will support their decision(s).

8. A well-run project will include . . .

    a. _____ efforts by the project manager to reduce the team's resistance to his decisions by indicating what they have to gain from them.

    b. _____ "give-and take" sessions to enable the project manager and team to explore more fully the implications of the project manager's decisions.

9. A good way to deal with people in a work situation is . . .

    a. _____ to present problems to your team as they arise, get suggestions, and then make a decision.

    b. _____ to permit the team to make decisions, with the understanding that the project manager will assist in implementing whatever decision they make.

10. A good project manager is one who takes . . .

    a. _____ the responsibility for locating problems and arriving at solutions, then tries to persuade his team to accept them.

    b. _____ the opportunity to collect ideas from his team about problems, then he makes his decision.

11. A project manager . . .

    a. _____ should make the decisions in his organization and tell his team to carry them out.

    b. _____ should work closely with his team in solving problems, and attempt to do so with a minimum of authority.

12. To do a good job, a project manager should . . .

   a. _____ present solutions for his team's reaction.

   b. _____ present the problem and collect from the team suggested solutions, then make a decision based on the best solution offered.

13. A good method for a project manager is . . .

   a. _____ to "tell" and then try to "sell" his decision.

   b. _____ to define the problem for his team, then pass them the right to make decisions.

14. On the job, a project manager . . .

   a. _____ need not give consideration to what his team will think or feel about his decisions.

   b. _____ should present his decisions and engage in a "give-and-take" session to enable everyone concerned to explore, more fully, the implications of the decisions.

15. A project manager . . .

   a. _____ should make all decisions himself.

   b. _____ should present the problem to his team, get suggestions, and then make a decision.

16. It is good . . .

   a. _____ to permit the team an opportunity to exert some influence on decisions, but the project manager should reserve final decisions for himself.

   b. _____ for the project manager to participate with his team in group decision making with as little authority as possible.

17. The project manager who gets the most from his team is the one who . . .

   a. _____ exercises direct authority.

   b. _____ seeks possible solutions from them and then makes a decision.

18. An effective project manager should . . .

   a. _____ make the decisions on his project and tell his team to carry them out.

   b. _____ make the decisions and then try to persuade his team to accept them.

19. A good way for a project manager to handle work problems is to . . .

   a. _____ implement decisions without giving any consideration to what his team will think or feel.

   b. _____ permit the team an opportunity to exert some influence on decisions but reserve the final decision for himself.

20. Project managers . . .

   a. _____ should seek to reduce the team's resistance to their decisions by indicating what they have to gain from them.

   b. _____ should seek possible solutions from their team when problems arise and then make a decision from the list of alternatives.

LEADERSHIP EFFECTIVENESS (B)

The Project

Your company has just won a contract for an outside customer. The contract is for one year, broken down as follows: R&D: six months; prototype testing: one month; manufacturing: five months. In addition to the risks involved in the R&D stage, both your management and the customer have stated that there will be absolutely no trade-offs on time, cost, or performance.

When you prepared the proposal six months ago, you planned and budgeted for a full-time staff of five people, in addition to the functional support personnel. Unfortunately, due to limited resources, your staff (i.e., the project office) will be as follows:

Tom: An excellent engineer, somewhat of a prima donna, but has worked very well with you on previous projects. You specifically requested Tom and were fortunate to have him assigned, although your project is not regarded as a high priority. Tom is recognized as both a technical leader and expert, and is considered as perhaps the best engineer in the company. Tom will be full-time for the duration of the project.

Bob: Started with the company a little over a year ago, and may be a little "wet behind the ears." His line manager has great expectations for him in the future but, for the time being, wants you to give him on-the-job-training as a project office team member. Bob will be full-time on your project.

Carol: She has been with the company for twenty years and does an acceptable job. She has never worked on your projects before. She is full-time on the project.

George: He has been with the company for six years, but has never worked on any of your projects. His superior tells you that he will be only half-time on your project until he finishes a crash job on another project. He should be available for full-time work in a month or two. George is regarded as an outstanding employee.

Management informs you that there is nobody else available to fill the fifth position. You'll have to spread the increased workload over the other members. Obviously, the customer may not be too happy about this.

LEADERSHIP QUESTIONNAIRE
Tabulation Form

	1	2	3	4	5
1	a	b			
2		a	b		
3				a	b
4	a				b
5			a		b
6			a	b	
7		a			b
8		a	b		
9				a	b
10	a		b		
11	a				b
12			a	b	
13		a			b
14	a		b		
15	a			b	
16			a		b
17	a			b	
18	a	b			
19	a		b		
20		a		b	
TOTAL	___	___	___	___	___

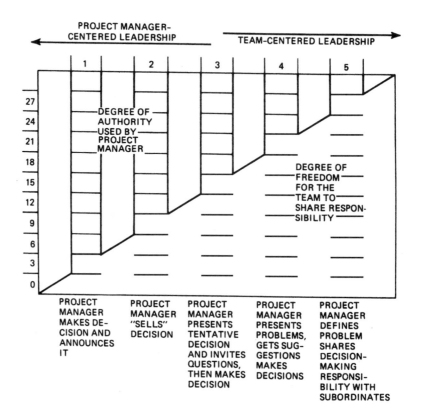

In each situation that follows, circle the best answer. The grading system will be provided later.

Remember: These staff individuals are "dotted" to you and "solid" to their line manager, although they are in your project office.

Situation 1: The project office team members have been told to report to you this morning. They have all received your memo concerning the time and place of the kickoff meeting. However, they have not been provided any specific details concerning the project except that the project will be at least one year in duration. For your company, this is regarded as a long-term project. A good strategy for the meeting would be:

A. The team must already be self-motivated or else they would not have been assigned. Simply welcome them and assign homework.
B. Motivate the employees by showing them how they will benefit: esteem, pride, self-actualization. Minimize discussion on specifics.
C. Explain the project and ask them for their input. Try to get them to identify alternatives and encourage group decision making.
D. Identify the technical details of the project: the requirements, performance standards, and expectations.

Situation 2: You give the team members a copy of the winning proposal and a "confidential" memo describing the assumptions and constraints you considered in developing the proposal. You tell your team to review the material and be prepared to perform detailed planning at the meeting you have scheduled for the following Monday. During Monday's planning meeting, you find that Tom (who has worked with you before) has established a take-charge role and has done some of the planning that should have been the responsibility of other team members. You should:

A. Do nothing. This may be a beneficial situation. However, you may wish to ask if the other project office members wish to review Tom's planning.
B. Ask each team member individually how he or she feels about Tom's role. If they complain, have a talk with Tom.
C. Ask each team member to develop his or her own schedules and then compare results.
D. Talk to Tom privately about the long-term effects of his behavior.

Situation 3: Your team appears to be having trouble laying out realistic schedules that will satisfy the customer's milestones. They keep asking you pertinent questions and seem to be making the right decisions, but with difficulty.

A. Do nothing. If the team is good, they will eventually work out the problem.
B. Encourage the team to continue but give some ideas as to possible alternatives. Let them solve the problem.
C. Become actively involved and help the team solve the problem. Supervise the planning until completion.
D. Take charge yourself and solve the problem for the team. You may have to provide continuous direction.

Situation 4: Your team has taken an optimistic approach to the schedule. The functional managers have reviewed the schedules and have sent your team strong memos stating that there is no way that they can support your schedules. Your team's morale appears to be very low. Your team expected the schedules to be returned for additional iterations and trade-offs, but not with such harsh words from the line managers. You should:

A. Take no action. This is common to these types of projects and the team must learn to cope.
B. Call a special team meeting to discuss the morale problem and ask the team for recommendations. Try to work out the problem.
C. Meet with each team member individually to reinforce his or her behavior and performance. Let members know how many other times this has occurred and been resolved through trade-offs and additional iterations. State your availability to provide advice and support.
D. Take charge and look for ways to improve morale by changing the schedules.

Situation 5: The functional departments have begun working, but are still criticizing the schedules. Your team is extremely unhappy with some of the employees assigned out of one functional department. Your team feels that these employees are not qualified to perform the required work. You should:

A. Do nothing until you are absolutely sure (with evidence) that the assigned personnel cannot perform as needed.

B. Sympathize with your team and encourage them to live with this situation until an alternative is found.

C. Assess the potential risks with the team and ask for their input and suggestions. Try to develop contingency plans if the problem is as serious as the team indicates.

D. Approach the functional manager and express your concern. Ask to have different employees assigned.

Situation 6: Bob's performance as a project office team member has begun to deteriorate. You are not sure whether he simply lacks the skills, cannot endure the pressure, or cannot assume part of the additional work that resulted from the fifth position in the project being vacant. You should:

A. Do nothing. The problem may be temporary and you cannot be sure that there is a measurable impact on the project.

B. Have a personal discussion with Bob, seek out the cause, and ask him for a solution.

C. Call a team meeting and discuss how productivity and performance are decreasing. Ask the team for recommendations and hope Bob gets the message.

D. Interview the other team members and see if they can explain Bob's actions lately. Ask the other members to assist you by talking to Bob.

Situation 7: George, who is half-time on your project, has just submitted for your approval his quarterly progress report for your project. After your signature has been attained, the report is sent to senior management and the customer. The report is marginally acceptable and not at all what you would have expected from George. George apologizes to you for the report and blames it on his other project, which is in its last two weeks. You should:

A. Sympathize with George and ask him to rewrite the report.

B. Tell George that the report is totally unacceptable and will reflect on his ability as a project office team member.

C. Ask the team to assist George in redoing the report since a bad report reflects on everyone.

D. Ask one of the other team members to rewrite the report for George.

Situation 8: You have completed the R&D stage of your project and are entering phase II: prototype testing. You are entering month seven of the twelve-month project. Unfortunately, the results of phase I R&D indicate that you were too optimistic in your estimating for phase II and a schedule slippage of at least two weeks is highly probable. The customer may not be happy. You should:

A. Do nothing. These problems occur and have a way of working themselves out. The end date of the project can still be met.

B. Call a team meeting to discuss the morale problem resulting from the slippage. If morale is improved, the slippage may be overcome.

    C. Call a team meeting and seek ways of improving productivity for phase II. Hopefully, the team will come up with alternatives.

    D. This is a crisis and you must exert strong leadership. You should take control and assist your team in identifying alternatives.

Situation 9: Your rescheduling efforts have been successful. The functional managers have given you adequate support and you are back on schedule. You should:

    A. Do nothing. Your team has matured and is doing what they are paid to do.

    B. Try to provide some sort of monetary or nonmonetary reward for your team (e.g., management-granted time off or a dinner team meeting).

    C. Provide positive feedback/reinforcement for the team and search for ideas for shortening phase III.

    D. Obviously, your strong leadership has been effective. Continue this role for the phase III schedule.

Situation 10: You are now at the end of the seventh month and everything is proceeding as planned. Motivation appears high. You should:

    A. Leave well enough alone.

    B. Look for better ways to improve the functioning of the team. Talk to them and make them feel important.

    C. Call a team meeting and review the remaining schedules for the project. Look for contingency plans.

    D. Make sure the team is still focusing on the goals and objectives of the project.

Situation 11: The customer unofficially informs you that his company has a problem and may have to change the design specifications before production actually begins. This would be a catastrophe for your project. The customer wants a meeting at your plant within the next seven days. This will be the customer's first visit to your plant. All previous meetings were informal and at the customer's facilities, with just you and the customer. This meeting will be formal. To prepare for the meeting, you should:

    A. Make sure the schedules are updated and assume a passive role since the customer has not officially informed you of his problem.

    B. Ask the team to improve productivity before the customer's meeting. This should please the customer.

    C. Call an immediate team meeting and ask the team to prepare an agenda and identify the items to be discussed.

    D. Assign specific responsibilities to each team member for preparation of handout material for the meeting.

Situation 12: Your team is obviously not happy with the results of the customer interface meeting because the customer has asked for a change in design specifications. The manufacturing plans and manufacturing schedules must be developed anew. You should:

    A. Do nothing. The team is already highly motivated and will take charge as before.

    B. Reemphasize the team spirit and encourage your people to proceed. Tell them that nothing is impossible for a good team.

    C. Roll up your shirt sleeves and help the team identify alternatives. Some degree of guidance is necessary.

    D. Provide strong leadership and close supervision. Your team will have to rely on you for assistance.

Situation 13: You are now in the ninth month. While your replanning is going on (as a result of changes in the specifications), the customer calls and asks for an assessment of the risks in cancelling this project right away and starting another one. You should:

    A. Wait for a formal request. Perhaps you can delay long enough for the project to finish.

    B. Tell the team that their excellent performance may result in a follow-on contract.

    C. Call a team meeting to assess the risks and look for alternatives.

    D. Accept strong leadership for this and with *minimum,* if any, team involvement.

Situation 14: One of the functional managers has asked for your evaluation of all of his functional employees currently working on your project (excluding project office personnel). Your project office personnel appear to be working closer with the functional employees than you are. You should:

    A. Return the request to the functional manager since this is not part of your job description.

    B. Talk to each team member individually telling them how important their input is and ask for their evaluations.

    C. As a team, evaluate each of the functional team members, and try to come to some sort of agreement.

    D. Do not burden your team with this request. You can do it yourself.

Situation 15: You are in the tenth month of the project. Carol informs you that she has the opportunity to be the project leader for an effort starting in two weeks. She has been with the company for twenty years and this is her first opportunity as a project leader. She wants to know if she can be released from your project. You should:

    A. Let Carol go. You do not want to stand in the way of her career advancement.

    B. Ask the team to meet in private and conduct a vote. Tell Carol you will abide by the team vote.

    C. Discuss the problem with the team since they must assume the extra workload, if necessary. Ask for their input into meeting the constraints.

    D. Counsel her and explain how important it is for her to remain. You are already short-handed.

Situation 16: Your team informs you that one of the functional manufacturing managers has built up a brick wall around his department and all information requests must flow through him. The brick wall has been in existence for two years. Your team members are having trouble with status reporting, but always get the information after catering to the functional manager. You should:

A. Do nothing. This is obviously the way the line manager wants to run his department. Your team is getting the information they need.

B. Ask the team members to use their behavioral skills in obtaining the information.

C. Call a team meeting to discuss alternative ways of obtaining the information.

D. Assume strong leadership and exert your authority by calling the line manager and asking for the information.

Situation 17: The executives have given you a new man to replace Carol for the last two months of the project. Neither you nor your team have worked with this man before. You should:

A. Do nothing. Carol obviously filled him in on what he should be doing and what is involved in the project.

B. Counsel the new man individually, bring him up to speed, and assign him Carol's work.

C. Call a meeting and ask each member to explain his or her role on the project to the new man.

D. Ask each team member to talk to this man as soon as possible and help him come on board. Request that individual conversations be used.

Situation 18: One of your team members wants to take a late-afternoon course at the local college. Unfortunately, this course may conflict with his workload. You should:

A. Postpone your decision. Ask the employee to wait until the course is offered again.

B. Review the request with the team member and discuss the impact on his performance.

C. Discuss the request with the team and ask for the team's approval. The team may have to cover for this employee's workload.

D. Discuss this individually with each team member to make sure that the task requirements will still be adhered to.

Situation 19: Your functional employees have used the wrong materials in making a production run test. The cost to your project was significant, but absorbed in a small "cushion" that you saved for emergencies such as this. Your team members tell you that the test will be rerun without any slippage of the schedule. You should:

A. Do nothing. Your team seems to have the situation well under control.

B. Interview the employees that created this problem and stress the importance of productivity and following instructions.

C. Ask your team to develop contingency plans for this situation should it happen again.

D. Assume a strong leadership role for the rerun test to let people know your concern.

Situation 20: All good projects must come to an end, usually with a final report. Your project has a requirement for a final report. This final report may very well become the basis for follow-on work. You should:

A. Do nothing. Your team has things under control and knows that a final report is needed.
B. Tell your team that they have done a wonderful job and there is only one more task to do.
C. Ask your team to meet and provide an outline for the final report.
D. You must provide some degree of leadership for the final report, at least the structure. The final report could easily reflect on your ability as a manager.

Fill in the table below. The answers appear in Appendix B.

Situation	Answer	Points	Situation	Answer	Points
1			11		
2			12		
3			13		
4			14		
5			15		
6			16		
7			17		
8			18		
9			19		
10			20		
				Total	

MOTIVATIONAL QUESTIONNAIRE

On the next several pages, you will find forty statements concerning what motivates you and how you try to motivate others. Beside each statement, circle the number that corresponds to your opinion. In the example below, the choice is "Slightly Agree."

−3	Strongly Disagree
−2	Disagree
−1	Slightly Disagree
0	No Opinion
(+1)	Slightly Agree
+2	Agree
+3	Strongly Agree

Part 1

The following twenty statements involve *what motivates you.* Please rate each of the statements as honestly as possible. Circle the rating that you think is correct, *not* the one you think the instructor is looking for:

1. My company pays me a reasonable salary for the work that I do. -3 -2 -1 0 $+1$ $+2$ $+3$

2. My company believes that every job that I do can be considered as a challenge. -3 -2 -1 0 $+1$ $+2$ $+3$

3. The company provides me with the latest equipment (i.e., hardware, software, etc.) so I can do my job effectively. -3 -2 -1 0 $+1$ $+2$ $+3$

4. My company provides me with recognition for work well done. -3 -2 -1 0 $+1$ $+2$ $+3$

5. Seniority on the job, job security, and vested rights are provided by the company. -3 -2 -1 0 $+1$ $+2$ $+3$

6. Executives provide managers with feedback of strategic or long-range information that may affect the manager's job. -3 -2 -1 0 $+1$ $+2$ $+3$

7. My company provides off-hour clubs and organizations so that employees can socialize, as well as sponsoring social events. -3 -2 -1 0 $+1$ $+2$ $+3$

8. Employees are allowed to either set their own work/performance standards or to at least approve/review standards set for them by management. -3 -2 -1 0 $+1$ $+2$ $+3$

9. Employees are encouraged to maintain membership in professional societies and/or attend seminars and symposiums on work-related subjects. -3 -2 -1 0 $+1$ $+2$ $+3$

10. The company often reminds me that the only way to have job security is to compete effectively in the marketplace.

11. Employees who develop a reputation for "excellence" are allowed to further enhance their reputation, if job related. -3 -2 -1 0 $+1$ $+2$ $+3$

12. Supervisors encourage a friendly, cooperative working environment for employees. -3 -2 -1 0 $+1$ $+2$ $+3$

13. My company provides me with a -3 -2 -1 0 $+1$ $+2$ $+3$
    detailed job description, identifying
    my role and responsibilities.

14. My company gives *automatic* wage -3 -2 -1 0 $+1$ $+2$ $+3$
    and salary increases for the em-
    ployees.

15. My company gives me the opportu- -3 -2 -1 0 $+1$ $+2$ $+3$
    nity to do what I do best.

16. My job gives me the opportunity -3 -2 -1 0 $+1$ $+2$ $+3$
    to be truly creative, to the point
    where I can solve complex
    problems.

17. My efficiency and effectiveness is -3 -2 -1 0 $+1$ $+2$ $+3$
    improving because the compnay
    provided me with better physical
    working conditions (i.e., lighting,
    low noise, temperature, rest-
    rooms, etc.)

18. My job gives me constant self-de- -3 -2 -1 0 $+1$ $+2$ $+3$
    velopment.

19. Our supervisors have feelings for -3 -2 -1 0 $+1$ $+2$ $+3$
    employees rather than simply treat-
    ing them as "inanimate tools."

20. Participation in the company's -3 -2 -1 0 $+1$ $+2$ $+3$
    stock option/retirement plan is
    available to employees.

Part 2

Statements 21–40 involve how project managers motivate team members. Again, it
is important that your ratings honestly reflect the way you think that *you*, as project
manager, try to motivate employees. Do *not* indicate the way others or the instructor
might recommend motivating the employees. Your thoughts are what are important
in this exercise.

21. Project managers should encourage -3 -2 -1 0 $+1$ $+2$ $+3$
    employees to take advantage of
    company benefits such as stock op-
    tion plans and retirement plans.

22. Project managers should make sure -3 -2 -1 0 $+1$ $+2$ $+3$
    that team members have a good
    work environment (i.e., heat, light-
    ing, low noise, restrooms, cafete-
    ria, etc.).

23. Project managers should assign team members work that can enhance each team member's reputation. -3 -2 -1 0 $+1$ $+2$ $+3$

24. Project managers should create a relaxed, cooperative environment for the team members. -3 -2 -1 0 $+1$ $+2$ $+3$

25. Project managers should *continually* remind the team that job security is a function of competitiveness, staying within constraints, and good customer relations. -3 -2 -1 0 $+1$ $+2$ $+3$

26. Project managers should try to convince team members that each new assignment is a challenge. -3 -2 -1 0 $+1$ $+2$ $+3$

27. Project managers should be willing to reschedule activities, if possible, around the team's company and out-of-company social functions. -3 -2 -1 0 $+1$ $+2$ $+3$

28. Project managers should continually remind employees of how they will benefit, monetarily, by successful performance on your project. -3 -2 -1 0 $+1$ $+2$ $+3$

29. Project managers should be willing to "pat people on the back" and provide recognition where applicable. -3 -2 -1 0 $+1$ $+2$ $+3$

30. Project managers should encourage the team to maintain constant self-development with each assignment. -3 -2 -1 0 $+1$ $+2$ $+3$

31. Project managers should allow team members to set their own standards, where applicable. -3 -2 -1 0 $+1$ $+2$ $+3$

32. Project managers should assign work to functional employees according to seniority on the job. -3 -2 -1 0 $+1$ $+2$ $+3$

33. Project managers should allow team members to use the informal, as well as formal, organization to get work accomplished. -3 -2 -1 0 $+1$ $+2$ $+3$

34. As a project manager, I would like   −3   −2   −1   0   +1   +2   +3
    to control the salaries of the full-
    time employees on my project.

35. Project managers should share in-   −3   −2   −1   0   +1   +2   +3
    formation with the team. This in-
    cludes project information that may
    not be directly applicable to the
    team member's assignment.

36. Project managers should encourage   −3   −2   −1   0   +1   +2   +3
    team members to be creative and
    to solve their own problems.

37. Project managers should provide   −3   −2   −1   0   +1   +2   +3
    detailed job descriptions for team
    members, outlining the team mem-
    ber's role and responsibility.

38. Project managers should give each   −3   −2   −1   0   +1   +2   +3
    team member the opportunity to do
    what the team member can do best.

39. Project managers should be willing   −3   −2   −1   0   +1   +2   +3
    to interact informally with the team
    members and get to know them, as
    long as there exists sufficient time
    on the project.

40. Most of the employees on my proj-   −3   −2   −1   0   +1   +2   +3
    ect earn a salary commensurate
    with their abilities.

Part 1 Scoring Sheet (What Motivates You?) Place your answers (the numerical values you circled) to questions 1–20 in the corresponding spaces in the chart below.

Basic Needs		*Safety Needs*		*Belonging Needs*	
#1	_____	#5	_____	#7	_____
#3	_____	#10	_____	#9	_____
#14	_____	#13	_____	#12	_____
#17	_____	#20	_____	#19	_____
Total	_____	Total	_____	Total	_____

Esteem/Ego Needs		*Self-Actualization Needs*	
#4	_____	#2	_____
#6	_____	#15	_____
#8	_____	#16	_____
#11	_____	#18	_____
Total	_____	Total	_____

Transfer your total score in each category to the table on page 324 by placing an "X" in the appropriate area for motivational needs.

Part 2 Scoring Sheet (How Do You Motivate?)

Place your answers (the numerical values you circled) to questions 21–40 in the corresponding spaces in the chart below.

Basic Needs		*Safety Needs*		*Belonging Needs*	
#22	____	#21	____	#24	____
#28	____	#25	____	#27	____
#34	____	#32	____	#33	____
#40	____	#37	____	#39	____
Total	____	Total	____	Total	____

Esteem/Ego Needs		*Self-Actualization Needs*	
#23	____	#26	____
#29	____	#30	____
#31	____	#36	____
#35	____	#38	____
Total	____	Total	____

Transfer your total score in each category to the table on page 324 by placing an "X" in the appropriate area for motivational needs.

QUESTIONS 1–20

Points																									
Needs	−12	−11	−10	−9	−8	−7	−6	−5	−4	−3	−2	−1	0	+1	+2	+3	+4	+5	+6	+7	+8	+9	+10	+11	+12
Self-Actualization																									
Esteem/Ego																									
Belonging																									
Safety																									
Basic																									

QUESTIONS 21–40

Points																									
Needs	−12	−11	−10	−9	−8	−7	−6	−5	−4	−3	−2	−1	0	+1	+2	+3	+4	+5	+6	+7	+8	+9	+10	+11	+12
Self-Actualization																									
Esteem/Ego																									
Belonging																									
Safety																									
Basic																									

Time Management

6.0 INTRODUCTION

Managing projects within time, cost, and performance is easier said than done. The project management environment is extremely turbulent, and is composed of numerous meetings, report writing, conflict resolution, continuous planning and replanning, communications with the customer, and crisis management. Ideally, the effective project manager is a manager, not a doer. But in the "real world," project managers often find themselves compromising their time between managing and doing, mainly because of the uncertain nature of the project environment.

In such situations, it is extremely critical that the project manager effectively manage his own time. It is often said that if the project manager cannot control his own time (see Figure 6–1), then he will control nothing else on the project. Disciplined time management is one of the keys to effective project management. Figures 6–2 and 6–3 represent the lack of disciplined time management.

6.1 UNDERSTANDING TIME MANAGEMENT[1]

For most people, time is a resource that, when lost or misplaced, is gone forever. For a project manager, however, time is more of a constraint, and effective time management principles must be employed to make it a resource.

---

1. Sections 6.1, 6.2, and 6.3 are adapted from David Cleland and Harold Kerzner, *Engineering Team Management* (Melbourne, Florida: Krieger, 1986), Chapter 8.

FIGURE 6–1. Time management.

FIGURE 6–2. Effective time management?

FIGURE 6–3. Effective time management?

Most executives prefer to understaff projects, in the mistaken belief (or, should we say, hope) that the project manager will assume the additional workload. Unfortunately, this is easier said than done. The project manager may already be heavily burdened with meetings, report preparation, internal and external communications, conflict resolution, and planning/replanning for crises. And yet, each project manager somehow manages to manipulate his time so that the work will get done.

Inexperienced project managers often work large amounts of overtime, with the faulty notion that this is the only way to get the job done. While this may be true, experienced personnel soon learn to delegate tasks and to employ effective time management principles.

The major problem with time management is getting people to realize that there exists a time management problem and that solutions are possible. The following questions should make the reader realize that each of us has room for improvement.

- Do you have trouble completing work within the allocated deadlines?
- How long can you work at your desk before being interrupted? How many interruptions are there each day?
- Do you have a procedure for handling interruptions?
- If you need a large block of uninterrupted time, is it available? With or without overtime?
- How do you handle drop-in visitors and phone calls?
- How is incoming mail handled?

- Are you accomplishing more or less than you were three months ago? Six months ago?
- How difficult is it for you to say no?
- How do you approach detail work?
- Do you perform work that should be handled by your subordinates?
- Do you have sufficient time each day for personal interests?
- Do you still think about your job when away from the office?
- Do you make a list of things to do? If yes, is the list prioritized?
- Does your schedule have some degree of flexibility?
- Do you have established procedures for routine work?

While it may not be possible to cope with all of these questions, the more one can deal with, the greater the opportunity for the project manager to convert time from being a constraint to becoming a resource.

6.2 TIME ROBBERS

Project managers are not merely managers, but are doers as well. As a result, they suffer from the time robbers of both the managers and the doers. If the project manager is not careful, and overemphasizes his role as a doer rather than a manager, the impact of time robbers may become monumental.

The most challenging problem facing the project manager is his inability to say no. Consider the situation in which an employee comes into your office with a problem. The employee may be sincere when he says that he simply wants your advice but, more often than not, the employee wants to take the monkey off of his back and put it onto yours. If the latter is, in fact, the real truth, then the employee's problem is now *your* problem.

The correct way to handle a situation such as this is first to screen out the problems with which you do not wish to get involved. Second, if the situation does necessitate your involvement, then you must make sure that when the employee leaves your office, the employee realizes that the problem is still his, not yours. Third, if you find that the problem will require your continued attention, remind the employee that all future decisions will be joint decisions and that the problem will still be on the employee's shoulders. Once employees realize that they cannot put their problems on your shoulders, then they soon learn how to make decisions and your time demands may ease up.

There are numerous time robbers in the project management environment. These include:

- Incomplete work
- A job poorly done that must be done over
- Poor communications channels
- Uncontrolled telephone calls
- Lack of adequate responsibility and commensurate authority
- Poor functional performance
- Changes without direct notification/explanation

- Casual visitors
- Waiting for people
- Failure to delegate, or unwise delegation
- Poor retrieval systems
- Lack of information in a ready-to-use format
- Day-to-day administration
- Spending more time than anticipated in answering questions
- Lack of sufficient clerical support
- Late appointments
- Impromptu tasks
- Union grievances
- Having to explain "thinking" to superiors
- Too many levels of review
- Too many people in a small area
- Office casual conversations
- Misplaced information
- Sorting mail
- Record keeping
- Shifting priorities
- Indecision or delaying decisions
- Procrastination
- Proofreading correspondence
- Setting up appointments
- Too many meetings
- Monitoring delegated work
- Unclear roles/job descriptions
- Unnecessary crisis intervention
- Overcommitted outside activities
- Executive meddling
- Budget adherence requirements
- Poorly educated customers
- Need to get involved in details to get job done
- Not enough proven or trustworthy managers
- Vague goals and objectives
- Lack of a job description
- Too many people involved in minor decision making
- Lack of technical knowledge
- Disorganization of superiors
- Lack of authorization to make judgment decisions
- Poor functional status reporting
- Inability to use one's full potential
- Overeducated for daily tasks
- Work overload
- Unreasonable time constraints
- Lack of commitment from higher authorities
- Not being responsible for the full scope
- Indecision on the part of higher management
- Too much travel
- Lack of adequate project management tools
- Poor functional communications/writing skills
- Departmental "buck passing"
- Meetings with executives
- Inability to relate to peers in a personal way
- Rush into decisions/beat the deadlines
- People being overpaid for their work
- Lack of reward ("a pat on the back can do wonders")
- Expecting too much from one's people and oneself
- Multiple time constraints
- Nonsupportive family
- Company political power struggles
- Going from crisis to crisis
- Conflicting directives
- Line management acting as a "father" figure
- Fire drills
- Lack of privacy
- Lack of challenge in job duties
- Project manager not involved/unknowledgeable about decision making
- Bureaucratic roadblocks ("ego")
- Empire-building line managers

- No communication between sales and engineering
- Too much work for one person to handle effectively
- Excessive paperwork
- Lack of clerical/administrative support
- Workload growing faster than capacity
- Dealing with unreliable subcontractors
- Reeducating project managers
- Lack of new business
- Personnel not willing to take risks
- Demand for short-term results
- Lack of long-range planning
- Being overdirected
- Changing company systems, which requires relearning
- Overreacting management
- Poor lead time on projects
- Disregard for company or personal things
- Documentation (reports/red tape)
- Large number of projects
- Inadequate or inappropriate requirements
- Desire for perfection
- Lack of dedication by technical experts
- Poor salary compared to contemporaries
- Lack of project organization
- Constant pressure
- Constant interruptions
- Problems coming in waves
- Severe home constraints
- Project monetary problems
- Shifting of functional personnel
- Lack of employee discipline
- Lack of qualified manpower

Sometimes, the project manager's inability to effectively handle a time robber will create additional time robbers. Consider the following list of "how not to get something done."[2]

- Profess to not having the answer. That lets you out of having any answer.
- Say that we must not move too rapidly. That avoids the necessity of getting started.
- For every proposal, set up an opposite and conclude that the middle ground (no motion whatever) represents the wisest course of action.
- When in a tight place, say something that the group cannot understand.
- Look slightly embarrassed when the problem is brought up. Hint that it is in bad taste, or too elementary for mature consideration, or that any discussion of it is likely to be misinterpreted by outsiders.
- Say that the problem cannot be separated from other problems. Therefore, no problem can be solved until all other problems have been solved.
- Point out that those who see the problem do so because they are unhappy—rather than vice versa.
- Ask what is meant by the question. When it is sufficiently clarified, there will be no time left for the answer.
- Move away from the problem into endless discussion of various ways to study it.

---

2. Source unknown.

- Put off recommendations until every related problem has been definitively settled by scientific research.
- Carry the problem into other fields; show that it exists everywhere; hence, everyone will just have to live with it.
- Introduce analogies and discuss *them* rather than the problem.
- Explain and clarify over and over again what you have already said.
- As soon as any proposal is made, say that you have been doing it for ten years.
- Wait until some expert can be consulted.
- Say, "That is not on the agenda; we'll take it up later." This may be extended ad infinitum.
- Conclude that we have all clarified our thinking on the problem, even though no one has thought of any way to solve it.
- Point out that some of the greatest minds have struggled with this problem, implying that it does us credit to have even thought of it.

6.3 TIME MANAGEMENT FORMS

There are two basic forms that project managers and project engineers can use for practicing better time management. The first form is the "to do" pad as shown in Figure 6–4. The project manager or secretary prepares the list of things to do. The project manager then decides which activities he must perform himself and assigns the appropriate priorities.

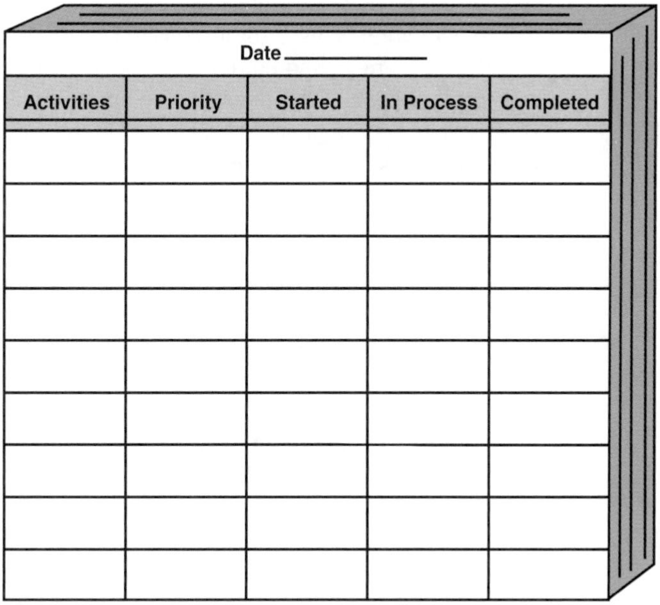

Date _____				
Activities	**Priority**	**Started**	**In Process**	**Completed**

FIGURE 6–4. "To-do" pad.

Date ______		
Time	**Activity**	**Priority**
8:00-9:00		
9:00-10:00		
10:00-11:00		
11:00-12:00		
12:00-1:00		
1:00-2:00		
2:00-3:00		
3:00-4:00		
4:00-5:00		

FIGURE 6–5. Daily calendar log.

The activities with the highest priorities are then transferred to the "daily calendar log," as shown in Figure 6–5. The project manager assigns these activities to the appropriate time blocks based on his own energy cycle. Unfilled time blocks are then used for unexpected crises or for lower-priority activities.

If there are more priority elements than time slots, the project manager may try to schedule well in advance. This is normally not a good practice, because it is very easy to create a backlog of high-priority activities to such a degree that schedule slippages are inevitable. In addition, an activity that today may be a "B" priority could easily become an "A" priority in a day or two. The moral here is do not postpone until tomorrow what you or your team can do today.

6.4 INTRODUCTION TO STRESS AND BURNOUT[3]

Everyone who works knows that on-the-job pressure is one of the major sources of stress in daily life. Project managers are subject to stress due to several different facets of their jobs. This can manifest itself in a variety of ways, such as:

3. The remaining sections are adapted from Mary Khosh and Harold Kerzner, "Stress and Burnout in Project Management," presented at the Annual Seminar/Symposium on Project Management, sponsored by the Project Management Institute, Philadelphia, October 8–10, 1984.

1. *Being tired.* Being tired is a result of being drained of strength and energy, perhaps through physical exertion, boredom, or impatience. The definition here applies more to a short-term, rather than long-term, effect. Typical causes for feeling tired include meetings, report writing, and other forms of document preparation.

2. *Feeling depressed.* Feeling depressed is an emotional condition usually characterized by discouragement or a feeling of inadequacy. There are several sources of depression in a project environment: Management or the client considers your report unacceptable, you are unable to get timely resources assigned, the technology is not available, or the constraints of the project are unrealistic and may not be met.

A state of depression in a project environment is usually the result of a situation that is beyond the control or capabilities of the project manager. This situation can exist indefinitely because the project manager has a great deal of responsibility and very little authority, and has no direct control over the staffing or assignment of personnel.

3. *Having a good day.* For most people, having a good day implies that something has gone right. In a project management environment, every project may be inherently different, and a good day may simply be the result of the project manager's ability to attack and resolve difficult problems, even if the final result is detrimental to the project. Sometimes it is truly amazing how decision making and looking at the "means to the end" rather than the end itself equals a good day. An experienced project manager once commented: "If I sit at my desk and do not have problems to resolve, then I go out and look for (or even create) problems to solve. That's my definition of having a good day."

4. *Being physically exhausted.* Project managers are both managers and doers. It is quite common for project managers to perform a great deal of the work themselves, either because they consider the assigned personnel unqualified to perform the work or because they are impatient and consider themselves capable of performing the work faster. In addition, project managers often work a great deal of "self-inflicted" overtime.

5. *Being emotionally exhausted.* The most common cause of emotional exhaustion is report writing and the preparation of handouts for interchange meetings. Sometimes the project manager finds himself performing these functions for line personnel, but more often than not, line employees procrastinate and force this function on project managers. Since data preparation is a continuous project function, one might expect this effect to occur frequently.

6. *Being happy.* Happiness generally suggests a feeling of pleasure and contentment. Most project managers view project management as a lifetime profession and are usually quite happy, even under situations of stress. A senior construction project manager commented on why he has not accepted a promotion to vice president: "I can take my children and grandchildren into ten countries in the world and show them projects that I either built or helped build. What do I show them as a vice president? My bank account? The size of my office? The stockholder's report?" Obviously, not all people would respond like this. The work

challenge associated with the project environment is a strong driving force toward happiness. There are very few positions where an employee can see an activity through from beginning to end.

7. *Wiped out.* Feeling wiped out is normally a combination of physical and emotional exhaustion. It is a short-term effect and may be caused by short spurts of intense overtime; nearness of deadlines on the time, cost, and performance constraints; or simply lengthy customer review meetings.

8. *Burned out.* Being burned out is more than just a feeling; it is a condition. Being burned out implies that one is totally exhausted, both physically and emotionally, and that rest, recuperation, or vacation time may not remedy the situation. The most common cause is prolonged overtime, or the need thereof, and an inability to endure or perform under continuous pressure and stress. The solution is almost always a change in job assignment, preferably with another company.

Burnout can occur almost overnight, often with very little warning. In one company, a project manager who was managing a high-technology project (and was on the fast track in the organization) burned out and accepted a job as the manager of quality control for a small company that manufactures brooms. In the termination interview, the project manager stated that his reason for leaving was because he felt burned out.

9. *Being unhappy.* There are several factors that produce unhappiness in project management. Such factors include highly optimistic planning, unreasonable expectations by management, management cutting resources because of a "buy-in," or simply customer demands for additional data items. A major source of unhappiness is the frustration caused by having limited authority that is not commensurate with the assigned responsibility.

10. *Feeling run down.* Feeling run down is a temporary condition caused by exhaustion, overwork, or simply poor physical conditioning. The run-down feeling usually occurs following "panics," especially as one nears the project constraints.

11. *Feeling trapped.* The most common situation where project managers feel trapped is when they have no control over the assigned resources on the project and feel as though they are at the mercy of the line managers. Employees tend to favor the manager who can offer them the most rewards, and that is usually the line manager. Providing the project manager with some type of direct reward power can remedy the situation.

Another instance of feeling trapped is when the project manager and line managers work together to develop realistic costs and schedules for a proposal and senior management arbitrarily slashes the price to remain competitive. Now, if the project is awarded to the company, the project manager feels trapped into accepting constraints that are not really his.

12. *Feeling worthless.* Feeling worthless implies that one is without worth or merit, that is, valueless. This situation occurs when project managers feel that they are managing projects beneath their dignity. Most project managers look forward to the death of their project right from the onset, and expect their next proj-

ect to be more important, perhaps twice the cost, and more complex. Unfortunately, there are always situations where one must take a step backwards.

13. *Being weary.* Being weary is a combination of several of the previous feelings. This includes tiredness, lack of energy, a worn out feeling, and perhaps impatience. Weariness is usually the transition stage between being tired and being burned out.

14. *Being troubled.* The two major causes for a project manager to be troubled are optimistic planning (which has since turned "sour") and approaching the constraints of the project with little hope for correction. The latter case is not a really serious problem, because most project managers pride themselves on their ability to perform trade-offs.

15. *Feeling resentful and disillusioned about people.* This situation occurs most frequently in the project manager's dealings (i.e., negotiations) with the line managers. During the planning stage of a project, line managers often make promises concerning future resource commitments, but renege on their promises during execution. Disillusionment then occurs and can easily develop into serious conflict. Another potential source of these feelings is when line managers appear to be making decisions that are not in the best interest of the project.

16. *Feeling weak and helpless.* A weak and helpless feeling is a common result of feeling disillusioned. Again, the cause of this feeling depends on the working relationship that project managers have with executives and line managers.

17. *Feeling hopeless.* The most common source of hopelessness are R&D projects where the ultimate objective is beyond the reach of the employee or even of the state-of-the-art technology. Hopelessness means showing no signs of a favorable outcome. Hopelessness is more a result of the performance constraint than of time or cost.

18. *Feeling rejected.* Feeling rejected can be the result of a poor working relationship with executives, line managers, or clients. Rejection often occurs when people with authority feel that their options or opinions are better than those of the project manager. Rejection has a demoralizing effect on the project manager because he feels that he is the "president" of the project and the true "champion" of the company.

19. *Feeling optimistic.* Almost all project managers feel optimistic, even in time of trouble. Project managers often have more faith in themselves and others than other people perceive. Optimism is usually a desired trait in a project manager.

20. *Feeling energetic.* The work challenge created by the project environment usually brings with it an energetic feeling, where the individual accepts the daily challenge of problem-solving and troubleshooting. The exact degree of energy may depend, of course, on the time of day, the day of the week, or simply the age of the project manager.

21. *Feeling anxious.* Almost all project managers have some degree of "tunnel vision," where they look forward to the end of the project, even when the project is in its infancy. This anxious feeling is not only to see the project end, but to see it completed successfully.

Stress is not necessarily negative. Without certain amounts of stress, reports would never get written or distributed, time deadlines would never be met, and in fact, no one would ever even get to work on time. However, stress can also be a powerful force resulting in illness and even fatal disease, and must be understood and managed if it is to be controlled and utilized for constructive purposes.

The mind, body, and emotions are not the separate entities they were once thought to be. They are one integrated system. One affects the other, sometimes in a positive way, and sometimes in a negative way. Stress becomes detrimental only when it is prolonged beyond what an individual can comfortably handle. In a project environment, with continually changing requirements, impossible deadlines, and each project being considered as a unique entity in itself, we must ask, How much prolonged stress can a project manager handle comfortably?

Business people deal with these stresses in different ways. It is not unusual to find high-powered, successful executives dropping out and buying farms in Vermont. Nor is it unusual to find a project manager turning bicycle shop owner or house painter. When questioned, they will often say that they did it because the pressures of their old jobs "weren't worth it."

Others are opting for early retirement at age fifty-five rather than continue to face the pressures of a demanding job. They may have successfully moved in their career to a point of having responsibility for large projects involving millions of dollars and interfacing with all kinds of people. However, by then they might prefer not to take on another vast project. They often reach a plateau or develop a neurotic suspicion that every subordinate is competing for their job. In project management, peers may become subordinates. Responsibility increases threefold. Project managers may be caught in a vise of conflicting demands: demands from above to get more done with fewer people, and demands to work harder and longer to meet time constraints.

6.5 STRESS IN PROJECT MANAGEMENT

The factors that serve to make any occupation especially stressful are responsibility without the authority or ability to exert control, a necessity for perfection, the pressure of deadlines, role ambiguity, role conflict, role overload, the crossing of organizational boundaries, responsibility for the actions of subordinates, and the necessity to keep up with the information explosions or technological breakthroughs. Project managers have all of these factors included in their jobs.

A project manager has his resources controlled by line management, yet the responsibilities of bringing a project to completion by a prescribed deadline are his. A project manager may be told to increase the work output, while the work force is simultaneously being cut. Project managers are expected to get work out on schedule, but are often not permitted to pay overtime. One project manager described it this way: "I have to implement plans I didn't design, but if the project fails, I'm responsible."

Project managers, unlike line managers or top executives, do not have the power or facilities to accomplish many of their objectives alone. They must depend on superiors, subordinates, and peers for the cooperation and efforts to make their projects successful, as they are constantly crossing organizational boundaries. Maintaining these three levels of interpersonal relationships is a juggling game that may make a consistent pattern of behavior almost impossible.

The project manager's superior is interested only in what is accomplished and may not be interested in hearing the specifics of how it was accomplished. The executive will hand down a list of required results, but it is the project manager's responsibility to translate that list into an organized system of behaviors that will produce the desired results. Whereas some levels of management have accessibility to a scapegoat if desired performance is not reached, the project manager has to assume full responsibility. He is evaluated on the results of the total operation and is solely responsible for whatever happens.

Additional high-intensity stressors in project management include unrealistic and inflexible time, cost, and performance constraints, unrealistic customer and environmental constraints, no direct input into the staffing process, no direct control or authority over resources after the project begins, no control over subordinates' salaries, and having to share key personnel with other projects.

The stresses of project management may seem excessive for whatever rewards the position may offer. However, the project manager who is aware of the stresses inherent in the job and knows stress management techniques can face this challenge objectively and make it a rewarding experience.

6.6 TIME MANAGEMENT SURVEY

In March/April 1981, a survey was conducted of more than 300 project managers in twenty-four different industries to identify the problems that exist in trying to obtain effective project time management.[4] The survey was conducted with written questionnaires and personal interviews. Fifteen areas were investigated:

- Employee's background (age, project time span, and dollar value of project)
- Energy cycle per day
- Energy cycle per week
- Daily/weekly work schedule
- Overtime
- Productivity
- Meetings

---

4. Although we refer to the respondents as project managers, the list also includes assistant project manager, project engineers, and other project office personnel.

TABLE 6–1. SURVEY BASE

Industry	Number of People		Average Age, Years	Span of Projects	Value of Projects
	Male	Female			
Utilities (electric)	9	2	40–45	2 mos–4 yrs	$2M–200M
Automotive equipment	39	0	35–40	1–7 yrs	1M–100M
Utilities (telephone)	10	0	35–40	1 mo–2 yrs	10K–500K
Oil	10	0	35–50	1–5 yrs	25M–2.5B
Banking	5	3	25–30	2 wks–6 mos	10K–100K
Manufacturing	7	0	25–35	6 mos–1 yr	1M–9M
Construction	57	2	30–40	6 mos–5 yrs	1M–500M
Communications	9	0	30–35	6 mos–2 yrs	50K–25M
Computers	2	1	25–30	6 mos–2yrs	100K–175K
Steel	7	1	25–30	3 mos–1 yr	10K–1M
Chemical	4	0	30–40	3 mos–1 yr	25K–5M
Government	38	3	45–55	3 mos–2 yrs	100K–25M
Batteries	10	0	30–35	6 mos–1 yr	100K–2M
Rubber	3	0	45–50	2 mos–1 yr	100K–500K
Nuclear	4	1	30–35	6 mos–5 yrs	100K–50M
Consulting (engineering)	9	0	30–35	1 mo–2 yrs	25K–500K
Health care	7	3	30–35	1 mo–3 yrs	25K–2M

- Time robbers
- Time away from desk
- Priorities
- Communications
- Conflict management
- Planning/replanning
- Community service
- Delegation

Table 6–1 identifies the survey base for the questionnaires. The respondents were surveyed according to gender, average age, project time span, and dollar value of project. The seventeen industries shown in Table 6–1 were representative of the survey. Most of the projects fell into the one- to two-year time period except for banking and manufacturing. The banking projects were predominantly data processing-oriented, and the manufacturing projects were capital equipment projects for modification and improvement of existing facilities. This accounts for the relatively short time periods.

The average age of the project managers appears to be consistent with published data.[5,6] The average age of all project managers appears to fall in the range

5. Harold Kerzner, "Formal Training for Project Managers," *Project Management Quarterly*, June 1979, pp. 38–44.

6. Harold Kerzner, "The Educational Path to Training Systems Managers," *Journal of Systems Management*, December 1978, pp. 23–27.

of thirty–forty years. The younger project managers are usually found in computer-oriented projects, such as in banking. Two surprises were found in the age brackets. In manufacturing companies today the trend is to give more responsibility to the younger manufacturing engineers for the capital equipment projects, and the steel industry appears to be hiring younger project managers and providing them with sufficient training in project management. Unfortunately, the sample size of the survey in these two areas makes these statements more assumptions than facts.

It should be mentioned that in some project-driven organizations such as construction, the project managers are generally older than the thirty–forty years identified in Table 6–1. The thirty–forty years reported reflects ages of project office personnel and assistant project managers.

Energy Cycle per Day

The exact amount of energy that an employee possesses is usually a function of such variables as fatigue, efficiency of work, concentration, amount of work, listlessness, eagerness, and alertness. Unfortunately, these individual energy flow variables are extremely difficult to measure. Because of the difficulty in measuring these parameters, the project managers were asked simply to rate their energy level per hour (per work day) on a scale from 1 to 10, with 10 being the best rating. Figure 6–6 illustrates the average energy cycle. Most respondents identified a primary and a secondary peak.

The energy cycle per day per industry is identified in Table 6–2. Most employees identified primary and secondary peaks as in Figure 6–6, with the first peak at 9–11 A.M. and the second peak at 1–4 P.M. However, there were some unusual results. Both NASA and construction project managers identified their secondary peaks as being higher than their primary peaks, a suggestion that these people do their more productive work in the afternoon rather than the morning. Another interesting result is in the magnitude of the energy level. Several respondents indicated that they never achieve an energy level of 10. Generally, project-driven organizations and those that use well-established historical standards for work appear to have the highest overall levels of energy.

All employees identified a minimum level at noon, the time for their lunch hour. However, because some employees work through lunch, the energy levels were never assigned a scale value of 1. Probably the most interesting result was that most project managers and project engineers know their own energy cycle. Many people believe, for example, that they do their most effective writing in the morning and save their reading for the afternoon. It is very important to know one's own energy cycle.

Energy Cycle per Week

Most employees do not perform at the same energy level each day of the week. In order to verify this, the respondents were asked again to rate their energy on a scale of 1 to 10, but for each day of the week. The results are shown in Table 6–3. Most respondents felt that their peak performance days were Wednesday and

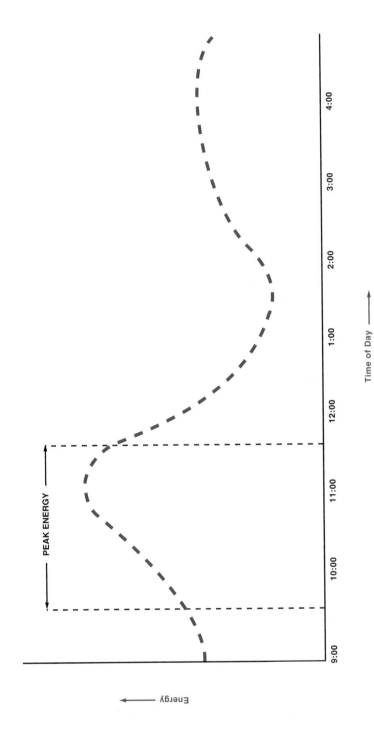

FIGURE 6-6. Energy cycle.

340

TABLE 6–2. ENERGY CYCLE PER DAY (8 A.M. TO 5 P.M.)

Industry Type	First Peak		Minimum		Second Peak	
	Time	Range	Time	Range	Time	Range
NASA	9–12	8.6–9.2	8–9 12–1	7.7	1–3	9.2
EDP	9–12	8.75	12–1	6.5	2–4	8.6
Auto manu. (primary)	9–11	8.0–8.3	12–1	7.0	2–3, 4–5	8.1
Auto manu. (subcontractors)	9–11	9.5	12–1	3.3	1–3	8.75
Construction*	8–11	8.6	12–1	6.2	1–3	8.75
Construction**	7–4	8.5	—	—	—	—
Oil	9–11	9.4	12–1	6.2	2–5	8.1
Primary batteries	9–11	8.4	12–1	5.2	1–2	7.0
Manu. engineering	9–12	9.0–9.2	12–1	7.5	1–5	7.8–8.0
Government	9–10	9.60	12–1	5.9	2–4	7.7–7.8
Others	10–12	8.8	12–1	5.4	2–4	7.2

*These personnel felt that their energy fluctuated per hour.
**These personnel felt that their energy cycle was virtually constant for the entire day.

Thursday. Construction and oil industries had the highest overall energy level per week.

Several people identified energy levels for Saturday and Sunday because of the necessity for overtime. In most cases, the energy level for Saturday was lower than that of the weekdays, and Sunday was lower than Saturday. Surprisingly, respondents from the automobile manufacturers, manufacturing engineering, and construction industries stated that they maintain at least 90 percent of their peak energy on Saturday. Unfortunately, there was no discussion as to whether this was due to mandatory workload, overtime pay, or other such arguments. However, the high Sunday energy level for the construction respondents indicates that, at least for the construction industry, the pressure of the time, cost, and performance con-

TABLE 6–3. ENERGY CYCLE PER WEEK

Industry	Monday	Tuesday	Wednesday	Thursday	Friday	Saturday	Sunday
NASA	8.25	9.25	9.75	9.63	7.14	5.0	
EDP	7.1	8.7	8.65	8.85	8.2	7.4	5.0
Auto. manu. (primary)	8.1	8.2	7.5	8.1	8.6	8.9	6.9
Auto. manu. (subcontractors)	8	9	9	8.7	7		
Construction	8.6	8.8	8.8	9.1	8.9	8.0	7.8
Oil	8.2	9.5	9.5	9.5	8.1		
Primary batteries	6.7	8.4	8.5	7.9	6.0	4.3	3.5
Manu. engineering	7.3	8.4	8.9	9.0	8.5	8.3	6.9
Others	8.1	8.9	8.6	8.1	6.4	3.8	

straints make prolonged overtime a necessity, and employees are expected to perform at a high energy level continuously.

Daily–Weekly Work Schedule

The majority of the people surveyed began work between 7:30 and 8:00 A.M. and finished between 4:00 and 5:00 P.M. Several government employees operated on a flex-time schedule. This meant that their energy cycle per day had to be adjusted to a common starting time. The employees who were under the flex-time system were required to work a minimum of 8.5 hours per day and *had* to be in the plant between 9:00 A.M. and 3:30 P.M. (core time). The employees could begin their workday any time between 7:00 and 9:00 A.M. With the adjustment of a common starting point due to flex-time, almost all government employees exhibited the daily energy cycle shown in Table 6–2.

This concept of flex-time is often used in project management. For example, it is common for East Coast companies to have their procurement specialists maintain a noon to 8:30 P.M. workday so as to coincide with the normal workday of West Coast distributors and vendors. Remote-location projects often create a need for flex-time for home office communications.

Overtime

Project-driven organizations tend to require a great deal of overtime due to underemployment, rather than to have to terminate people because of overemployment. These companies believe that if you have sufficient resources for all of your projects, then your organization is overstaffed. Non–project-driven organizations also require overtime but not to the same degree as in the project-driven organization. When respondents were asked about overtime, the following responses were obtained:

- Ninety percent of the government project managers worked an average of four–eight hours of overtime per week.
- Almost 100 percent of the construction workers claimed that overtime was a necessity, at 14.9 hours per week.
- The oil industry project managers equated the necessity and amount of overtime with the size of the project.
- Automotive equipment manufacturers and primary batteries managers also equated overtime with the size of the project, and said that overtime is usually required on all of the large projects.
- Health care/health services personnel work an average of six hours of overtime per week on their data processing/MIS projects.
- Nuclear power personnel stated that overtime is required on 50 percent of their projects, and the overtime is usually accomplished on Saturdays rather than weekdays.

Overtime can be good for the company as long as productivity levels are maintained. However, if overtime is prolonged, then employees may end up giving the same output in twelve hours that they would produce in a normal eight-hour day. In addition, if the overtime is prolonged, employees may get used to the overtime pay and may "create" the need for additional overtime if they feel that the additional money may be terminated.

Productivity

An individual can have a large amount of energy, but the productive use of this energy may be low. The average employee is usually productive about six hours in an eight-hour workday. The reason for this 70–80 percent productivity level is that various items "steal" time needed for the completion of a task. The following such items were identified by project managers:[7]

- Lack of information in a ready format
- Phone calls
- Day-to-day administration
- Spending more time than anticipated in answering questions
- Lack of sufficient clerical support
- Late appointments
- Impromptu tasks
- Unscheduled appointments or "drop-ins"
- Union grievances
- Having to explain "thinking" to superiors
- Too many levels of review
- Too many people in a small area
- Office casual conversations

The last two items require further clarification. More and more organizations are finding that white-collar productivity is directly related to the working environment. If employees are provided a relatively secluded place to work, productivity will increase. A company employing 1,700 people found that their white-collar productivity was five hours out of a nine-hour day. This low productivity was attributed to the fact that the employees' desks were so close together that casual conversations were continually occurring, and employees had to work overtime to get their normal workload completed.

Table 6–4 shows the way that the various project managers and project office personnel responded to questions about effective productive hours per day. The majority of the people felt that they were productive at least six hours per day. Productivity lower than this is probably the result of increased time robbers, or an inability to handle time robbers.

Most of the respondees felt that their productivity was at least the same on overtime. However, several comments were made that prolonged or continuous overtime would have a direct bearing on efficiency.

---

7. Some of these items are found in the "time robbers" list of Section 6.2.

TABLE 6–4. PRODUCTIVITY PER DAY*

Industry	Productive Hours per Day							
	2 hrs	3 hrs	4 hrs	5 hrs	6 hrs	7 hrs	8 hrs	9 hrs
Rubber/chemical			5.6		33.3	11.1	22.2	27.8
Government		10.0		40.0	40.0	10.0		
Automotive equipment					20.0	40.0	40.0	
Automotive (subcontracts)	6.25		12.5	12.5	37.5	12.5	18.75	
Construction					75.0	25.0		
Health care				44.4	55.6			
Utilities (electrical)					50.0	20.0	30.0	
Banking					100**			
Batteries				33.3	33.3	33.4		

*Table identifies percentage of industry personnel selecting each choice.
**Only average figures available.

Meetings

Meetings become a way of life in project management and project engineering. Unfortunately, meetings can become unproductive and a total waste of time, especially if the project manager:

- Spends too much time on trivial items
- Neglects sending out an agenda
- Holds too many team meetings
- Holds too few team meetings
- Neglects inviting personnel with decision-making authority

If functional employees are unhappy with the way that the project is progressing, they can easily tie up valuable time in team meetings by arguing about trivial items. This is often the case when team members wish to avoid making a decision. Team meetings are ideal for routine activities such as schedule updating and status reporting. However, if decision making is necessary, the project manager may have a problem because the functional team members may not have the authority to make a decision without first checking with their line managers. The project managers *must* learn, at the beginning of the project, which team members actually represent their line groups in decision making. One employee responded: "A letter would be just as effective as a team meeting but would require less time. Many meetings are just communications, not decision making."

Functional managers would like nothing better than to be able to attend project team meetings, but they do not have the time. Functional managers argue that they cannot spend two hours or more in a project team meeting simply to participate in a fifteen-minute conversation. If the project manager sends out an agenda and identifies the approximate time when each major topic will be discussed, then he may find more decision makers attending his meetings, and the meetings can easily become more productive.

Table 6–5 lists seven industry responses regarding the amount of time per week spent in meetings and how productive the meetings are. In general, the project-driven organizations appear to spend more time in meetings than the non–project-driven organizations, and the productivity of the former meetings seems to be higher. This may be attributed to the pressure of the project-driven organization as well as the experience and maturity of the project-driven organization.

Team meetings are supposedly meetings of the mind where information giving and receiving and listening take place. Unfortunately, many meetings are conducted using the methodology of Figure 6–7. Unless they are effective, team meetings become time management pitfalls. The project manager must ensure that meetings are valuable and necessary for the exchange of information. General guidelines for conducting effective meetings are given in Chapter 5 (Section 5.13).

Time Robbers

In the previous discussions, identification was made of the most common time robbers in a project environment; they are listed in Table 6–6.

The project managers were queried as to which of these time robbers commonly occur on their projects, and how much time is usually spent per week on each time robber. The results are shown in Table 6–6. Delayed decisions and poor communications were the most commonly identified items. Most of the industries appear to have two or three predominant time robbers, except for the construction project managers.

Most respondents identified "other" items that detracted from their performance. Seventy percent of the major automotive equipment manufacturer respondents identified such items. The following "other" items were listed in this survey:

- Lack of information in a ready format
- Too many people in a small area
- Casual office conversations
- Day-to-day administration
- Spending more time than anticipated answering questions
- Lack of sufficient clerical support
- Late appointments

TABLE 6–5. MEETINGS

Industry	Approx. Hours per Week	Productivity Level of Meetings
Oil	10	No response
NASA	6–11	75%
Government	8	75%
Batteries	1	50%
Automotive	1	50%
Health care (MIS)	13	No response
Nuclear	8	80%

FIGURE 6–7. How to conduct an effective meeting.

- Impromptu tasks
- Having to explain thinking to superiors
- Too many levels of review
- Union grievances

Several project managers felt that they should be divorced from the parent company's administrative responsibilities. Although this point may be arguable, the author contends that all projects are still attached to the parent company administratively, and thus project personnel must assume their share of responsibility for company administrative requirements.

Also shown in Table 6–6 is the average number of hours spent per week on each time robber. This identifies the magnitude of the time management problem. One project manager in the nuclear power industry estimated that he spends fourteen hours per week on the time robbers. If 30 to 40 percent of his time is spent on the time robbers, then this limits him to a maximum of 70 percent productivity in each time period. Another project manager felt that time robbers are simply part of a project manager's responsibility: "I'm not sure that I have a lot of time robbers, just a lot of work."

TABLE 6–6. TIME ROBBERS ANALYSIS*

	Industries								
Time Robbers	Automotive Equipment	Automotive Subcontractors	Construction	Utilities (Electrical)	NASA	Batteries	Communications	Others	Range of Hours per Week
Incomplete work	40	40	30	50	30	40	70	50	1–2
Jobs done over	40	70	10	50	50	30	60	50	1–5
Delayed decisions	80	100	50	90	100	60	80	70	1–4
Poor communication	50	80	50	80	50	80	70	70	1–10
Telephone calls	70	100	30	40	20	60	70	60	$1/_2$–10
Casual visits	50	70	20	60	30	40	30	40	$1/_2$–5
Waiting for people	70	70	50	30	40	70	70	60	$1/_2$–5
Failure to delegate	20	30	10	60	20	10	30	20	2–5
Poor retrieval system	30	50	40	20	30	20	70	30	1–5
Others	70	10	20	20	30	10	10	10	1–3

*Table identifies percentage of the respondees that selected each item.

Time Away from Desk

The project managers were asked to identify how much time they spend away from their desks. The results are shown in Table 6–7. The majority of the respondents indicated that 5 to 30 percent of their time is spent away from their desks on such items as:

- Vendor visits/communications
- Team meetings
- Time robbers
- Traveling
- Supervising functional work

TABLE 6–7. TIME AWAY FROM DESK*

	Time Away from Desk (%)												
Industry	0	1–3	5	10	15	20	25	30	35	40	50	60	70
Oil			10	20	10	10	10	10		20		10	
Chemical/ rubber	10		10	25	10	5		20		20			
Government	5	45		10	5	15	5			5			
NASA			10	15	5	10	15	10	5	10	15		5
Construction	5			20	5	35	5	10		10	5	5	
Batteries			10	10		30	30	10			10		
Health care			25	75									

*Table shows percentage of industry respondees that selected each category.

Priorities

The purpose of the priorities question was to determine how project priorities were established, and by whom. Here, we are referring to the activities on the project, not necessarily for new projects. Most of the project managers were at either one end of the spectrum or the other; namely, either they establish the priorities, or top management does it. The following responses were typical of the survey results:

● *Oil industry:* 100 percent of project managers felt that they establish their own priorities.
● *Construction industry:* Priorities are established by either the customer or in-house top-level management.
● *Primary batteries:* Priorities are established by either the results of the cost-benefit analysis or top-level management.
● *Nuclear:* Project managers set all priorities, but 50 percent do it with top management approval.
● *Health care:* "Everyone except the project managers appears to be establishing the priorities."

The majority of the project managers appeared to be unfamiliar with the methods used by top management to establish priorities.

Communications

The project managers were asked how they prefer to communicate on the project, and were asked to select from these forms of communication:

● Written formal
● Written informal
● Oral formal
● Oral informal

Several respondents felt that they could not answer the question without specifying whether the communications were with superiors, subordinates, or the client. The results are shown in Table 6–8. Most people seemed to prefer oral communications, especially informal ones.

As part of the survey, the project managers were asked how much time they spend each week trying to resolve conflicts. The results are shown in Table 6–9. It was anticipated that the project managers in project-driven organizations would spend more time resolving conflicts than those in non–project-driven organizations. The results of the survey, however, are not conclusive enough to support this hypothesis.

Planning/ Replanning Time

The project managers were asked how many hours they spend each week either planning (originally unplanned) project activities for a project already started, or replanning current activities. The results are shown in Table 6–10. Most project

TABLE 6–8. COMMUNICATIONS*

Communications With	Communications Form	Oil	Electric Utilities	NASA	Automotive	Batteries	Banking	Construction
Superior	Written formal		20	26	42	23	50	
	Written informal		18	23	10	23		50
	Oral formal		15	20	27	16		
	Oral informal		47	31	21	38	50	50
Subordinate	Written formal	20	20	26	19	23	50	
	Written informal		18	23	35	23		50
	Oral formal		15	20	11	16		
	Oral informal	80	47	31	35	38	50	50
Client	Written formal				42			50
	Written informal				3			
	Oral formal				28			50
	Oral informal				27			

*Table shows percentage of respondees that selected each item.

managers felt that at least ten hours per week are spent on planning/replanning. Several project managers tried to distinguish between planning and replanning, and commented that planning requires at least twice as much time as replanning. However, it was felt that some of these people may have misunderstood the nature of the question.

Community Service   People in a project environment, especially project managers, have very little if any time available for community service work. The average response for all in-

TABLE 6–9. CONFLICT MANAGEMENT TIME

Industry	Average Hours per Week Resolving Conflicts
Rubber/chemical	2
Oil	10
Electronic utilities	9.9
NASA	4.3
Automotive	6.3
Construction	13.8
Banking (MIS)	12
Health care	10
Communications	12
Government	6

TABLE 6–10. PLANNING/REPLANNING TIME

Industry	Average Hours per Week Spent Planning/Replanning Project
Oil	10
Construction	3 (small projects), 10 (large projects)
NASA	6
Automotive	4.8
Banking	14.4
Health care	10
Communications	12.4
Government	8

TABLE 6–11. DELEGATION TIME

Industry	Percentage of Project Manager's Work Load Delegated
Rubber/chemical	18
Oil	57
Electrical utility	20–70, varies with project
Construction	22
Banking	40
Health care	20
Comunications	80 administrative/20 technical
Government	25
NASA	56

dustries was approximately four hours per week spent in such work, with most of that time going to religious organizations. There was no distinction in the responses between project- and non–project-driven organizations.

Delegation

The project managers were asked what percentage of their own work they try to delegate to subordinates. The results are shown in Table 6–11. Most project managers said that they try to delegate as much work as possible while delegating virtually no authority. Ideally, if the project manager delegated all of the work, the result would resemble Figure 6–8. Unfortunately, there will always be paperwork to create the situation shown in Figure 6–9.

We can now summarize the major time management problems for the project managers. These include:

- Meetings (eight hours/week, from Table 6–5)
- Time robbers (ten hours/week, from Table 6–6)[8]

8. This assumes that 50 percent of the time robbers will occur, requiring the mean time from Table 6–6.

FIGURE 6–8. Project management: effective resource utilization.

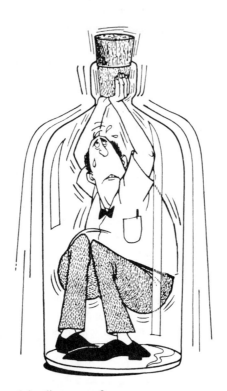

FIGURE 6–9. Is paperwork bottling you up?

- Conflicts (twelve hours/week, from Table 6–9)
- Planning/replanning (ten hours/week, from Table 6–10)

Summing up these hours, we find that it is entirely possible for project managers to spend forty hours or more each week on these problems—a calculation that neglects the possibility that the project manager's overall efficiency may be only 70 to 80 percent!

6.7 EFFECTIVE TIME MANAGEMENT

There are several techniques that project managers can practice in order to make better use of their time:[9]

- Delegate.
- Follow the schedule.
- Decide fast.
- Decide who should attend.
- Learn to say no.
- Start now.
- Do the tough part first.
- Travel light.
- Work at travel stops.
- Avoid useless memos.
- Refuse to do the unimportant.
- Look ahead.
- Ask: Is this trip necessary?
- Know your energy cycle.
- Control telephone time.
- Send out the meeting agenda.
- Shut off in-house visits.
- Overcome procrastination.
- Manage by exception.

As we learned in Chapter 5, the project manager, to be effective, must establish time management rules and then ask himself four questions:

- Rules for time management
  - Conduct a time analysis (time log).
  - Plan solid blocks for important things.
  - Classify your activities.

---

9. Source unknown.

- Establish priorities.
- Establish opportunity cost on activities.
- Train your system (boss, subordinate, peers).
- Practice delegation.
- Practice calculated neglect.
- Practice management by exception.
- Focus on opportunities—not on problems.
- Questions
  - What am I doing that I don't have to be doing at all?
  - What am I doing that can be done better by someone else?
  - What am I doing that could be done as well by someone else?
  - Am I establishing the right priorities for my activities?

The following recommendations are given to project managers:

- Know the weekly and daily energy cycle of your people as well as your own. Be sure to assign or perform work that is compatible with this energy cycle.
- If you have employees who come and go on flex-time schedules, be sure to account for this arrangement in assigning work and understanding their energy cycle.
- Understand the productivity levels of your people, and make sure that the project's performance standards are compatible with the productivity level of your people.
- Do not schedule overtime unnecessarily unless you know that overtime is needed and that efficiency will be maintained. It is possible for employees to "save themselves for overtime" and thereby produce the same work in twelve hours that they would in eight hours.
- Try to monitor your own workload closely and see if there is any work that could be done effectively by someone else. If necessary, refuse to do the unimportant work. Avoid procrastination and try to work on the most difficult tasks first. Start now and look for ways to buy additional time. Be prepared to make quick decisions.
- Do not schedule meetings unless they are cost-effective and necessary. Assist your people in preparation for the meeting. Prepare an agenda and make sure that key personnel are informed well in advance of any major problems to be discussed.
- Conduct the meeting effectively and efficiently. Start the meeting on time, get right to the point, and end the meeting on time. Try to get all attendees to express their views, and avoid prolonged discussions of trivial tasks.
- Decide whether it is absolutely necessary for you to attend a given meeting, especially if it requires travel time. If travel time is required, be prepared to work at travel stops.
- Try to minimize the amount of time you spend away from your desk. Be willing to delegate. Plan solid blocks of time for important work. Classify

your objectives, and get to the point at once. Learn how to say no. Be willing to delegate and employ the management-by-exception concept.

- Time robbers can destroy a good project schedule. Control telephone time and be willing to let your secretary take messages. Get rid of casual visitors. If necessary, find a way to work in seclusion.
- Establish proper priorities for yourself, your project, and your people.
- Avoid time-consuming communication processes. Avoid memos. If memos or letters are necessary, make them short and summary-type in nature. If you have lengthy reports to read, it is best to take them with you on long trips.
- Train your boss, peers, and subordinates how to work with you. Be willing to assert your rights.
- If conflict resolution is necessary, obtain the necessary information as fast as possible and make a decision. Establishing procedures for conflict resolution may be helpful.
- Follow your schedules closely, especially items on the critical path. You may find it necessary to monitor critical items yourself rather than wait for periodic feedback.
- Be willing to delegate work to subordinates and peers. Do not try to be a "nice guy" and do it all yourself, lest you place yourself in the position of doing work that is normally the responsibility of the functional departments or other project office personnel.

Project managers typically understand the role of the project manager at project conception, but seem to forget it during project execution. This loss of understanding, which creates time management problems for the project manager, is usually caused by the project manager's:

- Waiting for someone else to make a decision that is his own responsibility
- Neglecting to "keep his door open" and "walk the halls" to find out what's going on
- Neglecting to use the experts correctly and trying to do it all himself
- Being concerned about his previous technical discipline or profession rather than the best interest of the company
- Being too interested in methods rather than in results
- Trying to do the work himself rather than delegating it to someone who works more slowly
- Wasting time in project team meetings discussing one-on-one problems
- Failing to recognize that his boss is there to help

Project managers must understand that even though they have the authority, responsibility, and accountability for a project, there are still parent company administrative duties that must be accepted. These items are usually additional work that the project manager has not considered.

Project management may not be the best system for managing resources, but it is better than anything we have had in the past. Effective time management may very well be the most important weapon in the project manager's arsenal for obtaining proper resource control.

6.8 MANAGEMENT PITFALLS

The project environment offers numerous opportunities for project managers and team members to get into trouble, above and beyond time management traps. These problem-causing activities are referred to as management pitfalls. Common types of management pitfalls are:

- Lack of planning
- Lack of self-control (knowing oneself)
- Activity traps
- Managing versus doing
- People versus task skills
- Ineffective communications
- Management bottlenecks

These management pitfalls are discussed in detail in Chapter 5 (Section 5.12), to which the reader is referred.

6.9 PROJECT COMMUNICATIONS

Proper communications are vital to project success. The subject of communications was discussed in Chapter 5 (Section 5.13) and will be reviewed only briefly here. The four types of communication are:

- Written formal
- Written informal
- Oral formal
- Oral informal

Noise, from our own personality screens and from our perception screens, may distort or destroy information, causing ambiguity. Such ambiguity:

- Causes us to hear what we want to hear
- Causes us to hear what the group wants
- Causes us to relate to past experiences without being discriminatory
- Causes situations like those depicted in Figure 6–10

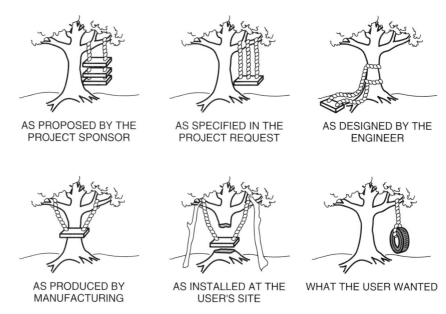

AS PROPOSED BY THE   AS SPECIFIED IN THE   AS DESIGNED BY THE
PROJECT SPONSOR   PROJECT REQUEST   ENGINEER

AS PRODUCED BY   AS INSTALLED AT THE   WHAT THE USER WANTED
MANUFACTURING   USER'S SITE

FIGURE 6–10. A breakdown in communications. (Source unknown)

The reader should consult Section 5.13 for the six simple steps for communicating, techniques used to improve communication, and barriers to communication. The following admonitions from Section 5.13 are well worth repeating:

- Don't assume that the message you sent will be received in the form you sent it.
- The swiftest and most effective communications take place among people with common points of view. The manager who fosters a good relationship with his associates will have little difficulty in communicating with them.
- Communications must be established early in the project.

Communication is also listening (see Figure 6–11). The advantages of being a good listener, both professionally and personally, are that:

- Subordinates know you are sincerely interested.
- You obtain feedback.
- Employee acceptance is fostered.

Ask yourself these questions:

- Do I make it easy for employees to talk to me?
- Am I sympathetic to their problems?

FIGURE 6–11. Listen to everything.

- Do I attempt to improve human relations?
- Do I make an extra effort to remember names and faces?

6.10 PROJECT MANAGEMENT BOTTLENECKS

Poor communications can produce communications bottlenecks, in both the parent and client organizations. The most common problems in information flow were discussed in Chapter 5 (see Section 5.13). Table 5–4 shows typical communications policies that can be employed to avoid bottlenecks.

PROBLEMS

6–1   Should time robbers be added to direct labor standards for pricing out work?

6–2   Is it possible for a project manager to improve his time management skills by knowing the "energy cycle" of his people? Can this energy cycle be a function of the hour of the day, day of the week, or whether overtime is required?

CASE STUDIES

THE RELUCTANT WORKERS

Tim Aston had changed employers three months ago. His new position was project manager. At first he had stars in his eyes about becoming the best project manager that his company had ever seen. Now, he wasn't sure if project management was worth the effort. He made an appointment to see Phil Davies, director of project management.

Tim Aston: "Phil, I'm a little unhappy about the way things are going. I just can't seem to motivate my people. Every day, at 4:30 P.M., all of my people clean off their desks and go home. I've had people walk out of late afternoon team meetings because they were afraid that they'd miss their car pool. I have to schedule morning team meetings."

Phil Davies: "Look, Tim. You're going to have to realize that in a project environment, people think that they come first and that the project is second. This is a way of life in our organizational form."

Tim Aston: "I've continually asked my people to come to me if they have problems. I find that the people do not think that they need help and, therefore, do not want it. I just can't get my people to communicate more."

Phil Davies: "The average age of our employees is about forty-six. Most of our people have been here for twenty years. They're set in their ways. You're the first person that we've hired in the past three years. Some of our people may just resent seeing a thirty-year-old project manager."

Tim Aston: "I found one guy in the accounting department who has an excellent head on his shoulders. He's very interested in project management. I asked his boss if he'd release him for a position in project management, and his boss just laughed at me, saying something to the effect that as long as that guy is doing a good job for him, he'll never be released for an assignment elsewhere in the company. His boss seems more worried about his personal empire than he does in what's best for the company.

"We had a test scheduled for last week. The customer's top management was planning on flying in for firsthand observations. Two of my people said that they had programmed vacation days coming, and that they would not change, under any conditions. One guy was going fishing and the other guy was planning to spend a few days working with fatherless children in our community. Surely, these guys could change their plans for the test."

Phil Davies: "Many of our people have social responsibilities and outside interests. We encourage social responsibilities and only hope that the outside interests do not interfere with their jobs.

"There's one thing you should understand about our people. With an average age of forty-six, many of our people are at the top of their pay grades and have no place to go. They must look elsewhere for interests. These are the people you have to work with and motivate. Perhaps you should do some reading on human behavior."

TIME MANAGEMENT FOR PROJECT MANAGERS

Effective time management is one of the most difficult chores facing even the most experienced managers. For a manager who manages well-planned repetitive tasks, effective time management can be accomplished without very much pain. But for a project manager who must plan, schedule, and control resources and activities on unique, one-of-a-kind projects or tasks, effective time management may not be possible because of the continuous stream of unexpected problems that develop.

This exercise is designed to make you aware of the difficulties of time management both in a traditional organization and in a project environment. Before beginning the exercise, you must make the following assumptions concerning the nature of the project:

- You are the project manager on a project for an outside customer.
- The project is estimated at $3.5 million with a time span of two years.
- The two-year time span is broken down into three phases: Phase I—one year, beginning February 1; Phase II—six months; Phase III—six months. You are now at the end of Phase I. (Phases I and II overlap by approximately two weeks. You are now in the Monday of the next to the last week of Phase I.) Almost all of the work has been completed.
- Your project employs thirty-five to sixty people, depending on the phase that you are in.
- You, as the project manager, have three full-time assistant project managers that report directly to you in the project office; an assistant project manager each for engineering, cost control, and manufacturing. (Material procurement is included as part of the responsibilities of the manufacturing assistant project manager.)
- Phase I appears to be proceeding within the time, cost, and performance constraints.
- You have a scheduled team meeting for each Wednesday from 10 A.M.–12 noon. The meeting will be attended by all project office team members and the functional team members from all participating line organizations. Line managers are not team members and therefore do not show up at team meetings. It would be impossible for them to show up at the team meetings for all projects and still be able to function as a line manager. Even when requested, they may not show up at the team meeting because it is not effective time management for them to show up for a two-hour meeting simply to discuss ten minutes of business. (Disregard the possibility that a team meeting agenda could resolve this problem.)

It is now Monday morning and you are home eating breakfast, waiting for your car pool to pick you up. As soon as you enter your office, you will be informed about problems, situations, tasks, and activities that have to be investigated. Your problem will be to accomplish effective time management for this entire week based on the problems and situations that occur.

You will take each day one at a time. You will be given ten problems and/or situations that will occur for each day, and the time necessary for resolution. You must try to optimize your time for each of the next five days and get the maximum amount of productive work accomplished. Obviously, the word "productive" can take on several meanings. You must determine what is meant by productive work. For the sake of simplicity, let us assume that your energy cycle is such that you can do eight hours of productive work in an eight-hour day. You do not have to schedule idle time, except for lunch. However, you must be aware that in a project environment, the project manager occasionally becomes the catchall for all work that line managers, line personnel, and even executives do not feel like accomplishing.

Following the ten tasks for each day, you will find a worksheet that breaks down each day into half-hour blocks between 9:00 A.M. and 5:00 P.M. Your job will be to determine which of the tasks you wish to accomplish during each half-hour block. The following assumptions are made in scheduling work:

- Because of car pool requirements, overtime is not permitted.
- Family commitments for the next week prevent work at home. Therefore, you will not schedule any work after 5:00 P.M.
- The project manager is advised of the ten tasks as soon as he arrives at work.

The first step in the solution to the exercise is to establish the priorities for each activity based on:

- *Priority A:* This activity is urgent and must be completed today. (However, some A priorities can be withheld until the team meeting.)
- *Priority B:* This activity is important but not necessarily urgent.
- *Priority C:* This activity can be delayed, perhaps indefinitely.

Fill in the space after each activity as to the appropriate priority. Next, you must determine which of the activities you have time to accomplish for this day. You have either seven or seven and one-half hours to use for effective time management, depending on whether you want a half-hour or a full hour for lunch.

You have choices as to how to accomplish each of the activities. These choices are shown below:

- You can do the activity *yourself* (Symbol = Y).
- You can *delegate* the responsibility to one of your assistant project managers (Symbol = D). If you use this technique, you can delegate only one hour's worth of *your* work to each of your assistants without incurring a penalty. The key word here is that you are delegating *your* work. If the task that you wish to delegate is one that the assistant project manager would normally perform, then it does *not* count toward the one hour's worth of your work. This type of work is transmittal work and will be discussed below. For example, if you wish to delegate five hours of work to one of your assistant project managers and four of those hours are activities that would normally be his responsibility, then no penalty will be assessed. You are actually transmitting four hours and delegating one. You may assume that whatever work you assign to an assistant project manager will be completed on the day it is assigned, regardless of the priority.
- Many times, the project manager and his team are asked to perform work that is normally the responsibility of someone else, say, an executive or a line manager. As an example, a line employee states that he doesn't have sufficient time to write a report and he wants you to do it, since you are the project manager. These types of requests can be returned to the requestor since they normally do not fall within the project manager's responsibilities. You may, therefore, select one of the following four choices:
  - You can *return* the activity request back to the originator, whether line manager, executive, or subordinate, since it is not your responsibility (Symbol = R). Of course, you might want to do this activity, if you have time, in order to build up good will with the requestor.
  - Many times, work that should be requested of an assistant project manager is automatically sent to the project manager. In this case, the project manager will automatically *transmit* this work to the appropriate assistant proj-

ect manager (Symbol = T). As before, if the project manager feels that he has sufficient time available or if his assistants are burdened, he may wish to do the work himself. Work that is normally the responsibility of an assistant project manager is transmitted, not delegated. Thus the project manager can transmit four hours of work (T) and still delegate one hour of work (D) to the same assistant project manager without incurring any penalty.

- You can *postpone* work from one day to the next (Symbol = P). As an example, you decide that you want to accomplish a given Monday activity but do not have sufficient time. You can postpone the activity until Tuesday. If you do not have sufficient time on Tuesday, you may then decide to transmit (T) the activity to one of your assistants, delegate (D) the activity to one of your assistants, return (R) the activity to the requestor, or postpone (P) the activity another day. Postponing activities can be a trap. On Monday you decide to postpone a category B priority. On Tuesday, the activity may become a category A priority and you have no time to accomplish it. If you make a decision to postpone an activity from Monday to Tuesday and find that you have made a mistake by not performing this activity on Monday, you *cannot* go back in time and correct the situation.
- You can simply consider the activity as unnecessary and *avoid* doing it (Symbol = A).

After you have decided which activities you will perform each day, place them in the appropriate time slot based on your own energy cycle. Later we will discuss energy cycles and the order of the activities accomplished each day. You will find one worksheet for each day. The worksheets follow the ten daily situations and/or problems.

Repeat the procedure for each of the five days. Remember to keep track of the activities that are carried over from the previous days. Several of the problems can be resolved by more than one method. If you are thoroughly trapped between two or more choices on setting priorities or modes of resolution, then write a note or two to justify your answer in space beneath each activity.

Scoring System

Briefly look at the work plan for one of the days. Under the column labeled "priority," the ten activities for each day are listed. You must first identify the priorities for each activity. Next, under the column labeled "method," you must select the method of accomplishment according to the legend at the bottom of the page. At the same time, you must fill in the activities you wish to perform yourself under the "accomplishment" column in the appropriate time slot because your method for accomplishment may be dependent on whether you have sufficient time to accomplish the activity.

Notice that there is a space provided for you to keep track of activities that have been carried over. This means that if you have three activities on Monday's list that you wish to carry over until Tuesday, then you must turn to Tuesday's work plan and record these activities so that you will not forget.

You will not score any points until you complete Friday's work plan. Using the scoring sheets that follow Friday's work plan, you can return to the daily work plans and fill in the appropriate points. You will receive either positive points or negative points for each decision that you make. Negative points should be subtracted when calculating totals.

After completing the work plans for all five days, fill in the summary work plan that follows and be prepared to answer the summary questions.

You will not be told at this time how the scoring points will be awarded because it may affect your answers.

Monday's Activities

Activity	*Description*	*Priority*
1.	The detailed schedules for Phase II must be updated prior to Thursday's meeting with the customer. (Time = 1 hr)	_____
2.	The manufacturing manager calls you and states that he cannot find a certain piece of equipment for tomorrow's production run test. (Time = ½ hr)	_____
3.	The local university has a monthly distinguished lecturer series scheduled for 3–5 P.M. today. You have been directed by the vice president to attend and hear the lecture. The company will give you a car. Driving time to the university is one hour. (Time = 3 hrs)	_____
4.	A manufacturer's representative wants to call on you today to show you why his product is superior to the one that you are now using. (Time = ½ hr)	_____
5.	You must write a two-page weekly status report for the vice president. Report is due on his desk by 1:00 P.M. Wednesday. (Time = 1 hr)	_____
6.	A vice president calls you and suggests that you contact one of the other project managers about obtaining a uniform structure for the weekly progress reports. (Time = ½ hr)	_____
7.	A functional manager calls to inform you that, due to a schedule slippage on another project, your beginning milestones on Phase II may slip to the right because his people will not be available. He wants to know if you can look at the detailed schedules and modify them. (Time = 2 hr)	_____
8.	The director of personnel wants to know if you have reviewed the three resumes that he sent you last week. He would like your written comments by quitting time today. (Time = 1 hr)	_____
9.	One of your assistant project managers asks you to review a detailed Phase III schedule that appears to have errors. (Time = 1 hr)	_____
10.	The procurement department calls with a request that you tell them approximately how much money you plan to spend on raw materials for Phase III. (Time = ½ hr)	_____

WORK PLAN

Day _____Monday_____

Priority			Method		Accomplishment		
Activity	Priority	Points	Method of Accomplishment	Points	Time	Activity	Points
1					9:00–9:30		
2					9:30–10:00		
3					10:00–10:30		
4					10:30–11:00		
5					11:00–11:30		
6					11:30–12:00		
7					12:00–12:30		
8					12:30–1:00		
9					1:00–1:30		
10					1:30–2:00		
	Total		Total		2:00–2:30		
					2:30–3:00		
					3:00–3:30		
					3:30–4:00		
					4:00–4:30		
					4:30–5:00		
					Total		

Activities Postponed Until Today	Today's Priority

Points	
Priority Points	
Method Points	
Accomplishment Points	
Today's Points	

Legend

Method of Accomplishment:

Y = you
D = delegate
T = transmit
R = return
A = avoid
P = postpone

Tuesday's Activities

Activity	*Description*	*Priority*
11.	A functional manager calls you wanting to know if his people should be scheduled for overtime next week. (Time = ½ hr)	_____
12.	You have a safety board meeting today from 1–3 P.M. and must review the agenda. (Time = 2½ hrs)	_____
13.	Because of an impending company cash flow problem, your boss has asked you for the detailed monthly labor expenses for the next three months. (Time = 2 hrs)	_____
14.	The vice president has just called to inform you that two congressmen will be visiting the plant today and you are requested to conduct the tour of the facility from 3–5 P.M. (Time = 2 hrs)	_____
15.	You have developed a new policy for controlling overtime costs on Phase II. You must inform your people either by memo, phone, or team meeting. (Time = ½ hr)	_____
16.	You must sign and review twenty-five purchase order requisitions for Phase III raw materials. It is company policy that the project manager sign all forms. Almost all of the items require a three-month lead time. (Time = 1 hr)	_____
17.	The engineering division manager has asked you to assist one of his people this afternoon in the solution of a technical problem. You are not required to do this. It would be as a personal favor for the engineering manager, a man to whom you reported for the six years that you were an engineering functional manager. (Time = 2 hrs)	_____
18.	The data processing department manager informs you that the company is trying to eliminate unnecessary reports. He would like you to tell him which reports you can do without. (Time = ½ hr)	_____
19.	The assistant project manager for cost informs you that he does not know how to fill out the revised corporate project review form. (Time = ½ hr)	_____
20.	One of the functional managers wants an immediate explanation of why the scope of effort for Phase II was changed this late into the project and why he wasn't informed. (Time = 1 hr)	_____

WORK PLAN

Day _____ Tuesday _____

Priority			Method		Accomplishment		
Activity	**Priority**	**Points**	**Method of Accomplishment**	**Points**	**Time**	**Activity**	**Points**
11					9:00–9:30		
12					9:30–10:00		
13					10:00–10:30		
14					10:30–11:00		
15					11:00–11:30		
16					11:30–12:00		
17					12:00–12:30		
18					12:30–1:00		
19					1:00–1:30		
20					1:30–2:00		
Total			Total		2:00–2:30		
					2:30–3:00		
					3:00–3:30		
					3:30–4:00		
					4:00–4:30		
					4:30–5:00		
					Total		

Activities Postponed Until Today	Today's Priority

Points	
Priority Points	
Method Points	
Accomplishment Points	
Today's Points	

Legend
Method of Accomplishment:
Y = you
D = delegate
T = transmit
R = return
A = avoid
P = postpone

Wednesday's Activities

Activity	Description	Priority
21.	A vice president calls you stating that he has just read the rough draft of your Phase I report and wants to discuss some of the conclusions with you before the report is submitted to the customer on Thursday. (Time = 2 hrs)	_____
22.	The reproduction department informs you that they are expecting the final version of the in-house quarterly report for your project by noon today. The report is on your desk waiting for final review. (Time = 1 hr)	_____
23.	The manufacturing department manager calls to say that they may have to do more work than initially defined in Phase II. A meeting is requested. (Time = 1 hr)	_____
24.	Quality control sends you a memo stating that, unless changes are made, they will not be able to work with the engineering specifications developed for Phase III. A meeting will be required with all assistant project managers in attendance. (Time = 1 hr)	_____
25.	A functional manager calls to tell you that the raw data from yesterday's tests are terrific and invites you to come up to the laboratory and see the results yourself. (Time = 1 hr)	_____
26.	Your assistant project manager is having trouble resolving a technical problem. The functional manager wants to deal with you directly. This problem must be resolved by Friday or else a major Phase II milestone might slip. (Time = 1 hr)	_____
27.	You have a technical interchange meeting with the customer scheduled for 1–3 P.M. on Thursday, and must review the handout before it goes to publication. The reproduction department has requested at least twelve hours' notice. (Time = 1 hr)	_____
28.	You have a weekly team meeting from 10–12 A.M. (Time = 2 hrs)	_____
29.	You must dictate minutes to your secretary concerning your weekly team meeting which is held on Wednesday 10–12 A.M. (Time = ½ hr)	_____
30.	A new project problem has occurred in the manufacturing area and your manufacturing functional team members are reluctant to make a decision. (Time = 1 hr)	_____

WORK PLAN

Day _____Wednesday_____

Priority			Method		
Activity	Priority	Points	Method of Accomplishment	Points	
21					
22					
23					
24					
25					
26					
27					
28					
29					
30					
	Total		Total		

Accomplishment		
Time	Activity	Points
9:00–9:30		
9:30–10:00		
10:00–10:30		
10:30–11:00		
11:00–11:30		
11:30–12:00		
12:00–12:30		
12:30–1:00		
1:00–1:30		
1:30–2:00		
2:00–2:30		
2:30–3:00		
3:00–3:30		
3:30–4:00		
4:00–4:30		
4:30–5:00		
Total		

Activities Postponed Until Today	Today's Priority

Legend	
Method of Accomplishment:	
Y = you	
D = delegate	
T = transmit	
R = return	
A = avoid	
P = postpone	

Points	
Priority Points	
Method Points	
Accomplishment Points	
Today's Points	

Thursday's Activities

Activity	Description	Priority
31	The electrical engineering department informs you that they have completed some Phase II activities ahead of schedule and want to know if you wish to push any other activities to the left. (Time = 1 hr)	_____
32.	The assistant project manager for cost informs you that the corporate overhead rate is increasing faster than anticipated. If this continues, severe cost overruns will occur in Phases II and III. A schedule and cost review is necessary. (Time = 2 hrs)	_____
33.	Your insurance man is calling to see if you wish to increase your life insurance. (Time = ½ hr)	_____
34.	You cannot find one of last week's manufacturing line manager's technical reports as to departmental project status. You'll need it for the customer technical interchange meeting. (Time = ½ hr)	_____
35.	One of your car pool members wants to talk to you concerning next Saturday's golf tournament. (Time = ½ hr)	_____
36.	A functional manager calls to inform you that, due to a change in his division's workload priorities, people with the necessary technical expertise may not be available for next week's Phase II tasks. (Time = 2 hrs)	_____
37.	An employee calls you stating that he is receiving conflicting instructions from one of your assistant project managers and his line manager. (Time = 1 hr)	_____
38.	The customer has requested bimonthly instead of monthly team meetings for Phase II. You must decide whether to add an additional project office team member to support the added workload. (Time = ½ hr)	_____
39.	Your secretary reminds you that you must make a presentation to the Rotary Club tonight on how your project will affect the local economy. You must prepare your speech. (Time = 2 hrs)	_____
40.	The bank has just called you concerning your personal loan. The information is urgent to get loan approval in time. (Time = ½ hr)	_____

WORK PLAN

Day _____Thursday_____

Priority			Method				Accomplishment		
Activity	Priority	Points	Method of Accomplishment	Points		Time	Activity	Points
31						9:00–9:30		
32						9:30–10:00		
33						10:00–10:30		
34						10:30–11:00		
35						11:00–11:30		
36						11:30–12:00		
37						12:00–12:30		
38						12:30–1:00		
39						1:00–1:30		
40						1:30–2:00		
	Total		Total			2:00–2:30		
						2:30–3:00		
						3:00–3:30		
						3:30–4:00		
						4:00–4:30		
						4:30–5:00		
						Total		

Activities Postponed Until Today	Today's Priority

Points	
Priority Points	
Method Points	
Accomplishment Points	
Today's Points	

Legend
Method of Accomplishment:
Y = you D = delegate T = transmit R = return A = avoid P = postpone

Friday's Activities

Activity	Description	Priority
41.	An assistant project manager has asked for your solution to a recurring problem. (Time = ½ hr)	_____
42.	A functional employee is up for a merit review. You must fill out a brief checklist form and discuss it with the employee. The form must be on the functional manager's desk by next Tuesday. (Time = ½ hr)	_____
43.	The personnel department wants you to review the summer vacation schedule for your project office personnel. (Time = ½ hr)	_____
44.	The vice president calls you into his office stating that he has seen the excellent test results from this week's work, and feels that a follow-on contract should be considered. He wants to know if you can develop reasonable justification for requesting a follow-on contract at this early date. (Time = 1 hr)	_____
45.	The travel department says that you'll have to make your own travel arrangements for next month's trip to one of the customers, since you are taking a planned vacation trip in conjunction with the customer visit. (Time = ½ hr)	_____
46.	The personnel manager has asked if you would be willing to conduct a screening interview for an applicant who wants to be an assistant project manager. The applicant will be available this afternoon 1–2 P.M. (Time = 1 hr)	_____
47.	Your assistant project manager wants to know why you haven't approved his request to take MBA courses this quarter. (Time = ½ hr)	_____
48.	Your assistant project manager wants to know if he has the authority to visit vendors without informing procurement. (Time = ½ hr)	_____
49.	You have just received your copy of *Engineering Review Quarterly* and would like to look it over. (Time = ½ hr)	_____
50.	You have been asked to make a statement before the grievance committee (this Friday, 10–12 A.M.) because one of the functional employees has complained about working overtime on Sunday mornings. You'll have to be in attendance for the entire meeting. (Time = 2 hrs)	_____

WORK PLAN

Day   Friday

Priority			Method		Accomplishment		
Activity	Priority	Points	Method of Accomplishment	Points	Time	Activity	Points
41					9:00–9:30		
42					9:30–10:00		
43					10:00–10:30		
44					10:30–11:00		
45					11:00–11:30		
46					11:30–12:00		
47					12:00–12:30		
48					12:30–1:00		
49					1:00–1:30		
50					1:30–2:00		
Total			Total		2:00–2:30		
					2:30–3:00		
					3:00–3:30		
					3:30–4:00		
					4:00–4:30		
					4:30–5:00		
					Total		

Activities Postponed Until Today	Today's Priority

Legend
Method of Accomplishment:
Y = you D = delegate T = transmit R = return A = avoid P = postpone

Points	
Priority Points	
Method Points	
Accomplishment Points	
Today's Points	

Rationale and Point Awards

In the answers that follow, your recommendations may differ from those of the author because of the type of industry or the nature of the project. You will be given the opportunity to defend your answers at a later time.

   a. If you selected the correct priority according to the table on pages 375–376, then the following system should be employed for awarding points:

Priority	Points
A	10
B	5
C	3

   b. If you selected the correct accomplishment mode according to the table on pages 375–376, then the following system should be employed for assigning points:

Method of Accomplishment	Points
Y	10
T	10
P	8
D	8
A	6

   c. You will receive 10 bonus points for each correctly postponed or delayed activity accomplished during the team meeting.
   d. You will receive 5 points for each half-hour time slot in which you perform a priority A activity (one that is correctly identified as priority A).
   e. You will receive a 10-point penalty for any activity that is split.
   f. You will receive a 20-point penalty for each priority A or B activity not accomplished by you or your team by Friday at 5:00 P.M.

Activity	*Rationale*
1.	The updating of schedules, especially for Phase II, should be of prime importance because of the impact on functional resources. These schedules can be delegated to assistant project managers. However, with a team meeting scheduled for Wednesday, it should be an easy task to update the schedules when all of the players are present. The updating of the schedules should *not* be delayed until Thursday. Sufficient time must be allocated for close analysis and reproduction services.
2.	This must be done immediately. Your assistant project manager for manufacturing should be able to handle this activity.
3.	You must handle this yourself.
4.	Here, we assume that the representative is available only today. The assistant project managers can handle this activity. This activity may be important if you were unaware of this vendor's product.
5.	This could be delegated to your assistants provided that you allow sufficient time for personal review on Wednesday.
6.	Delaying this activity for one more week should not cause any problems. This activity can be delegated.
7.	You must take charge at once.

Activity	*Rationale*
8.	Even though your main concern is the project, you still must fulfill your company's administrative requirements.
9.	This can be delayed until Wednesday's team meeting, especially since these are Phase III schedules. However, there is no guarantee that line people will be ready or knowledgeable to discuss Phase III this early. You will probably have to do this yourself.
10.	The procurement request must be answered. Your assistant project manager for manufacturing should have this information available.
11.	This is urgent and should *not* be postponed until the team meeting. Good project managers will give functional managers as much information as possible as early as possible for resource control. This task can be delegated to the assistant project managers, but it is notrecommended.
12.	This belongs to the project manager. The agenda review and the meeting can be split, but it is not recommended.
13.	This must be done immediately. The results could severely limit your resources (especially if overtime would normally be required). Although your assistant project managers will probably be involved, the majority of the work is yours.
14.	Most project managers hate a request like this but know that situations such as this are inevitable.
15.	Project policies should be told by the project manager himself. Policy changes should be announced as early as possible. Team meetings are appropriate for such actions.
16.	Obviously, the project manager must do this task himself. Fortunately, there is sufficient time if the lead times are accurate.
17.	The priority of this activity is actually your choice, but an A priority is preferred if you have time. This activity cannot be delegated.
18.	This activity must be done, but the question is when. Parts of this task can be delegated, but the final decision must be made by the project manager.
19.	Obviously you must do this yourself. Your priority, of course, depends on the deadline on the corporate project review form.
20.	The project manager must perform this activity immediately.
21.	Top-level executives from both the customer and contractor often communicate project status among themselves. Therefore, since the conclusions in the report reflect corporate policy, this activity should be accomplished immediately.
22.	The reproduction department considers each job as a project and therefore you should try not to violate their milestones. This activity can be delegated, depending on the nature of the report.
23.	This could have a severe impact on your program. Although you could delegate this to one of your assistants, you should do this yourself because of the ramifications.
24.	This must be done, and the team meeting is the ideal place.
25.	You, personally, should give the functional manager the courtesy of showing you his outstanding results. However, it is not a high priority and could even be delegated or postponed since you'll see the data eventually.

Activity	*Rationale*
26.	The question here is the importance of the problem. The problem must be resolved by Thursday in case an executive meeting needs to be scheduled to establish company direction. Waiting until the last minute can be catastrophic here.
27.	The project manager should personally review all data presented to the customer. Check Thursday's schedule. Did you forget the interchange meeting?
28.	This is your show.
29.	This should be done immediately. Nonparticipants need to know the project status. The longer you wait, the greater the risk that you will neglect something important. This activity can be delegated, but it is not recommended.
30.	You may have to solve this yourself even though you have an assistant project manager for manufacturing. The decision may affect the schedule and miletones.
31.	Activities such as this do not happen very often. But when they do, the project manager should make the most of them, as fast as he can. These are gold mine activities. They can be delegated, but not postponed.
32.	If this activity is not accomplished immediately, the results can be catastrophic. Regardless of the project manager's first inclination to delegate, this activity should be done by the project manager himself.
33.	This activity can be postponed or even avoided, if necessary.
34.	Obviously, if the report is that important, then your assistant project managers should have copies of the report and the activity can be delegated.
35.	This activity should be discussed in the car pool, not on company time.
36.	This is extremely serious. The line manager would probably prefer to work directly with the project manager on this problem.
37.	This is an activity that you should handle. Transmitting this to one of your assistants may aggravate the situation further. Although it is possible that this activity could be postponed, it is highly unlikely that time would smooth out the conflict.
38.	This is a decision for the project manager. Extreme urgency may not be necessary.
39.	Project managers also have a social responsibility.
40.	The solution to this activity is up for grabs. Most companies realize that employees occasionally need company time to complete personal business.
41.	Why is he asking you about a recurring problem? How did he solve it last time? Let him do it again.
42.	You must do this personally, but it can wait until Monday.
43.	This activity is not urgent and can be accomplished by your assistant project managers.
44.	This could be your lucky day.
45.	Although most managers would prefer to delegate this activity to their secretaries, it is really the responsibility of the project manager since it involves personal business.

PRIORITY/ACCOMPLISHMENT MODE

Activity	Monday Prior.	Monday Accom.	Tuesday Prior.	Tuesday Accom.	Wednesday Prior.	Wednesday Accom.	Thursday Prior.	Thursday Accom.	Friday Prior.	Friday Accom.
1	B	D,Y,T,P	B	D,Y,T,P	A	D,Y,T				
2	A	D,Y,T								
3	A	Y								
4	A/B	D,Y,T								
5	B	D,Y,P	B	D,Y,P	A	D,Y				
6	B	D,Y,P	B	D,Y,P	B	D,Y,P	B	D,Y,P	B	D,Y,P
7	A	Y								
8	A	Y								
9	B	Y,P	B	Y,P	A	Y				
10	B	Y,T,P	B	Y,T,P	B	Y,T,P	B	Y,T,P	B	Y,T,P
11			A	D,Y,T						
12			A	Y						
13			A	Y,P						
14			A	Y						
15			B	P,Y	A	Y				
16			B	Y,P	B	Y,P	B	Y,P	B	Y,P
17			C	A,Y						
18			B/C	D,Y,P	B	D,Y,P	B	D,Y,P	B	D,Y,P
19			A/B	Y,P	A/B	Y,P	A/B	Y,P	A/B	Y,P
20			A	Y						
21					A	Y				
22					A	D,Y				
23					A	D,Y,T				

(continues)

#						
24	A	Y	B	Y,T,P,D	B	Y,T,P,R
25	B	Y,T,P,D	A	Y		
26	B	Y				
27	A	Y				
28	A	Y				
29	A	Y,D				
30	A	Y,T				
31			A	Y,D		
32			A	Y		
33			C	Y,P	C	Y,P
34			A	Y,T		
35			C	A,P	C	A,P
36			A	Y,T		
37			A	Y		
38			B	Y,P	B	Y,P
39			A	Y		
40			A	Y		
41					A/B	R
42					B	Y,P
43					B	Y,P,D
44					A	Y
45					B	Y,P
46					A	Y,T,D
47					A	Y
48					B	Y,T,P,D,R
49					C	Y,P,A
50					A	Y

Activity	*Rationale*
46.	This is an example of an administrative responsibility that is required of all personnel regardless of the job title or management level. This activity must be accomplished today, if time permits.
47.	Although you might consider this as a B priority or one that can be postponed, you must remember that your assistant project manager considers this as an A priority and would like an answer today. You are morally obligated to give him the answer today.
48.	Why can't he get the answer himself? Whether or not you handle this activity might depend on the priority and how much time you have available.
49.	How important is it for you to review the publication?
50.	This is mandatory attendance on your behalf. You have total responsibility for all overtime scheduled on your project. You may wish to bring one of your assistant project managers with you for moral support.

Now take the total points for each day and complete the following table:

Summary Work Plan	
Day	**Points**
Monday	
Tuesday	
Wednesday	
Thursday	
Friday	
Total	

Conclusions and Summary Questions

1. Project managers have a tendency to want to carry the load themselves, even if it means working sixty hours a week. You were told to do everything within your normal working day. But, as a potentially good project manager, you probably have the natural tendency of wanting to postpone some work until a later date so that you can do it yourself. Doing the activities, when they occur, even through transmittal or delegation, is probably the best policy. You might wish to do the same again at a later time and see if you can beat your present score. Only this time, try to do as many tasks as possible on each day, even if it means delegation.

2. Several of the activities were company, not project, requests. Project managers have a tendency to avoid administrative responsibilities unless it deals directly with their project. This process of project management "tunnel vision" can lead to antagonism and conflicts if the proper attitude is not developed on the part of the project manager. This can easily carry down to his assistants as well.

3. Several of the activities could have been returned to the requestor. However, in a project environment where the project manager cannot be successful without the functional manager's support, most project managers would never turn away a line employee's request for assistance.

4. Make a list of the activities where your answers differ from those of the answer key and where you feel that there exists sufficient justification for your interpretation.

5. Quite often self-productivity can be increased by knowing one's own energy cycle. Are your more important meetings in the mornings or afternoons? What time of day do you perform your most productive work? When do you do your best writing? Does your energy cycle vary according to the day of the week?

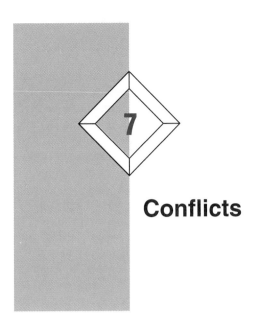

Conflicts

7.0 INTRODUCTION

In discussing the project environment, we have purposely avoided discussion of what may be its single most important characteristic: conflicts. Opponents of project management assert that the major reason why many companies avoid changeover to a project management organizational structure is either fear or an inability to handle the resulting conflicts. Conflicts are a way of life in a project structure and can generally occur at any level in the organization, usually as a result of conflicting objectives.

The project manager has often been described as a conflict manager. In many organizations the project manager continually fights fires and crises evolving from conflicts, and delegates the day-to-day responsibility of running the project to the project team members. Although this is not the best situation, it cannot always be prevented, especially after organizational restructuring or the initiation of projects requiring new resources.

The ability to handle conflicts requires an understanding of why they occur. Four questions can be asked, the answers to which should be beneficial in handling, and possibly preventing, conflicts.

- What are the project objectives and can they be in conflict with other projects?
- Why do conflicts occur?
- How do we resolve conflicts?
- Is there any type of preliminary analysis that could identify possible conflicts before they occur?

7.1 OBJECTIVES

Each project identified as such by management must have at least one objective. The objectives of the project must be made known to all project personnel and all managers, at every level of the organization. If this information is not communicated accurately, then it is entirely possible that upper-level managers, project managers, and functional managers may all have a different interpretation of the ultimate objective, a situation that invites conflicts to occur. As an example, company X has been awarded a $100,000 government contract for surveillance of a component that appears to be fatiguing. Top management might view the objective of this project to be discovering the cause of the fatigue and eliminating it in future component production. This might give company X a "jump" on the competition. The division manager might just view it as a means of keeping people employed, with no follow-on possibilities. The department manager can consider the objective as either another job that has to be filled, or a means of establishing new surveillance technology. The department manager, therefore, can staff the necessary positions with any given degree of expertise, depending on the importance and definition of the objective.

Projects are established with objectives in mind. Project objectives must be:

- Specific, not general
- Not overly complex
- Measurable, tangible, and verifiable
- Appropriate level, challenging
- Realistic and attainable
- Established within resource bounds
- Consistent with resources available or anticipated
- Consistent with organizational plans, policies, and procedures

Unfortunately, the above characteristics are not always evident, especially if we consider that the project might be unique to the organization in question. As an example, research and development projects sometimes start out general, rather than specific. Research and development objectives are reestablished as time goes on because the initial objective may not be attainable. As an example, company Y believes that they can develop a high-energy rocket-motor propellant. A proposal is submitted to the government, and, after a review period, the contract is awarded. However, as is the case with all R&D projects, there always exists the question of whether the objective is attainable within time, cost, and performance constraints. It might be possible to achieve the initial objective, but at an incredibly high production cost. In this case, the specifications of the propellant (i.e., initial objectives) may be modified so as to align them closer to the available production funds.

Reestablishment of objectives occurs most frequently during the definition phase of system/project development. If resources are not available, then alternatives must be considered. This type of analysis exists during the initial stages of feasibility studies, construction, design, and estimates, and new facility and equipment purchases.

Once the total project objective is set, subobjectives are defined in order that cost and performance may be tracked. (This procedure will be described in later chapters.) Subobjectives are a vital link in establishing proper communications between the project and functional managers. In a project environment, employees are evaluated according to accomplishment rather than according to how they spend their time. Since the project manager has temporarily assigned personnel, many of whom may have never worked for him either part-time or full-time, it is vital that employees have clearly defined objectives and subobjectives. In order to accomplish this effectively, without wasting valuable time, employees should have a part in setting their own objectives and subobjectives.

Many projects are directed and controlled using a management-by-objective (MBO) approach based upon effective project/functional communications and working relations as stated above. The philosophy of management by objectives:

- Is proactive rather than reactive management
- Is results oriented, emphasizing accomplishment
- Focuses on change to improve individual and organizational effectiveness

Management by objectives is a systems approach for aligning project goals with organizational goals, project goals with the goals of other subunits of the organization, and project goals with individual goals. Furthermore, management by objectives can be regarded as a:

- Systems approach to planning and obtaining project results for an organization
- Strategy of meeting individual needs at the same time that project needs are met
- Method of clarifying what each individual and organizational unit's contribution to the project should be

MBO professes to have a framework that can promote the effective utilization of time and other project resources. Many organizations, however, do not utilize the MBO philosophy. Whether or not MBO is utilized, project objectives must be set.

- If you do not have the right objectives, you may not have any idea of whether you are on the right road.
- Without objectives it is difficult to measure results against prior expectations.
- Objectives are utilized to determine individual goals that will provide maximum effectiveness of the whole.

7.2 THE CONFLICT ENVIRONMENT

In the project environment, conflicts are inevitable. However, as described in Chapter 5, conflicts and their resolution can be planned for. For example, conflicts can easily develop out of a situation where members of a group have a misunderstanding of each other's roles and responsibilities. Through documentation, such as linear responsibility charts, it is possible to establish formal organizational procedures (either at the project level or company-wide). Resolution means collaboration in which people must rely on one another. Without this, mistrust will prevail and activity documentation can be expected to increase.

The most common types of conflicts involve:

- Manpower resources
- Equipment and facilities
- Capital expenditures
- Costs
- Technical opinions and trade-offs
- Priorities
- Administrative procedures
- Scheduling
- Responsibilities
- Personality clashes

Each of these conflicts can vary in relative intensity over the life cycle of a project. The relative intensity can vary as a function of:

- Getting closer to project constraints
- Having only two constraints instead of three (i.e., time and performance, but not cost)
- The project life cycle itself
- The person with whom the conflict occurs

Sometimes conflict is "meaningful" and produces beneficial results. These meaningful conflicts should be permitted to continue as long as project constraints are not violated and beneficial results are being received. An example of this would be two technical specialists arguing that each has a better way of solving a problem, and each trying to find additional supporting data for his hypothesis.

Some conflicts are inevitable and continually reoccur. As an example, let us consider the raw material and finished goods inventory. Manufacturing wants the largest possible inventory of raw materials on hand so as not to shut down production; sales and marketing want the largest finished goods inventory so that customer demands will be met; and, finally, finance and accounting want the smallest raw material and finished goods inventory so the books will look better and no cash flow problems will occur.

Conflicts appear differently depending on the organizational structure. In the traditional structure, conflict should be avoided; in the project structure, conflict is part of change and therefore inevitable. In the traditional structure, conflict is the result of troublemakers and egoists; in the project structure, conflict is determined by the structure of the system and relationship among components. In the traditional structure, conflict is bad; in the project structure, conflict may be beneficial.

Conflicts can occur with anyone and over anything. Some people contend that personality conflicts are the most difficult to resolve. Below are several situations. The reader might consider what he or she would do if placed in the situations.

- Two of your functional team members appear to have personality clashes and almost always assume opposite points of view during decision making. They are both from the same line organization. Conflicts are inevitable.
- Two of your line managers continuously argue as to who should perform a certain test. You know that this situation exists, and that the department managers are trying to work it out themselves, often with great pain. However, you are not sure for how long they will be able to resolve the problem themselves.
- Manufacturing says that they cannot produce the end-item according to engineering specifications.
- R&D quality control and manufacturing operations quality control argue as to who should perform a certain test on an R&D project. R&D postulates that it is their project, and manufacturing argues that it will eventually go into production and that they wish to be involved as early as possible.
- During contract negotiations, a disagreement occurs. The vice president of company A orders his director of finance, the contract negotiator, to break off negotiations with company B because the contract negotiator for company B does not report directly to a vice president.
- Mr. X is the project manager of a $65 million project of which $1 million is subcontracted out to another company in which Mr. Y is the project manager. Mr. X does not consider Mr. Y as his counterpart and continually communicates with the director of engineering in Mr. Y's company.

Ideally, the project manager should report high enough so that he can get timely assistance in resolving conflicts. Unfortunately, this is easier said than done. Therefore, project managers must plan for conflict resolution. As examples of this:

- The project manager might wish to concede on a low-intensity conflict if he knows that a high-intensity conflict is expected to occur at a later point in the project.
- Jones Construction Company has recently won a $120 million effort for a local company. The effort includes three separate construction projects, each one beginning at the same time. Two of the projects are twenty-four months in duration, and the third is thirty-six months. Each project has its

own project manager. When resource conflicts occur between the projects, the customer is usually called in.

- Richard is a department manager who must supply resources to four different projects. Although each project has an established priority, the project managers continually argue that departmental resources are not being allocated effectively. Richard now holds a monthly meeting with all four of the project managers and lets them determine how the resources should be allocated.

Many executives feel that the best way of resolving conflicts is by establishing priorities. This may be true as long as priorities are not continually shifted around. As an example, Minnesota Power and Light establishes priorities as:

- Level 0: no completion date
- Level 1: to be completed on or before a specific date
- Level 2: to be completed in or before a given fiscal quarter
- Level 3: to be completed within a given year

This type of technique will work as long as we do not have a large number of projects in any one group, say level 1. How would we then distinguish between projects?

Executives are responsible for establishing priorities and often make the mistake of not telling the project managers the reasons for the priority level. There may be sound reasons for concealing this information, but this practice should be avoided whenever possible.

The most common factors influencing the establishment of project priorities include:

- The technical risks in development
- The risks that the company will incur, financially or competitively
- The nearness of the delivery date and the urgency
- The penalties that can accompany late delivery dates
- The expected savings, profit increase, and return on investment
- The amount of influence that the customer possesses, possibly due to the size of the project
- The impact on other projects
- The impact on affiliated organizations
- The impact on a particular product line

The ultimate responsibility for establishing priorities rests with top-level management. Yet even with priority establishment, conflicts still develop. David Wilemon has identified several reasons why conflicts still occur:[1]

---

1. David L. Wilemon, "Managing Conflict in Temporary Management Situations," *The Journal of Management Studies,* 1973, pp. 282–296.

- The greater the diversity of disciplinary expertise among the participants of a project team, the greater the potential for conflict to develop among members of the team.
- The lower the project manager's degree of authority, reward, and punishment power over those individuals and organizational units supporting his project, the greater the potential for conflict to develop.
- The less the specific objectives of a project (cost, schedule, and technical performance) are understood by the project team members, the more likely it is that conflict will develop.
- The greater the role of ambiguity among the participants of a project team, the more likely it is that conflict will develop.
- The greater the agreement on superordinate goals by project team participants, the lower the potential for detrimental conflict.
- The more the members of functional areas perceive that the implementation of a project management system will adversely usurp their traditional roles, the greater the potential for conflict.
- The lower the percent need for interdependence among organizational units supporting a project, the greater the potential for dysfunctional conflict.
- The higher the managerial level within a project or functional area, the more likely it is that conflicts will be based upon deep-seated parochial resentments. By contrast, at the project or task level, it is more likely that cooperation will be facilitated by the task orientation and professionalism that a project requires for completion.

7.3 MANAGING CONFLICT

Temporary management situations produce conflicts. This is a natural occurrence resulting from the differences in the organizational behavior of individuals, the differences in the way that functional and project managers view the work required, and the lack of time necessary for project managers and functional personnel to establish ideal working relationships.

Regardless of how well planning is developed, project managers must be willing to operate in an environment that is characterized by constant and rapid change. This turbulent environment can be the result of changes in the scope of work, a shifting of key project and functional personnel due to new priorities, and other unforeseen developments. The success or failure of a project manager is quite often measured by the ability to deal with change.

In contrast to the functional manager who works in a more standardized and predictable environment, the project manager must live with constant change. In his effort to integrate various disciplines across functional lines, he must learn to cope with the pressures of the changing work environment. He has to foster a climate that promotes the ability of his personnel to adapt to this continuously changing work environment. Demanding compliance to rigid rules, principles, and techniques is often counter-productive. In such situations, an environment conducive to effective project management is missing and the project leader too often suffers the same fate as heart-transplant patients—rejection![2]

There is no one method that will suffice for managing all conflicts in temporary management situations because:

- There exist several types of conflicts.
- Each conflict can assume a different relative intensity over the life cycle of the project.

The detrimental aspects of these conflicts can be minimized if the project manager can anticipate their occurrence and understand their composition. The prepared manager can then resort to one of several conflict resolution modes in order to more effectively manage the disagreements that can occur.[3]

Thamhain and Wilemon surveyed 150 project managers on conflict management. Their research tried to determine the type and magnitude of the particular type of conflict that is most common at specific life-cycle stages, regardless of the particular nature of the project. For the purpose of their paper the authors stated the following definitions:

> Conflict is defined as the behavior of an individual, a group, or an organization which impedes or restricts (at least temporarily) another party from attaining its desired goals. Although conflict may impede the attainment of one's goals, the consequences may be beneficial if they produce new information which, in turn, enhances the decision-making process. By contrast, conflict becomes dysfunctional if it results in poor project decision-making, lengthy delays over issues which do not importantly affect the outcome of the project, or a disintegration of the team's efforts.[4]

---

2. H. S. Dugan, H. J. Thamhain, and D. L. Wilemon, "Managing Change in Project Management," *Proceedings of the Ninth Annual International Seminar/Symposium on Project Management,* Chicago, October 22–26, 1977, pp. 178–188.

3. The remainder of Section 7.3 is devoted to Hans J. Thamhain and David L. Wilemon, "Conflict Management in Project Life Cycles," *Sloan Management Review,* Summer 1975, pp. 31–50. Reprinted by permission of publisher. Copyright © 1975 by Sloan Management Review Association; all rights reserved.

4. H. J. Thamhain and D. L. Wilemon, "Conflict Management in Project-Oriented Work Environments," *Proceedings of the Sixth International Meeting of the Project Management Institute,* Washington, D.C., September 18–21, 1974.

The study presented in their paper was part of an ongong and integrated research effort on conflict in the project-oriented work environment.[4-8]

Project managers frequently indicate that one of the requirements for effective performance is the ability to effectively manage various conflicts and disagreements that invariably arise in task accomplishment. While several research studies have reported on the general nature of conflict in project management, few studies have been devoted to the cause and management of conflict in specific project life-cycle stages. If project managers are aware of some of the major causes of disagreements in the various project life-cycle phases, there is a greater likelihood that the detrimental aspects of these potential conflict situations can be avoided or minimized.

This study first investigates the mean intensity of seven potential conflict determinants frequently thought to be prime causes of conflict in project management. Next, the intensity of each conflict determinant is viewed from the perspective of individual project life-cycle stages. An examination is then made of various conflict-handling modes used by project managers, which leads to a number of suggestions for minimizing the detrimental effects of conflict over the proj-ect life cycle.

Research Design

Approximately 150 managers from a variety of technology-oriented companies were asked to participate in this comprehensive research project. A usable sample of 100 project managers was eventually selected for this study.

A questionnaire was used as the principal data collection instrument. In addition, discussions were held with a number of project managers on the subject under investigation to supplement the questionnaire data and the resulting conclusions. This process proved helpful in formulating a number of recommendations for minimizing detrimental conflicts.

The development of the questionnaire relied on several pilot studies. It was designed to measure values on three variables: (1) the average intensity of seven potential conflict determinants over the entire project life cycle; (2) the intensity of each of the seven conflict sources in the four project life-cycle phases; and (3) the conflict resolution modes used by project managers.

---

4. H. J. Thamhain and D. L. Wilemon, "Conflict Management in Project-Oriented Work Environments," *Proceedings of the Sixth International Meeting of the Project Management Institute,* Washington, D.C., September 18–21, 1974.

5. "Diagnosing Conflict Determinants in Project Management," *IEEE Transactions on Engineering Management,* Vol. 22, 1975, pp. 35–44.

6. D. L. Wilemon and J. P. Cicero, "The Project Manager—Anomalies and Ambiguities," *Academy of Management Journal,* Fall 1970, pp. 269–282.

7. D. L. Wilemon, "Project Management Conflict: A View from Apollo," *Proceedings of the Third Annual Symposium of the Project Management Institute,* Houston, Texas, October 1971.

8. D. L. Wilemon, "Project Management and Its Conflicts: A View from Apollo," *Chemical Technology,* Vol. 2, No. 9, 1972, pp. 527–534.

Mean Conflict Intensity

The average conflict intensity perceived by the project managers was measured for various conflict sources and for various phases of the project life cycle. Project managers were asked to rank the intensity of conflict they experienced for each of seven potential conflict sources on a standard four-point scale. The seven potential sources are:

- *Conflict over project priorities.* The views of project participants often differ over the sequence of activities and tasks that should be undertaken to achieve successful project completion. Conflict over priorities may occur not only between the project team and other support groups but also within the project team.
- *Conflict over administrative procedures.* A number of managerial and administrative-oriented conflicts may develop over how the project will be managed; i.e., the definition of the project manager's reporting relationships, definition of responsibilities, interface relationships, project scope, operational requirements, plan of execution, negotiated work agreements with other groups, and procedures for administrative support.
- *Conflict over technical opinions and performance trade-offs.* In technology-oriented projects, disagreements may arise over technical issues, performance specifications, technical trade-offs, and the means to achieve performance.
- *Conflict over manpower resources.* Conflicts may arise around the staffing of the project team with personnel from other functional and staff support areas or from the desire to use another department's personnel for project support even though the personnel remain under the authority of their functional or staff superiors.
- *Conflict over cost.* Frequently, conflict may develop over cost estimates from support areas regarding various project work breakdown packages. For example, the funds allocated by a project manager to a functional support group might be perceived as insufficient for the support requested.
- *Conflict over schedules.* Disagreements may develop around the timing, sequencing, and scheduling of project-related tasks.
- *Personality conflict.* Disagreements may tend to center on interpersonal differences rather than on "technical" issues. Conflicts often are "ego-centered."

Intensity of Specific Conflict Sources by Project Life-Cycle Stage

The conflict intensity experienced by project managers for each source over the four life-cycle stages was measured on a special grid. The x-axis of the grid identifies four standard life-cycle phases: project formation, project buildup, main program phase, and phaseout. The y-axis delineates the seven potential sources of conflict. The respondents were asked to indicate on a standard four-point scale the intensity of the conflict they experienced for each of the seven potential sources of conflict within each of the four project life-cycle stages.

Conflict-Handling Modes

A number of research studies indicate that managers approach and resolve conflicts by utilizing various conflict resolution modes. Blake and Mouton,[9] for example, have delineated five modes for handling conflicts:

- *Withdrawal.* Retreating or withdrawing from an actual or potential disagreement.
- *Smoothing.* De-emphasizing or avoiding areas of difference and emphasizing areas of agreement.
- *Compromising.* Bargaining and searching for solutions that bring some degree of satisfaction to the parties in a dispute. Characterized by a "give-and-take" attitude.
- *Forcing.* Exerting one's viewpoint at the potential expense of another. Often characterized by competitiveness and a win-lose situation.
- *Confrontation.* Facing the conflict directly, which involves a problem-solving approach whereby affected parties work through their disagreements.[10]

Aphorisms or statements of folk wisdom were used as surrogates for each conflict resolution model.[11] The project managers were asked to rank the accuracy of each proverb in terms of how accurately it reflected the actual way in which they handled disagreements in the project environment. Fifteen proverbs were selected to match the five conflict-handling modes identified by Blake and Mouton.[12,13] This analysis provides an insight into the perceived conflict-handling mode of the project managers.

Analysis of Results

The results of the study are presented in three parts.

The mean intensity experienced for each of the potential conflict sources over the entire life of projects is presented in Figure 7–1. As indicated, relative to other situations, disagreements over schedules result in the most intense conflict over the

---

9. R. R. Blake and J. S. Mouton, *The Managerial Grid* (Houston: Gulf Publishing, 1964).

10. For a fuller description of these definitions, see R. J. Burke, "Methods of Resolving Interpersonal Conflict," *Personal Administration,* July–August 1969, pp. 48–55. Also see H. J. Thamhain and D. L. Wilemon, "Conflict Management in Project-Oriented Work Environments," *Proceedings of the Sixth International Meeting of the Project Management Institute,* Washington, D.C., September 18–21, 1974.

11. Specifically, the measurements rely on the research of P. R. Lawrence and J. W. Lorsch, "New Management Job: The Integrator," *Harvard Business Review,* November–Decembeer 1967, pp. 142–152.

12. See note 9.

13. These proverbs have been used in other research of a similar nature to avoid the potential bias that might be introduced otherwise by the use of social science jargon. For further details, see R. J. Burke, "Methods of Managing Superior–Subordinate Conflict," *Canadian Journal of Behavioral Science,* Vol. 2, No. 2, 1970, pp. 124–135.

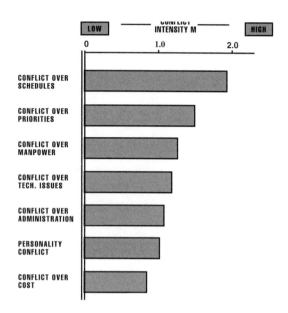

FIGURE 7–1. Mean conflict intensity profile over project life cycle. *Source.* Hans J. Thamhain and David L. Wilemon, "Conflict Management in Project Life Cycles," *Sloan Management Review,* Summer 1975, pp. 31–50. Reprinted by permission.

total project. Scheduling conflicts often occur with other support departments over which the project manager may have limited authority and control. Scheduling problems and conflicts also often involve disagreements and differing perceptions of organizational departmental priorities. For example, an issue urgent to the project manager may receive a low-priority treatment from support groups and/or staff personnel because of a different priority structure in the support organization. Conflicts over schedules frequently result from the technical problems and manpower resources.

Conflict over project priorities ranked second highest over the project life cycle. In our discussion with project managers, many indicated that this type of conflict frequently develops because the organization did not have prior experience with a current project undertaking. Consequently, the pattern of project priorities may change from the original forecast, necessitating the reallocation of crucial resources and schedules, a process that is often susceptible to intense disagreements and conflicts. Similarly, priority issues often develop into conflict with other support departments whose established schedules and work patterns are disturbed by the changed requirements.

Conflict over manpower resources was the third most important source of conflict. Project managers frequently lament when there is little "organizational slack" in terms of manpower resources, a situation in which they often experience intense conflicts. Project managers note that most of the conflicts over personnel resources occur with those departments that either assign personnel to the project or support the project internally.

The fourth strongest source of conflict involved disagreements over technical opinions and trade-offs. Often the groups who support the project are primarily responsible for technical inputs and performance standards. The project manager, on the other hand, is accountable for the cost, schedule, and performance objectives. Since support areas are usually responsible for only parts of the project, they may not have the broad management overview of the total project. The project manager, for example, may be presented with a technical problem. Often he must reject the technical alternative owing to cost or schedule restraints. In other cases, he may find that he disagrees with the opinions of others on strictly technical grounds.

Conflict over administrative procedures ranked fifth in the profile of seven conflict sources. It is interesting to note that most of the conflict over administrative procedures that occurs is almost uniformly distributed with functional departments, project personnel, and the project manager's superior.[14] Examples of conflict originating over administrative issues may involve disagreements over the project manager's authority and responsibilities, reporting relationships, administrative support, status reviews, or interorganizational interfacing. For the most part, disagreements over administrative procedures involve issues of how the project manager will function and how he relates to the organization's top management.

Personality conflict was ranked low in intensity by the project managers. Our discussions with project managers indicated that while the intensity of personality conflicts may not be as high as some of the other sources of conflict, they are among the most difficult to deal with effectively. Personality issues also may be obscured by communication problems and technical issues. A support person, for example, may stress the technical aspect of a disagreement with the project manager when, in fact, the real issue is a personality conflict.

Cost, like schedules, is often a basic performance measure in project management. As a conflict source, cost ranked lowest. Disagreements over cost frequently develop when project managers negotiate with other departments that will perform subtasks on the project. Project managers with tight budget constraints often want to minimize cost, while support groups may want to maximize their part of the project budget. In addition, conflicts may occur as a result of technical problems or schedule slippages that may increase costs.

Conflict Sources and Intensity in the Project Life Cycle

While it is important to examine some of the principal determinants of conflict from an aggregate perspective, more specific and useful insights can be gained by exploring the intensity of various conflict sources in each life-cycle stage, namely, project formation, project buildup, main program phase, and phaseout (see Figure 7–2).

---

14. See Thamhain and Wilemon in note 10.

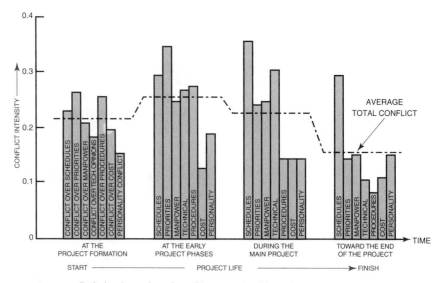

FIGURE 7–2. Relative intensity of conflict over the life cycle of projects. *Source.* Hans J. Thamhain and David L. Wilemon, "Conflict Management in Project Life Cycles," *Sloan Management Review,* Summer 1975, pp. 31–50. Reprinted by permission.

    1. *Project formation.* As Figure 7–2 illustrates, during the project formation stage, the following conflict sources (listed in order of rank) were found:[15]

    1. Project priorities
    2. Administrative procedures
    3. Schedules
    4. Manpower
    5. Cost
    6. Technical
    7. Personality

Unique to the project formation phase are some characteristics not typical of the other life-cycle stages. The project manager, for example, must launch his project within the larger "host" organization. Frequently, conflict develops between the priorities established for the project and the priorities that other line and staff groups believe important. To eliminate or minimize the detrimental consequences

---

15. Conflict intensity is computed as the total frequency (F) × magnitude (M) of conflict experienced within the sample of project managers, when $0 \leq M \leq 3$. For example, if the average conflict intensity experienced by project managers on schedules with all interfaces was M = 1.65 (considerable) and F = 14% of all project managers indicated that "most" of this conflict occurred during the project formation phase, then "conflict over schedules" would be M × F = 1.65 × 0.14 = 0.23 during project formation.

that could result, project managers must carefully evaluate and plan for the impact of their projects on the groups that support them. This should be accomplished as early as possible in the program life cycle. The source of conflict ranked second was administrative procedures, which are concerned with several critically important management issues; for example: How will the project organization be designed? Who will the project manager report to? What is the authority of the project manager? Does the project manager have control over manpower and material resources? What reporting and communication channels will be used? Who establishes schedules and performance specifications? Most of these areas are negotiated by the project manager, and conflict frequently occurs during the process. To avoid prolonged problems over these issues, it is important to clearly establish these procedures as early as possible.

Schedules typify another area where established groups may have to accommodate the newly formed project organization by adjusting their own operations. Most project managers attest that this adjustment is highly susceptible to conflict, even under ideal conditions, since it may involve a reorientation of present operating patterns and "local" priorities in support departments. These same departments might be fully committed to other projects. For similar reasons, negotiations over support personnel and other resources can be an important source of conflict in the project formation stage. Thus, effective planning and negotiation over these issues at the beginning of a project appear important.

2. *Project buildup.* The conflict sources for the project buildup are listed below in order of rank:

1. Project priorities
2. Schedules
3. Administrative procedures
4. Technical
5. Manpower
6. Personality
7. Cost

Disagreements over project priorities, schedules, and administrative procedures continue as important determinants of conflict. Some of these sources of conflict appear as an extension from the previous program phase. Additional conflicts surface during negotiations with other groups in the buildup phase. It is interesting to note that while schedules ranked third in conflict intensity in the project formation phase, they are the second major conflict determinant in the buildup phase. Many of the conflicts over schedules arise in the first phase because of the disagreements that develop over the establishment of schedules. By contrast, in the buildup phase, conflict may develop over the enforcement of schedules according to objectives of the overall project plan.

An important point is that conflict over administrative procedures becomes less intense in the buildup phase, indicating the diminishing magnitude and frequency of administrative problems. It also appears that it is important to resolve potential conflicts, such as administrative disagreements, in the earlier phase of a project to avoid a replication of the same problems in the more advanced project life-cycle phases.

Conflict over technical issues also becomes more pronounced in the buildup phase, rising from the sixth-ranked conflict source in the project formation phase to fourth in the buildup phase. Often this results from disagreements with a support group that cannot meet technical requirements or wants to enhance the technological input for which it is responsible. Such action can adversely affect the project manager's cost and schedule objectives.

Project managers emphasized that personality conflicts are particularly difficult to handle. Even apparently small and infrequent personality conflicts might be more disruptive and detrimental to overall program effectiveness than intense conflicts over nonpersonal issues, which can often be handled on a more rational basis. Many project managers also indicated that conflict over cost in the buildup phase generally tends to be low for two primary reasons. First, conflict over the establishment of cost targets does not appear to create intense conficts for most project managers. Second, some projects are not yet mature enough in the buildup phase to cause disagreements over cost between the project manager and those who support him.

3. *Main program.* The main program phase reveals a different conflict pattern. The seven potential causes of conflict are listed in rank order below:

1. Schedules
2. Technical
3. Manpower
4. Priorities
5. Procedures
6. Cost
7. Personality

In the main program phase, the meeting of schedule commitments by various support groups becomes critical to effective project performance. In complex task management, the interdependency of various support groups dealing with complex technology frequently gives rise to slippages in schedules. When several groups of organizations are involved, this in turn can cause a "whiplash" effect throughout the project. In other words, a slippage in schedule by one group may affect other groups if they are on the critical path of the project.

As noted, while conflicts over schedules often develop in the earlier project phases, they are frequently related to the establishment of schedules. In the main program phase, our discussions with project managers indicated that conflicts frequently develop over the "management and maintenance" of schedules. The latter, as indicated in Figure 7–2, produces more intense conflicts.

Technical conflicts are also one of the most important sources of conflict in the main program phase. There appear to be two principal reasons for the rather high level of conflict in this phase. First, the main program phase is often characterized by the integration of various project subsystems for the first time, such as configuration management. Owing to the complexities involved in this integration process, conflicts frequently develop over lack of subsystem integration and poor technical performance of one subsystem, which may, in turn, affect other components and subsystems. Second, the fact that a component can be designed in prototype does not always assure that all the technical anomalies will be eliminated. In extreme cases, the subsystem may not even be producible in the main program phase. Disagreements also may arise in the main program phase over reliability and quality control standards, various design problems, and testing procedures. All these problems can have a severe impact on the project and cause intense conflicts for the project manager.

Manpower resources ranked third as a determinant of conflict. The need for manpower reaches the highest levels in the main program phase. If support groups also are providing personnel to other projects, severe strains over manpower availability and project requirements frequently develop.

Conflict over priorities continued its decline in importance as a principal cause of conflict. Again, project priorities tend to be a form of conflict most likely to occur in the earlier project phases. Finally, administrative procedures, cost, and personality were about equal as the lowest-ranked conflict sources.

4. *Phaseout.* The final stage, project phaseout, illustrates an interesting shift in the principal cause of conflict. The ranking of the conflict sources in this final project phase are:

1. Schedules
2. Personality
3. Manpower
4. Priorities
5. Cost
6. Technical
7. Procedures

Schedules are again the most likely form of conflict to develop in project phaseout. Project managers frequently indicated that many of the schedule slippages that developed in the main program phase tended to carry over to project phaseout. Schedule slippages often become cumulative and affect the project most severely in the final stage of a project.

Somewhat surprisingly, personality conflict was the second-ranked source of conflict. It appears that much of the personality-oriented conflict can be explained in two ways. First, it is not uncommon for project participants to be tense and concerned with future assignments. Second, project managers frequently note that interpersonal relationships may be quite strained during this period owing to the pressure on project participants to meet stringent schedules, budgets, and performance specifications and objectives.

Somewhat related to the personality issue are the conflicts that arise over manpower resources, the third-ranked conflict source. Disagreements over manpower resources may develop due to new projects phasing in, hence creating competition for personnel during the critical phaseout stage. Project managers, by contrast, also may experience conflicts over the absorption of surplus manpower back into the functional areas where they affect the budgets and organizational variables.

Conflict over priorities in the phaseout stage often appears to be directly or indirectly related to competition with other project start-ups in the organization. Typically, newly organized projects or marketing support activities might require urgent, short-notice attention and commitments that have to be squeezed into tight schedules. At the same time, personnel might leave the project organization prematurely because of prior commitments that conflict with a slipped schedule on the current project or because of a sudden opportunity for a new assignment elsewhere. In either case, the combined pressure on schedules, manpower, and personality creates a climate that is highly vulnerable to conflicts over priorities.

As noted in Figure 7–2, cost, technical, and administrative procedures tend to be ranked lowest as conflict sources. Cost, somewhat surprisingly, was not a major determinant of conflict. Discussions with project personnel suggest that while cost control can be troublesome in this phase, intense conflicts usually do not develop. Most problems in this area develop gradually and provide little ground for arguments.[16] The reader should be cautioned, however, that the low level of conflict is by no means indicative of the importance of cost performance to overall rating of a project manager. During discussions with top management, it was repeatedly emphasized that cost performance is one of the key evaluation measures in judging the performance of project managers.

Technical and administrative procedures ranked lowest in project phaseout. When a project reaches this stage, most of the technical issues are usually resolved. A similar argument holds for administrative procedures.

A graphical summary of the relative conflict intensity over the four conflict stages is provided in Figure 7–3. The diagram, an abstract of Figures 7–1 and 7–2, shows the change of relative conflict intensity over the project life for each of the seven conflict sources.

It is important to note that while a determinant conflict may be ranked relatively low in a specific life-cycle stage, it can, nevertheless, cause severe problems. A project manager, for example, may have serious ongoing problems with schedules throughout his project, but a single conflict over a technical issue can be equally detrimental and could jeopardize his performance to the same extent

---

16. Depending on the work environment and particular business, there might be various reasons why conflicts over cost are low. First, some of the project components may be purchased externally on a fixed-free basis. In such cases the contractor would bear the burden of costs. Second, costs are one of the most difficult project variables to control throughout the life cycle of a project, and budgets are frequently adjusted for increase in material and manpower costs over the life of the project. These incremental cost adjustments frequently eliminate some of the "sting" in cost when they exceed the original estimates of the project manager. Moreover, some projects in the high-technology area are managed on a cost-plus basis. In some of these projects precise cost estimates cannot always be rigidly adhered to.

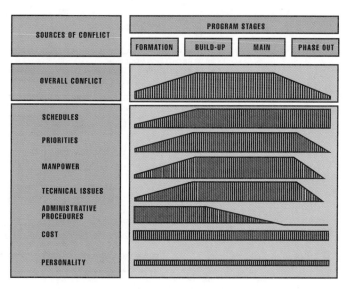

FIGURE 7–3. Trend of conflict intensity over the four project life-cycle stages. *Source.* Hans J. Thamhain and David L. Wilemon, "Conflict Management in Project Life Cycles," *Sloan Management Review,* Spring 1975, pp. 31–50. Reprinted by permission.

as schedule slippages. This point should be kept in mind in any discussion on project management conflict. Moreover, problems may develop that are virtually "conflict-free" (i.e., technological anomalies or problems with suppliers) but may be just as troublesome to the project manager as any of the conflict issues discussed.

The problem that now should be addressed is how these various conflict sources and the situations they create are managed.

Use of Conflict-Handling Modes

The investigation into the conflict-handling modes of project managers developed a number of interesting patterns. The actual style of project managers was determined from their scores on the aphorisms. As indicated in Figure 7–4, confrontation was most frequently utilized as a problem-solving mode. This mode was favored by approximately 70 percent of the project managers.[17] The compromise approach, which is characterized by trade-offs and a give-and-take attitude, ranked second, followed by smoothing. Forcing and withdrawal ranked as the fourth and fifth most favored resolution modes, respectively.

In terms of the most and least favored conflict resolution modes, the project managers had similar rankings for the conflict-handling method used between

17. Quantitatively, this means that 70 percent of the project managers in the sample indicated that the proverbs that are representative of this mode (i.e., confrontation) describe the actual way the manager is resolving conflict "accurately" or "very accurately" as related to his project situations.

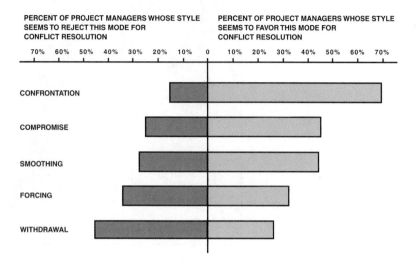

FIGURE 7–4. Conflict resolution profile. The various modes of conflict resolution actually used to manage conflict in project-oriented work environments. *Source.* Hans J. Thamhain and David L. Wilemon, "Conflict in Project Life Cycles," *Sloan Management Review,* Summer 1975, pp. 31–50. Reprinted by permission.

himself and his personnel, his superior, and his functional support departments except in the cases of confrontation and compromise. While confrontation was the most favored mode for dealing with superiors, compromise was more favored in handling disagreements with functional support departments. The various modes of conflict resolution used by project managers are summarized in the profile of Figure 7–4.

Implications

A number of ideas evolved for improving conflict management effectiveness in project-oriented environments from this research. As the data on the mean conflict intensities indicate, the three areas most likely to cause problems for the project manager over the entire project life cycle are disagreements over schedules, project priorities, and manpower resources. One reason these areas are apt to produce more intense disagreements is that the project manager may have limited control over other areas that have an important impact on these areas, particularly the functional support departments. These three areas (schedules, project priorities, and manpower resources) require careful surveillance throughout the life cycle of a project. To minimize detrimental conflict, intensive planning prior to actual launching of the project is recommended. Planning can help the project manager anticipate many potential sources of conflict before they occur.

Scheduling, priority-setting, and resource allocation require effective planning to avoid problems later in the project. In our discussions with project managers who have experienced problems in these areas, almost all maintain that these problems frequently originate from lack of effective preproject planning.

Managing projects involves managing change. It is not our intention to suggest that all such problems can be eliminated by effective planning. A more realistic view is that many potential problems can be minimized. There always will be random, unpredictable situations that defy forecasting in project environments.

Some specific suggestions are summarized in Table 7–1. The table provides an aid to project managers in recognizing some of the most important sources of conflict that are most likely to occur in various phases of projects. The table also suggests strategies for minimizing their detrimental consequences.

As one views the seven potential sources of disagreements over the life of a project, the dynamic nature of each conflict source is revealed. Frequently, areas that are most likely to foster disagreements early in a project become less likely to induce severe conflicts in the maturation of a project. Administrative procedures, for example, continually lose importance as an intense source of conflict during project maturation. By contrast, personality conflict, which ranks lowest in the project formation stage, is the second most important source of conflict in project phaseout. In summary, it is posted that if project managers are aware of the importance of each potential conflict source by project life cycle, then more effective conflict minimization strategies can be developed.

In terms of the means by which project managers handle conflicts and disagreements, the data revealed that the confrontation or problem-solving mode was the most frequent method utilized. While our study did not attempt to explore the effectiveness of each mode separately, in an earlier research project, Burke[18] suggests that the confrontation approach is the most effective conflict-handling mode.[19]

In some contrast to studies of general management, the findings of our research in project-oriented environments suggest that it is less important to search for a best mode of effective conflict management. It appears to be more significant that project managers, in their capacity as integrators of diverse organizational resources, employ the full range of conflict resolution modes. While confrontation was found as the ideal approach under most circumstances, other approaches may be equally effective depending on the situational content of the disagreement. Withdrawal, for example, may be used effectively as a temporary

---

18. R. J. Burke, "Methods of Resolving Interpersonal Conflict," *Personnel Administration,* July–August 1969, pp. 48–55.

19. Although Burke's study was conducted on general management personnel, it offers an interesting comparison to our research. Burke's paper notes that "Compromising" and "Forcing" were effective in 11.3 percent and 24.5 percent of the cases, while "Withdrawal" or "Smoothing" approaches were found mostly ineffective in the environment under investigation.

TABLE 7–1. MAJOR CONFLICT SOURCE AND RECOMMENDATIONS FOR MINIMIZING DYSFUNCTIONAL CONSEQUENCES

Project Life-Cycle Phase	Conflict Source	Recommendations
Project formation	Priorities	Clearly defined plans. Joint decision-making and/or consultation with affected parties.
	Procedures	Develop detailed administrative operating procedures to be followed in conduct of project. Secure approval from key administrators. Develop statement of understanding or charter.
	Schedules	Develop schedule commitments in advance of actual project commencement. Forecast other departmental priorities and possible impact on project.
Buildup phase	Priorities	Provide effective feedback to support areas on forecasted project plans and needs via status review sessions.
	Schedules	Schedule work breakdown packages (project subunits) in cooperation with functional groups.
	Procedures	Contingency planning on key administrative issues.
Main program	Schedules	Continually monitor work in progress. Communicate results to affected parties. Forecast problems and consider alternatives. Identify potential "trouble spots" needing closer surveillance.
	Technical	Early resolution of technical problems. Communication of schedule and budget retraints to technical personnel. Emphasize adequate, early technical testing. Facilitate early agreement on final designs.
	Manpower	Forecast and communicate manpower requirements early. Establish manpower requirements and priorities with functional and staff groups.
Phaseout	Schedules	Close schedule monitoring in project life cycle. Consider reallocation of available manpower to critical project areas prone to schedule slippages. Attain prompt resolution of technical issues which may impact schedules.
	Personality and Manpower	Develop plans for reallocation of manpower upon project completion. Maintain harmonious working relationships with project team and support groups. Try to loosen up "high-stress" environment.

Source: Hans J. Thamhain and David L. Wilemon, "Conflict Management in Project Life Cycles," *Sloan Management Review.* Summer 1975, pp. 31–50. Reprinted by permission.

measure until new information can be sought, or to "cool off" a hostile reaction from a colleague. As a basic long-term strategy, however, withdrawal may actually escalate a disagreement if no resolution is eventually sought.[20]

In other cases, compromise and smoothing might be considered effective strategies by the project manager, if they do not severely affect the overall project objectives. Forcing, on the other hand, often proves to be a win–lose mode. Even though the project manager may win over a specific issue, effective working arrangements with the "forced" party may be jeopardized in future relationships. Nevertheless, some project managers find that forcing is the only viable mode in some situations. Confrontation, or the problem-solving mode, may actually encompass all conflict-handling modes to some extent. A project manager, for example, in solving a conflict may use withdrawal, compromise, forcing, and smoothing to eventually get an effective resolution. The objective of confrontation, however, is to find a solution to the issue in question whereby all affected parties can live with the eventual outcome.

In summary, conflict is fundamental to complex task management. It is important for project managers not only to be cognizant of the potential sources of conflict, but also to know when in the life cycle of a project they are most likely to occur. Such knowledge can help the project manager avoid the detrimental aspects of conflict and maximize its beneficial aspects. Conflict can be beneficial when disagreements result in the development of new information that can enhance the decision-making process. Finally, when conflicts do develop, the project manager needs to know the advantages and disadvantages of each resolution mode for conflict resolution effectiveness.

7.4 CONFLICT RESOLUTION

Although each project within the company may be inherently different, the company may wish to have the resulting conflicts resolved in the same manner. The four most common methods are:

1. The development of company-wide conflict resolution policies and procedures
2. The establishment of project conflict resolution procedures during the early planning activities
3. The use of hierarchical referral
4. The requirement of direct contact

---

20. H. J. Thamhain and D. L. Wilemon, "Conflict Management in Project-Oriented Work Environments," *Proceedings of the Sixth International Meeting of the Project Management Institute,* Washington, D.C., September 1974, pp. 18–21.

With each of the above methods, the project manager may still select any of the conflict resolution modes discussed in the previous section.

Many companies have attempted to develop company-wide policies and procedures for conflict resolution. Results have shown that this method is doomed to failure because each project is different and not all conflicts can be handled the same way. Furthermore, project managers, by virtue of their individuality, and sometimes differing amounts of authority and responsibility, prefer to resolve conflicts in their own fashion.

A second method for resolving conflicts, and one that is often very effective, is to "plan" for conflicts during the planning activities. This can be accomplished through the use of linear responsibility charts. Planning for conflict resolution is similar to the first method except that each project manager can develop his own policies, rules, and procedures.

Hierarchial referral for conflict resolution, in theory, appears as the best method because neither the project manager nor the functional manager will dominate. Under this arrangement, the project and functional managers agree that for a proper balance to exist their common superior must resolve the conflict to protect the company's best interest. Unfortunately, this is not a realistic course of action because the common superior cannot be expected to continually resolve lower-level conflicts. Going to the "well" too often gives the impression that the functional and project managers cannot resolve their own problems.

The last method is direct contact, which is an outgrowth of the policies and procedures methods where established guidelines dictate that conflicting parties meet face-to-face and resolve their disagreement. Unfortunately, this method does not always work and, if continually stressed, can result in conditions where individuals will either suppress the identification of problems or develop new ones during confrontation.

Many conflicts can be either reduced or eliminated by constant communication of the project objectives to the team members. Many times this continual repetition will prevent individuals from going too far into the "wrong" and thus avoid the creation of a conflict situation.

7.5 UNDERSTANDING SUPERIOR, SUBORDINATE, AND FUNCTIONAL CONFLICTS[21]

In order for the project manager to be effective, an understanding of how to work with the various employees who must interface with the project is necessary. These various employees include upper-level management, subordinate project

---

21. The majority of this section, including the figures, was adapted from *Seminar in Project Management Workbook,* © 1977 by Hans J. Thamhain. Reproduced by permission of Dr. Hans J. Thamhain.

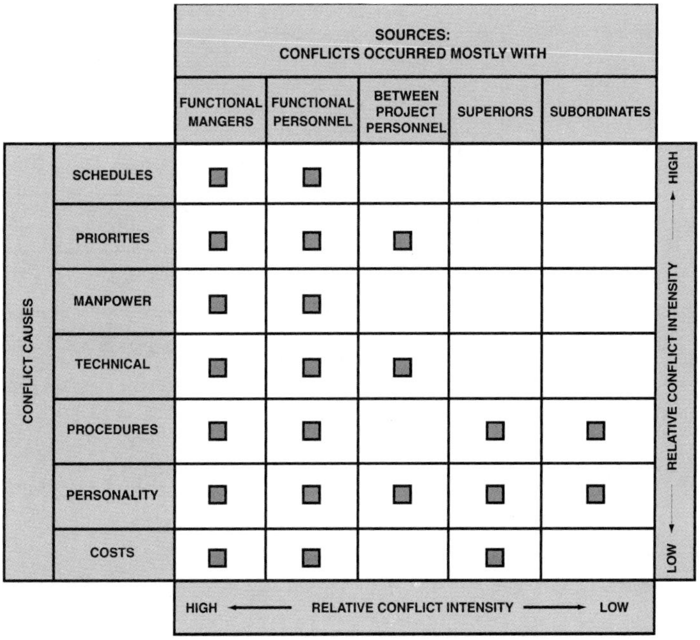

FIGURE 7–5. Relationship between conflict causes and sources.

team members, and functional personnel. Quite often, especially when conflicts are possible, the project manager must demonstrate an ability for continuous adaptability by creating a different working environment with each group of employees. The need for this was shown in the previous section by the fact that the relative intensity of conflicts can vary in the life cycle of a project.

The type and intensity of conflicts can also vary with the type of employee with whom the project manager must interface, as shown in Figure 7–5. Both conflict causes and sources are rated according to relative conflict intensity. Any conflict that the project manager has with a functional manager can also occur with the functional employee, and vice versa. The data in Figure 7–5 were obtained for a 75 percent confidence level.

In the previous section we discussed the five basic resolution modes for handling conflicts. The specific type of resolution mode that a project manager will use might easily depend on whom the conflict is with, as shown in Figure 7–6. The data in Figure 7–6 do not necessarily show the modes that project managers would prefer, but rather identify the modes that will increase or decrease the potential conflict intensity. For example, although project managers consider, in general, that withdrawal is their least favorite mode, it can be used quite effectively with functional managers. In dealing with superiors, project managers would rather be ready for an immediate compromise than for face-to-face confrontation that could easily result in having the resolution forced in favor of upper-level management.

(The figure shows only those associations which are statistically significant at the 95 percent level)

INTENSITY OF CONFLICT PERCEIVED BY PROJECT MANAGERS (P.M.)	ACTUAL CONFLICT RESOLUTION STYLE				
	FORCING	CONFRONTA-TION	COMPROMISE	SMOOTHING	WITHDRAWAL
BETWEEN P.M. AND HIS PERSONNEL	■	▲	▲	▲	■
BETWEEN P.M. AND HIS SUPERIOR		■	▲		
BETWEEN P.M. AND FUNCTIONAL SUPPORT DEPARTMENTS	■	■			▲

▲　STRONGLY FAVORABLE ASSOCIATION WITH REGARD TO LOW CONFLICT ($-\tau$)

■　STRONGLY UNFAVORABLE ASSOCIATION WITH REGARD TO LOW CONFLICT ($+\tau$)

• KENDALL τ CORRELATION

FIGURE 7–6. Association between perceived intensity of conflict and mode of conflict resolution.*

Figure 7–7 identifies the various influence styles that project managers find effective in helping to reduce potential conflicts. Penalty power, authority, and expertise are considered as strongly unfavorable associations with respect to low conflicts. As expected, work challenge and promotions (if the project manager has the authority) are strongly favorable associations with his personnel.

Therefore, for the project manager to be truly effective, he should understand

(The figure shows only those associated which are statistically significant at the 95 percent level)

INTENSITY OF CONFLICT PERCEIVED BY PROJECT MANAGER (P.M.)	INFLUENCE METHODS AS PERCEIVED BY PROJECT MANAGERS						
	EXPERTISE	AUTHORITY	WORK CHALLENGE	FRIENDSHIP	PROMOTION	SALARY	PENALTY
BETWEEN P.M. AND HIS PERSONNEL	■	■	▲		▲		■
BETWEEN P.M. AND HIS SUPERIOR			▲				■
BETWEEN P.M. AND FUNCTIONAL SUPPORT DEPARTMENTS		■					■

▲　STRONGLY FAVORABLE ASSOCIATION WITH REGARD TO LOW CONFLICT ($-\tau$)

■　STRONGLY UNFAVORABLE ASSOCIATION WITH REGARD TO LOW CONFLICT ($+\tau$)

• KENDALL τ CORRELATION

FIGURE 7–7. Association between influence methods of project managers and their perceived conflict intensity.*

not only what types of conflicts are possible in the various stages of the life cycle, but with whom these conflicts can occur and how to deal with them effectively.

7.6 THE MANAGEMENT OF CONFLICTS[22]

Good project managers realize that conflicts are inevitable and that procedures or techniques must be developed for their resolution. If the project manager is not careful, he could easily worsen the conflict by not knowing how to manage it. Once a conflict occurs, the project manager must observe certain preliminaries, including:

- Studying the problem and collecting all available information
- Developing a situational approach or methodology
- Setting the appropriate atmosphere or climate

In setting the appropriate atmosphere, the project manager must establish a willingness to participate for himself as well as the other participants. The manager must clearly state the objectives of the forthcoming meeting, establish the credibility of the meeting, and sanction the meeting.

If a confrontation meeting is necessary between conflicting parties, then the project manager should be aware of the logical steps and sequence of events that should be taken. These include:

- Setting the climate: establishing a willingness to participate
- Analyzing the images: how do you see yourself and others, and how do they see you?
- Collecting the information: getting feelings out in the open
- Defining the problem: defining and clarifying all positions
- Sharing the information: making the information available to all
- Setting the appropriate priorities: developing working sessions for setting priorities and timetables
- Organizing the group: forming cross-functional problem-solving groups
- Problem-solving: obtaining cross-functional involvement, securing commitments, and setting the priorities and timetable
- Developing the action plan: getting commitment
- Implementing the work: taking action on the plan
- Following up: obtaining feedback on the implementation for the action plan

Once the conflict has been defined and a meeting is necessary, the project manager or team leader should understand the conflict minimization procedures.

---

22. See note 21.

These include:

- Pausing and thinking before reacting
- Building trust
- Trying to understand the conflict motives
- Keeping the meeting under control
- Listening to all involved parties
- Maintaining a give-and-take attitude
- Educating others tactfully on your views
- Being willing to say when you were wrong
- Not acting as a superman and leveling the discussion only once in a while

We can now sum up these actions by defining the role of the effective manager in conflict problem-solving. The effective manager:

- Knows the organization
- Listens with understanding rather than evaluation
- Clarifies the nature of the conflict
- Understands the feelings of others
- Suggests the procedures for resolving differences
- Maintains relationships with disputing parties
- Facilitates the communications process
- Seeks resolutions

7.7 CONFLICT RESOLUTION MODES

The management of conflicts places the project manager in the precarious situation of having to select a conflict resolution mode. Previously, in Section 7.3, we briefly defined the five commonly used conflict resolution modes. Based upon the situation, the type of conflict, and whom the conflict is with, any of these modes could be justified.

Confronting (or Collaborating)

This is a problem-solving approach whereby the conflicting parties meet face-to-face and try to work through their disagreements. This approach should focus more on solving the problem and less on being combative. This approach is collaboration and integration where both parties need to win. This method should be used:

- When you and the conflicting party can both get at least what you wanted and maybe more
- To reduce cost
- To create a common power base

- To attack a common foe
- When skills are complementary
- When there is enough time
- When there is trust
- When you have confidence in the other person's ability
- When the ultimate objective is to learn

Compromising

To compromise is to bargain or to search for solutions such that both parties leave with some degree of satisfaction. Compromising is often the end result of confrontation. Some people argue that compromise is a "give and take" approach, which leads to a "win-win" position. Others argue that compromise is a "lose-lose" position, since neither party gets everything he/she wants or needs. Compromise should be used:

- When both parties need to be winners
- When you can't win
- When others are as strong as you are
- When you haven't time to win
- To maintain your relationship with your opponent
- When you are not sure you are right
- When you get nothing if you don't
- When stakes are moderate
- To avoid giving the impression of "fighting"

Smoothing (or Accommodating)

This approach is an attempt to reduce the emotions that exist in a conflict. This is accomplished by emphasizing areas of agreement and de-emphasizing areas of disagreement. An example of smoothing would be to tell someone, "We have agreed on three of the five points and there is no reason why we cannot agree on the last two points." Smoothing does not necessarily resolve a conflict, but tries to convince both parties to remain at the bargaining table because a solution is possible. In smoothing, one may sacrifice one's own goals in order to satisfy the needs of the other party. Smoothing should be used:

- To reach an overarching goal
- To create obligation for a trade-off at a later date
- When the stakes are low
- When liability is limited
- To maintain harmony
- When any solution will be adequate
- To create goodwill (be magnanimous)
- When you'll lose anyway
- To gain time

Forcing (or Competing, Being Uncooperative, Being Assertive)

This is what happens when one party tries to impose the solution on the other party. Conflict resolution works best when resolution is achieved at the lowest possible levels. The higher up the conflict goes, the greater the tendency for the conflict to be forced, with the result being a "win-lose" situation in which one party wins at the expense of the other. Forcing should be used:

- When you are right
- When a do-or-die situation exists
- When stakes are high
- When important principles are at stake
- When you are stronger (never start a battle you can't win)
- To gain status or to gain power
- In short-term, one-shot deals
- When the relationship is unimportant
- When it's understood that a game is being played
- When a quick decision must be made

Avoiding (or Withdrawing)

Avoidance is often regarded as a temporary solution to a problem. The problem and the resulting conflict can come up again and again. Some people view avoiding as cowardice and an unwillingness to be responsive to a situation. Avoiding should be used:

- When you can't win
- When the stakes are low
- When the stakes are high, but you are not ready yet
- To gain time
- To unnerve your opponent
- To preserve neutrality or reputation
- When you think the problem will go away
- When you win by delay

PROBLEMS _____

7–1 Is it possible to establish formal organizational procedures (either at the project level or company-wide) for the resolution of conflicts? If a procedure is established, what can go wrong?

7–2 Under what conditions would a conflict result between members of a group over misunderstandings of each other's roles?

7–3 Is it possible to have a situation in which conflicts are not effectively controlled, and yet have a decision-making process that is not lengthy or cumbersome?

7–4 If conflicts develop into a situation where mistrust prevails, would you expect activity documentation to increase or decrease? Why?

7–5 If a situation occurs that can develop into meaningful conflict, should the project manager let the conflict continue as long as it produces beneficial contributions, or should he try to resolve it as soon as possible?

7–6 Consider the following remarks made by David L. Wilemon ("Managing Conflict in Temporary Management Situations," *Journal of Management Studies,* October 1973, p. 296):

> The value of the conflict produced depends upon the effectiveness of the project manager in promoting beneficial conflict while concomitantly minimizing its potential dysfunctional aspects. A good project manager needs a "sixth sense" to indicate when conflict is desirable, what kind of conflict will be useful, and how much conflict is optimal for a given situation. In the final analysis he has the sole responsibility for his project and how conflict will impact the success or failure of his project.

Based upon these remarks, would your answer to Problem 7–5 change?

7–7 Mr. X is the project manager of a $65 million project of which $1 million is subcontracted out to another company in which Mr. Y is project manager. Unfortunately, Mr. X does not consider Mr. Y as his counterpart and continually communicates with the director of engineering in Mr. Y's company. What type of conflict is that, and how should it be resolved?

7–8 Contract negotiations can easily develop into conflicts. During a disagreement, the vice president of company A ordered his director of finance, the contract negotiator, to break off contract negotiations with company B because the contract negotiator of company B did not report directly to a vice president. How can this situation be resolved?

7–9 For each part below there are two statements; one represents the traditional view and the other the project organizational view. Identify each one.

    a. Conflict should be avoided; conflict is part of change and is therefore inevitable.
    b. Conflict is the result of troublemakers and egoists; conflict is determined by the structure of the system and the relationship among components.
    c. Conflict may be beneficial; conflict is bad.

7–10 Using the modes for conflict resolution defined in Section 7.7, which would be strongly favorable and strongly unfavorable for resolving conflicts between:

    a. Project manager and his project office personnel?
    b. Project manager and the functional support departments?
    c. Project manager and his superiors?
    d. Project manager and other project managers?

7–11 Which influence methods should increase and which should decrease the opportunities for conflict between the following:

- Project manager and his project office personnel?
- Project manager and the functional support departments?
- Project manager and his superiors?
- Project manager and other project managers?

7–12 Would you agree or disagree with the statement that "Conflict resolution through collaboration needs trust; people must rely on one another."

7–13 Davis and Lawrence (*Matrix,* © 1977 by Addison-Wesley Publishing Company, Inc. Reprinted by permission of the publisher) identify several situations common to the matrix that can easily develop into conflicts. For each situation, what would be the recommended cure?

a. Compatible and incompatible personnel must work together
b. Power struggles break the balance of power
c. Anarchy
d. Groupitis (people confuse matrix behavior with group decision-making)
e. A collapse during economic crunch
f. Decision strangulation processes
g. Forcing the matrix organization to the lower organizational levels
h. Navel-gazing (spending time ironing out internal disputes instead of developing better working relationships with the customer)

7–14 Determine the best conflict resolution mode for each of the following situations:

a. Two of your functional team members appear to have personality clashes and almost always assume opposite points of view during decision making.
b. R&D quality control and manufacturing operations quality control continually argue as to who should perform testing on an R&D project. R&D postulates that it's their project, and manufacturing argues that it will eventually go into production and that they wish to be involved as early as possible.
c. Two functional department managers continually argue as to who should perform a certain test. You know that this situation exists, and that the department managers are trying to work it out themselves, often with great pain. However, you are not sure that they will be able to resolve the problem themselves.

7–15 Forcing a confrontation to take place assures that action will be taken. Is it possible that, by using force, a lack of trust among the participants will develop?

7–16 With regard to conflict resolution, should it matter to whom in the organization the project manager reports?

7–17 One of the most common conflicts in an organization occurs with raw materials and finished goods. Why would finance/accounting, marketing/sales, and manufacturing have disagreements?

7–18 Explain how the relative intensity of a conflict can vary as a function of:

a. Getting closer to the actual constraints
b. Having only two constraints instead of three (i.e., time and performance, but not cost)
c. The project life cycle
d. The person with whom the conflict occurs

7–19 The conflicts shown in Figure 7–1 are given relative intensities as perceived in project-driven organizations. Would this list be arranged differently for non–project-driven organizations?

7–20 Consider the responses made by the project managers in Figures 7–5 through 7–7. Which of their choices do you agree with, and which do you disagree with? Justify your answers.

7–21 As a good project manager, you try to plan for conflict avoidance. You now have a low-intensity conflict with a functional manager and, as in the past, handle the conflict with confrontation. If you knew that there would be a high-intensity conflict shortly thereafter, would you be willing to use the withdrawal mode for the low-intensity conflict in order to lay the groundwork for the high-intensity conflict?

7–22 Jones Construction Company has recently won a $120 million effort for a local company. The effort includes three separate construction projects, each one beginning at the same time. Two of the projects are eighteen months in duration and the third one is thirty months. Each project has its own project manager. How do we resolve conflicts when each project may have a different priority but they are all for the same customer?

7–23 Minnesota Power and Light establishes priorities as follows:

> Level 0: no priority
> Level 1: to be completed on or before a specific date
> Level 2: to be completed in or before a given fiscal quarter
> Level 3: to be completed within a given year

How do you feel about this system of establishing priorities?

7–24 Richard is a department manager who must supply resources to four different projects. Although each project has an established priority, the project managers continually argue that departmental resources are not being allocated effectively. Richard has decided to have a monthly group meeting with all four of the project managers and to let them determine how the resources should be allocated. Can this technique work? If so, under what conditions?

CASE STUDIES

FACILITIES SCHEDULING AT MAYER MANUFACTURING

Eddie Turner was elated with the good news that he was being promoted to section supervisor in charge of scheduling all activities in the new engineering research laboratory. The new laboratory was a necessity for Mayer Manufacturing. The engineering, manufacturing, and quality control directorates were all in desperate need of a new testing facility. Upper-level management felt that this new facility would alleviate many of the problems that previously existed.

The new organizational structure (as shown in Exhibit 7–1) required a change in policy over use of the laboratory. The new section supervisor, on approval from his department manager, would have full authority for establishing priorities for the use of the new facility. The new policy change was a necessity because upper-level management felt that there would be inevitable conflict between manufacturing, engineering, and quality control.

Exhibit 7–1. Mayer Manufacturing Organizational Structure

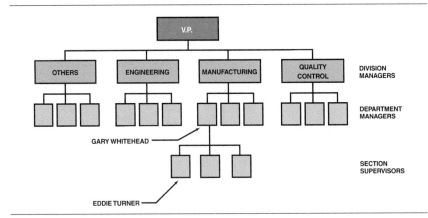

After one month of operations, Eddie Turner was finding his job impossible, so Eddie has a meeting with Gary Whitehead, his department manager.

Eddie: "I'm having a hell of a time trying to satisfy all of the department managers. If I give engineering prime-time use of the facility, then quality control and manufacturing say that I'm playing favorites. Imagine that! Even my own people say that I'm playing favorites with other directorates. I just can't satisfy everyone."

Gary: "Well, Eddie, you know that this problem comes with the job. You'll get the job done."

Eddie: "The problem is that I'm a section supervisor and have to work with department managers. These department managers look down on me like I'm their servant. If I were a department manager, then they'd show me some respect. What I'm really trying to say is that I would like you to send out the weekly memos to these department managers telling them of the new priorities. They wouldn't argue with you like they do with me. I can supply you with all the necessary information. All you'll have to do is to sign your name."

Gary: "Determining the priorities and scheduling the facilities is your job, not mine. This is a new position and I want you to handle it. I know you can because I selected you. I do not intend to interfere."

During the next two weeks, the conflicts got progressively worse. Eddie felt that he was unable to cope with the situation by himself. The department managers did not respect the authority delegated to him by his superiors. For the next two weeks, Eddie sent memos to Gary in the early part of the week asking whether Gary agreed with the priority list. There was no response to the two memos. Eddie then met with Gary to discuss the deteriorating situation.

Eddie: "Gary, I've sent you two memos to see if I'm doing anything wrong in establishing the weekly priorities and schedules. Did you get my memos?"

Gary: "Yes, I received your memos. But as I told you before, I have enough problems to worry about without doing your job for you. If you can't handle the work let me know and I'll find someone who can."

Eddie returned to his desk and contemplated his situation. Finally, he made a decision. Next week he was going to put a signature block under his for Gary to sign, with carbon copies for all division managers. "Now, let's see what happens," remarked Eddie.

SCHEDULING THE SAFETY LAB

"Now see here, Tom, I understand your problem well," remarked Dr. Polly, director of the Research Laboratories. "I pay you a good salary to run the safety labs. That salary also includes doing the necessary scheduling to match our priorities. Now, if you can't handle the job, I'll get someone who can."

Tom: "Every Friday morning your secretary hands me a sheet with the listing of priorities for the following week. Once, just once, I'd like to sit in on the director's meeting and tell you people what you do to us in the safety lab when you continually shuffle around the priorities from week to week.

"On Friday afternoons, my people and I meet with representatives from each project to establish the following week's schedules."

Dr. Polly: "Can't you people come to an agreement?"

Tom: "I don't think you appreciate my problem. Two months ago, we all sat down to work out the lab schedule. Project X-13 had signed up to use the lab last week. Now, mind you, they had been scheduled for the past two months. But the Friday before they were to use it, your new priority list forced them to reschedule the lab at a later date, so that we could give the use of the lab to a higher-priority project. We're paying an awful lot of money for idle time and the redoing of network schedules. Only the project managers on the top-priority projects end up smiling after our Friday meetings."

Dr. Polly: "As I see your problem, you can't match long-range planning with the current priority list. I agree that it does create conflicts for you. But you have to remember that we, upstairs, have many other conflicts to resolve. I want that one solved at your level, not mine."

Tom: "Every project we have requires use of the safety lab. This is the basis for our problem. Would you consider letting us modify your priority list with regard to the safety lab?"

Dr. Polly: "Yes, but you had better have the agreement of all of the project managers. I don't want them coming to see me about your scheduling problems."

Tom: "How about if I let people do long-range scheduling for the lab, for three out of four weeks each month? The fourth week will be for the priority projects."

Dr. Polly: "That might work. You had better make sure that each project manager informs you immediately of any schedule slippages so that you can reschedule accordingly. From what I've heard, some of the project managers don't let you know until the last minute."

Tom: "That has been part of the problem. Just to give you an example, Project VX-161 was a top-priority effort and had the lab scheduled for the first week in March. I was never informed that they had accelerated their schedule by two weeks. They walked into my office and demanded use of the lab for the third week in February. Since they had the top priority, I had to grant them their request. However, Project BP-3 was planning on using the lab during that week and was bumped back three weeks. That cost them a pile of bucks in idle time pay and, of course, they're blaming me."

Dr. Polly: "Well Tom, I'm sure you'll find a solution to your problem."

TELESTAR INTERNATIONAL

On November 15, 1978, the Department of Energy Resources awarded Telestar a $475,000 contract for the developing and testing of two waste treatment plants. Telestar had spent the better part of the last two years developing waste treatment technology under its own R&D activities. This new contract would give Telestar the opportunity to "break into a new field"—that of waste treatment.

The contract was negotiated at a firm-fixed price. Any cost overruns would have to be incurred by Telestar. The original bid was priced out at $847,000. Telestar's management, however, wanted to win this one. The decision was made that Telestar would "buy in" at $475,000 so that they could at least get their foot into the new marketplace.

The original estimate of $847,000 was very "rough" because Telestar did not have any good man-hour standards, in the area of waste treatment, on which to base their man-hour projections. Corporate management was willing to spend up to $400,000 of their own funds in order to compensate the bid of $475,000.

By February 15, 1979, costs were increasing to such a point where overrun would be occurring well ahead of schedule. Anticipated costs to completion were now $943,000. The project manager decided to stop all activities in certain functional departments, one of which was structural analysis. The manager of the structural analysis department strongly opposed the closing out of the work order prior to the testing of the first plant's high-pressure pneumatic and electrical systems.

Structures Manager: "You're running a risk if you close out this work order. How will you know if the hardware can withstand the stresses that will be imposed during the test? After all, the test is scheduled for next month and I can probably finish the analysis by then."

Project Manager: "I understand your concern, but I cannot risk a cost overrun. My boss expects me to do the work within cost. The plant design is similar to one that we have tested before, without any structural problems being detected. On this basis I consider your analysis unnecessary."

Structures Manager: "Just because two plants are similar does not mean that they will be identical in performance. There can be major structural deficiencies."

Project Manager: "I guess the risk is mine."

Structures Manager: "Yes, but I get concerned when a failure can reflect on the integrity of my department. You know, we're performing on schedule and within the time and money budgeted. You're setting a bad example by cutting off our budget without any real justification."

Project Manager: "I understand your concern, but we must pull out all the stops when overrun costs are inevitable."

Structures Manager: "There's no question in my mind that this analysis should be completed. However, I'm not going to complete it on my overhead budget. I'll reassign my people tomorrow. Incidentally, you had better be careful; my people are not very happy to work for a project that can be canceled immediately. I may have trouble getting volunteers next time."

Project Manager: "Well, I'm sure you'll be able to adequately handle any future work. I'll report to my boss that I have issued a work stoppage order to your department."

During the next month's test, the plant exploded. Postanalysis indicated that the failure was due to a structural deficiency.

a. Who is at fault?
b. Should the structures manager have been dedicated enough to continue the work on his own?
c. Can a functional manager, who considers his organization as strictly support, still be dedicated to total project success?

THE PROBLEM WITH PRIORITIES

For the past several years, Kent Corporation had achieved remarkable success in winning R&D contracts. The customers were pleased with the analytical capabilities of the R&D staff at Kent Corporation. Theoretical and experimental results were usually within 95 percent agreement. But many customers still felt that 95 percent was too low. They wanted 98–99 percent.

In 1989, Kent updated their computer facility by purchasing a large computer. The increased performance with the new computer encouraged the R&D group to attempt to convert from two-dimensional to three-dimensional solutions to their theoretical problems. Almost everyone except the director of R&D thought that this would give better comparison between experimental and theoretical data.

Kent Corporation had tried to develop the computer program for three-dimensional solutions with their own internal R&D programs, but the cost was too great. Finally, after a year of writing proposals, Kent Corporation convinced the federal government to sponsor the project. The project was estimated at $750,000, to begin January 2, 1991, and to be completed by December 20, 1991. Dan McCord was selected as project manager. Dan had worked with the EDP department on other projects and knew the people and the man-hour standards.

Kent Corporation was big enough to support 100 simultaneous projects. With so many projects in existence at one time, continual reshuffling of resources was necessary. The corporation directors met every Monday morning to establish project priorities. Priorities were not enforced unless project and functional managers could not agree on the allocation and distribution of resources.

Because of the R&D director's persistence, the computer project was given a low priority. This posed a problem for Dan McCord. The computer department manager refused to staff the project with his best people. As a result, Dan had severe skepticism about the success of the project.

In July, two other project managers held a meeting with Dan to discuss the availability of the new computer model.

"We have two proposals that we're favored to win, providing that we can state in our proposal that we have this new computer model available for use," remarked one of the project managers.

"We have a low priority and, even if we finish the job on time, I'm not sure of the quality of work because of the people we have assigned," said Dan.

"How do you propose we improve our position?" asked a project manager.

"Let's try to get in to see the director of R&D," asserted Dan.

"And what are we going to say in our defense?" asked one of the project managers.

HANDLING CONFLICT IN PROJECT MANAGEMENT

The next several pages contain a six-part case study in conflict management. Read the instructions carefully on how to keep score and use the boxes in the table on page 417 as the worksheet for recording your choice and the group's choice; after the case study has been completed, your instructor will provide you with the proper grading system for recording your scores.

Part 1: Facing the Conflict

As part of his first official duties, the new department manager informs you by memo that he has changed his input and output requirements for the MIS project (on which you are the project manager) because of several complaints by his departmental employees. This is contradictory to the project plan that you developed with the previous manager and are currently working toward. The department manager states that he has already discussed this with the vice president and general manager, a man to whom both of you report, and feels that the former department manager made a poor decision and did not get sufficient input from the employees who would be using the system as to the best system specifications. You telephone him and try to convince him to hold off on his request for change until a later time, but he refuses.

Changing the input–output requirements at this point in time will require a major revision and will set back total system implementation by three weeks. This will also affect other department managers who expect to see this system operational according to the original schedule. You can explain this to your superiors, but the increased project costs will be hard to absorb. The potential cost overrun might be difficult to explain at a later date.

At this point you are somewhat unhappy with yourself at having been on the search committee that found this department manager and especially at having recommended him for this position. You know that something must be done, and the following are your alternatives:

A. You can remind the department manager than you were on the search committee that recommended him and then ask him to return the favor, since he "owes you one."

B. You can tell the department manager that you will form a new search committee to replace him if he doesn't change his position.

C. You can take a tranquilizer and then ask your people to try to perform the additional work within the original time and cost constraints.

D. You can go to the vice president and general manager and request that the former requirements be adhered to, at least temporarily.

E. You can send a memo to the department manager explaining your problem and asking him to help you find a solution.

F. You can tell the department manager that your people cannot handle the request and his people will have to find alternate ways of solving their problems.

G. You can send a memo to the department manager requesting an appointment, at his earliest convenience, to help you resolve your problem.

H. You can go to the department manager's office later that afternoon and continue the discussion further.

I. You can send the department manager a memo telling him that you have decided to use the old requirements but will honor his request at a later time.

Line	Part	Personal		Group	
		Choice	Score	Choice	Score
1	1. Facing the Conflict				
2	2. Understanding Emotions	/////		/////	
3	3. Establishing Communications				
4	4. Conflict Resolution	/////		/////	
5	5. Understanding Your Choices				
6	6. Interpersonal Influences				
	TOTAL	/////		/////	

Although other alternatives exist, assume that these are the only ones open to you at the moment. Without discussing the answer with your group, record the letter representing your choice in the appropriate space on line 1 of the worksheet under "Personal."

As soon as all of your group have finished, discuss the problem as a group and determine that alternative that the group considers to be best. Record this answer on line 1 of the worksheet under "Group." Allow ten minutes for this part.

**Part 2:
Understanding
Emotions**

Never having worked with this department manager before, you try to predict what his reactions will be when confronted with the problem. Obviously, he can react in a variety of ways:

  A. He can *accept* your solution in its entirety without asking any questions.
  B. He can discuss some sort of justification in order to *defend* his position.
  C. He can become extremely annoyed with having to discuss the problem again and demonstrate *hostility.*
  D. He can demonstrate a willingness to *cooperate* with you in resolving the problem.
  E. He can avoid making any decision at this time by *withdrawing* from the discussion.

	Your Choice					Group Choice				
	Acc.	Def.	Host.	Coop.	With.	Acc.	Def.	Host.	Coop.	With.
A. I've given my answer. See the general manager if you're not happy.										
B. I understand your problem. Let's do it your way.										
C. I understand your problem, but I'm doing what is best for my department.										
D. Let's discuss the problem. Perhaps there are alternatives.										
E. Let me explain to you why we need the new requirements.										
F. See my section supervisors. It was their recommendation.										
G. New managers are supposed to come up with new and better ways, aren't they?										

In the table above are several possible statements that could be made by the department manager when confronted with the problem. Without discussion with your group, place a check mark beside the appropriate emotion that could describe this statement. When each member of the group has completed his choice, determine the group choice. Numerical values will be assigned to your choices in the discussion that follows. Do not mark the worksheet at this time. Allow ten minutes for this part.

Part 3: Establishing Communications

Unhappy over the department manager's memo and the resulting follow-up phone conversation, you decide to walk in on the department manager. You tell him that you will have a problem trying to honor his request. He tells you that he is too busy with his own problems of restructuring his department and that your schedule and cost problems are of no concern to him at this time. You storm out of his office, leaving him with the impression that his actions and remarks are not in the best interest of either the project or the company.

The department manager's actions do not, of course, appear to be those of a dedicated manager. He should be more concerned about what's in the best interest of the company. As you contemplate the situation, you wonder if you could have received a better response from him had you approached him differently. In other words, what is your best approach to opening up communications between you and the department manager? From the list of alternatives shown below, and working alone, select the alternative that best represents how you would handle this situation. When all members of the group have selected their personal choices, repeat the process and make a group choice. Record your personal and group choices on line 3 of the worksheet. Allow ten minutes for this part.

    A. Comply with the request and document all results so that you will be able to defend yourself at a later date in order to show that the department manager should be held accountable.

    B. Immediately send him a memo reiterating your position and tell him that at a later time you will reconsider his new requirements. Tell him that time is of utmost importance, and you need an immediate response if he is displeased.

    C. Send him a memo stating that you are holding him accountable for all cost overruns and schedule delays.

    D. Send him a memo stating you are considering his request and that you plan to see him again at a later date to discuss changing the requirements.

    E. See him as soon as possible. Tell him that he need not apologize for his remarks and actions, and that you have reconsidered your position and wish to discuss it with him.

    F. Delay talking to him for a few days in hopes that he will cool off sufficiently and then see him in hopes that you can reopen the discussions.

    G. Wait a day or so for everyone to cool off and then try to see him through an appointment; apologize for losing your temper, and ask him if he would like to help you resolve the problem.

Part 4: Conflict Resolution Modes

Having never worked with this manager before, you are unsure about which conflict resolution mode would work best. You decide to wait a few days and then set up an appointment with the department manager without stating what subject matter will be discussed. You then try to determine what conflict resolution mode appears to be dominant based on the opening remarks of the department manager. Neglecting the fact that your conversation with the department manager might already be considered as confrontation, for each statement shown below, select the conflict resolution mode that the *department manager* appears to prefer. After each member of the group has recorded his personal choices in the table on page 420, determine the group choices. Numerical values will be attached to your answers at a later time. Allow ten minutes for this part.

A. *Withdrawal* is retreating from a potential conflict.
B. *Smoothing* is emphasizing areas of agreement and de-emphasizing areas of disagreement.
C. *Compromising* is the willingness to give and take.
D. *Forcing* is directing the resolution in one direction or another, a win-or-lose position.
E. *Confrontation* is a face-to-face meeting to resolve the conflict.

	Personal Choice					Group Choice				
	With.	Smooth.	Comp.	Forc.	Conf.	With.	Smooth.	Comp.	Forc.	Conf.
A. The requirements are my decision, and we're doing it my way.										
B. I've thought about it and you're right. We'll do it your way.										
C. Let's discuss the problem. Perhaps there are alternatives.										
D. Let me again explain why we need the new requirements.										
E. See my section supervisors; they're handling it now.										
F. I've looked over the problem and I might be able to ease up on some of the requirements.										

**Part 5:
Understanding
Your Choices**

Assume that the department manager has refused to see you again to discuss the new requirements. Time is running out, and you would like to make a decision before the costs and schedules get out of hand. From the list below, select your personal choice and then, after each group member is finished, find a group choice.

A. Disregard the new requirements, since they weren't part of the original project plan.
B. Adhere to the new requirements, and absorb the increased costs and delays.
C. Ask the vice president and general manager to step in and make the final decision.
D. Ask the other department managers who may realize a schedule delay to try to convince this department manager to ease his request or even delay it.

Record your answer on line 5 of the worksheet. Allow five minutes for this part.

**Part 6:
Interpersonal
Influences**

Assume that upper-level management resolves the conflict in your favor. In order to complete the original work requirements you will need support from this department manager's organization. Unfortunately, you are not sure as to which type of interpersonal influence to use. Although you are considered as an expert in your field, you fear that this manager's functional employees may have a strong allegiance to the department manager and may not want to adhere to your requests. Which of the following interpersonal influence styles would be best under the given set of conditions?

    A.   You threaten the employees with penalty power by telling them that you will turn in a bad performance report to their department manager.

    B.   You can use reward power and promise the employees a good evaluation, possible promotion, and increased responsibilities on your next project.

    C.   You can continue your technique of trying to convince the functional personnel to do your bidding because you are the expert in the field.

    D.   You can try to motivate the employees to do a good job by convincing them that the work is challenging.

    E.   You can make sure that they understand that your authority has been delegated to you by the vice president and general manager and that they must do what you say.

    F.   You can try to build up friendships and off-work relationships with these people and rely on referent power.

Record your personal and group choices on line 6 of the worksheet. Allow ten minutes for completion of this part.

The solution to this exercise appears in Appendix A.

Special Topics

8.0 INTRODUCTION

Some situations or special topics could be discussed in every chapter. However, since most of the special topics span several chapters, the information is condensed here for the sake of clarity. The special topics include:

- Rewards and evaluation
- Managing small projects
- Managing mega projects
- R&D project management
- Ethics in project management

8.1 PERFORMANCE MEASUREMENT ON THE HORIZONTAL LINE

When functional employees are assigned to a new project, their first concern is that their functional manager be informed when they have performed well on their new assignment. A good project manager will make it immediately clear to all new functional employees that if they perform well in the project, then he (the project manager) will inform the functional manager of their progress and achievements. This assumes that the functional manager is not providing close supervision over the functional employees and is, instead, passing on some of the responsibility to the project manager—a common situation in project management organization structures. Obviously, if the functional manager has a small span of control and/or sufficient time for closely monitoring the work of his subordinates, then the project manager's need for indirect reward power is minimal.

Many good projects as well as project management structures have failed because of the inability of the system to evaluate properly the functional employee's performance. This problem is, unfortunately, one of the most often overlooked trouble spots in project management.

In a project management structure, there are basically six ways that a functional employee can be evaluated on a project:

- *The project manager prepares a written, confidential evaluation and gives it to the functional manager.* The functional manager will evaluate the validity of the project manager's comments and prepare his own evaluation. Only the line manager's evaluation is shown to the employee. The use of confidential forms is not preferred because, first, it may be contrary to government regulations, and, second, it does not provide the necessary feedback for an employee to improve.

- *The project manager prepares a nonconfidential evaluation and gives it to the functional manager.* The functional manager prepares his own evaluation form and shows both evaluations to the functional employee. This is the technique preferred by most project and functional managers. However, there are several major difficulties with this technique. If the functional employee is an average or below-average worker, and if this employee is still to be assigned to this project after his evaluation, then the project manager might rate the employee as above average simply to prevent any sabotage or bad feelings downstream. In this situation, the functional manager might want a confidential evaluation instead, knowing that the functional employee will see both evaluation forms. Functional employees tend to blame the project manager if they receive a below-average merit pay increase, but give credit to the functional manager if the increase is above average. The best bet here is for the project manager periodically to tell the functional employees how well they are doing, and to give them an honest appraisal. Several companies that use this technique allow the project manager to show the form to the line manager first (to avoid conflict later) and then show it to the employee.

- *The project manager provides the functional manager with an oral evaluation of the employee's performance.* Although this technique is commonly used, most functional managers prefer documentation on employee progress. Again, lack of feedback may prevent the employee from improving.

- *The functional manager makes the entire evaluation without any input from the project manager.* In order for this technique to be effective, the functional manager must have sufficient time to supervise each subordinate's performance on a continual basis. Unfortunately, most functional managers do not have this luxury because of their broad span of control and must therefore rely heavily on the project manager's input.

● *The project manager makes the entire evaluation for the functional manager.* This technique can work if the functional employee spends 100 percent of his time on one project, or if he is physically located at a remote site where he cannot be observed by his functional manager.

● *All project and functional managers jointly evaluate all project functional employees at the same time.* This technique should be limited to small companies with fewer than fifty or so employees; otherwise the evaluation process might be time-consuming for key personnel. A bad evaluation will be known by everyone.

In five of the six techniques, the project manager has either a direct or an indirect input into the employee's evaluation process.

Since most project managers prefer written, nonconfidential evaluations, we must determine what the evaluation forms look like and when the functional employee will be evaluated. The indirect evaluation process will be time-consuming. This is of paramount importance on large projects where the project manager may have as many as 200 part-time functional employees assigned to his activities.

The evaluation forms can be filled out either when the employee is up for evaluation or after the project is completed. If the evaluation form is to be filled out when the employee is eligible for promotion or a merit increase, then the project manager should be willing to give an *honest* appraisal of the employee's performance. Of course, the project manager should not fill out the evaluation form if he has not had sufficient time to observe the employee at work.

The evaluation form can be filled out at the termination of the project. This, however, may produce a problem in that the project may end the month after the employee is considered for promotion. The advantage of this technique is that the project manager may have been able to find sufficient time both to observe the employee in action and to see the output.

Figure 8–1 represents, in a humorous way, how project personnel perceive the evaluation form. Unfortunately, the evaluation process is very serious and can easily have a severe impact on an individual's career path with the company even though the final evaluation rests with the functional manager.

Figure 8–2 shows a simple type of evaluation form on which the project manager identifies the best description of the employee's performance. The project manager may or may not make additional comments. This type of form is generally used whenever the employee is up for evaluation, provided that the project manager has had sufficient time to observe the employee's performance.

Figure 8–3 shows another typical form that can be used to evaluate an employee. In each category, the employee is rated on a subjective scale. In order to minimize time and paperwork, it is also possible to have a single evaluation form at project termination for evaluation of all employees. This is shown in Figure 8–4. All employees are rated in each category on a scale of 1 to 5. Totals are obtained to provide a relative comparison of employees.

PERFORMANCE FACTORS	EXCELLENT (1 OUT OF 15)	VERY GOOD (3 OUT OF 15)	GOOD (8 OUT OF 15)	FAIR (2 OUT OF 15)	UNSATISFACTORY (1 OUT OF 15)
	FAR EXCEEDS JOB REQUIREMENTS	EXCEEDS JOB REQUIREMENTS	MEETS JOB REQUIREMENTS	NEEDS SOME IMPROVEMENT	DOES NOT MEET MINIMUM STANDARDS
QUALITY	LEAPS TALL BUILDINGS WITH A SINGLE BOUND	MUST TAKE RUNNING START TO LEAP OVER TALL BUILDING	CAN ONLY LEAP OVER A SHORT BUILDING OR MEDIUM ONE WITHOUT SPIRES	CRASHES INTO BUILDING	CANNOT RECOGNIZE BUILDINGS
TIMELINESS	IS FASTER THAN A SPEEDING BULLET	IS AS FAST AS A SPEEDING BULLET	NOT QUITE AS FAST AS A SPEEDING BULLET	WOULD YOU BELIEVE A SLOW BULLET?	WOUNDS HIMSELF WITH THE BULLET
INITIATIVE	IS STRONGER THAN A LOCOMOTIVE	IS STRONGER THAN A BULL ELEPHANT	IS STRONGER THAN A BULL	SHOOTS THE BULL	SMELLS LIKE A BULL
ADAPTABILITY	WALKS ON WATER CONSISTENTLY	WALKS ON WATER IN EMERGENCIES	WASHES WITH WATER	DRINKS WATER	PASSES WATER IN EMERGENCIES
COMMUNICATIONS	TALKS WITH GOD	TALKS WITH ANGELS	TALKS TO HIMSELF	ARGUES WITH HIMSELF	LOSES THE ARGUMENT WITH HIMSELF

FIGURE 8–1. Guide to performance appraisal.

Obviously, evaluation forms such as that shown in Figure 8–4 have severe limitations, as a one-to-one comparison of all project functional personnel is of little value if the employees are from different departments. How can a project engineer be compared to a cost accountant? If the project engineer receives a total score of 40 and the cost accountant receives a score of 30, does this mean that the project engineer is of more value or a better employee? Employees should have the right to challenge any item in a nonconfidential evaluation form.

Several companies are using this form by assigning coefficients of importance to each topic. For example, under a topic of technical judgment, the project engineer might have a coefficient of importance of 0.90, whereas the cost accountant's coefficient might be 0.25. These coefficients could be reversed for a topic on cost consciousness. Unfortunately, such comparisons have questionable validity, and this type of evaluation form is usually of a confidential nature.

Even though the project manager fills out an evaluation form, there is no guarantee that the functional manager will believe the project manager's evaluation. There are always situations in which the project and functional managers disagree as to either quality or direction of work. This disagreement can easily alienate the project manager enough that he will recommend a poor evaluation regardless of how well the employee has performed. If a functional employee

EMPLOYEE'S NAME			DATE	
EMPLOYEE ASSIGNMENT				
EMPLOYEE'S TOTAL TIME TO DATE ON PROJECT			EMPLOYEE'S REMAINING TIME ON PROJECT	

TECHNICAL JUDGEMENT:

☐ Quickly reaches sound conclusions ☐ Usually makes sound conclusions ☐ Marginal decision making ability ☐ Needs technical assistance ☐ Makes faulty conclusions

WORK PLANNING:

☐ Good planner ☐ Plans well with help ☐ Occasionally plans well ☐ Needs detailed instructions ☐ Cannot plan at all

COMMUNICATIONS:

☐ Always understands instructions ☐ Sometimes needs clarification ☐ Always needs clarifications ☐ Needs follow-up ☐ Needs constant instruction

ATTITUDE:

☐ Always job interested ☐ Shows interest most of the time ☐ Shows no job interest ☐ More interested in other activities ☐ Does not care about job

COOPERATION:

☐ Always enthusiastic ☐ Works well until job is completed ☐ Usually works well with others ☐ Works poorly with others ☐ Wants it done his/her way

WORK HABITS:

☐ Always project oriented ☐ Most often project oriented ☐ Usually consistent with requests ☐ Works poorly with others ☐ Always works alone

ADDITIONAL COMMENTS: _____

FIGURE 8–2. Project work assignment appraisal.

spends most of his time working alone, the project manager may give an average evaluation even if the employee's performance is superb. Also, the project manager may know the employee personally and allow personal feelings to influence his decision.

Another problem may exist in the situation where the project manager is a "generalist," say at a grade-7 level, and requests that the functional manager assign his best employee to the project. The functional manager agrees to the request and assigns his best employee, a grade-10 specialist. One solution to this problem is to have the project manager evaluate the expert only in certain categories such as communications, work habits, and problem-solving, but not in the area of his technical expertise. The functional manager might be the only person qualified to evaluate functional personnel on technical abilities and expertise.

As a final note, it is sometimes argued that functional employees should have some sort of indirect input into a project manager's evaluation. This raises rather

EMPLOYEE'S NAME		DATE	
PROJECT TITLE		JOB NUMBER	
EMPLOYEE ASSIGNMENT			
EMPLOYEE'S TOTAL TIME TO DATE ON PROJECT		EMPLOYEE'S REMAINING TIME ON PROJECT	

	EXCELLENT	ABOVE AVERAGE	AVERAGE	BELOW AVERAGE	INADEQUATE
TECHNICAL JUDGEMENT					
WORK PLANNING					
COMMUNICATIONS					
ATTITUDE					
COOPERATION					
WORK HABITS					
PROFIT CONTRIBUTION					

ADDITIONAL COMMENTS: _____

FIGURE 8–3. Project work assignment appraisal.

interesting questions as to how far we can go with the indirect evaluation procedure.

From a top-management perspective, the indirect evaluation process brings with it several headaches. Wage and salary administrators readily accept the necessity for using different evaluation forms for white-collar and blue-collar workers. But now, we have a situation in which there can be more than one type of evaluation system for white-collar workers alone. Those employees who work in project-driven functional departments will be evaluated directly and indirectly, but based on formal procedures. Employees who charge their time to overhead accounts and non–project-driven departments might simply be evaluated by a single, direct evaluation procedure.

Many wage and salary administrators contend that they cannot live with a white-collar evaluation system and therefore have tried to combine the direct and indirect evaluation forms into one, as shown in Figure 8–5. Some administrators have even gone so far as to adopt a single form company-wide, regardless of whether an individual is a white- or blue-collar worker.

The design of the employee's evaluation form depends on what evaluation method or procedure is being used. Generally speaking, there are nine methods available for evaluating personnel:

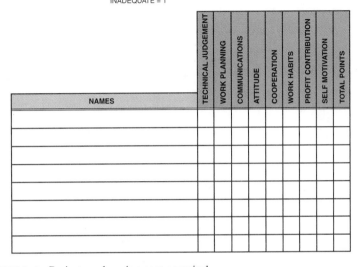

| PROJECT TITLE | | JOB NUMBER |
| EMPLOYEE ASSIGNMENT | | DATE |

CODE:

EXCELLENT = 5
ABOVE AVERAGE = 4
AVERAGE = 3
BELOW AVERAGE = 2
INADEQUATE = 1

NAMES	TECHNICAL JUDGEMENT	WORK PLANNING	COMMUNICATIONS	ATTITUDE	COOPERATION	WORK HABITS	PROFIT CONTRIBUTION	SELF MOTIVATION	TOTAL POINTS

FIGURE 8–4. Project work assignment appraisal.

- Essay appraisal
- Graphic rating scale
- Field review
- Forced-choice review
- Critical incident appraisal
- Management by objectives
- Work standards approach
- Ranking methods
- Assessment center

Descriptions of these methods can be found in almost any text on wage and salary administration. Which method is best suited for a project-driven organizational structure? To answer this question, we must analyze the characteristics of the organizational form as well as those of the personnel who must perform there. An an example, project management can be described as an arena of conflict. Which of the above evaluation procedures can best be used to evaluate an employee's ability to work and progress in an atmosphere of conflict? Figure 8–6 compares the above nine evaluation procedures against the six most common project conflicts. This type of analysis must be carried out for all variables and characteristics that describe the project management environment. Most compensation

I. <u>EMPLOYEE INFORMATION:</u>

1. NAME _____ 2. DATE OF EVALUATION _____

3. JOB ASSIGNMENT _____ 4. DATE OF LAST EVALUATION _____

5. PAY GRADE _____

6. EMPLOYEE'S IMMEDIATE SUPERVISOR _____

7. SUPERVISOR'S LEVEL: ☐ SECTION ☐ DEPT. ☐ DIVISION ☐ EXECUTIVE

II. <u>EVALUATOR'S INFORMATION:</u>

1. EVALUATOR'S NAME _____

2. EVALUATOR'S LEVEL: ☐ SECTION ☐ DEPT. ☐ DIVISION ☐ EXECUTIVE

3. RATE THE EMPLOYEE ON THE FOLLOWING:

	EXCELLENT	VERY GOOD	GOOD	FAIR	POOR
ABILITY TO ASSUME RESPONSIBILITY					
WORKS WELL WITH OTHERS					
LOYAL ATTITUDE TOWARD COMPANY					
DOCUMENTS WORK WELL AND IS BOTH COST AND PROFIT CONSCIOUS					
RELIABILITY TO SEE JOB THROUGH					
ABILITY TO ACCEPT CRITCISM					
WILLINGNESS TO WORK OVERTIME					
PLANS JOB EXECUTION CAREFULLY					
TECHNICAL KNOWLEDGE					
COMMUNICATIVE SKILLS					
OVERALL RATING					

4. RATE THE EMPLOYEE IN COMPARISON TO HIS CONTEMPORARIES:

LOWER 10%	LOWER 25%	LOWER 40%	MIDWAY	UPPER 40%	UPPER 25%	UPPER 10%

5. RATE THE EMPLOYEE IN COMPARISON TO HIS CONTEMPORARIES:

SHOULD BE PROMOTED AT ONCE	PROMOTABLE NEXT YEAR	PROMOTABLE ALONG WITH CONTEMPORARIES	NEEDS TO MATURE IN GRADE	DEFINITELY NOT PROMOTABLE

6. EVALUATOR'S COMMENTS: _____

_____

_____

SIGNATURE _____

III. <u>CONCURRENCE SECTION:</u>

1. NAME _____

2. POSITION: ☐ DEPARTMENT ☐ DIVISION ☐ EXECUTIVE

3. CONCURRENCE ☐ AGREE ☐ DISAGREE

4. COMMENTS: _____

_____

_____

_____

SIGNATURE _____

IV. <u>PERSONNEL SECTION:</u> (to be completed by the Personnel Department only)

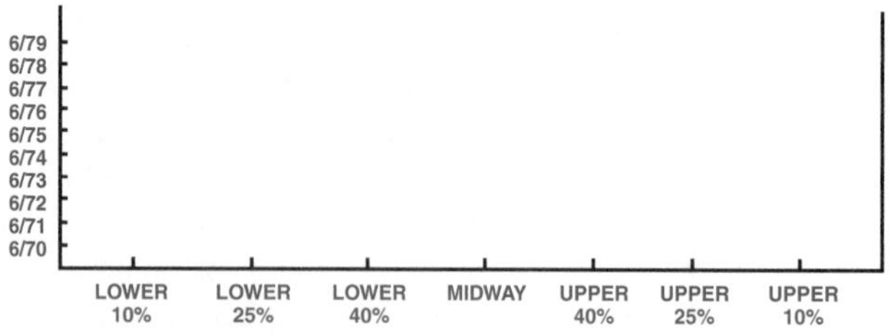

6/79
6/78
6/77
6/76
6/75
6/74
6/73
6/72
6/71
6/70

LOWER 10% | LOWER 25% | LOWER 40% | MIDWAY | UPPER 40% | UPPER 25% | UPPER 10%

V. <u>EMPLOYEE'S SIGNATURE:</u> _____ DATE: _____

FIGURE 8–5. Job evaluation.

	Essay Appraisal	Graphic Rating Scale	Field Review	Forced-Choice Review	Critical Incident Appraisal	Management By Objectives	Work Standards Approach	Ranking Methods	Assessment Center
Conflict over schedules	●	●		●	●		●	●	
Conflict over priorities	●	●		●	●		●	●	
Conflict over technical issues	●			●			●		
Conflict over administration	●	●	●	●			●	●	●
Personality conflict	●	●		●			●		
Conflict over cost	●		●	●	●		●	●	●

Circles define areas where evaluation technique may be difficult to implement.

FIGURE 8–6. Rating evaluation techniques against types of conflict.

managers would agree that the management by objectives (MBO) technique offers the greatest promise for a fair and equitable evaluation of all employees. Although MBO implies that functional employees will have a say in establishing their own goals and objectives, this may not be the case. In project management, maybe the project manager or functional manager will set the objectives, and the functional employee will be told that he has to live with that. Obviously, there will be advantages and disadvantages to whatever evaluation procedures are finally selected.

Having identified the problems with employee evaluation in a project environment, we can now summarize the results and attempt to predict the future. Project managers must have some sort of either direct or indirect input into an employee's evaluation. Without this, project managers may find it difficult to motivate people adequately on the horizontal line. The question is, of course, how should this input take place? Most wage and salary administrators appear to be pushing for a single procedure to evaluate all white-collar employees. At the same time, however, administrators recognize the necessity for an indirect input by the project manager and, therefore, are willing to let the project and functional managers (and possibly functional personnel) determine the exact method of input, which can be different for each employee and each project. This implies that the indirect input might be oral for one employee and written for another, with both employees reporting to the functional manager. Although this technique may seem confusing, it may be the only viable alternative for the future.

Sometimes, project management can create severe evaluation problems. As an example, Gary has been assigned as a part-time assistant project manager. He must function as both an assistant project manager and a functional employee. In addition, Gary reports both vertically to his functional manager and horizontally to a project manager. As part of his project responsibilities, Gary must integrate activities between his department and two other departments within his division.

His responsibilities also include writing a nonconfidential performance evaluation for all functional employees from all three departments who are assigned to his project. Can Gary effectively and honestly evaluate functional employees in his own department, people with whom he will be working side by side when the project is over? The answer to this question is no; the project manager should come to the rescue. If Gary were the project manager instead of the assistant project manager, then the line manager should come to his rescue.

8.2 FINANCIAL COMPENSATION AND REWARDS

Proper financial compensation and rewards are important to the morale and motivation of people in any organization. Projects are no exception. However, there are several issues that often make it necessary to treat compensation practices of project personnel separately from the rest of the organization:

- *Job classification and job descriptions* for project personnel are usually not compatible with those existing for other professional jobs. It is often difficult to pick an existing classification and adapt it to project personnel. Without proper adjustment, the small amount of formal authority of the project and the small number of direct reports may distort the position level of project personnel in spite of their broad range of business responsibilities.
- *Dual accountability* and dual reporting relationships of project personnel raise the question of who should assess performance and control the rewards.
- *Bases for financial rewards* are often difficult to establish, quantify, and administer. The criteria for "doing a good job" are difficult to quantify.
- *Special compensations* for overtime, extensive travel, or living away from home should be considered in addition to bonus pay for preestablished results. Bonus pay is a particularly difficult and delicate issue because often many people contribute to the results of such incentives. Discretionary bonus practices can be demoralizing to the project team.

Some specific guidelines are provided in this book to help business managers establish compensation systems for their project organizations. The foundations of these compensation practices are based on four systems: (1) job classification, (2) base pay, (3) performance appraisals, and (4) merit increases.

Job Classifications and Job Descriptions

Every effort should be made to fit the new classifications for project personnel into the existing standard classification that has already been established for the organization.

The first step is to define job titles for various project personnel and their corresponding responsibilities. Titles are very noteworthy. They imply certain re-

TABLE 8–1. SAMPLE JOB DESCRIPTION

**Job Description: Lead Project
Engineer of Processor Development**

Overall Responsibility
Responsible for directing the technical development of the new Central Processor including managing the technical personnel assigned to this development. The Lead Project Engineer has dual responsibility, (1) to his/her functional superior for the technical implementation and engineering quality and (2) to the project manager for managing the development within the established budget and schedule.

Specific Duties and Responsibilities
1. Provide necessary program direction for planning, organizing, developing and integrating the engineering effort, including establishing the specific objectives, schedules and budgets for the processor subsystem.
2. Provide technical leadership for analyzing and establishing requirements, preliminary designing, designing, prototyping and testing of the processor subsystem.
3. Divide the work into discrete and clearly definable tasks. Assign tasks to technical personnel within the Lead Engineer's area of responsibility and other organizational units.
4. Define, negotiate and allocate budgets and schedules according to the specific tasks and overall program requirements.
5. Measure and control cost, schedule and technical performance against program plan.
6. Report deviations from program plan to program office.
7. Replan trade-off and redirect the development effort in case of contingencies such as to best utilize the available resources toward the overall program objectives.
8. Plan, maintain and utilize engineering facilities to meet the long-range program requirements.

Qualifications
1. Strong technical background in state-of-the-art central processor development.
2. Prior task management experience with proven record for effective cost and schedule control of multi-disciplinary technology-based task in excess of SIM.
3. Personal skills to lead, direct and motivate senior engineering personnel.
4. Excellent communication skills, both orally and in writing.

sponsibilities, position power, organizational status, and pay level. Furthermore, titles may indicate certain functional responsibilities, as does, for example, the title of task manager.[1] Therefore, titles should be carefully selected and each of them supported by a formal job description.

The job description provides the basic charter for the job and the individual in charge of it. Therefore, the job description should be written not just for one individual but more generically for all individuals who fit the respective job classification. A good job description is brief and concise, not exceeding one page. Typically, it is broken down into three sections: (1) overall responsibilities, (2) specific duties, and (3) qualifications. A sample job description is given in Table 8–1.

---

1. In most organizations the title of task manager indicates being responsible for managing the technical content of a project subsystem within a functional unit, having dual accountabilities to the functional superior and the project office.

Base-Pay Classifications and Incentives

After the job descriptions have been developed, one can delineate pay classes consistent with the responsibilities and accountabilities for business results. If left to the personnel specialist, these pay scales often have a tendency to slip toward the lower end of an equitable compensation. This is understandable because, on the surface, project positions look less senior than their functional counterparts, as formal authority over resources and direct reports are often less necessary for project positions than for traditional functional positions. The impact of such a skewed compensation system is that the project organization will attract less qualified personnel than the functional units. Moreover, project management may be seen as an inferior career that at best may serve as a stepping stone for getting into functional management.

Many companies that have struggled with this problem have solved it by (1) working out compensation schemes as a team of senior managers and personnel specialists, and (2) applying criteria of responsibility and business/profit accountability to setting pay scales for project personnel in accord with other jobs in their organization. Once the proper range of compensation has been set, fine-tuning is a built-in feature. That is, managers who are hiring can choose a salary from the established range based on their judgment of actual position responsibilities, the candidate's qualifications, the available budget, and other considerations. Valuable guidance and perspective can be obtained from the personnel specialist.

Performance Appraisals

Traditionally, the purpose of the performance appraisal is to:

- Assess the employee's work performance, preferably against preestablished objectives
- Provide a justification for salary actions
- Establish new goals and objectives for the next review period
- Identify and deal with work-related problems
- Serve as a basis for career discussions

In reality, however, the first two objectives are in conflict. As a result, traditional performance appraisals essentially become a salary discussion with the objective to justify subsequent managerial actions.[2] In addition, discussions dominated by salary actions are usually not conducive for future goal setting, problem-solving, or career planning.

In order to get around this dilemma, many companies have separated the salary discussion from the other parts of the performance appraisal. Moreover, successful managers have carefully considered the complex issues involved and

---

2. For detailed discussions, see The Conference Board, *Matrix Organizations of Complex Businesses* 1979; plus some basic research by H. H. Meyer, E. Kay, and J. R. P. French, "Split Roles in Performance Appraisal," *Harvard Business Review,* January–February 1965.

have built a performance appraisal system solidly based on content, measurability, and source of information.

The first challenge is in content, that is, to decide "what to review" and "how to measure performance." Modern management practices try to individualize accountability as much as possible. Furthermore, subsequent incentive or merit increases are tied to profit performance. Although most companies apply these principles to their project organizations, they do it with a great deal of skepticism. Practices are often modified to assure balance and equity for jointly performed responsibilities. A similar dilemma exists in the area of profit accountability. The comment of a project manager at the General Electric Company is typical of the situation faced by business managers: "Although I am responsible for business results of a large program, I really can't control more than 20 percent of its cost." Acknowledging the realities, organizations are measuring performance of their *project managers,* in at least two areas:

- *Business results* as measured by profits, contribution margin, return on investment, new business, and income; also, on-time delivery, meeting contractual requirements, and within-budget performance.
- *Managerial performance* as measured by overall project management effectiveness, organization, direction and leadership, and team performance.

The first area applies only if the project manager is indeed responsible for business results such as contractual performance or new business acquisitions. Many project managers work with company-internal sponsors, such as a company-internal new product development or a feasibility study. In these cases, producing the results within agreed-on schedule and budget constraints becomes the primary measure of performance. The second area is clearly more difficult to assess. Moreover, if handled improperly, it will lead to manipulation and game playing. Table 8–2 provides some specific measures of project management performance. Whether the sponsor is company-internal or external, project managers are usually being assessed on how long it took to organize the team, whether the project is moving along according to agreed-on schedules and budgets, and how closely they meet the global goals and objectives set by their superiors.

On the other side of the project organization, resource managers or project personnel are being assessed primarily on their ability to direct the implementation of a specific project subsystem:

- *Technical implementation* as measured against requirements, quality, schedules, and cost targets
- *Team performance* as measured by ability to staff, build an effective task group, interface with other groups, and integrate among various functions

Specific performance measures are shown in Table 8–3. In addition, the actual project performance of both project managers and their resource personnel should

TABLE 8–2. PERFORMANCE MEASURES FOR PROJECT MANAGERS

Who Performs Appraisal
  Functional superior of project manager

Source of Performance Data
  Functional superior, resource managers, general managers

Primary Measures
  1. Project manager's success in leading the project toward preestablished global objectives
     - Target costs
     - Key milestones
     - Profit, net income, return on investment, contribution margin
     - Quality
     - Technical accomplishments
     - Market measures, new business, follow-on contract
  2. Project manager's effectiveness in overall project direction and leadership during all phases, including establishing:
     - Objectives and customer requirements
     - Budgets and schedules
     - Policies
     - Performance measures and controls
     - Reporting and review system

Secondary Measures
  1. Ability to utilize organizational resources
     - Overhead cost reduction
     - Working with existing personnel
     - Cost-effective make-buy decisions
  2. Ability to build effective project team
     - Project staffing
     - Interfunctional communications
     - Low team conflict complaints and hassles
     - Professionally satisfied team members
     - Work with support groups
  3. Effective project planning and plan implementation
     - Plan detail and measurability
     - Commitment by key personnel and management
     - Management involvement
     - Contingency provisions
     - Reports and reviews
  4. Customer/client satisfaction
     - Perception of overall project performance by sponsor
     - Communications, liaison
     - Responsiveness to changes
  5. Participation in business management
     - Keeping mangement informed of new project/product/business opportunities
     - Bid proposal work
     - Business planning, policy development

Additional Considerations
  1. Difficulty of tasks involved
     - Technical tasks
     - Administrative and orgnizational complexity
     - Multidisciplinary nature
     - Staffing and start-up

(continues)

TABLE 8–2. PERFORMANCE MEASURES FOR PROJECT MANAGERS (*Continued*)

2. Scope of the project
   - Total project budget
   - Number of personnel involved
   - Number of organizations and subcontractors involved
3. Changing work environment
   - Nature and degree of customer changes and redirections
   - Contingencies

be assessed on the conditions under which it was achieved: the degree of task difficulty, complexity, size, changes, and general business conditions.

Finally, one needs to decide who is to perform the performance appraisal and to make the salary adjustment. Where dual accountabilities are involved, good practices call for inputs from both bosses. Such a situation could exist for project managers who report functionally to one superior but are also accountable for specific business results to another person. While dual accountability of project managers is an exception for most organizations, it is common for project resource personnel who are responsible to their functional superior for the quality of the work and to their project manager for meeting the requirements within budget and schedule. Moreover, resource personnel may be shared among many projects. Only the functional or resource manager can judge overall performance of resource personnel.

Merit Increases and Bonuses

Professionals have come to expect merit increases as a reward for a job well done. However, under inflationary conditions, which we have experienced for many years, pay adjustments seldom keep up with cost-of-living increases. To deal with this salary compression and to give incentive for management performance, companies have introduced bonuses uniformly to all components of their organizations. The problem is that these standard plans for merit increases and bonuses are based on individual accountability while project personnel work in teams with shared accountabilities, responsibilities, and controls. It is usually very difficult to credit project success or failure to a single individual or a small group.

Most managers with these dilemmas have turned to the traditional remedy of the performance appraisal. If done well, the appraisal should provide particular measures of job performance that assess the level and magnitude at which the individual has contributed to the success of the project, including the managerial performance and team performance components. Therefore, a properly designed and executed performance appraisal that includes input from all accountable management elements, and the basic agreement of the employee with the conclusions, is a sound basis for future salary reviews. Often more important than the actual increase is the size of the salary adjustment relative to that of other employees. Equitable pay for performance and position is crucial to employee morale and satisfactory productivity, a very important area that deserves careful management attention.

TABLE 8–3. PERFORMANCE MEASURES FOR PROJECT PERSONNEL

Who Performs Appraisal
    Functional superior of project person

Source of Performance Data
    Project manager and resource managers

Primary Measures
  1. Success in directing the agreed-on task toward completion
- Technical implementation according to requirements
- Quality
- Key milestones/schedules
- Target costs, design-to-cost
- Innovation
- Trade-offs

  2. Effectiveness as a team member or team leader
- Building effective task team
- Working together with others, participation, involvement
- Interfacing with support organizations and subcontractors
- Interfunctional coordination
- Getting along with others
- Change orientation
- Making commitments

Secondary Measures
  1. Success and effectiveness in performing functional tasks in addition to project work in accordance with functional charter
- Special assignments
- Advancing technology
- Developing organization
- Resource planning
- Functional direction and leadership

  2. Administrative support services
- Reports and reviews
- Special task forces and committees
- Project planning
- Procedure development

  3. New business development
- Bid proposal support
- Customer presentations

  4. Professional development
- Keeping abreast in professional field
- Publications
- Liaison with society, vendors, customers, and educational institutions

Additional Considerations
  1. Difficulty of tasks involved
- Technical challenges
- State-of-the-art considerations
- Changes and contingencies

  2. Managerial responsibilities
- Task leader for number of project personnel
- Multi-functional integration
- Budget responsibility
- Staffing responsibility
- Specific accountabilities

  3. Multi-project involvement
- Number of different projects
- Number and magnitude of functional task and duties
- Overall workload

8.3 EFFECTIVE PROJECT MANAGEMENT IN THE SMALL BUSINESS ORGANIZATION

The acceptance of project management in large companies has been relatively easy because of the abundance of published literature identifying its potential pitfalls and problems. The definition of a small project could be:

- Total duration is usually three to twelve months.
- Total dollar value is $5,000 to $1.5 million (upper limit is usually capital equipment projects).
- There is continuous communication between team members, and no more than three or four cost centers are involved.
- Manual rather than computerized cost control may be acceptable.
- Project managers work closely with functional personnel and managers on a daily basis, so time-consuming detail reporting is not necessary.
- The work breakdown structure does not go beyond level three.

Here, we are discussing project management in both small companies and small organizations within a larger corporation. In small organizations, major differences from large companies must be accounted for:

- *In small companies, the project manager has to wear multiple hats and may have to act as a project manager and line manager at the same time.* Large companies may have the luxury of a single full-time project manager for the duration of a project. Smaller companies may not be able to afford a full-time project manager and therefore may require that functional managers wear two hats. This poses a problem in that the functional managers may be more dedicated to their own functional unit than to the project, and the project may suffer. There is also the risk that when the line manager also acts as project manager, the line manager may keep the best resources for his own project. The line manager's project may be a success at the expense of all the other projects that he must supply resources for.

In the ideal situation, the project manager works horizontally and has project dedication, whereas the line manager works vertically and has functional (or company) dedication. If the working relationship between the project and functional managers is a good one, then decisions will be made in a manner that is in the best interest of both the project and the company. Unfortunately, this may be difficult to accomplish in small companies when an individual wears multiple hats.

- *In a small company, the project manager handles multiple projects, perhaps each with a different priority.* In large companies, project managers normally handle only one project at a time. Handling multiple projects becomes a serious problem if the priorities are not close together. For this reason, many small companies avoid the establishment of priorities for fear that the lower-priority activities will never be accomplished.

● *In a small company, the project manager has limited resources.* In a large company, if the project manager is unhappy with resources that are provided, he may have the luxury of returning to the functional manager to either demand or negotiate for other resources. In a small organization, the resources assigned may be simply the only resources available.

● *In a small company, project managers must generally have a better understanding of interpersonal skills than in a larger company.* This is a necessity because a project manager in the small company has limited resources and must provide the best motivation that he can.

● *In the smaller company, the project manager generally has shorter lines of communications.* In small organizations project managers almost always report to a top-level executive, whereas in larger organizations the project managers can report to any level of management. Small companies tend to have fewer levels of management.

● *Small companies do not have a project office.* Large companies, especially in aerospace or construction, can easily support a project office of twenty to thirty people, whereas in the smaller company the project manager may have to be the entire project office. This implies that the project manager in a small company may be required to have more general and specific information about all company activities, policies, and procedures than his counterparts in the larger companies.

● *In a small company, there may be a much greater risk to the total company with the failure of as little as one project.* Large companies may be able to afford the loss of a multimillion-dollar program, whereas the smaller company may be in serious financial trouble. For example, a machine tool company in the Midwest has almost 70 percent of its business generated by one of the big three automotive manufacturers. The risk to the small company occurs when one project represents a large percentage of its business. Thus many smaller companies avoid bidding on projects that could place the company in such a delicate position; for, with the acceptance of such a project, the company would have to hire additional resources or give up some of its smaller accounts.

● *In a small company, there might be tighter monetary controls but with less sophisticated control techniques.* Because the smaller company incurs greater risk with the failure (or cost overrun) of as little as one project, costs are generally controlled much more tightly and more frequently than in larger companies. However, smaller companies generally rely on manual or partially computerized systems, whereas larger organizations rely heavily on sophisticated software packages. Today, more and more small companies are being forced to completely computerize their cost control procedures to adhere to requirements imposed by customers and prime contractors.

● *In a small company, there usually exists more upper-level management interference.* This is expected because in the small company there is a much greater risk with the failure of a single project. In addition, executives in smaller companies "meddle" more than executives in larger companies, and quite often delegate as little as possible to project managers.

- *Evaluation procedures for individuals are usually easier in a smaller company.* This holds true because the project manager gets to know the people better, and, as stated above, there exists a greater need for interpersonal skills on the horizontal line in a smaller company.
- *In a smaller company, project estimating is usually more precise and based on either history or standards.* This type of planning process is usually manual as opposed to computerized. In addition, functional managers in a small company usually feel obligated to live up to their commitments, whereas in larger companies, much more lip service is given.

The arguments presented here are not necessarily meant to discourage the small company, but to identify problems that may be encountered and must be resolved. Project management, when implemented correctly, will generate a smoother flow of work and better control of resources, on both horizontal and vertical lines.

8.4 MEGA PROJECTS

Mega projects may have a different set of rules and guidelines from those of smaller projects. For example, in large projects:

- Vast amounts of people may be required, often for short or intense periods of time.
- Continuous organizational restructuring may be necessary as each project goes through a different life-cycle phase.
- The matrix and project organizational form may be used interchangeably.
- The following elements are critical for success.
  - Training in project management
  - Rules and procedures clearly defined
  - Communications at all levels
  - Quality front-end planning

Many companies dream of winning mega project contracts only to find disaster rather than a pot of gold. The difficulty in managing mega projects stems mainly from resource restraints:

- Lack of available on-site workers (or local labor forces)
- Lack of skilled workers
- Lack of properly trained on-site supervision
- Lack of raw materials

As a result of such problems, the company immediately assigns its best employees to the mega project, thus creating severe risks for the smaller projects, many of which could lead to substantial follow-on business. Overtime is usually required, on a prolonged basis, and this results in lower efficiency and unhappy employees.

As the project schedule slips, management hires additional home-office personnel to support the project. By the time that the project is finished, the total organization is overstaffed, many smaller customers have taken their business elsewhere, and the company finds itself in the position of needing another mega project in order to survive and support the existing staff.

Mega projects are not always as glorious as people think they are. Organizational stability, accompanied by a moderate growth rate, may be more important than quantum steps to mega projects. The lesson here is that mega projects should be left to those companies that have the facilities, expertise, resources, and management know-how to handle the situation.

8.5 R&D PROJECT MANAGEMENT

One of the most difficult tasks in any organization is the management of R&D activities. These R&D activities are usually headed by scientists, engineers, managers, employees, or even executives. All of these people, at one time or another, may act as R&D project managers. They start out with an idea and are asked to lay out a detailed schedule, cost summary, set of specifications, and resource requirements so that the idea can become a reality. Unfortunately, this is easier said than done.

Project management is an attempt to obtain more efficient utilization of resources within an organization by getting work to flow horizontally as well as vertically. Furthermore, all projects must be completed within the constraints of time, cost, and performance. If the project is for an outside customer, then there exists a fourth constraint—good customer relations. Without proper training and understanding, R&D project managers might easily manage their projects within time, cost, and performance, but alienate the outside customer to such a degree that follow-on (or production-type) contracts are nonexistent.

R&D personnel were probably the first true project managers in the world. Unfortunately, very little training was available until the vanguard of modern project management occurred in the late fifties in aerospace, defense, and construction companies. Even today, twenty-five years later, very little project management training is provided for R&D personnel.

R&D personnel are technically trained perfectionists who believe that cost and time are unimportant when it comes to improving the state of the art. R&D personnel would rather crawl on their hands and knees and beg for more money and time than admit defeat on an R&D project. The more degrees an individual has, the more reluctant he is to accept defeat.

R&D personnel have been stereotyped and subjected to more criticism than any other employees, even engineers. R&D personnel are considered to be egocentric, spoon-fed, coddled individuals, sitting in small corners of laboratories, who are provided with hand calculators so that they can get excited once in a while. The stereotypical R&D project managers avoid people contact whenever possible. They cannot communicate well, write reports, or make presentations. They are illiterate except when it comes to complex graphs and equations. And yet they are consistently placed in charge of projects. In most project-driven organizations, there is usually strong representation of former project managers in top echelons of management, but how many senior corporate executives or CEOs have come out of the R&D ranks? Could it be that this inappropriate stereotyping has prevented R&D personnel from rising to the top?

The R&D Environment

Very few people in an organization truly understand the R&D environment and the problems facing the R&D project manager. We continually ask the R&D project manager to achieve an objective that even science fiction writers haven't thought of, and that requires technology that hasn't been discovered yet. We further ask him to lay out a detailed schedule, with established milestones and predetermined costs set forth by some executive, and then inform him that he may have trouble obtaining the resources that he needs.

After he establishes his schedule, executives change the milestones because the schedule affects their Christmas bonuses. And when the project finally gets on track, marketing pushes the end milestone to the left because they wish to have earlier introduction of the project into the marketplace in order to either beat or keep up with the competition.

The project manager therefore finds that he must do his work in seclusion, avoiding meddling from executives, marketing, and manufacturing. The avoidance of the manufacturing group ultimately leads to the R&D project manager's downfall because he finds out too late that manufacturing cannot mass-produce the item according to the R&D specifications. Who gets blamed? The R&D project manager, of course! He should have been communicating with everyone.

The R&D environment might very well be the most difficult and turbulent environment in which to manage a project. The remainder of this section describes this problem in R&D project management in hopes that readers will better appreciate those individuals who accept R&D project management as a career.

Detail Scheduling: Fact or Fantasy?

Scheduling activities for R&D projects is extremely difficult because of the problems mentioned above. Many R&D people believe that if you know how long it will take to complete an objective, you do not need R&D. Most R&D schedules are not detailed but are composed of major milestones where executives can decide whether additional money or resources should be committed. Some executives and R&D managers believe in this philosophy:

I'll give you "so much time" to get an answer.

In R&D project management, failure is often construed as an acceptable answer.

There are two schools of thought on R&D scheduling, depending of course on the type of project, time duration, and resources required. The first school involves tight R&D scheduling. This may occur if the project is a one-person activity. R&D personnel are generally highly optimistic and believe that they can do anything. Therefore, they tend to lay out rather tight, optimistic schedules. This type of optimism is actually a good trait. Where would we be without it? How many projects would be prematurely canceled without optimistic R&D personnel?

Tight schedules occur mostly on limited-resource projects. Project managers tend to avoid tight schedules if they feel that there exists a poor "window" in the functional organization for a timely commitment of resources. Also, R&D personnel know that in time of crisis or fire fighting on manufacturing lines, which are yielding immediate profits, they may lose their key functional project employees, perhaps for an extended period.

The second school of thought believes that R&D project management is not mechanical like other forms of project management, so all schedules must be loose. Scientists do not like or want tight structuring because they feel that they cannot be creative without having sufficient freedom to do their job. Many good results have been obtained from spinoffs and other activities where R&D project managers have deviated from predetermined schedules. Of course, too much freedom can spell disaster because the individual might try to be overly creative and "reinvent the wheel."

This second school says that R&D project managers should not focus on limited objectives. Rather, the project manager should be able to realize that other possible objectives can be achieved with further exploration of some of the activities.

Two special types of projects are generally performed without any schedules: the "grass roots" project and the "bootleg" project. Each type is simply an idea that, with one or two good data points, could become a full-blown, well-funded activity. The major difference between the two is that the grass roots project is normally funded with some sort of "seed" money, whereas the bootleg project is accomplished piecemeal and on the sly. With the bootleg project, employees charge their time to other activities while performing the bootleg R&D.

Working with Executives

Executives earn high salaries because they can perform long-range planning and formulate policy. In general, meddling by project management executives is a way of life because of conflict resolution and the continuing need to reassess project priorities. In R&D, the problem of executive meddling becomes more pronounced because, in addition to the above reasons for his involvement, the executive might still consider himself to be a technical specialist or might develop a sense of executive pride of ownership because the project was his idea. If an executive continually provides technical advice, it is entirely possible that an atmosphere of stifled creativity will develop. If the executive is considered to be an expert in the field, then everyone, including the R&D project manager, may let the executive do it all—and both the project and the executive's duties may suffer.

There is nothing wrong with an executive's demonstrating pride of ownership for a project as long as he does not assert that "this project will be mine, all the way," and meddle continuously. The R&D project manager should still be permitted to run the show with timely, structured feedback of information to the executive. If executives meddle continuously, then the R&D project manager may adopt a policy of "avoidance management," in which executives are continuously avoided unless problems arise.

In general project management, executives should actively interface a project only during the conception and planning stages. The same holds true in R&D project management but with much more emphasis on the conceptual stage than the planning stage. The executive should work closely with the R&D project manager in defining:

- Needs
- Requirements
- Objectives
- Success factors
- Realistic end date

The executive should then step out of the way and let the R&D project manager establish his own timetable. One cannot expect executive meddling to be entirely eliminated from R&D activities because each R&D activity could easily have a direct bearing on the strategic planning that the executive must perform as part of his daily routine.

R&D activities have a direct bearing on the organization's strategic planning. Executives should therefore provide some sort of feedback to R&D managers. The following comments were made by an R&D project manager:

> I know that there is planning going on now for activities which I will be doing three months from now. How should I plan for this? I don't have any formal or informal data on planning as yet. What should I tell my boss?

Executives should not try to understaff the R&D function. Forcing R&D personnel and project managers to work on too many projects at once can drastically reduce creativity. This does not imply that personnel should be used on only one project at a time. Most companies do not have this luxury. However, this situation of multiproject project management should be carefully monitored.

Finally, executives must be very careful about how much control they exercise over R&D project managers. Too much control can drastically reduce bootleg research, and, in the long run, the company may suffer.

Working with Marketing

In most organizations, either R&D drives marketing, or marketing drives R&D. The latter is more common. Well-managed organizations maintain a proper balance between marketing and R&D. Marketing-driven organizations can create havoc, especially if marketing continually requests information faster than R&D can deliver, and if bootleg R&D is eliminated. In this case, all R&D activities must be approved by marketing. In some organizations, R&D funding comes out of the marketing budget.

In order to stimulate creativity, R&D should have control over at least a portion of its own budget. This is a necessity because not all R&D activities are designed to benefit marketing. Some activities are intended simply to improve technology or create a new way of doing business.

Marketing support, if needed, should be available to all R&D projects, whether they originate in marketing or R&D. An R&D project manager at a major food manufacturer made the following remarks:

> A few years ago, one of our R&D people came up with an idea and I was assigned as the project manager. When the project was completed, we had developed a new product, ready for market introduction and testing. Unfortunately, R&D does not maintain funds for the market testing of a new product. The funds come out of marketing. Our marketing people either did not understand the product or placed it low on their priority list. We, in R&D, tried to talk to them. They were reluctant to test the new product because the project was our idea. Marketing lives in their own little world. To make a long story short, last year one of our competitors introduced the same product into the marketplace. Now, instead of being the leader, we are playing catch-up. I know R&D project managers are not trained in market testing, but what if marketing refuses to support R&D-conceived projects? What can we do?

Several organizations today have R&D project managers reporting directly to a new business group, business development group, or marketing. Engineering-oriented R&D project managers continually express their displeasure at being evaluated for promotion by someone in marketing who may not understand the technical difficulties in managing an R&D project. Yet, executives have valid arguments for this arrangement, asserting that the high-technology R&D project managers are so in love with their project that they don't know how and when to cancel it. Marketing executives contend that projects should be canceled when:

- Costs become excessive, causing product cost to be noncompetitive
- Return on investment will occur too late
- Competition is too stiff and not worth the risk

and so on. Of course, the question arises, "Should marketing have a vote in the cancellation of each R&D project or only those that are marketing-driven?" Some organizations cancel projects with the consensus of the project team.

Location of the R&D Function

R&D project management in small organizations is generally easier than similar functions in large organizations. In small companies, there usually exists a single R&D group responsible for all R&D activities. In large companies, each division may have its own R&D function. The giant corporations try to encourage decentralized R&D under the supervision of a central research (or corporate research) group. The following problems were identified by a central research group project manager:

- "I have seen parallel projects going on at the same time."
- "We have a great duplication of effort because each division has its own R&D and quality control functions. We have a very poor passing of information between divisions."
- "Central research was originally developed to perform research functions that could not be effectively handled by the divisions. Although we are supposed to be a service group, we still bill each division for the work we do for them. Some pay us and some don't. Last year, several divisions stopped using us because they felt that it was cheaper to do the work themselves. Now, we are funded entirely by corporate and have more work than we can handle. Everyone can think of work for us to do when it is free."

Priority Setting

Priorities create colossal managerial headaches for the R&D project manager because R&D projects are usually prioritized on a different list from all of the other projects. Functional managers must now supply resources according to two priority lists. Unfortunately, the R&D priority list is usually not given proper attention.

As an example of this, the director of R&D of a Fortune 25 corporation made the following remarks:

> Each of our operating divisions have their own R&D projects and priorities. Last year corporate R&D had a very high R&D project geared toward cost improvement in the manufacturinig areas. Our priorities were based on the short-run requirements. Unfortunately, the operating divisions that had to supply resources to our project felt that the benefits would not be received until the long run and therefore placed support for our project low on their priority list.

Communication of priorities is often a problem in the R&D arena. Setting of priorities on the divisional level may not be passed down to the departmental level, and vice versa. There must be early feedback of priorities so that functional managers can make their own plans.

Written Communications

R&D project managers are not different from other project managers in that they are expected to have superior writing skills but actually do not. R&D project managers quickly become prolific writers if they feel that they will receive recognition through their writings.

Most R&D projects begin with a project request form that includes a feasibility study and cost-benefit analysis. The report can vary from five to fifty pages. The project manager must identify benefits that the company will receive if it allocates funds to this activity. In many non-R&D activities project managers are not required to perform such feasibility studies.

Because of the lack of professional writing skills, executives should try to reduce the number of interim reports, since report writing can seriously detract from an individual's more important R&D functions. In addition, most interim reports are more marketing oriented than R&D oriented.

Many of today's companies have weekly or bimonthly status review meetings where each R&D project manager provides a five-minute (or shorter) oral briefing on the status of his project, without getting involved in technical details. Of course, at project completion or termination, a comprehensive written report is still required.

Salaries and Performance Evaluation

R&D groups have one of the highest salary ranges in a company. R&D groups are generally the first to establish a dual-ladder system where employees can progress on a technical pay scale to high salary positions without having to accept a position in management. In the R&D environment, it is quite common for some functional employees to be at a higher salary level than the R&D project manager or even their own functional managers. This arrangement is necessary in order to maintain a superior technical community and to select managers based on their managerial expertise, not technical superiority.

The R&D group of a Fortune 25 corporation recently adopted a dual-ladder system and found that it created strange problems. Several scientists began fighting over the size of their office, type of desk, and who should have their own secretaries.

The evaluation process of R&D personnel can be very difficult. R&D project managers can have either direct or indirect control over an employee's evaluation for promotion. Generally speaking, project managers, even R&D project managers, can only make recommendations to the functional managers, who in turn assess the validity of the recommendations and make the final assessments. Obviously, not all R&D projects are going to produce fruitful results. In such a case, should the employee be graded down because the project failed? This is a major concern to managers.

Motivation

R&D project managers have no problem with self-motivation, especially on one-person projects. But how does a project manager motivate project team members, especially when you, the R&D project manager, may have no say in the performance or evaluation? How do you get all of your employees to focus on the correct information? How do you motivate employees when their time is fragmented over several activities? How can you prevent employees from picking up bad habits that can lead to missed opportunities?

R&D project managers would rather motivate employees through work challenge and by demonstrating their own expertise. Most R&D project managers prefer not to use formal authority. One R&D project manager summed up his problem as follows:

> I have only implied authority and cannot always force the project participants to perform my way. We have used task forces both effectively and ineffectively. We are always confronted with authority and priority problems when it comes to motivating people. Functional managers resent R&D project managers who continuously demonstrate their project authority. Our best results are obtained when the task force members visualize this project as part of their own goals.

Executives must take a hard look at how they are managing their R&D projects. In general, all R&D personnel are project managers and should be trained accordingly, as any other project manager would be. If executives wish to develop an organization that will retain superior personnel and stimulate creativity and freedom, then they must recognize the need for effective organizational communications and alleviate meddling by marketing and the executive level of the organization. R&D project managers are actually the architects of the conceptual phase of the corporation's long-range plans, and it appears that their value to the organization finally is being recognized by management.

Management[3]

The primary responsibility for success in any organization is in its management. Possibly in research and development, more than any other function, true success depends on upper-level management and other functional managers rather than its own functional management. This dependence on other levels of management is a result of the information and resources required by the R&D function being supplied by other organizational units, which, for example, establish organizational needs for R&D, influence program priorities, control budgets, and coordinate activities outside the R&D structure. Since most upper-level and functional management is not familiar with the systems approach, especially in small companies, the perspective of line and staff management is greatly influenced by functional parochialism and consideration of R&D as a cost center rather than a profit center. In part, this view of R&D as a cost center leads to a commonly implied, if not expressed, feeling that "in good times, who needs R&D because we are successful in what we are doing, and, in bad times, who can afford it?" Another important factor affecting the way management views R&D is the short-term perspective of most of today's managers. Concern for short-term profits rather than long-term objectives such as growth and diversification has a considerable impact on the programs and priorities recommended and supported by

---

3. The remainder of Section 8.5 is adapted from a course paper by Dr. John J. Miller, "Problems of Informal Project Management in R&D in Small Companies."

functional management. In many cases, functional parochialism and short-term perspectives are reinforced by empire-building attitudes and possibly feelings of inferiority. These attitudes and feelings are, generally, more pronounced when a functional manager has risen from the ranks. This type of manager, although very experienced, may be afraid of new technology and dependent on closefisted control that has been successful in the past.

Within this environment, the R&D manager or director in the traditional organizational structure must be a strong individual. An informal project management system requires that the manager of the R&D organization provide a forceful representation of the function within the company. However, this requires an individual who can conduct a critical balancing game. If the manager is too forceful, he will alienate the organization. Projects that must interface with other functions will receive little assistance or support from these functions. If the R&D manager is weak, the direction of projects will be essentially controlled by the functional groups. R&D projects would then tend to be very short term. There would be many more support programs oriented toward process and quality control. The balancing game played by the manager or director of R&D becomes very time-consuming, and little time is left for technical and administrative responsibilities. In fact, much of the manager's time is spent justifying and rejustifying R&D programs to other functional groups.

Coordination

A nonstructured or informal approach to project management has a major shortcoming in that coordination between R&D and other functional groups cannot be formally established. There is no structure for this formal coordination. Cooperation and assistance from other functional groups on R&D projects is a "beg, borrow, or steal" situation. Although cooperation on programs cannot be effectively mandated even in a formal project management structure, the problem is magnified in an informal project system. Two major factors hinder effective cooperation and coordination in the informal project management system. First, there is little preplanned communication with the functional units. Therefore, the functional units have little knowledge of the project objectives or understanding of how the project, if successful, fits into the goals and objectives of the company. Second, there is no higher authority designated to encourage the coordination of R&D and functional units or to provide conflict resolution.

Training

A handicap of the informal project management approach is that its users lack training and development in project management concepts. There is little or no emphasis on systems theory, systems analysis, and systems management. Without this type of knowledge and training, it is difficult for users of the informal project management approach to obtain or maintain a successful track record, especially in the critical area of the transfer of technology from the laboratory to production. This lack of emphasis on systems and project management concepts is also, at least in many cases, reflected by a lack of concern for the thorough development of the individuals employed in the R&D department. Generally, professional development is focused only on technical areas. Training in nontechnical areas is usually not encouraged and may, in fact, be discouraged. This applies not only to formal training programs, but to informal in-house training programs. This is one reason why technically oriented individuals in the R&D environment have little familiarity with business strategies and business tools. Without some of these business basics, the individuals in the R&D unit can be severely handicapped. First, the R&D project leaders must depend on others in the organization for basic business and financial analyses. Second, communication with administration and other functional units is thwarted, since the individuals involved do not speak the same language. Not only might the technical people not understand the type of information required for business analyses, but also comments made by the engineers or scientists might easily be misinterpreted by the business analysts. Finally, persons with little business background or experience have little chance for advancement outside the R&D environment. This can be an especially difficult problem in a small company where chances for advancement are few and far between. Opportunity for advancement can enhance the spirit of the organization and motivation of employees.

Some individuals within this environment will attempt to learn on their own about the operation of other units or functions of the organization and basic business tools; but, in spite of this type of initiative, learning in such an atmosphere is slow. Unfortunately, these efforts may be interpreted by R&D management and other functional managers as overaggressiveness or meddling. Further self-learning may then be quickly discouraged.

Planning

One of the most crucial aspects of management in any organization is planning. With an informal project management approach in the R&D organization, planning may not be optimized. Without a systems approach, planning tends to be segmented, with concentration on aspects of the project that can be accomplished within the R&D unit. Little effort is applied to involving functional units in the planning process, and there is a general lack of integration of the project plans with the operational units.

Although R&D projects are difficult to plan and schedule because of the large numbers of unknowns, planning in R&D units of small companies tends to be very short term, for only one to twelve months. Without formal planning tools, such as statement of work, work breakdown schedules, linear responsibility charts, and PERT networks, planning tends to be simplified, but important details, responsibilities, and interfaces may easily be omitted. In certain respects the shorter-range planning, although not identifying the need for future resources, does not commit resources to a schedule that is or can be very tentative. There actually may be an advantage to short-term planning, since project plans that interface with other functional units can be more realistic with respect to the amount of support needed, amount and type of work to be done, and schedules, although the functional personnel must have sufficient notification of plans or needs to be able to act and react to these plans without undue strain on their schedules and resources. Of course, this advantage can be utilized in a formal planning procedure by constant updating of plans and schedules so that the functional units are aware of the progress of the project, especially as their work or assistance comes into the near-term planning horizon.

A common mistake made during the planning phase in the informal type of project management is that the functional managers are not included in the planning of the project, even when the project involves work performed in their department. Time, costs, and procedures may be established for the functional department by the project manager without input from the functional manager. The functional manager can be difficult to work with, once he learns that something else has planned his involvement and that he is supposed to adhere to these plans.

Communications

Lack of effective communications may be a major reason why R&D does not include functional managers in project planning, and why, once plans are established and approved, functional managers are not aware of the progress of a project. There is no doubt that functional managers need to be aware of potential and real changes in schedules, resources, and work scope that may affect their department. Without effective communications neither the project manager nor the functional manager knows what the other is doing, or what the current problems are. In fact, planning, coordination, and management cannot be performed effectively and efficiently without effective communications. However, communication on the horizontal or project level is not the only problem that the informal project management system has; all communication with upper management is filtered through the director of R&D. This may be an effective route for upward communication, but in downward communication two problems are common. First, because R&D is often considered a necessary evil, much of the information on business plans and strategies is not communicated to R&D. Second, since the director of R&D is the filter of downward-moving information from upper management, he may omit information he feels is not important or does not want his people to know. This lack of information on what the company is doing or going to do has a negative effect on the morale of the R&D group. Moreover, the reverse may also be true—R&D may have to toot their horn instead of relying on the results to "speak for themselves."

Problem Solutions

A number of the problems presented could be markedly improved or resolved by adopting a formal project management organizational structure in the entire company or just in the R&D unit. The R&D organization is probably an excellent proving ground for the introduction of project management to the company. A major reorganization such as the introduction of project management, preferably as a matrix type of structure, is a difficult task. The implementation of such a reorganization must be carefully planned, and a formal implementation program must be prepared. Generally, the success of such a major organizational change will depend not only on effective planning and implementation, but also on the degree of commitment of upper management. A well-planned project management approach should include solutions to the problems present in informal project management.

Although this discussion has centered on the problems commonly present in informal project management in small-company R&D laboratories, many successful projects can be, and have been, completed in this environment. Efforts by individuals to solve or minimize these problems personally have produced very acceptable program results. However, in these cases, success depends on the management skills of the individual and his or her understanding of the business environment. Personal experience indicates that many scientists and engineers, especially those involved in development projects, are at least cognizant of many of the business considerations that can affect the implementation of their development projects, such as costs, acceptable versus superior performance, and time constraints.[4] This observation may be influenced by the small-company environment that allows one to obtain a good perspective of the entire business more easily than in a larger company. In fact, the small company may be a good training environment for project managers because of this more accessible vista of the overall organization, and because, since resources are usually limited, the small-company engineer or scientist must be more self-reliant and learn to perform a number of varied skills using a wide range of tools.

8.6 CODE OF ETHICS

Professional organizations such as the Project Management Institute are taking a serious look at developing the requirements for a professional project manager. In a paper by Ireland, Pike, and Schrock, this subject was described by an ethics obligation matrix (see Figure 8–7) and a code of ethics (see Table 8–4).[5] The reader can expect to see more published literature in the near future on topics such as this.

---

4. This observation is in conflict with the observations of Harold Kerzner, "The R&D Project Manager," *Project Management Quarterly,* June 1981, pp. 20–24.

5. L. R. Ireland, W. J. Pike, and J. L. Schrock, "Ethics for Project Managers," *Proceedings of the 1982 PMI Seminar/Symposium*

OBLIGATIONS	TO WHOM OWNED						
	EMPLOYER	CLIENT/ CUSTOMER	TEAM MEMBERS	STUDENT APPRENTICE	PROFESSIONAL SOCIETY	PUBLIC IN GENERAL	GOVERNMENT
1. Support Code of Ethics					X		
2. Support Professional Society					X		
3. Guard Privileged Information	X	X					
4. Accept Responsibility for Actions	X	X	X	X	X	X	X
5. Proper Use of Authority	X		X	X			
6. Maintain Expertise in State-of-Art	X	X	X	X	X		
7. Build and Maintain Public Confidence					X		
8. Support, Respect and Abide by Laws						X	X
9. Avoid Gift Exchange	X	X					
10. Conservation of Resources (Productivity)	X	X				X	
11. Avoid Conflict of Interest	X	X					
12. Equal Opportunity Employment						X	
13. Health and Safety			X			X	
14. Promote Project Management Profession					X		
15. Honesty in Dealing With Employer and Client	X	X					
16. Professional Interface	X	X	X	X	X	X	

FIGURE 8–7. Ethics obligation matrix.

PROBLEMS

8–1 Beta Company has decided to modify its wage and salary administration program whereby line managers are evaluated for promotion and merit increases based on how well they have lived up to the commitments that they made to the project managers. What are the advantages and disadvantages of this approach?

8–2 How should a project manager handle a situation in which the functional employee (or functional manager) appears to have more loyalty to his profession, discipline, or expertise than to the project? Can a project manager also have this loyalty, say, on an R&D project?

8–3 Most wage and salary administrators contend that project management organizational structures must be "married" to the personnel evaluation process because personnel are always concerned with how they will be evaluated. Furthermore, converting from a traditional structure to a project management structure cannot be accomplished without first considering performance evaluation. What are your feelings on this?

TABLE 8–4. CODE OF ETHICS FOR PROJECT MANAGERS

PREAMBLE: Project Managers, in the pursuit of their profession, affect the quality of life for all people in our society. Therefore, it is vital that Project Managers conduct their work in an ethical manner to earn and maintain the confidence of team members, colleagues, employees, clients and the public.

ARTICLE I: Project Managers shall maintain high standards of personal and professional conduct.
  a. Accept responsibility for their actions.
  b. Undertake projects and accept responsibility only if qualified by training or experience, or after full disclosure to their employers or clients of pertinent qualifications.
  c. Maintain their professional skills at the state-of-the-art and recognize the importance of continued personal development and education.
  d. Advance the integrity and prestige of the profession by practicing in a dignified manner.
  e. Support this code and encourage colleagues and co-workers to act in accordance with this code.
  f. Support the professional society by actively participating and encouraging colleagues and co-workers to participate.
  g. Obey the laws of the country in which work is being performed.

ARTICLE II: Project Managers shall, in their work:
  a. Provide the necessary project leadership to promote maximum productivity while striving to minimize costs.
  b. Apply state-of-the-art management tools and techniques to ensure schedules are met and the project is appropriately planned and coordinated.
  c. Treat fairly all project team members, colleagues and co-workers, regardless of race, religion, sex, age or national origin.
  d. Protect project team members from physical and mental harm.
  e. Provide suitable working conditions and opportunities for project team members.
  f. Seek, accept and offer honest criticism of work, and properly credit the contibution of others.
  g. Assist project team members, colleagues and co-workers in their professional development.

ARTICLE III: Project Managers shall, in their relations with employers and clients:
  a. Act as faithful agents or trustees for their employers or clients in professional or business matters.
  b. Keep information on the business affairs or technical processes of an employer or client in confidence while employed, and later, until such information is properly released.
  c. Inform their employers, clients, professional societies or public agencies of which they are members or to which they may make any presentations, of any circumstances that could lead to a conflict of interest.
  d. Neither give nor accept, directly or indirectly, any gift, payment or service of more than nominal value to or from those having business relationships with their employers or clients.
  e. Be honest and realistic in reporting project cost, schedule and performance.

ARTICLE IV: Project Managers shall, in fulfilling their responsibilities to the community:
  a. Protect the safety, health and welfare of the public and speak out against abuses in those areas affecting the public interest.
  b. Seek to extend public knowledge and appreciation of the project management profession and its achievements.

8–4 As part of the evaluation process for functional employees, each project manager submits a written, confidential evaluation report to the employee's department manager who, in turn, makes the final judgment. The employee is permitted to see only the evaluation from his department manager. Assume that the average department merit increase is 7 percent, and that the employee could receive the merit increases shown in the following table. How would he respond in each case?

Project Manager's Evaluation	Merit Increase, %	Credit or Blame to		Reason
		P.M.	Fct. Mgr.	
Excellent	5			
Excellent	7			
Excellent	9			
Average	5			
Average	7			
Average	9			
Poor	5			
Poor	7			
Poor	9			

8–5 Should the evaluation form in Figure 8–4 be shown to the employees?

8–6 Does a functional employee have the right to challenge any items in the project manager's nonconfidential evaluation form?

8–7 Some people contend that functional employees should be able to evaluate the effectiveness of the project manager after project termination. Design an evaluation form for this purpose.

8–8 Some executives feel that evaluation forms should not include cooperation and attitude. The executives feel that a functional employee will always follow the instructions of the functional manager, and therefore attitude and cooperation are unnecessary topics. Does this kind of thinking also apply to the indirect evaluation forms that are filled out by the project managers?

8–9 Consider a situation in which the project manager (a generalist) is asked to provide an evaluation of a functional employee (a specialist). Can the project manager effectively evaluate the functional employee on technical performance? If not, then on what information can the project manager base his evaluation? Can a grade-7 generalist evaluate a grade-12 specialist?

8–10 Gary has been assigned as a part-time, assistant project manager. Gary's duties are split between assistant project management and being a functional employee. In addition, Gary reports both vertically to his functional manager and horizontally to a project manager. As part of his project responsibilities, Gary must integrate activities between his department and two other departments within his divison. His responsibilities also include writing a nonconfidential performance evaluation for all functional employees from all three departments that are assigned to his project. Can Gary effectively and honestly evaluate functional employees in his own department—people with whom he will be working side by side when the project is over? Should the project manager come to his rescue? Suppose Gary is a part-time project manager instead of a part-time assistant project manager. Can anyone come to his rescue now?

8–11 The following question was asked of executives: How do you know when to cut off research? The answers given: That's a good question, a very good question, and some people don't know when to cut it off. You have to have a feel; in some cases it depends on how much resource you have and whether you have enough resources to take a chance on sustaining research that may appear to be heading for a dead end. You don't know sometimes whether you're heading down the wrong path or not; sometimes it's pretty obvious you ought to shift directions—you've gone about as far as you can or you've taken it far enough that you can demonstrate to your own satisfaction that you just can't get there from here, or it's going to be very costly. You may discover that there are more productive ways to get around the barrier; you're always looking for faster ways. And it depends entirely on how creative the person is, whether he has tunnel vision, a very narrow vision, or whether he is fairly flexible in his conceptual thinking so that he can conceive of better ways to solve the problem. Discuss the validity of these remarks.

8–12 In a small company, can a functional manager act as director of engineering and director of project management at the same time?

8–13 In 1982, an electrical equipment manufacturer decentralized the organization, allowing each division manager to set priorities for the work in his division. The division manager of the R&D division selected as his number one priority project the development of low-cost methods for manufacturing. This project required support from the manufacturing division. The division manager for manufacturing did not assign proper resources, claiming that the results of such a project would not be realized for at least five years, and that he (the manufacturing manager) was worried only about the immediate profits. Can this problem be resolved and divisional decentralization still be maintained?

8–14 The executives of a company that produces electro-optical equipment for military use found it necessary to implement project management using a matrix. The project managers reported to corporate sales, and the engineers with the most expertise were promoted to project engineering. After the first year of operation, it became obvious to the executives that the engineering functional managers were not committed to the projects. The executives then made a critical decision. The functional employees selected by the line managers to serve on projects would report as a solid line to the project engineer and dotted to the line manager. The project engineers, who were selected for their technical expertise, were allowed to give technical direction and monetary rewards to the employees. Can this situation work? What happens if an employee has a technical question? Can he go to his line manager? Should the employees return to their former line managers at project completion? What are the authority/responsibility problems with this structure? What are the long-term implications?

8–15 Consider the four items listed on page 137 that describe what happens when a matrix goes out of control. Which of these end up creating the greatest difficulty for the company? for the project managers? for the line managers? for executives?

8–16 As a functional employee, the project manager tells you, "Sign these prints or I'll fire you from this project." How should this situation be handled?

8–17 How efficient can project management be in a unionized, immobile manpower environment?

8–18 Corporate salary structures and limited annual raise allocations often prevent proper project management performance rewards. Explain how each of the following could serve as motivational factors:

a. Job satisfaction
b. Personal recognition
c. Intellectual growth

CASE STUDIES

AMERICAN ELECTRONICS INTERNATIONAL

On February 13, 1994, American Electronics International (AEI) was awarded a $30 million contract for R&D and production qualification for an advanced type of guidance system. During an experimental program that preceded this award and was funded by the same agency, AEI identified new materials with advanced capabilities, which could easily replace existing field units. The program, entitled The Mask Project, would be thirty months in length, requiring the testing of fifteen units. The Mask Project was longer than any other project that AEI had ever encountered. AEI personnel were now concerned about what kind of staffing problems there would be.

Background

In June 1992, AEI won a one-year research project for new material development. Blen Carty was chosen as project manager. He had twenty-five years of experience with the company in both project management and project engineering positions. During the past five years Blen had successfully performed as the project manager on R&D projects.

AEI used the matrix approach to structuring project management. Blen was well aware of the problems that can be encountered with this organizational form. When it became apparent that a follow-on contract would be available, Blen felt that functional managers would be reluctant to assign key personnel full-time to his project and lose their services for thirty months. Likewise, difficulties could be expected in staffing the project office.

During the proposal stage of the Mask Project, a meeting was held with Blen Carty, John Wallace, the director of project management, and Dr. Albert Runnels, the director of engineering. The purpose of the meeting was to satisfy a customer requirement that all key project members be identified in the management volume of the proposal.

John Wallace: "I'm a little reluctant to make any firm commitment. By the time your program gets off the ground, four of our other projects are terminating, as well as several new projects starting up. I think it's a little early to make firm selections."

Blen Carty: "But we have a proposal requirement. Thirty months is a long time to assign personnel for. We should consider this problem now."

Dr. Runnels: "Let's put the names of our top people into the proposal. We'll add several Ph.D.s from our engineering community. That should beef up our management volume. As soon as we're notified of contract go-ahead, we'll see who's available and make the necessary assignments. This is a common practice in the industry."

<table>
<tr><td>

Completion of the Material Development Project

</td><td>

The material development program was a total success. From its inception, everything went smoothly. Blen staffed the project office with Richard Flag, a Ph.D. in engineering, to serve as project engineer. This was a risky move at first, because Richard had been a research scientist during his previous four years with the company. During the development project, however, Richard demonstrated that he could divorce himself from R&D and perform the necessary functions of a project engineer assigned to the project office. Blen was pleased with the way that Richard controlled project costs and directed activities.

</td></tr>
</table>

Richard had developed excellent working relations with development lab personnel and managers. Richard permitted lab personnel to work at their own rate of speed provided that schedule dates were kept. Richard spent ten minutes each week with each of the department managers informing them of the status of the project. The department managers liked this approach because they received firsthand (nonfiltered) information concerning the total picture, not necessarily on their own activities, and because they did not have to spend "wasted hours" in team meetings.

When it became evident that a follow-up contract might be available, Blen spent a large percentage of his time traveling to the customer, working out the details for future business. Richard then served as both project manager and project engineer.

The customer's project office was quite pleased with Richard's work. Information, both good and bad, was transmitted as soon as it became available. Nothing was hidden or disguised. Richard became familiar with all of the customer's project office personnel through the monthly technical interchange meetings.

At completion of the material development project, Blen and John decided to search for project office personnel and make recommendations to upper-level management. Blen wanted to keep Richard on board as chief project engineer. He would be assigned six engineers and would have to control all engineering activities within time, cost, and performance. Although this would be a new experience for him, Blen felt that he could easily handle it.

Unfortunately, the grapevine was saying that Larry Gilbert was going to be assigned as chief project engineer for the Mask Project.

Selection Problems

On November 15, Dr. Runnels and Blen Carty had a meeting to select the key members of the project team.

Dr. Runnels: "Well, Blen, the time has come to decide on your staff. I want to assign Larry Gilbert as chief engineer. He's a good man and has fifteen years' experience. What are your feelings on that?"

Blen Carty: "I was hoping to keep Richard Flag on. He has performed well, and the customer likes working with him."

Dr. Runnels: "Richard does not have the experience necessary for that position. We can still assign him to Larry Gilbert and keep him in the project office."

Blen Carty: "I'd like to have Larry Gilbert working for Richard Flag, but I don't suppose that we'd ever get approval to have a grade-9 engineer working for a grade-7 engineer. Personally, I'm worried about Gilbert's ability to work with people. He has been so regimented in his ways that our people in the functional units have refused to work with him. He treats them as kids, always walking around with a big stick. One department manager said that if Gilbert becomes the boss, then it will probably result in cutting the umbilical cord between the project office and his department. His people refuse to work for a dictator. I have heard the same from other managers."

Dr. Runnels: "Gilbert gets the job done. You'll have to teach him how to be a Theory Y manager. You know, Blen, we don't have very many grade-9 engineering positions in this company. I think we should have a responsibility to our employees. I can't demote Gilbert into a lower slot. If I were to promote Flag, and the project gets canceled, where would I reassign him? He can't go back to functional engineering. That would be a step down."

Blen Carty: "But Gilbert is so set in his ways. He's just totally inflexible. In addition, thirty months is a long time to maintain a project office. If he screws up we'll never be able to replace positions in time without totally upsetting the customer. There seem to be an awful lot of people volunteering to work on the Mask Project. Is there anyone else available?"

Dr. Runnels: "People always volunteer for long-duration projects because it gives them a feeling of security. This even occurs among our dedicated personnel. Unfortunately we have no other grade-9 engineers available. We could reassign one from another program, but I hate to do it. Our engineers like to carry a project through from start to finish. I think you had better spend some time with the functional managers making sure that you get good people."

Blen Carty: "I've tried that and am having trouble. The functional managers will not surrender their key people full-time for thirty months. One manager wants to assign two employees to our project so that they can get on-the-job training. I told him that this project is considered as strategic by our management and that we must have good people. The manager just laughed at me and walked away."

Dr. Runnels: "You know, Blen, you cannot have all top people. Our other projects must be manned. Also, if you were to use all seasoned veterans, the cost would exceed what we put into the proposal. You're just going to have to make do with what you can get. Prepare a list of the people you want and I'll see what I can do."

As Blen left the office, he wondered if Dr. Runnels would help him in obtaining key personnel.

a. Whose responsibility is it to staff office?
b. What should be Blen Carty's role, as well as that of Dr. Runnels?
c. Should Larry Gilbert be assigned?
d. How would you negotiate with the functional managers?

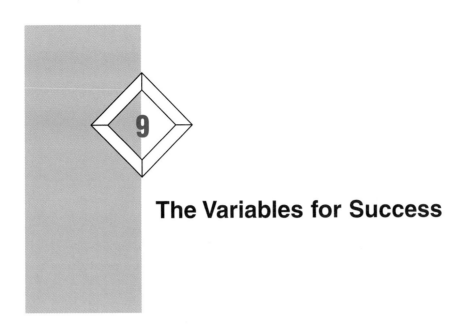

9

The Variables for Success

9.0 INTRODUCTION

Project management cannot succeed unless the project manager is willing to employ the systems approach to project management by analyzing those variables that lead to success and failure. This chapter briefly discusses the dos and don'ts of project management as well as providing a "skeleton" checklist of the key success variables. The following four topics are included:

- Predicting project success
- Project management effectiveness
- Expectations
- Force field analysis

9.1 PREDICTING PROJECT SUCCESS

One of the most difficult tasks is predicting whether the project will be successful. Most goal-oriented managers look only at the time, cost, and performance parameters. If an out-of-tolerance condition exists, then additional analysis is required to identify the cause of the problem. Looking only at time, cost, and performance might identify immediate contributions to profits, but will not identify whether the project itself was managed correctly. This takes on paramount importance if the survival of the organization is based on a steady stream of successfully managed projects. Once or twice a program manager might be able to

461

force a project to success by continually swinging a large baseball bat. After a while, however, either the effect of the big bat will become tolerable, or people will avoid working on his projects.

Project success is often measured by the "actions" of three groups: the project manager and team, the parent organization, and the customer's organization. There are certain actions that the project manager and team can take in order to stimulate project success. These actions include:

- Insist on the right to select key project team members.
- Select key team members with proven track records in their fields.
- Develop commitment and a sense of mission from the outset.
- Seek sufficient authority and a projectized organizational form.
- Coordinate and maintain a good relationship with the client, parent, and team.
- Seek to enhance the public's image of the project.
- Have key team members assist in decision making and problem solving.
- Develop realistic cost, schedule, and performance estimates and goals.
- Have backup strategies in anticipation of potential problems.
- Provide a team structure that is appropriate, yet flexible and flat.
- Go beyond formal authority to maximize influence over people and key decisions.
- Employ a workable set of project planning and control tools.
- Avoid overreliance on one type of control tool.
- Stress the importance of meeting cost, schedule, and performance goals.
- Give priority to achieving the mission or function of the end-item.
- Keep changes under control.
- Seek to find ways of assuring job security for effective project team members.

In Chapter 4 we stated that a project cannot be successful unless it is recognized as a project and has the support of top-level management. Top-level management must be willing to commit company resources and provide the necessary administrative support so that the project easily adapts to the company's day-to-day routine of doing business. Furthermore, the parent organization must develop an atmosphere conducive to good working relationships between the project manager, parent organization, and client organization.

With regard to the parent organization, there exist a number of variables that can be used to evaluate parent organization support. These variables include:

- A willingness to coordinate efforts
- A willingness to maintain structural flexibility
- A willingness to adapt to change
- Effective strategic planning
- Rapport maintenance
- Proper emphasis on past experience

- External buffering
- Prompt and accurate communications
- Enthusiastic support
- Identification to all concerned parties that the project does, in fact, contribute to parent capabilities

The mere identification and existence of these variables do not guarantee project success in dealing with the parent organization. Instead, they imply that there exists a good foundation with which to work so that if the project manager and team, and the parent organization, take the appropriate actions, project success is likely. The following actions must be taken:

- Select at an early point, a project manager with a proven track record of technical skills, human skills, and administrative skills (in that order) to lead the project team.
- Develop clear and workable guidelines for the project manager.
- Delegate sufficient authority to the project manager, and let him make important decisions in conjunction with key team members.
- Demonstrate enthusiasm for and commitment to the project and team.
- Develop and maintain short and informal lines of communication.
- Avoid excessive pressure on the project manager to win contracts.
- Avoid arbitrarily slashing or ballooning the project team's cost estimate.
- Avoid "buy-ins."
- Develop close, not meddling, working relationships with the principal client contact and project manager.

Both the parent organization and the project team must employ proper managerial techniques to ensure that judicious and adequate, but not excessive, use of planning, controlling, and communications systems can be made. These proper management techniques must also include preconditioning, such as:

- Clearly established specifications and designs
- Realistic schedules
- Realistic cost estimates
- Avoidance of "buy-ins"
- Avoidance of overoptimism

The client organization can have a great deal of influence on project success by minimizing team meetings, making rapid responses to requests for information, and simply letting the contractor "do his thing" without any interference. The variables that exist for the client organization include:

- A willingness to coordinate efforts
- Rapport maintenance
- Establishment of reasonable and specific goals and criteria

- Well-established procedures for changes
- Prompt and accurate communications
- Commitment of client resources
- Minimization of red tape
- Providing sufficient authority to the client contact (especially for decision making)

With these variables as the basic foundation, it should be possible to:

- Encourage openness and honesty from the start from all participants
- Create an atmosphere that encourages healthy competition, but not cut-throat situations or "liars'" contests
- Plan for adequate funding to complete the entire project
- Develop clear understandings of the relative importance of cost, schedule, and technical performance goals
- Develop short and informal lines of communication and a flat organizational structure
- Delegate sufficient authority to the principal client contact, and allow prompt approval or rejection of important project decisions
- Reject "buy-ins"
- Make prompt decisions regarding contract award or go-ahead
- Develop close, not meddling, working relationships with project participants
- Avoid arms-length relationships
- Avoid excessive reporting schemes
- Make prompt decisions regarding changes

By combining the relevant actions of the project team, parent organization, and client organization, we can identify the fundamental lessons for management. These include:

- When starting off in project management, plan to go all the way.
  - Recognize authority conflicts—resolve.
  - Recognize change impact—be a change agent.
- Match the right people with the right jobs.
  - No system is better than the people who implement it.
- Allow adequate time and effort for laying out the project groundwork and defining work:
  - Work breakdown structure
  - Network planning
- Ensure that work packages are the proper size:
  - Manageable, with organizational accountability
  - Realistic in terms of effort and time
- Establish and use planning and control systems as the focal point of project implementation.
  - Know where you're going.

- Know when you've gotten there.
- Be sure information flow is realistic.
  - Information is the basis for problem solving and decision making.
  - Communication "pitfalls" are the greatest contributor to project difficulties.
- Be willing to replan—do so.
  - The best-laid plans can often go astray.
  - Change is inevitable.
- Tie together responsibility, performance, and rewards.
  - Management by objectives
  - Key to motivation and productivity
- Long before the project ends, plan for its end.
  - Disposition of personnel
  - Disposal of material and other resources
  - Transfer of knowledge
  - Closing out work orders
  - Customer/contractor financial payments and reporting

The last lesson, project termination, has been the downfall for many good project managers. As projects near completion, there is a natural tendency to minimize costs by transferring people as soon as possible and by closing out work orders. This often leaves the project manager with the responsibility for writing the final report and transferring raw materials to other programs. Many projects require one or two months after work completion simply for administrative reporting and final cost summary.

Having defined project success, we can now identify some of the major causes for the failure of project management:

- *Selection of a concept that is not applicable.* Since each application is unique, selecting a project that does not have a sound basis, or forcing a change when the time is not appropriate, can lead to immediate failure.
- *Selection of the wrong person as project manager.* The individual selected must be more of a manager than a doer. He must place emphasis on all aspects of the work, not merely the technical.
- *Upper management that is not supportive.* Upper management must concur in the concept and must behave accordingly.
- *Inadequately defined tasks.* There must exist an adequate system for planning and control such that a proper balance between cost, schedule, and technical performance can be maintained.
- *Misused management techniques.* There exists the inevitable tendency in technical communities to attempt to do more than is initially required by contract. Technology must be watched, and individuals must buy only what is needed.
- *Project termination that is not planned.* By definition, each project must stop. Termination must be planned so that the impact can be identified.

It is often said that more can be learned from failure than from success. The lessons that can be learned from project failure include:[1]

- When starting off in project management, plan to go all the way.
- Don't skimp on the project manager's qualifications.
- Do not spare time and effort in laying out the project groundwork and defining work.
- Ensure that the work packages in the project are of proper size.
- Establish and use network planning techniques, having the network as the focal point of project implementation.
- Be sure that the information flow related to the project management system is realistic.
- Be prepared to replan jobs continually to accommodate frequent changes on dynamic programs.
- Whenever possible, tie together responsibility, performance, and rewards.
- Long before a project ends, provide some means for accommodating the employees' personal goals.
- If mistakes in project implementation have been made, make a fresh try.

9.2 PROJECT MANAGEMENT EFFECTIVENESS[2]

Project managers interact continually with upper-level management, perhaps more so than with functional managers. Not only the success of the project, but even the career path of the project manager can depend on the working relationships and expectations established with upper-level management. There are four key variables in measuring the effectiveness of dealing with upper-level management. These variables are credibility, priority, accessibility, and visibility:

- Credibility
  - Credibility comes from the image of a sound decision maker.
  - It is normally based on experience in a variety of assignments.
  - It is refueled by the manager and the status of his project.
  - Making success visible to others increases credibility.
  - To be believable, emphasize facts rather than opinions.
  - Give credit to others; they may return this favor.
- Priority
  - Sell the specific importance of the project to the objectives of the total organization.
  - Stress the competitive aspect, if relevant.

---

1. Ivars Avots, "Why Does Project Management Fail?" *California Management Review,* Vol. 12, 1969, pp. 77–82.

2. This section and Section 9.3 are adapted from *Seminar in Project Management Workbook,* copyright 1977 by Hans J. Thamhain. Reproduced by permission of Dr. Hans J. Thamhain.

- Stress changes for success.
- Secure testimonial support from others—functional departments, other managers, customers, independent sources.
- Emphasize "spin-offs" that may result from projects.
- Anticipate "priority problems."
- Sell priority on a one-to-one basis.
- Accessibility
  - Accessibility involves the ability to communicate directly with top management.
  - Show that your proposals are good for the total organization, not just the project.
  - Weigh the facts carefully; explain the pros and cons.
  - Be logical and polished in your presentations.
  - Become personally known by members of top management.
  - Create a desire in the "customer" for your abilities and your project.
  - Make curiosity work for you.
- Visibility
  - Be aware of the amount of visibility you really need.
  - Make a good impact when presenting the project to top management.
  - Adopt a contrasting style of management when feasible and possible.
  - Use team members to help regulate the visibility you need.
  - Conduct timely "informational" meetings with those who count.
  - Use available publicity media.

9.3 EXPECTATIONS

In the project management environment, the project managers, team members, and upper-level managers each have expectations of what their relationships should be with the other parties. To illustrate this, top management expects project managers to:

- Assume total accountability for the success or failure to provide results
- Provide effective reports and information
- Provide minimum organizational disruption during the execution of a project
- Present recommendations, not just alternatives
- Have the capacity to handle most interpersonal problems
- Demonstrate a self-starting capacity
- Demonstrate growth with each assignment

At first glance, it may appear that these qualities are expected of all managers, not necessarily project managers. But this is not true. The first four items are different. The line managers are not accountable for total project success, just for that portion performed by their line organization. Line managers can be promoted on their technical ability, not necessarily on their ability to write effective reports. Line managers cannot disrupt an entire organization, but the project manager can. Line managers do not necessarily have to make decisions, just provide alternatives and recommendations.

Just as top management has expectations of project managers, project managers have certain expectations of top management. Project management expects top management to:

- Provide clearly defined decision channels
- Take actions on requests
- Facilitate interfacing with support departments
- Assist in conflict resolution
- Provide sufficient resources/charter
- Provide sufficient strategic/long-range information
- Provide feedback
- Give advice and stage-setting support
- Define expectations clearly
- Provide protection from political infighting
- Provide the opportunity for personal and professional growth

The project team also has expectations from their leader, the project manager. The project team expects the project manager to:

- Assist in the problem-solving process by coming up with ideas
- Provide proper direction and leadership
- Provide a relaxed environment
- Interact informally with team members
- Stimulate the group process
- Facilitate adoption of new members
- Reduce conflicts
- Defend the team against outside pressure
- Resist changes
- Act as the group spokesperson
- Provide representation with higher management

In order to provide high task efficiency and productivity, a project team should have certain traits and characteristics. A project manager expects the project team to:

- Demonstrate membership self-development
- Demonstrate the potential for innovative and creative behavior
- Communicate effectively
- Be committed to the project

- Demonstrate the capacity for conflict resolution
- Be results oriented
- Be change oriented
- Interface effectively and with high morale

Team members want, in general, to fill certain primary needs. The project manager should understand these needs before demanding that the team live up to his expectations. Members of the project team need:

- A sense of belonging
- Interest in the work itself
- Respect for the work being done
- Protection from political infighting
- Job security and job continuity
- Potential for career growth

Project managers must remember that team members may not always be able to verbalize these needs, but they do exist nevertheless.

9.4 FORCE FIELD ANALYSIS

Project managers must live in a dynamic environment in which constant and rapid change becomes a way of life. To operate effectively under these circumstances, the project manager must be able to diagnose the situation, design alternatives that will remedy it, provide the necessary leadership so that these changes can be implemented, and develop an atmosphere that helps the employees to adapt readily to these changes.

One of the early pioneers in developing theories for managing change was Kurt Lewin.[3] Lewin believed that at any point in time during the life cycle of a project there will exist driving forces that will push the project toward success and restraining forces that may induce failure. In a steady-state environment, the driving and restraining forces are in balance. However, if the driving forces increase or the restraining forces decrease, whether they act independently or together, change is likely to take place. The formal analysis of these forces is commonly referred to as force field analysis. This type of analysis can be used to:[4]

- Monitor the project team and measure potential deficiencies
- Audit the project on an ongoing basis
- Involve project personnel, which can be conducive to team building
- Measure the sensitivity of proposed changes

---

3. Kurt Lewin, "Frontiers in Group Dynamics," *Human Relations,* Vol. 1, No. 1, 1947; Also, *Field Theory in Social Science* (New York: Harper, 1951).

4. See note 3.

Current studies in force field analysis have been conducted by Dugan et al.,[5] whose research involved 125 project managers in approximately seventy different technology-oriented companies. The research study and questionnaire were personally explained to the participating project managers to minimize potential communications problems.

The researchers obtained information in several areas, including:

- Personal drive, motivation, and leadership
- Team motivation
- Management support
- Functional support
- Technical expertise
- Project objectives
- Financial resources
- Client support and commitment

The research study categorized each of the above areas according to project life-cycle phase. However, for simplicity's sake, only a brief synopsis of each of these areas will be presented. The reader is directed to the reference article for a more detailed description.

Personal drive, motivation, and leadership were found to provide the strongest driving forces, and were important attributes of the project manager and team members and important in all project life-cycle phases. The lack of personal drive, motivation, and leadership was found to result in strong restraining forces. The force field analysis gave the following results for personal drive, motivation, and leadership:

- Driving forces
  - Desire for accomplishment
  - Interest in project
  - Work challenge
  - Group acceptance
  - Common objectives
  - Experience in task management
  - Providing proper direction
  - Assistance in problem-solving
  - Team builder
  - Effective communications
- Restraining forces
  - Inexperienced project leader
  - Uncertain roles
  - Lack of technical knowledge
  - Personality problems

---

5. H. S. Dugan, H. J. Thamhain, and D. L. Wilemon, "Managing Change in Project Management," *Proceedings of the Ninth Annual International Seminar/Symposium on Project Management,* The Project Management Institute, 1977, pp. 178–188.

- Lack of self-confidence and credibility
- Poor project control
- First project management experience

Team motivation was identified as having the strongest overall influence on project success, and as an important factor in all phases of the project. Team motivation was a strong driver and, if lacking, became a strong restraint. The following results for team motivation were found:

- Driving forces
  - Good interpersonal relations
  - Desire to achieve
  - Expertise
  - Common goal
  - Integration of team and project objectives
  - Agreement and distribution of work
  - Clear role definition
  - Professional interest in project
  - Challenge of project
  - Project visibility and rewards
- Restraining forces
  - Poor team organization
  - Communication barriers
  - Poor leadership
  - Uncertain rewards
  - Uncertain objectives
  - Resistance to project management approach
  - Little commitment or ownership in project
  - Team members overloaded
  - Limited prior team experience
  - Unequal talent distribution

Management support was found to have important driving and restraining qualities, and was associated with all project phases. The following results were obtained:

- Driving forces
  - Sufficient resources
  - Proper priorities
  - Authority delegation
  - Management interest
- Restraining forces
  - Unclear objectives
  - Insufficient resources
  - Changing priorities
  - Insufficient authority/charter
  - Management indifference
  - Poor direction

- Excessive preoccupation with minor details
- Wanting support
- Unresponsive management
- Continuous change in scope
- Poor project organization

Functional support was identified as important during project buildup, main phase, and phaseout, as well as being a must for successful project completion. Functional support was affected by top-management support, funding, and organizational structure. The forces behind functional support were found to be:

- Driving forces
  - Clear goals and priorities
  - Proper planning
  - Adequate task integrators
- Restraining forces
  - Priority conflicts
  - Funding restraints
  - Poor project organization
  - Resistance to project objectives
  - Unclear roles

Technical expertise was particularly important during project formation and buildup. The forces identified were:

- Driving forces
  - Ability to manage technology
  - Prior track record
  - Low-risk project
- Restraining forces
  - Lack of technical information
  - Unexpected technical problems
  - Inability to cope with change

Project objectives were most important during project formation and start-up. The forces identified were:

- Driving forces
  - Clear goals
  - Clear expectations/responsibilities
  - Clear interface relationships
  - Clear specifications
  - Workable project plan
- Restraining forces
  - Conflict over objectives (i.e., no project plan)
  - Customer uncertainties
  - Power plays
  - Technical problems

The last two items are financial resources and client support and commitment. Under *financial resources* are:

- Driving forces
  - Necessary financial resources
  - Financial control capability
- Restraining forces
  - Budget restraints
  - Lack of authority to commit funds
  - Manpower problems
  - Facilities unavailable
  - Insufficient planning

Under *client support and commitment* are:

- Driving forces
  - Good working relations
  - Clear objectives
  - Timely client feedback
  - Client support and commitment
  - Regular meetings/reviews
  - Help and concern
- Restraining forces
  - Lack of information on client needs
  - Lack of sustained interest
  - Conflict within client organization
  - Changing requirements
  - Funding problems

The authors then summarized their results as follows:

- Implications for project managers
  - Understand interaction of organizational and behavioral elements to build an effective team.
  - Show concern for team members—know their needs.
  - Provide work challenge.
  - Communicate objectives clearly.
- Plan effectively and early in the project cycle.
- Establish a contingency plan.
- Implications for top management
  - Poor organizational climate has a negative effect on project performance.
  - Project leader abilities are crucial to effective project management. Program management selection should be carefully considered. Formal training and development may be necessary.
  - Senior management support is important.
  - Clearly defined decision channels and priorities may improve operating effectiveness with functional departments.
  - Smooth project start-up and phaseout procedures help to ease personnel problems and power plays.

9.5 LESSONS LEARNED

Lessons can be learned from each and every project, even if the project is a failure. Most companies do not document lessons learned because employees are reluctant to sign their names to documents that indicate that lessons were learned from mistakes that were made. Employees end up repeating the mistakes that others have made and end up learning from their own mistakes rather than those of other people.

How to implement lessons learned is a key problem. Recently, a company successfully completed a project that required several innovative decisions and approaches in the way business was being conducted. During the postimplementation meeting, senior management decided that the entire company should benefit from the knowledge gained on this project. The executive sponsor then dismantled the project team and assigned each team member to a different unit of the company thinking that this knowledge would carry over. The experiment failed and soon all lessons learned were forgotten.

Today, emphasis is being placed on documenting lessons learned. Boeing maintains diaries of lessons learned on each airplane project. Another company conducts a postimplementation meeting where the team is required to prepare a three- to five-page case study documenting the successes and failures on the project. The case studies are then used by the training department in preparing individuals to become future project managers. Some companies even go to extremes, mandating that project managers keep project notebooks documenting all decisions as well as a project file with all project correspondence. On large projects, this may be impractical.

Most companies seem to prefer postimplementation meetings and case study documentation. The problem is when to hold the postimplementation meeting. One company uses project management for new product development and production. When the first production run is complete, the company holds a postimplementation meeting to discuss what was learned. Approximately six months later, the company conducts a second postimplementation meeting to discuss customer reaction to the product. There have been situations where the reaction of the customer indicated that what the company thought they did right turned out to be a wrong decision. A follow-up case study is now prepared during the second meeting.

PROBLEMS

9–1   What is an effective working relationship between project managers themselves?

9–2   Must everyone in the organization understand the "rules of the game" for project management to be effective?

9–3   Defend the statement that the first step in making project management work must be a complete definition of the boundaries across which the project manager must interact.

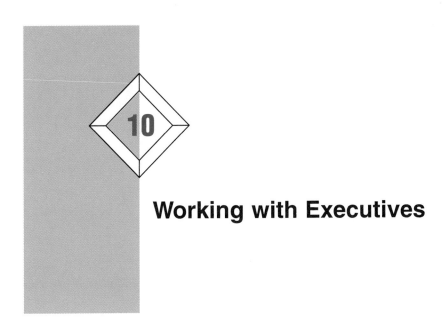

Working with Executives

10.0 INTRODUCTION

In any project management environment, project managers must continually interface with executives during both the planning and execution stages. Unless the project manager understands the executive's role and thought process, a poor working relationship will develop. In order to understand the executive–project interface, three topics are discussed:

- The project sponsor
- The in-house representatives
- Selling executives on project management

10.1 THE PROJECT SPONSOR

For more than two decades, the traditional role of senior management, as far as projects were concerned, has been to function as project sponsors. The project sponsor usually comes from the executive levels and has the primary responsibility of maintaining executive–client contact. The sponsor ensures that the correct information from the contractor's organization is reaching executives in the customer's organization, that there is no filtering of information from the contractor to the customer, and that someone at the executive levels is making sure that the customer's money is being spent wisely. The project sponsor will normally transmit cost and deliverables information to the customer, whereas schedule and performance status data comes from the project manager.

In addition to executive–client contact, the sponsor also provides guidance on:

- Objective setting
- Priority setting
- Project organizational structure
- Project policies and procedures
- Project master planning
- Up-front planning
- Key staffing
- Monitoring execution
- Conflict resolution

The role of the project sponsor takes on a different dimension based on which life-cycle phase the project is in. During the planning/initiation phase of a project, the sponsor normally functions in an active role, which includes such activities as:

- Assisting the project manager in establishing the correct objectives for the project
- Providing the project manager with information on the environmental/ political factors that could influence the project's execution
- Establishing the priority for the project (either individually or through consultation with other executives) and informing the project manager of the established priority and the *reason* for the priority
- Providing guidance for the establishment of policies and procedures by which to govern the project
- Functioning as the executive–client contact point

During the initiation or kickoff phase of a project, the project sponsor must be actively involved in objective setting and priority setting. It is absolutely mandatory that the executives establish the priorities in both business and technical terms. Historically, objectives were mistakenly established in technical terms only. In this case, the project manager's definition of success was technical success (i.e.: Did it work?), irrespective of the cost or schedule. Today, objectives are defined in both business and technical terms.

During the execution phase of the project, the role of the executive sponsor is more passive than active. The sponsor will provide assistance to the project manager on an as-needed basis except for routine status briefings.

During the execution stage of a project, the sponsor must be *selective* in the problems that he or she wishes to help resolve. Trying to get involved in every problem will not only result in severe micromanagement, but will undermine the project manager's ability to get the job done. This could also detract from the amount of time the executive should spend performing his normal function.

The role of the sponsor is similar to that of a referee. Table 10–1 shows the working relationship between the project manager and the line managers in both mature and immature organizations. When conflicts or problems exist in the

TABLE 10–1. THE PROJECT-LINE INTERFACE

Immature Organization	Mature Organization
• Project manager is vested with power/authority over the line managers. • Project manager negotiates for best people. • Project manager works directly with functional employees. • Project manager has no input into employee performance evaluations. • Leadership is project manager-centered.	• Project and line managers share authority and power. • Project manager negotiates for line manager's commitment. • Project manager works through line managers. • Project manager makes recommendations to the line managers. • Leadership is team-centered.

project-line interface and cannot be resolved at that level, the sponsor might find it necessary to step in and provide assistance. Table 10–2 shows the mature and immature ways that a sponsor interfaces with the project.

It should be understood that the sponsor exists for everyone on the project, including the line managers and their employees. Project sponsors must maintain open-door policies, even though maintaining an open-door policy can have detri-

TABLE 10–2. THE EXECUTIVE INTERFACE

Immature Organization	Mature Organization
• Executive is actively involved in projects. • Executive acts as the project champion. • Executive questions the project manager's decisions. • Priority shifting occurs frequently. • Executive views project management as a necessary evil. • There is very little project management support. • Executive discourages bringing problems upstairs. • Executive is not committed to project sponsorship. • Executive support exists only during project startup. • Executive encourages project decisions to be made. • No procedures exist for assigning project sponsors. • Executives seek perfection. • Executive discourages use of a project charter. • Executive is not involved in charter preparation. • Executive does not understand what goes into a charter. • Executives do not believe that the project team is performing.	• Executive involvement is passive. • Executive acts as the project sponsor. • Executive trusts the project manager's decisions. • Priority shifting is avoided. • Executive views project management as beneficial. • There is visible, ongoing support. • Executive encourages bringing problems upstairs. • Executive is committed to sponsorship (and ownership). • Executive support exists on a continuous basis. • Executive encourages business decisions to be made. • Sponsorship assignment procedures are visible. • Executives seek what is possible. • Executive recognizes the importance of a charter. • Executive takes responsibility for charter preparation. • Executive understands the content of a charter. • Executives trust that performance is taking place.

mental effects. First, employees may try to flood the sponsor with trivial items. Second, employees may feel that they can bypass levels of management and converse directly with the sponsor. The moral here is that employees must be encouraged to be careful about how many times and under what circumstances they "go to the well." The project manager also should not go to the project sponsor without a valid reason. Going to the sponsor too often may reflect unfavorably on the project manager's ability to manage or make decisions.

In addition to his/her normal functional job, the sponsor must be available to provide as needed assistance to the projects. Any given executive may find it necessary to act as a sponsor on several projects at the same time. Sponsorship can become a time-consuming effort, especially if problems occur. Therefore, executives are limited as to how many projects they can sponsor effectively at the same time.

As an organization matures in project management, executives begin to trust middle- and lower-level management to function as sponsors. There are several reasons for supporting this:

- Executives do not have time to function as sponsors on each and every project.
- Not all projects require sponsorship from the executive levels.
- Middle management is closer to where the work is being performed.
- Middle management is in a better position to provide advice on certain risks.
- Project personnel have easier access to middle management.

Sometimes executives refuse to act as project sponsors because of the nature of their job. Senior managers in large diversified corporations are extremely busy with strategic planning activities and often simply do not have the time to properly function as a sponsor as well. In such cases, sponsorship falls one level below senior management.

Figure 10–1 shows the major functions of a project sponsor. At the onset of a project, a senior committee meets to decide whether a given project should be deemed as priority or nonpriority. If the project is critical or strategic, then the committee may assign a senior manager as the sponsor, perhaps even a member of the committee. It is common practice for steering committee executives to function as sponsors for the projects that the steering committee oversees.

For projects that are routine, maintenance, or noncritical, a sponsor could be assigned from the middle-management levels. One organization that strongly prefers to have middle management assigned as sponsors cites the benefit of generating an atmosphere of management buy-in at the critical middle levels. Middle management is often criticized for not properly supporting or buying into a project, or even into project management as a methodology.

Not all projects need a project sponsor. Sponsorship is generally needed on those projects that require a multitude of resources or a large amount of integration between functional lines or that have the potential for disruptive conflicts or

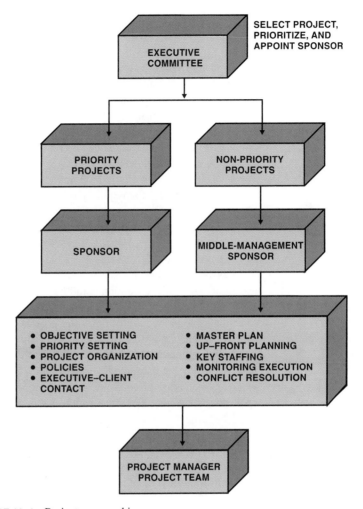

FIGURE 10–1. Project sponsorship.

the need for strong customer communications. This last item requires further comment. Quite often customers wish to make sure that the contractor's project manager is spending funds prudently. Customers therefore feel pleased when an executive sponsor is identified, and when that sponsor's responsibility includes the supervision of the project manager's funding allocation.

It is common practice for companies that are heavily involved in competitive bidding to identify in their proposal not only the resumé of the project manager, but the resumé of the executive project sponsor as well. This may give the bidder a competitive advantage, all other things being equal. Customers are now convinced that they have a direct path of communications to executive management.

One such contractor identified the functions of the executive project sponsor as follows:

- Major participation in sales effort and contract negotiations
- Establishes and maintains top-level client relationships
- Assists project manager in getting the project underway (planning, procedures, staffing, etc.)
- Maintains current knowledge of major project activities (receives copies of major correspondence and reports, attends major client and project review meetings, visits project regularly, etc.)
- Handles major contractual matters
- Interprets company policy for the project manager
- Assists project manager in identifying and solving major problems
- Keeps general management and company management advised of major problems

Consider a project that is broken down into two life-cycle phases: planning and execution. (Actually, execution could be subdivided into several other phases.) For short-duration projects, say two years or less, it is advisable for the project sponsor to be the same individual for the entire project. For long-term projects of, say, five years or so, it is possible to have a different project sponsor for each life-cycle phase, but preferably from the same level of management. The sponsor does not have to come from the same line organization as the one where the majority of the work will be taking place. Some companies even go so far as demanding that the sponsor come from a line organization that has no vested interest in the project.

The project sponsor is actually a "big brother" or advisor for the project manager. Under *no* circumstances should the project sponsor try to function as the project manager as well. History has shown that this will do more harm than good. The project sponsor should assist the project manager in solving those problems that the project manager cannot resolve by himself. The sponsor generally works his magic in " mahogany row" behind closed doors, rather than interacting directly with the team members.

In one government organization, the project manager wanted to open up a new position on his project. The project manager already had a young woman identified to fill the position. Unfortunately, the size of the government project office was constrained by a unit-manning document that dictated the number of available positions.

The project manager obtained the assistance of an executive sponsor who, working with human resources and personnel management, created a new position within thirty days. Without executive sponsorship, the bureaucratic system creating a new position would have taken months. By that time, the project would have been over.

In a second case study, the president of a medium-sized manufacturing company, a subsidiary of a larger corporation, wanted to act as sponsor on a special project. The project manager decided to make full use of this high-ranking sponsor by assigning him certain critical functions. As part of the project's schedule, four months were allocated to obtain corporate approval for tooling dollars. The project manager "assigned" this task to the project sponsor, who reluctantly agreed to fly to corporate headquarters. He returned two days later with authorization for tooling. The company actually reduced project completion time by four months, thanks to the project sponsor.

Figure 10–2 represents a situation where there were two project sponsors for one project. Alpha Company received a $25 million prime contractor project from the Air Force and subcontracted out $2 million to Beta Company. The project manager in Alpha Company earned $95,000 per year and refused to communicate directly with the project manager of Beta Company because his salary was only $65,000 per year. After all, as one executive said, "Elephants don't communicate with mice." The Alpha Company project manager instead sought out someone at Beta in his own salary range to act as the project sponsor, and the burden fell on the director of engineering.

The Alpha Company project manager reported to an Air Force colonel. The Air Force colonel considered his counterpart in Beta Company to be the vice president and general manager. Here, power and title were more important than the $100,000 differential in their salaries. Thus, there was one project sponsor for the prime contractor and a second project sponsor for the customer.

In some industries, such as construction, the project sponsor is identified in the proposal, and thus everyone know who it is. Unfortunately, there are situations where the project sponsor is "hidden," and the project manager may not realize who it is, or know if the customer realizes who it is.

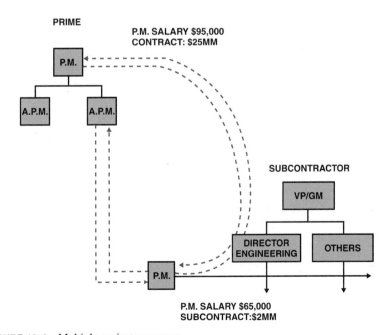

FIGURE 10–2. Multiple project sponsors.

Convincing executives of the necessity of project management is usually easier than getting them to provide ongoing, visible support by acting as a project sponsor. An unfortunate situation occurs when senior management becomes an invisible sponsor. This concept of invisible sponsorship occurs most frequently at the executive level and is referred to as absentee sponsorship.

There are several ways that invisible sponsorship can occur. The first is when the manager who is appointed as a sponsor refuses to act as a sponsor for fear that poor decisions or an unsuccessful project could have a negative impact on his or her career. In this case, invisibility is a result of fear.

The second type of invisible sponsorship results when an executive is appointed as a sponsor who really does not understand either sponsorship or project management. In this case, invisibility because of ignorance, the executive simply provides lip service to the sponsorship function.

The third way involves an executive who is already overburdened with a normal workload being asked to take on additional responsibilities by acting as a sponsor on several projects at one time. As a result, the executive simply does not have the time to perform meaningfully as a sponsor. Of course, this could be the result of the executive's lack of understanding of the additional workload of sponsorship when accepting the assignments.

The fourth way of creating an invisible sponsor occurs when the project manager refuses to keep the sponsor informed and involved. The sponsor may believe that everything is flowing smoothly and that he is not needed. This method creates further difficulties when problems occur because the sponsor may now feel helpless in assisting the project.

Some people contend that the best way for the project manager to work with an invisible sponsor is for the project manager to make the decision and then send a memo to the sponsor stating "This is the decision that I have made and, unless I hear back from you in the next 48 hours, I will assume that you agree with my decision."

The opposite extreme is the sponsor who micromanages. Sponsors who micromanage often do not understand the damage that they incur for the project manager. Some people contend that the best way for the project manager to handle this situation is to bury the sponsor with work in hopes that he will let go. Unfortunately this could lead to a detrimental situation for the project manager if it ends up reinforcing the sponsor's belief that what he is doing is correct.

The better alternative for handling a micromanaging sponsor is to ask for role clarification. The project manager should try working with the sponsor to define the roles of project manager and project sponsor more clearly. Sometimes executives are appointed as sponsors without understanding the sponsorship role. It is not uncommon for the project manager to end up educating the sponsor on role expectations.

The invisible sponsor and the overbearing sponsor are not as detrimental as the "can't-say-no" sponsor. In one company, the executive sponsor conducted executive–client communications on the golf course by playing golf with customer's sponsor. After every golf game, the executive sponsor would return with customer requests, which were actually scope changes that were considered as no-cost changes by the customer. When a sponsor continuously says "yes" to the customer, everyone in the contractor's organization eventually suffers.

Sometimes the existence of a sponsor can do more harm than good, especially if the sponsor focuses on the wrong objectives around which to make decisions. The following two remarks were made by two project managers at an appliance manufacturer:

- Projects here emphasize time measures: deadlines! We should emphasize milestones reached and quality. We say, "We'll get you a system by a deadline." When we should be saying, "We'll get you a good system."
- Upper management may not allow true project management to occur. Too many executives are "date-driven" rather than "requirements-driven." Original target dates should be for broad planning only. Specific target dates should be set utilizing the full concept of project management (i.e., available resources, separation of basic requirements from enhancements, technical and hardware constraints, unplanned activities, contingencies, etc.)

These comments illustrate the necessity of having a sponsor who understands project management rather than one who simply assists in decision-making. The goals and objectives of the sponsor must be aligned with the goals and objectives of the project, and they must be realistic. When such alignment occurs, it is common practice for the project manager to purposely treat the executive as an invisible sponsor.

If sponsorship is to exist at the executive levels, the sponsor must be visible and constantly informed concerning the project status. Absentee sponsorship may force critical decisions to be made at the wrong levels of management. If invisible sponsorship exists, then the project manager may have to act as his own sponsor.

Committee Sponsorship

For years companies have assigned a single individual as the sponsor for a project. Companies always ran the risk that the sponsor would show favoritism to his line group and suboptimal decision-making would occur. Recently, companies have begun looking at sponsorship by committee.

Committee sponsorship is becoming quite common in those organizations committed to concurrent engineering and shortening product development time. Committee membership is filled from the middle-management ranks and, at a minimum, should include one representative each from marketing, R&D, and operations. The idea behind this approach is that the committee will be able to make decisions in the best interest of the company more easily than a single individual could. This is particularly important for concurrent engineering projects where marketing, R&D, and production activities may be occurring at the same time.

Committee sponsorship also has its limitations. At the executive levels, it is almost impossible to find time blocks when senior managers can convene. Even at the middle levels of management, difficulties occur. It may be impossible for the committee members to serve on several committees at the same time. Therefore, the company may have to be selective (or set up some type of criteria) in deciding which projects require committee sponsorship and which do not. For a company with a large number of projects, committee sponsorship may not be a viable approach.

In time of crisis, project managers may need immediate access to their sponsors. If the sponsor is a committee, then how does the project manager get the committee to convene such that project delays will be minimal? This is further complicated by the fact that individual project sponsorship may carry with it more dedication than committee sponsorship.

Committee sponsorship has been shown to work well if one, and only one, member of the committee acts as the prime sponsor for a given project. One organization has a sponsorship committee of six members. Out of some 90 projects occurring at the same time, the committee sponsored 28 projects and each member served as the prime sponsor for some 5 projects. Each project manager's superior sponsored the remaining projects.

When to Seek Help

During status reporting, a project manager can wave either a red, yellow, or green flag. This is known as the "traffic light" reporting system, thanks in part to color printers. For each element in the status report, the project manager will illuminate one of three lights according to the following criteria:

- *Green light:* Work is progressing as planned. Sponsor involvement is not necessary.
- *Yellow light:* A potential problem may exist. The sponsor is informed but no action by the sponsor is necessary at this time.
- *Red light:* A problem exists that may affect time, cost, scope, or quality. Sponsor involvement is necessary.

Yellow flags are warnings that should be resolved at the middle levels of management or lower. There is nothing wrong with the executive being informed of the problem, but he should not be expected to actively participate in the solution. Sponsors must be willing to say to a project manager, "This is your problem and you handle it."

If the project manager waves a red flag, then the sponsor will more than likely wish to be actively involved. Red flags generally indicate that a problem exists that can affect the time, cost, or performance constraints of the project and that an immediate decision must be made. The main function of the sponsor is to assist in making the best possible decision in a timely fashion. Executives who are unable to make timely decisions should not be allowed to function as project sponsors. This problem occurred in one company where the sponsor refused to make decisions and delays occurred.

Consider a situation where the project manager and one of the line managers are having a conflict over a critical technical issue affecting the project, and the problem is brought up to the sponsor for resolution. The sponsor must first make sure that *all* other avenues of resolution have been exhausted before getting actively involved. Second, the sponsor must solicit input from all conflicting parties as to the nature of the problem and alternatives being considered. Third, sponsors must understand their own capabilities as to their ability to make qualified decisions. If the sponsor is not qualified to make such a decision, then the sponsor must have the authority to convene the proper resources such that a timely decision can be made, and finally, the sponsor must see that a timely decision is made. If the sponsor did not exist, then the conflicting parties would have to climb the chain of command until a common superior could be found. Sponsors, therefore, eliminate wasted time and useless memos and minimize the number of people necessary to make a decision.

Both project sponsors and project managers should not encourage employees to come to them with problems unless the employees also bring with them alternatives and recommendations. Usually, employees will solve most of their own problems once they prepare alternatives and recommendations. As for those problems that must be brought upstairs, resolution is quickest when alternatives and recommendations are also available.

Good corporate cultures bring problems to the surface quickly for resolution. The quicker the potential problem is identified, the more opportunities are available for resolution. People must not be punished for bringing problems to the surface. Also, executives must not micromanage when they see a red or yellow light. They must allow the project manager sufficient time to manage the problem.

A current problem plaguing executives is who determines the color of the light. Consider the following problem: A department manager had planned to perform 1000 hours of work in a given time frame but has completed only 500 hours at the end of the period. According to the project manager's calculation, the project is behind schedule, and he would prefer to have the traffic light colored yellow or red. The line manager, however, feels that he still has enough "wiggle room" in his schedule and that his effort will still be completed within time and cost. Hence the line manager wants the traffic light colored green and does not see this as a problem as yet.

Coloring the light yellow or red may create a false impression that a problem exists and this may create unnecessary executive involvement. Although it is sometimes argumentative as to who colors the light, most executives seem to favor the line manager who has the responsibility for the deliverable. Line managers must provide an honest appraisal of the color of the light. Although the project manager has the final say on the color of traffic light, it is most often based upon the previous working relationship between the two and how well the project manager trusts the line manager's opinion.

As a final note, some companies use more than three colors to indicate project status. One company uses red, yellow and green lights as defined above, but also has an orange light. The orange light represents an activity that is still being performed after the target milestone date for the activity has passed.

The New Role of the Executive

As stated previously, as project management matures, executives decentralize project sponsorship to middle- and lower-level management. Senior management then takes on the new role of strategic planning for project management excellence. In this regard, executives take on the role of:

- Establishing a Center for Excellence in project management
- Establishing a project office or centralized project management function
- Creating a project management career path
- Creating a mentorship program for newly appointed project managers
- Creating an organization committed to benchmarking best practices in project management in other organizations
- Providing strategic information for risk management

This last bullet requires further comment. Because of the pressure placed upon the project manager for schedule compression, risk management could very well become the single most critical skill for project managers for the first decade of the twenty-first century. Executive sponsorship support for risk management will take on paramount importance. Executives will find it necessary to provide project management with strategic business intelligence, assist in risk identification, and evaluate or prioritize risk-handling options.

Managing Scope Creep

Technically oriented team members are motivated not only by meeting specifications, but also by exceeding them. Unfortunately, exceeding specifications can be quite costly. Project managers must monitor scope creep and develop plans for controlling scope changes.

But what if it is the project manager who initiates scope creep? The project sponsor must remain in close contact with the project manager on a periodic basis in addition to gate review meetings. Part of the periodic review process should cover the scope baseline changes. If senior management does not monitor the changes, then the changes may occur without authorization and significant cost increases will result, as shown in Situation 10–1 below:

Situation 10–1: Pine Lake Amusement Park.   After six years of debate, the board of directors of Pine Lake Amusement Park finally came to an agreement on the park's new aquarium. The aquarium would be built, at an estimated cost of $30 million and, between fundraising and bank loans, financing was possible.

After the drawings were completed and approved the project was estimated as a two-year construction effort. Because of the project's complexity, a decision was made to have the project manager brought on board from the beginning of the design efforts, and to remain until six months after opening day. The project manager assigned was well known for his emphasis on details and his strong feelings for the aesthetic beauty of a ride or show.

The drawings were completed and a detailed construction cost estimate was undertaken. When the final cost estimate of $40 million was announced, the board of directors was faced with three alternatives: cancel the project, seek an additional $10 million in financing, or descope (i.e., reduce functionality of) the project. Additional funding was unacceptable and years of publicity on the future aquarium would be embarrassing for the board if the project were to be cancelled. The only reasonable alternative was to reduce the project's scope.

After two months of intensive replanning, the project team proposed a $32 million aquarium. The board of directors agreed to the new design and the construction phase of the project began. The project manager was given specific instructions that cost overruns would not be tolerated.

At the end of the first year, more than $22 million had been spent. Not only had the project manager reinserted the scope that had been removed during the descoping efforts, but also additional scope creep had increased to the point where the final cost would now exceed $62 million. The new schedule now indicated a three-year effort. By the time that management held its review meetings with the project team, the changes had been made.

The Executive Champion

Previously we stated that the executives, when functioning as a sponsor, should maintain an as-needed posture. The exception to this when the executive must act a champion and be actively involved on project on a daily basis.

Executive champions are needed for those activities that require the implementation of change, perhaps even a cultural change, and often with speed. An example of this would be the implementation of a corporate methodology for project management. Executive champions are needed to "drive" the implementation of project management from the top down to the bottom of the organization. Executive champions can accelerate the acceptance of the methodology because their involvement implies executive-level support and interest.

The executive champion must provide the guidance pressure and drive for the organization to develop a strategic competency in project management. This is shown in Figure 10–3. The executive champion must be the driving force behind each of the boxes in Figure 10–3 such that the organization will surpass maturity to the point where the organization's project management capabilities become a sustained competitive weapon.

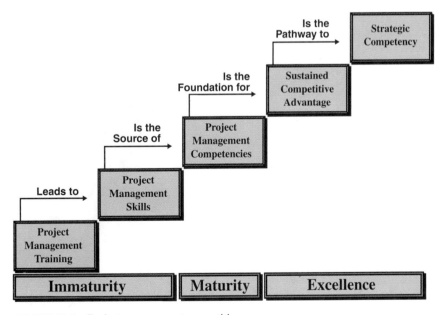

FIGURE 10–3. Project management competitiveness.

10.2 THE IN-HOUSE REPRESENTATIVES

On high-risk, high-priority projects or during periods of mistrust, customers may wish to place in-house representatives in the contractor's plant. These in-house representatives do not always appear as in Figure 10–4. (The in-house representative is the one on top!) These representatives, if treated properly, are like additional project office personnel who are not supported by your budget. They are invaluable resources for reading rough drafts of reports and making recommendations as to how their company may wish to see the report organized.

In-house representatives are normally not situated in or near the contractor's project office because of the project manager's need for some degree of privacy. The exception to the rule would be in the design phase of a construction project, where it is imperative to design what the customer wants and to obtain quick decisions and approvals.

Most in-house representatives know where their authority begins and ends. Some companies demand that in-house representatives have a project office escort when touring the plant, talking to functional employees, or simply observing the testing and manufacturing of components.

FIGURE 10–4. The in-house representative.

Contrary to popular belief, it is possible to have an in-house representative removed from the company because of a disruptive nature. This removal usually requires strong support from the project sponsor in the contractor's shop. The important point to be made here is that executives and project sponsors must maintain proper contact with and control over the in-house representatives, perhaps more so than the project manager.

10.3 SELLING EXECUTIVES ON PROJECT MANAGEMENT

Executives of the 1990s are much more inquisitive about matrix implementation than their predecessors were, even though the advantages and disadvantages of matrix structures have been published extensively in the literature. This section deals with questions asked of the author by executives. Usually the executives questioned the author in a closed session, as quite often executives do not wish functional employees to hear either such questions or their answers. In each of these cases, the executive was contemplating a change to a matrix organizational structure. When reading the questions, it is important to understand that executives of the 1990s are operating under greater pressure and more risk and uncertainty than the executives of either the 1970s or the 1980s, and therefore must be "sold" on the project management approach.[1]

- *Can our people be part-time project managers?* The nature of the question suggests that the executives wanted to manage the projects within the existing resource base of the company. The answer to the question depends, of course, on the size, nature, and complexity of the project. It is generally better to have a full-time project manager responsible for several small projects than to have many part-time project managers. Executives, as well as functional personnel, will never be convinced that the matrix will work until they see it in action. Therefore, it is strongly recommended that the first few projects be "breakthrough" projects with full-time project managers. This implies that, initially, these project managers will be staff to a top-level manager rather than within a newly developed line group for project managers.
- *If we go to project (matrix) management, must we increase resources, especially the number of project managers?* The reason for this question is obvious, namely, that the executives do not wish to increase the manpower base or overhead rate. Matrix management is designed to get better control of functional resources such that more work can be completed

---

1. It should be noted that the conceptual phase of project management implementation begins with functional managers who identify the need for project management because of their problems with resource control. The next step, therefore, is to sell top management on the concept. This is usually best accomplished through outside consultants, whom executives trust to give an impartial view.

in less time, with less money, and with potentially fewer people. Unfortunately, these results may not become evident for a year or two.

Initially, executives prefer to select project managers from within the organization with the argument that project managers must know the people and the operation of the organization. Even today, some companies require that all project managers first spend at least eighteen months in the functional areas prior to becoming project managers. However, there are also good reasons for filling project management positions from outside the company. Sometimes newly transferred project managers still maintain loyal ties to their former functional department and impartial project decision making is not possible.

● *Let's assume that we set up a separate staff function called project administration that is staff to one of our executives. Can we then use our functional people as part-time project managers who report vertically to a line manager and horizontally to project administration?* With proper preparation and training, most employees can learn how to report effectively to multiple managers. However, the process is more complicated if the employee acts as a project manager and functional employee at the same time. When a conflict occurs over what is best for the horizontal or the vertical line, the employee will usually bend in the direction that will put more pay into his pocket. In other words, if the (part-time or perhaps even full-time) project manager always makes decisions in the best interest of his line manager, the project will suffer. The most practical way to solve this problem is to let the functional employee act as a part-time assistant project manager rather than as a part-time project manager because now the functional employee has someone else to plead his case for him, and he is no longer caught in the middle.

This question has serious impacts on how employees are treated. If an employee reports to multiple managers and some managers treat him as though he is Theory Y while others treat him as Theory X, decisions will almost always be made in favor of the Theory Y managers. People who report to multiple managers must understand that, even if they are Theory Y employees, in time of crisis they will be treated as though they are Theory X. This type of understanding and training must be given to all employees who perform in a project environment.

● *Which vice president should be responsible for the project administration function?* Assuming that the company does not want to create a separate position for a vice president of projects, we must find out whether there exists a dominant percentage of people (on all projects) who come from one major functional group. If, say, 60 to 70 percent of all project employees come from engineering, then the vice president for engineering should also control the project administration function because there now exists a common superior for the resolution of the majority of project conflicts. Having to go up two or three levels of management to find a common superior for conflict resolution can create a self-defeating attitude within the matrix.

The assignment will become more difficult if functional dominance does not exist. We must now decide who dominates the decision-making process of the company (i.e., is the company marketing-driven, engineering-driven, etc?). The project administrative function will then fall under the control of this line function. Without either of these degrees of dominance and assuming a project-driven organization, it is not uncommon to find all project managers reporting under marketing with the vice president for marketing acting as the project sponsor.

- *Is it true that most project managers consider their next step to be that of a vice president?* Most project managers view the organization of the company with the project managers on top and executives performing horizontally. Therefore, project managers already consider themselves to be executives on the project and naturally expect their next step to be as executives in the company.

However, we should mention that many project managers are so in love with their jobs that money is not an important factor, and they may wish to stay in project management. Project managers are self-motivated by work challenge and therefore many have refused top-level promotions because they did not consider the work to be as challenging at this level, in comparison with project management.

- *Can we give our employees (especially engineers) a rotation period of six to eighteen months in the project office and then return them to the functional departments, where they should be more well-rounded individuals with a better appreciation and understanding of project management?* On paper, this technique looks good and may have some merit. But in the real world, the results may be disastrous. There are four detrimental effects of this arrangement. First, employees who know that they will be returning to their line function will not be dedicated to project management and will still try to maintain a strong allegiance to their line function. The result, of course, will be that the project will suffer. Second, when the employee knows that his assignment is temporary and brief, he usually walks the straight and narrow path and avoids risk whenever possible. Risky decisions are left to other project office personnel or even his replacement. Third, depending on the rate at which technology changes, the employee may find himself technically obsolete when he returns to his functional group. The fourth and last point is the most serious. The employee may find himself so attracted to the project management function that he wants to stay. If the company forces him to return to his functional department, there is always the risk that the employee will update his resume and begin reading the job-market section of the Tuesday *Wall Street*

Journal. Simply stated, a company should not place people in project management unless the company is willing to offer these people a career path there.

- *How much control should a project manager have over costs and budgets?* Executives in the areas of accounting and finance are very reluctant to delegate total cost control to project managers. Project managers cannot be effective unless they have the right to control costs by opening and closing work orders in accordance with the established project plan. However, if the project manager redirects the project activities in a manner that causes a major deviation in the cash flow position of the project, then he must coordinate his activities with top management in order to prevent a potential company cash flow problem.

- *What role should a project manager have in strategic and operational planning?* First of all, project managers are concerned primarily with the immediate execution of an operational plan. Therefore, they are operational planners. However, because of the company-wide knowledge that the project manager obtains on functional operations and integration, he becomes an invaluable asset to executives during strategic planning, but primarily as a resource person. Project managers are not known for their corporate strategic planning posture, but for their strategic project planning capability.

- *What working relationships should exist between executives and the project manager?* The answer to this question involves two things: internal meddling and customer communications. Executives are expected to work closely with the project manager and take an active role during the conceptual and planning stages of a project. However, after the project enters the implementation phase, active participation by executives equates to executive meddling and can do more harm than good. After planning is completed, executives should step back and let the project manager run the show. There will still be structured feedback from the project office to the executive, and the executive will still be actively involved in priority-setting and conflict resolution. The exception to this occurs when the executive is required to act as the project sponsor. In this case, the client wants to be sure that his project is receiving executive attention and feels confident when he sees one of the contractor's executives looking over the project. The project sponsor exists primarily as the executive–client contact link but can also serve as an invaluable staff resource.

Executives must not be blinded by the partial success they may achieve with executive meddling during the early days of matrix implementation. The overall, long-term effect on the company could be disastrous if executives feel that they can effectively control vertical and horizontal resources at the same time.

- *Where do we find good project managers?* First of all, project management is both an art and a science. The science aspect includes the quantitative tools and techniques for planning, scheduling, and controlling. The art aspect involves dealing with a wide variety of people. The science portion can be learned in the classroom, whereas the art portion can come only from on-the-job experience. Perhaps the most important characteristics are interpersonal skills and communicative skills.

Most companies have qualified people within the organization, and often they produce disastrous results by "forcing" such people to unwillingly accept a project management assignment. Project management generally works best if it is a voluntary assignment, which usually brings with it loyalty and dedication. Unfortunately, many people enter project management without fully understanding the job description of the project manager. If employees are promoted into project management and then "want out" or fail, the company may have no place for them at their new salary. Sometimes it is better to transfer employees to project management laterally, under the stipulation that rewards will follow if they produce.

- *What percentage of a total project budget should be available for project management and administrative support?* The answer to this question depends upon the nature of the project. Management support may run from a low of 2 percent to a high of 15 percent.
- *My company has fifty projects going on at once. The project managers handle multiple projects, each with a different priority, and can report to anyone in the company. Will a matrix give better control?* The matrix will alleviate a lot of these problems, provided that all of the project managers report to one line group. This will give uniform control of projects and will make it easier to establish priorities. If it becomes necessary to get better control over the project managers, then the projects should be grouped according to the customer or to similar technologies, not necessarily dollar value.
- *In a matrix, people are often assigned full-time to a project. What happens if a functional manager complains that pulling a good employee out of his department will leave a large gap?* In a matrix the employee is still physically and administratively attached to his functional group. And even with a full-time project assignment, the employee will probably still find sufficient slack time to assist in another project, even if only in a consultant capacity.
- *On some of our projects the first step is a cost-benefit analysis to see if the project is a feasible undertaking. Who will do this in a matrix?* On some projects, the job-related characteristics are more important than the project manager's personal characteristics. In this case, it may be better to have project managers who are trained in this area rather than having the cost-benefit analysis performed by another group. Project managers should be actively involved in any planning or decision making that may be bottom-line oriented.

- *How do we make sure that everyone in the company knows what the priorities are?* Priorities should be transmitted to both the project and functional departments through the traditional structure within the matrix. Even with the establishment of priorities, project managers will still fight for what they believe to be in the best interest of their project. This is to be expected. Initially, during the implementation of the matrix, it may be necessary to have all priorities documented.

There is a risk within the matrix that the slippage of as little as one project could cause reestablishment of all other project priorities. Even though some project managers may control their project so closely that they can obtain daily status reports, continually changing priorities on a daily or even weekly basis can destroy the functioning of the matrix because the functional managers may now be forced to continually shift resources from project to project.

- *We have had an explosion of operations support systems (the minicomputer era). How do we manage these projects? Can we use matrix management?* Matrix management works best for projects that cut across more than one functional group. Multifunctional MIS and database packages can be very effectively managed using a matrix. Banks are a prime example of industries where matrix management may exist primarily for such projects.

One major risk should be considered. There is always controversy over whether the programmers or the users should be the project managers. The usual arguments are that the programmers don't understand the user's needs and the user doesn't understand why it takes so long to write a program. Many companies have established a project management group to handle such conflicts. Each project is headed by a project manager and two assistant project managers, one from programming and one to represent the users. Conflicts and problems are now resolved horizontally rather than vertically. In this situation, it is possible for one project manager to handle several projects at once.

- *How does top management control the responsibilities that each person will have on a project?* Neither top management nor project management controls the responsibilities. The functional managers still control their own people. Project managers can fill out a linear responsibility chart (LRC) to make sure that every work breakdown structure element is accounted for. However, the functional managers should still approve the amount of authority and responsibility that the project manager wishes to delegate to functional employees. The reason for this is that the project manager should not be able to upgrade functional employees without the consent of the functional manager. The exception would be the project office personnel, who may report full-time to the project manager and also be evaluated by him. During the implementation phase of a matrix, the executives may wish to be actively involved in the LRC establishment, since, in fact, it is part of the planning process, and executives are expected to be closely associated with the project at this time.

- *How do we ensure effective and timely communications to all levels?* The project manager, being the focal point for all project activities, should be able to provide timely project information to everyone, including executives, at a faster rate than the traditional structure itself. The ability to provide effective and timely communications should be part of every project manager's job description.

- *How do we get top management committed to project management?* Regardless of how much literature exists in the area of effective project management, executives will not become committed until they see the system operating effectively and producing the expected dollar value of profit on the bottom line of the project. In order to effectively observe and comprehend the problems, executives must understand their new role in a project management environment and should attend the same "therapy" training sessions as middle management.

- *We need an awful lot of front-end work (i.e., planning) on projects. We are living in a world of limited resources. We need commitments from our people, not just promises. How do we get that?* When the functional managers realize that project management is designed for them, and not for executives or project managers, then the functional managers will start giving commitments that they will live up to. The functional managers must be convinced that the matrix is not simply an attempt on the part of the project manager to control the functional manager's empire, but that in fact the project manager and matrix exist to support the functional managers in getting better control over their own resources such that future commitments can be kept.

- *How do we resolve problems in which there is a lack of knowledge of project team members concerning their own rules?* The responsibility here rests on the shoulders of both the project and functional managers. Planning tools, such as the linear responsibility charts, can be used, but the bottom line is still effective communications. This is why one of the major prerequisites for a project manager is to be an effective communicator and integrator.

- *How do we convince people to disclose problems and not bury them?* In a matrix organization, the critical point is the project-functional interface. Both the project and functional managers must be willing to disclose problems and ask for help, especially on the horizontal line. When the project manager gets into trouble, he goes first to the functional manager to discuss project resources. When the functional manager gets into trouble, he goes to the project manager seeking additional time, additional funding, or a change in specifications. Project personnel must realize that the project is a team effort, and everyone should pitch in when problems occur.

Many people refuse to reveal problems for fear that the identification of the problem will be reflected in their evaluation for promotion. The matrix structure is designed not only to put forth the best team for accomplishing the objectives, but also to resolve problems. Because the matrix approach encourages the sharing of key people, employees may find that the best corporate resources are now available to assist them temporarily.

Executives and functional managers must encourage people to bring forth problems, especially during matrix implementations. This encouragement should probably be done orally, with personal contact, rather than through memos.

- *Is it true that if we go to a matrix, many of our functional people will start communicating directly with our customers?* When you have a matrix structure, customers are very reluctant to have all information flow from your project office to their project office for fear that your project office is filtering the information. Therefore, the customer may request (or even demand) that his technical people be permitted to talk to your technical people on a one-on-one basis. This should be permitted as long as the customer fully understands that:
  - Functional employees reflect their own personal opinion. Official company position can come only through the project office or through the project sponsor.
  - Functional employees cannot commit to additional work that may be beyond the scope of the contract. Any changes in work must be approved by the project office.

Functionally, employees should contact the project office after each communication and relate to the project office what was discussed. The project office will then consider whether a memo should be written to document the results of the discussion.

The purpose of the question–answer session is to convince the executives that a change might be for the better. With matrix management styles, the following are the most common arguments that executives give for avoiding change:[2]

- Why change?
  - I must be doing something right to get where I am. I may have to start working differently. Can I succeed?
- Balance of power
  - I understand the balance of power and my role within top management. Why change it? I might lose my present power.
- Loss of control
  - I presently generate change on projects and in policy areas. Why change it? I won't be able to control recommended changes.
- Need for contact with projects
  - I will lose my ability to perceive appropriate adjustments in organization policies when I lose detail involvement in projects. Why change it?

---

2. Adapted from John M. Tettemer, "Keeping Your Boss Happy While Implementing Project Management—A Management View," *Proceedings of the Tenth Annual Seminar/Symposium of the Project Management Institute,* Los Angeles, October 8–11, 1978, pp. IA-1 through 1A-4.

- Excessive delegation
  - It is not good practice to have key decisions delegated below the top men. Why change?
- Coordination
  - Coordination responsibility is a key management job. Why delegate it to project managers?

If the executives are willing to accept change, then the next step is to discuss the methods for implementation. The executives must understand the following strategies and tactics for implementation to be effective:

- Top management must delegate authority and responsibility to the project manager.
- Top management must delegate total cost control to the project manager.
- Top management must rely on the project manager for total project planning and scheduling.
- Only the project managers must fully understand advanced scheduling techniques such as PERT/CPM. This may require additional training. Functional managers may use other scheduling techniques for resource control.
- Top management must encourage functional managers to resolve problems and conflicts at the lowest organizational levels and not always run "upstairs."
- Top management must not consider functional departments as merely support groups for a project. Functional departments still control the company resources, and, contrary to popular belief, the project managers actually work for the functional managers, not vice versa.
- Top management must provide sufficient training for functional employees on how to report to and interact with multiple project managers.
- Top management must take an interest in how project management should work.
- Top management must not fight among themselves as to who should control the project management function.

The project manager also has strategies and tactics that should be understood during implementation. The following key points should be carefully considered by the project manager:[3]

- Breakthrough project
  - Start with a breakthrough project that the administration can keep pace with in the new project management format.

---

3. Adapted from John M. Tettemer, "Keeping Your Boss Happy While Implementing Project Management—A Management View," *Proceedings of the Tenth Annual Seminar/Symposium of the Project Management Institute,* Los Angeles, October 8–11, 1978, pp. IA-1 through IA-4.

- Traditional information for top management
  - The new project manager must be sure that traditional types of functional and project information are available to top management for traditional problem solving. He should take this information forward voluntarily, ahead of top-management's knowledge of the problem, preferably more quickly than the traditional line of communication.
- Retention of power
  - Allow every administrator to retain his traditional power within the hierarchy during the implementation phase.
- Policy recommendations
  - Project managers should carefully and thoughtfully develop only policy recommendations that can be easily accepted by the administration as being in concert with the organization's goals and objectives, and that are easy to implement and readily accepted by those outside the organization.
- Slow down
  - It is necessary for project managers to push for change but not at a rate that in itself builds opposition.
- Schedules aren't the end of the world
  - Project managers should keep schedules and other tools in the background of their involvement with top management. (The tools of project management are of far less interest to top management than the results obtained through them.)
- Decode all information
  - It is extremely important that project managers decode all their reporting documents to meet the style of the executive with whom they are trying to communicate.
- Use broad perspective
  - Project managers should be sure to recommend as general policy changes only those items that are applicable to a broad range of projects. Exceptions should be clearly indicated as exceptions to meet clearly defined project objectives.

It should be readily apparent from these key points that during implementation the project managers could easily frighten executives to such a degree that all thoughts of matrix implementation will be forgotten.

The last point that should be emphasized is that some executives face "blockages" even after the implementation phase is completed. These executive blockages may be avoided as follows:

- Top management directly interfaces a project only during its idea development and planning phases. Once the project is initiated, the executives should maintain a monitoring perspective via structured feedback from the project manager.
- Top management still establishes corporate direction and must make sure that the project managers fully understand its meaning.

- Top management must try to control environmental factors that may be beyond the control of the project manager. These factors include such items as external communications, joint-venture relationships, providing internal support, and providing environmental ongoing intelligence.
- Top management must have confidence in project managers and must be willing to give them both difficult and easy projects.
- Top management must understand that in order for work to flow horizontally in a company, a "dynamic" organizational structure is necessary. Not all activities can flow in parallel with the main activities of the company.
- Upper-level management must not want to take an active role in this "new" concept called project management.
- Upper-level management must be familiar with its new responsibilities and interface relationships in a project environment.

There is no surefire method today for the successful acceptance and implementation of matrix management. The best approach appears to be an early education process (including questions and answers) whereby executives, project managers, and functional personnel will be willing at least to give the system a chance. This type of early educational approach may be acceptable to all types of companies and in all industries where the matrix is applicable.

PROBLEMS

10–1 Should age have a bearing on how long it takes an executive to accept project management?

10–2 You have been called in by the executive management of a major utility company and asked to give a "selling" speech on why the company should go to project management. What are you going to say? What areas will you stress? What questions would you expect the executives to ask? What fears do you think the executives might have?

10–3 Some executives would prefer to have their project managers become tunnel-vision workaholics, with the project managers falling in love with their jobs and living to work instead of working to live. How do you feel about this?

10–4 Project management is designed to make effective and efficient use of resources. Most companies that adopt project management find it easier to underemploy and schedule overtime than to overemploy and either lay people off or drive up the overhead rate. A major electrical equipment manufacturer contends that with proper utilization of the project management concept, the majority of the employees who leave the company through either termination or retirement do not have to be replaced. Is this rationale reasonable?

10–5 The director of engineering services of R. P. Corporation believes that a project organizational structure of some sort would help resolve several of his problems. As part of the discussion, the director has made the following remarks: "All of our activities (or so-called projects if you wish) are loaded with up-front engineering. We have found in the past that time is the important parameter, not quality control or cost.

Sometimes we rush into projects so fast that we have no choice but to cut corners, and, of course, quality must suffer."

What questions, if any, would you like to ask before recommending a project organizational form? Which form will you recommend?

10–6 How should a project manager react when he finds inefficiency in the functional lines? Should executive management become involved?

10–7 An electrical equipment manufacturing company has just hired you to conduct a three-day seminar on project management for sixty employees. The president of the company asks you to have lunch with him on the first day of the seminar. During lunch, the executive remarks, "I inherited the matrix structure when I took over. Actually I don't think it can work here, and I'm not sure how long I'll support it." How should you continue at this point?

10–8 Should project managers be permitted to establish prerequisites for top management regarding standard company procedures?

10–9 During the implementation of project management, you find that line managers are reluctant to release any information showing utilization of resources in their line function. How should this situation be handled, and by whom?

10–10 Corporate engineering of a large corporation usually assumes control of all plant expansion projects in each of its plants for all projects over $25 million. For each case below, discuss the ramifications of this, assuming that there are several other projects going on in each plant at the same time as the plant expansion project.

   a. The project manager is supplied by corporate engineering and reports to corporate engineering, but all other resources are supplied by the plant manager.
   b. The project manager is supplied by corporate but reports to the plant manager for the duration of the project.
   c. The plant manager supplies the project manager, and the project manager reports "solid" to corporate and "dotted" to the plant manager for the duration of the project.

10–11 An aircraft company requires seven years from initial idea to full production of a military aircraft. Consider the following facts: engineering design requires a minimum of two years of R&D; manufacturing has a passive role during this time; and engineering builds its own prototype during the third year.

   a. To whom in the organization should the program manager, project manager, and project engineering report? Does your answer depend on the life-cycle phase?
   b. Can the project engineers be "solid" to the project manager and still be authorized by the engineering vice president to provide technical direction?
   c. What should be the role of marketing?
   d. Should there be a project sponsor?

10–12 Does a project sponsor have the right to have an in-house representative removed from his company?

10–13 An executive once commented that his company was having trouble managing projects, not because of a lack of tools and techniques, but because they (employees) did not know how to manage what they had. How does this relate to project management?

10–14 Ajax National is the world's largest machine tool equipment manufacturer. Its success is based on the experience of its personnel. The majority of its department managers are forty-five to fifty-five-year-old, nondegreed people who have come up from the ranks. Ajax has just hired several engineers with bachelors' and masters' degrees to control the project management and project engineering functions. Can this pose a problem? Are advanced-degreed people required because of the rapid rate of change of technology?

10–15 When does project management turn into overmanagement?

10–16 *Brainstorming at United Central Bank (Part I):* As part of the 1989 strategic policy plan for United Central Bank, the president, Joseph P. Keith, decided to embark on weekly "brainstorming meetings" in hopes of developing creative ideas that could lead to solutions to the bank's problems. The bank's executive vice president would serve as permanent chairman of the brainstorming committee. Personnel representation would be randomly selected under the constraint that 10 percent must be from division managers, 30 percent from department managers, 30 percent from section-level supervisors, and the remaining 30 percent from clerical and nonexempt personnel. President Keith further decreed that the brainstorming committee would criticize all ideas and submit only those that successfully passed the criticism test to upper-level management for review.

After six months, with only two ideas submitted to upper-level management (both ideas were made by division managers), Joseph Keith formed an inquiry committee to investigate the reasons for the lack of interest by the brainstorming committee participants. Which of the following statements might be found in the inquiry committee report? (More than one answer is possible.)

    a. Because of superior–subordinate relationships (i.e., pecking order), creativity is inhibited.

    b. Criticism and ridicule have a tendency to inhibit spontaneity.

    c. Good managers can become very conservative and unwilling to stick their necks out.

    d. Pecking orders, unless adequately controlled, can inhibit teamwork and problem solving.

    e. All seemingly crazy or unconventional ideas were ridiculed and eventually discarded.

    f. Many lower-level people, who could have had good ideas to contribute, felt inferior.

    g. Meetings were dominated by upper-level management personnel.

    h. The meetings were held at inappropriate places and times.

    i. Many people were not given adequate notification of meeting time and subject matter.

10–17 *Brainstorming at United Central Bank (Part II):* After reading the inquiry committee report, President Keith decided to reassess his thinking about brainstorming by listing the advantages and disadvantages. What are the arguments for and against brainstorming? If you were Joseph Keith, would you vote for or against the continuation of the brainstorming sessions?

10–18 *Brainstorming at United Central Bank (Part III):* President Keith evaluated all of the data and decided to give the brainstorming committee one more chance. What changes can Joseph Keith implement in order to prevent the previous problems from recurring?

10–19 Explain the meaning of the following proverb: "The first 10 percent of the work is accomplished with 90 percent of the budget. The second 90 percent of the work is accomplished with the remaining 10 percent of the budget."

10–20 You are a line manager, and two project managers (each reporting to a divisional vice president) enter your office soliciting resources. Each project manager claims that his project is top priority as assigned by his own vice president. How should you, as the line manager, handle this situation? What are the recommended solutions to keep this situation from recurring repeatedly?

10–21 Figure 10–5 shows the organizational structure for a new Environmental Protection Agency project. Alpha Company was one of three subcontractors chosen for the contract. Because this was a new effort, the project manager reported "dotted" to the board chairman, who was acting as the project sponsor. The vice president was the immediate superior to the project manager.

Because the project manager did not believe that Alpha Company maintained the expertise to do the job, he hired an outside consultant from one of the local colleges. Both the EPA and the prime contractor approved of the consultant, and the consultant's input was excellent.

The project manager's superior, the vice president, disapproved of the consultant, continually arguing that the company had the expertise internally. How should you, the project manager, handle this situation?

10–22 You are the customer for a twelve-month project. You have team meetings scheduled with your subcontractor on a monthly basis. The contract has a contractual

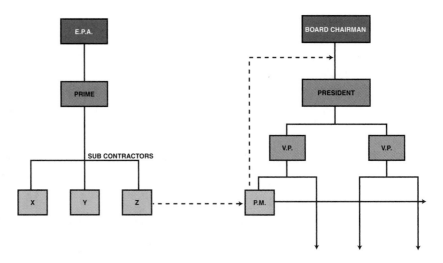

FIGURE 10–5. Organizational chart for EPA project.

requirement to prepare a twenty-five- to thirty-page handout for each team meeting. Are there any benefits for you, the customer, to see these handouts at least three to four days prior to the team meeting?

10–23 You have a work breakdown structure (WBS) that is detailed to level 5. One level-5 work package requires that a technical subcontractor be selected to support one of the technical line organizations. Who should be responsible for customer–contractor communications: the project office or line manager? Does your answer depend on the life-cycle phase? The level of the WBS? Project manager's "faith" in the line manager?

10–24 Should a client have the right to communicate directly to the project staff (i.e., project office) rather than directly to the project manager, or should this be at the discretion of the project manager?

10–25 Your company has assigned one of its vice presidents to function as your project sponsor. Unfortunately, your sponsor refuses to make any critical decisions, always "passing the buck" back to you. What should you do? What are your alternatives and the pros and cons of each? Why might an executive sponsor act in this manner?

CASE STUDIES

THE BLUE SPIDER PROJECT[4]

"This is impossible! Just totally impossible! Ten months ago I was sitting on top of the world. Upper-level management considered me one of the best, if not the best, engineer in the plant. Now look at me! I have bags under my eyes, I haven't slept soundly in the last six months, and here I am, cleaning out my desk. I'm sure glad they gave me back my old job in engineering. I guess I could have saved myself a lot of grief and aggravation had I not accepted the promotion to project manager."

History

Gary Anderson had accepted a position with Parks Corporation right out of college. With a Ph.D. in mechanical engineering, Gary was ready to solve the world's most traumatic problems. At first, Parks Corporation offered Gary little opportunity to do the pure research that he eagerly wanted to undertake. However, things soon changed. Parks grew into a major electronics and structural design corporation during the big boom of the late fifties and early sixties when Department of Defense (DoD) contracts were plentiful.

Parks Corporation grew from a handful of engineers to a major DoD contractor, employing some 6,500 people. During the recession of the late sixties, money became scarce and major layoffs resulted in lowering the employment level to 2,200 employ-

---

4. Copyright © 1978 by Harold Kerzner.

ees. At that time, Parks decided to get out of the R&D business and compete as a low-cost production facility while maintaining an engineering organization solely to support production requirements.

After attempts at virtually every project management organizational structure, Parks Corporation selected the matrix form. Each project had a program manager who reported to the director of program management. Each project also maintained an assistant project manager—normally a project engineer—who reported directly to the project manager and indirectly to the director of engineering. The program manager spent most of his time worrying about cost and time, whereas the assistant program manager worried more about technical performance.

With the poor job market for engineers, Gary and his colleagues began taking coursework toward an MBA degree should the job market deteriorate further.

In 1975, with the upturn in DoD spending, Parks had to change its corporate strategy. Parks had spent the last seven years bidding on the production phase of large programs. But now, with the new evaluation criteria set forth for contract awards, those companies winning the R&D and qualification phases had a definite edge on being awarded the production contract. The production contract was where the big profits could be found. In keeping with this new strategy, Parks began to beef up its R&D engineering staff. By 1978, Parks had increased in size to 2,700 employees. The increase was mostly in engineering. Experienced R&D personnel were difficult to find for the salaries that Parks was offering. Parks was, however, able to lure some employees away from the competitors, but relied mostly upon the younger, inexperienced engineers fresh out of college.

With the adoption of this corporate strategy, Parks Corporation administered a new wage and salary program that included job upgrading. Gary was promoted to senior scientist, responsible for all R&D activities performed in the mechanical engineering department. Gary had distinguished himself as an outstanding production engineer during the past several years, and management felt that his contribution could be extended to R&D as well.

In January 1978, Parks Corporation decided to compete for Phase I of the Blue Spider Project, an R&D effort that, if successful, could lead into a $500 million program spread out over twenty years. The Blue Spider Project was an attempt to improve the structural capabilities of the Spartan missile, a short-range tactical missile used by the Army. The Spartan missile was exhibiting fatigue failure after six years in the field. This was three years less than what the original design specifications called for. The Army wanted new materials that could result in a longer age life for the Spartan missile.

Lord Industries was the prime contractor for the Army's Spartan Program. Parks Corporation would be a subcontractor to Lord if they could successfully bid and win the project. The criteria for subcontractor selection were based not only on low bid, but also on technical expertise as well as management performance on other projects. Park's management felt that they had a distinct advantage over most of the other competitors because they had successfully worked on other projects for Lord Industries.

The Blue Spider Project Kickoff

On November 3, 1977, Henry Gable, the director of engineering, called Gary Anderson into his office.

Henry Gable: "Gary, I've just been notified through the grapevine that Lord will be issuing the RFP for the Blue Spider Project by the end of this month, with a thirty-day response period. I've been waiting a long time for a project like this to come along so that I can experiment with some new ideas that I have. This project is going to be my baby all the way! I want you to head up the proposal team. I think it must be an engineer. I'll make sure that you get a good proposal manager to help you. If we start working now, we can get close to two months of research in before proposal submittal. That will give us a one-month's edge on our competitors."

Gary was pleased to be involved in such an effort. He had absolutely no trouble in getting functional support for the R&D effort necessary to put together a technical proposal. All of the functional managers continually remarked to Gary, "This must be a biggy. The director of engineering has thrown all of his support behind you."

On December 2, the RFP was received. The only trouble area that Gary could see was that the technical specifications stated that all components must be able to operate normally and successfully through a temperature range of −65 °F to 145 °F. Current testing indicated the Parks Corporation's design would not function above 130 °F. An intensive R&D effort was conducted over the next three weeks. Everywhere Gary looked, it appeared that the entire organization was working on his technical proposal.

A week before the final proposal was to be submitted, Gary and Henry Gable met to develop a company position concerning the inability of the preliminary design material to be operated above 130 °F.

Gary Anderson: "Henry, I don't think it is going to be possible to meet specification requirements unless we change our design material or incorporate new materials. Everything I've tried indicates we're in trouble."

Henry Gable: "We're in trouble only if the customer knows about it. Let the proposal state that we expect our design to be operative up to 155 °F. That'll please the customer."

Gary Anderson: "That seems unethical to me. Why don't we just tell them the truth?"

Henry Gable: "The truth doesn't always win proposals. I picked you to head up this effort because I thought that you'd understand. I could have just as easily selected one of our many moral project managers. I'm considering you for program manager after we win the program. If you're going to pull this conscientious crap on me like the other project managers do, I'll find someone else. Look at it this way; later we can convince the customer to change the specifications. After all, we'll be so far downstream that he'll have no choice."

After two solid months of sixteen-hour days, the proposal was submitted. On February 10, 1978, Lord Industries announced that Parks Corporation would be awarded the Blue Spider Project. The contract called for a ten-month effort, negotiated at $2.2 million at a firm-fixed price.

Selecting the Project Manager

Following contract award, Henry Gable called Gary in for a conference.

Henry Gable: "Congratulations, Gary! You did a fine job. The Blue Spider Project has great potential for ongoing business over the next ten years, provided that we perform well during the R&D phase. Obviously you're the most qualified person in the plant to head up the project. How would you feel about a transfer to program management?"

Gary: "I think it would be a real challenge. I could make maximum use of the MBA degree I earned last year. I've always wanted to be in program management."

Henry Gable: "Having several masters' degrees, or even doctorates for that matter, does not guarantee that you'll be a successful project manager. There are three requirements for effective program management: You must be able to communicate both in writing and orally; you must know how to motivate people; and you must be willing to give up your car pool. The last one is extremely important in that program managers must be totally committed and dedicated to the program, regardless of how much time is involved.

"But this is not the reason why I asked you to come here. Going from project engineer to program management is a big step. There are only two places you can go from program management—up the organization or out the door. I know of very, very few engineers that failed in program management and were permitted to return."

Gary: "Why is that? If I'm considered to be the best engineer in the plant, why can't I return to engineering?"

Henry Gable: "Program management is a world of its own. It has its own formal and informal organizational ties. Program managers are outsiders. You'll find out. You might not be able to keep the strong personal ties you now have with your fellow employees. You'll have to force even your best friends to comply with your standards. Program managers can go from program to program, but functional departments remain intact.

"I'm telling you all this for a reason. We've worked well together the past several years. But if I sign the release so that you can work for Grey in program management, you'll be on your own, like hiring into a new company. I've already signed the release. You still have some time to think about it."

Gary: "One thing I don't understand. With all of the good program managers we have here, why am I given this opportunity?"

Henry Gable: "Almost all of our program managers are over forty-five years old. This resulted from our massive layoffs several years ago when we were forced to lay off the younger, inexperienced program managers. You were selected because of your age and because all of our other program managers have worked on only production-type programs. We need someone at the reins who knows R&D. Your counterpart at Lord Industries will be an R&D type. You have to fight fire with fire.

"I have an ulterior reason for wanting you to accept this position. Because of the division of authority between program management and project engineering, I need someone in program management whom I can communicate with concerning R&D work. The program managers we have now are interested only in time and cost. We need a manager who will bend over backwards to get performance also. I think you're that man. You know the commitment we made to Lord when we submitted that proposal. You have to try to achieve that. Remember, this program is my baby. You'll get all the support you need. I'm tied up on another project now. But when it's over, I'll be following your work like a hawk. We'll have to get together occasionally and discuss new techniques.

"Take a day or two to think it over. If you want the position, make an appointment to see Elliot Grey, the director of program management. He'll give you the same speech I did. I'll assign Paul Evans to you as chief project engineer. He's a seasoned veteran and you should have no trouble working with him. He'll give you good advice. He's a good man."

The Work Begins

Gary accepted the new challenge. His first major hurdle occurred in staffing the project. The top priority given to him to bid the program did not follow through for staffing. The survival of Parks Corporation depended on the profits received from the production programs. In keeping with this philosophy Gary found that engineering managers (even his former boss) were reluctant to give up their key people to the Blue Spider Program. However, with a little support from Henry Gable, Gary formed an adequate staff for the program.

Right from the start Gary was worried that the test matrix called out in the technical volume of the proposal would not produce results that could satisfy specifications. Gary had ninety days after go-ahead during which to identify the raw materials that could satisfy specification requirements. Gary and Paul Evans held a meeting to map out their strategy for the first few months.

Gary Anderson: "Well, Paul, we're starting out with our backs against the wall on this one. Any recommendations?"

Paul Evans: "I also have my doubts in the validity of this test matrix. Fortunately, I've been through this before. Gable thinks this is his project and he'll sure as hell try to manipulate us. I have to report to him every morning at 7:30 A.M. with the raw data results of the previous day's testing. He wants to see it before you do. He also stated that he wants to meet with me alone.

"Lord will be the big problem. If the test matrix proves to be a failure, we're going to have to change the scope of effort. Remember, this is an FFP contract. If we change the scope of work and do additional work in the earlier phases of the program, then we should prepare a trade-off analysis to see what we can delete downstream so as to not overrun the budget."

Gary Anderson: "I'm going to let the other project office personnel handle the administrating work. You and I are going to live in the research labs until we get some results. We'll let the other project office personnel run the weekly team meetings."

For the next three weeks Gary and Paul spent virtually twelve hours per day, seven days a week, in the research and development lab. None of the results showed any promise. Gary kept trying to set up a meeting with Henry Gable but always found him unavailable.

During the fourth week, Gary, Paul, and the key functional department managers met to develop an alternate test matrix. The new test matrix looked good. Gary and his team worked frantically to develop a new workable schedule that would not have impact on the second milestone, which was to occur at the end of 180 days. The second milestone was the final acceptance of the raw materials and preparation of production runs of the raw materials to verify that there would be no scale-up differences between lab development and full-scale production.

Gary personally prepared all of the technical handouts for the interchange meeting. After all, he would be the one presenting all of the data. The technical interchange meeting was scheduled for two days. On the first day, Gary presented all of the data, including test results, and the new test matrix. The customer appeared displeased with the progress to date and decided to have its own in-house caucus that evening to go over the material that was presented.

The following morning the customer stated its position: "First of all, Gary, we're quite pleased to have a project manager who has such a command of technology. That's good. But every time we've tried to contact you last month, you were unavailable or had to be paged in the research laboratories. You did an acceptable job presenting the technical data, but the administrative data was presented by your project office personnel. We, at Lord, do not think that you're maintaining the proper balance between your technical and administrative responsibilities. We prefer that you personally give the administrative data and your chief project engineer present the technical data.

"We did not receive any agenda. Our people like to know what will be discussed, and when. We also want a copy of all handouts to be presented at least three days in advance. We need time to scrutinize the data. You can't expect us to walk in here blind and make decisions after seeing the data for ten minutes.

"To be frank, we feel that the data to date are totally unacceptable. If the data do not improve, we will have no choice but to issue a work stoppage order and look for a new contractor. The new test matrix looks good, especially since this is a firm-fixed-price contract. Your company will burden all costs for the additional work. A trade-off with later work may be possible, but this will depend on the results presented at the second design review meeting, ninety days from now.

"We have decided to establish a customer office at Parks to follow your work more closely. Our people feel that monthly meetings are insufficient during R&D activities. We would like our customer representative to have daily verbal meetings with you or your staff. He will then keep us posted. Obviously, we had expected to review much more experimental data than you have given us.

"Many of our top-quality engineers would like to talk directly to your engineering community, without having to continually waste time by having to go through the project office. We must insist on this last point. Remember, your effort may be only $2.2 million, but our total package is $100 million. We have a lot more at stake than you people do. Our engineers do not like to get information that has been filtered by the project office. They want to help you.

"And last, don't forget that you people have a contractual requirement to prepare complete minutes for all interchange meetings. Send us the original for signature before going to publication."

Although Gary was unhappy with the first team meeting, especially with the requests made by Lord Industries, he felt that they had sufficient justification for their comments. Following the team meeting, Gary personally prepared the complete minutes. "This is absurd," thought Gary. "I've wasted almost one entire week doing nothing more than administrative paperwork. Why do we need such detailed minutes? Can't a rough summary suffice? Why is it that customers want everything documented? That's like an indication of fear. We've been completely cooperative with them. There has been no hostility between us. If we've gotten this much paperwork to do now, I hate to imagine what it will be like if we get into trouble."

A New Role

Gary completed and distributed the minutes to the customer as well as to all key team members.

For the next five weeks testing went according to plan, or at least Gary thought that it had. The results were still poor. Gary was so caught up in administrative paperwork that he hadn't found time to visit the research labs in over a month. On a Wednesday morning, Gary entered the lab to observe the morning testing. Upon arriving in the lab, Gary found Paul Evans, Henry Gable, and two technicians testing a new material, JXB-3.

Henry Gable: "Gary, your problems will soon be over. This new material, JXB-3, will permit you to satisfy specification requirements. Paul and I have been testing it for two weeks. We wanted to let you know, but were afraid that if the word leaked out to the customer that we were spending their money for testing materials that were not called out in the program plan, they would probably go crazy and might cancel the contract. Look at these results. They're super!"

Gary Anderson: "Am I supposed to be the one to tell the customer now? This could cause a big wave."

Henry Gable: "There won't be any wave. Just tell them that we did it with our own IR&D funds. That'll please them because they'll think we're spending our own money to support their program."

Before presenting the information to Lord, Gary called a team meeting to present the new data to the project personnel. At the team meeting, one functional manager spoke out: "This is a hell of a way to run a program. I like to be kept informed about everything that's happening here at Parks. How can the project office expect to get support out of the functional departments if we're kept in the dark until the very last minute? My people have been working with the existing materials for the last two months and you're telling us that it was all for nothing. Now you're giving us a material that's so new that we have no information on it whatsoever. We're now going to have to play catch-up, and that's going to cost you plenty."

One week before the 180-day milestone meeting, Gary submitted the handout package to Lord Industries for preliminary review. An hour later the phone rang.

Customer: "We've just read your handout. Where did this new material come from? How come we were not informed that this work was going on? You know, of course, that our customer, the Army, will be at this meeting. How can we explain this to them? We're postponing the review meeting until all of our people have analyzed the data and are prepared to make a decision.

"The purpose of a review or interchange meeting is to exchange information when *both* parties have familiarity with the topic. Normally, we (Lord Industries) require almost weekly interchange meetings with our other customers because we don't trust them. We disregard this policy with Parks Corporation based on past working relationships. But with the new state of developments, you have forced us to revert to our previous position, since we now question Parks Corporation's integrity in communicating with us. At first we believed this was due to an inexperienced program manager. Now, we're not sure."

Gary Anderson: "I wonder if the real reason we have these interchange meetings isn't to show our people that Lord Industries doesn't trust us. You're creating a hell of a lot of work for us, you know."

Customer: "You people put yourself in this position. Now you have to live with it."

Two weeks later Lord reluctantly agreed that the new material offered the greatest promise. Three weeks later the design review meeting was held. The Army was definitely not pleased with the prime contractor's recommendation to put a new untested material into a multimillion-dollar effort.

**The
Communications
Breakdown**

During the week following the design review meeting Gary planned to make the first verification mix in order to establish final specifications for selection of the raw materials. Unfortunately, the manufacturing plans were a week behind schedule, primarily because of Gary, since he had decided to reduce costs by accepting the responsibility for developing the bill of materials himself.

A meeting was called by Gary to consider rescheduling of the mix.

Gary Anderson: "As you know we're about a week to ten days behind schedule. We'll have to reschedule the verification mix for late next week."

Production Manager: "Our resources are committed until a month from now. You can't expect to simply call a meeting and have everything reshuffled for the Blue Spider Program. We should have been notified earlier. Engineering has the responsibility for preparing the bill of materials. Why aren't they ready?"

Engineering Integration: "We were never asked to prepare the bill of materials. But I'm sure that we could get it out if we work our people overtime for the next two days."

Gary: "When can we remake the mix?"

Production Manager: "We have to redo at least 500 sheets of paper every time we reschedule mixes. Not only that, we have to reschedule people on all three shifts. If we are to reschedule your mix, it will have to be performed on overtime. That's going to increase your costs. If that's agreeable with you, we'll try it. But this will be the first and last time that production will bail you out. There are procedures that have to be followed."

Testing Engineer: "I've been coming to these meetings since we kicked off this program. I think I speak for the entire engineering division when I say that the role that the director of engineering is playing in this program is suppressing individuality among our highly competent personnel. In new projects, especially those involving R&D, our people are not apt to stick their necks out. Now our people are becoming ostriches. If they're impeded from contributing, even in their own slight way, then you'll probably lose them before the project gets completed. Right now I feel that I'm wasting my time here. All I need are minutes of the team meetings and I'll be happy. Then I won't have to come to these pretend meetings anymore."

The purpose of the verification mix was to make a full-scale production run of the material to verify that there would be no material property changes in scale-up from the small mixes made in the R&D laboratories. After testing, it became obvious that the wrong lots of raw materials were used in the production verification mix.

A meeting was called by Lord Industries for an explanation of why the mistake had occurred and what the alternatives were.

Lord: "Why did the problem occur?"

Gary: "Well, we had a problem with the bill of materials. The result was that the mix had to be made on overtime. And when you work people on overtime, you have to be willing to accept mistakes as being a way of life. The energy cycles of our people are slow during the overtime hours."

Lord: "The ultimate responsibility has to be with you, the program manager. We, at Lord, think that you're spending too much time doing and not enough time managing.

As the prime contractor, we have a hell of a lot more at stake than you do. From now on we want documented weekly technical interchange meetings and closer interaction by our quality control section with yours."

Gary: "These additional team meetings are going to tie up our key people. I can't spare people to prepare handouts for weekly meetings with your people."

Lord: "Team meetings are a management responsibility. If Parks does not want the Blue Spider Program, I'm sure we can find another subcontractor. All you (Gary) have to do is give up taking the material vendors to lunch and you'll have plenty of time for handout preparation."

Gary left the meeting feeling as though he had just gotten raked over the coals. For the next two months, Gary worked sixteen hours a day, almost every day. Gary did not want to burden his staff with the responsibility of the handouts, so he began preparing them himself. He could have hired additional staff, but with such a tight budget, and having to remake verification mix, cost overruns appeared inevitable.

As the end of the seventh month approached, Gary was feeling pressure from within Parks Corporation. The decision-making process appeared to be slowing down and Gary found it more and more difficult to motivate his people. In fact, the grapevine was referring to the Blue Spider Project as a loser, and some of his key people acted as though they were on a sinking ship.

By the time the eighth month rolled around, the budget had nearly been expended. Gary was tired of doing everything himself. "Perhaps I should have stayed an engineer," thought Gary. Elliot Grey and Gary Anderson had a meeting to see what could be salvaged. Grey agreed to get Gary additional corporate funding to complete the project. "But performance must be met, since there is a lot riding on the Blue Spider Project," asserted Grey. He called a team meeting to identify the program status.

Gary: "It's time to map out our strategy for the remainder of the program. Can engineering and production adhere to the schedule that I have laid out beforeyou?"

Team Member: Engineering: "This is the first time that I've seen this schedule. You can't expect me to make a decision in the next ten minutes and commit the resources of my department. We're getting a little unhappy being kept in the dark until the last minute. What happened to effective planning?"

Gary: "We still have effective planning. We must adhere to the original schedule, or at least try to adhere to it. This revised schedule will do that."

Team Member: Engineering: "Look, Gary! When a project gets in trouble it is usually the functional departments that come to the rescue. But if we're kept in the dark, then how can you expect us to come to your rescue? My boss wants to know, well in advance, every decision that you're contemplating with regard to our departmental resources. Right now, we . . . "

Gary: "Granted, we may have had a communications problem. But now we're in trouble and have to unite forces. What is your impression as to whether your department can meet the new schedule?"

Team Member: Engineering: "When the Blue Spider Program first got in trouble, my boss exercised his authority to make all departmental decisions regarding the program himself. I'm just a puppet. I have to check with him on everything."

Team Member: Production: "I'm in the same boat, Gary. You know we're not happy having to reschedule our facilities and people. We went through this once before. I also have to check with my boss before giving you an answer about the new schedule."

The following week the verification mix was made. Testing proceeded according to the revised schedule, and it looked as though the total schedule milestones could be met, provided that specifications could be adhered to.

Because of the revised schedule, some of the testing had to be performed on holidays. Gary wasn't pleased with asking people to work on Sundays and holidays, but he had no choice, since the test matrix called for testing to be accomplished at specific times after end-of-mix.

A team meeting was called on Wednesday to resolve the problem of who would work on the holiday, which would occur on Friday, as well as staffing Saturday and Sunday. During the team meeting Gary became quite disappointed. Phil Rodgers, who had been Gary's test engineer since the project started, was assigned to a new project that the grapevine called Gable's new adventure. His replacement was a relatively new man, only eight months with the company. For an hour and a half, the team members argued about the little problems and continually avoided the major question, stating that they would first have to coordinate commitments with their bosses. It was obvious to Gary that his team members were afraid to make major decisions and therefore "ate up" a lot of time on trivial problems.

On the following day, Thursday, Gary went to see the department manager responsible for testing, in hopes that he could use Phil Rodgers this weekend.

Department Manager: "I have specific instructions from the boss (director of engineering) to use Phil Rodgers on the new project. You'll have to see the boss if you want him back."

Gary Anderson: "But we have testing that must be accomplished this weekend. Where's the new man you assigned yesterday?"

Department Manager: "Nobody told me you had testing scheduled for this weekend. Half of my department is already on an extended weekend vacation, including Phil Rodgers and the new man. How come I'm always the last to know when we have a problem?"

Gary Anderson: "The customer is flying down his best people to observe this weekend's tests. It's too late to change anything. You and I can do the testing."

Department Manager: "Not on your life. I'm staying as far away as possible from the Blue Spider Project. I'll get you someone, but it won't be me. That's for sure!"

The weekend's testing went according to schedule. The raw data were made available to the customer under the stipulation that the final company position would be announced at the end of the next month, after the functional departments had a chance to analyze it.

Final testing was completed during the second week of the ninth month. The initial results looked excellent. The materials were within contract specifications, and although they were new, both Gary and Lord's management felt that there would be little difficulty in convincing the Army that this was the way to go. Henry Gable visited Gary and congratulated him on a job well done.

All that now remained was the making of four additional full-scale verification mixes in order to determine how much deviation there would be in material properties between full-sized production-run mixes. Gary tried to get the customer to concur (as part of the original trade-off analysis) that two of the four production runs could be deleted. Lord's management refused, insisting that contractual requirements must be met at the expense of the contractor.

The following week, Elliot Grey called Gary in for an emergency meeting concerning expenditures to date.

Elliot Grey: "Gary, I just received a copy of the financial planning report for last quarter in which you stated that both the cost and performance of the Blue Spider Project were 75 percent complete. I don't think you realize what you've done. The target profit on the program was $200,000. Your memo authorized the vice president and general manager to book 75 percent of that, or $150,000, for corporate profit spending for stockholders. I was planning on using all $200,000 together with the additional $300,000 I personally requested from corporate headquarters to bail you out. Now I have to go back to the vice president and general manager and tell them that we've made a mistake and that we'll need an additional $150,000."

Gary Anderson: "Perhaps I should go with you and explain my error. Obviously, I take all responsibility."

Elliot Grey: "No, Gary. It's our error, not yours. I really don't think you want to be around the general manager when he sees red at the bottom of the page. It takes an act of God to get money back once corporate books it as profit. Perhaps you should reconsider project engineering as a career instead of program management. Your performance hasn't exactly been sparkling, you know."

Gary returned to his office quite disappointed. No matter how hard he worked, the bureaucratic red tape of project management seemed always to do him in. But late that afternoon, Gary's disposition improved. Lord Industries called to say that, after consultation with the Army, Parks Corporation would be awarded a sole-source contract for qualification and production of Spartan missile components using the new longer-life raw materials. Both Lord and the Army felt that the sole-source contract was justified, provided that continued testing showed the same results, since Parks Corporation had all of the technical experience with the new materials.

Gary received a letter of congratulations from corporate headquarters, but no additional pay increase. The grapevine said that a substantial bonus was given to the director of engineering.

During the tenth month, results were coming back from the accelerated aging tests performed on the new materials. The results indicated that although the new materials would meet specifications, the age life would probably be less than five years. These numbers came as a shock to Gary. Gary and Paul Evans had a conference to determine the best strategy to follow.

Gary Anderson: "Well, I guess we're now in the fire instead of the frying pan. Obviously, we can't tell Lord Industries about these tests. We ran them on our own. Could the results be wrong?"

Paul Evans: "Sure, but I doubt it. There's always margin for error when you perform accelerated aging tests on new materials. There can be reactions taking place that we know nothing about. Furthermore, the accelerated aging tests may not even correlate well with actual aging. We must form a company position on this as soon as possible."

Gary Anderson: "I'm not going to tell anyone about this, especially Henry Gable. You and I will handle this. It will be my throat if word of this leaks out. Let's wait until we have the production contract in hand."

Paul Evans: "That's dangerous. This has to be a company position, not a project office position. We had better let them know upstairs."

Gary Anderson: "I can't do that. I'll take all responsibility. Are you with me on this?"

Paul Evans: "I'll go along. I'm sure I can find employment elsewhere when we open Pandora's box. You had better tell the department managers to be quiet also."

Two weeks later, as the program was winding down into the testing for the final verification mix and final report development, Gary received an urgent phone call asking him to report immediately to Henry Gable's office.

Henry Gable: "When this project is over, you're through. You'll never hack it as a program manager, or possibly a good project engineer. We can't run projects around here without honesty and open communications. How the hell do you expect top management to support you when you start censoring bad news to the top? I don't like surprises. I like to get the bad news from the program manager and project engineers, not secondhand from the customer. And of course, we cannot forget the cost overrun. Why didn't you take some precautionary measures?"

Gary Anderson: "How could I when you were asking our people to do work such as accelerated aging tests that would be charged to my project and was not part of program plan? I don't think I'm totally to blame for what's happened."

Henry Gable: "Gary, I don't think it's necessary to argue the point any further. I'm willing to give you back your old job, in engineering. I hope you didn't lose too many friends while working in program management. Finish up final testing and the program report. Then I'll reassign you."

Gary returned to his office and put his feet up on the desk. "Well," thought Gary, "perhaps I'm better off in engineering. At least I can see my wife and kids once in a while." As Gary began writing the final report, the phone rang:

Functional Manager: "Hello, Gary. I just thought I'd call to find out what charge number you want us to use for experimenting with this new procedure to determine accelerated age life."

Gary Anderson: "Don't call me! Call Gable. After all, the Blue Spider Project is his baby."

GREYSON CORPORATION

Greyson Corporation was formed in 1940 by three scientists from the University of California. The major purpose of the company was research and development for advanced military weaponry. Following World War II, Greyson became a leader in the field of Research and Development. By the mid-1950s, Greyson employed over 200 scientists and engineers.

The fact that Greyson handled only R&D contracts was advantageous. First of all, all of the scientists and engineers were dedicated to R&D activities, not having to share their loyalties with production programs. Second, a strong functional organization was established. The project management function was the responsibility of the functional manager whose department would perform the majority of the work. Working relationships between departments were excellent.

By the late fifties Greyson was under new management. Almost all R&D programs called for establishment of qualification and production planning as well. As a result, Greyson decided to enter into the production of military weapons as well, and capture some of the windfall profits of the production market. This required a major reorganization from a functional to a matrix structure. Personnel problems occurred, but none that proved major catastrophes.

In 1964 Greyson entered into the aerospace market with the acquisition of a subcontract for the propulsion unit of the Hercules missile. The contract was projected at $200 million over a five-year period, with excellent possibilities for follow-on work. Between 1964 and 1968 Greyson developed a competent technical staff composed mainly of young, untested college graduates. The majority of the original employees who were still there were in managerial positions. Greyson never had any layoffs. In addition, Greyson had excellent career development programs for almost all employees.

Between 1967 and 1971 the Department of Defense procurement for new weapons systems was on the decline. Greyson relied heavily on their two major production programs, Hercules and Condor II, both of which gave great promise for continued procurement. Greyson also had some thirty smaller R&D contracts as well as two smaller production contracts for hand weapons.

Because R&D money was becoming scarce, Greyson's management decided to phase out many of the R&D activities and replace them with lucrative production contracts. Greyson believed that they could compete with anyone in regard to low-cost production. Under this philosophy, the R&D community was reduced to minimum levels necessary to support in-house activities. The director of engineering froze all hiring except for job-shoppers with special talents. All nonessential engineering personnel were transferred to production units.

In 1972, Greyson entered into competition with Cameron Aerospace Corporation for development, qualification, and testing of the Navy's new Neptune missile. The competition was an eight-motor shoot-off during the last ten months of 1973. Cameron Corporation won the contract owing to technical merit. Greyson Corporation, however, had gained valuable technical information in rocket motor development and testing. The loss of the Neptune Program made it clear to Greyson's management that aerospace technology was changing too fast for Greyson to maintain a passive position. Even though funding was limited, Greyson increased the technical staff and soon found great success in winning research and development contracts.

By 1975, Greyson had developed a solid aerospace business base. Profits had increased by 30 percent. Greyson Corporation expanded from a company with 200 employees in 1964 to 1,800 employees in 1975. The Hercules Program, which began in 1964, was providing yearly follow-on contracts. All indications projected a continuation of the Hercules Program through 1982.

Cameron Corporation, on the other hand, had found 1975 a difficult year. The Neptune Program was the only major contract that Cameron Corporation maintained.

The current production buy for the Neptune missile was scheduled for completion in August 1975 with no follow-on work earlier than January 1976. Cameron Corporation anticipated that overhead rates would increase sharply prior to next buy. The cost per motor would increase from $55,000 to $75,000 for a January procurement, $85,000 for a March procurement, and $125,000 for an August procurement.

In February 1975, the Navy asked Greyson Corporation if they would be interested in submitting a sole-source bid for production and qualification of the Neptune missile. The Navy considered Cameron's position as uncertain, and wanted to maintain a qualified vendor should Cameron Corporation decide to get out of the aerospace business.

Greyson submitted a bid of $30 million for qualification and testing of thirty Neptune motors over a thirty-month period beginning in January 1976. Current testing of the Neptune missile indicated that the minimum motor age life would extend through January 1979. This meant that production funds over the next thirty months could be diverted toward requalification of a new vendor and still meet production requirements for 1979.

In August 1975, on delivery of the last Neptune rocket to the Navy, Cameron Corporation announced that without an immediate production contract for Neptune follow-on work it would close its doors and get out of the aerospace business. Cameron Corporation invited Greyson Corporation to interview all of their key employees for possible work on the Neptune Requalification Program.

Greyson hired thirty-five of Cameron's key people to begin work in October 1975. The key people would be assigned to ongoing Greyson programs to become familiar with Greyson methods. Greyson's lower-level management was very unhappy about bringing in these thirty-five employees for fear that they would be placed in slots that could have resulted in promotions for some of Greyson's people. Management then decreed that these thirty-five people would work solely on the Neptune Program, and other vacancies would be filled, as required, from the Hercules and Condor II programs. Greyson estimated that the cost of employing these thirty-five people was approximately $150,000 per month, almost all of which was being absorbed through overhead. Without these thirty-five people, Greyson did not believe that they would have won the contract as sole-source procurement. Other competitors could have "grabbed" these key people and forced an open-bidding situation.

Because of the increased overhead rate, Greyson maintained a minimum staff to prepare for contract negotiations and document preparation. To minimize costs, the directors of engineering and program management gave the Neptune program office the authority to make decisions for departments and divisions that were without representation in the program office. Top management had complete confidence in the program office personnel because of their past performances on other programs and years of experience.

In December 1975, the Department of Defense announced that spending was being curtailed sharply and that funding limitations made it impossible to begin the qualification program before July 1976. To make matters worse, consideration was being made for a compression of the requalification program to twenty-five motors in a twenty-month period. However, long-lead funding for raw materials would be available.

After lengthy consideration, Greyson decided to maintain its present position and retain the thirty-five Cameron employees by assigning them to in-house programs. The Neptune program office was still maintained for preparations to support contract negotiations, rescheduling of activities for a shorter program, and long-lead procurement.

In May 1976, contract negotiations began between the Navy and Greyson. At the beginning of contract negotiations, the Navy stated the three key elements for negotiations:

1. Maximum funding was limited to the 1975 quote for a thirty-motor/thirty-month program.
2. The amount of money available for the last six months of 1976 was limited to $3.7 million.
3. The contract would be cost plus incentive fee (CPIF).

After three weeks of negotiations there appeared a stalemate. The Navy contended that the production man-hours in the proposal were at the wrong level on the learning curves. It was further argued that Greyson should be a lot "smarter" now because of the thirty-five Cameron employees and because of experience learned during the 1971 shoot-off with Cameron Corporation during the initial stages of the Neptune Program.

Since the negotiation teams could not agree, top-level management of the Navy and Greyson Corporation met to iron out the differences. An agreement was finally reached on a figure of $28.5 million. This was $1.5 million below Greyson's original estimate to do the work. Management, however, felt that, by "tightening our belts," the work could be accomplished within budget.

The program began on July 1, 1976, with the distribution of the department budgets by the program office. Almost all of the department managers were furious. Not only were the budgets below their original estimates, but the thirty-five Cameron employees were earning salaries above the department mean salary, thus reducing total man-hours even further. Almost all department managers asserted that cost overruns would be the responsibility of the program office and not the individual departments.

By November 1976, Greyson was in trouble. The Neptune Program was on target for cost but 35 percent behind for work completion. Department managers refused to take responsibility for certain tasks that were usually considered to be joint department responsibilities. Poor communication between program office and department managers provided additional discouragement. Department managers refused to have their employees work on Sunday.

Even with all this, program management felt that catch-up was still possible. The thirty-five former Cameron employees were performing commendable work equal to their counterparts on other programs. Management considered that the potential cost overrun situation was not in the critical stage, and that more time should be permitted before considering corporate funding.

In December 1976, the Department of Defense announced that there would be no further buys of the Hercules missile. This announcement was a severe blow to Greyson's management. Not only were they in danger of having to lay off 500 employees, but overhead rates would rise considerably. There was an indication last year that there would be no further buys, but management did not consider the indications positive enough to require corporate strategy changes.

Although Greyson was not unionized, there was a possibility of a massive strike if Greyson career employees were not given seniority over the thirty-five former Cameron employees in the case of layoffs.

By February 1977, the cost situation was clear:

1. The higher overhead rates threatened to increase total program costs by $1 million on the Neptune Program.

2. Because the activities were behind schedule, the catch-up phases would have to be made in a higher salary and overhead rate quarter, thus increasing total costs further.
3. Inventory costs were increasing. Items purchased during long-lead funding were approaching shelf-life limits. Cost impact might be as high as $1 million.

The vice president and general manager considered the Neptune Program critical to the success and survival of Greyson Corporation. The directors and division heads were ordered to take charge of the program. The following options were considered:

1. Perform overtime work to get back on schedule.
2. Delay program activities in hopes that the Navy can come up with additional funding.
3. Review current material specifications in order to increase material shelf life, thus lowering inventory and procurement costs.
4. Begin laying off noncritical employees.
5. Purchase additional tooling and equipment (at corporate expense) so that schedule requirements can be met on target.

On March 1, 1977, Greyson gave merit salary increases to the key employees on all in-house programs. At the same time, Greyson laid off 700 employees, some of whom were seasoned veterans. By March 15, Greyson employees formed a union and went out on strike.

CORWIN CORPORATION

By June 1983, Corwin Corporation had grown into a $150 million per year corporation with an international reputation for manufacturing low-cost, high-quality rubber components. Corwin maintained more than a dozen different product lines, all of which were sold as off-the-shelf items in department stores, hardware stores, and automotive parts distributors. The name "Corwin" was now synonymous with "quality." This provided management with the luxury of having products that maintained extremely long life cycles.

Organizationally, Corwin had maintained the same structure for more than fifteen years (see Exhibit 10–1). The top management of Corwin Corporation was highly conservative and believed in a marketing approach to find new markets for existing product lines rather than to explore for new products. Under this philosophy, Corwin maintained a small R&D group whose mission was simply to evaluate state-of-the-art technology and its application to existing product lines.

Corwin's reputation was so good that they continually received inquiries about the manufacturing of specialty products. Unfortunately, the conservative nature of Corwin's management created a "do not rock the boat" atmosphere opposed to taking any type of risks. A management policy was established to evaluate all specialty-product requests. The policy required answering the following questions:

● Will the specialty product provide the same profit margin (20 percent) as existing product lines?

Exhibit 10–1. Organizational Chart for Corwin Corporation

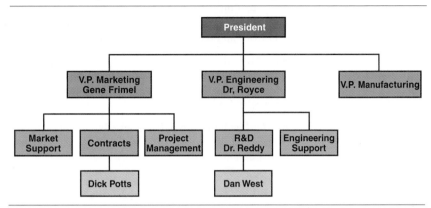

- What is the total projected profitability to the company in terms of follow-on contracts?
- Can the specialty product be developed into a product line?
- Can the specialty product be produced with minimum disruption to existing product lines and manufacturing operations?

These stringent requirements forced Corwin to no-bid more than 90 percent of all specialty-product inquiries.

Corwin Corporation was a marketing-driven organization, although manufacturing often had different ideas. Almost all decisions were made by marketing with the exception of product pricing and estimating, which was a joint undertaking between manufacturing and marketing. Engineering was considered as merely a support group to marketing and manufacturing.

For specialty products, the project managers would always come out of marketing even during the R&D phase of development. The company's approach was that if the specialty product should mature into a full product line, then there should be a product line manager assigned right at the onset.

The Peters Company Project

In 1980, Corwin accepted a specialty-product assignment from Peters Company because of the potential for follow-on work. In 1981 and 1982, and again in 1983, profitable follow-on contracts were received, and a good working relationship developed, despite Peter's reputation for being a difficult customer to work with.

On December 7, 1982, Gene Frimel, the vice president of marketing at Corwin, received a rather unusual phone call from Dr. Frank Delia, the marketing vice president at Peters Company.

Delia: "Gene, I have a rather strange problem on my hands. Our R&D group has $250,000 committed for research toward development of a new rubber product material, and we simply do not have the available personnel or talent to undertake the project. We have to go outside. We'd like your company to do the work. Our testing and R&D facilities are already overburdened."

Frimel: "Well, as you know, Frank, we are not a research group even though we've done this once before for you. And furthermore, I would never be able to sell our management on such an undertaking. Let some other company do the R&D work and then we'll take over on the production end."

Delia: "Let me explain our position on this. We've been burned several times in the past. Projects like this generate several patents, and the R&D company almost always requires that our contracts give them royalties or first refusal for manufacturing rights."

Frimel: "I understand your problem, but it's not within our capabilities. This project, if undertaken, could disrupt parts of our organization. We're already operating lean in engineering."

Delia: "Look, Gene! The bottom line is this: We have complete confidence in your manufacturing ability to such a point that we're willing to commit to a five-year production contract if the product can be developed. That makes it extremely profitable for you."

Frimel: "You've just gotten me interested. What additional details can you give me?"

Delia: "All I can give you is a rough set of performance specifications that we'd like to meet. Obviously, some trade-offs are possible."

Frimel: "When can you get the specification sheet to me?"

Delia: "You'll have it tomorrow morning. I'll ship it overnight express."

Frimel: "Good! I'll have my people look at it, but we won't be able to get you an answer until after the first of the year. As you know, our plant is closed down for the last two weeks in December, and most of our people have already left for extended vacations."

Delia: "That's not acceptable! My management wants a signed, sealed, and delivered contract by the end of this month. If this is not done, corporate will reduce our budget for 1983 by $250,000, thinking that we've bitten off more than we can chew. Actually, I need your answer within forty-eight hours so that I'll have some time to find another source."

Frimel: "You know, Frank, today is December 7, Pearl Harbor Day. Why do I feel as though the sky is about to fall in?"

Delia: "Don't worry, Gene! I'm not going to drop any bombs on you. Just remember, all that we have available is $250,000, and the contract must be a firm-fixed-price effort. We anticipate a six-month project with $125,000 paid on contract signing and the balance at project termination."

Frimel: "I still have that ominous feeling, but I'll talk to my people. You'll hear from us with a go or no-go decision within forty-eight hours. I'm scheduled to go on a cruise in the Caribbean, and my wife and I are leaving this evening. One of my people will get back to you on this matter."

Gene Frimel had a problem. All bid and no-bid decisions were made by a four-man committee composed of the president and the three vice presidents. The president and the vice president for manufacturing were on vacation. Frimel met with Dr. Royce, the vice president of engineering, and explained the situation.

Royce: "You know, Gene, I totally support projects like this because it would help our technical people grow intellectually. Unfortunately, my vote never appears to carry any weight."

Frimel: "The profitability potential as well as the development of good customer relations makes this attractive, but I'm not sure we want to accept such a risk. A failure could easily destroy our good working relationship with Peters Company."

Royce: "I'd have to look at the specification sheets before assessing the risks, but I would like to give it a shot."

Frimel: "I'll try to reach our president by phone."

By late afternoon, Frimel was fortunate enough to be able to contact the president and received a reluctant authorization to proceed. The problem now was how to prepare a proposal within the next two or three days and be prepared to make an oral presentation to Peters Company.

Frimel: "The Boss gave his blessing, Royce, and the ball is in your hands. I'm leaving for vacation, and you'll have total responsibility for the proposal and presentation. Delia wants the presentation this weekend. You should have his specification sheets tomorrow morning."

Royce: "Our R&D director, Dr. Reddy, left for vacation this morning. I wish he were here to help me price out the work and select the project manager. I assume that, in this case, the project manager will come out of engineering rather than marketing."

Frimel: "Yes, I agree. Marketing should not have any role in this effort. It's your baby all the way. And as for the pricing effort, you know our bid will be for $250,000. Just work backwards to justify the numbers. I'll assign one of our contracting people to assist you in the pricing. I hope I can find someone who has experience in this type of effort. I'll call Delia and tell him we'll bid it with an unsolicited proposal."

Royce selected Dan West, one of the R&D scientists, to act as the project leader. Royce had severe reservations about doing this without the R&D director, Dr. Reddy, being actively involved. With Reddy on vacation, Royce had to make an immediate decision.

On the following morning, the specification sheets arrived and Royce, West, and Dick Potts, a contracts man, began preparing the proposal. West prepared the direct labor man-hours, and Royce provided the costing data and pricing rates. Potts, being completely unfamiliar with this type of effort, simply acted as an observer and provided legal advice when necessary. Potts allowed Royce to make all decisions even though the contracts man was considered the official representative of the president.

Finally completed two days later, the proposal was actually a ten-page letter that simply contained the cost summaries (see Exhibit 10–2) and the engineering intent. West estimated that *thirty tests* would be required. The test matrix described only the test conditions for the first five tests. The remaining twenty-five test conditions would be determined at a later date, jointly by Peters and Corwin personnel.

Exhibit 10–2. Proposal Cost Summaries

Direct labor and support	$ 30,000
Testing (30 tests at $2,000 each)	60,000
Overhead at 100%	90,000
Materials	30,000
G&A (general and administrative, 10%)	21,000
Total	$231,000
Profit	19,000
Total	$250,000

On Sunday morning, a meeting was held at Peters Company, and the proposal was accepted. Delia gave Royce a letter of intent authorizing Corwin Corporation to begin working on the project immediately. The final contract would not be available for signing until late January, and the letter of intent simply stated that Peters Company would assume all costs until such time that the contract was signed or the effort terminated.

West was truly excited about being selected as the project manager and being able to interface with the customer, a luxury that was usually given only to the marketing personnel. Although Corwin Corporation was closed for two weeks over Christmas, West still went into the office to prepare the project schedules and to identify the support he would need in the other areas, thinking that if he presented this information to management on the first day back to work, they would be convinced that he had everything under control.

The Work Begins . . .

On the first working day in January 1983, a meeting was held with the three vice presidents and Dr. Reddy to discuss the support needed for the project. (West was not in attendance at this meeting, although all participants had a copy of his memo.)

Reddy: "I think we're heading for trouble in accepting this project. I've worked with Peters Company previously on R&D efforts, and they're tough to get along with. West is a good man, but I would never have assigned him as the project leader. His expertise is in managing internal rather than external projects. But, no matter what happens, I'll support West the best I can."

Royce: "You're too pessimistic. You have good people in your group and I'm sure you'll be able to give him the support he needs. I'll try to look in on the project every so often. West will still be reporting to you for this project. Try not to burden him too much with other work. This project is important to the company."

West spent the first few days after vacation soliciting the support that he needed from the other line groups. Many of the other groups were upset that they had not been informed earlier and were unsure as to what support they could provide. West met with Reddy to discuss the final schedules.

Reddy: "Your schedules look pretty good, Dan. I think you have a good grasp on the problem. You won't need very much help from me. I have a lot of work to do on other activities, so I'm just going to be in the background on this project. Just drop me a note every once in a while telling me what's going on. I don't need anything formal. Just a paragraph or two will suffice."

By the end of the third week, all of the raw materials had been purchased, and initial formulations and testing were ready to begin. In addition, the contract was ready for signature. The contract contained a clause specifying that Peters Company had the right to send an in-house representative into Corwin Corporation for the duration of the project. Peters Company informed Corwin that Patrick Ray would be the in-house representative, reporting to Delia, and would assume his responsibilities on or about February 15.

By the time Pat Ray appeared at Corwin Corporation, West had completed the first three tests. The results were not what was expected, but gave promise that Corwin was heading in the right direction. Pat Ray's interpretation of the tests was completely opposite to that of West. Ray thought that Corwin was "way off base," and redirection was needed.

Ray: "Look, Dan! We have only six months to do this effort and we shouldn't waste our time on marginally acceptable data. These are the next five tests I'd like to see performed."

West: "Let me look over your request and review it with my people. That will take a couple of days, and, in the meanwhile, I'm going to run the other two tests as planned."

Ray's arrogant attitude bothered West. However, West decided that the project was too important to "knock heads" with Ray and simply decided to cater to Ray the best he could. This was not exactly the working relationship that West expected to have with the in-house representative.

West reviewed the test data and the new test matrix with engineering personnel, who felt that the test data were inconclusive as yet and preferred to withhold their opinion until the results of the fourth and fifth tests were made available. Although this displeased Ray, he agreed to wait a few more days if it meant getting Corwin Corporation on the right track.

The fourth and fifth tests appeared to be marginally acceptable just as the first three were. Corwin's engineering people analyzed the data and made their recommendations.

West: "Pat, my people feel that we're going in the right direction and that our path has greater promise than your test matrix."

Ray: "As long as we're paying the bills, we're going to have a say in what tests are conducted. Your proposal stated that we would work together in developing the other test conditions. Let's go with my test matrix. I've already reported back to my boss that the first five tests were failures and that we're changing the direction of the project."

West: "I've already purchased $30,000 worth of raw materials. Your matrix uses other materials and will require additional expenditures of $12,000."

Ray: "That's your problem. Perhaps you shouldn't have purchased all of the raw materials until we agreed on the complete test matrix."

During the month of February, West conducted fifteen tests, all under Ray's direction. The tests were scattered over such a wide range that no valid conclusions could be drawn. Ray continued sending reports back to Delia confirming that Corwin was not producing beneficial results and there was no indication that the situation would reverse itself. Delia ordered Ray to take any steps necessary to ensure a successful completion of the project.

Ray and West met again as they had done for each of the past forty-five days to discuss the status and direction of the project.

Ray: "Dan, my boss is putting tremendous pressure on me for results, and thus far I've given him nothing. I'm up for promotion in a couple of months and I can't let this project stand in my way. It's time to completely redirect the project."

West: "Your redirection of the activities is playing havoc with my scheduling. I have people in other departments who just cannot commit to this continual rescheduling. They blame me for not communicating with them when, in fact, I'm embarrassed to."

Ray: "Everybody has their problems. We'll get this problem solved. I spent this morning working with some of your lab people in designing the next fifteen tests. Here are the test conditions."

West: "I certainly would have liked to be involved with this. After all, I thought I was the project manager. Shouldn't I have been at the meeting?"

Ray: "Look, Dan! I really like you, but I'm not sure that you can handle this project. We need some good results immediately, or my neck will be stuck out for the next four months. I don't want that. Just have your lab personnel start on these tests, and we'll get along fine. Also, I'm planning on spending a great deal of time in your lab area. I want to observe the testing personally and talk to your lab personnel."

West: "We've already conducted twenty tests, and you're scheduling another fifteen tests. I priced out only thirty tests in the proposal. We're heading for a cost-overrun condition."

Ray: "Our contract is a firm-fixed-price effort. Therefore, the cost overrun is your problem."

West met with Dr. Reddy to discuss the new direction of the project and potential cost overruns. West brought along a memo projecting the costs through the end of the third month of the project (see Exhibit 10–3).

Dr. Reddy: "I'm already overburdened on other projects and won't be able to help you out. Royce picked you to be the project manager because he felt that you could do the job. Now, don't let him down. Send me a brief memo next month explaining the situation, and I'll see what I can do. Perhaps the situation will correct itself."

During the month of March, the third month of the project, West received almost daily phone calls from the people in the lab stating that Pat Ray was interfering with their job. In fact, one phone call stated that Ray had changed the test conditions from what was agreed on in the latest test matrix. When West confronted Ray on his meddling, Ray asserted that Corwin personnel were very unprofessional in their attitude and that he thought this was being carried down to the testing as well. Furthermore, Ray demanded that one of the functional employees be removed immediately from

Exhibit 10–3. Projected Cost Summary at the End of the Third Month

	Original Proposal Cost Summary for Six-Month Project	Total Project Costs Projected at End of Third Month
Direct labor/support	$ 30,000	$ 15,000
Testing	60,000 (30 tests)	70,000 (35 tests)
Overhead	90,000 (100%)	92,000 (120%)*
Materials	30,000	50,000
G&A	21,000 (10%)	22,700 (10%)
Totals	$231,000	$249,700

*Total engineering overhead was estimated at 100%, whereas the R&D overhead was 120%.

the project because of incompetence. West stated that he would talk to the employee's department manager. Ray, however, felt that this would be useless and said, "Remove him or else!" The functional employee was removed from the project.

By the end of the third month, most Corwin employees were becoming disenchanted with the project and were looking for other assignments. West attributed this to Ray's harassment of the employees. To aggravate the situation even further, Ray met with Royce and Reddy, and demanded that West be removed and a new project manager be assigned.

Royce refused to remove West as project manager, and ordered Reddy to take charge and help West get the project back on track.

Reddy: "You've kept me in the dark concerning this project, West. If you want me to help you, as Royce requested, I'll need all the information tomorrow, especially the cost data. I'll expect you in my office tomorrow morning at 8:00 A.M. I'll bail you out of this mess."

West prepared the projected cost data for the remainder of the work and presented the results to Dr. Reddy (see Exhibit 10–4). Both West and Reddy agreed that the project was now out of control, and severe measures would be required to correct the situation, in addition to more than $250,000 in corporate funding.

Reddy: "Dan, I've called a meeting for 10:00 A.M. with several of our R&D people to completely construct a new test matrix. This is what we should have done right from the start."

West: "Shouldn't we invite Ray to attend this meeting? I'm sure he'd want to be involved in designing the new test matrix."

Reddy: "I'm running this show now, not Ray!! Tell Ray that I'm instituting new policies and procedures for in-house representatives. He's no longer authorized to visit the labs at his own discretion. He must be accompanied by either you or me. If he doesn't like these rules, he can get out. I'm not going to allow that guy to disrupt our organization. We're spending our money now, not his."

West met with Ray and informed him of the new test matrix as well as the new policies and procedures for in-house representatives. Ray was furious over the new

Exhibit 10–4. Estimate of Total Project Completion Costs

Direct labor/support	$ 47,000*
Testing (60 tests)	120,000
Overhead (120%)	200,000
Materials	103,000
G&A	47,000
	$517,000
Peters contract	250,000
Overrun	$267,000

*Includes Dr. Reddy.

turn of events and stated that he was returning to Peters Company for a meeting with Delia.

On the following Monday, Frimel received a letter from Delia stating that Peters Company was officially canceling the contract. The reasons given by Delia were as follows:

1. Corwin had produced absolutely no data that looked promising.
2. Corwin continually changed the direction of the project and did not appear to have a systematic plan of attack.
3. Corwin did not provide a project manager capable of handling such a project.
4. Corwin did not provide sufficient support for the in-house representative.
5. Corwin's top management did not appear to be sincerely interested in the project and did not provide sufficient executive-level support.

Royce and Frimel met to decide on a course of action in order to sustain good working relations with Peters Company. Frimel wrote a strong letter refuting all of the accusations in the Peters letter, but to no avail. Even the fact that Corwin was willing to spend $250,000 of their own funds had no bearing on Delia's decision. The damage was done. Frimel was now thoroughly convinced that a contract should not be accepted on "Pearl Harbor Day."

THE BOEING 767: FROM CONCEPT TO PRODUCTION (A)[5]

Introduction

In August 1981, eleven months before the first scheduled delivery of Boeing's new airplane, the 767, Dean Thornton, the program's vice president-general manager, faced a critical decision. For several years, Boeing had lobbied the Federal Aviation Administration (FAA) for permission to build wide-bodied aircraft with two-, rather than three-person cockpits. Permission had been granted late in July. Unfortunately,

5. Copyright © 1988 by the President and Fellows of Harvard College. Harvard Business School case 688-040. This case was prepared by Janet Simpson, Lee J. Field, and David A. Garvin as the basis for class discussion rather than to illustrate either effective or ineffective handling of an administrative situation. Reprinted by permission of the Harvard Business School.

the 767 had originally been designed with a three-person cockpit, and thirty of those planes were already in various stages of production.

Thornton knew that the planes had to be converted to models with two-person cockpits. But what was the best way to proceed? Should the changes be made in-line, inserting new cockpits into the thirty planes without removing them from the flow of production, or off-line, building the thirty planes with three-person cockpits as originally planned and then retrofitting them with two-person cockpits in a separate rework area? Either way, Thornton knew that a decision had to be made quickly. Promised delivery dates were sacred at Boeing, and the changes in cockpit design might well impose substantial delays.

The Airframe[6] Industry

Commercial aircraft manufacturing was an industry of vast scale and complexity. A typical 767 contained 3.1 million individual parts; federal regulations required that many be documented and traceable. There were eighty-five miles of wiring alone. Manufacturers employed thousands of scientists and engineers to develop new technologies and production systems, and also to attack design problems. Facilities were on a similarly grand scale. Boeing assembled the 747, its largest commercial airplane, in the world's largest building—sixty-two acres under a single roof—with a work force of 28,600 people.

Few companies were able to marshal such massive resources. In 1981 the industry had only three major players: the American manufacturers Boeing and McDonnell Douglas, and the European consortium Airbus. A fourth manufacturer, Lockheed, left the commercial airplane industry in 1981 after its wide-bodied jet, the L-1011, had incurred losses of $2.5 billion. Boeing and McDonnell Douglas were competitors of longstanding; Airbus, on the other hand, made its commercial debut in May 1974. It was not generally regarded as a serious competitive threat until 1978, the date of its first large sale to a U.S. airline. By 1981, Airbus had sold 300 planes to forty-one airlines, and had options for 200 more. It received direct financing and subsidies from the French, Spanish, German, and British governments.

Airframe manufacturing was a business of enormous risks, for in no other industry was so much capital deployed with so much uncertainty. Launching a new plane meant up-front development costs of $1.5–2 billion, lead times of up to four years from go-ahead to first delivery, and the qualification and management of thousands of subcontractors.

Projects of this scale could put a company's entire net worth on the line. For that reason, industry executives were sometimes characterized as "gamblers," sporting participants in a highstakes game. Side bets—actual wagers between manufacturers and airlines regarding airplane performance, features, or delivery dates—occasionally accompanied purchase negotiations. The odds against a successful new product were large. According to one industry expert, in the past thirty years only two new plane programs, the Boeing 707 and 727, actually made money.[7] (According to Boeing, the 737 and 747 programs have also been profitable.) If a new program were successful,

---

6. An airframe is an airplane without engines. Technically, Boeing competed in the airframe industry. In this case, however, the terms airframe, airplane, and aircraft are used interchangeably.

7. John Newhouse, *The Sporty Game* (New York: Alfred A. Knopf, 1982), p. 4.

however, the potential returns were enormous. A successful new plane could lock up its chosen market segment for as long as twenty years, producing sales of $25–45 billion and huge profits. It was also likely to bring great prestige, power, and influence to the company and managers that created it.

Success required a long-term view. Competitive pricing was essential. Pricing practices, however, contributed risks of their own. New plane prices were based not on the cost of producing the first airplane, but on the average cost of 300 to 400 planes, when required labor hours had declined because of learning. This effect, the so-called learning curve, was hardly unique to airframe manufacturing. But small annual volumes and long manufacturing cycles—even during peak periods Boeing planned to build only eight 767s per month—meant that break-even points stretched further into the future in airframe manufacturing than was typical of most other industries, where mass production was the norm.

Manufacturers were therefore anxious to build orders for new planes as quickly as possible. Buyers—primarily the fifty leading airlines around the world—used that knowledge to enhance their bargaining positions, often delaying orders until the last possible moment. Negotiations on price, design modifications, and after-sales parts and service became especially aggressive in the 1970s, when airlines that had been making steady profits began losing large sums of money. Cost savings became a dominant concern. As Richard Ferris, the CEO of United Airlines, remarked: "Don't bug me about interior design or customer preference, just guarantee the seat-mile performance."[8]

The Boeing Company

Boeing was the sales leader of the airframe industry, as well as one of America's leading exporters. It had built more commercial airplanes than any other company in the world. Sales in 1981 were $9.2 billion; of the total, $5.1 billion were ascribed to the Boeing Commercial Airplane Company, the firm's aircraft manufacturing division. Other divisions produced missiles, rockets, helicopters, space equipment, computers, and electronics.

History   The Boeing Company was founded in 1916 by William E. Boeing, the son of a wealthy timber man who had studied engineering at Yale. In its earliest days, the company built military aircraft for use in World War I. It began to prosper in the 1920s and 1930s, when the civil aviation market expanded, primarily because of the demand for mail carrying. At about that time, William Boeing issued a challenge that has remained the company's credo:

> Our job is to keep everlastingly at research and experimentation, to adapt our laboratories to production as soon as possible, and to let no new improvement in flying and flying equipment pass us by.

To meet this challenge, Boeing originally relied on extensive vertical integration. It not only manufactured entire planes itself, but also provided engines through its Pratt & Whitney subsidiary, and bought and flew planes through its United Air Lines

---

8. Seat-mile performance is the cost of operating a plane divided by the product of miles flown and the number of seats available.

subsidiary. A government mandate separated the three entities in 1934. As the costs of developing and producing new aircraft grew ever larger, the company became even more focused. By the late 1970s and early 1980s, Boeing no longer assumed all development costs itself, nor did it fabricate entire airplanes. Instead, it carefully selected partners, some of whom participated on a risk-sharing basis, who were then subcontracted portions of each plane and developed and built parts and subassemblies that Boeing later assembled. The primary exceptions were the nose section and wings, which Boeing continued to build in-house. One manager summarized the situation in the 1970s by saying: "Today Boeing is an assembler who makes wings."

In part, such efforts to limit up-front investment and reduce risks were prompted by Boeing's near disastrous experiences with its first wide-bodied jet, the 747. In 1969, when the company was introducing the 737 as well as the 747, management problems, declining productivity, steep development costs and unanticipated problems with the engine, plus cutbacks in commercial and government orders, produced a severe cash crunch. Boeing was close to bankruptcy. In the next three years, the company's work force fell from 150,000 to 50,000; unemployment in Seattle, Boeing's home base, rose to 14 percent. Eventually, such belt tightening, plus efforts to resolve problems with the 737 and 747 programs, carried the day, and Boeing emerged from the crisis leaner and stronger, but with a renewed sense of the inherent risks of major development programs.

Strategy   Ever since the 707 was introduced in 1955, Boeing had competed by selling families of planes. Each new generation of aircraft was created with several variations in mind, drawing on the same base airframe concept. By 1987 the 747, for example, was being offered in eleven varieties, including the 747-100B (standard), 747-200B (long range), 747F (freighter), and 747C (convertible to either passenger or cargo configurations). Flexible designs with inherent growth potential were essential to this approach. Modifications such as a stretched fuselage to increase capacity had to be accommodated without wholesale revisions in design or the need to start up entirely separate development programs.

A more efficient design and development process was only one benefit of the family of planes concept. There were manufacturing benefits as well. A common family of planes, produced on a common assembly line, ensured that learning was not lost as new models were added. Experience accumulated rapidly, as Thornton observed:

> We're good partly because we build lots of airplanes. And each new plane absorbs everything we have learned from earlier models.

One result of this approach was break-even points that were reached far earlier than they would have been without shared designs.

Other cornerstones of Boeing's strategy were expertise in global marketing, technological leadership, customer support, and production skills. Large centralized facilities were coupled with sophisticated manufacturing systems and tools for project management. The result, according to informed observers, was the industry's low-cost producer. Or as one aerospace analyst summarized the company's reputation: "If someone hired me to rebuild the Great Pyramid, I'd ask . . . Boeing to assemble it."[9]

---

9. John Newhouse, *The Sporty Game* (New York: Alfred A. Knopf, 1982) p. 139.

Culture   Boeing managers believed that the company had a distinct corporate identity. Teamwork was especially valued, as was interfunctional cooperation. According to Dexter Haas, a manager in corporate planning:

> At Boeing, employees are expected to be both competent and capable of working as members of a team. We feel that technically brilliant but uncooperative individuals can do as much harm to a program as cooperative but mediocre team members.

Such concerns were especially acute on new plane programs, which were a prime vehicle for management development. Programs required close cooperation among managers for five to ten years, often under intense time pressures and 60–70 hour work weeks. To make these programs work, Thornton commented, "You don't necessarily select the best people, you select the best team."

Once selected, teams were granted considerable autonomy. But a disciplined decision-making process was expected, as was detailed planning. Both were viewed by managers as characteristic Boeing traits. According to Fred Cerf, director of systems and equipment:

> A part of Boeing's culture is absolute dedication to commitments—from individuals within the company and from suppliers. We expect people to honor their commitments and adhere to plans. We don't regard plans as exercises, but as forecasted events.

Meeting schedules was an especially high priority for managers. A variety of tools, several of them unique to Boeing, were used to develop realistic schedules and monitor them over time. Among them were a Master Phasing Plan, which mapped out the entire development cycle, including critical milestones, for each new plane program; parametric estimating techniques, which estimated costs and established relationships between critical sections of a schedule, such as the time at which engineering drawings were released and the start-up of production, by using historical data drawn from earlier plane programs; and a management visibility system, which was designed to surface problems before they became serious enough to cause delays. Regular communication was encouraged, even if it meant bringing bad news. According to John Schmick, director of planning:

> Early exposure of problems is not a sin at Boeing. We tend not to kill our managers for taking that approach. Here, it's much worse if you bury the problem.

The 767 Program   In 1969, Boeing assembled a New Airplane Program (NAP) study group. Its goal was not to develop a new plane, but to review the company's past experiences with each of its major programs—the 707, 727, 737, and 747—so that problems, such as those incurred by the 737 and 747 programs, would not be repeated. As Neil Standal, a member of the NAP group who later became the 767 program manager, observed:

> We knew that we were going to have another commercial airplane. But we didn't know what, or when, it was going to be. Our objective was to provide lessons for the future, to look at our history and decide what we had done right and what we had done wrong.

This process, called Project Homework, took three years and produced a long list of "lessons learned," as well as a reasonable idea of the costs of developing the next-generation airplane.

Meanwhile, pressures were beginning to mount within Boeing to launch a new airplane program. Salespeople were especially insistent, as T. A. ("T") Wilson, Boeing's chairman, recalled:

> Our salespeople kept saying, "We need a new product." They didn't really care what it was, as long as it was new.

Because the company's last new plane, the 747, had been launched in 1966, there was also concern among the board of directors that Boeing's next generation of leaders was not being trained in the best way possible: by developing a new plane of their own.

In 1973, at Wilson's behest, Boeing initiated a new airplane study, naming it the 7X7 (X stood for development model). Key team members, including J. F. Sutter, the program's first leader, and Dean Thornton, who replaced Sutter after he was promoted to vice president of operations and development, were handpicked by Wilson. The team was given a broad charter: to define and, if approved, to develop, Boeing's next generation airplane.

Program Definition

The first stage of the process, called program definition, extended from May 1973 to December 1977 (see Exhibit 10–5). During this period, Boeing worked the puzzle of market, technology, and cost. Team members projected airline needs into the future to see if there were holes in the market not met by existing planes; considered alternative plane configurations; examined new technologies to see what might be available within the next few years; and estimated, in a preliminary fashion, likely development and production costs.

Market Assessment   Forecasting the airframe market for the 1980s and 1990s was a complex and challenging risk. Market analysts began by talking directly with the major airlines to get their estimates of future needs. That information was then combined with econometric models to generate three forecasts—optimistic, conservative, and expected—for each market segment. Segments were defined by range of travel—short (less than 1,500 nautical miles), medium (1,500–3,000 nautical miles), and long (greater than 3,000 nautical miles)—and all forecasts were based on the following assumptions: continued regulation of the airline industry; continued airline preferences for routes that directly linked pairs of major cities; steadily rising fuel prices; and no new competition from other airframe manufacturers in the medium-range market. Complete forecasts were run annually and readjusted quarterly.

Boeing's expected forecast for 1990 was a total market of $100 billion. The critical medium range segment—the expected target of the new airplane—was estimated at $19 billion. In that segment, Boeing expected to capture 100 percent of domestic sales. Continued production of the 727 would meet most replacement needs, and the 7X7 would be positioned for market growth.

Configuration   While these forecasts were being developed, another group was working on design specifications. After a year or two of study, the basics were de-

Exhibit 10–5. Critical Program Decisions and Reviews

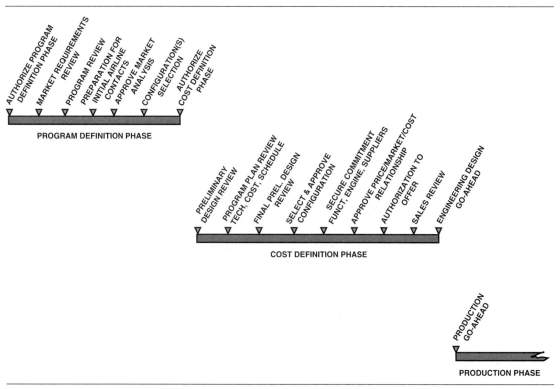

cided. Market research indicated that the new plane should carry approximately 200 passengers; have a one-stop, U.S. transcontinental range; and offer minimal fuel burn. The last requirement was regarded as especially important. With the rise in oil prices that followed the 1973 Arab oil embargo, fuel costs had become an ever-larger portion of airlines' operating expenses. Moreover, airline preferences were changing, as Frank Shrontz, president and CEO, observed:

> In the old days, airlines were infatuated with technology for its own sake. Today the rationale for purchasing a new plane is cost savings and profitability.

Market needs were thus reasonably clear, at least within broad outlines. Designers, however, still faced a number of critical choices. All involved some aspect of the plane's basic shape.

The most vexing question was whether to design the 7X7 with two or three engines. A two-engine version would be lighter and more fuel efficient; a three-engine version would offer greater range. But exactly what were the trade-offs? And how far was engine technology likely to advance in the next few years? Boeing, after all, did not build its own engines, but bought them from one of three manufacturers: General Electric, Pratt & Whitney, and Rolls Royce. Airlines paid separately for airframes and engines; however, they could only choose engines that were offered for the airplane. (This was necessary because Boeing guaranteed the performance of every plane it sold.) Early in the 7X7 program, managers chose to offer engines from both General Electric and Pratt & Whitney, despite the additional time and expense that Boeing would incur. This decision was a direct outgrowth of the company's experiences with the 747. Managers felt that continued competition among engine manufacturers was essential to moderate costs. Equally important, competition was expected to provide a steady stream of improvements in engine technology.

The certification decision proved to be far easier than the choice between a two- and three-engine plane. In fact, for most of the program definition phase, the 7X7 team worked simultaneously on two- and three-engine models. Eventually, fuel efficiency won out—as one manager put it, "in those days, an engineer would shoot his mother-in-law for a tenth of a percent improvement in fuel savings"—and the two-engine version was selected.

Other key configuration decisions involved the wings and tail. Both decisions showed the family of planes concept in action, and the need for designs that were adaptable to future needs. The 7X7 was conceived originally as a medium-range aircraft; however, later additions to the 7X7 family were expected to target longer-range flights. Engineers therefore selected a wing size—3,000 square feet—that was larger than necessary for short- and medium-range flights. It added weight to the basic design, with some loss of fuel efficiency. But the design was highly adaptable: It could be used, without modification, on longer-range versions and stretched models with greater carrying capacity.

Because they were so complex, configuration decisions required the close coordination of marketing, engineering, and production personnel. The airlines were also intimately involved. After a new configuration was developed, Boeing's marketing managers brought it to the airlines, who reviewed, among other things, its flight characteristics, range, cruising speed, interior, cockpit, systems and operating costs. Their reactions were then fed back to designers, and the process was repeated. Haas observed:

> Designing airplanes to best meet the unique requirements of customers is a difficult process. Each airline would prefer that it was designed a bit differently—a little longer, a little shorter, a few more people, a few less. Therefore, the configuration changes constantly.

Technology   Configuration decisions could not be made without assessing the technology that was then available. What was desired by the market might not be possible or economical given the current state of knowledge.

Technology development was an ongoing process at Boeing, and included such areas as structures, flight systems, aircraft systems (hydraulic and electrical), and aerodynamics. Each area had its own chief engineer, who was responsible for overseeing research, development, and application of the technology. The last requirement was regarded as especially critical, as David Norton, chief of technology, pointed out:

> There is nothing that brings me up quicker than thinking of how long we have to live with our decisions. At Boeing, applying a new technology is as important as developing it. We had better be right.

When a new plane was proposed, engineers first reviewed all existing technology projects to see if any were appropriate. They asked three questions of every project:

(1) What is its ultimate value to the customer? (2) Is it an acceptable technological risk? and (3) Can it be incorporated within schedule and cost? Responsibility for answering these questions was divided among the chief engineers of each technology and a chief engineer in charge of the plane program. Line engineers therefore reported through a matrix, and were accountable to two bosses: the chief engineer of their technology and the chief engineer of the program. The former was more concerned with technical questions (e.g., What is the most efficient approach? Will we have a technologically superior product?), while the latter had more practical concerns (e.g., What will the airlines think of the new technology? How will its initial costs compare with the reduced maintenance costs expected over the plane's lifetime? What will be the program's cost and schedule?).

A number of the "new" technologies considered for the 7X7 had, in fact, already been employed elsewhere, primarily on space vehicles. They were therefore regarded as proven, with few technological risks. For example, digital avionics prototype systems in the cockpit, which replaced the traditional analog systems, had originally been developed for the SST program in 1969. Because it offered improved reliability, more accurate flight paths, lower maintenance costs, and the potential for a two-person cockpit, it was incorporated into the 7X7 with little debate.

Decisions involving unproven technologies were considerably more difficult. As Everette Webb, the 7X7's chief engineer, pointed out: "In such cases, deciding what is an acceptable risk is largely a judgment call." Composites provide an example of Boeing's approach.

Composites are complex materials, formed by combining two or more complementary substances. They appeal to airframe manufacturers because they combine great strength with light weight. In the 1960s and 1970s, Boeing engineers conducted a number of laboratory tests on large, composite panels; eventually, they found a promising material, a mixture of graphite and kevlar. Laboratory tests, however, were not regarded as representative of the "real-world airline environment." To gather such data, Boeing worked with a small number of airlines and conducted limited, inservice tests. Boeing fabricated structural parts, such as wing control surfaces or spoiler panels, using composites; had them installed on a plane then in production; and monitored the material's performance as the plane underwent normal airline use. These tests soon indicated a problem with water absorption in environments of high heat and humidity, such as Brazil. A layer of fiberglass was added to the composite panels to solve the problem, and tests continued through the early 1970s. Yet, despite the tests, engineers decided against using composites for the 7X7's primary structure, and recommended instead that they be used only for secondary parts, where the safety risks were lower. Norton explained: "We push technology very hard, but we're conservative about implementation."

Audit Teams   Audit teams were also active during the program definition phase, starting in September 1976. Teams were staffed by experienced Boeing managers, and were assigned to review every significant element of the 7X7 program, including technology, finance, manufacturing, and management. Teams acted as "devil's advocates," and a typical audit took three months. According to Standal:

> In the past, we occasionally used outside consultants as auditors. But we found that, for the most part, we do a better job with our own people. We isolate them organizationally and give them a separate reporting line straight to T. Wilson.

Cost Definition

In September 1977, the 7X7 program was renamed the 767, and in January 1978, the cost definition phase began (see Exhibit 10–5). This shift was a major step: It indicated escalating program commitment and required the authorization of the president of the Boeing Commercial Airplane Company. Approximately $100 million had already been spent on the 7X7; most of it, however, was regarded as part of ongoing research and development. Now the critical decision was at hand: Would Boeing commit to building a new plane and, in the process, incur up-front costs of several billion dollars?

Only the board of directors could make such a decision. First, however, detailed cost estimates were necessary; they, in turn, had to be based on a single configuration. Cost definition forced engineers and marketing managers to stand up and say, "We want to offer *this* airplane." The 767's basic design, including the long-delayed choice between two and three engines, was finally frozen in place in May 1978 (see Exhibit 10–6).

Parametric Estimates   Once the basic design was established, costs could be estimated using a parametric estimating technique. This method, adapted by Boeing, had been developed by the New Airplane Program study group from comparisons of the 707, 727, 737, and 747. It predicted the costs of a new plane from design characteristics, such as weight, speed, and length, and historical relationships, such as the number of parts per airplane, that were known well in advance of production.

The critical calculation involved assembly labor hours. Managers began with data from a benchmark (and profitable) program, the 727, and noted, for every major section of the plane, the number of labor hours per pound required to build the first unit. That number was then multiplied by the expected weight of the same section of the 767; this result, in turn, was multiplied by a factor that reflected Boeing's historical experience in improving the relationship between labor hours and weight as it moved to the next-generation airplane. Totaling the results for all plane sections provided an estimate of the labor hours required to build the first 767. A learning curve was then applied to estimate the number of labor hours required to build subsequent planes.

Engineers believed that the historical relationships underlying these calculations remained valid for long periods. According to Dennis Wilson, manager of scheduling for the 767:

> Unless we drastically change the way we do business, we will be able to use the same parametrics to compare programs. After all, an airplane is an airplane.

Parametric estimates were, however, carefully fine-tuned to account for differences in plane programs. Adjustments could go in either direction. Improved equipment and management control systems, as enforced reduction in engineering change orders, and heavy use of Computer Aided Design and Computer Aided Manufacturing (CAD/CAM) suggested that the 767 would require fewer hours than predicted by parametrics derived from the 727; increased product complexity and a larger variety of customers suggested that more hours would be required. These factors were combined to form a final, adjusted estimate of total assembly hours.

A similar process was used to develop the Master Phasing Plan, which established the program schedule and identified major milestones (see Exhibit 10–7). The

Exhibit 10–6. Airline Configuration

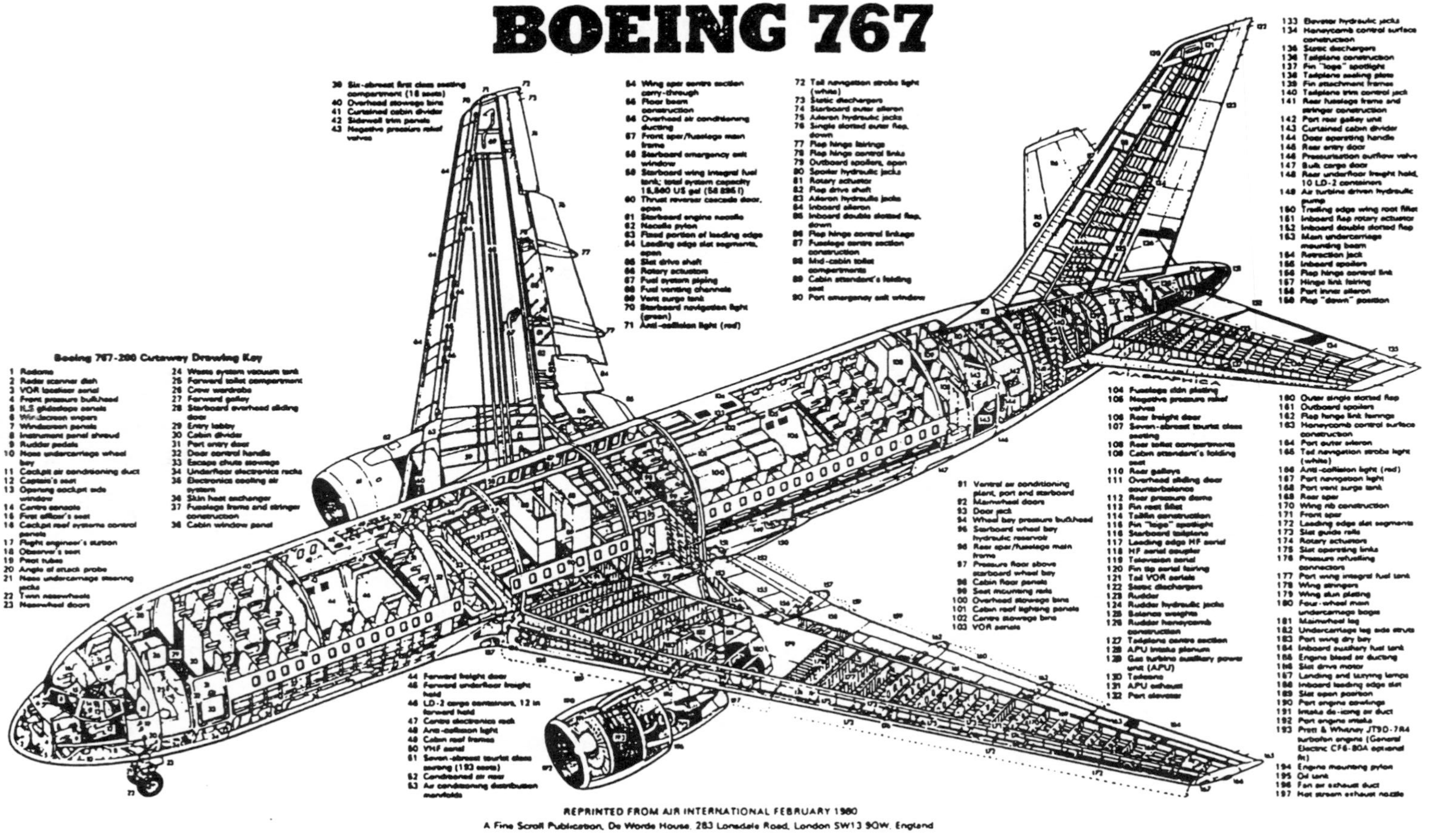

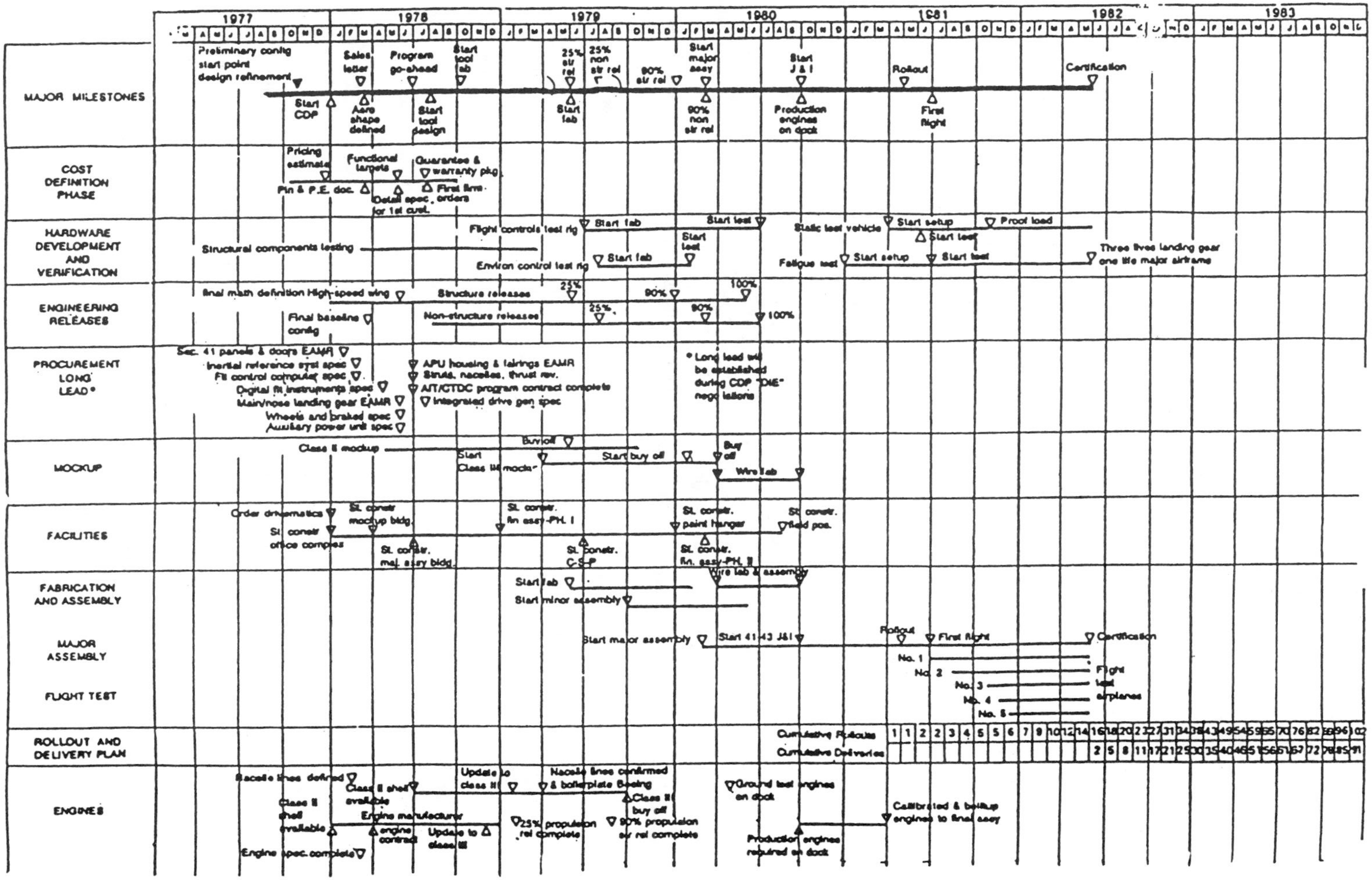

Exhibit 10-7. Program Master Phasing Plan—December 2, 1977—Initial Model

critical task was linking the schedules of interdependent groups, such as engineering and production, to avoid schedule compression or delays. Parametrics were used for that purpose. For example, comparisons of the 727 and 747 programs suggested that, if problems were to be avoided, fabrication should not begin until 25 percent of structural engineering drawings were complete, and that major assembly should not begin until 90 percent of engineering drawings were complete. Such values became the baseline for the 767's Master Phasing Plan. The initial plan was completed in October 1977, and was revised repeatedly as more up-to-date information became available.

The Go/No-Go Decision   In February 1978, Boeing's board of directors was asked to commit to the 767. Prior to that time, Wilson and the 767 team had briefed them, reviewing all aspects of the program. The board agreed to authorize the new plane, but only if two conditions were met: commitments to purchase were received from one foreign and two domestic airlines, and preproduction orders totaled at least 100 planes.

On July 14, 1978, United Airlines placed a $1 billion order for thirty 767s, making it Boeing's first customer. Being the first customer had certain tasks—the offer to sell was conditional, and could be canceled at a later date—but offered advantages as well. Prices were lower, and the first buyer had an opportunity to help shape the plane's final configuration. By November 1978, American and Delta Airlines had also placed orders, bringing the total to eighty planes, with an additional seventy-nine on option. The board then committed Boeing to full production of the 767. The cost definition phase had ended in July 1978; meanwhile, teams began to flesh out the details of supplier and production management.

Supplier Management

A complete 767 consisted of 3.1 million parts, which were supplied by 1,300 vendors. Of these, the most important were the two program participants and four major subcontractors, who built such critical parts as body structures, tail sections, and landing gear. Program participants were, in effect, risk-sharing partners who bore a portion of the costs of design, development, and tooling; major subcontractors were similar, but took on a smaller share of the work. Both were necessary because new airplane programs had become too big for Boeing, or any other single company, to handle alone. On the 767, Aeritalia, the Italian aircraft manufacturer, and the Japan Aircraft Development Company (JADC), a consortium made up of Mitsubishi, Kawasaki, and Fuji Industries, were the two program participants. Both were contracted with in September 1978.

In the late 1960s and 1970s, Aeritalia had worked with Boeing on several proposed airplane designs, including one plane with short-field takeoff and landing capacity. Based on that experience, Aeritalia asked to participate in future work with Boeing. Cerf recalled:

> Boeing honored Aeritalia's request. We decided that they would produce the 767's wing control surfaces and tail, parts which were considered to be significant but which were less critical than body panels to the final assembly line. As it turned out, materials technology advanced in the meantime, and most of the control surface parts were changed from aluminum structure to graphite composites. That helped to make them one of the more complex jobs on the airplane.

JADC, on the other hand, was responsible for the several large body sections. The Japanese participants had been interested in working with Boeing for years and had done progressively more important work on other aircraft. Now, their workmanship was considered exacting enough to meet Boeing standards for the production of major sections of structure.

Technology Transfer Boeing worked closely with all of its subcontractors, from initial planning to final delivery. Cerf observed:

> Generally, at Boeing we do not contract with suppliers and then walk away. We feel responsible for them and *have* to make it work. This was especially true of the 767 program participants. Because the content of their work was so significant, a failure would have precluded our ability to salvage an industrial operation of this size.

To begin, the Italian and Japanese participants were asked to work together with Boeing engineers. Engineering management helped to select the Italian and Japanese engineers who would participate in the 767 program, and rated them according to their skill levels. The Italian and Japanese engineers then worked alongside Boeing engineers in Seattle. At the 25 percent structures release point (a critical milestone, at which point stress analyses had been completed), they returned to their home companies, accompanied by their Boeing engineering counterparts, who were then integrated into the Italian and Japanese engineering organizations. At the same time, in mid-1978, Boeing established residence teams in Italy and Japan, consisting of some of Boeing's best operations people. The operations teams evaluated and helped to establish participants' facilities, training, and manufacturing processes, and also certified their quality assurance processes. If problems arose, rapid communication with Seattle was often necessary; this was assured by a private telephone network connecting Boeing to each participant.

An Example of Supplier Management: The Japanese Transportation Plan
Initially, JADC had argued that transporting body sections from its factories in Japan to Boeing's assembly plant near Seattle would present few problems. Boeing, to be absolutely certain, had insisted that scale models of all sections be built and carried along the proposed route. The parts proved to be too large for Japan's narrow, rural roads; as a result, an old steel factory, located closer to shipping facilities, was converted by one Japanese company to assemble major sections. Another company constructed a final assembly plant located directly on the water. As insurance, Boeing also requested that the body sections be air transportable, and their designs were sized accordingly.

Boeing then put one of its transportation specialists to work with his Japanese counterparts to develop a transportation plan. This effort took several months, as Cerf recalled:

> We went through a major exercise to prove that all of the Japanese companies could support our assembly schedule in Seattle. We brought their representatives to see the complete plan, which covered the walls of a huge meeting room, and worked with them carefully to plan what would be on their shipping docks, what would be on the high seas, and what would be in our plants at any one time.
>
> The level of detail was quite astounding. We kept asking them representative questions, such as "Do you have the right permits and who will get them? What does the

transportation container look like and has it been stressed properly for transport by sea?" Surprisingly, the Japanese didn't object to this process at all. They weren't just cooperative; they were used to working at this level of detail and wanted to learn all we knew.

All of this was a good thing because there was no backup once the decision was made to build the major body sections in Japan. We were committed because our plants at Boeing were working at capacity.

Production Management

Part fabrication began in July 1979, minor (subsection) assembly in April 1980, and major assembly in July 1980. Such long lead times were necessary to meet the planned rollout of the first 767 in August 1981. Flight tests began immediately after rollout, and FAA certification was expected in July 1982.

All 767s were assembled in Everett, Washington, in the same facility used for 747s. Half of the building was devoted to assembly of major subsections; the other half to final assembly. In the final stages of assembly, a line flow process was used, with seven major work stations (see Exhibit 10–8 for a rough sequence of manufacturing operations). Every four days, partially completed planes were moved, using large overhead cranes, from one work station to the next. At each work station, teams of skilled employees positioned a single plane in massive tools and fixtures, and then riveted, wired, and connected parts and pieces.

During the assembly stage, managers faced two critical tasks: maintaining schedule, and ensuring that learning curve goals were met. Both were complicated by a key difference between airframe manufacturing and other industries: the difficulty of managing a large number of engineering change orders. Haas observed:

> An airplane is not something you design, turn over to manufacturing, and then forget. The configuration is constantly changing. So you commit to a schedule, and then incorporate changes and improvements as they come.

This task was especially critical because cost estimates assumed that assembly labor hours would decline predictably over time, following a preset learning curve. Managers therefore had to ensure that learning goals were met at the same time that they were accommodating unanticipated changes.

Scheduling and Change Control   Requests for changes came from internal and external sources. Some, such as the color of carpeting or seating arrangements, were negotiated by airline customers; others, such as parts or wiring changes, were proposed by engineers. In total, the two sources generated 12,000 changes on the first 767.

Managers tracked these changes carefully. Even before the plane's basic design was frozen, all major changes had to be filed using the same formal procedure. This was done to ensure that specifications remained accurate. Once assembly began, a Production Change Board, chaired by the operations department, reviewed all engineering change requests and assessed their likely impact on schedule and cost. If the changes were approved, an implementation plan was then developed. Three general approaches were used: incorporating changes into the normal flow of production; installing old parts as originally planned and then retrofitting new parts off-line, outside the normal flow of production; and expediting changes by assigning additional workers, a process known as "blue streak."

Exhibit 10–8. 767-200 Manufacturing Sequence

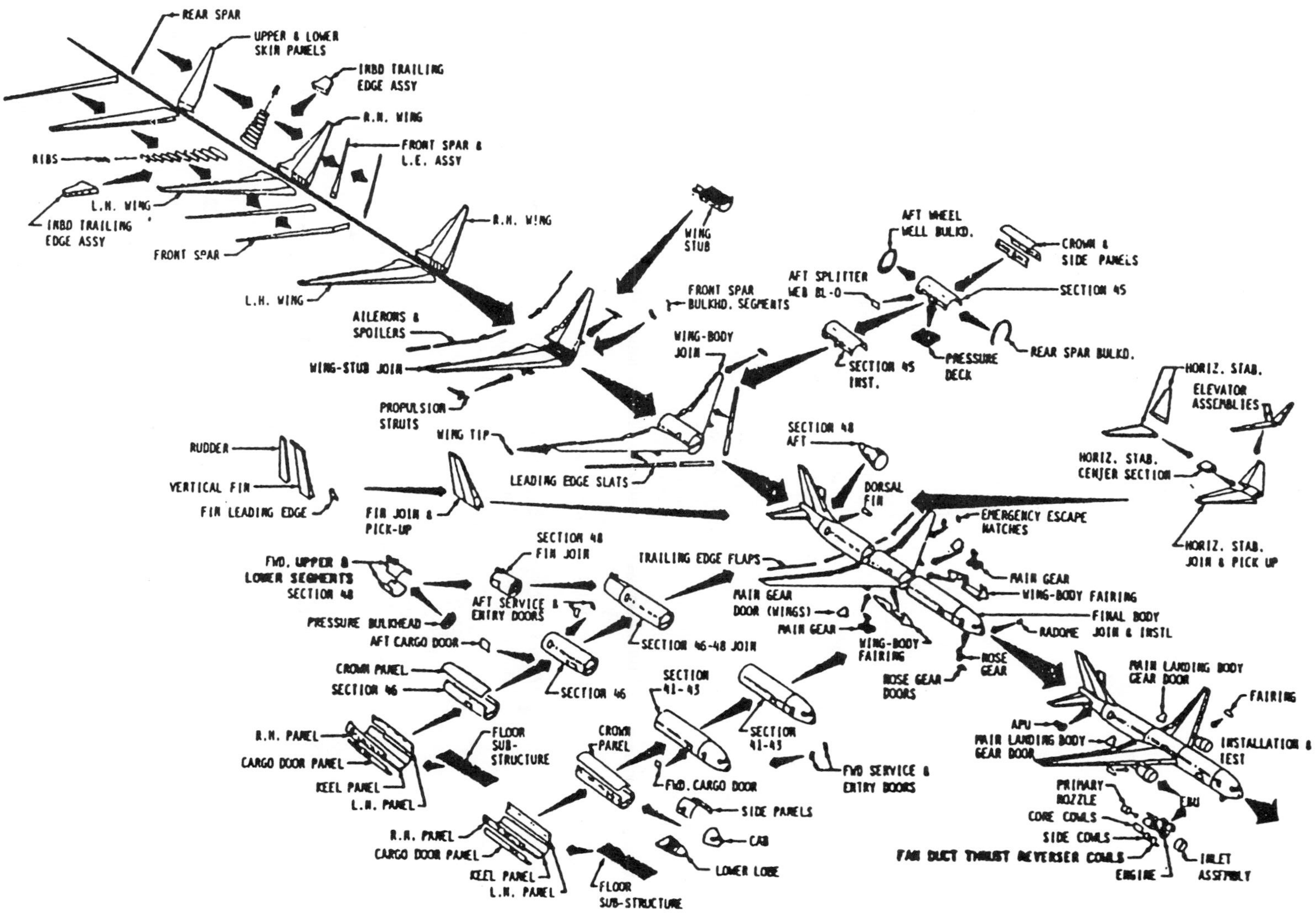

541

In all cases, a primary concern was maintaining schedule. Boeing faced substantial penalties if a plane was delivered even one day late, because airlines planned their schedules around promised delivery dates and expected a new plane to be flying immediately. According to Haas:

> For a long time, we have stressed the importance of schedule performance. The airplane *will* move [from one work station to the next] on the day that it is supposed to move. Management will get in a lot more trouble for not moving an airplane, assembly, or part on schedule than for a budget overrun. Over the years, budgets have gained significantly in importance, but not at the expense of schedules.

To ensure that schedules were maintained, Boeing employed a management visbility system. Schedules were prominently posted, and marathon status meetings, which were attended by representatives of all affected departments, were held weekly to review slippages and highlight potential problems. Every manager discussed what he or she was doing and what he or she was owed by others. The emphasis was on early notification, as Dennis Wilson observed:

> If I'm at a status meeting and I find that someone has missed a critical milestone, the first question I ask is, "Why didn't you tell me about the problem last week?," not, "Why did you miss the milestone?"

In June 1981, as assembly of the first 767 moved into its final stages, a First Flight Committee was established. The committee reported directly to Dean Thornton and met daily during the six weeks before the plane's first test flight. At that point, the test pilot had final say in setting priorities and selecting the tasks to be completed.

Learning Curves   Learning curves were also used to manage the assembly process. Based on historical experience, Boeing had developed learning curves for every major work center. Machining, assembly, and sheet metal fabrication had curves of their own, each with a different slope. However, curves were used in the same way at all centers.

To begin, an optimum crew size was defined for the operation, based on available work space, engineering guidelines, and tooling to be employed. For example, the optimal size for forward body section assembly was eight people. A parametric estimate was then made of the number of labor hours needed to assemble that section of the very first 767. The total (in this case, 6,000 hours) was then divided by the number of labor hours available each day (in this case, 128 hours, equal to eight people working eight hours per shift, two shifts per day) to give the number of days to complete the very first assembly (forty-seven days).

At this point, a learning curve was invoked. The next assembly would be scheduled not for forty-seven days but for a lesser number, to reflect the historical rate of learning on that operation. The same number of people would be employed, but they would work faster and more efficiently. (When precise calculations were impossible, Boeing varied staffing levels within minimum and maximum values, rather than sticking to a single, optimal crew size.)

Learning curves were also applied to change management. Work centers were initially staffed to reflect a large number of changes. For example, of the eight people assigned to forward body section assembly, three might initially be responsible for incorporating changes. But because the number of changes fell sharply as more planes were produced—the first 767 had 12,000 changes, while the seventieth 767 had only 500—fewer people would be needed for the activity as time passed, and staffing would be reduced over time.

Such improvements did not come automatically. Three tools were used to ensure that targets were met: specific work station goals; stand-up meetings with first-line supervisors; and the management visibility system discussed earlier. Hourly goals were set for every employee and displayed prominently on bar charts by their work stations. The game, as one manager put it, then became "worker versus bar chart." Stand-up meetings were held only if targets were not met. First-line supervisors had to stand up at these meetings and identify what was impeding their ability to meet learning curve goals. Managers were then responsible for solving the problems.

Three-Crew to Two-Crew Conversion

In the late 1970s, airframe manufacturers, led by Boeing, proposed a switch from three- to two-person cockpits. Advanced technology, they argued, had made a three-person crew unnecessary. The Air Line Pilots Association (ALPA) objected strongly to these arguments, claiming that safety levels were certain to fall if the number of crew members was reduced. To resolve the debate, a presidential task force was convened; both parties agreed to accept its findings. In July 1981, the task force concluded that two-person cockpits presented no unusual safety problems, and that manufacturers could offer them on all planes.

Airlines, including those that had already ordered 767s, soon expressed an interest in having their planes delivered with two-person cockpits. Boeing had anticipated such a response and, years earlier, had conducted preliminary studies to determine how best to convert the 767 from its original, three-person cockpit design to a two-person model (see Exhibit 10–9 for a comparison of the two cockpits). Further studies were immediately begun; their goal was to identify the number of planes then in process that would require rework or modification to become two-crew models, and the likely impact of these changes on cost and schedule. Engineers concluded that the thirty-first 767 was still far enough from completion that it, and all subsequent planes, could be built with two-person cockpits without modification. Thirty planes, however, were in relatively advanced stages of production. Some were nearly ready to be rolled out and flown; others had complete cockpits but were not yet tested; others had bare cockpits without any electronics installed. But since all thirty were being built according to the plane's original, three-person cockpit design, all would require some modification.

Customers were notified of the additional cost and delivery delay they could expect on these thirty planes. The impact was not large: a small percentage increase in costs and on average delay of one month from promised delivery dates. All but one airline chose to have their planes built with two-person cockpits.

In August 1981, a special task force, reporting directly to Thornton, was formed to determine the best way of modifying these planes. It soon narrowed the choice to two alternatives: (1) building the thirty airplanes as they had originally been designed, with three-person cockpits, and then converting them to two-person cockpits after they had left the production floor (but before delivery to customers), and (2) modifying the production plans for the thirty airplanes so that conversion would take place during production and no parts would be installed only to be removed later (which

Exhibit 10–9. Three-Crew and Two-Crew Cockpit Designs

FLIGHT DECK ARRANGEMENTS

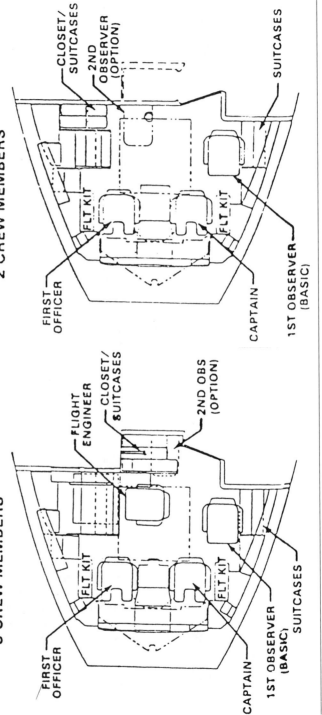

3 CREW MEMBERS

FLIGHT ENGINEER

CLOSET/ SUITCASES

2ND OBS (OPTION)

FIRST OFFICER

FLT KIT

FLT KIT

CAPTAIN

1ST OBSERVER (BASIC)

SUITCASES

2 CREW MEMBERS

CLOSET/ SUITCASES

2ND OBSERVER (OPTION)

SUITCASES

FIRST OFFICER

FLT KIT

FLT KIT

CAPTAIN

1ST OBSERVER (BASIC)

meant leaving some cockpits temporarily unfinished while drawings and parts for two-person cockpits were being developed).

Completion of Production and Subsequent Modification   In this approach, production would continue as planned, without delay. Neither learning curves nor schedules would be disrupted by attempts to modify airplanes during the assembly process. The modification program would be managed as a separate, tightly controlled activity, apart from the normal flow of production, and special teams of "modification experts," skilled at parts removal, modification, and repair, would be assigned to it. Approximately one million additional labor hours were thought to be required if this method were used.

The primary advantage of this approach was that flaps, ailerons, landing gear, hydraulics, and other airplane systems would be functionally tested during the final assembly process, as originally planned. Problems would be identified and corrected on the spot, rather than hidden or disguised by subsequent assembly activities. And because the airplane that rolled out of production would be fully tested and functional, any problems identified after installation of the two-person cockpit could be isolated, with some assurance, to the cockpit area.

The risk of this approach was the potential "loss of configuration" (i.e., when the plane was actually built, the integrity of the overall design might be compromised). Parts required for three-person cockpits would be installed firmly in place, only to be removed and replaced later by modification experts. (Because these parts had been ordered months before and were already on hand and paid for, this option did not impose greater scrap costs than the other option.) If the modification was not done carefully, many of the plane's operating systems might be disrupted. Boeing experts, however, believed that the management controls used for modification would prevent this from occurring. To minimize the risk, additional functional testing would be required after modification.

Space was also a problem. There was not enough room within the factory to modify all thirty planes. Work would therefore have to be done outside, but even then space was limited. A special parking plan would have to be developed, and the planes being modified would have to be parked extremely close together. The required arrangement would violate fire regulations, so special fire control plans and waivers would be necessary.

Several managers had reservations about this approach, for they objected to its underlying philosophy. The end result would be an airplane that had been modified, after the fact, to accommodate a two-person cockpit. As Standal put it: "It goes against our grain and better judgment to roll out an aircraft and then tear the guts out."

Modification During Production   In this approach, all modification of the thirty planes would be done during production, rather than after the fact. No parts would be installed only to be removed later. Instead, all panels, instruments, and switches that were associated with three-person cockpits would be identified and their installation halted. Meanwhile, production would continue on other sections of the plane. Once plans and parts were available for two-person cockpits, they would be incorporated within the flow of production.

This was the traditional method of making engineering and design changes. It was used routinely for the thousands of configuration changes on every new airplane. The primary advantage of this approach was that all parts were installed only once.

Because there would be no installation and subsequent removal, the configuration was more likely to remain secure. Moreover, because modification would occur during production, all activities would be controlled by normal management procedures, rather than by a separate program.

The primary disadvantage of this approach was that the original production plan would be disrupted. Separate plans would have to be developed for the first thirty airplanes, which required modification, and all subsequent planes. Learning curves would be disrupted as well, because a large number of additional workers would have to be added temporarily, at selected work stations, to complete the modification of the first thirty planes. If this method were used, modification was expected to require approximately two million additional labor hours.

Because all cockpit work would be deferred until engineering drawings and parts were available for two-crew models, test procedures would also have to change. Traditionally, functional testing was done sequentially, with each system (flaps, ailerons, etc.) tested as it became operational. That approach would be impossible here because all cockpit work would be deferred until complete plans and drawings were available. Functional testing would therefore have to be done after the two-person cockpit was fully installed. Problems might not be detected and corrected immediately and might well be hidden by systems that were installed later, making problem diagnosis much more difficult.

Thornton knew that it was time to make a choice between the two approaches so that production could continue. The risks, however, were great; as his staff kept telling him, the decision was a potential "show-stopper." He wondered: "Should I authorize after-the-fact conversion of planes or modification during production? And for what reasons?"

THE BOEING 767: FROM CONCEPT TO PRODUCTION (B)[10]

Thornton elected to retrofit the thirty 767s with two-person cockpits, rather than installing them in-line. The project was managed as a separate production program with its own schedule and learning curves, and the storage problem was solved by special parking arrangements in the large stalls normally used for 747s. Managers were greatly pleased with the results. In August 1981, the first 767 was rolled out as planned, and only a few deliveries were delayed by as much as a month.

Six years later, the world of airframe manufacturing had changed. By August 1987, Boeing had received orders for 263 767s; of these, 181 had been delivered. But the monthly production rate was down from the planned level of eight to two, and forecasts had not been fully met. One reason was that most U.S. airlines had developed different needs because of deregulation. Routes that had previously been limited to a small number of carriers had been opened up. The resulting competition had depressed ticket prices and profits and led ultimately to both bankruptcies and mergers.

---

10. Copyright © 1988 by the President and Fellows of Harvard College. Harvard Business School case 688-041. This case was prepared by Lee Field, Janet Simpson, and David A. Garvin as the basis for class discussion rather than to illustrate either effective or ineffective handling of an administrative situation. Reprinted by permission of the Harvard Business School.

At the same time, airlines had altered their route structures, moving from the traditional pattern of direct connections between city pairs to hub and spoke systems that encouraged shorter flights.

Airbus had also proved to be a formidable competitor. By 1987, it had captured 20 percent of the world market and 30 percent of the market outside the United States. Airbus continued to receive support from the French, British, Spanish, and German governments, and was actively seeking new members for its consortium.

In this environment, Boeing was preparing to launch its newest plane program, the 7J7, an advanced technology airplane targeted for the 150-seat market. The plane was based on a radically new engine, the prop-fan, that promised fuel savings of up to 50 percent over turbofan engines, as well as a new airframe and new optical fiber and hydraulics technologies. McDonnell Douglas, by contrast, was also planning a new plane, but it had decided to combine prop-fan engines with an existing airframe. Both companies were hoping that their planes, scheduled to appear in 1992, would take sales from Airbus' A-320, a 150-seat model, due in 1988, that was without the new engine technology.

To Boeing the challenge was clear. To be successful, the 7J7 had to offer an operating cost advantage over the A-320 while providing the airlines with enhanced revenue-generating capability. The question was, how? Technology was one route. But should the 7J7 program also be managed differently than its predecessor, the 767?

Planning

The most important responsibilities of a project manager are planning, integrating, and executing plans. Almost all projects, because of their relatively short duration and often prioritized control of resources, require formal, detailed planning. The integration of the planning activities is necessary because each functional unit may develop its own planning documentation with little regard for other functional units.

Planning, in general, can best be described as the function of selecting the enterprise objectives and establishing the policies, procedures, and programs necessary for achieving them. Planning in a project environment may be described as establishing a predetermined course of action within a forecasted environment. The project's requirements set the major milestones, and the line managers hope that they can meet them. If the line manager cannot commit because the milestones are perceived as unrealistic, the project manager may have to develop alternatives, one of which may be to move the milestones. Upper-level management must become involved in the selection of alternatives during the planning stage. Planning is, of course, decision making, since it involves choosing among alternatives. Planning is a required management function to facilitate the comprehension of complex problems involving interacting factors.

The project manager is the key to successful project planning. It is desirable that the project manager be involved from project conception through execution. Project planning must be *systematic, flexible* enough to handle unique activities, *disciplined* through reviews and controls, and capable of accepting *multifunctional* inputs. Successful project managers realize that project planning is an iterative process and must be performed throughout the life of the project.

One of the objectives of project planning is to completely define all work required (possibly through the development of a documented project plan) so that it will be readily identifiable to each project participant. This is a necessity in a project environment because:

- If the task is well understood prior to being performed, much of the work can be preplanned.
- If the task is not understood, then during the actual task execution more knowledge is gained that, in turn, leads to changes in resource allocations, schedules, and priorities.
- The more uncertain the task, the greater the amount of information that must be processed in order to ensure effective performance.

These considerations are important in a project environment because each project can be different from the others, requiring a variety of different resources, but having to be performed under time, cost, and performance constraints with little margin for error. Figure 11–1 identifies the type of project planning required to establish an effective monitoring and control system. The boxes in the upper portion of the curve represent the planning activities, and the lower portion identifies the "tracking" or monitoring of the planned activities.

Without proper planning, programs and projects can start off "behind the eight ball" because of poorly defined requirements during the initial planning phase. Below is a list of the typical consequences of poor planning:

- Project initiation
- Wild enthusiasm
- Disillusionment
- Chaos
- Search for the guilty
- Punishment of the innocent
- Promotion of the nonparticipants
- Definition of the requirements

Obviously, the definition of the requirements should have been the first step.

There are four basic reasons for project planning:

- To eliminate or reduce uncertainty
- To improve efficiency of the operation
- To obtain a better understanding of the objectives
- To provide a basis for monitoring and controlling work

There are involuntary and voluntary reasons for planning. Involuntary reasons can be internally mandatory functions of the organizational complexity and an organizational lag in response time; or they can be externally correlated to environmental fluctuations, uncertainty, and discontinuity. The voluntary reasons for planning are attempts to secure efficient and effective operations.

Planning is decision making based upon futurity. It is a continuous process of making entrepreneurial decisions with an eye to the future, and methodically organizing the effort needed to carry out these decisions. Furthermore, systematic planning allows an organization of set goals. The alternative to systematic planning is decision making based on history. This generally results in reactive management leading to crisis management, conflict management, and fire fighting.

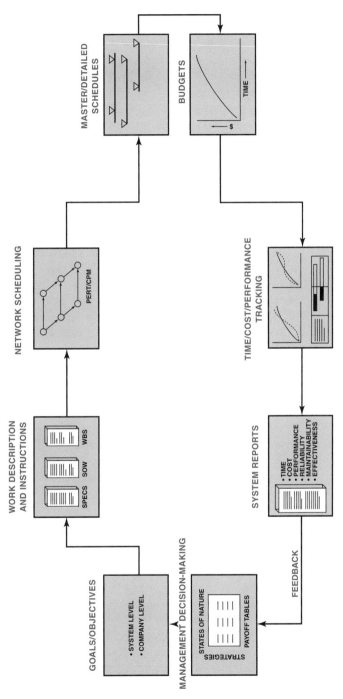

FIGURE 11–1. The project planning and control system.

11.1 GENERAL PLANNING

Planning is determining what needs to be done, by whom, and by when, in order to fulfill one's assigned responsibility. There are nine major components of the planning phase:

- *Objective:* a goal, target, or quota to be achieved by a certain time
- *Program:* the strategy to be followed and major actions to be taken in order to achieve or exceed objectives
- *Schedule:* a plan showing when individual or group activities or accomplishments will be started and/or completed
- *Budget:* planned expenditures required to achieve or exceed objectives
- *Forecast:* a projection of what will happen by a certain time
- *Organization:* design of the number and kinds of positions, along with corresponding duties and responsibilities, required to achieve or exceed objectives
- *Policy:* a general guide for decision making and individual actions
- *Procedure:* a detailed method for carrying out a policy
- *Standard:* a level of individual or group performance defined as adequate or acceptable

Several of these factors require additional comment. Forecasting what will happen may not be easy, especially if predictions of environmental reactions are required. For example, planning is customarily defined as either strategic, tactical, or operational. Strategic planning is generally for five years or more, tactical can be for one to five years, and operational is the here and now of six months to one year. Although most projects are operational, they can be considered as strategic, especially if spin-offs or follow-up work is promising. Forecasting also requires an understanding of strengths and weaknesses as found in:

- The competitive situation
- Marketing
- Research and development
- Production
- Financing
- Personnel
- The management structure

If project planning is strictly operational, then these factors may be clearly definable. However, if strategic or long-range planning is necessary, then the future economic outlook can vary, say, from year to year, and replanning must be accomplished at regular intervals because the goals and objectives can change. (The procedure for this can be seen in Figure 11–1.)

The last three factors, policies, procedures, and standards, can vary from project to project because of their uniqueness. Each project manager can establish project policies, provided that they fall within the broad limits set forth by top management. Policies are predetermined general courses or guides based on the following principles:[1]

- Subordinate policies are supplementary to superior policies.
- Policies are based upon known principles in the operative areas.
- Policies should be definable, understandable, and preferably in writing.
- Policies should be both flexible and stable.
- Policies should be reasonably comprehensive in scope.

Project policies must often conform closely to company policies, and are usually similar in nature from project to project. Procedures, on the other hand, can be drastically different from project to project, even if the same activity is performed. For example, the signing off of manufacturing plans may require different signatures on two selected projects even though the same end-item is being produced.

Planning varies at each level of the organization. At the individual level, planning is required so that cognitive simulation can be established before irrevocable actions are taken. At the working group or functional level, planning must include:

- Agreement on purpose
- Assignment and acceptance of individual responsibilities
- Coordination of work activities
- Increased commitment to group goals
- Lateral communications

All the organizational or project level, planning must include:

- Recognition and resolution of group conflict of goals
- Assignment and acceptance of group responsibilities
- Increased motivation and commitment to organizational goals
- Vertical and lateral communications
- Coordination of activities between groups

The logic of planning requires answers to several questions in order for the alternatives and constraints to be fully understood. An outline for a partial list of questions would include:

- Prepare environmental analysis
  - Where are we?
  - How and why did we get here?

---

1. Edwin Flippo and Garry Munsinger, *Management,* 3rd edition (Boston: Allyn and Bacon, 1975), p. 83.

- Set objectives
  - Is this where we want to be?
  - Where would we like to be? In a year? In five years?
- List alternative strategies
  - Where will we go if we continue as before?
  - Is that where we want to go?
  - How could we get to where we want to go?
- List threats and opportunities
  - What might prevent us from getting there?
  - What might help us to get there?
- Prepare forecasts
  - Where are we capable of going?
  - What do we need to take us where we want to go?
- Select strategy portfolio
  - What is the best course for us to take?
  - What are the potential benefits?
  - What are the risks?
- Prepare action programs
  - What do we need to do?
  - When do we need to do it?
  - How will we do it?
  - Who will do it?
- Monitor and control
  - Are we on course? If not, why?
  - What do we need to do to be on course?
  - Can we do it?

One of the most difficult activities in the project environment is to keep the planning on target. Below are typical procedures that can assist project managers during planning activities:

- Let functional managers do their own planning. Too often operators are operators, planners are planners, and never the twain shall meet.
- Establish goals before you plan. Otherwise short-term thinking takes over.
- Set goals for the planners. This will guard against the nonessentials and places your effort where there is payoff.
- Stay flexible. Use people-to-people contact, and stress fast response.
- Keep a balanced outlook. Don't overreact, and position yourself for an upturn.
- Welcome top-management participation. Top management has the capability to make or break a plan, and may well be the single most important variable.
- Beware of future spending plans. This may eliminate the tendency to underestimate.

- Test the assumptions behind the forecasts. This is necessary because professionals are generally too optimistic. Do not depend solely on one set of data.
- Don't focus on today's problems. Try to get away from crisis management and fire fighting.
- Reward those who dispel illusions. Avoid the Persian messenger syndrome (i.e., beheading the bearer of bad tidings). Reward the first to come forth with bad news.

11.2 IDENTIFYING STRATEGIC PROJECT VARIABLES

For long-range or strategic projects, the project manager must continually monitor the external environment in order to develop a well-structured program that can stand up under pressure. These environmental factors play an integral part in planning. The project manager must be able to identify and evaluate these strategic variables in terms of the future posture of the organization with regard to constraints on existing resources.

In the project environment, strategic project planning is performed at the horizontal hierarchy level, with final approval by upper-level management. There are three basic guidelines for strategic project planning:

- Strategic project planning is a job that should be performed by managers, not for them.
- It is extremely important that upper-level management maintain a close involvement with project teams, especially during the planning phase.
- Successful strategic planning must define the authority, responsibility, and roles of the strategic planning personnel.

For the project to be successful, all members of the horizontal team must be aware of those strategic variables that can influence the success or failure of the project plan. The analysis begins with the environment, subdivided as internal, external, and competitive, as shown below:

- Internal environment
  - Management skills
  - Resources
  - Wage and salary levels
  - Government freeze on jobs
  - Minority groups
  - Layoffs
  - Sales forecasts
- External environment
  - Legal

- Political
- Social
- Economic
- Technological
- Competitive environment
  - Industry characteristics
  - Company requirements and goals
  - Competitive history
  - Present competitive activity
  - Competitive planning
    —Return on investment
    —Market share
    —Size and variety of product lines
- Competitive resources

Once the environmental variables are defined, the planning process continues with the following:

- Identification of company strengths and weaknesses
- Understanding personal values of top management
- Identification of opportunities
- Definition of product market
- Identification of competitive edge
- Establishment of goals, objectives, and standards
- Identification of resource deployment

Complete identification of all strategic variables is not easily obtainable at the program level. Internal, or operating, variables are readily available to program personnel by virtue of the structure of the organization. The external variables are normally tracked under the perceptive eyes of top management. This presents a challenge for the organization of the system. In most cases, those in the horizontal hierarchy of a program are more interested in the current operational plan than in external factors and tend to become isolated from the environment after the program begins, losing insight into factors influencing the rapidly changing external variables in the process. Proper identification of these strategic variables requires that communication channels be established between top management and the project office.

Top-management support must be available for identification of strategic planning variables so that effective decision making can occur at the program level. The participation of top management in this regard has not been easy to implement. Many top-level officers consider this process a relinquishment of some of their powers and choose to retain strategic variable identification for the top levels of management.

The systems approach to management does not attempt to decrease top management's role in strategic decision making. The maturity, intellect, and wisdom

TABLE 11–1. STRATEGIC PLANNING VARIABLES IN THE TIRE INDUSTRY

Internal	External
• Operating • Product changes • Volume (economies of scale) • Wages vs. automation • R&D • Legal • Product quality • Union and safety considerations • Economic • Market indicators • Division of market • Production runs (timing) • Pricing/promotion policy • Sociopolitical • Allocation of resources • Raw material price/availability • Feasibility of exporting • Productivity levels	• Operating • Customer requirements • Capacity of plants • Borrowing expenses • Technological advances • Legal • OSHA noise levels • Product liabilities • DoT requirements • Economic • Forecast of industry • Inventory (on hand/dealers) • Steel and chemical output • Competition • Sociopolitical • Produce what is profitable • Primarily third world • Threat of imports • Stability of free market

of top management cannot be replaced. Ultimately, decision making will always rest at the upper levels of management, regardless of the organizational structure.

Identification and classification of the strategic variables are necessary to establish relative emphasis, priorities, and selectivity among the alternatives, to anticipate the unexpected, and to determine the restraints and limitations of the program. Universal classification systems are nonexistent because of the varied nature of organizations and projects. However, variables can be roughly categorized as internal and external, as shown in Table 11–1.

A survey of fifty companies was conducted to determine if lower-level and middle management, as well as project managers, knew what variables in their own industry were considered by top management as important planning variables. The following results were obtained:[2]

- Top management considered fewer variables as being strategic than did middle managers.
- Middle management and top management in project-driven companies had better agreement on strategic variable identification than did managers in non–project-driven companies.
- Top executives within the same industry differed as to the identification of strategic variables, even within companies having almost identical business bases.
- Very little attempt was made by top management to quantify the risks involved with each strategic variable.

2. Harold Kerzner, "Survey of Strategic Planning Variables," unpublished report, Project/Systems Management Research Institute, Baldwin-Wallace College, 1977.

As an example of the differences between the project manager and upper-level management, consider the six strategic variables, listed below, that are characteristic of the machine tool industry:

- Business markets and business cycles
- Product characteristics
- Pricing and promotion policies
- Technology changes
- Labor force and available skills
- Customer organization restructuring

Both project managers and upper-level management agreed on the first four variables. The last two were identified by upper-level management. Since many products are now made of materials other than steel, the question arises as to the availability of qualified workers. This poses a problem in that many customers perform a make-or-buy analysis before contracting with machine tool companies. The machine tool companies surveyed felt that it is the responsibility of upper-level management to communicate continually with all customers to ascertain if they are contemplating developing or enlarging their machine tool capabilities. Obviously, the decision of a prime customer to develop its own machine shop capabilities could have a severe impact on the contractor's growth potential, business base, and strategic planning philosophy.

11.3 LIFE-CYCLE PHASES

Project planning takes place at two levels. The first level is the corporate cultural approach; the second method is the individual's approach. The corporate cultural approach breaks the project down into life-cycle phases, such as those shown in Table 2–5. The life-cycle phase approach is *not* an attempt to put handcuffs on the project manager but to provide a methodology for uniformity in project planning. Many companies, including government agencies, prepare checklists of activities that should be considered in each phase. These checklists are for consistency in planning. The project manager can still exercise his own planning initiatives within each phase.

A second benefit of life-cycle phases is control. At the end of each phase there is a meeting between the project manager, sponsor, senior management, and even the customer, to assess the accomplishments of this life-cycle phase and to get approval for the next phase. These meetings are often called critical design reviews, "on-off ramps," and "gates." In some companies, these meetings are used to firm up budgets and schedules for the follow-on phases. In addition to monetary considerations, life-cycle phases can be used for manpower deployment and equipment/facility utilization. Some companies go so far as to prepare project management policy and procedure manuals where all information is subdivided according to life-cycle phasing. Life-cycle phase decision points eliminate the problem where project managers do not ask for phase funding, but rather ask for funds for the whole project before the true scope of the project is known. Several companies have even gone so far as to identify the types of decisions that can be made at each end-of-phase review meeting. They include:

- Proceed with the next phase based on an approved funding level
- Proceed to the next phase but with a new or modified set of objectives
- Postpone approval to proceed based on a need for additional information
- Terminate project

Consider a company that utilizes the following life-cycle phases:

- Conceptualization
- Feasibility
- Preliminary planning
- Detail planning
- Execution
- Testing and commissioning

The conceptualization phase includes brainstorming and common sense and involves two critical factors: (1) identify and define the problem, and (2) identify and define potential solutions.

In a brainstorming session, *all* ideas are recorded and none are discarded. The brainstorming session works best if there is no formal authority present and if the time duration is no more than thirty to sixty minutes. Sessions over sixty minutes in length will produce ideas that may begin to resemble science fiction.

The feasibility study phase considers the technical aspects of the conceptual alternatives and provides a firmer basis on which to decide whether to undertake the project.

The purpose of the feasibility phase is to:

- Plan the project development and implementation activities.
- Estimate the probable elapsed time, staffing, and equipment requirements.
- Identify the probable costs and consequences of investing in the new project.

If practical, the feasibility study results should evaluate the alternative conceptual solutions along with associated benefits and costs.

The objective of this step is to provide management with the predictable results of implementing a specific project and to provide generalized project requirements. This, in the form of a feasibility study report, is used as the basis on which to decide whether to proceed with the costly requirements, development, and implementation phases.

User involvement during the feasibility study is critical. The user must supply much of the required effort and information, and, in addition, must be able to judge the impact of alternative approaches. Solutions must be operationally, technically, and economically feasible. Much of the economic evaluation must be substantiated by the user. Therefore, the primary user must be highly qualified and intimately familiar with the workings of the organization and should come from the line operation.

The feasibility study also deals with the technical aspects of the proposed project and requires the development of conceptual solutions. Considerable experience and technical expertise are required to gather the proper information, analyze it, and reach practical conclusions.

Improper technical or operating decisions made during this step may go undetected or unchallenged throughout the remainder of the process. In the worst case, such an error could result in the termination of a valid project—or the continuation of a project that is not economically or technically feasible.

In the feasibility study phase, it is necessary to define the project's basic approaches and its boundaries or scope. A typical feasibility study checklist might include:

- Summary level
    - Evaluate alternatives
    - Evaluate market potential
    - Evaluate cost effectiveness
    - Evaluate producibility
    - Evaluate technical base
- Detail level
    - A more specific determination of the problem
    - Analysis of the state-of-the-art technology
    - Assessment of in-house technical capabilities
    - Test validity of alternatives
    - Quantify weaknesses and unknowns
    - Conduct trade-off analysis on time, cost, and performance
- Prepare initial project goals and objectives
- Prepare preliminary cost estimates and development plan

The end result of the feasibility study is a management decision on whether to terminate the project or to approve its next phase. Although management can stop the project at several later phases, the decision is especially critical at this point, because later phases require a major commitment of resources. All too often, management review committees approve the continuation of projects merely because termination at this point might cast doubt on the group's judgment in giving earlier approval.

The decision made at the end of the feasibility study should identify those projects that are to be terminated. Once a project is deemed feasible and is approved for development, it must be prioritized with previously approved projects waiting for development (given a limited availability of capital or other resources). As development gets under way, management is given a series of checkpoints to monitor the project's actual progress as compared to the plan.

The third life-cycle phase is either preliminary planning or "defining the requirements." This is the phase where the effort is officially defined as a project. In this phase, we should consider the following:

- General scope of the work
- Objectives and related background
- Contractor's tasks
- Contractor end-item performance requirements
- Reference to related studies, documentation, and specifications
- Data items (documentation)
- Support equipment for contract end-item
- Customer-furnished property, facilities, equipment, and services
- Customer-furnished documentation
- Schedule of performance
- Exhibits, attachments, and appendices

These elements can be condensed into four core documents, as will be shown in Section 11.6. Also, it should be noted that the word "customer" can be an internal customer, such as the user group or your own executives.

The table below shows the percentage of *direct* labor hours/dollars that are spent in each phase:

Phase	Percent of Direct Labor Dollars
Conceptualization	5
Feasibility study	10
Preliminary planning	15
Detail planning	20
Execution	40
Commissioning	10

The interesting fact from this table is that as much as 50 percent of the direct labor hours and dollars can be spent before execution begins. The reason for this is simple: Quality must be planned for and designed in. Quality cannot be inspected into the project. Companies that spend less than these percentages usually find quality problems in execution.

11.4 PROPOSAL PREPARATION

The question always exists of what to do with a project manager between assignments. For companies that survive on competitive bidding, the assignment is clear: The project manager writes proposals for future work. This takes place during the feasibility study, when the company must decide whether to bid on the job. There are four ways in which proposal preparation can occur:

- *Project manager prepares entire proposal.* This occurs frequently in small companies. In large organizations, the project manager may not have access to all available data, some of which may be company proprietary, and it may not be in the best interest of the company to have the project manager spend all of his time doing this.
- *Proposal manager prepares entire proposal.* This can work as long as the project manager is allowed to review the proposal before delivery to the customer and feels committed to its direction.
- *Project manager prepares proposal but is assisted by a proposal manager.* This is common, but again places tremendous pressure on the project manager.
- *Proposal manager prepares proposal but is assisted by a project manager.* This is the preferred method. The proposal manager maintains maximum authority and control until such time as the proposal is sent to the customer, at which point the project manager takes charge. The project manager is on board right from the start, although his only effort may be solely in preparing the technical volume of the proposal and perhaps part of the management volume.

Project-driven companies provide project managers with release time for proposal preparation. If there exists a large time span between proposal submittal and contract award, then the company may be forced to assign a project manager who had no input into the proposal activities. This can lead to poor performance due to lack of commitment.

11.5 UNDERSTANDING PARTICIPANTS' ROLES

Planning simply does not happen by itself. Companies that have histories of successful plans also have employees who fully understand their roles in the planning process. Good up-front planning may not eliminate the need for changes, but may reduce the number of changes required. The responsibilities of the major players are as follows:

- Project manager will define:
  - Goals and objectives
  - Major milestones
  - Requirements
  - Ground rules and assumptions
  - Time, cost, and performance constraints
  - Operating procedures

- Administrative policy
- Reporting requirements
- Line manager will define:
  - Detailed task descriptions to implement objectives, requirements, and milestones
  - Detailed schedules and manpower allocations to support budget and schedule
  - Identification of areas of risk, uncertainty, and conflict
- Senior management (project sponsor) will:
  - Act as the negotiator for disagreements between project and line management
  - Provide clarification of critical issues
  - Provide communication link with customer's senior management

Successful planning requires that project, line, and senior management are in agreement with the plan.

11.6 PROJECT PLANNING

Successful project management, whether it be in response to an in-house project or a customer request, must utilize effective planning techniques. The quantitative and qualitative tools for project planning must be identified (see Figure 11–2). From a systems point of view, management must make effective utilization of re-

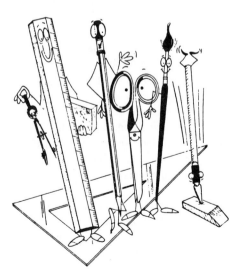

FIGURE 11–2. Tools for project planning.

sources. This effective utilization over several different types of projects requires a systematic plan in which the entire company is considered as one large network subdivided into smaller ones.

The first step in total program scheduling is understanding the project objectives. These goals may be to develop expertise in a given area, to become competitive, to modify an existing facility for later use, or simply to keep key personnel employed.

The objectives are generally not independent; they are all interrelated, both implicitly and explicitly. Many times it is not possible to satisfy all objectives. At this point, management must prioritize the objectives as to which are strategic and which are not. Typical problems with developing objectives include:

- Project objectives/goals are not agreeable to all parties.
- Project objectives are too rigid to accommodate changing priorities.
- Insufficient time exists to define objectives well.
- Objectives are not adequately quantified.
- Objectives are not documented well enough.
- Efforts of client and project personnel are not coordinated.
- Personnel turnover is high.

Once the objectives are clearly defined, four questions must be considered:

- What are the major elements of the work required to satisfy the objectives, and how are these elements interrelated?
- Which functional divisions will assume responsibility for accomplishment of these objectives and the major-element work requirements?
- Are the required corporate and organizational resources available?
- What are the information flow requirements for the project?

If the project is large and complex, then careful planning and analysis must be accomplished by both the direct- and indirect-labor-charging organizational units. The project organizational structure must be designed to fit the project; work plans and schedules must be established so that maximum allocation of resources can be made; resource costing and accounting systems must be developed; and a management information and reporting system must be established.

Effective total program planning cannot be accomplished unless all of the necessary information becomes available at project initiation. These information requirements are:

- The statement of work (SOW)
- The project specifications
- The milestone schedule
- The work breakdown structure (WBS)

The statement of work (SOW) is a narrative description of the work to be accomplished. It includes the objectives of the project, a brief description of the work, the funding constraint if one exists, and the specifications and schedule. The schedule is a "gross" schedule and includes such things as the:

- Start date
- End date
- Major milestones
- Written reports (data items)

Written reports should always be identified so that if functional input is required, the functional manager will assign an individual who has writing skills. After all, it is no secret who would write the report if the line people did not.

The last major item is the work breakdown structure. The WBS is the breaking down of the statement of work into smaller elements so that better visibility and control will be obtained. Each of these planning items is described in the following sections.

11.7 THE STATEMENT OF WORK

The statement of work (SOW) is a narrative description of the work required for the project. The complexity of the SOW is determined by the desires of top management, the customer, and/or the user groups. For projects internal to the company, the SOW is prepared by the project office with input from the user groups. The reason for this is that user groups tend to write in such scientific terms that only the user groups understand their meaning. Since the project office is usually composed of personnel with writing skills, it is only fitting that the project office prepare the SOW and submit it to the user groups for verification and approval.

For projects external to the organization, as in competitive bidding, the contractor may have to prepare the SOW for the customer because the customer may not have a team of people trained in SOW preparation. In this case, as before, the contractor would submit the SOW to the customer for approval. It is also quite common for the project manager to rewrite a customer's SOW so that the contractor's line managers can price out the effort.

In a competitive bidding environment, the reader should be aware of the fact that there are two SOWs—the SOW used in the proposal and a contract statement of work (CSOW). There might also be a proposal WBS and a contract work breakdown structure (CWBS). Special care must be taken by contract and negotiation teams that all discrepancies between the SOW/WBS and CSOW/CWBS are discovered, or additional costs may be incurred. A good (or winning) proposal is *no guarantee* that the customer or contractor understands the SOW. For large projects, fact-finding is usually required before final negotiations because it is *essential* that both the customer and the contractor understand and agree on the SOW, what work is required, what work is proposed, the factual basis for the costs, and other related elements. In addition, it is imperative that there be agreement between the final CSOW and CWBS.

SOW preparation is not as easy as it sounds. Consider the following:

- The SOW says that you are to conduct a *minimum* of fifteen tests to determine the material properties of a new substance. You price out twenty tests just to "play it safe." At the end of the fifteenth test, the customer says that the results are inconclusive and that you must run another fifteen tests. The cost overrun is $40,000.
- The Navy gives you a contract in which the SOW states that the prototype must be tested in "water." You drop the prototype into a swimming pool to test it. Unfortunately, the Navy's definition of "water" is the Atlantic Ocean, and it costs you $1 million to transport all of your test engineers and test equipment to the Atlantic Ocean.
- You receive a contract in which the SOW says that you must transport goods across the country using "aerated" boxcars. You select boxcars that have open tops so that air can flow in. During the trip, the train goes through an area of torrential rains, and the goods are ruined. The customer wanted boxcars that were aerated from below. The court is currently deciding who should be blamed for misinterpretation of the word "aerated."

The above three examples show that misinterpretations of the SOW can result in losses of hundreds of millions of dollars a year. Common causes of misinterpretation are:

- Mixing tasks, specifications, approvals, and special instructions
- Using imprecise language ("nearly," "optimum," "approximately," etc.)
- No pattern, structure, or chronological order
- Wide variation in size of tasks
- Wide variation in how to describe details of the work
- Failing to get third-party review

Misinterpretations of the statement of work can and will occur no matter how hard the quest for perfection during the definition phase. The result is creeping scope, or, as one telecommunications company calls it, "creeping elegance." The best way to control creeping scope is with a good definition of the requirements up front. Unfortunately, this is not always possible.

In some industries, such as aerospace, defense, and MIS, creeping scope had become a way of life until recently. In the Information Technology Group of a major appliance manufacturer, the project manager made it clear that she would not accept any scope changes once the definition of the requirement (prepared by the user group) was completed. Midway through the project, the user group tried to change the requirements. The project manager refused to accept the changes and, against the wishes of the user group, put all requests for changes into a follow-on enhancement project that would be budgeted for and scheduled *after* the initial project was completed. When the initial project was completed and installed at the user's location, the users stated that they could live with the original package, and the enhancement project was neither funded nor approved.

Today, both private industry and government agencies are developing manuals on SOW preparation. The following is adapted from a NASA publication on SOW preparation:[3]

- The project manager or his designees should review the documents that authorize the project and define its objectives, and also review contracts and studies leading to the present level of development. As a convenience, a bibliography of related studies should be prepared together with samples of any similar SOWs, and compliance specifications.
- A copy of the WBS should be obtained. At this point coordination between the CWBS elements and the SOW should commence. Each task element of the preliminary CWBS should be explained in the SOW, and related coding should be used.
- The project manager should establish a SOW preparation team consisting of personnel he deems appropriate from the program or project office who are experts in the technical areas involved, and representatives from procurement, financial management, fabrication, test, logistics, configuration management, operations, safety, reliability, and quality assurance, plus any other area that may be involved in the contemplated procurement.
- Before the team actually starts preparation of the SOW, the project manager should brief program management as to the structure of the preliminary CWBS and the nature of the contemplated SOW. This briefing is used as a baseline from which to proceed further.
- The project manager may assign identified tasks to team members and identify compliance specifications, design criteria, and other requirements documentation that must be included in the SOW and assign them to responsible personnel for preparation. Assigned team members will identify and obtain copies of specifications and technical requirements documents, engineering drawings, and results of preliminary and/or related studies that may apply to various elements of the proposed procurement.
- The project manager should prepare a detailed checklist showing the mandatory items and the selected optional items as they apply to the main body or the appendixes of the SOW.
- The project manager should emphasize the use of preferred parts lists; standard subsystem designs, both existing and under development; available hardware in inventory; off-the-shelf equipment; component qualification data; design criteria handbooks; and other technical information available to design engineers to prevent deviations from the best design practices.
- Cost estimates (manning requirements, material costs, software requirements, etc.) developed by the cost-estimating specialists should be reviewed by SOW contributors. Such reviews will permit early trade-off consideration on the desirability of requirements that are not directly related to essential technical objectives.

---

3. Adapted from *Statement of Work Handbook* NHB5600.2, National Aeronautics and Space Administration, February 1975.

- The project manager should establish schedules for submission of coordinated SOW fragments from each task team member. He must assure that these schedules are compatible with the schedule for the RFP issuance. The statement of work should be prepared sufficiently early to permit full project coordination and to ensure that all project requirements are included. It should be completed in advance of RFP preparation.

SOW preparation manuals also contain guides for editors and writers:[4]

- Every SOW that exceeds two pages in length should have a table of contents conforming to the CWBS coding structure. There should rarely be items in the SOW that are not shown on the CWBS; however, it is not absolutely necessary to restrict items to those cited in the CWBS.
- Clear and precise task descriptions are essential. The SOW writer should realize that his or her efforts will have to be read and interpreted by persons of varied background (such as lawyers, buyers, engineers, cost estimators, accountants, and specialists in production, transportation, security, audit, quality, finance, and contract management). A good SOW states precisely the product or service desired. The clarity of the SOW will affect administration of the contract, since it defines the scope of work to be performed. Any work that falls outside that scope will involve new procurement with probable increased costs.
- The most important thing to keep in mind when writing a SOW is the most likely effect the written work will have upon the reader. Therefore, every effort must be made to avoid ambiguity. All obligations of the government should be carefully spelled out. If approval actions are to be provided by the government, set a time limit. If government-furnished equipment (GFE) and/or services, etc., are to be provided, state the nature, condition, and time of delivery, if feasible.
- Remember that any provision that takes control of the work away from the contractor, even temporarily, may result in relieving the contractor of responsibility.
- In specifying requirements, use active rather than passive terminology. Say that the contractor shall conduct a test rather than that a test should be conducted. In other words, when a firm requirement is intended, use the mandatory term "shall" rather than the permissive term "should."
- Limit abbreviations to those in common usage. Provide a list of all pertinent abbreviations and acronyms at the beginning of the SOW. When using a term for the first time, spell it out and show the abbreviation or acronym in parentheses following the word or words.
- When it is important to define a division of responsibilities between the contractor, other agencies, etc., a separate section of the SOW (in an appropriate location) should be included and delineate such responsibilities.
- Include procedures. When immediate decisions cannot be made, it may be possible to include a procedure for making them (e.g., "as approved by the contracting officer," or "the contractor shall submit a report each time a failure occurs").

---

4. See note 3.

- Do not overspecify. Depending upon the nature of the work and the type of contract, the ideal situation may be to specify results required or end-items to be delivered and let the contractor propose his best method.
- Describe requirements in sufficient detail to assure clarity, not only for legal reasons, but for practical application. It is easy to overlook many details. It is equally easy to be repetitious. Beware of doing either. For every piece of deliverable hardware, for every report, for every immediate action, do not specify that something be done "as necessary." Rather, specify whether the judgment is to be made by the contractor or by the government. Be aware that these types of contingent actions may have an impact on price as well as schedule. Where expensive services, such as technical liaison, are to be furnished, do not say "as required." Provide a ceiling on the extent of such services, or work out a procedure (e.g., a level of effort, pool of man-hours) that will ensure adequate control.
- Avoid incorporating extraneous material and requirements. They may add unnecessary cost. Data requirements are common examples of problems in this area. Screen out unnecessary data requirements, and specify only what is essential and when. It is recommended that data requirements be specified separately in a data requirements appendix or equivalent.
- Do not repeat detailed requirements or specifications that are already spelled out in applicable documents. Instead, incorporate them by reference. If amplification, modification, or exceptions are required, make specific reference to the applicable portions and describe the change.

Some preparation documents also contain checklists for SOW preparation.[5] A checklist is furnished below to provide considerations that SOW writers should keep in mind in preparing statements of work:

- Is the SOW (when used in conjunction with the preliminary CWBS) specific enough to permit a contractor to make a tabulation and summary of manpower and resources needed to accomplish each SOW task element?
- Are specific duties of the contractor stated so he will know what is required, and can the contracting officer's representative, who signs the acceptance report, tell whether the contractor has complied?
- Are all parts of the SOW so written that there is no question as to what the contractor is obligated to do, and when?
- When it is necessary to reference other documents, is the proper reference document described? Is it properly cited? Is all of it really pertinent to the task, or should only portions be referenced? Is it cross-referenced to the applicable SOW task element?
- Are any specifications or exhibits applicable in whole or in part? If so, are they properly cited and referenced to the appropriate SOW element?
- Are directions clearly distinguishable from general information?
- Is there a time-phased data requirement for each deliverable item? If elapsed time is used, does it specify calendar or work days?

---

5. See note 3.

- Are proper quantities shown?
- Have headings been checked for format and grammar? Are subheadings comparable? Is the text compatible with the title? Is a multidecimal or alphanumeric numbering system used in the SOW? Can it be cross-referenced with the CWBS?
- Have appropriate portions of procurement regulations been followed?
- Has extraneous material been eliminated?
- Can SOW task/contract line items and configuration item breakouts at lower levels be identified and defined in sufficient detail so they can be summarized to discrete third-level CWBS elements?
- Have all requirements for data been specified separately in a data requirements appendix or its equivalent? Have all extraneous data requirements been eliminated?
- Are security requirements adequately covered if required?
- Has its availability to contractors been specified?

Finally, there should be a management review of the SOW preparation interpretation:[6]

> During development of the Statement of Work, the project manager should ensure adequacy of content by holding frequent reviews with project and functional specialists to determine that technical and data requirements specified do conform to the guidelines herein and adequately support the common system objective. The CWBS/SOW matrix should be used to analyze the SOW for completeness. After all comments and inputs have been incorporated, a final team review should be held to produce a draft SOW for review by functional and project managers. Specific problems should be resolved and changes made as appropriate. A final draft should then be prepared and reviewed with the program manager, contracting officer, or with higher management if the procurement is a major acquisition. The final review should include a briefing on the total RFP package. If other program offices or other Government agencies will be involved in the procurement, obtain their concurrence also.

11.8 PROJECT SPECIFICATIONS

A specification list as shown in Table 11–2 is separately identified or called out as part of the statement of work. Specifications are used for man-hour, equipment, and material estimates. Small changes in a specification can cause large cost overruns.

Another reason for identifying the specifications is to make sure that there are no surprises for the customer downstream. The specifications should be the most current revision. It is not uncommon for a customer to hire outside agencies

---

6. *Statement of Work Handbook* NHB5600.2, National Aeronautics and Space Administration, February 1975.

to evaluate the technical proposal and to make sure that the proper specifications are being used.

Specifications are, in fact, standards for pricing out a proposal. If specifications either do not yet exist or are not necessary, then work standards should be included in the proposal. The work standards can also appear in the cost volume

TABLE 11–2. SPECIFICATION FOR STATEMENT OF WORK

Description	Specification No.
Civil	100 (Index)
• Concrete	101
• Field equipment	102
• Piling	121
• Roofing and siding	122
• Soil testing	123
• Structural design	124
Electrical	200 (Index)
• Electrical testing	201
• Heat tracing	201
• Motors	209
• Power systems	225
• Switchgear	226
• Synchronous generators	227
HVAC	300 (Index)
• Hazardous environment	301
• Insulation	302
• Refrigeration piping	318
• Sheetmetal ductwork	319
Installation	400 (Index)
• Conveyors and chutes	401
• Fired heaters and boilers	402
• Heat exchangers	403
• Reactors	414
• Towers	415
• Vessels	416
Instruments	500 (Index)
• Alarm systems	501
• Control valves	502
• Flow instruments	503
• Level gages	536
• Pressure instruments	537
• Temperature instruments	538
Mechanical equipment	600 (Index)
• Centrifugal pumps	601
• Compressors	602
• High-speed gears	603
• Material handling equipment	640
• Mechanical agitators	641
• Steam turbines	642
Piping	700 (Index)
• Expansion joints	701
• Field pressure testing	702
• Installation of piping	703
• Pipe fabrication specs	749
• Pipe supports	750
• Steam tracing	751

TABLE 11–2. SPECIFICATION FOR STATEMENT OF WORK
(*Continued*)

Description	Specification No.
Project administration	800 (Index)
• Design drawings	801
• Drafting standards	802
• General requirements	803
• Project coordination	841
• Reporting procedure	842
• Vendor data	843
Vessels	900 (Index)
• Fireproofing	901
• Painting	902
• Reinforced tanks	948
• Shell and tube heat exchangers	949
• Steam boilers	950
• Vessel linings	951

of the proposal. Labor justification backup sheets may or may not be included in the proposal, depending on RFP/RFQ requirements.

Several years ago, a government agency queried contractors as to why some government programs were costing so much money. The main culprit turned out to be the specifications. The government began streamlining specifications and allowed the contractors to have more of a say as to "how" the work would be done provided that the end-item performance criteria was still met.

Typical specifications contain twice as many pages as necessary, do not stress quality enough, are loaded with unnecessary designs and schematics, are difficult to read and update, and are obsolete before they are published. Streamlining existing specifications is a costly and time-consuming effort. The better alternative is to educate those people involved in specification preparation as to correctness so that all future specifications will be reasonably correct.

11.9 MILESTONE SCHEDULES

Project milestone schedules contain such information as:

- Project start date
- Project end date
- Other major milestones
- Data items (deliverables or reports)

Project start and end dates, if known, must be included. Other major milestones such as review meetings, prototype available, procurement, testing, and so on, should also be identified. The last topic, data items, is often overlooked. There are two good reasons for preparing a separate schedule for data items. First, the separate schedule will indicate to line managers that personnel with writing skills may have to be assigned. Second, data items require direct-labor man-hours for writing, typing, editing, proofing, retyping, graphic arts, and reproduction. Many companies identify on the data item schedules the approximate number of pages per data item, and each data item is priced out at a cost per page, say $500/page. Pricing out data items separately often induces customers to require fewer reports.

The steps required to prepare a report, after the initial discovery work or collection of information, includes:

- Organizing the report
- Writing
- Typing
- Proofing
- Editing
- Retyping
- Graphic arts
- Submittal for approvals
- Reproduction and distribution

Typically, 6–8 hours of work are required per page. At a burdened hourly rate of $80/hour, it is easy for the cost of documentation to become exorbitant.

11.10 WORK BREAKDOWN STRUCTURE

The successful accomplishment of both contract and corporate objectives requires a plan that defines all effort to be expended, assigns responsibility to a specially identified organizational element, and establishes schedules and budgets for the accomplishment of the work. The preparation of this plan is the responsibility of the program manager, who is assisted by the program team assigned in accordance with program management system directives. The detailed planning is also established in accordance with company budgeting policy before contractual efforts are initiated.

In planning a project, the project manager must structure the work into small elements that are:

- Manageable, in that specific authority and responsibility can be assigned
- Independent, or with minimum interfacing with and dependence on other ongoing elements
- Integratable so that the total package can be seen
- Measurable in terms of progress

The first major step in the planning process after project requirements definition is the development of the work breakdown structure (WBS). A WBS is a product-oriented family tree subdivision of the hardware, services, and data required to produce the end product. The WBS is structured in accordance with the way the work will be performed and reflects the way in which project costs and data will be summarized and eventually reported. Preparation of the WBS also considers other areas that require structured data, such as scheduling, configuration management, contract funding, and technical performance parameters. The WBS is the single most important element because it provides a common framework from which:

- The total program can be described as a summation of subdivided elements.
- Planning can be performed.
- Costs and budgets can be established.
- Time, cost, and performance can be tracked.
- Objectives can be linked to company resources in a logical manner.
- Schedules and status-reporting procedures can be established.
- Network construction and control planning can be initiated.
- The responsibility assignments for each element can be established.

The work breakdown structure acts as a vehicle for breaking the work down into smaller elements, thus providing a greater probability that every major and minor activity will be accounted for. Although a variety of work breakdown structures exist, the most common is the six-level indented structure shown below:

	Level	Description
Managerial levels	1	Total program
	2	Project
	3	Task
Technical levels	4	Subtask
	5	Work package
	6	Level of effort

Level 1 is the total program and is composed of a set of projects. The summation of the activities and costs associated with each project must equal the total program. Each project, however, can be broken down into tasks, where the summation of all tasks equals the summation of all projects, which, in turn, comprises the total program. The reason for this subdivision of effort is simply ease of control. Program management therefore becomes synonymous with the integration of activities, and the project manager acts as the integrator, using the work breakdown structure as the common framework.

Careful consideration must be given to the design and development of the WBS. From Figure 11–3, the work breakdown structure can be used to provide the basis for:

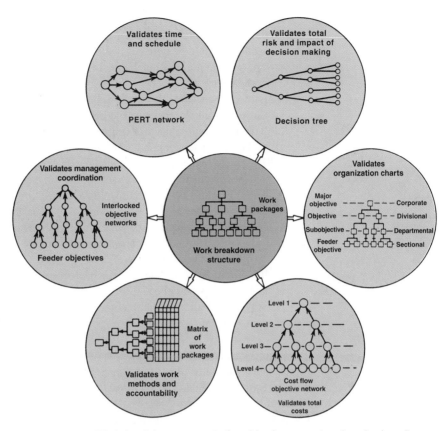

FIGURE 11–3. Work breakdown structure for objective control and evaluation. *Source:* Paul Mali, *Managing by Objectives* (New York: Wiley, 1972) p. 163. Copyright © 1972 by John Wiley & Sons, New York. Reprinted by permission of the publisher.

- The responsibility matrix
- Network scheduling
- Costing
- Risk analysis
- Organizational structure
- Coordination of objectives
- Control (including contract administration)

The upper three levels of the WBS are normally specified by the customer (if part of an RFP/RFQ) as the summary levels for reporting purposes. The lower levels are generated by the contractor for in-house control. Each level serves a vital purpose: Level 1 is generally used for the authorization and release of all work, budgets are prepared at level 2, and schedules are prepared at level 3. Certain characteristics can now be generalized for these levels:

- The top three levels of the WBS reflect integrated efforts and should not be related to one specific department. Effort required by departments or sections should be defined in subtasks and work packages.
- The summation of all elements in one level must be the sum of all work in the next lower level.
- Each element of work should be assigned to one and only one level of effort. For example, the construction of the foundation of a house should be included in one project (or task), not extended over two or three. (At level 5, the work packages should be identifiable and homogeneous.)
- The level at which the project is managed is generally called the work package level. Actually, the work package can exist at any level below level one.
- The WBS must be accompanied by a description of the scope of effort required, or else only those individuals who issue the WBS will have a complete understanding of what work has to be accomplished. It is common practice to reproduce the customer's statement of work as the description for the WBS.
- It is often the best policy for the project manager, regardless of his technical expertise, to allow all of the line managers to assess the risks in the SOW. After all, the line managers are usually the recognized experts in the organization.

Project managers normally manage at the top three levels of the WBS and prefer to provide status reports to management at these levels also. Some companies are trying to standardize reporting to management by requiring the top three levels of the WBS to be the same for every project, the only differences being in levels 4–6. For companies with a great deal of similarity among projects, this approach has merit. For most companies, however, the differences between projects make it almost impossible to standardize the top levels of the WBS.

The work package is the critical level for managing a work breakdown structure as shown in Figure 11–4. However, it is possible that the actual management of the work packages are supervised and performed by the line managers with status reporting provided to the project manager at higher levels of the WBS.

Work packages are natural subdivisions of cost accounts and constitute the basic building blocks used by the contractor in planning, controlling, and measuring contract performance. A work package is simply a low-level task or job assignment. It describes the work to be accomplished by a specific performing organization or a group of cost centers and serves as a vehicle for monitoring and reporting progress of work. Documents that authorize and assign work to a performing organization are designated by various names throughout industry. "Work package" is the generic term used in the criteria to identify discrete tasks that have definable end results. Ideal work packages are 80 hours and less than 2–4 weeks. However, this may not be possible on large projects.

It is not necessary that work package documentation contain complete, stand-alone descriptions. Supplemental documentation may augment the work package descriptions. However, the work package descriptions must permit cost

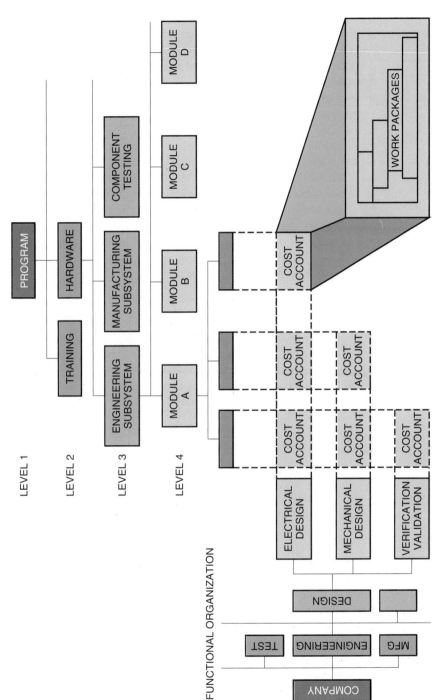

FIGURE 11–4. The cost account intersection.

account managers and work package supervisors to understand and clearly distinguish one work package effort from another. In the review of work package documentation, it may be necessary to obtain explanations from personnel routinely involved in the work, rather than requiring the work package descriptions to be completely self-explanatory.

A key feature from the standpoint of evaluation accomplishment is the desirability of having short-term work packages. This requirement is not intended to force arbitrary cutoff points simply to have short-term work packages. Work packages should be natural subdivisions of effort planned according to the way the work will be done. However, when work packages are relatively short, little or no assessment of work-in-process is required and the evaluation of status is possible mainly on the basis of work package completions. The longer the work packages, the more difficult and subjective the work-in-process assessment becomes unless the packages are subdivided by objective indicators such as discrete milestones with preassigned budget values or completion percentages.

In setting up the work breakdown structure, tasks should:

- Have clearly defined start and end dates
- Be usable as a communications tool in which results can be compared with expectations
- Be estimated on a "total" time duration, not when the task must start or end
- Be structured so that a minimum of project office control and documentation (i.e., forms) is necessary

For large projects, planning will be time phased at the work package level of the WBS. The work package has the following characteristics:

- Represents units of work at the level where the work is performed
- Clearly distinguishes one work package from all others assigned to a single functional group
- Contains clearly defined start and end dates that are representative of physical accomplishment
- Specifies a budget in terms of dollars, man-hours, or other measurable units
- Limits the work to be performed to relatively short periods of time to minimize the work-in-process effort

Table 11–3 shows a simple work breakdown structure with the associated numbering system following the work breakdown. The first number represents the total program (in this case, it is represented by 01), the second number represents the project, and the third number identifies the task. Therefore, number 01-03-00 represents project 3 of program 01, whereas 01-03-02 represents task 2 of project 3. This type of numbering system is not standard; each company may have its own system, depending on how costs are to be controlled.

TABLE 11–3. WORK BREAKDOWN STRUCTURE FOR NEW PLANT CONSTRUCTION AND START-UP

Program: New Plant Construction and Start-up	01-00-00
Project 1: Analytical Study	01-01-00
Task 1: Marketing/Production Study	01-01-01
Task 2: Cost Effectiveness Analysis	01-01-02
Project 2: Design and Layout	01-02-00
Task 1: Product Processing Sketches	01-02-01
Task 2: Product Processing Blueprints	01-02-02
Project 3: Installation	01-03-00
Task 1: Fabrication	01-03-01
Task 2: Setup	01-03-02
Task 3: Testing and Run	01-03-03
Project 4: Program Support	01-04-00
Task 1: Management	01-04-01
Task 2: Purchasing Raw Materials	01-04-02

The preparation of the work breakdown structure is not easy. The WBS is a communications tool, providing detailed information to different levels of management. If it does not contain enough levels, then the integration of activities may prove difficult. If too many levels exist, then unproductive time will be made to have the same number of levels for all projects, tasks, and so on. Each major work element should be considered by itself. Remember, the WBS establishes the number of required networks for cost control.

For many programs, the work breakdown structure is established by the customer. If the contractor is required to develop a WBS, then certain guidelines must be considered. A partial list is as follows:

- The complexity and technical requirements of the program (i.e., the statement of work)
- The program cost
- The time span of the program
- The contractor's resource requirements
- The contractor's and customer's internal structure for management control and reporting
- The number of subcontracts

Applying these guidelines serves only to identify the complexity of the program. These data must then be subdivided and released, together with detailed information, to the different levels of the organization. The WBS should follow specified criteria because, although preparation of the WBS is performed by the program office, the actual work is performed by the doers, not the planners. Both the doers and the planners must be in agreement as to what is expected. A sample listing of criteria for developing a work breakdown structure is shown below:

- The WBS and work description should be easy to understand.
- All schedules should follow the WBS.

- No attempt should be made to subdivide work arbitrarily to the lowest possible level. The lowest level of work should not end up having a ridiculous cost in comparison to other efforts.
- Since scope of effort can change during a program, every effort should be made to maintain flexibility in the WBS.
- The WBS can act as a list of discrete and tangible milestones so that everyone will know when the milestones were achieved.
- The level of the WBS can reflect the "trust" you have in certain line groups.
- The WBS can be used to segregate recurring from nonrecurring costs.
- Most WBS elements (at the lowest control level) range from 0.5 to 2.5 percent of the total project budget.

11.11 WBS DECOMPOSITION PROBLEMS

There is a common misconception that WBS decomposition is an easy task to perform. In the development of the WBS, the top three levels or management levels are usually roll-up levels. Preparing templates at these levels is becoming common practice. However, at levels 4–6 of the WBS, templates may not be appropriate. There are reasons for this.

- Breaking the work down to extremely small and detailed work packages may require the creation of hundreds or even thousands of cost accounts and charge numbers. This could increase the management, control, and reporting costs of these small packages to a point where the costs exceed the benefits. Although a typical work package may be 200–300 hours and approximately two weeks in duration, consider the impact on a large project, which may have more than one million direct labor hours.
- Breaking the work down to small work packages can provide accurate cost control if, and only if, the line managers can determine the costs at this level of detail. Line managers must be given the right to tell project managers that costs *cannot* be determined at the requested level of detail.
- The work breakdown structure is the basis for scheduling techniques such as the Arrow Diagramming Method and the Precedence Diagramming Method. At low levels of the WBS, the interdependencies between activities can become so complex that meaningful networks cannot be constructed.

One solution to the above problems is to create "hammock" activities, which encompass several activities where exact cost identification cannot or may not be accurately determined. Some projects identify a "hammock" activity called management support (or project office), which includes overall project management, data items, management reserve, and possibly procurement. The advantage of this type of hammock activity is that the charge numbers are under the *direct* control of the project manager.

There is a common misconception that the typical dimensions of a work package are approximately 80 hours and less than two weeks to a month. Although this may be true on small projects, this would necessitate millions of work packages on large jobs and this may be impractical, even if line managers could control work packages of this size.

From a cost control point of view, cost analysis down to the fifth level is advantageous. However, it should be noted that the cost required to prepare cost analysis data to each lower level may increase exponentially, especially if the customer requires data to be presented in a specified format that is not part of the company's standard operating procedures. The level-5 work packages are normally for in-house control only. Some companies bill customers separately for each level of cost reporting below level 3.

The WBS can be subdivided into subobjectives with finer divisions of effort as we go lower into the WBS. By defining subobjectives, we add greater understanding and, it is hoped, clarity of action for those individuals who will be required to complete the objectives. Whenever work is structured, understood, easily identifiable, and within the capabilities of the individuals, there will almost always exist a high degree of confidence that the objective can be reached.

Work breakdown structures can be used to structure work for reaching such objectives as lowering cost, reducing absenteeism, improving morale, and lowering scrap factors. The lowest subdivision now becomes an end-item or subobjective, not necessarily a work package as described here. However, since we are describing project management, for the remainder of the text we will consider the lowest level as the work package.

Once the WBS is established and the program is "kicked off," it becomes a very costly procedure to either add or delete activities, or change levels of reporting because of cost control. Many companies do not give careful forethought to the importance of a properly developed WBS, and ultimately they risk cost control problems downstream. One important use of the WBS is that it serves as a cost control standard for any future activities that may follow on or may just be similar. One common mistake made by management is the combining of direct support activities with administrative activities. For example, the department manager for manufacturing engineering may be required to provide administrative support (possibly by attending team meetings) throughout the duration of the program. If the administrative support is spread out over each of the projects, a false picture is obtained as to the actual hours needed to accomplish each project in the program. If one of the projects should be canceled, then the support manhours for the total program would be reduced when, in fact, the administrative and support functions may be constant, regardless of the number of projects and tasks.

Quite often work breakdown structures accompanying customer RFPs contain much more scope of effort as specified by the statement of work than the existing funding will support. This is done intentionally by the customer in hopes that a contractor may be willing to "buy in." If the contractor's price exceeds the customer's funding limitations, then the scope of effort must be reduced by eliminating activities from the WBS. By developing a separate project for administrative and indirect support activities, the customer can easily modify his costs by eliminating the direct support activities of the canceled effort.

Before we go on, there should be a brief discussion of the usefulness and applicability of the WBS system. Many companies and industries have been successful in managing programs without the use of work breakdown structures, especially on repetitive-type programs. As was the case with the SOW, there are also preparation guides for the WBS:[7]

- Develop the WBS structure by subdividing the total effort into discrete and logical subelements. Usually a program subdivides into projects, major systems, major subsystems, and various lower levels until a manageable-size element level is reached. Wide variations may occur, depending upon the type of effort (e.g., major systems development, support services, etc.). Include more than one cost center and more than one contractor if this reflects the actual situation.
- Check the proposed WBS and the contemplated efforts for completeness, compatibility, and continuity.
- Determine that the WBS satisfies both functional (engineering/manufacturing/test) and program/project (hardware, services, etc.) requirements, including recurring and nonrecurring costs.
- Check to determine if the WBS provides for logical subdivision of all project work.
- Establish assignment of responsibilities for all identified effort to specific organizations.
- Check the proposed WBS against the reporting requirements of the organizations involved.

There are also checklists that can be used in the preparation of the WBS:[8]

- Develop a preliminary WBS to not lower than the top three levels for solicitation purposes (or lower if deemed necessary for some special reason).
- Assure that the contractor is required to extend the preliminary WBS in response to the solicitation, to identify and structure all contractor work to be compatible with his organization and management system.
- Following negotiations, the CWBS included in the contract should not normally extend lower than the third level.
- Assure that the negotiated CWBS structure is compatible with reporting requirements.

---

7. Source: *Handbook for Preparation of Work Breakdown Structures,* NHB5610.1, National Aeronautics and Space Administration, February 1975.

8. See note 7.

- Assure that the negotiated CWBS is compatible with the contractor's organization and management system.
- Review the CWBS elements to ensure correlation with:
  - The specification tree
  - Contract line items
  - End-items of the contract
  - Data items required
  - Work statement tasks
  - Configuration management requirements
- Define CWBS elements down to the level where such definitions are meaningful and necessary for management purposes (WBS dictionary).
- Specify reporting requirements for selected CWBS elements if variations from standard reporting requirements are desired.
- Assure that the CWBS covers measurable effort, level of effort, apportioned effort, and subcontracts, if applicable.
- Assure that the total costs at a particular level will equal the sum of the costs of the constituent elements at the next lower level.

On simple projects, the WBS can be constructed as a "tree diagram" (see Figure 11–5) or according to the logic flow. In Figure 11–5, the tree diagram can follow the work or even the organizational structure of the company (i.e., division, department, section, unit). The second method is to create a logic flow (see Figure 12–19) and cluster certain elements to represent tasks and projects. In the tree method, lower-level functional units may be assigned to one, and only one,

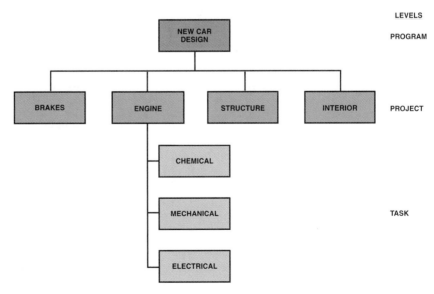

FIGURE 11–5. WBS tree diagram.

work element, whereas in the logic flow method the lower-level functional units may serve several WBS elements.

A tendency exists today to develop guidelines, policies, and procedures for project management, but not for the development of the WBS. Since the work breakdown structure must have flexibility built into it, the tendency is to avoid limiting the way the WBS must be developed. Some companies have been marginally successful in developing a "generic" methodology for levels 1, 2, and 3 of the WBS. In other words, the top three levels of the WBS are the same for all projects. The differences appear in levels 4, 5, and 6.

The table below shows the three most common methods for structuring the WBS:

| | Method | | |
Level	Flow	Life Cycle	Organization
Program	Program	Program	Program
Project	System	Life cycle	Division
Task	Subsystem	System	Department
Subtask	People	Subsystem	Section
Work package	People	People	People
Level of effort	People	People	People

The flow method breaks the work down into systems and major subsystems. This method is well suited for projects less than two years in length. For longer-duration projects, we use the life-cycle method, which is similar to the flow method. The organization method is used for projects that may be repetitive or require very little integration between functional units.

11.12 ROLE OF THE EXECUTIVE IN PROJECT SELECTION

A prime responsibility of senior management (and possibly project sponsors) is the selection of projects. Most organizations have an established selection criteria, which can be subjective, objective, quantitative, qualitative, or simply a seat-of-the-pants guess. In any event, there should be a valid reason for selecting the project.

From a financial perspective, project selection is basically a two-part process. First, the organization will conduct a feasibility study to determine whether the project *can* be done. The second part is to perform a benefit-to-cost analysis to see whether the company *should* do it.

The purpose of the feasibility study is to validate that the project meets feasibility of cost, technological, safety, marketability, and ease of execution requirements. It is possible for the company to use outside consultants or subject matter experts (SMEs) to assist in both feasibility studies and benefit-to-cost analyses. A project manager may not be assigned until after the feasibility study is completed.

As part of the feasibility process during project selection, senior management often solicits input from SMEs and lower level managers through rating models. The rating models normally identify the business and/or technical criteria against which the ratings will be made. Figure 11–6 shows a scaling model for a single project. Figure 11–7 shows a checklist rating system to evaluate three projects at once. Figure 11–8 shows a scoring model for multiple projects using weighted averages.

If the project is deemed feasible and a good fit with the strategic plan, then the project is prioritized for development along with other projects. Once feasibility is determined, a benefit-to-cost analysis is performed to validate that the project will, if executed correctly, provide the required financial and nonfinancial benefits. Benefit-to-cost analyses require significantly more information to be scrutinized than is usually available during a feasibility study. This can be an expensive proposition.

Estimating benefits and costs in a timely manner is very difficult. Benefits are often defined as:

- Tangible benefits for which dollars may be reasonably quantified and measured.
- Intangible benefits that may be quantified in units other than dollars or may be identified and described subjectively.

Costs are significantly more difficult to quantify, at least in a timely and inexpensive manner. The minimum costs that must be determined are those that specifically are used for comparison to the benefits. These include:

- The current operating costs or the cost of operating in today's circumstances.
- Future period costs that are expected and can be planned for.
- Intangible costs that may be difficult to quantify. These costs are often omitted if quantification would contribute little to the decision-making process.

There must be careful documentation of all known constraints and assumptions that were made in developing the costs and the benefits. Unrealistic or unrecognized assumptions are often the cause of unrealistic benefits. The go or no-go decision to continue with a project could very well rest upon the validity of the assumptions.

Table 11–4 shows the major differences between feasibility studies and benefit-to-cost analyses.

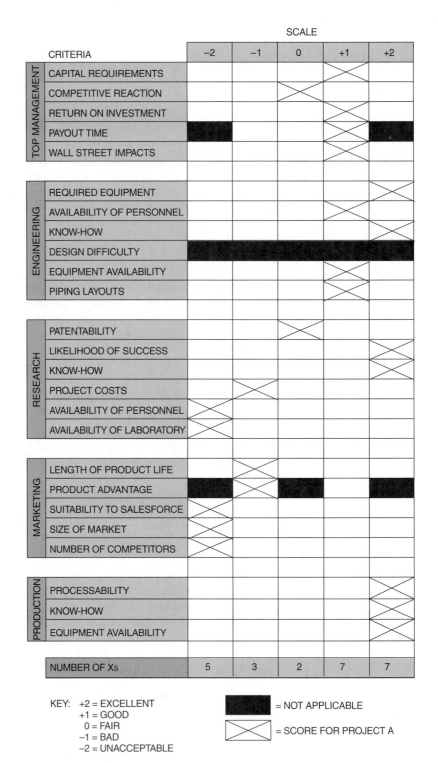

FIGURE 11–6. Illustration of a scaling model for one project, Project A. *Source:* William E. Souder, *Project Selection and Economic Appraisal,* p. 66.

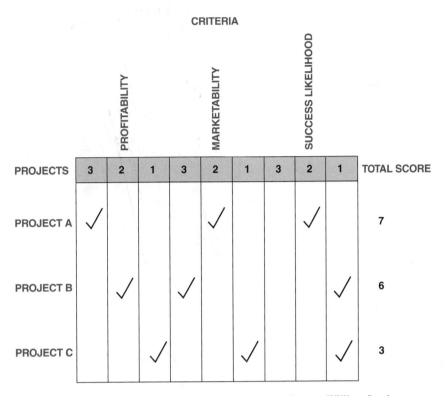

FIGURE 11–7. Illustration of a checklist for three projects. *Source:* William Souder, *Project Selection and Economic Appraisal*, p. 68.

11.13 ROLE OF THE EXECUTIVE IN PLANNING

Many project managers view the first critical step in planning as obtaining the support of top management because once it becomes obvious to the functional managers that top management is expressing an interest in the project, they (the functional managers) are more likely to respond favorably to the project team's request for support, partly to protect themselves.

Executives are also responsible for selecting the project manager, and the person chosen should have planning expertise. Not all technical specialists are good planners. As Rogers points out:[9]

> The technical planners, whether they are engineers or systems analysts, must be experts at designing the system, but seldom do they recognize the need to "put

---

9. Lloyd A. Rogers, "Guidelines for Project Management Teams," *Industrial Engineering*, December 12, 1974. Published and copyright 1974 by the Institute of Industrial Engineers, 25 Technology Park, Norcross, GA 30092.

CRITERIA	PROFITABILITY	PATENTABILITY	MARKETABILITY	PRODUCEABILITY
CRITERION WEIGHTS	4	3	2	1

PROJECTS	CRITERION SCORES*				TOTAL WEIGHTED SCORE
PROJECT D	10	6	4	3	69
PROJECT E	5	10	10	5	75
PROJECT F	3	7	10	10	63

TOTAL WEIGHTED SCORE = Σ (CRITERION SCORE X CRITERION WEIGHT)

*SCALE: 10 = EXCELLENT; 1 = UNACCEPTABLE

FIGURE 11–8. Illustration of a scoring model. *Source:* William Souder, *Project Selection and Economic Appraisal,* p. 69.

on another hat" when system design specifications are completed and design the project control or implementation plan. If this is not done, setting a project completion target date of a set of management checkpoint milestones is done by guesswork at best. Management will set the checkpoint milestones, and the technical planners will hope they can meet the schedule.

Executives must not arbitrarily set unrealistic milestones and then "force" line managers to fulfill them. Both project and line managers should try to adhere to unrealistic milestones, but if a line manager says he cannot, executives should

TABLE 11–4. FEASIBILITY STUDY AND BENEFIT-COST ANALYSIS

	Feasibility Study	**Benefit-Cost Analysis**
Basic Question	*Can we do it?*	*Should we do it?*
Life Cycle Phase	Preconceptual	Conceptual
P.M. Selected	Usually not yet	Usually identified but partial involvement
Analysis	Qualitative	Quantitative
Critical Factors for Go/No-Go	• Technical	• Net present value
	• Cost	• Discounted cash flow
	• Quality	• Internal rate of return
	• Safety	• Return on investment
	• Ease of performance	• Probability of success
	• Economical	• Reality of assumptions and constraints
	• Legal	
Executive Decision Criteria	Strategic fit	Benefits exceed costs by required margin

comply because the line manager is supposedly the expert. Sometimes, executives lose sight of what they are doing. As an example, a bank executive took the six-month completion date milestone and made it three months. The project and line managers rescheduled all of the other projects to reach this milestone. The executive then did the same thing on three other projects, and again the project and line managers came to his rescue. The executive began to believe that the line people did not know how to estimate and that they probably loaded up every schedule with "fat." So, the executive changed the milestones on all of the other projects to what his "gut feeling" told him was realistic. The reader can imagine the chaos that followed.

Executives should interface with project and line personnel during the planning stage in order to define the requirements and establish reasonable deadlines. Executives must realize that creating an unreasonable deadline may require the reestablishment of priorities, and, of course, changing priorities can push milestones backward instead of forward.

11.14 THE PLANNING CYCLE

In Section 2.9, we stated that perhaps the most important reason for structuring projects into life-cycle phases is to provide management with control of the critical decision points in order to:

- Avoid commitment of major resources too early
- Preserve future options
- Maximize benefits of each project in relation to all other projects
- Assess risks

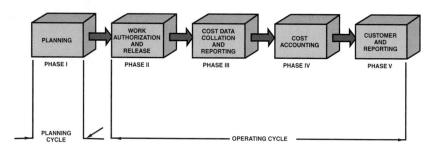

FIGURE 11–9. Phase of a management cost and control system.

On long-term projects, phasing can be overdone, with resultant extra costs and delays in achieving objectives. To prevent such a situation, many project-driven companies resort to other types of systems, such as a management cost and control system (MCCS). No program or project can be efficiently organized and managed without some form of management cost and control system. Figure 11–9 shows the five phases of a management cost and control system. The first phase constitutes the planning cycle, and the next four phases identify the operating cycle.

Figure 11–10 shows the activities included in the planning cycle. The work breakdown structure serves as the initial control from which all planning em-

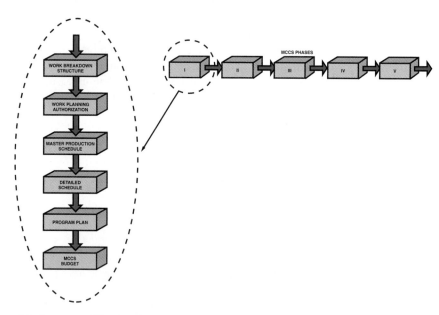

FIGURE 11–10. The planning cycle of a management cost and control system.

anates. The WBS acts as a vital artery for both communications and operations, not only for the planning cycle, but for all other phases as well. A comprehensive analysis of management cost and control systems is presented in Chapter 15.

11.15 WORK PLANNING AUTHORIZATION

After receipt of a contract, some form of authorization is needed before work can begin, even in the planning stage. Both work authorization and work planning authorization are used to release funds, but for different purposes. Work planning authorization releases funds (primarily for functional management) so that scheduling, costs, budgets, and all other types of plans can be prepared prior to the release of operational cycle funds, which hereafter shall be referred to simply as work authorization. Both forms of authorization require the same paperwork. In many companies this work authorization is identified as a subdivided work description (SWD), which is a narrative description of the effort to be performed by the cost center (division-level minimum). This package establishes the work to be performed, the period of performance, and possibly the maximum number of hours available. The SWD is multipurpose in that it can be used to release contract funds, authorize planning, describe activities as identified in the WBS, and, last but not least, release work.

The SWD is one of the key elements in the planning of a program as shown in Figure 11–10. Contract control and administration releases the contract funds by issuing a SWD, which sets forth general contractual requirements and authorizes program management to proceed. Program management issues the SWD to set forth the contractual guidelines and requirements for the functional units. The SWD specifies how the work will be performed, which functional organizations will be involved, and who has what specific responsibilities, and authorizes the utilization of resources within a given time period.

The SWD authorizes both the program team and functional management to begin work. As shown in Figure 11–10, the SWD provides direct input to Phase II of the MCCS. Phase I and Phase II can and do operate simultaneously because it is generally impossible for program office personnel to establish plans, procedures, and schedules without input from the functional units.

The subdivided work description package is used by the operating organizations to further subdivide the effort defined by the WBS into small segments or work packages.

Many people contend that if the data in the work authorization document are different from what was originally defined in the proposal, the project is in trouble right at the start. This may not be the case, because most projects are priced out assuming "unlimited" resources, whereas the hours and dollars in the work authorization document are based upon "limited" resources. This situation is common for companies that thrive on competitive bidding.

11.16 WHY DO PLANS FAIL?

No matter how hard we try, planning is not perfect, and sometimes plans fail (Figure 11–11). Typical reasons why plans fail include:

- Corporate goals are not understood at the lower organizational levels.
- Plans encompass too much in too little time.
- Financial estimates were poor.
- Plans were based on insufficient data.
- No attempt was made to systematize the planning process.
- Planning was performed by a planning group.
- No one knows the ultimate objective.
- No one knows the staffing requirements.
- No one knows the major milestone dates, including written reports.
- Project estimates are best guesses, and are not based on standards or history.
- Not enough time was given for proper estimating.
- No one bothered to see if there would be personnel available with the necessary skills.
- People are not working toward the same specifications.
- People are consistently shuffled in and out of the project with little regard for schedule.

FIGURE 11–11.   Why always on my project?

Why do these situations occur, and who should be blamed? If corporate goals are not understood, it is because corporate executives were negligent in providing the necessary strategic information and feedback. If a plan fails because of extreme optimism, then the responsibility lies with both the project and line managers for not assessing risk. Project managers should ask the line managers if the estimates are optimistic or pessimistic, and expect an honest answer. Erroneous financial estimates are the responsibility of the line manager. If the project fails because of a poor definition of the requirements, then the project manager is totally at fault.

Project managers must be willing to accept failure. Sometimes, a situation occurs that can lead to failure, and the problem rests with either upper-level management or some other group. As an example, consider the major utility company with a planning group that prepares budgets (with the help of functional groups) and selects projects to be completed within a given time period. A project manager on one such project discovered that the project should have started "last month" in order to meet the completion date. In cases like this, project managers will not become dedicated to the projects unless they are active members during the planning and know what assumptions and constraints were considered in development of the plan.

Sometimes, the project manager is part of the planning group and as part of a feasibility study is asked to prepare, with the assistance of functional managers, a schedule and cost summary for a project that will occur three years downstream, if it is approved at all. Suppose that three years downstream the project is approved. How does the project manager get functional managers to accept the schedule and cost summary that they themselves prepared three years before? It cannot be done, because technology may have changed, people may be working higher or lower on the learning curve, and salary and raw material escalation factors are inaccurate.

Sometimes project plans fail because simple details are forgotten or overlooked. Examples of this might be:

- Neglecting to tell a line manager early enough that the prototype is not ready and that rescheduling is necessary.
- Neglecting to see if the line manager can still provide additional employees for the next two weeks because it was possible to do so six months ago.

Sometimes plans fail because the project manager "bites off more than he can chew," and then something happens, such as his becoming ill. Even if the project manager is effective at doing a lot of the work, overburdening is unnecessary. Many projects have failed because the project manager was the only one who knew what was going on and then got sick.

11.17 STOPPING PROJECTS

There are always situations in which projects have to be stopped. Below are nine reasons for stopping:

- Final achievement of the objectives
- Poor initial planning and market prognosis
- A better alternative is found
- A change in the company interest and strategy
- Allocated time is exceeded
- Budgeted costs are exceeded
- Key people leave the organization
- Personal whims of management
- Problem too complex for the resources available

Today most of the reasons why projects are not completed on time and within cost are behavioral rather than quantitative considerations. They include:

- Poor morale
- Poor human relations
- Poor labor productivity
- No commitment by those involved in the project

The last item appears to be the cause of the first three items in many situations.

Once the reasons for cancellation are defined, the next problem concerns how to stop the project. Some of the ways are:

- Orderly planned termination
- The "hatchet" (withdrawal of funds and removal of personnel)
- Reassignment of people to higher priority
- Redirection of efforts toward different objectives
- Burying it or letting it die on the vine (i.e., not taking any official action)

There are three major problem areas to be considered in stopping projects:

- Worker morale
- Reassignment of personnel
- Adequate documentation and wrap-up

Sometimes executives do not realize the relationship between projects and what happens if one is canceled prematurely. As an example, the following remarks were made by an executive concerning data processing operations:

When 75–80 percent of the resource commitment is obtained, there is the point of no return and the benefits to be obtained from the project are anticipated. However, project costs, once forecast, are seldom adjusted during the project life cycle. Adjustments, when made, are normally to increase costs prior to or during conversion. Increases in cost are always in small increments and usually occur when the corporation is "committed," i.e., 75–80 percent of the actual costs are expended; however, total actual costs are not known until the project is over.

Projects can and sometimes should be canceled at any point in the project life cycle. Projects are seldom canceled because costs exceed forecasts. More often, resources are drained from successful projects. The result of the action is the corporation as a whole becomes marginally successful in bringing all identified projects on line. One might assume individual projects can be analyzed to determine which projects are successful and which are unsuccessful. However, the corporate movement of resources makes the determination difficult without elaborate computer systems. For example, as project A appears to be successful, resources are diverted to less successful project B. The costs associated with project A increase dramatically as all remaining activities become critical to project A completion. Increasing costs for project A are associated with overtime, traveling, etc. Costs for project B are increasing at a straight time rate and more activities are being accomplished because more manpower can be expended. Often resources, particularly manpower working on project B, are charged to project A because the money is in the budget for project A. The net result is projects A and B overrun authorized budgets by about the same percentage. In the eyes of top corporate management, neither project team has done well nor have the teams performed poorly. This mediocrity in performance is often the goal of corporate project management technique.

11.18 HANDLING PROJECT PHASEOUTS AND TRANSFERS

By definition, projects have an end point. Closing out is a very important phase in the project life cycle, which should follow particular disciplines and procedures with the objective of:

- Effectively bringing the project to closure according to agreed-on contractual requirements
- Preparing for the transition of the project into the next operational phase, such as from production to field installation, field operation, or training
- Analyzing overall project performance with regard to financial data, schedules, and technical efforts
- Closing the project office, and transferring or selling off all resources originally assigned to the project, including personnel
- Identifying and pursuing follow-on business

Although most project managers are completely cognizant of the necessity for proper planning for project start-up, many project managers neglect planning for project termination. Planning for project termination includes:

- Transferring responsibility
- Completion of project records
  - Historic reports
  - Post project analysis

- Documenting results to reflect "as built" product or installation
- Acceptance by sponsor/user
- Satisfying contractual requirements
- Releasing resources
  - Reassignment of project office team members
  - Disposition of functional personnel
  - Disposition of materials
- Closing out work orders (financial closeout)
- Preparing for financial payments

Project success or failure often depends on management's ability to handle personnel issues properly during this final phase. If job assignments beyond the current project look undesirable or uncertain to project team members, a great deal of anxiety and conflict may develop that diverts needed energy to job hunting, foot dragging, or even sabotage. Another problem is that project personnel engage in job searches on their own and may leave the project prematurely. This creates a glaring void that is often difficult to patch, always costing additional time and money, and often eroding the already strained morale of the remaining project team.

Given the business realities, it is often difficult to transfer project personnel under ideal conditions for all parties involved. However, some suggestions are delineated below that can increase organizational effectiveness in closing out a project and can minimize personal stress for all parties involved:

- Carefully plan the project closeout on the part of both project and functional managers. Use a checklist to assist in the preparation of the closeout plan.
- Establish a simple project closeout procedure that identifies the major steps and responsibilities.
- Treat the closeout phase like any other project, with clearly delineated tasks, agreed-on responsibilities, schedules, budgets, and deliverable items or results.
- Understand the interaction of behavioral and organizational elements in order to build an environment conducive to teamwork during this final project phase.
- Emphasize the overall goals, applications, and utilities of the project as well as its business impact. This will boost the morale of the team and enhance the desire to participate up to final closure and success.
- Secure top-management involvement and support.
- Be aware of conflict, fatigue, shifting priorities, and technical or logistic problems. Try to identify and deal with these problems when they start to develop. Maintaining an effective flow of communications is the key to managing these problems. Regularly scheduled status meetings can be an important vehicle for maintaining effective communications.
- If at all possible, keep project personnel informed of upcoming job op-

portunities. Resource managers should discuss and negotiate new assignments with their personnel and, ideally, start involving their people already in the next project.

- Be aware of rumors. If a reorganization or layoff is inevitable at the end of a project, the situation should be described in a professional manner. If it is left to the imagination, project personnel will assume the worst, resulting in a demoralized team, work slowdowns, and sporadic departure of key team members.
- Assign a contract administrator dedicated to company-oriented projects. He will protect your financial position and business interests by following through on customer sign-offs and final payment.

11.19 DETAILED SCHEDULES AND CHARTS

The scheduling of activities is the first major requirement of the program office after program go-ahead. The program office normally assumes full responsibility for activity scheduling if the activity is not too complex. For large programs, functional management input is required before scheduling can be completed. Depending on program size and contractual requirements, it is not unusual for the program office to maintain, at all times, a program staff member whose responsibility is that of a scheduler. This individual continuously develops and updates activity schedules to provide a means of tracking program work. The resulting information is then supplied to the program office personnel, functional management, and team members, and, last but not least, is presented to the customer.

Activity scheduling is probably the single most important tool for determining how company resources should be integrated so that synergy is produced. Activity schedules are invaluable for projecting time-phased resource utilization requirements as well as providing a basis for visually tracking performance. Most programs begin with the development of schedules so that accurate cost estimates can be made. The schedules serve as master plans from which both the customer and management have an up-to-date picture of operations.

Certain guidelines should be followed in the preparation of schedules, regardless of the projected use or complexity:

- All major events and dates must be clearly identified. If a statement of work is supplied by the customer, those dates shown on the accompanying schedules must be included. If for any reason the customer's milestone dates cannot be met, the customer should be notified immediately.
- The exact sequence of work should be defined through a network in which interrelationships between events can be identified.
- Schedules should be directly relatable to the work breakdown structure. If the WBS is developed according to a specific sequence of work, then

it becomes an easy task to identify work sequences in schedules using the same numbering system as in the WBS. The minimum requirement should be to show where and when all tasks start and finish.

● All schedules must identify the time constraints and, if possible, should identify those resources required for each event.

Although these four guidelines relate to schedule preparation, they do not define how complex the schedules should be. Before preparing schedules, three questions should be considered:

● How many events or activities should each network have?
● How much of a detailed technical breakdown should be included?
● Who is the intended audience for this schedule?

Most organizations develop multiple schedules: summary schedules for management and planners and detailed schedules for the doers and lower-level control. The detailed schedules may be strictly for interdepartmental activities. Program management must approve all schedules down through the first three levels of the work breakdown structure. For lower-level schedules (i.e., detailed interdepartmental), program management may or may not request a sign of approval.

The need for two schedules is clear. According to Martin:[10]

In larger complicated projects, planning and status review by different echelons are facilitated by the use of detailed and summary networks. Higher levels of management can view the entire project and the interrelationships of major tasks without looking into the detail of the individual subtasks. Lower levels of management and supervision can examine their parts of the project in fine detail without being distracted by those parts of the project with which they have no interface.

One of the most difficult problems to identify in schedules is a hedge position. A hedge position is a situation in which the contractor may not be able to meet a customer's milestone date without incurring a risk, or may not be able to meet activity requirements following a milestone date because of contractual requirements. To illustrate a common hedge position, consider Example 11–1 below.

Example 11–1. Condor Corporation is currently working on a project that has three phases: design, development, and qualification of a certain component. Contractual requirements with the customer specify that no components will be fabricated for the development phase until the design review meeting is held fol-

---

10. Reprinted, with permission of the publisher, from *Project Management: How to Make It Work* (p. 137) by Charles Martin, © 1976 AMACOM, a division of the American Management Association. All rights reserved.

lowing the design phase. Condor has determined that if it does not begin component fabrication prior to the design review meeting, then the second and third phases will slip. Condor is willing to accept the risk that should specifications be unacceptable during the design review meeting, the costs associated with preauthorization of fabrication will be incurred. How should this be shown on a schedule? (The problems associated with performing unauthorized work are not being considered here.)

The solution to Example 11–1 is not an easy one. Condor must play an honest game and show on the master production schedule that component fabrication will begin early, at the contractor's risk. This should be followed up by a contractual letter in which both the customer and contractor understand the risks and implications.

Example 11–1 also raises the question of whether this hedge position could have been eliminated with proper planning. Hedge positions are notorious for occurring in research and development or design phases of a program. Condor's technical community, for example, may have anticipated that each component could be fabricated in one week based on certain raw materials. If new raw materials were required or a new fabrication process had to be developed, it is then possible that the new component fabrication time could have increased from one week to two or three weeks, thus creating an unanticipated hedge position.

Detailed schedules are prepared for almost every activity. It is the responsibility of the program office to marry all of the detailed schedules into one master schedule to verify that all activities can be completed as planned. The preparation sequence for schedules (and also for program plans) is shown in Figure 11–12. The program office submits a request for detailed schedules to the functional

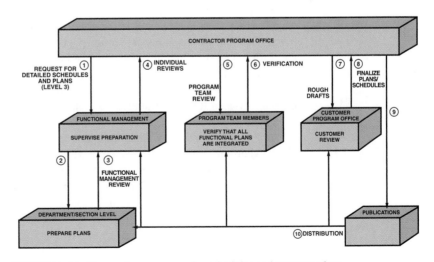

FIGURE 11–12. Preparation sequence for schedules and program plans.

managers. The request may be in the form of a planning work authorization document. The functional managers then prepare summary schedules, detailed schedules, and, if time permits, interdepartmental schedules. Each functional manager then reviews his schedules with the program office. The program office, together with the functional program team members, integrates all of the plans and schedules and verifies that all contractual dates can be met.

Before the schedules are submitted to publications, rough drafts of each schedule and plan should be reviewed with the customer. This procedure accomplishes the following:

- Verifies that nothing has fallen through the cracks
- Prevents immediate revisions to a published document and can prevent embarrassing moments
- Minimizes production costs by reducing the number of early revisions
- Shows customers early in the program that you welcome their help and input into the planning phase

After the document is published, it should be distributed to all program office personnel, functional team members, functional management, and the customer.

The exact method of preparing the schedules is usually up to the individual performing the activity. All schedules, however, must be approved by the program office. The schedules are normally prepared in a format that is suitable to both the customer and contractor and is easily understood by all. The schedules may then be used in-house as well as for customer review meetings, in which case the contractor can "kill two birds with one stone" by tracking cost and performance on the original schedules. Examples of detailed schedules are shown in Chapter 13.

In addition to the detailed schedules, the program office, with input provided by functional management, must develop organization charts. The organizational charts tell all active participants in the project who has responsibility for each activity. (Examples were shown in Section 4.11.) The organizational charts display the formal (and often the informal) lines of communication.

The program office may also establish linear responsibility charts (LRCs). In spite of the best attempts by management, many functions in an organization may overlap between functional units. Also, management might wish to have the responsibility for a certain activity given to a functional unit that normally would not have that responsibility. This is a common occurrence on short-duration programs where management desires to cut costs and red tape.

Care must be taken that project personnel do not forget the reason why the schedule was developed. The primary objective of detailed schedules is usually to coordinate activities into a master plan in order to complete the project with the:

- Best time
- Least cost
- Least risk

Of course, the objective can be constrained by:

- Calendar completion dates
- Cash or cash flow restrictions
- Limited resources
- Approvals

There are also secondary objectives of scheduling:

- Studying alternatives
- Developing an optimal schedule
- Using resources effectively
- Communicating
- Refining the estimating criteria
- Obtaining good project control
- Providing for easy revisions

11.20 MASTER PRODUCTION SCHEDULING

The release of the planning SWD, as shown in Figure 11–10, authorizes the manufacturing units to prepare a master production schedule from which detailed analysis of the utilization of company resources can be seen and tracked.

Master production scheduling is not a new concept. Earliest material control systems used a "quarterly ordering system" to produce a master production schedule (MPS) for plant production. This system uses customer order backlogs to develop a production plan over a three-month period. The production plan is then exploded manually to determine what parts must be purchased or manufactured at the proper time. However, rapidly changing customer requirements and fluctuating lead times, combined with a slow response to these changes, can result in the disruption of master production scheduling.[11]

Master Production Schedule Definition

A *master production schedule* is a statement of what will be made, how many units will be made, and when they will be made. It is a production plan, not a sales plan. The MPS considers the total demand on a plant's resources, including finished product sales, spare (repair) part needs, and interplant needs. The MPS must also consider the capacity of the plant and the requirements imposed on vendors. Provisions are made in the overall plan for each manufacturing facility's operation. All planning for materials, manpower, plant, equipment, and financing for the facility is driven by the master production schedule.

---

11. The master production schedule is being discussed here because of its importance in the planning cycle. The MPS cannot be fully utilized without effective inventory control procedures.

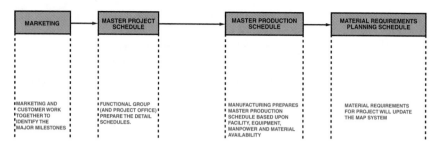

FIGURE 11–13. Material requirements planning interrelationships.

Objectives of the MPS

Objectives of master production scheduling are:

- To provide top management with a means to authorize and control manpower levels, inventory investment, and cash flow
- To coordinate marketing, manufacturing, engineering, and finance activities by a common performance objective
- To reconcile marketing and manufacturing needs
- To provide an overall measure of performance
- To provide data for material and capacity planning

The development of a master production schedule is a very important step in a planning cycle. Master production schedules directly tie together personnel, materials, equipment, and facilities as shown in Figure 11–13. Master production schedules also identify key dates to the customer, should he wish to visit the contractor during specific operational periods.

11.21 PROGRAM PLAN

Fundamental to the success of any project is documented planning in the form of a program plan. In an ideal situation, the program office can present the functional manager with a copy of the program plan and simply say "accomplish it." The concept of the program plan came under severe scrutiny during the 1960s when the Department of Defense required all contractors to submit detailed planning to such extremes that many organizations were wasting talented people by having them serve as writers instead of doers. Since then, because of the complexity of large programs, requirements imposed on the program plan have been eased.

For large and often complex programs, customers may require a program plan that documents all activities within the program. The program plan then serves as a guideline for the lifetime of the program and may be revised as often as once a month, depending on the circumstances and the type of program (i.e., research and development programs require more revisions to the program plan than manufacturing or construction programs). The program plan provides the following framework:

- Eliminates conflicts between functional managers
- Eliminates conflicts between functional management and program management
- Provides a standard communications tool throughout the lifetime of the program. (It should be geared to the work breakdown structure.)
- Provides verification that the contractor understands the customer's objectives and requirements
- Provides a means for identifying inconsistencies in the planning phase
- Provides a means for early identification of problem areas and risks so that no surprises occur downstream
- Contains all of the schedules defined in Section 11.19 as a basis for progress analysis and reporting

Development of a program plan can be time-consuming and costly. The input requirements for the program plan depend on the size of the project and the integration of resources and activities. All levels of the organization participate. The upper levels provide summary information, and the lower levels provide the details. The program plan, like activity schedules, does not preclude departments from developing their own planning.

The program plan must identify how the company resources will be integrated. Finalization of the program is an iterative process similar to the sequence of events for schedule preparation, shown in Figure 11–12. Since the program plan must explain the events in Figure 11–12, additional iterations are required, which can cause changes in a program. This can be seen in Figure 11–14.

The program plan is a standard from which performance can be measured, not only by the customer, but by program and functional management as well. The plan serves as a cookbook for the duration of the program by answering these questions for all personnel identified with the program:

- What will be accomplished?
- How will it be accomplished?
- Where will it be accomplished?
- When will it be accomplished?
- Why will it be accomplished?

The answers to these questions force both the contractor and the customer to take a hard look at:

- Program requirements
- Program management

- Program schedules
- Facility requirements
- Logistic support
- Financial support
- Manpower and organization

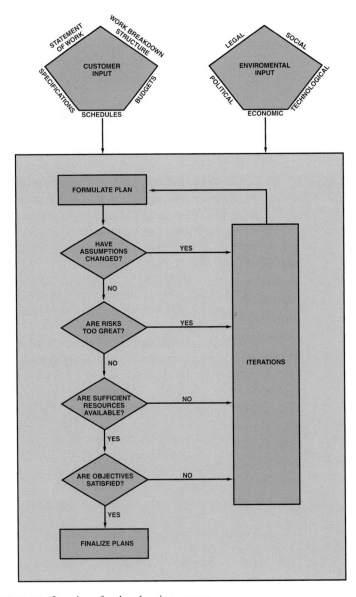

FIGURE 11–14. Iterations for the planning process.

The program plan is more than just a set of instructions. It is an attempt to eliminate crisis by preventing anything from "falling through the cracks." The plan is documented and approved by both the customer and the contractor to determine what data, if any, are missing and the probable resulting effect. As the program matures, the program plan is revised to account for new or missing data. The most common reasons for revising a plan are:

- "Crashing" activities to meet end dates
- Trade-off decisions involving manpower, scheduling, and performance
- Adjusting and leveling manpower requests

Maturity of a program usually implies that crisis will decrease. Unfortunately, this is not always the case.

The makeup of the program plan may vary from contractor to contractor.[12] Most program plans can be subdivided into four main sections: introduction, summary and conclusions, management, and technical. The complexity of the information is usually up to the discretion of the contractor, provided that customer requirements, as may be specified in the statement of work, are satisfied.

The introductory section contains the definition of the program and the major parts involved. If the program follows another, or is an outgrowth of similar activities, this is indicated, together with a brief summary of the background and history behind the project.

The summary and conclusion section identifies the targets and objectives of the program and includes the necessary "lip service" on how successful the program will be and how all problems can be overcome. This section must also include the program master schedule showing how all projects and activities are related. The total program master schedule should include the following:

- An appropriate scheduling system (bar charts, milestone charts, network, etc.)
- A listing of activities at the project level or lower
- The possible interrelationships between activities (can be accomplished by logic networks, critical path networks, or PERT networks)
- Activity time estimates (a natural result of the item above)

The summary and conclusion chapter is usually the second section in the program plan so that upper-level customer management can have a complete overview of the program without having to search through the technical information.

The management section of the program plan contains procedures, charts, and schedules as follows:

---

12. Cleland and King define fourteen subsections for a program plan. This detail appears more applicable to the technical and management volumes of a proposal. They do, however, provide a more detailed picture than presented here. See David I. Cleland and William R. King, *Systems Analysis and Project Management* (New York: McGraw-Hill, 1975), pp. 371–380.

- The assignment of key personnel to the program is indicated. This usually refers only to the program office personnel and team members, since under normal operations these will be the only individuals interfacing with customers.
- Manpower, planning, and training are discussed to assure customers that qualified people will be available from the functional units.
- A linear responsibility chart might also be included to identify to customers the authority relationships that will exist in the program.

Situations exist in which the management section may be omitted from the proposal. For a follow-up program, the customer may not require this section if management's positions are unchanged. Management sections are also not required if the management information was previously provided in the proposal or if the customer and contractor have continuous business dealings.

The technical section may include as much as 75 to 90 percent of the program plan, especially if the effort includes research and development. The technical section may require constant updating as the program matures. The following items can be included as part of the technical section:

- A detailed breakdown of the charts and schedules used in the program master schedule, possibly including schedule/cost estimates.
- A listing of the testing to be accomplished for each activity. (It is best to include the exact testing matrices.)
- Procedures for accomplishment of the testing. This might also include a description of the key elements in the operations or manufacturing plans as well as a listing of the facility and logistic requirements.
- Identification of materials and material specifications. (This might also include system specifications.)
- An attempt to identify the risks associated with specific technical requirements (not commonly included). This assessment tends to scare management personnel who are unfamiliar with the technical procedures, so it should be omitted if at all possible.

The program plan, as used here, contains a description of all phases of the program. For many programs, especially large ones, detailed planning is required for all major events and activities. Table 11–5 identifies the type of individual plans that may be required in place of a (total) program plan. However, the amount of detail must be controlled, for too much paperwork can easily inhibit successful management of a program.

The program plan, once agreed on by the contractor and customer, is then used to provide program direction. This is shown in Figure 11–15. If the program plan is written clearly, then any functional manager or supervisor should be able to identify what is expected of him.

The program plan should be distributed to each member of the program team, all functional managers and supervisors interfacing with the program, and

TABLE 11–5. TYPES OF PLANS

Type of Plan	Description
Budget	How much money is allocated to each event?
Configuration management	How are technical changes made?
Facilities	What facilities resources are available?
Logistics support	How will replacements be handled?
Management	How is the program office organized?
Manufacturing	What are the time-phase manufacturing events?
Procurement	What are my sources? Should I make or buy? If vendors are not qualified, how shall I qualify them?
Quality assurance	How will I guarantee specifications will be met?
Research/development	What are the technical activities?
Scheduling	Are all critical dates accounted for?
Tooling	What are my time-phased tooling requirements?
Training	How will I maintain qualified personnel?
Transportation	How will goods and services be shipped?

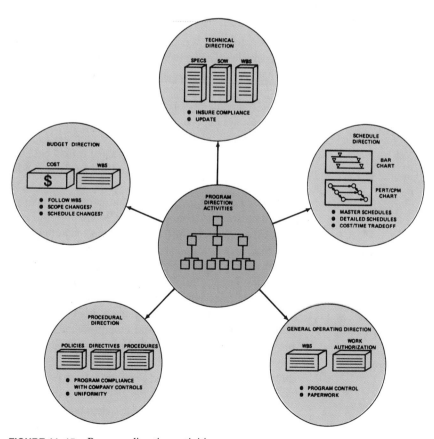

FIGURE 11–15. Program direction activities.

all key functional personnel. The program plan does not contain all of the answers, for if it did, there would be no need for a program office. The plan serves merely as a guide.

One final note need be mentioned concerning the legality of the program plan. The program plan may be specified contractually to satisfy certain requirements as identified in the customer's statement of work. The contractor retains the right to decide how to accomplish this, unless, of course, this is also identified in the SOW. If the SOW specifies that quality assurance testing will be accomplished on fifteen end-items from the production line, then fifteen is the minimum number that must be tested. The program plan may show that twenty-five items are to be tested. If the contractor develops cost overrun problems, he may wish to revert to the SOW and test only fifteen items. Contractually, he may do this without informing the customer. In most cases, however, the customer is notified, and the program is revised.

11.22 TOTAL PROJECT PLANNING

The difference between the good project manager and the poor project manager is often described in one word: planning. Unfortunately, people have a poor definition of what project planning actually involves. Project planning involves planning for:

- Schedule development
- Budget development
- Project administration (see Section 5.3)
- Leadership styles (interpersonal influences; see Section 5.4)
- Conflict management (see Chapter 7)

The first two items involve the quantitative aspects of planning. Planning for project administration includes the development of the linear responsibility chart.

Although each project manager has the authority and responsibility to establish project policies and procedures, they must fall within the general guidelines established by top management. Guidelines can also be established for planning, scheduling, controlling, and communications.

Linear responsibility charts can result from customer-imposed requirements above and beyond normal operations. For example, the customer may require as part of his quality control requirements that a specific engineer supervise and approve all testing of a certain item, or that another individual approve all data released to the customer over and above program office approval. Customer requirements similar to those identified above require LRCs and can cause disruptions and conflicts within an organization.

Several key factors affect the delegation of authority and responsibility both from upper-level management to project management, and from project management to functional management. These key factors include:

- The maturity of the project management function
- The size, nature, and business base of the company
- The size and nature of the project
- The life cycle of the project
- The capabilities of management at all levels

Once agreement has been reached on the project manager's authority and responsibility, the results may be documented to delineate that role regarding:

- Focal position
- Conflict between the project manager and functional managers
- Influence to cut across functional and organizational lines
- Participation in major management and technical decisions
- Collaboration in staffing the project
- Control over allocation and expenditure of funds
- Selection of subcontractors
- Rights in resolving conflicts
- Input in maintaining the integrity of the project team
- Establishment of project plans
- Provisions for a cost-effective information system for control
- Provisions for leadership in preparing operational requirements
- Maintenance of prime customer liaison and contact
- Promotion of technological and managerial improvements
- Establishment of project organization for the duration
- Elimination of red tape

Documenting the project manager's authority is necessary in some situations because:

- All interfacing must be kept as simple as possible.
- The project manager must have the authority to "force" functional managers to depart from existing standards and possibly incur risk.
- Gaining authority over those elements of a program that are not under the project manager's control is essential. This is normally achieved by earning the respect of the individuals concerned.
- The project manager should not attempt to fully describe the exact authority and responsibilities of the project office personnel or team members. Problem solving rather than role definition should be encouraged.

Although documenting project authority is undesirable, it may be a necessary prerequisite, especially if project initiation and planning require a formal project chart. In such a case, a letter such as that shown in Table 11–6 may suffice.

Power and authority are often discussed as though they go hand in hand. Authority comes from people above you, perhaps by delegation, whereas power comes from people below you. You can have authority without power or power without authority.

TABLE 11–6. PROJECT CHARTER

ELECTRODYNAMICS
12 Oak Avenue
Cleveland, Ohio 44114

11 June 1983

To: Distribution
From: L. White, Executive Vice President
Subject: Project Charter for the Acme Project

Mr. Robert L. James has been assigned as the Project Manager for the Acme Project.

Responsibility

Mr. James will be responsible for ensuring that all key milestones are met within the time, cost, and performance constraints of his project, while adhering to proper quality control standards. Furthermore, the project manager must work closely with line managers to ensure that all assigned resources are used effectively and efficiently, and that the project is properly staffed. Additionally, the project manager will be responsible for:

1. All formal communications between the customer and contractor.
2. Preparation of a project plan that is realistic, and acceptable by both the customer and contractor.
3. Preparation of all project data items.
4. Keeping executive management informed as to project status through weekly (detailed) and monthly (summary) status reporting.
5. Ensuring that all functional employees and managers are kept informed as to their responsibilities on the project and all revisions imposed by the customer or parent organization.
6. Comparing actual to predicted cost and performance, and taking corrective action when necessary.
7. Maintaining a plan that continuously displays the project's time, cost, and performance as well as resource commitments made by the functional managers.

Authority

To ensure that the project meets its objectives, Mr. James is authorized to manage the project and issue directives in accordance to the policies and procedures section of the company's *Project Management Manual*. Additional directives may be issued through the office of the executive vice-president.

The program manager's authority also includes:

1. Direct access to the customer on all matters pertaining to the Acme Project.
2. Direct access to Electrodynamics' executive management on all matters pertaining to the Acme Project.
3. Control and distribution of all project dollars, including procurement, such that company and project cash flow limitations are adhered to.
4. To revise the project plan as needed, and with customer approval.
5. To require periodic functional status reporting.
6. To monitor the time, cost, and performance activities in the functional departments and ensure that all problems are promptly identified, reported, and solved.
7. To cut across all functional lines and to interface with all levels of management as necessary to meet project requirements.
8. To renegotiate with functional managers for changes in personnel assignments.
9. Delegating responsibilities and authority to functional personnel, provided that the line manager is in approval that the employee can handle this authority/responsibility level.

Any questions regarding the above policies should be directed to the undersigned.

L. White
Executive Vice-President

In a traditional organizational structure, most individuals maintain position power. The higher up you sit, the more power you have. But in project management, the reporting level of the project might be irrelevant, especially if a project sponsor exists. In project management, the project manager's power base emanates from his

- Expertise (technical or managerial)
- Credibility with employees
- Sound decision-making ability

The last item is usually preferred. If the project manager is regarded as a sound decision maker, then the employees normally give the project manager a great deal or power over them.

Leadership styles refer to the interpersonal influence modes that a project manager can use. Project managers may have to use several different leadership styles, depending on the makeup of the project personnel. Conflict management is important because if the project manager can predict what conflicts will occur and when they are most likely to occur, he may be able to plan for the resolution of the conflicts through project administration.

Figure 11–16 shows the complete project planning phase for the quantitative portions. The object, of course, is to develop a project plan that shows complete distribution of resources and the corresponding costs. The figure represents an iterative process. The project manager begins with a coarse (arrow diagram) network and then decides on the work breakdown structure. The WBS is essential to the arrow diagram and should be constructed so that reporting elements and levels are easily identifiable. Eventually, there will be an arrow diagram and detailed chart for each element in the WBS. If there exists too much detail, the project manager can refine the diagram by combining all logic into one plan and can then decide on the work assignments. There is a risk here that, by condensing the diagrams as much as possible, there may be a loss of clarity. As shown in Figure 11–16, all the charts and schedules can be integrated into one summary-level figure. This can be accomplished at each WBS level until the desired plan is achieved.

Finally, project, line, and executive management must analyze other internal and external variables before finalizing these schedules. A partial listing of these variables includes:

- Introduction or acceptance of the product in the marketplace
- Present or planned manpower availability
- Economic constraints of the project
- Degree of technical difficulty
- Manpower availability
- Availability of personnel training
- Priority of the project

In small companies and projects, certain items in Figure 11–16 may be omitted, such as the LRCs.

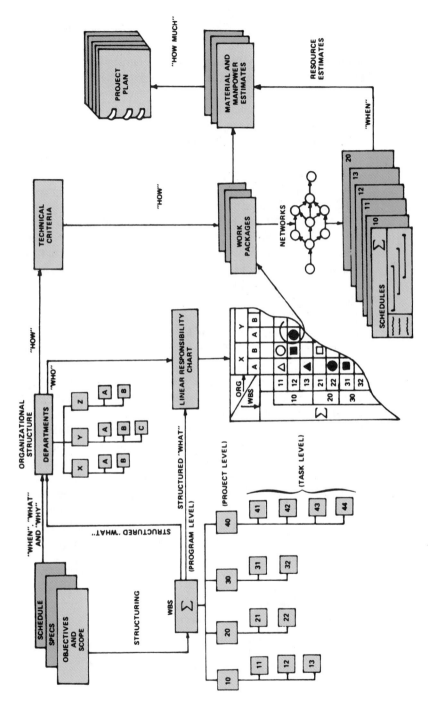

FIGURE 11–16. Project planning.

11.23 THE PROJECT CHARTER

The original concept behind the project charter was to document the project manager's authority and responsibility, especially for projects implemented away from the home office. Today, the project charter has been expanded to become more of an internal legal document identifying to the line managers and his personnel not only the project manager's authority and responsibility, but the management- and/or customer-approved scope of the project.

Theoretically, the sponsor prepares the charter and affixes his/her signature, but in reality, the project manager may prepare it for the sponsor's signature. At a minimum, the charter should include:

- Identification of the project manager and his/her authority to apply resources to the project
- The business purpose that the project was undertaken to address, including all assumptions and constraints
- Summary of the conditions defining the project

The charter is a "legal" agreement between the project manager and the company. Some companies supplement the charter with a "contract" that functions as an agreement between the project and the line organizations.

Within the last two years or so, some companies have converted the charter into a highly detailed document containing:

- The scope baseline/scope statement
  - Scope and objectives of the project (SOW)
  - Specifications
  - WBS (template levels)
  - Timing
  - Spending plan (S-curve)
- The management plan
  - Resource requirements and manloading (if known)
  - Resumés of key personnel
  - Organizational relationships and structure
  - Responsibility assignment matrix
  - Support required from other organizations
  - Project policies and procedures
  - Change management plan
  - Management approval of above

When the project charter contains a scope baseline and management plan, the project charter may function as the project plan. This is not really an effective use of the charter, but it may be acceptable on certain types of projects for internal customers.

TABLE 11–7. PLANNING AND REQUIREMENTS POLICIES

Program Manager	Functional Manager	Relationship
Requests the preparation of the program master schedules and provides for integration with the division composite schedules. Defines work to be accomplished through preparation of the subdivided work description package. Provides program guidance and direction for the preparation of program plans that establish program cost, schedule, and technical performance; and that define the major events and tasks to ensure the orderly progress of the program.	Develops the details of the program plans and requirements in conjunction with the program manager. Provides proposal action in support of program manager requirements and the program master schedule. With guidance furnished by the program manager, participates in the preparation of program plans, schedules, and work release documents which cover cost, schedule, and technical performance; and which define major events and tasks. Provides supporting detail plans and schedules.	Program planning and scheduling is a functional specialty; the program manager utilizes the services of the specialist organizations. The specialists retain their own channels to the general manager but must keep the program manager informed. Program planning is also a consultative operation and is provided guidelines by the program manager. Functional organizations initiate supporting plans for program manager approval, or react to modify plans to maintain currency. Functional organizations also initiate planning studies involving trade-offs and alternative courses of action for presentation to the program manager.
Establishes priorities within the program. Obtains relative program priorities between programs managed by other programs from the director, program management, manager, marketing and product development, or the general manager as specified by the policy.	Negotiates priorities with program managers for events and tasks to be performed by his organization.	The program manager and program team members are oriented to his program, whereas the functional organizations and the functional managers are "function" and multiprogram oriented. The orientation of each director, manager, and team member

Approves program contractual data requirements.

Remains alert to new contract requirements, government regulations and directives that might affect the work, cost, or management of the program.

Provides early technical requirements definitions, and substantiates make-or-buy recommendations. Participates in the formulation of the make-or-buy plan for the program.

Approves the program bill of material for need and compliance with program need and requirements.

Directs data management including maintenance of current and historical files on programmed contractual data requirements.

Conducts analysis of contractual data requirements. Develops data plans including contractor data requirements list and obtains program manager approval.

Remains alert to new contract requirements, government regulations, and directives that might affect the work, cost, or management of his organization on any program.

Provides the necessary make-or-buy data; substantiates estimates and recommendations in the area of functional specialty.

Prepares the program bill of material.

must be mutually recognized to preclude unreasonable demands and conflicting priorities. Priority conflicts that cannot be resolved must be referred to the general manager.

Make-or-buy concurrence and approvals are obtained in accordance with current Policies and Procedures.

615

11.24 MANAGEMENT CONTROL

Because the planning phase provides the fundamental guidelines for the remainder of the project, careful management control must be established. In addition, since planning is an ongoing activity for a variety of different programs, management guidelines must be established on a company-wide basis in order to achieve unity and coherence.

All functional organizations and individuals working directly or indirectly on a program are responsible for identifying, to the project manager, scheduling and planning problems that require corrective action during both the planning cycle and the operating cycle. The program manager bears the ultimate and final responsibility for identifying requirements for corrective actions. Management policies and directives are written specifically to assist the program manager in defining the requirements. Without clear definitions during the planning phase, many projects run off in a variety of directions.

Many companies establish planning and scheduling management policies for the project and functional managers, as well as a brief description of how they should interface. Table 11–7 identifies a typical management policy for planning and requirements, and Table 11–8 describes scheduling management policies.

11.25 THE PROJECT MANAGER–LINE MANAGER INTERFACE

The utilization of management controls, such as those outlined in Section 11.24, does not necessarily guarantee successful project planning. Good project planning, as well as other project functions, requires a good working relationship between the project and line managers. At this interface:[13]

- The project manager answers these questions:
  - What is to be done? (using the SOW, WBS)
  - When will the task be done? (using the summary schedule)
  - Why will the task be done? (using the SOW)
  - How much money is available? (using the SOW)
- The line manager answers these questions:
  - How will the task be done? (i.e., technical criteria)
  - Where will the task be done? (i.e., technical criteria)
  - Who will do the task? (i.e., staffing)

---

13. Adapted from David I. Cleland and William R. King, *Systems Analysis and Project Management* (New York: McGraw-Hill), p. 237. Copyright © 1968, 1975 by McGraw-Hill. Used with permission of McGraw-Hill Book Company.

TABLE 11–8. SCHEDULING POLICIES

Program Manager	Functional Manager	Relationship
Provides contractual data requirements and guidance for construction of program master schedules.	The operations directorate shall construct the program master schedule. Data should include but not be limited to engineering plans, manufacturing plans, procurement plans, test plans, quality plans, and provide time spans for accomplishment of work elements defined in the work breakdown structure to the level of definition visible in the planned subdivided work description package.	The operations directorate constructs the program master schedule with data received from functional organizations and direction from the program manager. Operations shall coordinate program master schedule with functional organizations and secure program manager's approval prior to release.
Concurs with detail schedules construction by functional organizations. Provides corrective action decisions and direction as required at any time a functional organization fails to meet program master schedule requirements or when, by analysis, performance indicated by detail schedule monitoring threatens to impact the program master schedule.	Constructs detail program schedules and working schedules in consonance with program manager–approved program master schedule. Secures program manager concurrence and forwards copies to the program manager.	Program manager monitors the functional organizations detail schedules for compliance with program master schedules and reports variance items that may impact division operations to the director, program management.

Project managers may be able to tell line managers "how" and "where," provided that the information appears in the SOW as a requirement for the project. Even then, the line manager can take exception based on his technical expertise.

Figures 11–17 and 11–18 show what can happen when project managers overstep their bounds. In Figure 11–17, the manufacturing manager built a brick wall to keep the project managers away from his personnel because the project managers were telling his line people how to do their job. In Figure 11–18, the subproject managers (for simplicity's sake, equivalent to project engineers) would have, as their career path, promotions to assistant project managers (A.P.M.s). Unfortunately, the A.P.M.s still felt that they were technically competent enough to give technical direction, and this created havoc for the engineering managers.

The simplest solution to all of these problems is for the project manager to provide the technical direction *through* the line managers. After all, the line managers are supposedly the true technical experts.

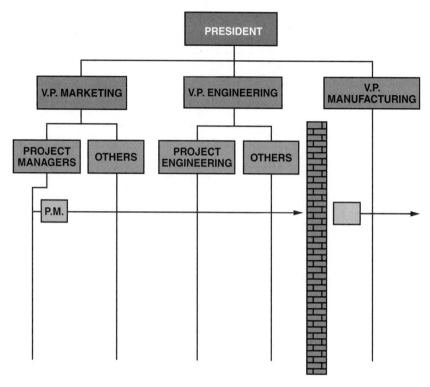

FIGURE 11–17. The brick wall.

11.26 FAST-TRACKING

Sometimes, no matter how well we plan, something happens that causes havoc on the project. Such is the case when either the customer or management changes the project's constraints. Consider Figure 11–19 and let us assume that the execution time for the construction of the project is one year. To prepare the working drawings and specifications down through level 5 of the WBS would require an additional 35 percent of the expected execution time, and if a feasibility study is required, then an additional 40 percent will be added on. In other words, if the execution phase of the project is one year, then the entire project is almost two years.

Now, let us assume that management wishes to keep the end date fixed but the start date is delayed because of lack of adequate funding. How can this be accomplished *without* sacrificing the quality? The answer is to fast-track the project. Fast-tracking a project means that activities that are normally done in series are done in parallel. An example of this is when construction begins before detail design is completed. (See Table 2–5 on life-cycle phases, on p. 83).

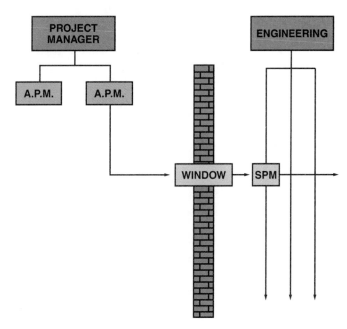

FIGURE 11–18. Modification of the brick wall.

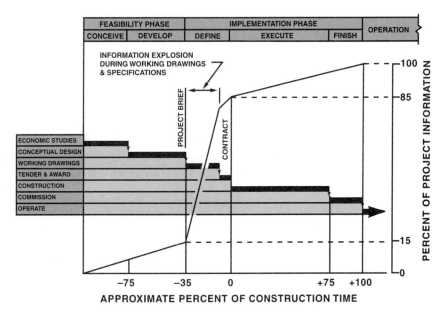

FIGURE 11–19. The information explosion. *Source:* R. M. Wideman, *Cost Control of Capital Projects* (Vancouver, B.C.: A.E.W. Services of Canada, 1983), p. 22.

Fast-tracking a job can accelerate the schedule but requires that additional risks be taken. If the risks materialize, then either the end date will slip or expensive rework will be needed. Almost all project-driven companies fast-track projects. The danger, however, is when fast-tracking becomes a way of life on all projects.

11.27 CONFIGURATION MANAGEMENT

One of the most critical tools employed by a project manager is configuration management or configuration change control. As projects progress downstream through the various life-cycle phases, the cost of engineering changes can grow boundlessly. It is not uncommon for companies to bid on proposals at 40 percent below their own cost hoping to make up the difference downstream with engineering changes. It is also quite common for executives to "encourage" project managers to seek out engineering changes because of their profitability.

Configuration management is a control technique, through an orderly process, for formal review and approval of configuration changes. If properly implemented, configuration management provides

- Appropriate levels of review and approval for changes
- Focal points for those seeking to make changes
- A single point of input to contracting representatives in the customer's and contractor's office for approved changes

At a minimum, the configuration control committee should include representation from the customer, contractor, and line group initiating the change. Discussions should answer the following questions:

- What is the cost of the change?
- Do the changes improve quality?
- Is the additional cost for this quality justifiable?
- Is the change necessary?
- Is there an impact on the delivery date?

Changes cost money. Therefore, it is imperative that configuration management be implemented correctly. The following steps can enhance the implementation process:

- Define the starting point or "baseline" configuration
- Define the "classes" of changes
- Define the necessary controls or limitations on both the customer and contractor

- Identify policies and procedures, such as
  - Board chairman
  - Voters/alternatives
  - Meeting time
  - Agenda
  - Approval forums
  - Step-by-step processes
  - Expedition processes in case of emergencies

Effective configuration control pleases both customer and contractor. Overall benefits include:

- Better communication among staff
- Better communication with the customer
- Better technical intelligence
- Reduced confusion for changes
- Screening of frivolous changes
- Providing a paper trail

As a final note, it must be understood that configuration control, as used here, is not a replacement for design review meetings or customer interface meetings. These meetings are still an integral part of all projects.

11.28 PROCEDURAL DOCUMENTATION

People communicate in many ways. Often communications get filtered and somewhat distorted. For many reasons, agreements in a project environment must be in writing. Project management believes in the philosophy that only what is on paper is really important.

Another important facet of any project management system is to provide the people in the organization with procedural guidelines for how to conduct project-oriented activities and how to communicate in such a multidimensional environment. The project management policies, procedures, forms, and guidelines can provide some of these tools for delineating the process, as well as a format for collecting, processing, and communicating project-related data in an orderly, standardized format. Project planning and tracking, however, involves more than just the generation of paperwork. It requires the participation of the entire project team, including support departments, subcontractors, and top management. It is this involvement of the entire team that fosters a unifying team environment oriented toward the project goals, and ultimately to the personal commitment of the team members to the various tasks within time and budget constraints. The specific benefits of procedural documents, including forms and checklists, are that they help to:

- Provide guidelines and uniformity
- Encourage documentation
- Communicate clearly and effectively
- Standardize data formats
- Unify project teams
- Provide a basis for analysis
- Document agreements for future reference
- Refuel commitments
- Minimize paperwork
- Minimize conflict and confusion
- Delineate work packages
- Bring new team members on board
- Build an experience track and method for future projects

Done properly, the process of project planning must involve both the performing and the customer organizations. This involvement creates new insight into the intricacies of a project and its management methods. It also leads to the visibility of the project at various organizational levels, management involvement, and support. It is this involvement at all organizational levels that stimulates interest in the project and the desire for success, and fosters a pervasive reach for excellence that unifies the project team. It leads to commitment toward establishing and reaching the desired project objectives and to a self-forcing management system where people want to work toward these established objectives.

Few companies have introduced project management procedures with ease. Most have experienced problems ranging from skepticism to sabotage of the procedural system. Realistically, however, program managers do not have much of a choice, especially for the larger, more complex programs. Every project manager who believes in project management has his own success story. It is interesting to note, however, that many use incremental approaches to develop and implement their project management system.

Developing and implementing such a system incrementally is a multifaceted challenge to management. The problem is seldom to understand the techniques involved, such as budgeting and scheduling, but to involve the project team in the process, to get their input, support, and commitment, and to establish a supportive environment. Furthermore, project personnel must have the feeling that the policies and procedures of the project management system facilitate communication, are flexible and adaptive to a changing environment, and provide an early-warning system through which project personnel obtain assistance rather than punishment in case of a contingency.

The procedural guidelines and forms of an established project management system can be especially useful during the project planning/definition phase. Not only does it help to delineate and communicate the four major sets of variables for organizing and managing the project—tasks, timing, resources, and responsibilities—it also helps to define measurable milestones, as well as report and review requirements. This provides the ability to measure project status and performance, and supplies crucial inputs for controlling the project toward the desired results.

However, none of these systems will really control project performance or rectify a problem unless the project plan has received approval and commitment from the people behind it. Such a self-forcing project control system[14] is based on the following six key components:

1. *Objectives and measurability.* Existence of a sound system of standards and tools for planning and tracking the project effort, such as procedures and forms.
2. *Involvement* of all key personnel during project planning.
3. *Agreement and commitment* by all key personnel to the project plan and its specific results and performance measures.
4. *Senior management commitment* and continuous *involvement.*
5. *Availability of quality personnel.*
6. *Proper project direction and leadership.*

Some of the strongest drives toward high project performance are derived from an interesting and professionally stimulating work environment. For example, Thamhain and Wilemon found, in various field studies,[15] that project success is directly associated with personal commitment, involvement, and top-management support. These factors are the strongest in a professional, stimulating work environment, characterized by interesting, challenging work, visibility and recognition for achievements, growth potential, and good project leadership. Furthermore, the same conditions are associated with other criteria for project success. Specifically, the more professionally stimulating and interesting the work environment is perceived to be by the project team, the more involved and committed are the people, and the more innovative, creative, and change oriented they are being perceived by top management.

In summary, developing an effective project management system takes more than just a set of policies and procedures. It also requires the integration of these guidelines and standards into the culture and value system of the organization. Management must lead the overall efforts and foster an environment conducive to teamwork. The greater the team spirit, trust, commitment, and quality of information exchange among team members, the more likely the team will develop effective decision-making processes, making individual and group commitments, focus on problem solving and operate in a self-forcing, self-correcting control

---

14. The concept of self-enforcing project control was first discussed in detail by Leonard R. Sayles and Margaret K. Chandler in *Managing Large Systems* (New York: Harper & Row, 1971).

15. For more detail see articles by Hans J. Thamhain and David L. Wilemon, "Managing Engineers Effectively," *IEEE Transactions on Engineering Management,* August 1983, "Team Building in Project Management," *Project Management Quarterly,* June 1983, and "Anatomy of a High Performing New Product Team," *Proceedings of the Annual Symposium of the Project Management Institutte,* 1984.

mode. These are the characteristics that will support and pervade the formal project management system and make it work for you. When understood and accepted by the team members, such a system provides the formal standards, guidelines, and measures needed to direct a project toward specific results within the given time and resource constraints.

11.29 ESTABLISHED PRACTICES

Although project managers have the right to establish their own policies and procedures, many companies have taken the route of designing project control forms that can be used uniformly on all projects to assist in the communications process. Project control forms serve two vital purposes by establishing a common framework from which (1) the project manager will communicate with executives, functional employees, and clients; and (2) executives and the project manager can make meaningful decisions concerning the allocation of resources.

Success or failure of a project depends on the ability of key personnel to have sufficient data for decision making. Project management is often considered to be both an art and a science. It is an art because of the strong need for interpersonal skills, and the project planning and control forms attempt to convert part of the "art" into a science.

Many companies tend not to realize until too late the necessity of good planning and control forms. Today, some of the larger companies with mature project management structures maintain a separate functional unit for forms controls. This is quite common in the aerospace and defense industries, and is also becoming common practice in other industries. Yet some executives believe that forms are needed only when the company grows to a point where a continuous stream of unique projects necessitates some sort of uniform control mechanism.

In some small or non–project-driven organizations, each project can have its own forms. But for most other organizations, unformity is a must. Quite often, the actual design and selection of the forms is made by individuals other than the users.

PROBLEMS

11–1 Under what conditions would each of the following either not be available or not be necessary for initial planning?

    a. Work breakdown structure
    b. Statement of work
    c. Specifications
    d. Milestone schedules

11–2 What planning steps should precede total program scheduling? What steps are necessary?

11–3 How does a project manager determine how complex to make a program plan or how many schedules to include?

11–4 Can objectives always be identified and scheduled?

11–5 Can a WBS always be established for attaining an objective?

11–6 Who determines the work necessary to accomplish an objective?

11–7 What roles does a functional manager play in establishing the first three levels of the WBS?

11–8 Should the length of a program have an impact on whether to set up a separate project or task for administrative support? How about for raw materials?

11–9 Is it possible for the WBS to be designed so that resource allocation is easier to identify?

11–10 If the scope of effort of a project changes during execution of activities, what should be the role of the functional manager?

11–11 What types of conflicts can occur during the planning cycle, and what modes should be used for their resolution?

11–12 What would be the effectiveness of Figure 11–3 if the work packages were replaced by tasks?

11–13 Under what situations or projects would work planning authorization not be necessary?

11–14 On what types of projects could hedge positions be easily identified on a schedule?

11–15 Can activities 5 and 6 of Figure 11–12 be eliminated? What risks does a project manager incur if these activities are eliminated?

11–16 Where in the planning cycle should responsibility charts be prepared? Can you identify this point in Figure 11–12?

11–17 For each one of the decision points in Figure 11–14, who makes the decision? Who must input information? What is the role of the functional manager and the functional team member? Where are strategic variables identified?

11–18 Consider a project in which all project planning is performed by a group. After all planning is completed, including the program plan and schedules, a project manager is selected. Is there anything wrong with this arrangement? Can it work?

11–19 How do the customer and contractor know if each one completely understands the statement of work, the work breakdown structure, and the program plan?

11–20 Should a good project plan formulate methods for anticipating problems?

11–21 Some project managers schedule staff meetings as the primary means for planning and control. Do you agree with this philosophy?

11–22 Paul Mali (*Management by Objectives,* New York: John Wiley, 1972, p. 12) defines MBO as a five-step process:

- Finding the objective
- Setting the objective

- Validating the objective
- Implementing the objective
- Controlling and reporting status of the objective

How can the work breakdown structure be used to accomplish each of the above steps? Would you agree or disagree that the more levels the WBS contains, the greater the understanding and clarity of those steps necessary to complete the objectives?

11–23 Many textbooks on management state that you should plan like you work, by doing one thing at a time. Can this same practice be applied at the project level, or must a project manager plan all activities at once?

11–24 Is it true that project managers set the milestones and functional managers hope they can meet them?

11–25 You have been asked to develop a work breakdown structure for a project. How should you go about accomplishing this? Should the WBS be time-phased, department-phased, division-phased, or some combination?

11–26 You have just been instructed to develop a schedule for introducing a new product into the marketplace. Below are the elements that must appear in your schedule. Arrange these elements into a work breakdown structure (down through level 3), and then draw the arrow diagram. You may feel free to add additional topics as necessary.

- Production layout
- Market testing
- Analyze selling cost
- Analyze customer reactions
- Storage and shipping costs
- Select salespeople
- Train salespeople
- Train distributors
- Literature to salespeople
- Literature to distributors
- Print literature
- Sales promotion
- Sales manual
- Trade advertising
- Review plant costs
- Select distributors
- Lay out artwork
- Approve artwork
- Introduce at trade show
- Distribute to salespeople
- Establish billing procedure
- Establish credit procedure
- Revise cost of production
- Revise selling cost
- Approvals*
- Review meetings*
- Final specifications
- Material requisitions

(*Approvals and review meetings can appear several times.)

11–27 Once a project begins, a good project manager will set up checkpoints. How should this be accomplished? Will the duration of the project matter? Can checkpoints be built into a schedule? If so, how should they be identified?

11–28 Detailed schedules (through WBS levels 3, 4, 5, . . .) are prepared by the functional managers. Should these schedules be shown to the customer?

11–29 The project start-up phase is complete, and you are now ready to finalize the operational plan. Below are six steps that are often part of the finalization procedure. Place them in the appropriate order.

1. Draw diagrams for each individual WBS element.
2. Establish the work breakdown structure and identify the reporting elements and levels.

3. Create a coarse (arrow-diagram) network and decide on the WBS.
4. Refine the diagram by combining all logic into one plan. Then decide on the work assignments.
5. If necessary, try to condense the diagram as much as possible without losing clarity.
6. Integrate diagrams at each level until only one exists. Then begin integration into higher WBS levels until the desired plan is achieved.

11–30 Below are seven factors that must be considered before finalizing a schedule. Explain how a base case schedule can change as a result of each of these:

- Introduction or acceptance of the product in the marketplace
- Present or planned manpower availability
- Economic constraints of the project
- Degree of technical difficulty
- Manpower availability
- Availability of personnel training
- Priority of the project

11–31 You are the project manager of a nine-month effort. You are now in the fifth month of the project and are more than two weeks behind schedule, with very little hope of catching up. The dam breaks in a town near you, and massive flooding and mudslides take place. Fifteen of your key functional people request to take off three days from the following week to help fellow church members dig out. Their functional managers, bless their hearts, have left the entire decision up to you. Should you let them go?

11–32 Once the functional manager and project manager agree on a project schedule, who is responsible for getting the work performed? Who is accountable for getting the work performed? Why the difference, if any?

11–33 Discuss the validity of the following two statements on authority:

a. A good project manager will have more authority than his responsibility calls for.
b. A good project manager should not hold a subordinate responsible for duties that he (the project manager) does not have the authority to enforce.

11–34 Below are twelve instructions. Which are best described as planning, and which are best described as forecasting?

a. Give a complete definition of the work.
b. Lay out a proposed schedule.
c. Establish project milestones.
d. Determine the need for different resources.
e. Determine the skills required for each WBS task or element.
f. Change the scope of the effort and obtain new estimates.
g. Estimate the total time to complete the required work.
h. Consider changing resources.
i. Assign appropriate personnel to each WBS element.
j. Reschedule project resources.
k. Begin scheduling the WBS elements.
l. Change the project priorities.

11–35 A major utility company has a planning group that prepares budgets (with the help of functional groups) and selects the projects to be completed within a given time period. you are assigned as a project manager on one of the projects and find out that it should have been started "last month" in order to meet the completion date. What can you, the project manager, do about this? Should you delay the start of the project to replan the work?

11–36 The director of project management calls you into his office and informs you that one of your fellow project managers has had a severe heart attack midway through a project. You will be taking over his project, which is well behind schedule and overrunning costs. The director of project management then "orders" you to complete the project within time and cost. How do you propose to do it? Where do you start? Should you shut down the project to replan it?

11–37 Planning is often described as establishing, budgeting, scheduling, and resource allocation. Identify these four elements in Figure 11–1.

11–38 A company is undertaking a large development project that requires that a massive "blueprint design tree" be developed. What kind of WBS outline would be best to minimize the impact of having two systems, one for blueprints and one for WBS work?

11–39 A company allows each line organization to perform its own procurement activities (through a centralized procurement office) as long as the procurement funds have been allocated during the project planning phase. The project office does not sign off on these functional procurement requisitions and may not even know about them. Can this system work effectively? If so, under what conditions?

11–40 As part of a feasibility study, you are asked to prepare, with the assistance of functional managers, a schedule and cost summary for a project that will occur three years downstream, if the project is approved at all. Suppose that three years downstream the project is approved. How does the project manager get functional managers to accept the schedule and cost summary that they themselves prepared three years before?

11–41 "Expecting trouble." Good project managers know what type of trouble can occur at the various stages in the development of a project. The activities in the numbered list below indicate the various stages of a project. The lettered list that follows identifies major problems. For each project stage, select and list all of those problems that are applicable.

      1. Request for proposal _____
      2. Submittal to customer _____
      3. Contract award _____
      4. Design review meetings _____
      5. Testing the product _____
      6. Customer acceptance _____

a. Engineering does not request manufacturing input for end-item producibility.

b. The work breakdown structure is poorly defined.

e. The project–functional infertace definition is poor.

f. Improper systems integration had created conflicts and a communications breakdown.

c. Customer does not fully realize the impact that a technical change will have upon cost and schedule.

d. Time and cost constraints are not compatible with the state of the art.

g. Several functional managers did not realize that they were responsible for certain risks.

h. The impact of design changes is not systematically evaluated.

11–42 Table 11–9 identifies twenty-six steps in project planning and control. Below is a description of each of the twenty-six steps. Using this information, fill in columns 1 and 2 (column 2 is a group response). After your instructor provides you with column 3, fill in the remainder of the table.

1. *Develop the linear responsibility chart.* This chart identifies the work breakdown structure and assigns specific authority/responsibility to various individuals as groups in order to be sure that all WBS elements are accounted for. The linear responsibility chart can be prepared with either the titles or names of individuals. Assume that this is prepared after you negotiate for qualified personnel, so that you know either the names or capabilities of those individuals who will be assigned.

2. *Negotiate for qualified functional personnel.* Once the work is decided on, the project manager tries to identify the qualifications for the desired personnel. This then becomes the basis for the negotiation process.

3. *Develop specifications.* This is one of the four documents needed to initially define the requirements of the project. Assume that these are either performance or material specifications, and are provided to you at the initial planning stage by either the customer or the user.

4. *Determine the means for measuring progress.* Before the project plan is finalized and project execution can begin, the project manager must identify the means for measuring progress; specifically, what is meant by an out-of-tolerance condition and what are the tolerances/variances/thresholds for each WBS base case element?

5. *Prepare the final report.* This is the final report to be prepared at the termination of the project.

6. *Authorize departments to begin work.* This step authorizes departments to begin the actual execution of the project, *not* the planning. This step occurs generally after the project plan has been established, finalized, and perhaps even approved by the customer or user group. This is the initiation of the work orders for project implementation.

7. *Develop the work breakdown structure.* This is one of the four documents required for project definition in the early project planning stage. Assume that WBS is constructed using a bottom-up approach. In other words, the WBS is constructed from the logic network (arrow diagram) and checkpoints which will eventually become the basis for the PERT/CPM charts (see Activity 25).

8. *Close out functional work orders.* This is where the project manager tries to prevent excessive charging to his project by closing out the functional work orders (i.e., Activity 6) as work terminates. This includes cancelling all work orders except those needed to administer the termination of the project and the preparation of the final report.

9. *Develop scope statement and set objectives.* This is the statement of work and is one of the four documents needed in order to identify the require-

TABLE 11–9. STEPS IN PROJECT PLANNING AND CONTROL

Activity	Description	Column 1: Your sequence	Column 2: Group sequence	Column 3: Expert's sequence	Column 4: Difference between 1 & 3	Column 5: Difference between 2 & 3
1.	Develop linear responsibility chart					
2.	Negotiate for qualified functional personnel					
3.	Develop specifications					
4.	Determine means for measuring progress					
5.	Prepare final report					
6.	Authorize departments to begin work					
7.	Develop work breakdown structure					
8.	Close out functional work orders					
9.	Develop scope statement and set objectives					
10.	Develop gross schedule					
11.	Develop priorities for each project element					
12.	Develop alternative courses of action					
13.	Develop PERT network					
14.	Develop detailed schedules					
15.	Establish functional personnel qualifications					
16.	Coordinate ongoing activities					
17.	Determine resource requirements					
18.	Measure progress					
19.	Decide upon a basic course of action					
20.	Establish costs for each WBS element					

(continues)

TABLE 11–9. STEPS IN PROJECT PLANNING AND CONTROL (*Continued*)

Activity	Description	Column 1: Your sequence	Column 2: Group sequence	Column 3: Expert's sequence	Column 4: Difference between 1 & 3	Column 5: Difference between 2 & 3
21.	Review WBS costs with each functional manager					
22.	Establish a project plan					
23.	Establish cost variances for base case elements					
24.	Price out WBS					
25.	Establish logic network with checkpoints					
26.	Review "base case" costs with director					

ments of the project. Usually, the WBS is the structuring of the statement of work.

10. *Develop gross schedule.* This is the summary or milestone schedule needed at project initiation in order to define the four requirements documents for the project. The gross schedule includes start and end dates (if known), other major milestones, and data items.

11. *Develop priorities for each project element.* After the base case is identified and alternative courses of action are considered (i.e., contingency planning), the project team performs a sensitivity analysis for each element of the WBS. This may require assigning priorities for each WBS element, and the highest priorities may *not* necessarily be assigned to elements on the critical path.

12. *Develop alternative courses of action.* Once the base case is known and detailed courses of action (i.e., detailed scheduling) are prepared, project managers conduct "what if" games to develop possible contingency plans.

13. *Develop PERT network.* This is the finalization of the PERT/CPM network and becomes the basis from which detailed scheduling will be performed. The logic for the PERT network can be conducted earlier in the planning cycle (see Activity 25), but the finalization of the network, together with the time durations, are usually based on who has been (or will be) assigned, and the resulting authority/responsibility of the individual. In other words, the activity time duration is a function not only of the performance standard, but also of the individual's expertise and authority/responsibility.

14. *Develop detailed schedules.* These are the detailed project schedules, and are constructed from the PERT/CPM chart and the capabilities of the assigned individuals.

15. *Establish functional personnel qualifications.* Once senior management reviews the base case costs and approves the project, the project manager begins the task of conversion from rough to detail planning. This includes identification of the required resources, and then the respective qualifications.

16. *Coordinate ongoing activities.* These are the ongoing activities for project execution, not project planning. These are the activities that were authorized to begin in Activity 6.

17. *Determine resource requirements.* After senior management approves the estimated base case costs obtained during rough planning, detailed planning begins by determining the resource requirements, including human resources.

18. *Measure progress.* As the project team coordinates ongoing activities during project execution, the team monitors progress and prepares status reports.

19. *Decide on a basic course of action.* Once the project manager obtains the rough cost estimates for each WBS element, the project manager puts together all of the pieces and determines the basic course of action.

20. *Establish costs for each WBS element.* After deciding on the base case, the project manager establishes the base case cost for each WBS element in order to prepare for the senior management pricing review meeting. These costs are usually the same as those that were provided by the line managers.

21. *Review WBS costs with each functional manager.* Each functional manager is provided with the WBS and told to determine his role and price out his functional involvement. The project manager then reviews the WBS costs to make sure that everything was accounted for and without duplication of effort.

22. *Establish project plan.* This is the final step in detail planning. Following this step, project execution begins. (Disregard the situation where project plan development can be run concurrently with project execution.)

23. *Establish cost variances for base case elements.* Once the priorities are known for each base case element, the project manager establishes the allowable cost variances that will be used as a means for measuring progress. Cost reporting is minimum as long as the actual costs remain within these allowable variances.

24. *Price out the WBS.* This is where the project manager provides each functional manager with the WBS for initial activity pricing.

25. *Establish logic network with checkpoints.* This is the bottom-up approach that is often used as the basis for developing both the WBS and later the PERT/CPM network.

26. *Review base case costs with director.* Here the project manager takes the somewhat rough costs obtained during the WBS functional pricing and review and seeks management's approval to begin detail planning.

11–43 Consider the work breakdown structure shown in Figure 11–20. Can the project be managed from this one sheet of paper assuming that, at the end of each month, the project manager also receives a cost and percent-complete summary?

11–44 During 1992 and 1993, General Motors saved over $2 billion due to the cost-cutting efforts of Mr. Lopez. Rumors spread throughout the auto industry that General

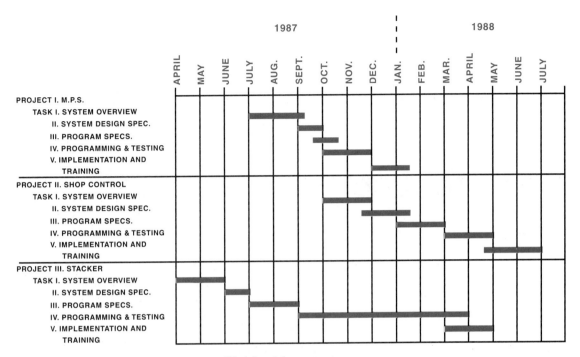

FIGURE 11–20. Work breakdown structure.

Motors was considering a plan to offer subcontractors ten-year contracts in exchange for a 20 percent cost reduction.

These long-term contracts provided both GM and the subcontractors the chance to develop an informal project management relationship based on trust, effective communications, and minimum documentation requirements.

 a. Is it conceivable that the cost savings of 20 percent could have been realized entirely from the decrease in formalized documentation?

 b. Philosophically, what do you think happened when Mr. Lopez departed GM in the spring of 1993 for a senior position at Volkswagen? Did his informal project management system continue without him? Explain your answer.

11–45 During the recession of 1989–1993, the auto industry began taking extreme cost-cutting measures by downsizing its organizations. The downsizing efforts created project management problems for the project engineers in the manufacturing plants. With fewer resources available, more and more of the work had to be out-sourced, primarily for services. The manufacturing plants had years of experience in negotiations for parts, but limited experience in negotiations for services. As a result, the service contracts were drastically overrun with engineering changes and schedule slippages. What is the real problem and your recommendation for a solution?

11–46 When to bring the project manager on board has always been a problem. For each of the following situations, identify the advantages and disadvantages.

a. The project manager is brought on board at the beginning of the conceptual phase but acts only as an observer. The project manager neither answers questions nor provides his ideas until the brainstorming session is completed.

b. When brainstorming is completed during the conceptual phase, senior management appoints one of the brainstorming team members to serve as the project manager.

CASE STUDIES

THE TWO-BOSS PROBLEM

On May 15, 1991, Brian Richards was assigned full-time to Project Turnbolt by Fred Taylor, manager of the thermodynamics department. All work went smoothly for four and one-half of the five months necessary to complete this effort. During this period of successful performance Brian Richards had good working relations with Edward Compton (the Turnbolt Project Engineer) and Fred Taylor.

Fred treated Brian as a Theory Y employee. Once a week Fred and Brian would chat about the status of Brian's work. Fred would always conclude their brief meeting with, "You're doing a fine job, Brian. Keep it up. Do anything you have to do to finish the project."

During the last month of the project Brian began receiving conflicting requests from the project office and the department manager as to the preparation of the final report. Compton told Brian Richards that the final report was to be assembled in view-graph format (i.e., "bullet" charts) for presentation to the customer at the next technical interchange meeting. The project did not have the funding necessary for a comprehensive engineering report.

The thermodynamics department, on the other hand, had a policy that all engineering work done on new projects would be documented in a full and comprehensive report. This new policy had been implemented about one year ago when Fred Taylor became department manager. Rumor had it that Fred wanted formal reports so that he could put his name on them and either publish or present them at technical meetings. All work performed in the thermodynamics department required Taylor's signature before it could be released to the project office as an official company position. Upper-level management did not want its people to publish and therefore did not maintain a large editorial or graphic arts department. Personnel desiring to publish had to get the department manager's approval and, on approval, had to prepare the entire report themselves, without any "overhead" help. Since Taylor had taken over the reins as department head, he had presented three papers at technical meetings.

A meeting was held between Brian Richards, Fred Taylor, and Edward Compton.

Edward: "I don't understand why we have a problem. All the project office wants is a simple summary of the results. Why should we have to pay for a report that we don't want or need?"

Fred: "We have professional standards in this department. All work that goes out must be fully documented for future use. I purposely require that my signature be attached to all communications leaving this department. This way we obtain uniformity and standarization. You project people must understand that, although you can institute or own project policies and procedures (within the constraints and limitations of company policies and procedures), we department personnel also have standards. Your work must be prepared within our standards and specifications."

Edward: "The project office controls the purse strings. We (the project office) specified that only a survey report was necessary. Furthermore, if you want a more comprehensive report, then you had best do it on your own overhead account. The project office isn't going to foot the bill for your publications."

Fred: "The customary procedure is to specify in the program plan the type of report requested from the departments. Inasmuch as your program plan does not specify this, I used my own discretion as to what I thought you meant."

Edward: "But I told Brian Richards what type of report I wanted. Didn't he tell you?"

Fred: "I guess I interpreted the request a little differently from what you had intended. Perhaps we should establish a new policy that all program plans must specify reporting requirements. This would alleviate some of the misunderstandings, especially since my department has several projects going on at one time. In addition, I am going to establish a policy for my department that all requests for interim, status, or final reports be given to me directly. I'll take personal charge of all reports."

Edward: "That's fine with me! And for your first request I'm giving you an order that I want a survey report, not a detailed effort."

Brian: "Well, since the meeting is over, I guess I'll return to my office (and begin updating my résumé just in case)."

PROJECT OVERRUN

The Green Company production project was completed three months behind schedule and at a cost overrun of approximately 60 percent. Following submittal of the final report, Phil Graham, the director of project management, called a meeting to discuss the problems encountered on the Green Project.

Phil Graham: "We're not here to point the finger at anyone. We're here to analyze what went wrong and to see if we can develop any policies and/or procedures that will prevent this from happening in the future. What went wrong?"

Project Manager: "When we accepted the contract, Green did not have a fixed delivery schedule for us to go by because they weren't sure when their new production plant would be ready to begin production activities. So, we estimated 3,000 units per month for months five through twelve of the project. When they found that the production plant would be available two months ahead of schedule, they asked us to accelerate our production activities. So, we put all of our production people on overtime in order to satisfy their schedule. This was our mistake, because we accepted a fixed delivery date and budget before we understood everything."

Functional Manager: "Our problem was that the customer could not provide us with a fixed set of specifications, because the final set of specifications depended on OSHA and EPA requirements, which could not be confirmed until initial testing of the new plant. Our people, therefore, were asked to commit to man-hours before specifications could be reviewed.

"Six months after project go-ahead, Green Company issued the final specifications. We had to remake 6,000 production units because they did not live up to the new specifications."

Project Manager: "The customer was willing to pay for the remake units. This was established in the contract. Unfortunately, our contract people didn't tell me that we were still liable for the penalty payments if we didn't adhere to the original schedule."

Phil Graham: "Don't you feel that misinterpretation of the terms and conditions is your responsibility?"

Project Manager: "I guess I'll have to take some of the blame."

Functional Manager: "We need specific documentation on what to do in case of specification changes. I don't think that our people realize that user approval of specification is not a contract agreed to in blood. Specifications can change, even in the middle of a project. Our people must understand that, as well as the necessary procedures for implementing change."

Phil Graham: "I've heard that the functional employees on the assembly line are grumbling about the Green Project. What's their gripe?"

Functional Manager: "We were directed to cut out all overtime on all projects. But when the Green Project got into trouble, overtime became a way of life. For nine months, the functional employees on the Green Project had as much overtime as they wanted. This made the functional employees on other projects very unhappy.

"To make matters worse, the functional employees got used to a big take-home paycheck and started living beyond their means. When the project ended, so did their overtime. Now, they claim that we should give them the opportunity for more overtime. Everybody hates us."

Phil Graham: "Well, now we know the causes of the problem. Any recommendations for cures and future prevention activities?"

MARGO COMPANY

"I've called this meeting, gentlemen, because that paper factory we call a computer organization is driving up our overhead rates," snorted Richard Margo, president, as he looked around the table at the vice presidents of project management, engineering, manufacturing, marketing, administration, and information systems. "We seem to be developing reports faster than we can update our computer facility. Just one year ago, we updated our computer and now we're operating three shifts a day, seven days a week. Where do we go from here?"

V.P. Information: "As you all know, Richard asked me, about two months ago, to investigate this gigantic increase in the flow of paperwork. There's no question that we're getting too many reports. The question is, are we paying too much money for the information that we get? I've surveyed all of our departments and their key personnel. Most of the survey questionnaires indicate that we're getting too much information. Only a small percentage of each report appears to be necessary. In addition, many of the reports arrive too late. I'm talking about scheduled reports, not planning, demand, or exception reports."

V.P. Project Management: "Every report may people receive is necessary for us to make decisions effectively with regard to planning, organizing, and controlling each project. My people are the biggest users and we can't live with fewer reports."

V.P. Information: "Can your people live with less information in each report? Can some of the reports be received less frequently?"

V.P. Project Management: "Some of our reports have too much information in them. But we need them at the frequency we have now."

V.P. Engineering: "My people utilize about 20 percent of the information in most of our reports. Once our people find the information they want, the report is discarded. That's because we know that each project manager will retain a copy. Also, only the department managers and section supervisors read the reports."

V.P. Information: "Can engineering and manufacturing get the information they need from other sources, such as the project office?"

V.P. Project Management: "Wait a minute! My people don't have time to act as paper pushers for each department manager. We all know that the departments can't function without these reports. Why should we assume the burden?"

V.P. Information: "All I'm trying to say is that many of our reports can be combined into smaller ones and possibly made more concise. Most of our reports are flexible enough to meet changes in our operating business. We have two sets of reports: one for the customer and one for us. If the customer wants the report in a specific fashion, he pays for it. Why can't we act as our own customer and try to make a reporting system that we can all use?"

V.P. Engineering: "Many of the reports obviously don't justify the cost. Can we generate the minimum number of reports and pass it on to someone higher or lower in the organization?"

V.P. Project Management: "We need weekly reports, and we need them on Monday mornings. I know our computer people don't like to work on Sunday evenings, but we have no choice. If we don't have those reports on Monday mornings, we can't control time, cost, and performance."

V.P. Information: "There are no reports generated from the pertinent data in our original computer runs. This looks to me like every report is a one-shot deal. There has to be room for improvement.

"I have prepared a checklist for each of you with four major questions. Do you want summary or detailed information? How do you want the output to look? How many copies do you need? How often do you need these reports?"

Richard Margo: "In project organizational forms, the project exists as a separate entity except for administrative purposes. These reports are part of that administrative purpose. Combining this with the high cost of administration in our project structure, we'll never remain competitive unless we lower our overhead. I'm going to leave it up to you guys. Try to reduce the number of reports, but don't sacrifice the necessary information you need to control the projects and your resources."

DENVER INTERNATIONAL AIRPORT (DIA)

Background

How does one convert a $1.2 billion project into a $5.0 billion project? It's easy. Just build a new airport in Denver. The decision to replace Denver's Stapleton Airport with Denver International Airport (DIA) was made by well-intentioned city officials. The city of Denver would need a new airport eventually, and it seemed like the right time to build an airport that would satisfy Denver's needs for at least 50–60 years. DIA could become the benchmark for other airports to follow.

A summary of the critical events is listed below:

1985: Denver Mayor Federico Pena and Adams County officials agree to build a replacement for Stapleton International Airport.
Project estimate: $1.2 billion

1986: Peat Marwick, a consulting firm, is hired to perform a feasibility study including projected traffic. Their results indicate that, depending on the season, as many as 50 percent of the passengers would change planes. The new airport would have to handle this smoothly. United and Continental object to the idea of building a new airport, fearing the added cost burden.

May, 1989: Denver voters pass an airport referendum.
Project estimate: $1.7 billion

March, 1993: Denver Mayor Wellington Webb announces the first delay. Opening day would be postponed from October, 1993 to December, 1993. (Federico Pena becomes Secretary of Transportation under Clinton).
Project estimate: $2.7 billion

October, 1993: Opening day is to be delayed to March, 1994. The problems were the fire and security systems in addition to the inoperable baggage handling system.
Project estimate: $3.1 billion

December, 1993: The airport is ready to open, but without an operational baggage handling system. Another delay is announced.

February, 1994: Opening day is to be delayed to May 15, 1994 because of baggage handling system.

May, 1994: Airport misses the fourth deadline.

August, 1994: DIA finances a backup baggage handling system. Opening day is delayed indefinitely.
Project estimate: $4 billion plus.

December, 1994: Denver announces that DIA was built on top of an old Native-American burial ground. An agreement is reached to lift the curse.

Airports and Airline Deregulation

Prior to the Airline Deregulation Act of 1978, airline routes and airfare were established by the Civil Aeronautics Board (CAB). Airlines were allowed to charge whatever they wanted for airfare, based upon CAB approval. The cost of additional aircraft was eventually passed on to the consumer. Initially, the high cost for airfare restricted travel to the businessperson and the elite who could afford it.

Increases in passenger travel were moderate. Most airports were already underutilized and growth was achieved by adding terminals or runways on existing airport sites. The need for new airports was not deemed critical for the near term.

Following deregulation, the airline industry had to prepare for open market competition. This meant that airfares were expected to decrease dramatically. Airlines began purchasing hoards of planes, and most routes were "free game." Airlines had to purchase more planes and fly more routes in order to remain profitable. The increase in passenger traffic was expected to come from the average person who could finally afford air travel.

Deregulation made it clear that airport expansion would be necessary. While airport management conducted feasibility studies, the recession of 1979–1983 occurred. Several airlines such as Braniff filed for bankruptcy protection under Chapter 11 and the airline industry headed for consolidation through mergers and leveraged buyouts.

Cities took a wait-and-see attitude rather than risk billions in new airport development. Noise abatement policies, environmental projection acts, and land acquisition were viewed as headaches. The only major airport built in the last 20 years was Dallas-Ft. Worth, which was completed in 1974.

Does Denver Need a New Airport?

In 1974, even prior to deregulation, Denver's Stapleton Airport was experiencing such rapid growth that Denver's Regional Council of Governments concluded that Stapleton would not be able to handle the necessary traffic expected by the year 2000. Modernization of Stapleton could have extended the inevitable problemto 2005. But were the headaches with Stapleton better cured through modernization or by building a new airport? There was no question that insufficient airport capacity would cause Denver to lose valuable business. Being 500 miles from other major cities placed enormous pressure upon the need for air travel in and out of Denver.

In 1988, Denver's Stapleton International Airport ranked as the fifth busiest with 30 million passengers. The busiest airports were Chicago, Atlanta, Los Angeles, and Dallas-Ft. Worth. By the year 2000, Denver anticipated 66 million passengers, just below Dallas-Ft. Worth's 70 million and Chicago's 83 million estimates.

Delays at Denver's Stapleton Airport caused major delays at all other airports. By one estimate, bad weather in Denver caused up to $100 million in lost income to the airlines each year because of delays, rerouting, canceled flights, putting travelers into hotels overnight, employee overtime pay, and passengers switching to other airlines. Denver's United Airlines and Continental comprise 80% of all flights in and out of Denver. Exhibit 11–1 shows the current service characteristics of United and Continental between December, 1993 and April, 1994. Exhibit 11–2 shows all of the airlines serving Denver as of June, 1994. Exhibit 11–3 shows the cities that are serviced from Denver. It should be obvious that delays in Denver could cause delays in each of these cities. Exhibit 11–4 shows the top ten domestic passenger origin-destination markets from Denver Stapleton.

Stapleton was ranked as one of the 10 worst air traffic bottlenecks in the United States. Even low clouds at Denver Stapleton could bring delays of 30 to 60 minutes.

Exhibit 11–1. Current Service Characteristics: United Airlines and Continental Airlines, December 1993 and April 1994

	Enplaned passengers (a)	Scheduled seats (b)	Boarding load factor	Scheduled departures (b)	Average seats per departure
December 1993					
United Airlines	641,209	1,080,210	59%	7,734	140
United Express	57,867	108,554	53%	3,582	30
Continental Airlines	355,667	624,325	57%	4,376	143
Continental Express	52,680	105,800	50%	3,190	33
Other	236,751	357,214	66%	2,851	125
Total	1,344,174	2,276,103	59%	21,733	105
April 1994					
United Airlines	717,093	1,049,613	68%	7,743	136
United Express	44,451	92,880	48%	3,395	27
Continental Airlines	275,948	461,168	60%	3,127	147
Continental Express	24,809	92,733	27%	2,838	33
Other	234,091	354,950	66%	2,833	125
Total	1,296,392	2,051,344	63%	19,936	103

(a) Airport management records.
(b) Official Airline Guides, Inc. (online data base); for periods noted.

Stapleton has two parallel north-south runways that are close together. During bad weather where instrument landing conditions exist, the two runways are considered as only one. This drastically reduces the takeoffs and landings each hour.

The new airport would have three north-south runways initially with a master plan calling for eight eventually. This would triple or quadruple instrument flights occurring at the same time to 104 aircraft per hour. Currently, Stapleton can handle only 30 landings per hour under instrument conditions with a *maximum* of 80 aircraft per hour during clear weather.

The runway master plan called for ten 12,000 foot and two 16,000 foot runways. By opening day, three north-south and one east-west 12,000 foot runways would be in operation and one of the 16,000 foot north-south runways would be operational shortly thereafter.

The airfield facilities also included a 327 foot FAA air traffic control tower (the nation's tallest) and base building structures. The tower's height allowed controllers to visually monitor runway thresholds as much as three miles away. The runway/taxiway lighting system, with lights imbedded in the concrete pavement to form centerlines and stopbars at intersections, would allow air traffic controllers to signal pilots to wait on taxiways and cross active runways, and to lead them through the airfield in poor visibility.

Due to shifting winds, runway operations were shifted from one direction to another. At the new airport, the changeover would require four minutes as opposed to the 45 minutes at Stapleton.

Sufficient spacing was provided for in the concourse design such that two FAA Class 6 aircraft (i.e. 747-XX) could operate back-to-back without impeding each other.

Exhibit 11–2. Airlines Serving Denver June 1994

Major/national airlines	*Regional/commuter airlines*
America West Airlines	Air Wisconsin (United Express) (b)
American Airlines	Continental Express
Continental Airlines	GP Express Airlines
Delta Air Lines	Great Lakes Aviation (United Express)
Markair	Mesa Airlines (United Express)
Midway Airlines	Midwest Express (b)
Morris Air (a)	
Northwest Airlines	*Cargo airlines*
Trans World Airlines	
United Airlines	Airborne Express
USAir	Air Vantage
	Alpine Air
Charter airlines	American International Airways
	Ameriflight
Aero Mexico	Bighorn Airways
American Trans Air	Burlington Air Express
Casino Express	Casper Air
Express One	Corporate Air
Great American	DHL Worldwide Express
Private Jet	Emery Worldwide
Sun Country Airlines	Evergreen International Airlines
	EWW Airline/Air Train
Foreign flag airlines (scheduled)	Federal Express
	Kitty Hawk
Martinair Holland	Majestic Airlines
Mexicana de Aviacion	Reliant Airlines
	United Parcel Service
	Western Aviators

(a) Morris Air was purchased by Southwest Airlines in December 1993. The airline has announced that it will no longer serve Denver as of October 3, 1994.

(b) Air Wisconsin and Midwest Express have both achieved the level of operating revenues needed to qualify as a national airline as defined by the FAA. However, for purposes of this report, these airlines are referred to as regional airlines.

Source: Airport management, June 1994.

Even when two aircraft (one from each concourse) have pushed back at the same time, there could still exist room for a third FAA Class 6 aircraft to pass between them.

City officials believed that Denver's location, being equidistant from Japan and Germany, would allow twin-engine, extended range transports to reach both countries nonstop. The international opportunities were there. Between late 1990 and early 1991, Denver was entertaining four groups of leaders per month from Pacific Rim countries to look at DIA's planned capabilities.

In the long term, Denver saw the new airport as a potential hub for Northwest or USAir. This would certainly bring more business to Denver. Very few airports in the world can boast of multiple hubs.

The Enplaned Passenger Market

Perhaps the most critical parameter that illustrates the necessity for a new airport is the enplaned passenger market. (An enplaned passenger is one who gets on a flight, either an origination flight or connecting flight.)

Exhibit 11–3. U.S. Airports Served Nonstop from Denver

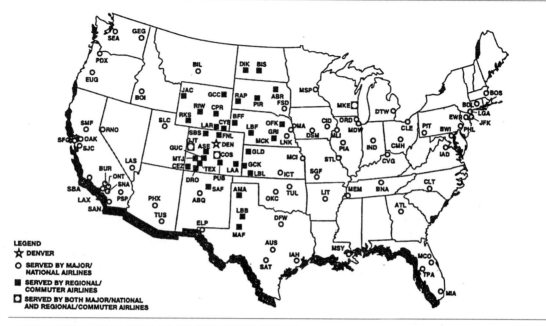

LEGEND
★ DENVER
O SERVED BY MAJOR/
    NATIONAL AIRLINES
■ SERVED BY REGIONAL/
    COMMUTER AIRLINES
◨ SERVED BY BOTH MAJOR/NATIONAL
    AND REGIONAL/COMMUTER AIRLINES

SOURCE: OFFICIAL AIRLINE GUIDES, INC. (ONLINE DATA BASE), JUNE 1994.

Exhibit 11–5, shown below, identifies the enplaned passengers for individual airlines servicing Denver Stapleton for 1992 and 1993.

Connecting passengers were forecast to decrease about 1,000,000 between 1993 and 1995 before returning to a steady 3.0% per year growth, totaling 8,285,500 in 2000. As a result, the number of connecting passengers is forecast to represent a smaller share (46%) of total enplaned passengers at the Airport in 2000 than in 1993 (50%). Total enplaned passengers at Denver are forecast to increase from 16,320,472 in 1993 to 18,161,000 in 2000—an average increase of 1.5% per year (decreasing slightly from 1993 through 1995, then increasing 2.7% per year after 1995).

The increase in enplaned passengers will necessitate an increase in the number of aircraft departures. Since landing fees are based upon aircraft landed weight, more arrivals and departures will generate more landing fee revenue. Since airport revenue is derived from cargo operations as well as passenger activities, it is important to recognize that enplaned cargo is also expected to increase.

Land Selection[16]

The site selected was a 53-square-mile area 18 miles northeast of Denver's business district. The site would be larger than the Chicago O'Hare and Dallas Ft. Worth air-

---

16. Adapted from David A. Brown, "Denver Aims for Global Hub Status with New Airport Under Construction," *Aviation Week and Space Technology,* March 11, 1991; p. 44

**Exhibit 11–4. Top 10 Domestic Passenger Origin-Destination Markets
and Airline Service, Stapleton International Airport
(for the 12 months ended September 30, 1993)**

City of orgin or destination (a)	Air miles from Denver	Percentage of certificated airline passengers	Average daily nonstop departures (b)
1. Los Angeles (c)	849	6.8	34
2. New York (d)	1,630	6.2	19
3. Chicago (e)	908	5.6	26
4. San Francisco (f)	957	5.6	29
5. Washington, D.C. (g)	1,476	4.9	12
6. Dallas/Forth Worth	644	3.5	26
7. Houston (h)	864	3.2	15
8. Phoenix	589	3.1	19
9. Seattle	1,019	2.6	14
10. Minneapolis	693	2.3	16
Cities listed		43.8	210
All others		56.2	241
Total		100.0	451

(a) Top 10 cities based on total inbound and outbound passengers (on large certificated airlines) at Stapleton International Airport in 10% sample for the 12 months ended September 30, 1993.
(b) Official Airline Guides, Inc. (online data base), April 1994. Includes domestic flights operated at least four days per week by major/national airlines and excludes the activity of foreign-flag and commuter/regional airlines.
(c) Los Angeles International, Burbank-Glendale-Pasadena, John Wayne (Orange County), Ontario International, and Long Beach Municipal Airports.
(d) John F. Kennedy International, LaGuardia, and Newark International Airports.
(e) Chicago-O'Hare International and Midway Airports.
(f) San Francisco, Metropolitan Oakland, and San Jose International Airports.
(g) Washington Dulles International, Washington National, and Baltimore/Washington International Airports.
(h) Houston Intercontinental and William P. Hobby Airports.
Sources: U.S. Department of Transportation/Air Transport Association of America, "Origin-Destination Survey of Airline Passenger Traffic, Domestic," third quarter 1993, except as noted.

ports combined. Unfortunately, a state law took effect prohibiting political entities from annexing land without the consent of its residents. The land was in Adams County. Before the vote was taken, Adams County and Denver negotiated an agreement limiting noise and requiring the creation of a buffer zone to protect surrounding residents. The agreement also included continuous noise monitoring, as well as limits on such businesses as airport hotels that could be in direct competition with existing services provided in Adams County. The final part of the agreement limited DIA to such businesses as airline maintenance, cargo, small package delivery, and other such airport-related activities.

With those agreements in place, Denver annexed 45 square miles and purchased an additional 8 square miles for noise buffer zones. Denver rezoned the buffer area to prohibit residential development within a 65 LDN (Level Day/Night) noise level. LDN is a weighted noise measurement intended to determine perceived noise in both day and night conditions. Adams County enacted even stiffer zoning regulations calling for no residential development with an LDN noise level of 60.

Exhibit 11–5. Enplaned Passengers by Airline 1992–1993,
Stapleton International Airport

Enplaned passengers	1992	1993
United	6,887,936	7,793,246
United Express(1)	470,841	578,619
	7,358,777	8,371,865
Continental	5,162,812	4,870,861
Continental Express	514,293	532,046
	5,677,105	5,402,907
American Airlines	599,705	563,119
America West Airlines	176,963	156,032
Delta Air Lines	643,644	634,341
MarkAir	2,739	93,648
Northwest Airlines	317,507	320,527
Trans World Airlines	203,096	182,502
US Air	201,949	197,095
Other	256,226	398,436
	2,401,829	2,545,700
Total	15,437,711	16,320,472

(1) Includes Mesa Airlines, Air Wisconsin, Great Lakes Aviation and Westair Airlines.
(Source: Department of Aviation managment records.)

Most of the airport land embodied two ranches. About 550 people were relocated. The site had overhead power lines and gas wells, which were relocated or abandoned. The site lacked infrastructure development and there were no facilities for providing water, power, sewage disposal, or other such services.

Front Range Airport   Located 2.5 miles southeast of DIA is Front Range Airport, which had been developed to relieve Denver's Stapleton Airport of most nonairline traffic operations. As a satellite airport to DIA, Front Range Airport had been offering six aviation business services by 1991.

- Air cargo and air freight, including small package services. (This is direct competition for DIA.)
- Aircraft manufacturing.
- Aircraft repair. (This is direct competition for DIA.)
- Fixed base operators to service general (and corporate) aviation.
- Flight training.
- Military maintenance and training.

The airport was located on a 4800-acre site and was surrounded by a 12,000-acre industrial park. The airport was owned and operated by Adams County, which had completely different ownership than DIA. By 1991, Front Range Airport had two east-west runways: a 700-foot runway for general aviation use and an 8000-foot runway to be extended to 10,000 feet. By 1992, the general plans called for two more runways to be built, both north-south. The first runway would be 10,000 feet initially with expansion capability to 16,000 feet to support wide body aircraft. The second runway would be 7000 feet to service general aviation.

Opponents of DIA contended that Front Range Airport could be enlarged significantly, thus reducing pressure on Denver's Stapleton Airport, and that DIA would not be necessary at that time. Proponents of DIA argued that Front Range should be used to relieve pressure on DIA if and when DIA became a major international airport as all expected. Both sides were in agreement that initially, Front Range Airport would be a competitor to DIA.

Airport Design

The Denver International Airport was based upon a "Home-on-the-Range" design. The city wanted a wide open entry point for visitors. In spring of 1991, the city began soliciting bids.

To maintain a distinctive look that would be easily identified by travelers, a translucent tent-like roof was selected. The roof was made of two thicknesses of translucent, Teflon-coated glass fiber material suspended from steel cables hanging from the structural supports. The original plans for the roof called for a conventional design using 800,000 tons of structural steel. The glass fiber roof would require only 30,000 tons of structural steel, thus providing substantial savings on construction costs. The entire roof would permit about 10% of the sunlight to shine through, thus providing an open, outdoors-like atmosphere.

The master plan for the airport called for four concourses, each with a maximum of 60 gates. However, only three concourses would be built initially, and none would be full size. The first, Concourse A, would have 32 airline gates and six commuter gates. This concourse would be shared by Continental and any future international carriers. Continental had agreed to give up certain gate positions if requested to do so in order to accommodate future international operations. Continental was the only long-haul international carrier with one daily flight to London. Shorter international flights were to Canada and Mexico.

Concourses B and C would each have 20 gates initially for airline use plus six commuter gates. Concourse B would be the United Concourse. Concourse C would be for all carriers other than Continental or United.

All three concourses would provide a total of 72 airline gates and 18 commuter gates. This would be substantially less than what the original master plan called for.

Although the master plan identified 60 departure gates for each concourse, cost became an issue. The first set of plans identified 106 departure gates (not counting commuter gates) and was then scaled down to 72 gates. United Airlines originally wanted 45 departure gates, but settled for 20. The recession was having its effect.

The original plans called for a train running through a tunnel beneath the terminal building and the concourses. The train would carry 6000 passengers per hour. Road construction on and adjacent to the airport was planned to take one year. Runway construction was planned to take one year but was deliberately scheduled for two years in order to save on construction costs.

The principal benefits of the new airport compared to Stapleton were:

- A significantly *improved airfield configuration* that allowed for triple simultaneous instrument landings in all weather conditions, improved the efficiency and safety of airfield operations, and reduced taxiway congestion

● *Improved efficiency in the operation of the regional airspace,* which, coupled with the increased capacity of the airfield, was supposed to significantly reduce aircraft delays and airline operating costs both at Denver and system-wide

● *Reduced noise impacts* resulting from a large site that was situated in a relatively unpopulated area

● *A more efficient terminal/concourse/apron layout* that minimized passenger walking distance, maximized the exposure of concessions to passenger flows, provided significantly greater curbside capacity, and allowed for the efficient maneuvering of aircraft in and out of gates

● *Improved international facilities* including longer runway lengths for improved stage length capability for international flights and larger Federal Inspection Services (FIS) facilities for greater passenger processing capability

● *Significant expansion capability* of each major functional element of the airport

● *Enhanced efficiency of airline operations* as a result of new baggage handling, communications, de-icing, fueling, mail sorting, and other specialty systems

One of the problems with the airport design related to the high wind shears that would exist where the runways were placed. This could eventually become a serious issue.

Project Management

The city of Denver selected two companies to assist in the project management process. The first was Greiner Engineering, an engineering, architecture, and airport planning firm. The second company was Morrison-Knudsen Engineering (MKE) which is a design-construct firm. The city of Denver and Greiner/MKE would function as the Project Management Team (PMT) responsible for schedule coordination, cost control, information management, and administration of approximately 100 design contracts, 160 general contractors, and more than 2000 subcontractors.

In the selection of architects, it became obvious that there would be a split between those who would operate the airport and the city's aspirations. Airport personnel were more interested in an "easy-to-clean" airport and convinced the city to hire a New Orleans-based architectural firm with whom Stapleton personnel had worked previously. The city wanted a "thing of beauty" rather than an easy-to-clean venture.

In an unusual split of responsibilities, the New Orleans firm was contracted to create standards that would unify the entire airport and to take the design of the main terminal only through schematics and design development, at which point it would be handed off to another firm. This sharing of the wealth with several firms would later prove more detrimental than beneficial.

The New Orleans architectural firm complained that the direction given by airport personnel focused on operational issues rather than aesthetic values. Furthermore, almost all decisions seemed to be made in reaction to maintenance or technical issues. This created a problem for the design team because the project's requirements specified that the design reflect a signature image for the airport, one that would capture the uniqueness of Denver and Colorado.

The New Orleans team designed a stepped-roof profile supported by an exposed truss system over a large central atrium, thus resembling the structure of train sheds. The intent was to bring the image of railroading, which was responsible for Denver's early growth, into the jet age.

The mayor, city council, and others were concerned that the design did not express a $2 billion project. A blue-ribbon commission was formed to study the matter. The city council eventually approved the design.

Financial analysis of the terminal indicated that the roof design would increase the cost of the project by $48 million and would push the project off schedule. A second architectural firm was hired. The final design was a peaked roof with Teflon-coated fabric designed to bring out the image of the Rocky Mountains. The second architectural firm had the additional responsibility to take the project from design development through to construction. The cost savings from the new design was so substantial that the city upgraded the floor finish in the terminal and doubled the size of the parking structure to 12,000 spaces.

The effectiveness of the project management team was being questioned. The PMT failed to sort out the differences between the city's aspirations and the maintenance orientation of the operators. It failed to detect the cost and constructability issues with the first design even though both PMT partners had vast in-house expertise. The burden of responsibility was falling on the shoulders of the architects. The PMT also did not appear to be aware that the first design may not have met the project's standards.

Throughout the design battle, no one heard from the airlines. Continental and United controlled 80% of the flights at Stapleton. Yet the airlines refused to participate in the design effort, hoping the project would be canceled. The city ordered the design teams to proceed for bids without any formal input from the users.

With a recession looming in the wings and Contential fighting for survival, the city needed the airlines to sign on. To entice the airlines to participate, the city agreed to a stunning range of design changes while assuring the bond rating agencies that the 1993 opening date would be kept. Continental convinced Denver to move the international gates away from the north side of the main terminal to terminal A, and to build a bridge from the main terminal to terminal A. This duplicated the function of a below-ground people-mover system. A basement was added the full length of the concourses. Service cores, located between gates, received a second level.

United's changes were more significant. It widened concourse B by 8 feet to accommodate two moving walkways in each direction. It added a second level of service cores, and had the roof redesigned to provide a clerestory of natural light. Most important, United wanted a destination-coded vehicle (DCV) baggage handling system where bags could be transferred between gates in less than 10 minutes, thus supporting short turnaround times. The DCV was to be on Concourse B (United) only. Within a few weeks thereafter, DIA proposed that the baggage handling system be extended to the entire airport. Yet even with these changes in place, United and Continental *still* did not sign a firm agreement with DIA, thus keeping bond interest expense at a higher than anticipated level. Some people contended that United and Continental were holding DIA hostage.

From a project management perspective, there was no question that disaster was on the horizon. Nobody knew what to do about the DCV system. The risks were unknown. Nobody realized the complexity of the system, especially the software requirements. By one account, the launch date should have been delayed by at least two years. The contract for DCV hadn't been awarded yet, and terminal construction was already under way. Everyone wanted to know why the design (and construction) was not delayed until after the airlines had signed on. How could DIA install and maintain the terminal's baseline design without having a design for the baggage handling system? Everyone felt that what they were now building would have to be ripped apart.

There were going to be massive scope changes. DIA persisted in its belief that the airport would open on time. Work in process was now $130 million per month. Acceleration costs, because of the scope changes, would be $30–$40 million. Three shifts were running at DIA with massive overtime. People were getting burned out to the point where they couldn't continue.

To reduce paperwork and maintain the schedule, architects became heavily involved during the construction phase, which was highly unusual. The PMT seemed to be abdicating control to the architects who would be responsible for coordination. The trust that had developed during the early phases began evaporating.

Even the car rental companies got into the act. They balked at the fees for their in-terminal location and said that servicing within the parking structures was inconvenient. They demanded and finally received a separate campus. Passengers would now be forced to take shuttle buses out of the terminal complex to rent or return vehicles.

The Baggage Handling System

DIA's $200 million baggage handling system was designed to be state-of-the-art. Conventional baggage handling systems are manual. Each airline operates its own system. DIA opted to buy a single system and lease it back to the airlines. In effect, it would be a one-baggage-system-fits-all configuration.

The system would contain 100 computers, 56 laser scanners, conveyor belts, and thousands of motors. As designed, the system would contain 400 fiberglass carts, each carrying a single suitcase through 22 miles of steel tracks. Operating at 20 miles per hour, the system could deliver 60,000 bags per hour from dozens of gates. United was worried that passengers would have to wait for luggage since several of their gates were more than a mile from the main terminal. The system design was for the luggage to go from the plane to the carousel in 8–10 minutes. The luggage would reach the carousel before the passengers.

The baggage handling system would be centered on track-mounted cars propelled by linear induction motors. The cars slow down, but don't stop, as a conveyor ejects bags onto their platform. During the induction process, a scanner reads the bar-coded label and transmits the data through a programmable logic controller to a radio frequency identification tag on a passing car. At this point, the car knows the destination of the bag it is carrying, as does the computer software that routes the car to its destination. To illustrate the complexity of the situation, consider 4000 taxicabs in a major city, all without drivers, being controlled by a computer through the streets of a city.

1989

Construction began without a signed agreement from Continental and United.

Early Risk Analysis

By March of 1991, the bidding process was in full swing for the main terminal, concourses, and tunnel. Preliminary risk analysis involved three areas: cost, human resources, and weather.

- *Cost:* The grading of the terminal area was completed at about $5 million under budget and the grading of the first runway was completed at about $1.8 million under budget. This led management to believe that the original construction cost estimates were accurate. Also, many of the construction bids being received were below the city's own estimates.

● *Human Resources:* The economic recession hit Denver a lot harder than the rest of the nation. DIA was at that time employing about 500 construction workers. By late 1992, it was anticipated that 6000 construction workers would be needed. Although more than 3000 applications were on file, there remained the question of available, qualified labor. If the recession were to be prolonged, then the lack of qualified suppliers could be an issue as well.

● *Bad Weather:* Bad weather, particularly in the winter, was considered as the greatest risk to the schedule. Fortunately, the winters of 1989–1990 and 1990–1991 were relatively mild, which gave promise to future mild winters. Actually, more time was lost due to bad weather in the summer of 1990, than in either of the two previous winters.

March 1991

By early March, 1991, Denver had already issued more than $900 million in bonds to begin construction of the new airport. Denver planned to issue another $500 million in bonds the following month. Standard & Poor's Corporation lowered the rating on the DIA bonds from BBB to BBB–, just a notch above the junk grade rating. This could prove to be extremely costly to DIA because any downgrading in bond quality ratings would force DIA to offer higher yields on their new bond offerings, thus increasing their yearly interest expense.

Denver was in the midst of an upcoming mayoral race. Candidates were calling for the postponement of the construction, not only because of the lower ratings, but also because Denver *still* did not have a firm agreement with either Continental or United Airlines that they would use the new airport. The situation became more intense because three months earlier, in December of 1990, Continental had filed for bankruptcy protection under Chapter 11. Fears existed that Continental might drastically reduce the size of its hub at DIA or even pull out altogether.

Denver estimated that cancelation or postponement of the new airport would be costly. The city had $521 million in contracts that could not be canceled. Approximately $22 million had been spent in debt service for the land, and $38 million in interest on the $470 million in bond money was already spent. The city would have to default on more than $900 million in bonds if it could not collect landing fees from the new airport. The study also showed that a two year delay would increase the total cost by $2 billion to $3 billion and increase debt service to $340 million per year. It now appeared that the point of no return was at hand.

Fortunately for DIA, Moody's Investors Service, Inc. did *not* lower their rating on the $1 billion outstanding of airport bonds. Moody's confirmed their conditional Baa1 rating, which was slightly higher than the S & P rating of BBB–. Moody's believed that the DIA effort was a strong one and that even at depressed airline traffic levels, DIA would be able to service its debt for the scaled-back airport. Had both Moody's and S & P lowered their ratings together, DIA's future might have been in jeopardy.

April 1991

Denver issued $500 million in serial revenue bonds with a maximum yield of 9.185% for bonds maturing in 2023. A report by Fitch Investors Service estimated that the airport was ahead of schedule and 7% below budget. The concerns of the investor community seemed to have been tempered despite the bankruptcy filing of Continental Airlines. However, there was still concern that no formal agreement existed between DIA and either United Airlines or Continental Airlines.

May 1991

The city of Denver and United Airlines finally reached a tentative agreement. United would use 45 of the potential 90–100 gates at Concourse B. This would be a substantial increase from the 26 gates DIA had originally thought that United would require. The 50% increase in gates would also add 2000 reservations jobs. United also expressed an interest in building a $1 billion maintenance facility at DIA employing 6000 people.

United stated later that the agreement did not constitute a firm commitment but was contingent upon legislative approval of a tax incentive package of $360 million over 30 years plus $185 million in financing and $23 million in tax exemptions. United would decide by the summer in which city the maintenance facility would be located. United reserved the right to renegotiate the hub agreement if DIA was not chosen as the site for the maintenance facility.

Some people believed that United had delayed signing a formal agreement until it was in a strong bargaining position. With Continental in bankruptcy and DIA beyond the point of no return, United was in a favorable position to demand tax incentives of $200 million in order to keep their hub in Denver and build a maintenance facility. The state legislature would have to be involved in approving the incentives. United Airlines ultimately located the $1 billion maintenance facility at the Indianapolis Airport.

August 1991

Hotel developers expressed concern about building at DIA, which is 26 miles from downtown compared to 8 miles from Stapleton to downtown Denver. DIA officials initially planned for a 1000-room hotel attached to the airport terminal, with another 300–500 rooms adjacent to the terminal. The 1000-room hotel had been scaled back to 500–700 rooms and was not likely to be ready when the airport would open in October, 1993. Developers had expressed resistance to build close to DIA unless industrial and office parks were also built near the airport. Even though ample land existed, developers were putting hotel development on the back burner until after 1993.

November 1991

Federal Express and United Parcel Service (UPS) planned to move cargo operations to the smaller Front Range Airport rather than to DIA. The master plan for DIA called for cargo operations to be at the northern edge of DIA, thus increasing the time and cost for deliveries to Denver. Shifting operations to Front Range Airport would certainly have been closer to Denver but would have alienated northern Adams County cities that counted on an economic boost in their areas. Moving cargo operations would have been in violation of the original agreement between Adams County and Denver for the annexation of the land for DIA.

The cost of renting at DIA was estimated at $0.75 per square foot compared to $0.25 per square foot at Front Range. DIA would have higher landing fees of $2.68 per 1000 pounds compared to $2.15 for Front Range. UPS demanded a cap on landing fees at DIA if another carrier were to go out of business. Under the UPS proposal, area landholders and businesses would set up a fund to compensate DIA if landing fees were to exceed the cap. Cargo carriers at Stapleton were currently paying $2 million in landing fees and rental of facilities per year.

As the "dog fight" over cargo operations continued, the Federal Aviation Administration (FAA) issued a report calling for cargo operations to be collocated with passenger operations at the busier metropolitan airports. This included both full cargo carriers as well as passenger cargo (i.e., "belly cargo") carriers. Proponents of Front Range argued that the report didn't preclude the use of Front Range because of its proximity to DIA.

December 1991

United Airlines formally agreed to a 30-year lease for 45 gates at Concourse B. With the firm agreement in place, the DIA revenue bonds shot up in price almost $30 per $1000 bond. Earlier in the year, Continental signed a five-year lease agreement.

Other airlines also agreed to service DIA. Exhibit 11–6, shown below, sets forth the airlines that either executed use and lease agreements for, or indicated an interest in leasing, the 20 gates on Concourse C on a first-preferential-use basis.

January 1992

BAE was selected to design and build the baggage handling system. The airport had been under construction for three years before BAE was brought on board. BAE agreed to do eight years of work in two years to meet the October, 1993 opening date.

June 1992

DIA officials awarded a $24.4 million conract for the new airport's telephone services to U.S. West Communication Services. The officials of DIA had considered controlling its own operations through shared tenant service, which would allow the airport to act as its own telephone company. All calls would be routed through an airport-owned computer switch. By grouping tenants together into a single shared entity, the airport would be in a position to negotiate discounts with long distance providers, thus enabling cost savings to be passed on to the tenants.

By one estimate, the city would generate $3 million to $8 million annually in new, nontax net revenue by owning and operating its own telecommunication network. Unfortunately, DIA officials did not feel that sufficient time existed for them to operate their own system. The city of Denver was unhappy over this lost income.

Exhibit 11–6. Airline Agreements

Airline	Term (Years)	No. of Gates
American Airlines	5	3
Delta Air Lines(1)	5	4
Frontier Airlines	10	2
MarkAir	10	5
Northwest Airlines	10	2
Trans World Airlines	10	2
USAir(1)	5	2
TOTAL		20

(1) The City has entered into Use and Lease Agreements with these airlines. the USAir lease is for one gate on Concourse C and USAir has indicated its interest in leasing a second gate on Concourse C.

September 1992   By September, 1992, the city had received $501 million in Federal Aviation Administration grants and $2.3 billion in bonds with interest rates of 9.0%–9.5% in the first issue to 6% in the latest issue. The decrease in interest rates due to the recession was helpful to DIA. The rating agencies also increased the city's bond rating one notch.

The FAA permitted Denver to charge a $3 departure tax at Stapleton with the income earmarked for construction of DIA. Denver officials estimated that over 34 years, the tax would generate $2.3 billion.

The cities bordering the northern edge of DIA (where the cargo operations were to be located) teamed up with Adams County to file lawsuits against DIA in its attempt to relocate cargo operations to the southern perimeter of DIA. This relocation would appease the cargo carriers and hopefully end the year-long battle with Front Range Airport. The Adams County Commissioner contended that relocation would violate the Clean Air Act and the National Environmental Policy Act and would be a major deviation from the original airport plan approved by the FAA.

October 1992   The city issued $261 million of Airport Revenue Bonds for the construction of facilities for United Airlines. (See Exhibit A at the end of this case study).

March 1993   The city of Denver announced that the launch date for DIA would be pushed back to December 18 rather than the original October 30 date in order to install and test all of the new equipment. The city wanted to delay the opening until late in the first quarter of 1994 but deemed it too costly because the airport's debt would have to be paid without an adequate stream of revenue. The interest on the bond debt was now at $500,000 per day.

The delay to December 18 angered the cargo carriers. This would be their busiest time of the year, usually twice their normal cargo levels, and a complete revamping of their delivery service would be needed. The Washington-based Air Freight Association urged the city to allow the cargo carriers to fly out of Stapleton through the holiday period.

By March 1993, Federal Express, Airborne Express, and UPS (reluctantly) had agreed to house operations at DIA after the city pledged to build facilities for them at the south end of the airport. Negotiations were also underway with Emery Worldwide and Burlington Air Express. The "belly" carriers, Continental and United, had already signed on.

UPS had wanted to create a hub at Front Range Airport. If Front Range Airport were a cargo-only facility, it would free up UPS from competing with passenger traffic for runway access even though both Front Range and DIA were in the same air traffic control pattern. UPS stated that it would not locate a regional hub at DIA. This would mean the loss of a major development project that would have attracted other businesses that relied on UPS delivery.

For UPS to build a regional hub at Front Range would have required the construction of a control tower and enlargement of the runways, both requiring federal funds. The FAA refused to free up funds for Front Range largely due to a lawsuit by United Airlines and environmental groups.

United's lawsuit had an ulterior motive. Adams County officials repeatedly stated that they had no intention of building passenger terminals at Front Range. However, once federal funds were given to Front Range, a commercial passenger plane could not be prevented from setting up shop in Front Range. The threat to United was the low-cost carriers such as Southwest Airlines. Because costs were fixed, fewer passengers traveling through DIA meant less profits for the airlines. United simply did not want any airline activities removed from DIA!

August 1993

Plans for a train to connect downtown Denver to DIA were underway. A $450,000 feasibility study and federal environmental assessment were being conducted, with the results due November 30, 1993. Union Pacific had spent $350,000 preparing a design for the new track, which could be constructed in 13 to 16 months.

The major hurdle would be the financing, which was estimated between $70 million and $120 million, based upon hourly trips or 20-minute trips. The more frequent the trips, the higher the cost.

The feasibility study also considered the possibility of baggage check-in at each of the stops. This would require financial support and management assistance from the airlines.

September 1993

Denver officials disclosed plans for transfering airport facilities and personnel from Stapleton to DIA. The move would be stage-managed by Larry Sweat, a retired military officer who coordinated troop movements for Operation Desert Shield. Bechtel Corporation would be responsible for directing the transport and setup of machinery, computer systems, furniture, and service equipment, all of which had to be accomplished overnight since the airport had to be operational again in the morning.

October 1993

DIA, which was already $1.1 billion over budget, was to be delayed again. The new opening date would be March 1994. The city blamed the airlines for the delays, citing the numerous scope changes required. Even the fire safety system hadn't been completed.

Financial estimates became troublesome. Airlines would have to charge a $15 per person tax, the largest in the nation. Fees and rent charged the airlines would triple from $74 million at Stapleton to $247 million at DIA.

January 1994

Front Range Airport and DIA were considering the idea of being designated as one system by the FAA. Front Range could legally be limited to cargo only. This would also prevent low cost carriers from paying lower landing fees and rental space at Front Range.

February 1994

Southwest Airlines, being a low cost-no frills carrier, said that it would not service DIA. Southwest wanted to keep its airport fees below $3 a passenger. Current projections indicated that DIA would have to charge between $15 and $20 per passenger in order to service its debt. This was based upon a March 9 opening day.

Continental announced that it would provide a limited number of low-frill service flights in and out of Denver. Furthermore, Continental said that because of the high landing fees, it would cancel 23% of its flights through Denver and relocate some of its maintenance facilities.

United Airlines expected its operating cost to be $100 million more per year at DIA than at Stapleton. With the low-cost carriers either pulling out or reducing service to Denver, United was under less pressure to lower airfares.

March 1994

The city of Denver announced the fourth delay in opening DIA, from March 9 to May 15. The cost of the delay, $100 million, would be paid mostly by United and Continental. As of March, only Concourse C, which housed the carriers other than United and Continental, was granted a temporary certificate of occupancy (TCO) by the city.

As the fingerpointing began, blame for this delay was given to the baggage handling system, which was experiencing late changes, restricted access flow, and a slowdown in installation and testing. A test by Continental Airlines indicated that only 39% of baggage was delivered to the correct location. Other problems also existed. As of December 31 1993, there were 2100 design changes. The city of Denver had taken out insurance for construction errors and omissions. The city's insurance claims cited failure to coordinate design of the ductwork with ceiling and structure, failure to properly design the storm draining systems for the terminal to prevent freezing, failure to coordinate mechanical and structural designs of the terminal, and failure to design an adequate subfloor support system.

Consultants began identifying potential estimating errors in DIA's operations. The runways at DIA were six times longer than the runways at Stapleton, but DIA had purchased only 25% more equipment. DIA's cost projections would be $280 million for debt service and $130 million for operating costs, for a total of $410 million per year. The total cost at Stapleton was $120 million per year.

April 1994

Denver International Airport began having personnel problems. According to DIA's personnel officer, Linda Rubin Royer, moving 17 miles away from its present site was creating serious problems. One of the biggest issues was the additional 20-minute drive that employees had to bear. To resolve this problem, she proposed a car/van pooling scheme and tried to get the city bus company to transport people to and from the new airport. There was also the problem of transfering employees to similar jobs elsewhere if they truly disliked working at DIA. The scarcity of applicants wanting to work at DIA was creating a problem as well.

May 1994

Standard and Poor's Corporation lowered the rating on DIA's outstanding debt to the noninvestment grade of BB, citing the problems with the baggage handling system and no immediate cure in sight. Denver was currently paying $33.3 million per month to service debt. Stapleton was generating $17 million per month and United Airlines had agreed to pay $8.8 million in cash for the next three months only. That left a current shortfall of $7.5 million each month that the city would have to fund. Beginning in August 1994, the city would be burdened with $16.3 million each month.

BAE Automated Systems personnel began to complain that they were pressured into doing the impossible. The only other system of this type in the world was in Frankfurt, Germany. That system required six years to install and two years to debug. BAE was asked to do it all in two years.

BAE underestimated the complexity of the routing problems. During trials, cars crashed into one another, luggage was dropped at the wrong location, cars that were needed to carry luggage were routed to empty waiting pens, and some cars traveled in the wrong direction. Sensors became coated with dirt, throwing the system out of alignment, and luggage was dumped prematurely because of faulty latches, jamming cars against the side of a tunnel. By the end of May, BAE was conducting a world-wide search for consultants who could determine what was going wrong and how long it would take to repair the system.

BAE conducted an end-of-month test with 600 bags. Outbound (terminal to plane), the sort accuracy was 94% and inbound the accuracy was 98%. The system had a zero down-time for both inbound and outbound testing. The specification requirements called for 99.5% accuracy.

BAE hired three technicians from Germany's Logplan, which helped solve similar problems with the automated system at Frankfurt, Germany. With no opening date set, DIA contemplated opening the east side of the airport for general aviation and air cargo flights. That would begin generating at least some revenue.

June 1994

The cost for DIA was now approaching $3.7 billion and the jokes about DIA appeared everywhere. One common joke as that when you fly to Denver, you will have to stop in Chicago to pick up your luggage. Other common jokes included the abbreviation, DIA. Exhibit B at the end of this case study provides a listing of some of the jokes.

The people who did not appear to be laughing at these jokes were the concessionaires, including about 50 food service operators, who had been forced to rehire, retrain, and reequip at considerable expense. Several small businesses were forced to call it quits because of the eight-month delay. Red ink was flowing despite the fact that the $45-a-square foot rent would not have to be paid until DIA officially opened. Several of the concessionaires had requested that the rent be cut by $10 a square foot for the first six months or so, after the airport opened. A merchant's association was formed at DIA to fight for financial compensation.

The Project's Work Breakdown Structure (WBS)

The city had managed the design and construction of the project by grouping design and construction activities into seven categories or "areas":

Area #0   Program management/preliminary design
Area #1   Site development
Area #2   Roadways and on-grade parking
Area #3   Airfield
Area #4   Terminal complex
Area #5   Utilites and specialty systems
Area #6   Other

Since the fall of 1992, the project budget had increased by $224 million (from $2,700 million to $2,924 million) principally as a result of scope changes.

- Structural modifications to the terminal buildings (primarily in the Landside Terminal and Concourse B) to accommodate the automated baggage system
- Changes in the interior configuration of Concourse B

- Increases in the scope of various airline tenant finished, equipment, and systems, particularly in Concourse B
- Grading, drainage, utilities, and access costs associated with the relocation of air cargo facilities to the south side of the airport
- Increases in the scope and costs of communication and control systems, particularly premises wiring
- Increases in the costs of runway, taxiway, and apron paving and change orders as a result of changing specifications for the runway lighting system
- Increased program management costs because of schedule delays

Yet even with all of these design changes, the airport was ready to open except for the baggage handling system.

July 1994

The Securities and Exchange Commission (SEC) disclosed that DIA was one of 30 municipal bond issuers that were under investigation for improper contributions to the political campaigns of Pena and his successor, Mayor Wellington Webb. Citing public records, Pena was said to have received $13,900 and Webb's campaign fund increased by $96,000. The SEC said that the contributions may have been in exchange for the right to underwrite DIA's muncipal bond offerings. Those under investigation included Merrill Lynch, Goldman Sachs & Co., and Lehman Brothers, Inc.

August 1994

Continental confirmed that as of November 1, 1994, it would reduce its flights out of Denver from 80 to 23. At one time, Continental had 200 flights out of Denver.

Denver announced that it expected to sell $200 million in new bonds. Approximately $150 million would be used to cover future interest payments on existing DIA debt and to replenish interest and other money paid due to the delayed opening.

Approximately $50 million would be used to fund the construction of an interim baggage handling system of the more conventional tug-and-conveyor type. The interim system would require 500–600 people rather than the 150–160 people needed for the computerized system. Early estimates said that the conveyor belt/tug-and-cart system would be at least as fast as the system at Stapleton and would be using proven technology and off-the-shelf parts. However, modifications would have to be made to both the terminal and the concourses.

United Airlines asked for a 30-day delay in approving the interim system for fear that it would not be able to satisfy their requirements. The original lease agreement with DIA and United stipulated that on opening day there would be a fully operational automated baggage handling system in place. United had 284 flights a day out of Denver and had to be certain that the interim system would support a 25-minute turn-around time for passenger aircraft.

The city's District Attorney's Office said it was investigating accusations of falsified test data and shoddy workmanship at DIA. Reports had come in regarding fraudulent construction and contracting practices. No charges were filed at that time.

DIA began repairing cracks, holes, and fissures that had emerged in the runways, ramps, and taxiways. Officials said that the cracks were part of the normal settling problems and might require maintenance for years to come.

United Airlines agreed to invest $20 million and act as the project manager to the baggage handling system at Concourse B. DIA picked February 28, 1995 as the new opening date as long as either the primary or secondary baggage handling systems were operational.

United Benefits from Continental's Downsizing

United had been building up its Denver hub since 1991, increasing its total departures 9% in 1992, 22% in 1993, and 9% in the first six months of 1994. Stapleton is United's second largest connecting hub after Chicago O'Hare (ORD) ahead of San Francisco (SFO), Los Angeles (LAX), and Washington Dulles (IAD) International Airports, as shown in Exhibit 11–7.

In response to the downsizing by Continental, United is expected to absorb a significant portion of Continental's Denver traffic by means of increased load factors and increased service (i.e. capacity), particularly in larger markets where significant voids in service might be left by Continental. United served 24 of the 28 cities served by Continental from Stapleton in June, 1994, with about 79% more total available seats to those cities—23,937 seats provided by United compared with 13,400 seats provided by Continental. During 1993, United's average load factor from Denver was 63%, indicating that, with its existing service and available capacity, United had the ability to absorb many of the passengers abandoned by Continental. In addition, United had announced plans to increase service at Denver to 300 daily flights by the end of the calendar year.

Exhibit 11–7. *Comparative United Airlines Service at Hub Airports, June 1993 and June 1994*

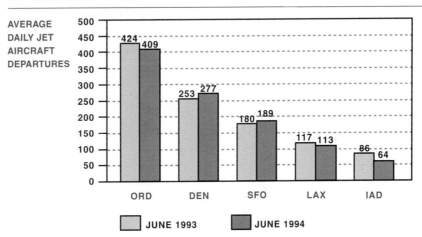

NOTE: DOES NOT INCLUDE ACTIVITY BY UNITED EXPRESS.

SOURCE: OFFICIAL AIRLINE GUIDES, INC.
(ONLINE DATA BASE), FOR PERIODS SHOWN.

As a result of its downsizing in Denver, Continental was forecasted to lose more than 3.9 million enplaned passengers from 1993 to 1995—a total decrease of 80%. However, this decrease was expected to be largely offset by the forecasted 2.2 million increase in enplaned passengers by United and 1.0 million by the other airlines, resulting in a total of 15,877,000 enplaned passengers at Denver in 1995. As discussed earlier, it was assumed that, in addition to a continuation of historical growth, United and the other airlines would pick up much of the traffic abandoned by Continental through a combination of added service, larger average aircraft size, and increased load factors.

From 1995 to 2000, the increase in total enplaned passengers is based on growth rates of 2.5% per year in originating passengers and 3.0% per year in connecting passengers. Between 1995 and 2000, United's emerging dominance at the airport (with almost twice the number of passengers of all other airlines combined) should result in somewhat higher fare levels in the Denver markets, and therefore may dampen traffic growth. As shown in Exhibit 11–8, of the 18.2 million forecasted enplaned passengers in 2000, United and United Express together are forecasted to account for 70% of total passengers at the airport—up from about 51% in 1993—while Continental's share, including GP Express, is forecasted to be less than 8%—down from about 33% in 1993.

Exhibit 11–8. Enplaned Passenger Market Shares
Denver Airport

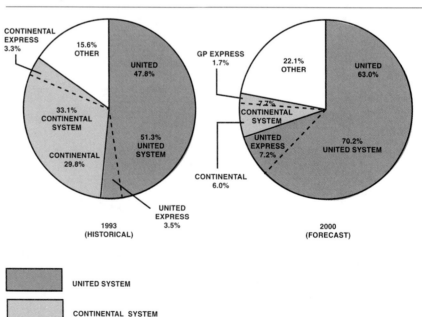

SOURCES: 1993: AIRPORT MANAGEMENT RECORDS.

Total connecting passengers at Stapleton increased from about 6.1 million in 1990 to about 8.2 million in 1993—an average increase of about 10% per year. The number of connecting passengers was forecast to decrease in 1994 and 1995, as a result of the downsizing by Continental, and then return to steady growth of 3.0% per year through 2000, reflecting expected growth in passenger traffic nationally and a stable market share by United in Denver. Airline market share of connecting passengers in 1993 and 1995 are shown in Exhibit 11–9.

September 1994

Denver began discussions with cash-strapped MarkAir of Alaska to begin service at DIA. For an undercapitalized carrier, the prospects of tax breaks, favorable rents, and a $30 million guaranteed city loan were enticing.

DIA officials estimated an $18 per person charge on opening day. Plans to allow only cargo carriers and general aviation to begin operations at DIA were canceled.

Exhibit 11–9. Connecting Passenger Market Shares Denver Airport

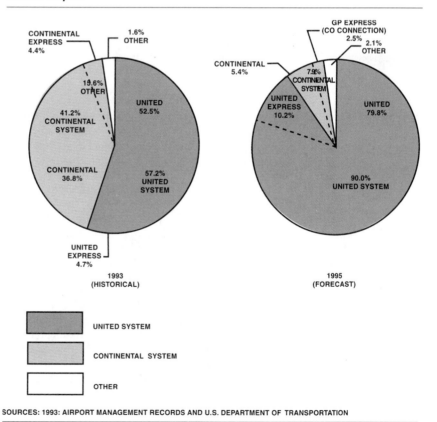

SOURCES: 1993: AIRPORT MANAGEMENT RECORDS AND U.S. DEPARTMENT OF TRANSPORTATION

Total construction cost for the main terminal exceeded $455 million (including the parking structure and the airport office building).

General site expenses, commission	$38,667,967
Sitework, building excavations	15,064,817
Concrete	89,238,296
Masonry	5,501,608
Metals	40,889,411
Carpentry	3,727,408
Thermal, moisture protection	8,120,907
Doors and windows	13,829,336
Finishes	37,025,019
Specialties	2,312,691
Building equipment	227,720
Furnishings	3,283,852
Special construction	39,370,072
Conveying systems	23,741,336
Mechanical	60,836,566
Electrical	73,436,575
TOTAL	$455,273,581

October 1994

A federal grand jury convened to investigate faulty workmanship and falsified records at DIA. The faulty workmanship had resulted in falling ceilings, buckling walls, and collapsing floors.

November 1994

The baggage handling system was working, but only in segments. Frustration still existed in not being able to get the whole system to work at the same time. The problem appeared to be with the software required to get computers to talk to computers. The fact that a mere software failure could hold up Denver's new airport for more than a year put in question the project's risk management program.

Jerry Waddles was the risk manager for Denver. He left that post to become risk manager for the State of Colorado. Eventually the city found an acting risk manager, Molly Austin Flaherty, to replace Mr. Waddles, but for the most part, DIA construction over the past several months had continued without a full-time risk manager.

The failure of the baggage handling system had propelled DIA into newspaper headlines around the country. The U.S. Securities and Exchange Commission had launched a probe into whether Denver officials had deliberately deceived bondholders about how equipment malfunctions would affect the December 19 1993 opening. The allegations were made by Denver's KCNC-TV. Internal memos indicated that in the summer of 1993 city engineers believed it would take at least until March 1994 to get the system working. However, Mayor Wellington Webb did not announce the delayed opening until October 1993. The SEC was investigating whether the last postponement misled investors holding $3 billion in airport bonds.

Under a new agreement, the city agreed to pay BAE an additional $35 million for modifications *if* the system was working for United Airlines by February 28, 1995. BAE would then have until August, 1995 to complete the rest of the system for the other tenants. If the system was not operational by February 28, the city could withhold payment of the $35 million.

BAE lodged a $40 million claim against the city, alleging that the city caused the delay by changing the system's baseline configuration after the April 1, 1992 deadline. The city filed a $90 million counterclaim blaming BAE for the delays.

The lawsuits were settled out of court when BAE agreed to pay $12,000 a day in liquidated damages dating from December 19 1993 to February 28, 1995, or approximately $5 million. The city agreed to pay BAE $6.5 million to cover some invoices submitted by BAE for work already done to repair the system.

Under its DIA construction contract, BAE's risks were limited. BAE's liability for consequential damages resulting from its failure to complete the baggage handling system on time was capped at $5 million. BAE had no intention of being held liable for changes to the system. The system as it was at the time was not the system that BAE was hired to install.

Additional insurance policies also existed. Builder's risk policies generally pay damages caused by defective parts or materials, but so far none of the parts used to construct the system had been defective. BAE was also covered for design errors or omissions. The unknown risk at that point was who would be responsible if the system worked for Concourse B (i.e., United) but then failed when it was expanded to cover all concourses.

A study was underway to determine the source of respiratory problems suffered by workers at the construction site. The biggest culprit appeared to be the use of concrete in a confined space.

The city and DIA were also protected from claims filed by vendors whose businesses were put on hold because of the delays under a hold-harmless agreement in the contracts. However, the city had offered to permit the concessionaires to charge higher fees and also to extend their leases for no charge to make up for lost income due to the delays.

December 1994

The designer of the baggage handling system was asked to reexamine the number of bags per minute that the BAE system was required to accommodate as per the specifications. The contract called for departing luggage to Concourse A to be delivered at a peak rate of 90 bags per minute. The designer estimated peak demand at 25 bags per minute. Luggage from Concourse A was contracted for at 223 bags per minute but again, the designer calculated peak demand at a lower rate of 44 bags per minute.

Airport Debt

By December 1994, DIA was more than $3.4 billion in debt, as shown below.

Series 1984 Bonds	$103,875,000
Series 1985 Bonds	175,930,000
Series 1990A Bonds	700,003,843
Series 1991A Bonds	500,003,523
Series 1991D Bonds	600,001,391
Series 1992A Bonds	253,180,000
Series 1992B Bonds	315,000,000
Series 1992C Bonds	392,160,000
Series 1992D–G Bonds	135,000,000
Series 1994A Bonds	257,000,000
	$3,432,153,757

Airport Revenue   Airports generally have two types of contracts with their tenants. The first type is the residual contract where the carriers guarantee that the airport will remain solvent. Under this contract, the carriers absorb the majority of the risk. The airport maintains the right to increase rents and landing fees to cover operating expenses and debt coverage. The second type of contract is the compensatory contract where the airport is at risk. DIA has a residual contract with its carriers.

Airports generate revenue from several sources. The most common breakdown includes landing fees and rent from the following entities: airline carriers, passenger facilities rental car agencies, concessionary stores, food and beverage services, retail shops, and parking garages. Retail shops and other concessionary stores also pay a percent of sales.

Airline Costs per Enplaned Passenger   Revenues derived from the airlines are often expressed on a per enplaned passenger basis. The average airline cost per enplaned passenger at Stapleton in 1993 was $5.02. However, this amount excludes costs related to major investments in terminal facilities made by United Airlines in the mid-1980s and, therefore, understates the true historical airline cost per passenger.

Average airline costs per enplaned passenger at the airport in 1995 and 2000 are forecast to be as follows:

Total average airline costs per enplaned passenger

Year	Current dollars	1990 dollars
1995	$18.15	$14.92
2000	17.20	11.62

The forecasted airline costs per enplaned passenger at the airport are considerably higher than costs at Stapleton today and the highest of any major airport in the United States. (The cost per enplaned passenger at Cleveland Hopkins is $7.50). The relatively high airline cost per passenger is attributable, in part, to (1) the unusually large amount of tenant finishes, equipment, and systems costs being financed as part of the project relative to other airport projects and (2) delayed costs incurred since the original opening date for purposes of the Plan of Financing (January 1, 1994).

The City estimates that, as a result of the increased capacity and efficiency of the airfield, operation of the airport will result in annual delay savings to the airlines of $50 million to $100 million per year (equivalent to about $3 to $6 per enplaned passenger), and that other advanced technology and systems incorporated into the design of the airport will result in further operational savings. In the final analysis, the cost effectiveness of operating at the airport is a judgment that must be made by the individual airlines in deciding to serve the Denver market.

It is assumed for the purposes of this analysis that the city and the airlines will resolve the current disputes regarding cost allocation procedures and responsibility for delay costs, and that the airlines will pay rates generally in accordance with the procedures of the use and lease agreements as followed by the city and as summarized in the accompanying exhibits.

February 28, 1995   The airport opened as planned on February 28, 1995. However, several problems became apparent. First, the baggage handling system did have "bad days." Passengers traveling to and from Denver felt more comfortable carrying bags than having them transfered by the computerized baggage handling system. Large queues began to form at the end of the escalators in the main terminal going down to the concourse trains. The trains were not running frequently enough, and the number of cars in each train did not appear to be sufficient to handle the necessary passenger traffic.

The author flew from Dallas-Ft. Worth to Denver in one hour and 45 minutes. It then took one hour and 40 minutes to catch the airport shuttles (which stop at all the hotels) and arrive at the appropriate hotel in downtown Denver. Passengers began to balk at the discomfort of the remote rental car facilities, the additional three dollar tax per day for each rental car, and the fact that the nearest gas station was 15 miles away. How does one return a rental car with a full tank of gas?

Departing passengers estimated it would take two hours to drive to the airport from downtown Denver, unload luggage, park their automobile, check in, and take the train to the concourse.

Faults in the concourse construction were becoming apparent. Tiles that were supposed to be 5/8 inches thick were found to be 1/2 inch thick. Tiles began to crack. During rainy weather, rain began seeping in through the ceiling.

EXHIBIT A[17]
MUNICIPAL BOND PROSPECTUS

$261,415,000
CITY AND COUNTY OF DENVER, COLORADO
6.875% SPECIAL FACILITIES AIRPORT REVENUE BONDS
(UNITED AIRLINES PROJECT)
Series 1992A
Date: October 1, 1992
Due: October 1, 2032
Rating: Standard & Poor's BBB-
Moody's Baa2

Introduction

This official statement is provided to furnish information in connection with the sale by the City and County of Denver, Colorado (the "City") of 6.875% Special Facilities Airport Revenue Bonds (United Airlines Project) series 1992A in the aggregate principle amount of $261,415,000 (the "Bonds"). The bonds will be dated, mature, bear interest, and be subject to redemption prior to maturity as described herein.

The Bonds will be issued pursuant to an Ordinance of the City and County of Denver, Colorado (the "Ordinance").

The proceeds received by the City from the sale of the Bonds will be used to acquire, construct, equip, or improve (or a reimbursement of payments for the acquisition, construction, equipping, or improvement of) certain terminals, Concourse B, aircraft maintenance, ground equipment maintenance, flight kitchen, and air freight facilities (the "Facilities") at the new Denver International Airport (the "New Airport").

The City will cause such proceeds to be deposited, distributed, and applied in accordance with the terms of a Special Facilities and Ground Lease, dated as of October

---

17. Only excerpts from the prospectus are included here.

1, 1992 (the "Lease") between United Airlines and the City. Under the Lease, United has agreed to make payments sufficient to pay the principal, premium, if any, and interest on the Bonds. Neither the Facilities nor the ground rental payments under the Lease are pledged as security for the payment of principal, premium, if any, and interest on the bonds.

Agreement between United and the City

On June 26, 1991, United and the City entered into an agreement followed by a second agreement on December 12, 1991, which, among other things, collectively provide for the use and lease by United of certain premises and facilities at the New Airport. In the United Agreement, United agrees among other things, to (1) support the construction of the New Airport, (2) relocate its present air carrier operations from Stapleton to the New Airport, (3) occupy and lease certain facilities at the New Airport, including no less than 45 gates on Concourse B within two years of the date of beneficial occupancy as described in the United Agreement, and (4) construct prior to the date of beneficial occupancy, a regional reservation center at a site at Stapleton.

In conjunction with the execution of the United Agreement, United also executes a 30-year use and lease agreement. United has agreed to lease, on a preferential use basis, Concourse B, which is expected to support 42 jet aircraft with up to 24 commuter aircraft parking positions at the date of beneficial occupancy, and, on an exclusive use basis, certain ticket counters and other areas in the terminal complex of the New Airport.

The Facilities

The proceeds of the bonds will be used to finance the acquisition, construction, and equipping of the Facilities, as provided under the Lease. The Facilities will be located on approximately 100 acres of improved land located within the New Airport, which United will lease from the City. The Facilities will include an aircraft maintenance facility capable of housing ten jet aircraft, a ground equipment support facility with 26 maintenance bays, an approximately 55,500-square-foot air freight facility, and an approximately 155,000-square-foot flight kitchen. Additionally, the proceeds of the Bonds will be used to furnish, equip, and install certain facilities to be used by United in Concourse B and in the terminal of the New Airport.

Redemption of Bonds

The Bonds will be subject to optional and mandatory redemption prior to maturity in the amounts, at the times, at the prices, and in the manner as provided in the Ordinance. If less than all of the Bonds are to be redeemed, the particular Bonds to be called for redemption will be selected by lot by the Paying Agent in any manner deemed fair and reasonable by the Paying Agent.

The bonds are subject to redemption prior to maturity by the City at the request of United, in whole or in part, by lot, on any date on or after October 1, 2002 from an account created pursuant to the Ordinance used to pay the principal, premium, if any, and interest on the Bonds (the "Bond Fund") and from monies otherwise available for such purpose. Such redemptions are to be made at the applicable redemption price shown below as a percentage of the principal amount thereof, plus interest accrued to the redemption date:

Redemption Period	Optional Redemption Price
October 1, 2002 through September 30, 2003	102%
October 1, 2003 through September 30, 2004	101%
October 1, 2004 and thereafter	100%

The Bonds are subject to optional redemption prior to maturity, in whole or in part by lot, on any date, upon the exercise by United of its option to prepay Facilities Rentals under the Lease at a redemption price equal to 100% of the principal amount thereof plus interest accrued to the redemption date, if one or more of the following events occurs with respect to one or more of the units of the Leased Property:

(a) the damage or destruction of all or substantially all of such unit or units of the Leased Property to such extent that, in the reasonable opinion of United, repair and restoration would not be economical and United elects not to restore or replace such unit or units of the Leased Property; or,

(b) the condemnation of any part, use, or control of so much of such unit or units of the Leased Property that such unit or units cannot be reasonably used by United for carrying on, at substantially the same level or scope, the business theretofore conducted by United on such unit or units.

In the event of a partial extraordinary redemption, the amount of the Bonds to be redeemed for any unit of the Leased Property with respect to which such prepayment is made shall be determined as set forth below (expressed as a percentage of the original principal amount of the Bonds) plus accrued interest on the Bonds to be redeemed to the redemption date of such Bonds provided that the amount of Bonds to be redeemed may be reduced by the aggregate principal amount (valued at par) of any Bonds purchased by or on behalf of United and delivered to the Paying Agent for cancelation:

Terminal Concourse B Facility	Aircraft Maintenance Facility	Ground Equipment Maintenance Facility	Flight Kitchen	Air Freight Facility
20%	50%	10%	15%	5%

The Bonds shall be subject to mandatory redemption in whole prior to maturity, on October 1, 2023, at a redemption price equal to 100% of the principal amount thereof, plus accrued interest to the redemption date if the term of the Lease is not extended to October 1, 2032 in accordance with the provisions of the Lease and subject to the conditions in the Ordinance.

Limitations

Pursuant to the United Use and Lease Agreement, if costs at the New Airport exceed $20 per revenue enplaned passenger, in 1990 dollars, for the preceding calendar year, calculated in accordance with such agreement, United can elect to terminate its Use and Lease Agreement. Such termination by United would not, however, be an event of default under the Lease.

If United causes an event of default under the Lease and the City exercises its remedies there under and accelerates Facilities Rentals, the City is not obligated to relet the Facilities. If the City relets the Facilities, it is not obligated to use any of the payments received to pay principal, premium, if any, or interest on the Bonds.

Application of the Bond Proceeds

It is estimated that the proceeds of the sale of the Bonds will be applied as follows:

Cost of Construction	$226,002,433
Interest on Bonds During Construction	22,319,740
Cost of Issuance Including Underwriters' Discount	1,980,075
Original Issue Discount	11,112,742
Principal Amount of the Bonds	261,415,000

Tax Covenant

Under the terms of the lease, United has agreed that it will not take or omit to take any action with respect to the Facilities or the proceeds of the bonds (including any investment earnings thereon), insurance, condemnation, or any other proceeds derived in connection with the Facilities, which would cause the interest on the Bonds to become included in the gross income of the Bondholder for federal income tax purposes.

Other Material Covenants

United has agreed to acquire, construct, and install the Facilities to completion pursuant to the terms of the Lease. If monies in the Construction Fund are insufficient to pay the cost of such acquisition, construction, and installation in full, then United shall pay the excess cost without reimbursement from the City, the Paying Agent, or any Bondholder.

United has agreed to indemnify the City and the Paying Agent for damages incurred in connection with the occurrence of certain events, including without limitation, the construction of the Facilities, occupancy by United of the land on which the Facilities are located, and violation by United of any of the terms of the Lease or other agreements related to the Leased Property.

During the Lease Term, United has agreed to maintain its corporate existence and its qualifications to do business in the state. United will not dissolve or otherwise dispose of its assets and will not consolidate with or merge into another corporation provided, however, that United may, without violating the Lease, consolidate or merge into another corporation.

Additional Bonds

At the request of United, the City may, at its option, issue additional bonds to finance the cost of special Facilities for United upon the terms and conditions in the Lease and the Ordinance.

The Guaranty

Under the Guaranty, United will unconditionally guarantee to the Paying Agent, for the benefit of the Bondholders, the full and prompt payment of the principal, premium, if any, and interest on the Bonds, when and as the same shall become due whether at the stated maturity, by redemption, acceleration, or otherwise. The obligations of United under the Guaranty are unsecured, but are stated to be absolute and unconditional, and the Guaranty will remain in effect until the entire principal, premium, if any, and interest on the Bonds has been paid in full or provision for the payment thereof has been made in accordance with the Ordinance.

DENVER—The Denver International Airport, whose opening has been delayed indefinitely because of snafus, has borne the brunt of joke writers.

Punsters in the aviation and travel community have done their share of work on one particular genre, coming up with new variations on the theme of DIA, the star-crossed airport's new and as-yet-unused city code.

Here's what's making the rounds on electronic bulletin boards; it originated in the May 15 issue of the Boulder (Colo.) Camera newspaper:

1. Dis Is Awful
2. Doing It Again
3. Dumbest International Airport
4. Dinosaur In Action
5. Debt In Arrival
6. Denver's Intense Adventure
7. Darn It All
8. Dollar Investment Astounding
9. Delay It Again
10. Denver International Antique
11. Date Is AWOL
12. Denver Intellects Awry
13. Dance Is Autumn
14. Dopes In Authority
15. Don't Ice Attendance
16. Drop In Asylum
17. Don't Immediately Assume
18. Don't Ignore Aspirin
19. Dittohead Idle Again
20. Doubtful If Atall
21. Denver In Action
22. Deces, l'Inaugural Arrivage (means "dead on arrival" in French)
23. Dummies In Action
24. Dexterity In Action
25. Display In Arrogance
26. Denver Incomplete Act
27. D'luggage Is A'coming
28. Defect In Automation
29. Dysfunctional Itinerary Apparatus
30. Dis Is Absurd
31. Delays In Abundance

32. Did It Arrive?
33. Denver's Infamous Air-or-port (sounds like "error")
34. Dopes In Action
35. Doubtful Intermittent Access
36. Don't Intend Atall
37. Damned Inconvenient Airport
38. Duped In Anticipation
39. Delay In Action
40. Delirious In Accounting
41. Date Indeterminate, Ah?
42. Denver's Indisposed Access
43. Detained Interphase Ahead
44. Denver's Interminably Aground
45. Deceit In Action
46. Delay Institute America
47. Denver's Intractable Airport
48. Delayed Indefinitely Again
49. Delayed Introduction Again
50. Disaster In Arrears
51. Denver International Amusementpark
52. Debacle In Action
53. Deadline (of) Incomprehensible Attainment
54. Duffel Improbable Arrival
55. Delay In America
56. Dying In Anticipation
57. Dazzling Inaccessible Absurdity
58. Damned Intractable Automation
59. Da Infamous Annoyance
60. Dare I Ask?
61. Done In Arrears
62. Done In Ancestral
63. Denver International Accident
64. Dumb Idea Anyway
65. Diversion In Accounting
66. Doesn't Include Airlines
67. Disparate Instruments in Action
68. Delay International Airport
69. Dumb Idea Askew

70. Delayed Indefinitely Airport
71. Delays In Arrival
72. Deja In Absentee
73. Done In Aminute
74. Done In August
75. Denver's Inordinate Airport
76. Denver's Imaginary Airport
77. Debentures In Arrears
78. Denver Isn't Airborne
79. Descend Into Abyss
80. Done In April 2000
81. Disaster In Aviation
82. Denver's Interminable Airport
83. Denver In Arrears
84. Dallying Is Aggravating
85. Don't In Angst
86. Distress Is Acute
87. Development Is Arrested
88. Darned Inevitable Atrocity
89. Debt In Airport
90. Devastation In Aviation
91. Debacle In Automation
92. Denver's Inconstructable Airport
93. Denver Is Awaitin'
94. DIsAster
95. Denver's Inoperable Airport
96. Delay, Impede, Await
97. Date Isn't Available
98. Delayed International Airport
99. Denver Irrational Airport
100. Denver Irate Association
101. Denver's Ignominious Atrocity
102. Daytrippers Invitational Airport
103. Delay Is Anticipated
104. Doofis, Interruptness, Accidentalis
105. Denver International Arrival
106. Denver's Interminable Apparition
107. Distance Is Astronomical
108. Doubtful It's Able
109. Dreadfully Ineffective Automation
110. Do It Again
111. Did it, Installed it, Ate it
112. Drowned In Apoplexy

113. Dodo International Airport (the dodo is an extinct, flightless bird)
114. Dead In the Air
115. Denouement In Ambiguity
116. Deserted, Inactive Airport
117. Definitely Incapable of Activation
118. Democracy In Action
119. Dysfunction Imitating Art
120. Design In Alabaster
121. Desperately In Arrears
122. Dazzling, If Anything
123. Delays In Aeternum
124. Delighted If Actualized
125. Destination: Imagine Arabia
126. Dumb Idea: Abandoned?
127. Deem It Apiary
128. Dollars In Action
129. Definitely Iffy Achievement
130. Dreadfully Incompetent Architects
131. Denver International Ain't
132. Delayed In Automation
133. Dragging Its Ass
134. Driving Is Advantageous
135. Dang It All
136. Druggies Installing Automation
137. Dumb Idea Approved
138. Didn't Invite Airplanes
139. Died In April
140. Deplane In Albuquerque
141. Departure Is Agonizing
142. Denver's Infuriating Abscess
143. Denver's Ill-fated Airport
144. Domestic International Aggravation
145. Duffels In Anchorage
146. Denver's Indeterminate Abomination
147. Damn It All
148. Darn Idiotic Airport
149. Delay Is Acceptable
150. Denver's Idle Airport
151. Does It Arrive?
152. Damned Inconvenient Anyway

[18]Boulder (Colorado) Camera Newspaper, May 15, 1991.

Bibliography (in Chronological Order)

1. Brown, David A., "Denver Aims for Global Hub Status with New Airport Under Construction," *Aviation Week & Space Technology,* March 11, 1991, pp. 42–45
2. "Satellite Airport to Handle Corporate, General Aviation for Denver Area," *Aviation Week & Space Technology,* March 11, 1991, pp. 44–45
3. "Denver to Seek Bids This Spring for Wide-Open Terminal Building," *Aviation Week & Space Technology,* March 11, 1991, p. 50
4. "Denver City Council Supports Airport Despite Downgrade," *The Wall Street Journal,* March 20, 1991, p. A1D
5. "Denver Airport Bonds' Rating is Confirmed by Moody's Investors," *The Wall Street Journal,* March 22, 1991, p. C14
6. "Bonds for Denver Airport Priced to Yield up to 9.185%," *New York Times,* April 10, 1991, p. D16
7. Charlier, Marj, "Denver Reports a Tentative Agreement with United over Hub at New Airport," *The Wall Street Journal,* May 3, 1991, p. B2
8. Smith, Brad, "New Airport Has Its Ups and Downs," *Los Angeles Times,* July 9, 1991, p. A5
9. Wood, Christopher, "Hotel Development at New Airport Not Likely Until after '93," *Denver Business Journal,* August 2, 1991, p. 8S
10. Wood, Christopher, "FAA: Link Air Cargo, Passengers," *Denver Business Journal,* November 1–7, 1991, p. 3
11. Wood, Christopher, "Airport May Move Cargo Operations, Offer Reserve Funds," *Denver Business Journal,* December 6–12, 1991, p. 1, 34
12. "UAL in Accord on Denver," *New York Times,* December 7, 1991, p. 39L
13. Fisher, Thomas, "Projects Flights of Fantasy," *Progressive Architecture,* March, 1992, p. 103
14. Locke, Tom, "Disconnected," *Denver Business Journal,* June 12–18, 1992, p. 19
15. "Big Ain't Hardly The Word for It," *ENR,* September 7, 1992, pp. 28–29
16. Wood, Christopher, "Adams Seeks Action," *Denver Business Journal,* September 4–10, 1992, p. 1, 13
17. "Denver Airport Rises under Gossamer Roof," *The Wall Street Journal,* November 17, 1992, p. B1
18. Solomon, Mark B., "Denver Airport Delay Angers Cargo Carriers," *Journal of Commerce,* March 17 1993, p. 3B
19. "Denver Airport Opening Delayed Until December," *Aviation Week & Space Technology,* May 10 1993, p. 39
20. Svaldi, Aldo, "DIA Air Train Gathering Steam as Planners Shift Possible Route," *Denver Business Journal,* August 27–September 2 1993, p. 74
21. Johnson, Dirk, "Opening of New Denver Airport is Delayed Again," *The New York Times,* October 26 1993, p. A19
22. "Denver's Mayor Webb Postpones Opening International Airport," *The Wall Street Journal,* October 26 1993, p. A9
23. "An Airport Comes to Denver," *Skiing,* December 1993, p. 66
24. Booker, Ellis, "Airport Prepares for Takeoff," *Computerworld,* January 10, 1994
25. Svaldi, Aldo, "Front Range, DIA Weigh Merging Airport Systems," *Denver Business Journal,* January 21–27, 1994, p. 3
26. Phillips, Don, "$3.1 Billion Airport at Denver Preparing for a Rough Takeoff," *Washington Post,* February 13, 1994, p. A10
27. "New Denver Airport Combines Several State-of-the-Art Systems," *Travel Weekly,* February 21, 1994, p. 20
28. Munford, Steve, "Options in Hard Surface Flooring," *Buildings,* March, 1994, p. 58
29. Charles, Mars, "Denver's New Airport, Already Mixed in Controversy, Won't Open Next Week," *The Wall Street Journal,* March 2, 1994, p. B1, B7

30. "Denver Grounded for Third Time," *ENR,* March 7, 1994, p. 6

31. Peters, Shannon, "Denver's New Airport Creates HR Challenges," *Personnel Journal,* April 1994, p. 21

32. Del Rosso, Laura, "Denver Airport Delayed Indefinitely," *Travel Weekly,* May 5, 1994, p. 37

33. "DIA Bond Rating Cut," *Aviation Week & Space Technology,* May 16, 1994, p. 33

34. Scheler, Robert, "Software Snafu Grounds Denver's High-Tech Airport," *PC Week,* May 16, 1994, p. 1

35. Dodge, John, "Architects Take a Page from Book on Denver Airport-Bag System," *PC Week,* May 16, 1994, p. 3

36. Bozman, Jean S., "Denver Airport Hits Systems Layover," *Computerworld,* May 16, 1994, p. 30

37. Woodbury, Richard, "The Bag Stops Here," *Time,* May 16, 1994, p. 52

38. "Consultants Review Denver Baggage Problems," *Aviation Week & Space Technology,* June 6, 1994, p. 38

39. "Doesn't It Amaze? The Delay that Launched a Thousand Gags," *Travel Weekly,* June 6, 1994, p. 16

40. Romano, Michael, "This Delay Is Costing Business a Lot of Money," *Restaurant Business,* June 10, 1994, p. 26

41. Armstrong, Scott, "Denver Builds New Airport, Asks 'Will Planes Come?'," *The Christian Science Monitor,* June 21, 1994, p. 1

42. Weiser, Benjamin, "SEC Turns Investigation to Denver Airport Financing," *The Washington Post,* July 13, 1994, p. D1

43. Knill, Bernie, "Flying Blind at Denver International Airport," *Material Handling Engineering,* July, 1994, p. 47

44. Dubay, Keith, "Denver Airport Seeks Compromise on Baggage Handling," *American Banker Washington Watch,* July 25, 1994, p. 10

45. Johnson, Dirk, "Denver May Open Airport in Spite of Glitches," *New York Times,* July 27, 1994, p. A14

46. Leib, Jeffrey, "Investors Want a Plan," *The Denver Post,* August 2, 1994, p. A1

47. Charlier, Marj, "Denver Plans Backup Baggage System for Airport's Troubled Automated One," *The Wall Street Journal,* August 5, 1994, p. B2

48. Sahagun, Louis, "Denver Airport to Bypass Balky Baggage Mover," *Los Angeles Times,* August 5, 1994, p. A1

49. Morgan, Len, "Airports Have Growing Pains," *Flying,* August, 1994, p. 104

50. Bryant, Adam, "Denver Goes Back to Basics for Baggage," *New York Times,* August 6, 1994, p. 5N, 6L

51. "Prosecutors Scrutinize New Denver Airport," *New York Times,* August 21, 1994, p. 36L

52. Flynn, Kevin, "Panic Drove New DIA Plan," *Rocky Mountain News,* August 7, 1994, p. 5A

53. Hughes, David, "Denver Airport Still Months from Opening," *Aviation Week & Space Technology,* August 8, 1994, p. 30

54. "Airport May Open in Early '95," *Travel Weekly,* August 8, 1994, p. 57

55. Meyer, Michael and Glick, Daniel, "Still Late for Arrival," *Newsweek,* August 22, 1994, p. 38

56. Bary, Andrew, "A $3 Billion Joke," *Barron's,* August 22, 1994, p. MW10

57. Bozman, Jean, "Baggage System Woes Costing Denver Airport Millions," *Computerworld,* August 22, 1994, p. 28

58. Phillips, Edward, "Denver, United Agree on Baggage System Fixes," *Aviation Week & Space Technology,"* August 29, 1994

59. Rifkin, Glenn, "What Really Happened at Denver's Airport," *Forbes,* August 29, 1994, p. 110

60. Bary, Andrew, "New Denver Airport Bond Issue Could Face Turbulence from Investors," *Barron's,* August 29, 1994, p. MW9

61. Bary, Andrew, "Denver Airport Bonds Take Off as Investors Line Up for Higher Yields," *Barron's,* August 29, 1994, p. MW9

62. Carey, Susan, "Alaska's Cash-Strapped MarkAir Is Wooed by Denver," *The Wall Street Journal,* September 1, 1994, p. B6

63. Henderson, Dana K., "It's in the Bag(s)," *Air Transport World,* September, 1994, p. 54

64. Johnson, Dirk, "Late Already, Denver Airport Faces More Delays," *The New York Times,* September 25, 1994, p. 26L

65. Wright, Gordon, "Denver Builds a Field of Dreams," *Building Design and Construction,* September 1994, p. 52

66. Jabez, Alan, "Airport of the Future Stays Grounded," *Sunday Times,* October 9, 1994, Features Section

67. Bozman, Jean, "United to Simplify Denver's Troubled Baggage Project," *Computerworld,* October 10, 1994, p. 76

68. "Denver Aide Tells of Laxity in Airport Job," *The New York Times,* October 17, 1994, p. A12

69. Murray, Brendan, "In the Bags: Local Company to Rescue Befuddled Denver Airport," *Marietta Daily Journal,* October 21, 1994, p. C1

70. Wojcik, Joanne, "Airport in Holding Pattern, Project Is Insured, but Denver to Retain Brunt of Delay Costs," *Business Insurance,* November 7, 1994, p. 1

71. Russell, James S., "Is This Any Way to Build an Airport?", *Architectural Record,* November, 1994, p. 30

Network Scheduling Techniques

12.0 INTRODUCTION

Management is continually seeking new and better control techniques to cope with the complexities, masses of data, and tight deadlines that are characteristic of many industries and their highly competitive environments today, as well as seeking better methods for presenting technical and cost data to customers.

Scheduling techniques have taken on paramount importance since World War II. The most common techniques are shown below:

- Gantt or bar charts
- Milestone charts
- Line of balance[1]
- Networks
  - Program Evaluation and Review Technique (PERT)
  - Arrow Diagram Method (ADM) [Sometimes called the Critical Path Method (CPM)][2]
  - Precedence Diagram Method (PDM)
  - Graphical Evaluation and Review Technique (GERT)

---

1. Line of balance is more applicable to manufacturing operations for production line activities. However, it can be used for project management activities where a finite number of deliverables must be produced in a given time period. The reader need only refer to the multitude of texts on production management for more information on this technique.

2. The text uses the term CPM instead of ADM. The reader should understand that they are interchangeable.

Perhaps the best known of all the relatively new techniques is the program evaluation and review technique. PERT has several distinguishing characteristics:

- It forms the basis for all planning and predicting and provides management with the ability to plan for best possible use of resources to achieve a given goal within time and cost limitations.
- It provides visibility and enables management to control "one-of-a-kind" programs as opposed to repetitive situations.
- It helps management handle the uncertainties involved in programs by answering such questions as how time delays in certain elements influence project completion, where slack exists between elements, and what elements are crucial to meet the completion date. This provides management with a means for evaluating alternatives.
- It provides a basis for obtaining the necessary facts for decision making.
- It utilizes a so-called time network analysis as the basic method to determine manpower, material, and capital requirements as well as providing a means for checking progress.
- It provides the basic structure for reporting information.
- It reveals interdependencies of activities.
- It facilitates "what if" exercises.
- It identifies the longest path or critical paths.
- It allows us to perform scheduling risk analysis.

These advantages apply to all network scheduling techniques, not just PERT.

PERT was originally developed in 1958 and 1959 to meet the needs of the "age of massive engineering" where the techniques of Taylor and Gantt were inapplicable. The Special Projects Office of the U.S. Navy, concerned with performance trends on large military development programs, introduced PERT on its Polaris Weapon System in 1958, after the technique had been developed with the aid of the management consulting firm of Booz, Allen, and Hamilton. Since that time, PERT has spread rapidly throughout almost all industries. At about the same time the Navy was developing PERT, the DuPont Company initiated a similar technique known as the critical path method (CPM), which also has spread widely, and is particularly concentrated in the construction and process industries.

In the early 1960s, the basic requirements of PERT/time as established by the Navy were as follows:

- All of the individual tasks to complete a given program must be visualized in a manner clear enough to be put down in a network, which comprises events and activities; i.e., follow the work breakdown structure.
- Events and activities must be sequenced on the network under a highly logical set of ground rules that allow the determination of important critical and subcritical paths. Networks can have up to one hundred or more events, but not less than ten or twenty.
- Time estimates must be made for each activity of the network on a three-way basis. Optimistic, most likely, and pessimistic elapsed-time figures are estimated by the person(s) most familiar with the activity involved.
- Critical path and slack times are computed. The critical path is that sequence of activities and events whose accomplishment will require the greatest expected time.

A big advantage of PERT is the kind of planning required to create a major network. Network development and critical path analysis reveal interdependencies and problem areas that are neither obvious nor well defined by other planning methods. The technique therefore determines where the greatest effort should be made for a project to stay on schedule.

The second advantage of PERT is that one can determine the probability of meeting specified deadlines by development of alternative plans. If the decision maker is statistically sophisticated, he can examine the standard deviations and the probability of accomplishment data. If there exists a minimum of uncertainty, one may use the single-time approach, of course, while retaining the advantage of network analysis.

A third advantage is the ability to evaluate the effect of changes in the program. For example, PERT can evaluate the effect of a contemplated shift of resources from the less critical activities to the activities identified as probable bottlenecks. Other resources and performance trade-offs may also be evaluated. PERT can also evaluate the effect of a deviation in the actual time required for an activity from what had been predicted.

Finally, PERT allows a large amount of sophisticated data to be presented in a well-organized diagram from which both contractor and customer can make joint decisions.

PERT, unfortunately, is not without its disadvantages. The complexity of PERT adds to the implementation problems. There exist more data requirements for a PERT-organized MCCS reporting system than for most others. PERT, therefore, becomes an item that is expensive to maintain and is utilized most often on large, complex programs.

In recent years, many companies have taken a hard look at the usefulness of PERT on small projects. The literature contains many diversified approaches toward applying PERT to other than large and complex programs. The result has been the PERT/LOB procedures, which, when applied properly, can do the following job:

- Cut project costs and reduce time scale
- Coordinate and expedite planning
- Eliminate idle time
- Provide better scheduling and control of subcontractor activities
- Develop better troubleshooting procedures
- Cut the time required for routine decisions, but allow more time for decision making

Even with these advantages, many companies should ask themselves whether they actually need PERT. Incorporation of PERT may not be easy, even if canned software packages are available. One of the biggest problems with incorporating PERT occurred in the 1960s when the Department of Defense requested that DoD customers adopt PERT/cost for relating cost and schedules. This resulted in the expenditure of considerable cost and effort on behalf of the contractor to overcome the numerous cost-accounting problems. Many contractors eventually went to two sets of books; one set was for program control (which was in compliance with standard company cost control procedures), and a second set was created for customer reporting. Therefore, before accepting a PERT system, management must perform a trade-off study to determine if the results are worth the cost.

The criticism that most people discover when using PERT includes:

- Time and labor intensive effort is required.
- Upper-level management decision-making ability is reduced.
- There exists a lack of functional ownership in estimates.
- There exists a lack of historical data for time–cost estimates.
- The assumption of unlimited resources may be inappropriate.
- There may exist the need for too much detail.

An in-depth study of PERT would require a course or two by itself. The intent of this chapter is to familiarize the reader with the terminology, capability, and applications of networks.

12.1 NETWORK FUNDAMENTALS

The major discrepancy with Gantt, milestone, or bubble charts is the inability to show the interdependencies between events and activities. These interdependencies must be identified so that a master plan can be developed that provides an up-to-date picture of operations at all times and is easily understood by all.

Interdependencies are shown through the construction of networks. Network analysis can provide valuable information for planning, integration of plans, time studies, scheduling, and resource management. The primary purpose of network planning is to eliminate the need for crisis management by providing a pictorial representation of the total program. The following management information can be obtained from such a representation:

- Interdependencies of activities
- Project completion time
- Impact of late starts
- Impact of early starts
- Trade-offs between resources and time
- "What if" exercises
- Cost of a crash program
- Slippages in planning/performance
- Evaluation of performance

Networks are composed of events and activities. An event is defined as the starting or ending point for a group of activities, and an activity is the work required

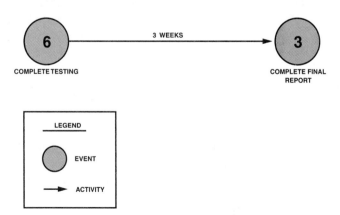

FIGURE 12–1. Standard PERT nomenclature.

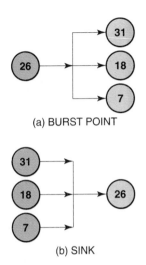

(a) BURST POINT

(b) SINK

FIGURE 12–2. PERT sources (burst points) and sinks.

to proceed from one event or point in time to another. Figure 12–1 shows the standard nomenclature for PERT networks. The circles represent events, and arrows represent activities. The numbers in the circles signify the specific events or accomplishments. The number over the arrow specifies the time needed (hours, days, months), to go from event 6 to event 3. The events need not be numbered in any specific order. However, event 6 must take place before event 3 can be completed (or begin). In Figure 12–2a, event 26 must take place prior to events 7, 18, and 31. In Figure 12–2b, the opposite holds true, and events 7, 18, and 31 must take place prior to event 26. Figure 12–2b is similar to "and gates" used in logic diagrams.[3]

Elsewhere we have summarized the advantages and disadvantages of Gantt and milestone charts. These charts, however, can be used to develop the PERT network, as shown in Figure 12–3. The bar chart in Figure 12–3a can be converted to the milestone chart in Figure 12–3b. By then defining the relationship between the events on different bars in the milestone chart, we can construct the PERT chart in Figure 12–3c.

PERT is basically a management planning and control tool. It can be considered as a road map for a particular program or project in which all of the major elements (events) have been completely identified together with their corresponding interrelations.[4] PERT charts are often constructed from back to front because, for many projects, the end date is fixed and the contractor has front-end flexibility.

---

3. PERT diagrams can, in fact, be considered as logic diagrams. Many of the symbols used in PERT have been adapted from logic flow nomenclature.

4. These events in the PERT charts should be broken down to at least the same reporting levels as defined in the work breakdown structure.

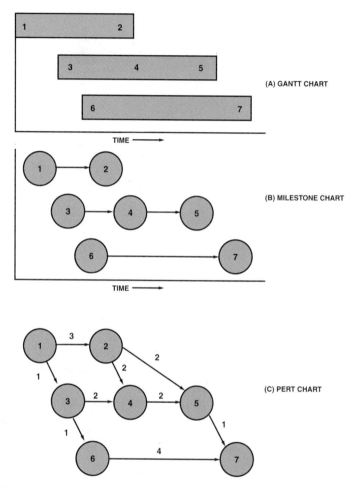

FIGURE 12–3. Conversion from bar chart to PERT chart.

One of the purposes of constructing the PERT chart is to determine how much time is needed to complete the project. PERT, therefore, uses time as a common denominator to analyze those elements that directly influence the success of the project, namely, time, cost, and performance. The construction of the network requires two inputs. First, a selection must be made as to whether the events represent the start or the completion of an activity. Event completions are generally preferred. The next step is to define the sequence of events, as shown in Table 12–1, which relates each event to its immediate predecessor. Large projects can easily be converted into PERT networks once the following questions are answered:

TABLE 12–1. SEQUENCE OF EVENTS

Activity	Title	Immediate Predecessors	Activity Time, Weeks
1–2	A	—	1
2–3	B	A	5
2–4	C	A	2
3–5	D	B	2
3–7	E	B	2
4–5	F	C	2
4–8	G	C	3
5–6	H	D,F	2
6–7	I	H	3
7–8	J	E,I	3
8–9	K	G,J	2

- What job immediately precedes this job?
- What job immediately follows this job?
- What jobs can be run concurrently?

Figure 12–4 shows a typical PERT network. The bold line in Figure 12–4 represents the critical path, which is established by the longest time span through the total system of events. The critical path is composed of events 1–2–3–5–6–7–8–9. The critical path is vital for successful control of the project because it tells management two things:

- Because there is no slack time in any of the events on this path, any slippage will cause a corresponding slippage in the end date of the program unless this slippage can be recovered during any of the downstream events (on the critical path).
- Because the events on this path are the most critical for the success of the project, management must take a hard look at these events in order to improve the total program.

Using PERT we can now identify the earliest possible dates on which we can expect an event to occur, or an activity to start or end. There is nothing overly mysterious about this type of calculation, but without a network analysis the information might be hard to obtain.

PERT charts can be managed from either the events or the activities. For levels 1–3 of the WBS, the project manager's prime concerns are the milestones, and therefore, the events are of prime importance. For levels 4–6 of the WBS, the project manager's concerns are the activities.

The principles that we have discussed thus far apply not only to PERT, but to CPM as well. The nomenclature is the same for both, and both techniques are often referred to as arrow diagramming methods, or activity-on-arrow networks. The differences between PERT and CPM are as follows:

- PERT uses three time estimates (optimistic, most likely, and pessimistic as shown in Section 12.7). From these estimates, an expected time can be derived. CPM uses one time estimate that represents the normal time (i.e., better estimate accuracy with CPM).
- PERT is probabilistic in nature, based on a beta distribution for each activity time and a normal distribution for expected time duration (see Section 12.7). This allows us to calculate the "risk" in completing a project. CPM is based on a single time estimate and is deterministic in nature.
- Both PERT and CPM permit the use of dummy activities in order to develop the logic.
- PERT is used for R&D projects where the risks in calculating time durations have a high variability. CPM is used for construction projects that are resource dependent and based on accurate time estimates.
- PERT is used on those projects, such as R&D, where percent complete is almost impossible to determine except at completed milestones. CPM is used for those projects, such as construction, where percent complete can be determined with reasonable accuracy and customer billing can be accomplished based on percent complete.

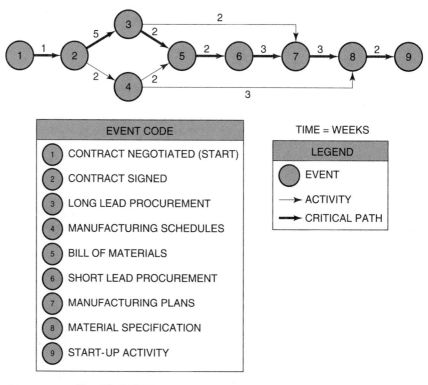

FIGURE 12–4. Simplified PERT network.

12.2 GRAPHICAL EVALUATION AND REVIEW TECHNIQUE (GERT)

Graphical evaluation and review techniques are similar to PERT but have the distinct advantages of allowing for looping, branching, and multiple project end results. With PERT one cannot easily show that if a test fails, we may have to repeat the test several more times. With PERT, we cannot show that, based upon the results of a test, we can select one of several different branches to continue the project. These problems are easily overcome using GERT.

12.3 DEPENDENCIES

There are three basic types of interrelationships or dependencies:

- Mandatory dependencies (i.e., hard logic): These are dependencies that cannot change, such as erecting the walls of a house before putting up the roof.
- Discretionary dependencies (i.e., soft logic): These are dependencies that may be at the discretion of the project manager or may simply change from project to project. As an example, one does not need to complete the entire bill of materials prior to beginning procurement.
- External dependencies: These are dependencies that may be beyond the control of the project manager such as having contractors sit on your critical path.

Sometimes, it is impossible to draw network dependencies without including dummy activities. Dummy activities are artificial activities, represented by a dotted line, and do not consume resources or require time. They are added into the network simply to complete the logic.

In Figure 12–5, the dummy activity is required to show that D is preceded by A and B.

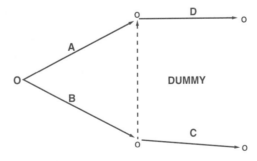

FIGURE 12–5. Dummy activity.

12.4 SLACK TIME

Since there exists only one path through the network that is the longest, the other paths must be either equal in length to or shorter than that path. Therefore, there must exist events and activities that can be completed before the time when they are actually needed. The time differential between the scheduled completion date and the required date to meet critical path is referred to as the slack time. In Figure 12–4, event 4 is not on the crucial path. To go from event 2 to event 5 on the critical path requires seven weeks taking the route 2–3–5. If route 2–4–5 is taken, only four weeks are required. Therefore, event 4, which requires two weeks for completion, should begin anywhere from zero to three weeks after event 2 is complete. During these three weeks, management might find another use for the resources of people, money, equipment, and facilities required to complete event 4.

The critical path is vital for resource scheduling and allocation because the project manager, with coordination from the functional manager, can reschedule those events not on the critical path for accomplishment during other time periods when maximum utilization of resources can be achieved, provided that the critical path time is not extended. This type of rescheduling through the use of slack times provides for a better balance of resources throughout the company, and may possibly reduce project costs by eliminating idle or waiting time.

Slack can be defined as the difference between the latest allowable date and the earliest expected data based on the nomenclature below:

T_E = the earliest time (date) on which an event can be expected to take place
T_L = the latest date on which an event can take place without extending the completion date of the project
Slack time = $T_L - T_E$

The calculation for slack time is performed for each event in the network, as shown in Figure 12–6, by identifying the earliest expected date and the latest starting date. For event 1, $T_L - T_E = 0$. Event 1 serves as the reference point for the network and could just as easily have been defined as a calendar date. As before, the critical path is represented as a bold line. The events on the critical path have no slack (i.e., $T_L = T_E$) and provide the boundaries for the noncritical path events.[5] Since event 2 is critical, $T_L = T_E = 3 + 7 = 10$ for event 5. Event 6 terminates the critical path with a completion time of fifteen weeks.

The earliest time for event 3, which is not on the critical path, would be two weeks ($T_E = 0 + 2 = 2$), assuming that it started as early as possible. The latest allowable date is obtained by subtracting the time required to complete the activity from events 3 to 5 from the latest starting date of event 5. Therefore, T_L (for event 3) = $10 - 5 = 5$ weeks. Event 3 can now occur anywhere between weeks

---

5. There are special situations where the critical path may include some slack. These cases are not considered here.

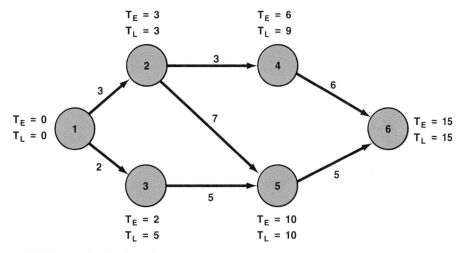

FIGURE 12–6. PERT network with slack time.

2 and 5 without interfering with the scheduled completion date of the project. This same procedure can be applied to event 4, in which case $T_E = 6$ and $T_L = 9$.

Figure 12–6 contains a simple PERT network, and therefore the calculation of slack time is not too difficult. For complex networks containing multiple paths, the earliest starting dates must be found by proceeding from start to finish through the network, while the latest allowable starting date must be calculated by working backward from finish to start.

The importance of knowing exactly where the slack exists cannot be overstated. Proper use of slack time permits better technical performance. Donald Marquis has observed that those companies making proper use of slack time were 30 percent more successful than the average in completing technical requirements.[6]

Because of these slack times, PERT networks are often not plotted with a time scale. Planning requirements, however, can require that PERT charts be reconstructed with time scales, in which case a decision must be made as to whether we wish early or late time requirements for slack variables. This is shown in Figure 12–7 for comparison with total program costs and manpower planning. Early time requirements for slack variables are utilized in this figure.

The earliest times and late times can be combined to determine the probability of successfully meeting the schedule. A sample of the required information is shown in Table 12–2. The earliest and latest times are considered as random variables. The original schedule refers to the schedule for event occurrences that were established at the beginning of the project. The last column in Table 12–2 gives

6. Donald Marquis, "Ways of Organizing Projects," *Innovation,* 1969.

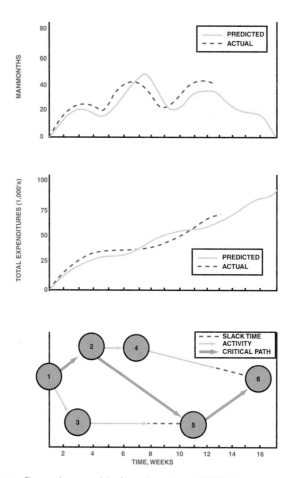

FIGURE 12–7. Comparison models for a time-phase PERT chart.

the probability that the earliest time will not be greater than the original schedule time for this event. The exact method for determining this probability, as well as the variances, is described in Section 12.5.

In the example shown in Figure 12–6, the earliest and latest times were calculated for each event. Some people prefer to calculate the earliest and latest times for each activity instead. Also, the earliest and latest times were identified simply as the time or date when an event can be expected to take place. To make full use of the capabilities of PERT/CPM, we could identify four values:

- The earliest time when an activity can start (ES)
- The earliest time when an activity can finish (EF)
- The latest time when an activity can start (LS)
- The latest time when an activity can finish (LF)

TABLE 12–2. PERT CONTROL OUTPUT INFORMATION

Event Number	Earliest Time		Latest Time		Slack	Original Schedule	Probability of Meeting Schedule
	Expected	Variance	Expected	Variance			

Figure 12–8 shows the earliest and latest times identified on the activity.

To calculate the earliest starting times, we must make a forward pass through the network (i.e., left to right). The earliest starting time of a successor activity is the latest of the earliest finish dates of the predecessors. The latest starting time is the total of the earliest starting time and the activity duration.

To calculate the finishing times, we must make a *backward* pass through the network by calculating the latest finish time. Since the activity time is known, the latest starting time can be calculated by subtracting the activity time from the latest finishing time. The latest finishing time for an activity entering a node is the earliest finishing time of the activities exiting the node. Figure 12–9 shows the earliest and latest starting and finishing times for a typical network.

The identification of slack time can function as an early warning system for the project manager. As an example, if the total slack time available begins to decrease from one reporting period to the next, that could indicate that work is taking longer than anticipated or that more highly skilled labor is needed. A new critical path could be forming.

Looking at the earliest and latest start and finish times can identify slack. As an example, look at the two situations below:

[20, 26]	[30, 36]
[24, 30]	[25, 31]
Situation a	Situation b

In Situation a, the slack is easily identified as four work units, where the work units can be expressed in hours, days, weeks, or even months. In Situation b, the slack is *negative* five units of work. This is referred to as negative slack or negative float.

What can cause the slack to be negative? Look at Figure 12–10. When performing a forward pass through a network, we work from left to right beginning at the customer's starting milestone (position 1). The backward pass, however, begins at the customer's end date milestone (position 2), *not* (as is often taught in the classroom) where the forward pass ends. If the forward pass ends at position 3, which is before the customer's end date, it is possible to have slack on the crit-

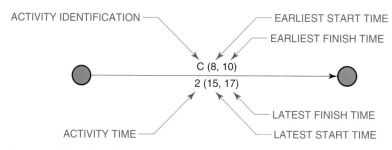

FIGURE 12–8. Slack identification.

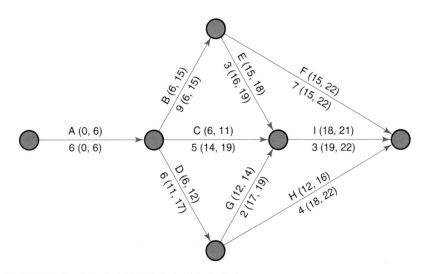

FIGURE 12–9. A typical PERT chart with slack times.

ical path. This slack is often called reserve time and may be added to other activities or filled with activities such as report writing so that the forward pass will extend to the customer's completion date.

Negative slack usually occurs when the forward pass extends beyond the customer's end date, as shown by position 4 in the figure. However, the backward pass is still measured from the customer's completion date, thus creating negative slack. This is most likely to result when:

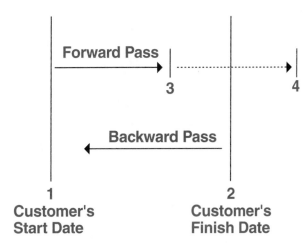

FIGURE 12–10. Slack time.

- The original plan was highly optimistic, but unrealistic
- The customer's end date was unrealistic
- One or more activities slipped during project execution
- The assigned resources did not possess the correct skill levels
- The required resources would not be available until a later date

In any event, negative slack is an early warning indicator that corrective action is needed to maintain the customer's end date.

12.5 NETWORK REPLANNING

Once constructed, the PERT/CPM charts provide the framework from which detailed planning can be initiated and costs can be controlled and tracked. Many iterations, however, are normally made during the planning phase before the PERT/CPM chart is finished. Figure 12–11 shows this iteration process. The slack times form the basis from which additional iterations, or network replanning, can be performed. Network replanning is performed either at the conception of the program in order to reduce the length of the critical path, or during the program, should the unexpected occur. If all were to go according to schedule, then the original PERT/CPM chart would be unchanged for the duration of the project. But, how many programs or projects follow an exact schedule from start to finish?

Suppose that activities 1–2 and 1–3 in Figure 12–6 require manpower from the same functional unit. Upon inquiry by the project manager, the functional manager asserts that he can reduce activity 1–2 by one week if he shifts resources from activity 1–3 to activity 1–2. Should this happen, however, activity 1–3 will increase in length by one week. Reconstructing the PERT/CPM network as shown in Figure 12–12, the length of the critical path is reduced by one week, and the corresponding slack events are likewise changed.

There are two network replanning techniques based almost entirely upon resources: resource leveling and resource allocation.

- Resource leveling is an attempt to eliminate the manpower peaks and valleys by smoothing out the period-to-period resource requirements. The ideal situation is to do this without changing the end date. However, in reality, the end date moves out and additional costs are incurred.
- Resource allocation is an attempt to find the shortest possible critical path based upon the available or fixed resources. The problem with this approach is that the employees may not be qualified technically to perform on more than one activity in a network.

Unfortunately, not all PERT/CPM networks permit such easy rescheduling of resources. Project managers should make every attempt to reallocate resources so

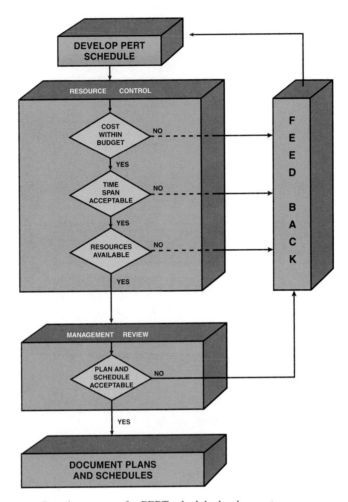

FIGURE 12–11. Iteration process for PERT schedule development.

as to reduce the critical path, provided that the slack was not intentionally planned as a safety valve.

Transferring resources from slack paths to more critical paths is only one method for reducing expected project time. Several other methods are available:

● Elimination of some parts of the project
● Addition of more resources
● Substitution of less time-consuming components or activities
● Parallelization of activities
● Shortening critical path activities
● Shortening early activities

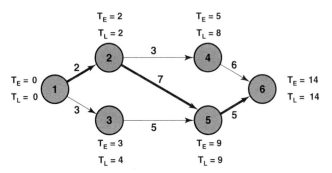

FIGURE 12–12. Network replanning of Figure 12–6.

- Shortening longest activities
- Shortening easiest activities
- Shortening activities that are least costly to speed up
- Shortening activities for which you have more resources
- Increasing the number of work hours per day

Under the ideal situation, the project start and end dates are fixed, and performance within this time scale must be completed within the guidelines described by the statement of work. Should the scope of effort have to be reduced in order to meet other requirements, the contractor incurs a serious risk in that the project may be canceled, or performance expectations may no longer be possible.

Adding resources is not always possible. If the activities requiring these added resources also call for certain expertise, then the contractor may not have qualified or experienced employees, and may avoid the risk. The contractor might still reject this idea, even if time and money were available for training new employees, because on project termination he might not have any other projects to which to assign these additional people. However, if the project is the construction of a new facility, then the labor-union pool may be large enough that additional experienced manpower can be hired.

Parallelization of activities can be regarded as accepting a risk by assuming that a certain event can begin in parallel with a second event that would normally be in sequence with it. This is shown in Figure 12–13. One of the biggest headaches at the beginning of any project is the purchasing of tooling and raw materials. As shown in Figure 12–13, four weeks can be saved by sending out purchase orders after contract negotiations are completed, but before the one-month waiting period necessary to sign the contract. Here the contractor incurs a risk. Should the effort be canceled or the statement of work change prior to the signing of the contract, the customer incurs the cost of the termination liability expenses from the vendors. This risk is normally overcome by the issuance of a long-lead procurement letter immediately following contract negotiations.

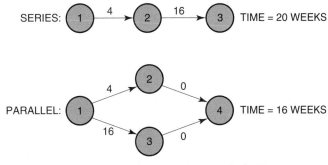

NOTE: EVENT 4 IS A DUMMY EVENT AND IS INCLUDED WITH A ZERO ACTIVITY TIME
IN ORDER TO CONSTRUCT A COMPLETE NETWORK

LEGEND
① CONTRACT NEGOTIATIONS COMPLETED
② CONTRACT SIGNED
③ MATERIAL/TOOLING PURCHASED
④ DUMMY EVENT

FIGURE 12–13. Parallelization of PERT activities.

There are two other types of risk that are common. In the first situation, engineering has not yet finished the prototype, and manufacturing must order the tooling in order to keep the end date fixed. In this case, engineering may finally design the prototype to fit the tooling. In the second situation, the subcontractor finds it difficult to perform according to the original blueprints. In order to save time, the customer may allow the contractor to work without blueprints, and the blueprints are then changed to represent the as-built end-item.

Because of the complexities of large programs, network replanning becomes an almost impossible task when analyzed on total program activities. It is often better to have each department or division develop its own PERT/CPM networks, on approval by the project office, and based on the work breakdown structure. The individual PERT charts are then integrated into one master chart to identify total program critical paths, as shown in Figure 12–14. The reader should not infer from Figure 12–14 that department D does not interact with other departments or that department D is the only participant for this element of the project.

Segmented PERT charts can also be used when a number of contractors work on the same program. Each contractor (or subcontractor) develops his own PERT chart. It then becomes the responsibility of the prime contractor to integrate all of the subcontractors' PERT charts to ensure that total program requirements can be met.

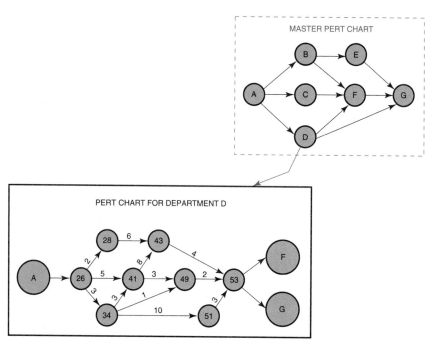

FIGURE 12–14. Master PERT chart breakdown by department.

12.6 ESTIMATING ACTIVITY TIME

Determining the elapsed time between events requires that responsible functional managers evaluate the situation and submit their best estimates. The calculations for critical paths and slack times in the previous sections were based on these best estimates.

In this ideal situation, the functional manager would have at his disposal a large volume of historical data from which to make his estimates. Obviously, the more historical data available, the more reliable the estimate. Many programs, however, include events and activities that are nonrepetitive. In this case, the functional managers must submit their estimates using three possible completion assumptions:

- *Most optimistic completion time.* This time assumes that everything will go according to plan and with a minimal amount of difficulties. This should occur approximately 1 percent of the time.
- *Most pessimistic completion time.* This time assumes that everything will not go according to plan and that the maximum potential difficulties will develop. This should also occur approximately 1 percent of the time.

● *Most likely completion time.* This is the time that, in the mind of the functional manager, would most often occur should this effort be reported over and over again.[7]

Before these three times can be combined into a single expression for expected time, two assumptions must be made. The first assumption is that the standard deviation, σ, is one-sixth of the time requirement range. This assumption stems from probability theory, where the end points of a curve are three standard deviations from the mean. The second assumption requires that the probability distribution of time required for an activity be expressible as a beta distribution.[8]

The expected time between events can be found from the expression:

$$t_e = \frac{a + 4m + b}{6}$$

where t_e = expected time, a = most optimistic time, b = most pessimistic time, and m = most likely time.

As an example, if $a = 3$, $b = 7$, and $m = 5$ weeks, then the expected time, t_e, would be 5 weeks. This value for t_e would then be used as the activity time between two events in the construction of a PERT chart. This method for obtaining best estimates contains a large degree of uncertainty. If we change the variable times to $a = 2$, $b = 12$, and $m = 4$ weeks, then t_e will still be 5 weeks. The latter case, however, has a much higher degree of uncertainty because of the wider spread between the optimistic and pessimistic times. Care must be taken in the evaluation of risks in the expected times.

12.7 ESTIMATING TOTAL PROGRAM TIME

In order to calculate the probability of completing the project on time, the standard deviations of each activity must be known. This can be found from the expression:

$$\sigma_{t_e} = \frac{b - a}{6}$$

where σ_{t_e} is the standard deviation of the expected time, t_e. Another useful expression is the variance, v, which is the square of the standard deviation. The vari-

---

7. It is assumed that the functional manager performs all of the estimating. The reader should be aware that there are exceptions where the program or project office would do their own estimating.

8. See F. S. Hillier and G. J. Lieberman, *Introduction to Operations Research* (San Francisco: Holden-Day, 1967), p. 229.

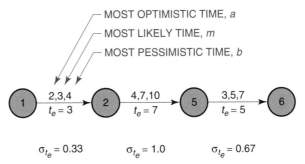

FIGURE 12–15. Expected time analysis for critical path events in Figure 12–5.

ance is primarily useful for comparison to the expected values. However, the standard deviation can be used just as easily, except that we must identify whether it is a one, two, or three sigma limit deviation. Figure 12–15 shows the critical path of Figure 12–6, together with the corresponding values from which the expected times were calculated, as well as the standard deviations. The total path standard deviation is calculated by the square root of the sum of the squares of the activity standard deviations using the following expression:

$$\sigma_{\text{total}} = \sqrt{\sigma_{1\text{-}2}^2 + \sigma_{2\text{-}5}^2 + \sigma_{5\text{-}6}^2}$$
$$= \sqrt{(0.33)^2 + (1.0)^2 + (0.67)^2}$$
$$= 1.25$$

12.8 TOTAL PERT/CPM PLANNING

Before we continue, it is necessary to discuss the methodology for preparing PERT schedules. PERT scheduling is a six-step process. Steps one and two begin with the project manager laying out a list of activities to be performed and then placing these activities in order of precedence, thus identifying the interrelationships. These charts drawn by the project manager are called either logic charts, arrow diagrams, work flow, or simply networks. The arrow diagrams will look like Figure 12–6 with two exceptions: The activity time is not identified, and neither is the critical path.

Step three is reviewing the arrow diagrams with the line managers (i.e., the true experts) in order to obtain their assurance that neither too many nor too few activities are identified, and that the interrelationships are correct.

In step four the functional manager converts the arrow diagram to a PERT chart by identifying the time duration for each activity. It should be noted here that the time estimates that the line managers provide are based on the *assumption of unlimited resources* because the calendar dates have not yet been defined.

Step five is the first iteration on the critical path. It is here that the project manager looks at the critical calendar dates in the definition of the project's requirements. If the critical path does not satisfy the calendar requirements, then the project manager must try to shorten the critical path using methods explained in Section 12.3 or by asking the line managers to take the "fat" out of their estimates.

Step six is often the most overlooked step. Here the project manager places calendar dates on each event in the PERT chart, thus converting from planning under unlimited resources to planning with *limited resources*. Even though the line manager has given you a time estimate, there is no guarantee that the correct resources will be available when needed. That is why this step is crucial. If the line manager cannot commit to the calendar dates, then replanning will be necessary. Most companies that survive on competitive bidding lay out proposal schedules based on unlimited resources. After contract award, the schedules are analyzed again because the company now has limited resources. After all, how can a company bid on three contracts simultaneously and put a detailed schedule into each proposal if it is not sure how many contracts, if any, it will win? For this reason customers require that formal project plans and schedules be provided thirty to ninety days after contract award.

Finally, PERT replanning should be an ongoing function during project execution. The best project managers are those individuals who continually try to assess what can go wrong and perform perturbation analysis on the schedule. (This should be obvious because the constraints and objectives of the project can change during execution.) Primary objectives on a schedule are:

- Best time
- Least cost
- Least risk

Secondary objectives include:

- Studying alternatives
- Optimum schedules
- Effective use of resources
- Communications
- Refinement of the estimating process
- Ease of project control
- Ease of time or cost revisions

Obviously, these objectives are limited by such constraints as:

- Calendar completion
- Cash or cash flow restrictions
- Limited resources
- Management approvals

12.9 CRASH TIMES

In the preceding sections, no distinction was made between PERT and CPM. The basic difference between PERT and CPM lies in the ability to calculate percent complete. PERT is used in R&D or just development activities, where a percent-complete determination is almost impossible. Therefore, PERT is event oriented rather than activity oriented. In PERT, funding is normally provided for each mile-stone (i.e., event) achieved because incremental funding along the activity line has to be based on percent complete. CPM, on the other hand, is activity oriented be-cause, in activities such as construction, percent complete along the activity line can be determined. CPM can be used as an arrow diagram network without PERT. The difference between the two methods lies in the environments in which each one evolved and how each one is applied. According to Archibald and Villoria:[9]

> The environmental factors which had an important role in determining the elements of the CPM techniques were:
> (a) Well-defined projects
> (b) One dominant organization
> (c) Relatively small uncertainties
> (d) One geographical location for a project

The CPM (activity-type network) has been widely used in the process industries, in construction, and in single-project industrial activities. Common problems include no place to store early arrivals of raw materials and project delays for late arrivals.

Using strictly the CPM approach, project managers can consider the cost of speeding up, or crashing, certain phases of a project. In order to accomplish this, it is necessary to calculate a crashing cost per unit time as well as the normal ex-pected time for each activity. CPM charts, which are closely related to PERT charts, allow visual representation of the effects of crashing. There are these re-quirements:

- For a CPM chart, the emphasis is on activities, not events. Therefore, the PERT chart should be redrawn with each circle representing an activity rather than an event.
- In CPM, both time and cost of each activity are considered.[10]
- Only those activities on the critical path are considered, starting with the activities for which the crashing cost per unit time is the lowest.

Figure 12–16 shows a CPM network with the corresponding crash time for all activities both on and off the critical path. The activities are represented by cir-

9. R. D. Archibald and R. L. Villoria, *Network-Based Management Systems (PERT/CPM)* (New York: John Wiley, 1967), p. 14.

10. Although PERT considers mainly time, modifications through PERT/cost analysis can be made to consider the cost factors.

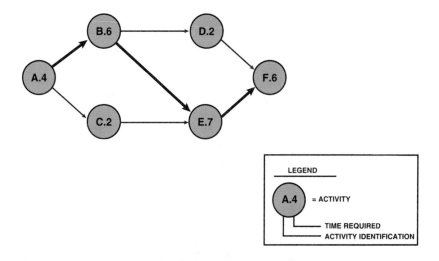

FIGURE 12–16. CPM network.

	TIME REQUIRED, WEEKS		COST $		CRASHING COST
ACTIVITY	NORMAL	CRASH	NORMAL	CRASH	PER WEEK, $
A	4	2	10,000	14,000	2,000
B	6	5	30,000	42,500	12,500
C	2	1	8,000	9,500	1,500
D	2	1	12,000	18,000	6,000
E	7	5	40,000	52,000	6,000
F	6	3	20,000	29,000	3,000

cles and include an activity identification number and the estimated time. The costs expressed in the figure are usually direct costs only.

To determine crashing costs we begin with the lowest weekly crashing cost, activity A, at $2,000 per week. Although activity C has a lower crashing cost, it is not on the critical path. Only critical path activities are considered for crashing. Activity A will be the first to be crashed for a maximum of two weeks at $2,000 per week. The next activity to be considered would be F at $3,000 per week for a maximum of three weeks. These crashing costs are additional expenses above the normal estimates.

A word of caution concerning the selection and order of the activities that are to crash: There is a good possibility that as each activity is crashed, a new critical path will be developed. This new path may or may not include those elements that were bypassed because they were not on the original critical path.

Returning to Figure 12–16 (and assuming that no new critical paths are developed), activities A, F, E, and B would be crashed in that order. The crashing cost would then be an increase of $37,500 from the base of $120,000 to $157,500. The corresponding time would then be reduced from twenty-three weeks to fifteen weeks. This is shown in Figure 12–17 to illustrate how a trade-off between time and cost can be obtained. Also shown in Figure 12–17 is the increased cost of crashing elements not on the critical path. Crashing these elements would result in a cost increase of $7,500 without reducing the total project time. There is also the possibility that this figure will represent unrealistic conditions because sufficient resources are not or cannot be made available for the crashing period.

The purpose behind balancing time and cost is to avoid the useless waste of resources. If the direct and indirect costs can be accurately obtained, then a region of feasible budgets can be found, bounded by the early-start (crash) and late-start (or normal) activities. This is shown in Figure 12–18.

Since the direct and indirect costs are not necessarily expressible as linear functions, time–cost trade-off relationships are made by searching for the lowest possible total cost (i.e., direct and indirect) that likewise satisfies the region of feasible budgets. This method is shown in Figure 12–19.

Like PERT, CPM also contains the concept of slack time, the maximum amount of time that a job may be delayed beyond its early start without delaying the project completion time. Figure 12–20 shows a typical representation of slack time using a CPM chart. In addition, the figure shows how target activity costs can be identified. Figure 12–20 can be modified to include normal and crash times as

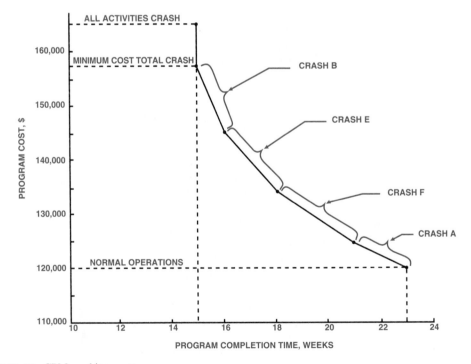

FIGURE 12–17. CPM crashing costs.

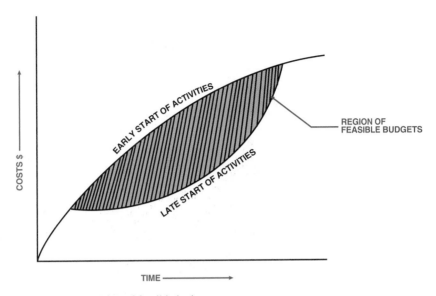

FIGURE 12–18. Region of feasible budgets.

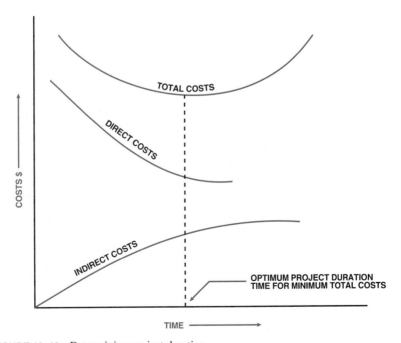

FIGURE 12–19. Determining project duration.

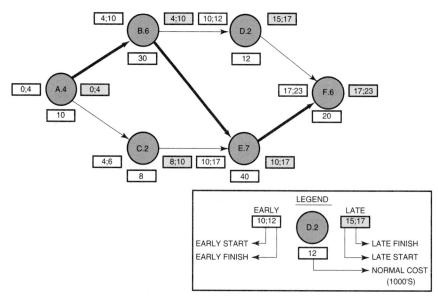

FIGURE 12–20. CPM network with slack.

well as normal and crash costs. In this case, the cost box in the figure would contain two numbers: The first number would be the normal cost, and the second would be the crash cost. These numbers might also appear as running totals.

12.10 PERT/CPM PROBLEM AREAS

PERT/CPM models are not without their disadvantages and problems. Even the largest organizations with years of experience in using PERT and CPM have the same ongoing problems as newer or smaller companies.

Many companies have a difficult time incorporating PERT systems because PERT is end-item oriented. Many upper-level managers feel that the adoption of PERT/CPM removes a good part of their power and ability to make decisions. This is particularly evident in companies that have been forced to accept PERT/CPM as part of contractual requirements.

There exists a distinct contrast in PERT systems between the planners and the doers. This human element must be accounted for in order to determine where the obligation actually lies. In most organizations PERT planning is performed by the program office and functional management. Yet once the network is constructed, the planners and managers become observers and rely on the doers to accomplish the job within time and cost limitations. Management must convince the doers that they have an obligation toward the successful completion of the established PERT/CPM plans.

Unless the project is repetitive, there usually exists a lack of historical information on which to base the cost estimates of most optimistic, most pessimistic, and most likely times. Problems can also involve poor predictions for overhead costs, other indirect costs, material and labor escalation factors, and crash costs. It is also possible that each major functional division of the organization has its own method for estimating costs. Engineering, for example, may use historical data, whereas manufacturing operations may prefer learning curves. PERT works best if all organizations have the same method for predicting costs and performance.

PERT networks are based on the assumption that all activities start as soon as possible. This assumes that qualified personnel and equipment are available. Regardless of how well we plan, there almost always exist differences in performance times from what would normally be acceptable for the model selected. For the selected model, time and cost should be well-considered estimates, not a spur-of-the-moment decision.

Cost control presents a problem in that the project cost and control system may not be compatible with company fiscal planning policies. Project-oriented costs may be meshed with non-PERT-controlled jobs in order to develop the annual budget. This becomes a difficult chore for cost reporting, especially when each project may have its own method for analyzing and controlling costs.

Many people have come to expect too much of PERT-type networks. Figure 12–21 illustrates a PERT/CPM network broken down by work packages with identification of the charge numbers for each activity. Large projects may contain hundreds of charge numbers. Subdividing work packages (which are supposedly the lowest element) even further by identifying all subactivities has the advantage that direct charge numbers can be easily identified, but the time and cost for this

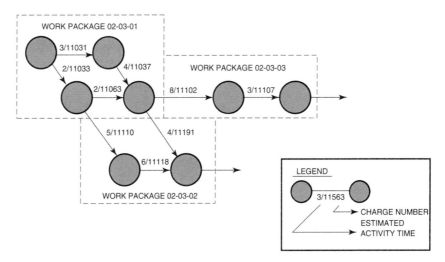

FIGURE 12–21. Using PERT for work package control.

form of detail may be prohibitive. PERT/CPM networks are tools for program control, and managers must be careful that the original game plan of using networks to identify prime and supporting objectives is still met. Additional detail may mask this all-important purpose. Remember, networks are constructed as a means for understanding program reports. Management should not be required to read reports in order to understand PERT/CPM networks.

12.11 ALTERNATIVE PERT/CPM MODELS

Because of the many advantages of PERT/time, numerous industries have found applications for this form of network. A partial list of these advantages includes capabilities for:

- Trade-off studies for resource control
- Providing contingency planning in the early stages of the project
- Visually tracking up-to-date performance
- Demonstrating integrated planning
- Providing visibility down through the lowest levels of the work breakdown structure
- Providing a regimented structure for control purposes to ensure compliance with the work breakdown structure and the statement of work
- Increasing functional members' ability to relate to the total program, thus providing participants with a sense of belonging

Even with these advantages, in many situations PERT/time has proved ineffective in controlling resources. In the beginning of this chapter we defined three parameters necessary for the control of resources: time, cost, and performance. With these factors in mind, companies began reconstructing PERT/time into PERT/cost and PERT/performance models.

PERT/cost is an extension of PERT/time and attempts to overcome the problems associated with the use of the most optimistic and most pessimistic time for estimating completion. PERT/cost can be regarded as a cost accounting network model based on the work breakdown structure and capable of being subdivided down to the lowest elements, or work packages. The advantages of PERT/cost are that it:

- Contains all the features of PERT/time
- Permits cost control at any WBS level

The primary reason for the development of PERT/cost was so that project managers could identify critical schedule slippages and cost overruns in time for corrective action to be taken.

Many attempts have been made to develop effective PERT/schedule models. In almost all cases, the charts are constructed from left to right.[11] An example of such current attempts is the accomplishment/cost procedure (ACP). As described by Block:[12]

ACP reports cost based on schedule accomplishment, rather than on the passage of time. To determine how an uncompleted task is progressing with respect to cost, ACP compares (a) cost/progress relationship budgeting with (b) the cost/progress relationship expended for the task. It utilizes data accumulated from periodic reports and from the same data base generates the following:

● The relationship between cost and scheduled performance
● The accounting relationships between cost and fiscal accounting requirements
● The prediction of corporate cash flow needs

Unfortunately, the development of PERT/schedule techniques is still in its infancy. Although their applications have been identified, many companies feel locked in with their present method of control, whether it be PERT, CPM, or some other technique.

12.12 PRECEDENCE NETWORKS

Over the past ten years there has been an explosion in project management software packages. Small packages may sell for a few thousand dollars, whereas the price for larger packages may be $70,000. Computerized project management can provide answers to such questions as:

● How will the project be affected by limited resources?
● How will the project be affected by a change in the requirements?
● What is the cash flow for the project (and for each WBS element)?
● What is the impact of overtime?
● What additional resources are needed to meet the constraints of the project?
● How will a change in the priority of a certain WBS element affect the total project?

---

11. See Gary E. Whitehouse, "Project Management Techniques," *Industrial Engineering,* March 1973, pp. 24–29, for a description of the technique.

12. Ellery B. Block, "Accomplishment/Cost: Better Project Control," *Harvard Business Review,* May–June 1971, pp. 110–124. Copyright © 1971 by the President and Fellows of Harvard College; all rights reserved.

The more sophisticated packages can provide answers to schedule and cost based on:

- Adverse weather conditions
- Weekend activities
- Unleveled manpower requirements
- Variable crew size
- Splitting of activities
- Assignment of unused resources

Regardless of the sophistication of computer systems, printers and plotters prefer to draw straight lines rather than circles. Most software systems today use precedence networks, as shown in Figure 12–22, which attempt to show interrelationships on bar charts. In Figure 12–22, task 1 and task 2 are related because of the solid line between them. Task 3 and task 4 can begin when task 2 is half finished. (This cannot be shown easily on PERT without splitting activities.) The dotted lines indicate slack. The critical path can be identified either by putting an asterisk (*) beside the critical elements, by making the critical connections in a different-colored ink, or by making the critical path a boldface type.

The more sophisticated software packages display precedence networks in the format shown in Figure 12–23. In each of these figures, work is accomplished during the activity. This is sometimes referred to as the activity-on-node method. The arrow represents the relationship or constraint between activities.

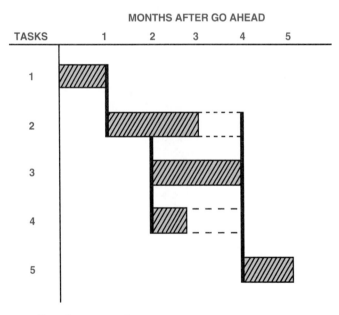

FIGURE 12–22. Precedence network.

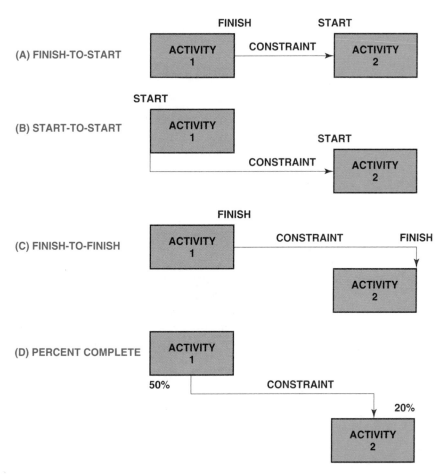

FIGURE 12–23. Typical precedence relationships.

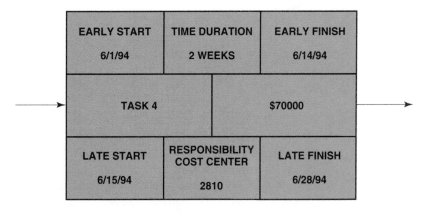

FIGURE 12–24. Computerized information flow.

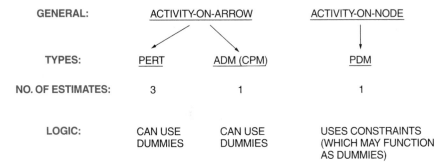

FIGURE 12–25. Comparison of networks.

Figure 12–23A illustrates a finish-to-start constraint. In this figure, activity 2 can start no earlier than the completion of activity 1. Figure 12-23B illustrates a start-to-start constraint. Activity 2 cannot start prior to the start of activity 1. Figure 12-23C illustrates a finish-to-finish constraint. In this figure, activity 2 cannot finish until activity 1 finishes. Figure 12-23D illustrates a percent-complete constraint. In this figure, the last 20 percent of activity 2 cannot be started until 50 percent of activity 1 has been completed.

Figure 12–24 shows the typical information that appears in each of the activity boxes shown in Figure 12–23. The box identified as "responsibility cost center" could also have been identified as the name, initials, or badge number of the person responsible for this activity.

Figure 12–25 shows the comparison of three of the different network techniques.

12.13 LAG

The time period between the early start or finish of one activity and the early start or finish of another activity in the sequential chain is called lag. Lag is most commonly used in conjunction with precedence networks. Figure 12–26 shows five different ways to identify lag on the constraints.

12.14 UNDERSTANDING PROJECT MANAGEMENT SOFTWARE

Efficient project management requires more than good planning, it requires that relevant information be obtained, analyzed, and reviewed in a timely manner. This can provide early warning of pending problems and impact assessments on other activities, which can lead to alternate plans and management actions. Today, project managers have a large array of software available to help in the difficult task of

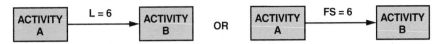

(A) FINISH-TO-START (FS) RELATIONSHIP. THE START OF B MUST LAG 6 DAYS AFTER THE FINISH OF A.

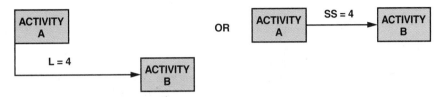

(B) START-TO-START (SS) RELATIONSHIP. THE START OF B MUST LAG 4 DAYS AFTER THE START OF A.

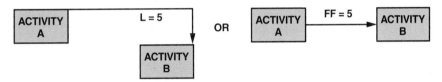

(C) FINISH-TO-FINISH (FF) RELATIONSHIP. THE FINISH OF B MUST LAG 5 DAYS AFTER THE FINISH OF A.

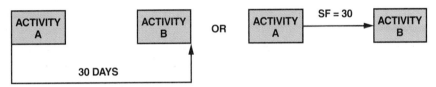

(D) START-TO-FINISH (SF) RELATIONSHIP. THE FINISH OF B MUST LAG 30 DAYS AFTER THE START OF A.

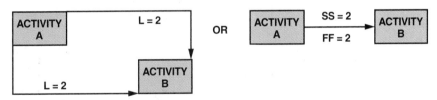

(E) COMPOSITE START-TO-START AND FINISH-TO-FINISH RELATIONSHIP. THE START OF B MUST LAG 2 DAYS AFTER THE START OF A, AND THE FINISH OF B MUST LAG 2 DAYS AFTER THE FINISH OF A.

FIGURE 12–26. Precedence charts with lag.

tracking and controlling projects. While it is clear that even the most sophisticated software package is not a substitute for competent project leadership—and by itself does not identify or correct any task-related problems—it can be a terrific aid to the project manager in tracking the many interrelated variables and tasks that come into play with a modern project. Specific examples of these capabilities are:

- Project data summary: expenditure, timing, and activity data
- Project management and business graphics capabilities
- Data management and reporting capabilities
- Critical path analysis
- Customized, as well as standard, reporting formats
- Multiproject tracking
- Subnetworking
- Impact analysis (what if . . .)
- Early-warning systems
- On-line analysis of recovering alternatives
- Graphical presentation of cost, time, and activity data
- Resource planning and analysis
- Cost analysis, variance analysis
- Multiple calendars
- Resource leveling

Further, many of the more sophisticated software packages that, until the mid-1980s, needed mainframe computer support, are now available for personal computers. This offers many advantages ranging from true user interaction, to ready access and availability, to simpler and more user-friendly interfaces, to often considerably lower software cost. Yet the biggest impact might be to smaller businesses and projects that in the past could not afford the luxury of mainframe computers, but now have access to computer-aided project management systems.

12.15 SOFTWARE FEATURES OFFERED

Project management software capabilities and features vary a great deal among the many products available. However, the variation is more in the depth and sophistication of the feature, such as its storage, display, analysis, interoperability, and user friendliness, rather than in the type of features offered, which are very similar for most software programs. Specifically, the following features are being offered by most project management software packages:

1. *Planning, tracking, and monitoring.* These most common features provide for planning and tracking of the projects' tasks, resources, and costs. The data format for describing the project to the computer is usually based on standard network typologies such as the Critical Path Method (CPM), Program Evaluation and Review Technique (PERT), or Precedence Diagram Method (PDM). Task elements, with their estimated start and finish times, their assigned resources, and actual cost data, can be entered

and updated as the project progresses. The software provides an analysis of the data and documents the technical and financial status of the project against its schedule and original plan. Usually, the software also provides impact assessments of plan deviations and resource and schedule projections. Many systems also provide resource leveling, a feature that averages out available resources to determine task duration and generates a leveled schedule for comparison. The specific analysis reports are described next.

2. *Reports.* Project reporting is usually achieved via a menu-driven report writer system that allows the user to request several standard reports in a standard format. The user can also modify these reports or create new ones. Depending on the sophistication of the system and its peripheral hardware, these reports are supported by a full range of Gantt charts, network diagrams, tabular summaries, and business graphics. A sample of reporting capabilities available today includes:

- Budgeted cost for work scheduled (BCWS) report
- Budgeted cost for work performed (BCWP) report
- Actual versus planned expenditure report
- Earned value analysis
- Cost and schedule performance indices
- Cash-flow reports
- Critical path analysis
- Change order reports
- Standard government reports (DoD, DoE, NASA), formatted for the performance monitoring system (PMS)

In addition, many software packages feature a user-oriented, free-format report writer for styled project reporting.

3. *Project calendar.* This feature allows the user to establish work weeks based on actual workdays. Hence, the user can specify nonwork periods such as weekends, holidays, and vacations. The project calendar can be printed out in detail or in a summary format and is automatically the basis for all computer-assisted resource scheduling.

4. *What-if analysis.* Some software is designed to make what-if analyses easy. A separate, duplicate project database is established and the desired changes are entered. Then the software performs a comparative analysis and displays the new against the old project plan in tabular or graphical form for fast and easy management review and analysis.

5. *Multiproject analysis.* Some of the more sophisticated software packages feature a single, comprehensive database that facilitates cross-project analysis and reporting. Cost and schedule modules share common files that allow integration among projects and minimize problems of data inconsistencies and redundancies.

12.16 SOFTWARE CLASSIFICATION

For purposes of easy classification, project management software products have been divided into three categories based on the type of functions and features they provide.[13]

Level I software. Designed for single-project planning, these software packages are simple, easy to use, and their outputs are easy to understand. They do provide, however, only a limited analysis of the data. They do not provide automatic rescheduling based on specific changes. Therefore, deviations from the original project plan require complete replanning of the project and a complete new data input to the computer.

Level II software. Designed for single project management, these software packages aid project leaders in the planning, tracking, and reporting of projects. They provide a comprehensive analysis of the project, progress reports, and plan revisions, based on actual performance. This type of software is designed for managing projects beyond the planning stage, and for providing semiautomatic project control.

Level III software. These packages feature multiproject planning, monitoring, and control by utilizing a common database and sophisticated cross-project monitoring and reporting software.

Most software packages at levels II and III have the following extensive capabilities for project monitoring and control:

1. *System capacity.* The number of activities and/or number of subnetworks that may be used.
2. *Network schemes.* The network schemes are activity diagram (AD) and/or precedence relationship (PRE).
3. *Calendar dates.* An internal calendar is available to schedule the project's activities. The variations and options of the different calendar algorithms are numerous.
4. *Gantt or bar charts.* A graphic display of the output on a time scale is available if desired.
5. *Flexible report generator.* The user can specify within defined guidelines the format of the output.
6. *Updating.* The program will accept revised time estimates and completion dates and recompute the revised schedule.
7. *Cost control.* The program accepts budgeted cost figures for each activity and then the actual cost incurred, and summarizes the budgeted and actual figures on each updating run. The primary objective is to help management produce a realistic cost plan before the project is started and to assist in the control of the project expenditures as the work progresses.

---

13. Some standards were initially set by *PC Magazine,* "Project Management with the PC," Vol. 3, No. 24, December 11, 1984.

8. *Scheduled dates.* A date is specified for the completion of any of the activities for purposes of planning and control. The calculations are performed with these dates as constraints.

9. *Sorting.* The program lists the activities in a sequence specified by the user.

10. *Resource allocation.* The program attempts to allocate resources optimally using one of many heuristic algorithms.

11. *Plotter availability.* A plotter is available to plot the network diagram.

12. *Machine requirements.* This is the minimum hardware memory requirement for the program (in units of bytes).

13. *Cost.* Indicates whether the program is sold and/or leased and the purchase price and/or lease price (where available).

12.17 PROJECT SOFTWARE EVALUATION

From the middle 1970s to the early 1980s, companies invested heavily in mainframe project management software with costs varying between $75,000 and $125,000. Acceptance of these packages was difficult because only an elite few truly understood the jargon and were capable of using the programs. Turnaround of information was measured in days. Comprehensive evaluation of these programs was difficult because of the complexity of the operating instructions, most of which were not very user-friendly.

Today there exist more than 200 software packages on program management ranging from the large $100,000+ mainframe packages to the small $10 diskette that simply calculates the critical path. The majority of these programs are now user-friendly and capable of running on PCs. Many of the software packages priced between $500–$1,000 have capabilities equivalent to earlier generation mainframe packages.

The ease of use of these packages has allowed organizations to develop very sophisticated evaluation mechanisms for comparing software programs. The National Software Testing Laboratories (NSTL) of Conshohoken, Pennsylvania, utilizes the following methodology for comparing software programs:[14]

- Performance
  - Print GANTT to LaserJet
  - Print PERT to LaserJet
  - Print GANTT to PaintJet
  - Print PERT to PaintJet
  - Change views
  - Recalculate schedule
  - Level resources
- Quality
  - GANTT chart on LaserJet
  - PERT chart on LaserJet
  - GANTT chart on PaintJet
  - PERT chart on PaintJet
  - Resource leveling
- Versatility
  - Project calendar (see Figure 12–27)

---

14. Project Management Programs, *Software Digest,* Volume 7, November 16 © 1990 by NSTL, Plymouth Corporate Center, Plymouth Meeting, Pennsylvania, 19462. (880)-223-7093.

- Scheduling constraints
- Task durations (see Figure 12–28)
- Precedence relationships
- Other scheduling features
- Outlining
- Resource information (see Figure 12–29)
- Resource/cost allocations
- Leveling
- Task tracking
- Resource allocation tracking
- GANTT charts (see Figure 12–30)
- PERT charts
- Schedule reporting (see Figure 12–31)
- Resource schedule reporting
- Resource profile reporting
- Cost reporting (see Figuer 12–32)
- Cash flow reporting
- Earned value analysis
- Sorting
- Selecting

- Output
- Import/export
- Networking
- Multiple project support
- Miscellaneous
- Ease of learning
- Manuals and learning aids
- General program interface
- Project set-up
- Editing a project
- Tracking progress
- Preparing reports
- File management and printing
- General ease of learning
- Ease of use
  - Manuals and learning aids
  - General program interface
  - Project set-up
  - Editing a project
  - Tracking progress
  - Preparing reports
  - File management and printing
  - General ease of use

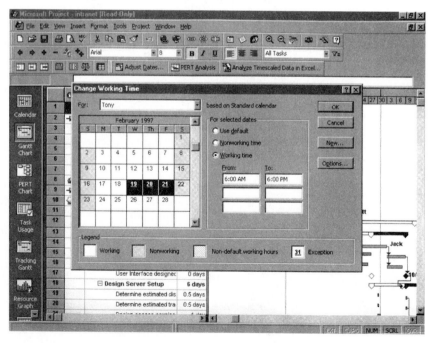

FIGURE 12–27. Project calendar.

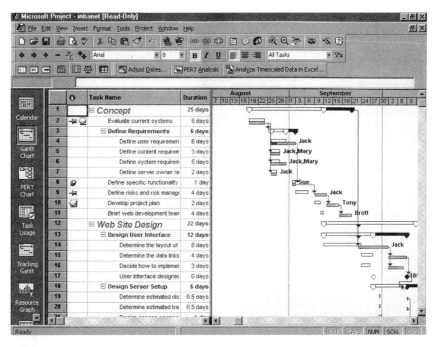

FIGURE 12–28. Task durations.

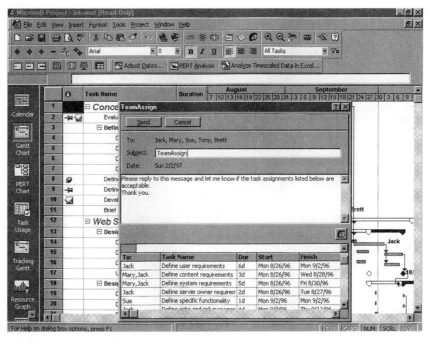

FIGURE 12–29. Resource information.

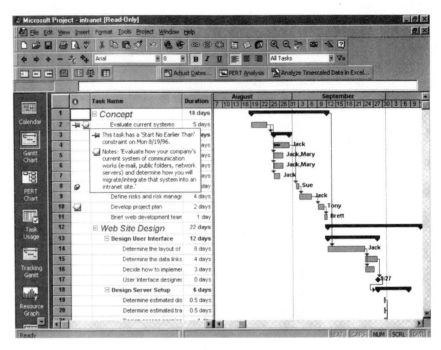

FIGURE 12–30. GANTT charts.

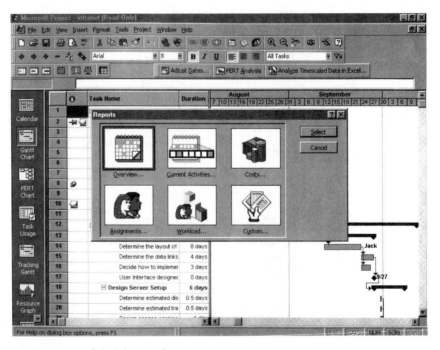

FIGURE 12–31. Schedule reporting.

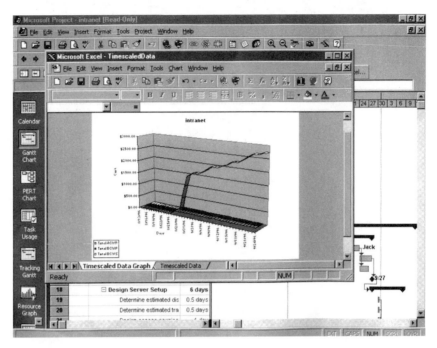

FIGURE 12–32. Cost reporting.

12.18 IMPLEMENTATION PROBLEMS

Generally speaking, mainframe software packages are more difficult to implement than smaller packages, because everyone is requested to use the same package, perhaps even the same way. The following are common difficulties during implementation:

- *Upper-level management may not like the reality of the output.* The output usually shows top management that more time and resources are needed than originally anticipated. This can also be a positive note for the project manager, who is forced to deal with severe resource constraints.
- *Upper-level management may not use the packages for planning, budgeting, and decision making.* Upper-level personnel generally prefer the more traditional methods, or simply refuse to look at reality because of politics. As a result, the plans they submit to the board are based on an eye-pleasing approach for quick acceptance, rather than reality.
- *Day-to-day project planners may not use the packages for their own projects.* Project managers often rely on other planning methods and tools from previous assignments. They rely heavily on instinct and trial and error.
- *Upper-level management may not demonstrate support and commitment to training.* Ongoing customized training is mandatory for successful implementation, even though each project may vary.

- *Use of mainframe software requires strong internal communications lines for support.* Managers who share resources must talk to one another continually.
- *Clear, concise reports are lacking.* Large mainframe packages can generate volumes of data, even if the package has a report writer package.
- *Mainframe packages do not always provide for immediate turnabout of information.* This is often the result of not understanding how to utilize the new systems.
- The business entity may not have any project management standards in place prior to implementation. This relates to a lack of WBS numbering schemes, no life-cycle phases, and a poor understanding of task dependencies.
- *Implementation may highlight middle management's inexperience in project planning and organizational skills.* Fear of its use is a key factor in not obtaining proper support.
- *The business environment and organizational structure may not be appropriate to meet project management/planning needs.* If extensive sharing of resources exists, then the organizational structure should be a formal or informal matrix. If the organization is deeply entrenched in a traditional structure, then organizational mismatch exists and the software system may not be accepted.
- *Sufficient/extensive resources (staff, equipment, etc.) are required.* Large mainframe packages consume a significant amount of resources in the implementation phase.
- *The business entity must determine the extent of, and appropriate use of, the systems within the organization.* Should it be used by all organizations? Should it be used only on high-priority projects?
- *The system may be viewed as a substitute for the extensive interpersonal skills required by the project manager.* Software systems do not replace the need for project managers with strong communications and negotiation skills.
- *Software implementation is less likely to succeed if the organization does not have sufficient training in project management principles.* This barrier is perhaps the underlying problem for all of the other barriers.

PROBLEMS

12–1 Should a PERT/CPM network become a means of understanding reports and schedules, or should it be vice versa?

12–2 Before PERT diagrams are prepared, should the person performing the work have a clear definition of the requirements and objectives, both prime and supporting? Is it an absolute necessity?

12–3 Who prepares the PERT diagrams? Who is responsible for their integration?

12–4 Should PERT networks follow the work breakdown structure?

12–5 How can a PERT network be used to increase functional ability to relate to the total program?

12–6 What problems are associated with applying PERT to small programs?

12–7 Should PERT network design be dependent on the number of elements in the work breakdown structure?

12–8 Can bar charts and PERT diagrams be used to smooth out departmental manpower requirements?

12–9 Should key milestones be established at points where trade-offs are most likely to occur?

12–10 Would you agree or disagree that the cost of accelerating a project rises exponentially, especially as the project nears completion?

12–11 What are the major difficulties with PERT, and how can they be overcome?

12–12 Is PERT/cost designed to identify critical schedule slippages and cost overruns early enough that corrective action can be taken?

12–13 Draw the network and identify the critical path. Also calculate the earliest–latest starting and finishing times for each activity:

Activity	Preceding Activity	Time (Weeks)
A	—	7
B	—	8
C	—	6
D	A	6
E	B	6
F	B	8
G	C	4
H	D, E	7
I	F, G, H	3

12–14 Draw the network and identify the critical path. Also calculate the earliest–latest starting and finishing times for each activity:

Activity	Preceding Activity	Time (Weeks)
A	—	4
B	—	6
C	A, B	7
D	B	8
E	B	5
F	C	5
G	D	7
H	D, E	8
I	F, G, H	4

12–15 Consider the following network for a small maintenance project (all times are in days; network proceeds from node 1 to node 7):

    a. Draw an arrow diagram representing the project.
    b. What is the critical path and associated time?

| Job | Network | | Optimistic | Pessimistic | Most |
(Activity)	Initial Node	Final Node	Time	Time	Likely
A	1	2	1	3	2
B	1	4	4	6	5
C	1	3	4	6	5
D	2	6	2	4	3
E	2	4	1	3	2
F	3	4	2	4	3
G	3	5	7	15	9
H	4	6	4	6	5
I	4	7	6	14	10
J	4	5	1	3	2
K	5	7	2	4	3
L	6	7	6	14	10

    c. What is the total slack time in the network?

    d. What is the expected time for 68, 95, and 99 percent completion limits?

    e. If activity G had an estimated time of fifteen days, what impact would this have on your answer to part b?

12–16 Consider the following network for a small MIS project (all times are in days; network proceeds from node 1 to node 10):

| Job (Activity) | Network | | Estimated Time |
	Initial Node	Final Node	
A	1	2	2
B	1	3	3
C	1	4	3
D	2	5	3
E	2	9	3
F	3	5	1
G	3	6	2
H	3	7	3
I	4	7	5
J	4	8	3
K	5	6	3
L	6	9	4
M	7	9	4
N	8	9	3
O	9	10	2

    a. Identify the critical path.

    b. Calculate the total network slack time.

    c. Suppose that activities A, B, and C all utilize the same manpower base, and shortening any one of these three activities causes one of the other two to increase by the same amount. Can network replanning, only for these three activities, shorten the length of the critical path?

    d. Repeat parts a, b, and c assuming that the estimated time for job C is 4.

12–17 On May 1, Arnie Watson sent a memo to his boss, the director of project management, stating that the MX project would require thirteen weeks for completion according to the figure shown below.

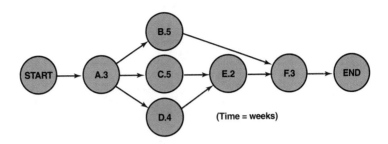

Arnie realized that the customer wanted the job completed in less time. After discussions with the functional managers, Arnie developed the table shown below:

	Normal		Crash		
Activity	Time	Cost	Time	Cost	Additional (Crash) Cost/Week
A	3	6,000	2	8,000	2,000
B	5	12,000	4	13,500	1,500
C	5	16,000	3	22,000	3,000
D	4	8,000	2	10,000	1,000
E	2	6,000	1	7,500	1,500
F	3	14,000	1	20,000	3,000
		$62,000			

   a. According to the contract, there is a penalty payment of $5,000 per week for every week over six. What is the minimum amount of additional funding that Arnie should request?

   b. Suppose your answer to part a gives you the same additional minimum cost for both an eight-week and a nine-week project. What factors would you consider before deciding whether to do it in eight or nine weeks?

12–18 On March 1, the project manager received three status reports indicating resource utilization to date. Shown below are the three reports as well as the PERT diagram.

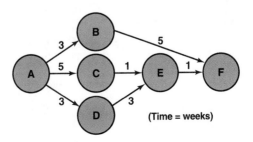

PERCENT-COMPLETION REPORT

Activity	Date Started	% Completed	Time to Complete
AB	2/1	100%	—
AC	2/1	60%	2
AD	2/1	100%	—
DE*	not started	—	3
BF	2/14	40%	3

*Note: Because of priorities, resources for activity DE will not be available until 3/14. Management estimates that this activity can be crashed from 3 weeks to 2 weeks at an additional cost of $3,000

PROJECT PLANNING BUDGET: WEEKS AFTER GO-AHEAD

Activity	1	2	3	4	5	6	7	8	Total $
AB	2,000	2,000	2,000	—	—	—	—	—	6,000
AC	3,000	4,000	4,000	4,000	5,000	—	—	—	20,000
AD	2,000	3,000	2,500	—	—	—	—	—	7,500
BF	—	—	—	2,000	3,000	4,000	3,000	3,000	15,000
CE	—	—	—	—	—	2,500	—	—	2,500
DE	—	—	—	3,500	3,500	3,500	—	—	10,500
EF	—	—	—	—	—	—	3,000	—	3,000
Total	7,000	9,000	8,500	9,500	11,500	10,000	6,000	3,000	64,500

COST SUMMARY

Activity	Week Ending Budget Cost	Week Ending Actual	Week Ending (Over) Under	Cumulative to Date Budget Cost	Cumulative to Date Actual	Cumulative to Date (Over) Under
AB	—	—	—	6,000	6,200	(200)
AC	4,000	4,500	(500)	15,000	12,500	2,500
AD	—	2,400	(2,400)	7,500	7,400	100
BF	2,000	2,800	(800)	2,000	4,500	(2,500)
DE	3,500	—	3,500	3,500	—	3,500
Total	9,500	9,700	(200)	34,000	30,600	3,400

a. As of the end of week 4, how much time is required to complete the project (i.e., time to complete)?

b. At the end of week 4, are you over/under budget, and by how much, for the work (either partial or full) that has been completed to date? (This is *not* a cost to complete.)

c. At what point in time should the decision be made to crash activities?

d. Either construct a single table by which cost and performance data are more easily seen, or modify the above tables accordingly.

To solve this problem, you must make an assumption about the relationship between percent complete and time/cost. In the project planning budget table, assume that percent complete is *linear* with time and *nonlinear* with cost (i.e., cost must be read from table.).

12–19 Can PERT charts have more depth than the WBS?

12–20 Estimating activity time is not an easy task, especially if assumptions must be made. State whether each item identified below can be accounted for in the construction of a PERT/CPM network:

   a. Consideration of weather conditions
   b. Consideration of weekend activities
   c. Unleveled manpower requirements
   d. Checking of resource allocations
   e. Variable crew size
   f. Splitting (or interrupting) of activities
   g. Assignment of unused resources
   h. Accounting for project priorities

12–21 Scheduling departmental manpower for a project is a very difficult task, even if slack time is available. Many managers would prefer to supply manpower at a constant rate rather than continually shuffle people in and out of a project.

   a. Using the information shown below, construct the PERT network, identify the critical path, and determine the slack time for each node.

Activity	Weeks	Personnel Required (Full-time)
A–B	5	3
A–C	3	3
B–D	2	4
B–E	3	5
C–E	3	5
D–F	3	5
E–F	6	3

   b. The network you have just created is a departmental PERT chart. Construct a weekly manpower plot assuming that all activities begin as early as possible. (Note: Overtime cannot be used to shorten the activity time.)
   c. The department manager wishes to assign eight people full-time for the duration of the project. However, if an employee is no longer needed on the project, he can be assigned elsewhere. Using the base of eight people, identify the standby (or idle) time and the overtime periods.
   d. Determine the standby and overtime costs, assuming that each employee is paid $300 per week and overtime is paid at time and a half. During standby time the employee draws his full salary.
   e. Repeat parts c and d and try to consider slack time in order to smooth out the manpower curve. (Hint: Some activities should begin as early as possible, while others begin as late as possible.) Identify the optimum manpower level so as to minimize the standby and overtime costs. Assume all employees must work full-time.

f. Would your answer to parts d and e change if the employees must remain for the full duration of the project, even if they are no longer required?

12–22 How does a manager decide whether the work breakdown structure should be based on a "tree" diagram or the PERT diagram?

12–23 Using Table 12–3, draw the CPM chart for the project. In this case, make all identifications on the arrows (activities) rather than the events. Show that the critical path is twenty-one weeks.

Using Table 12–4, draw the precedence chart for the project, showing interrelationships. Try to use a different color or shade for the critical path.

Calculate the *minimum* cash flow needed for the first four weeks of the project, assuming the following distribution.

Activity	Total Cost for Each Activity
A–H	16,960
I–P	5,160
Q–V	40,960
W	67,200
X	22,940

Furthermore, assume that *all* costs are linear with time, and that the activity X cost must be spent in the first two weeks. Prove that the minimum cash flow is $92,000.

TABLE 12–3.   DATA FOR PROJECT CPM CHART

Activity	Preceding Activity	Normal Time (Weeks)
A	—	4
B	A	6
C	B,U,V,N	3
D	C	2
E	C	2
F	C	7
G	C	7
H	D,E	4
I	—	2
J	I,R	1
K	J	1
L	K	2
M	L	1
N	M	1
O	N	2
P	O	1
Q	—	4
R	Q	1
S	—	1
T	—	1
U	S	2
V	T	2
W*	—	*
X	—	2

*Stands for total length of project. This is management support.

TABLE 12–4. PROJECT PRECEDENCE CHART*

Weeks

Activity	1	2	3	4	5	6	7	8	9	10	11	12	13	14	15	16	17	18	19	20	21
A																					
B																					
C																					
D																					
E																					
F																					
G																					
H																					
I																					
J																					
K																					
L																					
M																					
N																					
O																					
P																					
Q																					
R																					
S																					
T																					
U																					
V																					
W																					
X																					

*Draw the appropriate bar charts into the figure, assuming that such activity starts as early as possible (identify slack). Try to show the interrelationships as in a precedence network.

CASE STUDIES

CROSBY MANUFACTURING CORPORATION

"I've called this meeting to resolve a major problem with our management cost and control system (MCCS)," remarked Wilfred Livingston, president. "We're having one hell of a time trying to meet competition with our antiquated MCCS reporting procedures. Last year we were considered nonresponsive to three large government contracts because we could not adhere to the customer's financial reporting requirements. The government has recently shown a renewed interest in Crosby Manufacturing Corporation. If we can computerize our project financial reporting procedure, we'll be in great shape to meet the competition head-on. The customer might even waive the financial reporting requirements if we show our immediate intent to convert."

Crosby Manufacturing was a $50-million-a-year electronics component manufacturing firm in 1985, at which time Wilfred "Willy" Livingston became president. His first major act was to reorganize the 700 employees into a modified matrix structure. This reorganization was the first step in Livingston's long-range plan to obtain large government contracts. The matrix provided the customer focal point policy that government agencies prefer. After three years, the matrix seemed to be working. Now they could begin the second phase, an improved MCCS policy.

On October 20, 1988, Livingston called a meeting with department managers from project management, cost accounting, MIS, data processing, and planning.

Livingston: "We have to replace our present computer with a more advanced model so as to update our MCCS reporting procedures. In order for us to grow, we'll have to develop capabilities for keeping two or even three different sets of books for our customers. Our present computer does not have this capability. We're talking about a sizable cash outlay, not necessarily to impress our customers, but to increase our business base and grow. We need weekly, or even daily, cost data so as to better control our projects."

MIS Manager: "I guess the first step in the design, development, and implementation process would be the feasibility study. I have prepared a list of the major topics which are normally included in a feasibility study of this sort" (see Exhibit 12–1).

Exhibit 12–1. Feasibility Study

- Objectives of the study
- Costs
- Benefits
- Manual or computer-based solution?
- Objectives of the system
- Input requirements
- Output requirements
- Processing requirements
- Preliminary system description
- Evaluation of bids from vendors
- Financial analysis
- Conclusions

Exhibit 12–2. Typical Schedule (in Months)

Activity	Normal Time to Complete	Crash Time to Complete
Management go-ahead	0	0
Release of preliminary system specs.	6	2
Receipt of bids on specs.	2	1
Order hardware and systems software	2	1
Flow charts completed	2	2
Applications programs completed	3	6
Receipt of hardware and systems software	3	3
Testing and debugging done	2	2
Documentation, if required	2	2
Changeover completed	22	15*

*This assumes that some of the activities can be run in parallel, instead of series.

Livingston: "What kind of costs are you considering in the feasibility study?"

MIS Manager: "The major cost items include input–output demands; processing; storage capacity; rental, purchase or lease of a system; nonrecurring expenditures; recurring expenditures; cost of supplies; facility requirements; and training requirements. We'll have to get a lot of this information from the EDP department."

EDP Manager: "You must remember that, for a short period of time, we'll end up with two computer systems in operation at the same time. This cannot be helped. However, I have prepared a typical (abbreviated) schedule of my own (see Exhibit 12–2). You'll notice from the right-hand column that I'm somewhat optimistic as to how long it should take us."

Livingston: "Have we prepared a checklist on how to evaluate a vendor?"

EDP Manager: "Besides the 'benchmark' test, I have prepared a list of topics that we must include in evaluation of any vendor (see Exhibit 12–3). We should plan to call on or visit other installations that have purchased the same equipment and see the sys-

Exhibit 12–3. Vendor Support Evaluation Factors

- Availability of hardware and software packages
- Hardware performance, delivery, and past track record
- Vendor proximity and service-and-support record
- Emergency backup procedure
- Availability of applications programs and their compatibility with our other systems
- Capacity for expansion
- Documentation
- Availability of consultants for systems programming and general training
- Who burdens training cost?
- Risk of obsolescence
- Ease of use

tem in action. Unfortunately, we may have to commit real early and begin developing software packages. As a matter of fact, using the principle of concurrency, we should begin developing our software packages right now."

Livingston: "Because of the importance of this project, I'm going to violate our normal structure and appoint Tim Emary from our planning group as project leader. He's not as knowledgeable as you people are in regard to computers, but he does know how to lay out a schedule and get the job done. I'm sure your people will give him all the necessary support he needs. Remember, I'll be behind this project all the way. We're going to convene again one week from today, at which time I expect to see a detailed schedule with all major milestones, team meetings, design review meetings, etc., shown and identified. I'd like the project to be complete in eighteen months, if possible. If there are risks in the schedule, identify them. Any questions?"

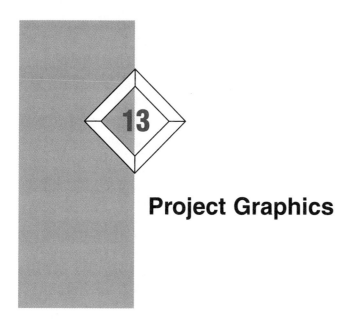

Project Graphics

13.0 INTRODUCTION

In Chapter 11, we defined the steps involved in establishing a formal program plan with detailed schedules such that the total program can be effectively managed. Once the need has arisen to commit the plan to paper via the master program plan, suitable notations must be adapted. Any plan, schedule, drawing, or specification that will be read by more than one person must be regarded as a vehicle for the communication of information. If effective communication is to be established and maintained in compliance with the requirements, this information must be expressed in a language that is understood by all recipients.

The ideal situation is to construct charts and schedules in suitable notation that can be used for both in-house control and out-of-house customer status reporting. Unfortunately, this is easier said than done. Whenever a project has to be accomplished according to a time or date deadline, then both the customer and contractor must have an accurate picture of the relations between the time allowed and the time needed. Both the customer and contractor are interested mainly in the three vital control parameters:

- Time
- Cost
- Performance

All schedules and charts should consider these three parameters and their relationship to corporate resources.

Information must be available such that proper project evaluation can be made. There are four methods for project evaluation:

- Firsthand observation
- Oral and written reports

- Review and technical interchange meetings
- Graphical displays

Firsthand observations are an excellent tool for obtaining nonfiltered information. Many times, functional managers get a deep sense of pride when they see key project personnel observing work, provided that these personnel are, in fact, observing and not providing direction. Firsthand observation may not be possible on large projects.

Although oral and written reports are a way of life, they often contain either too much or not enough detail. Significant information may be disguised. Most organizations do not have standardized reporting procedures, which further complicates the situation.

Review and technical interchange meetings provide face-to-face communications between all concerned parties, a situation that can often result in immediate agreement on problem definitions or solutions, such as changing a schedule. The difficult problem is in the selection of attendees from the customer's and the contractor's organizations.

Graphical displays are the prime means for tracking cost, schedule, and performance. Good graphics usually makes the information easy to identify. Unfortunately, not all information can be displayed, and quite often any additional information requests require additional cost and effort. Proper graphical displays can result in:

- Cutting project costs and reducing the time scale
- Coordinating and expediting planning
- Eliminating idle time
- Obtaining better scheduling and control of subcontractor activities
- Developing better troubleshooting procedures
- Cutting time for routine decisions, but allowing more time for decision making

13.1 CUSTOMER REPORTING

There exist between thirty and forty different visual methods for the representation of activities. The exact method chosen should depend on the intended audience. For example, upper-level management may be interested in costs and integration of activities, with very little detail. Summary-type charts normally suffice for this purpose. Daily practitioners, on the other hand, may require that as much detail as possible be included in activity schedules. If the schedule is to be presented to the customer, then the presentation should include cost and performance data.

The presentation of cost and performance data must be considered as both a science and an art. As a science, the figures and graphs should be describable in terms of symbols and expressions that are easily understandable. As an art, the diagram should rapidly bring across the intended message or objective. In many organizations, each department or division may have its own method of showing scheduling activities. Research and development organizations prefer to show the logic of activities rather than the integration of activities that would normally be representative of a manufacturing plant.

The ability to communicate is a definite prerequisite for successful management of a program. Program review meetings, technical interchange meetings, customer summary meetings, and in-house management control meetings all require different representative forms of current program performance status. The final form of the schedule may be bar charts, graphs, tables, bubble charts, or logic diagrams. In the sections that follow, a variety of charting techniques, together with the associated limitations, are described for various types of a program. The reader should be able to realize the advantages and disadvantages of each chart in relation to his own program activities.

13.2 BAR (GANTT) CHART

The most common type of display is the bar or Gantt chart, named for Henry Gantt, who first utilized this procedure in the early 1900s. The bar chart is a means of displaying simple activities or events plotted against time or dollars. An activity represents the amount of work required to proceed from one point in time to another. Events are described as either the starting or ending point for either one or several activities.

Bar charts are most commonly used for exhibiting program progress or defining specific work required to accomplish an objective. Bar charts often include such items as listings of activities, activity duration, schedule dates, and progress-to-date. Figure 13–1 shows nine activities required to start up a production line for a new product. Each bar in the figure represents a single activity. Figure 13–1 is a typical bar chart that would be developed by the program office at program inception.

Bar charts are advantageous in that they are simple to understand and easy to change. They are the simplest and least complex means of portraying progress (or the lack of it) and can easily be expanded to identify specific elements that may be either behind or ahead of schedule.

Bar charts provide only a vague description of how the entire program or project reacts as a system. There are three major discrepancies in the use of a bar chart. First, bar charts do not show the interdependencies of the activities, and therefore do not represent a "network" of activities. This relationship between activities is crucial for controlling program costs. Without this relationship, bar charts have little predictive value. For example, does the long-lead procurement activity in Figure 13–1 require that the contract be signed before procurement can begin? Can the manufacturing plans be written without the material specifications activity being completed? The second major discrepancy is that the bar chart cannot show the results of either an early or a late start

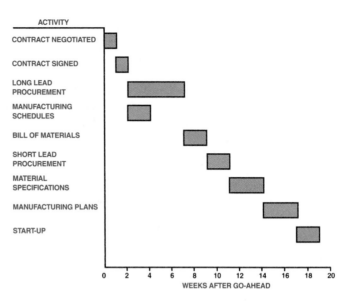

FIGURE 13–1. Bar chart for single activities.

in activities. How will a slippage of the manufacturing schedules activity in Figure 13–1 affect the completion date of the program? Can the manufacturing schedules activity begin two weeks later than shown and still serve as an input to the bill of materials activity? What will be the result of a crash program to complete activities in sixteen weeks after go-ahead instead of the originally planned nineteen weeks? Bar charts do not reflect true project status because elements behind schedule do not mean that the program or project is behind schedule. The third limitation is that the bar chart does not show the uncertainty involved in performing the activity and, therefore, does not readily admit itself to sensitivity analysis. For instance, what is the shortest time that an activity might take? What is the longest time? What is the average or expected time to activity completion?

Even with these limitations, bar charts do, in fact, serve as a useful tool for program analysis. Even the earliest form of bar chart, as developed by Henry Gantt, still has merit under certain circumstances. Figure 13–2 shows the conventional usage for work scheduled in a production facility for twelve days in January. On Thursday of the first week, the production facility was idle owing to lack of materials. By the end of the workday on Friday of the first week, only 280 out of the planned 300 units were produced. The production line was not available on either Saturday or Sunday, and operations resumed Monday. On Tuesday, the production line was down for repairs and did not resume operations until Thursday. Operations were sporadic on Thursday and Friday, and by the end of the day, only 340 out of a scheduled 400 units were completed. These types of ap-

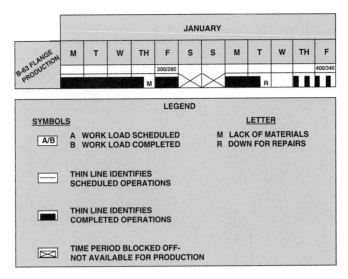

FIGURE 13–2. Manufacturing schedule for Model B-63 flanges.

plications are commonly used for equipment layout and usage, department loading, and progress tracking.[1]

Some of the limitations of bar charts can be overcome by combining single activities as shown in Figure 13–3. The weakness in this method is that the numbers representing each of the activities do not indicate whether this is the beginning or the end of the activity. Therefore, the numbers should represent events rather than activities, together with proper identification. As before, no distinction is made as to whether even 2 must be completed prior to the start of event 3 or event 4. The chart also fails to define clearly the relationship between the multiple activities on a single bar. For example, must event 3 be completed prior to event 5? Often, combined activity bar charts can be converted to milestone bar charts by placing small triangles at strategic locations in the bars to indicate completion of certain milestones within each activity or grouping of activities, as shown in Figure 13–4. The exact definition of a milestone differs from company to company, but usually implies some point where major activity either begins or ends, or cost data become critical.

Bar charts can be converted to partial interrelationship charts by indicating (with arrows) the order in which activities must be performed. Figure 13–5 represents the partial interrelationship of the activities in Figures 13–1 and 13–3. A full interrelationship schedule is included under the discussion of PERT networks in Chapter 12.

---

1. A. C. Laufer, *Operations Management* (Cincinnati: Southwestern Publishing Co., 1975); see pp. 106–108 for examples of Gantt charts and nomenclature.

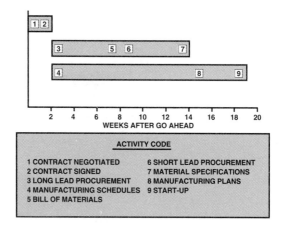

FIGURE 13–3. Bar chart for combined activities.

The most common method of presenting data to both in-house management and the customer is through the use of bar charts. Care must be taken not to make the figures overly complex so that more than one interpretation can exist. A great deal of information and color can be included in bar charts. Figure 13–6 shows a grouped bar chart for comparison of three projects performed during different years. Care must be taken when using different shading techniques that each area is easily definable and that no major contrast between shaded areas exists, except for possibly the current project. When grouped bars appear on one chart, non-shaded bars should be avoided. Each bar should have some sort of shading, whether it be cross-hatched or color-coded.

Contrasting shaded to nonshaded areas is normally used for comparing projected progress to actual progress as shown in Figure 13–7. The tracking date line indicates the time when the cost data/performance data was analyzed. Project 1 is behind schedule, project 2 is ahead of schedule, and project 3 is on target.

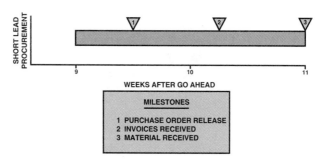

FIGURE 13–4. Bar/milestone chart.

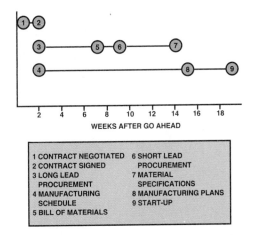

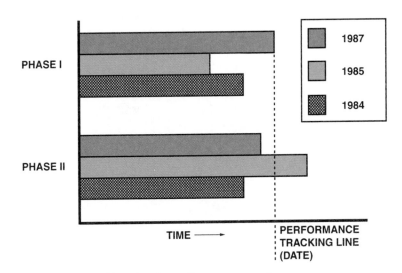

FIGURE 13–5. Partial interrelationship chart.

Unfortunately, the upper portion of Figure 13–7 does not indicate the costs attributed to the status of the three projects. By plotting the total program costs against the same time axis (as shown in Figure 13–7), a comparison between cost and performance can be made. From the upper section of Figure 13–7 it is impossible to tell the current program cost position. From the lower section, however, it becomes evident that the program is heading for a cost overrun, possibly due to project 1. It is generally acceptable to have the same shading technique

FIGURE 13–6. Grouped bar chart for performance comparison.

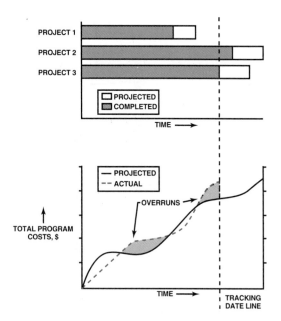

FIGURE 13–7. Cost and performance tracking schedule.

represent different situations, provided that clear separation between the shaded regions appears, as in Figure 13–7.

Another common means for comparing activities or projects is through the use of step arrangement bar charts. Figure 13–8 shows a step arrangement bar chart for a cost percentage breakdown of the five projects included within a pro-

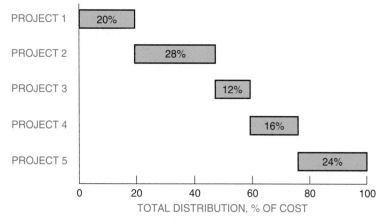

FIGURE 13–8. Step arrangement bar chart for total cost as a percentage of the five program projects.

gram. Figure 13–8 can also be used for tracking, by shading in certain portions of the steps that identify each project. This is not normally done, however, since this type of step arrangement tends to indicate that each step must be completed before the next step can begin.

Bar charts need not be represented horizontally. Figure 13–9 indicates the comparison between the 1989 and 1991 costs for the total program and raw materials. Again, care must be taken to make proper use of shading techniques. Three-dimensional vertical bar charts are often the most beautiful to behold. Figure 13–10 shows a typical three-dimensional bar chart for direct and indirect labor and material cost breakdowns.

Bar charts can be made quite colorful and appealing to the eye by combining them with other graphic techniques. Figure 13–11 shows a quantitative-pictorial bar chart for the distribution of total program costs. Figure 13–12 shows the same cost distribution as in Figure 13–11, but represented with the commonly used pie technique. Figure 13–13 illustrates how two quantitative bar charts can be used side by side to create a quick comparison. The right-hand side shows the labor hour percentages. Figure 13–13 works best if the scale of each axis is the same; otherwise the comparisons may appear distorted when, in fact, they are not.

The figures shown in this section have been previously used by the author for customer interchange meetings and do not, by any means, represent the only method of presented data in bar chart format. Several other methods exist, some of which are shown in the sections that follow.

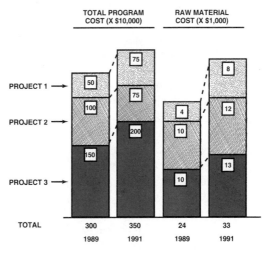

FIGURE 13–9. Cost comparison, 1989 versus 1991.

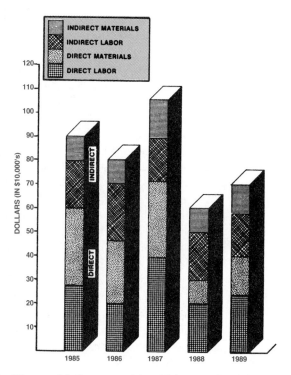

FIGURE 13–10. Direct and indirect material and labor cost breakdowns for all programs per year.

13.3 OTHER CONVENTIONAL PRESENTATION TECHNIQUES

Bar charts serve as a useful tool for presenting data at technical meetings. Unfortunately, programs must be won competitively or organized in-house before technical meeting presentations can be made. Competitive proposals or in-house project requests should contain descriptive figures and charts, not necessarily representing activities, but showing either planning, organizing, tracking, or technical procedures designed for the current program or used previously on other programs. Proposals generally contain figures that require either some interpolation or extrapolation. Figure 13–14 shows the breakdown of total program costs. Although this figure would also normally require interpretation, a monthly cost table accompanies it. If the table is not too extensive, then it can be included with the figure. This is shown in Figure 13–15. During proposal activities, the actual and cumulative delivery columns, as well as the dotted line in Figure 13–15, would be omitted, but would be included after updating for use in technical interchange meetings. It is normally a good practice to use previous figures and tables whenever possible because management becomes accustomed to the manner in which data are presented.

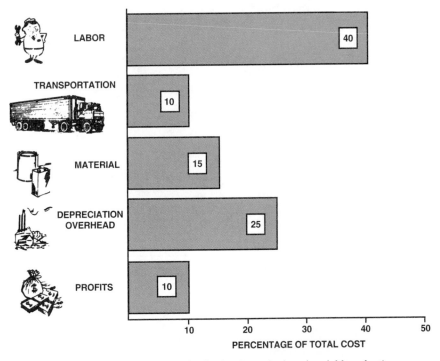

FIGURE 13–11. Total program cost distribution (quantitative-pictorial bar chart).

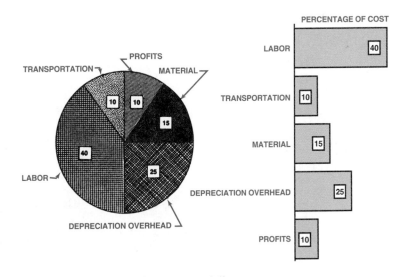

FIGURE 13–12. Distribution of the program dollar.

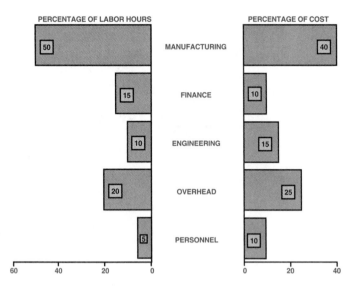

FIGURE 13–13. Divisional breakdown of costs and labor hours.

Another commonly used technique is schematic models. Organizational charts are schematic models that depict the interrelationships between individuals, organizations, or functions within an organization. One organizational chart normally cannot suffice for describing total program interrelationships. Figure 4–10 identified the Midas Program in relation to other programs within Dalton

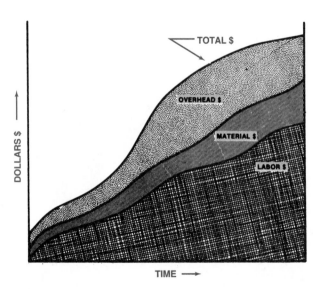

FIGURE 13–14. Total program cost breakdown.

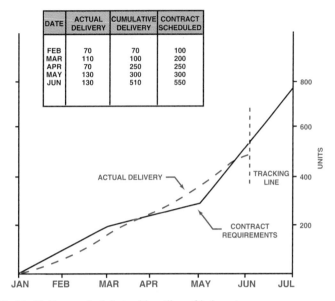

DATE	ACTUAL DELIVERY	CUMULATIVE DELIVERY	CONTRACT SCHEDULED
FEB	70	70	100
MAR	110	100	200
APR	70	250	250
MAY	130	300	300
JUN	130	510	550

FIGURE 13–15. Delivery schedule tracking (line of balance).

Corporation. The Midas Program is indicated by the bold lines. The program manager for the Midas Program was placed at the top of the column, even though his program may have the lowest priority. Each major unit of management for the Midas Program should be placed as close as possible to top-level management to indicate to the customer the "implied" relative importance of the program.

Another type of schematic representation is the work flow chart, synonymous with the application of flowcharting for computer programming. Flow charts are designed to describe, either symbolically or pictorially, the sequence of events required to complete an activity. Figure 13–16 shows the logic flow for production of molding VZ-3. The symbols shown in Figure 13–16 are universally accepted by several industries.

Pictorial representation, although often a costly procedure, can add color and quality to any proposal. Pictorial sketches provide the customer with a document easier to identify with than a logic or bubble chart. Customers may request tours during activities to relate to the pictorial figures. If at all possible, program management should avoid pictorial representation of activities that may be closed off to customer viewing, possibly due to security or safety.

Block diagrams can also be used to describe the flow of activities. Figures 4–12 and 4–13 are examples of block diagrams. Block diagrams can be used to show how information is distributed throughout an organization or how a process or activity is assembled. Figure 13–17 shows the testing matrix for propellant samples. Figures similar to this are developed when tours are scheduled during the production or testing phase of a program. Figure 13–17 shows the customer not only where the testing will take place, but what tests will be conducted.

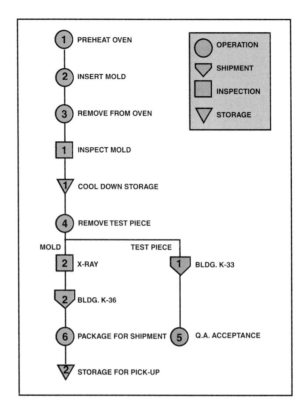

FIGURE 13–16. Logic flow for production of molding VZ-3.

Block diagrams, schematics, pictorials, and logic flows all fulfill a necessary need for describing the wide variety of activities within a company. The figures and charts are more than descriptive techniques. They can also provide management with the necessary tools for decision making.

13.4 LOGIC DIAGRAMS/NETWORKS

Probably the most difficult figure to construct is the logic diagram. Logic diagrams are developed to illustrate the inductive and deductive reasoning necessary to achieve some objective within a given time frame. The major difficulty in developing logic diagrams is the inability to answer such key questions as: What happens if something goes wrong? Can I quantify any part of the diagram's major elements?

Logic diagrams are constructed similar to bar charts on the supposition that nothing will go wrong and are usually accompanied by detailed questions, possi-

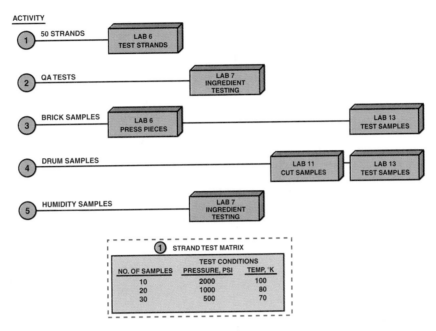

FIGURE 13–17. Propellant samples testing matrix.

bly in a checklist format, that require answering. The following questions would be representative of those that might accompany a logic diagram for a research and development project:

- What documentation is released to start the described activity and possibly the elements within each activity?
- What information is required before this documentation can be released? (What prior activities must be completed, work designed, studies finalized, etc?)
- What are the completion, or success, criteria for the activity?
- What are the alternatives for each phase of the program if success is not achieved?
- What other activities are directly dependent on the result of this activity?
- What other activities or inputs are required to perform this activity?
- What are the key decision points, if any, during the activity?
- What documentation signifies completion of the activity (i.e., report, drawing, etc.)?
- What management approval is required for final documentation?

These types of questions are applicable to many other forms of data presentation, not necessarily logic diagrams.

13–1 For each type of schedule defined in this chapter answer the following questions:

    a. Who prepares the schedule?
    b. Who updates the schedule?
    c. Who should present the data to the customers?

13–2 Should the customers have the right to dictate to the contractor how the schedule should be prepared and presented? What if this request contradicts company policies and procedures?

13–3 Should a different set of schedules and charts be maintained for out-of-house as well as in-house reporting? Should separate schedules be made for each level of management? Is there a more effective way to ease these types of problems?

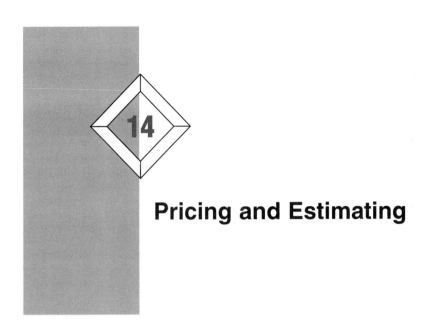

Pricing and Estimating

14.0 INTRODUCTION

With the complexities involved, it is not surprising that many business managers consider pricing an art. Having the right intelligence information on customer cost budgets and competitive pricing would certainly help. However, the reality is that whatever information is available to one bidder is generally available to the others. Even more important, intelligence sources are often unreliable. The only thing worse than missing information is wrong or misleading information. When it comes to competitive pricing, the old saying still applies: "Those who talk don't know; and those who know don't talk!" It is true, partially, that pricing remains an art. However, a disciplined approach certainly helps one to develop all the input for a rational pricing recommendation. A side benefit of using a disciplined management process is that it leads to the documentation of the many factors and assumptions involved at a later point in time. These can be compared and analyzed, contributing to the learning experiences that make up the managerial skills needed for effective business decisions.

Estimates are *not* blind luck. They are well-thought-out decisions based on either the best available information, some type of cost estimating relationship, or some type of cost model. Cost estimating relationships (CERs) are generally the output of cost models. Typical CERs might be:

- Mathematical equations based on regression analysis
- Cost–quantity relationships such as learning curves
- Cost–cost relationships
- Cost–noncost relationships based on physical characteristics, technical parameters, or performance characteristics

741

14.1 GLOBAL PRICING STRATEGIES

Specific pricing strategies must be developed for each individual situation. Frequently, however, one of two situations prevails when one is pursuing project acquisitions competitively. First, the new business opportunity may be a one-of-a-kind program with little or no follow-on potential, a situation classified as type I acquisition. Second, the new business opportunity may be an entry point to a larger follow-on or repeat business, or may represent a planned penetration into a new market. This acquisition is classified as type II.

Clearly, in each case, we have specific but different business objectives. The objective for type I acquisition is to win the program and execute it profitably and satisfactorily according to contractual agreements. The type II objective is often to win the program and perform well, thereby gaining a foothold in a new market segment or a new customer community in place of making a profit. Accordingly, each acquisition type has its own, unique pricing strategy, as summarized in Table 14–1.

Comparing the two pricing strategies for the two global situations (as shown in Table 14–1) reveals a great deal of similarity for the first five points. The fundamental difference is that for a profitable new business acquisition the bid price is determined according to actual cost, whereas in a "must-win" situation the price is determined by the market forces. It should be emphasized that one of the most crucial inputs in the pricing decision is the cost estimate of the proposed baseline. The design of this baseline to the minimum requirements should be started early, in accordance with well-defined ground rules, cost models, and established cost targets. Too often the baseline design is performed in parallel with the proposal development. At the proposal stage it is too late to review and fine-tune the baseline for minimum cost. Also, such a late start does not allow much of an option for a final bid decision. Even if the price appears outside the competitive range, it makes little sense to terminate the proposal development. As all the resources have been sent anyway, one might just as well submit a bid in spite of the remote chance of winning.

Clearly, effective pricing begins a long time before proposal development. It starts with preliminary customer requirements, well-understood subtasks, and a top-down estimate with should-cost targets. This allows the functional organization to design a baseline to meet the customer requirements and cost targets, and gives management the time to review and redirect the design before the proposal is submitted. Furthermore, it gives management an early opportunity to assess the chances of winning during the acquisition cycle, at a point in time when additional resources can be allocated or the acquisition effort can be terminated before too many resources are committed to a hopeless effort.

The final pricing review session should be an integration and review of information already well known in its basic context. The process and management tools outlined here should help to provide the framework and discipline for deriving pricing decisions in an orderly and effective way.

TABLE 14–1. TWO GLOBAL PRICING STRATEGIES

Type I Acquisition: One-of-a-Kind Program with Little or No Follow-On Business	Type II Acquisition: New Program with Potential for Large Follow-On Business or Representing a Desired Penetration into New Markets
1. Develop cost model and estimating guidelines; design proposed project/program baseline for minimum cost, to minimum customer requirements.	1. Design proposed project/program baseline compliant with customer requirements, with innovative features but minimum risks.
2. Estimate cost realistically for minimum requirements.	2. Estimate cost realistically.
3. Scrub the baseline. Squeeze out unnecessary costs.	3. Scrub baseline. Squeeze out unnecessary costs.
4. Determine realistic minimum cost. Obtain commitment from performing organizations.	4. Determine realistic minimum cost. Obtain commitment from performing organizations.
5. Adjust cost estimate for risks.	5. Determine "should-cost" including risk adjustments.
6. Add desired margins. Determine the price.	6. Compare your final cost estimate to customer budget and the "most likely" winning price.
7. Compare price to customer budget and competitive cost information.	7. Determine the gross profit margin necessary for your winning proposal. This margin could be negative!
8. Bid only if price is within competitive range.	8. Decide whether the gross margin is acceptable according to the must-win desire.
	9. Depending on the strength of your desire to win, bid the "most likely" winning price or lower.
	10. If the bid price is below cost, it is often necessary to provide a detailed explanation to the customer of where the additional funding is coming from. The source could be company profits or sharing of related activities. In any case, a clear resource picture should be given to the customer to ensure cost credibility.

14.2 TYPES OF ESTIMATES

Projects can range from a feasibility study, through modification of existing facilities, to complete design, procurement, and construction of a large complex. Whatever the project may be, whether large or small, the estimate and type of information desired may differ radically.

The first type of estimate is an *order-of-magnitude* analysis, which is made without any detailed engineering data. The order-of-magnitude analysis may have an accuracy of ± 35 percent within the scope of the project. This type of estimate may use past experience (not necessarily similar), scale factors, parametric curves or capacity estimates (i.e., $/# of product or $/KW electricity).

Next, there is the *approximate estimate* (or top-down estimate), which is also made without detailed engineering data, and may be accurate to ±15 percent. This type of estimate is prorated from previous projects that are similar in scope and capacity, and may be titled as estimating by analogy, parametric curves, rule of thumb, and indexed cost of similar activities adjusted for capacity and technology. In such a case, the estimator may say that this activity is 50 percent more difficult than a previous (i.e., reference) activity and requires 50 percent more time, man-hours, dollars, materials, and so on.

The *definitive estimate,* or grassroots buildup estimate, is prepared from well-defined engineering data including (as a minimum) vendor quotes, fairly complete plans, specifications, unit prices, and estimate to complete. The definitive estimate, also referred to as detailed estimating, has an accuracy of ±5 percent.

Another method for estimating is the use of *learning curves.* Learning curves are graphical representations of repetitive functions in which continuous operations will lead to a reduction in time, resources, and money. The theory behind learning curves is usually applied to manufacturing operations.

Each company may have a unique approach to estimating. However, for normal project management practices, Table 14–2 would suffice as a starting point.

Many companies try to standardize their estimating procedures by developing an *estimating manual.* The estimating manual is then used to price out the effort, perhaps as much as 90 percent. Estimating manuals usually give better estimates than industrial engineering standards because they include groups of tasks and take into consideration such items as downtime, cleanup time, lunch, and breaks. Table 14–3 shows the table of contents for a construction estimating manual.

Estimating manuals, as the name implies, provide estimates. The question, of course, is "How good are the estimates?" Most estimating manuals provide accuracy limitations by defining the type of estimates (shown in Table 14–3). Using Table 14–3, we can create Tables 14–4, 14–5, and 14–6, which illustrate the use of the estimating manual.

Not all companies can use estimating manuals. Estimating manuals work best for repetitive tasks or similar tasks that can use a previous estimate adjusted by a degree-of-difficulty factor. Activities such as R&D do not lend themselves to the use of estimating manuals other than for benchmark, repetitive laboratory tests. Proposal managers must carefully consider whether the estimating manual

TABLE 14–2. STANDARD PROJECT ESTIMATING

Estimating Method	Generic Type	WBS Relationship	Accuracy	Time to Prepare
Parametric	ROM*	Top down	−25% to +75%	Days
Analogy	Budget	Top down	−10% to +25%	Weeks
Engineering (grass roots)	Definitive	Bottom up	−5% to +10%	Months

*ROM = Rough order of magnitude.

TABLE 14–3. ESTIMATING MANUAL TABLE OF CONTENTS

Introduction
  Purpose and types of estimates
Major Estimating Tools
  Cataloged equipment costs
  Automated investment data system
  Automated estimate system
  Computerized methods and procedures
Classes of Estimates
  Definitive estimate
  Capital cost estimate
  Appropriation estimate
  Feasibility estimate
  Order of magnitude
  Charts—estimate specifications quantity and pricing guidelines
Data Required
  Chart—comparing data required for preparation of classes of estimates
Presentation Specifications
  Estimate procedure—general
  Estimate procedure for definitive estimate
  Estimate procedure for capital cost estimate
  Estimate procedure for appropriation estimate
  Estimate procedure for feasibility estimate

is a viable approach. The literature abounds with examples of companies that have spent millions trying to develop estimating manuals for situations that just do not lend themselves to the approach.

During competitive bidding, it is important that the type of estimate be consistent with the customer's requirements. For in-house projects, the type of estimate can vary over the life cycle of a project:

- *Conceptual stage:* venture guidance or feasibility studies for the evaluation of future work. This estimating is often based on minimum-scope information.
- *Planning stage:* estimating for authorization of partial or full funds. These estimates are based on preliminary design and scope.
- *Main stage:* estimating for detailed work.
- *Termination stage:* reestimation for major scope changes or variances beyond the authorization range.

TABLE 14–4. CLASSES OF ESTIMATES

Class	Types	Accuracy
I	Definitive	±5%
II	Capital cost	±10–15%
III	Appropriation (with some capital cost)	±15–20%
IV	Appropriation	±20–25%
V	Feasibility	±25–35%
VI	Order of magnitude	> ± 35%

TABLE 14–5. CHECKLIST FOR WORK NORMALLY REQUIRED FOR THE VARIOUS CLASSES (I–VI) OF ESTIMATES

Item	I	II	III	IV	V	VI
1. Inquiry	X	X	X	X	X	X
2. Legibility	X	X	X			
3. Copies	X	X				
4. Schedule	X	X	X	X		
5. Vendor inquiries	X	X	X			
6. Subcontract packages	X	X				
7. Listing	X	X	X	X	X	
8. Site visit	X	X	X	X		
9. Estimate bulks	X	X	X	X	X	
10. Labor rates	X	X	X	X	X	
11. Equipment and subcontract selection	X	X	X	X	X	
12. Taxes, insurance, and royalties	X	X	X	X	X	
13. Home office costs	X	X	X	X	X	
14. Construction indirects	X	X	X	X	X	
15. Basis of estimate	X	X	X	X	X	X
16. Equipment list	X					
17. Summary sheet	X	X	X	X	X	
18. Management review	X	X	X	X	X	X
19. Final cost	X	X	X	X	X	X
20. Management approval	X	X	X	X	X	X
21. Computer estimate	X	X	X	X		

14.3 PRICING PROCESS

This activity schedules the development of the work breakdown structure and provides management with two of the three operational tools necessary for the control of a system or project. The development of these two tools is normally the responsibility of the program office with input from the functional units.

The integration of the functional unit into the project environment or system occurs through the pricing-out of the work breakdown structure. The total program costs obtained by pricing out the activities over the scheduled period of performance provide management with the third tool necessary to successfully manage the project. During the pricing activities, the functional units have the option of consulting program management about possible changes in the activity schedules and work breakdown structure.

The work breakdown structure and activity schedules are priced out through the lowest pricing units of the company. It is the responsibility of these pricing units, whether they be sections, departments, or divisions, to provide accurate and meaningful cost data (based on historical standards, if possible). All information is priced out at the lowest level of performance required, which, from the assumption of Chapter 11, will be the task level. Costing information is rolled up to the project level and then one step further to the total program level.

Under ideal conditions, the work required (i.e., man-hours) to complete a given task can be based on historical standards. Unfortunately, for many indus-

TABLE 14–6. DATA REQUIRED FOR PREPARATION OF ESTIMATES

	Classes of Estimates					
	I	II	III	IV	V	VI
General						
Product	X	X	X	X	X	X
Process description	X	X	X	X	X	X
Capacity	X	X	X	X	X	X
Location—general					X	X
Location—specific	X	X	X	X		
Basic design criteria	X	X	X	X		
General design specifications	X	X	X	X		
Process						
Process block flow diagram						X
Process flow diagram (with equipment size and material)				X	X	
Mechanical P&I's	X	X	X			
Equipment list	X	X	X	X	X	
Catalyst/chemical specifications	X	X	X	X	X	
Site						
Soil conditions	X	X	X	X		
Site clearance	X	X	X			
Geological and meteorological data	X	X	X			
Roads, paving, and landscaping	X	X	X			
Property protection	X	X	X			
Accessibility to site	X	X	X			
Shipping and delivery conditions	X	X	X			
Major cost is factored					X	X
Major Equipment						
Preliminary sizes and materials			X	X	X	
Finalized sizes, materials, and appurtenances	X	X				
Bulk Material Quantities						
Finalized design quantity take-off		X				
Preliminary design quantity take-off	X	X	X	X		
Engineering						
Plot plan and elevations	X	X	X	X		
Routing diagrams	X	X	X			
Piping line index	X	X				
Electrical single line	X	X	X	X		
Fire protection	X	X	X			
Sewer systems	X	X	X			
Pro-services—detailed estimate	X	X				
Pro-services—ratioed estimate			X	X	X	
Catalyst/chemicals quantities	X	X	X	X	X	
Construction						
Labor wage, F/B, travel rates	X	X	X	X	X	
Labor productivity and area practices	X	X				
Detailed construction execution plan	X	X				
Field indirects—detailed estimate	X	X				
Field indirects—ratioed estimate			X	X	X	
Schedule						
Overall timing of execution				X	X	
Detailed schedule of execution	X	X	X			
Estimating preparation schedule	X	X	X			

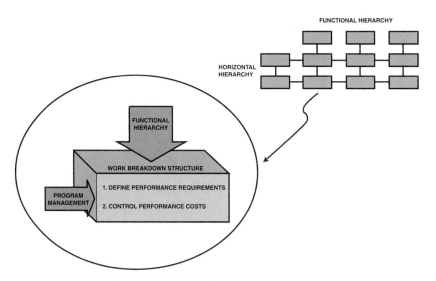

FIGURE 14–1. The vertical–horizontal interface.

tries, projects and programs are so diversified that realistic comparison between previous activities may not be possible. The costing information obtained from each pricing unit, whether or not it is based on historical standards, should be regarded only as an estimate. How can a company predict the salary structure three years from now? What will be the cost of raw materials two years from now? Will the business base (and therefore overhead rates) change over the duration of the program? The final response to these questions shows that costing data are explicitly related to an environment that cannot be predicted with any high degree of certainty. The systems approach to management, however, provides for a more rapid response to the environment than less structured approaches permit.

Once the cost data are assembled, they must be analyzed for their potential impact on the company resources of people, money, equipment, and facilities. It is only through a total program cost analysis that resource allocations can be analyzed. The resource allocation analysis is performed at all levels of management, ranging from the section supervisor to the vice president and general manager. For most programs, the chief executive must approve final cost data and the allocation of resources.

Proper analysis of the total program costs can provide management (both program and corporate) with a strategic planning model for integration of the current program with other programs in order to obtain a total corporate strategy. Meaningful planning and pricing models include analyses for monthly manloading schedules per department, monthly costs per department, monthly and yearly total program costs, monthly material expenditures, and total program cash-flow and man-hour requirements per month.

Previously we identified several of the problems that occur at the nodes where the horizontal hierarchy of program management interfaces with the vertical hierarchy of functional management. The pricing-out of the work breakdown structure provides the basis for effective and open communication between functional and program management where both parties have one common goal. This is shown in Figure 14–1. After the pricing effort is completed, and the program is initiated, the work breakdown structure still forms the basis of a communications tool by documenting the performance agreed on in the pricing effort, as well as establishing the criteria against which performance costs will be measured.

14.4 ORGANIZATIONAL INPUT REQUIREMENTS

Once the work breakdown structure and activity schedules are established, the program manager calls a meeting for all organizations that will be required to submit pricing information. It is imperative that all pricing or labor-costing representatives be present for the first meeting. During this "kickoff" meeting, the work breakdown structure is described in depth so that each pricing unit manager will know exactly what his responsibilities are during the program. The kickoff meeting also resolves the struggle-for-power positions of several functional managers whose responsibilities may be similar to overlap on certain activities. An example of this would be quality control activities. During the research and development phase of a program, research personnel may be permitted to perform their own quality control efforts, whereas during production activities the quality control department or division would have overall responsibility. Unfortunately, one meeting is not always sufficient to clarify all problems. Follow-up or status meetings are held, normally with only those parties concerned with the problems that have arisen. Some companies prefer to have all members attend the status meetings so that all personnel will be familiar with the total effort and the associated problems. The advantage of not having all program-related personnel attend is that time is of the essence when pricing out activities. Many functional divisions carry this policy one step further by having a divisional representative together with possibly key department managers or section supervisors as the only attendees at the kickoff meeting. The divisional representative then assumes all responsibility for assuring that all costing data are submitted on time. This arrangement may be beneficial in that the program office need contact only one individual in the division to learn of the activity status, but it may become a bottleneck if the representative fails to maintain proper communication between the functional units and the program office, or if the individual simply is unfamiliar with the pricing requirements of the work breakdown structure.

During proposal activities, time may be extremely important. There are many situations in which a request for proposal (RFP) requires that all responders submit their bids no later than a specific date, say within thirty days. Under a proposal environment, the activities of the program office, as well as those of the functional units, are under a schedule set forth by the proposal manager. The proposal manager's schedule has very little, if any, flexibility and is normally under tight time constraints so that the proposal may be typed, edited, and published prior to the date of submittal. In this case, the RFP will indirectly define how much time the pricing units have to identify and justify labor costs.

The justification of the labor costs may take longer than the original cost estimates, especially if historical standards are not available. Many proposals often require that comprehensive labor justification be submitted. Other proposals, especially those that request an almost immediate response, may permit vendors to submit labor justification at a later date.

In the final analysis, it is the responsibility of the lowest pricing unit supervisors to maintain adequate standards, if possible, so that an almost immediate response can be given to a pricing request from a program office.

14.5 LABOR DISTRIBUTIONS

The functional units supply their input to the program office in the form of man-hours as shown in Figure 14–2. The input may be accompanied by labor justification, if required. The man-hours are submitted for each task, assuming that the task is the lowest pricing element, and are time-phased per month. The man-hours per

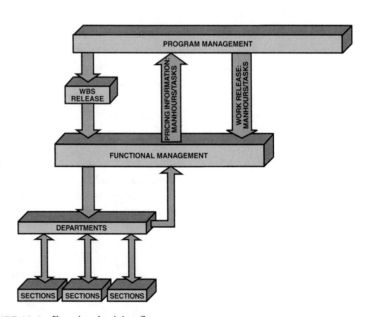

FIGURE 14–2. Functional pricing flow.

month per task are converted to dollars after multiplication by the appropriate labor rates. The labor rates are generally known with certainty over a twelve-month period, but from then on are only estimates. How can a company predict salary structures five years hence? If the company underestimates the salary structure, increased costs and decreased profits will occur. If the salary structure is overestimated, the company may not be competitive; if the project is government funded, then the salary structure becomes an item under contract negotiations.

The development of the labor rates to be used in the projection is based on historical costs in business base hours and dollars for the most recent month or quarter. Average hourly rates are determined for each labor unit by direct effort within the operations at the department level. The rates are only averages, and include both the highest-paid employees and lowest-paid employees, together with the department manager and the clerical support.[1] These base rates are then escalated as a percentage factor based on past experience, budget as approved by management, and the local outlook and similar industries. If the company has a predominant aerospace or defense industry business base, then these salaries are negotiated with local government agencies prior to submittal for proposals.

The labor hours submitted by the functional units are quite often overestimated for fear that management will "massage" and reduce the labor hours while attempting to maintain the same scope of effort. Many times management is forced to reduce man-hours either because of insufficient funding or just to remain competitive in the environment. The reduction of man-hours often causes heated discussions between the functional and program managers. Program managers tend to think in terms of the best interests of the program, whereas functional managers lean toward maintaining their present staff.

The most common solution to this conflict rests with the program manager. If the program manager selects members for the program team who are knowledgeable in man-hour standards for each of the departments, then an atmosphere of trust can develop between the program office and the functional department so that man-hours can be reduced in a manner that represents the best interests of the company. This is one of the reasons why program team members are often promoted from within the functional ranks.

The man-hours submitted by the functional units provide the basis for total program cost analysis and program cost control. To illustrate this process, consider Example 14–1 below.

Example 14–1. On May 15, Apex Manufacturing decided to enter into competitive bidding for the modification and updating of an assembly line program. A work breakdown structure was developed as shown below:

---

1. Problems can occur if the salaries of the people assigned to the program exceed the department averages. Methods to alleviate this problem are discussed later. Also, in many companies department managers are included in the overhead rate structure, not in direct labor, and therefore their salaries are not included as part of the department average.

PROGRAM (01-00-00): Assembly Line Modification
  PROJECT 1 (01-01-00): Initial Planning
    Task 1 (01-01-01): Engineering Control
    Task 2 (01-01-02): Engineering Development
  PROJECT 2 (01-02-00): Assembly
    Task 1 (01-02-01): Modification
    Task 2 (01-02-02): Testing

On June 1, each pricing unit was given the work breakdown structure together with the schedule shown in Figure 14–3. According to the schedule developed by the proposal manager for this project, all labor data must be submitted to the program office for review no later than June 15. It should be noted here that, in many companies, labor hours are submitted directly to the pricing department for submittal into the base case computer run. In this case, the program office would "massage" the labor hours only after the base case figures are available. This procedure assumes that sufficient time exists for analysis and modification of the base case. If the program office has sufficient personnel capable of critiquing the labor input prior to submittal to the base case, then valuable time can be saved, especially if two or three days are required to obtain computer output for the base case.

During proposal activities, the proposal manager, pricing manager, and program manager must all work together, although the program manager has the final say. The primary responsibility of the proposal manager is to integrate the proposal activities into the operational system so that the proposal will be submitted to the requestor on time. A typical schedule developed by the proposal manager is shown in Figure 14–4. The schedule includes all activities necessary to "get the proposal out of the house," with the first major step being the submittal of man-hours by the pricing organizations. Figure 14–4 also indicates the tracking of proposal costs. The proposal activity schedule is usually accompanied

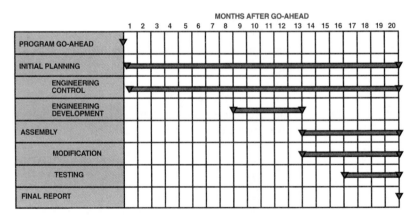

FIGURE 14–3. Activity schedule for assembly line updating.

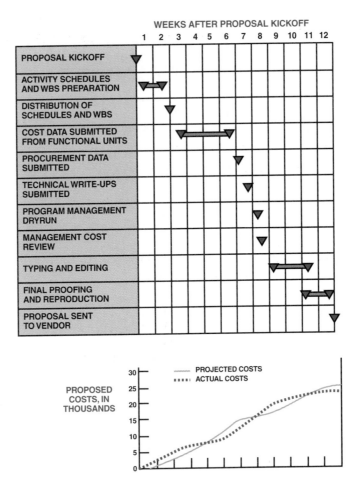

FIGURE 14–4. Proposal activity schedule.

by a time schedule with a detailed estimates checklist if the complexity of the proposal warrants one. The checklist generally provides detailed explanations for the proposal activity schedule.

After the planning and pricing charts are approved by program team members and program managers, they are entered into an electronic data processing (EDP) system as shown in Figure 14–5. The computer then prices the hours on the planning charts using the applicable department rates for preparation of the direct budget time plan and estimate-at-completion reports. The direct budget time plan reports, once established, remain the same for the life of the contract except for customer-directed or approved changes or when contractor management determines that a reduction in budget is advisable. However, if a budget is reduced by management, it cannot be increased without customer approval.

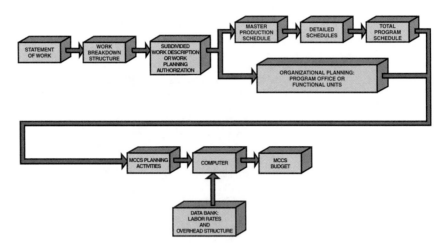

FIGURE 14–5. Labor planning flow chart.

The time plan is normally a monthly mechanical printout of all planned effort by work package and organizational element over the life of the contract, and serves as the data bank for preparing the status completion reports.

Initially, the estimate-at-completion report is identical to the budget report, but it changes throughout the life of a program to reflect degradation or improvement in performance or any other events that will change the program cost or schedule.

14.6 OVERHEAD RATES

The ability to control program costs involves more than tracking labor dollars and labor hours. Overhead dollars can be one of the biggest headaches in controlling program costs and must be tracked along with labor hours and dollars. Although most programs have an assistant program manager for cost whose responsibilities include monthly overhead rate analysis, the program manager can drastically increase the success of his program by insisting that each program team member understand overhead rates. For example, if overhead rates apply only to the first forty hours of work, then, depending on the overhead rate, program dollars can be saved by performing work on overtime where the increased salary is at a lower burden. This can be seen in Example 14–2 below.

Example 14–2. Assume that ApexManufacturing must write an interim report for task 1 of project 1 during regular shift or on overtime. The project will require 500 man-hours at $15.00 per hour. The overhead burden is 75 percent on regular shift but only 5 percent on overtime. Overtime, however, is paid at a rate of time and a half. Assuming that the report can be written on either time, which is cost-effective—regular time or overtime?

- On regular time the total cost is:

  (500 hours) $\times$ ($15.00/hour) $\times$ (100% + 75% burden) = $13,125

- On overtime, the total cost is:

$$(500 \text{ hours}) \times (\$15.00/\text{hour} \times 1.5 \text{ overtime}) \times (100\% + 5\% \text{ burden})$$
$$= \$11,812.50$$

Therefore, the company can save $1,312.50 by performing the work on overtime. Scheduling overtime can produce increased profits if the overtime overhead rate burden is much less than the regular time burden. This difference can be very large in manufacturing divisions, where overhead rates between 300 and 450 percent are common.

Regardless of whether one analyzes a project or a system, all costs must have associated overhead rates. Unfortunately, many program managers and systems managers consider overhead rates as a magic number pulled out of the air. The preparation and assignment of overheads to each of the functional divisions is a science. Although the *total dollar pool* for overhead rates is relatively constant, management retains the option of deciding how to distribute the overhead among the functional divisions. A company that supports its R&D staff through competitive bidding projects may wish to keep the R&D overhead rate as low as possible. Care must be taken, however, that other divisions do not absorb additional costs so that the company no longer remains competitive on those manufactured products that may be its bread and butter.

The development of the overhead rates is a function of three separate elements: direct labor rates, direct business base projections, and projection of overhead expenses. Direct labor rates have already been discussed. The direct business base projection involves the determination of the anticipated direct labor hours and dollars along with the necessary direct materials and other direct costs required to perform and complete the program efforts included in the business base. Those items utilized in the business base projection include all contracted programs as well as the proposed or anticipated efforts. The foundation for determination of the business base required for each program can be one or more of the following:

- Actual costs to date and estimates to completion
- Proposal data
- Marketing intelligence
- Management goals
- Past performance and trends

The projection of the overhead expenses is made by an analysis of each of the elements the constitute the overhead expense. A partial listing of those items that constitute overhead expenses is shown in Table 14–7. Projection of expenses within the individual elements is then made based on one or more of the following:

- Historical direct/indirect labor ratios
- Regression and correlation analysis
- Manpower requirements and turnover rates
- Changes in public laws
- Anticipated changes in company benefits
- Fixed costs in relation to capital asset requirements
- Changes in business base
- Bid and proposal (B&P) tri-service agreements
- IR&D tri-service agreements

For many industries, such as aerospace and defense, the federal government funds a large percentage of the B&P and IR&D activities. This federal funding is a necessity since many companies could not otherwise be competitive within the industry. The federal government employs this technique to stimulate research and competition. Therefore, B&P and IR&D are included in the above list.

The prime factor in the control of overhead costs is the annual budget. This budget, which is the result of goals and objectives established by the chief executive officer, is reviewed and approved at all levels of management. It is established at department level, and the department manager has direct responsibility for identifying and controlling costs against the approved plan.

The departmental budgets are summarized, in detail, for higher levels of management. This summarization permits management, at these higher organizational levels, to be aware of the authorized indirect budget in their area of responsibility.

TABLE 14–7.   ELEMENTS OF OVERHEAD RATES

Building maintenance	New business directors
Building rent	Office supplies
Cafeteria	Payroll taxes
Clerical	Personnel recruitment
Clubs/associations	Postage
Consulting services	Professional meetings
Corporate auditing expenses	Reproduction facilities
Corporate salaries	Retirement plans
Depreciation of equipment	Sick leave
Executive salaries	Supplies/hand tools
Fringe benefits	Supervision
General ledger expenses	Telephone/telegraph facilities
Group insurance	Transportation
Holiday	Utilities
Moving/storage expenses	Vacation

Reports are published monthly indicating current month and year-to-date budget, actuals, and variances. These reports are published for each level of management, and an analysis is made by the budget department through coordination and review with management. Each directorate's total organization is then reviewed with the budget analyst who is assigned the overhead cost responsibility. A joint meeting is held with the directors and the vice president and general manager, at which time overhead performance is reviewed.

14.7 MATERIALS/SUPPORT COSTS

The salary structure, overhead structure, and labor hours fulfill three of four major pricing input requirements. The fourth major input is the cost for materials and support. Six subtopics are included under materials/support: materials, purchased parts, subcontracts, freight, travel, and other. Freight and travel can be handled in one of two ways, both normally dependent on the size of the program. For small-dollar-volume programs, estimates are made for travel and freight. For large-dollar-volume programs, travel is normally expressed as between 3 and 5 percent of the direct labor costs, and freight is likewise between 3 and 5 percent of all costs for material, purchased parts, and subcontracts. The category labeled "other support costs" may include such topics as computer hours or special consultants.

Determination of the material costs is very time-consuming, more so than cost determination for labor hours. Material costs are submitted via a bill of materials that includes all vendors from whom purchases will be made, projected costs throughout the program, scrap factors, and shelf lifetime for those products that may be perishable.

Upon release of the work statement, work breakdown structure, and subdivided work description, the end-item bill of materials and manufacturing plans are prepared as shown in Figure 14–6. End-item materials are those items identified as an integral part of the production end-item. Support materials consist of those materials required by engineering and operations to support the manufacture of end-items, and are identified on the manufacturing plan.

A procurement plan/purchase requisition is prepared as soon as possible after contract negotiations (using a methodology as shown in Figure 14–7). This plan is used to monitor material acquisitions, forecast inventory levels, and identify material price variances.

Manufacturing plans prepared upon release of the subdivided work descriptions are used to prepare tool lists for manufacturing, quality assurance, and engineering. From these plans a special tooling breakdown is prepared by tool engineering, which defines those tools to be procured and the material requirements of tools to be fabricated in-house. These items are priced by cost element for input on the planning charts.

The materials/support costs are submitted by month for each month of the program. If long-lead funding of materials is anticipated, then they should be as-

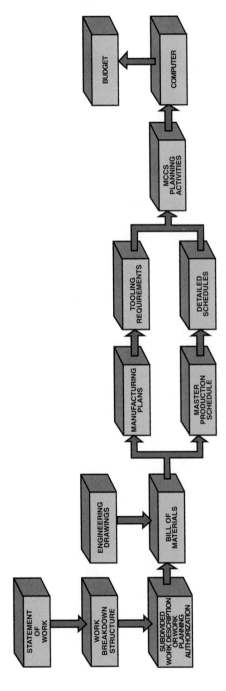

FIGURE 14–6. Material planning flow chart.

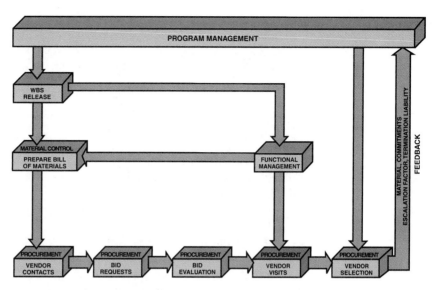

FIGURE 14–7. Procurement activity.

signed to the first month of the program. In addition, an escalation factor for costs of materials/support items must be applied to all materials/support costs. Some vendors may provide fixed prices over time periods in excess of a twelve-month period. As an example, vendor Z may quote a firm-fixed price of $130.50 per unit for 650 units to be delivered over the next eighteen months if the order is placed within sixty days. There are additional factors that influence the cost of materials.

14.8 PRICING OUT THE WORK

Logical pricing techniques are available in order to obtain detailed estimates. The following thirteen steps provide a logical sequence in order to better control the company's limited resources. These steps may vary from company to company.

Step 1: Provide a complete definition of the work requirements.
Step 2: Establish a logic network with checkpoints.
Step 3: Develop the work breakdown structure.
Step 4: Price out the work breakdown structure.
Step 5: Review WBS costs with each functional manager.
Step 6: Decide on the basic course of action.
Step 7: Establish reasonable costs for each WBS element.
Step 8: Review the base case costs with upper-level management.
Step 9: Negotiate with functional managers for qualified personnel.

Step 10: Develop the linear responsibility chart.
Step 11: Develop the final detailed and PERT/CPM schedules.
Step 12: Establish pricing cost summary reports.
Step 13: Document the result in a program plan.

Although the pricing of a project is an iterative process, the project manager must still burden himself at each iteration point by developing cost summary reports so that key project decisions can be made during the planning. Detailed pricing summaries are needed at least twice: in preparation for the pricing review meeting with management and at pricing termination. At all other times it is possible that "simple cosmetic surgery" can be performed on previous cost summaries, such as perturbations in escalation factors and procurement cost of raw materials. The list identified below shows the typical pricing reports:

- *A detailed cost breakdown for each WBS element.* If the work is priced out at the task level, then there should be a cost summary sheet for each task, as well as rollup sheets for each project and the total program.
- *A total program manpower curve for each department.* These manpower curves show how each department has contracted with the project office to supply functional resources. If the departmental manpower curves contain several "peaks and valleys," then the project manager may have to alter some of his schedules to obtain some degree of manpower smoothing. Functional managers always prefer manpower-smoothed resource allocations.
- *A monthly equivalent manpower cost summary.* This table normally shows the fully burdened cost for the average departmental employee carried out over the entire period of project performance. If project costs have to be reduced, the project manager performs a parametric study between this table and the manpower curve tables.
- *A yearly cost distribution table.* This table is broken down by WBS element and shows the yearly (or quarterly) costs that will be required. This table, in essence, is a project cash-flow summary per activity.
- *A functional cost and hour summary.* This table provides top management with an overall description of how many hours and dollars will be spent by each major functional unit, such as a division. Top management would use this as part of the forward planning process to make sure that there are sufficient resources available for all projects. This also includes indirect hours and dollars.
- *A monthly labor hour and dollar expenditure forecast.* This table can be combined with the yearly cost distribution, except that it is broken down by month, not activity or department. In addition, this table normally includes manpower termination liability information for premature cancellation of the project by outside customers.
- *A raw material and expenditure forecast.* This shows the cash flow for raw materials based on vendor lead times, payment schedules, commitments, and termination liability.

● *Total program termination liability per month.* This table shows the customer the monthly costs for the entire program. This is the customer's cash flow, not the contractor's. The difference is that each monthly cost contains the termination liability for man-hours and dollars, on labor and raw materials. This table is actually the monthly costs attributed to premature project termination.

These tables are used by both project managers and upper-level executives. The project managers utilize these tables as the basis for project cost control. Top-level management utilizes them for selecting, approving, and prioritizing projects.

14.9 SMOOTHING OUT DEPARTMENT MAN-HOURS

The dotted curve in Figure 14–8 indicates projected manpower requirements for a given department as a result of a typical program manloading schedule. Department managers, however, attempt to smooth out the manpower curve as shown by the solid line in Figure 14–8. Smoothing out the manpower requirements is always beneficial to the department managers by eliminating the necessity for scheduling fractional man-hours per day. The program manager must understand that if departments are permitted to eliminate peaks, valleys, and small-step functions in manpower planning, small project and task man-hour (and cost) variances can occur, but should not, in general, affect the total program cost significantly.

One important question that needs to be asked by program management as well as by functional management is whether the department has sufficient personnel available to fulfill manpower requirements. Another important question that management must be concerned with is the rate at which the functional departments can staff the program. For example, project engineering requires approximately twenty-three

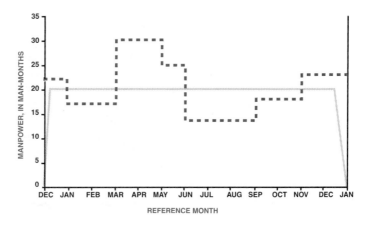

FIGURE 14–8. Typical manpower loading.

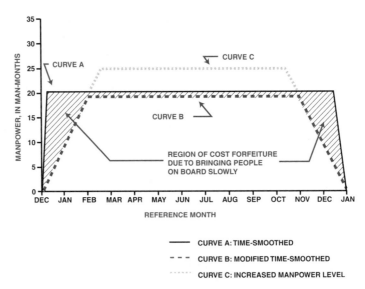

FIGURE 14–9. Linearly increased manpower loading.

people during January 1984. The functional manager, however, may have only fifteen people available for immediate reassignment, with the remainder to be either transferred from other programs or hired from outside the company. The same situation occurs during activity termination. Will project engineering still require twenty-two people in August 1984, or can some of these people begin being phased to other programs, say, as early as June 1984? This question, specifically addressed to support and administrative tasks/projects, must be answered prior to contract negotiations. Figure 14–9 indicates the types of problems that can occur. Curve A shows the manpower requirements for a given department after time-smoothing. Curve B represents the modification to the time-phase curve to account for reasonable program manning and demanning rates. The difference between these two curves (i.e., the shaded area) therefore reflects the amount of money the contractor may have to forfeit owing to manning and demanning activities. This problem can be partially overcome by increasing the manpower levels after time-smoothing (see Curve C) such that the difference between curves B and C equals the amount of money that would be forfeited from curves A and B. Of course, program management would have to be able to justify this increase in average manpower requirements, especially if the adjustments are made in a period of higher salaries and overhead rates.

14.10 THE PRICING REVIEW PROCEDURE

The ability to project and analyze problem costs so that a basis can be formed for program control requires coordination and control of all pricing information and obtaining agreement and cooperation between the functional units and upper-level management. A typical company policy for cost analysis and review is shown in Figure 14–10. Corporate management may be required to initiate or authorize activities, if corporate/company resources are or may be strained by the program, if capital expenditures are required for new facilities or equipment, or simply if corporate approval is required for all projects in excess of a certain dollar amount.

Upper-level management, upon approval by the chief executive officer of the company, approves and authorizes the initiation of the project or program. The

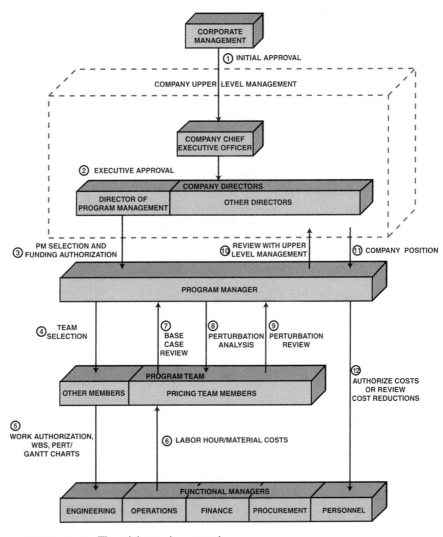

FIGURE 14–10. The pricing review procedure.

actual performance activities, however, do not begin until the director of program management selects a program manager. The director of program management also authorizes, at this point, either the bid and proposal budget (if the program is competitive) or project planning funds.

The newly appointed program manager then selects this program team's members. These team members, who are also members of the program office, may come from other programs, in which case the program manager may find it necessary to negotiate with other program managers, as well as with upper-level management, in order to obtain the individuals whom he thinks are essential to the success of his program. The members of the program office are normally support-type individuals. In order to obtain team members representing the functional departments, the program manager must negotiate directly with the functional managers. Functional team members may not be selected or assigned to the program until the actual work is contracted for. Many proposals, however, require that all functional team members be identified, in which case selection must be made during the proposal stage of a program.

The first responsibility of the program office (not necessarily including functional team members) is the development of the activity schedules and the work breakdown structure. The program office then provides work authorization for the functional units to price out the activities. The functional units then submit the labor hours, material costs, and justification, if required, to the pricing team member. The pricing team member is normally attached to the program office until the final costs are established. The pricing member also becomes part of the negotiating team if the project is competitive.

Once the base case is formulated, the pricing team member, together with the other program office team members, performs perturbation analyses in order to answer any questions that may come up during the final management review. The perturbation analysis is designed as a systems approach to problem solving where alternatives are developed in order to respond to any questions that management may wish to consider during the final review.

The base case, with the perturbation analysis costs, is then reviewed with upper-level management in order to formulate a company position for the program as well as to take a hard look at the allocation of resources required for the program. The company position may be to cut costs, authorize work, or submit a bid. If the program is competitive, corporate approval may be required if the company's chief executive office has a ceiling on the dollar bids he can authorize to go out of house.

If labor costs must be cut, the program manager must negotiate with the functional managers as to the size and method for the cost reductions. Otherwise, this step would simply entail authorization for the functional managers to begin the activities.

Figure 14–10 represents the system approach toward determining total program costs. This procedure normally creates a synergistic environment, provides open channels of communication between all levels of management, and ensures agreement among all individuals as to program costs.

14.11 SYSTEMS PRICING

The basis of successful program management is the establishment of an accurate cost package from which all members of the organization can both project and track costs. The cost data must be represented in such a manner that maximum allocation of the corporate resources of people, money, and facilities can be achieved.

The systems approach to pricing out the activity schedules and the work breakdown structure provides a means for obtaining unity within the company. The flow of information readily admits the participation of all members of the organization in the program, even if on a part-time basis. Functional managers obtain a better un-

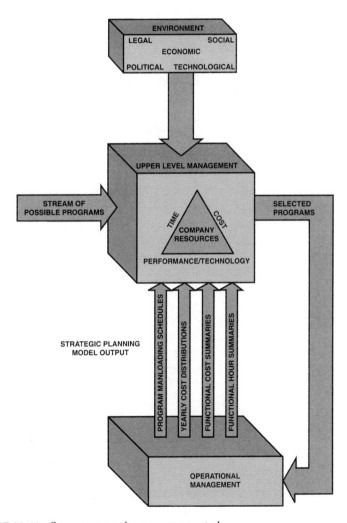

FIGURE 14–11. System approach to resource control.

derstanding of how their labor fits into the total program and how their activities interface with those of other departments. For the first time, functional managers can accurately foresee how their activity can lead to corporate profits.

The project pricing model (sometimes called a strategic project planning model) acts as a management information system, forming the basis for the systems approach to resource control, as shown in Figure 14–11. The summary sheets from the computer output of the strategic pricing model provide management with the necessary data from which the selection of possible programs can be made so that maximum utilization of resources will follow.

The strategic pricing model also provides management with an invaluable tool for performing perturbation analysis on the base case costs. This perturbation analysis provides management with sufficient opportunity for design and evaluation of contingency plans, should a deviation from the original plan be required.

14.12 DEVELOPING THE SUPPORTING/BACKUP COSTS

Not all cost proposals require backup support, but for those that do, the backup support should be developed along with the pricing. Extreme caution must be exercised to make sure that the itemized prices are compatible with the supporting data. Government pricing requirements are a special case.

Most supporting data come from external (subcontractor or outside vendor) quotes. Internal data must be based on historical data, and these historical data must be updated continually as each new project is completed. The supporting data should be traceable by itemized charge numbers.

Customers may wish to audit the cost proposal. In this case, the starting point might be with the supporting data. It is not uncommon on sole-source proposals to have the supporting data audited before the final cost proposal is submitted to the customer.

Not all cost proposals require supporting data; the determining factor is usually the type of contract. On a fixed-price effort, the customer may not have the right to audit your books. However, for a cost-reimbursable package, your costs are an open book, and the customer usually compares your exact costs to those of the backup support.

Most companies usually have a choice of more than one estimate to be used for backup support. In deciding which estimate to use, consideration must be given to the possibility of follow-on work:

- If your actual costs grossly exceed your backup support estimates, you may lose credibility for follow-on work.
- If your actual costs are less than the backup costs, you must use the new actual costs on follow-on efforts.

The moral here is that backup support costs provide future credibility. If you

TABLE 14-8. OPERATIONS SKILLS MATRIX

Functional areas of expertise	Able, J.	Baker, P.	Cook, D.	Dirk, L.	Easley, P.	Franklin, W.	Green, C.	Henry, L.	Imhoff, R.	Jules, C.	Klein, W.	Ledger, D.	Mayer, Q.	Newton, A.	Oliver, G.	Pratt, L.
Administrative management	b	a				a		a			a	a			a	b
Control and communications			b	b	b		b	b		b	b	b		b	b	b
Environmental impact assessment	c	c	c						c		c		c			
Facilities management		d					d				d		d			
Financial management	e					e			e	e	e				e	e
Human resources mangement	f							f				f				
Industrial engineering	g				g					g						
Intelligence and security								h				h		h		
Inventory control	i						i								i	i
Logistics			j		j			j				j				
OSHA	k									k			k			
Project management	l			l		l					l				l	
Quality control		m	m			m	m	m	m							
R&D		n	n	n							n		n			n
Wage and salary administration		o			o				o	o		o		o	o	

767

TABLE 14–9. CONTRACTOR'S MANPOWER AVAILABILITY

	Number of Personnel			
	Total Current Staff		Available for This Project and Other New Work 1/93 Permanent + Agency	Anticipated Growth by 1/93 Permanent + Agency
	Permanent Employees	Agency Personnel		
Process engineers	93	—	70	4
Project managers/engineers	79	—	51	4
Cost estimating	42	—	21	2
Cost control	73	—	20	2
Scheduling/scheduling control	14	—	8	1
Procurement/ purchasing	42	—	20	1
Inspection	40	—	20	2
Expediting	33	—	18	1
Home office construction management	9	—	6	0
Piping	90	13	67	6
Electrical	31	—	14	2
Instrumentation	19	—	3	1
Vessels/exchangers	24	—	19	1
Civil/structural	30	—	23	2
Other	13	—	8	0

have well-documented, "livable" cost estimates, then you may wish to include them in the cost proposal even if they are not required.

Since both direct and indirect costs may be negotiated separately as part of a contract, supporting data such as those in Tables 14–8 through 14–11 and Figure 14–12 may be necessary to justify any costs that may differ from company (or customer-approved) standards.

TABLE 14–10. STAFF TURNOVER DATA

	For Twelve-Month Period 1/1/92 to 1/1/93	
	Number Terminated	Number Hired
Process engineers	5	2
Project managers/engineers	1	1
Cost estimating	1	2
Cost control	12	16
Scheduling/scheduling control	2	5
Procurement/purchasing	13	7
Inspection	18	6
Expediting	4	5
Home office construction management	0	0
Design and drafting—total	37	29
Engineering specialists—total	26	45
Total	119	118

TABLE 14–11. STAFF EXPERIENCE PROFILE

	Number of Years' Employment with Contractor				
	0–1	1–2	2–3	3–5	5 or more
Process engineers	2	4	15	11	18
Project managers/engineers	1	2	5	11	8
Cost estimating	0	4	1	5	7
Cost control	5	9	4	7	12
Scheduling and scheduling control	2	2	1	3	6
Procurement/purchasing	4	12	13	2	8
Inspection	1	2	6	14	8
Expediting	6	9	4	2	3
Piping	9	6	46	31	22
Electrical	17	6	18	12	17
Instrumentation	8	8	12	13	12
Mechanical	2	5	13	27	19
Civil/structural	4	8	19	23	16
Environmental control	0	1	1	3	7
Engineering specialists	3	3	3	16	21
Total	64	81	161	180	184

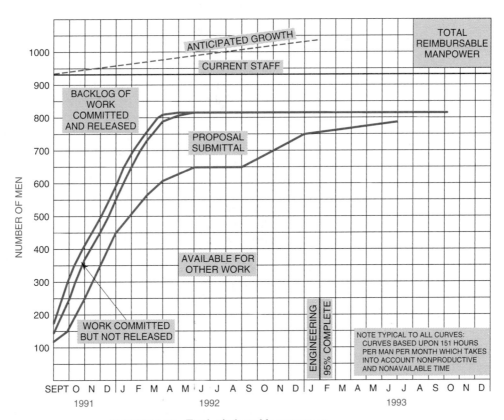

FIGURE 14–12. Total reimbursable manpower.

14.13 THE LOW-BIDDER DILEMMA

There is little argument about the importance of the price tag to the proposal. The question is, what price will win the job? Everyone has an answer to this question. The decision process that leads to the final price of your proposal is highly complex with many uncertainties. Yet proposal managers, driven by the desire to win the job, may think that a very low-priced proposal will help. But, hopefully, winning is only the beginning. Companies have short- and long-range objectives on profit, market penetration, new product development, and so on. These objectives may be incompatible with or irrelevant to a low-price strategy per se; for example:

- A suspiciously low price, particularly on cost-plus type proposals, might be perceived by the customer as unrealistic, thus affecting the bidder's cost credibility or even the technical ability to perform.
- The bid price may be unnecessarily low, relative to the competition and customer budget, thus eroding profits.
- The price may be irrelevant to the bid objective, such as entering a new market. Therefore, the contractor has to sell the proposal in a credible way, e.g., using cost sharing.
- Low pricing without market information is meaningless. The price level is always relative to (1) the competitive prices, (2) the customer budget, and (3) the bidder's cost estimate.
- The bid proposal and its price may cover only part of the total program. The ability to win phase II or follow-on business depends on phase I performance and phase II price.
- The financial objectives of the customer may be more complex than just finding the lowest bidder. They may include cost objectives for total system life-cycle cost (LCC), for design to unit production cost (DTUPC), or for specific logistic support items. Presenting sound approaches for attaining these system cost–performance parameters and targets may be just as important as, if not more important than, a low bid for the system's development.

Further, it is refreshing to note that in spite of customer pressures toward low cost and fixed price, the lowest bidder is certainly not an automatic winner. Both commercial and governmental customers are increasingly concerned about cost realism and the ability to perform under contract. A compliant, sound, technical and management proposal, based on past experience with realistic, well-documented cost figures, is often chosen over the lowest bidder, who may project a risky image regarding technical performance, cost, or schedule.

14.14 SPECIAL PROBLEMS

There are always special problems that, although often overlooked, have a severe impact on the pricing effort. As an example, pricing must include an understanding of cost control—specifically, how costs are billed back to the project. There are three possible situations:

- *Work is priced out at the department average, and all work performed is charged to the project at the department average salary, regardless of who accomplished the work.* This technique is obviously the easiest, but encourages project managers to fight for the highest salary resources, since only average wages are billed to the project.
- *Work is priced out at the department average, but all work performed is billed back to the project at the actual salary of those employees who perform the work.* This method can create a severe headache for the project manager if he tries to use only the best employees on his project. If these employees are earning substantially more money than the department average, then a cost overrun will occur unless the employees can perform the work in less time. Some companies are forced to use this method by government agencies and have estimating problems when the project that has to be priced out is of a short duration where only the higher-salaried employees can be used. In such a situation it is common to "inflate" the direct labor hours to compensate for the added costs.
- *The work is priced out at the actual salary of those employees who will perform the work, and the cost is billed back the same way.* This method is the ideal situation as long as the people can be identified during the pricing effort.

Some companies use a combination of all three methods. In this case, the project office is priced out using the third method (because these people are identified early), whereas the functional employees are priced out using the first or second method.

14.15 ESTIMATING PITFALLS

Several pitfalls can impede the pricing function. Probably the most serious pitfall, and the one that is usually beyond the control of the project manager, is the "buy-in" decision, which is based on the assumption that there will be "bail-out" changes or follow-on contracts later. These changes and/or contracts may be for spares, spare parts, maintenance, maintenance manuals, equipment surveillance, optional equipment, optional services, and scrap factors. Other types of estimating pitfalls include:

- Misinterpretation of the statement of work
- Omissions or improperly defined scope
- Poorly defined or overly optimistic schedule
- Inaccurate work breakdown structure
- Applying improper skill levels to tasks

- Failure to account for risks
- Failure to understand or account for cost escalation and inflation
- Failure to use the correct estimating technique
- Failure to use forward pricing rates for overhead, general and administrative, and indirect costs

Unfortunately, many of these pitfalls do not become evident until detected by the cost control system, well into the project.

14.16 ESTIMATING HIGH-RISK PROJECTS

The major difference between high-risk and low-risk projects depends on the validity of the historical estimate. Construction companies have well-defined historical standards, which therefore makes their risk lower, whereas many R&D and MIS projects are high risk. Typical accuracies for each level of the WBS are shown in Table 14–12.

One of the most common techniques used to estimate high-risk projects is the "rolling wave" or "moving window" approach. This is shown in Figure 14–13 for a high-risk R&D project. The project lasts for twelve months. The R&D effort to be accomplished for the first six months is well defined and can be estimated to level 5 of the WBS. However, the effort for the last six months is based on the results of the first six months and can be estimated at level 2 only, thus incurring a high risk. Now consider part B of Figure 14–13, which shows a six-month moving window. At the end of the first month, in order to maintain a six-month moving window (at level 5 of the WBS), the estimate for month seven must be improved from a level-2 to a level-5 estimate. Likewise, in parts C and D of Figure 14–13, we see the effects of completing the second and third months.

There are two key points to be considered in utilizing this technique. First, the length of the moving window can vary from project to project, and usually increases in length as you approach downstream life-cycle phases. Second, this technique works best when upper-level management understands how the tech-

TABLE 14–12. LOW- VERSUS HIGH-RISK ACCURACIES

WBS		Accuracy	
Level	Description	Low-Risk Projects	High-Risk Projects
1	Program	±35	±75–100
2	Project	20	50–60
3	Task	10	20–30
4	Subtask	5	10–15
5	Work package	2	5–10

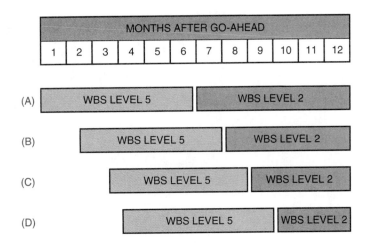

FIGURE 14–13. The moving window/rolling wave concept.

nique works. All too often senior management hears only one budget and schedule number during project approval and might not realize that at least half of the project might be time/cost accurate to only 50–60 percent. Simply stated, when using this technique, the word "rough" is not synonymous with the word "detailed."

Methodologies can be developed for assessing risk. Figures 14–14, 14–15, and Table 14–13 show such methodologies.

14.17 PROJECT RISKS

Project plans are "living documents" and are therefore subject to change. Changes are needed in order to prevent or rectify unfortunate situations. These unfortunate situations can be called project risks.

Risk refers to those dangerous activities or factors that, if they occur, will *increase* the probability that the project's goals of time, cost, and performance will not be met. Many risks can be anticipated and controlled. Furthermore, risk management must be an integral part of project management throughout the entire life cycle of the project.

Some common risks include:

- Poorly defined requirements
- Lack of qualified resources
- Lack of management support
- Poor estimating
- Inexperienced project manager

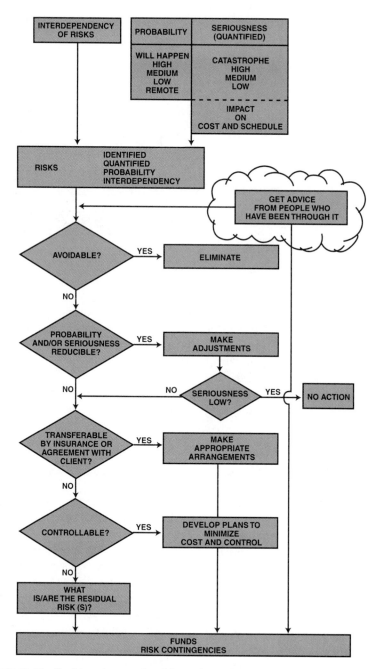

FIGURE 14–14. Decision elements for risk contingencies.

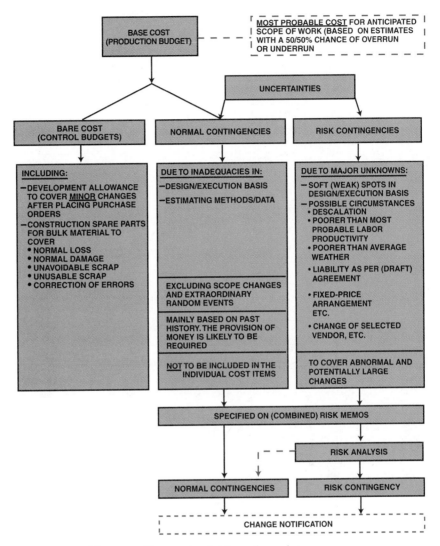

FIGURE 14–15. Elements of base cost and risk contingencies.

Risk identification is an art. It requires the project manager to probe, penetrate, and analyze all data. Tools that can be used by the project manager include:

- Decision support systems
- Expected value measures
- Trend analysis/projections
- Independent reviews and audits

TABLE 14–13. STANDARD FORM FOR PROJECT RISK ANALYSIS AND RISK CONTINGENCIES

PROJECT RISK ANALYSIS & RISK CONTINGENCY REF: PROCEDURE 0110E

RISK CONTINGENCY = 2 EXPECTED VALUES

Proposal/Order No. ____ Div./Dept. ____ Date ____ Issue No. ____

Sequence	Item	Value	Risk: Yes/No	Description of Risk of Maximum Possible Change of Item Value in %	Maximum Risk — Amount	Probability	Possible Outcome — Amount	Interdependency	Seriousness Cat./High/Med./Low	Make Adjustments	Insurance	Agreement	Subcontractor or Vendor	Exclusion from Scope	Inclusion in Estimate	Development Allowance	Construction Spares	Plan to Control	Accept as Residual Risk	Normal Contingency	RISK — Expected Value

(columns under "Transfer to": Insurance, Agreement, Subcontractor or Vendor, Exclusion from Scope, Inclusion in Estimate, Development Allowance, Construction Spares, Plan to Control, Accept as Residual Risk, Normal Contingency)

776

Managing project risks is not as difficult as it may seem. There are six steps in the risk management process:

- Identification of the risk
- Quantifying the risk
- Prioritizing the risk
- Developing a strategy for managing the risk
- Project sponsor/executive review
- Taking action

Figures 14–14 and 14–15 and Table 14–13 identify the process of risk evaluation on capital projects. In all three exhibits, it is easily seen that the attempt is to quantify the risks, possibly by developing a contingency fund.

14.18 THE DISASTER OF APPLYING THE 10 PERCENT SOLUTION TO PROJECT ESTIMATES

Economic crunches can and do create chaos in all organizations. For the project manager, the worst situation is when senior management arbitrarily employs "the 10 percent solution," which is a budgetary reduction of 10 percent for each and every project, especially those that have already begun. The 10 percent solution is used to "create" funds for additional activities for which budgets are nonexistent. The 10 percent solution very rarely succeeds. For the most part, the result is simply havoc on top of havoc, resulting in schedule slippages, a degradation of quality and performance, and eventual budgetary increases rather than the expected decreases.

Most projects are initiated through an executive committee, governing committee, or screening committee. The two main functions of these committees are to select the projects to be undertaken and to prioritize the efforts. Budgetary considerations may also be included, as they pertain to project selection. The real budgets, however, are established from the middle-management levels and sent upstairs for approvals.

Although the role of executive committee is often ill-defined with regard to budgeting, the real problem is that the committee does not realize the impact of adopting the 10 percent solution. If the project budget is an honest one, then a reduction in budget *must* be accompanied by a trade-off in either time or performance. It is often said that 90 percent of the budget generates the first 10 percent of the desired service or quality levels, and that the remaining 10 percent of the budget will produce the last 90 percent of the target requirements. If this is true, then a 10 percent reduction in budget must be accompanied by a loss of performance much greater than the target reduction in cost.

It is true that some projects have "padded" estimates, and the budgetary reduction will force out the padding. Most project managers, however, provide realistic estimates and schedules with marginal padding. Likewise, a trade-off between time and cost is unlikely to help, since increasing the duration of the project will increase the cost.

Cost versus Quality

Everyone knows that reducing cost quite often results in a reduction of quality. Conversely, if the schedule is inflexible, then the only possible trade-offs available to the project manager may be cost versus quality. If the estimated budget for a project is too high, then executives often are willing to sacrifice some degree of quality to keep the budget in line. The problem, of course, is to decide how much quality degradation is acceptable.

All too often, executives believe that cost and quality are linearly related: if the budget is cut by 10 percent, then we will have an accompanying degradation of quality by 10 percent. Nothing could be further from the truth. In the table below we can see the relationship between cost, quality, and time.

Project Costs	85–90%	10–15%
Tangible Quality	10%	90%

Time ⟶

The first 85–90 percent of the budget (i.e., direct labor budget) is needed to generate the first 10 percent of the quality. The last 10–15 percent of the budget often produces the remaining 90 percent of the quality. One does not need an advanced degree in mathematics to realize that a 10 percent cost reduction could easily be accompanied by a 50 percent quality reduction, depending, of course, where the 10 percent was cut.

The following scenario shows the chain of events as they might occur in a typical organization:

- At the beginning of the fiscal year, the executive committee selects those projects to be undertaken, such that *all* available resources are consumed.
- Shortly into the fiscal year, the executive committee authorizes additional projects that must be undertaken. These projects are added to the queue.
- The executive committee recognizes that the resources available are insufficient to service the queue. Since budgets are tight, hiring additional staff is ruled out. (Even if staff could be hired, the project deadline would be at hand before the new employees were properly trained and up to speed.)
- The executive committee refuses to cancel any of the projects and takes the "easy" way out by adopting the 10 percent solution on each and every project. Furthermore, the executive committee asserts that original performance *must* be adhered to at all costs.

- Morale in the project and functional areas, which may have taken months to build, is now destroyed overnight. Functional employees lose faith in the ability of the executive committees to operate properly and make sound decisions. Employees seek transfers to other organizations.
- Functional priorities are changed on a daily basis, and resources are continuously shuffled in and out of projects, with very little regard for the schedule.
- As each project begins to suffer, project managers begin to hoard resources, refusing to surrender the people to other projects, even if the work is completed.
- As quality and performance begin to deteriorate, managers at all levels begin writing "protection" memos.
- Schedule and quality slippages become so great that several projects are extended into the next fiscal year, thus reducing the number of new projects that can be undertaken.

The 10 percent solution simply does not work. However, there are two viable alternatives. The first alternative is to use the 10 percent solution, but only on selected projects and *after* an "impact study" has been conducted, so that the executive committee understands the impact on the time, cost, and performance constraints. The second choice, which is by far the better one, is for the executive committee to cancel or descope selected projects. Since it is impossible to reduce budget without reducing scope, canceling a project or simply delaying it until the next fiscal year is a viable choice. After all, why should all projects have to suffer?

Terminating one or two projects within the queue allows existing resources to be used more effectively, more productively, and with higher organizational morale. However, it does require strong leadership at the executive committee level for the participants to terminate a project rather than to "pass the buck" to the bottom of the organization with the 10 percent solution. Executive committees often function best if the committee is responsible for project selection, prioritization, and tracking, with the middle managers responsible for budgeting.

14.19 LIFE-CYCLE COSTING (LCC)

For years, many R&D organizations have operated in a vacuum where technical decisions made during R&D were based entirely on the R&D portion of the plan, with little regard for what happens after production begins. Today, industrial firms are adopting the life-cycle costing approach that has been developed and used by military organizations. Simply stated, LCC requires that decisions made during the R&D process be evaluated against the total life-cycle cost of the system. As an example, the R&D group has two possible design configurations for a new product. Both design configurations will require the same budget for R&D and the same costs for manufacturing. However, the maintenance and support costs may be substantially greater for one of the products. If these downstream costs are not considered in the R&D phase, large unanticipated expenses may result at a point where no alternatives exist.

Life-cycle costs are the total cost to the organization for the ownership and acquisition of the product over its full life. This includes the cost of R&D, production, operation, support, and, where applicable, disposal. A typical breakdown description might include:

- *R&D costs:* The cost of feasibility studies; cost-benefit analyses; system analyses; detail design and development; fabrication, assembly, and test of engineering models; initial product evaluation; and associated documentation.
- *Production cost:* The cost of fabrication, assembly, and testing of production models; operation and maintenance of the production capability; and associated internal logistic support requirements, including test and support equipment development, spare/repair parts provisioning, technical data development, training, and entry of items into inventory.
- *Construction cost:* The cost of new manufacturing facilities or upgrading existing structures to accommodate production and operation of support requirements.
- *Operation and maintenance cost:* The cost of sustaining operational personnel and maintenance support; spare/repair parts and related inventories; test and support equipment maintenance; transportation and handling; facilities, modifications, and technical data changes; and so on.
- *Product retirement and phaseout cost:* The cost of phasing the product out of inventory due to obsolescence or wearout, and subsequent equipment item recycling and reclamation as appropriate.

Life-cycle cost analysis is the systematic analytical process of evaluating various alternative courses of action early on in a project, with the objective of choosing the best way to employ scarce resources. Life-cycle cost is employed in the evaluation of alternative design configurations, alternative manufacturing methods, alternative support schemes, and so on. This process includes:

- Defining the problem (what information is needed)
- Defining the requirements of the cost model being used
- Collecting historical data–cost relationships
- Developing estimate and test results

Successful application of LCC will:

- Provide downstream resource impact visibility
- Provide life-cycle cost management
- Influence R&D decision making
- Support downstream strategic budgeting

There are also several limitations to life-cycle cost analyses. They include:

- The assumption that the product, as known, has a finite life-cycle
- A high cost to perform, which may not be appropriate for low-cost/low-volume production
- A high sensitivity to changing requirements

Life-cycle costing requires that early estimates be made. The estimating method selected is based on the problem context (i.e., decisions to be made, required accuracy, complexity of the product, and the development status of the product) and the operational considerations (i.e., market introduction date, time available for analysis, and available resources).

The estimating methods available can be classified as follows:

- Informal estimating methods
  - Judgment based on experience
  - Analogy
  - SWAG method
  - ROM method
  - Rule-of-thumb method
- Formal estimating methods
  - Detailed (from industrial engineering standards)
  - Parametric

Table 14–14 shows the advantages/disadvantages of each method.

Figure 14–16 shows the various life-cycle phases for Department of Defense projects. At the end of the demonstration and validation phase (which is the completion of R&D) 85 percent of the decisions affecting the total life-cycle cost will have been made, and the cost reduction opportunity is limited to a maximum of 22 percent (excluding the effects of learning curve experiences). Figure 14–17 shows that, at the end of the R&D phase, 95 percent of the cumulative life-cycle cost is committed by the government. Figure 14–18 shows that, for every $12 that DoD puts into R&D, $28 are needed downstream for production and $60 for operation and support.

Life-cycle cost analysis is an integral part of strategic planning since today's decision will affect tomorrow's actions. Yet there are common errors made during life-cycle cost analyses:

- Loss or omission of data
- Lack of systematic structure
- Misinterpretation of data
- Wrong or misused techniques
- A concentration on insignificant facts
- Failure to assess uncertainty
- Failure to check work
- Estimating the wrong items

TABLE 14–14.   ESTIMATING METHODS

Estimating Technique	Application	Advantages	Disadvantages
Engineering estimates (empirical)	Reprocurement Production Development	• Most detailed technique • Best inherent accuracy • Provides best estimating base for future program change estimates	• Requires detailed program and product definition • Time-consuming and may be expensive • Subject to engineering bias • May overlook system integration costs
Parametric estimates and scaling (statistical)	Production Development	• Application is simple and low cost • Statistical data base can provide expected values and prediction intervals • Can be used for equipment or systems prior to detail design or program planning	• Requires parametric cost relationships to be established • Limited frequently to specific subsystems or functional hardware of systems • Depends on quantity and quality of the data • Limited by data and number of independent variables
Equipment/ subsystem analogy estimates (comparative)	Reprocurement Production Development Program planning	• Relatively simple • Low cost • Emphasizes incremental program and product changes • Good accuracy for similar systems	• Requires analogous product and program data • Limited to stable technology • Narrow range of electronic applications • May be limited to systems and equipment built by the same firm
Expert opinion	All program phases	• Available when there are insufficient data, parametric cost relationships, or program/product definition	• Subject to bias • Increased product or program complexity can degrade estimates • Estimate substantiation is not quantifiable

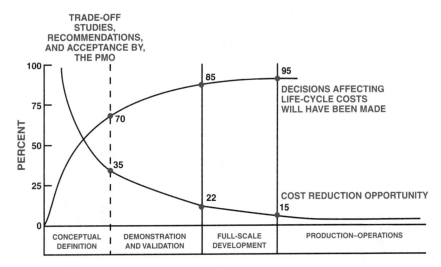

FIGURE 14–16. Department of Defense life-cycle phases.

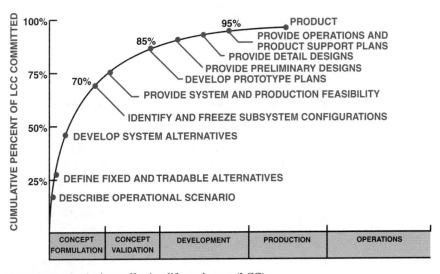

FIGURE 14–17. Actions affecting life-cycle cost (LCC).

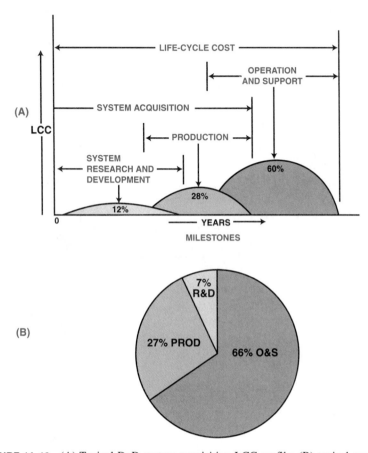

FIGURE 14–18. (A) Typical DoD system acquisition LCC profile; (B) typical communication system acquisition LCC profile.

14.20 LOGISTICS SUPPORT

There exists a class of projects called "material" projects where the project's deliverable may require maintenance, service, and support after development. This support will continue throughout the life cycle of the deliverable. Providing service to these deliverables is referred to as logistics support.

In the previous section we showed that approximately 85 percent of the deliverable's life-cycle cost has been committed by the end of the design phase (see Figures 14–16 and 14–17). We also showed that the majority of the total life-cycle cost of a system is in operation and support, and could account for well above 60 percent of the total cost. Clearly, the decisions with the greatest chance of affecting life-cycle cost and identifying cost savings are those influencing the design of the deliverable. Simply stated, proper planning and design can save a company hundreds of millions of dollars once the deliverable is put into use.

The two key parameters used to evaluate the performance of materiel systems are supportability and readiness. Supportability is the ability to maintain or acquire the necessary human and nonhuman resources to support the system. Readiness is a measure of how good we are at keeping the system performing as planned and how quickly we can make repairs during a shutdown. Clearly, proper planning during the design stage of a project can reduce supportability requirements, increase operational readiness, and minimize or lower logistics support costs.

The ten elements of logistics support are shown in Figure 14–19 and include:

- *Maintenance planning:* The process conducted to evolve and establish maintenance concepts and requirements for the lifetime of a materiel system.
- *Manpower and personnel:* The identification and acquisition of personnel with the skills and grades required to operate and support a materiel system over its lifetime.
- *Supply support:* All management actions, procedures, and techniques used to determine requirements to acquire, catalog, receive, store, transfer, issue, and dispose of secondary items. This includes provisioning for initial support as well as replenishment supply support.
- *Support equipment:* All equipment (mobile or fixed) required to support the operation and maintenance of a materiel system. This includes associated multiuse end-items; ground-handling and maintenance equipment; tools, metrology, and calibration equipment; and test and automatic test equipment. It includes the acquisition of logistics support for the support and test equipment itself.
- *Technical data:* Recorded information regardless of form or character (such as manuals and drawings) of a scientific or technical nature. Computer programs and related software are not technical data; documentation of computer programs and related software are: Also other information related to contract administration.
- *Training and training support:* The processes, procedures, techniques, training devices, and equipment used to train personnel to operate and support a materiel system. This includes individual and crew training; new equipment training; initial, formal, and on-the-job training; and logistic support planning for training equipment and training device acquisitions and installations.
- *Computer resource support:* The facilities, hardware, software, documentation, manpower, and personnel needed to operate and support embedded computer systems.
- *Facilities:* The permanent or semipermanent real property assets required to support the materiel system. Facilities management includes conducting studies to define types of facilities or facility improvement, locations, space needs, environment requirements, and equipment.

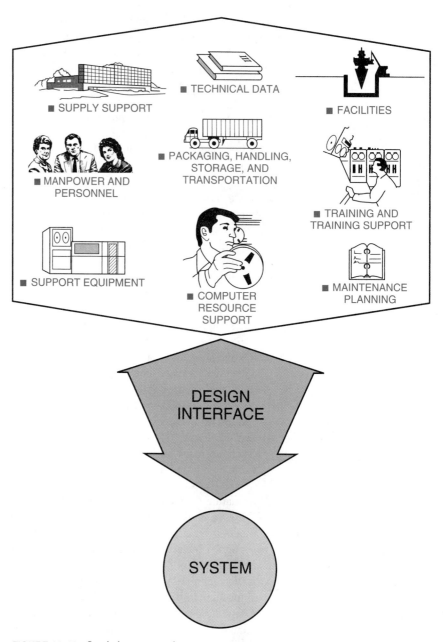

FIGURE 14–19. Logistic support elements.

- *Packaging, handling, storage, and transportation:* The resources, processes, procedures, design considerations, and methods to ensure that all system, equipment, and support items are preserved, packaged, handled, and transported properly. This includes environmental considerations and equipment preservation requirements for short- and long-term storage and transportability.
- *Design interface:* The relationship of logistics-related design parameters to readiness and support resource requirements. These logistics-related design parameters are expressed in operational terms rather than as inherent values and specifically relate to system readiness objectives and support costs of the materiel system.

14.21 ECONOMIC PROJECT SELECTION CRITERIA: CAPITAL BUDGETING

Project managers are often called upon to be active participants during the benefit-to-cost analysis of project selection. It is highly unlikely that companies will approve a project where the costs exceed the benefits. Benefits can be measured in either financial or nonfinancial terms.

The process of identifying the financial benefits is called capital budgeting, which may be defined as the *decision-making process* by which organizations evaluate projects that include the purchase of major fixed assets such as buildings, machinery, and equipment. Sophisticated capital budgeting techniques take into consideration depreciation schedules, tax information, and cash flow. Since only the principles of capital budgeting will be discussed in this text, we will restrict ourselves to the following topics:

- Payback Period
- Discounted Cash Flow (DCF)
- Net Present Value (NPV)
- Internal Rate of Return (IRR)

14.22 PAYBACK PERIOD

The payback period is the exact length of time needed for a firm to recover its initial investment as calculated from cash inflows. Payback period is the *least* precise of all capital budgeting methods because the calculations are in dollars and not adjusted for the time value of money. Table 14–15 shows the cash flow stream for Project A.

From Table 14–15, Project A will last for exactly five years with the cash inflows shown. The payback period will be exactly four years. If the cash inflow in Year 4 were $6,000 instead of $5,000, then the payback period would be three years and 10 months.

TABLE 14–15. CAPITAL EXPENDITURE DATA FOR PROJECT A

Initial Investment	Expected Cash Inflows				
	Year 1	Year 2	Year 3	Year 4	Year 5
$10,000	$1000	$2000	$2000	$5000	$2000

The problem with the payback method is that $5,000 received in Year 4 is not worth $5,000 today. This unsophisticated approach mandates that the payback method be used as a supplemental tool to accompany other methods.

14.23 THE TIME VALUE OF MONEY

Everyone knows that a dollar today is worth more than a dollar a year from now. The reason for this is because of the time value of money. To illustrate the time value of money, let us look at the following equation:

$$FV = PV(1 + k)^n$$

where FV = Future value of an investment
PV = Present value
k = Investment interest rate (or cost of capital)
n = Number of years

Using this formula, we can see that an investment of $1,000 today (i.e., PV) invested at 10% (i.e., k) for one year (i.e., n) will give us a future value of $1,100. If the investment is for two years, then the future value would be worth $1,210.

Now, let us look at the formula from a different perspective. If an investment yields $1,000 a year from now, then how much is it worth *today* if the cost of money is 10%? To solve the problem, we must discount future values to the present for comparison purposes. This is referred to as "discounted cash flows."

The previous equation can be written as:

$$PV = \frac{FV}{(1 + k)^n}$$

Using the data given:

$$PV = \frac{\$1,000}{(1 + 0.1)^1} = \$909$$

Therefore, $1,000 a year from now is worth only $909 today. If the interest rate, k, is known to be 10%, then you should *not* invest more than $909 to get the

$1,000 return a year from now. However, if you could purchase this investment for $875, your interest rate would be more than 10%.

Discounting cash flows to the present for comparison purposes is a viable way to assess the value of an investment. As an example, you have a choice between two investments. Investment A will generate $100,000 two years from now and investment B will generate $110,000 three years from now. If the cost of capital is 15%, which investment is better?

Using the formula for discounted cash flow, we find that:

$$PV_A = \$75,614$$
$$PV_B = \$72,327$$

This implies that a return of $100,000 in two years is worth more to the firm than a $110,000 return three years from now.

14.24 NET PRESENT VALUE (NPV)

The net present value (NPV) method is a sophisticated capital budgeting technique that equates the discounted cash flows against the initial investment. Mathematically,

$$NPV = \sum_{t=1}^{n} \left[\frac{FV_t}{(1 + k)^t} \right] - II$$

where FV is the future value of the cash inflows, II represents the initial investment, and k is the discount rate equal to the firm's cost of capital.

Table 14–16 calculates the NPV for the data provided previously in Table 14–15 using a discount rate of 10%.

TABLE 14–16. NPV CALCULATION FOR PROJECT A

Year	Cash Inflows	Present Value
1	$1,000	$ 909
2	2,000	1,653
3	2,000	1,503
4	5,000	3,415
5	2,000	1,242
	Present value of cash inflows	$ 8,722
	Less investment	10,000
	Net Present Value	<1,278>

This indicates that the cash inflows discounted to the present will *not* recover the initial investment. This, in fact, is a bad investment to consider. Previously, we stated that the cash flow stream yielded a payback period of four years. However, using discounted cash flow, the actual payback is greater than five years, assuming that there will be cash inflow in years 6 and 7.

If in Table 14–16 the initial investment was $5,000, then the net present value would be $3,722. The decision-making criteria using NPV are as follows:

- If the NPV is greater than or equal to zero dollars, accept the project.
- If the NPV is less than zero dollars, reject the project.

A positive value of NPV indicates that the firm will earn a return equal to or greater than its cost of capital.

14.25 INTERNAL RATE OF RETURN (IRR)

The internal rate of return (IRR) is perhaps the most sophisticated capital budgeting technique and also more difficult to calculate than NPV. The internal rate of return is the discount rate where the present value of the cash inflows exactly equals the initial investment. In other words, IRR is the discount rate when NPV = 0. Mathematically

$$\sum_{t=1}^{n} \left[\frac{FV_t}{(1 + IRR)^t} \right] - II = 0$$

The solution to problems involving IRR is basically a trial-and-error solution. Table 14–17 shows that with the cash inflows provided, and with a $5,000 initial investment, an IRR of 10% yielded a value of $3,722 for NPV. Therefore, as a second guess, we should try a value greater than 10% for IRR to generate a zero value for NPV. Table 14–17 shows the final calculation.

The table implies that the cash inflows are equivalent to a 31% return on investment. Therefore, if the cost of capital were 10%, this would be an excellent investment. Also, this project is "probably" superior to other projects with a lower value for IRR.

TABLE 14–17. IRR CALCULATION FOR PROJECT A CASH INFLOWS

IRR	NPV
10%	$3722
20%	1593
25%	807
30%	152
31%	34
32%	<78>

TABLE 14–18. CAPITAL PROJECTS

Project	IRR	Payback Period with DCF
A	10%	1 year
B	15%	2 years
C	25%	3 years
D	35%	5 years

14.26 COMPARING IRR, NPV, AND PAYBACK

For most projects, both IRR and NPV will generate the same accept-reject decision. However, there are differences that can exist in the underlying assumptions that can cause the projects to be ranked differently. The major problem is the differences in the magnitude and timing of the cash inflows. NPV assumes that the cash inflows are reinvested at the cost of capital, whereas IRR assumes reinvestment at the project's IRR. NPV tends to be a more conservative approach.

The timing of the cash flows is also important. Early year cash inflows tend to be at a lower cost of capital and are more predictable than later year cash inflows. Because of the downstream uncertainty, companies prefer larger cash inflows in the early years rather than the later years.

Magnitude and timing are extremely important in the selection of capital projects. Consider Table 14–18.

If the company has sufficient funds for one and only one project, the natural assumption would be to select Project D with a 35% IRR. Unfortunately, companies shy away from long-term payback periods because of the relative uncertainties of the cash inflows after Year 1. One chemical/plastics manufacturer will not consider any capital projects unless the payback period is less than one year and has an IRR in excess of 50%!

14.27 RISK ANALYSIS

Suppose you have a choice between two projects, both of which require the same initial investment, have identical net present values, and require the same yearly cash inflows to break even. If the cash inflow of the first investment has a probability of occurrence of 95% and that of the second investment is 70%, then risk analysis would indicate that the first investment is better.

Risk analysis refers to the chance that the selection of this project will prove to be unacceptable. In capital budgeting, risk analysis is almost entirely based upon how well we can predict cash inflows since the initial investment is usually known with some degree of certainty. The inflows, of course, are based upon sales projections, taxes, cost of raw materials, labor rates, and general economic conditions.

TABLE 14–19. SENSITIVITY ANALYSIS

Initial Investment	Project A $10,000	Project B $10,000
	Annual Cash Inflows	
optimistic	$ 8,000	$10,000
most likely	5,000	5,000
pessimistic	3,000	1,000
range	$ 5,000	$ 9,000
	Net Present Values	
optimistic	$20,326	$27,908
most likely	8,954	8,954
pessimistic	1,342	<6,209>
range	$18,984	$34,117

Sensitivity analysis is a simple way of assessing risk. A common approach is to estimate NPV based upon an optimistic (best case) approach, most likely (expected) approach, and pessimistic (worst case) approach. This can be illustrated using the table below. Both Projects A and B require the same initial investment of $10,000, with a cost of capital of 10%, and with expected five-year annual cash inflows of $5,000/year.

In Table 14–19, the range for Project A's NPV is substantially less than that of Project B, thus implying that Project A is less risky. A risk lover might select Project B because of the potential reward of $27,908, whereas a risk avoider would select Project A, which offers perhaps no chance for loss.

14.28 CAPITAL RATIONING

Capital rationing is the process of selecting the best group of projects such that the highest overall net present value will result without exceeding the total budget available. An assumption with capital rationing is that the projects under consideration are mutually exclusive. There are two approaches often considered for capital rationing.

The internal rate of return approach plots the IRRs in descending order against the cumulative dollar investment. The resulting figure is often called an investment opportunity schedule. As an example, suppose a company has $300,000 committed for projects and must select from the projects identified in Table 14–20. Furthermore, assume that the cost of capital is 10%.

Figure 14–20 shows the investment opportunity schedule. Project G should not be considered because the IRR is less than the firm's cost of capital. From Figure 14–20, we should select Projects, A, B, and C, which will consume $280,000 out of a total budget of $300,000. This allows us to have the three largest IRRs.

TABLE 14–20. PROJECTS UNDER CONSIDERATION

Project	Investment	IRR	Discounted cash flows at 10%
A	$ 50,000	20%	$116,000
B	120,000	18%	183,000
C	110,000	16%	147,000
D	130,000	15%	171,000
E	90,000	12%	103,000
F	180,000	11%	206,000
G	80,000	8%	66,000

The problem with the IRR approach is that it does not guarantee that the projects with the largest IRRs will maximize the total dollar returns. The reason for this is because not all of the funds have been consumed.

A better approach is the net present value method. In this method, the projects are again ranked according to their IRRs, but the combination of projects selected will be based upon the highest net present value. As an example, the selection of Projects A, B, and C from Table 14–20 requires an initial investment of $280,000 with resulting discounted cash flows of $446,000. The net present value of Projects A, B, and C is, therefore, $166,000. This assumes that unused portions of the original budget of $300,000 do not gain or lose money. However, if we now select Projects A, B, and D, we will invest $300,000 with a net present value of $170,000 ($470,000 less $300,000). Selection of Projects A, B, and D will, therefore, maximize net present value.

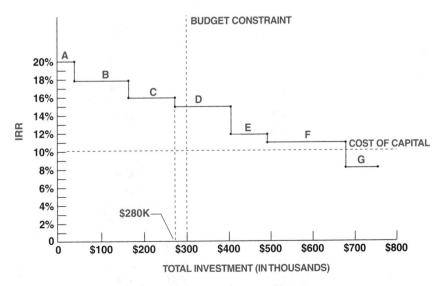

FIGURE 14–20. Investment Opportunity Schedule (IOS) for Table 14-20.

14–1 How does a project manager price out a job in which the specifications are not prepared until the job is half over?

14–2 Beta Corporation is in the process of completing a contract to produce 150 units for a given customer. The contract consisted of R&D, testing and qualification, and full production. The industrial engineering department had determined that the following number of hours were required to produce certain units:

Unit	Hours Required Per Unit
1	100
2	90
4	80
8	70
16	65
32	60
64	55
128	50

a. Plot the data points on regular graph paper with the Y-axis as hours and the X-axis as number of units produced.
b. Plot the data points on log–log paper and determine the slope of the line.
c. Compare parts a and b. What are your conclusions?
d. How much time should it take to manufacture the 150th unit?
e. How much time should it take to manufacture the 1,000th unit? Explain your answer. Is it realistic? If not, why?
f. As you are producing the 150th unit, you receive an immediate follow-on contract for another 150 units. How many manufacturing hours should you estimate for the follow-on effort (using only the learning curves)?
g. Let's assume that industrial engineering determines that the optimum number of hours (for 100 percent efficiency) of manufacturing is forty-five. At what efficiency factor are you now performing at the completion of unit number 150? After how many units in the follow-on contract will you reach the optimum level?
h. At the end of the first follow-on contract, your team and personnel are still together and performing at a 100 percent efficiency position (of part g). You have been awarded a second follow-on contract, but the work will not begin until six months from now. Assuming that you can assemble the same team, how many man-hours/unit will you estimate for the next 150-unit follow-on?
i. Would your answer to part h change if you could not assemble the same team? Explain your answer quantitatively.
j. You are now on the contract negotiation team for the second follow-on contract of 150 units (which is not scheduled to start for six months). Based on the people available and the "loss of learning" between contracts, your industrial engineering department estimates that you will be performing at a 60 percent efficiency factor. The customer says that your efficiency factor should be at least 75 percent. If your company is burdened at $40/hour, how much money is involved between the 60 and 75 percent efficiency factors?

k. What considerations should be made in deciding where to compromise in the efficiency factor?

14–3 With reference to Figure 14–10, under what conditions could *each* of the following situations occur:

a. Program manager and program office determine labor hours by pricing out the work breakdown structure without coordination with functional management.
b. Upper-level management determines the price of a bid without forming a program office or consulting functional management.
c. Perturbations on the base case are not performed.
d. The chief executive officer selects the program manager without consulting his directors.
e. Upper-level management does not wish to have a cost review meeting prior to submittal of a bid.

14–4 Can Figure 14–21 be used effectively to price out the cost of preparing reports?

14–5 Answer the following questions with reference to Figure 14–10.

a. The base case for a program is priced out at $22 million. The company's chief executive officer is required to obtain written permission from corporate to bid on programs in excess of $20 million. During the price review meeting the chief executive states that the bid will be submitted at $19.5 million. Should you, as program manager, question this?

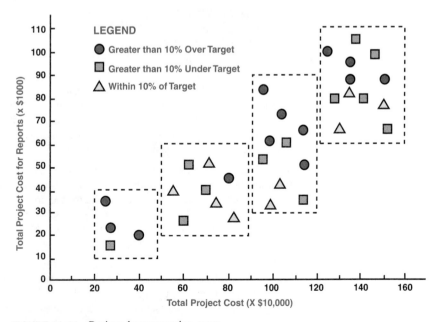

FIGURE 14–21. Project documentation costs.

    b. Would your answer to part a change if this program were a follow-on to an earlier program?

    c. Proposals normally consist of management, technical, and cost volumes. Indicate in Figure 14–10 where these volumes can go to press, assuming each can be printed independently.

14–6 Under what kind of projects would each of the following parameters be selected:

    a. Salary escalation factor of 0 percent.

    b. Materiel termination liability of 0 percent or 100 percent.

    c. Materiel commitments for twenty months of a twenty-four-month program.

    d. Demanning ratio of 0 percent or 100 percent of following months' labor.

14–7 How can upper-level management use the functional cost and hour summary to determine manpower planning for the entire company? How would you expect management to react if the functional cost and hour summary indicated a shortage or an abundance of trained personnel?

14–8 Which of the figures presented in this chapter should program management make available to the functional managers? Explain your answer.

14–9 The Jennings Construction Company has decided to bid on the construction for each of the two phases of a large project. The bidding requirements are that the costs for each phase be submitted separately together with a transition cost for turning over the first phase of the program to a second contractor should Jennings not receive both awards or perform unsatisfactorily on the first phase. The evaluation for the award of the second phase will not be made until the first phase is near completion. How can the transition costs be identified in the strategic planning model?

14–10 Two contractors decide to enter into a joint venture on a project. What difficulties can occur if the contractors have decided on who does what work, but changes may take place if problems occur? What happens if one contractor has higher salary levels and overhead rates?

14–11 The Jones Manufacturing Company is competing for a production contract that requires that work begin in January 1979. The cost package for the proposal must be submitted by July 1978. The business base, and therefore the overhead rates, are uncertain because Jones has the possibility of winning another contract, to be announced in September 1978. How can the impact of the announcement be included in the proposal? How would you handle a situation where another contract may not be renewed after January 1979, i.e., assume that announcement would not be made until March?

14–12 Many competitive programs contain two phases: research and development, and production. Production profits far exceed R&D profits. The company that wins the R&D contract normally becomes a favorite for the production contract, as well as for any follow-on work. How can the dollar figures attached to follow-on work influence the cost package that you submit for the R&D phase? Would your answer change if the man-hours submitted for the R&D phase become the basis for the production phase?

14–13 During initial pricing activities, one of the functional managers discovers that the work breakdown structure requires costing data at a level that is not normally made, and will undoubtedly incur additional costs. How should you, as a program manager, respond to this situation? What are your alternatives?

14–14 Should the project manager give the final manpower loading curves to the functional managers? If so, at what point in time?

14–15 You have been asked to price out a project for an outside customer. The project will run for eight months. Direct labor is $100,000 for each month and the overhead rate is fixed at 100 percent per month. Termination liability on the direct labor and overhead rate is 80 percent of the following month's expenses. Material expenses are as follows:

Material A: Cost is $100,000 payable 30 days net. Material is needed at the end of the fifth month. Lead time is four months with termination liability expenses as follows:

> 30 days: 25%
> 60 days: 75%
> 90 days: 100%

Material B: Cost is $200,000, payable on delivery. Material is needed at the end of the seventh month. Lead time is three months with termination liability as follows:

> 30 days: 50%
> 60 days: 100%

Complete the table below, neglecting profits.

14–16 Should a project manager be appointed in the bidding stage of a project? If so, what authority should he have, and who is responsible for winning the contract?

	Month							
	1	2	3	4	5	6	7	8
Direct labor								
Overhead								
Materiel								
Monthly cash flow								
Cumulative cash flow								
Monthly termination liability: labor								
Cumulative termination liability: labor								
Monthly termination liability: materiel								
Cumulative termination liability: materiel								
Total project termination liability								

14–17 Explain how useful each of the following can be during the estimating of project costs:

    a. Contingency planning and estimating
    b. Using historical databases (see Figure 15–12)
    c. Usefulness of computer estimating
    d. Usefulness of performance factors to account for inefficiencies and uncertainties.

CASE STUDIES

POLYPRODUCTS INCORPORATED

Polyproducts Incorporated, a major producer of rubber components, employs 800 people and is organized with a matrix structure. Exhibit 14–1 shows the salary structure for the company, and Exhibit 14–2 identifies the overhead rate projections for the next two years.

Polyproducts has been very successful at maintaining its current business base with approximately 10 percent overtime. Both exempt and nonexempt employees are paid overtime at the rate of time and a half. All overtime hours are burdened at an overhead rate of 30 percent.

On April 16, Polyproducts received a request for proposal from Capital Corporation (see Exhibit 14–3). Polyproducts had an established policy for competitive bidding. First, they would analyze the marketplace to see whether it would be advantageous for them to compete. This task was normally assigned to the marketing group (which operated on overhead). If the marketing group responded favorably, then Polyproducts would go through the necessary pricing procedures to determine a bid price.

On April 24, the marketing group displayed a prospectus on the four companies that would most likely be competing with Polyproducts for the Capital contract. This is shown in Exhibit 14–4.

At the same time, top management of Polyproducts made the following projections concerning the future business over the next eighteen months:

1. Salary increases would be given to all employees at the beginning of the thirteenth month.
2. If the Capital contract was won, then the overhead rates would go down 0.5 percent each quarter (assuming no strike by employees).
3. There was a possibility that the union would go out on strike if the salary increases were not satisfactory. Based on previous experience, the strike would last between one and two months. It was possible that, due to union demands, the overhead rates would increase by 1 percent per quarter for each quarter after the strike (due to increased fringe benefit packages).
4. With the current work force, the new project would probably have to be done on overtime. (At least 75 percent of all man-hours were estimated to be performed on overtime). The alternative would be to hire additional employees.

Exhibit 14–1. Salary Structure

Pay Scale	
Grade	Hourly Rate
1	8.00
2	9.00
3	11.00
4	12.00
5	14.00
6	18.00
7	21.00
8	24.00
9	28.00

	Number of Employees per Grade									
Department	*1*	*2*	*3*	*4*	*5*	*6*	*7*	*8*	*9*	*Total*
R&D			5	40	20	10	12	8	5	100
Design		3	5	40	30	10	10	2		100
Project engineering						30	15	10	5	60
Project management							10	10	10	30
Cost accounting				20	10	10	10	10		60
Contracts						3	4	2	1	10
Publications		3	5	3	3	3	3			20
Computers				2	3	3	1	1		10
Manufacturing engineering			2	7	7	3	1			20
Industrial engineering					4	3	2	1		10
Facilities					8	9	10	7	1	35
Quality control				3	4	5	5	2	1	20
Production line				55	50	50	30	10	5	200
Traffic				2	2	1				5
Procurement				2	2	2	2	1	1	10
Safety						2	2	1		5
Inventory control	2	2		2	2	1	1			10

5. All materials could be obtained from one vendor. It can be assumed that raw materials cost $200/unit (without scrap factors) and that these raw materials are new to Polyproducts.

On May 1, Roger Henning was selected by Jim Grimm, the director of project management, to head the project.

Grimm: "Roger, we've got a problem on this one. When you determine your final bid, see if you can account for the fact that we may lose our union. I'm not sure exactly how that will impact our bid. I'll leave that up to you. All I know is that a lot of our people are getting unhappy with the union. See what numbers you can generate."

Henning: "I've read the RFP and have a question about inventory control. Should I look at quantity discount buying for raw materials?"

Exhibit 14–2. Overhead Structure

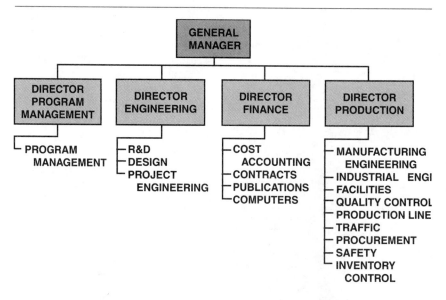

Division	Quarter							
	1	*2*	*3*	*4*	*5*	*6*	*7*	*8*
Engineering	75	75	76	76	76	76	77	78
Program management	100	100	100	100	100	100	100	100
Finance	50	50	50	52	54	54	55	55
Production	175	176	177	177	177	178	178	178
Overhead rates per quarter, %.								

Grimm: "Yes. But be careful about your assumptions. I want to know all of the assumptions you make."

Henning: "How stable is our business base over the next eighteen months?"

Grimm: "You had better consider both an increase and a decrease of 10 percent. Get me the costs for all cases. Incidentally, the grapevine says that there might be follow-on contracts if we perform well. You know what that means."

Henning: "Okay. I get the costs for each case and then we'll determine what our best bid will be."

On May 15, Roger Henning received a memo from the pricing department summing up the base case man-hour estimates. (This is shown in Exhibits 14–5 and 14–6.) Now Roger Henning wondered what people he could obtain from the functional departments and what would be a reasonable bid to make.

Exhibit 14–3. Request for Proposal

Capital Corporation is seeking bids for 10,000 rubber components that must be manufactured according to specifications supplied by the customer. The contractor will be given sufficient flexibility for material selection and testing provided that all testing include latest developments in technology. All material selection and testing must be within specifications. All vendors selected by the contractor must be (1) certified as a vendor for continuous procurement (follow-on contracts will not be considered until program completion), and (2) operating with a quality control program that is acceptable to both the customer and contractor.

The following timetable must be adhered to:

Month after Go-ahead	Description
2	R&D completed and preliminary design meeting held
4	Qualification completed and final design review meeting held
5	Production setup completed
9	Delivery of 3,000 units
13	Delivery of 3,500 units
17	Delivery of 3,500 units
18	Final report and cost summary

The contract will be firm-fixed-price and the contractor can develop his own work breakdown structure on final approval by the customer.

SMALL PROJECT COST ESTIMATING AT PERCY COMPANY

Paul graduated from college in June 1970 with a degree in industrial engineering. He accepted a job as a manufacturing engineer in the Manufacturing Division of Percy Company. His prime responsibility was performing estimates for the Manufacturing Division. Each estimate was then given to the appropriate project office for consideration. The estimation procedure history had shown the estimates to be valid.

In 1975, Paul was promoted to project engineer. His prime responsibility was the

Exhibit 14–4. Prospectus

Company	Business Base $ Million	Growth Rate Last Year (%)	Profit %	R&D Personnel	Contracts In-House	Number of Employees	Overtime (%)	Personnel Turnover (%)
Alpha	10	10	5	Below avg.	6	30	5	1.0
Beta	20	10	7	Above avg.	15	250	30	0.25
Gamma	50	10	15	Avg.	4	550	20	0.50
Polyproducts	100	15	10	Avg.	30	800	10	1.0

Exhibit 14–5.

To: Roger Henning
From: Pricing Department
Subject: Rubber Components Production

1. All man-hours in the Exhibit (14–12) are based upon performance standards for a grade-7 employee. For each grade below 7, add 10 percent of the grade-7 standard and subtract 10 percent of the grade standard for each employee above grade 7. This applies to all departments as long as they are direct labor hours (i.e., not administrative support as in project 1).
2. Time duration is fixed at 18 months.
3. Each production run normally requires four months. The company has enough raw materials on hand for R&D, but must allow 2 months lead time for purchases that would be needed for a production run. Unfortunately, the vendors cannot commit large purchases, but will commit to monthly deliveries up to a maximum of 1,000 units of raw materials per month. Furthermore, the vendors will guarantee a fixed cost of $200 per raw material unit during the first 12 months of the project only. Material escalation factors are expected at month 13 due to renegotiation of the United Rubber Workers contracts.
4. Use the following work breakdown structure:

> Program: Rubber Components Production
>> Project 1: Support
>>> TASK 1: Project office
>>> TASK 2: Functional support
>> Project 2: Preproduction
>>> TASK 1: R&D
>>> TASK 2: Qualification
>> Project 3: Production
>>> TASK 1: Setup
>>> TASK 2: Production

---

coordination of all estimates for work to be completed by all of the divisions. For one full year Paul went by the book and did not do any estimating except for project office personnel manager. After all, he was now in the project management division, which contained job descriptions including such words as "coordinating and integrating."

In 1976, Paul was transferred to small program project management. This was a new organization designed to perform low-cost projects. The problem was that these projects could not withstand the expenses needed for formal divisional cost estimates. For five projects, Paul's estimates were "right on the money." But the sixth project incurred a cost overrun of $20,000 in the Manufacturing Division.

In November 1977, a meeting was called to resolve the question of "Why did the overrun occur?" The attendees included the general manager, all division managers and directors, the project manager, and Paul. Paul now began to worry about what he should say in his defense.

Exhibit 14–6.   Program: Rubber Components Production

Project	Task	Department	1	2	3	4	5	6	7	8	9	10	11	12	13	14	15	16	17	18
1	1	Proj. Mgt.	480	480	480	480	480	480	480	480	480	480	480	480	480	480	480	480	480	480
1	2	R&D	16	16	16	16	16	16	16	16	16	16	16	16	16	16	16	16	16	16
		Proj. Eng.	320	320	320	320	320	320	320	320	320	320	320	320	320	320	320	320	320	320
		Cost Acct.	80	80	80	320	320	320	320	320	320	320	320	320	320	320	320	320	320	320
		Contracts	320	320	320	320	320	x320	320	320	320	320	320	320	320	320	320	320	320	320
		Manu. Eng.	320	320	320	320	320	320	320	320	320	320	320	320	320	320	320	320	320	320
		Quality Cont.	160	160	160	160	160	160	160	160	160	160	160	160	160	160	160	160	160	160
		Production	160	160	160	160	160	160	160	160	160	160	160	160	160	160	160	160	160	160
		Procurement	80	80	80	80	80	80	80	80	80	80	80	80	80	80	80	80	80	80
		Publications	80	80	80	80	80	80	80	80	80	80	80	80	80	80	80	80	80	80
		Invent. Cont.	80	80	80	80	80	80	80	80	80	80	80	80	80	80	80	80	80	80
2	1	R&D	480	480																
		Proj. Eng.	160	160																
		Manu. Eng.	160	160																
2	2	R&D			80	80														
		Proj. Eng.			160	160														
		Manu. Eng.			160	160														
		Ind. Eng.			40	40														
		Facilities			20	20														
		Quality Cont.			160	160														
		Production			600	600														
		Safety			20	20														
3	1	Proj. Eng.					160													
		Manu. Eng.					160													
		Facilities					80													
		Quality Cont.					160													
		Production					320													
3	2	Proj. Eng.						160	160	160	160	160	160	160	160	160	160	160	160	160
		Manu. Eng.						320	320	320	320	320	320	320	320	320	320	320	320	320
		Quality Cont.						320	320	320	320	320	320	320	320	320	320	320	320	320
		Production						1600	1600	1600	1600	1600	1600	1600	1600	1600	1600	1600	1600	1600
		Safety						20	20	20	20	20	20	20	20	20	20	20	20	20

CAPITAL INDUSTRIES

In the summer of 1976, Capital Industries undertook a material development program to see if a hard plastic bumper could be developed for medium-sized cars. By January 1977, Project Bumper (as it was called by management) had developed a material that endured all preliminary laboratory testing.

One more step was required before full-scale laboratory testing: a three-dimensional stress analysis on bumper impact collisions. The decision to perform the stress analysis was the result of a concern on the part of the technical community that the bumper might not perform correctly under certain conditions. The cost of the analysis would require corporate funding over and above the original estimates. Since the current costs were identical to what was budgeted, the additional funding was a necessity.

Frank Allen, the project engineer in the Bumper Project Office, was assigned control of the stress analysis. Frank met with the functional manager of the engineering analysis section to discuss the assignment of personnel to the task.

Functional Manager: "I'm going to assign Paul Troy to this project. He's a new man with a Ph.D. in structural analysis. I'm sure he'll do well."

Frank Allen: "This is a priority project. We need seasoned veterans, not new people, regardless of whether or not they have Ph.D.'s. Why not use some other project as a testing ground for your new employee?"

Functional Manager: "You project people must accept part of the responsibility for on-the-job training. I might agree with you if we were talking about blue-collar workers on an assembly line. But this is a college graduate, coming to us with a good technical background."

Frank Allen: "He may have a good background, but he has no experience. He needs supervision. This is a one-man task. The responsibility will be yours if he fouls up."

Functional Manager: "I've already given him our book for cost estimates. I'm sure he'll do fine. I'll keep in close communication with him during the project."

Frank Allen met with Paul Troy to get an estimate for the job.

Paul Troy: "I estimate that 800 hours will be required."

Frank Allen: "Your estimate seems low. Most three-dimensional analyses require at least 1,000 hours. Why is your number so low?"

Paul Troy: "Three-dimensional analysis? I thought that it would be a two-dimensional analysis. But no difference; the procedures are the same. I can handle it."

Frank Allen: "O.K. I'll give you 1,100 hours. But if you overrun it, we'll both be sorry."

Frank Allen followed the project closely. By the time the costs were 50 percent completed, performance was only 40 percent. A cost overrun seemed inevitable. The functional manager still asserted that he was tracking the job and that the difficulties were a result of the new material properties. His section had never worked with materials like these before.

Six months later Troy announced that the work would be completed in one week, two months later than planned. The two-month delay caused major problems in facility and equipment utilization. Project Bumper was still paying for employees who were "waiting" to begin full-scale testing.

On Monday mornings, the project office would receive the weekly labor monitor report for the previous week. This week the report indicated that the publications and graphics art department had spent over 200 man-hours (last week) in preparation of the final report. Frank Allen was furious. He called a meeting with Paul Troy and the functional manager.

Frank Allen: "Who told you to prepare a formal report? All we wanted was a go or no-go decision as to structural failure."

Paul Troy: "I don't turn in any work unless it's professional. This report will be documented as a masterpiece."

Frank Allen: "Your 50 percent cost overrun will also be a masterpiece. I guess your estimating was a little off!"

Paul Troy: "Well, this was the first time that I had performed a three-dimensional stress analysis. And what's the big deal? I got the job done, didn't I?"

PAYTON CORPORATION

Payton Corporation had decided to respond to a government RFP for the R&D phase on a new project. The statement of work specified that the project must be completed within ninety days after go-ahead, and that the contract would be at a fixed cost and fee.

The majority of the work would be accomplished by the development lab. According to government regulations, the estimated cost must be based on the *average* cost of the entire department, which was $19.00 per hour (unburdened).

Payton won the contract for a total package (cost plus fee) of $305,000. After the first weekly labor report was analyzed, it became evident that the development lab was spending $28.50 per hour. The project manager decided to discuss the problem with the manager of the development lab.

Project Manager: "Obviously you know why I'm here. At the rate that you're spending money, we'll overrun our budget by 50 percent."

Lab Manager: "That's your problem, not mine. When I estimate the cost to do a job, I submit only the hours necessary based on historical standards. The pricing department converts the hours to dollars based on department averages."

Project Manager: "Well, why are we using the most expensive people? Obviously there must be lower-salaried people capable of performing the work."

Lab Manager: "Yes, I do have lower-salaried people, but none who can complete the job within the two months required by the contract. I have to use people high on the learning curve, and they're not cheap. You should have told the pricing department to increase the average cost for the department."

Project Manager: "I wish I could, but government regulations forbid this. If we were ever audited, or if this proposal were compared to other salary structures in other proposals, we would be in deep trouble. The only legal way to accomplish this would be to set up a new department for those higher-paid employees working on this project. Then the average department salary would be correct.

"Unfortunately the administrative costs of setting up a temporary unit for only two months is prohibitive. For long-duration projects, this technique is often employed.

"Why couldn't you have increased the hours to compensate for the increased dollars required?"

Lab Manager: "I have to submit labor justifications for all hours I estimate. If I were to get audited, my job would be on the line. Remember, we had to submit labor justification for all work as part of the proposal.

"Perhaps next time management might think twice before bidding on a short-duration project. You might try talking to the customer to get his opinion."

Project Manager: "His response would probably be the same regardless of whether I explained the situation to him before we submitted the proposal or now, after we have negotiated it. There's a good chance that I've just lost my Christmas bonus."

    a. What is the basis for the problem?
    b. Who is at fault?
    c. How can the present situation be corrected?
    d. Is there any way this situation can be prevented from recurring?
    e. How would you handle this situation on a longer-duration project, say one year, assuming that multiple departments are involved and that no new departments were established other than possibly the project office?
    f. Should a customer be willing to accept monetary responsibility for this type of situation, possibly by permitting established standards to be deviated from? If so, then how many months should be considered as a short-duration project?

CORY ELECTRIC

"Frankly speaking, Jeff, I didn't think that we would stand a chance in winning this $20 million program. I was really surprised when they said that they'd like to accept our bid and begin contract negotiations. As chief contract administrator, you'll head up the negotiating team," remarked Gus Bell, vice president and general manager of Cory Electric. "You have two weeks to prepare your data and line up your team. I want to see you when you're ready to go."

Jeff Stokes was chief contract negotiator for Cory Electric, a $250-million-a-year electrical components manufacturer serving virtually every major U.S. industry. Cory Electric had a well-established matrix structure that had withstood fifteen years of testing. Job casting standards were well established, but did include some "fat" upon the discretion of the functional manager.

Two weeks later, Jeff met with Gus Bell to discuss the negotiation process:

Gus Bell: "Have you selected an appropriate team? You had better make sure that you're covered on all sides."

Jeff: "There will be four, plus myself, at the negotiating table; the program manager, the chief project engineer who developed the engineering labor package; the chief manufacturing engineer who developed the production labor package; and a pricing specialist who has been on the proposal since the kickoff meeting. We have a strong team and should be able to handle any questions."

Gus Bell: "Okay, I'll take your word for it. I have my own checklist for contract negotiations. I want you to come back with a guaranteed fee of $1.6 million for our stockholders. Have you worked out the possible situations based on the negotiated costs?"

Jeff: "Yes! Our minimum position is $20 million plus an 8 percent profit. Of course, this profit percentage will vary depending on the negotiated cost. We can bid the program at a $15 million cost; that's $5 million below our target, and still book a $1.6 million profit by overrunning the cost-plus-incentive-fee contract. Here is a list of the possible cases (see Exhibit 14–7)."

Gus Bell: "If we negotiate a cost overrun fee, make sure that cost accounting knows about it. I don't want the total fee to be booked as profit if we're going to need it later to cover the overrun. Can we justify our overhead rates, general and administrative costs, and our salary structure?"

Jeff: "That's a problem. You know that 20 percent of our business comes from Mitre Corporation. If they fail to renew our contract for another two-year follow-on effort, then our overhead rates will jump drastically. Which overhead rates should I use?"

Gus Bell: "Let's put in a renegotiation clause to protect us against a drastic change in our business base. Make sure that the customer understands that as part of the terms and conditions. Are there any unusual terms and conditions?"

Exhibit 14–7. Cost Positions

Negotiated Cost	%	Negotiated Fee			
		Target Fee	Overrun Fee	Total Fee	Total Package
15,000,000	14.00	1,600,000	500,000	2,100,000	17,100,000
16,000,000	12.50	1,600,000	400,000	2,000,000	18,000,000
17,000,000	11.18	1,600,000	300,000	1,900,000	18,900,000
18,000,000	10.00	1,600,000	200,000	1,800,000	19,800,000
19,000,000	8.95	1,600,000	100,000	1,700,000	20,700,000
20,000,000	8.00	1,600,000	0	1,600,000	21,600,000
21,000,000	7.14	1,600,000	−100,000	1,500,000	*22,500,000
22,000,000	6.36	1,600,000	−200,000	1,400,000	23,400,000
23,000,000	5.65	1,600,000	−300,000	1,300,000	24,300,000
24,000,000	5.00	1,600,000	−400,000	1,200,000	25,200,000

Assume total cost will be spent:

21,000,000	7.61		
22,000,000	7.27	Minimum position	= $20,000,000
23,000,000	6.96	Minimum fee	= 1,600,000 = 8% of minimum position
24,000,000	6.67	Sharing ratio	= $^{90}/_{10}$ %

Jeff: "I've read over all terms and conditions, and so have all of the project office personnel as well as the key functional managers. The only major item is that the customer wants us to qualify some new vendors as sources for raw material procurement. We have included in the package the cost of qualifying two new raw material suppliers."

Gus Bell: "Where are the weak points in our proposal? I'm sure we have some."

Jeff: "Last month, the customer sent in a fact-finding team to go over all of our labor justifications. The impression that I get from our people is that we're covered all the way around. The only major problem might be where we'll be performing on our learning curve. We put into the proposal a 45 percent learning curve efficiency. The customer has indicated that we should be up around 50 to 55 percent efficiency, based on our previous contracts with him. Unfortunately, those contracts the customer referred to were four years old. Several of the employees who worked on those programs have left the company. Others are assigned to ongoing projects here at Cory. I estimate that we could put together about 10 percent of the people we used previously. That learning curve percentage will be a big point for disagreements. We finished off the previous programs with the customer at a 35 percent learning curve position. I don't see how they can expect us to be smarter, given these circumstances."

Gus Bell: "If that's the only weakness, then we're in good shape. It sounds like we have a foolproof audit trail. That's good! What's your negotiation sequence going to be?"

Jeff: "I'd like to negotiate the bottom line only, but that's a dream. We'll probably negotiate the raw materials, the man-hours and the learning curve, the overhead rate, and, finally, the profit percentage. Hopefully, we can do it in that order."

Gus Bell: "Do you think that we'll be able to negotiate a cost above our minimum position?"

Jeff: "Our proposal was for $22.2 million. I don't foresee any problem that will prevent us from coming out ahead of the minimum position. The 5 percent change in learning curve efficiency amounts to approximately $1 million. We should be well covered.

"The first move will be up to them. I expect that they'll come in with an offer of $18 to $19 million. Using the binary chop procedure, that'll give us our guaranteed minimum position."

Gus Bell: "Do you know the guys who you'll be negotiating with?"

Jeff: "Yes, I've dealt with them before. The last time, the negotiations took three days. I think we both got what we wanted. I expect this one to go just as smoothly."

Gus Bell: "Okay, Jeff. I'm convinced we're prepared for negotiations. Have a good trip."

The negotiations began at 9:00 A.M. on Monday morning. The customer countered the original proposal of $22.2 million with an offer of $15 million. After six solid hours of arguments, Jeff and his team adjourned. Jeff immediately called Gus Bell at Cory Electric:

Jeff: "Their counteroffer to our bid is absurd. They've asked us to make a counteroffer to their offer. We can't do that. The instant we give them a counteroffer, we are in fact giving credibility to their absurd bid. Now, they're claiming that, if we don't give them a counteroffer, then we're not bargaining in good faith. I think we're in trouble."

Gus Bell: "Has the customer done their homework to justify their bid?"

Jeff: "Yes. Very well. Tomorrow we're going to discuss every element of the proposal, task by task. Unless something drastically changes in their position within the next day or two, contract negotiations will probably take up to a month."

Gus Bell: "Perhaps this is one program that should be negotiated at the top levels of management. Find out if the person that you're negotiating with reports to a vice president and general manager, as you do. If not, break off contract negotiations until the customer gives us someone at your level. We'll negotiate this at my level, if necessary."

CAMDEN CONSTRUCTION CORPORATION

"For five years I've heard nothing but flimsy excuses from you people as to why the competition was beating us out in the downtown industrial building construction business," remarked Joseph Camden, president. "Excuses, excuses, excuses; that's all I ever hear! Only 15 percent of our business over the past five years has been in this area, and virtually all of that was with our established customers. Our growth rate is terrible. Everyone seems to just barely outbid us. Maybe our bidding process leaves something to be desired. If you three vice presidents don't come up with the answers then we'll have three positions to fill by midyear.

"We have a proposal request coming in next week, and I want to win it. Do you guys understand that?"

Background

Camden Construction Corporation matured from a $1 million to a $26 million construction company between 1969 and 1979. Camden's strength was in its ability to work well with the customer. Their reputation for quality work far exceeded the local competitor's reputation.

Most of Camden's contracts in the early seventies were with long-time customers who were willing to go sole-source procurement and pay the extra price for quality and service. With the recession of 1975, Camden found that, unless it penetrated the competitive bidding market, its business base would decline.

In 1976, Camden was "forced" to go union in order to bid government projects. Unionization drastically reduced Camden's profit margin, but offered a greater promise for increased business. Camden had avoided the major downtown industrial construction market. But with the availability of multimillion-dollar skyscraper projects, Camden wanted its share of the pot of gold at the base of the rainbow.

Meeting of the Minds

On January 17, 1979, the three vice presidents met to consider ways of improving Camden's bidding technique.

V.P. Finance: "You know, fellas, I hate to say it, but we haven't done a good job in developing a bid. I don't think that we've been paying enough attention to the competition. Now's the time to begin."

V.P. Operations: "What we really need is a list of who our competitors have been on each project over the last five years. Perhaps we can find some bidding trends."

Exhibit 14–8. Proposal Data Summary (Cost in Tens of Thousands)

Year	Acme	Ajax	Pioneer	Camden Bid	Camden Cost
1970	270	244	260	283	260
1970	260	250	233	243	220
1970	355	340	280	355	300
1971	836	830	838	866	800
1971	300	288	286	281	240
1971	570	560	540	547	500
1972	240*	375	378	362	322
1972	100*	190	180	188	160
1972	880	874	883	866	800
1973	410	318	320	312	280
1973	220	170	182	175	151
1973	400	300	307	316	283
1974	408	300*	433	449	400
1975	338	330	342	333	300
1975	817	808	800	811	700
1975	886	884	880	904	800
1976	384	385	380	376	325
1976	140	148	158	153	130
1977	197	193	188	200	165
1977	750	763	760	744	640

*Buy-in contracts

V.P. Engineering: "I think the big number we need is to find out the overhead rates of each of the companies. After all, union contracts specify the rate at which the employees will work. Therefore, except for the engineering design packages, all of the companies should be almost identical in direct labor man-hours and union labor wages for similar jobs."

V.P. Finance: "I think I can hunt down past bids by our competitors. Many of them are in public records. That'll get us started."

V.P. Operations: "What good will it do? The past is past. Why not just look toward the future?"

V.P. Finance: "What we want to do is to maximize our chances for success and maximize profits at the same time. Unfortunately, these two cannot be met at the same time. We must find a compromise."

V.P. Engineering: "Do you think that the competition looks at our past bids?"

V.P. Finance: "They're stupid if they don't. What we have to do is to determine their target profit and target cost. I know many of the competitors personally and have a good feel for what their target profits are. We'll have to assume that their target direct costs equals ours; otherwise we will have a difficult time making a comparison."

V.P. Engineering: "What can we do to help you?"

V.P. Finance: "You'll have to tell me how long it takes to develop the engineering design packages, and how our personnel in engineering design stack up against the competition's salary structure. See if you can make some contacts and find out how much money the competition put into some of their proposals for engineering design activities. That'll be a big help.

"We'll also need good estimates from engineering and operations for this new project we're suppose to bid. Let me pull my data together, and we'll meet again in two days, if that's all right with you two."

Reviewing the Data   The executives met two days later to review the data. The vice president for finance presented the data on the three most likely competitors (see Exhibit 14–8). These companies were Ajax, Acme, and Pioneer. The vice president for finance made the following comments:

1. In 1973, Acme was contract-rich and had a difficult time staffing all of its projects.
2. In 1970, Pioneer was in danger of bankruptcy. It was estimated that it needed to win one or two in order to hold its organization together.
3. Two of the 1972 companies were probably buy-ins based on the potential for follow-on work.
4. The 1974 contract was for an advanced state-of-the-art project. It is estimated that Ajax bought in so that it could break into a new field.

The vice presidents for engineering and operations presented data indicating that the total project cost (fully burdened) was approximately $5 million. "Well," thought the vice president of finance, "I wonder what we should bid so it we will have at least a reasonable chance of winning the contract?"

15

Cost Control

15.0 INTRODUCTION

Cost control is equally important to all companies, regardless of size. Small companies generally have tighter monetary controls, mainly because of the risk with the failure of as little as one project, but with less sophisticated control techniques. Large companies may have the luxury to spread project losses over several projects, whereas the small company may have few projects.

Too many people have a poor definition of cost control, with the final result shown in Figure 15–1. Cost control is not only "monitoring" of costs and recording perhaps massive quantities of data, but also analyzing of the data in order to take corrective action before it is too late. Cost control should be performed by all personnel who incur costs, not merely the project office.

Cost control implies good cost management, which must include:

- Cost estimating
- Cost accounting
- Project cash flow
- Company cash flow
- Direct labor costing
- Overhead rate costing
- Others, such as incentives, penalties, and profit-sharing

Cost control is actually a subsystem of the management cost and control system (MCCS) rather than a complete system per se. This is shown in Figure 15–2, where the MCCS is represented as a two-cycle process: a planning cycle and an operating cycle. The operating cycle is what is commonly referred to as the cost control system. Failure of a cost control system to accurately describe the true status of a project

FIGURE 15–1. Do you control costs, or do costs control you?

does not necessarily imply that the cost control system is at fault. Any cost control system is only as good as the original plan against which performance will be measured. It is more common for the plan to be at fault than the control system. Therefore, the designing of a company's planning system must take into account the cost control system as well. For this reason, it is common for the planning cycle to be referred to as planning and control, whereas the operating cycle is referred to as cost and control.

The planning and control system selected must be able to satisfy management's needs and requirements in order that they can accurately project the status toward objective completion. The purpose of any management cost and control system is to establish policies, procedures, and techniques that can be used in the day-to-day management and control of projects and programs. The planning and control system must, therefore, provide information that:

- Gives a picture of true work progress
- Will relate cost and schedule performance
- Identifies potential problems with respect to their sources.
- Provides information to project managers with a practical level of summarization
- Demonstrates that the milestones are valid, timely, and auditable

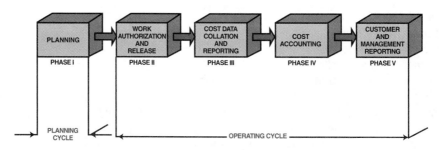

FIGURE 15–2. Phases of a management cost and control system.

The planning and control system, in addition to being a tool by which objectives can be defined (i.e., hierarchy of objectives and organization accountability), exists as a tool to develop planning, measure progress, and control change. As a tool for planning, the system must be able to:

- Plan and schedule work
- Identify those indicators that will be used for measurement
- Establish direct labor budgets
- Establish overhead budgets
- Identify management reserve

The project budget that is the final result of the planning cycle of the MCCS must be reasonable, attainable, and based on contractually negotiated costs and the statement of work. The basis for the budget is either historical cost, best estimates, or industrial engineering standards. The budget must identify planned manpower requirements, contract-allocated funds, and management reserve.

Establishing budgets requires that the planner fully understand the meaning of standards. There are two categories of standards. Performance results standards are quantitative measurements and include such items as quality of work, quantity of work, cost of work, and time-to-complete. Process standards are qualitative, including personnel, functional, and physical factors relationships. Standards are advantageous in that they provide a means for unity, a basis for effective control, and an incentive for others. The disadvantage of standards is that performance is often frozen, and employees are quite often unable to adjust to the differences.

As a tool for measuring progress and controlling change, the systems must be able to:

- Measure resources consumed
- Measure status and accomplishments
- Compare measurements to projections and standards
- Provide the basis for diagnosis and replanning

In using the MCCS, the following guidelines usually apply:

- The level of detail is specified by the project manager with approval by top management.
- Centralized authority and control over each project are the responsibility of the project management division.
- For large projects, the project manager may be supported by a project team for utilization of the MCCS.

Almost all project planning and control systems have identifiable design requirements. These include:

- A common framework from which to integrate time, cost, and technical performance
- Ability to track progress of significant parameters
- Quick response
- Capability for end-value prediction
- Accurate and appropriate data for decision making by each level of management
- Full exception reporting with problem analysis capability
- Immediate quantitative evaluation of alternative solutions

MCCS planning activities include:

- Contract receipt (if applicable)
- Work authorization for project planning
- Work breakdown structure
- Subdivided work description
- Schedules
- Planning charts
- Budgets

MCCS planning charts are worksheets used to create the budget. These charts include planned labor in hours and material dollars.

MCCS planning is accomplished in one of these ways:

- One level below the lowest level of the WBS
- At the lowest management level
- By cost element or cost account

Even with a fully developed planning and control system, there are numerous benefits and costs. The appropriate system must consider a cost-benefit analysis, and include such items as:

- Project benefits
  - Planning and control techniques facilitate:
    - —Derivation of output specifications (project objectives)
    - —Delineation of required activities (work)
    - —Coordination and communication between organizational units
    - —Determination of type, amount, and timing of necessary resources
    - —Recognition of high-risk elements and assessment of uncertainties
    - —Suggestions of alternative courses of action
    - —Realization of effect of resource level changes on schedule and output performance
    - —Measurement and reporting of genuine progress
    - —Identification of potential problems
    - —Basis for problem solving, decision making, and corrective action
    - —Assurance of coupling between planning and control
- Project cost
  - Planning and control techniques require:
    - —New forms (new systems) of information from additional sources and incremental processing (managerial time, computer expense, etc.)
    - —Additional personnel or smaller span of control to free managerial time for planning and control tasks (increased overhead)
    - —Training in use of techniques (time and materials)

A well-disciplined MCCS will produce the following results:

- Policies and procedures that will minimize the ability to distort reporting
- Strong management emphasis on meeting commitments

- Weekly team meetings with a formalized agenda, action items, and minutes.
- Top-management periodic review of the technical and financial status
- Simplified internal audit for checking compliance with procedures

For MCCS to be effective, both the scheduling and budgeting systems must be disciplines and formal in order to prevent inadvertent or arbitrary budget or schedule changes. This does *not* mean that the baseline budget and schedule, once established, is static or inflexible. Rather, it means that changes must be controlled and result only from deliberate management actions.

Disciplined use of MCCS is designed to put pressure on the project manager to perform exceptionally good project planning so that changes will be minimized. As an example, government subcontractors may not:

- Make retroactive changes to budgets or costs for work that has been completed.
- Rebudget work-in-progress activities
- Transfer work or budget independently of each other
- Reopen closed work packages

In some industries, the MCCS must be used on all contracts of $2 million or more, including firm-fixed-price efforts. The fundamental test of whether to use the MCCS is to determine whether the contracts have established end-item deliverables, either hardware or computer software, that must be accomplished through measurable efforts.

Two new programs are currently being used by the government and industry in conjunction with the MCCS as an attempt to improve effectiveness in cost control. The zero-base budgeting program was established to provide better estimating techniques for the verification portion of control. The design-to-cost program assists the decision-making part of the control process by identifying a decision-making framework from which replanning can take place.

15.1 UNDERSTANDING CONTROL

Effective management of a program during the operating cycle requires that a well-organized cost and control system be designed, developed, and implemented so that immediate feedback can be obtained, whereby the up-to-date usage or resources can be compared to target objectives established during the planning cycle. The requirements for an effective control system (for both cost and schedule/performance) should include:[1]

- Thorough planning of the work to be performed to complete the project
- Good estimating of time, labor, and costs
- Clear communication of the scope of required tasks
- A disciplined budget and authorization of expenditures

1. Russell D. Archibald, *Managing High-Technology Programs and Projects* (New York: John Wiley & Sons, 1976), p. 191.

- Timely accounting of physical progress and cost expenditures
- Periodic reestimation of time and cost to complete remaining work
- Frequent, periodic comparison of actual progress and expenditures to schedules and budgets, both at the time of comparison and at project completion

Management must compare the time, cost, and performance of the program to the budgeted time, cost, and performance, not independently but in an integrated manner. Being within one's budget at the proper time serves no useful purpose if performance is only 75 percent. Likewise, having a production line turn out exactly 200 items, when planned, loses its significance if a 50 percent cost overrun is incurred. All three resource parameters (time, cost, and performance) must be analyzed as a group, or else we might "win the battle but lose the war." The use of the expression "management cost and control system" is vague in that the implication is made that only costs are controlled. This is not true—an effective control system monitors schedule and performance as well as costs by setting budgets, measuring expenditures against budgets and identifying variances, assuring that the expenditures are proper, and taking corrective action when required.

Previously we defined the work breakdown structure as the element that acts as the source from which all costs and controls must emanate. The WBS is the total project broken down into successively lower levels until the desired control levels are established. The work breakdown structure therefore serves as the tool from which performance can be subdivided into objectives and subobjectives. As work progresses, the WBS provides the framework on which costs, time, and schedule/performance can be compared against the budget for each level of the WBS.

The first purpose of control therefore becomes a verification process accomplished by the comparison of actual performance to date with the predetermined plans and standards set forth in the planning phase. The comparison serves to verify that:

- The objectives have been successfully translated into performance standards.
- The performance standards are, in fact, a reliable representation of program activities and events.
- Meaningful budgets have been established such that actual versus planned comparisons can be made.

In other words, the comparison verifies that the correct standards were selected, and that they are properly used.

The second purpose of control is that of decision making. Three useful reports are required by management in order to make effective and timely decisions:

- The project plan, schedule, and budget prepared during the planning phase.
- A detailed comparison between resources expended to data and those predetermined. This includes an estimate of the work remaining and the impact on activity completion.
- A projection of resources to be expended through program completion.

These reports are then supplied to both the managers and the doers. Three useful results arise through the use of these three reports, generated during a thorough decision-making stage of control:

- Feedback to management, the planners, and the doers
- Identification of any major deviations from the current program plan, schedule, or budget
- The opportunity to initiate contingency planning early enough that cost, performance, and time requirements can undergo corrected action without loss of resources

These reports, if properly prepared, provide management with the opportunity to minimize downstream changes by making proper corrections here and now. As shown in Figures 15–3 and 15–4, possible cost reductions are usually available more readily in the early project phases, but are reduced as we go further into the project life-cycle phases. Downstream the cost for changes could easily exceed the original cost of the project. This is an example of the "iceberg" syndrome, where problems become evident too late in the project to be solved easily, resulting in a very high cost to correct them.

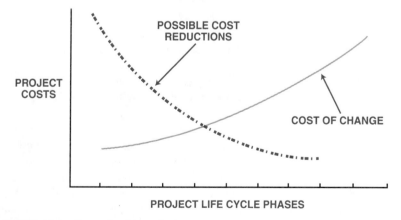

FIGURE 15–3. Cost reduction analysis.

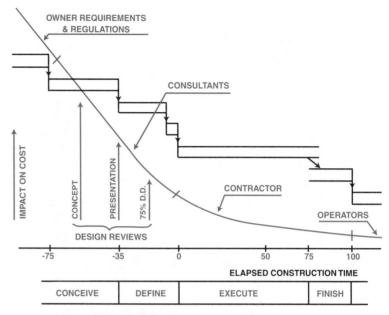

FIGURE 15–4. Ability to influence cost. *Source.* Max Wideman, "Managing Project Development for Better Results," *Project Management Quarterly,* September 1981, p. 16.

15.2 THE OPERATING CYCLE

The management cost and control system (MCCS) takes on paramount importance during the operating cycle of the project. The operating cycle is composed of four phases:

- Work authorization and release (phase II)
- Cost data collection and reporting (phase III)
- Cost analysis (phase IV)
- Reporting: customer and management (phase V)

These four phases, when combined with the planning cycle (phase I), constitute a closed system network that forms the basis for the management cost and control system.

Phase II is considered as work release. After planning is completed and a contract is received, work is authorized via a work description document. The work description, or project work authorization form, is a contract that contains the narrative description, organization, and time frame for *each* WBS level. This multipurpose form is used to release the contract, authorize planning, record detail description of the work outlined in the work breakdown structure, and release work to the functional departments.

Contract services may require a work description form to release the contract. The contractual work description form sets forth general contractual requirements and authorizes program management to proceed.

Program management may then issue a subdivided work description form to the functional units so that work can begin. The subdivided work description may also be issued through the combined efforts of the project team, and may be revised or amended when either the scope of time frame changes. The subdivided work description generally is not used for efforts longer than ninety days and must be "tracked" as if a project in itself. This subdivided work description form sets forth contractual requirements and planning guidelines for the applicable performing organizations. The subdivided work description package established during the proposal and updated after negotiations by the program team is incrementally released by program management to the work control centers in manufacturing engineering, publications, and program management as the authority for release of work orders to the performing organizations. The subdivided work description specifies how contractual requirements are to be accomplished, the functional organizations involved, and their specific responsibilities, and authorizes the expenditure of resources within a particular time frame.

The work control center assigns a work order number to the subdivided work description form, if no additional instructions are required, and releases the document to the performing organizations. If additional instructions are required, the work control center can prepare a more detailed work-release document (shop traveler, tool order, work order release), assign the applicable work order number, and release it to the performing organization.

A work order number is required for all in-house direct and indirect charging. The work order number also serves as a cross-reference number for automatic assignment of the indentured work breakdown structure number to labor and material data records in the computer.

Small companies can avoid this additional paperwork cost by going directly from an awarded contract to a single work order, which may be the only work order needed for the entire contract.

15.3 COST ACCOUNT CODES

Since project managers control resources through the line managers rather than directly, project managers end up controlling direct labor costs by opening and closing work orders. Work orders define the charge numbers for each cost account. By definition, a cost account is an identified level at a natural intersection point of the work breakdown structure and the organizational breakdown structure (OBS) at which functional responsibility for the work is assigned, and actual direct labor, material, and other direct costs are compared with actual work performed for management control purposes.

Cost accounts are the focal point of the MCCS and may comprise several work packages, as shown in Figure 15–5. Work packages are detailed short-span

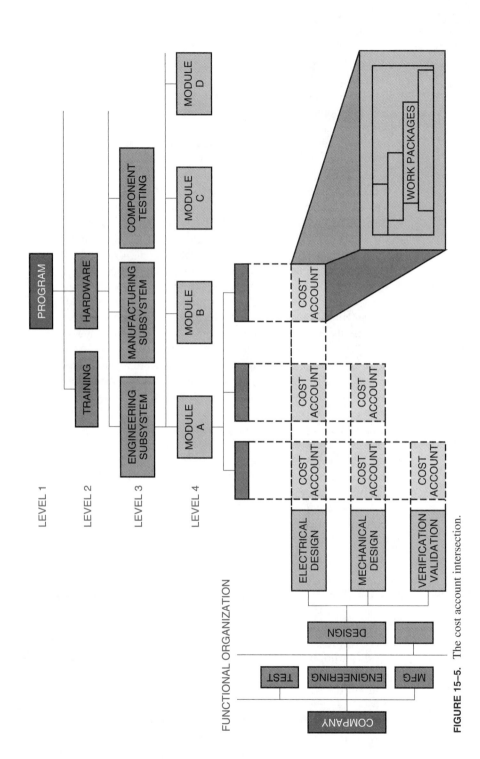

FIGURE 15–5. The cost account intersection.

job or material items identified for the accomplishment of required work. To illustrate this, consider the cost account code breakdown shown in Figure 15–6 and the work authorization form shown in Figure 15–7. The work authorization form specifically identifies the cost centers that are "open" for this charge number, the man-hours available for each cost center, and the operational time period for the charge number. Because the exact dates of operation are completely defined, the charge number can be assigned perhaps as much as a year in advance of the work-begin date. This can be shown pictorially, as in Figure 15–8.

If the man-hours are assigned to Cost Center 2400, then any 24xx cost center can use this charge number. If the work authorization form specifies Cost Center 2610, then any 261x cost center can use the charge number. However, if Cost Center 2623 is specified, then no lower cost accounts exist, and this is the only cost center that can use this work order charge number. In other words, if a charge number is opened up at the department level, then the department manager has the right to subdivide the assigned man-hours among the various sections and subsections. Company policy usually identifies the permissible cost center levels that can be assigned in the work authorization form. These permissible levels are related to the work breakdown structure level. For example, Cost Center 5000 (i.e., divisional) can be assigned at the project level of the work breakdown structure, but only department, sectional, or subsectional cost accounts can be assigned at the task level of the work breakdown structure.

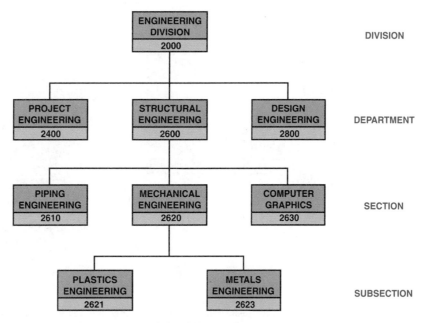

FIGURE 15–6. Cost account code breakdown.

WORK AUTHORIZATION FORM

WBS NO: 31-03-02   WORK ORDER NO: D1385

DATE OF ORIGINAL RELEASE: 3 FEB 93

DATE OF REVISION: : 18 MAR 93

REVISION NUMBER: :   C

DESCRIPTION	COST CENTERS	HOURS	WORK BEGINS	WORK ENDS
TEST MATERIAL VB-2 IN ACCORDANCE WITH THE PROGRAM PLAN AND MIL STANDARD G1483-52. THIS TASK INCLUDES A WRITTEN REPORT.	2400 2610 2621 2623 5000*	150 160 140 46 600	1 AUG 93 ↓	15 SEPT 93 ↓

PROJECT OFFICE AUTHORIZATION SIGNATURE _____

*NOTE: SOME COMPANIES DO NOT PERMIT DIVISION COST CENTERS
  TO CHARGE AT LEVEL 3 OF THE WBS

FIGURE 15–7. Work authorization form.

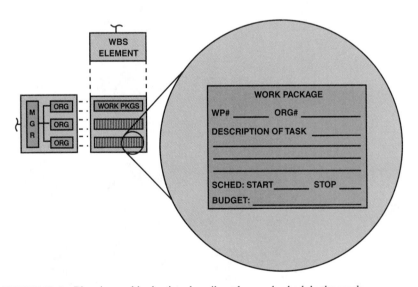

FIGURE 15–8. Planning and budgeting describe, plan, and schedule the work.

If a cost center needs additional time or additional man-hours, then a cost account change notice form must be initiated, usually by the requesting cost center, and approved by the project office. Figure 15–9 shows a typical cost account change notice form.

Large companies have computerized cost control and reporting systems. Small companies have manual or partially computerized systems. The major difficulty in using the cost account code breakdown and the work authorization form (Figures 15–6 and 15–7) is related to whether the employees fill out time cards, and frequency with which the time cards are filled out. Project-driven organizations fill out time cards at least once a week, and the cards are inputted to a computerized system. Non–project-driven organizations fill out time cards on a monthly basis, with computerization depending on the size of the company.

CACN No. _____ Revision to Cost Account No. _____ Date_____

DESCRIPTION OF CHANGE:

_____

_____

_____

_____

_____

_____

REASON FOR CHANGE:

_____

_____

_____

_____

_____

_____

	Requested Budget	**Authorized Budget**	
Labor Hours	_____	_____	**Period of Performance:**
Material $	_____	_____	From _____
Indirect $	_____	_____	To _____

BUDGET SOURCE:

☐ Funded Contract Change
☐ Management Reserve
☐ Undistributed Budget
☐ Other _____

APPROVALS: **Program Mgr.** _____

INITIATED BY: _____ **Prog. Control** _____

FIGURE 15–9. Cost account change notice (CACN).

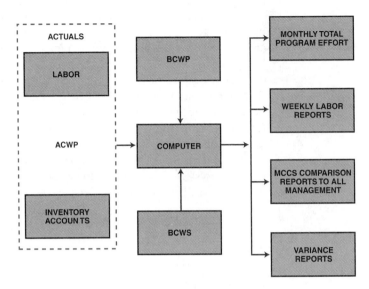

FIGURE 15–10. Cost data collection and reporting flow chart.

Cost data collection and reporting constitute the second phase of the operating cycle of the MCCS. Actual cost (ACWP) and the budgeted cost for work performed (BCWP) for each contract or in-house project are accumulated in detailed cost accounts by cost center and cost element, and reported in accordance with the flow charts shown in Figure 15–10. These detailed elements, for both actual costs incurred and the budgeted cost for work performed, are usually printed out monthly for all levels of the work breakdown structure. In addition, weekly supplemental direct labor reports can be printed showing the actual labor charge incurred, and can be compared to the predicted efforts.

Table 15–1 shows a typical weekly labor report. The first column identifies the WBS number.[2] If more than one work order were assigned to this WBS element, then the work order number would appear under the WBS number. This procedure would be repeated for all work orders under the same WBS number. The second column contains the cost centers charging to this WBS element (and possibly work order numbers). Cost Center 41xx represents department 41 and is a rollup of Cost Centers 4110, 4115, and 4118. Cost Center 4xxx represents the entire division and is a rollup of all 4000-level departments. Cost Center xxxx represents the total for all divisions charging to this WBS element. The weekly labor reports must list all cost centers authorized to charge to this WBS element, whether or not they have incurred any costs over the last reporting period.

---

2. Only three levels of cost reporting are assumed here. If work packages were used, then the WBS number would identify all five levels of control.

TABLE 15–1. WEEKLY LABOR REPORT

WBS No:	Cost Center	H $	Weekly Actual	Current Month Subtotal	Previous Month		Year to Date			Total EAC	Work Order Release
					ACWP	BCWP	ACWP	BCWP	BCWS		
01-03-06	4110	H	200	300	300	300	1000	1000	1000	1000	1000
		$	1000	1500	1500	1500	5000	5000	5000	5000	
	4115	H	200	300	300	300	1000	1000	1000	2000	2000
		$	1000	1500	1500	1500	5000	5000	5000	10000	
	4118	H	200	300	300	300	1000	1000	1000	2000	1800
		$	1000	1500	1500	1500	5000	5000	5000	10000	
	41XX	H	600	900	900	900	900	900	900	5000	4800
		$	3000	4500	4500	4500	4500	4500	4500	25000	
	4443	H	100	200	400	360	800	700	1400	2000	1800
		$	600	1200	2400	2260	4800	4200	8400	12000	
	4446	H	200	400	1000	1200	2000	2000	2300	3000	2500
		$	800	1600	4000	4800	8000	8000	9200	12000	
	4448	H	300	600	1000	1200	2000	2000	2300	3000	3000
		$	1500	3000	5000	6000	10000	10000	11500	15000	
	44XX	H	600	1200	2400	2760	4800	4700	6000	8000	7300
		$	2900	5800	11400	13060	22800	22200	29100	39000	
	4XXX	H	1200	2100	3300	3660	5700	5600	6900	13000	12100
		$	5900	10300	15900	17560	27300	26700	33600	64000	
	XXXX	H	8000	18000	20000	19000	50000	48000	47000	61000	58000
		$	56000	126000	140000	133000	350000	336000	329000	427000	

Note. See Table 15–4 and text for explanation of abbreviations.

Most weekly labor reports provide current month subtotals and previous month totals. Although these also appear on the detailed monthly report, they are included in the weekly report for a quick-and-dirty comparison. Year-to-date totals are usually not on the weekly report unless the users request them for an immediate comparison to the estimate at completion (EAC) and the work order release.

Weekly labor output is a vital tool for members of the program office in that these reports can indicate trends in cost and performance in sufficient time for contingency plans to be established and implemented. If these reports are not available, then cost and labor overruns would not be apparent until the following month when the detailed monthly labor, cost, and materials output was obtained.

In Table 15–1, Cost Center 4110 has spent its entire budget. The work appears to be completed on schedule. The responsible program office team may wish to eliminate this cost center's authority to continue charging to this WBS element by issuing a new SWD or work order canceling this department's efforts. Cost Center 4115 appears to be only halfway through. If time is becoming short, then Cost Center 4115 must add resources in order to meet requirements. Cost Center 4443 appears to be heading for an overrun. This could also indicate a management reserve. In this case the responsible program team member feels that the work can be accomplished in fewer hours.

Work order releases are used to authorize certain cost centers to begin charging their time to a specific cost reporting element. Work orders specify hours, not dollars. The hours indicate the "targets" that the program office would like to have the department shoot for. If the program office wished to be more specific and "compel" the departments to live within these hours, then the budgeted cost for work scheduled (BCWS) should be changed to reflect the reduced hours.

Four categories of cost data are normally accumulated:

- Labor
- Material
- Other direct charges
- Overhead

Project managers can maintain reasonable control over labor, material, and other direct charges. Overhead costs, on the other hand, are calculated yearly or monthly and applied retroactively to all applicable programs. Management reserves are often used to counterbalance the effects of adverse changes in overhead rates.

15.4 BUDGETS

The project budget, which is the final result of the planning cycle of the MCCS, must be reasonable, attainable, and based on contractually negotiated costs and the statement of work. The basis for the budget is either historical cost, best estimates, or industrial engineering standards. The budget must identify planned manpower requirements, contract allocated funds, and management reserve.

All budgets must be traceable through the budget "log," which includes:

- Distributed budget
- Management reserve
- Undistributed budget
- Contract changes

Management reserve is the dollar amount established by the project office to budget for all categories of unforeseen problems and contingencies resulting in out-of-scope work to the performers. Management reserve should be used for tasks or dollars, such as rate changes, and not to cover up bad planning estimates or budget overruns. When a significant change occurs in the rate structure, the total performance budget should be adjusted.

In addition to the "normal" performance budget and the management reserve budget, there also exists the following:

- Undistributed budget, which is that budget associated with contract changes where time constraints prevent the necessary planning to incorporate the change into the performance budget. (This effort may be time-constrained.)
- Unallocated budget, which represents a logical grouping of contract tasks that have not yet been identified and/or authorized.

15.5 VARIANCE AND EARNED VALUE

A variance is defined as any schedule, technical performance, or cost deviation from a specific plan. Variances are used by all levels of management to verify the budgeting system and the scheduling system. The budgeting and scheduling system variance must be compared together because:

- The cost variance compares deviations only from the budget and does not provide a measure of comparison between work scheduled and work accomplished.
- The scheduling variance provides a comparison between planned and actual performance but does not include costs.

There are two primary methods of measurement:

- *Measurable efforts:* discrete increments of work with a definable schedule for accomplishment, whose completion produces tangible results.
- *Level of effort:* work that does not lend itself to subdivision into discrete scheduled increments of work, such as project support and project control.

Variances are used on both types of measurement.

In order to calculate variances we must define the three basic variances for budgeting and actual costs for work scheduled and performed. Archibald defines these variables:[3]

- Budgeted cost for work scheduled (BCWS) is the budgeted amount of cost for work scheduled to be accomplished plus the amount or level of effort or apportioned effort scheduled to be accomplished in a given time period.
- Budget cost for work performed (BCWP) is the budgeted amount of cost for completed work, plus budgeted for level of effort or apportioned effort activity completed within a given time period. This is sometimes referred to as "earned value."
- Actual cost for work performed (ACWP) is the amount reported as actually expended in completing the work accomplished within a given time period.

These costs can then be applied to any level of the work breakdown structure (i.e., program, project, task, subtask, work package) for work that is completed, in-program, or anticipated. Using these definitions, the following variance definitions are obtained:

- Cost variance (CV) calculation:

$$CV = BCWP - ACWP$$

A negative variance indicates a cost-overrun condition.

- Schedule variance (SV) calculation:

$$SV = BCWP - BCWS$$

A negative variance indicates a behind-schedule condition.

In the analysis of both cost and schedule, costs are used as the lowest common denominator. In other words, the schedule variance is given as a function of cost. To alleviate this problem, the variances are usually converted to percentages:

$$\text{Cost variance \% (CVP)} = \frac{CV}{BCWP}$$

$$\text{Schedule variance \% (SVP)} = \frac{SV}{BCWS}$$

The schedule variance may be represented by hours, days, weeks, or even dollars.

---

3. Russell D. Archibald, *Managing High-Technology Programs and Projects* (New York: John Wiley & Sons, 1976), p. 176.

As an example, consider a project that is scheduled to spend $100K for each of the first four weeks of the project. The actual expenditures at the end of week four are $325K. Therefore, BCWS = $400K and ACWP = $325K. From these two parameters alone, there are several possible explanations as to project status. However, if BCWP is now known, say $300K, then the project is behind schedule and overrunning costs.

Variances are almost always identified as critical items and are reported to all organizational levels. Critical variances are established for each level of the organization in accordance with management policies.

Not all companies have a uniform methodology for variance thresholds. Permitted variances may be dependent on such factors as:

- Life-cycle phase
- Length of life-cycle phase
- Length of project
- Type of estimate
- Accuracy of estimate

Variance controls may be different from program to program. Table 15–2 identifies sample variance criteria for program X.

For many programs and projects, variances are permitted to change over the duration of the program. For strict manufacturing programs (product management), variances may be fixed over the program time span using criteria as in Table 15–2. For programs that include research and development, larger deviations may be permitted during the earlier phases than during the later phases. Figure 15–11 shows time-phased cost variances for a program requiring research and development, qualification, and production phases. Since the risk should decrease as time goes on, the variance boundaries are reduced. Figure 15–12 shows that the variance envelope in such a case may be dependent on the type of estimate.

By using both cost and schedule variance, we can develop an integrated cost/schedule reporting system that provides the basis for variance analysis by

TABLE 15–2. VARIANCE CONTROL FOR PROGRAM X

Organizational Level	Variance Thresholds*
Section	Variances greater than $750 that exceed 25% of costs
Section	Variances greater than $2500 that exceed 10% of costs
Section	Variances greater than $20,000
Department	Variances greater than $2000 that exceed 25% of costs
Department	Variances greater than $7500 that exceed 10% of costs
Department	Variances greater than $40,000
Division	Variances greater than $10,000 that exceed 10% of costs

*Thresholds are usually tighter within company reporting system than required external to government. Thresholds for external reporting are usually adjusted during various phases of program (% lower at end).

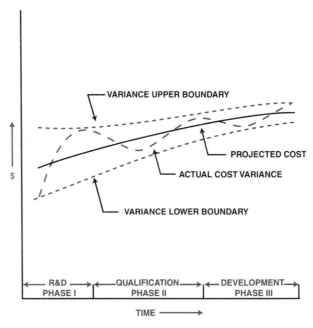

FIGURE 15–11. Project variance projection.

measuring cost performance in relation to work accomplished. This system ensures that both cost budgeting and performance scheduling are constructed on the
same database.

In addition to calculating the cost and schedule variances in terms of dollars
or percentages, we also want to know how efficiently the work has been accomplished. The formulas used to calculate the performance efficiency as a percentage of BCWP are:

$$\text{Cost performance index (CPI)} = \frac{\text{BCWP}}{\text{ACWP}}$$

$$\text{Schedule performance index (SPI)} = \frac{\text{BCWP}}{\text{BCWS}}$$

If CPI = 1.0, we have perfect performance. If CPI > 1.0, we have exceptional performance. If CPI < 1.0, we have poor performance. The same analysis
can be applied to the SPI.

LIFE CYCLE PHASE	MANPOWER REQUIRED	$ REQUIRED	TIME DURATION	TYPE OF ESTIMATE	ACCURACY	PERMITTED VARIANCE
MAIN	16,000 HRS.	1,285,600	6 MOS	HISTORY	±5%	±2%

FIGURE 15–12. Methodology to variance.

The cost and schedule performance index is most often used for trend analysis as shown in Figure 15–13. Companies use either three-month, four-month, or six-month moving averages to predict trends. The usefulness of trend analysis is to take corrective action to alleviate unfavorable trends by having an early warning system. Unfortunately, effective use of trend analysis may be restricted to long-term projects because of the time needed to correct the situation.

Figure 15–14 shows an integrated cost/schedule system. The figure identifies a performance slippage to date. This might not be a bad situation if the costs are proportionately underrun. However, from the upper portion of Figure 15–14, we find that costs are overrun (in comparison to budget costs), thus adding to the severity of the situation.

Also shown in Figure 15–14 is the management reserve. This is identified as the difference between the contracted cost for projected performance to date and the budgeted cost. Management reserves are the contingency funds established by

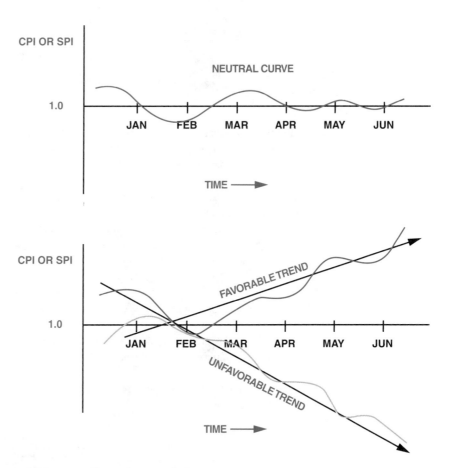

FIGURE 15–13. The performance index.

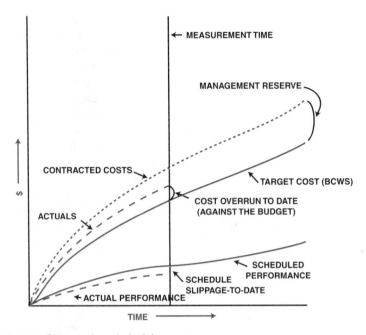

FIGURE 15–14. Integrated cost/schedule system.

the program manager to counteract unavoidable delays that can affect the project's critical path. Management reserves cover unforeseen events *within* a defined project scope that experience has shown are likely to occur. Management reserves are not used for unlikely major force events or changes in scope. These changes are funded separately, perhaps through management-established contingency funds. Actually, there is a difference between management reserves (which come from project budgets) and contingency funds (which come from external sources) although most people do not differentiate. It is a natural tendency for a functional manager (and some project managers) to substantially inflate estimates to protect the particular organization and provide a certain amount of cushion. Furthermore, if the inflated budget is approved, managers will undoubtedly use all of the allocated funds, including reserves. According to Parkinson:[4]

- The work at hand expands to fill the time available.
- Expenditures rise to meet budget.

Managers must identify all such reserves for contingency plans, in time, cost, and performance (i.e., PERT slack time).

---

4. C. N. Parkinson, *Parkinson's Law* (Boston: Houghton Mifflin, 1957).

The line indicated as actual cost in Figure 15–14 shows a cost overrun compared to the budget. However, costs are still within the contractual requirement if we consider the management reserve. Therefore, things may not be as bad as they seem.

Government subcontractors are required to have a government-approved cost/schedule control system. The information requirements that must be demonstrated by such a system include:

- Budgeted cost for work scheduled (BCWS)
- Budgeted cost for work performed (BCWP)
- Actual cost for work performed (ACWP)
- Estimated cost at completion
- Budgeted cost at completion
- Cost and schedule variances/explanations
- Traceability

The last two items imply that standardized policies and procedures should exist for reporting and controlling variances.

When permitted variances are exceeded, cost account variance analysis reports, as shown in Figure 15–15, are required. Signature approval of these reports may be required by:

- The functional employees responsible for the work
- The functional managers responsible for the work
- The cost accountant and/or the assistant project manager for cost control
- The project manager, work breakdown structure element manager, or someone with signature authority from the project office.

For variance analysis, the goal of the cost account manager (whether project officer or functional employee) is to take action that will correct the problem within the original budget or justify a new estimate.

Five questions must be addressed during variance analysis:

- What is the problem causing the variance?
- What is the impact on time, cost, and performance?
- What is the impact on other efforts, if any?
- What corrective action is planned or under way?
- What are the expected results of the corrective action?

One of the key parameters used in variance analysis is the "earned value" concept, which is the same as BCWP. Earned value (or whatever other name might be used in the literature) is a forecasting variable used to predict whether the project will finish over or under the budget. As an example, on June 1, the budget showed that 800 hours should have been expended for a given task. However, only 600 hours appeared on the labor report. Therefore, the performance is (800/600) × 100, or 133 percent, and the task is underrunning in per-

COST ACCOUNT NO/CAM						REPORTING LEVEL		
WBS/DESCRIPTION						AS OF		
COST PERF. DATA			VARIANCE			AT COMPLETION		
	BCWS	BCWP	ACWP	SCH	COST	BUDGET	EAC	VAR.
MONTH TO DATE ($)								
CONTRACT TO DATE ($K)								
PROBLEM CAUSE AND IMPACT								
CORRECTIVE ACTION (INCLUDE EXPECTED RECOVERY DATE)								
COST ACCOUNT MANAGER	DATE	COST CENTER MGR.		DATE	WBS ELEMENT MANAGER	DATE		DATE

FIGURE 15–15. Cost account variance analysis report.

formance. If the actual hours were 1,000, the performance would be 80 percent, and an overrun would be occurring.

The difficulty in performing variance analysis is the calculation of BCWP because one must predict the percent complete. To eliminate this problem, many companies use standard dollar expenditures for the project, regardless of percent complete. For example, we could say that 10 percent of the costs are to be "booked" for each 10 percent of the time interval. Another technique, and perhaps the most common, is the 50/50 rule:

> Half of the budget for each element is recorded at the time that the work is scheduled to begin, and the other half at the time that the work is scheduled to be completed. For a project with a large number of elements, the amount of distortion from such a procedure is minimal. (Figures 15–16 and 15–17 illustrate this technique.)

One advantage of using the 50/50 rule is that it eliminates the necessity for the continuous determination of the percent complete. However, if percent com-

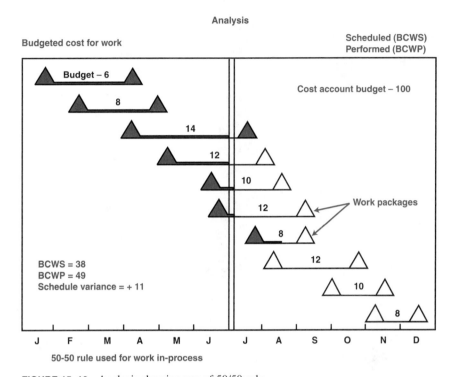

FIGURE 15–16. Analysis showing use of 50/50 rule.

plete can be determined, then percent complete can be plotted against time expended, as shown in Figure 15–18.

There are techniques available other than the 50/50 rule:[5]

- 0/100—Usually limited to work packages (activities) of small duration (i.e., less than one month). No value is earned until the activity is complete.
- Milestone—This is used for long work packages with associated interim milestones, or a functional group of activities with a milestone established at identified control points. Value is earned when the milestone is completed. In these cases, a budget is assigned to the milestone rather than the work packages.
- Percent complete—Usually invoked for long-duration work packages (i.e., three months or more) where milestones cannot be identified. The value earned would be the reported percent of the budget.

---

5. These techniques, in addition to the 50/50 method for determining work in progress, are available in software packages. The reader might wish to contact AGS Management Systems, 800 First Avenue, King of Prussia, PA 19406.

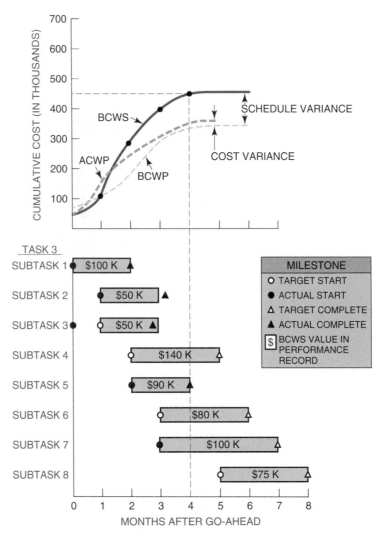

FIGURE 15–17. Project Z, task 3 cost data (contractual).

- Equivalent units—Used for multiple similar-unit work packages, where earnings are on completed units, rather than labor.
- Cost formula (80/20)—A variation of percent complete for long-duration work packages.
- Level of effort—This method is based on the passage of time, often used for supervision and management work packages. The value earned is based on time expended over total scheduled time. It is measured in terms of resources consumed over a given period of time and does not result in a final product.

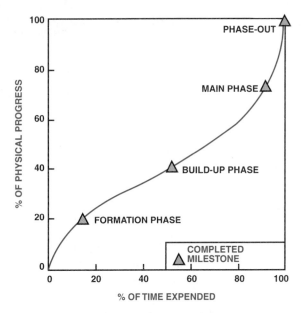

FIGURE 15–18. Physical progress versus time expended.

- Apportioned effort—A rarely used technique, for special related work packages. As an example, a production work package might have an apportioned inspection work package of 20 percent. There are only a few applications of this technique. Many people will try to use this for supervision, which is not a valid application. This technique is used for effort that is not readily divisible into short-span work packages but that is in proportion to some other measured effort.

Generally speaking, the concept of earned value may not be an effective control tool if used in the lower levels of the WBS. Task levels and above are normally worth the effort for the calculation of earned value. As an example, consider Figure 15–17, which shows the contractual cost data for task 3 of project Z, and Table 15–3, which shows the cost data status at the end of the fourth month. The following is a brief summary of the cost data for each subtask in task 3 at the end of the fourth month:

- Subtask 1: All contractual funds were budgeted. Cost/performance was on time as indicated by the milestone position. Subtask is complete.
- Subtask 2: All contractual funds were budgeted. A cost overrun of $5,000 was incurred, and milestone was completed later than expected. Subtask is completed.
- Subtask 3: Subtask is completed. Costs were underrun by $10,000, probably because of early start.

TABLE 15–3. PROJECT Z, TASK 3 COST DATA STATUS AT END OF FOURTH MONTH (COST IN THOUSANDS)

Subtasks	Status	BCWS	BCWP	ACWP
1	Completed	100	100	100
2	Completed	50	50	55
3	Completed	50	50	40
4	Not started	70	0	0
5	Completed	90	90	140
6	Not started	40	0	0
7	Started	50	50	25
8	Not started	—	—	—
Total		450	340	360

Note. The data assume a 50/50 ratio for planned and earned values of budget.

- Subtask 4: Work is behind schedule. Actually, work has not yet begun.
- Subtask 5: Work is completed on schedule, but with a $50,000 cost overrun.
- Subtask 6: Work has not yet started. Effort is behind schedule.
- Subtask 7: Work has begun and appears to be 25 percent complete.
- Subtask 8: Work has not yet started.

To complete our analysis of the status of a project, we must determine the budget at completion (BAC) and the estimate at completion (EAC)? Table 15–4 shows the parameters for variance analysis.

- The budget at completion is the sum of all budgets (BCWS) allocated to the project. This is often synonymous with the project baseline. This is what the total effort should cost.
- The estimate at completion identifies either the dollars or hours that represent a realistic appraisal of the work when performed. It is the sum of all direct and indirect costs to date plus the estimate of all authorized work remaining (EAC = cumulative actuals + the estimate-to-complete).

TABLE 15–4. THE PARAMETERS FOR VARIANCE ANALYSIS

Question	Answer	Acronym
How much work *should* be done?	Budgeted cost of work scheduled	BCWS
How much work *is* done?	Budgeted cost of work performed	BCWP
How much *did* the "is done" work cost?	Actual cost of work performed (actuals)	ACWP
What was the total job *supposed* to cost?	Budget at completion (total budget)	BAC
What do we *now* expect the total job to cost?	Estimate at completion or latest revised estimate	EAC LRE

Using the above definitions, we can calculate the variance at completion (VAC):

$$VAC = BAC - EAC$$

The estimate at completion (EAC) is the best estimate of the total cost at the completion of the project. The EAC is a periodic evaluation of the project status, usually on a monthly basis or until a significant change has been identified. It is usually the responsibility of the performing organization to prepare the EAC.

The calculation of a new EAC and subsequent revision does not imply that corrective action has been taken. Consider a three-month task that is 99 percent complete and was budgeted to spend \$400K (BCWS). The actual costs to date (ACWP) are \$395K. Using the 50/50 rule, BCWP is \$200K. The estimated cost-to-complete (EAC) ratio is \$395K/\$200K, which implies that we are heading for a 100 percent cost overrun. Obviously, this is not the case.

Using the data in Table 15–5, we can calculate the estimate at completion (EAC) by the expression

$$
\begin{aligned}
EAC &= (ACWP/BCWP) \times BAC = BAC/CPI \\
&= (360/340) \times 579,000 \\
&= \$613,059
\end{aligned}
$$

where BAC is the value of BCWS at completion.

The discussion of what value to use for BAC is argumentative. In the above calculation, we used burdened direct labor dollars. Some people prefer to use nonburdened labor with the argument that the project manager controls only direct labor hours and dollars. Also, the calculation for EAC did not include material costs or G & A.

The above calculation of EAC implies that we are overrunning labor costs by 6.38% and that the final burdened labor cost will exceed the budgeted burdened

TABLE 15–5. PROJECT Z, TASK 3 COST SUMMARY FOR WORK COMPLETED OR IN PROGRESS (COST IN THOUSANDS)

		Cumulative to Date			Cost	Schedule
	Contractual	BCWS	BCWP	ACWP	Variance	Variance
Direct labor hours	8650	6712	5061	4652	409	
Direct labor dollars	241	187	141	150	(9)	(46)
Labor overhead (140%)	338	263	199	210	(11)	(64)
Subtotal	579	450	340	360	(20)	
Material dollars	70	66	26	30	(4)	
Subtotal	649					
G&A (10%)	65					
Subtotal	714					
Fee (12%)	86					
Total	800					

Notes. 1. This table assumes a 50/50 ratio for planned and earned values of budget.

labor cost by $34,059. For a more precise calculation of EAC we would need to include material cost (assumed at $70,000) and G & A. This would give us a final cost, excluding profit, of $751,365, which is an overrun of $37,365. The resulting profit would be $86,000 less $37,365, or $48,635. The final analysis is that work is being accomplished almost on schedule except for Subtask 4 and Subtask 6, but costs are being overrun.

The question that remains to be answered is, "Where is the cost overrun occurring?" To answer this question, we must analyze the cost summary sheet for project Z, task 3. Table 15–5 represents a hypothetical case for the cost elements of project Z, task 3. From Table 15–5 we see that negative (overrun) variances exist for labor dollars, overhead dollars, and material costs. Because labor overhead is measured as a percentage of direct labor dollars, the problem appears to be in the direct labor dollars.

From the contractual column in Table 15–5 the project was estimated at $27.86 per hour direct labor ($241,000/8650 hours), but actuals to date are $150,000/4652 hours, or $32.24 per hour. Therefore, higher-salaried people than anticipated are being employed. This salary increase is partially offset by the fact that there exists a positive variance of 409 direct labor hours, indicating that these higher-salaried employees are performing at a more favorable position than expected on the learning curve. Since the milestones (from Figure 15–17) appear to be on target, work is progressing as planned, except for subtask 4.

The labor overhead rate has not changed. The contractual, BCWS, and BCWP overhead rates were estimated at 140 percent. The actuals, obtained from month-end reports, indicate that the true overhead rate is as predicted.

The following conclusions can be drawn:

- Work is being performed as planned (almost on schedule, although at a more favorable position on the learning curve), except for subtask 4, which is giving us a schedule delay.
- Direct labor costs are increasing through the use of higher-salaried employees.
- Overhead rates are as anticipated.
- Direct labor hours must be reduced even further to compensate for increased costs, or else profits will be drastically reduced.

This type of analysis could have been carried out to one more level by identifying exactly which departments were using the more expensive employees. This step should probably be completed anyway to see if lower-paid employees are available and can work at the required position on the learning curve. Had the labor costs been a result of increased labor hours, this step would have definitely been necessary to identify the reason for the overrun in-house. Perhaps poor estimating was the cause.

In Table 15–5, there also appears a positive variance in materials. This likewise should undergo further analysis. The cause may be the result of improperly identified hardware, material escalation costs increasing beyond what was planned, increased scrap factors, or a change in subcontractors.

It should be obvious from the above analysis that a detailed investigation into the cause of variances appears to be the best method for identifying causes. The concept of earned value, although a crude estimate, identifies trends concerning the status of specific WBS elements. Using this concept, the budgeted cost for work scheduled (BCWS) may be called planned earned value (PEV), and the budgeted cost for work performed (BCWP) may be referred to as actual earned value (AEV). Earned values are used to determine whether costs are being incurred faster or slower than planned. However, cost overruns do not necessarily mean that there will be an eventual overrun, because the work may be getting done faster than planned.

There are several formulas that can be used to calculate EAC. Using the data shown below, we can illustrate how each of three different formulas can give a different result. Assume that your project consists of these three activities only.

Activity	% Complete	BCWS	BCWP	ACWP
A	100	1000	1000	1200
B	50	1000	500	700
C	0	1000	0	0

Formula I. $\text{EAC} = \dfrac{\text{ACWP}}{\text{BCWP}} \times \text{BAC}$

$= \dfrac{1900}{1500} (3000) = \$3800$

Formula II. $\text{EAC} = \dfrac{\text{ACWP}}{\text{BCWP}} \times \begin{bmatrix} \text{Work completed} \\ \text{and in progress} \end{bmatrix} + \begin{bmatrix} \text{Actual (or revised) cost} \\ \text{of work packages not} \\ \text{yet begun} \end{bmatrix}$

$= \dfrac{1900}{1500} (2000) + \$1000 = \$3533$

Formula III. $\text{EAC} = [\text{Actual to date}] + \begin{bmatrix} \text{All remaining work to be at planned} \\ \text{cost including remaining work in} \\ \text{progress} \end{bmatrix}$

$= 1900 + [500 + 1000] = \$3400$
$\uparrow \uparrow$
$\text{B} \text{C}$

Advantages and disadvantages exist for each formula. Formula I assumes that the burn rate (i.e., ACWP/BCWP) will be the same for the remainder of the project. This is the easiest formula to use. The burn rate is updated each reporting period.

Formula II assumes that all work packages not yet opened will be completed at the planned cost. However, it is possible for planned cost to be revised based upon history from completed work packages.

Formula III assumes that all remaining work is independent of the burn rate incurred thus far. This may be unrealistic unless all remaining work can be reestimated if necessary.

Other techniques are available for determining final completion costs.[6] The value of the technique selected is based upon the dollar value of the project, the risk, the quality of the cost accounting system, and the accuracy of the estimates. The estimating techniques here use only labor costs. Material costs can be added into each equation to obtain total cost.

There exist thirteen cases for comparing planned versus actual performance. These thirteen cases are shown in Table 15–6. Each case is described below using the relationships:

- Cost variance = actual earned value − actuals
- Schedule/performance variances = actual earned value − planned earned value

Case 1: This is the ideal planning situation where everything goes according to schedule.

Case 2: Costs are behind schedule, and the program appears to be underrunning. Work is being accomplished at less than 100 percent, since actuals exceed AEV (or BCWP). This indicates that a cost overrun ran be anticipated. This situation grows even worse when we see that we are 50 percent behind schedule also. This is one of the worst possible cases.

Case 3: In this case there exists good news and bad news. The good news is that we are performing the work efficiently (efficiency exceeds 100 percent). The bad news is that we are behind schedule.

Case 4: The work is not being accomplished according to schedule (i.e., is behind schedule), but the costs are being maintained for what has been accomplished.

Case 5: The costs are on target with the schedule, but the work is 25 percent behind schedule because the work is being performed at 75 percent efficiency.

Case 6: Because we are operating at 125 percent efficiency, work is ahead of schedule by 25 percent but within scheduled costs. We are performing at a more favorable position on the learning curve.

Case 7: We are operating at 100 percent efficiency and work is being accomplished ahead of schedule. Costs are being maintained according to budget.

Case 8: Work is being accomplished properly, and costs are being underrun.

Case 9: Work is being accomplished properly, but costs are being overrun.

6. Fleming, W. Q. and Koppelman J. M; "Forecasting the Final Cost and Schedule Results," *PM Network,* January 1996, pp. 13–18.

TABLE 15–6. VARIANCE ANALYSIS CASE STUDIES

Case	Planned earned Value (BCWS)	Actuals (ACWP)	Actual Earned Value (BCWP)
1	800	800	800
2	800	600	400
3	800	400	600
4	800	600	600
5	800	800	600
6	800	800	1,000
7	800	1,000	1,000
8	800	600	800
9	800	1,000	800
10	800	1,000	600
11	800	600	1,000
12	800	1,200	1,000
13	800	1,000	1,200

Case 10: Costs are being overrun while underaccomplishing the plan. Work is being accomplished inefficiently. This situation is very bad.

Case 11: Performance is ahead of schedule, and the costs are lower than planned. This situation results in a big Christmas bonus.

Case 12: Work is being done efficiently, and a possible cost overrun can occur. However, performance is ahead of schedule. The overall result may be either an overrun in cost or an underrun in schedule.

Case 13: Although costs are greater than those budgeted, performance is ahead of schedule, and work is being accomplished very efficiently. This is also a good situation.

In each of these cases, the concept of earned value was used to predict trends in cost and variance analysis. This method has its pros and cons. According to Martin:[7]

> The usefulness of earned value measurements in project management is controversial. The most enthusiastic managers regard it as the best way to prevent surprises and as a most workable tool. Others consider the information helpful in managing the project but not worth the cost of obtaining it. Still others say the information becomes available too late or there are better ways to obtain it. The most critical managers view it as a complete waste of time.

Each of the critical variances (or earned values) identified usually requires a formal analysis to determine the cause of the variance, the corrective action to be taken, and the effect on the estimate to completion. These analyses are performed by the organization that was assigned the budget (BCWS) at the level of accumulation directed by program management.

---

7. Reprinted, with permission of the publisher, from *Project Management: How to Make It Work* by Charles Martin, © 1976 AMACOM, a division of the American Management Association. All rights reserved.

**Organization-Level
Analysis**

Each critical variance identified on the organizational MCCS reports may require the completion of MCCS variance analysis procedures by the supervisor of the cost center involved. Analyzing both the work breakdown and organizational structure, the supervisor systematically concentrates his efforts on cost and schedule problems appearing within his organization.

Analysis begins at the lowest organizational level by the supervisor involved. Critical variances are noted at the cost account on the MCCS report. If a schedule variance is involved and the subtask consists of a number of work packages, the supervisor may refer to a separate report that breaks down each cost account into the various work packages that are ahead or behind schedule. The supervisor can then analyze the variance on the basis of the work package involved and determine with the aid of supporting organizations the cause of the variance, the corrective action that can be taken, or the possible effect on associated or future planned effort.

Cost variances involving labor are analyzed by the supervisor on the basis of the performance of his organization in accomplishing the work assigned, within the budgeted man-hours and planned labor rate. The cause of any variance to this performance is determined, and corrective action is then implemented.

Cost variances on nonlabor efforts are analyzed by the supervisor with the aid of the program team member and other supporting organizations.

All material variance analyses are normally initiated by cost accounting as a service to the using organization. These variance analyses are completed, including cause and corrective action, to the extent that can be explained by cost accounting. They are then sent to the using organization, which reviews the analyses and completes those resulting from schedule performance or usage. If a variance is recognized as a change in the material acquisition price, this information is supplied by cost accounting to the responsible organization and a change to the estimate-to-complete is initiated by the using organization.

The supervisor should forward copies of each completed MCCS variance analysis/EAC change form to his higher-level manager and the program team member.

**Program Team
Analysis**

The program team member may receive a team critical variance report that lists variances in his organization at the lowest level of the work breakdown structure at the division cost center level by cost element. Upon request of the program manager, analyses of variances contributing to the variances on the team critical variance report are summarized by the responsible program team member and reviewed with the program manager.

The preparation of status reports, whether they be for internal management or for the customer, should, at a minimum, answer two fundamental questions:

● Where are we today (with respect to time and cost)?
● Where will we end up (with respect to time and cost)?

The information necessary to answer these questions can be obtained from the following formulas:

- Where are we today?
  - Cost variances (in dollars/hours and percent complete)
  - Schedule variances (in dollars/hours and percent complete)
  - Percent complete
  - Percent money spent
- Where will we end up?
  - Estimate at completion (EAC)
  - The remaining critical path
  - SPI (trend analysis)
  - CPI (trend analysis)

Percent complete and percent money spent can be obtained from the following formulas:

$$\text{Percent complete} = \frac{\text{BCWP}}{\text{BAC}}$$

$$\text{Percent money spent} = \frac{\text{ACWP}}{\text{BAC}}$$

where BAC is the budget at completion.

The program manager uses this information to review the program status with upper-level management. This review is normally on a monthly basis on large projects. In addition, the results of these analyses are used to explain variances in the contractually required reports to the customer.

After the analyses of the variances have been made, reports must be developed for both the customer and in-house (upper-level) management. Customer reporting procedures and specifications can be more detailed than in-house reporting and are often governed by the contract. Contractual requirements specify the reports required, the frequency of submission and distribution, and the customer regulation that specifies the preparation instructions for the report.

The types of reports required by the customer and management depend on the size of the program and the magnitude of the variance. Most reports usually contain the tracking of the vital technical parameters. These might include:

- The major milestones necessary for project success
- Comparison to specifications
- Types or conditions of testing
- Correlation of technical performance to the activity network and the work breakdown structure

One final note need be mentioned concerning reports. To facilitate time and money savings, each of these reports might be no more than one or two pages. In many cases, the reports are merely fill-in-the-blank types. When necessary, explanations can be provided by additional pages.

15.6 RECORDING MATERIAL COSTS USING EARNED VALUE MEASUREMENT

Using "earned value" measurement, the actual cost for work performed represents those direct and indirect costs identified specifically for the project (contract) at hand. Both the *recorded* and *reported* costs must relate specifically to this effort at hand. Recording direct labor costs usually presents no problem in this regard since labor costs are normally recorded as the labor is accomplished. Therefore, recorded and reported labor will be the same.

Material costs, on the other hand, may be recorded at various points in time. Material costs can be recorded as commitments, expenditures, accruals, and applied costs. All provide useful information and are important for control purposes.

Because of the choices available for material cost analysis, material costs should be reported *separately* from the standard labor hour/labor dollar earned value report. For example, cost variances associated with the procurement of material may be determined at the time that the purchase orders are negotiated and placed with the vendors since this information provides the *earliest* visibility of potential cost variance problems. Significant variances in the anticipated and actual costs of materials can have a serious effect on the total contract cost and should be reflected promptly in the estimated cost at completion (EAC) and explained in the narrative part of the project status report.

Separating labor from material costs is essential. Consider the following example:

Example 15–1. You are budgeted to spend $1,000,000 in burdened labor and $600,000 in material. At the end of the first month of your project, the following information is made available to you:

$$Labor: \quad ACWP = \$90,000$$
$$BCWP = \$100,000$$
$$BAC = \$1,000,000$$
$$Material: \quad ACWP = \$450,000$$
$$BCWP = \$400,000$$
$$BAC = \$600,000$$

For simplicity's sake, let us use the following formula for EAC:

$$EAC = (ACWP/BCWP) \times BAC$$

Therefore,

$$EAC(labor) = \$900,000$$

$$EAC(material) = \$675,000$$

If we add together both EACs, the estimated cost at completion will be $1,575,000, which is $25,000 *below* the planned budget. If the costs are combined before we calculate EAC, then

$$EAC = [(\$450,000 + \$90,000)/\$500,000] \times (\$1,600,000) = \$1,728,000$$

which is a $128,000 *overrun*. Therefore, it is usually best to separate material from labor in status reporting.

Another major problem is how to account for the costs of material placed on order. The cost of material on order does *not* reflect the cost of work completed and is not normally used in status reporting. For performance measurement purposes, it is desirable that material costs be recorded at the time that the materials are received, paid for, or used rather than as of the time that they are ordered. Therefore, the actual costs reported for materials should be derived in accordance with established procedures, and normally will be recorded for earned value measurement purposes at or after time of material receipt. In addition, costs should always be recorded on the same basis as budgets are prepared in order to make comparisons between budgeted and actual costs meaningful. For example, material should not be budgeted on the basis of when it is used and then have its costs collected/reported on the basis of when it is received. Consider the following situations:

Situation I: An equipment manufacturer receives a contract to build five machines for the *same* customer, but each machine is slightly different. The manufacturer purchases and receives five of the same electric motors, one for each machine. What is the earliest time that the manufacturer should take credit for the electric motors?

    a. When ordered
    b. When received
    c. When paid for
    d. When withdrawn from inventory
    e. When installed

Situation II: The same manufacturer has purchased large quantities of steel plate for the five machines as well as for machines for other customers. By ordering in large quantities, the manufacturer received a substantial price break. What is the earliest time the manufacturer should take credit for the steel plate?

  a. When ordered
  b. When received
  c. When paid for
  d. When withdrawn from inventory
  e. When installed

Situation III: Assume that the manufacturer in Situation II purchases the steel plate for a single customer rather than for multiple customers. What is the earliest time the manufacturer should take credit for the steel plate?

  a. When ordered
  b. When paid for
  c. When received
  d. When applied

In Situations I and III, the recommended answer is "when received." In Situation II, any answer can be argued, but the preferred answer is "when installed."

15.7 THE MATERIAL ACCOUNTING CRITERION[8]

At a minimum, the contractor's material accounting system must provide for the following:

  a. Accurate cost accumulation and assignment of costs to cost accounts in a manner consistent with budgets using recognized, acceptable costing techniques.
  b. Determination of material price variances by comparing planned versus actual commitments.
  c. Cost performance measurement at the point in time most suitable for the category of material involved, but no earlier than the time of actual receipt of material.
  d. Determination of material cost variances attributable to the excess usage of material.
  e. Determination of unit or lot costs when applicable.
  f. Full accountability for all material purchased for the project, including residual inventory.

---

8. Adapted from Quenton W. Fleming, *Cost/Schedule Control Systems Criteria* (Chicago: Probus Publishers, 1992), pp. 144–145

In order to satisfy these six system requirements, the following accounting practices should be adhered to:

a. The material cost actuals (ACWP) must equate to its material plans (BCWS), and be carried down to the cost account level of the WBS.
b. The material price variances must be determinable by comparing planned commitments (estimated material value) to actual commitments (actual cost of the material).
c. Physical work progress or earned value (BCWP) must be determinable, but not before the materials have been received.
d. Usage cost variances (to be discussed in the next section) must be determinable from excess material usage.
e. Material unit costs and/or lot costs must be determinable, as applicable.
f. There must be full accountability of all materials purchased, including any residual material inventory.

Although this appears difficult on the surface, the organization may find the task easy if the organization focuses on the following two areas:

1. **The material plans (BCWS).** These frequently start at the point at which engineering or manufacturing or others have provided a definition sufficient to initiate an order for the items, regardless of when such items are actually ordered or received.
2. **The material actuals (ACWP).** This is ordinarily the point at which the costs of the parts are recorded on the firm's accounting books, that is, when the bill is paid.

Those firms that have a material commitment system in use as part of the material accounting system are usually able to establish and update the costs for their purchased goods at multiple points: as an estimated liability when engineering or manufacturing defines the requirements; still as an estimated liability when someone formally initiates the request; updated to an accrued liability when an order is placed by purchasing; later updated to an actual liability when parts are received and accepted; and updated a final time when the bill is paid and the costs are recorded on the accounting books.

15.8 MATERIAL VARIANCES: PRICE AND USAGE[9]

One of the requirements of a material accounting system that is generally consistent with that of normal procurement practices is the matter of determining just why

---

9. Adapted from Quenton W. Fleming, *Cost/Schedule Control Systems Criteria* (Chicago: Probus Publishers, 1992), pp. 151–152

material budgets were exceeded, called variance analysis. When the actual material costs exceed a material budget, the fault can normally be traced to two causes:

1. The articles purchased cost more than was planned, called a "price variance."
2. More articles were consumed than were planned, called a "usage variance."

When material budgets are exceeded, typically, some combination of these two occurs.

Price variances (PV) occur when the budgeted price value (BCWS) of the material was different than what was actually experienced (ACWP). This condition can arise for a host of reasons: poor initial estimates, inflation, different materials used than were planned, too little money available to budget, and so on.

The formula for price variance (PV) is:

$$PV = (\text{Budgeted price} - \text{Actual price}) \times (\text{Actual quantity})$$

Price variance is the difference between the budgeted cost for the bill of materials, and the price paid for the bill of materials.

By contrast, usage variances (UV) occur when a greater quantity of materials is consumed than were planned. The formula for usage variance (UV) is:

$$UV = (\text{Budgeted quantity} - \text{Actual quantity}) \times (\text{Budgeted price})$$

Normally, usage variances are the resulting costs of materials used over and above the quantity called for in the bill of materials.

Consider the following example: The project manager establishes a material budget of 100 units (which includes 10 units for scrap factor) at a price of $150 per unit. Therefore, the material budget was set at $15,000. At the end of the short project, material actuals (ACWP) came in at $15,950, which was $950 over budget. What happened?

Applying the formulas defined previously,

$$
\begin{aligned}
\text{Price variance (PV)} &= (\text{BCWS price} - \text{ACWP price}) \times \text{Actual quantity} \\
&= (\$150 \text{ per unit} - \$145 \text{ per unit}) \times 110 \text{ units} \\
&= \$550 \text{ favorable} \\
\text{Usage variance (UV)} &= (\text{BCWP qty} - \text{ACWP qty}) \times \text{BCWS price} \\
&= (100 \text{ units} - 110 \text{ units}) \times \$150 \text{ per unit} \\
&= \$1,500 \text{ unfavorable}
\end{aligned}
$$

The analysis indicates that your purchase price was less than you anticipated, thus generating a cost savings. However, you used 10 units more than planned for, thus generating an unfavorable usage variance. Further investigation indicated that your line manager had increased the scrap factor from 10 to 20 units.

Good business practices indicate that such variance analyses take place to determine why actual material costs exceed the budgeted material values.

15.9 SUMMARY VARIANCES

Summary variances can be calculated for both labor and material. Consider the information shown below:

	Direct Material	Direct Labor
Planned price/unit	$ 30.00	$ 24.30
Actual units	$ 17,853	$ 9,000
Actual priceunit	$ 31.07	$ 26.24
Actual cost	$554,630	$236,200

We can now calculate the total price variance for direct material and the rate cost variance

- *Total* price variance for direct material
    = Actual units $\times$ (BCWP $-$ ACWP)
    = 17,853 $\times$ ($30.00 $-$ $31.07)
    = $19,102.71 (unfavorable)
- Labor *rate* cost variance
    = Budgeted rate $-$ Actual rate
    = $24.30 $-$ $26.24
    = $1.94 (unfavorable)

15.10 STATUS REPORTING

One of the best ways of reducing or even eliminating executive meddling on projects is to provide executives with frequent, meaningful status reports so that they can accurately realize the true status of the project. Figure 15–19 shows a relatively simple status report based upon data accumulation in the form of Figures 15–20 and 15–21. These types of status reports should be short and concise, containing pertinent information only. Status can also be shown graphically as in Figure 15–22. The difference between Figure 15–22 and 15–17 is that at-completion estimates have been identified.

Reporting procedures for variance analysis should be as brief as possible. The reason for this is simple: the shorter and more concise the report, the faster that feedback can be generated and responses developed. The time parameter be-

1. VARIANCE ANALYSIS (cost in thousands)

Subtask	Milestone Status	Budgeted Cost Work Schedule	Budgeted Cost Work Performed	Actual Cost	Variance, %	
					Schedule	Cost
1	Completed	100	100	100	0	0
2	Completed	50	50	55	0	−10
3	Completed	50	50	40	0	20
4	Not started	70	0	0	−100	—
5	Completed	90	90	140	0	−55.5
6	Not started	40	0	0	−100	—
7	Started	50	50	25	0	50
8	Not started	0	0	0	—	—
Total		450	340	360	−24.4	−5.9

2. ESTIMATE AT COMPLETION (EAC)

$$EAC = (360/340) \times \$579,000 = \$613,059$$
$$Overrun = 613,059 - 579,000 = \$34,059$$

3. COST SUMMARY

Costs are running approximately 5.9% over budget because of higher-salaried labor.

4. SCHEDULE SUMMARY

The 24.4% behind-schedule condition is due to subtasks 4 and 6, which have not yet begun owing to lack of raw materials and the 50/50 method for booking costs. Overtime will get us back on schedule but at an additional cost of 2.5% of direct labor costs.

5. MILESTONE REPORT

Milestone/Subtask	Scheduled Completion	Projected Completion	Actual Completion
1	4/1/94		4/1/94
2	5/1/94		5/8/94
3	5/1/94		4/23/94
4	7/1/94	7/1/94	
5	6/1/94		6/1/94
6	8/1/94	8/1/94	
7	9/1/94	9/1/94	
8	10/1/94	10/1/94	

6. EVENT REPORT

Current Problem	Potential Impact	Corrective Action
(a) Lack of raw materials.	Cost overrun and behind schedule condition.	Overtime is scheduled. We will try to use lower-salaried people. Raw materials are expected to be on dock next week.
(b) Customer unhappy with test results, and wants additional work.	May need additional planning.	Customer will provide us with revised statement of work on 6/15/94.

Gary Anderson, Project Manager

FIGURE 15–19. Blue Spider Project, monthly project report #4.

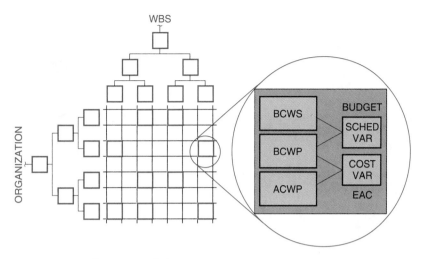

FIGURE 15–20. Data accumulation.

comes critical if rescheduling must be accomplished with limited resources. The two most common situations providing constraints on resource rescheduling are that:

● The end date is fixed
● The resources available are constant (or limited)

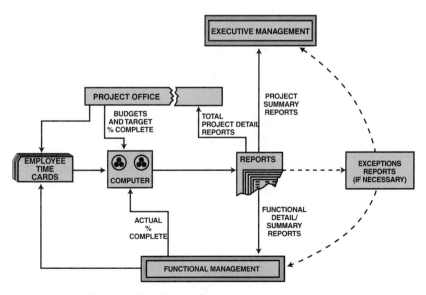

FIGURE 15–21. Cost control and report flow.

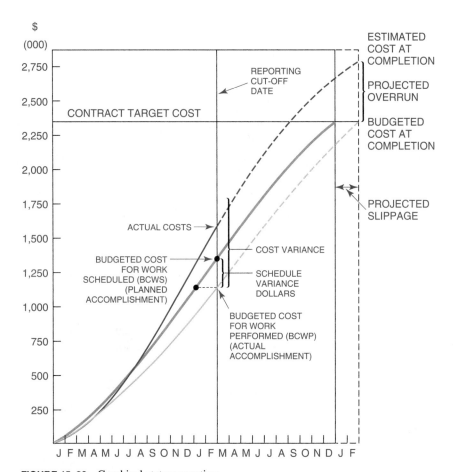

FIGURE 15–22. Graphical status reporting.

With a fixed end date, program rescheduling generally requires that additional resources be supplied. In the second situation, program slippage may be the only alternative unless a constant sum of resources can be redistributed so as to shorten the length of the critical path.

Once the variance analysis is completed, both project and functional management must diagnose the problem and search for corrective actions. This includes:

- Finding the cure for the problem
- Developing a plan to recover the position

This by no means implies that all variances require corrective action. There are four major responses to a variance report:

- Ignoring it
- Functional modification
- Replanning
- System redesign

Permissible variances exist for all levels of the organization. If the variance is within these permitted deviations, then there will be no response, and the variance may be ignored. In some situations where the variance is marginal (or even within limits), corrective action may be required. This would normally occur at the functional level and might simply involve using another test procedure or possibly considering some alternative not delineated in the program plan.

If major variances occur, then either replanning or system redesign must take place. The replanning process requires the redefining and reestablishing of project goals as work progresses, but always within system specifications. This might include making trade-offs in time, cost, and performance or defining new project activities and methods of pursuing the project, such as new PERT networks. If resources are limited, then a proper redistribution or reallocation must be made. If resources are not limited, the additional personnel, financing, equipment, facilities, or information may be required.

If replanning cannot be accomplished without system redesign, then system specifications may have to be changed.[10] This is the worst possible case because performance may have to be sacrificed to satisfy the constraints of time and money.

Whenever companies operate on a matrix structure, job descriptions, responsibilities, and management directives must be carefully prepared and distributed to all key individuals in the organization. This is an absolute necessity when a multitude of people must interact to control company resources. Management policies must establish the decision-making policies associated with management cost and control systems. Otherwise, dual standards can occur within the same organization, and the decision-making process becomes a tedious flow of red tape. The following might be a management policy guide for a program or project manager:

- Approving all estimates, and negotiating all estimates and the definition of work requirements with the respective organizations.
- Approving the budget, and directing distribution and budgeting of available funds to all organizational levels by program element.
- Defining the work required and the schedule.
- Authorizing work release. The manager may not, however, authorize work beyond the scope of the contract.
- Approving the program bill-of-materials, detailed plans, and program schedules for need and compliance with program requirements.

---

10. Here we are discussing system specifications. Functional modification responses can also require specification changes, but not on the system level. Examples of functional modifications might be changes in tolerances for testing or for purchasing raw materials.

TABLE 15–7. PROGRAM CONTROLS INTERRELATIONSHIPS

Program Manager	Functional Manager	Relationship
Makes or approves all decisions that affect the contractually committed target time, cost, and performance requirements or objectives of the program.	Assembles and furnishes the information needed to assist the program manager in making decisions. Submits to the program manager all proposed changes that affect program cost, schedule targets, and technical requirements and objectives through the program team member.	Management controls, contract administration, budgeting, estimating, and financial controls are a functional specialty. The program manager utilizes the services of the specialist organizations. The specialists retain their own channels to the general manager but must keep the program manager informed through the program team member.
Approves all engineering change control decisions that affect the contractually committed target time, cost, and performance requirements or objectives of the program.	Implements engineering change decisions approved by the program manager. Advises him of any resulting programming impasses and negotiates adjustments through the program team member.	
Establishes program budgets in conjunction with the cognizant program team members; monitors and negotiates changes.		In all matters pertaining to budget and cost control, the program manager utilizes the services of the program team member representing the cognizant financial control organization.
Authorizes release of the budget and work authorization for the performance of approved work, and negotiates any intradirectorate reallocation above section level with the affected functional organizations through the program team members.	Within the allocated budget, provides manpower skills, facilities, and other resources pertaining to his functional specialty to the degree and level necessary to meet program schedule, cost, and technical performance requirements of the contract.	

858

Requests the assignment of program team members to the program, and approves the release of the team member from the program.

Establishes report requirements and controls necessary for evaluation of all phases of program performance consistent with effective policies and procedures.

Measures and evaluates performance of tasks against the established plan. Identifies current and potential problems. Decides upon and authorizes corrective action.

Appraises the program team members and/or functional organizations of program changes affecting their function.

Assures the establishment, coordination, and execution of support programs to the extent required or permitted by the contract.

Coordinates with the program manager in the selection and assignment of a program team member to the program or release of the program team member from the program.

Works in concert with other functional organizations to ensure that he and they are proceeding satisfactorily in the completion of mutually interdependent program tasks and events.

Follows-up all activities of his organization to ensure satisfactory performance to program requirements. Detects actual or potential problems. Takes timely corrective action in his organization, and when such problems involve interface with other functional organizations, notifies them and coordinates the initiation of mutually satisfactory remedial action. Keeps the program manager advised (through the program team member) of conditions affecting the program, existing, or expected problems, problems solved, and corrective action required or performed.

Program manager does not hire or fire functional personnel. Program team members should not be removed from the program without the concurrence of the program manager.

Insofar as possible, program controls must be satisfied from existing data and controls as defined by division policies and procedures.

The program manager directs or redirects activities of functional organizations only through the cognizant program team member. Functional managers are responsible for the performance of their organizations. Functional managers do not implement decisions involving increased total program costs, changes in schedule, or changes in technical performance without prior approval of the program team members and the program manager.

This includes such programs as value engineering, data management, and configuration management.

- Approving the procuring work statement, the schedules, the source selection, the negotiated price, and the type of contract on major procurement.
- Monitoring the functional organization's performance against released budgets, schedules, and program requirements.
- When cost performance is unacceptable, taking appropriate action with the affected organization to modify the work requirements or to stimulate corrective action within the functional organization so as to reduce cost without changing the contracted scope of work.
- Being responsible for all communications and policy matters on contracted programs so that no communicative directives shall be issued without the signature or concurrence of the program manager.

Describing the responsibilities of a manager is only a portion of the management policy or management guideline package. Because the program manager must cross over functional boundaries to accomplish all of the above, it is also necessary to describe the role and responsibility of the functional manager as well as the relationship between functional and program management for major program activities. Table 15–7 defines the responsibilities for the program manager and the functional manager and their relationship (i.e., interaction) for development and implementations of a management cost and control system. Similar tables can be developed for planning and scheduling, communications, customer relations, and contract administration.

15.11 COST CONTROL PROBLEMS

No matter how good the cost and control system is, problems can occur, as shown in Figure 15–23. Below are common causes of cost problems:

- Poor estimating techniques and/or standards, resulting in unrealistic budgets
- Out-of-sequence starting and completion of activities and events
- Inadequate work breakdown structure
- No management policy on reporting and control practices
- Poor work definition at the lower levels of the organization
- Management reducing budgets or bids to be competitive or to eliminate "fat"
- Inadequent formal planning that results in unnoticed, or often uncontrolled, increases in scope of effort
- Poor comparison of actual and planned costs
- Comparison of actual and planned costs at the wrong level of management
- Unforeseen technical problems
- Schedule delays that require overtime or idle time costing
- Material escalation factors that are unrealistic

Cost overruns can occur in any phase of project development. Below are the most common causes for cost overruns.

FIGURE 15–23. Was there a reason for the cost overrun?

- Proposal phase
  - Failure to understand customer requirements
  - Unrealistic appraisal of in-house capabilities
  - Underestimating time requirements
- Planning phase
  - Omissions
  - Inaccuracy of the work breakdown structure
  - Misinterpretation of information
  - Use of wrong estimating techniques
  - Failure to identify and concentrate on major cost elements
  - Failure to assess and provide for risks
- Negotiation phase
  - Forcing a speedy compromise
  - Procurement ceiling costs
  - Negotiation team that must "win this one"
- Contractual phase
  - Contractual discrepancies
  - SOW different from RFP requirements
  - Proposal team different from project team
- Design phase
  - Accepting customer requests without management approval
  - Problems in customer communications channels and data items
  - Problems in design review meetings
- Production phase
  - Excessive material costs
  - Specifications that are not acceptable
  - Manufacturing and engineering disagreement

15–1 Do cost overruns just happen, or are they caused?

15–2 Cemeteries are filled with projects that went out of control. Below are several causes that can easily develop into out-of-control conditions. In which phase of a project should each of these conditions be detected and, if possible, remedied?

  a. Customer's requirements not understood
  b. Project team formed after bid was prepared
  c. Accepting unusual terms and conditions
  d. Permitting a grace period for changing specifications
  e. Lack of time to research specifications
  f. Overestimation of company's capabilities

15–3 Below are several factors that can result in project delays and cost overruns. Explain how these problems can be overcome.

  a. Poorly defined milestones
  b. Poor estimating techniques
  c. A missing PERT/CPM chart
  d. Functional managers not having a clear understanding of what has to be done
  e. Poor programming procedures and techniques
  f. Changes constantly being made deep in the project's life cycle

15–4 Under what circumstances would each of the figures in Chapter 13 be applicable for customer reporting? In-house reporting? Reporting to top-level management?

15–5 What impact would there be on BCWS, BCWP, ACWP, and cost and schedule variances as a result of the:

  a. Early state of an activity on a PERT chart?
  b. Late start of an activity on a PERT chart?

15–6 Alpha Company has implemented a plan whereby functional managers will be held totally responsible for all cost overruns against their (the functional managers') original estimates. Furthermore, all cost overruns must come out of the functional managers' budgets, whether they be overhead or otherwise, not the project budget. What are the advantages and disadvantages of this approach?

15–7 Karl has decided to retain a management reserve on a $400,000 project that includes a $60,000 profit. At the completion of the project, Karl finds that the management reserve fund contains $40,000. Should Karl book the management reserve as excess profits (i.e., $100,000), or should he just book the target profit of $60,000 and let the functional managers "sandbag" on the slush fund until it is depleted?

15–8 ABC Corporation has recently given out a nine-month contract to a construction subcontractor. At the end of the first month, it becomes obvious that the subcontractor is not reporting costs according to an appropriate WBS level. ABC Corporation asks the subcontractor to change its cost reporting procedures. The subcontractor states that this cannot be done without additional funding. This problem has occurred with other subcontractors as well. What can ABC Corporation do about this?

15–9 What would be the result if all project managers decided to withhold a management reserve? What criteria should be used for determining when a management reserve is necessary?

15–10 Alpha Company, a project-driven organization, pays its department managers a quarterly bonus that is dependent on two factors: the departmental overhead rate and direct labor dollars. The exact value of the bonus is proportional to how much these two factors are underrun.

Department man-hours are priced out against the department average, which does not include the department manager's salary. His salary is included under his departmental overhead rate, but he does have the option of charging his own time as direct labor to the projects for which he must supply resources.

What do you think of this method? Is it adequate inducement for a functional manager to control resources more effectively? How would you feel, as a project manager, knowing that the functional managers got quarterly bonuses and you got none?

15–11 Many executives are reluctant to let project managers have complete control of project costs because then the project managers must know the exact salaries of almost all project personnel. Can this situation be prevented if the contract requires reporting costs as actuals?

15–12 How can a country's inflation rate influence the contractual payment policy?

15–13 Consider a situation in which several tasks may be for one to two years rather than the 200 hours normally used in the work-package level of the WBS.

    a. How will this affect cost control?

    b. Can we still use the 50/50 rule?

    c. How frequently should costs be updated?

15–14 By now you should be familiar with the various tools that can be used for planning, controlling, scheduling, and directing project activities. Table 15–8 contains

TABLE 15–8. PROJECT PLANNING, CONTROLLING, AND DIRECTING

	Useful for			
Tool	**Planning**	**Controlling**	**Directing**	**Interface Relationships**
Project organizational charts				
Work breakdown structure				
Task descriptions				
Work packages				
Project budget				
Project plan				
Charts/schedules				
Progress reports				
Review meetings				

○ somewhat useful
● very useful

a partial list of such tools and how they relate to specific project management functions. Complete the table (using the legend at the bottom) to indicate which are very useful and which are somewhat useful.

Obviously there will be some questions about what is very useful and what is somewhat useful. Be able to defend your answers.

15–15 Complete the table below and plot the EAC as a function of time. What are your conclusions?

	Cumulative Cost, in Thousands			Variance $		
Week	BCWS	BCWP	ACWP	Schedule	Cost	EAC
1	50	50	25			
2	70	60	40			
3	90	80	67			
4	120	105	90			
5	130	120	115			
6	140	135	130			
7	165	150	155			
8	200	175	190			
9	250	220	230			
10	270	260	270			
11	300	295	305			
12	350	340	340			
13	380	360	370			
14	420	395	400			
15	460	460	450			

15–16 Using the information in Chapter 12, problem 12–18, complete Table 15–9.

15–17 On June 12, 1990, Delta Cooperation was awarded a $160,000 contract for testing a product. The contract consisted of $143,000 for labor and materials, and the remaining $17,000 was profit. The contract had a scheduled start date of July 3. The network logic, as defined by the project manager and approved by the customer, consisting of the following:

Activity	Time (Weeks)
AB	7
AC	10
AD	8
BC	4
BE	2
CF	3
DF	5
EF	2
FG	1

TABLE 15–9. PROJECT COSTS

1	2	3	4	5	6	7
Activity	Percent Complete	Budgeted Cost for Work Scheduled	Budgeted Cost for Work Performed	Actual Cost for Work Performed	Cost Variance = 4 – 5	Schedule Variance = 4 –3
Total						

Cost variance ($) = Column 4 – Column 5 = _____

Schedule variance ($) = Column 4 – Column 3 = _____

Schedule variance (weeks) = $\dfrac{\text{Schedule variance (\$)}}{\text{Average weekly budgeted \$}}$ = $\dfrac{\text{Column 3} \div 4 \text{ weeks}}{}$ = _____

Time-to-complete = _____

Cost-at-completion = rate of spending × Total budget = $\dfrac{\text{Column 5}}{\text{Column 4}}$ (_____) = _____

Cost-to-complete = (Cost-at-completion) – ACWP = _____

On August 27, 1990, the executive steering committee received the following report indicating the status of the project at the end of the eighth week:

Activity	% Complete	Actual Cost	Time Remaining (Weeks)
AB	100	$23,500	0
AC	60	19,200	4
AD	87.5	37,500	1
BC	50	8,000	2
BE	50	5,500	1

The steering committee could not identify the real status of the project from this brief report. Even after comparing this brief status report with the project planning budget (see Table 15–10), the real status was not readily apparent.

Management instructed the project manager to prepare a better status report that depicted the true status of the project, as well as the amount of profit that could be expected at project completion. Your assignment is to prepare a table such as Table 15–9.

15–18 *The Alpha Machine Tool Project*

Acme Corporation has received a contractual order to build a new tooling machine for Alpha Corporation. The project started several months ago. Table 15–11 is the Monthly Cost Summary for June, 1988. Some of the entries in the table have been purposely omitted, but the following additional information is provided to help you answer the questions below:

    A. Assume that the overhead of 100% is fixed over the period of performance.

    B. The report you are given is at a month end, June 30, 1988.

    C. The 80/20 sharing ratio says that the customer (i.e., Alpha) will pay 80 percent of the dollars above the target cost and up to the ceiling cost. Likewise, 80 percent of the cost savings below the target cost go back to Alpha.

    D. The revised BCWS is revised from the released BCWS.

    E. The ceiling price is based on cost (i.e., without profit).

Answer the following questions by extracting data from the Alpha Machine Tool Project's monthly summary report.

    1. What is the total *negotiated* target value of the contract? _____

    2. What is the budgeted target value for *all work authorized* under this contract? _____

    3. What is the total budgetary amount that Acme had originally allocated/released to the Alpha Project? _____

    4. What is the new/revised total budgetary amount that Acme has released to the Alpha Project? _____

TABLE 15–10. PROJECT PLANNING BUDGET

Activity	Week														
	1	2	3	4	5	6	7	8	9	10	11	12	13	14	15
AB	2000	2000	3000	3000	4000	4000	3000								
AC	3000	3000	3000	4000	4000	4000	4000	2000	2000	1000					
AD	5000	5000	6000	4000	4000	4000	3000	1000							
BC								3000	4000	4000	5000				
BE								6000	6000						
CF												2000	3000	3000	
DF									3000	3000	3000	4000	4000		
EF											2000	2000			
FG															3000

Note: Table 15–10 assumes that percent is *linear* with time and *nonlinear* with cost.

TABLE 15–11. MONTHLY COST SUMMARY—JUNE 1988

Contract:	Alpha Machine Tool	Negotiated Cost:	$2,500,000	Sharing Ratio:	80/20
PM:	Gary Jones	Target Fee:	12%	Ceiling:	3,000,000 on cost (= $3.2 M on price)
Reporting Period:	June 1 - June 30, 1988	Target Price:	2,800,000	Contract:	fixed price incentive fee
Contract Period:	Feb. 1 - Oct. 30, 1988				

Level 2 WBS Items	Current Month, $					Cumulative to Date, $					At Completion, $			
	BCWS	BCWP	ACWP	SV	CV	BCWS	BCWP	ACWP	SV	CV	Contracted BCWS	Original Released BCWS	Revised BCWS	Var.
Program mgt.	19300	19300	19300	0	0	108000	108000	108000	0	0	200000	200000	200000	
Subsystem A	23000	16600	24200	<6400>	<7600>	158000	181700	234700	23700	<53000>	250000	200000	225000	<25000>
Subsystem B	14000	15200	16800	1200	<1600>	96000	94200	93000	<1800>	1200	200000	200000	200000	
Subsystem C	0	0	0	0	0	0					300000	275000	275000	
Manu. support	11600	10400	12000	<1200>	<1600>	73000	74300	75600	1300	<1300>	200000	190000	190000	
Quality control	5900	6000	6000	100	0	5900	6000	6000	100	0	100000	100000	100000	
TOTAL DIRECT	73800	67500	78300								1250000	1165000	1190000	
OVERHEAD, 100%	73800	67500	78300								1250000	1165000	1190000	
TOTAL	147600	135000	156600								2500000	2330000	2380000	

5. How much money, if any, had Acme set aside as a management reserve based upon the original released budget? (burdened)

6. Has the management reserve been revised, and if so, by how much? (burdened)

7. Which level-2 WBS elements make up the revised management reserve?

8. Based upon the reviewed BCWS completion costs, how much profit can Acme expect to make on the Alpha Project? (Hint: Don't forget sharing ratio)

9. How much of the distributed budget that has been identified for accomplishment of work is only *indirectly* attributed to this contract? (i.e., *overhead*)

Answer the Following Questions for Direct Labor Only

10. Of the total direct effort budgeted for on this contract, how much work did Acme *schedule* to be performed this month?

11. How much of the work scheduled for accomplishment this month was actually earned (i.e., earned value)?

12. Did Acme do more or less work than planned for this month? How much was the schedule variance (SV)? [$ and %]

13. What did it actually cost Acme for the work performed this month?

14. What is the difference between the amount that Acme budgeted for the work performed this month and what the actual cost was? (i.e., CV) [$ and %]

15. Which WBS level-2 elements are the primary causes for this month's cost and schedule variances?

16. How much cost variance has Acme experienced to date? [$ and %]

17. How much schedule variance has Acme experienced to date? [$ and %]

18. Is the cost variance improving or getting worse?

19. Is the schedule variance improving or getting worse?

20. Does it appear that the scheduled end date will be met?

21. What is the new estimated burdened cost at completion? _____
22. How much profitability/loss can Acme expect from the new estimated cost at completion? _____
23. If Acme's final burdened cost for the program was $3,150,000, how much profit/loss would it experience? _____

15–19 Calculate the total price variance for direct labor and the labor rate cost variance from the following data:

	Direct Material	Direct Labor
Planned price/unit	$ 10.00	$ 22.00
Actual units	$ 9,300	$ 12,000
Actual price/unit	$ 9.25	$ 22.50
Actual cost	$86,025,00	$270,000

15–20 One of your assistant project managers has given you an earned value report that is only partially complete. Can you fill in the missing information?

(All numbers are in thousands of dollars)

WBS Work Packages	BCWS	BCWP	ACWP	SV	CV
A	103	115	___	12	<91>
B	0	___	40	___	___
D	42	12	33	<30>	<21>
H	66	___	94	189	161
P	87	77	116	<10>	<39>
S	175	___	184	<115>	<124>
	473	___	___	___	<144>

15–21 The following problem requires an understanding of the WBS, the cost account elements, and cost control analysis. Assume that all costs are in thousands of dollars.

Given the partial WBS shown below, what is the total cost for the WBS element 4.0? Assume that the costs provided are direct labors costs only and that the overhead rate is 100 percent.

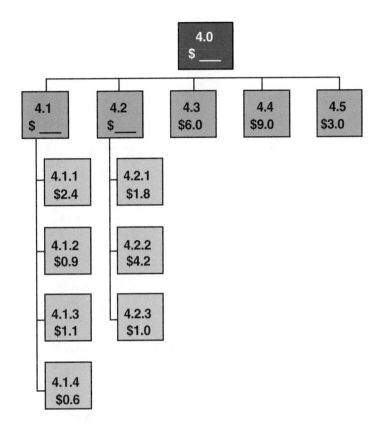

Which of the following is the value of WBS element 4.0?

    a. $60.0
    b. $30.0
    c. $24.0
    d. $54.0

Using the data in Figure 15–24, and the actual costs given below for WBS elements 5.1 through 5.4 and elements 4.1 and 4.2, answer the questions shown below:

	Actual Costs
E-1–5.1	$1.0
E-1–5.3	$1.5
E-2–5.2	$1.0
E-2–5.4	$2.0
E-3–5.1	$1.0
E-3–5.3	$2.5
E-4–5.3	$3.0
E-4–5.2	$3.5

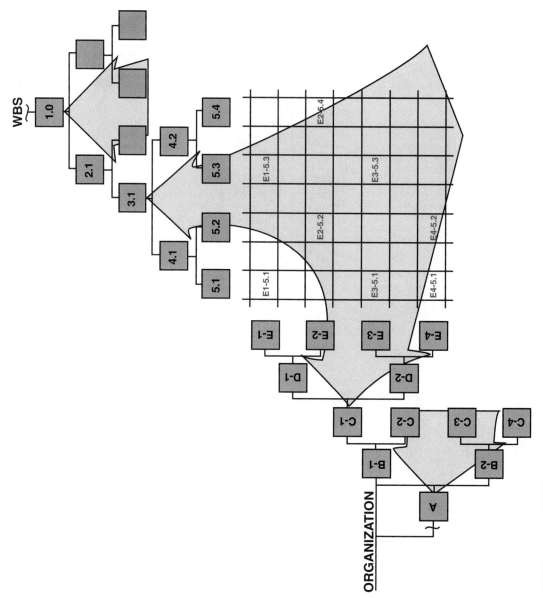

FIGURE 15–24. Exhibit of cost accounts.

WBS element 5.1	$____
WBS element 5.2	$____
WBS element 5.3	$____
WBS element 5.4	$____
WBS element 4.1	$____
WBS element 4.2	$____
Functional element E-1	$____
Functional element E-2	$____
Functional element E-3	$____
Functional element E-4	$____
Functional element D-1	$____
Functional element D-2	$____

CASE STUDIES

THE BATHTUB PERIOD

The award of the Scott contract on January 3, 1987, left Park Industries elated. The Scott Project, if managed correctly, offered tremendous opportunities for follow-on work over the next several years. Park's management considered the Scott Project as strategic in nature.

The Scott Project was a ten-month endeavor to develop a new product for Scott Corporation. Scott informed Park Industries that sole-source production contracts would follow, for at least five years, assuming that the initial R&D effort proved satisfactory. All follow-on contracts were to be negotiated on a year-to-year basis.

Jerry Dunlap was selected as project manager. Although he was young and eager, he understood the importance of the effort for future growth of the company. Dunlap was given some of the best employees to fill out his project office as part of Park's matrix organization. The Scott Project maintained a project office of seven full-time people, including Dunlap, throughout the duration of the project. In addition, eight people from the functional department were selected for representation as functional project team members, four full-time and four half-time.

Although the workload fluctuated, the manpower level for the project office and team members was constant for the duration of the project at 2,080 hours per month. The company assumed that each hour worked incurred a cost of $60.00 per person, fully burdened.

At the end of June, with four months remaining on the project, Scott Corporation informed Park Industries that, owing to a projected cash flow problem, follow-on work would not be awarded until the first week in March (1988). This posed a tremendous problem for Jerry Dunlap because he did not wish to break up the project office. If he permitted his key people to be assigned to other projects, there would be no guarantee that he could get them back at the beginning of the follow-on work. Good project office personnel are always in demand.

Jerry estimated that he needed $40,000 per month during the "bathtub" period to support and maintain his key people. Fortunately, the bathtub period fell over Christmas and New Year's, a time when the plant would be shut down for seventeen days. Between the vacation days that his key employees would be taking, and the small special projects that this people could be temporarily assigned to on other programs, Jerry revised his estimate to $125,000 for the entire bathtub period.

At the weekly team meeting, Jerry told the program team members that they would have to "tighten their belts" in order to establish a management reserve of $125,000. The project team understood the necessity for this action and began rescheduling and replanning until a management reserve of this size could be realized. Because the contract was firm-fixed-price, all schedules for administrative support (i.e., project office and project team members) were extended through February 28 on the supposition that this additional time was needed for final cost data accountability and program report documentation.

Jerry informed his boss, Frank Howard, the division head for project management, as to the problems with the bathtub period. Frank was the intermediary between Jerry and the general manager. Frank agreed with Jerry's approach to the problem and requested to be kept informed.

On September 15, Frank told Jerry that he wanted to "book" the management reserve of $125,000 as excess profit since it would influence his (Frank's) Christmas bonus. Frank and Jerry argued for a while, with Frank constantly saying, "Don't worry! You'll get your key people back. I'll see to that. But I want those uncommitted funds recorded as profit and the program closed out by November 1."

Jerry was furious with Frank's lack of interest in maintaining the current organizational membership.

   a. Should Jerry go to the general manager?
   b. Should the key people be supported on overhead?
   c. If this were a cost-plus program, would you consider approaching the customer with your problem in hopes of relief?
   d. If you were the customer of this cost-plus program, what would your response be for additional funds for the bathtub period, assuming cost overrun?
   e. Would your previous answer change if the program had the money available as a result of an underrun?
   f. How do you prevent this situation from recurring on all yearly follow-on contracts?

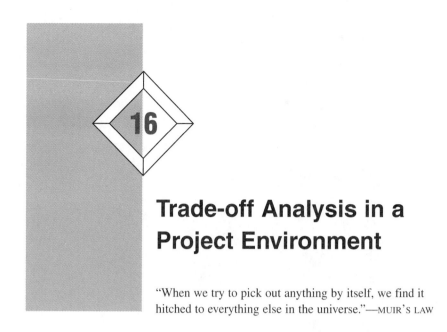

Trade-off Analysis in a Project Environment

"When we try to pick out anything by itself, we find it hitched to everything else in the universe."—MUIR'S LAW

16.0 INTRODUCTION

Successful project management is both an art and a science and attempts to control corporate resources within the constraints of time, cost, and performance. Most projects are unique, one-of-kind activities for which there may not have been reasonable standards for forward planning. As a result, the project manager may find it extremely difficult to stay within the time-cost-performance triangle of Figure 16–1.

The time-cost-performance triangle is the "magic combination" that is continuously pursued by the project manager throughout the life cycle of the project. If the project were to flow smoothly, according to plan, there might not be a need for trade-off analysis. Unfortunately, most projects eventually find crises where this delicate balance necessary to attain the desired performance within time and cost is no longer possible.

This is shown in Figure 16–2, where the Δ's represent deviations from the original estimates. The time and cost deviations are normally overruns, whereas the performance error will be an underrun. No two projects are ever exactly alike, and trade-off analysis would appear to be an ongoing effort throughout the life of the project, continuously influenced by both the internal and the external environment. Experienced project managers may have predetermined trade-offs in reserve as appropriate crises arise, recognizing that trade-offs are part of a continuous thought process, as shown in Figure 16–3. Inexperienced project managers may consider trade-off analysis as shown in Figure 16–4.

Trade-offs are always based on the constraints of the project. Table 16–1 illustrates the types of constraints commonly imposed. Situations A and B are the typical trade-offs encountered in project management. For example, situation A-3 portrays most research and development projects. The performance of an R&D project is usually well defined, and it is cost and time that may be allowed to go beyond budget and schedule. The determination of what to sacrifice is based on the available alternatives. If there are no alternatives to the product being developed and the potential usage is great, then cost and time are the trade-offs.

875

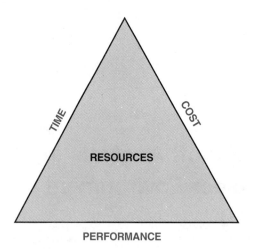

FIGURE 16–1. Overview of project management.

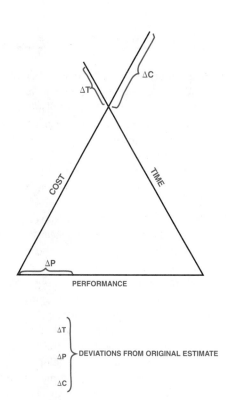

FIGURE 16–2. Project management with trade-offs.

FIGURE 16–3. Trade-off analysis.

FIGURE 16–4. Is this how you solve project problems?

TABLE 16–1.   CATEGORIES OF CONSTRAINTS

	Time	Cost	Performance
A. One Element Fixed at a Time			
A-1	Fixed	Variable	Variable
A-2	Variable	Fixed	Variable
A-3	Variable	Variable	Fixed
B. Two Elements Fixed at a Time			
B-1	Fixed	Fixed	Variable
B-2	Fixed	Variable	Fixed
B-3	Variable	Fixed	Fixed
C. Three Elements Fixed or Variable			
C-1	Fixed	Fixed	Fixed
C-2	Variable	Variable	Variable

Most capital equipment projects would fall into situation A-1 or B-2, where time is of the essence. The sooner the piece of equipment gets into production, the sooner the return of investment can be realized. Often there exist performance constraints that determine the profit potential of the project. If the project potential is determined to be great after all alternatives have been established, cost will be the slippage factor, as in situation B-2.

Non-process-type equipment, such as air pollution control equipment, usually develops a scenario around situation B-3. Performance is fixed by the Environmental Protection Agency. The deadline for compliance can be delayed through litigation, but if the lawsuits fail, most firms then try to comply with the least expensive equipment that will meet the minimum requirements.

The professional consulting firm operates primarily under situation B-1. In situation C, the trade-off analysis will be completed based on the selection criteria and constraints. If everything is fixed (C-1), there

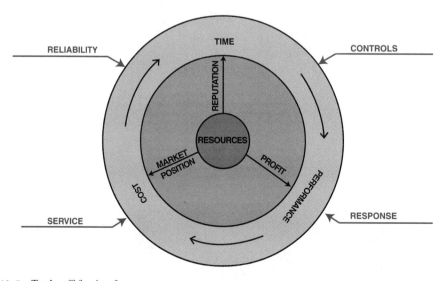

FIGURE 16–5. Trade-off forcing factors.

is no room for any outcome other than total success, and if everything is variable (C-2), there are no constraints and thus no trade-off.

Many factors go into the decision to sacrifice either time, cost, or performance. It should be noted, however, that it is not always possible to sacrifice one of these items without affecting the others. For example, reducing the time could have a serious impact on performance and cost (especially if overtime is required).

There are several factors, such as those shown in Figure 16–5, that tend to "force" trade-offs. Poorly written documents (e.g., statements of work, contracts, and specifications) are almost always inward forces for conflict in which the project manager tends to look for performance relief. In many projects, the initial sale and negotiation, as well as the specification writing, are done by highly technical people who are driven to create a monument rather than meet the operational needs of the customer, the operator of the system. When the operating forces dominate outward from the project to the customer, project managers may tend to seek cost relief.

16.1 METHODOLOGY FOR TRADE-OFF ANALYSIS

Any process for managing time, cost, and performance trade-offs should emphasize the systems approach to management by recognizing that even the smallest change in a project or system could easily affect all of the organization's systems. A typical systems model is shown in Figure 16–6. Because of this, it is often better to develop a process for decision-making/trade-off analysis rather than to maintain hard-and-fast rules on trade-offs. The following six steps might be a representative method for managing project time, cost, and performance trade-offs:

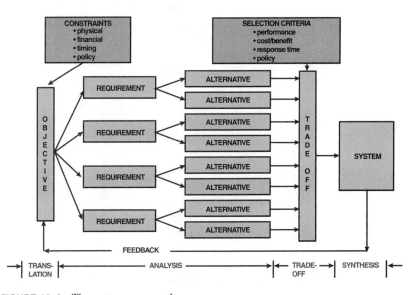

FIGURE 16–6. The systems approach.

- Recognizing and understanding the basis for project conflicts
- Reviewing the project objectives
- Analyzing the project environment and status
- Identifying the alternative courses of action
- Analyzing and selecting the best alternative
- Revising the project plan

The first step in any decision-making process must be recognition and understanding of the conflict. Most projects have management cost and control systems that compare actual versus planned results, scrutinize the results through variance analyses, and provide status reports so that corrective action can be taken to resolve the problems. Project managers must carefully evaluate project problems because information concerning a potential problem may not always be what it appears to be. The source of the early warning and the validity of the intelligence data should first be tested. Management control of a project team organization is usually quite sensitive to both the accuracy and timeliness of data communications. Typical questions that should be asked at this point might be:

- Is the information pertinent?
- Is the information current?
- Are the data complete?
- Who has determined that this situation exists?
- How does he know this information is correct?
- If this information is true, what are the implications for the project?

The major reason for this first step is to understand the potential cause for the conflict, and thus for trade-offs. Most causes can be categorized as human errors or failures, uncertain problems, and totally unexpected problems. This is shown below:

- Human errors/failures
  - Impossible schedule commitments
  - Poor control of design changes
  - Poor project cost accounting
  - Machine failures
  - Test failures
  - Failure to receive a critical input
  - Failure to receive anticipated approvals
- Uncertain problems
  - Too many concurrent projects
  - Labor contract expiration
  - Change in project leadership
  - Possibility of project cancellation
- Unexpected problems
  - Overcommitted company resources

- Conflicting project priorities
- Cash flow problems
- Labor contract disputes
- Delay in material shipment
- "Fast-track" people having been promoted off the project
- "Temporary" employees having to be returned to their home base
- Inaccurate original forecast
- Change in market conditions
- New standards having been developed

The second step in the decision-making process is a complete review of the project objectives. This review must include an analysis of these objectives as seen by the various participants in the projects, ranging from top management to project team members. These objectives and/or priorities were originally set with many environmental factors being considered. These factors must be reviewed because they may have changed over the lifetime of the project.

The nature of these objectives will usually determine the degree of rigidity that has been established between time, cost, and performance. This may very well require review of all project documentation, including:

- Project objectives
- Project integration into sponsor's objectives and strategic plan
- Statement of work
- Schedule, cost, and performance specifications
- Resources consumed and projected

The third step in the methodology is the analysis of the project environment and status. This step includes a detailed measurement of the actual time, cost, and performance results with the original or revised project plan. This step should not turn into a "witch hunt" but instead should focus on project results, problems, and roadblocks. Factors such as financial risk, potential follow-up contracts, the status of other projects, and relative competitive positions are just a few of the environmental factors that should be reviewed. Some companies have established policies toward trade-off analysis, such as "never compromise performance." Even these policies, however, have been known to change when environmental factors add to the financial risk of the company. The following topics may be applicable under step 3:

- Discuss the project with the project management office to:
  - Determine relative priorities for time, cost, and performance
  - Determine impact on firm's profitability and strategic plan
  - Get a management assessment (even a hunch as to what the problems are)
- If the project is a contract with an outside customer, meet with the customer's project manager to assess his views relative to project status and assess the customer's priorities for time, cost, and performance.

- Meet with the functional managers to determine their views on the problem and to gain an insight regarding their commitment to a successful project. Where does this project sit in their priority list?
- Review in detail the status of each project work package. Obtain a clear and detailed appraisal by the responsible project office personnel as to:
  - Time to complete
  - Cost to complete
  - Work to complete
- Review past data to assess credibility of cost and schedule information in the previous step.

The project manager may have sufficient background to quickly assess the significance of a particular variance and the probable impact of that variance on project team performance. Knowledge of the project requirements (possibly with the assistance of the project sponsor) will usually help a project manager determine whether corrective action must be taken at all, or whether the project should simply be permitted to continue as originally conceived.

Whether or not immediate action is required, a quick analysis of why a potential problem has developed is in order. Obviously, it will not help to "cure the symptoms" if the "disease" itself is not remedied. The project manager must remain objective in such problem identification, since he himself is a key member of the project team and may be personally responsible for problems that are occurring. Suspect areas typically include:

- Inadequate planning. Either planning was not done in sufficient detail or controls were not established to determine that the project is proceeding according to the approved plan.
- Scope changes. Cost and schedule overruns are the normal result of scope changes that are permitted without formal incorporation in the project plan or increase in the resources authorized for the project.
- Poor performance. Because of the high level of interdependencies that exist within any project team structure, unacceptable performance by one individual may quickly undermine the performance of the entire team.
- Excess performance. Frequently an overzealous team member will unintentionally distort the planned balance between cost, schedule, and performance on the project.
- Environmental restraints—particularly on projects involving "third-party approvals" or dependent on outside resources. Changes, delays, or nonperformance by parties outside the project team may have an adverse impact on the team performance.

Some projects appear to be out of tolerance when, in fact, they are not. For example, some construction projects are so front-loaded with costs that there appears to be a major discrepancy when one actually does not exist. The front-end loading of cost was planned for.

The fourth step in the project trade-off process is to list alternative courses of action. This step usually means brainstorming the possible methods of completing the project by compromising some combination of time, cost, or performance. Hopefully, this step will refine these possible alternatives into the three or four most likely scenarios for project completion. At this point, some intuitive decision making may be required to keep the list of alternatives at a manageable level.

In order fully to identify the alternatives, the project manager must have specific answers to key questions involving time, cost, and performance:

- Time
  - Is a time delay acceptable to the customer?
  - Will the time delay change the completion date for other projects and other customers?
  - What is the cause for the time delay?
  - Can resources be recommitted to meet the new schedule?
  - What will be the cost for the new schedule?
  - Will the increased time give us added improvement?
  - Will an extension of this project cause delays on other projects in the customer's house?
  - What will the customer's response be?
  - Will the increased time change our learning curve?
  - Will this hurt our company's ability to procure future contracts?
- Cost
  - What is causing the cost overrun?
  - What can be done to reduce the remaining costs?
  - Will the customer accept an additional charge?
  - Should we absorb the extra cost?
  - Can we renegotiate the time or performance standards to stay within cost?
  - Are the budgeted costs for the remainder of the project accurate?
- Will there be any net value gains for the increased funding?
  - Is this the only way to satisfy performance?
  - Will this hurt our company's ability to procure future contracts?
  - Is this the only way to maintain the schedule?
- Performance
  - Can the original specifications be met?
  - If not, at what cost can we guarantee compliance?
  - Are the specifications negotiable?
  - What are the advantages to the company and customer for specification changes?
  - What are the disadvantages to the company and customer for performance changes?
  - Are we increasing or decreasing performance?
  - Will the customer accept a change?
  - Will there be a product or employee liability incurred?

- Will the change in specifications cause a redistribution of project resources?
- Will this change hurt our company's ability to procure future contracts?

Once the answers to the above questions are obtained, it is often best to plot the results graphically. Graphical methods have been used during the past two decades to determine crashing costs for shortening the length of a project. To use the graphical techniques, we must decide on which of the three parameters to hold fixed.

Situation 1: Performance Is Held Constant (to Specifications)

With performance fixed, cost can be expressed as a function of time. Sample curves appear in Figures 16–7 and 16–8. In Figure 16–7, the circled X indicates the target cost and target time. Unfortunately, the cost to complete the project at the target time is higher than the budgeted cost. It may be possible to add resources and work overtime so that the time target can be met. Depending upon the way that overtime is burdened, it may be possible to find a minimum point in the curve where further delays will cause the total cost to escalate.

Curve A in Figure 16–8 shows the case where "time is money," and any additional time will increase the cost to complete. Factors such as management support time will always increase the cost to complete. There are, however, some situations where the increased costs occur in plateaus. This is shown in curve B of Figure 16–8. This could result from having to wait for temperature conditioning of a component before additional work can be completed, or simply waiting for nonscheduled resources to be available. In the latter case, the trade-off decision points may be at the end of each plateau.

With performance fixed, there are four methods available for constructing and analyzing the time/cost curves:

- Additional resources may be required. This will usually drive up the cost very fast. Assuming that the resources are available, cost control problems can occur as a result of adding resources after initial project budgeting.
- The scope of work may be redefined and some work deleted without changing the project performance requirements. Performance standards may have been set too high, or the probability of success demanded of the project team may have been simply unrealistic. Reductions in cost and improvements in schedules would typically result from relaxing performance specifications, provided that the lower quality level will still meet the requirements of the customer.
- Available resources may be shifted in order to balance project costs or to speed up activities that are on the "critical" path work element that is trailing. This process of replanning shifts elements from noncritical to critical activities.

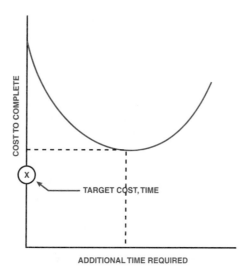

FIGURE 16–7. Trade-offs with fixed performance.

● Given a schedule problem, a change in the logic diagram may be needed to move from the current position to the desired position. Such a change could easily result in the replanning and reallocation of resources. An example of this would be to convert from "serial" to "parallel" work efforts. This often requires that a large risk be incurred.

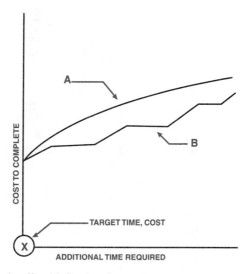

FIGURE 16–8. Trade-offs with fixed performance.

Trade-offs with fixed performance levels must take into account the dependence of the firm on the customer, priority of the project within the firm, and potential for future business. A basic assumption here is that the firm may never sacrifice its reputation by delivering a product that performs to less than the specifications called for. The exception might be a recommended engineering change that would enhance performance capability to such a degree that the scope change would allow the contractor to pull the project back on schedule. This is always worth investigating before entering into time–cost trade-offs.

Time and cost are interrelated in a labor-intensive project. As delivery slips, cost growth usually occurs. Slipping delivery schedules and minimizing cost growth through the use of overtime usually constitute the recommended alternative for projects in which the dependence of the firm on the customer, the priority of the project within the firm's stream of projects, and the future business potential in terms of sales represent a low- to medium-risk area. Even in some high-risk situations, the contractor may have to absorb the additional cost himself. This decision is often based on estimating the future projects from this customer so that the loss is amortized against future business. Not all projects are financial successes.

A company's reputation for excellence is often hard to establish and can be extremely fragile. It is probably a contractor's greatest asset. This is particularly true in high-liability contracts, where the consequences of failure are extremely serious. There are companies that have been very successful in aerospace and advanced technology contracting but have seldom been the low bidder. Where the government is the contractor, performance is rated far above cost. An example here would be contracting for the U.S. Navy's nuclear reactor components. The costs incurred in the Navy's work could not be tolerated in commercial nuclear reactor components. (This has been true, but after the Three Mile Island incident, commercial nuclear energy interests may have to adopt the higher standards of quality and reliability—and cost—that characterize the Navy's nuclear energy programs.)

The consequences of a commercial aircraft crash are of such magnitude that the cost and time are relatively insignificant compared with precision manufacturing and extremely high reliability. As fuel costs rise, demands become even more stringent, with efficiency assuming greater importance along with the already extremely high reliability requirements.

Sometimes projects may have fixed time and costs, leaving only the performance variable for trade-offs. However, as shown in the following scenario, the eventual outcome may be to modify the "fixed" cost constraint.

The hypothetical situation involves a government hardware subcontract, fixed-price, with delivery to the major government contractor. The major contractor had a very tight schedule, and the hardware being supplied had only a one-week "window" in which to be delivered, or the major contractor would suffer a major delay. Any delay at this point would place the general contractor in serious trouble. Both the government contracting officer and the purchasing manager of the general contractor had "emphasized" the importance of making the delivery schedule. There was no financial penalty for being late, but the contracting officer had stated in writing that any follow-on contracts, which were heavily counted on by the company's top management, would be placed with other vendors if delivery was not made on time.

Quality (performance) was critical but had never been a serious problem. In fact, performance had exceeded the contractual requirements because it had been company policy to be the "best" in the industry. This policy had, at times, caused cost problems, but it had ensured follow-on orders.

This project was in trouble at the halfway point, three months into the six-month schedule. The latest progress report indicated that the delivery would be delayed by three weeks. Costs were on target to date, but the shipping delay was expected to result in extra costs that would amount to 20 percent of the planned profit.

The project got off schedule when the flow of raw materials from a major vendor was interrupted for three weeks by a quality problem that was not discovered until the material was placed in production. Since the manufacturing time was process controlled, it was very difficult to make up lost time.

The first decision was that everything possible would be done to make delivery within one week of the original schedule. The potential lost revenue from future orders was so great that delivery must be made "at all costs," to quote the company president.

The quality system was then thoroughly investigated. It appeared that by eliminating two redundant inspection operations, one week could be saved in the total schedule. These two time-consuming inspection operations had been added when a quality problem developed on a former contract. The problem had been solved, and with present controls there was no reason to believe the inspections were still necessary. They would be eliminated with no determinable risk in performance.

Another two weeks were made up by working three production people seven days a week for the remainder of the project. This would permit delivery on the specified date of the contract, and would allow one week for other unforeseen problems so there would be a high probability of delivery within the required "window."

The cost of the seven-day-per-week work had the net effort of reducing the projected profit by 40 percent. Eliminating the two inspection operations saved 10 percent of the profit.

The plan outlined above met the time and performance specifications with increased cost that eventually reduced profit by an estimated 30 percent. The key to this situation was that only the labor, material, and overhead costs of the project were fixed, and the contractor was willing to accept a reduced profit.

Situation 2: Cost Is Fixed

With cost fixed, performance will vary as a function of time, as shown in Figure 16–9. The decision of whether to adhere to the target schedule data is usually determined by the level of performance. In curve A, performance may increase rapidly to the 90 percent level at the beginning of the project. A 10 percent increase in time may give a 20 percent increase in performance. After a certain point, a 10 percent increase in time may give only a 1 percent increase in performance. The company may not wish to risk the additional time necessary to attain

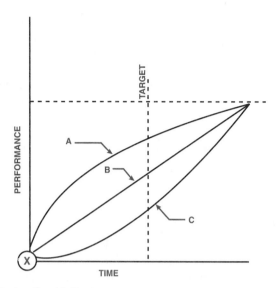

FIGURE 16–9. Trade-offs with fixed cost.

the 100 percent performance level if it is possible to do so. In curve C, the additional time must be sacrificed because it is unlikely that the customer will be happy with a 30 to 40 percent performance level. Curve B is the most difficult curve to analyze unless the customer has specified exactly which level of performance will be acceptable.

If cost is fixed, then it is imperative that the project have a carefully worded and understood contract with clear specifications as to the required level of performance and very clear statements of inclusion and exclusion. Careful attention to costs incurred because of customer changes or additional requirements can help reduce the possibility of a cost overrun. Experience in contracting ensures that costs that may be overlooked by the inexperienced project manager are included. Careful and skillful negotiations going in are essential to have all costs included in the contract and hopefully minimize the need for such trade-offs downstream. Common items that are often overlooked and can drive up costs include:

- Excessive detailed reporting
- Unnecessary documentation
- Excessive tracking documentation for time, cost, and performance
- Detailed specification development for equipment that could be purchased externally for less cost
- Wrong type of contract for this type of project

Often with a fixed-cost constraint, the first item that is sacrificed to meet that constraint is performance. But such an approach to trade-offs can contain hidden disasters over the life of a project if those performance specifications that were given up prove to have been essential to meeting some unspecified requirement such as long-term maintenance. In the long run, a degraded performance can actually increase costs rather than decrease them. Therefore, the project manager and his assistants should be sure they have a good analysis and understanding of the real costs associated with any trade-offs in performance.

Situation 3: Time Is Fixed

Figure 16–10 identifies the situation in which time is fixed and cost varies with performance. Figure 16–10 is similar to Figure 16–9 in that the rate of change of performance with cost is the controlling factor. If performance is at the 90 percent level with the target cost, then the contractor may request performance relief. This is shown in curve A. However, if the actual situation reflects curve B or C, additional costs must be incurred with the same considerations of situation 1—namely, how important is the customer and what emphasis should be placed on his follow-on business?

Completing the project on schedule can be extremely important in certain cases. For example, if an aircraft pump is not delivered when the engine is ready for shipment, it can hold up the engine manufacturer, the airframe manufacturer, and ultimately the customer. All three can incur substantial losses due to the delay of a single component. Moreover, customers who are unable to perform and who incur large unanticipated costs tend to have long memories. An irate vice

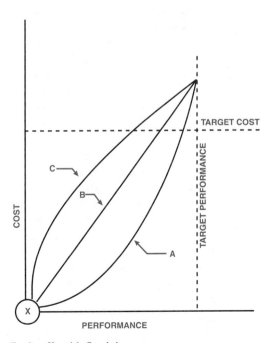

FIGURE 16–10. Trade-offs with fixed time.

president at a high level in the customer's shop can kill further contracts out of all proportion to the real failure to deliver on time.

Sometimes, even though time is supposedly fixed, there may be latitude without inconvenience to the customer. This could come about because the entire program (of which your project is just one subcontract) is behind schedule, and the customer is not ready for your particular project.

Another aspect of the time factor is that "early warning" of a time overrun can often mitigate the damage to the customer and greatly increase his favorable response. Careful planning and tracking, close coordination with all functions involved, and realistic dealing with time schedules before and during the project can ensure early notification to the customer and the possible negotiation of a trade-off of time and dollars or even technical performance. The last thing that a customer ever wants is to have a favorable progress report right up to the end of scheduled time and then to be surprised with a serious schedule overrun.

When time is fixed, the customer may find that he has some flexibility in determining how to arrive at the desired performance level. As shown in Figure 16–11, the contractor may be willing to accept additional costs to maximize employee safety.

Situation 4: No Constraints Are Fixed

Another common situation is that in which neither time, cost, nor performance is fixed. The best method for graphically showing the trade-off relationships is to develop parametric curves as in Figure 16–12. Cost and time trade-offs can now be analyzed for various levels of performance. The curves can also be redrawn for various cost levels (i.e., 100, 120, 150 percent of target cost) and schedule levels.

Another method for showing a family of curves is illustrated in Figure 16–13. Here, the contractor may have several different cost paths for achieving the desired time and performance constraints. The final path selected depends on the size of the risk that the contractor wishes to take.

There have been several attempts to display the three-dimensional trade-off problem graphically. Unfortunately, such a procedure is quite complex and difficult to follow. A more common approach is to use some sort of computer model and handle the trade-off as though it were a linear programming or dynamic programming problem. This too is often difficult to perform and manage.

Trade-offs can also be necessary at any point in time during the life cycle of a project. It is quite possible, and probable, for the criteria for the trade-offs to change over the life cycle of the project. Figure 16–14 identifies how the relative importance of the constraints of time, cost, and performance can change over the life cycle of the project. At project initiation, costs may not have accrued to a point where they are important. On the other hand, project performance may very well be overstressed until it becomes even more important than the schedule. At this point, additional performance can be "bought." As the project nears termination, the relative importance of the cost constraint may increase drastically, especially if project profits are the company's major source of revenue. Likewise, it is probable that the impact of performance and schedule will be lower.

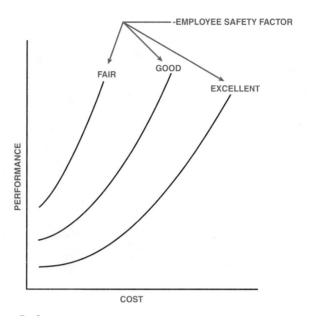

FIGURE 16–11. Performance versus cost.

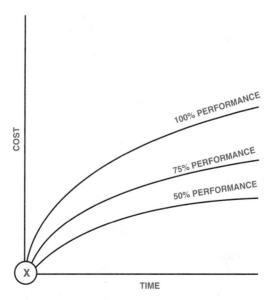

FIGURE 16–12. Trade-off analysis with family of curves.

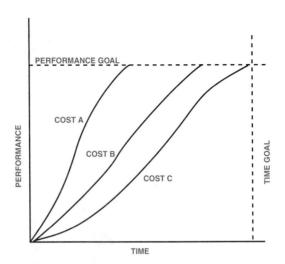

FIGURE 16–13. Cost–time–performance family of curves.

Once the alternative courses of action are determined, step 5 in the methodology is employed in order to analyze and select the feasible alternatives. Analyzing the alternatives should include the preparation of the revised project objectives for cost, performance, and time, along with an analysis of the required resources, general schedules, and revised project plans necessary to support each scenario. It is then the function of top management in conjunction with the project and functional managers to choose the solution that minimizes the overall

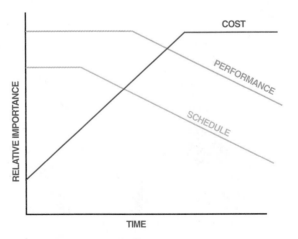

FIGURE 16–14. Life-cycle trade-offs. (Schedule not necessarily typical.)

impact to the company. This impact need not be measured just in short-term financial results, but should also include long-term strategic and market considerations.

The following tasks can be included in this step:

- Prepare a formal project update report including alternative work scopes, schedules, and costs to achieve.
  - Minimum cost overrun
  - Conformance to project objectives
  - Minimum schedule overrun
- Construct a decision tree including costs, work objectives, and schedules, and an estimate of the probability of success for each condition leading to the decision point.
- Present to internal and external project management the several alternatives along with an estimate of success probability.
- With management's agreement, select the appropriate completion strategy, and begin implementation. This assumes that management does not insist on an impossible task.

The last item requires further clarification. Many companies use a checklist to establish the criteria for alternative evaluation as well as for assessment of potential future problems. The following questions may be part of such a checklist:

- Will other projects be affected?
- Will rework be required in previous tasks?
- Are repair and/or maintenance made more difficult?
- Will additional tasks be required in the future?
- How will project personnel react?
- What is the effect on the project life cycle?
- Will project flexibility be reduced?
- What is the effect on key employees?
- What is the effect on the customer(s)?

The probability of occurrence and severity should be assessed for all potential future problems. If there is a high probability that the problem will recur and a high probability that the severity will be critical, a plan should be developed to reduce the probability of recurrence and severity. Internal restrictions such as manpower, materials, machines, money, management, time, policies, quality, and changing requirements can cause problems throughout the life cycle of a project. External restrictions of capital, completion dates, and liability also limit project flexibility.

One of the best methods for comparing the alternatives is to list them and then rank them in order of perceived importance relative to certain factors such as customer, potential follow-on business, cost deficit, and loss of goodwill. This is shown in Table 16–2. In the table each of the objectives is weighted according to

TABLE 16–2. WEIGHING THE ALTERNATIVES

Objectives / Weights / Alternatives	Increase Future Business	Ready on Time	Meet Current Cost	Meet Current Specs	Maximize Profits
	0.4	0.25	0.10	0.20	.05
Add resources	100%	90%	30%	90%	10%
Reduce scope of work	60%	90%	90%	30%	95%
Reduce specification change	90%	80%	95%	5%	80%
Complete project late	80%	0%	20%	95%	0%
Bill customer for added cost	30%	85%	0%	60%	95%

some method established by management. The percentages represent the degree of satisfactory completion for each alternative. This type of analysis, often referred to as decision making under risk, is commonly taught in operations research and management science coursework. Weighting factors are often used to assist in the decision-making process. Unfortunately, this can add mass confusion to the already confused process.

Table 16–3 shows that some companies perform trade-off analysis by equating all alternatives to a lowest common denominator—dollars. Although this conversion can be very difficult, it does ensure that we are comparing "apples with apples." All resources such as capital equipment can be expressed in terms of dollars. Difficulties arise in assigning dollar values to such items as environmental pollution, safety standards, or the possible loss of life.

There are often several types of corrective action that can be utilized. Below are a number of examples:

- Overtime
- Double shifts
- Expediting

TABLE 16–3. TRADE-OFF ANALYSIS FOR IMPROVING PERFORMANCE CAPABILITY

Assumption	Description	Capital Expenditure $	Time to Complete, Months	Project Profit, $	Ranking in Profit $
1	No change	0	6	100,000	5
2	Hire higher-salaried people	0	5	105,000	3
3	Refurbish equipment	10,000	7	110,000	2
4	Purchase new equipment	85,000	9	94,000	6
5	Change specifications	0	6	125,000	1
6	Subcontract	0	6	103,000	4

- Additional manpower
- More money
- Change of vendors
- Change of specifications
- Shift of project resources
- Waiving equipment inspections
- Change in statement of work
- Change in work breakdown structure
- Substitution of equipment
- Substitution of materials
- Use of outside contractors
- Providing bonus payments to contractors
- Single-sourcing
- Waiving drawing approvals

The corrective actions defined above can be used for time, cost, and performance. However, there are specific alternatives for each area. Assuming that a PERT/CPM analysis was done initially to schedule the project, then the following options are available for schedule manipulation:

- Prioritize all tasks and see the effect on the critical path of eliminating low-priority efforts.
- Use resource leveling.
- Carry the work breakdown structure to one more level, and reassess the time estimates for each task.

Performance trade-offs can be obtained as follows:

- Excessive or tight specifications that are not critical to the project may be eased. (Many times standard specifications such as mil-specs are used without regard for their necessity.)
- Requirements for testing can be altered to accommodate automation (such as accelerated life testing) to minimize costs.
- Set an absolute minimum acceptable performance requirement below which you will not pursue the project. This gives a bound at the low end of performance that can't be crossed in choosing between trade-off alternatives.
- Only give up those performance requirements that have little or no bearing on the overall project goals (including implied goals) and their achievement. This may require the project manager to itemize and prioritize major and minor objectives.
- Consider absorbing tasks with dedicated project office personnel. This is a resource trade-off that can be effective when the tasks to be performed require in-depth knowledge of the project. An example would be the use of dedicated project personnel to perform information gathering on reha-

bilitation-type projects. The improved performance of these people in the design and testing phases due to their strong background can save considerable time and effort.

The most promising areas for cost analysis include:

- Incremental costing (using sensitivity analysis)
- Reallocation of resources
- Material substitution where lower-cost materials are utilized without changing project specifications

Depending on the magnitude of the problem, the timeliness of its identification, and the potential impact on the project results, it may be that no actions exist that will bring the project in on time, within budget, and at an acceptable level of performance. The following viable alternatives usually remain:

- A renegotiation of project performance criteria could be attempted with the project sponsor. Such action would be based on a pragmatic view of the acceptability of the probable outcome. Personal convenience of the project manager is not a factor. Professional and legal liability for the project manager, project team, or parent organization may be very real concerns.
- If renegotiation is not considered a viable alternative, or if it is rejected, the only remaining option is to "stop loss" in completing the project. Such planning should involve both line and project management, since the parent organization is at this point seeking to defend itself. Options include:
  - Completing the project on schedule, to the minimum quality level required by the project sponsor. This results in cost overruns (financial loss) but should produce a reasonably satisfied project sponsor. (Project sponsors are not really comfortable when they know a project team is operating in a "stop-loss" mode!)
  - Controlling costs and performance, but permitting the schedule to slide. The degree of unhappiness this generates with the project sponsor will be determined by the specific situation. Risks include loss of future work or consequential damages.
  - Maintaining schedule and cost performance by allowing quality to slip. The high-risk approach has a low probability of achieving total success and a high probability of achieving total failure. Quality work done on the project will be lost if the final results are below minimum standards.
  - Seeking to achieve desired costs, schedule, and performance results in the light of impossible circumstances. This approach "hopes" that the inevitable won't happen, and offers the opportunity to fail simultaneously in all areas. Criminal liability could become an issue.

- Project cancellation, in an effort to limit exposure beyond that already encountered. This approach might terminate the career of a project manager but could enhance the career of the staff counsel!

The sixth and final step in the methodology of the management of project trade-offs is to obtain management approval and replan the project. The project manager usually identifies the alternatives and prepares his recommendation. He then submits his recommendation to top management for approval. Top-management involvement is necessary because the project manager may try to make corrective action in a vacuum. Top management normally makes decisions based on the following:

- The firm's policies on quality, integrity, and image
- The ability to develop a long-term client relationship
- Type of project (R&D, modernization, new product)
- Size and complexity of the project
- Other projects underway or planned
- Company's cash flow
- Bottom line—ROI
- Competitive risks
- Technical risks
- Impact on affiliated organizations

After choosing a new course of action from the list of alternatives, management and especially the project team must focus on achieving the revised objectives. This may require a detailed replanning of the project, including new schedules, PERT charts, work breakdown structures, and other key benchmarks. The entire management team (i.e., top management, functional managers, and project managers) must all be committed to achieving the revised project plan.

16.2 CONTRACTS: THEIR INFLUENCE ON PROJECTS

The final decision on whether to trade-off cost, time, or performance can vary depending on the type of contract. Table 16–4 identifies seven common types of contracts and the order in which trade-offs will be made.

The firm-fixed-price contract. Time, cost, and performance are all specified within the contract, and all the contractor's responsibility. Because all constraints are equally important with respect to this type of contract, the sequence of resources sacrificed is the same as for the project-driven organization shown previously in Table 16–1.

The fixed-price-incentive-fee contract. Cost is measured to determine the incentive fee, and thus is the last constraint to be considered for trade-off. Because performance is usually more important than schedule for project completion, time is considered the first constraint for trade-off, and performance is the second.

TABLE 16–4. SEQUENCE OF RESOURCES SACRIFICED BASED ON TYPE OF CONTRACT

	Firm-Fixed-Price (FFP)	Fixed-Price-Incentive-Fee (FPIF)	Cost Contract	Cost Sharing	Cost-Plus-Incentive-Fee (CPIF)	Cost-Plus-Award-Fee (CPAF)	Cost-Plus-Fixed-Fee (CPFF)
Time	2	1	2	2	1	2	2
Cost	1	3	3	3	3	1	1
Performance	3	2	1	1	2	3	3

1 = first to be sacrificed.
2 = second to be sacrificed.
3 = third to be sacrificed.

The cost-plus-incentive-fee contract. The costs are reimbursed and measured for determination of the incentive fee. Thus, cost is the last constraint to be considered for trade-off. As with the FPIF contract, performance is usually more important than schedule for project completion, and so the sequence is the same as for the FPIF contract.

The cost-plus-award-fee contract. The costs are reimbursed to the contractor, but the award fee is based on performance by the contractor. Thus, cost would be the first constraint to be considered for trade-off, and performance would be the last constraint to be considered.

The cost-plus-fixed-fee contract. Costs are reimbursed to the contractor. Thus, cost would be the first constraint to be considered for trade-off. Although there are no incentives for efficiency in time or performance, there may be penalties for bad performance. Thus, time is the second constraint to be considered for trade-off, and performance is the third.

16.3 INDUSTRY TRADE-OFF PREFERENCES

Table 16–5 identifies twenty-one industries that were surveyed on their preferential process for trade-offs. Obviously, there are variables that affect each decision. The data in the table reflect the interviewees' general responses, neglecting external considerations. External variables probably would alter the order of preference. For example, plastics manufacturing rated performance the first choice for trade-offs. This assumes that a low-liability item is being manufactured. Utilities rated cost as the last item for trade-off, whereas prior to 1970, performance would have been the last item, with cost ranking second.

Table 16–6 shows the relative grouping of Table 16–5 into four categories: project-driven, non-project-driven, nonprofit, and banks.

In all projects in the banking industry, whether regulated or nonregulated, cost is the first resource to be sacrificed. The major reason for this trade-off is that

TABLE 16–5. INDUSTRY GENERAL PREFERENCE FOR TRADE-OFFS

Industry	Time	Cost	Performance
Construction	1	3	2
Chemical	2	1	3
Electronics	2	3	1
Automotive manu.	2	1	3
Data processing	2	1	3
Government	2	1	3
Health (nonprofit)	2	3	1
Medicine (profit)	1	3	2
Nuclear	2	1	3
Manu. (plastics)	2	3	1
Manu. (metals)	1	2	3
Consulting (mgt.)	2	1	3
Consulting (eng.)	3	1	2
Office products	2	1	3
Machine tool	2	1	3
Oil	2	1	3
Primary batteries	1	3	2
Utilities	1	3	2
Aerospace	2	1	3
Retailing	3	2	1
Banking	2	1	3

Note: Numbers in table indicate the order (first, second, third) in which the three parameters are sacrificed.

banks in general do not have a quantitative estimation of what actual costs they incur in providing a given service. One example of this phenomenon is that a number of commercial banks heavily emphasize the use of *Functional Cost Analysis,* a publication of the Federal Reserve, for pricing their services. This publication is a summary of data received from member banks, of which the user is one. This results in questionable output because of inaccuracies of the input.

TABLE 16–6. SPECIAL CASES

	Type of Organization					
	Project-Driven Organizations				Banks	
	Early Life-Cycle Phases	Late Life-Cycle Phases	Non-Project-Driven Organizations	Nonprofit Organizations	Leader	Follower
Time	2	1	1	2	3	2
Cost	1	3	3	3	1	1
Performance	3	2	2	1	2	3

In cases where federal regulations prescribe time constraints, cost is the only resource of consideration, since performance standards are also delineated by regulatory bodies.

In nonregulated banking projects the next resource to be sacrificed depends on the competitive environment. When other competitors have developed a new service or product that a particular bank does not yet offer, then the resource of time will be less critical than the performance criteria. A specific case in point is the development of the automatic teller machine (ATM). After the initial introduction of the system by some banks (leaders), the remainder of the competitors (followers) chose to provide a more advanced ATM with little consideration for the time involved for procurement and installation. On the other hand, with the introduction of negotiable order of withdrawal (NOW) accounts, the January 1, 1981, change in federal regulations allowed banks and savings and loans to offer interest-bearing checking accounts. The ensuing scramble to offer the service by that date led to varying performance levels, especially on the part of savings and loans. In this instance the competitors sacrificed performance in order to provide a timely service.

In some banking projects, the time factor is extremely important. A number of projects depend on federal laws. The date that a specific law goes into effect sets the deadline for the project.

Generally, in a nonprofit organization, performance is the first resource that will be compromised. The United Way, free clinics, March of Dimes, American Cancer Society, and Goodwill are among the many nonprofit agencies that serve community needs. They derive their income from donations and/or federal grants, and this funding mechanism places a major constraint on their operations. Cost overruns are prohibited by the very nature of the organization.

For example, the services offered by a free clinic are dependent on the quality and expertise of the physicians it can attract. Usually two major types of doctors will work at such a clinic. The first group includes young, inexperienced doctors who are using the clinic as a vehicle for gaining needed practical experience and exposure in the community, whereas the second group includes established physicians who feel morally obligated to render services to the needy. Because of inexperience and time constraints, the two groups provide services that often fall short of the quality obtainable from private medical practices. Additionally, much of the medical equipment bought or received by the clinic is inferior to what can be found in medical centers.

The time resource is compromised again in the area of customer service. The free clinic will require its clerical and medical staff to work longer hours to obtain a performance level that could be achieved in a shorter period of time in a private medical facility. The inexperience of the staff and lack of funds necessitate the time trade-off.

The non-project-driven organization is structured along the lines of the traditional vertical hierarchy. Functional managers in areas such as marketing, engineering, accounting, and sales are involved in planning, organizing, staffing, and controlling their functional areas. Many projects that materialize, specifically in a manufacturing concern, are a result of a need to improve a product or process and can be initiated by customer request, competitive climate, or internal operations.

The first resource to be sacrificed in the non-project-driven organization is time, followed by performance and cost, respectively. The Battery Products Division of a major corporation is a non-project-driven organization that in 1980 became involved in a plant expansion program. In response to the economic downturn that affected market conditions, the facility expansion was delayed.

In most manufacturing concerns, budgetary constraints outweigh performance criteria. The proposed expansion described above now specifies less floor space and less sophisticated machinery, resulting in decreased production capacity (decreased performance).

In a non-project-driven organization, new projects will take a back seat to the day-to-day operations of the functional departments. The organizational funds are allocated to individual departments rather than to the project itself. When functional managers are required to maintain a certain productivity level in addition to supporting projects, their main emphasis will be on operations at the expense of project development. When it becomes necessary for the firm to curtail costs, special projects will be deleted in order to maintain corporate profit margins.

Resource trade-offs in a project-driven organization depend on the life-cycle phase of a given project. During the conceptual, definition, and production phases and into the operational phase of the project, the trade-off priorities are cost first, then time, and finally performance. In these early planning phases the project is being designed to meet certain performance and time standards. At this point the cost estimates are based on the figures supplied to the project manager by the functional managers.

During the operational phase the cost factor increases in importance over time and performance, both of which begin to decrease. In this phase the organization attempts to recover its investment in the project and therefore emphasizes cost control. The performance standards may have been compromised, and the project may be behind schedule, but management will analyze the cost figures to judge the success of the project.

The project-driven organization is unique in that the resource trade-offs may vary in priority, depending on the specific project. Research and development projects may have a fixed performance level, whereas construction projects normally are constrained by a date of completion.

16.4 CONCLUSION

It is obvious from the above discussion that a project manager does have options to control a project during its execution. Project managers must be willing to control minor trade-offs as well as major ones. However, the availability of specific options is a function of the particular project environment.

Probably the greatest contribution a project manager makes to a project team organization is through the stability he can impart as adverse conditions are encountered. Interpersonal relationships have a great deal to do with the alternatives available and their probability of success. Normally, solution of a potential performance problem requires a team solution, since it is team performance that is demanded. Through a combination of management skill and sensitivity, project managers can make the trade-offs, encourage the team members, and reassure the project sponsor in order to produce a satisfactory project.

Risk Management[1]

17.0 INTRODUCTION

In the early days of project management on many commercial programs, the majority of project decisions heavily favored cost and schedule. This favoritism occurred because we knew more about cost and scheduling than we did about technical risks. Technology forecasting was very rarely performed other than by extrapolating past technical knowledge into the present.

Today, the state of the art of technology forecasting is being pushed to the limits. For projects with a time duration of less than one year, we normally assume that the environment is known and stable, particularly the technological environment. For projects over a year or so in length, technology forecasting must be considered. Computer technology doubles in performance about every two years. Engineering technology is said to double every three or so years. How can a project manager accurately define and plan the scope of a three- or four-year project without expecting engineering changes resulting from technology improvements? What are the risks?

A Midwest manufacturing company embarked on an eight-year project to design the manufacturing factory of the future. The plant is scheduled to go into the construction phase in the year 2000. How do we design the factory of the future without forecasting the technology? What computer technology will exist? What types of materials will exist and what types of components will our customers require? What production rate will we need and will technology exist to support this production level?

Economists and financial institutions forecast interest rates. The forecasts appear in public newspapers and journals. Yet, every company involved in high tech does some form of technology forecasting, but ap-

1. This chapter was updated by Dr. Edmund H. Conrow CMC, PMP. Dr. Conrow has extensive experience in developing and implementing risk management on a wide variety of projects. He is the author of: *Effective Risk Management: Some Keys To Success,* American Institute of Aeronautics and Astronautics, Reston, VA, 2000. He can be reached at (310) 374-7975 and www.risk-services.com

pears very reluctant to publish the data. Technology forecasting is regarded as company proprietary information and may be part of the company's strategic planning process.

We read in the newspaper about cost overruns and schedule slips on a wide variety of large-scale development projects. Several issues within the control of the buyer, seller, or major stakeholders can lead to cost growth and schedule slippage on development projects. These causes include, but are not limited to:[2]

- Starting a project with a budget and/or schedule that is inadequate for the desired level of performance or scope (e.g., integration complexity).
- Having an overall development process (or key parts of that process) that favors performance (or scope) over cost and schedule.
- Establishing a design that is near the feasible limit of achievable performance or integration complexity at a given point in time.
- Making major project design decisions before the relationships between cost, performance, schedule, and risk are understood.

These four causes will contribute to uncertainty in forecasting technology and the associated design needed to meet performance requirements. And the inability to perfectly forecast technology and the associated design will contribute to a project's technical risk, and can also lead to cost and schedule risk.

Today, the competition for technical achievement has become fierce. Companies have gone through life-cycle phases of centralizing all activities, especially management functions, but are decentralizing technical expertise. By the mid 1980s, many companies recognized the need to integrate technical risks with cost and schedule risks, and other activities (e.g., quality). Risk management processes were developed and implemented where risk information was made available to key decision-makers.

The risk management process, however, should be designed to do more than just identify the risk. The process must also include: a formal *planning* activity, *analysis* to quantify the likelihood and predict the impact on the project, a *handling* strategy for selected risks, and the ability to *monitor* the progress in reducing these selected risks to the desired level.

A project, by definition, is something that we have not done previously and will not do again in the future. Because of this uniqueness, we have developed a "live with it" attitude on risk and attribute it as part of doing business. If risk management is set up as a continuous, disciplined process of planning, assessment (identification and analysis), handling, and monitoring, then the system will easily supplement other systems as organization, planning and budgeting, and cost control. Surprises that become problems will be diminished because emphasis will now be on proactive rather than reactive management.

Risk management can be justified on almost all projects. The level of implementation can vary from project to project, depending on such factors as size, type of project, who the customer is, relationship to the corporate strategic plan, and corporate culture. Risk management is particularly important when the overall stakes are high and a great deal of uncertainty exists. In the past, we treated risk as a "let's live with it." Today, risk management is a key part of overall project management. It forces us to focus on the future where uncertainty exists and develop suitable plans of action to prevent potential issues from adversely impacting the project.

---

2. Edmund H. Conrow, "Some Long-Term Issues and Impediments Affecting Military Systems Acquisition Reform," *Acquisition Review Quarterly,* Defense Acquisition University, Summer 1995.

17.1 DEFINITION OF RISK

Risk is a measure of the probability and consequence of not achieving a defined project goal. Most people agree that risk involves the notion of uncertainty. Can the specified aircraft range be achieved? Can the computer be produced within budgeted cost? Can the new product launch date be met? A probability measure can be used for such questions; for example, the probability of not meeting the new product launch date is 0.15. However, when risk is considered, the consequences or damage associated with occurrence must also be considered.

Goal A, with a probability of occurrence of only 0.05, may present a much more serious (risky) situation than goal B, with a probability of occurrence of 0.20, if the consequences of not meeting goal A are, in this case, more than four times more severe than failure to meet goal B. Risk is not always easy to assess, since the probability of occurrence and the consequence of occurrence are usually not directly measurable parameters and must be estimated by statistical or other procedures.

Risk has two primary components for a given event:

- A probability of occurrence of that event
- Impact of the event occurring (amount at stake)

Figure 17–1 shows the components of risk.

Conceptually, risk for each event can be defined as a function of likelihood and impact; that is,

$$\text{Risk} = f(\text{Likelihood, impact})$$

In general, as either the likelihood or impact increases, so does the risk. Both the likelihood and impact must be considered in risk management.

Risk constitutes a lack of knowledge of future events. Typically, future events (or outcomes) that are favorable are called opportunities, whereas unfavorable events are called risks.

Another element of risk is the cause of risk. Something, or the lack of something, can induce a risky situation. We denote this source of danger as the hazard. Certain hazards can be overcome to a great extent by knowing them and taking action to overcome them. For example, a large hole in a road is a much greater danger to a driver who is unaware of it than to one who travels the road frequently and knows enough to slow down and go around the hole. This leads to the second representation of risk:

$$\text{Risk} = f(\text{Hazard, safeguard})$$

Risk increases with hazard but decreases with safeguard. The implication of this equation is that good project management should be structured to identify hazards and to allow safeguards to be developed to overcome them. If enough safeguards are available, then the risk can be reduced to an acceptable level.

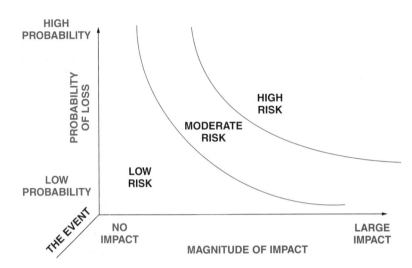

FIGURE 17–1. Overall risk is a function of its components.

17.2 TOLERANCE FOR RISK

There is no single textbook answer on how to manage risk. The project manager must rely upon sound judgment and the use of the appropriate tools in dealing with risk. The ultimate decision on how to deal with risk is based in part upon the project manager's tolerance for risk.

The three commonly used classifications of tolerance for risk appear in Figure 17–2. They include the risk averter or avoider, the neutral risk taker, and the risk seeker or lover. The Y axis in Figure 17–2 represents "utility," which can be defined as the amount of satisfaction or pleasure that the individual receives from a payoff. (This is also called the project manager's tolerance for risk.) The X axis in this case is the amount of money at stake.

The shape of a given decision maker's curve is derived from comparing response to alternative decision acts.

FIGURE 17–2. Risk preference and the utility function.

With the risk averter, utility rises at a *decreasing* rate. In other words, when more money is at stake, the project manager's satisfaction or tolerance diminishes. With the risk lover, the project manager's satisfaction increases when more money is at stake (i.e., an increasing slope to the curve). A risk averter prefers a more certain outcome and will demand a premium to accept risk. A risk lover prefers the more uncertain outcome and may be willing to pay a penalty to take a risk.

17.3 DEFINITION OF RISK MANAGEMENT

Risk management is the act or practice of dealing with risk. It includes *planning* for risk, *assessing* (*identifying and analyzing*) risk issues, developing *risk handling* options, and *monitoring* risks to determine how risks have changed.

Risk management is not a separate project office activity assigned to a risk management department, but rather is one aspect of sound project management. Risk management should be closely coupled with key project processes, including but not limited to: overall project management, systems engineering, cost, scope, quality, and schedule.

Proper risk management is proactive rather than reactive. As an example, an activity in a network requires that a new technology be developed. The schedule indicates six months for this activity, but project engineers think that nine months is closer to the truth. If the project manager is proactive, he might develop a Risk Handling Plan right *now*. If the project manager is reactive (e.g., a "problem solver"), then he will do nothing until the problem actually occurs. At that time the project manager must react rapidly to the crisis, and may have lost valuable time when contingencies could have been developed. Hence, proper risk management will attempt to reduce the likelihood of an event occurring and/or the magnitude of its impact.

17.4 CERTAINTY, RISK, AND UNCERTAINTY

Decision-making falls into three categories: certainty, risk, and uncertainty. Decision-making under certainty is the easiest case to work with. With certainty, we assume that all of the necessary information is available to assist us in making the right decision, and we can predict the outcome with a high level of confidence.

Decision-Making under Certainty

Decision-making under certainty implies that we know with 100 percent accuracy what the states of nature will be and what the expected payoffs will be for each state of nature. Mathematically, this can be shown with payoff tables.

To construct a payoff matrix, we must identify (or select) the states of nature over which *we have no control*. We then select our own action to be taken for each of the states of nature. Our actions are called strategies. The elements in the payoff table are the outcomes for each strategy.

A payoff matrix based on decision-making under certainty has two controlling features.

- Regardless of which state of nature exists, there will be one dominant strategy that will produce larger gains or smaller losses than any other strategy for all the states of nature.
- There are no probabilities assigned to each state of nature. (This could also be stated that each state of nature has an equal likelihood of occurring.)

Example 17–1. Consider a company wishing to invest $50 million to develop a new product. The company decides that the states of nature will be either a strong market demand, an even market demand, or a low market demand. The states of nature shall be represented as $N_1 = $ a strong market, $N_2 = $ an even market, and $N_3 = $ a low market demand. The company also has narrowed their choices to one of three ways to develop the product: either A, B, or C. There also exists a strategy S_4, not to develop the product at all, in which case there would be neither profit nor loss. We shall assume that the decision is made to develop the product. The payoff matrix for this example is shown in Table 17–1. Looking for the controlling features in Table 17–1, we see that regardless of how the market reacts, strategy S_3 will always yield larger profits than the other two strategies. The project manager will therefore always select strategy S_3 in developing the new product. Strategy S_3 is the best option to take.

Table 17–1 can also be represented in subscript notation. Let $P_{i,j}$ be the elements of the matrix, where P represents profit. The subscript i is the row (strategy), and j is the column (state of nature). For example, $P_{2,3} = $ the profit from choosing strategy 2 with N_3 state of nature occurring. It should be noted that there is no restriction that the matrix be square (i.e., the number of states of nature need not equal the number of possible strategies).

Decision-Making under Risk

In most cases, there usually does not exist one dominant strategy for all states of nature. In a realistic situation, higher profits are usually accompanied by higher risks and therefore higher probable losses. When there does not exist a dominant strategy, a probability must be assigned to the occurrence of each state of nature.

TABLE 17–1. PAYOFF MATRIX (PROFIT IN MILLIONS)

	States of Nature		
Strategy	$N_1 = $ **Up**	$N_2 = $ **Even**	$N_3 = $ **Low**
$S_1 = $ A	$50	$40	–$50
$S_2 = $ B	$50	$50	$60
$S_3 = $ C	$100	$80	$90

Risk can be viewed as outcomes (i.e., states of nature) that can be described within established confidence limits (i.e., probability distributions). These probability distributions are obtained from well-defined experimental distributions.

Consider Table 17–2, in which the payoffs for strategies 1 and 3 of Table 17–1 are interchanged for the state of nature N_3.

From Table 17–2, it is obvious that there does not exist one dominant strategy. When this occurs, probabilities must be assigned to the possibility of each state of nature occurring. The best choice of strategy is therefore the strategy with the largest expected value, where the *expected value* is the summation of the payoff times and the probability of occurrence of the payoff for each state of nature. In mathematical formulation,

$$E_i = \sum_{j=1}^{N} P_{i,j}\, p_j$$

where E_i is the expected payoff for strategy i, $P_{i,j}$ is the payoff element, and P_j is the probability of each state of nature occurring. The expected value for strategy S_1 is therefore

$$E_1 = (50)(0.25) + (40)(0.25) + (90)(0.50) = 67.50$$

Repeating the procedure for strategy 2 and 3, we find that $E_2 = 55$, and $E_3 = 20$. Therefore, based on the expected value, the project manager should always select strategy S_1. If two strategies of equal value occur, the decision should include other potential considerations (time to impact, frequency of occurrence, resource availability, etc.).

To quantify potential payoffs, we must identify the strategy we are willing to take, the expected outcome (element of the payoff table), and the probability that the outcome will occur. In the previous example, we should accept the risk associated with strategy S_1, since it gives us the greatest expected value. If the expected value is positive, then this risk should be considered. If the expected value is negative, then this risk should be proactively managed.

An important factor in decision-making under risk is the assigning of the probabilities for each of the states of nature. If the probabilities are erroneously

TABLE 17–2. PAYOFF TABLE (PROFIT IN MILLIONS)

	States of Nature*		
Strategy	N_1 0.25*	N_2 0.25*	N_3 0.50*
S_1	50	40	90
S_2	50	50	60
S_3	100	80	−50

*Numbers are assigned probabilities of occurrence for each state of nature.

assigned, different expected values will result, thus giving us a different perception of the best risk to take. Suppose in Table 17–2 that the assigned probabilities of the three states of nature are 0.6, 0.2, and 0.2. The respective expected values are:

$$E_1 = 56$$
$$E_2 = 52$$
$$E_3 = 66$$

In this case, the project manager would always choose strategy S_3.

Decision-Making under Uncertainty

The difference between risk and uncertainty is that under risk there are assigned probabilities, and under uncertainty meaningful assignments of probabilities are not possible. As with decision-making under risk, uncertainty also implies that there may exist no single dominant strategy. The decision-maker, however, does have at his disposal four basic criteria from which to make a management decision. The decision about which criterion to use will depend on the type of project as well as the project manager's tolerance to risk.

The first criterion is the Hurwicz criterion, often referred to as the maximax criterion. Under the Hurwicz criterion, the decision-maker is always optimistic and attempts to maximize profits by a go-for-broke strategy. This result can be seen from the example in Table 17–2. The maximax criterion says that the decision-maker will always choose strategy S_3 because the maximum profit is 100. However, if the state of nature were N_3, then strategy S_3 would result in a maximum loss instead of a maximum gain. The use of the maximax, or Hurwicz, criterion must then be based on how big a risk can be undertaken and how much one can afford to lose. A large corporation with strong assets may use the Hurwicz criterion, whereas the small private company might be more interested in minimizing the possible losses.

A small company would be more apt to use the Wald, or maximin, criterion, where the decision-maker is concerned with how much he can afford to lose. In this criterion, a pessimistic rather than optimistic position is taken with the viewpoint of minimizing the maximum loss.

In determining the Hurwicz criterion, we looked at only the maximum payoffs for each strategy in Table 17–2. For the Wald criterion, we consider only the minimum payoffs. The minimum payoffs are 40, 50, and −50 for strategies S_1, S_2, and S_3, respectively. Because the project manager wishes to minimize his maximum loss, he will always select strategy S_2 in this case. If all three minimum payoffs were negative, the project manager would select the smallest loss if these were the only options available. Depending on a company's financial position, there are situations where the project would not be undertaken if all three minimum payoffs were negative.

The third criterion is the Savage, or minimax, criterion. Under this criterion, we assume that the project manager is a sore loser. To minimize the regrets of the sore loser, the project manager attempts to minimize the maximum regret; that is, the minimax criterion.

The first step in the Savage criterion is to set up a regret table by subtracting all elements in each column from the largest element. Applying this approach to Table 17–2, we obtain Table 17–3.

The regrets are obtained for each column by subtracting each element in a given column from the largest column element. The maximum regret is the largest regret for each strategy, that is, in each row. In other words, if the project manager selects strategy S_1 or S_2, he will only be sorry for a loss of 50. However, depending on the state of nature, a selection of strategy S_3 may result in a regret of 140. The Savage criterion would select either strategy S_1 or S_2 in this example.

The fourth criterion is the Laplace criterion. The Laplace criterion is an attempt to transform decision-making under uncertainty into decision-making under risk. Recall that the difference between risk and uncertainty is a knowledge of the probability of occurrence of each state of nature. The Laplace criterion makes an *a priori* assumption based on Bayesian statistics, that if the probabilities of each state of nature are not known, then we can assume that each state of nature has an equal likelihood of occurrence. The procedure then follows decision-making value. Using the Laplace criterion applied to Table 17–2, we obtain Table 17–4. Using the Laplace criterion, the project manager would therefore choose strategy S_1.

The important conclusion to be drawn from decision-making under uncertainty is the risk that the project manager wishes to incur. For the four criteria previously mentioned, we have shown that any strategy can be chosen depending on how much money we can afford to lose and what risks we are willing to take.

The concept of expected value can also be combined with "probability" or "decision" trees to identify and quantify the potential risks. Another common term is the impact analysis diagram. Decision trees are used when a decision cannot be viewed as a single, isolated occurrence, but rather as a sequence of several interrelated decisions. In this case, the decision-maker makes an entire series of decisions simultaneously.

Consider the following problem. A product can be manufactured using Machine A or Machine B. Machine A has a 40 percent chance of being used and Machine B a 60 percent chance. Both machines use either Process C or D. When Machine A is selected, Process C is selected 80 percent of the time and Process D 20 percent. When Machine B is selected, Process C is selected 30 percent of

TABLE 17–3.   REGRET TABLE

Strategy	States of Nature			Maximum Regrets
	N_1	N_2	N_3	
S_1	50	40	0	50
S_2	50	30	30	50
S_3	0	0	140	140

TABLE 17–4. LAPLACE CRITERION

Strategy	Expected Value
S_1	60
S_2	160/3
S_3	130/3

the time and Process D 70 percent of the time. What is the probability of the product being produced by the various combinations?

Figure 17–3 shows the decision tree for this problem. The probability at the end of each branch (furthest to the right) is obtained by multiplying the branch probabilities together.

For more sophisticated problems, the process of constructing a decision tree can be complicated. Decision trees contain decision points, usually represented by a box or square, where the decision-maker must select one of several available alternatives. Chance points, designated by a circle, indicate that a chance event is expected at this point.

The following three steps are needed to construct a tree diagram:

- Build a logic tree, usually from left to right, including all decision points and chance points.
- Put the probabilities of the states of nature on the branches, thus forming a probability tree.
- Finally, add the conditional payoffs, thus completing the decision tree.

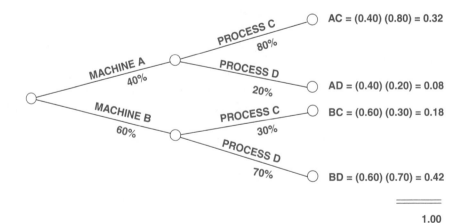

AC = (0.40) (0.80) = 0.32

AD = (0.40) (0.20) = 0.08

BC = (0.60) (0.30) = 0.18

BD = (0.60) (0.70) = 0.42

1.00

SUM OF THE PROBABILITIES MUST EQUAL 1.00.

FIGURE 17–3. Decision tree.

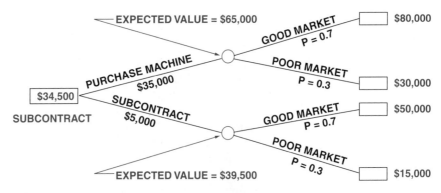

FIGURE 17–4. Expanded tree diagram.

Consider the following problem. You have the chance to make or buy certain widgets for resale. If you make the widgets yourself, you must purchase a new machine for $35,000. If demand is good, which is expected 70 percent of the time, an $80,000 profit will occur on the sale of the widgets. With poor market conditions, $30,000 in profits will occur, not including the cost of the machine. If we subcontract out the work, our contract administration costs will be $5,000. If the market is good, profits will be $50,000; for a poor market, profits will be $15,000. Figure 17–4 shows the tree diagram for this problem. In this case, the expected value of the strategy that subcontracts the widgets is both positive and $4,500 greater than the strategy that manufactures the widgets. Hence, here we should select the strategy that subcontracts the widgets.

17.5 RISK MANAGEMENT PROCESS

It is important that a risk management strategy is established early in a project and that risk is continually addressed throughout the project life cycle. Risk management includes several related actions involving risk: planning, assessment (identification and analysis), handling, and monitoring:[3]

---

3. This risk management structure, and some of the information in subsequent subsections, is derived from work performed by the Department of Defense in 1996–1998, and summarized in: "Risk Management Guide for DoD Acquisition," Defense Acquisition University and Defense Systems Management College, Second Edition, May 1999. *This is quite simply the best introductory document on risk management that exists and it is applicable, with suitable tailoring, to a wide variety of projects,* including commercial projects. (The URL to download this risk management guide free of charge at the time of this writing is: http://www.dsmc.dsm.mil/pubs/gdbks/risk_management.htm) Dr. Conrow's book, mentioned in note 2, uses this risk management process and explains some of the keys to tailor and implement it on a variety of projects.

- *Risk planning:* This is the process of developing and documenting an organized, comprehensive, and interactive strategy and methods for identifying and tracking risk issues, developing risk handling plans, performing continuous risk assessments to determine how risks have changed, and assigning adequate resources.
- *Risk assessment:* This process involves identifying and analyzing program areas and critical technical process risks to increase the likelihood of meeting cost, performance, and schedule objectives. *Risk identification* is the process of examining the program areas and each critical technical process to identify and document the associated risk. *Risk analysis* is the process of examining each identified risk issue or process to refine the description of the risk, isolate the cause, and determine the effects.
- *Risk handling:* This is the process that identifies, evaluates, selects, and implements options in order to set risk at acceptable levels given program constraints and objectives. This includes the specifics on what should be done, when it should be accomplished, who is responsible, and associated cost and schedule. Risk handling options include assumption, avoidance, control (also known as mitigation), and transfer. The most desirable handling option is selected, and a specific approach is then developed for this option.
- *Risk monitoring:* This is the process that systematically tracks and evaluates the performance of risk handling actions against established metrics throughout the acquisition process and provides inputs to updating risk handling strategies, as appropriate.

17.6 RISK PLANNING

Risk planning is the detailed formulation of a program of action for the management of risk. It is the process to:

- Develop and document an organized, comprehensive, and interactive risk management strategy.
- Determine the methods to be used to execute a program's risk management strategy.
- Plan for adequate resources.

Risk planning is iterative and includes the entire risk management process, with activities to assess (identify and analyze), handle, monitor (and document) the risk associated with a program. The result is often the risk management plan (RMP).

Planning begins by developing and documenting a risk management strategy. Early efforts establish the purpose and objective, assign responsibilities for specific areas, identify additional technical expertise needed, describe the assessment process and areas to consider, define a risk rating approach, delineate procedures for consideration of handling options, establish monitoring metrics (where possible), and define the reporting, documentation, and communication needs.

The RMP is the roadmap that tells the project team how to get from where the program is today to where the program manager wants it to be in the future. The key to writing a good RMP is to provide the necessary information so the program team knows the objectives, goals, and the risk management process. Since it is a roadmap, it may be specific in some areas, such as the assignment of responsibilities for project personnel and definitions, and general in other areas to allow users to choose the most efficient way to proceed. For example, a description of techniques that suggests several methods for evaluators to use to assess risk is appropriate, since every technique has advantages and disadvantages depending on the situation.

17.7 RISK ASSESSMENT

Risk assessment is the *problem definition* stage of risk management, the stage that identifies, analyzes, and quantifies program issues in terms of probability and consequences, and possibly other considerations (e.g., the time to impact). The results are a key input to many subsequent risk management actions. It is often a difficult and time-consuming part of the risk management process. There are no quick answers or shortcuts. Tools are available to assist evaluators in assessing risk, but none are totally suitable for any program and are often highly misleading if the user does not understand how to apply them or interpret the results. Despite its complexity, risk assessment is one of the most important phases of the risk management process because the caliber and quality of assessments can have a large impact on program outcomes.

The components of assessment—identification and analysis—are performed sequentially with identification being the first step.

Risk identification begins by compiling the program's risk issues. Project issues should be examined and identified by reducing them to a level of detail that permits an evaluator to understand the significance of any risk and its causes (e.g., risk issues). This is a practical way of addressing the large and diverse number of potential risks that often occur in moderate- to large-scale programs. For example, a WBS level 4 or 5 element may be made up of several risk issues associated with a specification or function.

Risk analysis is a technical and systematic process to examine identified risks, isolate causes, determine the relationship to other risks, and express the impact in terms of probability and consequence of occurrence.

17.8 RISK IDENTIFICATION

The second step in risk management is to identify all potential risk issues. This may include a survey of the program, customer, and users for concerns and problems.

Some degree of risk always exists in project, technical, test, logistics, production, and engineering areas. Project risks include cost, funding, schedule, contract relationships, and political risks. (Cost and schedule risks are often so fundamental to a project that they may be treated as stand-alone risk categories.) Technical risks, such as related to engineering and technology, may involve the risk of meeting a performance requirement, but may also involve risks in the feasibility of a design concept or the risks associated with using state-of-the-art equipment or software. Production risk includes concerns over packaging, manufacturing, lead times, and material availability. Support risks include maintainability, operability, and trainability concerns. The understanding of risks in these and other areas evolves over time. Consequently, risk identification must continue through all project phases.

The methods for identifying risk are numerous. Common practice is to classify project risk according to its source. Most sources are either objective or subjective.

- *Objective sources:* Recorded experience from past projects and the current project as it proceeds
  - Lessons learned files
  - Program documentation evaluations
  - Current performance data
- *Subjective sources:* Experiences based upon knowledgeable experts
  - Interviews and other data from subject matter experts

Risks can also be identified according to life-cycle phases, as shown in Figure 17–5. In the early life-cycle phases, the total project risk is high because of lack of information. In the later life-cycle phases, the financial risk is the greatest.

Any source of information that allows recognition of a potential problem can be used for risk identification. These include:

- Systems engineering documentation
- Life-cycle cost analysis
- Plan/WBS decomposition
- Schedule analysis
- Baseline cost estimates
- Requirements documents
- Lessons learned files
- Assumption analysis
- Trade studies/analyses
- Technical performance measurement (TPM) planning/analysis
- Models (influence diagrams)
- Decision drivers
- Brainstorming
- Expert judgment

Expert judgment techniques are applicable not only for risk identification, but also for forecasting and decision-making. Two expert judgment techniques are

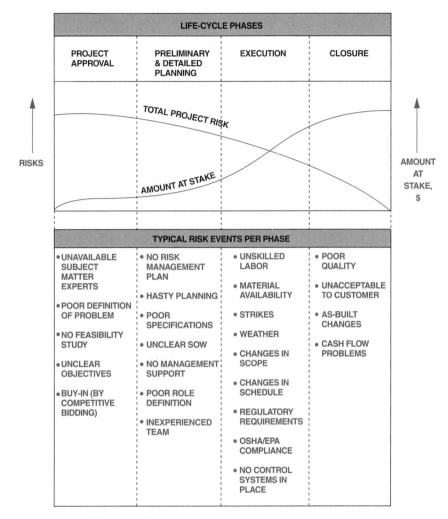

FIGURE 17–5. Life-cycle risk analysis.

the Delphi method and the nominal group technique. The Delphi method has the following general steps:

- *Step 1:* A panel of experts is selected from both inside and outside the organization. The experts do not interact on a face-to-face basis and may not even know who else sits on the panel.
- *Step 2:* Each expert is asked to make an anonymous prediction on a particular subject.

- *Step 3:* Each expert receives a composite feedback of the entire panel's answers and is asked to make new predictions based upon the feedback. The process is then repeated as necessary.

Closely related to the Delphi method is the nominal group technique, which allows for face-to-face contact and direct communication. The steps in the nominal group technique are as follows:

- *Step 1:* A panel is convened and asked to generate ideas in writing.
- *Step 2:* The ideas are listed on a board or a flip chart. Each idea is discussed among the panelists.
- *Step 3:* Each panelist prioritizes the ideas, which are then ranked mathematically. Steps 2 and 3 may be repeated as necessary.

Expert judgment techniques have the potential for bias in risk identification and analysis. Factors affecting the bias include:

- Overconfidence in one's ability
- Insensitivity to the problem or risk
- Proximity to project
- Motivation
- Recent event recall
- Availability of time
- Relationship with other experts

There exist numerous ways to classify risks. In a simple business context, risk can be defined as:

- Business risk
- Insurable risk

Business risks provide us with opportunities of profit and loss. Examples of business risk would be competitor activities, bad weather, inflation, recession, customer response, and availability of resources. Insurable risks provide us with only a chance for a loss. Insurable risks include such elements as:

- *Direct property damage:* This includes insurance for assets such as fire insurance, collision insurance, and insurance for project materials, equipment, and properties.
- *Indirect consequential loss:* This includes protection for contractors for indirect losses due to third-party actions, such as equipment replacement and debris removal.
- *Legal liability:* This is protection for legal liability resulting from poor product design, design errors, product liability, and project performance failure. This does not include protection from loss of goodwill.

- *Personnel:* This provides protection resulting from employee bodily injury (worker's compensation), loss of key employees, replacement cost of key employees, and several other types of business losses due to employee actions.

On construction projects, the owner/customer usually provides "wrap-up" or "bundle" insurance, which bundles the owner, contractor, and subcontractors into one insurable package. The contractor may be given the responsibility to provide the bundled package, but it is still paid for by the owner/customer.

The Project Management Institute categorizes risks as follows:

- *External–unpredictable:* Government regulations, natural hazards, and acts of God
- *External–predictable:* Cost of money, borrowing rates, raw material availability

The external risks are outside of the project manager's control but may affect the direction of the project.

- *Internal (nontechnical):* Labor stoppages, cash flow problems, safety issues, health and benefit plans

The internal risks may be within the control of the project manager and present uncertainty that may affect the project.

- *Technical:* Changes in technology, changes in state of the art, design issues, operations/maintenance issues

Technical risks relate to the utilization of technology and the impact it has on the direction of the project.

- *Legal:* Licenses, patent rights, lawsuits, subcontractor performance, contractual failure

To identify risk issues, evaluators should break down program elements to a level where they can perform valid assessments. The information necessary to do this varies according to the phase of the program. During the early phases, requirement and scope documents, and acquisition plans may be the only program-specific data available. They should be evaluated to identify issues that may have adverse consequences.

Another method of decomposition is to create a Work Breakdown Structure (WBS) as early as possible in a program, and use this in a structured approach to evaluate candidate risk categories against candidate system or lower level designs. To use this approach, each element at level three of the WBS is further broken down to the fourth or fifth level and is subjected to a risk analysis. Items at system, segment or group, or subsystem levels, as well as management items, are assessed using attributes such as maturity and complexity of hardware and software items or the dependency of the item on existing systems, facilities, or contractors to evaluate their risk levels.

Another approach is to evaluate risk associated with some key processes (e.g., design and manufacturing) that will exist on a project. Information on this approach is contained in the government DoD directive 4245.7-M, which provides a standard structure for identifying technical risk areas in the transition from development to production. The structure is geared toward programs that are mid-to-late in the development phase but, with modifications, could be used for other projects. The directive identifies a *template* for each major technical activity. Each template identifies potential areas of risk. Overlaying each template on a project allows identification of mismatched areas, which are then identified as "at risk." Having used all applicable templates, the program manager will have created a "watch list" of production transition risk areas and can prioritize control actions—many of which will be the responsibility of systems engineering. DoD Directive 4245.7-M describes technical methods for reducing the risk in each identified area.

High-risk areas may reflect missing capabilities in the project manager's organization or in supporting organizations. They may also reflect technical difficulties in the design or development process. In either case, "management" of risk involves using project management assets to reduce the identified risks.

The value in each of these approaches to risk identification lies in the methodical nature of the approach, which forces disciplined, consistent treatment of risk. However, using any method in a "cookbook" manner may cause unique risk aspects of the project to be overlooked. Before acting on the outcome of any assessment, the project manager must review the strengths and weaknesses of the approach and identify other factors that may introduce technical, schedule, cost, program, or other risks.

17.9 RISK ANALYSIS

Analysis begins with a detailed study of the risk issues that have been identified. The objective is to gather enough information about the risk issues to judge the probability of occurrence and cost, schedule, and technical consequences if the risk occurs.

Risk analyses are often based on detailed information that may come from:

- Comparisons with similar systems
- Relevant lessons-learned studies
- Experience
- Results from tests and prototype development
- Data from engineering or other models

- Specialist and expert judgments
- Analysis of plans and related documents
- Modeling and simulation
- Sensitivity analysis of alternatives

Each risk category (i.e., cost, schedule, and technical) includes a core set of evaluation tasks and is related to the other two categories. This relationship requires supportive analysis among areas to ensure the integration of the evaluation process. Some characteristics of cost, schedule, and technical evaluations follow:

Cost Evaluation
- Builds on technical and schedule evaluation results
- Translates technical and schedule risks into cost
- Derives cost estimate by integrating technical risk, schedule risk, and cost estimating uncertainty impacts to resources
- Documents cost basis and risk issues for the risk evaluation

Schedule Evaluation
- Evaluates baseline schedule inputs
- Reflects technical foundation, activity definition, and inputs from technical and cost areas
- Incorporates cost and technical evaluation and schedule uncertainty inputs to program schedule model
- Performs schedule analysis on program schedule
- Documents schedule basis and risk issues for the risk evaluation

Technical Evaluation
- Provides technical foundation
- Identifies and describes program risks (e.g., technology)
- Analyzes risks and relates them to other internal and external risks
- Prioritizes risks for program impact
- Quantifies associated program activities with both time duration and resources
- Quantifies inputs for cost evaluation and schedule evaluation
- Documents technical basis and risk issues for the risk evaluation

Describing and quantifying a specific risk and the magnitude of that risk usually requires some analysis or modeling. Typical tools for use in risk analysis are:

- Life-cycle cost analysis
- Network analysis
- Monte Carlo simulation
- Estimating relationships
- Risk scales (typically ordinal probability and consequence scales)
- Quick reaction rate/quantity impact analysis

- Probability analysis
- Graphical analysis
- Decision analysis
- Delphi techniques
- Work breakdown structure simulation
- Logic analysis
- Technology state-of-the-art trending
- Total risk-assessing cost analysis (TRACE)
- Defense science board templates (DoD Directive 4245.7-M)

Without any hard data, it may be necessary to use qualitative rather than quantitative data to assess potential damage. A common form of qualitative risk rating is as follows:

- *High risk:* Substantial impact on cost, schedule, or technical. Substantial action required to alleviate issue. High priority management attention is required.
- *Moderate risk:* Some impact on cost, schedule, or technical. Special action may be required to alleviate issue. Additional management attention may be needed.
- *Low risk:* Minimal impact on cost, schedule, or technical. Normal management oversight is sufficient.

Risk ratings are an indication of the potential impact of risks on a program. They are typically a measure of the likelihood of an issue occurring and the consequences of the issue, and often expressed as low, medium, and high. (Other factors that may significantly contribute to the importance of risk issues, such as frequency of occurrence, time sensitivity, and interdependence with other risk issues can also be noted and used either directly or indirectly in the rating methodology used.) The prioritization should be done based on a structured risk rating approach using relevant expert opinion and experience.

A major area of concern is how to arrive at a method for assigning risk levels. It is important to use agreed upon definitions (such as the "strawman" definitions above) and procedures for estimating risk levels, rather than subjectively assigning them, since each person could easily have a different understanding of words typically used to describe both probability distributions and risks. Figure 17–6 shows what some probability statements mean to different people. An important point to grasp from this figure is that a nontrivial variation in probability (e.g., 0.3) exists for more than half of the statements evaluated.

A risk viewed as easily manageable by some managers may be considered hard to manage by less experienced or less knowledgeable managers. Consequently, the terms "high," "medium," or "low" risk are relative terms. Some managers may be risk averse and choose to avoid recognized risk at all reasonable cost. Other managers may be risk seekers and actually prefer to take an approach with more risk. The terms "high," "medium," and "low" risk may change

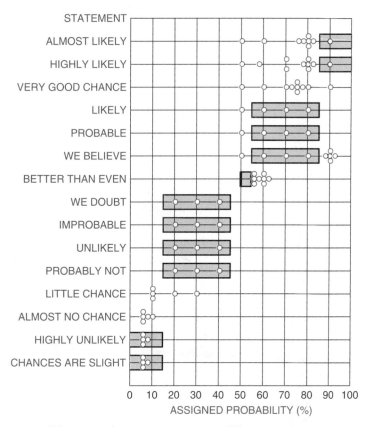

FIGURE 17–6. What uncertainty statements mean to different people.

with the turnover of managers and their superiors as much as with the project events.

Program managers can use risk ratings to identify issues requiring priority management (medium or higher risk). Risk ratings also help to identify the areas that should be reported within and outside the program. Thus, it is important that the ratings be portrayed as accurately as possible.

Previously, we showed that risk quantification could be found by use of an expected value calculation. However, there are more sophisticated approaches that involve templates combined with the expected value model. Here, ordinal scales (scales whose values are rank ordered) are commonly used to represent different aspects of the probability of occurrence (e.g., due to technology) and consequence of occurrence (e.g., cost, schedule, and technical). While such scales, tailored to your project, can be a useful methodology for estimating risk, great care must be taken in using them. A common abuse of such probability and consequence scales is performing mathematical operations on the results, which can

TABLE 17–5.   EXAMPLE OF ORDINAL TECHNOLOGY "PROBABILITY" MATURITY SCALE

Definition	Scale Level
Basic principles observed	E
Concept design analyzed for performance	D
Breadboard or brassboard validation in relevant environment	C
Prototype passes performance tests	B
Item deployed and operational	A

easily lead to erroneous results *because the true scale interval values are unknown* (e.g., a five level scale labeled 0.2, 0.4, 0.6, 0.8, and 1.0 almost certainly does not have values of equal 0.2 increments between adjacent scale levels).

The following simple example illustrates the proper use of ordinal scales in project risk analysis, and provides some recommendations for properly representing the results.[4] Please note, these scales should not be used on your project—they are only provided as an illustration.

Example 17–2.   A single "probability" of occurrence scale, related to technology maturity, is used, as shown in Table 17–5. In reality, technical risk will typically encompass a number of additional risk categories in addition to technology maturity, such as engineering, and so on. However, the use of a single risk category simplifies subsequent computations and is sufficient for illustration purposes. For the technology maturity "probability" scale, assume that low = scale levels A and B, medium = scale level C, and high = scale levels D and E. (Note: this information does not correspond to low, medium, and high risk, and is only an indicator of where breakpoints will occur when used in developing the risk mapping matrix later in this section. Letters are provided for scale levels instead of numbers to discourage you from attempting to perform invalid mathematical operations on the results.)

Three consequence of occurrence scales, for cost, schedule, and technical, are used and given in Table 17–6. For each of the three consequence of occurrence scales, assume that low = scale levels A and B, medium = scale levels C and D, and high = scale level E. (Note: this information does not correspond to low, medium, and high risk, and is only an indicator of where breakpoints will occur when used in developing the risk mapping matrix later in this section.)

Given the mapping information associated with the "probability" of occurrence and consequence of occurrence scales, a mapping matrix was developed and is given in Table 17–7. [Note: the interpretation of some of the levels is subjective given that three divisions were used for both the "probability" and consequence of

4. This example is from: Edmund H. Conrow, *Effective Risk Management: Some Keys To Success.* Reston, VA: American Institute of Aeronautics and Astronautics, 2000. Copyright ©1999, Edmund H. Conrow. Used with permission of the author.

TABLE 17–6.   EXAMPLE OF ORDINAL COST, SCHEDULE, AND TECHNICAL CONSEQUENCE OF OCCURRENCE SCALE

C_C	C_S	C_T	Scale Level
≥10%	Can't achieve key team or major program milestone	Unacceptable	E
7%–<10%	Major slip in key milestone or critical path impacted	Acceptable; no remaining margin	D
5%–<7%	Minor slip in key milestones, not able to meet need date	Acceptable with significant reduction in margin	C
<5%	Additional resources required able to meet need date	Acceptable with some reduction in margin	B
Minimal or no impact	Minimal or no impact	Minimal or no impact	A

occurrence scales versus the five possible levels (one per scale level), along with three resulting risk levels (low, medium, and high). A mapping matrix with different "probability" of occurrence and/or consequence of occurrence relationships (e.g., low = scale levels A and B, medium = scale levels C and D, and high = scale level E for both "probability" and consequence of occurrence scores), or five resulting risk levels (low, low medium, medium, medium high, and high), or a different risk mapping could also have been used for this example.]

We'll now evaluate two different items associated with a commercial high-grade digital camera, using the above risk analysis methodology. Remember, these risk issues are hypothetical and only used to illustrate how to apply the risk analysis methodology.

In the first case, a high performance commercial charge coupled device (CCD) exists that is in preprototype development. The CCD will be included in a high-grade digital camera. The risk issue is whether or not the desired signal to noise ratio can be achieved to meet low light operating requirements and avoid an increased level of image "grain" during operation. The potential cost conse-

TABLE 17–7.   EXAMPLE OF RISK MAPPING MATRIX

Probability \	Consequence ⟶ Higher	A	B	C	D	E
Higher ↑	E	M	M	H	H	H
	D	L	M	M	H	H
	C	L	L	M	M	H
	B	L	L	L	M	M
	A	L	L	L	L	M

quence of this occurring is a 6 percent cost impact for a third design, fabrication, and test iteration (two iterations are baselined). The potential schedule consequence of this occurring is additional resources required, but able to meet the need date. The potential technical consequence of this occurring is acceptable performance, but no remaining margin. In this example, the resulting probability of occurrence score from Table 17–5 is Level C (preprototype maturity), and from Table 17–6, C_C = Level C, C_S = Level B, and C_T = Level D. Given this information and the risk mapping matrix in Table 17–7, the risk levels relative to cost, schedule, and technical are medium, low, and medium, respectively, as illustrated in Table 17–8.

In the second case, a high density digital storage card is in the concept formulation stage. This storage card will be included in the same high grade digital camera as the CCD previously discussed. The risk issue is the ability to achieve the desired bit density for the card to store the desired number of very high resolution images. Here, the bit density is presumed to be a factor of five times greater than the existing state of the art. The potential cost consequence of not achieving the desired bit density is a 20 percent cost impact for additional technology advancement of the storage medium, plus one or more additional redesign, fabrication, and test iterations. The potential schedule consequence of this occurring is a major slip in introducing the digital camera with the desired high density storage card. The potential technical consequence of this occurring is unacceptable performance because the desired number of high resolution, high dynamic range images cannot be stored with existing density storage cards. (It is presumed here that multiple lower density storage cards cannot be substituted for a single high density card.) In this example, the resulting probability of occurrence score from Table 17–5 is Level D (concept design analyzed for performance), and from Table 17–6, C_C = Level E, C_S = Level D, and C_T = Level E. Given this information and the risk mapping matrix in Figure 17–7, the risk levels relative to cost, schedule, and performance are high, high, and high, respectively, as illustrated in Table 17–8.

Of the results for the two candidate risk issues given in Table 17–8, the higher risk item is the digital storage card. Note also that if the risk level is collapsed to a single value by taking the maximum of the three risk levels relative to cost, schedule, and technical consequence, then the CCD low light performance risk is medium, while the digital storage card bit density risk is high.

Had there been n technology risk categories instead of the one used here (technology maturity), then there would have been $n \times 3$ total scores to report for

TABLE 17–8. EXAMPLE OF RISK SCORING SUMMARY SHEET

| WBS Number | WBS Item/Issue | Risk Level | | |
		Cost	Schedule	Technical
1.1.1	CCD low light performance	M	L	M
1.2.3	Digital storage card bit density	H	H	H

each risk issue. If desired, this could be reduced to three risk scores per risk issue by using a conservative ranking approach and taking the maximum score for cost consequence, schedule consequence, and technical consequence. Similarly, if desired this could be reduced to one risk score per risk issue by using a conservative ranking approach and taking the maximum of all risk scores across cost, schedule, and technical consequence.

Finally, given that a medium or higher risk level exists for both the camera CCD low light performance and the digital storage card bit density, risk handling plans (discussed in Section 17.11) should be developed for both risk issues. (Note: All risk issues should be analyzed before selecting risk handling strategies.)

Another common product of risk analysis is a "watch list." Items placed on a "watch list" often include indicators of the start of the problem and consequences that are likely to occur. An example of this is the cost risk of production due to an immature technical data package. When production starts before the technical data package has been adequately engineered for producibility, the first unit cost may be higher than planned. A typical "watch list" is structured to show the trigger event or item (for example, long-lead items delayed), the related area of impact (production schedule), and later, as they are developed, the risk handling actions taken to reduce the potential for or impact from that event (such as ensuring early identification of long-lead items, placing contractor emphasis on early delivery, etc.).

The "watch list" is periodically reevaluated and items are added, modified, or deleted as appropriate. Should the trigger events occur for items on the "watch list" during a project, there would be immediate cause for risk assessments to be updated and risk handling methods to be selected.

17.10 THE MONTE CARLO PROCESS

The Monte Carlo process, as applied to risk management, is an attempt to create a series of probability distributions for potential risk items, randomly sample these distributions, and to then transform these numbers into useful information that reflects quantification of the potential risks of a real world situation. Monte Carlo simulation has been used to determine risks in design of service centers, time to complete an activity in a project, inventory management, and thousands of other applications.

A summary of the steps used in performing a Monte Carlo simulation for cost and schedule follows. Although the details of implementing the Monte Carlo simulation will vary between applications, many cases use a procedure similar to this.

1. Identify the lowest WBS or activity level for which probability distribution functions will be constructed. The level selected will depend on the program phase—lower levels will be selected as the project matures.

2. Develop the reference point estimate (e.g., cost or schedule duration) for each WBS element or activity contained within the model.
3. Identify which WBS elements or activities contain estimating uncertainty and/or risk. (For example, technical risk can be present in some cost estimate WBS elements and schedule activities.)
4. Develop suitable probability distributions for each WBS element or activity with estimating uncertainty and/or risk.
5. Aggregate the WBS element or activity probability distributions functions using a Monte Carlo simulation program. When performed for cost, the results of this step will typically be a WBS Level 1 cost estimate at completion and a cumulative distribution function (CDF) of cost versus probability. These outputs are then analyzed to determine the level of cost risk and to identify the specific cost drivers. When performed for schedule, the results of this step will be a schedule at the desired (WBS) level and CDFs of schedule versus probability. The CDFs will typically represent duration or finish date at the desired activity level, but can include other variables as well. These outputs are then analyzed to determine the level of schedule risk and to identify the specific schedule drivers.

Note: it should be recognized that the quality of Monte Carlo simulation results are only as good as the reference point estimates and associated probability distributions used in the simulation. If this data is not carefully obtained and accurate, the results can be misleading, if not erroneous.

Example 17-3.   The manager of a service center is contemplating the addition of a second service counter. He has observed that people are usually waiting in line. If the service center operates 12 hours per day and the cost of a checkout clerk is $60.00 (burdened) per hour, simulate the manager's problem using the Monte Carlo method, assuming that the loss of good will is approximately $50.00 per hour.

The first step in the process is to develop procedures for defining arrival rates and service rates. The use of simulation implies that the distribution expressions are either nonexistent for this type of problem or do not apply to this case. In either event, we must construct either expressions or charts for arrival and service rates.

The arrival and service rates are obtained from sample observations over a given period of time and transformed into histograms. Let us assume that we spend some time observing and recording data at the one service counter. The data recorded is the time between customer arrivals and the number of occurrences of these arrivals. The same procedure is repeated for servicing. We record the amount of time each person spends at the checkout facility and the number of times this occurs. This data is shown in Table 17–9 and transformed to histograms in Figures 17–7 and 17–8. From Table 17–9 and Figures 17–7 and 17–8, five people entered the store within one minute of previous customers. The five customers may have come at the same time or different times. Likewise 18 people entered

TABLE 17–9.   ARRIVAL AND SERVICE RATE DATA

Arrivals	
Arrival Time between Customers (Min.)	**Number of Occurrences**
0	5
5	7
8	1
10	9
12	12
15	20
16	18
18	10
20	9
25	5
30	4
	100

Services	
Service Time at Checkout Counter (Min.)	**Number of Occurrences**
10	5
12	10
14	15
16	20
18	20
20	15
22	15
	100

within 16 minutes of other customers. The service rates are handled in the same manner. Fifteen people required 14 minutes of service and 20 people required 18 minutes of service.

The second step transforms the arrival and service histograms into a step-function type chart in which for every number there corresponds one and only one arrival and service rate. To develop these charts, it is best to have 100 observances for both arrivals and services discussed in the first step and shown in Table 17–9.

The step-function charts are based upon 100 numbers. Consider the service data in Table 17–9. We let the numbers 1 through 5 represent 10 minutes of service since there were 5 observations. Ten observations were tabulated for 12 minutes of service. This is represented by the numbers 6 through 15. Likewise, the numbers 16 through 30 represent the 15 observations of 14 minutes of service. The remaining data can be tabulated in the same manner to complete the service chart. The service step-function chart is shown in Figure 17–9 and the arrival step-function chart is shown in Figure 17–10. Some points on these charts are plateau points, as the number 15 on the service chart. The number 15 refers to the

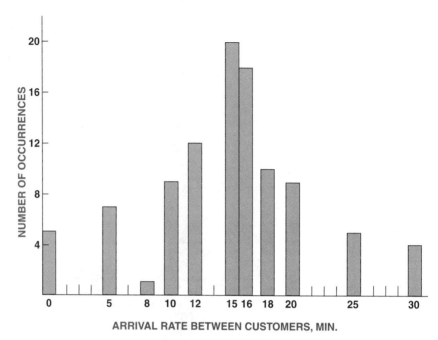

FIGURE 17–7. Arrival rate histogram.

left-hand most point. Therefore, 15 implies 12 minutes of service, not 14 minutes of service.

The third step requires the generation of random numbers and the analysis. (See Table 17–10.) The random numbers can be obtained either from random number tables or from computer programs that contain random number generators. These random numbers are used to simulate the arrival and service rates of customers from the step-function charts in Figures 17–9 and 17–10. Random numbers are generated between 0 and 1. However, it is common practice to multiply these numbers by 100 so as to have integers between 0 and 99 or 1 and 100. As an example, consider the following 10 random numbers: 1, 8, 32, 1, 4, 15, 53, 80, 68, and 82. The numbers are read in groups of two, with the first number representing arrivals and the second representing service. From Figure 17–10, the number 1 corresponds to a 0 arrival rate. From Figure 17–9, the number 8 corresponds to 12 minutes of service. Therefore, assuming that the store opens at 8:00 a.m., the first customer arrives at the checkout facility at approximately 8:00 a.m. and leaves at 8:12, after requiring 12 minutes of service at the checkout counter. The second pair of points are 32 and 1. The first number, 32, indicates that the second customer arrives 12 minutes after the first customer, at 8:12. But since the first customer is through the service facility at 8:12, the second customer will not have to wait. His 10 minutes of service at the checkout counter will begin at 8:12 and he will finish at 8:22. The third customer arrives at the same time as the sec-

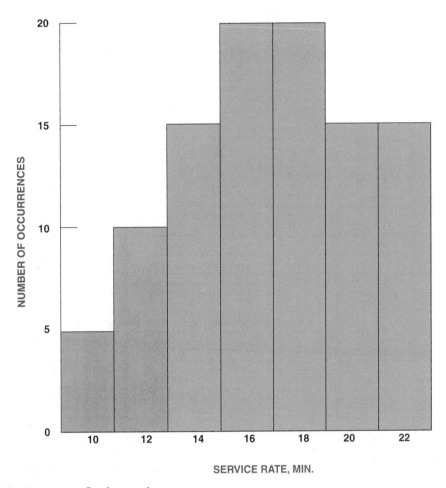

FIGURE 17–8. Service rate data.

ond customer and requires 12 minutes service. But since the second customer is in the service facility, the third customer must wait in the queue until 8:22 before entering the service facility. Therefore, his waiting time is 10 minutes and he leaves the service facility at 8:34 (8:22 + 12 minutes service). The fourth customer arrives 15 minutes after the third customer (at 8:27) and requires 20 minutes service. Since the service facility is occupied until the third customer leaves at 8:34, the fourth customer must wait seven minutes in the queue. This process is repeated for 16 customers and the results are shown in Table 17–10.

The fourth step in the process is the final analysis of the data. The data shown in Table 17–10 consisted of 16 customers processed in the first four hours. The summation of the waiting time for the four hours is 230 minutes. Since the store

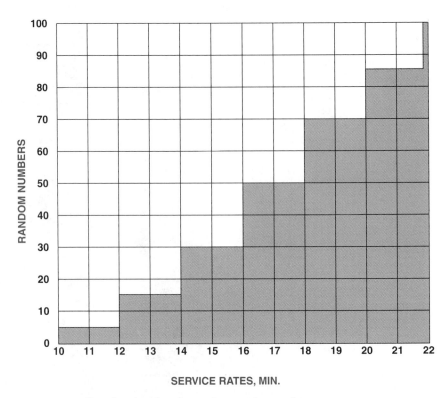

FIGURE 17–9. Step-function chart for random number service rates.

is opened for 12 hours, the total waiting time is 3 × 230, or 690 minutes. At $50.00 per hour loss of good will, the manager loses approximately $575 per 12-hour day because of waiting-line costs. The manager can put in a second service counter. If he pays the worker $60.00 per hour burdened for a 12-hour day, the cost will be $720.00. Therefore, it is more economical for the manager to allow people to wait than to put in a second checkout facility.

17.11 RISK HANDLING

Risk handling includes specific methods and techniques to deal with known risks, identifies who is responsible for the risk issue, and provides an estimate of the cost and schedule associated with reducing the risk, if any. It involves planning and execution with the objective of reducing risks to an acceptable level. The evaluators who assess risk should begin the process by identifying risks and developing handling options and approaches to propose to the program manager, who selects the appropriate one(s) for implementation. There are several factors that can influence our response to a risk, including but not limited to:

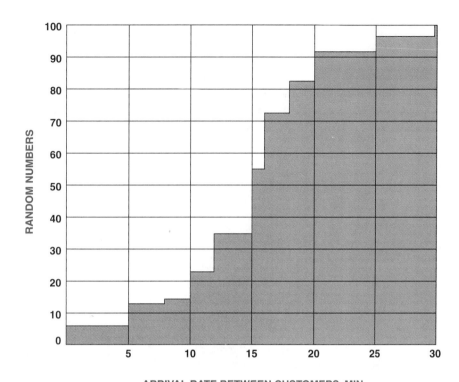

FIGURE 17–10. Step-function chart for random number arrival rates.

TABLE 17–10. SINGLE QUEUE MONTE CARLO SIMULATION MODEL

Random Number (Arrival)	Arrival Time Increment: Min.	Arrival Time	Random Number (Service)	Service Time Increment: Min.	Service Begins	Service Ends	Waiting Time (Min.)
1	0.0	8:00	8	12.00	8:00	8:12	0.0
32	12.00	8:12	1	10.00	8:12	8:22	0.0
4	0.0	8:12	15	12.00	8:22	8:34	10.00
53	15.00	8:27	80	20.00	8:34	8:54	7.00
68	16.00	8:43	82	20.00	8:54	9:14	11.00
87	20.00	9:03	83	20.00	9:14	9:34	11.00
17	10.00	9:13	47	16.00	9:34	9:50	21.00
32	12.00	9:25	64	18.00	9:50	10:08	25.00
99	30.00	9:55	10	12.00	10:08	10:20	13.00
72	16.00	10:11	39	16.00	10:20	10:36	9.00
82	18.00	10:29	41	16.00	10:36	10:52	7.00
7	5.00	10:34	65	18.00	10:52	11:10	18.00
30	12.00	10:46	92	22.00	11:10	11:32	24.00
77	18.00	11:04	32	16.00	11:32	11:48	28.00
96	25.00	11:29	82	20.00	11:48	12:08	19.00
30	12.00	11:41	41	16.00	12:08	12:24	27.00

Total waiting time = 230.00 minutes

- Amount and quality of information on the actual hazards that caused the risk (descriptive uncertainty)
- Amount and quality of information on the magnitude of the damage (measurement uncertainty)
- Amount and quality of information on probability of occurrence
- Personal benefit to project manager for accepting the risk (voluntary risk)
- Risk forced upon project manager (involuntary risk)
- Confusion and avoidability of the risk
- The existence of cost-effective alternatives (equitable risks)
- The existence of high-cost alternatives or possibly lack of options (inequitable risks)
- Length of exposure to the risk

Risk handling must be compatible with the RMP and any additional guidance the program manager provides. A critical part of risk handling involves refining and selecting the most appropriate handling option(s) and specific approach(es) for selected risk issues (often those with medium or higher risk levels).

Personnel who evaluate candidate risk handling options may use the following criteria as starting points for evaluation:

- Can the option be feasibly implemented and still meet the user's needs?
- What is the expected effectiveness of the handling option in reducing program risk to an acceptable level?
- Is the option affordable in terms of dollars and other resources (e.g., use of critical materials, and test facilities)?
- Is time available to develop and implement the option, and what effect does that have on the overall program schedule?
- What effect does the option have on the system's technical performance?

Risk handling options include: risk assumption, risk avoidance, risk control, and risk transfer. Although the control option (often called mitigation) is commonly used in many high technology programs, it should not automatically be chosen. All four options should be evaluated, and the best one chosen for each risk issue.

The options for handling risk fall into the following categories:

- *Risk assumption (i.e., retention):* The project manager says, "I know the risk exists and am aware of the possible consequences. I am willing to wait and see what happens. I accept the risk and its impact should it occur."
- *Risk avoidance:* The project manager says, "I will not accept this option because of the potentially unfavorable results."
- *Risk control (i.e., prevention or mitigation):* The project manager says, "I will take the necessary measures required to control this risk by continuously reevaluating it and developing contingency plans or fall-back positions. I will do what is expected."

- *Risk transfer:* The project manager says, "I will share this risk with others through insurance or a warranty, or transfer the entire risk to them. Perhaps I can convert the risk into an opportunity."

We now explore each of these risk handling options in somewhat greater detail.

Risk assumption is an acknowledgment of the existence of a particular risk situation and a conscious decision to accept the associated level of risk, without engaging in any special efforts to control it. However, a general cost and schedule reserve may be set aside to deal with any problems that may occur as a result of various risk assumption decisions. This risk handling option recognizes that not all identified program risks warrant special handling; as such, it is most suited for those situations that have been classified as low risk.

The key to successful risk assumption is twofold:

- Identify the resources (e.g., money, people, and time) that will be needed to overcome a risk if it materializes. This includes identifying the specific management actions (such as retesting, and additional time for further design activities) that may occur.
- Ensure that necessary administrative actions are taken to identify a management reserve to accomplish those management actions.

Risk avoidance involves a change in the concept, requirements, specifications, and/or practices to reduce risk to an acceptable level. Simply stated, it eliminates the sources of high or possibly medium risk and replaces them with a lower risk solution. This method may be used in parallel with the up-front requirements analysis, supported by cost/requirement trade-off studies. It may also be used later in the development phase when test results indicate that some requirements cannot be met, and the potential cost and/or schedule impact would be severe.

Risk control does not attempt to eliminate the source of the risk but seeks to reduce or mitigate the risk. It manages the risk in a manner that reduces the likelihood and/or consequence of its occurrence on the program. This option may add to the cost of a program, and the selected approach should provide an optimal mix among the candidate approaches of risk reduction, cost effectiveness, and schedule impact. A summary of some common risk control actions includes:

- **Alternative design:** Create a backup design option that uses a lower risk approach.
- **Demonstration events:** Demonstration events are points in the program (normally tests) that determine if risks are being successfully reduced.
- **Design of experiments:** This engineering tool identifies critical design factors that are sensitive, therefore potentially medium or higher risk, to achieve a particular user requirement.
- **Early prototyping:** Build and test prototypes early in the system development.

- **Incremental development:** This is design with the intent of upgrading system parts in the future.
- **Key parameter control boards:** The practice of establishing a control board for a parameter may be appropriate when a particular feature (such as system weight) is crucial to achieving the overall program requirements.
- **Manufacturing screening:** For programs in the mid- to late-development phases, various manufacturing screens (including environmental stress screening) can be incorporated into test article production and low rate initial production to identify deficient manufacturing processes.
- **Modeling/simulation:** Modeling and simulation can be used to investigate various design options and system requirement levels.
- **Multiple development efforts:** Create systems that meet the same performance requirements. (This approach is also known as parallel development.)
- **Open systems:** Use of carefully selected commercial specifications and standards can result in lower risk levels.
- **Process proofing:** Particular processes, especially manufacturing and support processes, are critical to achieving system requirements.
- **Reviews, walk-throughs, and inspections:** These three actions can be used to reduce the likelihood and potential consequences of risks through timely assessment of actual or planned events.
- **Robust design:** This approach uses advanced design and manufacturing techniques that promote quality and capability through design.
- **Technology maturation efforts:** Normally, technology maturation is used when the desired technology will replace an existing technology that is available for use in the system.
- **Test-analyze-and-fix (TAAF):** TAAF is the use of a period of dedicated testing to identify and correct deficiencies in a design.
- **Trade-off studies:** Arrive at a balance of engineering requirements in the design of a system. Ideally, this also includes cost, schedule, and risk considerations.
- **Use of mock-ups:** The use of mock-ups, especially man–machine interface mock-ups, can be utilized to conduct early exploration of design options.
- **Use of standard items/software reuse:** Use of existing and proven hardware and software, where applicable, can potentially reduce risks.

Risk transfer may reallocate risk from one part of the system to another, thereby reducing the overall system and/or lower-level risk. It may also redistribute risks between the buyer (e.g., government) and the seller (e.g., prime contractor), or within the buyer or seller teams. It should be considered as part of the requirements analysis process. Risk transfer is a form of risk sharing and not risk abrogation on the part of the buyer or seller, and it may influence cost objectives. An example is the transfer of a function from hardware implementation to software implementation or vice versa. (Risk transfer is also not deflecting a risk issue because insufficient information exists about it.) The effectiveness of risk transfer depends on the use of successful system design techniques. Modularity and functional partitioning are two design techniques that support risk transfer. In some cases, risk transfer may concentrate risk issues in one area of the design. This allows management to focus attention and resources on that area. Other examples of risk transfer include the use of insurance, warranties, bonding (e.g., bid, performance, or payment bonds), and similar agreements. These agreements are typically between the buyer and seller such that the consequent "costs" of failure will be assumed by the seller for some agreed to price. That price may be in terms of profit dollars, schedule changes, product performance modifications, or other considerations.

Risk handling options and the implemented approaches have broad cost implications. The magnitude of these costs are circumstance-dependent. The approval and funding of handling options and specific approaches should be done by the project manager or Risk Management Board (or equivalent) and be part of the process that establishes the program cost, and performance and schedule goals. The selected handling option and approach for each selected risk issue should be included in the program's acquisition strategy.

Once the acquisition strategy includes the risk handling strategy for each selected risk issue, the cost and schedule impacts can be identified and included in the program plan and schedule, respectively.

17.12 RISK MONITORING

The monitoring process systematically tracks and evaluates the effectiveness of risk handling actions against established metrics. Monitoring results may also provide a basis for developing additional risk handling options and approaches, or updating existing risk handling approaches, and reanalyzing known risks. In some cases monitoring results may also be used to identify new risks and revise some aspects of risk planning. The key to the risk monitoring process is to establish a cost, performance, and schedule management indicator system over the program that the program manager and other key personnel use to evaluate the status of the program. The indicator system should be designed to provide early warning of potential problems to allow management actions. Risk monitoring is not a problem-solving technique, but rather, a proactive technique to obtain objective information on the progress to date in reducing risks to acceptable levels. Some techniques suitable for risk monitoring that can be used in a program-wide indicator system include:

- **Earned value (EV):** This uses standard cost/schedule data to evaluate a program's cost performance (and provide an indicator of schedule performance) in an integrated fashion. As such, it provides a basis to determine if risk handling actions are achieving their forecasted results.
- **Program metrics:** These are formal, periodic performance assessments of the selected development processes, evaluating how well the develop-

ment process is achieving its objective. This technique can be used to monitor corrective actions that emerged from an assessment of critical program processes.

- **Schedule performance monitoring:** This is the use of program schedule data to evaluate how well the program is progressing to completion.
- **Technical performance measurement (TPM):** TPM is a product design assessment that estimates, through engineering analysis and tests, the values of essential performance parameters of the current design as effected by risk handling actions.

The indicator system and periodic reassessments of program risk should provide the program with the means to incorporate risk management into the overall program management structure. Finally, a well-defined test and evaluation program is often a key element in monitoring the performance of selected risk handling approaches and developing new risk assessments.

17.13 THE USE OF LESSONS LEARNED

Risk issues that are analyzed to be medium or higher must be handled to the extent assets allow, to reduce their potential to adversely affect the program. All levels of management must be sensitive to hidden "traps" that may induce a false sense of security. If properly interpreted, these signals really indicate a developing problem in a known area of risk. Each trap is usually accompanied by several "warning signs" that show an approaching problem and the likelihood of failing to treat the problem at its inception.

The ability to turn traps into advantages suggests that much of the technical risk in a program can be actively handled via the control or transfer option, not merely watched and resolved after a problem occurs. In some instances it may pay to watch and wait. If the probability that a certain problem will arise is low or if the cost exceeds the benefits of "fixing" the problem before it happens, a do-nothing alternative (assumption risk handling option) may be advisable. Effective risk management makes selection of the do-nothing alternative a conscious decision rather than an oversight and may trigger an appropriate addition to the risk "watch list".

"Best practices" acknowledges that all of the traps have not been identified for each risk issue. The traps are intended to be suggestive, and other potential issues should be examined as they arise. It is also important to recognize that sources and types of risk evolve over time. Risks may take a long time to mature into problems. Attention must be properly focused to examine risks and lessons learned.

Lessons learned should be documented so that future project managers can learn from past mistakes.

Experience is an excellent teacher in risk management. Yet, no matter how hard we try, risks will occur and projects may suffer. As an example, we have over forty years of knowledge in going from new product development to production.[5] We plan for risk management, identify and analyze risk issues, and develop ways of handling and monitoring risks, but some types of risk issues commonly occur on projects that are mid to late in the development phase. Some examples of these risk issues are now given.

Risk Issue: Design process.   The design process must reflect a sound design policy and proper engineering disciplines and practices—an integration of factors that influence the production, operation, and support of a system throughout its life cycle. Nevertheless, concepts are often selected, demonstrated, and validated with little thought given to the feasibility of producing a system employing those concepts. This omission is then carried forward into design, with voids appearing in manufacturing technology and absence of proven manufacturing methods and processes to produce the system within affordable cost. One of the most common sources of risk in the transition from development to production is failure to design for production. Some design engineers do not consider in their design the limitations in manufacturing personnel and processes. The predictable result is that an apparently successful design, assembled by engineers and highly skilled model shop technicians, goes to pieces in the factory environment when subjected to rate production. A design should not be produced if it cannot survive rate production without degradation.

Prevention.   The potential to produce a system must be investigated carefully during the planning phase by means of appropriate producibility analyses. Voids in manufacturing technology projects and manufacturing methods and processes peculiar to the design of the specific system, subsystem, and components must be addressed during engineering development.

Risk Issue: Design Reviews.   While most engineering development projects usually require formal design reviews, they often lack specific direction and discipline in the design review requirement, resulting in an unstructured review process that fails to fulfill either of the two main purposes of design review, which are (1) to bring additional knowledge to the design process to augment the basic program design and analytical activity and (2) to challenge the satisfactory accomplishment of specified design and analytical tasks needed for approval to proceed with the next step in the process.

Prevention:

- The customer and their contractors recognize that design reviews represent the "front line" where readiness for transition from development to production is decided ultimately. Design review policy, schedule, budget, agenda, participants, actions, and follow-up are decided in view of this foremost need.

---

5. Adapted from *Transition from Development to Production.* DoD 4245.7, Department of Defense, September 1985. These risk areas may occur on a variety of projects, but it may not be possible to take decisive action to deal with them until midway in the development phase.

- Design reviews should be included in all projects in accordance with existing customer requirements. A design review plan must be developed by the contractor and approved by the customer.

Risk Issue: Life. Life tests are intended to assess the adequacy of a particular equipment design when subjected to long-term exposure to certain operational environments. Due to the time-consuming nature of these tests, various methods have been used to accelerate test times by exposure to more stringent environments than those expected in actual operational use. These methods may give misleading results due to a lack of understanding of the acceleration factors involved.

Many projects are forced into conducting life tests after the systems are placed in use and before reliability requirements are achieved. As a result, life tests are performed after the start of production, and costly engineering change proposals (ECPs) and retrofit programs must be initiated in an attempt to "get well" with less than optimum design solutions.

Prevention:

- Include life testing in the overall system integrated test plan to ensure that testing is conducted in a cost-effective manner and to meet program schedules.
- Use test data from other phases of the test program to augment the system and subsystem life testing by reducing the time required to prove that reliability requirements are met.
- Use life test data from similar equipment, operating in the same environment, to augment the equipment life testing in order to gain confidence in the design.

Risk Issue: Manufacturing plan. Involvement of production and manufacturing engineering only *after* the design process has been completed is a fundamental error and a major transition risk. Consequences of late involvement are: (1) an extended development effort required for redesign and retest of the end-item for compatibility with the processes and procedures necessary to produce the item and (2) lower and inefficient rates of production due to excessive changes in the product configuration introduced on the factory floor. Increased costs and schedule delays are the result of this approach.

Prevention. The following represent the key elements of a manufacturing plan:

- Master delivery schedule that identifies by each major subassembly the time spans, need dates, and who is responsible.
- Durable tooling requirements to meet increased production rates as the program progresses
- Special tools
- Special test equipment
- Assembly flowcharts

Risk Issue: Quality manufacturing process. The introduction of a recently developed item to the production line brings new processes and procedures to the factory floor. Changes in hardware or work flow through the manufacturing facility increase the possibility of work stoppage during rate production. Failure to qualify the manufacturing process before rate production with the same emphasis as design qualification—to confirm the adequacy of the production planning, tool design, manufacturing process and procedures—can result in increased unit costs, schedule slippage, and degraded production performance.

Prevention:

- The work breakdown structure, production statement of work, and transition and production plans do not contain any conflicting approaches. Any discrepancies among these documents are identified and resolved before production is started.
- A single-shift, eight-hour day, five-day workweek operation is planned for all production schedules during initial start-up. Subsequent manpower scheduling is adjusted to manufacturing capability and capacity consistent with rate production agreements.
- The drawing release system must be controlled and disciplined.
- The manufacturing flow must minimize tooling changes and machine adjustments and ensure that alternate flow plans have been developed.
- A mechanism must be established that ensures the delivery of critical items with long-lead time four to six weeks before required.
- All new equipment or processes that will be used to produce the item must be identified.

Risk Issue: Manpower and personnel. Product development and support systems must be designed with as complete an understanding as possible of user manpower and personnel skill profiles. A mismatch yields reduced field reliability, increased equipment training, technical manual costs, and redesign as problems in these areas are discovered during demonstration tests and early fielding. Discovery of increased skill and training requirements late in the acquisition process creates a difficult catch-up problem and often leads to poor system performance.

Prevention:

- Manpower and skill requirements must be based on formal analysis of previous experience on comparable systems and maintenance concepts.
- Manpower cost factors used in design and support trade-off analyses must take into account costs to train or replace experienced personnel, as well as the true overhead costs.

Risk Issue: Training, materials, and equipment. On some programs, training requirements are not addressed adequately, resulting in great difficulty in operation and support of the hardware. Training programs, materials, and equipment such as simulators may be more complex and costly than the hardware they support. Delivery of effective training materials and equipment depends on the understanding of final production design configuration, maintenance concepts, and skill levels of personnel to be trained. On many programs, training materials and equipment delivery schedules are overly ambitious. The results include poor training, inaccuracies in technical content of materials, and costly redesign and modification of training equipment:

Prevention:

- Contractors must be provided with clear descriptions of user personnel qualifications and current training programs of comparable systems, to be used in prime hardware and training systems design and development.
- On-the-job training capability must be incorporated in the prime equipment design as a method to reduce the need for additional training equipment.

PROBLEMS

17–1 You have $1,000,000 worth of equipment at the job site and wish to minimize your risk of direct property damage by taking out an insurance policy. The insurance company provides you with their statistical data as shown below:

Type of Damage	Probability (%)	Amount of Damage (Loss) (%)
Total	0.02	100
Medium	0.08	40
Low	0.10	20
No Damage	99.8	0

If the insurance company uses expected value to calculate premiums, then how much would you expect the premium to be, assuming the insurance company adds on $300 for handling and profit?

17–2 You have been asked to use the expected-value model to assess the risk in developing a new product. Each strategy requires a different sum of money to be invested and produces a different profit payoff as shown below:

| Strategy | States of Nature | | |
	Complete Failure	Partial Success	Total Success
S_1	<$50K>	<30K>	70K
S_2	<80K>	20K	40K
S_3	<70K>	0	50K
S_4	<200K>	<50K>	150K
S_5	0	0	0

Assume that the probabilities for each state are 30 percent, 50 percent, and 20 percent, respectively.

a. Using the concept of expected value, what risk (i.e., strategy) should be taken?
b. If the project manager adopts a go-for-broke attitude, what strategy should be selected?
c. If the project manager is a pessimist and does not have the option of strategy S_5, what risk would be taken?
d. Would your answer to part C change if strategy S_5 were an option?

17–3 Your company has asked you to determine the financial risks of manufacturing 6,000 units of a product rather than purchasing them from a vendor at $66.50 per unit. The production line will handle exactly 6,000 units and requires a one-time setup cost of $50,000. The production cost is $60/unit.

Your manufacturing personnel inform you that some of the units may be defective, as shown below:

% defective	0	1	2	3	4
probability of occurrence (%)	40	30	20	6	4

Defective items must be removed and replaced at a cost of $145/defective unit. However, 100 percent of units purchased from vendors are defect-free.

Construct a payoff table, and using the expected-value model, determine the financial risk and whether the make or buy option is best.

17–4 Below are four categories of risk and ways that a company is currently handling the risks. According to Section 17.11, which risk handling options are being used? More than one answer may apply.

a. A company is handling its high R&D financial risk by taking on partners and hiring subcontractors. The partners/subcontractors are expected to invest some of their own funds in the R&D effort in exchange for sole-source, long-term production contracts if the product undergoes successful commercialization.
b. A company has decided to handle its marketing risks by offering a family of products to its customer base. Different features exist for each product offered.
c. A company has product lines with a life expectancy of ten years or more. The company is handling its technical risks by performing extensive testing on new components and performing parallel technical development efforts for downstream enhancements.
d. A company has large manufacturing costs for its high tech products. The company will not begin production until it has a firm commitment for a certain quantity. The company uses learning curves and project management to control its costs.

17–5 A telecommunications firm believes that the majority of its income over the next ten years will come from organizations outside of the United States. More specifically, the income will come from third world nations that may have very little understanding or experience in project management. The company prepared Figure 17–11. What causes the increasing risks in Figure 17–11?

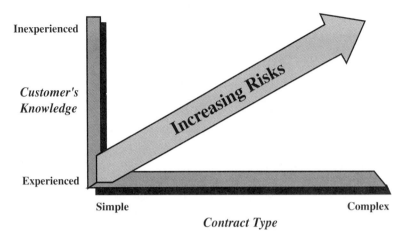

FIGURE 17–11. Future risks.

17–6 In the 1970s and 1980s, military organizations took the lead in developing ways to assess total program risk. One approach was to develop a rigorous process for identifying specific technical risk at the functional level and translating this detailed information through several steps. In this way, it was believed that risks could easily be monitored and corrected, as shown in Figure 17–12. Why is this method not being supported today?

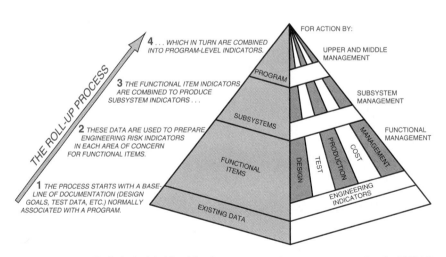

FIGURE 17–12. Technical risk identification at appropriate management levels (ONAS P 4855-X).

17–7 As an example of the situation in Problem 17–6, Figure 17–13 shows risk categories at the program, subsystem, and functional levels. Starting at the bottom, data are developed for five engineering indicators and rated according to "high," "medium," or "low" risk. Results of this assessment are then summarized for each subsystem to provide a system overview. This is often considered a template risk analysis method. What are the advantages and disadvantages of this approach? Why is this method not used extensively today?

17–8 With the explosion of computer hardware and software during the 1970s and 1980s, companies began developing models to assess the technical risk for the computer hardware and software effort. One such model is discussed in this problem. Although some people contend that there may still exist applicable use for this model, others argue that the model is obsolete and flawed with respect to current thinking. After reading the paragraphs below, explain why the model may have limited use today for technical risk management.

Previously, we showed that risk quantification could be found by use of an expected-value calculation. However, there are more sophisticated approaches that involve templates combined with the expected-value model. Here, we can develop mathematical expressions for failure and risk for *specific* types of projects.

Risk can be simply modeled as the interaction of two variables: probability of failure (P_f) and the effect or consequence of the failure (C_f). Consequences may be measured in terms of technical performance, cost, or schedule. A simple model can be used to highlight areas where the probability of failure (P_f) is high (even if there is

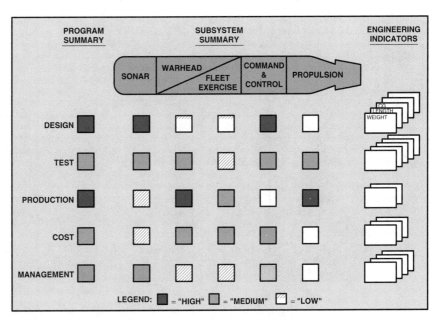

FIGURE 17–13. Variation of risk identification products with management level (ONAS P 4855-X).

a low probability of occurrence). Mathematically, this model can be expressed as the union of two sets, P_f and C_f. Table 17–11 shows a mathematical model for risk assessment on hardware–software projects. In other words, the risk factor (defined as $P_f \times C_f$) will be largest where both P_f and C_f are large, and may be high if either factor is large.

In this case, P_f is estimated by looking at hardware and software maturity, complexity, and dependency on interfacing items. The probability of failure, P_f, is then quantified from ratings similar to the factors in Table 17–11. C_f is calculated by looking at the technical, cost, and schedule implications of failure. For example, consider an item with the following characteristics:

TABLE 17–11. A MATHEMATICAL MODEL FOR RISK ASSESSMENT

$$(1)\ \text{Risk Factor} = P_f + C_f - P_f \cdot C_f$$

$$(2)\ P_f = a \cdot P_{M_{hw}} + b \cdot P_{M_{sw}} + c \cdot P_{C_{hw}} + d \cdot P_{C_{sw}} + e \cdot P_D$$

where:

$P_{M_{hw}}$ = Probability of failure due to degree of hardware maturity

$P_{M_{sw}}$ = Probability of failure due to degree of software maturity

$P_{C_{hw}}$ = Probability of failure due to degree of hardware complexity

$P_{C_{sw}}$ = Probability of failure due to degree of software complexity

P_D = Probability of failure due to dependency on other items

and where: a, b, c, d, and e are weighting factors whose sum equals one.

$$(3)\ C_f = f \cdot C_t + g \cdot C_c + h \cdot C_s$$

where:

C_t = Consequence of failure due to technical factors

C_c = Consequence of failure due to changes in cost

C_s = Consequence of failure due to changes in schedule

and where: f, g, and h are weighting factors whose sum equals one.

Magnitude	Maturity Factor (P_M)		Complexity Factor (P_C)		Dependency Factor (P_D)
	Hardware $P_{M_{hw}}$	Software $P_{M_{sw}}$	Hardware $P_{C_{hw}}$	Software $P_{C_{sw}}$	
0.1	Existing	Existing	Simple design	Simple design	Independent of existing system, facility, or associate contractor
0.3	Minor redesign	Minor redesign	Minor increases in complexity	Minor increases in complexity	Schedule dependent on existing system, facility, or associate contractor
0.5	Major change feasible	Major change feasible	Moderate increase	Moderate increase	Performance dependent on existing system performance, facility, or associate contractor
0.7	Technology available, complex design	New software, similar to existing	Significant increase	Significant increase/major increase in # of modules	Schedule dependent on new system schedule, facility, or associate contractor
0.9	State of art, some research complete	State of art, never done before	Extremely complex	Extremely complex	Performance dependent on new system schedule, facility, or associate contractor

(continues)

TABLE 17–11. A MATHEMATICAL MODEL FOR RISK ASSESSMENT (*Continued*)

Magnitude	Technical Factor (C_t)	Cost Factor (C_c)	Schedule Factor (C_s)
0.1 (low)	Minimal or no consequences, unimportant	Budget estimates not exceeded, some transfer of money	Negligible impact on program, slight development schedule change compensated by available schedule slack
0.3 (minor)	Small reduction in technical performance	Cost estimates exceed budget by 1 to 5 percent	Minor slip in schedule (less than 1 month), some adjustment in milestones required
0.5 (moderate)	Some reduction in technical performance	Cost estimates increased by 5 to 20 percent	Small slip in schedule
0.7 (significant)	Significant degradation in technical performance	Cost estimates increased by 20 to 50 percent	Development schedule slip in excess of 3 months
0.9 (high)	Technical goals cannot be achieved	Cost estimates increased in excess of 50 percent	Large schedule slip that affects segment milestones or has possible effect on system milestones

- Uses off-the-shelf hardware with minor modifications to software database
- Is based on simply-designed hardware
- Requires software of somewhat minor increase in complexity
- Involves a new database to be developed by a subcontractor

Using Table 17–11, the probability of failure, P_f, would be calculated as follows:
Assume that the weighting factors for *a, b, c, d,* and *e* are 20 percent, 10 percent, 40 percent, 10 percent, and 20 percent, respectively.

P_M (hardware)	= 0.1		$0.2\ P_M$ (h)	= 0.02
P_M (software)	= 0.3		$0.1\ P_M$ (s)	= 0.03
P_C (hardware)	= 0.1		$0.4\ P_C$ (h)	= 0.04
P_C (software)	= 0.3		$0.1\ P_C$ (s)	= 0.03
P_D	= 0.9		$0.2\ P_D$	= 0.18
				= 0.30

Then, assuming the weighting factors shown in equation (2) of Table 17–11 are as indicated above, the P_f on this item would be 0.30.

If the consequence of the item's failure because of technical factors would cause some problems of a correctable nature, but correction would result in an 8 percent cost increase and two-month schedule slip, the consequence of failure, C_f, would be calculated from Table 17–11 as follows:

C_t = 0.3			$0.4\ C_t$ = 0.12
C_c = 0.5			$0.5\ C_c$ = 0.25
C_s = 0.5			$0.1\ C_s$ = 0.12
			0.42

Then C_f for this item [assuming that the weighting factors in equation (3) of Table 17–11 are as indicated above] would be 0.42.

From equation (1) of Table 17–11, the risk factor would be

$$0.30 + 0.42 - (0.30)(0.42) = 0.594$$

In other words, the risk associated with this item is medium. Because most of the risk associated with this example arises from software changes, in particular the use of a subcontractor in this area, we can conclude that the risk can be reduced when the computer software developer is held "accountable for work quality and is subject to both incentives and penalties during all phases of the system life cycle."

Similar risk analyses would be performed for all other items and a risk factor would be obtained for each identified risk area. Risk areas would then be prioritized according to source of the risk (for example, are other items exhibiting excessive risk due to subcontractor software development?).

CASE STUDIES

TELOXY ENGINEERING (A)

Teloxy Engineering has received a onetime contract to design and build 10,000 units of a new product. During the proposal process, management felt that the new product could be designed and manufactured at a low cost. One of the ingredients necessary to build the product was a small component that could be purchased for $60 in the marketplace, including quantity discounts. Accordingly, management budgeted $650,000 for the purchasing and handling of 10,000 components plus scrap.

During the design stage, your engineering team informs you that the final design will require a somewhat higher-grade component that sells for $72 with quantity discounts. The new price is substantially higher than you had budgeted for. This will create a cost overrun.

You meet with your manufacturing team to see if they can manufacture the component at a cheaper price than buying it from the outside. Your manufacturing team informs you that they can produce a maximum of 10,000 units, just enough to fulfill your contract. The setup cost will be $100,000 and the raw material cost is $40 per component. Since Teloxy has never manufactured this product before, manufacturing expects the following defects:

% defective	0	10	20	30	40
probability of occurrence (%)	10	20	30	25	15

All defective parts must be removed and repaired at a cost of $120 per part.

1. Using expected value, is it economically better to make or buy the component?

2. Strategically thinking, why might management opt for other than the most economical choice?

TELOXY ENGINEERING (B)

Your manufacturing team informs you that they have found a way to increase the size of the manufacturing run from 10,000 to 18,000 units, in increments of 2,000 units. However, the setup cost will be $150,000 and defects will cost the same $120 for removal and repair.

1. Calculate the economic feasibility of make or buy.
2. Should the probability of defects change if we produce 18,000 units as opposed to 10,000 units?
3. Would your answer to question 1 change if Teloxy management believes that follow-on contracts will be forthcoming? What would happen if the probability of defects changes to 15 percent, 25 percent, 40 percent, 15 percent, and 5 percent due to learning-curve efficiencies?

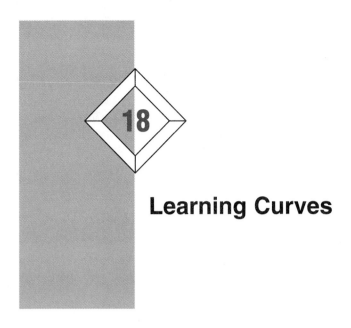

Learning Curves

18.0 INTRODUCTION

Competitive bidding has become an integral part of the project management responsibility in many industries. A multitude of estimating techniques are available in such fields as construction, aerospace, and defense to assist project managers in arriving at a competitive bid. If the final bid is too high, the company may not be competitive. If the bid is too low, the company may have to incur the cost of the overrun out of its own pocket. For a small firm, this overrun could lead to financial disaster.

Perhaps one of the most difficult projects to estimate are those that involve the development and ultimate manufacturing of a large quantity of units. As an example, a company is asked to bid on the development and manufacture of 15,000 components. The company is able to develop a cost for the manufacture of its first unit, but what will be the cost for the 10th, 100th, 1000th, or 10,000th unit? Obviously, the production cost of each successive unit should be less than the previous unit, but by how much? Fortunately for the project manager there exist highly accurate estimating techniques for these types of projects. These estimating techniques are referred to as "learning" or "experience" curves.

18.1 GENERAL THEORY

Experience curves are based on the old adage that practice makes perfect. A product can always be manufactured better and in a shorter time period not only the second time, but each succeeding time. This concept is highly applicable to labor-intensive projects such as those in manufacturing where labor forecasting has been a tedious and time-consuming effort.

951

The experience curve concept dates back to 1860 when Chauncey Jerome, a pioneer in clock manufacturing, wrote, "The business of manufacture of them has become so systematized of late that it has brought the price exceedingly low and it has long been the astonishment of the whole world how they could be made so cheap and yet so good."[1] Perhaps the earliest quantifiable effect of experience curves occurred in 1925, when the commander of Wright-Patterson Air Force Base found that the total hours required to assemble an aircraft decreased as the number of aircraft assembled increased. Not only did this fact result in a lower aircraft cost, but it also implied that, in time of war, more aircraft could be produced with the same resources and in a shorter period of time. Because of the high cost of building an aircraft, the effects of learning curves became more conspicuous in the aircraft industry than in any other industry.

It wasn't until the 1960s that the true implications of experience curves became evident. Personnel from the Boston Consulting Group showed that each time cumulative production doubled, the total manufacturing time and cost fell by a *constant* and *predictable* amount. Furthermore, the Boston Consulting Group showed that this experience effect was not limited to just the aircraft industry, but extended to other industries such as chemicals, metals, and electronic components.

Today's executives often measure the profitability of a corporation as a function of market share. As market share increases, profitability will increase, more because of lower production costs than increased margins. This is the experience curve effect. Large market shares allows companies to build large manufacturing plants so that the fixed capital costs are spread over more units, thus lowering the unit cost. This increase in efficiency is referred to as *economies of scale* and may be the main reason why large manufacturing organizations may be more efficient than smaller ones.

In certain industries, such as chemicals, mathematical expressions exist that clearly show the cost implications of economies of scale and learning curves.

Capital equipment costs follow the rule of six-tenths power of capacity. As an example, consider a plant that has the capacity of producing 35,000 units each year. The plant's construction cost was $10 million. If the company wishes to build a new plant with a capacity of 70,000 units, what will the construction cost be?

$$\frac{\$\ new}{\$\ old} = \left(\frac{70{,}000}{35{,}000}\right)^{0.6}$$

Solving for $ new, we find that the new plant will cost approximately $15 million, or one and one-half times the cost of the old plant. (For a more accurate determination, the costs must be adjusted for inflation.)

---

1. Chauncey Jerome, *History of the American Clock Business for the Past Sixty Years: Life of Chauncey Jerome, Written by Himself* (New Haven: F.C. Dayton Jr., 1860).

18.2 THE LEARNING CURVE CONCEPT

Learning curves stipulated that manufacturing man-hours (specifically direct labor) will decline each time a company doubles its output. Typically, learning curves produce a cost and time savings of 10 to 30 percent each time a company's experience at producing a product doubles. As an example, consider the data shown in Table 18–1, which represents a company operating on a 75 percent learning curve. The time for the second unit is 75 percent of the time of the first unit. The time for the fortieth unit is 75 percent of the time for the twentieth unit. The time for the 800th unit is 75 percent of the time for the 400th unit. Likewise, we can *forecast* the time for the 1,000th unit as being 75 percent of the time for the 500th unit. In this example, the time decreased by a fixed amount of 25 percent. Theoretically, this decrease could occur indefinitely.

In Table 18–1, we could have replaced the man-hours per production unit with the cost per production unit. It is more common to use man-hours because exact costs are either not always known or not publicly disclosed by the firm. Also, the use of costs implies the added complexity of considering escalation factors on salary, cost of living adjustments, and possibly the time value of money. For projects under a year or two, costs are often used instead of man-hours.

These types of costs are often referred to as value-added costs, and can also appear in the form of lower freight and procurement costs through bulk quanti-

TABLE 18–1. CUMULATIVE PRODUCTION AND LABOR-HOUR DATA

Cumulative Production	Hours This Unit	Cumulative Total Hours
1	812	812
2	609	1,421
10	312	4,538
12	289	5,127
15	264	5,943
20	234	7,169
40	176	11,142
60	148	14,343
75	135	16,459
100	120	19,631
150	101	25,116
200	90	29,880
250	82	34,170
300	76	38,117
400	68	45,267
500	62	51,704
600	57	57,622
700	54	63,147
800	51	68,349
840	50	70,354

ties. The value-added costs are actually cost savings for both the customer and contractor.

The learning curve was adapted from the historical observation that individuals performing repetitive tasks exhibit an improvement in performance as the task is repeated a number of times. Empirical studies of this phenomenon yielded three conclusions on which the current theory and practice is based:

- The time required to perform a task decreases as the task is repeated.
- The amount of improvement decreases as more units are produced.
- The rate of improvement has sufficient consistency to allow its use as a prediction tool.

The consistency in improvement has been found to exist in the form of a constant percentage reduction in time required over successive doubled quantities of units produced.

It's important to recognize the significance of using the learning curve for manufacturing projects. Consider a project where 75 percent of the total direct labor is in assembly (such as aircraft assembly) and the remaining 25 percent is machine work. With direct labor, learning improvements are possible, whereas with machine work, output may be restricted due to the performance of the machine. In the above example, with 75 percent direct labor and 25 percent machine work, a company may find itself performing on an 80 percent learning curve. But, if the direct labor were 25 percent and the machine work were 75 percent, then the company may find itself on a 90 percent learning curve.

18.3 GRAPHIC REPRESENTATION

Figure 18–1 shows the learning curve plotted from the data in Table 18–1. The horizontal axis represents the total number of units produced. The vertical axis represents the total labor hours (or cost) for each unit. The labor-hour graph in Figure 18–1 represents a hyperbola when drawn on ordinary graph paper (i.e., rectangular coordinates). The curve shows that the difference or amount of labor-hour reduction is *not* consistent. Rather, it declines by a continuously diminishing amount as the quantities are doubled. But the rate of change or decline has been found to be a constant percentage of the prior cost, because the decline in the base figure is proportionate to the decline in the amount of change. To illustrate this, we can use the data in Table 18–1, which was used to construct Figure 18–1. In doubling production from the first to the second unit, a reduction of 203 hours occurs. In doubling from 100 to 200 units, a reduction of thirty hours occurs. However in both cases, the percentage decrease was 25 percent. Again, in going from 400 to 800 units, a 25 percent reduction of seventeen hours results. We can therefore conclude that, as more units are produced, the rate of change remains constant but the magnitude of the change diminishes.

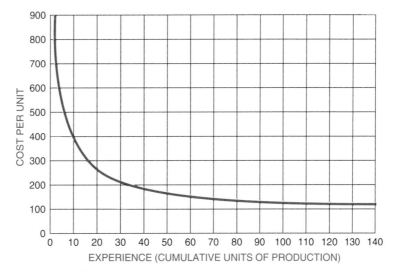

FIGURE 18–1. A 75 percent learning curve.

When the data from Figure 18–1 is plotted on log-log paper, the result is a straight line, which represents the learning curve as shown in Figure 18–2.

There are two fundamental models of the learning curve in general use; the unit curve and the cumulative average curve. Both are shown in Figure 18–2. The unit curve focuses on the hours or cost involved in specific units of production. The

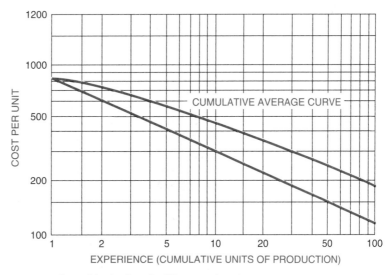

FIGURE 18–2. Logarithmic plot of a 75 percent learning curve.

theory can be stated as follows: As the total quantity of units produced doubles, the cost per unit decreases by some constant percentage. The constant percentage by which the costs of doubled quantities decrease is called the rate of learning.

The "slope" of the learning curve is related to the rate of learning. It is the difference between 100 percent and the rate of learning. For example, if the hours between doubled quantities are reduced by 20 percent (rate of learning), it would be described as a curve with an 80 percent slope.

To plot a straight line, one must know either two points or one point and the slope of the line. Generally speaking, the latter is more common. The question is whether the company knows the man-hours for the first unit or uses a projected number of man-hours for a target or standard unit to be used for pricing purposes.

The cumulative average curve in Figure 18–2 can be obtained from columns 1 and 3 in Table 18–1. Dividing column 3 by column 1, we find that the average hours for the first 100 units is 196 hours. For 200 units, the average is 149 hours. This becomes important in determining the cost for a manufacturing project.

18.4 KEY WORDS ASSOCIATED WITH LEARNING CURVES ───────────

To utilize learning curve theory, certain key phrases listed below are of importance:

- *Slope of the curve.* A percentage figure that represents the steepness (constant rate of improvement) of the curve. Using the unit curve theory, this percentage represents the value (e.g., hours or cost) at a doubled production quantity in relation to the previous quantity. For example, with an experience curve having 80 percent slope, the value of unit two is 80 percent of the value of unit one, the value of unit four is 80 percent of the value at unit two, the value at unit 1000 is 80 percent of the value of unit 500, and so on.
- *Unit one.* The first unit of product actually completed during a production run. This is not to be confused with a unit produced in any reproduction phase of the overall acquisition program.
- *Cumulative average hours.* The average hours expended per unit for all units produced through any given unit. When illustrated on a graph by a line drawn through each successive unit, the values form a cumulative average curve.
- *Unit hours.* The total direct labor hours expended to complete any specific unit. When a line is drawn on a graph through the values for each successive unit, the values form a unit curve.
- *Cumulative total hours.* The total hours expended for all units produced through any given unit. The data plotted on a graph with each point connected by a line form a cumulative total curve.

The greatest benefit of learning curves lies in the story they tell when plotted on log-log paper. As an example, consider the learning curve in Figure 18–3,

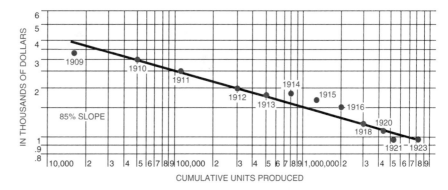

FIGURE 18–3. Price of Model T, 1909–1923 (average list price in 1958 dollars). Reprinted by permission of *Harvard Business Reviews*. An exhibit from "Limits of the Learning Curve," by William J. Abernathy and Kenneth Wayne, September–October 1974.

which shows the pricing for the Ford Model T. Other typical relationships can be seen in Figure 18–4.

18.5 THE CUMULATIVE AVERAGE CURVE

It is common practice to plot the learning curve on log-log paper but to calculate the cumulative average from the following formula:

$$T_x = T_1 X^{-K}$$

where

T_x = the direct labor hours for unit n
T_1 = the direct labor hours for the first unit (unit one)
X = the cumulative unit produced
$-K$ = a factor derived from the slope of the experience curve

Typical values for the exponent K are:

Learning curve %	K
100	0.0
95	0.074
90	0.152
85	0.235
80	0.322
75	0.415
70	0.515

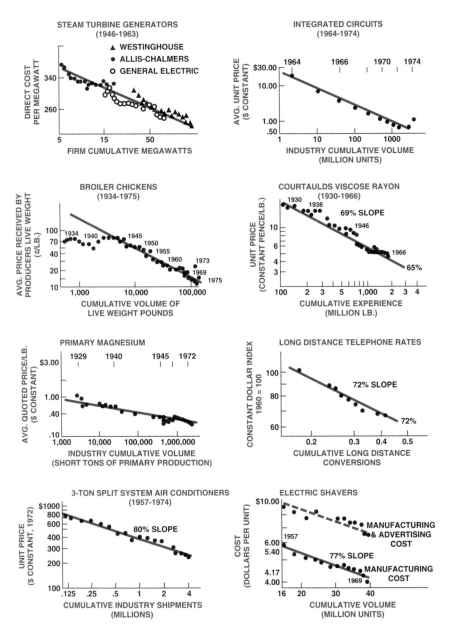

FIGURE 18–4. Some examples of experience curves. *Source.* The Boston Consulting Group.

As an example, consider a situation where the first unit requires 812 hours and the company is performing on a 75 percent learning curve. The man-hours required for the 250th unit would be:

$$T_{250} = (812)(250)^{-0.415}$$

$$= 82 \text{ hours}$$

This agrees with the data in Table 18–1.

Sometimes companies do not know the time for the first unit. Instead, they assume a target unit and accompanying target man-hours. As an example, consider a company that assumes that the standard for performance will be the 100th unit, which is targeted for 120 man-hours, and performs on a 75 percent learning curve. Solving for T_1 we have:

$$T_1 = T_x X^{-K}$$

$$= (120)(100)^{0.415}$$

$$= 811 \text{ hours}$$

This is in approximate agreement with the data in Table 18–1. The cumulative average number of labor hours can be *approximated* from the expression

$$T_c = \frac{T_1 X^{-K}}{1 - K}$$

where T_c = cumulative average labor hours for the Xth unit.

$$X = \text{cumulative units produced}$$
$$T_1 = \text{direct labor hours for first unit}$$

For the 250th unit,

$$T_c = \frac{(812)(250)^{-0.415}}{1 - 0.415}$$

$$= 135 \text{ hours}$$

From Table 18–1, the cumulative average for the 250th unit is 34,170 man-hours divided by 250, or 137 hours. We must remember that the above expression is merely an approximation. Significant errors can occur using this expression for less than 100 units. For large values of X, the error becomes insignificant.

It is possible to use the learning curve equation to develop Table 18–2, which shows typical cost reductions due to increased experience. Suppose that the production level is quadrupled and you are performing on an 80 percent learning curve. Using Table 18–2, the costs will be reduced by 36 percent.

TABLE 18–2. SAMPLE COST REDUCTIONS DUE TO INCREASED EXPERIENCE

Ratio of Old Experience to New Experience	Experience Curve					
	70%	75%	80%	85%	90%	95%
1.1	5%	4%	3%	2%	1%	1%
1.25	11	9	7	5	4	2
1.5	19	15	12	9	6	3
1.75	25	21	16	12	8	4
2.0	30	25	20	15	10	5
2.5	38	32	26	19	13	7
3.0	43	37	30	23	15	8
4.0	51	44	36	28	19	10
6.0	60	52	44	34	24	12
8.0	66	58	49	39	27	14
16.0	76	68	59	48	34	19

Source: Derek F. Abell and John S. Hammond, *Strategic Market Planning,* Upper Saddle River, NJ: Prentice-Hall, 1979, p. 109.

18.6 SOURCES OF EXPERIENCE

There are several factors that contribute to the learning curve phenomenon. None of the factors perform entirely independently, but are interrelated through a complex network. However, for simplicity's sake, these factors will be sorted out for discussion purposes.

● *Labor efficiency.* This is the most common factor, which says that we learn more each time we repeat a task. As we learn, the time and cost of performing the task should diminish. As the employee learns the task, less managerial supervision is required, waste and inefficiency can be reduced or even eliminated, and productivity will increase.

Unfortunately, labor efficiency does not occur automatically. Personnel management policies in the area of *workforce stability* and *worker compensation* are of vital importance. As workers mature and become more efficient, it becomes increasingly important to maintain this pool of skilled labor. Loss of a contract or interruption between contracts could force employees to seek employment elsewhere. In certain industries, like aerospace and defense, engineers are often regarded as migratory workers moving from contract to contract and company to company.

Upturns and downturns in the economy can have a serious impact on maintaining experience curves. During downturns in the economy, people work slower, trying to preserve their jobs. Eventually the company is forced into a position of having to reassign people to other activities or to lay people off. During upturns in the economy, massive training programs may be needed in order to accelerate the rate of learning.

If an employee is expected to get the job done in a shorter period of time, then the employee expects to be adequately compensated. Wage incentives can produce either a positive or negative effect based on how they are applied. Learning curves and productivity can become a bargaining tool by labor as it negotiates for greater pay.

Fixed compensation plans generally do not motivate workers to produce more. If an employee is expected to produce more at a lower cost, then the employee expects to receive part of the cost savings as either added compensation or fringe benefits.

The learning effect goes beyond the labor directly involved in manufacturing. Maintenance personnel, supervisors, and persons in other line and staff manufacturing positions also increase their productivity, as do people in marketing, sales, administration, and other functions.

- *Work specialization and methods improvements.*[2] Specialization increases worker proficiency at a given task. Consider what happens when two workers, who formerly did both parts of a two-stage operation, each specialize in a single stage. Each worker now handles twice as many items and accumulates experience twice as fast on the more specialized task. Redesign of work operations (methods) can also result in greater efficiency.
- *New production processes.* Process innovations and improvements can be an important source of cost reductions, especially in capital-intensive industries. The low-labor-content semiconductor industry, for instance, achieves experience curves at 70 percent to 80 percent from improved production technology by devoting a large percentage of its research and development to process improvements. Similar process improvements have been observed in refineries, nuclear power plants, and steel mills, to mention a few.
- *Getting better performance from production equipment.* When first designed, a piece of production equipment may have a conservatively rated output. Experience may reveal innovative ways of increasing its output. For instance, capacity of a fluid catalytic cracking unit typically "grows" by about 50 percent over a ten-year period.[3]
- *Changes in the resource mix.* As experience accumulates, a producer can often incorporate different or less expensive resources in the operation. For instance, less skilled workers can replace skilled workers or automation can replace labor.
- *Product standardization.* Standardization allows the replication of tasks necessary for worker learning. Production of the Ford Model T, for ex-

---

2. The next six elements are from Derek F. Abell and John S. Hammond, *Strategic Market Planning,* Prentice-Hall, 1979, pp. 112–113. Reprinted by permission of Prentice-Hall, Inc., Upper Saddle River, NJ.

3. Winfred B. Hirschmann, "Profit from the Learning Curve," *Harvard Business Review* 42, no. 1 (January–February 1964), p. 125.

ample, followed a strategy of deliberate standardization; as a result, from 1909 to 1923 its price was repeatedly reduced, following an 85 percent experience curve.[4] Even when flexibility and/or a wider product line are important marketing considerations, standardization can be achieved by modularization. For example, by making just a few types of engines, transmissions, chassis, seats, body styles, etc., an auto manufacturer can achieve experience effects due to specialization in each part. These in turn can be assembled into a wide variety of models.

- *Product redesign.* As experience is gained with a product, both the manufacturer and customers gain a clear understanding of its performance requirements. This understanding allows the product to be redesigned to conserve material, allow greater efficiency in manufacture, and substitute less costly materials and resources, while at the same time improving performance on relevant dimensions. The change from wooden to brass works of clocks in the early 1800s is a good example; so are the new designs and substitution of plastic, synthetic fiber, and rubber for leather in ski boots.

- *Incentives and disincentives.* Compensation plans and other sources of experience can be both incentives and disincentives. Incentives can change the slope of the learning curve, as shown in Figure 18–5. This is referred to as a "toe-down" learning curve where a more favorable learning process can occur. In Figure 18–6, we have a "toe-up," or "scallop," learning curve, which is the result of disincentives. After the toe-up occurs, the learning curve may have a new slope that was not as favorable as the original slope. According to Hirschmann,[5]

A rise in the curve can occur in the middle of a contract too, owing to a substantial interruption (such as that caused by introducing changes in a model, by moving operations to a new building, or by halting operations for a while so that forgetting occurs). Shortly after operations recommence and skill in handling changes is acquired, the curve declines rapidly to approach the old slope. Such a break in the curve occurs frequently enough to have acquired the descriptive term "scallop." In fact, if, instead of merely a change being made, a new model is introduced, or a new type of item is put into production, the scallop occurs initially and the curve essentially starts again. Thus, the direct labor input reverts back to what it had been when the first item of the preceding type was put into production (assuming that the two items were of similar type and configuration).

Worker dissatisfaction can also create a leveling off of the learning curve, as shown in Figure 18–7. This leveling off can also occur as a result of inefficien-

---

4. William J. Abernathy and Kenneth Wayne, "Limits of the Learning Curve," *Harvard Business Review,* 52, no. 5 (September–October 1974), pp. 109–119.

5. Winfred B. Hirschmann, "Profit from the Learning Curve," *Harvard Business Review,* January–February, 1964, p. 126.

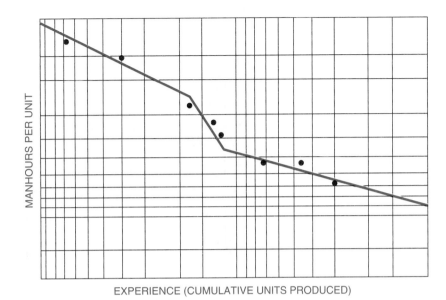

FIGURE 18–5. A "toe-down" learning curve.

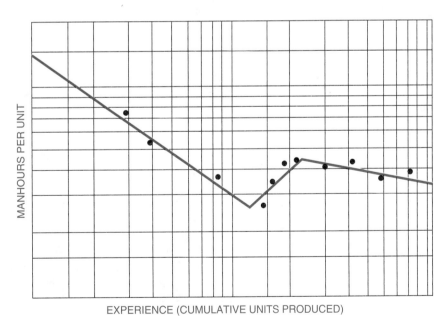

FIGURE 18–6. A "toe-up" learning curve.

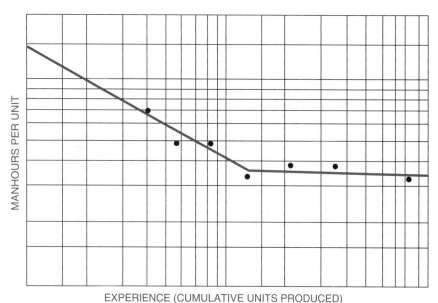

FIGURE 18–7. A leveling off of the learning curve.

cies due to closing out of a production line or transferring workers to other activities at the end of a contract.

18.7 DEVELOPING SLOPE MEASURES

Research by the Stanford Research Institute revealed that many different slopes were experienced by different manufacturers, sometimes on similar manufacturing programs. In fact, manufacturing data collected from the World War II aircraft manufacturing industry had slopes ranging from 69.7 percent to almost 100 percent. These slopes averaged 80 percent, giving rise to an industry average curve of 80 percent. Other research has developed measures for other industries, such as 95.6 percent for a sample of 162 electronics programs. Unfortunately, this industry average curve is frequently misapplied by practitioners who use it as a standard or norm. When estimating slopes without the benefit of data on the item being manufactured from the plant of the manufacturer, it is better to use learning curve slopes from similar items at the manufacturer's plant rather than the industry average.

The analyst needs to know the slope of the learning curve for a number of reasons. One is to facilitate communication, because it is part of the language of the learning curve theory. The steeper the slope (lower the percent), the more rapidly the resource requirements (hours) will decline as production increases.

Accordingly, the slope of the learning curve is usually an issue in production contract negotiation. The slope of the learning curve is also needed to project follow-on costs, using either learning tables or the computational assistance of a computer. Another need for a slope is that for many production situations, a given slope may be established as a standard based on reliable historical experience. Learning curves developed from actual experience on current production can then be compared against this standard slope to determine whether the improvement on a particular contract is or is not reasonable.

18.8 UNIT COSTS AND USE OF MIDPOINTS

The use of the learning curve is dependent on the methods of recording costs that companies employ. An accounting or statistical record system must be devised by a company so that data are available for learning curve purposes. Otherwise, it may be impossible to construct a learning curve. Costs, such as labor hours per unit or dollars per unit, must be identified with the unit of product. It is preferable to use labor hours rather than dollars, because the latter contain an additional variable—the effect of inflation or deflation (both wage-rate and material cost changes)—that the former does not contain. In any event, the record system must have definite cutoff points for such costs permitting identification of the costs with the units involved. Most companies use a lot-release system, whereby costs are accumulated on a job order in which the number of units completed are specified and the costs are cut off at the completion of the number of units. In this case, however, the costs are usually equated with equivalent units rather than actual units. Because the job order system is commonly used, the unit cost is not the actual cost per unit in the lot. This means that when lots are plotted on graph paper, the unit value corresponding with the average cost value must be found.

18.9 SELECTION OF LEARNING CURVES

Existing experience curves, by definition, reflect past experience. Trend lines are developed from accumulated data plotted on logarithmic paper (preferably) and "smoothed out" to portray the curve. The type of curve may represent one of several concepts. The data may have been accumulated by product, process, department, or by other functional or organizational segregations, depending on the needs of the user. But whichever experience curve concept or method of data accumulation is selected for use, based on suitability to the experience pattern, the data should be applied consistently in order to render meaningful information to management. Consistency in curve concept and data accumulation cannot be overemphasized, because existing experience curves play a major role in determining the project experience curve for a new item or product.

When selecting the proper curve for a new production item when only one point of data is available and the slope is unknown, the following, in decreasing order of magnitude, should be considered.

- Similarity between the new item and an item or items previously produced.
- Physical comparisons
  - Addition or deletion of processes and components
  - Differences in material, if any
  - Effect of engineering changes in items previously produced
- Duration of time since a similar item was produced
  - Condition of tooling and equipment
  - Personnel turnover
  - Changes in working conditions or morale
- Other comparable factors between similar items
  - Delivery schedules
  - Availability of material and components
  - Personnel turnover during production cycle of item previously produced
  - Comparison of actual production data with previously extrapolated or theoretical curves to identify deviations.

It is feasible to assign weights to these factors as well as to any other factors that are of a comparable nature in an attempt to quantify differences between items. These factors are again historical in nature and only comparison of several existing curves and their actuals would reveal the importance of these factors.

If at least two points of data are available, the slope of the curve may be determined. Naturally the distance between these two points must be considered when evaluating the reliability of the slope. The availability of additional points of data will enhance the reliability of the curve. Regardless of the number of points and the assumed reliability of the slope, comparisons with similar items are considered the most desirable approach and should be made whenever possible.

A value for unit one may be arrived at either by accumulation of data or statistical derivation. When production is underway, available data can be readily plotted, and the curve may be extrapolated to a desired unit. However, if production has yet to be started, actual unit-one data would not be available, and a theoretical unit-one value would have to be developed. This may be accomplished in one of three ways:

- A statistically derived relationship between the preproduction unit hours and first unit hours can be applied to the actual hours from the preproduction phase.
- A cost estimating relationship (CER) for first-unit cost based on physical or performance parameters can be used to develop a first-unit cost estimate.

- The slope and the point at which the curve and the labor standard value converge are known. In this case, a unit-one value can be determined. This is accomplished by dividing the labor standard by the appropriate unit value.

18.10 FOLLOW-ON ORDERS

Once the initial experience curve has been developed for either the initial order or production run, the values through the last unit on the cumulative average and unit curves can be determined. Follow-on orders and continuations of production runs, which are considered extensions of the original orders or runs, are plotted as extensions on the appropriate curve. However, the cumulative average value through the final point of the extended curve is not the cumulative average for the follow-on portion of that curve. It is the cumulative average for both portions of the curve, assuming no break in production. Thus, estimating the cost for the follow-on effort only requires evaluation of the differences between cumulative average costs for the initial run and the follow-on. Likewise, the last-unit value for both portions of the unit curve would represent the last-unit value for the combined curve.

18.11 MANUFACTURING BREAKS

The manufacturing break is the time lapse between the completion of an order or manufacturing run of certain units of equipment and the commencement of a follow-on order or restart of a manufacturing run for identical units. This time lapse disrupts the continuous flow of manufacturing and constitutes a definite cost impact. The time lapse under discussion here pertains to significant periods of time (weeks and months) as opposed to the minutes or hours for personnel allowances, machine delays, power failures, and the like.

It is logical to assume that because the experience curve has a time-cost relationship, a break will affect both time and cost. Therefore, the length of the break becomes as significant as the length of the initial order or manufacturing run. Because the break is quantifiable, the remaining factor to be determined is the cost of this lapse in manufacturing (that is, the additional cost incurred over and above that which would have been incurred had either the initial order or the run continued through the duration of the follow-on order or the restarted run).

When a manufacturer relies on experience curves as management information tools, it can be assumed that the necessary, accurate data for determining the initial curves have been accumulated, recorded, and properly validated. Therefore, if the manufacturer has experienced breaks, the experience curve data for the orders (lots) or runs involved should be available in such form that appropriate curves can be developed.

George Anderlohr, in the September 1969 issue of *Industrial Engineering,* suggests a method that assumes loss of learning is dependent on five factors:[6]

- *Manufacturing personnel learning.* In this area, the physical loss of personnel, either through regular movement or layoff, must be determined. The company's personnel records can usually furnish evidence on which to establish this learning loss. The percentage of learning lost by the personnel retained on other plant projects should also be ascertained. These people will lose their physical dexterity and familiarity with the product, and the momentum of repetition.

- *Supervisory learning.* Once again, a percentage of supervisory personnel will be lost as a result of the break in repetition. Management will make a greater effort to retain this higher caliber of personnel, so the physical loss, in the majority of cases, will be far less than in the area of production personnel. However, the supervisory personnel retained will lose their overall familiarity with the job, so that the guidance they can furnish will be reduced. In addition, because of the loss of production personnel, the supervisor will have no knowledge of the new hires and their individual personalities and capabilities.

- *Continuity of productivity.* This relates to the physical positioning of the line, the relationship of one work station to another, and the location of lighting, bins, parts, and tools within the work station. It also includes the position adjustment to optimize the individual's needs. In addition, a major factor affecting this area is the balanced line or the work-in-process buildup. Of all the elements of learning, the greatest initial loss is suffered in this area.

- *Methods.* This area is least affected by a break. As long as the method sheets are kept on file, learning can never be completely lost. However, drastic revisions to the method sheets may be required as a result of a change from soft to hard tooling.

- *Special tooling.* New and better tooling is a major contributor to learning. In relating loss in tooling area to learning, the major factors are wear, physical misplacement, and breakage. An additional consideration must be the comparison of short-tun, or so-called soft, tooling to long-run, or hard, tooling, and the effect of the transition from soft to hard tooling.

18.12 LEARNING CURVE LIMITATIONS

There are limitations to the use of learning curves, and care must be taken that erroneous conclusions do not result from their use. Typical limitations include:

---

6. "What Product Breaks Costs," George Anderlohr, *Industrial Engineering,* September 1969, pp. 34–36.

- The learning curve does not continue forever. The percentage decline in hours/dollars diminishes over time.
- The learning curve knowledge gained on one product may not be extendable to other products unless there exist shared experiences.
- Cost data may not be readily available in order to construct a meaningful learning curve. Other problems can occur if overhead costs are included with the direct labor cost, or if the accounting codes cannot separate work packages sufficiently in order to identify those elements that truly demonstrate experience effects.
- Quantity discounts can distort the costs and the perceived benefits of learning curves.
- Inflation must be expressed in constant dollars. Otherwise, the gains realized from experience may be neutralized.
- Learning curves are most useful on long-term horizons (i.e., years). On short-term horizons, benefits perceived may not be the result of learning curves.
- External influences, such as limitations on materials, patents, or even government regulations, can restrict the benefits of learning curves.
- Constant annual production (i.e., no growth)may have a limiting experience effect after a few years.

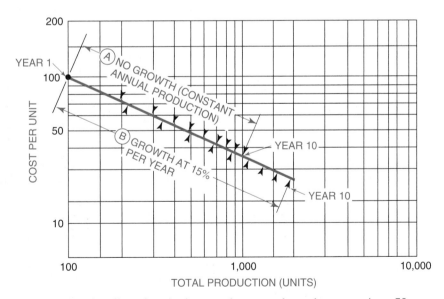

FIGURE 18–8. The effect of production growth on annual cost decreases using a 75 percent experience curve. *Source.* John S. Hammond and Gerald B. Allan, "Note on the Use of Experience Curves in Competitive Bidding," Boston: Harvard Business School Case 175-174. Copyright © 1975 by the President and Fellows of Harvard College. Reprinted by permission.

The last element requires further comment. Consider the example shown in Figure 18–8. With a constant production rate of 100 units per year for a ten-year horizon, and using a 75 percent learning curve, the percentage of cost decline goes from 25 percent in the first year to 1.7 percent in the tenth year. But with a 15 percent annual growth rate, the percentage of cost reduction goes from 27 percent the first year to 2.2 percent the tenth year.

Figure 18–8 also shows the competitive advantage of the 15 percent growth rate. The competitor with a 15 percent growth rate could have a competitive advantage of 30 percent or more after ten years. The moral here is that learning curves could indicate the necessity to exit a business if the company cannot match the competitor's growth rate.

18.13 PRICES AND EXPERIENCE

If the competitive marketplace is stable, then as cost decreases as a function of the learning curve experience, prices will decrease similarly. This assumes that profit margins are expressed as a percentage of price rather than in absolute dollar terms. Therefore, the gap between selling price and cost will remain a constant, as shown in Figure 18–9.

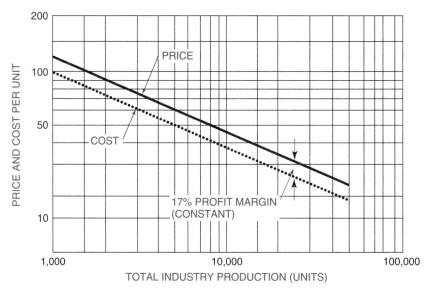

FIGURE 18–9. An idealized price–cost relationship when profit margin is constant. *Source.* Derek F. Abell and John S. Hammond, *Strategic Market Planning,* Prentice-Hall, © 1979, p. 115. Reprinted by permission of Prentice-Hall, Inc., Upper Saddle River, NJ.

Unfortunately, price and cost will most likely follow the relationship shown in Figure 18–10. Companies that use learning curves develop pricing policies based on either an industry average cost or an average cost based on a target production volume. In phase A, new product prices are less than the company cost, because the market would probably be reluctant to purchase the first few items at the *actual production cost*. As the company enters phase B, profits begin to materialize as the experience curve takes hold. Fixed costs are recovered. Price may remain firm because of market strategies adopted by the market leader.

The longer one remains in phase B, the greater the profits. Unfortunately, phase B is relatively unstable. One or more competitors will quickly drop their prices, because if the profit potential were too large, new entrants into the highly profitable marketplace would soon occur. In phase C, prices drop faster than costs, thus forcing a shakeout of the marketplace where marginal producers exit the market. The shakeout phase ends when prices begin to follow industry costs down the experience curve. This is phase D, which represents a stable market condition. Figure 18–11 shows examples for the semiconductor and chemical industries.

The average cost of the dominant market producers virtually regulates the industry. Whatever learning curve the industry leader uses, then so must the competitors. If the competitors' costs or volume cannot match the industry leader, then the slower rate of cost reductions will force profits to decrease or disappear, thus eliminating these competitors from the marketplace (i.e., Figure 18–8).

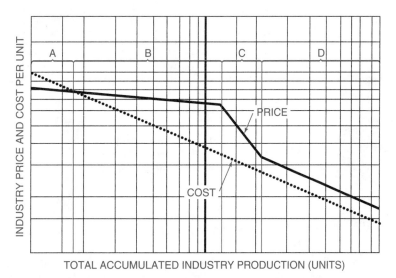

FIGURE 18–10. Typical price–cost relationships. *Source.* Derek F. Abell and John S. Hammond, *Strategic Market Planning,* Prentice-Hall, © 1979, p. 116. Reprinted by permission of Prentice-Hall, Inc., Upper Saddle River, NJ. Adapted from *Perspectives on Experience,* The Boston Consulting Group, 1972, p. 21.

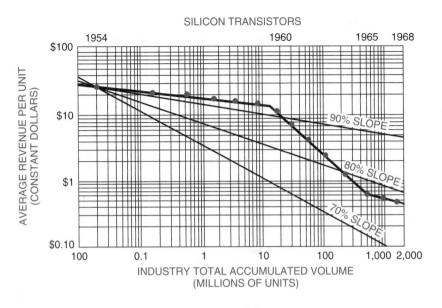

SILICON TRANSISTORS

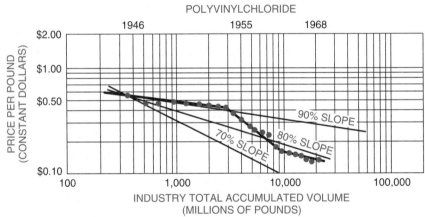

POLYVINYLCHLORIDE

FIGURE 18–11. Representative price–experience curves (each dot represents one year). *Source. Perspectives on Experience,* The Boston Consulting Group, Boston, Massachusetts, 1968, pp. 72, 85.

18.14 COMPETITIVE WEAPON

Learning curves are a strong competitive weapon, especially in developing a pricing strategy. The actual pricing strategy depends on the product life-cycle stage, the firm's market position, the competitor's available resources and market position, the time horizon, and the firm's financial position. To illustrate corporate philosophy toward pricing, although companies such as Texas Instruments (TI) and Digital

Equipment (DEC) have used "experience curve pricing" to achieve an early market share and a subsequent strong competitive position, companies such as Hewlett-Packard (HP) have used completely different approaches to achieve a commanding portion in the market. The focal point of TI's and DEC's strategy has been to price a new product in relation to the manufacturing costs that they expect to achieve when the product is mature. In contrast, HP, instead of competing on price, concentrates on developing products so advanced that customers are willing to pay a premium for them. Dr. David Packard, chairman of HP, drives the point home by saying,

> The main determinant of our growth is the effectiveness of our new product programs. . . . Anyone can build market share, and if you set your price low enough, you can get the whole damn market. But I will tell you it won't get you anywhere around here.[7]

From a project management perspective, learning curve pricing can be a competitive weapon. As an example, consider a company that is burdened at $60/hour and is bidding on a job to produce 500 units. Let us assume that the data in Table 18–1 apply. For 500 units of production, the cumulative total hours are 51,704, giving us an average rate of 103.4 hours per unit. The cost for the job would be 51,704 hours × $60/hour, or $3,102,240. If the target profit is 10 percent, then the final bid should be $3,412,464. This includes a profit of $310,224.

Even though a 10 percent profit is projected, the *actual* profit may be substantially less. Each product is priced out an average of 103.4 hours/unit. The first unit, however, will require 812 hours. The company will *lose* 708.6 hours × $60/hour, or $42,516, on the first unit produced. The 100th unit will require 120 hours, giving us a loss of $996 (i.e., [120 hours − 103.4 hours] × $60/hour). Profit will begin when the 150th unit is produced, because the hours required to produce the 150th unit are less than the average hour per unit of 103.4.

Simply stated, the first 150 units are a drain on cash flow. The cash-flow drain may require the company to "borrow" money to finance operations until the 150th unit is produced, thus lowering the target profit.

During competitive bidding, it is important to know where the competitors sit on the learning curve. Consider the situation shown in Figure 18–12, where three firms are competing for a new production contract. All three firms are performing on the same experience curve. Firm A has an advantage over firm B and a superior advantage over firm C. Firm C is also performing at a higher cost than the current market price. If firm C submits a bid at the current market price, then a substantial loss will occur. Therefore, it is not advisable for firm C to bid the job.

Both firms A and B could bid the job and make a profit, with firm A making more profit. However, if firm A lowers its price to a point *below* B's cost per unit, then A could drastically improve its changes of winning the contract, but at a lower profit.

---

7. "Hewlett-Packard: When Slower Growth is Smarter Management," *Business Week,* June 9, 1975, pp. 50–58.

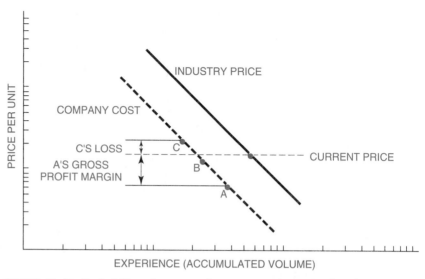

FIGURE 18–12. Profitability advantages of greater experience (market share). *Source.* Adapted from "The Experience Curve Revisited: I. The Concept," The Boston Consulting Group, 1974, *Perspectives,* no. 124.

PROBLEMS

18–1 When a learning curve is plotted on ordinary graph paper, the curve appears to level off. But when the curve is plotted on log-log paper, it appears that the improvements can go on forever. How do you account for the difference? Can the improvements occur indefinitely? If not, what factors could limit continuous improvement?

18–2 A company is performing on an 85 percent learning curve. If the first unit requires 620 hours, how much time will be required for the 300th unit?

18–3 A company working on a 75 percent learning curve has decided that the production standard should be 85 hours of production for the 100th unit. How much time should be required for the first unit? If the first unit requires more hours than you anticipated, does this mean that the learning curve is wrong?

18–4 A company has just received a contract for 700 units of a certain product. The pricing department has predicted that the first unit should require 2,250 hours. The pricing department believes that a 75 percent learning curve is justified. If the actual learning curve is 77 percent, how much money has the company lost? Assume that a fully burdened hour is $65. What percentage error in total hours results from a 2 percent increase in learning curve percentage?

18–5 If the first unit of production requires 1,200 hours and the 150th unit requires 315 hours, then what learning curve is the company performing at?

18–6 A company has decided to bid on a follow-on contract for 500 units of a product. The company has already produced 2,000 units on a 75 percent learning curve.

The 2000th unit requires 80 hours of production time. If a fully burdened hour is $80 and the company wishes to generate a 12 percent profit, how much should be bid?

18–7 Referrring to question 18–6, how many units of the follow-on contract must be produced before a profit is realized?

18–8 A manufacturing company wishes to enter a new market. By the end of next year, the market leader will have produced 16,000 units on an 80 percent learning curve, and the year-end price is expected to be $475/unit. Your manufacturing personnel tell you that the first unit will require $7,150 to produce and, with the new technology you have developed, you should be able to perform at a 75 percent learning curve. How many units must you produce and sell over the next year in order to compete with the leader at $475/unit at year end? Is your answer realistic, and what assumptions have you made?

18–9 Rylon Corporation is an assembler of electrical components. The company estimates that for the next year, the demand will be 800 units. The company is performing on an 80 percent learning curve. The company is considering purchasing some assembly machinery to accelerate the assembly time. Most assembly activities are 85–90 percent labor intensive. However, with the new machinery, the assembly activities will be only 25–45 percent labor intensive. If the company purchases and installs the new equipment, it will occur after the 200th unit is produced. Therefore, the remaining 600 units will be produced with the new equipment. The 200th unit will require 620 hours of assembly. However, the 201st unit will require only 400 hours of assembly but on a 90 percent learning curve.

    a. Will the new machine shorten product assembly time for all 800 units and, if so, by how many hours?

    b. If the company is burdened by $70 per hour, and the new equipment is depreciated over five years, what is the most money that the company should pay for the new equipment? What assumptions have you made?

CASE STUDIES

INSIGHT OPTICAL EQUIPMENT COMPANY[8]

On May 28th, Mr. William Thomas, manager of manufacturing of the Insight Optical Equipment Company was holding a meeting to discuss and evaluate plans for the assembly activities for the KD 780 photo-reconnaissance Air Force camera contract. These plans (Exhibit 18–1) had been developed during April and May by Mr. Robert

---

8. Copyright © 1975 by the President and Fellows of Harvard College. Harvard Business School case 675-168. This case was prepared by Steven C. Wheelwright as the basis for class discussion rather than to illustrate either effective or ineffective handling of an administrative situation. Reprinted by permission of the Harvard Business School.

Exhibit 18–1. Insight Optical Equipment Company Assembly Schedule

	Assembly Operators Added	Total Operators Available	Effective Labor Hours Available	Cameras Assembled during Month	Cumulative Total Cameras Assembled
June & July	0	4	1,280	2	2
August	25	29	3,440	12	14
September	25	54	7,440	59	73
October	0	54	8,640	120	193
November	0	54	8,640	173	366
December	0	54	8,640	223	589
January	0	54	8,640*	251*	840*

Source: Mr. Robert Phillips' KD 780 Camera Assembly Project File.
*665 effective labor hours available in January will not be needed to achieve the total production of 840 units.

Phillips, superintendent of the assembly of noncommercial products of the Insight factory at Cleveland, Ohio. Mr. Thomas and others at this meeting were not at all certain that Mr. Phillips' plans were feasible. The KD 780 camera job was Insight's first defense-product contract in the past decade, and Mr. Thomas was anxious for the manufacturing division to look good on this job to enhance prospects for more business with the Air Force.

The Insight Optical Equipment Company of Cleveland, Ohio, designed, manufactured, and sold optical equipment used in laboratories, factories, and medical facilities. Two years earlier the company had purchased a factory building and some machine tools, which had been declared surplus property by the U.S. Department of Defense. These new facilities provided about 25 percent more space and machining capacity than was to be required by optical equipment manufacturing, according to a ten-year forecast of sales. However, the price and especially the location of this former government property were so attractive and Insight's former plant space had been so inadequate that the added investment in the surplus plant and machine was easily justified. During the ensuing nine months, the move to the new plant had been completed and operations were running smoothly.

The previous September Mr. J. F. Pickering, president of the company, had decided to solicit government contracts to manufacture and assemble defense products in order to utilize the extra available plant space and machine tools more fully. No commitments were to be made for Insight to design or develop new products because Insight's engineers were fully occupied with optical equipment design work. Accordingly, a sales engineer and a production engineer had made a series of calls at various military equipment procurement offices. In December Insight was awarded a prime contract to manufacture 840 model KD 780 night-photo-reconnaissance cameras for the Air Force. Insight had been chosen among competitive bidders as the alternate prime source of supply of these cameras, which had previously been designed and produced by the Camtronic Instrument Company.

To prepare Insight's quotation for this contract, a group comprising a manufacturing engineer, a tool engineer, a cost estimator, and a purchasing agent had reviewed and analyzed over 600 Camtronic drawings of detail and assembly parts of the KD

780 camera. After Insight was awarded the contract, these drawings were thoroughly checked to insure that Insight had drawings showing the latest Camtronic engineering change information. Then, various make-buy decisions had been made and accordingly materials and tool orders placed with various vendors and/or with the machining and tool-making departments at the Insight plant. Air Force procurement officers had stated they desired these cameras as soon as possible. The contract stipulated that Insight was to ship the first KD 780 cameras in July, and, by October, Insight was to build up its camera output rate to at least 120 units per month until the 840 cameras had been produced and shipped.

Development of Mr. Phillips' Assembly Plan

By February Mr. Phillips received copies of the parts lists, assembly drawings, and test specifications, after the various procurement and parts manufacturing planning decisions had been made. Mr. Phillips turned these documents over to the assembly methods engineer on his staff, with instructions to plan the layout of the benches in the assembly area, to design and order necessary tools and fixtures, and to provide estimates of the standard hours per unit required at each assembly work station deemed necessary. The standard hour estimates were prepared by using predetermined methods and time standard data, and by presuming planned assembly work station layouts, methods, and carefully selected and fully trained assembly operators. Assisting the methods engineer were the project foreman and four "assembly-technicians" assigned as a "nucleus crew" to assemble the first, small production lot of cameras and to "debug" the assembly processing methods. The technicians were later to become working foremen and job leaders of new assembly personnel to be added to the assembly working force, as the assembly output rate was boosted to the minimum rate of 120 units per month. On April 15, the assembly methods planning group advised Mr. Phillips that after the assembly work force were skilled in using the planned methods, each camera would require a total eight-five standard labor hours to assemble completely. The eight-five standard labor hours was the sum of the standard labor hours per unit for different jobs involved in assembling one camera. They estimated that this standard of eight-five labor hours would be reached with the production of the ninetieth unit.

While his assembly methods planning group were engaged in their work, Mr. Phillips concentrated on how to approach the problems of programming the buildup of the assembly work force, and of controlling the rate of buildup in output of the cameras while new personnel were being hired and trained. He anticipated the possibilities of production delays and man-idleness during the entire period of assembling the 840 KD 780 cameras. He had heard of production delay problems in companies producing defense products, in which as much as 95 percent of the units ordered were delayed in shipment to the customer until the last month of a twelve-month planned period devoted to producing a particular defense project. This was an experience Mr. Phillips had hoped to avoid. He realized that a desirable approach was one enabling him to anticipate a specific quantitative pattern of output during the entire period the cameras were being assembled.

Mr. Phillips had decided that the best approach to his planning problem was to use a learning curve analysis (sometimes called a manufacturing progress function). A few years earlier, he had discovered that this method of quantifying cost experiences was frequency used by the Air Force as a guide in negotiating prices and delivery terms of contracts with manufacturers. Mr. Phillips had investigated a number of pieces of literature[9] on the subject and had talked to people who had used it before; as a result of his investigation and his persistence, Insight last year had utilized learning curve analysis fairly successfully to plan inventory and manpower needs for a new line of photo cells.

Learning curve analysis was basically founded on the premise that as production experience increases (as measured by number of units produced) costs can be reduced on a fairly predictable basis. A general rule of thumb that had been developed through application of the technique suggested that each time output doubled, labor hours (and therefore costs) could be reduced to between 70 percent and 90 percent of previous levels. Since Mr. Phillips had used this method once before, and since this was an Air Force contract, he felt the concept would provide a logical and sound base for planning his assembly operations.

As his first step in adapting the manufacturing progress function to his assembly activities, Mr. Phillips listed pertinent conditions that would affect his assembly program.

1. After lengthy discussion with his methods engineer and technicians, Mr. Phillips decided that 90 KD cameras would have been assembled by the time the assembly personnel had developed sufficient skill and experience to meet the standard rate of eight-five total labor hours per unit.

2. Starting with the nucleus crew of four assembly-technicians, it was decided that additional assembly personnel could be selected, hired, and effectively trained at the *maximum* rate of twenty-five new employees per month. To attempt to train more than twenty-five new operators would overtax training facilities and personnel, Mr. Phillips believed. The personnel manager, Mr. P. D. Kenworthy, had advised that all additional assembly personnel required for the KD 780 job would have to be recruited from the Cleveland area and would require Insight company orientation training as well as job methods training. During their first month on the KD 780 job, new employees were presumed to be 70 percent efficient (100 percent efficient meant that an operator completed the job in exactly the standard labor hours set for the assembly tasks assigned for him to complete). After the first month, all operators were presumed to be at least 100 percent efficient.

3. For purposes of developing these plans, Mr. Phillips assumed that there would be 160 assembly operating hours in any calendar month. Since a calendar month contained 4 1/3 weeks, this meant that every third month, a "margin of safety" of one week was available as a reserve for contingencies such as material shortages, quality problems, and other delays interfering with the flow of assembly work.

4. The KD 780 cameras contained over 800 parts. Plans for the process specified assembly work to be done at twenty-seven different work stations on four major subassemblies and thirty-five work stations in the final assembly area.

9. R. W. Conway and A. Schultz, Jr., "The Management Progress Function," *Journal of Industrial Engineering,* Jan.–Feb. 1959; W. B. Hirschmann, "Profit from the Learning Curve," *Harvard Business Review,* January–February 1964; S. L. Young, "Misapplication of the Learning Curve Concept," *Journal of Industrial Engineering,* August 1966; N. Baloff, "Startup Management," *IEEE Transactions on Engineering Management,* Vol. EM 17, no. 4 (Nov.), 1970, pp. 132–141; N. Baloff, "Startups in Machine-Intensive Production Systems," *Journal of Industrial Engineering,* Jan. 1960, pp. 25–32; *Perspectives on Experience,* The Boston Consulting Group, Boston, Massachusetts, 1970.

Standard times at these work stations were not uniform, and to insure reasonable continuity of flow of work, buffer stocks were to be provided and certain operators were to be shifted among several work stations. From these plans, Mr. Phillips estimated that the elapsed time for assembling a camera would be four weeks, two weeks for final and test, and two weeks for subassembly work.

5. The initial production-lot quantity planned was two cameras—just enough for the methods engineer and the four assembly-technicians to check out on the assembly methods, tools, and work place arrangements in the assembly area. The Air Force desired to make thorough acceptance tests of the performance of the first two units produced by Insight.

6. To use the manufacturing progress function, Mr. Phillips had to make an assumption of the measured rate of progress he could expect the growing labor force to achieve while assembling the 840 KD 780 cameras. He had noted in the literature that an 80–85 percent learning curve was rather widely used in the aircraft industry. Mr. Phillips had realized that to choose a progress rate parameter of 80 percent, 70 percent, or whatever, he would have to use good judgment in extrapolating from past experiences. He therefore examined blueprints, methods specifications, and labor time tickets for several optical equipment products assembled by Insight employees in the past. He chose products that all had some degree of similarity with the KD 780 job with respect to such factors as: the number of different parts to be assembled; the clearances between parts; the fragility of the parts; the number of different assembly operations required, and the total assembly hours required per unit.[10] By plotting learning curves for several such assembly activities in the past, Mr. Phillips had determined that the assembly progress-rate parameters for these past jobs had ranged from 70 percent to 75 percent. From this, Mr. Phillips had chosen 72 percent as the expected rate of progress that would be achieved on the KD 780 Air Force camera assembly job.

From these six presumed conditions, Mr. Phillips had developed his assembly production schedule and his manpower buildup schedule, shown in Exhibit 18–1. The detailed, step-by-step procedure Mr. Phillips followed to determine these schedules is summarized in Appendix A [of this case study]. Mr. Phillips had completed the work of determining these schedules on May 20.

During a regular KD 780 camera job-progress meeting of manufacturing management personnel held on May 25, Mr. Phillips had presented his assembly schedules, and had briefly described how he had derived them.

Mr. J. D. Jorgenson, KD 780 Camera Project Cost Supervisor: "Bob, using your data on labor hours and total units assembled and some cost figures I have, I estimate that we won't make any money on the KD 780 job until after we have shipped about 450 units. In fact, I don't think we will have absorbed out start-up costs directly incurred on this job until after we've shipped the 300th unit. We're committed to a fixed price on this job you know; we could not get the Air Force to go along with a cost-plus-fixed-fee price."

---

10. The photo-cell product with which Insight had used the learning curve analysis previously had not been as complex a product as the KD 780 camera.

Mr. Phillip D. Kenworthy, Manager of Personnel and Relations: "The union has been after me about wage-incentive procedures for this KD 780 camera assembly job. As you know, we normally put a newly hired man on the straight piecework incentive wage after he has been on the job for one month. As I see this learning curve plan, we are going to have a problem due to the inevitable built-in "looseness" in the time standards. It is pretty arbitrary where we choose to put the workers on incentive pay. If we put these KD 780 assembly personnel on an incentive basis too soon, their wages will get out of line with those of other personnel in the same labor class. If we don't put the operators on incentives soon enough, however, the union will gripe. We don't really know if your estimated 72 percent progress rate is realistic at this point. Since we haven't used learning curve planning on anything but the photo cells, we haven't had the extensive and uninterrupted opportunity for leaning on comparable optical equipment assembly jobs. If all your people are put on incentive wage rates by October, Bob, and if they progress the way you say they will along your 72 percent progress curve, they will be turning on the 840th camera in less than thirty hours. But if they start pegging rates, say, after the 150th camera (when standard hours are 85/66 = 128 percent of actual hours), won't this give you some trouble, Bob?"

Mr. Phillips: "There is a possible way inequity problem, Phil, and all I can say is that we'll have to take a good look at our whole wage payment policy and procedure, in light of this, before our next union contract negotiation. Meanwhile, I'm going to keep my methods engineer alerted to keep his methods and time standards up to date and to take more initiatives in revising them. There's nothing in the contract to prevent us from tightening the rates of jobs when we engineer the changes. But at the same time, I'm going to tell our people that there will be no tightening of standards when an operator makes a methods change that enables him to beat the rates we have set. I want the worker to participate in the success of the learning curve; improvements he makes help us in the long run. This type of incentive is really the backbone of the learning curve thesis anyway.

"I think there is really a great opportunity for us here to learn more about a planning tool that might be very valuable to us in the future. We have already learned in one case—the photo-cell production—that it is a workable approach to production planning. This project will allow us to experiment with it under much more rigorous conditions— conditions that are more representative of the majority of our production. And in any case, I am confident that we have the major problems anticipated; the minor ones like incentive wages can be dealt with as we, too, move down the learning curve."

Mr. William Thomas, Manager of Manufacturing: "Bob, this is quite a program you've planned. I had told Mr. Pickering I thought we wouldn't wind up this KD 780 job until May of next year. Now you show us shipping the last unit in January or February. If you're wrong, and we land another Air Force contract to work on in February, we'll really be in a bind. Are you sure you can make this schedule? Another thing, if you've planned that the standard will be 85 labor hours per unit, and the contract states that we have to ship 120 units per month, then I figure we should have a capacity of 85 × 120 = 10,200 standard labors hours per month. This is 10,200/160 = 64 operators. Yet you say you can do the whole job with 54 operators. (If this is true with assembly work, I wonder how this idea would go with our parts machining work.)"

Mr. Phillips: "Bill, I'm convinced we can do this. I'm telling my foremen exactly how I got the 72 percent progress curve, and that I am going to plot their actual progress each week to see how close they come to the curve. All I have to do is take the count of cameras coming off the package operation, and divide this into the total weekly direct labor hours per unit, I'll know something is wrong and find out what it is. I'd like to try to carry out these plans, and I hope you will approve them and give me the support I know I'll need."

Appendix A

Summary of the Procedure for Using the Manufacturing Function to Schedule Assembly Buildup on KD 780 Air Force Night-Photo-Reconnaissance Camera[11]

1. General Technical Specifications of the Manufacturing Progress Function
When empirical data on direct-labor per unit are plotted against the production count of units of product produced, the resulting curve appears, for example, as shown in Exhibit 18–2 for the KD 780 camera assembly operations. The curve depicts a phenomenon that makes strong intuitive sense, that is, *a job requires less effort as more experience is gained and as more methods improvements are made.* As production accumulates progress continues but at a decreasing rate, because further opportunities to improve the job become less and less obvious. This curve is just one of an almost infinite variety of such curves having the same "family-resemblance"; that is, the direct labor hours per unit decrease more or less sharply, but always steadily, as the number of units produced increases.

The algebraic statement of this progress phenomenon is

$$Y_i = ai^{-b}$$

where

Y_i is the direct labor hours required to produce the ith unit of product;
i is the production count, beginning with the first unit;
a is a parameter of the model, which is equal to the labor hours required for the first unit, Y_1 [for $i = 1$, $Y_1 = a(1)^{-b} = a$];
b is a measure of the *rate* at which the direct labor hours per unit are reduced as the production count increases.

When the labor hours/unit and production count data are plotted on logarithmic coordinate graph paper, or when the logarithms of these data are plotted on conventional arithmetic coordinate graph paper, the curve becomes a straight line. Algebraically this fact is stated by taking the logarithmic transformation of the equation above:

$$(\log Y_i) = (\log a) - b (\log i)$$

The rate of progress is nominally described by stating the complement of the percentage reduction in labor hours per unit when the production quantity is doubled.

---

11. *Source.* Mr. Robert Phillips' KD 780 Camera Assembly Project File.

Exhibit 18–2. Assembly Progress Curve

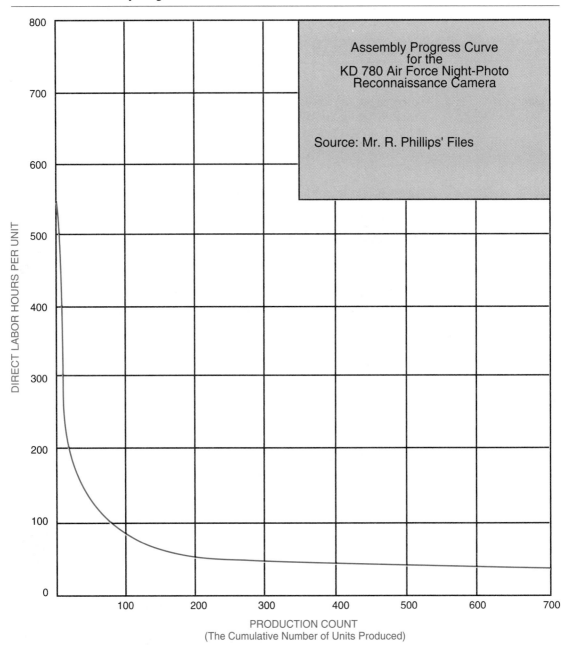

Assembly Progress Curve
for the
KD 780 Air Force Night-Photo
Reconnaissance Camera

Source: Mr. R. Phillips' Files

DIRECT LABOR HOURS PER UNIT

PRODUCTION COUNT
(The Cumulative Number of Units Produced)

This means that if i_2 and i_1 are any two different production counts and if i_2/i_1 always equals 2, then for an 80% progress curve, $b = 0.322$ because $2^{-0.322} = 0.80$; for a 72% progress curve, $b = 0.474$ because $2^{-0.474} = 0.72$.

The *cumulative* number of direct labor hours required to produce n units may be expressed as:

$$T_n = Y_1 + Y_2 + \ldots + Y_n = \sum_{i=1}^{n} Y_i$$

An approximation of this sum is given by the integral:

$$T_n \cong \int_0^n Y_i \, di \cong a \int_0^n i^{-b} \, di \cong a \left(\frac{n^{1-b}}{1-b} \right)$$

Dividing this expression by the cumulative number of unit (n) gives an approximation for the *cumulative average* number of labor hours:

$$A_n \cong \frac{a}{n} \left(\frac{n^{1-b}}{1-b} \right) \cong \frac{an^{-b}}{1-b}$$

These approximations typically yield insignificant errors at n values of 100 units or more, but large errors can occur for small values of n.

2. Method of Adapting the Manufacturing Progress Function to Plans for Assembling the KD 780 Camera

a. Assumptions made:

1. The 90th camera would require 85 direct labor hours to assemble. This was an estimate made by the assembly methods planning group.
2. The rate of progress in assembly methods improvements, and in development of skill by assembly personnel would conform to a 72% progress function (corresponding to a b parameter value of 0.474).

$$Y_i = a(i)^{-0.474}$$

b. The assembly progress curve (direct labor hours per unit). Using log-log graph paper, starting at 716 hours for the first unit, a straight line with a slope of -0.474 was drawn through this point (See Exhibit 18–3).
c. A cumulative average direct labor hours curve was also plotted on Exhibit 18–3 to ease calculations for the assembly output buildup schedule and for the operator buildup schedule. This curve was developed by calculating the cumulative average hours per unit for a variety of values of cumulative output (n and then plotting them on the graph. Note that the cumulative average curve becomes asymptotically parallel to the unit curve as the number of units completed increase.

The assembly operator buildup schedule required that subtotals of the cumulative assembly direct labor hours be related to cumulative production. These subtotals were

Exhibit 18–3. Graph of the 72 Percent Assembly Progress Curve

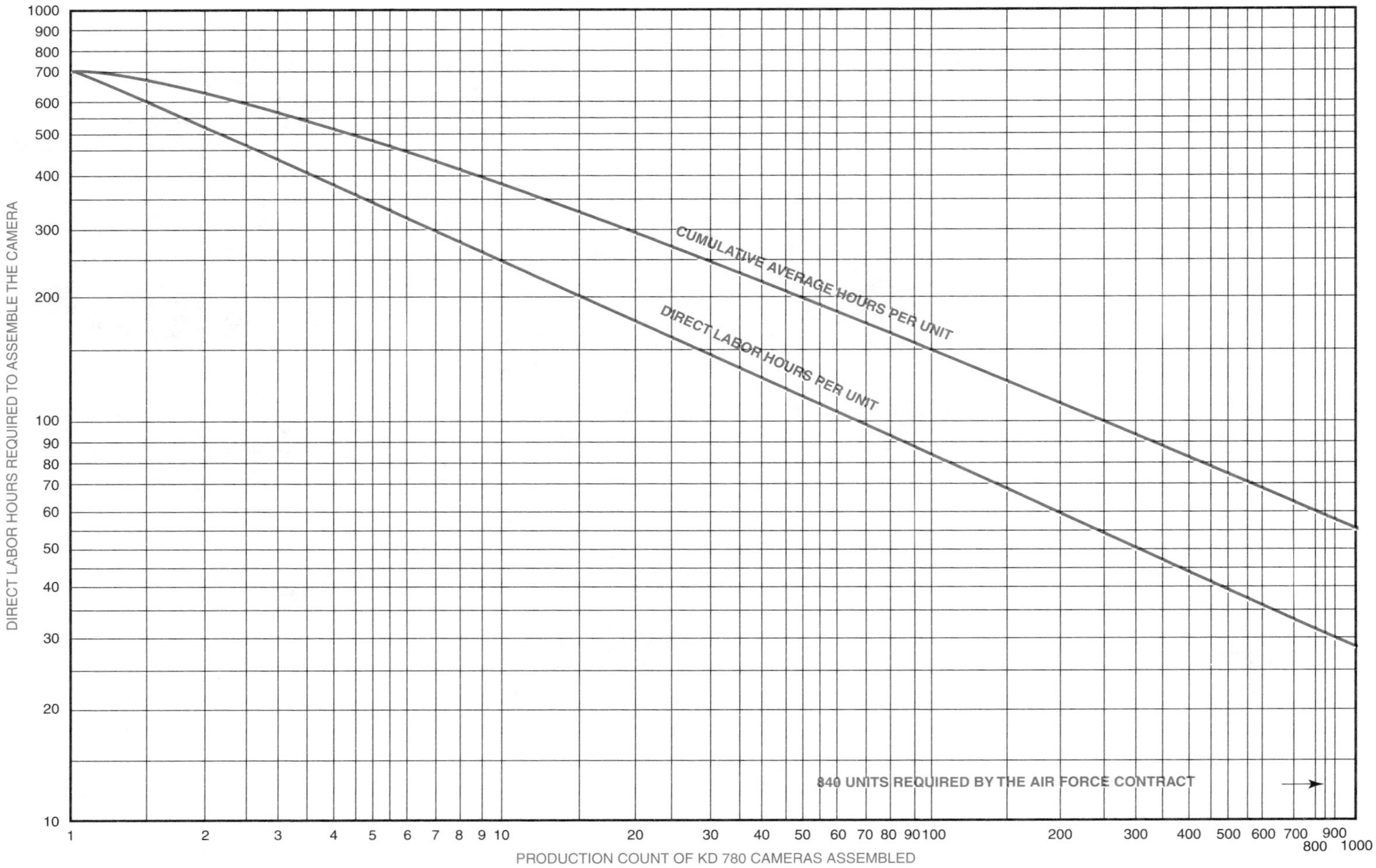
DIRECT LABOR HOURS REQUIRED TO ASSEMBLE THE CAMERA
1000
900
800
700
600
500
400
300
200
100
90
80
70
60
50
40
30
20
10
CUMULATIVE AVERAGE HOURS PER UNIT
DIRECT LABOR HOURS PER UNIT
840 UNITS REQUIRED BY THE AIR FORCE CONTRACT
1 2 3 4 5 6 7 8 9 10 20 30 40 50 60 70 80 90 100 200 300 400 500 600 700 800 900 1000
PRODUCTION COUNT OF KD 780 CAMERAS ASSEMBLED

easily calculated by multiplying the cumulative average direct labor hours per unit by the cumulative number of units assembled. Date on cumulative average direct-labor hours per unit were simply read from the curve. (Without having this curve, calculations for the manpower and output buildup schedules would have been more tedious.) From this curve a table could be determined (the actual values shown were computer calculated) (see Exhibit 18–4).

Sample Calculations for Assembly Output and Labor Schedules

June and July

Direct labor required for the first two units is approximately 1,240 labor hours.
Direct labor available: 4 at 160 hours/month × 2 months = 1,280 labor hours.

August

Direct labor: Add 25 new employees whose efficiency is 70%.

25 × 160 × 0.70 =	2,800	
Already available: 4 × 160	640	3,400 labor hours
Cumulative total labor hours through August		4,720

Output: Comparison of 4,720 with data in column 4 of Exhibit 18–4 shows that the 14th unit would have been produced by the end of August. During August, 14 − 2 = 12 units would have been completed.

Exhibit 18–4. *Table of Cumulative Production and Labor Hour Data*

Cumulative Production	Hours This Unit	Cumulative Average Hours per Unit	Cumulative Total Hours (Column 1 x Column 3)
1	716	716	716
2	516	616	1,232
10	240	371	3,714
12	221	347	4,165
15	198	319	4,780
20	173	285	5,692
40	125	214	8,564
60	103	180	10,806
75	93	163	12,262
100	81	144	14,412
150	67	120	18,054
200	58	106	21,153
250	52	96	23,903
300	48	88	26,402
400	42	77	30,868
500	38	70	34,830
600	35	64	38,431
700	32	60	41,757
800	30	56	44,864
840	29	55	46,055

September

Direct labor:	Add 25 new employees—efficiency 70%	2,800 labor hours
	Already available as of September 1:	
	$29 \times 160 =$	4,640
	Total labor hours expended in September	7,440
	Cumulative total labor hours through	
	August	4,720
	Cumulative total labor hours through	
	September	12,160
Output:	In Exhibit 18–4, comparison of 12,160 with	
	data in column 4 shows that about 73 units	
	would have been produced by the end of	
	September. During September, $73 - 14 = 59$	
	units would have been completed.	

October

Direct labor:	Available as of October 1: $54 \times 160 =$	8,640 labor hours
	Cumulative total expended through	
	September	12,160
	Cumulative total labor hours expended	20,800
	through October	
Output:	In Exhibit 18–4, comparison of 20,800	
	with data in column 4 shows that	
	approximately 193 units would have	
	been produced after expending 20,800	
	labor hours of assembly labor. During	
	the month of October, $193 - 73 = 120$	
	cameras would have been assembled.	

From October through January the output schedule was based on the 8,640 labor hours available each month and the data in Exhibit 18–4.

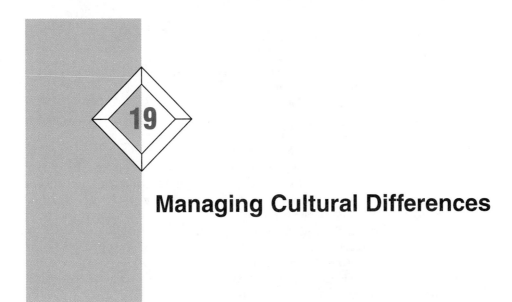

Managing Cultural Differences

19.0 INTRODUCTION

As companies endeavor to expand their business base globally, the need for multinational project management has escalated. This escalation has created enormous strains on our ability to understand and manage cultural differences. For simplicity's sake, cultural differences can be classified into two broad categories:

- *Multinational Cultural Differences:* These include differences that exist across various countries, all working on the same project.
- *Intracountry Cultural Differences:* These include the differences that exist within a single country. The cultural differences result from legislative actions, social groups, class structure, race, religious beliefs, and gender.

Multinational cultural differences are discussed by looking at the cultural impact on each part of project management body of knowledge (PMBOK). Intracountry differences are discussed by looking at the impact of legislation and the removal of apartheid on the management of projects in South Africa.

19.1 AN INTRODUCTION TO GLOBAL PROJECTS[1]

Global projects are those that cross the boundaries between countries. These projects can be staffed with team members from one, two, or more countries. Hence,

---

1. Sections 19.1 through 19.4 were provided by Al Zeitoun, Ph.D., PMP. Dr. Zeitoun is CPO and Vice President Global Project Management Services for the International Institute for Learning; E-mail: alzeitoun@aol.com

those working on such global projects deal with multicultural differences that in some cases can be very great and that can lead to unique issues, issues that can only be seen in these kinds of projects.

Dealing with global projects that involve multinationalities is not as rare as it may have been in the past. The world is becoming a global village where the accessibility to and the reliance upon other nations in business is becoming the norm, one of the ways for our business base to grow. Some projects designed to produce new technologies, for example, could involve manufacturers from five or six countries collaborating with one another in making a new technology work. Events that may impact one part of the global village can quickly impact other parts of the village, endangering a project's ultimate deliverable.

Global projects by their very nature require a higher degree of awareness and sensitivity. What seems acceptable in a local or national project may not be acceptable when boundaries are being crossed. Thus a strong cultural understanding may be the first key to success in building the relationships and the trust that is so fundamental to the success of international endeavors.

It is important to realize that not every individual and/or organization is prepared to manage across the globe. It requires certain skills, political understanding, and superior communication ability to break through the barriers that could hinder a project's chances for success.

19.2 UNIQUENESS AND TRENDS IN GLOBAL PROJECTS

The uniqueness of a global project stems from the fact that there seem to be different "driver" factors in different parts of the world. The globe can be divided into first, second, and third world nations. First world covers the United States, Canada, Australia, New Zealand, Japan, and the advanced nations of Western Europe. Second world covers the countries that have a balance between their needs and resources. Third world covers the countries with the worst economic conditions.

First world countries are driven by the idea of continuous improvement through high technology advancements. Second world countries are driven by the goal of catching up with the first world while still considering their limitations. Third world nations are attempting to build or rebuild their infrastructure so that the necessities of living can become a normal reality. This means that the project management approach used in each of these world sectors can be different, due to the different needs and nature of projects.

Some of the trends that are seen across all world sectors have to do with the growing population, the rising need for education and advanced skills, and the availability of cheap travel and telecommunications. This last trend is making it much easier to work globally, as well as opening the door to global mergers and acquisitions.

One fundamental trend stems from the realization that projects need to be managed in a formal fashion. This is a key to replicating success that is the trademark for maturity in project management. Several bodies of knowledge across the globe are contributing to this formality needed. Several professional organizations, such as the Project Management Institute (PMI) and the International Project Management Association (IPMA), have been taking the lead in giving the profession the respect that is needed. These organizations are also trying to establish formulas that will enable global organizations to support project management growth and project managers' needs.

19.3 CULTURAL CHALLENGES BROKEN DOWN BY KNOWLEDGE AREAS

There are nine knowledge areas in the PMBOK® Guide, covering five process areas of Initiating, Planning, Executing, Controlling, and Closing. These nine areas are Project Integration, Scope, Time, Cost, Procurement, Risk, Quality, Human Resource, and Communications Management. Managing global projects can create challenges in each of these knowledge areas. The following is a discussion of these possible global challenges and some of the recommendations that project managers managing global projects should follow.

Scope/Integration Management

There can be a slow reaction time to necessary scope changes due to slowly changing market conditions. The alternative is, if shortcuts are taken prematurely or too quickly, total project failure due to misunderstandings and faulty perceptions.

Project managers must, in some global projects, coordinate limited resources between government agencies. Developmental plans must be well researched. Lack of historical data can create difficulty in developing a good project plan. Difficulty can also exist in maintaining overall change control because inaccurate performance reports are viewed as saving face and are highly regarded in some cultures.

Scope planning may be impacted by the planners' faulty assumptions other cultures. Scope definition may be impacted if management fails to take the local country's constraints into account, constraints that which may be more limiting than the project's constraints. Different parties to the project may have differing project criteria, especially in their business reasons for performing the project. The project charter may not be detailed enough. The strategic plan and product descriptions may be poor or misunderstood. The feasibility may either be understated or overestimated. Cost-benefit analyses, if performed at all, may not be accurate and are often misunderstood. Differences may exist in accounting practices, which can lead to an inaccurate Work Breakdown Structure linkage to the performing organization's cost control systems.

The project plan may be developed without appropriate research. Language barriers mandate several iterations in finalizing the statement of work. Difficulty exists in gaining agreement and cooperation from diverse and scattered groups. A deficiency in problem-solving skills leads to poor reaction time to problems and elongated schedules. Little history exists and when it does, it is not usually documented in a common language for ease of use.

Organizational policies often reflect national laws that differ from nation to nation. Major time differences make it difficult to manage change requests efficiently, and cultural differences can distort change requests. Frequent status reviews are costly when international travel is required. Organizational procedures at the national level are often in the native language, a problem when they need to be read by the project manager in another nation. Project Management Information Systems are often written/implemented for a single national project. Product descriptions are sometimes prepared in metric system specifications. Not everyone may be on board for a strategic plan that will lead to a global or multinational effort.

Project charters are often crafted in secrecy, which may well cause resentment abroad. Expert judgment can be subjective and will cause many other "so-called" experts to surface in each nation. Many countries do not have a standard 8-hour workday. Multinational deliverables will normally be inspected by a multitude of people, each with different backgrounds and different exposure to the project. The language of the documentation may be prepared based upon culture and dialect.

Scope management is primarily concerned with defining and controlling what is or is not included in the project. Difficulties can occur when:

- The host does not agree with the project management methodology.
- There are language and educational issues.
- There are communication barriers.
- There are unrealistic objectives.

Historical data could be limited based on the extent of the prior usage of project management techniques in conducting business. The documents created in project plan development will be limited by the country's legal system and by the cultural acceptance of such documents. When staff in two different countries exchange information and collaborate on documents, both countries must communicate and assume the same constraints and outputs.

Consideration of assumptions based on cultural differences and interpretation will be imperative for knowledgeable documentation. Organizational policies need to be addressed concerning multiple country cultures and business practices. Scope change methodology documentation is imperative for basic understanding of all parties involved. The project manager's control or authority will need to be defined based on cultural differences.

The scope statement will need to be defined in terminology understandable by all parties involved when dealing internationally. Initiation of the project requires the commitment by all performing organizations. This commitment will be defined differently within various countries. The documents prepared prior to the contract will have different definitions based on each country's legal and cultural foundations.

Timing of the planning process is proportional to both the overall importance of the project and to the urgency status each country accords it. Tools and techniques used will be based on the education levels of the people involved with the project and the country's overall standards for education. The requirements for a college degree can vary from country to country. Previous data from successful projects is usually not available.

It is difficult to reach complete understanding between all participants about the planning, execution, and change control of the project; who makes which decision is often not clearly known. Cultural/social differences may adversely affect the scope of a project. Thorough investigation and analysis of the project and host country should be conducted prior to project commencement.

Time Management   Timelines may need to be extended. Planning, communication, and education must be a well-defined, deliberate process. Nothing can be assumed. Activity sequencing may be affected by late arrival of required goods and services due to a poor infrastructure. Local customs, holidays, religious beliefs, vacation days, and so on, may affect activity duration estimates.

Schedule control may be affected by inadequate performance reports due to a given local culture's disregard for time. Unrealistic schedules exist because local time planning tools are inaccurate or obsolete. Technology might not be available for familiar planning software. Culture differences exist in views on time (i.e., urgency). The words "long term" can have very different meanings in different cultures.

Inaccurate product descriptions lead to underestimating project requirements. Laws and regulations can differ and will most certainly change timelines. Language differences can cause requests for changes to be misunderstood, which can eventually lead to scope creep.

Time is not viewed as being that critical an issue in many cultures. First world project managers are often seen as being preoccupied with time. The ultimate project objective in several countries is more important than the duration spent on the project. Missed milestones and targets are not considered a major problem. As an example, the time it takes to build a new hospital in a Middle Eastern country is not as important as the fact that the hospital will eventually be completed.

Only a few multinational project templates exist. In most cultures, the distinction line between mandatory and discretionary dependencies may vary between nations and cultures. Roles and jobs may be different. Resource pools and the quality of the resources can vary greatly from nation to nation. Calendars are very different throughout the world in regards to holidays, vacations, and so on. There are considerable differences in how work is performed and when. Some cultures are used to waiting until the last minute to complete or execute a task.

Time management includes the processes required to ensure timely completion of the project. Project managers must:

- Realize that the perspective of time can differ from country to country
- Set schedules and completion dates based on the country's perspective of time
- Be aware of the *actual* time differences when scheduling meetings and deadlines

Documentation and understanding of specific employment laws and cultural restrictions will need to be assessed and integrated into the schedule. Activity definitions involving different languages and cultures may restrict the deliverables if they are not clear to both parties. Project compression may be limited to specific areas of the project based on the level of urgency and the team members' capabilities to assess and correct the time or monetary restrictions of the project. The project manager may need to "filter" estimations he receives in areas of time and costs, along with the qualifications of the team members, based on the different countries varying interpretations of each.

Cost Management

The skill levels of employees, quality of materials, and different equipment may impact resource planning. Cost estimating may be affected by currency conversion. Cost control may be made even more difficult by unstable government economies and high inflation rates.

Inaccuracies throughout certain systems make planning difficult. Estimations cost variance might be inaccurate, therefore causing overruns. Differing accounting systems will make costing and reconciling inaccurate. Policies of the client organization might change the labor forecasts and the Work Breakdown Structure.

Efficiency versus effectiveness may take on a new meaning. Labor is in great abundance in some countries, and the requirement of simply employing people can be more important than money, materials, and equipment in such cases. Status and stability may be more important to workers in some cultures than optimizing cost and maximizing profit. The goals we think of as common—optimizing revenue, minimizing cost, and maximizing profit—may be unfamiliar in international project management, and they could be replaced with status, stability, consensus, and so on.

The value system among various countries is also highly diverse. The volatility of a country's economic conditions will skew the budgets on long-term projects. Estimating has different meanings in various languages. Resource planning can be difficult based on the customs and cultures of the country where the project is being executed. Resource requirements can be complicated to predict based on the economic volatility of a country. In addition, the need to budget multiple currencies poses its own challenges, as does the variability in exchange rates. Monitoring of the budget requires a very accurate and attentive project manager.

Evaluation of the stability of the company conducting the project and the company paying for the project will need to be addressed for payment support. Cost control monitoring for variances and predicted changes is continual and may become overburdening. Time issues will affect the cost overruns in countries that do not have specified project completion time specifications.

All areas related to cost or value must be fully understood by the project manager. The host country may not share the same concerns. An aggressive project manager, too concerned about cost, may offend the host country, again jeopardizing both current and future projects.

| **Procurement Management** | Poor local infrastructure may lead to delayed and damaged goods. Quality of the goods may be unknown. Negotiating contracts must be done as per local customs. Legal enforcement of a contract may be severely limited. |

A major concern of a project is the country's infrastructure. One country may have an excellent infrastructure while its neighbors have an inadequate one. In Malaysia and Singapore, the infrastructure is excellent. Both countries have excellent ports, modern equipment for cargo loading, modern warehousing, excellent roads, good communication systems, good rail and air transportation systems, and so on. China, on the other hand, is lacking in these systems. In China, only a few of the ports are adequate. Ninety-five percent of the warehouses in China are government-owned. The warehouses are single-story block buildings. Products are not handled on skids but manually, and the products are stored directly on the floor. Flood damage to cargo is frequent.

In China, the roads are poor as well. Truck transportation is accomplished by two drivers using a stake bed truck. The drivers work 16 hours a day, averaging 23 miles an hour. The cargo, covered only with a tarp, is easily damaged. The air cargo system in China is inadequate for the needs of the country. The rail system is poor and has the additional constraint that during the harvest season, nothing moves on the trains but food goods. Products ordered at the wrong time might wait for three months to be shipped by rail.

In addition, the populations of Malaysia and Singapore are highly educated and are a skilled work force. The general population of China is not.

The phrase, "Think globally and act locally," is most appropriate in international project management. The expectations of customers are different in each country. An Arab, for example, will expect a gift lavish enough to enhance his status, but will also expect that the proposal will include the cost of the gift. In Malaysia, on the other hand, only a small token gift is expected. The gift is not to be expensive and will be welcomed even more if it is handmade. And in Brazil some government officials can still expect to receive bribes.

Specific to the project, in France the project manager had better be French. If the project language is English, it is important to work closely with the Germans and Italians. If left to themselves, they may translate the work instructions incorrectly. In Japan, additional training will be needed because the training will start with the top of the hierarchy and be inadequately passed down to the employees who do the work, requiring subsequent training. As project managers in a global environment, it is crucial that we bring our skills in project management with us, but we must also know the way to implement them that acknowledges and honors the host country's culture.

If there are inaccurate scope statements, needed resources may not be procured. Cultural differences must be understood during contract negotiations. Lack of accurate cost data will cause indecisiveness in make-or-buy decisions. Language will cause problems in developing accurate Statements of Work. Proposals might not be accurate with regard to technical expertise.

Limited contractor availability may restrict quality and timeliness of deliverables. Thorough understanding of the host's contracting procedures is mandatory. Leasing versus buying can have specialized tax issues within each country. Availability and supportability by vendors is a major concern in each country.

The word "often" varies in meaning between countries. There do not always exist black and white decisions because some cultures base their decision on such factors as the relationships with the salesman's family. Economic considerations and other regulations impact the procurement process in many countries. Examples include:

- The government of certain countries determines what will be produced and when.
- The project manager may be required to use local and limited resources.
- Contracts are awarded, in some cultures, on the basis of business relationships, gratuities, or kickbacks.
- Use of resources may have to be coordinated between various government agencies.
- Variations in the exchange rates can impact salaries and payments.

Procurement planning can be restricted by availability of resources and not by project requirements. Solicitation of resources will be restricted by culture in some countries' versus project need in others. Customers will affect the solicitation process with regards to bidding and quotations.

Source selection will be limited by cultural factors, not just by potential sellers. Contracts for procurement do not have legal ramifications in some countries. Buyer and seller rights are not necessarily a legal determinant in some countries. Cost overruns will be factored by cultural norms. Buyer-seller relationships are determined by a country's customs and policies. Legal differences will be a factor for closure of contracts among foreign countries.

Risk Management   Mixed perceptions may occur, especially in risk management. First world project managers are often seen as the "experts," with many tools and resources available to solve a problem. Inability to solve the problem may be seen as ineptness or withholding of information. Distrust and suspicion may occur. Differences will exist in what represents an acceptable risk level. Inaccurate descriptions and understanding will cloud the true risk that exists. Insurance might not be available or may be prohibitively expensive. Contractual agreements might not be enforceable, depending on legal systems.

Any predictions of external risks (weather, labor strikes, civil unrest, economic instability, etc.) can be inaccurate, and this is a huge area of concern when failure is not an option. There may be no second chance to succeed or repair the damage. Project risks may include:

- Travel constraints due to the country's infrastructure
- Labor strikes affecting the deliverables
- Extensive expected holidays
- Government intervention
- Changes in monetary policy and exchange rates

Risk determination is based more upon cultural factors than on quantitative data. Economics becomes a risk factor in some countries. The way in which a project manager responds to risk will be a reflection of his or her background and personal culture, and it may not be the best way on foreign projects. Quantification of risk will be affected by the country's policies. Predicting risk is volatile in some countries. Sources of risk vary by project but also by a country's policies and economic factors.

Expert judgment of risk may be contrary to the project manager's instincts when dealing with foreign projects. Monitoring factors that will affect the risk of a project could become constraints for time and cost. Planning for risk is contingent on the country's stability.

Quality Management

Skill levels of the local workers may not be adequate in some parts of the world, but the local government may mandate that they be used. Local building codes are different. Disasterous accidents, sometimes with large numbers of fatalities, are more likely to occur in some world regions, due to poor quality regulations. Local cultures may have limited measurement and inspection tools, and the methods of measurement used may not coincide with the desired standards. Different views on the definition of quality might or might not be the prevailing attitude: "Close is good enough" in some cultures. Benchmarking standards could differ.

Testing techniques can vary, causing differences in acceptable product variations. Measurements may not be precise or accurate. Operation steps can be defined differently. Certain countries are deficient in knowledge and practice of modern quality techniques and testing procedures. Lack of common language will often affect quality.

Possible deficiency exists in the ability to resolve quality issues. Often international quality policies are hard to agree upon. Regulations can vary internationally. Quality management difficulties can occur when:

- Countries have different standards for the definition of quality.
- Governments intervene.
- There are no established quality policies.

- Focus is more on cost than on quality.
- No formalized chain of command exists for the correction of quality problems.

When dealing with issues of quality control, the customs of the country may determine the standards for the project. Evaluation of quality may be difficult for a foreign project manager. Satisfying quality standards will be determined by cultural restraints. Understanding the customer's quality requirements will be awkward for a foreign project manager.

Monitoring the quality levels of the project will need to be based on the cultural foundation of the country. Addressing issues of unsatisfactory quality while dealing with cultural restrictions will be a challenge for the project manager. Encouraging foreign workers to employ quality control can be complicated in certain countries.

Customer satisfaction is relevant to each country's disciplines. Quality planning will be difficult at best for a foreign project manager. A successful project manager will understand the value of quality in the host country and adjust his/her approach accordingly. Too much emphasis on quality in a host country that does not share the same concern may be detrimental to the project's success. The project manager must fully understand the host country's methods of measuring quality.

Human Resource Management

The most important criteria for achieving success in international project management are well-developed people skills and a willingness to understand cultural diversity. A project manager needs to view manpower as one of the most valuable resources. Project managers need to understand and respect social and cultural values. They also need to understand the political climate that is inherent to the country they are dealing with, whether socialist or capitalist, and the government's role in private enterprise.

Rates of economic and cultural development vary greatly. There may be a very low standard of living. The culture may be agriculturally based rather than technology based. This may impact the quality or skill level of available resources. There may be a vast difference in educational levels and experience with automated processes.

World events and political uprisings may have an impact on an employee's views, especially if the views are based upon limited knowledge. Laws may be much more stringent in one country, with harsh penalties. What is accepted in one society may be taboo in another.

Environmental health and safety policies between countries may be different. Cultural differences exist in attitudes toward women and expected attire. Educational differences and level of cultural sophistication vary between countries. Not all college degrees are equal. Some countries are very informal and some management techniques, such as concurrent engineering, TQM, risk management, and change management, may be unknown concepts to some cultures.

There may be a difference in the importance of work to different cultures. Work may be just one facet in the life of a Brazilian and is well balanced with family time. A Japanese person lives and sometimes dies for his/her work. The Japanese employee expects to stay with a company for life, whereas Americans may jump from job to job.

Project management between cultures needs to take into account several nuances, some which are subtle and may be missed by a project manager, and some that are very evident. Some examples:

- Different work patterns—some cultures choose to arrive early and work through lunches in order to get the job done. Others will arrive late and take time for afternoon tea or a siesta.
- Type "A" personalities working with more laid-back personalities (for example, Japanese are very punctual; Brazilians are known for being late).
- Gestures that have different meanings—The American "A-OK" sign is highly offensive to the Brazilians.
- Differences in diet may be offensive to other cultures (for example, Brazil's Veijouda contains pork and beef, which would be offensive to Jewish or Indian cultures).
- Holiday observances may be many and rigorously observed, affecting some timeframes for project planning.
- Differences in negotiation patterns—Japanese and Americans want to get right down to business, whereas Brazilians must have a social process first, then will do business only if they like you.
- Management styles differ across cultures: autocratic versus democratic, micromanagement versus employee empowerment.

Logistical costs and difficulties can be incurred in bringing in team members from other countries, such as: the distance away from the rest of the family and familiar support systems, difficulty in duplicating the quality of home conditions, schools, and so on, in another country.

International project management covers a realm of variables, all of which are important in order to achieve success of the project. Failure to address any of the given areas can result in failure or serious delay and cost overruns. True skill levels of local labor may be unknown. Top-down management hierarchy may interfere with matrix planning. Managers may not understand their roles and responsibilities. Actions by some project managers may be in violation of workers' cultural and social norms.

Some project managers may have a misunderstanding of workers' reactions to managerial actions. The host's national workforce may be unwilling to accept the differences between the cultural and social background of the global project manager and themselves.

The project manager's definition of the client as only those who are at the host national workforce decision-making summit may be incorrect. Reluctance of project managers and engineers to accept manpower as a resource that is equally as important as, if not more important than, money, materials, time, and equipment can be offensive to the host country.

Lack of training for managers deployed in the areas of transcultural management and intercultural communications can create severe problems. There may exist an overly simplistic view of the variables affecting workforce attitude and feelings. The informal lifestyle of some cultures may conflict with structured management principles. Hierarchy and class structure is very important in many cultures. Multiple-boss reporting conflicts with cultures in many countries. Reputation is important. Command, control, and decision-making are more individualistic, and there are often fewer committees.

Fewer unions exist. Most workers stay with the same company for longer periods of time. Attitude is as important as availability and skill. Human resource practices are hard to standardize upon globally. Organizational charts are often very controversial within a multinational project when the bulk of management is based in one country. The project manager has even less control with the line managers.

Recruitment is difficult when it is centralized and has to be executed in more than one country. Rewards can be difficult when the project manager has even less involvement internationally. Colocation is not always possible in international projects.

Project managers must understand the cultural framework of the country, understand the validity of perceptions and feelings as data, and understand the typical management structure of the country. Staffing becomes an issue in countries where nepotism and customers rule the hiring practices of a company. Matrix organizational structures will not be applicable in many countries.

Team concepts are not priorities, or even developed, in some countries. Communication between team members will become awkward when language barriers are present. Employment regulations and laws vary between countries and may be a hindrance to project completion. Education levels of project team members will need to be closely evaluated in countries where team members are assigned based on cultural restrictions. A project manager's authority is based on customers and cultural restrictions. Time and cost for developing a productive team could be a major factor in reaching the project's completion. The successful project manager will select a cross-functional project team comprised of members from both the host country and his firm. Adequate training and education of the team regarding the project and the host country is vital to a successful project.

There are always differences of general business practices between countries, and they are often not well understood. The issues surrounding the relocation of the project managers and their families are more important in some countries than in others. Cultural differences affecting the project manager and his family can vary.

The difference in value systems between the project manager's country and the host country can strain relationships. The project manager can easily underestimate the importance of the workers' attitudes and feelings relating to the project. The lack of training in transcultural management and intercultural communications will affect performance.

Communications Management

Communications management provides the critical link among people, ideas, and information that is necessary for success. Protocol at customer interchange meetings may vary greatly. Members of some cultures tend to be very class or level sensitive, and will take it as a personal affront if a foreign project manager tries to circumvent the established system. Protocol will also impact the level of communication between upper and lower level workers and the resources needed to solve problems. Communications planning may be impacted by technological constraints.

Staff may not accurately be able to translate information into the standard "project language." Culture will dictate whether communications are formal or informal. In addition to the obvious language barriers existing between nations, communication technology might not be adequate for project needs. Time zone differences between the home company, project team, and client could cause communication delays. Archiving of past information might lead to loss of previous successes. Reporting difficulties and scope creep could cause differences in closure and deliverables.

There will be numerous communication challenges in the pursuit of projects in the international arena. This should not keep your company from pursuing these opportunities, but should caution you to step slowly. A typical first world executive will arrive with his/her accountants and lawyers to set up a deal. The executive will want to sit down and go over the fine print and then sign a contract that will hold both parties to their obligations. He/she will want to review, sign and notarize the deal and then leave. His/her agenda is all business. The problem arises because he thinks this contract is ironclad and will protect both parties, say in a Chinese court of law. The Chinese will want to socialize and entertain the executive, not just get down to business. This will frustrate the executive because he wants to just get the business deal done and not party. He has missed the point entirely. The Chinese court system is not nearly as organized or as powerful as the U.S. system. Even with a signed contract, there is no real protection against default or problems. The Chinese expect to have a personal relationship with their business partners. They must trust you to do business with you. If the entertaining is bypassed, they do not have a forum to evaluate the executive and establish a relationship. Only when a relationship is established can a deal can be forged out. Differences like these must be understood, evaluated, and planned for in order to do business in the international marketplace. We cannot demand that projects be done the same way as they occur in our countries.

Identification of reliable sources of information may be difficult; in fact, they may not exist. Lack of coordination between governing bodies and deficiencies in proper infrastructure can cause delays and misinformation. Language barriers will occur, even as an excuse not to perform work. Lack of common language creates more work. Some of the major communication difficulties can arise when:

- There are language and educational differences.
- There is not a clear understanding of the rules of the culture's speech etiquette.
- There is a lack of trust.
- There is a misinterpretation of body language.

Language differences will be a major obstacle among team members and with the customer.

Communication to stakeholders will be delivered at different levels and times, based on a country's culture. Distribution of information among team members, customer, and other company personnel will be based on the country's customs. When communicating between languages, delivery of information is done in the recipient's language. Translation can be costly and time consuming.

The choice of communication media will be determined by the cultural requirements of the country. Presentation body language varies between countries and will need to be addressed by the project manager for effective team communications. Meetings have cultural interpretations. Project record keeping may need to be documented in more than one language, making for a costly project factor.

19.4 THE PROJECT MANAGER'S CHECKLIST FOR GLOBAL PROJECTS

To conclude, here are some key elements for the project managers' checklist as they prepare for their global assignments:

- Recognize the differences between the first, second, and third worlds.
- Get help from the various project management professional organizations in regards to the acceptable practices in the management of projects in certain countries.
- Use the bodies of knowledge to provide the common language that is needed to break some of the project barriers.
- Watch for the assumptions that are made based on cultural differences.
- Be careful about the cultural differences in viewing time and urgency.
- Notice the impact of unstable governmental economies and high inflation rates on cost control possibility.
- Study the infrastructure of the country to avoid logistical surprises.
- Agree on what represents an acceptable risk level.
- Be ready with well-developed people skills and willingness to understand cultural diversity.
- Know that you must be trusted to do business across the world countries, so give the host the forum needed to establish this trust relationship.

19.5 MANAGING DURING POLITICAL, SOCIAL, AND ECONOMIC REFORM[2]

Managing projects within the uncertainties of time, cost, and quality creates havoc for even the most experienced project managers. But what happens if, at

---

2. The remainder of the chapter has been contributed by Dr. Lionel J. Smalley. Dr. Smalley is the Director, The School of Project Management, P.O. Box 28142, Sunnyside, 0132, South Africa. Web site address: http://www.spm.co.za

the same time, the country is going through political reform, social reform, economic uncertainties, and a host of legislative changes, all of which require a new way of managing projects? Such was the situation in South Africa with the elimination of apartheid. Social classes were changing. New legislative policies were designed to create employment opportunities for the many rather than the few. A culture that had existed for decades was being torn down. And yet projects still had to be completed within time, cost, and quality constraints.

19.6 AN INTRODUCTION TO PROJECT MANAGEMENT IN SOUTH AFRICA

Project management first gained prominence in South Africa within the building and construction industries, followed closely by the professional practices such as engineering, architecture, and quantity surveying. As the new millennium begins, many other industries are taking a serious look at the advantages of implementing project management principles and techniques. These new industries include marketing, utilities, telecommunications, banking, health care, manufacturing, information technology (IT), and leisure. Their interest in project management is in response to the ever-increasing competition in the marketplace and the desire for high-quality products and/or services that may provide import and export potential.

Management philosophies such as "diversity management," "change management," "performance management," and "reengineering management" are still on the increase in usage. Many organizations and companies are spending vast sums of money on implementing these philosophies. Although some of these concepts may merit these expenses, most organizations might be better off incurring the expense of implementing an effective corporate project management philosophy. The remainder of this chapter focuses on the current status of project management in South Africa within non–project-driven organizations and companies. These companies are either product-driven and/or service-driven, and this is where the greatest changes are appearing. The remaining sections also address those internal factors likely to push project management to successful implementation, as well as those external factors likely to impede successful implementation. In typical project-driven organizations and companies, project management is well established and on par with the management of similar projects in developed countries.

19.7 INTERNAL FACTORS AFFECTING PROJECT MANAGEMENT

Many product- and service-driven organizations and companies still regard project management as merely another form of functional management equal to marketing, finance, and human resource management. It is a common belief that project management addresses mainly planning and scheduling. Aspects such as effective communications, negotiations, finance, strategy formulation and implementation, conflict resolution methodologies, and decision-making are still regarded as being general management responsibilities having nothing to do with project management. This approach will definitely restrict the successful implementation of project management in the next decade.

Another critical aspect is the fact that in many organizations and companies there is no project sponsor in place. In addition, the roles of project champion and project sponsor are often misinterpreted. Many senior managers believe that their role is mainly in the area of strategic and scenario planning, and they do not get directly involved with the management of projects.

It is a common belief that many senior managers, usually above the level of general manager, feel this way primarily due to the formal business education they received at our traditional business schools. A typical expression from MBA graduates might be: "I know all about project management; it's merely a little bit of planning coupled with activity scheduling. I did this as part of my MBA degree, part of operations management." In fact, very few locally offered MBA programs contain any modules dealing exclusively with project management. In the United States and other developed countries there are complete MBA degree programs specializing in project management. In the United Kingdom there are two MBA degree programs specializing in project management. In the post-apartheid South Africa there are none, but this situation will soon change.

Another aspect worth mentioning is the existing human resource element in our organizations and companies. South Africa has a wealth of "people talent" that has to be developed to its full potential. Formal project management training in this regard is vital. The problem is that too few large organizations and companies provide effective training programs. One of the few who are providing effective project management training is Eskom, a large, well-managed utility company.

Eskom has adopted and implemented a culture of learning for their employees. This is based on a value-added policy. The employees are offered the opportunity of attending formal project management training programs and then applying their newly acquired knowledge within their respective cost or profit centers.

Problems encountered on projects are mainly due to ineffective cross-cultural communication resulting from individuals and groups having different perceptions, attitudes, and value/belief systems. Words mean different things to different racial groups. Many times, a colleague might interpret a remark made in jest as an offensive statement. It is vital that we understand, respect, and learn from each other's cultures.

Often, whenever activities on projects are late, it is due to something known as "African time," a common perception that it is quite acceptable to do tomorrow what can be easily done today. Although this may not really be the case, the perception can be damaging in terms of maintaining good race relations in the workplace.

South African project managers and team members, however, have one thing going for them–they have a natural ability to "duck and dive," or take calculated risks in order to complete the project within time, cost, and performance constraints. Amazingly, many project managers successfully complete their projects with the minimal use of formal project planning documentation and scheduling data.

Project managers in South Africa appear to rely too heavily on their immediate superiors for authorization to complete specified activities. In fact, many project managers in South Africa are appointed solely for their knowledge of computerized scheduling packages. A more appropriate focus would be on decision-making packages, leaving the scheduling activities to the team members who may be more qualified in playing "what-if" games.

19.8 EXTERNAL FACTORS AFFECTING PROJECT MANAGEMENT

Since the South African general elections in April 1994, South Africa has gone through tremendous transformational changes, some of which are regarded by the private sector as being essential for job and wealth creation, whereas other changes are regarded as unnecessary and relatively nonproductive. These changes must be seen in the context of organizational competitiveness in the marketplace and their influence on the management of existing and future projects. The changes referred to can be found in the following three areas:

- Legislated affirmative action in the workplace
- Creation of the Southern African Development Community (SADC)
- Impact on the South African suppliers and contractors

Legislated Affirmative Action in the Workplace

In order to overcome the imbalances of the past due to apartheid, soon after the April 1994 general elections, the newly elected government introduced affirmative action legislation, the purpose of which was to empower the previously disadvantaged community in both the public and private sectors. The latest act in this regard was the Employment Equity Bill (Act 55) legislated on October 12, 1998.[3] Its main purpose was to eliminate unfair discrimination in the workplace and to ensure that equity is implemented to redress the effects of racial discrimination. This caused a major change in the way projects were managed. It was felt that, since the 1994 general election, the implementation of affirmative action, especially in the private sector, had been far too slow. Hence, there existed the need for firmer measures.

---

3. Juta's Statutes Editors. *Employment Equity Act 55 of 1988.* Cape Town: Juta & Co., Ltd., 1999.

The intention of the Act was to make the workforce broadly representative of the demographics of the population in South Africa. This implies that approximately 70 percent of the workforce must be comprised of designated groups. These include black, female, and disabled employees. There is also the possibility that management and executive levels will have to include these groups on all future project teams. Hence, there exists a tremendous need for rapid development of these groups through effective project management training programs.

Designated employers are those organizations and companies employing 50 (or more) employees. A survey undertaken in 1997 by the Central Statistical Service indicates that there are at least 10,000 companies and organizations that can be regarded as designated employers. Also, it will be illegal for any company having more than 50 employees to divide itself into two separate smaller companies, each having less than 50 employees, in order to get around the Act.

The Act stipulates that within 18 months after its commencement designated employers must forward affirmative action plans to the Department of Labor for approval. These plans are aimed at uplifting the designated groups employed by organizations and companies. The time frame allowed for these plans should not exceed five years. During this period, designated employers must clearly show how they intend reaching the prescribed affirmative action quotas.

Those employers of less than 50 employees must also submit similar plans should their annual turnover either be equal to, or more than, the applicable turnover of a small business in terms of Section 4 of the Act. This amounts to an annual gross turnover of R10 million (or $1.67 million) for small manufacturing, utility, transport, storage, communication, and finance companies. For retail and motor trade services this equals R15 million (or $2.5 million), and R5 million (or $0.83 million) for construction companies.

In addition, the question of disproportionate income differentials has to be addressed. The Act makes provision for this by forcing designated employers to reduce the remuneration packages paid to senior management and executives should the difference between their packages and those of the general workers be more than a specified percentage. One solution might be that the difference in the packages would then be equally spread among the workers.

Although most organizations and companies have welcomed this legislation, there are some that feel that this will prove to be disruptive to their expansion plans and unproductive in terms of profits and return on equity for their stockholders.

Failure to comply with the conditions laid down by the Act will result in fines (or penalties) ranging from R500,000 (or $83K) for a first offense to R900,000 (or $150K) for four contravention's within a three-year period.

Affirmative action is definitely justified and warranted. Some companies believe that it should, however, be implemented purely on a merit basis rather than on a quota basis as called for by the terms of the legislation. Employing a person who is unqualified and inexperienced merely because he or she is of the "right" background may be doing both the project and the individual an injustice, unless the organization is committed to quality project management training for these individuals.

Often, a particular candidate for a post may have the necessary academic qualifications while lacking adequate on-the-job training and experience. In this case it makes more sense to allow this person time to gain the experience, attend approved training programs, and then be promoted to a more senior position if the situation warrants this.

Despite the obvious benefits of the Act, this could easily have negative consequences for medium-sized and small companies. These companies could easily have difficulty meeting the required quotas while still remaining competitive in the marketplace. This may also force them to shelve expansion plans, limit their new product development projects, and severely restrict their present and future cash flow. Some small operations may have to relocate to neighboring countries, such as Botswana or Swaziland, just to stay in business.

To illustrate this, consider a small manufacturing company situated outside Pretoria. The company employs approximately 70 employees plus 4 executives and produces high-precision parts for the automotive industry. The company has been in local operation for the past 20 years.

Due to the nature of its business the firm has had to rely on importing specialized staff from Germany. For the less specialized work, use is made of local employees. In compliance with the terms of the Act, this company will most definitely be one of the "designated companies" and be forced to comply with the quota system.

The question remains as to whether the company would still be able to remain competitive in the marketplace while satisfying the required quotas. The answer forwarded by the Managing Director was negative, not without some sort of restructuring, and possibly downsizing. And since this is illegal in terms of the Act, the only viable solution is to relocate to a neighboring state, keeping a small depot open in South Africa. This, of course, will most definitely result in a loss of existing jobs. The company also will not be able to divide itself into two smaller companies, each having less than 50 employees.

This Act will also affect the possible inflow of foreign investment into South Africa. Organizations and companies situated abroad, with a desire to invest locally, will not take too kindly to being told how to manage their South African operations. The focus of any investment is always the return on investment. To maximize this, foreign companies would surely wish to employ their own management teams and, in turn, pay them whatever the position merited. A quota system will not be looked upon favorably.

The Southern African Development Community (SADC)

The Declaration and Treaty for Southern African Development establishing the SADC was signed in Windhoek, Namibia, during August 1992. The primary objective was to achieve economic development and growth and in so doing promote self-reliance and interdependence between the 13 member states. These included South Africa, Mozambique, Namibia, Angola, Zimbabwe, Zambia, Tanzania, Mauritius, Botswana, Lesotho, Malawi, Swaziland, and the Democratic Republic of the Congo. South Africa was included as a full member in 1994, followed by Mauritius in 1995 and the Democratic Republic of the Congo in 1997.

The South African government announced, during October 1999, that the tariff protection currently in place between South Africa and its SADC trading partners would, over time, be phased out. This has interesting ramifications for designated organizations and companies forced to implement the Employment Equity Bill.

This could lead to partial disinvestment from South Africa and reinvestment in one of the other SADC countries. For example, a company operating in Pretoria may decide to close down its current operations, restrict any new development projects, maintain only a small regional office in Pretoria for distribution purposes, and relocate its main business or core competency to, say, Botswana or Swaziland, where fewer restrictions exist.

This would have the benefit, for the company, of decreased labor expenses and lower corporate and personal tax rates, coupled with the newly proposed gradual decrease in import tariffs, and with ease of getting the products and/or services back into the South African marketplace. From a South African perspective, this may result in increased job losses and lost tax revenue.

To illustrate just how attractive this relocation option is, consider the following example. Kelvinator is a large U.S. owned South African appliance manufacturer based in Johannesburg and employing approximately 900 workers. The company has been in operation in South Africa for approximately 30 years. However, a few years ago their position in the market place started eroding, primarily due to increased competition coupled with higher labor and material costs. During September 1999 the company was placed under liquidation.[4] They had lost R150 million ($25 million) coupled with a large slice of market share.

Their main competitor, Fridge Master, a Swaziland based appliance manufacturing company, presently occupies 50 percent of the refrigerator (icebox) market, compared with the 15 percent occupied by Kelvinator. Fridge Master had, over the past few years, been able to flood the local market with a wide range of very competitive and reliable products. They had not been faced with increasing labor and material costs similar to those of their South African competitors. In fact, their labor costs were only 25 percent of those in South Africa.

Even with the existing import tariffs in place, they had been able to offer their customers a reduced price, better than their local rivals had. Imagine how much easier this is going to be for companies such as Fridge Master when the import tariffs are eventually phased out.

As of December 1999, Kelvinator had been bought by Defy, another large South African appliance manufacturing company. This new company will have the remaining 50 percent of the refrigerator (icebox) market. In the process, 650 workers will be retrenched. In time, Defy too might feel the effect of the phased out import tariffs.

South African Suppliers and Contractors

Many South African projects are affected by poorly appointed and/or trained project managers, inadequate planning documentation, lack of sponsorship, and clients who continually seem to change the scope of work with complete disregard for the

---

4. *Business Report*, Monday, December 6, 1999, p.4.

schedule and budget. Projects are also influenced by suppliers and contractors who, often through no fault of their own, fail to deliver on time, deliver on time but to the incorrect physical address, or deliver faulty products. In many instances, there is no delivery at all even though a signed contract exists. There are many reasons why this is occurring, and equally as many suggestions on how to rectify the problem. However, it is a little more complicated than most people believe.

Since the 1994 general elections, newly formed empowerment groups replaced many regular suppliers and contractors to the larger organizations and companies in both the private and public sectors. Some of these groups were relatively new to the business. A senior executive of one large parastatal organization[5] commented that his firm had been instructed to appoint only newly formed empowerment suppliers and contractors. This, however, was not the major problem.

The issue revolves around whether or not the new suppliers can deliver on time and according to the required specifications. The project manager of this parastatal was of the impression that they could not satisfy these requirements, primarily due to the lack of experience and training. He felt that this could easily be rectified over time. However, this posed the following questions: Who will pay for the required training and can the country afford to let these contractors gain the necessary on-the-job experience at the expense of the current projects and possible future projects?

Many suppliers and contractors win tenders and merely subcontract to those companies previously appointed to get the project completed. This is not the way the game should be played. This approach will not solve the problem.

There are cases where the appointed suppliers and contractors are experienced and well trained but still fail to deliver. In this case, it is often due to the increasing crime wave in South Africa. Vehicles are hijacked, and armed robberies take place almost daily, resulting in employees being either injured or killed. Often, products are stolen directly from the premises. This is today referred to as "shrinkage." One large retail store recently announced that for the period June 1998–1999 it had experienced R100 million ($16.7 million) shrinkage. This practice appears to be on the increase rather than the decrease.

To illustrate the effect of bureaucratic bungling and supplier inefficiency, consider the following example:[6] The local education authorities in several provinces had not yet received the required textbooks for the students[7] for grades three to seven, required for the next academic year. This academic year would commence in January 2000. Appointed suppliers to the provincial education authorities had scheduled the textbooks for delivery during the period from October to November 1999. It is interesting to note that some of the newly appointed suppliers had never before been involved with the distribution of study material. In addition, some suppliers did not have sufficient cash flow to efficiently carry out their tasks.

---

5. Parastatal organizations are essentially public companies having the SA government as their only shareholder. Examples include Eskom, Telkom, and so on.

6. *Saturday Star,* December 11, 1999, pp. 1–2.

7. In South Africa, students are referred to as learners.

From the supplier's perspective, in many cases the main reason for the delay was that the orders for the textbooks placed by the local education authorities had been received too late for the necessary processing and delivery. Another complaint was that no delivery could be made without prompt payment.

Another example of bureaucratic bungling and contractor dissatisfaction was illustrated in a local newspaper story[8] concerning the construction of a large casino valued at R890 million ($148.33 million). The winner of the tender, a prominent contractor, intended to construct this casino at Umdloti, a site just north of Durban. Work was scheduled to continue throughout the traditional builder's holiday from mid December 1999 to mid January 2000. However, due to the failure by the local politicians to pass the long delayed Gambling Amendment Bill, construction could not continue and as a result approximately 200 workers will lose their jobs. The project is already one year behind schedule. Events like this are totally unnecessary and must be reduced or eliminated in the future if South Africa is to advance economically.

There is a light at the end of the tunnel. Hopefully, with more and more companies accepting the philosophy of project management, the major improvements everyone expects will become reality over the next decade. The critical issue is how quickly these South African companies will recognize the benefits of project management and see that effective project management practices will make them more competitive.

PROBLEMS

19–1 The successful implementation of project management requires overcoming several difficulties and problems. For each of the items listed below, state whether overcoming the obstacles would be easier for U.S. corporations, or developing countries, assuming both are interested in implementing project management:

a. Good forward-planning capability
b. Understanding the importance of project management
c. Availability of computers
d. Understanding of project management principles by remote-site personnel and subcontractors
e. Ability to update status as events are completed
f. Understanding the reasons for the need of trade-offs
g. Centralization of decision making
h. Short-term resource control
i. Ability to assimilate large amounts of data
j. Variety and frequency of political changes
k. Variety and frequency of economic changes
l. Governmental supporting-policy measures
m. Inadequacies of subcontractors
n. Lack of accurate information

8. *Sunday Tribune*, December 12, 1999, p. 3.

20

Strategic Planning for Excellence in Project Management

20.0 INTRODUCTION

Strategic planning for excellence in project management needs to consider all aspects of the company: from the working relationships among employees and managers and between staff and management, to the roles of the various players (especially the role of executive project sponsors), to the company's corporate structure and culture. Other aspects of project management must also be planned. Strategic planning is vital for every company's health. Effective strategic planning can mean the difference between long-term success and failure. Even career planning for individual project managers ultimately plays a part in a company's excellence in project management or its mediocrity. All of these subjects are discussed in this chapter.

20.1 INFLUENCE OF ECONOMIC CONDITIONS

During favorable economic times, changes in management style and corporate culture move very slowly, but favorable economic conditions don't last forever. The period between recognizing the need for change and garnering the ability to manage change is usually measured in years. As economic conditions deteriorate, change occurs more and more quickly in business organizations, but not fast enough to keep up with the economy.

Before the recession of 1989–1993, U.S. companies were willing to accept the implementation of project management at a tedious pace. Corporate managers in general believed that their guidance was sufficient to keep their companies healthy and outside consultants were brought in primarily to train production workers in

TABLE 20–1. EFFECTS OF THE 1989–1993 RECESSION ON THE IMPLEMENTATION OF PROJECT MANAGEMENT

Factor	Prior to the Recession	After the Recession
Strategic focus	Short-term	Long-term
Organizational structuring	To secure power, authority, and control	To get closer to customers
Management focus	To manage people	To manage work and deliverables
Sponsorship	Lip service sponsorship	Active
Training emphasis	Quantitative	Qualitative/behavioral
Risk analysis	Minimal effort	Concerted effort
Authority	In writing	Implied
Team building	Functional teams	Cross-functional teams

the principles of project management. Executive training sessions, even very short ones, were rarely offered. Executives believed that project management was simply a methodology to placate employees rather than a benefit to the business.

During the recession, senior managers came to realize that their knowledge of project management was not as comprehensive as they had once believed. Table 20–1 shows how the recession affected the development of project management systems.

By the end of the recession in 1993, companies finally recognized the importance of both strategic planning and project management, as well as the relationship between them. The relationship between project management and strategic planning can best be seen from Figure 20–1. Historically, a great deal of emphasis was placed on strategic formulation with little emphasis on strategic implementation. Now companies were recognizing that the principles of project management could be used for the implementation of strategic plans, as well as operational plans.

Another factor promoting project management was the acceptances of strategic business units (SBUs). The strategic business units found less resistance than in the parent corporation for the use of project management and for the necessity to obtain horizontal as well as vertical workflow. This is shown in Figure 20–2.[1] Project management was now recognized as a vehicle for the implementation of just about any type of plan for any type of project.

To address the far-reaching changes in the economic environment, senior managers began to ask a fundamental question: How do we plan for excellence in project management? In answering this question, it would be futile to expect managers to implement immediately all of the changes needed to set up modern project management in their companies. What senior managers needed was a plan like the one shown in Table 20–2, expressed in terms of three broad, critical success factors: qualitative factors, organizational factors, and quantitative factors. These factors are discussed in later sections.

---

1. Source unknown.

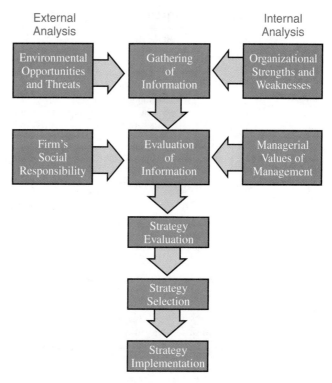

FIGURE 20–1. The traditional strategic planning model. *Source:* P. Rea and H. Kerzner, *Strategic Planning.* (New York: Wiley, 1997), p. 3.

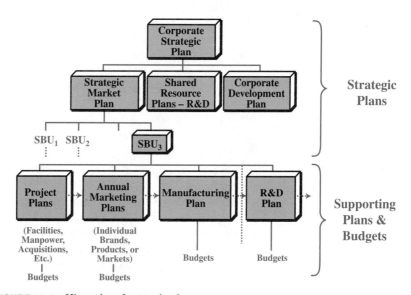

FIGURE 20–2. Hierarchy of strategic plans.

TABLE 20–2.   STRATEGIC FACTORS IN ACHIEVING EXCELLENCE

Factor	Short-Term Applications	Long-Term Implications
Qualitative	Provide educational training Dispel illusion of a need for authority Share accountability Commit to estimates and deliverables Provide visible executive support and sponsorship	Emphasize cross-functional working relationships and team building
Organizational	De-emphasize policies and procedures	Create project management career path
	Emphasize guidelines	Provide project managers with reward/penalty power
	Use project charters	Use nondedicated, cross-functional teams
Quantitative	Use a single tool for planning, scheduling, and controlling	Use estimating databases

20.2 WHAT IS GENERAL STRATEGIC PLANNING?

Strategic planning is the process of formulating and implementing decisions about an organization's future direction. This can be seen from Figure 20–1. This process is vital to every organization's survival because it is the process by which the organization adapts to its ever-changing environment and is applicable to all levels and types of organizations. The formulation process is the process of deciding where you want to go, what decisions must be made, and when they must be made in order to get there. It is the process of defining and understanding the business you are in. The outcome of this process results in the organization doing the right thing by producing goods or services for which there is a demand or need in the external environment. When this occurs, we say the organization has been effective as measured by market response, such as sales, market share, customer satisfaction and repeat business. All organizations must be effective or responsive to their environments to survive in the long run.

The formulation process is performed at the top levels of the organization. Here, top management values provide the ultimate decision template for directing the course of the firm.

Formulation

- Scans the external environment and industry environment for changing conditions
- Interprets the changing environment in terms of opportunities or threats
- Analyzes the firm's resource base for asset strengths and weaknesses
- Defines the mission of the business by matching environmental opportunities and threats with resource strengths and weaknesses
- Sets goals for pursuing the mission based on top management values and sense of responsibility

Implementation translates the formulated plan into policies and procedures for achieving the grand decision and involves all levels of management in moving the organization toward its mission. The process seeks to create a fit between the organization's formulated goal and its ongoing activities. Because it involves all levels of the organization, it results in the integration of all aspects of the firm. Middle- and lower-level managers spend most of their time on implementation activities. Effective implementation results in stated objectives, action plans, timetables, policies and procedures, and results in the organization moving efficiently toward its mission.

20.3 WHAT IS STRATEGIC PLANNING FOR PROJECT MANAGEMENT?

Strategic planning for project management is the *development of a standard methodology for project management,* which can be used over and over again, and which will produce a high likelihood of achieving the project's objectives. Although strategic planning and execution of the methodology does not guarantee profits or success, it does improve the chances of success.

One primary advantage of developing an implementation methodology is that it provides the organization with a consistency of action. As the number of interrelated units in organizations have increased, so have the benefits from the integrating direction afforded by the project management implementation process.

Methodologies need not be complex. Figure 20–3 shows the "skeleton" for the development of a simple project management methodology. The methodology

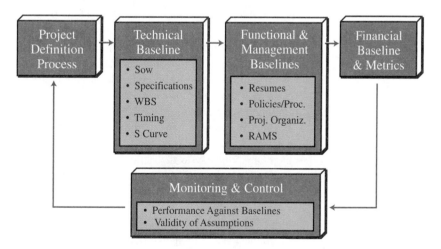

FIGURE 20–3. Methodology structuring.

begins with a project definition process that is broken down into a technical base-line, functional and management baseline, and financial baseline. The technical baseline includes, at a minimum:

- Statement of Work (SOW)
- Specifications
- Work breakdown structure (WBS)
- Timing (i.e., schedules)
- Spending curve (S curve)

The functional or management baseline indicates how you will manage the technical baseline. This includes:

- Resumés of the key players
- Project policies and procedures
- The organization for the project
- Responsibility assignment matrices (RAMs)

The financial baseline identifies how costs will be collected, analyzed, variances explained, and reports prepared. This will be covered separately in Section 20.8. Altogether, this is a simplistic process, which can be applied to each and every project.

Without this repetitive process, subunits tend to drift off in their own direction without regard to their role as a subsystem in a larger system of goals and objectives. The objective-setting and the integrating of the implementation process using the methodology assure that all of the parts of an organization are moving toward the same common objective. The methodology gives direction to diverse activities.

Another advantage of strategic project management planning is that it provides a vehicle for the communication of overall goals to all levels of management in the organization. It affords the potential of a vertical feedback loop from top to bottom, bottom to top, and functional unit to functional unit. The process of communication and its resultant understanding help reduce resistance to change. It is extremely difficult to achieve commitment to change when employees do not understand its purpose. The strategic project planning process gives all levels an opportunity to participate, thus reducing the fear of the unknown and eliminating resistance.

The final and perhaps the most important advantage is the thinking process required. Planning is a rational, logically ordered function. Many managers caught up in the day-to-day action of operations will appreciate the order afforded by a logical thinking process. Methodologies can be based upon sound, logical decisions. Figure 20–4 shows the logical decision-making process that could be part of the competitive bidding process for an organization. Checklists can be developed for each section of Figure 20–4 to simplify the process.

In the absence of an explicit project management methodology, decisions are made incrementally. A response to the crisis of the moment may result in a

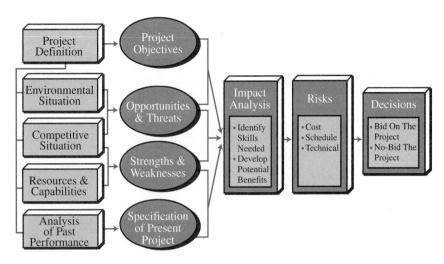

FIGURE 20–4. Competitive bidding process.

choice, that is unrelated and perhaps inconsistent with the choice made in the previous moment of crisis. Discontinuous choices serve to keep the organization from moving forward. Contradictory choices are a disservice to the organization and cause its demise. These discontinuous and contradictory choices occur when decisions are made independently to achieve different objectives. When the implementation process is made explicit, however, objectives, missions, and policies become visible guidelines, which produce logically consistent decisions.

Small companies usually have an easier time in performing strategic planning for project management excellence. Large companies with highly diversified product lines and multiple management styles find that institutionalizing changes in the way projects are managed can be very complex. Innovation and creativity in project management can be a daunting, but not impossible, task.

Effective strategic planning for project management is a never-ending effort. The two most common, continuous supporting strategies are the integration opportunities strategy and the performance improvement strategy. Figure 20–5 is the strategy for opportunities to integrate or combine the existing methodology with other types of management opportunities currently in use by the company. Such other methodologies available for integration include concurrent engineering, total quality management, scope management and risk management. Integrated strategies provide a synergistic effect.

The generic performance improvement strategy, shown in Figure 20–6, is designed to improve the efficiency of the existing methodology and to find new applications for the methodology. The integrated process strategies of Figure 20–5 are also part of the process improvement strategies. Process improvement will be discussed in Section 20.9 of this chapter.

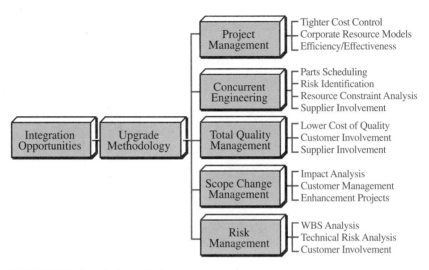

FIGURE 20–5. Generic integrated process strategies.

The goals of most organizations are to satisfy stakeholder expectations and to be more profitable than their competitors. There are both internal and external factors that are regarded as contributing sources to profitability. This is shown in Figure 20–7. Project management methodologies contribute to profitability through more efficient execution of the project and implementation of the

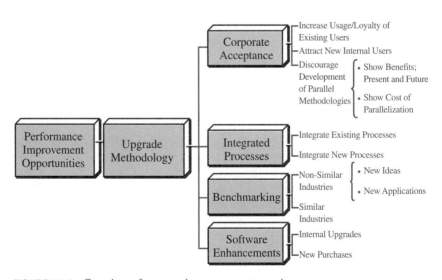

FIGURE 20–6. Generic performance improvement strategies.

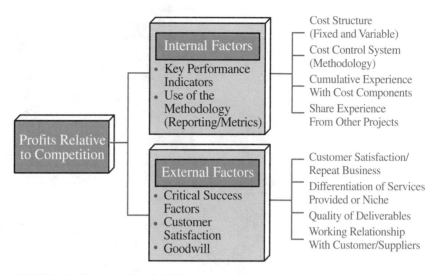

FIGURE 20–7. Sources of profitability.

methodology. This is another valid reason mandating continuous strategic planning for project management.

A good project management methodology will serve all of its stakeholders. Stakeholders are people who have a vested interest in the company's performance and who have claims on its performance. Figure 20–8 shows six commonly used categories of stakeholder: suppliers, customers, employees, creditors, shareholders, and even competitors. Organizations serve multiple stakeholders as customers, suppliers, government officials, shareholders, employees, and society at large. Methodologies for project management may indicate, when a problem exists, the order in which stakeholders will be satisfied. Good methodologies also include "standard practices" sections, which discuss morality and ethics when dealing with stakeholders.

20.4 CRITICAL SUCCESS FACTORS FOR STRATEGIC PLANNING

Critical success factors for strategic planning for project management include those activities that must be performed if the organization is to achieve its long-term objectives. Most businesses have only a handful of critical success factors. However, if even one of them were not executed successfully, the business's competitive position would be threatened.

The critical success factors in achieving project management excellence apply equally to all types of organizations, even those that have not fully imple-

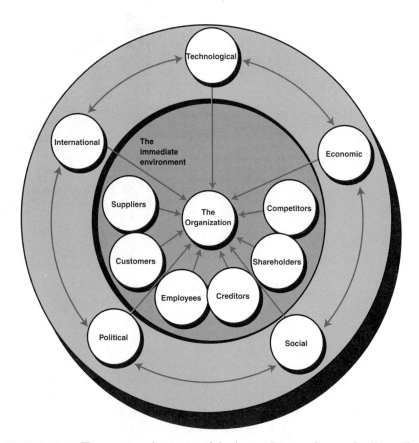

FIGURE 20–8. The macroenvironment of business. *Source:* Grover Starling, *The Changing Environment of Business,* 4th ed. (International Thomson Publishing, South Western College Publishing, Cincinnati, Ohio 1996, A Division of Thomson International Publishing, London, England, 1996), p. 19.

mented their project management systems. Though most organizations are sincere in their efforts to fully implement their systems, stumbling blocks are inevitable and must be overcome. Here's a list of common complaints from project teams:

- There's scope creep in every project and no way to avoid it.
- Completion dates are set before project scope and requirements have been agreed upon.
- Detailed project plans identifying all of the project's activities, tasks, and subtasks are not available.
- Projects emphasize deadlines. We should emphasize milestones and quality and not time.

- Senior managers don't always allow us to use pure project management techniques. Too many of them are still date-driven instead of requirements-driven. Original target dates should be used only for broad planning.
- Project management techniques from the 1960s are still being used on most projects. We need to learn how to manage from a plan and how to use shared resources.
- Sometimes we are pressured to cut estimates low to win a contract, but then we have to worry about how we'll accomplish the project's objectives.
- There are times when line personnel not involved in a project change the project budget to maintain their own chargeability. Management does the same.
- Hidden agendas come into play. Instead of concentrating on the project, some people are out to set precedents or score political points.
- We can't run a laboratory without equipment, and equipment maintenance is a problem because there's no funding to pay for the materials and labor.
- Budgets and schedules are not coordinated. Sometimes we have spent money according to the schedule but are left with only a small percentage of the project activities complete.
- Juggling schedules on multiple projects is sometimes almost impossible.
- Sometimes we filter information from reports to management because we fear sending them negative messages.
- There's a lot of caving in on budgets and schedules. Trying to be a good guy all the time is a trap.

With these comments in mind, let's look at the three critical success factors in achieving project management excellence.

Qualitative Factors   If excellence in project management is a continuous stream of successfully completed projects, then our first step should be to define *success*. Success in projects has traditionally been defined as achieving the project's objectives within the following constraints:

- Allocated time
- Budget cost
- Desired performance at technical or specification level
- Quality standards as defined by customers or users

In experienced organizations, the four preceding parameters have been extended to include the following:

- With minimal or mutually agreed upon scope changes
- Without disturbing the organization's corporate culture or values
- Without disturbing the organization's usual work flow

These last three parameters deserve further comment.

Organizations that eventually achieve excellence are committed to quality and up-front planning so that minimal scope changes are required as the project progresses. Those scope changes that are needed must be approved jointly by both the customer and the contractor. A well-thought-out process for handling scope changes is in place in such organizations. Even in large profit-making, project-driven industries such as aerospace, defense, and large construction, tremendous customer pressure can be expected to curtail any "profitable" scope changes introduced by the contractor.

Most organizations have well-established corporate cultures that have taken years to build. On the other hand, project managers may need to develop their own subcultures for their projects, particularly when the projects will require years to finish. Such temporary project cultures must be developed within the limitations of the larger corporate culture. The project manager should not expect senior officers of the company to allow the project manager free rein.

The same limitations affect organizational workflow. Most project managers working in organizations that are only partially project-driven realize that line managers in their organizations are committed to providing continuous support to the company's regular functional work. Satisfying the needs of time-limited projects may only be secondary. Project managers are expected to keep the welfare of their whole companies in mind when they make project decisions.

For companies to reach excellence in project management, executives must learn to define project success in terms of both what is good for the project and what is good for the organization.

Executives can support project managers by reminding them of this two-part responsibility by:

- Encouraging project managers to take on nonproject responsibilities such as administrative activities
- Providing project managers with information on the company's operations and not just information pertaining to their assigned projects
- Supporting meaningful dialogue among project managers
- Asking whether decisions made by project managers are in the best interest of the company as a whole.

Organizational Factors

Organizational behavior in project management is a delicate balancing act, something like sitting on a bar stool. Bar stools usually come with three legs to keep them standing. So does project management: one leg is the project manager, one is the line manager, and one is the project sponsor. If one of the legs is lost or unusable, the stool will be very difficult to balance.

Although line managers are the key to successful project management, they will have a lot of trouble performing their functions without effective interplay with the project's manager and corporate sponsor. In unsuccessful projects, the project manager has often been vested with power (authority) over the line managers involved. In more successful projects, project and line managers share authority. The project manager negotiates the line managers' commitment to the project and works through line managers rather than around them. Project managers provide recommendations regarding employee performance. And leadership is centered on the whole project team, not just the project manager.

In successful project management systems, the following equation always holds true:

$$\text{Accountability} = \text{Responsibility} + \text{Authority}$$

When project and line managers view each other as equals, they share equally in the management of the project, and thus they share equally the authority, responsibility, and accountability for the project's success. Obviously the sharing of authority makes sharing decision-making easier. A few suggestions for executive project sponsors follow:

- Do not increase the authority of the project manager at the expense of the line managers.
- Allow line managers to provide technical direction to their people if at all possible.
- Encourage line managers to provide realistic time and resource estimates and then work with the line managers to make sure they keep their promises.
- Above all, keep the line managers fully informed.

In organizations that have created effective project management systems, the role of the executive manager has changed along with project management. Early in the implementation of project management, executives were actively involved in the everyday project management process. But as project management has come into its own and general economic conditions have changed, executive involvement has become more passive, and they concentrate on long-term and strategic planning. They have learned to trust project managers' decisions and view project management as a central factor in their company's success.

Project sponsors provide visible, ongoing support. Their role is to act as a bodyguard for the project and the project manager. Unlike other executives on the senior management team, individual project sponsors may play a more active role in projects, depending on how far along the project is. Early in the project's functioning, for example, the project sponsor might help the project manager define the project's requirements. Once that is done, the sponsor resumes a less active role and receives project information only as needed.

In successful project management systems that carry a high volume of ongoing project work, an executive sponsor may not be assigned to low-dollar-value or low-priority projects. Middle managers may fill the sponsorship role in some cases. But no matter the size or value of the project, project sponsors today are responsible for the welfare of all members of their project teams and not just the project manager.

The existence of a project sponsor implies visible, ongoing executive support for project management. And executive support motivates project personnel to excel. Executive project sponsorship also supports the development of an organizational culture that fosters confidence in the organization's project management systems.

> *Conclusion: Executive project sponsorship must exist and be visible so that the project–line manager interface is in balance.*

Recommendations for obtaining maturity include:

- Educate the executives as to the benefits of project management.
- Convince the executives of the necessity for ongoing, visible support in the capacity of a project sponsor.
- Convince executives that they need not know all the details. Provide them with the least information that tells the most.

Quantitative Factors

The third factor in achieving excellence in project management is the implementation and acceptance of project management tools to support the methodology. Some companies are quick to implement PERT/CPM tools, but many are reluctant to accept other mainframe or personal computer network software for project planning, project cost estimating, project cost control, resource scheduling, project tracking, project audits, or project management information systems.

Mainframe project management tools have been resurrected in the past few years. These new mainframe products are being used mainly for total company project control. However, executives have been slow to accept these sophisticated tools. The reasons for this are:

- Upper management may not like the reality of the output.
- Upper management uses their own techniques rather than the system for the planning, budgeting, and decision-making process.
- Day-to-day planners may not use the packages for their own projects.
- Upper management may not demonstrate support and commitment to training.
- Use of sophisticated mainframe packages requires strong internal communication lines for support.
- Clear, concise reports are lacking even though report generators exist.

- Mainframe packages do not always provide for immediate turnaround of information.
- The business entity may not have any project management standards in place prior to implementation.
- Implementation may highlight middle management's inexperience in project planning and organizational skills.
- Sufficient/extensive resources required (staff, equipment, etc.) may not be in place.
- Business environment and organizational structure may not be appropriate to meet project management/planning needs.
- Software utilization training without project management training is insufficient.
- Software may be used inappropriately as a substitute for the extensive interpersonal and negotiation skills required by project management.
- The business entity may not have predetermined the extent and appropriate use of the software within the organization.

> *Conclusions:* *Project management education must precede software education. Also, executives must provide the same encouragement and support for the use of the software as they do for project management.*

The following recommendations are made to accelerate the maturity process:

- Educating people in the use of sophisticated software and having them accept its use is easier if the organization is already committed to project management.
- Executives must provide standards and consistency for the information they wish to see in the output.
- Executive knowledge (overview) in project management principles is necessary to provide meaningful support.
- Not everyone needs to become an expert in the use of the system. One or two individuals can act as support resources for multiple projects.

20.5 IDENTIFYING STRATEGIC RESOURCES

All businesses have corporate competencies and resources that distinguish them from their competitors. These competencies and resources are usually identified in terms of a company's strengths and weaknesses. Deciding upon what a company "should do" can only be achieved after assessing the strengths and weaknesses to determine what the company "can do." Strengths support windows of opportunities, whereas weaknesses create limitations. What a company "can do" is based upon the quality of its resources.

Strengths and weaknesses can be identified at all levels of management. Senior management may have a clearer picture of the overall company's position in relation to the external environment, whereas middle management may have a better grasp of the internal strengths and weaknesses. Unfortunately, most managers do not think in terms of strengths and weaknesses and, as a result, worry more about what they should do rather than what they can do.

Although all organizations have strengths and weaknesses, no organization is equally strong in all areas. Procter & Gamble, Budweiser, Coke, and Pepsi are all known for their advertising and marketing. Computer firms are known for technical strengths, whereas General Electric has long been regarded as the training ground for manufacturing executives. Large firms have vast resources with strong technical competency, but react slowly when change is needed. Small firms can react quickly but have limited strengths. The strengths and weaknesses can change over time and must, therefore, be closely monitored.

Strengths and weaknesses are internal measurements of what a company can do and must be based upon the quality of its resources. Consider the situation in Figure 20–9. A company with a world-class methodology in project management will not be able to close the gap in Figure 20–9 until the proper internal or subcontracted resources are available. Resources are necessary to execute methodologies, no matter how good the methodologies may be. Project management methodologies alone do not guarantee success. They simply increase the chances for success provided that (1) the objective is realistic and (2) the proper resources are available, along with the skills needed to achieve the objective.

Tangible Resources   In basic project management courses, the strengths and weaknesses of a firm are usually described in the terms of its tangible resources. The most common classification for tangible resources is:

- Equipment
- Facilities
- Manpower
- Materials
- Money
- Information/technology

Another representation of resources is shown in Figure 20–10. Unfortunately, these crude types of classification do not readily lend themselves to an accurate determination of internal strengths and weaknesses for project management. A more useful classification for strategic planning activities would be human resources, nonhuman resources, organizational resources, and financial resources.

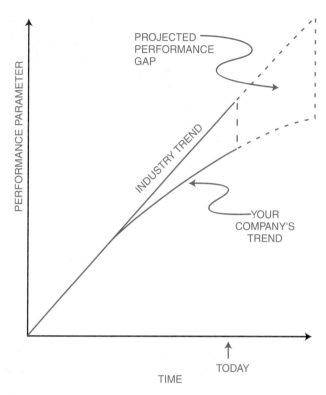

FIGURE 20–9. Projecting performance. *Source:* Grover Starling, *The Changing Environment of Business,* 4th ed. (International Thomson Publishing, South Western College Publishing, Cincinnati, Ohio 1996, A Division of Thomson International Publishing, London, England, 1996), p. 91.

Human Resources

Human resources are the knowledge, skills, capabilities, and talent of the firm's employees. This includes the board of directors, managers at all levels, and employees as a whole. The board of directors provides the company with considerable experience, political astuteness, and connections, and possibly sources of borrowing power. The board of directors is primarily responsible for selecting the CEO and representing the best interest of the diverse stakeholders as a whole.

Top management is responsible for developing the strategic mission and making sure that the strategic mission satisfies the shareholders. All too often, CEOs have singular strengths in one area of business such as marketing, finance, technology, or production.

The biggest asset of senior management is its decision-making ability, especially during project planning. Unfortunately, all too often senior management will delegate planning (and the accompanying decision-making process) to staff personnel. This may result in no effective project planning process within the organization and may lead to continuous replanning efforts.

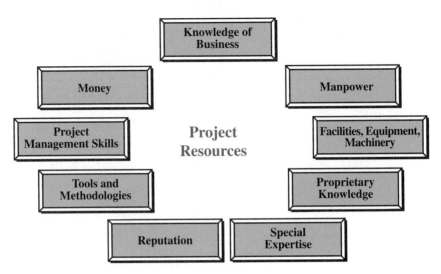

FIGURE 20–10. Project resources.

Another important role of a senior management is to define clearly its own managerial values and the firm's social responsibility. (See Figure 20–1.) A change in senior management could change the organization's managerial values and social responsibility overnight. This could cause an immediate update of the project management methodology.

Lower and middle management are responsible for developing and maintaining the "core" technical competencies of the firm. Every organization maintains a distinct collection of human resources. Middle management must develop some type of cohesive organization such that synergistic effects will follow. It is the synergistic effect that produces the core competencies that lead to sustained competitive advantages and a high probability of successful project execution.

Nonhuman Resources

Nonhuman resources are physical resources that distinguish one organization from another. Boeing and IBM both have sustained competitive advantages but have different physical resources. Physical resources include plant and equipment, distribution networks, proximity of supplies, availability of a raw material, land, and labor.

Companies with superior nonhuman resources may not have a sustained competitive advantage without having superior human resources. Likewise, a company with strong human resources may not be able to take advantage of windows of opportunities without having strong physical resources. An Ohio-based company had a 30-year history of sustained competitive advantage on R&D projects that were won through competitive bidding. Unfortunately, the megaprofits were in production, and in order to acquire physical production resources, the organization diluted some of its technical resources. The firm learned a hard lesson in that the management of human resources is not the same as the management of nonhuman resources. The firm also had to reformulate its project management methodology to account for manufacturing operations.

Firms that endeavor to develop superior manufacturing are faced with two critical issues. First, how reliable are the suppliers? Do the suppliers maintain quality standards? Are the suppliers cost effective? The second concern, and perhaps the more serious of the two, is the ability to cut costs quickly and efficiently to remain competitive. This usually leads to some form of vertical integration.

Organizational Resources

Organizational resources are the glue that holds all of the other resources together. Organizational resources include the organizational structure, the project office, the formal (and sometimes informal) reporting structure, the planning system, the scheduling system, the control system, and the supporting policies and procedures. Decentralization can create havoc in large firms where each strategic business unit (SBU), functional unit, and operating division can have its own policies, procedures, rules, and guidelines. Multiple project management methodologies can cause serious problems if resources are shared between SBUs.

Financial Resources

Financial resources are the firm's borrowing capability, credit lines, credit rating, ability to generate cash, and relationship with investment bankers. Companies with quality credit ratings can borrow money at a lower rate than companies with nonquality ratings. Companies must maintain a proper balance between equity and credit markets when raising funds. A firm with strong, continuous cash flow may be able to fund growth projects out of cash flow rather than through borrowing. This is the usual financial-growth strategy for a small firm.

Intangible Resources

Human, physical, organizational, and financial resources are regarded as tangible resources. There are also intangible resources that include the organizational culture, reputation, brand name, patents, trademarks, know-how, and relationships with customers and suppliers. Intangible resources do not have the visibility that tangible resources possess, but they can lead to a sustained competitive advantage. When companies develop a "brand name," it is nurtured through advertising and marketing and is often accompanied by a slogan. Project management methodologies can include paragraphs on how to protect the corporate image or brand name.

Social Responsibility

Social responsibility is also an intangible asset, although some consider it both intangible and tangible. Social responsibility is the expectation that the public perceives that a firm will make decisions that are in the best interest of the public as a whole. Social responsibility can include a broad range of topics from environmental protection to consumer safeguards to consumer honesty and employing the disadvantaged. An image of social responsibility can convert a potential disaster into an advantage. Johnson and Johnson earned high marks for social responsibility in the way it handled the two Tylenol tragedies in the 1980s. Nestlé, on the other hand, earned low marks for the infant-formula controversy.

20.6 STRATEGIC SELECTION OF PROJECTS

What a company wants to do is not always what it can do. The critical constraint is normally the availability and quality of the critical resources. Companies normally have an abundance of projects they would like to work on but, because of resource limitations, have to develop a prioritization system for the selection of projects.

A commonly used selection process is the portfolio classification matrix shown in Figure 20–11. Each project undergoes a situational assessment for strengths, weaknesses, opportunities, and threats. The projects are then ranked on the nine-square grid based upon the projects' benefits and the quality of resources needed to achieve those benefits. The characteristics of the benefits appear in Figure 20–12 and the characteristics of the resources needed are shown in Figure 20–13.

This technique allows for proper selection of projects, as well as providing the organization with the foundation for a capacity planning model to see how much work the organization can take on. Companies usually have little trouble

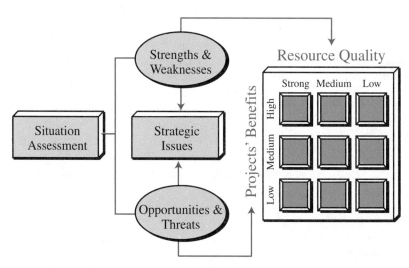

FIGURE 20–11. Portfolio classification matrix.

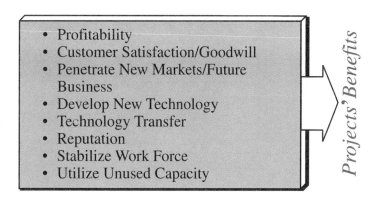

FIGURE 20–12. Characteristics of benefits.

deciding where to assign the highly talented people. The model, however, provides guidance on how to make the most effective utilization of the average and below average individuals as well.

The boxes in the nine-square grid of Figure 20–11 can then be prioritized according to strategic importance as shown in Figure 20–14. If resources are limited but funding is adequate, the boxes identified as "high priority" will be addressed first.

The nine-square grid in Figure 20–14 can also be used to identify the quality of the project management skills needed, in addition to the quality of functional employees. This is shown in Figure 20–15. As an example, the project managers with the best overall skills will be assigned to those projects that are needed to

- Knowledge of Business
- Manpower
- Facilities, Equipment, Machinery
- Proprietary Knowledge
- Special Expertise
- Reputation
- Relationship with Key Stakeholders
- Project Management Skills
- Money

Quality of Resources

FIGURE 20–13. Quality of resources needed.

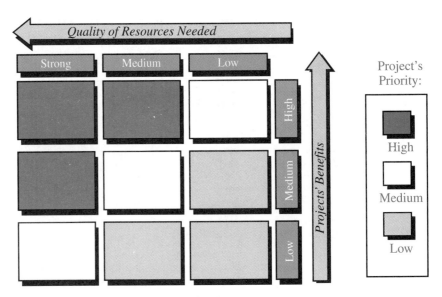

FIGURE 20–14. Strategic importance of projects.

protect the firm's current position. Each of the nine cells in Figure 20–15 can be described as follows:

- *Protect Position (High Benefits and High Quality of Resources):* These projects may be regarded as essential to the survival of the firm. These projects mandate professional project management, possibly certified

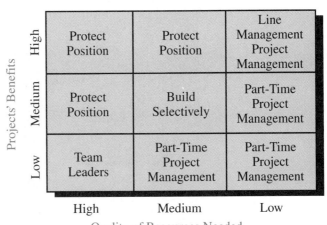

FIGURE 20–15. Strategic guide to allocating project resources.

project managers, and the organization considers project management as a career path position. Continuous improvement in project management is essential to make sure that the methodology is the best it can be.

- *Protect Position (High Benefits and Medium Quality of Resources):* These projects may require a full-time project manager, but not necessarily a certified one. An enhanced project management methodology is needed, with emphasis on reinforcing vulnerable areas of project management.
- *Protect Position (Medium Benefits and High Quality of Resources):* Emphasis is on training project managers with emphasis on leadership skills. The types of projects here usually emphasize customer value-added efforts rather than new product development.
- *Line Management Project Management (High Benefits and Low Quality of Resources):* These projects are usually process improvement efforts to support repetitive production. Minimum integration across functional lines is necessary, which allows line managers to function as project managers. These projects are characterized by short time frames.
- *Build Selectively (Medium Benefits and Medium Quality of Resources):* These projects are specialized, perhaps repetitive, and focus on a specific area of the business. Limited project management strengths are needed. Risk management may be needed, especially technical risk management.
- *Team Leaders (Low Benefits But High Quality of Resources):* These are normally small, short-term R&D projects that require strong technical skills. Since minimal integration is required, scientists and technical experts will function as team leaders. Minimal knowledge of project management is needed.
- *Part-Time Project Management (Medium Benefits and Low Quality Resources):* These are small capital projects that require only an introductory knowledge of project management. One project manager could end up managing multiple small projects.
- *Part-Time Project Management (Low Benefits and Medium Quality of Resources):* These are internal projects or very small capital projects. These projects have small budgets and perhaps a low to moderate risk.
- *Part-Time Project Management (Low Benefits and Low Quality of Resources):* These projects are usually planned by line managers but executed by project coordinators or project expediters.

20.7 PORTFOLIO SELECTION OF PROJECTS

Companies that are project-driven organizations must be careful about the type and quantity of projects they work on because of the available resources. Because of critical timing, it is not always possible to hire new employees and have them trained in time, or to hire subcontractors who have the needed skills.

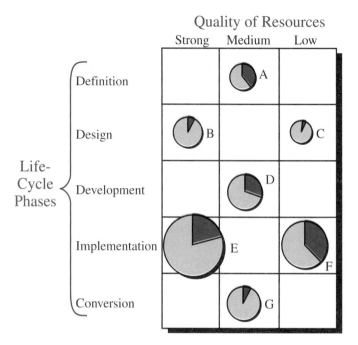

FIGURE 20–16. Life cycle portfolio model.

Figure 20–16 shows a typical project portfolio.[2] Each circle represents a project. The location of each circle represents the quality of resources and the life cycle phase that the project is in. The size of the circle represents the magnitude of the benefits relative to other projects, and the pie wedge represents the percentage of the project completed thus far.

In Figure 20–16, Project A, for example, has relatively low benefits and uses medium quality resources. Project A is in the definition phase. However, when Project A moves into the design phase, the quality of resources may change to low quality or strong quality. Therefore, this type of chart has to be updated frequently.

Figures 20–17, 20–18, and 20–19 show three types of portfolios. Figure 20–17 represents a high-risk project portfolio where strong resources are required on each project. This may be representative of project-driven organizations that have been awarded highly profitable, large projects. This could also be a company in the computer field that competes in an industry that has short product life cycles and where product obsolescence occurs six months down stream.

Figure 20–18 represents a conservative profit portfolio where an organization works on low-risk projects that require low quality resources. This could be representation of project portfolio selection in a service organization, or even a manufacturing firm that has projects designed mostly for product enhancement.

---

2. This type of portfolio was adapted from the life-cycle portfolio model used for strategic planning activities.

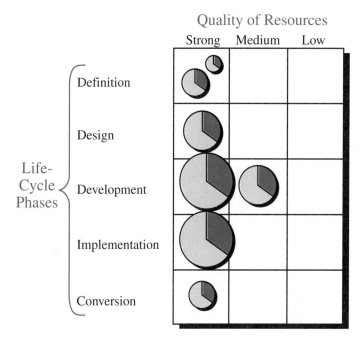

FIGURE 20–17. Typical high-risk project portfolio.

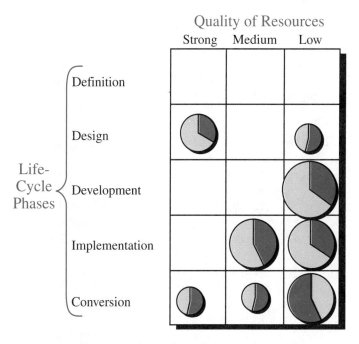

FIGURE 20–18. Typical conservative profit portfolio.

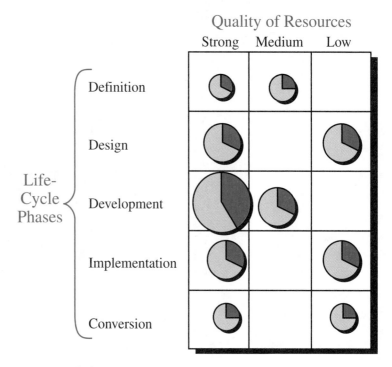

FIGURE 20–19. Typical balanced corporate portfolio.

Figure 20–19 shows a balanced portfolio with projects in each life cycle phase and where all quality of resources is being utilized, usually quite effectively. A very delicate juggling act is required to maintain this balance.

20.8 HORIZONTAL ACCOUNTING

In the early days of project management, project management was synonymous with scheduling. Project planning was simply laying out a schedule with very little regard for costs. After all, we know that costs will change (i.e., most likely increase) over the life of the project and that the final cost will never resemble the original budget. Therefore, why worry about cost control?

Recessions and poor economic times have put pressure on the average company for better cost control. Historically, costs were measured on a vertical basis only. This created a problem in that project managers had no knowledge of how many hours were actually being expended in the functional areas to perform the assigned project activities. Standards were very rarely updated and, if they were, it was usually without the project manager's knowledge.

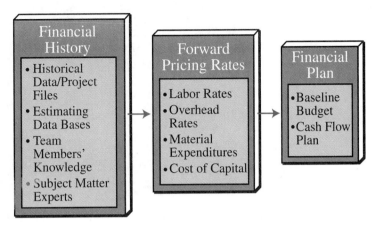

FIGURE 20–20. The evolution of integrated cost-schedule management. Phase I—budget-based planning.

Today, methodologies for project management mandate horizontal accounting using earned value measurement techniques. This is extremely important, especially if the project manager has the responsibility for profit and loss. Projects are now controlled through a series of charge numbers or cost account codes assigned to all of the work packages in the work breakdown structure.

Strategic planning for cost control on projects is a three-phase effort as shown in Figures 20–20 through 20–22. The three phases are:

● *Phase I—Budget-Base Planning (Figure 20–20):* This is the development of a project's baseline budget and cash flow based upon reasonably accurate historical data. The historical databases are updated at the end of each project.

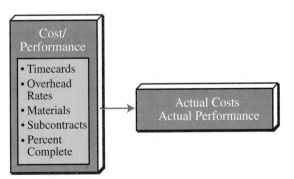

FIGURE 20–21. The evolution of integrated cost-schedule management. Phase II—Cost/performance determination.

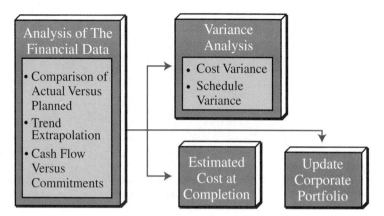

FIGURE 20–22. The evolution of integrated cost-schedule management. Phase III—updating and reporting.

- *Phase II—Cost/Performance Determination (Figure 20–21):* This is where the costs are determined for each work package and where the actual costs are compared against the actual performance in order to determine the true project status.
- *Phase III—Updating and Reporting (Figure 20–22):* This is the preparation of the necessary reports for the project team members, line managers, sponsors, and customer. At a minimum, these reports should address the questions of:
  - Where are we today (time and cost)?
  - Where will we end up (time and cost)?
  - What problems do we have now and will we have in the future, and what mitigation strategies have we come up with?

Good methodologies provide the framework for gathering the information to answer these questions.

20.9 CONTINUOUS IMPROVEMENT

Project management methodologies must undergo continuous improvement. This may be strategically important to stay ahead of the competition. Continuous improvements to a methodology can be internally driven by factors such as better software availability, a more cooperative corporate culture, or simply training and education in the use of the methodology. Externally driven factors include relationships with customers and suppliers, legal factors, social factors, technological factors, and even political factors.

Five areas for continuous improvement to the project management methodology are show in Figure 20–23.

Existing Process Improvements

- *Frequency of Use:* Has prolonged use of the methodology made it apparent that changes can be made?
- *Access to Customers:* Can we improve the methodology to get closer to our customers?
- *Substitute Products:* Are there new products (i.e., software) in the marketplace that can replace and improve part of our methodology?
- *Better Working Conditions:* Can changes in the working conditions cause us to eliminate parts of the methodology (i.e., paperwork requirements)?
- *Better Use of Software:* Will new or better use of the software allow us to eliminate some of our documentation and reports?

Integrated Process Improvements

- *Speed of Integration:* Are there ways to change the methodology to increase the speed of integrating activities?
- *Training Requirements:* Have changes in our training requirements mandated changes in our methodology?
- *Corporate-Wide Acceptance:* Should the methodology change in order to obtain corporate-wide acceptance?

Behavioral Issues

- *Changes in Organizational Behavior:* Have changes in behavior mandated methodology changes?

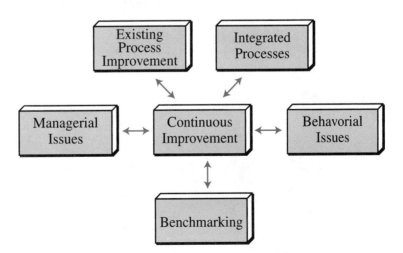

FIGURE 20–23. Factors to consider for continuous improvement.

- *Cultural Changes:* Has our culture changed (i.e., to a cooperative culture) such that the methodology can be enhanced?
- *Management Support:* Has management support improved to a point where fewer gate reviews are required?
- *Impact on Informal Project Management:* Is there enough of a cooperative culture such that informal project management can be used to execute the methodology?
- *Shifts in Power and Authority:* Do authority and power changes mandate a more rigid or looser methodology?
- *Safety Considerations:* Have safety or environmental changes occurred that will impact the methodology?
- *Overtime Requirements:* Do new overtime requirements mandate an updating of forms, policies, or procedures?

Benchmarking

- *Creation of a Project Management Center for Excellence:* Do we now have a "core" group responsible for benchmarking?
- *Cultural Benchmarking:* Do other organizations have better cultures than we do in project management execution?
- *Process Benchmarking:* What new processes are other companies integrating into their methodology?

Managerial Issues

- *Customer Communications:* Have there been changes in the way we communicate with our customers?
- *Resource Capability Versus Needs:* If our needs have changed, what has happened to the capabilities of our resources?
- *Restructuring Requirements:* Has restructuring caused us to change our sign-off requirements?
- *Growing Pains:* Does the methodology have to be updated to include our present growth in business (i.e., tighter or looser controls)?

The five factors considered above provide a company with a good framework for continuous improvement. The benefits of continuous improvement include:

- Better competitive positioning
- Corporate unity
- Improved cost analysis
- Customer value added
- Better management of customer expectations
- Ease of implementation

20.10 THE PROJECT OFFICE/CENTER FOR EXCELLENCE

During the late 1950s and early 1960s, the concept of a project office came into existence. The project office (PO) was initially used only by the construction industry and aerospace/defense contractors for large projects. The project office was the management team for the contractor and the focal point for all customer communications. The majority of the people in the project office were assigned full-time because customers felt better having projects overmanaged rather than run the risk of undermanagement. Suppose a $75,000 engineer was needed only 80 percent of the time in the project office. By assigning the engineer full-time, the overmanagement cost is 20 percent of $75,000, or $15,000. If, however, the individual were assigned only 80 percent of the time but was needed 100 percent of the time, the undermanagement cost could easily be an order of magnitude greater than the overmanagement cost.

Overstaffing the project office became the norm in the 1950s and 1960s. The government's use of cost-plus-percentage-of-cost contracts (which are illegal in the government today) encouraged empire building within the project office. On a large weapon systems contract, it was not uncommon for a project office to employ in excess of 100 people. Also, since the project was long-term in nature, say five to ten years or longer, the project office functioned as a colocated team in the same geographical area of the building as the project manager.

In the early days of project management, the project office was also called the "war room" for the project. It existed to support one and only one customer. The primary responsibilities of the project office were twofold: update the master project schedules, which were laid out like wallpaper covering all of the walls; and prepare customer documentation. Both of these primary functions were labor-intensive because computer technology was still in its infancy stages.

By the mid-1970s, the advent of mainframe computers with large main memories and sophisticated plotters created an opportunity for project management-related software. Unfortunately, the majority of the project management software packages were cumbersome to use, required mainframe support, and could be run only by individuals specially trained in the use of the software packages. It became obvious very quickly that it would be impossible to train everyone involved in projects in the use of the software. What was needed was a group of individuals, say three to six people, who would become corporate experts in the use of the software and who would function as support staff to all of the project managers and project offices. The role of the project office was about to change.

The original intent of the project office was to support a single customer, but now we had support staff that had to serve all customers. The role of the project office was now changed from a customer-focused project office to a corporate knowledge-based center for project information, but still serving all of the customers. The project office was now responsible for:

- Standardization in estimating
- Standardization in planning

- Standardization in scheduling
- Standardization in control
- Standardization in reporting
- Clarification of project management roles and responsibilities
- Preparation of job descriptions for project managers
- Preparation of archive data on lessons learned

By the late 1980s and early 1990s, the project office had accumulated enough history from lessons learned files to recommend changes in the way projects were being managed. Published literature and case studies on both project success and project failure became abundant. Software was now available for just about every facet of project management. The number and frequency of symposiums on project management began to grow. Companies began recognizing the importance of project management benchmarking. The roles of the project office once again began to change. The additional responsibilities of the project office now included:

- Benchmarking continuously
- Developing project management templates
- Developing a project management methodology
- Recommending and implementing changes and improvements to the existing methodology
- Identifying project standards
- Identifying best practices
- Coordinating and/or conducting project management training programs
- Transferring knowledge through coaching and mentorship
- Developing a corporate resource capacity/utilization plan
- Assessing risks
- Planning for disaster recovery

With these changes taking place, organizations began changing the name of the project office to the Center for Excellence (COE) in project management. The COE was mainly responsible for providing information to stakeholders rather than actually executing projects or making mid-course corrections to a plan.

20.11 WHY DOES STRATEGIC PLANNING FOR PROJECT MANAGEMENT FAIL?

We have developed a strong case in earlier sections of this chapter for the benefits of strategic planning for project management. Knowledge about this process is growing and new information is being disseminated rapidly. Why, then, does this process often fail? Following are some of the problems that occur during the strategic planning process. Each of these pitfalls must be examined carefully if the process is to be effective.

- *CEO Endorsement:* Any type of strategic planning process must originate with senior management. They must start the process and signal their own aspirations. A failure to endorse may signal line management that the process is unreal.
- *Failure to Reexamine:* Strategic planning for project management is not a one-shot process. It is a dynamic, continuous process of reexamination, feedback, and updating.
- *Being Blinded by Success:* Simply because a few projects are completed successfully does not mean that the methodology is correct, nor does it imply that improvements are not possible. Simply put, believing that "you can do no wrong" usually leads to failure.
- *Overresponsiveness to Information:* Too many changes in too short a time frame may leave employees with the impression that the methodology is flawed or that its use may not be worth the effort. The argument here is whether changes should be made continuously or at structured time frames.
- *Failure to Educate:* People cannot implement successfully and repetitively a methodology they do not understand. Training and education on the use of the methodology are essential.
- *Failure of Organizational Acceptance:* Company-wide acceptance of the methodology is essential. This may take time to achieve in large organizations. Strong, visible executive support may be essential for rapid acceptance.
- *Failure to Keep the Methodology Simple:* Simple methodologies based upon guidelines are ideal. Unfortunately, as more and more improvements are made, there is a tendency to go from informality using guidelines to formality using policies and procedures.
- *Blaming Failures on the Methodology:* Project failures are not always the result of poor methodology. Unrealistic objectives or poor executive expectations can lead to poor implementation. Good methodologies do not guarantee success, but they do imply that the project will be managed correctly.
- *Failure to Prioritize:* There can exist serious differences in the priorities assigned to strategic project objectives by different functional areas such as marketing and manufacturing. Figure 20–24 shows three projects and how they are viewed differently by marketing and manufacturing. A common, across-company prioritization system may be necessary.
- *Rapid Acquisitions:* Sometimes an organization will purchase another company as part of their long-term strategy for vertical integration. Backwards integration occurs when you purchase suppliers of components or raw materials to reduce your dependency upon them. Forward integration occurs when you purchase your forward channels of distribution for your products. In both cases, your projects now require more work, and this must be accounted for in the methodology. Changes may occur quickly.

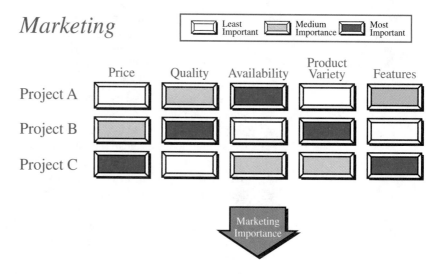

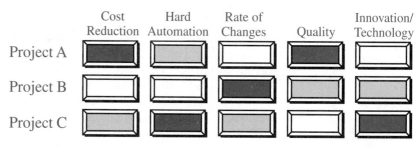

FIGURE 20–24. Differences in strategic importance as perceived by marketing and manufacturing.

20.12 ORGANIZATIONAL RESTRUCTURING

Effective project management cultures are based on trust, communication, cooperation, and teamwork. When the basis of project management is strong, organizational structure becomes almost irrelevant. Restructuring an organization only to add project management is unnecessary and perhaps even dangerous. Companies may need to be restructured for other reasons, such as making the customer more important. But successful project management can live within any structure, no matter how awful the structure looks on paper, just as long as the culture of the company promotes teamwork, cooperation, trust, and effective communication.

The organizations of companies excellent in project management can take almost any form. Today, small- to medium-size companies sometimes restructure to pool management resources. Large companies tend to focus on the strategic business unit as the foundation of their structures. Many companies still follow matrix management. Any can work with project management as long as they have the following traits:

- They are organized around nondedicated project teams.
- They have a flat organizational hierarchy.
- They practice informal project management.
- They do not consider the reporting level of project managers important.

The first point listed above may be somewhat controversial. Dedicated project teams have been a fact of life since the late 1980s. Although there have been many positive results from dedicated teams, there has also been a tremendous waste of manpower, coupled with duplication of equipment, facilities, and technologies. Today, most experienced organizations believe that they are scheduling resources effectively so that multiple projects can make use of scarce resources at the same time. And, they believe, nondedicated project teams can be just as creative as dedicated teams, and perhaps at a lower cost.

Although tall organizational structures with multiple layers of management were the rule when project management came on the scene in the early 1960s, today's organizations tend to be lean and mean, with fewer layers of management than ever. The span of control has been widened, and the results of that change have been mass confusion in some companies but complete success in others. The simple fact is that flat organizations work better. They are characterized by better internal communication, cooperation among employees and managers, and atmospheres of trust.

In addition, today's project management organizations, with only a few exceptions (purely project-driver companies), prefer to use informal project management. With formal project management systems, the authority and power of project managers must be documented in writing, formal project management policies and procedures are required, and documentation is required on even the simplest tasks. By contrast, in informal systems, paperwork is minimized. In the future I believe that even totally project-driven organizations will develop more informal systems.

The reporting level for project managers has fluctuated between top-level and lower-level managers. As a result, some line managers have felt alienated over authority and power disagreements with project managers. In the most successful organizations, the reporting level has stabilized, and project managers and line managers today report at about the same level. Project management simply works better when the managers involved view each other as peers. In large projects, however, project managers may report higher up, sometimes to the executive level. For such projects, a project office is usually set up for project team members at the same level as the line managers with whom they interact daily.

To sum it all up, effective cross-functional communication, cooperation, and trust are bound to generate organizational stability. Let's hope that organizational restructuring on the scale we've seen in recent years will no longer be necessary.

20.13 CAREER PLANNING

In organizations that successfully manage their projects, project managers are considered professionals and have distinct job descriptions. Employees usually are allowed to climb one of two career ladders: the management ladder or the technical ladder. (They cannot, however, jump back and forth between the two.) This presents a problem to project managers, whose responsibilities bridge the two ladders. To solve this problem, some organizations have created a third ladder, one that fills the gap between technology and management. It is a project management ladder with the same opportunities for advancement as the other two.

Modern Developments in Project Management

21.0 INTRODUCTION

As more and more industries accept project management as a way of life, the change in project management practices has taken place at an astounding rate. But what is even more important is the fact that these companies are sharing their accomplishments with other companies during benchmarking activities.

Eight recent interest areas are included in this chapter:

- The project management maturity model (PMMM)
- Developing effective procedural documentation
- Project management methodologies
- Continuous improvement
- Capacity planning
- Competency models
- Managing multiple projects
- End-of-phase review meetings

These eight topics appear to be the quickest paths to change as we enter the twenty-first century.

21.1 THE PROJECT MANAGEMENT MATURITY MODEL (PMMM)

All companies desire to achieve maturity and excellence in project management. Unfortunately, not all companies recognize that the time frame can be shortened by performing strategic planning for project management. The simple use of project management, even for an extended period of time, does *not* lead to excellence. Instead, it can result in repetitive mistakes and, what's worse, learning from your own mistakes rather than from the mistakes of others.

Companies such as Motorola, Nortel, Ericsson, and Compaq perform strategic planning for project management, and the results are self-explanatory. What Nortel and Ericsson have accomplished from 1992–1998, other companies have not achieved in twenty years of using project management.

Strategic planning for project management is unlike other forms of strategic planning in that it is most often performed at the middle-management level, rather than by executive management. Executive management is still involved, mostly in a supporting role, and provides funding together with employee release time for the effort. Executive involvement will be necessary to make sure that whatever is recommended by middle management will not result in unwanted changes to the corporate culture.

Organizations tend to perform strategic planning for new products and services by laying out a well-thought-out plan and then executing the plan with the precision of a surgeon. Unfortunately, strategic planning for project management, if performed at all, is done on a trial-by-fire basis. However, there are models that can be used to assist corporations in performing strategic planning for project management and achieving maturity and excellence in a reasonable period of time.

The foundation for achieving excellence in project management can best be described as the project management maturity model (PMMM), which is comprised of five levels, as shown in Figure 21–1. Each of the five levels represents a different degree of maturity in project management.

- *Level 1—Common Language:* In this level, the organization recognizes the importance of project management and the need for a good understanding of the basic knowledge on project management, along with the accompanying language/terminology.
- *Level 2—Common Processes:* In this level, the organization recognizes that common processes need to be defined and developed such that successes on one project can be repeated on other projects. Also included in this level is the recognition that project management principles can be applied to and support other methodologies employed by the company.
- *Level 3—Singular Methodology:* In this level, the organization recognizes the synergistic effect of combining all corporate methodologies into a singular methodology, the center of which is project management. The synergistic effects also make process control easier with a single methodology than with multiple methodologies.
- *Level 4—Benchmarking:* This level contains the recognition that process improvement is necessary to maintain a competitive advantage. Benchmarking must be performed on a continuous basis. The company must decide whom to benchmark and what to benchmark.

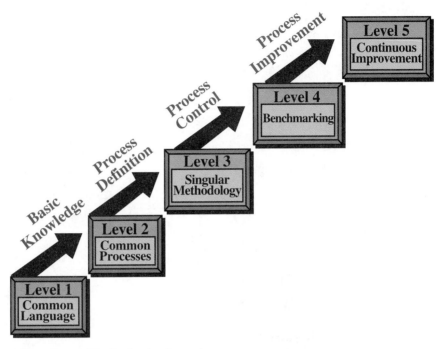

FIGURE 21–1. The five levels of maturity.

● *Level 5—Continuous Improvement:* In this level, the organization evaluates the information obtained through benchmarking and must then decide whether or not this information will enhance the singular methodology.

When we talk about levels of maturity (and even life-cycle phases), there exists a common misbelief that all work must be accomplished sequentially (i.e., in series). This is not necessarily true. Certain levels can and do overlap. The magnitude of the overlap is based upon the amount of risk the organization is willing to tolerate. For example, a company can begin the development of project management checklists to support the methodology while it is still providing project management training for the workforce. A company can create a center for excellence in project management before benchmarking is undertaken.

Although overlapping does occur, the order in which the phases are completed cannot change. For example, even though Level 1 and Level 2 can overlap, Level 1 *must* still be completed before Level 2 can be completed. Overlapping of several of the levels can take place, as shown in Figure 21–2.

● *Overlap of Level 1 and Level 2:* This overlap will occur because the organization can begin the development of project management processes either while refinements are being made to the common language or during training.

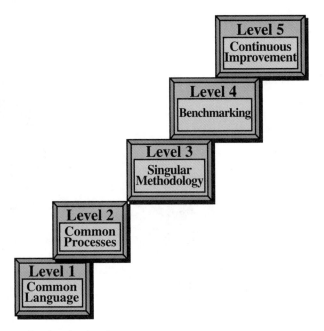

FIGURE 21–2. Overlapping levels.

- *Overlap of Level 3 and Level 4:* This overlap occurs because, while the organization is developing a singular methodology, plans are being made as to the process for improving the methodology.
- *Overlap of Level 4 and Level 5:* As the organization becomes more and more committed to benchmarking and continuous improvement, the speed by which the organization wants changes to be made can cause these two levels to have significant overlap. The feedback from Level 5 back to Level 4 and Level 3, as shown in Figure 21–3, implies that these three levels form a continuous improvement cycle, and it may even be possible for all three of these levels to overlap.

Level 2 and Level 3 generally do not overlap. It may be possible to begin some of the Level 3 work before Level 2 is completed, but this is highly unlikely. Once a company is committed to a singular methodology, work on other methodologies generally terminates. Also, companies can create a Center for Excellence in project management early in the life-cycle process, but will not receive the full benefits until later on.

Risks can be assigned to each level of the PMMM. For simplicity's sake, the risks can be labeled as low, medium, and high. The level of risk is most frequently associated with the impact on the corporate culture. The following definitions can be assigned to these three risks:

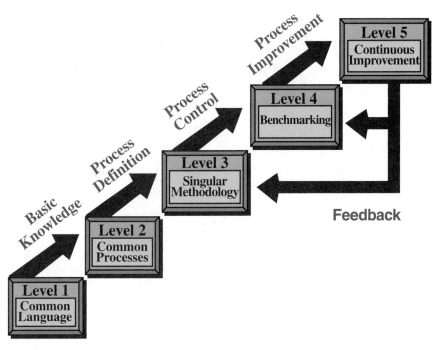

FIGURE 21–3. Feedback between the five levels of maturity.

- *Low Risk:* Virtually no impact upon the corporate culture, or the corporate culture is dynamic and readily accepts change.
- *Medium Risk:* The organization recognizes that change is necessary but may be unaware of the impact of the change. Multiple-boss reporting would be an example of a medium risk.
- *High Risk:* High risks occur when the organization recognizes that the changes resulting from the implementation of project management will cause a change in the corporate culture. Examples include the creation of project management methodologies, policies, and procedures, as well as decentralization of authority and decision-making.

Level 3 has the highest risk and degree of difficulty for the organization. This is shown in Figure 21–4. Once an organization is committed to Level 3, the time and effort needed to achieve the higher levels of maturity have a low degree of difficulty. Achieving Level 3, however, may require a major shift in the corporate culture.

These types of maturity models will become more common in the future, with generic models being customized for individual companies. These models will assist management in performing strategic planning for excellence in project management.

Level	Description	Degree of Difficulty
1	Common Language	Medium
2	Common Processes	Medium
3	Singular Methodology	High
4	Benchmarking	Low
5	Continuous Improvement	Low

FIGURE 21–4. Degrees of difficulty of the five levels of maturity.

21.2 DEVELOPING EFFECTIVE PROCEDURAL DOCUMENTATION

In the previous section, we showed the necessity of developing processes, and ultimately a singular methodology, for project management. Project management methodologies require a project management information system (PMIS), which is based upon procedural documentation. The procedural documentation can be in the form of policies, procedures, guidelines, forms, and checklists, or even a combination of these. Good procedural documentation will accelerate the project management maturity process, foster support at all levels of management, and greatly improve project communications. The type of procedural documentation selected can change over the years and is heavily biased on whether we wish to manage more formally or informally. In any event, procedural documentation supports effective communications, which in turn provides for better interpersonal skills.

An important facet of any project management methodology is to provide the people in the organization with procedural documentation on how to conduct project-oriented activities and how to communicate in such a multidimensional environment. The project management policies, procedures, forms, and guidelines can provide some of these tools for delineating the process, as well as a format for collecting, processing, and communicating project-related data in an orderly, standardized format. Project planning and tracking, however, involve more than just the generation of paperwork. They require the participation of the entire project team, including support departments, subcontractors, and top management. It is this involvement of the entire team that fosters a unifying team environment pervasive toward the project goals, and ultimately to the personal commitment to the various tasks within time and budget constraints. The specific benefits of procedural documents, including forms and checklists, are that they help to:

- Provide guidelines and uniformity
- Encourage useful, but minimum, documentation
- Communicate information clearly and effectively
- Standardize data formats
- Unify project teams
- Provide a basis for analysis
- Ensure document agreements for future reference
- Refuel commitments
- Minimize paperwork
- Minimize conflict and confusion
- Delineate work packages
- Bring new team members on board
- Build an experience track and method for future projects

Done properly, the process of project planning must involve both the performing and the customer organizations. This involvement creates a new insight into the intricacies of a project and its management methods. It also leads to visibility of the project at various organizational levels, management involvement, and support. It is this involvement at all organizational levels that stimulates interest in the project and the desire for success, and fosters a pervasive reach for excellence that unifies the project team. It leads to commitment toward establishing and reaching the desired project objectives and to a self-forcing management system where people want to work toward these established objectives.

The Challenges

Even though procedural documents can provide all these benefits, management is often reluctant to implement or fully support a formal project management system. Management concerns often center around four issues: overhead burden, start-up delays, stifled creativity, and reduced self-forcing control. First, the introduction of more organizational formality via policies, procedures, and forms might cost some money, and additional funding may be needed to support and maintain the system. Second, the system is seen, especially by action-oriented managers, as causing undesirable start-up delays by requiring the placing of certain stakes into the ground, in terms of project definition, feasibility, and organization, before the detailed implementation can start. Third and fourth, the system is often perceived as stifling creativity and shifting project control from the responsible individual to an impersonal process that enforces the execution of a predefined number of procedural steps and forms without paying attention to the complexities and dynamics of the individual project and its possibly changing objectives. The comment of one project manager may be typical for many situations: "My support personnel feel that we spend too much time planning a project up front; it creates a very rigid environment that stifles innovation. The only purpose seems to be establishing a basis for controls against outdated measures and for punishment rather than help in case of a contingency." This comment is echoed by many project managers. It also illustrates the potential misuse of formal project management systems to establish unrealistic controls and penalties for deviations from the program plan rather than to help to find solutions. Whether these fears are real or imaginary does not change the fact that they are felt. It is the perceived coercion that leads to the rejection of the project management system. An additional concern is the lack of management involvement and funding to implement the project management system. Often the customer or sponsor organization must also be involved and agree with the process for planning and controlling the project.

How to Make It Work

Few companies have introduced project management procedures with ease. Most have experienced problems ranging from skepticism to sabotage of the procedural system. Realistically, however, program managers have not much of a choice, especially for the larger, more complex programs. Every project manager who believes in project management has his or her own success story. It is interesting to note, however, that many use incremental approaches to develop and implement their project management methodology.

Developing and implementing such a methodology incrementally is a multifaceted challenge to management. The problem is seldom one of understanding the techniques involved, such as budgeting and scheduling, but rather a problem of involving the project team in the process, getting their inputs, support, and commitment, and establishing a supportive environment. Furthermore, project personnel must have the feeling that the policies and procedures of the project management system facilitate communication, are flexible and adaptive to the changing environment, and provide an early warning system through which project personnel obtain assistance rather than punishment in case of a contingency.

The procedural guidelines and forms of an established project management methodology can be especially useful during the project planning/definition phase. Not only does project management methodology help to delineate and communicate the four major sets of variables for organizing and managing the project—(1) tasks, (2) timing, (3) resources, and (4) responsibilities—it also helps to define measurable milestones, as well as report and review requirements. This provides project personnel the ability to measure project status and performance and supplies the crucial inputs for controlling the project toward the desired results.

Developing an effective project management methodology takes more than just a set of policies and procedures. It requires the integration of these guidelines and standards into the culture and value system of the organization. Management must lead the overall efforts and foster an environment conducive to teamwork. The greater the team spirit, trust, commitment, and quality of information exchange among team members, the more likely the team will be to develop effective decision-making processes, make individual and group commitments, focus on problem-solving, and operate in a self-forcing, self-correcting control mode. These are the characteristics that will support and pervade the formal project management system and make it work for you. When understood and accepted by the team members, such a system provides the formal standards, guidelines, and measures needed to direct a project toward specific results within the given time and resource constraints.

Established Practices

Although project managers may have the right to establish their own policies and procedures, many companies have taken the route of designing project control forms that can be used uniformly on all projects to assist in the communications process. Project control forms provide two vital purposes by establishing a common framework from which:

- The project manager will communicate with executives, functional managers, functional employees, and clients.
- Executives and the project manager can make meaningful decisions concerning the allocation of resources.

Success or failure of a project depends upon the ability of key personnel to have sufficient data for decision-making. Project management is often considered to be both an art and a science. It is an art because of the strong need for interpersonal skills, and the project planning and control forms attempt to convert part of the "art" into a science.

Many companies tend not to realize until too late the necessity of good planning and control forms. Today, some of the larger companies with mature project management structures maintain a separate functional unit for forms control. This is quite common in aerospace and defense, but is also becoming common practice in other industries. Yet, some executives believe that forms are needed only when the company grows to a point where a continuous stream of unique projects necessitates some sort of uniform control mechanism.

In some small or non–project-driven organizations, each project can have its own forms. But for most other organizations, uniformity is a must. Quite often, the actual design and selection of the forms is made by individuals other than the users. This can easily lead to disaster.

Large companies with a multitude of different projects do not have the luxury of controlling projects with three or four forms. There are different forms for planning, scheduling, controlling, authorizing work, and so on. It is not uncommon for companies to have 20 to 30 different forms, each dependent upon the type of project, length of project, dollar value, type of customer reporting, and other such arguments.

In project management, the project manager is often afforded the luxury of being able to set up his or her own administration for the project, a fact that could lead to irrevocable long-term damage if each project manager were permitted to design his or her own forms for project control. Many times this problem remains unchecked, and the number of forms grows exponentially with each project.

Executives can overcome this problem either by limiting the number of forms necessary for planning, scheduling, and controlling projects, or by establishing a separate department to do so. Neither of these ways is really practical or cost effective. The best method appears to be the task force concept, where both managers and doers will have the opportunity to interact and provide input. In the short run, this may appear to be ineffective and a waste of time and money. However, in the long run there should be large benefits.

To be effective, the following ground rules can be used:

● Task forces should include managers as well as doers.
● Task force members must be willing to accept criticism from other peers, superiors, and especially subordinates who must "live" with these forms.
● Upper-level management should maintain a rather passive (or monitoring) involvement.
● A minimum of signature approvals should be required for each form.
● Forms should be designed so that they can be updated periodically.
● Functional managers and project managers must be dedicated and committed to the use of the forms.

Categorizing the Broad Spectrum of Documents

The dynamic nature of project management and its multifunctional involvement create a need for a multitude of procedural documents to guide a project through the various phases and stages of integration. Especially for the larger organizations, the challenge is not only to provide management guidelines for each project activity, but also to provide a coherent procedural framework within which project leaders from all disciplines can work and communicate with each other. Specifically, each policy or procedure must be consistent with and accommodating to the various other functions that interface with the project over its life cycle. This complexity of intricate relations is illustrated in Figure 21–5.

One simple and effective way of categorizing the broad spectrum of procedural documents is by utilizing the work breakdown concept, as shown in Figure 21–6. Accordingly, the principal procedural categories are defined along the principal project life-cycle phases. Each category is then subdivided into (1) general management guidelines, (2) policies, (3) procedures, (4) forms, and (5) checklists. If necessary, the same concept can be carried forward one additional step to develop policies, procedures, forms, and checklists for the various project and functional sublevels of operation. Although this might be needed for very large programs, an effort should be made to minimize "layering" of policies and procedures, as the additional bureaucracy can cause new interface problems and additional overhead costs. For most projects, a single document covers all levels of project operations.

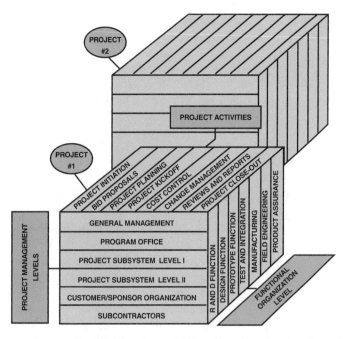

FIGURE 21–5. Interrelationship of project activities with various functional/organizational levels and project management levels.

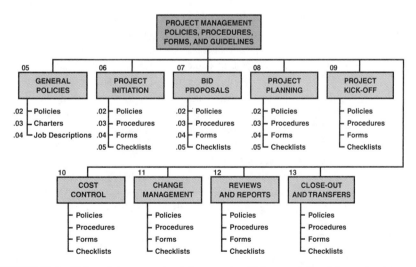

FIGURE 21–6. Categorizing procedural documents within a work breakdown structure.

As We Mature . . .   As companies become more mature in executing the project management methodology, project management policies and procedures are disregarded and replaced with guidelines, forms, and checklists. More flexibility is provided the project manager. Unfortunately, this takes time because executives must have faith in the ability of the project management methodology to work without the rigid controls provided by policies and procedures. Yet all companies seem to go through the evolutionary stages of policies and procedures before they get to guidelines, forms, and checklists.

21.3 PROJECT MANAGEMENT METHODOLOGIES

The ultimate purpose of any project management system is to drastically increase the likelihood that your organization will have a continuous stream of successfully managed projects. The best way to achieve this goal is with the development of a good project management methodology. Good project management methodologies are based upon guidelines and forms rather than policies and procedures. Methodologies must have enough flexibility that they can be adapted easily to each and every project. There are consulting companies that have created their own methodologies and that will try to convince you that the solution to most of your project management problems can be found with the purchase of their (often expensive) methodology. These consulting companies have as their primary goal the desire to turn problems into gold: *your problems into their gold!*

There exists a major hurdle that companies must overcome when developing or purchasing a project management methodology. A methodology is nothing more than a sheet of paper with instructions. What converts this sheet of paper into a successful methodology is the way the company accepts, supports, and executes the methodology. Methodologies should be designed to support the corporate culture, not vice versa. It is a fatal mistake to purchase a canned methodology package that mandates that you change your corporate culture to support it. If the methodology does not support the culture, the result will be a lack of acceptance of the methodology, sporadic use at best, inconsistent application of the methodology, poor morale, and perhaps even diminishing support for project management. What converts any methodology into a world-class methodology is its adaptability to the corporate culture. There is no reason why companies cannot develop their own methodology. Companies such as Compaq Services, Ericsson, Nortel Networks, Johnson Controls, and Motorola are regarded as having world-class methodologies for project management and, in each case, the methodology was developed internally. The amount of time and effort needed to develop a methodology will vary from company to company based upon such factors as the size and nature of the projects, the number of functional boundaries to be crossed, whether the organization is project-driven or non–project-driven, and competitive pressures.

Creating your own methodology need not be an expensive endeavor. Developing your own methodology internally to guarantee a fit with the corporate culture usually provides a much greater return on investment than purchasing canned packages that require massive changes.

Even the simplest methodology, if accepted by the organization and used correctly, can increase your chances of success. As an example, Matthew P. LoPiccolo, Director of I.S. Operations for Swagelok Company, describes the process Swagelok went through to develop its methodology:

> We developed our own version of an I.S. project management methodology in the early 90s. We had searched extensively and all we found were a lot of binders that we couldn't see being used effectively. There were just too many procedures and documents. Our answer was a simple checklist system with phase reviews. We called it Checkpoint.
>
> As strategic planning has become more important in our organization, the need for improved project management has risen as well. Project management has found its place as a key tool in executing tactical plans.
>
> As we worked to improve our Checkpoint methodology, we focused on keeping it simple. Our ultimate goal was to transform our methodology into a one-page matrix that was focused on deliverables within each project phase and categorized by key project management areas of responsibility. The key was to create something that would provide guidance in daily project direction and decision making. In order to gain widespread acceptance, the methodology needed to be easy to learn and quick to reference. The true test of its effectiveness is our ability to make decisions and take actions that are driven by the methodology.
>
> We also stayed away from the temptation to buy the solution in the form of a software package. Success is in the application of a practical methodology not in a piece of software. We use various software products as a tool set for scheduling, communicating, effort tracking, and storing project information such as time, budget, issues and lessons learned.

The summary description of the methodology developed by Swagelok is shown in Table 21–1. Swagelok also realized that training and education would be required to support both the methodology and project management in general. Table 21–2 shows the training plan created by Swagelok Company.

21.4 CONTINUOUS IMPROVEMENT

All too often complacency dictates the decision-making process. This is particularly true of organizations that have reached some degree of excellence in project management, become complacent, and then realize too late that they have lost their competitive advantage. This occurs when organizations fail to recognize the importance of continuous improvement.

Figure 21–7 illustrates why there is a need for continuous improvement. As companies begin to mature in project management and reach some degree of excellence, they achieve a sustained competitive advantage. The sustained compet-

TABLE 21–1. SWAGELOK COMPANY'S CHECKPOINT METHODOLOGY, VERSION 3

Project Management	Assessment	Initiate Define/Plan	Design Specify	Deliver Construct/Integrate	Close Deploy/Transition
Key deliverables	Feasibility report	Project charter Business requirements Technical requirements	Detailed business rqmts. Systems analysis Design prototype	System construction System integration pilot test Implementation plan	Project deliverables evaluation Operational transition Vendor performance report Project performance repor
Approval	Feasibility report review Assessment approval	Project approval	Design approval Prototype approval	Construct integrate approval Deployment approval	Project audit Completion approval
Scope	Scope boundaries	Scope/deliverables Benefits/value Assumptions & alternatives Strategic & tactical: impact/ priority/alignment	Change request procedures Issue management procedure	Change management Issue management	Manage delivered value
Human resource	Resource identification	Roles and responsibilities General resource capacity Training requirements Business sponsors	Resource impact & assignment Team training	Resource management Resource performance Knowledge transfer End-customer training	Resource performance evaluation
Time	"Window of opportunity"	Preliminary project schedule Time reporting database	Work breakdown structure Project plan	Execute & monitor plan	Verify activity/completion Close time buckets

1058

Cost	Cost projections	Capital budget Operating budget Return on investment	Budget details	Execute & monitor budget	Close cost centers
Procurement	Alternatives evaluation	Hardware Software Consulting services Vendor RFPs	Vendor selection Contract finalization	Purchase hardware & software Vendor performance report	Ongoing maintenance agreements Vendor performance evaluation
Quality	Vendor assessment Quality requirements	Quality plan Previous lessons learned	Test approach Config. management approach Review lessons learned Walkthroughs/reviews	Test plans Test (i.e., unit, integration, system, acceptance)	Process review Post-implementation review Capture to lessons learned
Risk	"Opportunity costs"	Risk assessment	Risk management plan	Risk mitigation	Capture to lessons learned
Technology	Architecture alignment	Architecture requirements	Architecture verification	Technology architecture	Architecture review
Communication	Inter- and intra-program coordination	Communication requirements project site	Progress reports Meetings schedule Project site update	Project site update	Administrative closure

TABLE 21–2. SWAGELOK COMPANY'S TRAINING PLAN

Project Management Toolset	Training Programs			
	Project Manager	Line Manager	Project Team Member	Executive Managment
1) Project management concepts	PMP class PMP certification PMO overview	PM 101 PM 102 — Small project management	PM 101	Executive overview
2) Checkpoint (methodology)	Teaching level	Basic understanding	Basic understanding	Overview
3) MS project (scheduling)	Knowledgeable to expect	Basic understanding	Not required	Not required
4) TSP (effort tracking)	Management level	Management level	Time entry	Not required
5) Budget DB (budget tracking)	Management of project budget	Owner of department budget	Not required	Not required
6) SICL DB (issues/changes/lessons' management)	Owner	How to view	How to view	Not required
7) Netmosphere (project communication)	Owner, publisher	How to view	How to view	How to view

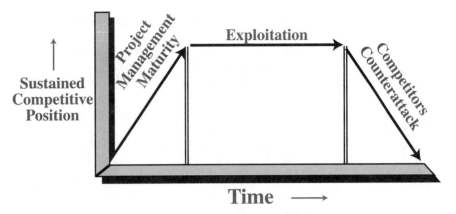

FIGURE 21–7. Why there is a need for continuous improvement.

itive advantage might very well be the single most important strategic objective of the firm. The firm will then begin the exploitation of its sustained competitive advantage.

Unfortunately, the competition is not sitting by idly watching you exploit your sustained competitive advantage. As the competition begins to counterattack, you may lose a large portion, if not all, of your sustained competitive advantage. To remain effective and competitive, the organization must recognize the need for continuous improvement, as shown in Figure 21–8. Continuous improvement allows a firm to maintain its competitive advantage even when the competitors counterattack.

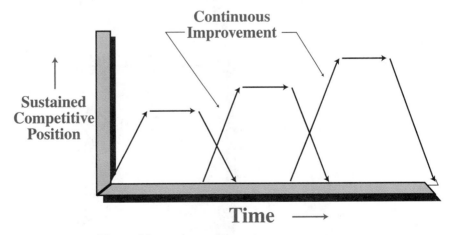

FIGURE 21–8. The need for continuous improvement.

21.5 CAPACITY PLANNING

As companies become excellent in project management, the benefits of performing more work in less time and with fewer resources becomes readily apparent. The question, of course, is how much more work can the organization take on? Companies are now struggling to develop capacity planning models to see how much new work can be undertaken within the existing human and nonhuman constraints.

Figure 21–9 illustrates the classical way that companies perform capacity planning. The approach outlined in this figure holds true for both project- and non–project-driven organizations. The "planning horizon" line indicates the point in time for capacity planning. The "proposals" line indicates the manpower needed for approved internal projects or a percentage (perhaps as much as 100 percent) for all work expected through competitive bidding. The combination of this line and the "manpower requirements" line, when compared against the current staffing, provides us with an indication of capacity. This technique can be effective if performed early enough such that training time is allowed for future manpower shortages.

The limitation to the above process for capacity planning is that only human resources are considered. A more realistic method would be to use the method shown in Figure 21–10, which can also be applied to both project-driven and non–project-driven organizations. From Figure 21–10, projects are selected based upon such factors as strategic fit, profitability, who the customer is, and corporate benefits. The objectives for the projects selected are then defined in both business and technical terms, because there can be both business and technical capacity constraints.

The next step is a critical difference between average companies and excellent companies. Capacity constraints are identified from the summation of the

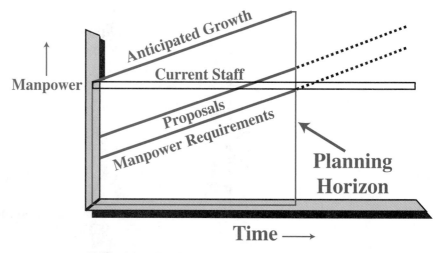

FIGURE 21–9. Classical capacity planning.

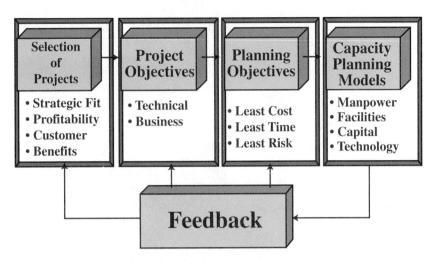

FIGURE 21–10. Improved capacity planning.

schedules and plans. In excellent companies, project managers meet with sponsors to determine the objective of the plan, which is different than the objective of the project. Is the objective of the plan to achieve the project's objective with the least cost, least time, or least risk? Typically, only one of these applies, whereas immature organizations believe that all three can be achieved on every project. This, of course, is unrealistic.

The final box in Figure 21–10 is now the determination of the capacity limitations. Previously, we considered only human resource capacity constraints. Now we realize that the critical path of a project can be constrained not only by time but also by available manpower, facilities, cash flow, and even existing technology. It is possible to have multiple critical paths on a project other than those identified by time. Each of these critical paths provides a different dimension to the capacity planning models, and each of these constraints can lead us to a different capacity limitation. As an example, manpower might limit us to taking on only four additional projects. Based upon available facilities, however we might only be able to undertake two more projects, and based upon available technology, we might be able to undertake only one new project.

21.6 COMPETENCY MODELS

In the twenty-first century, companies will replace job descriptions with competency models. Job descriptions for project management tend to emphasize the deliverables and expectations from the project manager, whereas competency models emphasize the specific skills needed to achieve the deliverables.

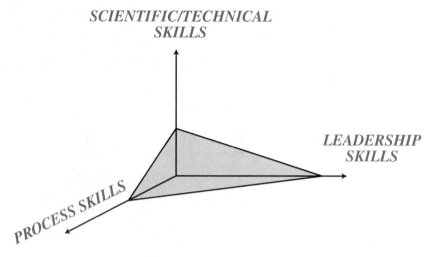

FIGURE 21–11. Competency model.

Figure 21–11 shows the competency model for Eli Lilly. Project managers are expected to have competencies in three broad areas:[1]

- Scientific/technical skills
- Leadership skills
- Process skills

For each of the three broad areas, there are subdivisions or grade levels. A primary advantage of a competency model is that it allows the training department to develop customized project management training programs to satisfy the skill requirements. Without competency models, most training programs are generic rather than customized. Also, a competency model makes it easier for an organization to develop a complete training curriculum rather than a single course.

Competency models focus on specialized skills in order to assist the project manager in making more efficient use of his or her time. Figure 21–12, although argumentative, shows that with specialized competency training, project managers can increase their time effectiveness by reducing time robbers and rework. Unfortunately, time robbers and rework cannot always be eliminated, only reduced.

Competency models make it easier for companies to develop a complete project management curriculum, rather than a singular course. This is shown in Figure 21–13. As companies mature in project management and develop a

---

1. A detailed description of the Eli Lilly competency model and the Ericsson competency model can be found in Harold Kerzner, *Applied Project Management* (New York: Wiley, 1999), pp. 266–283.

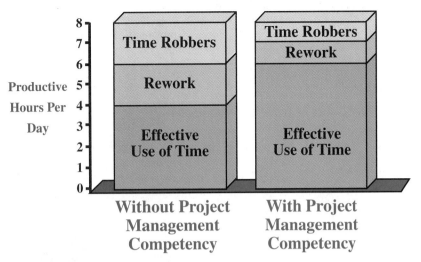

FIGURE 21–12. Core competency analysis.

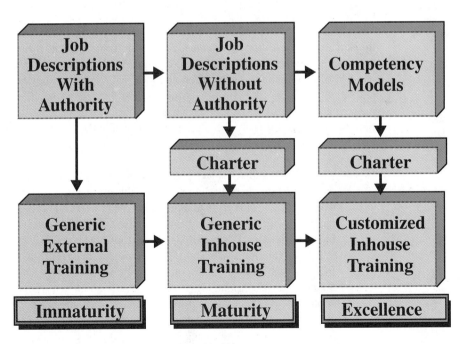

FIGURE 21–13. Competency models and training.

company-wide core competency model, an internal, custom-designed curriculum will be developed. Companies, especially large ones, will find it necessary to maintain a course architecture specialist on their staff.

21.7 MANAGING MULTIPLE PROJECTS

As organizations begin to mature in project management, there is a tendency toward having one person manage multiple projects. The initial impetus may come either from the company sponsoring the projects or from project managers themselves. There are several factors supporting the managing of multiple projects. First, the cost of maintaining a full-time project manager on all projects may be prohibitive. The magnitude and risks of each individual project dictate whether a full-time or part-time assignment is necessary. Assigning a project manager full-time on an activity that does not require it is an overmanagement cost. Overmanagement of projects was considered an acceptable practice in the early days of project management because we had little knowledge on how to handle risk management. Today, methods for risk management exist.

Second, line managers are now sharing accountability with project managers for the successful completion of the project. Project managers are now managing at the template levels of the WBS with the line managers accepting accountability for the work packages at the detailed WBS levels. Project managers now spend more of their time integrating work rather than planning and scheduling functional activities. With the line manager accepting more accountability, time may be available for the project manager to manage multiple projects.

Third, senior management has come to the realization that they must provide high quality training for their project managers if they are to reap the benefits of managing multiple projects. Senior managers must also change the way that they function as sponsors. There are six major areas where the corporation as a whole may have to change in order for the managing of multiple projects to succeed.

- *Prioritization:* If a project prioritization system is in effect, it must be used correctly such that employee credibility in the system is realized. There are downside risks to a prioritization system. The project manager, having multiple projects to manage, may favor those projects having the highest priorities. It is possible that no prioritization system at all may be the best solution. Also, not every project needs to be prioritized. Prioritization can be a time-consuming effort.
- *Scope Changes:* Managing multiple projects is almost impossible if the sponsors/customers are allowed to make continuous scope changes. When using multiple projects management, it must be understood that the majority of the scope changes may have to be performed through enhancement projects rather than through a continuous scope change effort. A major scope change on one project could limit the project manager's

available time to service other projects. Also, continuous scope changes will almost always be accompanied by reprioritization of projects, a further detriment to the management of multiple projects.

- *Capacity Planning:* Organizations that support the management of multiple projects generally have a tight control on resource scheduling. As a result, the organization must have knowledge of capacity planning, theory of constraints, resource leveling, and resource limited planning.
- *Project Methodology:* Methodologies for project management range from rigid policies and procedures to more informal guidelines and checklists. When managing multiple projects, the project manager must be granted some degree of freedom. This necessitates guidelines, checklists, and forms. Formal project management practices create excessive paperwork requirements, thus minimizing the opportunities to manage multiple projects. The project size is also critical.
- *Project Initiation:* Managing multiple projects has been going on for almost 40 years. One thing that we have learned is that it can work well as long as the projects are in relatively different life-cycle phases. The demands on the project manager's time are different for each life-cycle phase. Therefore, for the project manager to effectively balance his/her time among multiple projects, it would be best for the sponsor not to have the projects begin at exactly the same time.
- *Organizational Structures:* If the project manager is to manage multiple projects, then it is highly unlikely that the project manager will be a technical expert in all areas of all projects. Assuming that the accountability is shared with the line managers, the organization will most likely adopt a weak matrix structure.

21.8 END-OF-PHASE REVIEW MEETINGS

For more than 20 years, end-of-phase review meetings were simply an opportunity for executives to "rubber stamp" the project to continue on. The meetings were used to give the executives some degree of comfort concerning project status. Only good news was presented by the project team.

Executives very rarely cancelled projects from a selfish point of view; the executive was better off allowing the new product to be developed even though the executive knew full well that the product had no buyers or would be overpriced. Once the product was developed, the executive sponsor was "off the hook." Blame now rested on the shoulders of the marketing group: if customers could not be found, obviously the problem was with marketing.

Today, end-of-phase review meetings take on a different dimension. First and foremost, executives are no longer afraid to cancel projects, especially if the objectives have changed, if the objectives are unreachable, or if the resources can be used on other activities that have a greater likelihood of success. Executives now spend more time assessing the risks in the future rather than focusing on accomplishments in the past.

Since project managers are now becoming more business-oriented rather than technically oriented, the project managers are expected to present information on business risks, reassessment of the benefit-to-cost ratio, and any business decisions that could affect the ultimate objectives. Simply stated, the end-of-phase review meetings now focus more on business decisions, rather than on technical decisions.

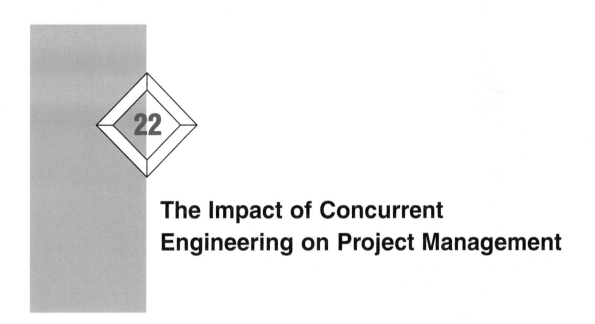

The Impact of Concurrent Engineering on Project Management

22.0 INTRODUCTION

Corporations today are finally chiseling away at the functional silos and smokestacks that have been in existence for years, as well as the walls separating these smokestacks. Companies are beginning to realize and accept the fact that isolated functional empires are not conducive to effective teamwork. Response to changes in the marketplace has become so slow that the organization's competitive advantage may be eroding

Over the years, project management has proven to be effective in integrating work across these functional silos *without* requiring organizational restructuring or shifts in the balance of power and authority. Line managers were allowed to hoard their power-generating information and provide it to the projects on an as-needed basis. Although this was not always the best way to operate, organizations adapted reasonably well. Once line managers felt that project management posed no threat to them, project management support slowly was forthcoming such that maturity could be realized.

Several studies have been conducted that provide management with an insight into what critical factors must be considered in order to achieve maturity in project management.[1-3] Typical maturity factors considered included:

1. D. I. Cleland and H. Kerzner, "The Best Managed Projects," *Proceedings of the Project Management Institute's 1985 Annual Seminar/Symposium on Project Management,* Denver, Colorado, October 7–9, 1985, Volume 2.

2. H. Kerzner, "In Search of Excellence in Project Management," *Journal of Systems Management,* February 1987, pp. 30–39.

3. H. Kerzner and J. Kerzner, "Planning for Excellence in Project Management: The Next Twenty Years," *Proceedings of the Project Management Institute's Annual Seminar/Symposium on Project Management,* San Francisco, September 17–21, 1988, pp. 407–413.

- A commitment of planning
- Effective risk management
- Management of creeping scope
- Development of policies, procedures, and guidelines
- Effective project staffing
- Project sponsorship
- Wage and salary administration program that includes project personnel
- Changes in organizational behavior
- Effective problem reporting and corrections

As companies mature toward excellence in project management, the above factors were effectively considered and incorporated into the project management culture. Unfortunately, new management practices are continuously surfacing that require rethinking and changes to the above factors. The most common management practices to surface are:

- Total quality management (TQM)
- Empowerment
- Self-directed work teams
- Life-cycle costing
- Concurrent engineering

Only the last item appears to have a *major* impact on how we manage projects. Concurrent engineering requires better teamwork and cooperation between the functional silos. Information must now be shared freely and in a timely manner. The traditional methods for managing projects and institutionalizing project management must change.

22.1 UNDERSTANDING CONCURRENT ENGINEERING

Corporations are under tremendous pressure to get products to the marketplace quicker. This is partially due to the shortening of product life cycles. To shorten the time from concept to production requires that work that is normally conducted in series now be conducted in parallel. This concept is referred to as concurrent or simultaneous engineering, where marketing, engineering, and production all work together at the same time, perhaps *throughout* the life cycle of the project.

Figure 22–1 illustrates a simplistic schedule for a small project. If the work is conducted in series, the time frame would be fifteen weeks. However, if the work is conducted in parallel, then it may be possible to complete the project in nine weeks, thus reducing the schedule by 40 percent. Concurrent engineering requires that additional risks be taken. In Figure 22–1, engineering design begins *before* planning is completed. By waiting for planning to be completed, we are simply lengthening the project.

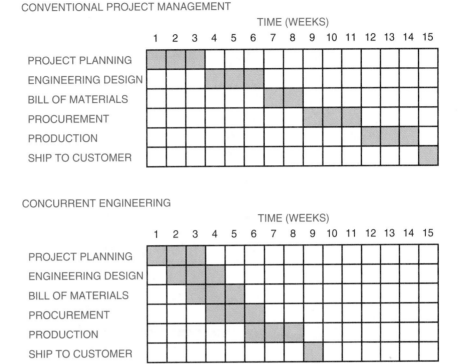

FIGURE 22–1. Comparison of conventional project management and concurrent engineering. © 1992 by Project Management Associates.

According to Reinertsen,[4] "Do just enough planning to begin design and then complete it early enough to support key design decisions." The preparation of the bill of material can begin early in the design stage. Procurement can begin when the bill of materials is partially prepared. However, complete procurement requires a complete bill of materials. Other typical activities that can be done in parallel are concept generation and product planning, and product and process engineering. Concurrent engineering tries to shrink the functional silos that advocate "over-the-fence" and "over-the-wall" engineering. Without concurrent engineering, designs were too far along into the manufacturing process for manufacturing personnel to recommend radical change to improve the quality or lower the manufacturing cost of the product. With concurrent engineering, manufacturing personnel are on board at day one.

---

4. D. E. Reinertsen, "The Mythology of Speed," *Machine Design,* March 26, 1992, p. 47.

John Hartley[5] has developed a list of benefits of concurrent engineering:

- Products that precisely match customer's needs
- Shorter time to market
- Earlier break-even point
- Fewer changes late in the program, reducing cost of development
- Simpler and cheaper manufacture
- Assured quality from Job One
- Low service cost throughout the life of the product
- Less risk of failure than normal

These benefits have been proven in such organizations as Digital Equipment Corporation, Northrup Corporation, and the U.S. Department of Defense. During concurrent engineering activities, the costs associated with rework and schedule slippages could be an order of magnitude greater than during conventional project management. Also, because of the complexities of parallel activities, contingency planning may not be possible.

22.2 PROJECT PLANNING

When a project manager plans a project, the project manager must determine the objective for the plan. (This is *not* the objective for the project, which is included in the statement [scope] of work.) There are three primary objectives for planning—to develop a plan

- In the least time
- With the least cost
- With the least risk

Most projects have one and only one primary planning objective.

Because of the conservative nature of many corporate decisions, most project managers have opted for the least risk, thus accepting a willingness to increase time and cost. With concurrent engineering, the primary planning constraint is now "least time," which requires risk-taking. As a result, concurrent engineering advocates that the project manager become a risk manager. The hard part is to decide which risk is worth taking and which is not.

In the past, downstream planning activities have always been delayed until upstream activities were 100 percent complete. This sequential work flow led to project planning at the microscopic levels of the work breakdown structure and

---

5. J. R. Hartley, *Concurrent Engineering* (Cambridge, Massachusetts: Productivity Press, 1992), p. 88.

with an affinity for excruciating detail. Project planning thus resided *on the critical path.* With concurrent engineering, project planning is never on the critical path.

The final project plan should be viewed as a living document and therefore subject to change. Unfortunately, every change increases the risks within the project and makes concurrent engineering more difficult to implement properly. Therefore, the project manager is faced with the dilemma of executing a project with an incomplete plan and knowing that changes probably will occur.

Another critical problem is that concurrent engineering almost always creates multiple critical paths. This increases the project's risk factors and forces continuous rather than periodic schedule updates. Rapid response must be taken when problems arise.

22.3 RISK MANAGEMENT

With the concurrent engineering, project managers are, first and foremost, managers of risk. They should therefore be compensated for identifying risks, quantifying risks, and deciding which risks are worth taking and which are not, always considering what is in the best interest of the company. With concurrent engineering, the risks can become so great that the project manager may have a difficult time in choosing between the best interest of the project and the best interest of the company.

The project manager has help in assessing risk. First of all, the line managers are probably the real technical experts in most organizations and are therefore the best people qualified to assess the risk. The project manager must make better utilization of the line managers, at least more so than with conventional project management. The project sponsor can also support the project manager by providing strategic information and helping make timely decisions such that work slowdowns do not occur.

Papers are now being published that expound on the risks involved in conventional project management. However, since project management with concurrent engineering is still in the embryonic state, not much has been published on these types of risks within concurrent engineering and their respective solutions.

22.4 CREEPING SCOPE

With concurrent engineering, creeping scope becomes a way of life. It simply may not be possible to identify and process all of the critical information in the early stages of the project. The ideal way to handle creeping scope is to freeze the specifications/scope and treat all further changes as a separate project with its own budget, schedule, and requirements. This project is later funded as an enhancement project. This approach is well and good *if* the specifications/scope can be frozen. Unfortunately, for projects involving new product development, the specifications may be the output of the project rather than the input. Frozen specifications may not be compatible with project management using concurrent engineering.

Creeping scope isn't all that bad if that's what it takes to satisfy the customer's requirements. The more serious problem is when creeping scope becomes creeping "elegance." In this case, the requirements of the project have been met but the employees appear to be seeking perfection.

For years creeping scope has occurred all the way from concept development to full manufacturing. Companies have tried unsuccessfully to establish a policy as to how late in a project creeping scope should be allowed to occur. Companies instituted change control boards to analyze the impact the change would have on the time, cost, and performance constraints of the project. With concurrent engineering, the project manager now has the task of identifying the risks associated with each change. This becomes a very critical activity since continuous scope changes may destroy the benefits of using concurrent engineering.

With concurrent engineering, more scope changes will evolve than with conventional project management. However, fewer downstream changes should be allowed because of the risks to the projects. Concurrent engineering advocates the identification of scope changes early on.

22.5 PROJECT MANAGEMENT GUIDELINES

Since the inception of project management, senior managers have been fearful that they would lose control of the organization because each project manager would be going off on a tangent doing his own thing. To alleviate this problem, management had to either accept fewer projects or find a better way to control projects. The first choice was impractical because companies were not about to turn away work. The second choice was then examined and selected.

In the early 1970s, companies opted for the development of well-structured life-cycle phases such as shown in Figure 22–2. There were two main benefits of this approach. First, a generic checklist of activities could be identified for each phase. This provided management with some degree of assurance that there would be consistency in the way each project would be planned, scheduled, and controlled. The second benefit was the establishment of end-of-phase reviews. This provided management with well-structured decision points on each and every project. Budgeting could be conducted on a phase-by-phase basis rather than for the entire project. Also, management found that well-structured end-of-phase reviews meant that they did not have to micromanage or meddle throughout each phase.

By the early 1980s, management began to reap the benefits of project management and recognized that more and more projects could be undertaken with-

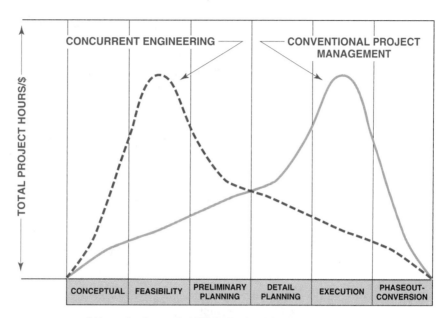

FIGURE 22–2. Life-cycle phases. © 1992 by Project Management Associates.

out substantially increasing the resource base. However, management became fearful that even with the use of life-cycle phases, additional controls were needed. Companies, therefore, developed policy and procedure manuals for project management, thus reducing the project manager's flexibility.

By the mid 1980s, the project-driven industries that undertook projects as their only means of survival began having second thoughts about using rigid policy and procedure manuals. These manuals now were looked upon as handcuffs rather than as benefits. In addition, the large diversity of projects, even within the same company, made it almost impossible to develop policies and procedures that covered every possible type of project. Companies, therefore, converted their policies and procedures to guidelines, thus giving more freedom to the project managers.

By the early 1990s, companies recognized that concurrent engineering was not a fad and will be one of the management practices that will endure well into the twenty-first century. Since project management and concurrent engineering work hand-in-hand, organizations now have to decide whether life-cycle phases, policies, procedures, guidelines, and end-of-phase reviews are still applicable. Life-cycle phases are still applicable but their usefulness is limited. Several life-cycle phases will be going on at the same time and it may not be possible to identify where one phase begins and another phase ends.

With concurrent engineering, the deployment of project resources will move the "bulge" of the resource curve in Figure 22–2 to the left into the earlier life-cycle phases as shown by the dotted curve. This requires a strong commitment by corporate management to understand that downstream cost savings will occur as a result of heavy up-front person-loading.

This overlapping of phases also limits the usefulness of end-of-phase reviews as the only checkpoints. Project policies and procedures are all but obsolete with concurrent engineering. It is truly a formidable task to develop a policy or procedure that can span several concurrent life-cycle phases and integrate work over a multitude of departments. Guidelines are still being used only because companies feel that something is needed and they are not sure what it is or will be. These guidelines are being transformed into "methodologies."

Large companies usually have "pockets" of project management where each operational unit has its own way of managing. One, and only one, project management culture is nonexistent. In this case, each pocket is allowed to develop its own methodology for handling projects. However, all of the methodologies must have common threads for integration, planning, scheduling, controlling, and documentation.

Figure 22–3 shows the direction in which organizations probably will go. With concurrent engineering, what makes most sense appears to be checklists and *periodic* checkpoints for project reviews, combined with some type of methodol-

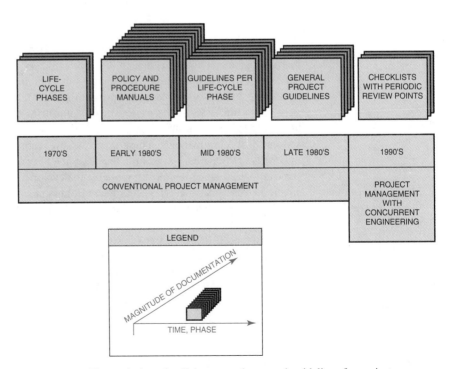

FIGURE 22–3. The evolution of policies, procedures, and guidelines for project management. © 1992 by Project Management Associates.

ogy. These periodic reviews should not be longer than two weeks and should be held in the presence of the project sponsor. Weekly reviews are preferable. The checklists can become detailed as companies begin to mature in project management and concurrent engineering.

22.6 SELECTING THE PROJECT MANAGER

Modern-day project management had its roots in the aerospace and defense fields in the late 1950s and early 1960s. Project managers were selected for their technical skill rather than their ability to get along with people. As project management matured and projects became large and complex, management began to realize that the project manager was a manager of people in addition to being a manager of work. Thus the project manager's behavioral skills became equally as important as his technical skills. On technically strong projects such as R&D, the project manager's behavioral skills were not considered as important as his technical skills.

With concurrent engineering, the *primary* skill of project managers should be their multidisciplinary knowledge of the business. The *secondary* skill should be the ability to analyze and assess risks, especially the risks associated with integration of work. Having worked in a variety of line positions within the organization is a definite plus. As concurrent engineering matures, we may once again reassess the importance of the project manager's behavioral skills. Behavioral skills will become of increasing importance.

Today, project management has matured in both project-driven and non–project-driven companies. Unfortunately, non–project-driven organizations will find it more difficult to maintain a mature project management system while performing concurrent engineering. First, in non–project-driven companies, it is common practice for line managers to wear multiple hats and serve as a project and line manager at the same time. Under concurrent engineering, this may very well be impossible. Non–project-driven companies will probably accept the culture of project-driven companies by making project management a career path. Table 22–1 shows the changes that will be required. Note that project-driven companies will find it easier to mature in project management with concurrent engineering than non–project-driven companies.

22.7 THE PROJECT OFFICE

Not all projects are large enough to justify or afford a project office. But those that are, find that concurrent engineering is imposing a different set of criteria for the selection of project office personnel. When project offices came into existence some thirty years ago, the people placed in the offices were most frequently those

TABLE 22–1. MAJOR CHANGES NEEDED TO INCORPORATE CONCURRENT ENGINEERING

	Present Organization		New Organization
	Project-Driven	**Non–Project-Driven**	**Concurrent Engineering**
Number of hats for the project manager	1	2	1
Availability	Full-time	Part-time	Full-time
Primary skill required	Understand technology, understand people	Technical expert, understand people	Knowledge of business, risk management, integration skills
Career path	Line Manager to project manager to executive	Project manager to line manager to executive	Multiple paths
Promotion ladders	Management, technical, project management	Management, technical	Management, technical, project management
Project management department	Yes	No	Yes
Certification required in the near future	Probably	No	Highly probable

individuals with the greatest technical skill. To add insult to injury, each project office technical specialist was provided with one or two assistants as backup protection (should sickness or termination from the company occur). Most of these individuals had expertise in one and only one area. Integration was time-consuming and costly. All work was performed sequentially.

Customers recognized that this was an overmanagement expense but were willing to pay for it because the cost for undermanagement (i.e., needing the people but having them unavailable) could be perhaps an order of magnitude more costly than the price for overmanagement. The project office became so strong technically that line personnel were taking technical direction from the project office rather than from their own line managers.

In the late 1970s and early 1980s, companies recognized the importance of maintaining strong technical skills within the line groups. The people now placed in the project office were generalists who *understood* the technology but did not possess a command of technology. Furthermore, project office personnel became backups for one another, thus reducing the overmanagement costs. If costs were really critical, project office personnel could perform on a part-time basis.

With concurrent engineering, staffing requirements for the project office will change. Like the project manager, project office personnel should have multidisciplinary backgrounds and therefore be generalists rather than experts (there are exceptions, however). They should understand the integration problems and the potential solutions. They should be assigned full-time *for the duration of the project* and require minimal supervision from the project manager and, if applicable, their respective line managers.

Professionalism for project office personnel will occur. If the company maintains a project management career path ladder for the project manager, then this same ladder should be available for project office personnel. This implies that project office personnel may not return to a line function but will go from project office to project office as a career path. Certification may eventually be a prerequisite for a career path for project office personnel. Project office personnel may be regarded as assistant project managers rather than simply as employees. This may occur primarily for the customer's benefit. Customers like talking to people with the title of manager.

One final note needs to be mentioned concerning project office staffing. The project manager's major concern in staffing the project office should be to negotiate for the *best team,* not necessarily the best workers. Sometimes, outstanding employees find it difficult to work in groups where they must "trust" someone else's numbers and equations. Mistrust in a project office during concurrent engineering will be disastrous.

22.8 THE FUNCTIONAL TEAM

With concurrent engineering, the organization's technical expertise rests in the line groups, not in the project office. The line manager is the true technical expert and perhaps best qualified to identify technical risks. This means that the line managers, rather than the project office, will provide technical direction to their people. The implication here is that the project manager should negotiate for deliverables rather than people. If the line manager commits to a deliverable, then the project manager must trust the line manager to perform as expected. Concurrent engineering requires a lot of trust.

This by no means implies that project managers divorce themselves from the functional staffing process. The project manager still has the right to question specific assignments and whether they will be team players. All critical employees should be assigned full-time, perhaps for the duration of the project. The noncritical skills can be matrixed into the project from the line groups.

The project manager will maintain full-time support from perhaps a large majority of the assigned personnel. By no means should the project manager force these people to sever their relationship with the rest of the organization. This is an argument for the project manager wanting his entire team under one roof and in one location. This could be more harmful than good especially if the line manager feels threatened with the loss of a key employee. Removing functional employees from their line manager usually encourages line managers to assign low-caliber or unwanted employees and to make commitments to deliverables hard to come by.

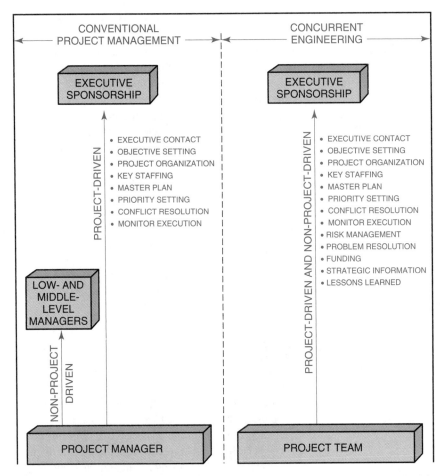

FIGURE 22–4. Comparison of the role of the project sponsor for high-priority–high-visibility projects. © 1992 by Project Management Associates.

22.9 PROJECT SPONSORSHIP

Perhaps the most difficult function that must change will be the role of the project sponsor. With conventional project management, the role of the project sponsor was primarily for executive–client contact even though other functions existed, as shown in Figure 22–4. Under concurrent engineering, the primary function for the sponsor may be the timely handling of internal problems involving integration. Today, sponsorship exists at all levels of management (as shown in Figure 22–4) based on the priority of the project. With concurrent engineering, sponsorship must exist at the top at least until the company matures in both project management and concurrent engineering.

Today, some organizations are already redefining the role of the project sponsor to include additional functions. First, because of the risks of certain projects, both the project sponsor and the project manager must encourage problems to be brought to the surface quickly so that they can be resolved. People should not feel threatened by exposing problems early. Second, more and more reporting will be done informally rather than formally. Formal reporting is not only costly because of paperwork preparation, but time-consuming for reviews. Third, sponsors must be actively involved in analyzing the impact of scope changes. Fourth, the sponsor must be willing to support the project manager in obtaining the necessary manpower funding in order to person-load the project correctly in the early project phases. Fifth, the sponsor must provide the project office with as much critical information as possible that could relate to the project. And sixth, it is imperative that executives conduct postaudit reviews so that "lessons learned" can be applied to other projects.

Today, project sponsors appear to get involved either too little or too much. The involvement is primarily a relationship between the project manager and the sponsor. With concurrent engineering, project sponsors must act as sponsors for the team and *must* be willing to be available for team members as well as attending team meeting during the early stages of a project.

With conventional engineering, sponsorship can change over the life cycle of the project. This probably will not occur under concurrent engineering. The downside risk of executive sponsorship is that the executive will view himself as the project manager as well.

As can be seen in Figure 22–4, executive sponsorship has more responsibilities under concurrent engineering. Therefore, until concurrent engineering matures, executives may find fewer projects requiring concurrent engineering and be more selective in choosing projects on which to serve as an executive sponsor. Concurrent engineering may very well occupy more of the executive's time than does conventional project management.

22.10 WAGE AND SALARY ADMINISTRATION

As stated previously, concurrent engineering professionalizes the role of a project manager. Companies must consider a project management career path ladder for both the project manager and project office personnel. The company must also develop a realistic evaluation process for employees assigned to concurrent engineering project teams. With conventional project management, functional employees may have to share their efforts among several projects simultaneously. The line manager provides the employee's evaluation with or without any input from the project manager. With concurrent engineering, the employees may be full-time on one project perhaps for the duration of the project. It is possible that the project manager *may* be the best-qualified person to evaluate the employee's performance. Employees must have a clear understanding right at the start of the project as to how they will be evaluated.

22.11 CONCLUSION

Given the fact that project sponsorship will be with us well into the twenty-first century, companies must change the way they manage projects. Project-driven companies will find it easier to make the changes. Non–project-driven organizations may have to prepare for cultural shock.

Changes will have to occur at all levels of the organization. This includes project managers, line managers, and executive sponsors. Risk management will become a way of life. Strong lines of communication, cooperation, and trust will be needed for effective risk management. Wage and salary programs will have to be reexamined for compatibility with effective concurrent engineering.

Quality Management[1]

1. Appreciation is given to Terry Fischer (PMP) and Dr. Frank Anbari (PMP) for their invaluable assistance in the preparation of this chapter.

23.0 INTRODUCTION

During the past twenty years, there has been a revolution toward improved quality. The improvements have occurred not only in product quality, but also in quality leadership and quality project management. The changing views of quality appear in Table 23–1.

Unfortunately, it takes an economic disaster or a recession to get management to recognize the need for improved quality. Prior to the recession of 1979–1982, Ford, General Motors, and Chrysler viewed each other as the competition rather than the Japanese. Prior to the recession of 1989–1994, high-tech engineering companies never fully recognized the need for shortening product development time and the relationship between project management, total quality management, and concurrent engineering.

The push for higher levels of quality appears to be customer driven. Customers are now demanding:

- Higher performance requirements
- Faster product development
- Higher technology levels
- Materials and processes pushed to the limit
- Lower contractor profit margins
- Fewer defects/rejects

One of the critical factors that can affect quality is market expectations. The variables that affect market expectations include:

TABLE 23–1. CHANGING VIEWS OF QUALITY

Past	Present
• Quality is the responsibility of blue-collar workers and direct labor employees working on the floor	• Quality is everyone's responsibility, including white-collar workers, the indirect labor force, and the overhead staff
• Quality defects should be hidden from the customers (and possibly management)	• Defects should be highlighted and brought to the surface for corrective action
• Quality problems lead to blame, faulty justification, and excuses	• Quality problems lead to cooperative solutions
• Corrections-to-quality problems should be accomplished with minimum documentation	• Documentation is essential for "lessons learned" so that mistakes are not repeated
• Increased quality will increase project costs	• Improved quality saves money and increases business
• Quality is internally focused	• Quality is customer focused
• Quality will not occur without close supervision of people	• People want to produce quality products
• Quality occurs during project execution	• Quality occurs at project initiation and must be planned for within the project

- Salability: the balance between quality and cost
- Produceability: the ability to produce the product with available technology and workers, and at an acceptable cost
- Social acceptability: the degree of conflict between the product or process and the values of society (i.e., safety, environment)
- Operability: the degree to which a product can be operated safely
- Availability: the probability that the product, when used under given conditions, will perform satisfactorily when called upon
- Reliability: the probability of the product performing without failure under given conditions and for a set period of time
- Maintainability: the ability of the product to be retained in or restored to a performance level when prescribed maintenance is performed

Customer demands are now being handled using total quality management (TQM). Total quality management is an ever-improving system for integrating various organizational elements into the design, development, and manufacturing efforts, providing cost-effective products or services that are fully acceptable to the ultimate customer. Externally, TQM is customer oriented and provides for more meaningful customer satisfaction. Internally, TQM reduces production line bottlenecks and operating costs, thus enhancing product quality while improving organizational morale.

23.1 DEFINITION OF QUALITY

Mature organizations today readily admit that they cannot accurately define quality. The reason for this is because quality is defined by the customer. The Kodak definition of quality is those products and services that are perceived to meet or exceed the needs and expectations of the customer at a cost that represents outstanding value. The ISO 9000 definition is "the totality of feature and characteristics of a product or service that bears on its ability to satisfy stated or implied needs." Terms such as fitness for use, customer satisfaction, and zero defects are goals rather than definitions.

Most organizations today view quality more as a process than a product. To be more specific, it is a continuously improving process where lessons learned are used to enhance future products and services in order to

- Retain existing customers
- Win back lost customers
- Win new customers

Therefore, companies today are developing quality improvement processes. Figure 23–1 shows the five quality principles that support Kodak's quality policy. Figure 23–2 shows a more detailed quality improvement process. These two fig-

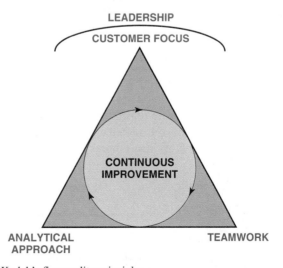

FIGURE 23–1. Kodak's five quality principles.

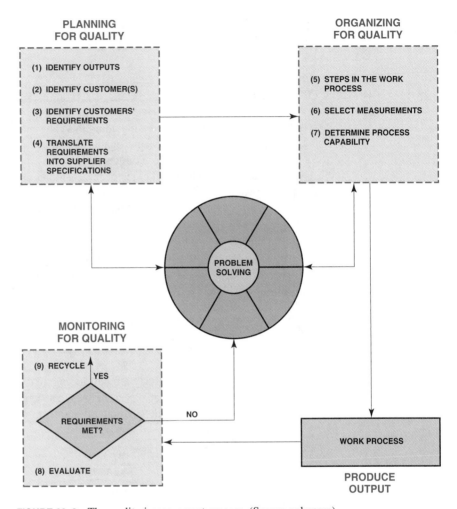

PLANNING
FOR QUALITY

(1) IDENTIFY OUTPUTS

(2) IDENTIFY CUSTOMER(S)

(3) IDENTIFY CUSTOMERS'
    REQUIREMENTS

(4) TRANSLATE
    REQUIREMENTS
    INTO SUPPLIER
    SPECIFICATIONS

ORGANIZING
FOR QUALITY

(5) STEPS IN THE WORK
    PROCESS

(6) SELECT MEASUREMENTS

(7) DETERMINE PROCESS
    CAPABILITY

PROBLEM
SOLVING

MONITORING
FOR QUALITY

(9) RECYCLE

YES

REQUIREMENTS
MET?

NO

(8) EVALUATE

WORK PROCESS

PRODUCE
OUTPUT

FIGURE 23–2. The quality improvement process. (Source unknown).

ures seem to illustrate that organizations are placing more emphasis on the quality process than on the quality product and, therefore, are actively pursuing quality improvements through a continuous cycle.

23.2 THE QUALITY MOVEMENT

During the past 100 years, the views of quality have changed dramatically. Prior to World War I, quality was viewed predominantly as inspection, sorting out the good items from the bad. Emphasis was on problem identification. Following

World War I and up to the early 1950s, emphasis was still on sorting good items from bad. However, *quality control* principles were now emerging in the form of:

- Statistical and mathematical techniques
- Sampling tables
- Process control charts

From the early 1950s to the late 1960s, quality control evolved into quality assurance, with its emphasis on problem avoidance rather than problem detection. Additional quality assurance principles emerged, such as:

- The cost of quality
- Zero-defect programs
- Reliability engineering
- Total quality control

Today, emphasis is being placed on strategic quality management, including such topics as:

- Quality is defined by the customer.
- Quality is linked with profitability on both the market and cost sides.
- Quality has become a competitive weapon.
- Quality is now an integral part of the strategic planning process.
- Quality requires an organization-wide commitment.

Although many experts have contributed to the success of the quality movement, the three most influential contributors in this country and internationally are W. Edwards Deming, Joseph M. Juran, and Phillip B. Crosby. Dr. Deming pioneered the use of statistics and sampling methods from 1927 to 1940 at the U.S. Department of Agriculture. During these early years, Dr. Deming was influenced by Dr. Shewhart. Later, Dr. Deming applied Dr. Shewhart's Plan/Do/Check/Act cycle to clerical tasks. Figure 23–3 shows the Deming Cycle for Improvement.

Deming believed that the reason why companies were not producing quality products was that management was preoccupied with "today" rather than worrying about the future. Deming postulated that 85 percent of all quality problems required management to take the initiative and change the process. Only 15 percent of the quality problems could be controlled by the workers on the floor. As an example, the workers on the floor were not at fault because of the poor quality of raw materials that resulted from management's decision to seek out the lowest cost suppliers. Management had to change the purchasing policies and procedures. Management had to develop long-term relationships with vendors.

Processes had to be placed under statistical analysis and control to demonstrate the repeatability of quality. Furthermore, the ultimate goals should be a continuous refinement of the processes rather than quotas. Statistical process control charts (SPCs) allowed for the identification of common cause and special (as-

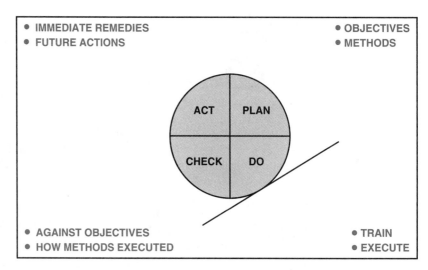

FIGURE 23–3. The Deming Cycle for Improvement.

signable) cause variations. Common cause variations are inherent in any process. They include poor lots of raw material, poor product design, work conditions being unsuitable, and equipment that cannot meet the design tolerances. These common causes are *beyond* the control of the workers on the floor and therefore, for improvement to occur, actions by management are necessary.

Special or assignable causes include lack of knowledge by workers, worker mistakes, or workers not paying attention during production. Special causes can be identified by workers on the shop floor and corrected. However, workers can eliminate *only* special cause variability. Management's decision to change the manufacturing process is still needed to reduce common cause variability.

Deming contended that workers simply cannot do their best. They had to be shown what constitutes acceptable quality and that continuous improvement is not only possible, but necessary. For this to be accomplished, workers had to be trained in the use of statistical process control charts. Realizing that even training required management's approval, Deming's lectures became more and more focused toward management and what they must do.

Dr. Juran began conducting quality control courses in Japan in 1954, four years after Dr. Deming. Dr. Juran developed his 10 Steps to Quality Improvement (see Table 23–2) as well as the Juran Trilogy: Quality Improvement, Quality Planning, and Quality Control. Juran stressed that the manufacturer's view of quality is adherence to specifications but the customer's view of quality is "fitness for use." Juran defined five attributes of "fitness for use."

● Quality of design: There may be many grades of quality
● Quality of conformance: Provide the proper training; products that maintain specification tolerances; motivation

TABLE 23–2. Various Approaches to Quality Improvement

Deming's 14 Points for Management	Juran's 10 Steps to Quality Improvement	Crosby's 14 Steps to Quality Improvement
1. Create constancy of purpose for improvement of product and service.	1. Build awareness of the need and opportunity for improvement.	1. Make it clear that management is committed to quality.
2. Adopt the new philosophy.	2. Set goals for improvement.	2. Form quality improvement teams with representatives from each department.
3. Cease dependence on inspection to achieve quality.	3. Organize to reach the goals (establish a quality council, identify problems, select projects, appoint teams, designate facilitators).	3. Determine where current and potential quality problems lie.
4. End the practice of awarding business on the basis of price tag alone. Instead, minimize total cost by working with a single supplier.	4. Provide training.	4. Evaluate the cost of quality and explain its use as a management tool.
5. Improve constantly and forever every process for planning, production, and service.	5. Carry out projects to solve problems.	5. Raise the quality awareness and personal concern of all employees.
6. Institute training on the job.	6. Report progress.	6. Take actions to correct problems identified through previous steps.
7. Adopt and institute leadership.	7. Give recognition.	7. Establish a committee for the zero-defects program.
8. Drive out fear.	8. Communicate results.	8. Train supervisors to actively carry out their part of the quality improvement program.
9. Break down barriers between staff areas.	9. Keep score	9. Hold a "zero-defects day" to let all employees realize that there has been a change.
10. Eliminate slogans, exhortations, and targets for the work force.	10. Maintain momentum by making annual improvement part of the regular systems and processes of the company.	10. Encourage individuals to establish improvement goals for themselves and their groups.
11. Eliminate numerical quotas for the workforce and numerical goals for management.		11. Encourage employees to communicate to management the obstacles they face in attaining their improvement goals.
12. Remove barriers that rob people of workmanship. Eliminate the annual rating or merit system.		12. Recognize and appreciate those who participate.
13. Institute a vigorous program of education and self-improvement for everyone.		13. Establish quality councils to communicate on a regular basis.
14. Put everybody in the company to work to accomplish the transformation.		14. Do it all over again to emphasize that the quality improvement program never ends.

- Availability: reliability (i.e., frequency of repairs) and maintainability (i.e. speed or ease of repair).
- Safety: The potential hazards of product use
- Field use: This refers to the way the product will be used by the customer

Dr. Juran also stressed the cost of quality (Section 23.7) and the legal implications of quality. The legal aspects of quality include:

- Criminal liability
- Civil liability
- Appropriate corporate actions
- Warranties

Juran believes that the contractor's view of quality is conformance to specification, whereas the customer's view of quality is fitness for use when delivered and value. Juran also admits that there can exist many grades of quality. The characteristics of quality can be defined as:

- Structural (length, frequency)
- Sensory (taste, beauty, appeal)
- Time-oriented (reliability, maintainability)
- Commercial (warrantee)
- Ethical (courtesy, honesty)

The third major contributor to quality was Phillip B. Crosby. Crosby developed his 14 Steps to Quality Improvement (see Table 23–2) and his Four Absolutes of Quality:

- Quality means conformance to requirements.
- Quality comes from prevention.
- Quality means that the performance standard is "zero defects."
- Quality is measured by the cost of nonconformance.

Crosby found that the cost of not doing things right the first time could be appreciable. In manufacturing, the price of nonconformance averages 40 percent of operating costs.

23.3 THE TAGUCHI APPROACH[2]

After World War II the allied forces found that the quality of the Japanese telephone system was extremely poor and totally unsuitable for long-term communication purposes. To improve the system the allied command recommended that

2. Taken from Ranjit Roy, *A Primer on the Taguchi Method* (Dearborn, Michigan: Society of Manufacturing Engineers, 1990), Chapter 2. Reproduced by permission.

Japan establish research facilities similar to the Bell Laboratories in the United States in order to develop a state-of-the-art communication system. The Japanese founded the Electrical Communication Laboratories (ECL) with Dr. Taguchi in charge of improving the R&D productivity and enhancing product quality. He observed that a great deal of time and money was expended in engineering experimentation and testing. Little emphasis was given to the process of creative brainstorming to minimize the expenditure of resources.

Dr. Taguchi started to develop new methods to optimize the process of engineering experimentation. He developed techniques that are now known as the Taguchi Methods. His greatest contribution lies not in the mathematical formulation of the design of experiments, but rather in the accompanying philosophy. His approach is more than a method to lay out experiments. His is a concept that has produced a unique and powerful quality improvement discipline that differs from traditional practices.

These concepts are:

1. Quality should be designed into the product and not inspected into it.
2. Quality is best achieved by minimizing the deviation from a target. The product should be so designed that it is immune to uncontrollable environmental factors.
3. The cost of quality should be measured as a function of deviation from the standard and the losses should be measured system-wide.

Taguchi built on W. E. Deming's observation that 85 percent of poor quality is attributable to the manufacturing process and only 15 percent to the worker. Hence, he developed manufacturing systems that were "robust" or insensitive to daily and seasonal variations of environment, machine wear, and other external factors. The three principles were his guides in developing these systems, testing the factors affecting quality production, and specifying product parameters.

Taguchi believed that the better way to improve quality was to design and build it into the product. Quality improvement starts at the very beginning, i.e., during the design stages of a product or a process, and continues through the production phase. He proposed an "off-line" strategy for developing quality improvement in place of an attempt to inspect quality into a product on the production line. He observed that poor quality cannot be improved by the process of inspection, screening, and salvaging. No amount of inspection can put quality back into the product; it merely treats a symptom. Therefore, quality concepts should be based upon, and developed around, the philosophy of prevention. The product design must be so robust that it is immune to the influence of uncontrolled environmental factors on the manufacturing processes.

His second concept deals with actual methods of effecting quality. He contended that quality is directly related to deviation of a design parameter from the target value, not to conformance to some fixed specifications. A product may be produced with properties skewed toward one end of an acceptance range yet show shorter life expectancy. However, by specifying a target value for the critical property and developing manufacturing processes to meet the target value with little deviation, the life expectancy may be much improved.

His third concept calls for measuring deviations from a given design parameter in terms of the overall life-cycle costs of the product. These cost would include the cost of scrap, rework, inspection, returns, warranty service calls, and/or product replacement. These costs provide guidance regarding the major parameters to be controlled.

Limitations

The most severe limitation of the Taguchi method is the need for timing with respect to product/process development. The technique can only be effective when applied early in the design of the product/process system. After the design variables are determined and their nominal values are specified, experimental design may not be cost-effective. Also, though the method has wide-ranging applications, there are situations in which classical techniques are better suited; in simulation studies involving factors that vary in a continuous manner, such as the torsional strength of a shaft as a function of its diameter, the Taguchi method may not be a proper choice.

Selecting Design Parameters for Reduced Variation

Taguchi strives to attain quality by reducing the variation around the target. In an effort to reduce variations, he searched for techniques that allow variability to be reduced without necessarily eliminating the causes of variation. Often in an industrial setting, totally removing the causes of variation can be expensive. A no-cost or low-cost solution may be achieved by adjusting the levels and controlling the variation of other factors. This is what Taguchi tries to do through his *parameter design* approach. There is no cost or low cost in reducing variability in parameter design. Furthermore, the cost savings realized far exceed the cost of additional experiments needed to reduce variations.

The Taguchi method is most effective when applied to experiments with multiple factors. But the concept of selecting the proper levels of design factors, and reducing the variation of performance around the optimum/target value, can be easily illustrated through an example.

Consider a baking process. Assume several bakers are given the same ingredients to bake a pound cake, the object being to produce the best-tasting cake. Within limits, they can adjust the amount of ingredients, but they can only use the ingredients provided. They are to make the best cake within available design parameters. Taguchi's approach would be to design an experiment considering all baking ingredients and other influencing factors such as baking temperature, baking time, oven type (if a variable), and so on.

The idea is to combine the factors at appropriate levels, each within the respective acceptable range, to produce the best result and yet exhibit minimum variation around the optimum result. To see how the Taguchi technique is used for many factors, consider once again the process of determining the best recipe for a pound cake (Figure 23–4). Our objective is to determine the right proportions

FIGURE 23–4. Cake baking experiment.

of the five major ingredients—eggs, butter, milk, flour, and sugar—so that the recipe will produce the best cake most of the time (Figure 23–5). Based on past experience, the working ranges of these factors are established at the levels shown in Figure 23–6. At this point we face the following questions. How do we determine the right combination? How many experiments do we need to run and in what combination? Figure 23–7 shows a Taguchi experiment flow diagram.

23.4 THE MALCOLM BALDRIGE NATIONAL QUALITY AWARD

To become a world-class competitor, companies need a model to integrate the continuous improvement tools into a system that involves participative cross-functional implementation. In 1987, this need was recognized at the national level

FIGURE 23–5. The desirable result of an optimized baking process.

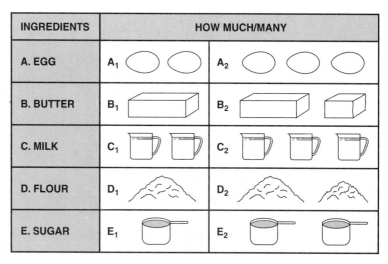

FIGURE 23–6. Factors and levels for a pound cake experiment.

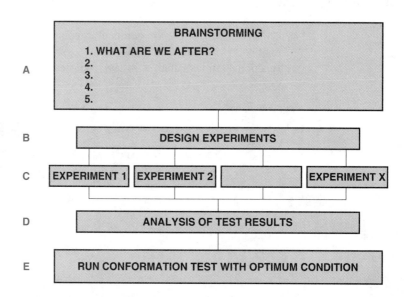

FIGURE 23–7. A Taguchi experiment flow diagram. *Source.* Ranjit Roy, *A Primer on the Taguchi Method* (Dearborn, Michigan: Society of Manufacturing Engineers, 1990), p. 231. Reproduced by permission.

with the establishment of the Malcolm Baldrige National Quality Award. The award is presented to those companies that have achieved a level of world-class competition through quality management of products and services.

The criteria for the award include:

- The <u>leadership</u> category examines primarily how the senior executives create and sustain a clear and visible quality value system along with a supporting management system to guide all activities of the company. Also examined are the senior executives' and the company's leadership and support of quality developments both inside and outside the company.
- The <u>strategic planning</u> category examines how the company sets strategic directions, and how it determines key action plans. Also examined is how the plans are translated into an effective performance management system.
- The <u>customer and market focus</u> category examines how the company determines requirements and expectations of customers and markets. Also examined is how the company enhances relationships with customers and determines their satisfaction.
- The <u>information and analysis</u> category examines the management and effectiveness of the use of data and information to support key company processes and the company's performance management system.
- The <u>human resource development and management</u> category examines how the workforce is enabled to develop and utilize its full potential, aligned with the company's objectives. Also examined are the company's efforts to build and maintain an environment conducive to performance excellence, full participation, and personal and organizational growth.
- The <u>process management</u> category examines the key aspects of process management, including customer-focused design, product and service delivery processes, support processes, and supplier and partnering processes involving all work units. The category examines how key processes are designed, effectively managed, and improved to achieve better performance.
- The <u>business results</u> category examines the company's performance and improvement in key business areas: customer satisfaction, financial and marketplace performance, human resource, supplier and partner performance, and operational performance. Also examined are performance levels relative to competitors.

Some companies that have been honored with the award include IBM, General Motors, Xerox, Kodak, AT&T, Westinghouse, Federal Express, Ritz-Carlton, Armstrong Building Products, and Motorola. Generally speaking, only two or three companies a year win the award.

23.5 ISO 9000

The International Organization for Standardization (ISO), based in Geneva, Switzerland, is a consortium of approximately 100 of the world's industrial nations. The American National Standards Institute (ANSI) represents the United States. ISO 9000 is *not* a set of standards for products or services, nor is it specific to any one industry. Instead, it is a quality system standard applicable to any product, service, or process anywhere in the world.

The information included in the ISO 9000 series includes:

ISO 9000: This defines the key terms and acts as a road map for the other standards within the series.

ISO 9001: This defines the model for a quality system when a contractor demonstrates the capability to design, produce, and install products or services.

ISO 9002: This is a quality system model for quality assurance in production and installation.

ISO 9003: This is a quality system model for quality assurance in final inspection and testing.

ISO 9004: This provides quality management guidelines for any organization wishing to develop and implement a quality system. Guidelines are also available to determine the extent to which each quality system model is applicable.

There are several myths concerning the ISO 9000 series. First, ISO 9000 is *not* a European standard, although it may be necessary to do business within the European Community. ISO 9000 is based on American quality standards that are still being used. Second, ISO 9000 is *not* a paperwork nightmare. Although documentation is a necessary requirement, the magnitude of the documentation is less than most people believe. Third, becoming ISO 9000 certified does *not* guarantee that your organization will produce quality products or services. Instead, it confirms that the appropriate system is in place.

ISO 9000 is actually a three-part, never-ending cycle including planning, controlling, and documentation. *Planning* is required to ensure that the objectives, goals, authority, and responsibility relationships of each activity are properly defined and understood. *Controlling* is required to ensure that the goals and objectives are met, and that problems are anticipated or averted through proper corrective actions. *Documentation* is used predominantly for feedback on how well the quality management system is performing to satisfy customer's needs and what changes may be necessary.

There always exists the question of how ISO 9000 relates to the Malcolm Baldrige Award. ISO 9000 requirements fall predominantly into the "quality assurance of products and services" section of the Malcolm Baldrige Award. It does touch the other six sections in varying degrees.

ISO 9000 provides minimum requirements needed for certification. The Malcolm Baldrige National Quality Award (MBNQA) tries to identify the "best in class." Organizations wishing to improve quality are encouraged to consider practices of and benchmark against past recipients of the MBNQA as "role models."

The International Organization for Standardization has recently developed the ISO 14000 series standards. ISO 14000 is an evolving series that provides business management with the structure for managing environmental impacts, including the basic management system, performance evaluation, auditing, labeling, and life-cycle assessment.

23.6 QUALITY MANAGEMENT CONCEPTS

The project manager has the ultimate responsibility for quality management on the project. Quality management has equal priority with cost and schedule management. However, the direct measurement of quality may be the responsibility of the quality assurance department or the assistant project manager for quality. For a labor-intensive project, management support (i.e., the project office) is typically 12–15 percent of the total labor dollars of the project. Approximately 3–5 percent can be attributed to quality management. Therefore, as much as 20–30 percent of all the labor in the project office could easily be attributed to quality management.

From a project manager's perspective, there are six quality management concepts that should exist to support each and every project. They include:

- Quality policy
- Quality objectives
- Quality assurance
- Quality control
- Quality audit
- Quality program plan

Ideally, these six concepts should be embedded within the corporate culture.

Quality Policy

The quality policy is a document that is typically created by quality experts and fully supported by top management. The policy should state the quality objectives, the level of quality acceptable to the organization, and the responsibility of the organization's members for executing the policy and ensuring quality. A quality policy would also include statements by top management pledging its support to the policy. The quality policy is instrumental in creating the organization's reputation and quality image.

Many organizations successfully complete a good quality policy but immediately submarine the good intentions of the policy by delegating the implementation of the policy to lower-level managers. The implementation of the quality policy is the responsibility of top management. Top management must "walk the walk" as well as "talk the talk." Employees will soon see through the ruse of a quality policy that is delegated to middle managers while top executives move onto "more crucial matters that really impact the bottom line."

A good quality policy will:

● Be a statement of principles stating what, not how
● Promote consistency throughout the organization and across projects
● Provide an explanation to outsiders of how the organization views quality
● Provide specific guidelines for important quality matters
● Provide provisions for changing/updating the policy

Quality Objectives

Quality objectives are a part of an organization's quality policy and consist of specific objectives and the time frame for completion of the stated objectives. The quality objectives must be selected carefully. Selecting objectives that are not naturally possible can cause frustration and disillusionment. Examples of acceptable quality objectives might be: to train all members of the organization on the quality policy and objectives before the end of the current fiscal year, to set up baseline measurements of specific processes by the end of the current quarter, to define the responsibility and authority for meeting the organization's quality objectives down to each member of the organization by the end of the current fiscal year, etc.

Good quality objectives should:

● Be obtainable
● Define specific goals
● Be understandable
● State specific deadlines

Quality Assurance

Quality assurance is the collective term for the formal activities and managerial processes that are planned and undertaken in an attempt to ensure that products and services that are delivered are at the required quality level. Quality assurance also includes efforts external to these processes that provide information for improving the internal processes. It is the quality assurance function that attempts to ensure that the project scope, cost, and time functions are fully integrated.

The Project Management Institute Guide to the Body of Knowledge (PMBOK)® refers to quality assurance as the management section of quality management. This is the area where the project manager can have the greatest impact on the quality of his project. The project manager needs to establish the administrative processes and procedures necessary to ensure and, often, prove that the scope statement conforms to the actual requirements of the customer. The project manager must work with his team to determine which processes they will use to ensure that all stakeholders have confidence that the quality activities will be properly performed. All relevant legal and regulatory requirements must also be met.

A good quality assurance system will:

● Identify objectives and standards
● Be multifunctional and prevention oriented
● Plan for collection and use of data in a cycle of continuous improvement
● Plan for the establishment and maintenance of performance measures
● Include quality audits

Quality Control

Quality control is a collective term for activities and techniques, within the process, that are intended to create specific quality characteristics. Such activities include continually monitoring processes, identifying and eliminating problem causes, use of statistical process control to reduce the variability and to increase the efficiency of processes. Quality control certifies that the organization's quality objectives are being met.

The PMBOK® refers to quality control as the technical aspect of quality management. Project team members who have specific technical expertise on the various aspects of the project play an active role in quality control. They set up the technical processes and procedures that ensure that each step of the project provides a quality output from design and development through implementation and maintenance. Each step's output must conform to the overall quality standards and quality plans, thus ensuring that quality is achieved.

A good quality control system will:

● Select what to control
● Set standards that provide the basis for decisions regarding possible corrective action
● Establish the measurement methods used
● Compare the actual results to the quality standards
● Act to bring nonconforming processes and material back to the standard based on the information collected
● Monitor and calibrate measuring devices
● Include detailed documentation for all processes

Quality Audit

A quality audit is an independent evaluation performed by qualified personnel that ensures that the project is conforming to the project's quality requirements and is following the established quality procedures and policies.

A good quality audit will ensure that:

● The planned quality for the project will be met.
● The products are safe and fit for use.
● All pertinent laws and regulations are followed.

- Data collection and distribution systems are accurate and adequate.
- Proper corrective action is taken when required.
- Improvement opportunities are identified.

Quality Plan

The quality plan is created by the project manager and project team members. The project quality plan is created by breaking down the project objectives into a work breakdown structure. Using a treelike diagramming technique, the project activities are broken down into lower-level activities until specific quality actions can be identified. The project manager then ensures that these actions are documented and implemented in the sequence that will meet the customer's requirements and expectations. This enables the project manager to assure the customer that he has a road map to delivering a quality product or service and therefore will satisfy the customer's needs.

A good quality plan will:

- Identify all of the organization's external and internal customers
- Cause the design of a process that produces the features desired by the customer
- Bring in suppliers early in the process
- Cause the organization to be responsive to changing customer needs
- Prove that the process is working and that quality goals are being met

23.7 THE COST OF QUALITY

To verify that a product or service meets the customer's requirements requires the measurement of the cost of quality. For simplicity's sake, the costs can be classified as "the cost of conformance" and "the cost of nonconformance." Conformance costs include items such as training, indoctrination, verification, validation, testing, maintenance, calibration, and audits. Nonconforming costs include items such as scrap, rework, warranty repairs, product recalls, and complaint handling.

Trying to save a few project dollars by reducing conformance costs could prove disastrous. For example, an American company won a contract as a supplier of Japanese parts. The initial contract called for the delivery of 10,000 parts. During inspection and testing at the customer's (i.e., Japanese) facility, two rejects were discovered. The Japanese returned *all* 10,000 components to the American supplier stating that this batch was not acceptable. In this example, the nonconformance cost could easily be an order of magnitude greater than the conformance cost. The moral is clear: *Build it right the first time.*

Another common method to classify costs includes the following:

- *Prevention costs* are the up-front costs oriented toward the satisfaction of customer's requirements with the first and all succeeding units of product produced without defects. Included in this are typically such costs as design review, training, quality planning, surveys of vendors, suppliers, and subcontractors, process studies, and related preventive activities.

- *Appraisal costs* are costs associated with evaluation of product or process to ascertain how well all of the requirements of the customer have been met. Included in this are typically such costs as inspection of product, lab test, vendor control, in-process testing, and internal–external design reviews.
- *Internal failure costs* are those costs associated with the failure of the processes to make products acceptable to the customer, before leaving the control of the organization. Included in this area are scrap, rework, repair, downtime, defect evaluation, evaluation of scrap, and corrective actions for these internal failures.
- *External failure costs* are those costs associated with the determination by the customer that his requirements have not been satisfied. Included are customer returns and allowances, evaluation of customer complaints, inspection at the customer, and customer visits to resolve quality complaints and necessary corrective action.

Figure 23–8 shows the expected results of the total quality management system on quality costs. Prevention costs are expected to actually rise as more time is

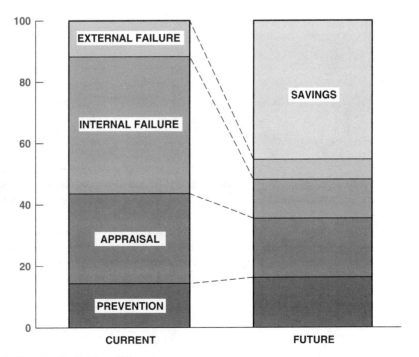

FIGURE 23–8. Total quality cost.

spent in prevention activities throughout the organization. As processes improve over the long run, appraisal costs will go down as the need to inspect in quality decreases. The biggest savings will come from the internal failure areas of rework, scrap, reengineering, redo, etc. The additional time spent in up-front design and development will really pay off here. And, finally, the external costs will also come down as processes yield first-time quality on a regular basis. The improvements will continue to affect the company on a long-term basis in both improved quality and lower costs. Also, as project management begins to mature, there should be further decreases in the cost of both maintaining quality and developing products.

Figure 23–8 shows that prevention costs can increase. This is not always the case. Prevention costs actually decrease without sacrificing the purpose of prevention if we can identify and eliminate the costs associated with waste, such as waste due to

- Rejects of completed work
- Design flaws
- Work in progress
- Improperly instructed manpower
- Excess or noncontributing management (who still charge time to the project)
- Improperly assigned manpower
- Improper utilization of facilities
- Excessive expenses that do not necessarily contribute to the project (i.e., unnecessary meetings, travel, lodgings, etc.)

Another important aspect of Figure 23–8 is that 50 percent or more of the total cost of quality can be attributed to the internal and external failure costs. Complete elimination of failures may seem like an ideal solution but may not be cost-effective. As an example, see Figure 23–9. There are assumptions in the development of this figure. First, the cost of failure (i.e., nonconformance) approaches zero as defects become fewer and fewer. Second, the conformance costs of appraisal and prevention approach infinity as defects become fewer and fewer.

If the ultimate goal of a quality program is to continuously improve quality, then from a financial standpoint, quality improvement may not be advisable if the positive economic return becomes negative. Juran argued that as long as the per unit cost for prevention and appraisal were less expensive than nonconformance costs, resources should be assigned to prevention and appraisal. But when prevention and appraisal costs begin to increase the per unit cost of quality, then the policy should be to maintain quality. The implication here is that zero defects may not be a practical solution since the total cost of quality would not be minimized.

Figure 23–8 shows that the external failure costs are much lower than the internal failure costs. This indicates that most of the failures are being discovered *before* they leave the functional areas or plants. This is particularly important if we consider the life-cycle cost model discussed in Section 14.19. We showed that typical life-cycle costs are:

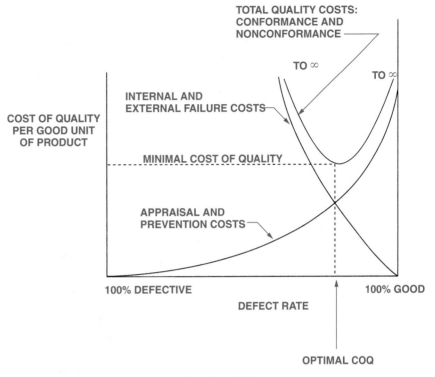

FIGURE 23–9. Minimizing the costs of quality (COQ).

- R&D: 12 percent
- Acquisition: 28 percent
- Operations and support: 60 percent

Since 60 percent of the life-cycle cost occurs *after* the product is put into service, then small increases in the R&D and acquisition areas could generate major cost savings in operation and support due to better design, higher quality, less maintenance, and so forth.

23.8 THE SEVEN QUALITY CONTROL TOOLS[3]

Over the years, statistical methods have become prevalent throughout business, industry, and science. With the availability of advanced, automated systems that collect, tabulate, and analyze data, the practical application of these quantitative

---

3. This section is taken from H. K. Jackson and N. L. Frigon, "Achieving the Competition Edge" (New York: John Wiley & Sons, Inc., 1996), Chapters 6 and 7. Reproduced by permission.

methods continues to grow. Statistics today plays a major role in all phases of modern business.

More important than the quantitative methods themselves is their impact on the basic philosophy of business. The statistical point of view takes decision making out of the subjective autocratic decision-making arena by providing the basis for objective decisions based on quantifiable facts. This change provides some very specific benefits:

- Improved process information
- Better communication
- Discussion based on facts
- Consensus for action
- Information for process changes

Statistical process control (SPC) takes advantage of the natural characteristics of any process. All business activities can be described as specific processes with known tolerances and measurable variances. The measurement of these variances and the resulting information provide the basis for continuous process improvement. The tools presented here provide both a graphical and measured representation of process data. The systematic application of these tools empowers business people to control products and processes to become world-class competitors.

The basic tools of statistical process control are data figures, Pareto analysis, cause-and-effect analysis, trend analysis, histograms, scatter diagrams, and process control charts. These basic tools provide for the efficient collection of data, identification of patterns in the data, and measurement of variability. Figure 23–10 shows the relationships among these seven tools and their use for the identification and analysis of improvement opportunities. We will review these tools and discuss their implementation and applications.

Data Tables

Data tables or data arrays, provide a systematic method for collecting and displaying data. In most cases, data tables are forms designed for the purpose of collecting specific data. These tables are used most frequently where data is available from automated media. They provide a consistent, effective, and economical approach to gathering data, organizing them for analysis, and displaying them for preliminary review. Data tables sometimes take the form of manual check sheets where automated data are not necessary or available. Data figures and check sheets should be designed to minimize the need for complicated entries. Simple-to-understand, straightforward tables are a key to successful data gathering.

Figure 23–11 is an example of an attribute (pass/fail) data figure for the correctness of invoices. From this simple check sheet several data points become apparent. The total number of defects is 34. The highest number of defects is from supplier A, and the most frequent defect is incorrect test documentation. We can

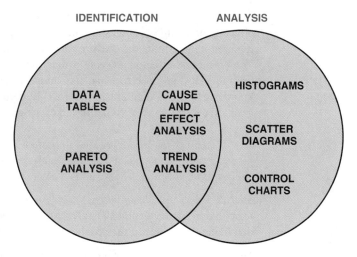

FIGURE 23–10. The seven quality control tools.

subject this data to further analysis by using Pareto analysis, control charts, and other statistical tools.

In this check sheet, the categories represent defects found during the material receipt and inspection function. The following defect categories provide an explanation of the check sheet:

- Incorrect invoices: The invoice does not match the purchase order.
- Incorrect inventory: The inventory of the material does not match the invoice.
- Damaged material: The material received was damaged and rejected.
- Incorrect test documentation: The required supplier test certificate was not received and the material was rejected.

DEFECT	SUPPLIER				
	A	**B**	**C**	**D**	**TOTAL**
INCORRECT INVOICE	////	/		//	7
INCORRECT INVENTORY	/////	//	/	/	9
DAMAGED MATERIAL	///		//	///	8
INCORRECT TEST DOCUMENTATION	/	///	////	//	10
TOTAL	13	6	7	8	34

FIGURE 23–11. Check sheet for material receipt and inspection.

Cause-and-Effect Analysis

After identifying a problem, it is necessary to determine its cause. The cause-and-effect relationship is at times obscure. A considerable amount of analysis often is required to determine the specific cause or causes of the problem.

Cause-and-effect analysis uses diagramming techniques to identify the relationship between an effect and its causes. Cause-and-effect diagrams are also known as fishbone diagrams. Figure 23–12 demonstrates the basic fishbone diagram. Six steps are used to perform a cause-and-effect analysis.

Step 1. Identify the problem. This step often involves the use of other statistical process control tools, such as Pareto analysis, histograms, and control charts, as well as brainstorming. The result is a clear, concise problem statement.

Step 2. Select interdisciplinary brainstorming team. Select an interdisciplinary team, based on the technical, analytical, and management knowledge required to determine the causes of the problem.

Step 3. Draw problem box and prime arrow. The problem contains the problem statement being evaluated for cause and effect. The prime arrow functions as the foundation for their major categories.

Step 4. Specify major categories. Identify the major categories contributing to the problem stated in the problem box. The six basic categories for the primary causes of the problems are most frequently personnel, method, materials, machinery, measurements, and environment, as shown in Figure 23–12. Other categories may be specified, based on the needs of the analysis.

Step 5. Identify defect causes. When you have identified the major causes contributing to the problem, you can determine the causes related to each of the major categories. There are three approaches to this analysis: the random method, the systematic method, and the process analysis method.

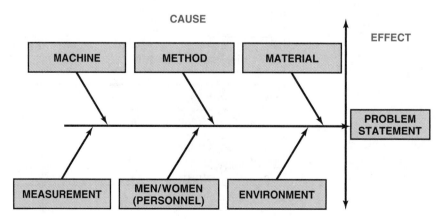

FIGURE 23–12. Cause-and-effect diagram.

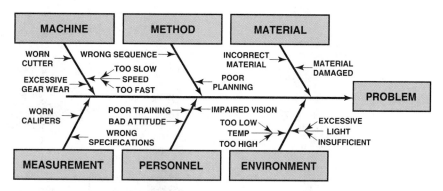

FIGURE 23–13. Random method.

Random method. List all six major causes contributing to the problem at the same time. Identify the possible causes related to each of the categories, as shown in Figure 23–13.

Systematic method. Focus your analysis on one major category at a time, in descending order of importance. Move to the next most important category only after completing the most important one. This process is diagrammed in Figure 23–14.

Process analysis method. Identify each sequential step in the process and perform cause-and-effect analysis for each step, one at a time. Figure 23–15 represents this approach.

Step 6. Identify corrective action. Based on (1) the cause-and-effect analysis of the problem and (2) the determination of causes contributing to each major category, identify corrective action. The corrective action analysis is performed in the same manner as the cause-and-effect analysis. The cause-and-effect diagram is simply reversed so that the problem box becomes the corrective action box. Figure 23–16 displays the method for identifying corrective action.

A histogram is a graphical representation of data as a frequency distribution. This tool is valuable in evaluating both attribute (pass/fail) and variable (measurement)

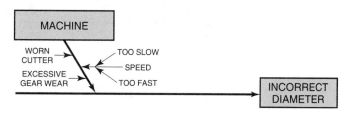

FIGURE 23–14. Systematic method.

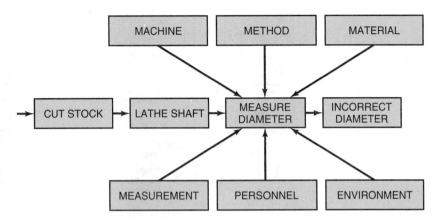

FIGURE 23–15. Process analysis method.

data. Histograms offer a quick look at the data at a single point in time; they do not display variance or trends over time. A histogram displays how the cumulative data looks *today*. It is useful in understanding the relative frequencies (percentages) or frequency (numbers) of the data and how that data are distributed. Figure 23–17 illustrates a histogram of the frequency of defects in a manufacturing process.

Pareto Analysis

A Pareto diagram is a special type of histogram that helps us to identify and prioritize problem areas. The construction of a Pareto diagram may involve data collected from data figures, maintenance data, repair data, parts scrap rates, or other sources. By identifying types of nonconformity from any of these data sources, the Pareto diagram directs attention to the most frequently occurring element.

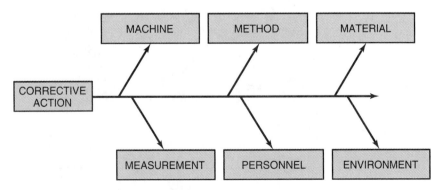

FIGURE 23–16. Identify corrective action.

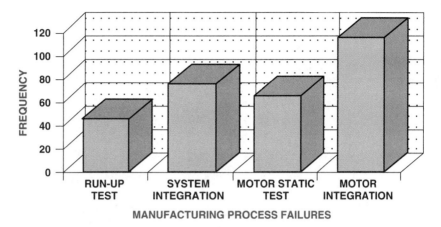

FIGURE 23–17. Histogram for variables.

There are three uses and types of Pareto analysis. The basic Pareto analysis identifies the vital few contributors that account for most quality problems in any system. The comparative Pareto analysis focuses on any number of program options or actions. The weighted Pareto analysis gives a measure of significance to factors that may not appear significant at first—such additional factors as cost, time, and criticality.

The basic Pareto analysis chart provides an evaluation of the most frequent occurrences for any given data set. By applying the Pareto analysis steps to the material receipt and inspection process described in Figure 23–18, we can pro-

MATERIAL RECEIPT AND INSPECTION FREQUENCY OF FAILURES			
SUPPLIER	**FAILING FREQUENCY**	**PERCENT FAILING**	**CUMULATIVE PERCENT**
A	13	38	38
B	6	17	55
C	7	20	75
D	9	25	100

FIGURE 23–18. Basic Pareto analysis.

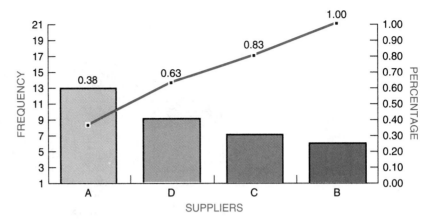

FIGURE 23–19. Basic Pareto analysis.

duce the basic Pareto analysis demonstrated in Figure 23–19. This basic Pareto analysis quantifies and graphs the frequency of occurrence for material receipt and inspection and further identifies the most significant, based on frequency.

A review of this basic Pareto analysis for frequency of occurrences indicates that supplier A is experiencing the most rejections with 37 percent of all the failures.

Pareto analysis diagrams are also used to determine the effect of corrective action, or to analyze the difference between two or more processes and methods. Figure 23–20 displays the use of this Pareto method to assess the difference in defects after corrective action.

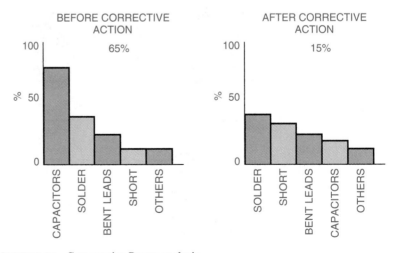

FIGURE 23–20. Comparative Pareto analysis.

FIGURE 23–21. Solder certification test scores.

Scatter Diagrams

Another pictorial representation of process control data is the scatter plot or scatter diagram. A scatter diagram organizes data using two variables: an independent variable and a dependent variable. These data are then recorded on a simple graph with *X* and *Y* coordinates showing the relationship between the variables. Figure 23–21 displays the relationship between two of the data elements from solder qualification test scores. The independent variable, experience in months, is listed on the *X*-axis. The dependent variable is the score, which is recorded on the *Y*-axis.

These relationships fall into several categories, as shown in Figure 23–22. In the first scatter plot there is no correlation—the data points are widely scattered

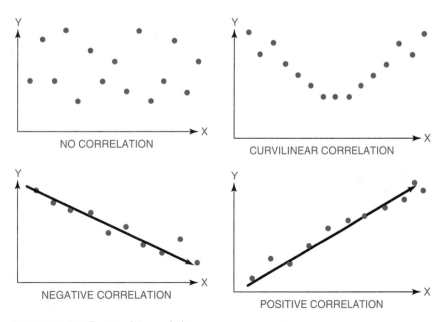

FIGURE 23–22. Scatter plot correlation.

with no apparent pattern. The second scatter plot shows a curvilinear correlation demonstrated by the U shape of the graph. The third scatter plot has a negative correlation, as indicated by the downward slope. The final scatter plot has a positive correlation with an upward slope.

From Figure 23–21 we can see that the scatter plot for solder certification testing is somewhat curvilinear. The least and the most experienced employees scored highest, whereas those with an intermediate level of experience did relatively poorly. The next tool, trend analysis, will help clarify and quantify these relationships.

Trend Analysis

Trend analysis is a statistical method for determining the equation that best fits the data in a scatter plot. Trend analysis quantifies the relationships of the data, determines the equation, and measures the fit of the equation to the data. This method is also known as curve fitting or least squares.

Trend analysis can determine optimal operating conditions by providing an equation that describes the relationship between the dependent (output) and independent (input) variables. An example is the data set concerning experience and scores on the solder certification test (see Figure 23–23).

The equation of the regression line, or trend line, provides a clear and understandable measure of the change caused in the output variable by every incremental change of the input or independent variable. Using this principle, we can predict the effect of changes in the process.

One of the most important contributions that can be made by trend analysis is forecasting. Forecasting enables us to predict what is likely to occur in the future. Based on the regression line we can forecast what will happen as the independent variable attains values beyond the existing data.

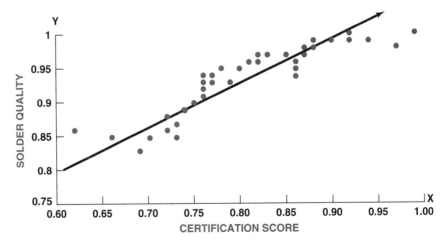

FIGURE 23–23. Scatter plot solder quality and certification score.

Control Charts

The use of control charts focuses on the prevention of defects, rather than their detection and rejection. In business, government, and industry, economy and efficiency are always best served by prevention. It costs much more to produce an unsatisfactory product or service than it does to produce a satisfactory one. There are many costs associated with producing unsatisfactory goods and services. These costs are in labor, materials, facilities, and the loss of customers. The cost of producing a proper product can be reduced significantly by the application of statistical process control charts.

Control Charts and the Normal Distribution   The construction, use, and interpretation of control charts is based on the normal statistical distribution as indicated in Figure 23–24. The centerline of the control chart represents the average or mean of the data $(\overline{X})$. The upper and lower control limits (UCL and LCL), respectively, represent this mean plus and minus three standard deviations of the data $(\overline{X} \pm 3s)$. Either the lowercase s or the Greek letter σ (sigma) represents the standard deviation for control charts.

The normal distribution and its relationship to control charts is represented on the right of the figure. The normal distribution can be described entirely by its mean and standard deviation. The normal distribution is a bell-shaped curve (sometimes called the Gaussian distribution) that is symmetrical about the mean, slopes downward on both sides to infinity, and theoretically has an infinite range. In the normal distribution 99.73 percent of all measurements lie within $\overline{X} + 3s$ and $\overline{X} - 3s$; this is why the limits on control charts are called three-sigma limits.

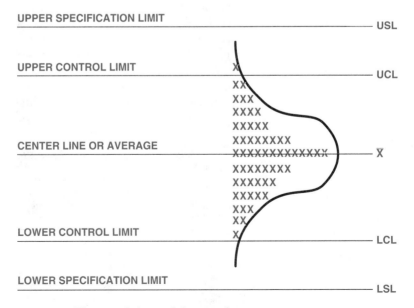

FIGURE 23–24.   The control chart and the normal curve.

Companies like Motorola have embarked upon a six-sigma limit rather than a three-sigma limit. The benefit is shown in Table 23–3. With a six-sigma limit, only two defects per billion are allowed. The cost to maintain a six-sigma limit can be extremely expensive unless the cost can be spread out over, say, 1 billion units produced.

Control chart analysis determines whether the inherent process variability and the process average are at stable levels, whether one or both are out of statistical control (not stable), or whether appropriate action needs to be taken. Another purpose of using control charts is to distinguish between the inherent, random variability of a process and the variability attributed to an assignable cause. The sources of random variability are often referred to as common causes. These are the sources that cannot be changed readily, without significant restructuring of the process. Special cause variability, by contrast, is subject to correction within the process under process control.

- *Common cause variability or variation:* This source of random variation is always present in any process. It is that part of the variability inherent in the process itself. The cause of this variation can be corrected only by a management decision to change the basic process.
- *Special cause variability or variation:* This variation can be controlled at the local or operational level. Special causes are indicated by a point on the control chart that is beyond the control limit or by a persistent trend approaching the control limit.

To use process control measurement data effectively, it is important to understand the concept of variation. No two product or process characteristics are exactly alike, because any process contains many sources of variability. The differences between products may be large, or they may be almost immeasurably small, but they are always present. Some sources of variation in the process can cause immediate differences in the product, such as a change in suppliers or the accuracy of an individual's work. Other sources of variation, such as tool wear, environmental changes, or increased administrative control, tend to cause changes in the product or service only over a longer period of time.

TABLE 23–3. ATTRIBUTES OF THE NORMAL (STANDARD) DISTRIBUTION

Specification Range (in ± Sigmas)	Percent within Range	Defective Parts Billion
1	68.27	317,300,000
2	95.45	45,400,000
3	99.73	2,700,000
4	99.9937	63,000
5	99.999943	57
6	99.9999998	2

To control and improve a process, we must trace the total variation back to its sources. Again the sources are common cause and special cause variability. Common causes are the many sources of variation that always exist within a process that is in a state of statistical control. Special causes (often called assignable causes) are any factors causing variation that cannot be adequately explained by any single distribution of the process output, as would be the case if the process were in statistical control. Unless all the special causes of variation are identified and corrected, they will continue to affect the process output in unpredictable ways.

The factors that cause the most variability in the process are the main factors found on cause-and-effect analysis charts: people, machines, methodology, materials, measurement, and environment. These causes can either result from special causes or be common causes inherent in the process.

- The theory of control charts suggests that if the source of variation is from chance alone, the process will remain within the three-sigma limits.
- When the process goes out of control, special causes exist. These need to be investigated, and corrective action must be taken.

Control Chart Types Just as there are two types of data, continuous and discrete, there are two types of control charts: variable charts for use with continuous data and attribute charts for use with discrete data. Each type of control chart can be used with specific types of data. Table 23–4 provides a brief overview of the types of control charts and their applications.

Variables charts. Control charts for variables are powerful tools that we can use when measurements from a process are variable. Examples of variable data are the diameter of a bearing, electrical output, or the torque on a fastener.

TABLE 23–4. TYPES OF CONTROL CHARTS AND APPLICATIONS

Variables Charts	Attributes Charts
$\overline{X}$ and R charts: To observe changes in the mean and range (variance) of a process.	p chart: For the fraction of attributes nonconforming or defective in a sample of varying size.
$\overline{X}$ and s charts: For a variable average and standard deviation.	np charts: For the number of attributes nonconforming or defective in a sample of constant size.
$\overline{X}$ and s^2 charts: for a variable average and variance.	c charts: For the number of attributes nonconforming or defects in a single item within a subgroup, lot, or sample area of constant size.
	u charts: For the number of attributes nonconforming or defects in a single item within a subgroup, lot, or sample area of varying size.

As shown in Table 23–4, $\overline{X}$ and R charts are used to measure control processes whose characteristics are continuous variables such as weight, length, ohms, time, or volume. The p and np charts are used to measure and control processes displaying attribute characteristics in a sample. We use p charts when the number of failures is expressed as a fraction, or np charts when the failures are expressed as a number. The c and u charts are used to measure the number or portion of defects in a single item. The c control chart is applied when the sample size or area is fixed, and the u chart when the sample size or area is not fixed.

Attribute charts. Although control charts are most often thought of in terms of variables, there are also versions for attributes. Attribute data have only two values (conforming/nonconforming, pass/fail, go/no-go, present/absent), but they can still be counted, recorded, and analyzed. Some examples are: the presence of a required label, the installation of all required fasteners, the presence of solder drips, or the continuity of an electrical circuit. We also use attribute charts for characteristics that are measurable, if the results are recorded in a simple yes/no fashion, such as the conformance of a shaft diameter when measured on a go/no-go gauge, or the acceptability of threshold margins to a visual or gauge check.

It is possible to use control charts for operations in which attributes are the basis for inspection, in a manner similar to that for variables but with certain differences. If we deal with the fraction rejected out of a sample, the type of control chart used is called a p chart. If we deal with the actual number rejected, the control chart is called an np chart. If articles can have more than one nonconformity, and all are counted for subgroups of fixed size, the control chart is called a c chart. Finally, if the number of nonconformities per unit is the quantity of interest, the control chart is called a u chart.

The power of control charts (Shewhart techniques) lies in their ability to determine if the cause of variation is a special cause that can be affected at the process level, or a common cause that requires a change at the management level. The information from the control chart can then be used to direct the efforts of engineers, technicians, and managers to achieve preventive or corrective action.

The use of statistical control charts is aimed at studying specific ongoing processes in order to keep them in satisfactory control. By contrast, downstream inspection aims to identify defects. In other words, control charts focus on prevention of defects rather than detection and rejection. It seems reasonable, and it has been confirmed in practice, that economy and efficiency are better served by prevention rather than detection.

Control Chart Components   All control charts have certain features in common (Figure 23–25). Each control chart has a centerline, statistical control limits, and the calculated attribute or control data. Additionally, some control charts contain specification limits.

The centerline is a solid (unbroken) line that represents the mean or arithmetic average of the measurements or counts. This line is also referred to as the X bar line ($\overline{X}$). There are two statistical control limits: the upper control limit for values greater than the mean and the lower control limit for values less than the mean.

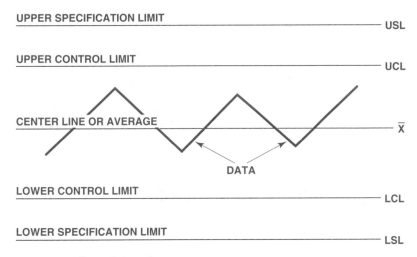

FIGURE 23–25. Control chart elements.

Specification limits are used when specific parametric requirements exist for a process, product, or operation. These limits usually apply to the data and are the pass/fail criteria for the operation. They differ from statistical control limits in that they are prescribed for a process, rather than resulting from the measurement of the process.

The data element of control charts varies somewhat among variable and attribute control charts. We will discuss specific examples as a part of the discussion on individual control charts.

Control Chart Interpretation There are many possibilities for interpreting various kinds of patterns and shifts on control charts. If properly interpreted, a control chart can tell us much more than simply whether the process is in or out of control. Experience and training can lead to much greater skill in extracting clues regarding process behavior, such as that shown in Figure 23–26. Statistical guidance is invaluable, but an intimate knowledge of the process being studied is vital in bringing about improvements.

A control chart can tell us when to look for trouble, but it cannot by itself tell us where to look, or what cause will be found. Actually, in many cases, one of the greatest benefits from a control chart is that it tells when to leave a process alone. Sometimes the variability is increased unnecessarily when an operator keeps trying to make small corrections, rather than letting the natural range of variability stabilize. The following paragraphs describe some of the ways the underlying distribution patterns can behave or misbehave.

Runs. When several successive points line up on one side of the central line, this pattern is called a run. The number of points in that run is called the length of the run. As a rule of thumb, if the run has a length of seven points, there is an abnormality in the process. Figure 23–27 demonstrates an example of a run.

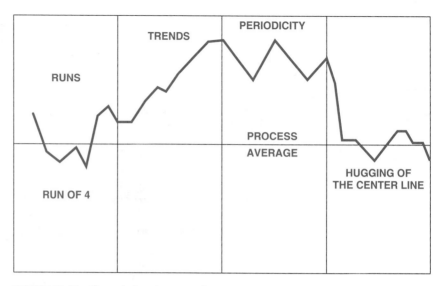

FIGURE 23–26. Control chart interpretation.

Trends. If there is a continued rise of all in a series of points, this pattern is called a trend. In general, if seven consecutive points continue to rise or fall, there is an abnormality. Often, the points go beyond one of the control limits before reaching seven. Figure 23–28 demonstrates an example of trends.

Periodicity. Points that show the same pattern of change (rise or fall) over equal intervals denote periodicity. Figure 23–29 demonstrates an example of periodicity.

Hugging the centerline or control limit. Points on the control chart that are close to the central line or to the control limit, are said to hug the line. Often, in

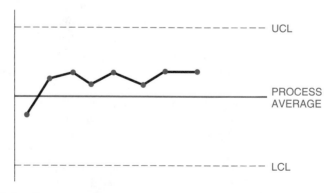

FIGURE 23–27. Process run.

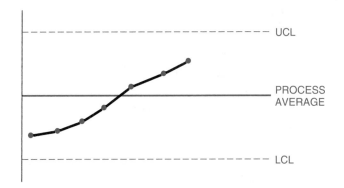

FIGURE 23–28. Control chart trends.

this situation, a different type of data or data from different factors have been mixed into the subgroup. In such cases it is necessary to change the subgrouping, reassemble the data, and redraw the control chart. To decide whether there is hugging of the center line, draw two lines on the control chart, one between the centerline and the UCL and the other between the center line and the LCL. If most of the points are between these two lines, there is an abnormality. To see whether there is hugging of one of the control limits, draw a line two-thirds of the distance between the center line and each of the control lines. There is abnormality if 2 out of 3 points, 3 out of 7 points, or 4 out of 10 points lie within the outer one-third zone. The abnormalities should be evaluated for their cause(s) and the corrective action taken. Figure 23–30 demonstrates data hugging the LCL.

Out of control. An abnormality exists when data points exceed either the upper or lower control limits. Figure 23–31 illustrates this occurrence.

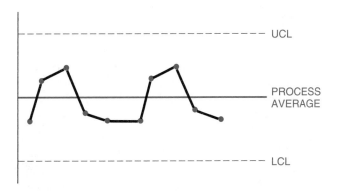

FIGURE 23–29. Control chart periodicity.

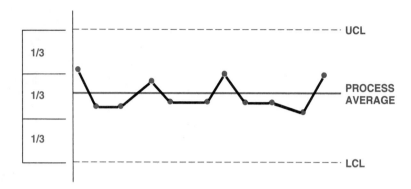

FIGURE 23–30. Hugging the centerline.

In control. No obvious abnormalities appear in the control chart. Figure 23–32 demonstrates this desirable process state.

23.9 PROCESS CAPABILITY (C_P)

Process capability, for a stable manufacturing process, is the ability to produce a product that conforms to design specifications. Because day-to-day variations can occur during manufacturing, process capability is a statement about product uniformity. Process capability, as measured by the quality characteristics of the prod-

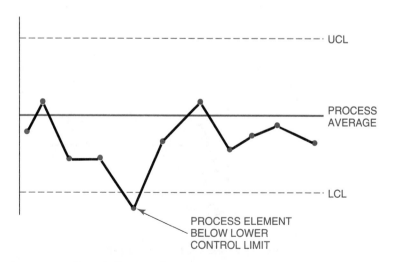

FIGURE 23–31. Control chart out of control.

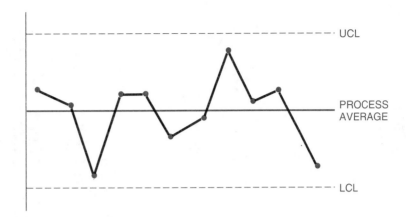

FIGURE 23–32. Process in control.

uct of the process, is expressed as the mean value plus or minus three standard deviations. Mathematically:

$$C_P = \frac{\text{USL} - \text{LSL}}{6\sigma}$$

It is desirable for C_P to be greater than one. This implies that the process of three-sigma limit is well within the customer's specification limits as shown in Figure 23–33.

The following are generally accepted rules for C_P:

- $C_P > 1.33$: The process is well within the customer's specifications requirements.
- $1.33 \geq C_P > 1.0$: The process is marginally acceptable. The process may not completely satisfy the customer's requirements. Improvements in process control are needed.
- $C_P \leq 1.0$: The process is unacceptable as is. Improvements are mandatory.

To illustrate the use of the formula, assume that your customer's requirements are to produce metal rods that are 10 inches ± .05 inches. Your manufacturing process has a sigma of 0.008.

$$C_P = \frac{\text{USL} - \text{LSL}}{6\sigma}$$
$$= \frac{0.05 + 0.05}{6(0.008)}$$
$$= 2.08$$

Looking at Figure 23-33, C_P is the relative spread of the process width within the specification width. Unfortunately, the spread of the process capability, even

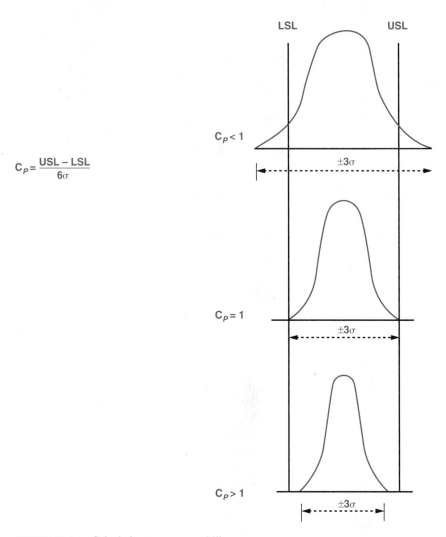

$$C_p = \frac{USL - LSL}{6\sigma}$$

FIGURE 23–33. Calculating process capability.

for very good values, could be poorly positioned within the specification width. The process width could easily be hugging either the USL or LSL. Today, process capability is measured by both C_P and C_{Pk}, where C_{Pk} is the capability index with correction (k) for noncentrality. According to Dr. Frank Anbari, the formula for C_{Pk} can be simplified as:

$$C_{Pk} = \left| \frac{CL - \text{Closest specification limit}}{3\sigma} \right|$$

where CL is the center of the specification width.

Dr. Anbari postulates that the C_P provides an upper limit for the C_{Pk}, which is reached when the process is fully centered around the nominal dimension.

23.10 ACCEPTANCE SAMPLING

Acceptance sampling is a statistical process of evaluating a portion of a lot for the purpose of accepting or rejecting the entire lot. It is an attempt to monitor the quality of the incoming product or material after the completion of production.

The alternatives to developing a sampling plan would be 100% inspection and 0% inspection. The costs associated with 100% are prohibitive, and the risks associated with 0% inspection are likewise large. Therefore, some sort of compromise is needed. The three most commonly used sampling plans are:

- Single sampling: This is the acceptance or rejection of a lot based upon one sampling run.
- Double sampling: A small sample size is tested. If the results are not conclusive, then a second sample is tested.
- Multiple sampling: This process requires the sampling of several small lots.

Regardless of what type of sampling plan is chosen, sampling errors can occur. A shipment of good-quality items can be rejected if a large portion of defective units are selected at random. Likewise, a bad-quality shipment can be accepted if the tested sample contains a disproportionately large number of quality items. The two major risks are identified below:

- Producer's risk: This is called the α (alpha) risk or type I error. This is the risk to the producer that a good lot will be rejected.
- Consumer's risk: This is called the β (beta) risk or type II error. This is the consumer's risk of accepting a bad lot.

When a lot is tested for quality, we can look at either "attribute" or "variable" quality data. Attribute quality data is either quantitative or qualitative data for which the product or service is designed and built. Variable quality data is a quantitative, continuous measurement process to either accept or reject the lot. The exact measurement can be either destructive or nondestructive testing.

23.11 OPERATING CHARACTERISTIC CURVES[4]

For large shipments consisting of many units, say 5,000, we must determine a sample size n and an acceptance number c such that we are sufficiently assured that our accept/reject decision, based on the sample, is correct. The choices for n

---

4. This section has been adapted from E. E. Adam and R. J. Ebert, *Production and Operations Management,* 5th ed. (New York: Prentice-Hall, 1992), pp. 653–655. Reproduced by permission of Everett Adam.

and *c* determine the characteristics of our sampling plan. Standard procedures are available for determining the sampling plan parameters, *n* and *c*, that will meet the performance requirements specified by the user. The performance requirements include the following four items of information: AQL, a conventional notation standing for "acceptable quality level" or "good quality"; LTPD, standing for "lot tolerance percent defective" or "poor quality level"; α, the producer's risk; and β, the consumer's risk. Assigning numeric values to these four parameters is largely a matter of managerial judgment. As soon as their numeric values have been assigned, values for *n* and *c* can be determined:

Example: A large medical clinic purchases shipments of pregnancy test kits (PTKs). A shipment contains 10,000 PTKs. It is important that the chemical composition of the PTK shipment be evaluated so that prescribing physicians are assured of valid tests.

Physicians have agreed that a shipment has acceptable quality if no more than 2 percent of the PTKs in the shipment have an incorrect chemical composition. They consider shipments having 5 percent or more defective PTKs to be an extremely bad-quality shipment. We want a sampling plan that affords a 0.95 probability of accepting good shipments but only a 0.10 probability of accepting extremely bad shipments. These performance specifications for the sampling plan are summarized on the left side of Table 23–5. A sampling plan was derived to meet these performance requirements. The plan calls for 308 PTKs to be sampled from each shipment (right side of Table 23–5). If more than 10 of these PTKs are defective, the entire shipment is rejected. If 10 or fewer PTKs are defective, the shipment is accepted. In this way, a shipment having 2 percent defective PTKs has only 5 chances out of 100 of being rejected, whereas a shipment having 5 percent defective has only 10 chances out of 100 of being accepted. This sampling plan includes procedures for determining the probability of accepting the shipment if its percent defective is between 2 and 5. These probabilities are shown in Figure 23–34.

The curves in Figure 23–34, called the *operating characteristic curves* or OC curves, reveal how sampling plans discriminate among shipments. If a shipment is of high quality (low percent defective), a good sampling plan yields a high probability of accepting the shipment. If a shipment is of poor quality (high percent defective), the plan yields a low probability of accepting the shipment.

You can see from the OC curve in Figure 23–34 that the desired probabilities of accepting good- and bad-quality PTK shipments have been obtained. The second

TABLE 23–5. SAMPLING PLAN AND SPECIFICATIONS FOR PTKs

Performance Specifications	Parameters of Sampling Plan
Good quality (AQL) = .02 or few defectives	
Desired probability of accepting a good quality shipment = .95	$n = 308$
Risk: probability of α errors = .05	$c = 10$
Bad quality (LTPD) = .05 or more defectives	
Desired probability of accepting a bad quality shipment = .10	
Risk: probability of β errors = .10	

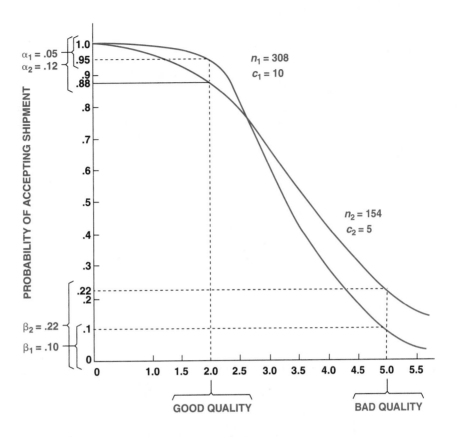

FIGURE 23–34. Probabilities of accepting a PTK shipment; OC curves.

OC curve represents a different sampling plan, $n = 154$ and $c = 5$, that does not meet desired performance specifications: It offers only a 0.88 probability of accepting a good-quality shipment, and a 0.22 probability of accepting a bad shipment.

A sampling plan specifying a unique pair of n and c has a unique OC curve. Sampling plans calling for a large sample size are more discriminating than plans calling for a small sample size. Figure 23–34 shows OC curves for two sampling plans with different samples sizes and acceptance numbers. Comparing plans, the ratio of the acceptance number c and the sample size n is constant. For plans with larger ns, the probability of accepting good-quality lots is higher than for plans with smaller ns; similarly, for plans with larger ns, the probability of accepting bad-quality lots is lower than for plans with smaller ns. Of course, these benefits are not obtained without incurring the higher inspection costs associated with large sample sizes.

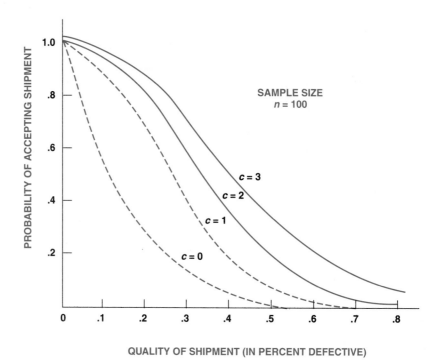

FIGURE 23–35. Effect of variations in c on OC curve.

The effect of increasing the acceptance number c (for a given value of n) is to increase the probability of accepting the shipment for all levels of percent defective other than zero (Figure 23–35). By increasing c, more defective units are allowed to pass inspection. By decreasing c, inspection is tightened.

In general, higher values of c allow "looser" performance, increasing the probability of accepting a shipment with a given percent of defective units. Increasing n results in greater confidence that we have correctly discriminated between good and bad shipments. However, inspection costs are also increased with larger values of n. The task of quality management is to find the proper balance between the costs and benefits of alternative sampling plans.

23.12 IMPLEMENTING SIX SIGMA[5]

Six Sigma is a business initiative first espoused by Motorola in the early 1990s. Recent Six Sigma success stories, primarily from the likes of General Electric, Sony, AlliedSignal, and Motorola, have captured the attention of Wall Street and

---

5. Adapted from Forrest W. Breyfogle, III, *Implementing Six Sigma* (New York: Wiley, 1999), pp. 5–7.

have propagated the use of this business strategy. The Six Sigma strategy involves the use of statistical tools within a structured methodology for gaining the knowledge needed to achieve products and services better, faster, and less expensively than the competition. The repeated, disciplined application of the master strategy on project after project, where the projects are selected based on key business issues, is what drives dollars to the bottom line, resulting in increased profit margins and impressive return on investment from the Six Sigma training. The Six Sigma initiative has typically contributed an average of six figures per project to the bottom line. The Six Sigma project executioners are sometimes called "black belts," "top guns," "change agents," or "trailblazers," depending on the company deploying the strategy. These people are trained in the Six Sigma philosophy and methodology and are expected to accomplish at least four projects annually, which should deliver at least $500,000 annually to the bottom line. A Six Sigma initiative in a company is designed to change the culture through breakthrough improvement by focusing on out-of-the-box thinking in order to achieve aggressive, stretch goals. Ultimately, Six Sigma, if deployed properly, will infuse intellectual capital into a company and produce unprecedented knowledge gains that translate directly into bottom line results.[6]

General Electric (GE) CEO Jack Welch describes Six Sigma as "the most challenging and potentially rewarding initiative we have ever undertaken at General Electric." The GE 1997 annual report states that Six Sigma delivered more than $300 million to its operating income. In 1998, they expected to more than double this operating profit impact. GE listed in their annual report the following to exemplify these Six Sigma benefits:

- Medical Systems described how Six Sigma designs have produced a 10-fold increase in the life of CT scanner X-ray tubes—increasing the "uptime" of these machines and the profitability and level of patient care given by hospitals and other health care providers.
- Superabrasives—our industrial diamond business—described how Six Sigma quadrupled its return on investment and, by improving yields, is giving it a full decade's worth of capacity despite growing volume—without spending a nickel on plant and equipment capacity.
- Our railcar leasing business described 62% reduction in turnaround time at its repair shops: an enormous productivity gain for our railroad and shipper customers and for a business that's now two or three times faster than its nearest rival because of Six Sigma improvements. In the next phase across the entire shop network, black belts and green belts, working with their teams, redesigned the overhaul process, resulting in a 50% further reduction in cycle time.
- The plastics business, through rigorous Six Sigma process work, added 300 million pounds of new capacity (equivalent to a "free plant"), saved $400 million in investment and will save another $400 by 2000.[7]

---

6. Information in this paragraph was contributed by J. Kiemele, Ph.D., of Air Academy Associates.

7. 1998 GE Annual Report.

A *USA Today* article presented differences of opinions about the value of Six Sigma in "Firms Air for Six Sigma Efficiency."[8] One stated opinion was that Six Sigma is "malarkey," while Larry Bossidy, CEO of AlliedSignal, counters: "The fact is, there is more reality with this (Six Sigma) than anything that has come down in a long time in business. The more you get involved with it, the more you're convinced." Some other quotes from the article are as follows:

- After four weeks of classes over four months, you'll emerge a Six Sigma "black belt." And if you're an average black belt, proponents say you'll find ways to save $1 million each year.
- Six Sigma is expensive to implement. That's why it has been a large-company trend. About 30 companies have embraced Six Sigma, including Bombardier, ABB (Asea Brown Boveri) and Lockheed Martin.
- Nobody gets promoted to an executive position at GE without Six Sigma training. All white-collar professionals must have started training by January. GE says it will mean $40 billion to $15 billion in increased annual revenue and cost savings by 2000 when Welch retires.
- Raytheon figures it spends 25% of each sales dollar fixing problems when it operates at four sigma, a lower level of efficiency. But if it raises its quality and efficiency to Six Sigma, it would reduce spending on fixes to 1%.
- It will keep the company (AlliedSignal) from having to build an $85 million plant to fill increasing demand for caperolactan used to make nylon, a total savings of $30–$50 million a year.
- Lockheed Martin used to spend an average of 200 work-hours trying to get a part that covers the landing gear to fit. For years, employees had brainstorming sessions which resulted in seemingly logical solutions. None worked. The statistical discipline of Six Sigma discovered a part that deviated by one-thousandth of an inch. Now corrected, the company saves $14,000 a jet.
- Lockheed Martin took a stab at Six Sigma in the early 1990s, but the attempt so foundered that it now calls its trainees "program managers" instead of black belts to prevent in-house jokes of skepticism. . . . Six Sigma is a success this time around. The company has saved $64 million with its first 40 projects.
- John Akers promised to turn IBM around with Six Sigma, but the attempt was quickly abandoned when Akers was ousted as CEO in 1993.
- Marketing will always use the number that makes the company look best. . . . Promises are made to potential customers around capability statistics that are not anchored in reality.
- Because manager's bonuses are tied to Six Sigma savings, it causes them to fabricate results, and savings turn out to be phantom.
- Six Sigma will eventually go the way of other fads, but probably not until Welch and Bossidy retire.

---

8. D. Jones, "Firms Air for Six Sigma Efficiency," *USA Today,* July 21, 1998, Money Section. Copyright © 1998 *USA Today;* reprinted with permission.

● History will prove those like Smith wrong, says Bossidy, who has been skeptical of other management fads. Six Sigma is not more fluff. At the end of the day, something has to happen.

23.13 QUALITY LEADERSHIP[9]

Consider for a moment the following seven items:

● Teamwork
● Strategic integration
● Continuous improvement
● Respect for people
● Customer focus
● Management-by-fact
● Structured problem-solving

Some people contend that these seven items are the principles of project management when, in fact, they are the seven principles of the total quality management program at Sprint. Project management and TQM have close similarity in leadership and team-based decision-making. According to Breyfogle,[10] American managers have often conducted much of their business through an approach that is sometimes called *management by results*. This type of management tends to focus only on the end result, that is, process yield, gross margin, sales dollars, return on investment, and so on. Emphasis is placed on a chain of command with a hierarchy of standards, objectives, controls, and accountability. Objectives are translated into work standards or quotas that guide the performance of employees. Use of these numerical goals can cause short-term thinking, misdirected focus, fear (e.g., of a poor job performance rating), fudging the numbers, internal conflict, and blindness to customer concerns. This type of management is said to be like trying to keep a dog happy by forcibly wagging its tail.

Quality leadership is an alternative that emphasizes results by working on methods. In this type of management, every work process is studied and constantly improved so that the final product or service not only meets but exceeds customer expectations. The principles of quality leadership are customer focus, obsession with quality, effective work structure, control yet freedom (e.g., man-

---

9. Adapted from Forrest W. Breyfogle, III, *Implementing Six Sigma* (New York: Wiley, 1999), pp. 28–29.

10. Adapted from Forrest W. Breyfogle, III, *Implementing Six Sigma* (New York: Wiley, 1999), pp. 28–29.

agement in control of employees yet freedom given to employees), unity of purpose, process defect identification, teamwork, and education and training. These principles are more conducive to long-term thinking, correctly directed efforts, and a keen regard for the customer's interest.

Quality leadership does have a positive effect on the return on investment. In 1950, Deming described this chain reaction of getting a greater return on investment as follows: improve quality → decrease costs → improve productivity → decrease prices → increase market share in business → provide jobs → increase return on investment. Quality is not something that can be delegated to others. Management must lead the transformation process.

To give quality leadership, the historical hierarchical management structure needs to be changed to a structure that has a more unified purpose using project teams. A single person can make a big difference in an organization. However, one person rarely has enough knowledge or experience to understand everything within a process. Major gains in both quality and productivity can often result when a team of people pool their skills, talents, and knowledge.

Teams need to have a systematic plan to improve the process that creates mistakes/defects, breakdowns/delays, inefficiencies, and variation. For a given work environment, management needs to create an atmosphere that supports team effort in all aspects of business. In some organizations, management may need to create a process that describes hierarchical relationships between teams, the flow of directives, how directives are transformed into action and improvements, and the degree of autonomy and responsibility of the teams. The change to quality leadership can be very difficult. It requires dedication and patience to transform an entire organization.

23.14 RESPONSIBILITY FOR QUALITY

Everyone in an organization plays an important role in quality management. In order for an organization to become a quality organization, all levels must actively participate, and, according to Dr. Edwards Deming, the key to successful implementation of quality starts at the top.

Top management must drive fear from the workplace and create an environment where cross-functional cooperation can flourish. The ultimate responsibility for quality in the organization lies in the hands of upper management. It is only with their enthusiastic and unwavering support that quality can thrive in an organization.

The project manager is ultimately responsible for the quality of the project. This is true for the same reason the president of the company is ultimately responsible for quality in a corporation. The project manager selects the procedures and policies for the project and therefore controls the quality. The project manager must create an environment that fosters trust and cooperation among the team members. The project manager must also support the identification and reporting of problems by team members and avoid at all costs a "shoot the messenger" mentality.

The project team members must be trained to identify problems, recommend solutions, and implement the recommended solutions. They must also have the authority to limit further processing when a process is outside of specified limits. In other words, they must be able to halt any activity that is outside of the quality limits set for the project and work toward a resolution of the problem at any point in the project.

23.15 QUALITY CIRCLES

Quality circles are small groups of employees who meet frequently to help resolve company quality problems and provide recommendations to management. Quality circles were initially developed in Japan and only recently have achieved some degree of success in the United States. The employees involved in quality circles meet frequently either at someone's home or at the plant before the shift begins. The group identifies problems, analyzes data, recommends solutions, and carries out management-approved changes. The success of quality circles is heavily based upon management's willingness to listen to employee recommendations.

The key elements of quality circles include:

- They give a team effort.
- They are completely voluntary.
- Employees are trained in group dynamics, motivation, communications, and problem solving.
- Members rely upon each other for help.
- Management support is active but as needed.
- Creativity is encouraged.
- Management listens to recommendations.

The benefits of quality circles include:

- Improved quality of products and services
- Better organizational communications
- Improved worker performance
- Improved morale

23.16 JUST-IN-TIME MANUFACTURING (JIT)

Just-in-time manufacturing is a process that continuously stresses waste reduction by optimizing the processes and procedures necessary to maintain a manufacturing operation. Part of this process is JIT purchasing or inventory where the materials needed appear just in time for use, thus eliminating costs associated with ma-

TABLE 23–6. COMPARATIVE ANALYSIS OF PURCHASING PRACTICE: TRADITIONAL U.S. AND JAPANESE JIT

Purchasing Activity	JIT Purchasing	Traditional Purchasing
Purchase lot size	Purchase in small lots with frequent deliveries	Purchase in large batch size with less frequent deliveries
Selecting supplier	Single source of supply for a given part in nearby geographical area with a long-term contract	Rely on multiple sources of supply for a given part and short-term contracts
Evaluating supplier	Emphasis is placed on product quality, delivery performance, and price, but *no* percentage of reject from supplier is acceptable	Emphasis is placed on product quality, delivery performance and price but about two percent reject from supplier is acceptable
Receiving inspection	Counting and receiving inspection of incoming parts is reduced and eventually eliminated	Buyer is responsible for receiving, counting, and inspecting all incoming parts
Negotiating and bidding process	Primary objective is to achieve product quality through a long-term contract and fair price	Primary objective is to get the lowest possible price
Determing mode of transportation	Concern for both inbound and outbound freight, and on-time delivery. Delivery schedule left to the buyer	Concern for outbound freight and lower outbound costs. Delivery schedule left to the supplier
Product specification tions	"Loose" specifications. The buyer relies more on performance specifications than on product design and the supplier is encouraged to be more innovative	"Rigid" specifications. The buyer relies more on design specifica- than on product performance and suppliers have less freedom in design specifications
Paperwork	Less formal paperwork. Delivery time and quantity level can be changed by telephone calls	Requires great deal of time and formal paperwork. Changes in delivery date and quantity require purchase orders
Packaging	Small standard containers used to hold exact quantity and to specify the precise specifications	Regular packaging for every part type and part number with no clear specifications on product content

Source: Sang M. Lee, and A. Ansari, "Comparative Analysis of Japanese Just-in-Time Purchasing and Traditional Purchasing Systems," *International Journal of Operations and Product Management* 5, no. 4 (1985), 5–14.

terial handling, storage, paperwork, and even inspection. In order to eliminate inspection, the customer must be convinced that the contractor has adhered to all quality requirements. In other words, JIT inventory pushes quality assurance and quality control for that product down to the contractor's level.

The customer benefits from JIT purchasing by developing long-term relationships with *fewer* suppliers, thus lowering subcontractor management costs. The contractor benefits by having long-term contracts. However, the contractor must agree to special conditions such as on-site inspections by the customer's executives, project manager, or quality team, or even allowing an on-site customer representative at the contractor's location.

JIT purchasing has been widely adopted in Japan, but only marginal success has occurred here in the United States. Table 23–6 shows the relative comparison of American versus Japanese quality practices.

Another part of JIT manufacturing is the identification and continuous reduction of waste. Shigeo Shingo of Toyota Motor Company has identified seven wastes that should be the targets of a continuous improvement process. These appear in Table 23–7.

Two new topics are now being discussed as part of JIT manufacturing: value-added manufacturing and stockless production. Value-added manufacturing advocates the elimination of any step in the manufacturing process that does not add value to the product for the customer. Examples include process delays, transporting materials, work-in-process inventories, and excessive paperwork. Stockless production promotes little inventories for raw materials, work in process, and finished goods. Everything ends up being made to order and then delivered as needed. Waste becomes nonexistent. The practicality and risks of this approach may not be feasible for either the company or the project manager.

TABLE 23–7.   THE SEVEN WASTES

1. *Waste of overproduction.* Eliminate by reducing setup times, synchronizing quantities and timing between processess, compacting layout, visibility, and so forth. Make only what is needed now.
2. *Waste of waiting.* Eliminate through synchronizing work flow as much as possible, and balance uneven loads by flexible workers and equipment.
3. *Waste of transportation.* Establish layouts and locations to make transport and handling unnecessary if possible. Then rationalize transport and material handling that cannot be eliminated.
4. *Waste of processing itself.* First question why this part or product should be made at all, then why each process is necessary. Extend thinking beyond economy of scale or speed.
5. *Waste of stocks.* Reduce by shortening setup times and reducing lead times, by synchronizing work flows and improving work skills, and even by smoothing fluctuations in demand for the product. Reducing all the other wastes reduces the waste of stocks.
6. *Waste of motion.* Study motion for economy and consistency. Economy improves productivity, and consistency improves quality. First improve the motions, then mechanize or automate. Otherwise there is danger of automating waste.
7. *Waste of making defective products.* Develop the production process to prevent defects from being made so as to eliminate inspection. At each process, accept no defects and make no defects. Make processes failsafe to do this. From a quality process comes a quality product—automatically.

Source: Hall, R, *Attaining Manufacturing Excellence.* Homewood, IL: Dow-Jones-Irwin, 1987. p. 26.

23.17 TOTAL QUALITY MANAGEMENT (TQM)[11]

There is no explicit definition of total quality management. Some people define it as providing the customer with quality products at the right time and at the right place. Others define it as meeting or exceeding customer requirements. Internally, TQM can be defined as less variability in the quality of the product and less waste.

Figure 23–36 shows the basic objectives and focus areas of a TQM process. Almost all companies have a primary strategy to obtain TQM, and the selected strategy is usually in place over the long term. The most common primary strategies are listed below. A summary of the seven primary improvement strategies mapped onto 17 corporations is shown in Table 23–8.

Primary strategies:

- Solicit ideas for improvement from employees.
- Encourage and develop teams to identify and solve problems.
- Encourage team development for performing operations and service activities resulting in participative leadership.
- Benchmark every major activity in the organization to ensure that it is done in the most efficient and effective way.
- Utilize process management techniques to improve customer service and reduce cycle time.
- Develop and train customer staff to be entrepreneurial and innovative in order to find ways to improve customer service.
- Implement improvements so that the organization can qualify as an ISO 9000 supplier.

There also exist secondary strategies that, over the long run, focus on operations and profitability. Typical secondary strategies are shown below, and Table 23–9 identifies the secondary improvement strategies by listed companies.

Secondary strategies:

- Maintain continuous contact with customers; understand and anticipate their needs.
- Develop loyal customers by not only pleasing them but by exceeding their expectations.
- Work closely with suppliers to improve their product/service quality and productivity.
- Utilize information and communication technology to improve customer service.
- Develop the organization into manageable and focused units in order to improve performance.

---

11. This section has been adapted from C. Carl Pegels, *Total Quality Management* (Boyd & Fraser, 1995), pp. 4–27.

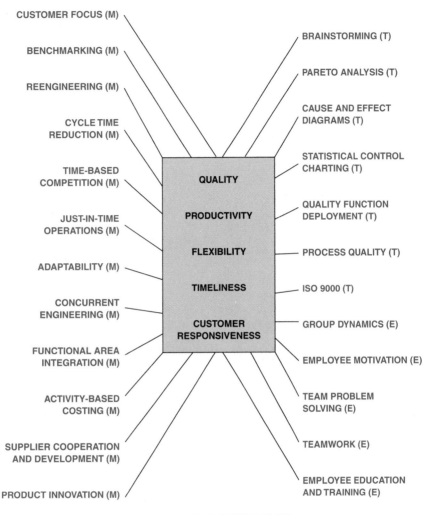

FIGURE 23–36. TQM objectives and focus areas. *Source:* C. Carl Pegels; *Total Quality Management* (Boyd & Fraser, 1995), p. 6.

- Utilize concurrent or simultaneous engineering.
- Encourage, support, and develop employee training and education programs.
- Improve timeliness of all operation cycles (minimize all cycle times).
- Focus on quality, productivity, and profitability.
- Focus on quality, timeliness, and flexibility.

TABLE 23–8.   PRIMARY IMPROVEMENT STRATEGIES EMPLOYED BY LISTED CORPORATIONS

	Strategy						
	P1	*P2*	*P3*	*P4*	*P5*	*P6*	*P7*
Asea, Brown, Boveri		X					
AT&T				X			
Cigna						X	
DuPont				X			
Eastman Kodak		X					
Eaton Corp.	X	X	X				
Ford Motor Company	X						
General Motors				X			
Goodyear Tire		X	X				
IBM Rochester							X
ICL Plc							X
Johnson Controls							X
Motorola				X			
New England Corp.					X		
New York Life		X	X				
Pratt and Whitney			X				
Xerox Corp.				X			

Source: C. Carl Pegels, *Total Quality Management* (Boyd & Fraser, 1995), p. 21.

TABLE 23–9.   SECONDARY IMPROVEMENT STRATEGIES EMPLOYED BY LISTED CORPORATIONS

	Strategy									
	S1	*S2*	*S3*	*S4*	*S5*	*S6*	*S7*	*S8*	*S9*	*S10*
AMP Corp.	X	X							X	X
Asea, Brown, Boveri	X	X								
British Telecom	X						X			
Chrysler Corp.					X				X	X
Coca-Cola									X	
Corning							X			
Eastman Kodak	X									
Eaton Corp.									X	
Fidelity Investment	X			X					X	
Ford Motor Company									X	
Fujitsu Systems	X		X						X	
General Motors					X				X	X
Holiday Inns			X							
IBM Rochester	X			X					X	X
ICL Plc		X								
Johnson Controls	X	X					X			
Motorola								X		
New England Corp.	X									
New York Life	X	X								
Pratt and Whitney						X				
Procter & Gamble		X							X	
The Forum Corp.	X									X
VF Corp.				X						X
Xerox Corp.	X									

Source: C. Carl Pegels, *Total Quality Management* (Boyd & Fraser, 1995).

TABLE 23–10. SUMMARY ILLUSTRATIONS OF QUANTIFIED IMPROVEMENTS ACHIEVED

AMP. On-time shipments improved from 65% to 95%, and AMP products have nationwide availability within three days or less on 50% of AMP sales.

Asea, Brown, Boveri. Every improvement goal customers asked for—better delivery, quality responsiveness, and so on—was met.

Chrysler. New vehicles are now being developed in 33 months versus as long as 60 months 10 years ago.

Eaton. Increased sales per employee from $65,000 in 1983 to about $100,000 in 1992.

Fidelity. Handles 200,000 information calls in 4 telephone centers; 1,200 representatives handle 75,000 calls, and the balance is automated.

Ford. Use of 7.25 man-hours of labor per vehicle versus 15 man-hours in 1980; Ford Taurus bumper uses 10 parts compared to 100 parts on similar GM cars.

General Motors. New vehicles are now being developed in 34 months versus 48 months in the 1980s.

IBM Rochester. Defect rates per million are 32 times lower than four years ago and on some products exceed six sigma (3.4 defects per million).

Pratt & Whitney. Defect rate per million was cut in half; a tooling process was shortened from two months to two days; part lead times were reduced by 43%.

VF Corp. Market response system enables 97% in-stock rate for retail stores compared to 70% industry average.

NCR. Checkout terminal was designed in 22 months versus 44 months and contained 85% fewer parts than its predecessor.

AT&T. Redesign of telephone switch computer completed in 18 months versus 36 months, manufacturing defects reduced by 87%.

Deere & Co. Reduced cycle time of some of its products by 60%, saving 30% of usual development costs.

Source: C. Carl Pegels, *Total Quality Management* (Boyd & Fraser, 1995), p. 27.

Quality improvements achieved by corporations are not easy to obtain. Most firms consider this information as confidential and usually do not like to publish for fear of providing an advantage to their competitors. As a result, the information in Table 23–10 is sketchy and limited. It largely consists of limited information that firms were willing to disclose. It is simply a snapshot of a limited number of quantitative performance improvements that were achieved by firms as part of their total quality management programs.

One of the more noteworthy achievements is Ford's reduction in man-hours to build a vehicle from 15 to 7.25. Although this took 10 years to achieve, it is still a sterling example of productivity improvement. IBM Rochester, Minnesota's reduction in defects per million by a factor of 32 over a 4-year period is worthy of note. And the ability of Chrysler and General Motors to reduce their design development times for new vehicles from 60 and 48 months to the current 33 and 34 months, respectively, is an achievement that indicates the return of competitiveness to the U.S. automobile industry.

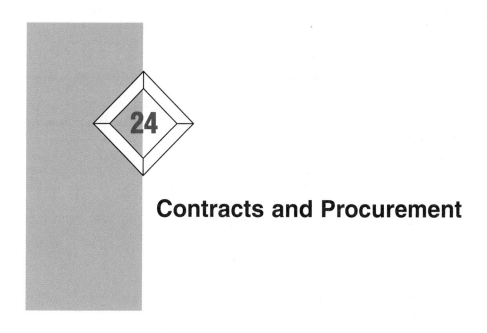

Contracts and Procurement

24.0 INTRODUCTION

In general, companies provide services or products based on the requirements of invitations for competitive bids issued by the client or the results of direct contract negotiations with the client. One of the most important factors in preparing a proposal and estimating the cost and profit of a project is the type of contract expected. The confidence by which a bid is prepared is usually dependent on how much of a risk the contractor will incur through the contract. Certain types of contracts provide relief for the contractor, since onerous risks[1] exist. The cost must therefore consider how well the contract type covers certain high- and low-risk areas.

Prospective clients are always concerned when, during a competitive bidding process, one bid is much lower than the others. The client may question the validity of the bid and whether the contract can be achieved for the low bid. In cases such as this, the client usually imposes incentive and penalty clauses in the contract for self-protection.

Because of the risk factor, competitors must negotiate not only for the target cost figures, but also for the type of contract involved, since risk protection is the predominant influential factor. The size and experience of the client's own staff, urgency of completion, availability of qualified contractors, and other factors must be carefully evaluated. The advantages and disadvantages of all basic contractual arrangements must be recognized to select the optimum arrangement for a particular project.

---

1. *Onerous risks* are unfair risks that the contractor may have to bear. Quite often, the contract negotiations may not reach agreement on what is or is not an onerous risk.

24.1 PROCUREMENT

Procurement can be defined as the acquisition of goods or services. Procurement (and contracting) is a process that involves two parties with different objectives who interact in a given market segment. Good procurement practices can increase corporate profitability by taking advantage of quantity discounts, minimizing cash flow problems, and seeking out quality suppliers. Because procurement contributes to profitability, procurement is often centralized, which results in standardized practices and lower paperwork costs.

All procurement strategies are frameworks by which an organization attains its objectives. There are two basic procurement strategies:

● Corporate procurement strategy: the relationship of specific procurement actions to the corporate strategy
● Project procurement strategy: the relationship of specific procurement actions to the operating environment of the project

Project procurement strategies can differ from corporate procurement strategies because of constraints, availability of critical resources, and specific customer requirements. Corporate strategies might promote purchasing small quantities from several qualified vendors, whereas project strategies may dictate sole source procurement.

Procurement planning usually involves the selection of one of the following as the primary objective:

● Procure all goods/services from a single source.
● Procure all goods/services from multiple sources.
● Procure only a small portion of the goods/services.
● Procure none of the goods/services.

Another critical factor is the environment in which procurement must take place. There are two environments: macro and micro. The macro environment includes the general external variables that can influence how and when we do procurement. These include recessions, inflation, cost of borrowing money, and unemployment. As an example, a foreign corporation had undertaken a large project that involved the hiring of several contractors. Because of the country's high unemployment rate, the decision was made to use only domestic suppliers/contractors and to give first preference to contractors in cities where unemployment was the greatest, even though there were other more qualified suppliers/contractors.

The micro environment is the internal environment of the firm, especially the policies and procedures imposed by either the firm, project, or client in the way that procurement will take place. This includes the procurement/contracting system, which contains five cycles:

● Requirement cycle: definition of the boundaries of the project
● Requisition cycle: analysis of sources

- Solicitation cycle: the bidding process
- Award cycle: contractor selection and contract award
- Contract administration cycle: managing the subcontractor until completion of the contract

There are several activities that are part of the procurement process and that overlap several of the cycles. These cycles can be conducted in parallel, especially requisition and solicitation.

24.2 REQUIREMENT CYCLE

The first step in the procurement process is the definition of project, specifically the requirement. This is referred to as the requirement cycle and includes the following:

- Defining the need for the project
- Development of the statement of work, specifications, and work breakdown structure
- Performing a make or buy analysis
- Laying out the major milestones and the timing/schedule
- Cost estimating, including life-cycle costing
- Obtaining authorization and approval to proceed

Previously, in Chapter 11, we discussed the statement of work. The SOW is a *narrative* description of the work to be accomplished and/or the resources to be supplied. The identification of resources to be supplied has taken on paramount importance during the last ten years or so. During the 1970s and 1980s, small companies were bidding on mega jobs only to subcontract out more than 99% of all of the work. Lawsuits were abundant and the solution was to put clauses in the SOW requiring that the contractor identify the names and resumes of the talented *internal* resources that would be committed to the project, including the percentage of their time on the project.

Specifications are written, pictorial, or graphic information that describe, define, or specify the services or items to be procured. There are three types of specifications:

- Design specifications: These detail what is to be done in terms of physical characteristics. The risk of performance is on the buyer.
- Performance specifications: These specify measurable capabilities the end product must achieve in terms of operational characteristics. The risk of performance is on the contractor.
- Functional specifications: This is when the seller describes the end use of the item to stimulate competition among commercial items, at a lower overall cost. This is a subset of the performance specification, and the risk of performance is on the contractor.

There are always options in the way the end item can be obtained. Feasible procurement alternatives include make or buy, lease or buy, buy or rent, and lease or rent. Buying domestic or international is also of critical importance, especially to the United Auto Workers Union. Factors involving the make or buy analysis are shown below:

- The make decision
  - Less costly (but not always!!)
  - Easy integration of operations
  - Utilize existing capacity that is idle
  - Maintain direct control
  - Maintain design/production secrecy
  - Avoid unreliable supplier base
  - Stabilize existing workforce
- The buy decision
  - Less costly (but not always!!)
  - Utilize skills of suppliers
  - Small volume requirement (not cost effective to produce)
  - Having limited capacity or capability
  - Augment existing labor force
  - Maintain multiple sources (qualified vendor list)
  - Indirect control

The lease or rent decision is usually a financial endeavor. Leases are usually longer term than renting. Consider the following example. A company is willing to rent you a piece of equipment at a cost of $100 per day. You can lease the equipment for $60 per day plus a one-time cost of $5000. What is the breakeven point, in days, where leasing and renting are the same?

$$\text{Let X be the number of days.}$$
$$\$100X = \$5000 + \$60X$$
$$\uparrow \qquad\qquad \uparrow$$
$$\text{renting} \qquad \text{leasing}$$
$$\text{Solving, X} = 125 \text{ days}$$

Therefore, if the firm wishes to use this equipment for more than 125 days, it would be more cost effective to sign a lease agreement rather than a rental agreement.

24.3 REQUISITION CYCLE

Once the requirements are identified, a requisition form is sent to procurement to begin the requisition process. The requisition cycle includes:

- Evaluating/confirming specifications (are they current?)
- Confirming sources
- Reviewing past performance of sources
- Producing solicitation package

The solicitation package is prepared during the requisition cycle but utilized during the solicitation cycle. In most situations, the same solicitation package must be sent to each possible supplier so that the playing field is level. A typical solicitation package would include:

- Bid documents (usually standardized)
- Listing of qualified vendors (expected to bid)
- Proposal evaluation criteria
- Bidder conferences
- How change requests will be managed
- Supplier payment plan

Standardized bid documents usually include standard forms for compliance with EEO, affirmative action, OSHA/EPA, minority hiring, etc. A listing of qualified vendors appears in order to drive down the cost. Quite often, one vendor will not bid on the job because it knows that it cannot submit a lower bid than one of the other vendors. The cost of bidding on a job is an expensive process.

Bidder conferences are used so that no single bidder has more knowledge than others. If a potential bidder has a question concerning the solicitation package, then it *must* wait for the bidders' conference to ask the question so that all bidders will be privileged to the same information. This is particularly important in government contracting. There may be several bidders' conferences between solicitation and award. Project management may or may not be involved in the bidders' conferences, either from the customer's side or the contractor's side.

24.4 SOLICITATION CYCLE

Selection of the acquisition method is the critical element in the solicitation cycle. There are three common methods for acquisition:

- Advertising
- Negotiation
- Small purchases (i.e., office supplies)

Advertising is when a company goes out for sealed bids. There are no negotiations. Competitive market forces determine the price and the award goes to the lowest bidder.

Negotiation is when the price is determined through a bargaining process. In such a situation, the customer may go out for a:

- Request for information (RFI)
- Request for quotation (RFQ)
- Request for proposal (RFP)

The RFP is the most costly endeavor for the vendor. Large proposals contain separate volumes for cost, technical performance, management history, quality, facilities, subcontractor management, and others. The negotiation process can be competitive or noncompetitive. Noncompetitive processes are called sole-source procurement.

On large contracts, the negotiation process goes well beyond negotiation of the bottom line. Separate negotiations can be made on price, quantity, quality, and timing. Vendor relations are critical during contract negotiations. The integrity of the relationship and previous history can shorten the negotiation process. The three major factors of negotiations are:

- Compromise ability
- Adaptability
- Good faith

Negotiations should be planned for. A typical list of activities would include:

- Develop objectives (i.e., min-max positions)
- Evaluate your opponent
- Define your strategy and tactics
- Gather the facts
- Perform a complete price/cost analysis
- Arrange "hygiene" factors

If you are the buyer, what is the *maximum* you will be willing to pay? If you are the seller, what is the *minimum* you are willing to accept? You must determine what motivates your opponent. Is your opponent interested in profitability, keeping people employed, developing a new technology, or using your name as a reference? This knowledge could certainly affect your strategy and tactics.

Hygiene factors include where the negotiations will take place. In a restaurant? Hotel? Office? Square table or round tables? Morning or afternoon? Who faces the windows and who faces the walls?

There should be a postnegotiation critique in order to review what was learned. The first type of postnegotiation critique is internal to your firm. The second type of postnegotiation critique is with all of the losing bidders to explain why they did not win the contract. Losing bidders may submit a "bid protest" where the customer may have to prepare a detailed report as to why this bidder did not win the contract. Bid protests are most common on government contracts.

24.5 AWARD CYCLE

The award cycle results in a signed contract. Unfortunately, there are several types of contracts. The negotiation process also includes the selection of the type of contract.

There are certain basic elements of most contracts.

- Mutual agreement: There must be an offer and acceptance.
- Consideration: There must be a down payment.
- Contract capability: The contract is binding only if the contractor has the capability to perform the work.

Conclusion: The objective of the award cycle is to negotiate a contract type and price that will result in reasonable contractor risk and provide the contractor with the greatest incentive for efficient and economic performance.

- Legal purpose: The contract must be for a legal purpose.
- Form provided by law: The contract must reflect the contractor's legal obligation, or lack of obligation, to deliver end products.

The two most common contract forms are completion contracts and term contracts.

- Completion contract: The contractor is required to deliver a definitive end product. Upon delivery and formal acceptance by the customer, the contract is considered complete, and final payment can be made.
- Term contract: The contract is required to deliver a specific "level of effort," not an end product. The effort is expressed in woman/man-days (months or years) over a specific period of time using specified personnel skill levels and facilities. When the contracted effort is performed, the contractor is under no further obligation. Final payment is made, irrespective of what is actually accomplished technically.

The final contract is usually referred to as a *definitive* contract, which follows normal contracting procedures such as the negotiation of all contractual terms, conditions, cost, and schedule prior to initiation of performance. Unfortunately, negotiating the contract and preparing it for signatures may require months of preparation. If the customer needs the work to begin immediately or if long-lead procurement is necessary, then the customer may provide the contractor with a *letter contract* or *letter of intent.* The letter contract is a preliminary written instrument authorizing the contractor to begin immediately the manufacture of supplies or the performance of services. The final contract price *may* be negotiated after performance begins, but the contractor may not exceed the "not to exceed" face value of the contract. The definitive contract must still be negotiated.

The type of contract selected is based upon the following:

- Overall degree of cost and schedule risk
- Type and complexity of requirement (technical risk)
- Extent of price competition
- Cost/price analysis
- Urgency of the requirements
- Performance period
- Contractor's responsibility (and risk)
- Contractor's accounting system (is it capable of earned value reporting?)
- Concurrent contracts (will my contract take a back seat to existing work?)
- Extent of subcontracting (how much work will the contractor outsource?)

24.6 TYPES OF CONTRACTS

Before analyzing the various types of contracts, one should be familiar with the terminology found in them.

- The *target cost* or *estimated cost* is the level of cost that the contractor will most likely obtain under normal performance conditions. The target cost serves as a basis for measuring the true cost at the end of production or development. The target cost may vary for different types of contracts even though the contract objectives are the same. The target cost is the most important variable affecting research and development.
- *Target* or *expected profit* is the profit value that is negotiated for, and set forth, in the contract. The expected profit is usually the largest portion of the total profit.
- *Profit ceiling* and *profit floor* are the maximum and minimum values, respectively, of the total profit. These quantities are often included in contract negotiations.
- *Price ceiling* or *ceiling price* is the amount of money for which the government is responsible. It is usually measured as a given percentage of the target cost, and is generally greater than the target cost.
- *Maximum* and *minimum fees* are percentages of the target cost and establish the outside limits of the contractor's profit.
- The *sharing arrangement* or *formula* gives the cost responsibility of the customer to the cost responsibility of the contractor for each dollar spent. Whether that dollar is an overrun or an underrun dollar, the sharing arrangement has the same impact on the contractor. This sharing arrangement may vary depending on whether the contractor is operating above or below target costs. The *production point* is usually that level of production above which the sharing arrangement commences.

● Point of total assumption is the point (cost or price) where the contractor assumes all liability for additional costs.

Because no single form of contract agreement fits every situation or project, companies normally perform work in the United States under a wide variety of contractual arrangements, such as:

● Cost-plus percentage fee
● Cost-plus fixed fee
● Cost-plus guaranteed maximum
● Cost-plus guaranteed maximum and shared savings
● Cost-plus incentive (award fee)
● Cost and cost sharing
● Fixed price or lump sum
● Fixed price with redetermination
● Fixed price incentive fee
● Fixed price with economic price adjustment
● Fixed price incentive with successive targets
● Fixed price for services, material, and labor at cost (purchase orders, blanket agreements)
● Time and material/labor hours only
● Bonus-penalty
● Combinations
● Joint venture

At one end of the range is the *cost-plus,* a fixed-fee type of contract where the company's profit, rather than price, is fixed and the company's responsibility, except for its own negligence, is minimal. At the other end of the range is the *lump sum* or *turnkey* type of contract under which the company has assumed full responsibility, in the form of profit or losses, for timely performance and for all costs under or over the fixed contract price. In between are various types of contracts, such as the guaranteed maximum, incentive types of contracts, and the bonus-penalty type of contract. These contracts provide for varying degrees of cost responsibility and profit depending on the level of performance. Contracts that cover the furnishing of consulting services are generally on a per diem basis at one end of the range and on a fixed-price basis at the other end of the range.

There are generally five types of contracts to consider: fixed-price (FP), cost-plus-fixed-fee (CPFF), or cost-plus-percentage-fee (CPPF), guaranteed maximum-shared savings (GMSS), fixed-price-incentive-fee (FPIF), and cost-plus-incentive-fee (CPIF) contracts. Each type is discussed separately.

● Under a *fixed-price* or *lump-sum contract,* the contractor must carefully estimate the target cost. The contractor is required to perform the work at the negotiated contract value. If the estimated target cost was low, the total profit is reduced and may even vanish. The contractor may not be able to underbid the competitors if the expected cost is overestimated. Thus, the contractor assumes a large risk.

This contract provides maximum protection to the owner for the ultimate cost of the project, but has the disadvantage of requiring a long period for preparation and adjudications of bids. Also, there is the possibility that because of a lack of knowledge of local conditions, all contractors may necessarily include an excessive amount of contingency. This form of contract should never be considered by the owner unless, at the time bid invitations are issued, the building requirements are known exactly. Changes requested by the owner after award of a contract on a lump sum basis lead to troublesome and sometimes costly extras.

● Traditionally, the *cost-plus-fixed-fee* contract has been employed when it was believed that accurate pricing could not be achieved any other way. In the CPFF contract, the cost may vary but the fee remains firm. Because, in a cost-plus contract, the contractor agrees only to use his best efforts to perform the work, good performance and poor performance are, in effect, rewarded equally. The total dollar profit tends to produce low rates of return, reflecting the small amount of risk that the contractor assumes. The fixed fee is usually a small percentage of the total or true cost. The cost-plus contract requires that the company books be audited.

With this form of contract the engineering-construction contractor bids a fixed dollar fee or profit for the services to be supplied by the contractor, with engineering, materials, and field labor costs to be reimbursed at actual cost. This form of bid can be prepared quickly at a minimal expense to contractor and is a simple bid for the owner to evaluate. Additionally, it has the advantage of establishing incentive to the contractor for quick completion of the job.

If it is a *cost-plus-percentage-fee* contract, it provides maximum flexibility to the owner and permits owner and contractor to work together cooperatively on all technical, commercial, and financial problems. However, it does not provide financial assurance of ultimate cost. Higher building cost may result, although not necessarily so, because of lack of financial incentive to the contractor compared with other forms. The only meaningful incentive that is evident today is the increased competition and prospects for follow-on contracts.

● Under the *guaranteed maximum-share savings* contract, the contractor is paid a fixed fee for his profit and reimbursed for the actual cost of engineering, materials, construction labor, and all other job costs, but only up to the ceiling figure established as the "guaranteed maximum." Savings below the guaranteed maximum are shared between owner and contractor, whereas contractor assumes the responsibility for any overrun beyond the guaranteed maximum price.

This contract form essentially combines the advantages as well as a few of the disadvantages of both lump sum and cost-plus contracts. This is the best form for a negotiated contract because it establishes a maximum price at the earliest possible date and protects the owner against being overcharged, even though the contract is awarded without competitive tenders. The guaranteed maximum-share savings contract is unique in that the owner and contractor share the financial risk and both have a real incentive to complete the project at lowest possible cost.

- *Fixed-price-incentive-fee* contracts are the same as fixed-price contracts except that they have a provision for adjustment of the total profit by a formula that depends on the final total cost at completion of the project and that has been agreed to in advance by both the owner and the contractor. To use this type of contract, the project or contract requirements must be firmly established. This contract provides an incentive to the contractor to reduce costs and therefore increase profit. Both the owner and contractor share in the risk and savings.
- *Cost-plus-incentive-fee* contracts are the same as cost plus contracts except that they have a provision for adjustment of the fee as determined by a formula that compares the total project costs to the target cost. This formula is agreed to in advance by both the owner and contractor. This contract is usually used for long-duration or R&D type projects. The company places more risk on the contractor and forces him to plan ahead carefully and strive to keep costs down. Incentive contracts are covered in greater detail in Section 24.7.

Other types of contracts that are not used frequently include:

- The *fixed-price incentive successive targets* contract is an infrequently used contract type. It has been used in the past in acquiring systems with very long lead time requirements where follow-on production contracts must be awarded before design or even production confirmation costs have been confirmed. Pricing data for the follow-on contract is inconclusive. This type of contract can be used in lieu of a letter contract or cost-plus arrangement.
- The *fixed-price with redetermination* contract can be either prospective or retroactive. The prospective type allows for future negotiations of two or more firm, fixed-price contracts at prearranged times. This is often used when future costs and pricing is expected to change significantly. The retroactive FPR contract allows for adjusting contract price after performance has been completed.
- *Cost* (CR) and *cost-sharing* (CS) contracts have limited use. Cost contracts have a "no fee" feature that has limited use except for nonprofit educational institutions conducting research. Cost sharing contracts are used for basic and applied research where the contractor is expected to benefit from the R & D by transferring knowledge to other parts of the business for commercial gain and to improve the contractor's competitive position.

Table 24–1 identifies the advantages and disadvantages of various contracting methods that are commonly used.

TABLE 24–1. CONTRACT COMPARISON

Contract Type	Advantages	Disadvantages
Cost-plus-fee	• Provides maximum flexibility to owner • Minimizes contractor profits • Minimizes negotiations and preliminary specification costs • Permits quicker start, earlier completion • Permits choice of best-qualified, not lowest-bidding, contractor • Permits use of same contractor from consultation to completion, usually increasing quality and efficiency	• No assurance of actual final cost • No financial incentive to minimize time and cost • Permits specification of high-cost features by owner's staff • Permits excessive design changes by owner's staff increasing time and costs
Guaranteed maximum-share savings	• Provides firm assurance of ultimate cost at earliest possible date • Insures prompt advice to owner of delays and extra costs resulting from changes • Provides incentive for quickest completion • Owner and contractor share financial risk and have mutual incentive for possible savings • Ideal contract to establish owner–contractor cooperation throughout execution of project	• Requires complete auditing by owner's staff • Requires completion of definitive engineering before negotiation of contract
Fixed price/lump sum	• Provides firm assurance of ultimate cost • Insures prompt advice to owner of delays and extra costs resulting from changes • Requires minimum owner follow-up on work • Provides maximum incentive for quickest completion at lowest cost • Involves minimal auditing by owner's staff	• Requires exact knowledge if what is wanted before contract award • Requires substantial time and cost to develop inquiry specs, solicit, and evaluate bids. Delays completion 3–4 months • High bidding costs and risks may reduce qualified bidders • Cost may be increased by excessive contingencies in bids to cover high-risk work

(continues)

TABLE 24-1. *(Continued)*

Contract Type	Advantages	Disadvantages
Fixed price for services, material and labor	• Essentially same as cost-plus-fee contract • Fixes slightly higher percentage of total cost • Eliminates checking and verifying contractor's services	• May encourage reduction of economic studies and detailing of drawings: produce higher costs for operation, construction, maintenance • Other same disadvantages as cost-plus-fee contract
Fixed price for imported goods and services, local costs reimbursable	• Maximum price assured for high percentage of plant costs • Avoids excessive contingencies in bids for unpredictable and highly variable local costs • Permits selection of local suppliers and subcontractors by owner	• Same extended time required for inquiry specs, quotations, and evaluation as fixed lump-sum for complete project • Requires careful definition of items supplied locally to insure comparable bids • No financial incentive to minimize field and local costs

The type of contract that is acceptable to the client and the company is determined by the circumstances of each individual project and the prevailing economic and competitive conditions. Generally, when work is hard to find, clients insist on fixed-price bids. This type of proposal is usually a burden to the contractor because of the proposal costs involved (about 1 percent of the total installed cost of the project), and the higher risk involved in the execution of the project on such a basis.

When there is an upsurge in business, clients are unable to insist on fixed-price bids and more work is awarded on a cost-plus basis. In fact, where a special capacity position exists, or where time is a factor, the client occasionally negotiates a cost-plus contract with only one contractor. Another technique used during a time of high workload is to award a project on a cost-plus basis with the understanding that the contract will be converted at a later date, when the scope has been better defined and unknowns identified, to another form, such as a lump sum for services. This approach is appealing to both the client and the contractor.

As we mentioned earlier, the client frequently has a standard form of contract that is used as the basis of negotiation or the basis of requests for proposals. A company should review the client's document carefully to assure itself that it understands how the client's document differs from what is its preferred position. Any additional duties or responsibilities assigned to your company merit careful scrutiny if the additional legal consequences and increased financial risks are to be evaluated properly.

It is important that you use an adequate and realistic description of the work to be undertaken and a careful evaluation and pricing of the scope of the work to be performed and the responsibilities and obligations assumed. The preparation of a proposal requires a clear understanding between the client and your company as to the rights, duties, and responsibilities of your company. The proposal defines what it intends to do and can do, what it neither intends doing nor is qualified to undertake, and the manner and basis of its compensation. Thorough analysis of these matters before, not after, submission of the proposal is essential.

24.7 INCENTIVE CONTRACTS

To alleviate some of the previously mentioned problem areas, clients, especially the government, have been placing incentive objectives into their contracts. The fixed-price-incentive-fee (FPIF) contract is an example of this. The essence of the incentive contract is that it offers a contractor more profit if costs are reduced or performance is improved and less profit if costs are raised or if performance goals are not met. Cost incentives take the form of a sharing formula generally expressed as a ratio. For example, if a 90/10 formula were negotiated, the government would pay for 90 cents and the contractor 10 cents for every dollar above the target cost. Thus, it benefits both the contractor and the government to reduce costs, because the contractor must consider that 10 percent of every dollar must be spent by the company. Expected profits can thus be increased by making maximum use of the contractor's managerial skills.

In the FPIF contract, the contractor agrees to perform a service at a given fixed cost. If the total cost is less than the target cost, than the contractor has made a profit according to the incentive-fee formula. If the total cost exceeds the target cost, then the contractor loses money.

Consider the following example, which appears in Figure 24–1. In Figure 24–1, the contractor has a target cost and target profit. However, there exists a price ceiling of $11,500, which is the maximum price that the contractor will be paid. If the contractor performs the work below the target cost of $10,000, then additional profit will be made. For example, by performing the work for $9,000, the contractor will receive a profit of $1,150, which is the target profit of $850 plus $300 for 30% of the underrun. The contractor will receive a total price of $10,150.

If the cost exceeds the target cost, then the contractor must pay 30% of the overrun out of the contractor's profits. However, the fixed price incentive fee (FPIF) contract has a point of total assumption. In this example, the point of total assumption is the point where all additional costs are burdened by the contractor. From Figure 24–1, the point of total assumption is when the cost reaches $10,928. At this point, the final price of $11,500 is reached. If the cost continues to increase, then all profits may disappear and the contractor may be forced to pay the majority of the overrun.

When the contract is completed, the contractor submits a statement of costs incurred in the performance of the contract. The costs are audited to determine al-

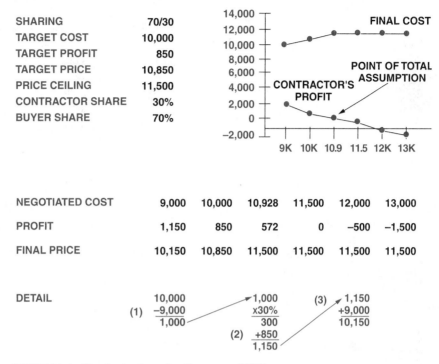

SHARING	70/30
TARGET COST	10,000
TARGET PROFIT	850
TARGET PRICE	10,850
PRICE CEILING	11,500
CONTRACTOR SHARE	30%
BUYER SHARE	70%

NEGOTIATED COST	9,000	10,000	10,928	11,500	12,000	13,000
PROFIT	1,150	850	572	0	–500	–1,500
FINAL PRICE	10,150	10,850	11,500	11,500	11,500	11,500

DETAIL

(1)
```
  10,000
  –9,000
   1,000
```

```
 1,000
 x30%
  300
```
(2)
```
 +850
 1,150
```

(3)
```
 1,150
 +9,000
 10,150
```

FIGURE 24–1. Fixed price incentive firm target (FPIF).

lowability and questionable charges are removed. This determines the negotiated cost. The negotiated cost is then subtracted from the target cost. This number is then multiplied by the sharing ratio. If the number is positive, it is added to the target profit. If it is negative, it is subtracted. The new number, the final profit, is then added to the negotiated cost to determine the final price. The final price never exceeds the price ceiling.

Figure 24–2 shows a typical cost-plus-incentive fee (CPIF) contract. In this contract, the contractor is reimbursed 100% of the costs. However, there exists a maximum fee (i.e., profit) of $1,350 and a minimum fee of $300. The final allowable profit will vary between the minimum and maximum fee. Because there appears more financial risk for the customer in a CPIF contract, the target fee is usually less than in an FPIF contract, and the contractor's portion of the sharing ratio is smaller.

24.8 CONTRACT TYPE VERSUS RISK

The amount of profit on a contract is most frequently based upon how the risks are to be shared between the contractor and the customer. For example, on a firm-fixed-price contract, the contractor absorbs 100 percent of the risks (especially fi-

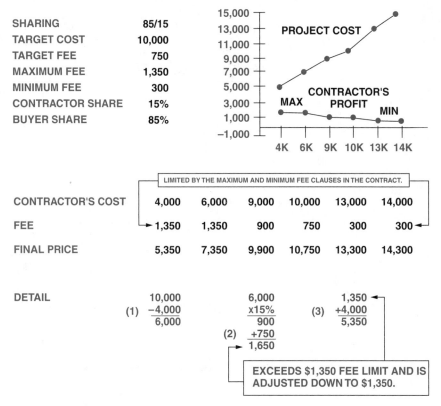

SHARING	85/15					
TARGET COST	10,000					
TARGET FEE	750					
MAXIMUM FEE	1,350					
MINIMUM FEE	300					
CONTRACTOR SHARE	15%					
BUYER SHARE	85%					

LIMITED BY THE MAXIMUM AND MINIMUM FEE CLAUSES IN THE CONTRACT.

CONTRACTOR'S COST	4,000	6,000	9,000	10,000	13,000	14,000
FEE	1,350	1,350	900	750	300	300
FINAL PRICE	5,350	7,350	9,900	10,750	13,300	14,300

DETAIL

(1) 10,000
    −4,000
     6,000

     6,000
    x15%
      900
(2) +750
    1,650

(3) 1,350
    +4,000
     5,350

EXCEEDS $1,350 FEE LIMIT AND IS ADJUSTED DOWN TO $1,350.

FIGURE 24–2. Cost-plus-incentive-fee (CPIF).

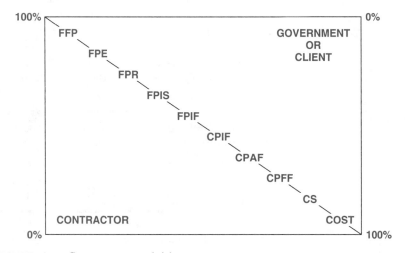

FIGURE 24–3. Contract types and risk types

nancial) and expects to receive a larger profit than on other types of contracts. On cost, cost-plus, and cost sharing contracts, the customer absorbs up to 100 percent of the risks and expects the contractor to work for a lower than expected profit margin or perhaps no profit at all.

All other types of contracts may have a risk sharing formula between the customer and the contractor. Figure 24–3 shows the relative degree of risk between the customer and the contractor for a variety of contracts.

24.9 CONTRACT ADMINISTRATION CYCLE

The contract administrator is responsible for compliance by the contractor to the contract's terms and conditions, and to make sure that the final product is fit for use. The functions of the contract administrator include:

- Change management
- Specification interpretation
- Adherence to quality
- Warranties
- Subcontractor management
- Production surveillance
- Waivers
- Contract breach
- Resolution of disputes
- Project termination
- Payment schedules
- Project closeout

The larger the contract, the greater the need for the contract administrator to resolve ambiguity in the contract. Sometimes, large contracts that are prepared by teams of attorneys contain an *order of precedence* clause. The order of precedence specifies that any inconsistency in the solicitation of the contract shall be resolved in a given order of procedure such as:

A. Specifications (first priority)
B. Other instructions (second priority)
C. Other documents, such as exhibits, attachments, appendices, SOW, contract data requirements list [CDRL], etc. (third priority)
D. Contract clauses (fourth priority)
E. The schedule (fifth priority)

Generally speaking, an ambiguous contract will be interpreted against the party who drafted the document. However, there is an offsetting rule called *Patent Ambiguity*. This includes the following:

- The offeror in a "bid" situation is expected to be knowledgeable about ordinary and normal industrial or construction practices pertinent to its work.
- The presumption is made that the offeror has made reasonable and complete review of the contractual documents before preparing and submitting them.
- Failure to notify of patent ambiguity works against the offeror if the claim is later submitted based on ambiguity.

Perhaps the majority of the contract administrator's time is spent handling changes. The following definitions describe the types of changes:

- Administrative change: A unilateral contractual change, in writing, that does not affect the substantive rights of the parties (i.e., a change in the paying office or the appropriation funding).
- Change order: A written order, signed by the contracting officer, directing the contractor to make a change.
- Contract modification: Any written change in the terms of the contract.
- Undefinitized contractual action: Any contractual action that authorizes the commencement of work prior to the establishment of a final definitive price.
- Supplemental agreement: A contract modification that is accompanied by the mutual action of both parties.
- Constructive change: Any effective change to the contract caused by the actions or inaction of personnel in authority, or by circumstances that cause a contractor to perform work differently than required by written contract. The contractor may file a claim for equitable adjustment in the contract.

Typical causes of constructive changes include:

- Defective specification with impossibility of performance
- Erroneous interpretation of contract
- Overinspection of work
- Failure to disclose superior knowledge
- Acceleration of performance
- Late or unsuitable owner or customer furnished property
- Failure to cooperate
- Improperly exercised options
- Misusing proprietary data

Based on the type of contract, terms, and conditions, the customer may have the right to terminate a contract for convenience at any time. However, the customer must compensate the contractor for his preparations and for any completed and accepted work relating to the terminated part of the contract.

The following are reasons for termination for convenience of the customer:

- Elimination of the requirement
- Technological advances in the state-of-the-art
- Budgetary changes
- Related requirements and/or procurements
- Anticipating profits not allowed

The following are reasons for termination for default due to contractor's actions:

- Contractor fails to make delivery on scheduled date.
- Contractor fails to make progress so as to endanger performance of the contract and its terms.
- Contractor fails to perform any other provisions of the contract.

If a contract is terminated due to default, then the contractor may not be entitled to compensation of work in progress but not yet accepted by the customer. The customer may even be entitled to repayment from the contractor of any advances or progress payments applicable to such work. Also, the contractor may be liable for any excess reprocurement costs. However, contractors can seek relief through negotiations, a Board of Contracts Appeals, or Claims Court.

The contract administrator, is responsible for performance control. This includes inspection, acceptance, and breach of contract/default. If the goods/services do not comply with the contract, then the contract administrator has the right to:

- Reject the entire shipment
- Accept the entire shipment (barring latent defects)
- Accept part of the shipment

In government contracts, the government has the right to have the goods repaired with the costs charged back to the supplier or fix the goods themselves and charge the cost of repairs to the supplier. If the goods are then acceptable to the government, then the government may reduce the contract amount by an appropriate amount to reflect the reduced value of the contract.

Project managers often do financial closeout once the goods are shipped to the customer. This poses a problem if the goods must be repaired. Billing the cost of repairs against a financially closed out project is called *backcharging*. Most companies do not perform financial closeout until at least 90 days after delivery of goods.

24.10 USING A CHECKLIST

To assist a company in evaluating inquiries and preparing proposals and contracts, a checklist of contract considerations and provisions can be helpful in the

TABLE 24–2. TYPICAL MAIN HEADING FOR A CONTRACT PROVISIONS CHECKLIST

I.	Definitions of contract terms
II.	Definition of project scope
III.	Scope of services and work to be performed
IV.	Facilities to be furnished by client (for service company use)
V.	Changes and extras
VI.	Warranties and guarantees
VII.	Compensation to service company
VIII.	Terms of payment
IX.	Definition of fee base (cost of the project)
X.	State sales and/or use taxes
XI.	Taxes (other than sales use taxes)
XII.	Insurance coverages
XIII.	Other contractual provisions (including certain general provisions)
XIV.	Miscellaneous general provisions

evaluation of each proposal and form of contract to insure that appropriate safeguards are incorporated. This checklist is also used for sales letters and brochures that may promise or represent a commercial commitment. The primary purpose of the checklist is to raise in the minds of those who use it the legal and commercial factors that should at least be considered in preparing proposals and contracts. Table 24–2 shows the typical major headings that would be considered in a checklist. A key word concept also provides an excellent checklist of the key issues to be considered for any contract. It will be useful as a reminder in preparation for contractor-client agreement discussions.

Contract provisions that would be critical in minimizing the major areas of inherent risk on projects, and that should be prepared for inclusion in proposals and contracts, are the following:

- Scope of services and description of project
- Contract administration
- Terms of payment
- Client obligation and supplied items
- Warranties and guarantees
- Liability limitation and consequential damages
- Indemnity
- Taxes
- Patent indemnification
- Confidential information
- Termination provisions
- Changes and extras
- Assignments
- Delays, including *force majeure*
- Insurance requirements
- Arbitration
- Escalation (lump sum)
- Time of completion

Because of the necessarily wide variations in detail among each proposal and contract, it is not feasible to prepare material specifically suited for each situation. It must also be realized that not only does each company have special situations and provisions that are applicable to its individual situation and clients, but in the changing world of today, new situations that require special handling arise constantly. Therefore, it is not practical to establish a standard form of contract and, only to a limited degree, standard provisions to be included in a contract.

However, under present-day conditions, an increasing number of clients have certain set ideas as to the content of the proposal and contract. In addition, many clients and prospective clients have their own contract forms that must be followed in order to be considered for project awards. Because the goal is a contract or proposal leading to maximum profit and minimum risk, it has not always been possible to differentiate between company policy, or commercial, technical, legal, financial, accounting, or other considerations. Therefore, it would be extremely helpful in a general approach to preparing proposals and contracts to develop a standard list and file of draft contract clauses that could be used with some modification for each bid. As these clauses are used and refined, the amount of changes required for each occasion will diminish. In addition, because clients occasionally ask for a "typical" contract, the draft clauses can be combined into a "typical" or "draft" contract that can be given to a client. Even though this "typical" contract agreement may not be sufficient for every situation, it can be a favorable starting place for your company. It would also be valuable to maintain a summary of commercially oriented company policies for reference in reviewing a client's contract provisions.

Negotiating for the type of contract is a two-way street. The contractor desires a certain type of contract to reduce risk. The client desires a certain type of contract to reduce costs. Often the client and contractor disagree. It is not uncommon in industry for prospective projects to be canceled because of lack of funds, disagreements in contract negotiations, or changing of priorities.

24.11 PROPOSAL-CONTRACTUAL INTERACTION

It is critical during the proposal preparation stage that contract terms and conditions be reviewed and approved before submission of a proposal to the client. The contracts (legal) representative is responsible for the preparation of the contract portion of the proposal. Generally, contracts with the legal department are handled through or in coordination with the proposal group. The contract representative determines or assists with the following:

- Type of contract
- Required terms and conditions
- Any special requirements
- Cash-flow requirements
- Patent and proprietary data

- Insurance and tax considerations
- Finance and accounting

The sales department, through the proposal group, has the final responsibility for the content and outcome of all proposals and contracts that it handles. However, there are certain aspects that should be reviewed with others who can offer guidance, advice, and assistance to facilitate the effort. In general, contract agreements should be reviewed by the following departments:

- Proposal
- Legal
- Insurance
- Tax
- Project management
- Engineering
- Estimating
- Construction (if required)
- Purchasing (if required)

Responsibility for collecting and editing contract comments rests with the proposal manager. In preparing contract comments, consideration should be given to comments previously submitted to the client for the same form of agreement, and also previous agreements signed with the client.

Contract comments should be reviewed for their substance and ultimate risk to the company. It must be recognized that in most instances, the client is not willing to make a large number of revisions to his proposed form of agreement. The burden of proof that a contract change is required rests with the company; therefore each comment submitted must have a good case behind it.

Occasionally, a company is confronted with a serious contract comment for which it is very difficult to express their position in words. In such instances, it is better to flag the item that the company would like to discuss further with the client, and take it up at the conference table. A good example of this is taxes on cost plus foreign projects. Normally, when submitting a proposal for such work, a company does not have sufficient definitive information to establish its position relative to how it would like to handle taxes; that is:

- What is the client's position on taxes?
- Will one or two agreements be used for the work? Who will the contracting parties be?
- Time will not permit nor is the cost justifiable for a complete tax assessment.
- Contract procedures have not been established. Would we buy in the name of the company or as agents without liability for the client?

Proposal personnel should become familiar with the legal considerations that should be taken into account in all proposals, contracts, and negotiations. Legal considerations are important because they can have financial impact.

Accordingly, effective communication between proposals and the legal department is essential so that legal consideration can be identified early and then minimized. To be effective, the legal department should be advised of information pertinent to their functions as promptly as possible as negotiations develop. Proposal personnel should also be familiar with the standard contract forms the company uses, its contract terms, and available conditions, including those developed jointly between sales and the legal department, as well as the functions, duties, and responsibilities of the legal department. In addition, key areas that are normally negotiated should be discussed so that proposal personnel have a better understanding of the commercial risks involved and why the company has certain positions.

By the time the client has reviewed the proposal, the company's legal position is fixed commercially if not legally. Therefore, sales and proposal personnel should understand and be prepared to put forward the company's position on commercially significant legal considerations, both in general and on specific issues that arise in connection with a particular project. In this way, sales will be in a position to assert, and sell, the company's position at the appropriate time.

Proposals should send all bid documents, including the client's form of contract, or equivalent information, along with the proposal outline or instructions to the legal department as soon as possible, usually upon receipt of documents from the client. The instructions or outline should indicate the assignment of responsibility and include background information on matters that are pertinent to sales strategy or specific problems such as guarantees, previous experience with client, and so on.

Proposals should discuss briefly with the legal department what is planned by way of the project, the sales effort, and commercial considerations. If there is a kickoff meeting, a representative of the legal department should attend if it is appropriate or advisable. The legal department should make a preliminary review of the documents before any such discussion or meeting.

The legal department reviews the documents and prepares a memorandum of comment and any required contract documents, obtaining input where necessary or advisable. If the client has included a contract agreement with the inquiry, the legal department reviews it to see if it has any flaws or is against some set policy of the company. Unless a lesser level of effort is agreed upon, this memorandum will cover all legal issues that the legal department determines. This does not necessarily mean that all such issues must be raised with the client.

The purpose of the memorandum is to alert the proposal department to such issues. The memorandum suggests solutions to the legal issues raised, usually in the form of contract comments. The memo may make related appropriate commercial suggestions. If required, the legal department will submit a proposed form of contract, joint venture agreement, and so on. Generally, the legal department follows standards that have been worked out with sales and uses standard forms and contract language that were found to be salable in the past and to offer sufficient protection.

At the same time, proposals reviews the documents and advises the legal department of any pertinent issues known by or determined by proposals. This is essential not only because proposals has the final responsibility but also because proposals is responsible for providing information to, and getting comments from, others, such as purchasing, engineering, and estimating.

Proposals reviews and arranges for any other necessary review of the legal department's comments and documents. Proposals suggests the final form of comments, contract documents, and other relevant documents including the offer letter. Proposals reviews proposed final forms with the legal department as promptly as possible and prior to any commercial commitment.

Normal practice is to validate proposals for a period of thirty to sixty days following date of submission. Validation of proposals for periods in excess of this period may be required by special circumstances and should be done only with management's concurrence. Occasionally, it is desirable to validate a bid for less than thirty days. The validity period is especially important on lump sum bids. On such bids, the validity period must be consistent with validity times of quotations received for major equipment items. If these are not consistent, additional escalation on equipment and materials may have to be included in the lump sum price, and the company's competitive position could thereby be jeopardized.

Occasionally, you may be requested to submit with your proposals a schedule covering hourly rate ranges to reimbursable personnel. For this purpose, you should develop a standard schedule covering hourly rate ranges and average rates for all personnel whom you consider to be in the reimbursable category. The hourly rate ranges are based on the lowest-paid person and the highest-paid person in any specific job classification. In this connection, if there are any oddball situations, the effect of such is not included. Average rates are based on the average of all personnel in any given job classification.

One area that is critical to the development of a good contract is the definition of the scope of work covered by the contract. This is of particular importance to the proposal manager, who is responsible for having the proper people prepared for the scope of work description. What is prepared during proposal production most likely governs the contract preparation and eventually becomes part of that contract. The degree to which the project scope of work must be described in a contract depends on the pricing mechanism and contract form used.

A contract priced on a straight per diem basis or on the basis of reimbursement of all costs plus a fee does not normally require a precise description of either the services to be performed or the work to be accomplished.

Usually, a general description is adequate. This, however, is not the case if the contract is priced by other methods, especially fixed price, cost sharing, or guaranteed maximum. For these forms of contracts, it is essential that considerable care be taken to set forth in the contract documents the precise nature of the work to be accomplished as well as the services to be performed.

In the absence of a detailed description of the work prepared by the client, you must be prepared to develop such a description for inclusion in your proposal. When preparing the description of the work for inclusion in the contract documents, the basic premise to be followed must be that the language in the contract will be strictly interpreted during various stages of performance. The proper preparation of the description of the work as well as the evaluation of the requirements thereof requires coordination among sales, administration, cost, and technical personnel both inside and outside the organization. Technical personnel within the organization or technical consultants from outside must inform management whether there is an in-house capability to undertake the work and successfully solve the proper and timely completion of the work. Determination also must be made of whether suitable subcontracts or purchase orders can be awarded. In the major areas, firm commitments should be obtained. Technical projections must be effected relative to a host of problems, including delivery or scheduling requirements, the possibility of changes in the proposed scope of work, client control over the work, quality control, and procedures.

An inadequate or unrealistic description of the work to be undertaken or evaluation of the project requirements marks the beginning of an unhappy contract experience.

24.12 SUMMARY

While it is essential that companies obtain good contracts with a minimum of risk provisions, it is equally important that administration of those contracts be effective in order to achieve optimum results. Under current competitive and demanding conditions, it is imperative that all modern techniques of good contract administration be initiated.

The following guidelines can aid a company in preparing its proposals and contracts and administering operations thereunder:

- Use of the checklist in the preparation of all proposals and contracts
- Evaluation of risks by reference to the suggested contract provisions wherever appropriate
- Review by the legal department prior to submission to the client of all major proposals and contracts and of other contracts with questionable provisions
- Appropriate pricing or insuring of risks under the contract
- Improving contract administration at appropriate levels
- Periodic review and updating of the entire contract procedure including basic risk areas, administration, and so on.

Solutions to the Project Management Conflict Exercise

Part One: Facing the Conflict

After reading the answers that follow, record your score on line 1 of the worksheet.

A. Although many project managers and functional managers negotiate by "returning" favors, this custom is not highly recommended. The department manager might feel some degree of indebtedness at first, but will surely become defensive in follow-on projects in which you are involved, and might even get the idea that this will be the only way that he will be able to deal with you in the future. If this was your choice, allow one point on line 1.

B. Threats can only lead to disaster. This is a surefire way of ending a potentially good arrangement before it starts. Allow no points if you selected this as your solution.

C. If you say nothing, then you accept full responsibility and accountability for the schedule delay and increased costs. You have done nothing to open communications with the department manager. This could lead into additional conflicts on future projects. Enter two points on line 1 if this was your choice.

D. Requesting upper-level management to step in at this point can only complicate the situation. Executives prefer to step in only as a last resort. Upper-level management will probably ask to talk to the department manager first. Allow two points on line 1 if this was your choice.

E. Although he might become defensive upon receiving your memo, it will become difficult for him to avoid your request for help. The question, of course, is when he will give you this help. Allow eight points on line 1 if you made this choice.

F. Trying to force your solution on the department manager will severely threaten him and provide the basis for additional conflict. Good project managers will always try to predict emotional reactions to whatever decisions they might be forced to make. For this choice, allow two points on line 1 of the worksheet.

G. Making an appointment for a later point in time will give both parties a chance to cool off and think out the situation further. He will probably find it difficult to refuse your request for help and will be forced to think about it between now and the appointment. Allow ten points for this choice.

H. An immediate discussion will tend to open communications or keep communication open. This will be advantageous. However, it can also be a disadvantage if emotions are running high and sufficient time has not been given to the selection of alternatives. Allow six points on line 1 if this was your choice.

I. Forcing the solution your way will obviously alienate the department manager. The fact that you do intend to honor his request at a later time might give him some relief especially if he understands your problem and the potential impact of his decision on other departments. Allow three points on line 1 for this choice.

Part Two: Understanding Emotions

Using the scoring table shown on page 1167, determine your total score. Record your total in the appropriate box on line 2 of the worksheet. There are no "absolutely" correct answers to this problem, merely what appears to be the "most" right.

Part Three: Establishing Communications

A. Although your explanations may be acceptable and accountability for excess costs may be blamed on the department manager, you have not made any attempt to open communications with the department manager. Further conflicts appear inevitable. If this was your choice, allow a score of zero on line 3 of the worksheet.

B. You are offering the department manager no choice but to elevate the conflict. He probably has not had any time to think about changing his requirements and it is extremely doubtful that he will give in to you since you have now backed him into a corner. Allow zero points on line 3 of the worksheet.

C. Threatening him may get him to change his mind, but will certainly create deteriorating working relationships both on this project and any others that will require that you interface with his department. Allow zero points if this was your choice.

D. Sending him a memo requesting a meeting at a later date will give him and you a chance to cool down but might not improve your bargaining position. The department manager might now have plenty of time to reassure himself that he was right because you probably aren't under such a terrible time constraint as you led him to believe if you can wait several days to see him again. Allow four points on line 3 of the worksheet if this was your choice.

E. You're heading in the right direction trying to open communications. Unfortunately, you may further aggravate him by telling him that he lost his cool and should have apologized to you when all along you may have been the one who lost your cool. Expressing regret as part of your opening remarks would benefit the situation. Allow six points on line 3 of the worksheet.

F. Postponing the problem cannot help you. The department manager might consider the problem resolved because he hasn't heard from you. The confrontation should not be postponed. Your choice has merit in that you are attempting to open up a channel for communications. Allow four points on line 3 if this was your choice.

G. Expressing regret and seeking immediate resolution is the best approach. Hopefully, the department manager will now understand the importance of this conflict and the need for urgency. Allow ten points on line 3 of the worksheet.

	Reaction	Personal or Group Score
A. I've given you my answer. See the general manager if you're not happy.	Hostile or Withdrawing	4
B. I understand your problem. Let's do it your way.	Accepting	4
C. I understand your problem, but I'm doing what is best for my department.	Defensive or Hostile	4
D. Let's discuss the problem. Perhaps there are alternatives.	Cooperative	4
E. Let me explain to you why we need the new requirements.	Cooperative or Defensive	4
F. See my section supervisors. It was their recommendation.	Withdrawing	4
G. New managers are supposed to come up with new and better ways, aren't they?	Hostile or Defensive	4
	Total: Personal	
	Total: Group	

Part Four: Conflict Resolution

Use the table shown on page 1168 to determine your total points. Enter this total on line 4 of the worksheet.

Part Five: Understanding Your Choices

A. Although you may have "legal" justification to force the solution your way, you should consider the emotional impact on the organization as a result of alienating the department manager. Allow two points on line 5 of the worksheet.

B. Accepting the new requirements would be an easy way out if you are willing to explain the increased costs and schedule delays to the other participants. This would certainly please the department manager and might even give him the impression that he has a power position and can always resolve problems in this fashion. Allow four points on line 5 of your worksheet.

C. If this situation cannot be resolved at your level, you have no choice but to request upper-level management to step in. At this point you must be pretty sure that a compromise is all but impossible and are willing to accept a go-for-broke position. Enter ten points on line 5 of the worksheet if this was your choice.

	Mode	Personal or Group Score
A. The requirements are my decision and we're doing it my way.	Forcing	4
B. I've thought about it and you're right. We'll do it your way.	Withdrawal or Smoothing	4
C. Let's discuss the problem. Perhaps there are alternatives.	Compromise or Confrontation	4
D. Let me explain why we need the new requirements.	Smoothing, Confrontation, or Forcing	4
E. See my section supervisors; they're handling it now.	Withdrawal	4
F. I've looked over the problem and I might be able to ease up on some of the requirements.	Smoothing or Compromise	4
	Total: Personal	
	Total: Group	

D. Asking other managers to plead your case for you is not a good situation. Hopefully upper-level management will solicit their opinions when deciding on how to resolve the conflict. Enter six points on line 5 if this was your choice, and hope that the functional managers do not threaten him by ganging up on him.

Part Six: Interpersonal Influences

A. Threatening the employees with penalty power will probably have no effect at all because your conflict is with the department manager, who at this time probably could care less about your evaluation of his people. Allow zero points on line 6 of the worksheet if you selected this choice.

B. Offering rewards will probably induce people toward your way of thinking provided that they feel that you can keep your promises. Promotions and increased responsibilities are functional responsibilities, not those of a project manager. Performance evaluation might be effective if the department manager values your judgment. In this situation it is doubtful that he will. Allow no points for this answer and record the results on line 6 of the worksheet.

C. Expert power, once established, is an effective means of obtaining functional respect provided that it is used for a relatively short period of time. For long-term efforts, expert power can easily create conflicts between project and functional managers. In this situation, although relatively short term, the department manager probably will not consider you as an expert, and this might carry on down to his functional subordinates. Allow six points on line 6 of the worksheet if this was your choice.

D. Work challenge is the best means of obtaining support and in many situations can overcome personality clashes and disagreements. Unfortunately, the problem occurred because of complaints by the functional personnel and it is therefore unlikely that work challenge would be effective here. Allow eight points on line 6 of the worksheet if this was your choice.

E. People who work in a project environment should respect the project manager because of the authority delegated to him from the upper levels of management. But this does not mean that they will follow his directions. When in doubt, employees tend to follow the direction of the person who signs their evaluation form, namely, the department manager. However, the project manager has the formal authority to "force" the line manager to adhere to the original project plan. This should be done only as a last resort, and here, it looks as though it may be the only alternative. Allow ten points if this was your answer and record the result on line 6 of the worksheet.

F. Referent power cannot be achieved overnight. Furthermore, if the department manager feels that you are trying to compete with him for the friendship of his subordinates, additional conflicts can result. Allow two points on line 6 of the worksheet if this was your choice.

APPENDIX B

Solution to Leadership Exercise

Situation 1

A. This technique may work if you have proven leadership credentials. Since three of these people have not worked for you before, some action is necessary.

B. The team should already be somewhat motivated and reinforcement will help. Team building must begin by showing employees how they will benefit. This is usually the best approach on long-term projects. (5 points)

C. This is the best approach if the employees already understand the project. In this case, however, you may be expecting too much out of the employees this soon. (3 points)

D. This approach is too strong at this time, since emphasis should be on team building. On long-term projects, people should be given the opportunity to know one another first. (2 points)

Situation 2

A. Do nothing. Don't overreact. This may improve productivity without damaging morale. See the impact on the team first. If the other members accept Tom as the informal leader, because he has worked for you previously, the results can be very favorable. (5 points)

B. This may cause the team to believe that a problem exists when, in fact, it does not.

C. This is duplication of effort and may reflect on your ability as a leader. Productivity may be impaired. (2 points)

D. This is a hasty decision and may cause Tom to overreact and become less productive. (3 points)

Situation 3

A. You may be burdening the team by allowing them to struggle. Motivation may be affected and frustration will result. (1 point)

B. Team members expect the project manager to be supportive and to have ideas. This will reinforce your relationship with the team. (5 points)

C. This approach is reasonable as long as your involvement is minimum. You must allow the team to evolve without expecting continuous guidance. (4 points)

D. This action is premature and can prevent future creativity. The team may allow you to do it all.

Situation 4

A. If, in fact, the problem does exist, action must be taken. These types of problems do not go away by themselves.

B. This will escalate the problem and may make it worse. It could demonstrate your support for good relations with your team, but could also backfire. (1 point)

C. Private meetings should allow you to reassess the situation and strengthen employee relations on a one-on-one basis. You should be able to assess the magnitude of the problem. (5 points)

D. This is a hasty decision. Changing the team's schedules may worsen the morale problem. This situation requires replanning, not a strong hand. (2 points)

Situation 5

A. Crisis management does not work in project management. Why delay until a crisis occurs and then waste time having to replan?

B. This situation may require your immediate attention. Sympathizing with your team may not help if they are looking toward you for leadership. (2 points)

C. This is the proper balance: participative management and contingency planning. This balance is crucial for these situations. (5 points)

D. This may seriously escalate the problem unless you have evidence that performance is substandard. (1 point)

Situation 6

A. Problems should be uncovered and brought to the surface for solution. It is true that this problem may go away, or that Bob simply does not recognize that his performance is substandard.

B. Immediate feedback is best. Bob must know your assessment of his performance. This shows your interest in helping him improve. (5 points)

C. This is not a team problem. Why ask the team to do your work? Direct contact is best.

D. As above, this is your problem, not that of the team. You may wish to ask for their input, but do not ask them to perform your job.

Situation 7

A. George must be hurting to finish the other project. George probably needs a little more time to develop a quality report. Let him do it. (5 points)

B. Threatening George may not be the best situation because he already understands the problem. Motivation by threatening normally is not good. (3 points)

C. The other team members should not be burdened with this unless it is a team effort.

D. As above, this burden should not be placed on other team members unless, of course, they volunteer.

Situation 8

A. Doing nothing in time of crisis is the worst decision that can be made. This may frustrate the team to a point where everything that you have built up may be destroyed.

B. The problem is the schedule slippage, not morale. In this case, it is unlikely that they are related.

C. Group decision making can work but may be difficult under tight time constraints. Productivity may not be related to the schedule slippage. (3 points)

D. This is the time when the team looks to you for strong leadership. No matter how good the team is, they may not be able to solve all of the problems. (5 points)

Situation 9

A. A pat on the back will not hurt. People need to know when they are doing well.

B. Positive reinforcement is a good idea, but perhaps not through monetary rewards. (3 points)

C. You have given the team positive reinforcement and have returned authority/responsibility to them for phase III. (5 points)

D. Your team has demonstrated the ability to handle authority and responsibility except for this crisis. Dominant leadership is not necessary on a continuous basis.

Situation 10

A. The best approach. All is well. (5 points)

B. Why disturb a good working relationship and a healthy working environment? Your efforts may be counterproductive.

C. If the team members have done their job, they have already looked for contingencies. Why make them feel that you still want to be in control? However, if they have not reviewed the phase III schedule, this step may be necessary. (3 points)

D. Why disturb the team? You may convince them that something is wrong or about to happen.

Situation 11

A. You cannot assume a passive role when the customer identifies a problem. You must be prepared to help. The customer's problems usually end up being your problems. (3 points)

B. The customer is not coming into your company to discuss productivity.

C. This places a tremendous burden on the team, especially since it is the first meeting. They need guidance.

D. Customer information exchange meetings are *your* responsibility and should not be delegated. You are the focal point of information. This requires strong leadership, especially during a crisis. (5 points)

Situation 12

A. A passive role by you may leave the team with the impression that there is no urgency.

B. Team members are motivated and have control of the project. They should be able to handle this by themselves. Positive reinforcement will help. (5 points)

C. This approach might work but could be counterproductive if employees feel that you question their abilities. (4 points)

D. Do not exert strong leadership when the team has already shown its ability to make good group decisions.

Situation 13   A. This is the worst approach and may cause the loss of both the existing and follow-on work.
                     B. This may result in overconfidence and could be disastrous if a follow-on effort does not occur.
                     C. This could be very demoralizing for the team, because members may view the existing program as about to be canceled. (3 points)
                     D. This should be entirely the responsibility of the project manager. There are situations where information may have to be withheld, at least temporarily. (5 points)

Situation 14   A. This is an ideal way to destroy the project-functional interface.
                     B. This consumes a lot of time, since each team member may have a different opinion. (3 points)
                     C. This is the best approach, since the team may know the functional personnel better than you do. (5 points)
                     D. It is highly unlikely that you can accomplish this.

Situation 15   A. This is the easiest solution, but the most dangerous if it burdens the rest of the team with extra work. (3 points)
                     B. The decision should be yours, not your team's. You are avoiding your responsibility.
                     C. Consulting with the team will gain support for your decision. It is highly likely that the team will want Carol to have this chance. (5 points)
                     D. This could cause a demoralizing environment on the project. If Carol becomes irritable, so could other team members.

Situation 16   A. This is the best choice. You are at the mercy of the line manager. He may ease up some if not disturbed. (5 points)
                     B. This is fruitless. They have obviously tried this already and were unsuccessful. Asking them to do it again could be frustrating. Remember, the brick wall has been there for two years already. (3 points)
                     C. This will probably be a wasted meeting. Brick walls are generally not permeable.
                     D. This will thicken the brick wall and may cause your team's relationship with the line manager to deteriorate. This should be used as a last resort *only* if status information cannot be found any other way. (2 points)

Situation 17   A. This is a poor assumption. Carol may not have talked to him or may simply have given him her side of the project.
                     B. The new man is still isolated from the other team members. You may be creating two project teams. (3 points)
                     C. This may make the new man uncomfortable and feel that the project is regimented through meetings. (2 points)
                     D. New members feel more comfortable one-on-one, rather than having a team gang up on them. Briefings should be made by the team, since project termination and phaseout will be a team effort. (5 points)

Situation 18
   A. This demonstrates your lack of concern for the growth of your employees. This is a poor choice.
   B. This is a personal decision between you and the employee. As long as his performance will not be affected, he should be allowed to attend. (5 points)
   C. This is not necessarily a problem open for discussion. You may wish to informally seek the team's opinion. (2 points)
   D. This approach is reasonable but may cause other team members to feel that you are showing favoritism and simply want their consensus.

Situation 19
   A. This is the best choice. Your employees are in total control. Do nothing. You must assume that the employees have already received feedback. (5 points)
   B. The employees have probably been counseled already by your team and their own functional manager. Your efforts can only alienate them. (1 point)
   C. Your team already has the situation under control. Asking them for contingency plans at this point may have a detrimental effect. They may have already developed contingency plans. (2 points)
   D. A strong leadership role now may alienate your team.

Situation 20
   A. A poor choice. You, the project manager, are totally accountable for all information provided to the customer.
   B. Positive reinforcement may be beneficial, but does nothing to guarantee the quality of the report. Your people may get overcreative and provide superfluous information.
   C. Soliciting their input has some merit, but the responsibility here is actually yours. (3 points)
   D. Some degree of leadership is needed for all reports. Project teams tend to become diffused during report writing unless guided. (5 points)

Author Index

Subject Index